RAYMOND A.
TRIBUTE E

MW00814047

OAHSPE

A Sacred History Of The Dominions Of The Higher And Lower Heavens Of The Earth For The Past 24,000 Years. Together With A Synopsis Of The Cosmogony Of The Universe, The Creation Of The Planets, The Creation of Man, The Unseen World, The Labor And Glory Of Gods And Goddesses In The Etherean Heavens.

VOLUME 1

OAHSPE
RAYMOND A. PALMER EDITION
JOHN BALLOU NEWBROUGH

Volume One of a Two Volume Set

Nonfiction

Timothy Green Beckley: Editorial Director
Carol Rodriguez: Publishers Assistant
Sean Casteel: Associate Editor
Cover Art: Tim R. Swartz

Printed in the United States of America

For free catalog write:
Global Communications
P.O. Box 753
New Brunswick, NJ 08903

Free Subscription to Conspiracy Journal E-Mail Newsletter
www.conspiracyjournal.com

Email: mrufo8@hotmail.com

Full color prints of the Prophets are available for $12 plus $5 shipping at the above address.

Paintings Of The Prophets

Zarathustra, lived over nine thousand years ago. Plato, Pliny and Aristotle wrote of him, stating unanimously, that he lived at least six thousand years before their time.

Po, lived about five thousand nine hundred years ago.
It was he who undermined the Han kingdom.

Abram, afterward called Abraham, lived approximately six thousand years ago. His heart was as gentle as a woman's, yet he was fierce to look upon.

Brahma and Yu-tiv

Ea-wah-tah, sometimes called Hiawatha, lived about six thousand years ago; a man of great stature, most beloved in the hearts of the Americas even unto this day in sacred dance in monotonous voice amongst the Native Americans.

Thothma, (Hojax) lived approximately five thousand years ago. He could hear and talk with the Gods and was the builder of the Great Pyramid in Egypt.

Capilya, lived three thousand five hundred years ago, similar to Moses in all respects, yet he had the greatest knowledge of governmental rule.

VIII

Moses, lived three thousand five hundred years ago, one of the greatest characters of history. He was great and wise as to corporeality, yet abiding in the essence of the Most High

Chine, of China, lived three thousand five hundred years ago. There is no person in all the nations of the world, past or present, that had attained to such unbelievable miracles.

Sakaya, sometimes erroneously called Buddha, lived two thousand six hundred years ago, established system and order regarding convents, nunneries and monastaries.

Ka-Yu, erroneously called Confucius, lived two thousand six hundred years ago. He was the greatest scholar ever recorded. He condensed eighteen thousand books into twenty volumes.

XII

Joshu, Jesus, the most controversial character of today. In fact, he did not die on the cross; according to Jewish custom of the day he had to be stoned to death. He reinstated the Mosiac Law saying: "I did not come to destroy the law but to restore it." The Most High is the law, governing the universe in word and power. As written, "I AM the law."

In using the words "the religion of Jesus," we simply mean the religion of Israel. We believe that Jesus of Nazareth was a Jew in every sense of the word. He did not establish a new religion, or preach a new doctrine in any shape or form. The preacher "from the mount, the prophet of the beatitudes, does not repeat with persuasive lips what the law-givers of his race proclaimed in mighty tones of command." (See T.W. Doane. Chap. XL)

OAHSPE:
THE WONDER BOOK OF ALL AGES

SPECIAL
RAYMOND A. PALMER TRIBUTE EDITION

WHAT IS IT?

Probably the best way to describe Oahspe is in the words of the book itself: "A sacred history of the dominions of the higher and lower heavens on the Earth for the past 24,000 years, beginning with the submersion of the continent of Pan in the Pacific Ocean, commonly called the Flood or Deluge, to the Kosmon (present) Era. Also a brief history of the preceding 55,000 years, together with a cosmogony of the Universe, the creation of the planets; the creation of man; the unseen worlds; the labor and glory of gods and goddesses in the etherean heavens; with the new commandments of Jehovih to man of the present day."

WHAT DOES IT CONTAIN?

Oahspe is best described as The Complete Book of The Cosmos and it might easily have been written by today's space scientists! Much of the science in OAHSPE has only recently been "discovered". Newbrough could not have "guessed" so rightly, especially in the face of all the authorities of his day. Today space satellites are discovering "how it is" out in space, while in 1882 OAHSPE contained the same information! As an instance, the now famous Van Allen radiation belts, complete as to nature and height! The scientific reader is overwhelmed by the science of OAHSPE.

Do you think flying saucers are new? Then read OAHSPE! A whole panorama of aerial and space vessels are described as though from today's newspapers. Do you wonder at Einstein's theories? Then read OAHSPE! 'He could have gotten his information there! Uncounted thousands of tons of meteorites fall to Earth each day, yet space is nearly empty of them. OAHSPE knew it in 1882! Space is dark, say our daring astronauts. So did OAHSPE in 1882, and tells us why! Archaeologists have made amazing discoveries of ancient races and dead cities and civilizations since 1882. They might have discovered them sooner had they read OAHSPE. Ancient languages are described in OAHSPE.

Just where is Heaven? What do you do there?

Is there anything for YOU to do when you get there - what kind of occupation? Is there really a hell?

Who manages the Earth, the Solar System, the Universe - and how? How do the different religions fit into God's one Universe? OAHSPE tells all this, and a thousand more answers to man's most difficult questions.

WHEN AND HOW WAS IT WRITTEN?

OAHSPE was written by a process known as automatic writing, on a Sholes typewriter (one of the very first), by John Ballou Newbrough, who was born on June 5, 1828, on a Springfield, Ohio farm. A college man, he specialized in medicine, particularly dentistry. After college he went to the goldfields of California and also to Australia. Afterward he became a dentist in New York City. One morning in 1870, Newbrough went to the home of his dearest friend Edwin Augustus Davis (to whose memoirs we owe this information), who lived on Sixth Avenue, near the old Hay Market, and said: "I've come for your advice; I had quite an experience about 4 am this morning. I was sleeping nicely when I felt a hand on my shoulder. A voice said: 'Wake up, doctor. Everything is all right. I only want to ask you a question and we will go.'"

"I sat up and answered: 'Yes, if I can.'

The voice said: 'Would you like to perform a mission for Jehovih?'

"I rubbed my eyes and I saw the room was lit up with pillars of light so pleasing to the eyes that is was indescribable. I saw great numbers of beautiful spirits or angels. They did not have wings.

"I spoke: 'What is the mission, so that I may know whether to say yes or no?' The answer came back: 'Jehovih would like you to live spiritually for ten years, and at the end of that time we will come back and tell you what it is that we desire, for your body and mind are not efficiently perceptible now.'

"'What do you mean by living spiritually?'"

"'We want you never to kill anything, or eat anything that breathes; meat, fish, birds, reptile. Live on nuts, fruit, vegetables. One other thing is very important: you must help people; give your services to people who need dental help without pay if they cannot pay. Do charity work," the voice said, and then the lights dimmed and went out, and the atmosphere changed back to its normal darkness. I got up and wrote down everything that had happened, then came over to talk to you."

Davis and Newbrough discussed the matter for hours, and during the conversation Newbrough revealed that he thought he had recognized three of the spirits, although he had not had a good look at them. He asked Davis if he thought the adventure was real, or only a dream.

"John," said Davis, "I don't believe it was a dream. I'd say, go ahead. Perhaps the ten year wait will he worth it, when you find out what it is that *you* are to do." At 4 a.m. in the morning late in 1880, John Newbrough was again awakened from his slumber to find the same mysterious and beautiful light filling his room. The same voice spoke, "You have done well. You have passed our test.

Now we want you to buy a typewriter and place it on this table. We wilt thereafter awaken you one hour before dawn each morning, and you will sit in this chair before the typewriter and put your hands on the keys. You will buy plenty of paper and keep it for always ready to use." "I don't know how to use a typewriter." "We will control your hands and arms, and perform the task for you, so don't worry. You must not look at what is written until it is finished."

There was further discussion and instruction, then the pillars of light dimmed and went out.

On the morning of January 1, 1881, having followed all instructions, the first writing session began at 4 a.m. As Newbrough, later told to his friend, Davis:

"To my amazement as I sat in the chair, my hands went up and started to pound at the keys. It seemed to me that I was half asleep, but I saw everything I was doing. I saw no spirits, but I knew they were using my body and thought. I looked at my hands and fingers and they were going like mad. "The papers seem to pile up fast on the right side of the typewriter. As the days went by, I was doing more and more. At first 1 was thinking what am I writing about? My mind seemed blank, but I had never felt better in my life. I always locked my door after me, and it was locked when I came back. I noticed, though that there was a blank paper over the pile I had finished, and a paperweight on top.

"As I left my room the next morning I took particular notice of how the paperweight lay on the stack of finished work. When I returned that evening, I wanted to see if it had been moved, but it had not. But to my surprise, my bed had been made. Everything had been dusted and cleaned and I said to myself: 'The spirits are certainly working hard around here!' "I heard a loud laugh, and the voice said: '"We are! We don't want you to worry about a thing. We are taking care of you and no harm can come to you. And already remember this.'"

Every morning, before sunrise, until December 15, 1881, John Ballou Newbrough wrote at a speed physically almost impossible considering the crudity of the first typewriter, and finally the manuscript was completed.

In 1882 the book was published, according to the instructions given Newbrough by his spirit authors. This is an authentic reproduction of the original 1882 edition, with added material that was located under strange circumstances, as well as reproductions of the oil paintings (first presented in the 1891 edition) of Zarathustra, Po, Abram, Brahma and his wife Yu-Tiv, Ea-wah-tah (Hiawatha), Thothma (builder of the Great Pyramid), Capilya, Moses, Chine, Sakaya, Ka'Vu (Confucius), and Joshu. These paintings were done by Newbrough in total darkness. They have never been published in color in any other edition of Oahspe

Timothy Green Beckley

WHO WAS RAYMOND A. PALMER, AND WHY IS THIS EDITION OF OAHSPE DEDICATED TO HIM?

Raymond A. Palmer (RAP for short) was a true pioneer, one of the most important individuals in the field of esoterica and arcane knowledge of the last 100 years. He was the editor of Amazing Stories, a futuristic "sci fi" magazine published in the mid 1940s which presented the fantastic stories of Richard Shaver and his subterranean worlds. Palmer was also one of the founders of FATE magazine and later started his own publishing empire with such titles as Mystic, Search, Forum and Space World.

He also issued reprints of hard to find works. For a while he possessed the only copy of a first edition of OAHSPE and issued 2000 copies in a private edition even at a financial loss just to get the word out about this amazing book which was one of his all time favorites. Said Palmer about OAHSPE:

> OAHSPE cannot be attacked as an expurgated and perverted book and summarily dismissed. In the light of present day science, the Book of Cosmology alone is evidence of a superior fore-knowledge that stands as a sturdy sentinel over the doctrinal portions. And in the light of present day anthropology and archaeology, its historical portions stand as remarkable evidence of that same superior fore-knowledge. OAHSPE is truly a gateway to understanding.

This in addition to the fact that Ray Palmer charged us with great enthusiasm in our earliest work and provided our first forums by way of columns in both Search and Flying Saucers magazine. This, the greatest edition of OAHSPE ever published, is a fitting tribute to RAP.

OAHSPE

OAHSPE

A

NEW BIBLE

IN THE

WORDS OF JEHOVIH

AND HIS

Angel Embassadors.

~~~~~~~~~~~~~~~~~

A SACRED HISTORY

OF THE DOMINIONS OF THE HIGHER AND LOWER HEAVENS ON THE EARTH.

FOR THE PAST

TWENTY - FOUR THOUSAND YEARS,

TOGETHER WITH

A SYNOPSIS OF THE COSMOGONY OF THE UNIVERSE; THE CREATION OF PLANETS; THE
CREATION OF MAN; THE UNSEEN WORLDS; THE LABOR AND GLORY OF
GODS AND GODDESSES IN THE ETHEREAN HEAVENS;

WITH THE

NEW COMMANDMENTS OF JEHOVIH TO MAN OF THE PRESENT DAY. WITH REVELATIONS FROM
THE SECOND RESURRECTION, FORMED IN WORDS IN THE THIRTY-
THIRD YEAR OF THE KOSMON ERA.

OAHSPE PUBLISHING ASSOCIATION,
NEW YORK AND LONDON.
—
(1882.)
ANNO KOSMON 34.

2

THE EDITOR'S PREFACE.

When a man holds up a book, and says, "You must believe this, because it says, 'Thus saith the Lord,'" should we not pity that man? Does he comprehend the liberty of man to acquire knowledge?

Any book that imparts knowledge of the life and destiny of man, is a good book. Any book that unfolds the character and person of Jehovih, and the wonder and glory of His creations, is a good book.

When a book gives us information of things we know not of, it should also give us a method of proving that information to be true. This book covers that ground.

The day has arrived, when man will not accept proclamations and assertions; he wants plausible reasons, or substantial proofs, that the authority be not merely a presence, but a demonstrable fact.

The time of man-worship is at an end; readers no longer accept a book as good and great, merely because any certain one wrote it. The book must have merits of its own, otherwise it will soon pass out of existence.

When a man says, "I heard the voice of Jehovih, saying," that part of his speech is worthless. When he says, "I heard the voice of Jehovih, saying: 'Do unto others as ye would that they should do unto you,'" then the words become valuable. His assertion of his authority is of no avail in this age of the world. The words purporting to be Jehovih's should, therefore, be the only consideration as to merit. And all men have a right to pass judgment thereon. Is it not the light of Jehovih within all men, that makes them conscious of wisdom and truth? If so, then man's expression of any truth or wisdom is Jehovih's expression.

If a book were to fall down from the sky with Jehovih's signature to it, man would not accept the book on that account. Why, then, should anything be said about how this book was written? It blows nobody's horn; it makes no leader. It is not a destroyer of old systems or religions. It reveals a new one, adapted to this age.

New York, 1882.

GLOSSARY

OF STRANGE WORDS USED IN THIS BOOK.

A'ji. Semi-dark. A dense region in etherea which sometimes descends to the earth. Less than nebula.

Agni. Fire or light, especially without combustion, as spirit lights. A pillar of fire by day, as with the Israelites going out of Egypt.

Algonquin. The United States of the North American Indians before their destruction by the Christians.

Anash. A wicked tongue; one of the Hebrew seven tetracts. See the word, satan.

Angel. A spirit man. Su, also, su-gan, and gans-spe. (The word, spirit, does not define whether man or animal, but is often erroneously used instead of angel.)

Anubi. God of the scales. Sometimes called, God of Justice

Aph. The God who submerged the continent of Pan. See Book of Aph, and account of the flood.

Apollo. The God to whose duty was assigned beautifying mortals in form and figure. See Book of Apollo. He had many names, as, Soodhga, So-Gow, Choo Choo, Sudghda, and so on, but the meaning is the same, whether in Chinese, Hindoo, Greek, Latin or English.

Archangel. Angels next in rank to Gods, who dwell in certain arcs in etherea. They generally come in the dawn of a cycle to give new inspiration to mortals. Whilst they remain with mortals, as during the last few years, good mortals become more angelic toward one another.

A'su. The first race of man. To crawl on the belly…. see Asu, Book of Jehovih.

Asaphs. Angels in heaven whose office it is to receive the spirit when a mortal dies, and bear it to the place prepared for it. They are in organic associations. Their rank is next below ashars.

Ashars. Guardian angels who are appointed over mortals, to be with them during life. They deliver the spirit in time of death into the hands of the asaphs. They also keep the record of the mortal, which is also given to the asaphs in heaven, along with the newborn spirit, which is called an es'yan, for a certain season. Ashars are next in rank to loo'is. See word loo'is.

Atmospherea. The earth's vortex. See Book of Cosmogony. Atmospherea comprises the places and dominions of the God of this planet. See the word God;

Aven. Evil actions. One of the seven Hebrew tetracts. See satan.

Babel. Confounded by compounding too many things together, as the Yi-haic language.

Beast. The animal man. The earthly part of man. Anything that is enforced as a religion.

Belyyaal. One of the seven Hebrew tetracts. Hypocrisy crawling. See satan.

BRAH, or BRAHMAN. Wisdom, knowledge. Brah was the founder of Brahmanism, and was cotemporaneous with Abram, or Abraham. See FIRST BOOK OF GOD, and Under the false God, Ennochissa, the word bra'hma became synonymous with warrior.

BRIDE AND BRIDEGROOM. The emancipated degree of angels in heaven; a title bequeathed to all such as have gone beyond the bound heavens, atmospherea, and who are free from the Gods and Saviors. As we say of man at twenty-one years, he is free from his father; he is strong enough to go alone.

BUDHA. Wisdom, knowledge. But afterward, under the false God, Kabalactes, the word budha became synonymous with warrior.

CAPILYA. A deliverer; a man of India, cotemporaneous with Moses. And, like Moses, he delivered the Faithists out of bondage, not by migration, but by establishing their freedom throughout India. He also wrought miracles. Sometimes spelt Capella; a star was named after him.

CORPOR. Whatever has length, breadth and thickness, and is tangible to sight, hearing and feeling; the extreme opposite condition from ether, or solution, or rarefaction.

CORPOREAN. A man of the earth; any man, all men. In contradistinction from an angel who is a man of es, a spirit.

CHAOTICS. Deranged angels; such as are killed in war or in anger.

CHINE. A deliverer; a man of China, cotemporaneous with Moses and Capilya. He was to China a great deliverer. He was an iesu by birth, and wrought miracles. The country, China, was named by him after himself. (After his death, and his body was reduced to ashes, Jehovih caused a wind to gather up the ashes, and restore Chine to life for seven days, during which time he preached before the kings and the people. Then Jehovih sent down a ship of light, and bore Chine up to heaven.) See doctrines of Chine, this work.

CHINVAT. The boundary between the rotating atmosphere of the earth and the ether beyond. Called also Bridge of Chinvat.

CHRIST, or KRISTE. Wisdom, knowledge, education. After the false God, Looeamong, falsely took this name, it became synonymous with warrior.

CHRISTIANS, or KRISTE·YANS. A brotherhood of warriors; they were named Christians, in derision, by the Hebrews. One who rushes into a multitude of rioters, and, with a sword, enforces peace, is a true Christian. A people whose faith is in arms and standing armies. (The following words are synonymous: Brahma, budha, christ, kriste, baal ashtaroth, dagon, vishnu, ashdod, knowledge, wisdom, chreshna, light, po, te'in, wah, manito, and, in fact, a score of others.)

CRUCIFY. To melt; to test by fire; to test by binding. The original form of testing a su'is or sar'gis (medium), was by binding him on a wheel.

DAN. Light. A cyclic dawn, as the Arc of Spe'ta or Arc of Bon. A dan comes once every three thousand years, and is preceded by spirit-manifestations and by signs and wonders. A dan lasts about thirty-three years. There are also sub-cycles, of 200, 400 and 600 years. Dan is synonymous with dang. See BOOK OF SAPHAH.

Daveas, or **Daevas.** Bad angels; spirits that deceive and tempt. A prince of liars. In the Vedic Scriptures, equivalent to devil, in English.

Deity, or **Dyaus.** One of the Gods of the lower heavens, who pretended to be the Creator. He was afterward cast into hell by his own subjects, the false God, Anuhasaj.

Dibbah. One of the Hebrew seven tetracts; a tattler. See satan.

Div, or **Diva,** or **Divinity.** A parliament of Lords in the lower heavens. The Divan laws were in use three thousand years. See Book of Divinity.

Druk. A low mortal; one who desires no spiritual light; one who can not understand spiritually. An evil man, a warrior.

Druj. Druj applies to an angel, the same as druk to a mortal; low, dark, evil, dangerous.

Eawahtah or **Hiawatha.** A North American Indian, a kind of Abraham, with whom he was cotemporaneous.

Es. The unseen worlds, i.e., unseen to mortals. This word is used in the feminine; synonymous with the spirit world. See Book of Jehovih.

Es'senaurs. Heavenly musicians, comprised of singers and instrumental players.

Es'yan. A newborn spirit. When a mortal dies, and his spirit departs into heaven, it is called an es'yan. An infant spirit. The name, es'yan, it retains as long as it is helpless, perhaps a year, or five years, or a hundred years. See the word purgatory.

Ethe. The solvent of corpor; as water is the solvent of a salt, so is ethe the solvent of corporeal substance, of which latter hydrogen is one of the most sublimated. As a corporeal man dwells on the earth, and as an es'yan dwells in atmospherea, so do the advanced angels dwell in ethe, in etherea.

Etherea. Beyond the atmosphere, the great firmament, where are situated the higher heavens, the homes of the Gods and Goddesses. Etherea, as a place, is nirvana.

Faith. A convinced belief; a condition of mind fully satisfied; next to actual knowledge. We have faith the sun will rise to-morrow morning, but the knowledge can not be actual until after sunrise.

Faithist. One who has faith in Jehovih being over all, and within all, to a wise and definite purpose. One who has not faith in anything but Jehovih. One who endeavors to make himself in unison with Jehovih by doing good unto others, and in striving to put away self-gratification. A non-resistant. The opposite from Uzian.

Fetal. A suckling; also one that gives suck. More especially, an absorbent. As a young child, sleeping with a very old person, is robbed of its vitality. The imperceptible nutrition; the unseen current of life that passes from one person to another. A healer gives haoma (fetal food) to the sick. A child that dies before birth, has a fetal spirit; it is fetaled on a mortal until it attains development. Many full-grown spirits (angels) fetal themselves on mortals, and so live. These are called vampire fetals. Persons who have been drunkards or gormandizers on flesh food, after death, fetal themselves on other mortals, living on their atmosphere, especially of drunkards and smokers and gross eaters.

6

FIRMAMENT. The world of space between the stars and planets.

FRAGAPATTI. A God of the highest rank, a nirvanian Chief. In the Hindoo Scriptures, he is denominated a Creator. See BOOK OF FRAGAPATTI.

GOD, or **IOD,** or **JOSS.** An angel, in rank next above Lord, and next below Orian Chief. One who is sufficiently wise and powerful to take charge of a planet and its atmospherean heavens. His assistant on the throne is called vice-God.

GOLGOTHA. A temple of skulls.

GREAT SPIRIT. The universe is earth (corpor), sky and spirit, the three (in one) are Jehovih. As the spirit of a man is to the man, so is the Great Spirit to Jehovih. Though Great Spirit is also used as synonymous with Jehovih.

GUATAMA. The cosmological name of America. Literally, the last spirit foundation; the last revelation. Sometimes spelt Gotama.

HAM. Cosmological name of Egypt. The followers of Abram bestowed that country's name on him, after they settled there. One who is black with sunburn.

HAOMA. Food; food for sacrament. Also spiritual food; unseen food. The unseen sustenance that passes from one to another; improperly called magnetism.

HELL. Anarchy in heaven, especially in hada, the lowest heaven, where angels torment one another. When an earthly tyrant dies, evil spirits seize his newborn spirit for vengeance's sake, and cast him into hell.

HIROM. A Zarathustrian hat; a hat red with blood; a rimless hat. Renowned by Habbak, a Faithist, who was cast into a den of lions. The hat was afterward recovered. The master in the lodge wears the hat, during which time he is saluted as cardinal, or Hi-rom, which is the Ahamic word for red hat.

IESU. A sexless person; one without the possibility of sexual passion. Some men, as Brahma, attain to iesu. Improperly called Iesus. The Hebraic word ieue was made from iesu; one who can hear the voice of the Great Spirit. Ieue has been improperly confounded with Jehovih. Men who attain iesu are said to have attained the state of woman, i.e., to have changed sex.

I'HINS. The race born of a'su and angels; the half-breeds, from whom we are the descendants.

I'HUAN. Half-breed between I'hins and druks. The copper-colored race.

I'HUA'MAZDA. God of Zarathustra. See BOOK OF GOD'S WORD.

ISAAH, or **ISAIAH.** I'sa'ah, a Chinese prophet. The word Isaiah is of modern Hebrew. Most likely the ancient Phoenicians disguised the Chinese name purposely. IS, faith, A', knowledge, AH, above the earth; a prophet. Is'aac is Faithist in something above the earth; Is'ra'al, faith in Jehovih. A pass-word in the fourth degree of a lodge of prophets. RA, however, in Hebrew, is evil.

JEHOVIH. One who can hear Jehovih's voice is Ieue or Iesu. Some scholars have (erroneously?) used the words Jehovih, Elohim and Ieue as synonymous.

Ji'ay. Pertaining to nebulae, but less dense. See tablet Se'moin, BOOK OF SAPHAH.

Judas. From the Persian name Zhoo'da, or Zhoo'das. Betrayer of Zarathustra. See BOOK OF GOD'S WORD.

Kingdom. Synonymous with jov, or an organic association with a head. The head on earth is king, in heaven, jovs, or God, or Jove, or Joss.

Kosmon era. Kosmon, universal knowledge, corpor and spirit. Universal fellowship in all nations.

Leotonas. Pharaoh's daughter, Moses' protectoress.

Loo'is. Angels who provide the pre-natal condition for such mortal births as are designed for especial work by the Gods or Lords. Synonymous with masters of generations; next in rank to Lords. Their smallest organization is one hundred thousand members. Next rank above ashars.

Lord. A God of the earth, or of part of the earth; next lower in rank than the God of heaven and earth. The first exalted rank an angel receives in heaven, is asaph; the second is ashar, the third loo'is, the fourth marshal, the fifth Lord, and the sixth God. Marshals are rather vice-Lords and are not titled. The first title is Lord, the second God. God sometimes appoints a Lord to a single city on earth; sometimes one to a nation. A Lord's minor dominion is one hundred million angels, and a major, several thousand millions. Lords must have passed beyond the second resurrection before eligibility.

Lord God. An angel that fulfills both offices.

Lord-self, or **False Lords.** As the name implies. (Any angel that announces himself to mortals as an officer in heaven, is false.)

Lusters. Angels who maintain sex in the es world by proximity to mortals. Nocturnal visitors for secret vice. (The cause of the evil habit in men, and also the producers of harlots amongst women.)

Moses. A basket baby; a "come by chance." See full history of Moses in the BOOK OF THE ARC OF BON.

Nubulae. A dense atmosphere of corporeal substance.

Nirvana. Emancipated; etherean heavens; beyond the earth's heavens; the higher heavens.

Oahspe. Sky, earth (corpor) and spirit. The all; the sum of corporeal and spiritual knowledge as at present.

Orian, Orian. Same as nirvana (nirvania).

Ormazd. OR, light; MAZD, master. Master Light; equivalent to Jehovih.

Osire, Osiris. Philosophy of measurement. One who maintains that only what can be measured or weighed is real knowledge. The sun is the largest, therefore, the SUN IS THE ALMIGHTIEST. Also a God. See BOOK OF OSIRIS. There was also a false God Osiris of latter date who inspired the building of the pyramids.

PAN. Original name of the earth, from AH; as, I see what I see; and, only what I see, is. (The name of a continent in the Pacific Ocean, submerged about 24,000 years ago.) See BOOK OF APH, the flood.

SACRIFICE. Worship; to give one's time, or property, or money, without an equivalent. Also to burn or destroy, for appeasing the Gods.

SATAN. The chief of the seven Hebrew tetracts. Reckoned the worst of all the human passions; a leader; the captain of the selfish passions; the real self; selfishness, per se, see BOOK OF GOD'S WORD.

SAR'GIS, SARGIS. Both, a materialized angel, or a person in whose presence the angels can take on the semblance of mortal forms.

SE'MU. Gelatin, the preceding substance of the living.

SE'MUAN AGE. Before the creation of animal life, or at the beginning of that time. See BOOK OF JEHOVIH.

SHEM. One of the ancient names of India. See submersion of Pan, BOOK OF APH, and THE LORDS' FIRST BOOK.

SHEPHERD KINGS. A nick-name to a wandering tribe who kept flocks of goats, in the south-west of Persia. They also migrated into Egypt, and became powerful. At first, they were mild and non-resistant, but afterward, they became savage warriors. Such of them as did not apostatize, but kept themselves holy, separated from the others, and became the founders of Ebra, which afterward became Hebrew, which afterward became Jew, from whom Abram was descended. These were, therefore, the cream of the ancient Zarathustrians of three thousand years before.

SHIRL. Spirit, a breath; and sometimes angel.

SPIRIT. Synonymous (but not correctly) with angel. (When we say, water, we may not mean the ocean; but when we say, ocean, we mean water. When we say, angel, we do mean a spirit; but when we say, spirit, we may not mean an angel.)

SU'IS, SUIS. Clairaudience and clairvoyance. A person who can see with the eyes closed, or one who can hear angel voices. Not imaginary, but that which can be proved by experiment.

TAU. Bull, force; opposite from cow, which is receptivity. A time of the zodiac, when nature enforces growth. In some countries, the church representative is a white bull; in others, as the Roman catholic, the pope issues a bull merely as an edict.

YESHUA. A heavenly kingdom. Yeshua is the original of iesu and ieue, and Joshua.

YU'TIV. Brahma's wife. "A stream of light pierced their graves, and brought them forth, and they ascended to heaven in a sea of fire!"

THE PUBLISHER'S SYNOPSIS AND INDEX
OF
OAHSPE, THE NEW BIBLE.

LIBERTY FIRST OF ALL; THEN DISCIPLINE AND HARMONY
AND THEN THE DEVELOPMENT OF ALL THE TALENTS JEHOVIH CREATED WITH ALL.

This is a book of books, namely:

bible of Moses; the original song of Moses; bible of Capilya; bible of Chine of China; Chine's death and resurrection from a field of ashes; his appearance after his resurrection; why the land was named after him; the reign of peace in China; how it became called the Flowery Kingdom; triumph of the Faithists; how and why Lika appointed the Faithists (Israelites) to go westward whilst their brethern held China and India to the All One.

God's Book of Ben. Page 720. The eight entities and Jehovih; science, philosophy, metaphysics, etc, etc.; the etherean Gods' re-appearance.

Book of Cosmogony and Prophecy. Page 751. The plans of the corporeal worlds; overthrow of the doctrine of attraction of gravitation; no force existing or extending from one planet to another; neither light nor heat comes from the sun to the earth; the atmospherean vortices; the solar vortex; the great serpent (phalanx); defection of man's measurements of heavenly bodies; defections of the observations; magnifying power of vortices; cause of the photospheres, polar lights, velocities, electricity, magnetism, life, growth; meteors, nebula, clouds, wind and wind currents; ocean currents; how to regulate the temperature of the earth by man; how to bring rain showers; cause of tornadoes, waterspouts; famines, epidemics, and how to prophesy by astronomical knowledge.

Book of Saphah. Page 791. Philology; origin of languages; how to prove them as to origin, duration, and kind of people who spoke them; hieroglyphs, and how to read them; tracing of language down from Panic, through Yi'ha, Chinese, Vedic, Sanskrit, Hebrew, and so on down to English; how to find what an English word would be in Panic; thorax words and their era; labial words and their era; nasal words and their era; how to determine what the language of the future will be; how to find original bibles; how to find the speech of an extinct race.

Bon's Book of Praise. Page 876. Somewhat in the style of Psalms of David, but relating mostly to the heavens of the earth and to etherea.

God's Book of Eskra. Page 893. A spiritual history from the time of Moses down to the discovery of America; also a history of the heavens of the earth for the same period of time; descriptions of the heavens of the Brahmins, of the Buddhists, of the Christians and of the Mohammedans, with rules and signs for determining the same.

Book of E's, Daughter of Jehovih. Page 983. A sacred history of man since the last four hundred years down to the present, and for some time in the future. The above books give an account of the lower heavens, or spirit world, during the same periods of time. They describe the first, second and third resurrections in atmospherea; tell what the angels do, how they live, give their training and discipline; describe wandering spirits, familiar spirits, vampire spirits, demon spirits, engrafting spirits who live on mortals, teaching re-incarnation; spirit powers over mortals; chaotic spirits on battle-fields; lost spirits in haunted houses; obsessions, entrancement, spirit manifestations, how to get them; how to determine what realm a spirit belongs to, and who he is; how spirits deceive mortals; how selfish spirits in the lower heavens make slaves of their dupes after death and entrance into heaven; how to acquire prophecy and seer-ship; the delusion of the magnetic sleep; of spirit control; how to know the nature of spiritual communications; how mortals are graded by the Gods, and their status known in heaven; how nations fall; why cities are burnt down; how spirits can cast pestilence and contagious diseases; how the offspring of mortals are controlled; how any one may determine into what realm of heaven he will

12

enter after death; how to determine the time of his bondage and of his emancipation; how to determine the place in heaven where a king or queen will go; where a rich man will go; the length of the time of bondage of any of them in the lower heavens; how any one may discover his own grade, as to where he will go; how they work themselves out of bondage in the lowest heavens; the necessity of purifying ourselves in flesh and in thoughts before we are companionable to pure angels; rites and ceremonies; discipline and communities in heaven; ships in the higher heavens that carry thousands of millions of angels in the etherean seas, and on excursions of thousands of years; the great firmament, etherea, filled with thousands of millions of etherean worlds, habitable within and without; the labors of Gods and Goddesses; the insignificance of earth and its heavens, atmospherea; what is meant by higher and lower heavens; how mortals can attain to receive communications from the first resurrection, from the second resurrection and from the third, and even from Gods and Goddesses; what is purification; how to purity one's self, in flesh, and in spirit; how to know when a spirit communication is from the second resurrection or from the first; how to raise children; the coming race; the cosmopolitan, in the words of God; who is God; who is Lord; what is liberty, and how to attain it. The false Kriste inspireth the destruction of the Quakers. Cotton Mather. Angels of the inquisitions; how appropriated by the Lord. The republic established. Of Thomas Paine, inspired by God. Washington protected by the angels of God. God casteth out the four false Gods. Jehovih judgeth the false Gods. Of the Mormons, Shakers, Swedenborgians. President Lincoln directed by the angels of Jehovih to liberate the slaves.

~~~~~~~~~~~~~~~~~~~~~~~~~

God said: "I come not, in this day, to teach man charity, nor yet to teach man as to what is right and wrong between men; these things were revealed before. I come to produce a new race, and show them how to fulfill the former commandments: to do unto others as they would be done by; to return good for evil; to give away all and fear not. Before, these things were preached; behold, I come now to put them in practice. By this shall man know who are the chosen of Jehovih. They have said: 'Thy kingdom come on earth, as it is in heaven!" Who are ready? Let them come, the Light of Jehovih is on hand. Beware of those that longer preach and pray for these things, but practice them not; they profane the name of the ALMIGHTY!"

INDEX OF PRINCIPAL PLATES.

OAHSPE.

1. After the creation of man, the Creator, Jehovih, said unto him: That thou shalt know thou art the work of My hand, I have given thee capacity for knowledge, power and dominion. This was the first era.

2. But man was helpless, crawling on his belly, and he understood not the voice of the Almighty. And Jehovih called his angels, who were older than the earth, and he said unto them: Go ye, raise man upright, and teach him to understand.

3. And the angels of heaven descended to the earth and raised man upright. And man wandered about on the earth. This was the second era.

4. Jehovih said to the angels that were with man: Behold, man hath multiplied on the earth. Bring ye them together; teach them to dwell in cities and nations.

5. And the angels of Jehovih taught the peoples of the earth to dwell together in cities and nations. This was the third era.

6. And in that same time the Beast (self) rose up before man and spake to him, saying: Possess thou whatsoever thou wilt, for all things are thine, and are good for thee.

7. And man obeyed the Beast; and war came into the world. This was the fourth era.

8. And man was sick at heart, and he called out to the Beast, saying: Thou saidst: Possess thyself of all things, for they are good for thee. Now, behold, war and death have encompassed me about on all sides. I pray thee, therefore, teach me peace!

9. But the Beast said: Think not I am come to send peace on the earth; I come not to send peace, but a sword. I come to set man at variance against his father; and a daughter against her mother. Whatsoever thou findest to eat, be it fish or flesh, eat thou thereof, taking no thought of tomorrow.

10. And man ate fish and flesh, becoming carnivorous, and darkness came upon him, and he no more heard the voice of Jehovih, or believed in Him. This was the fifth era.

11. And the Beast divided itself into four great heads, and possessed the earth about; and man fell down and worshipped them.

12. And the names of the heads of the Beast were BRAHAMIN, BUDDHIST, CHRISTIAN and MOHAMMEDAN. And they divided the earth, and apportioned it between themselves, choosing soldiers and standing armies for the maintenance of their earthly aggrandizement.

13. And the Brahmins had seven million soldiers; the Buddhists twenty millions; the Christians seven millions; and the Mohammedans two millions, whose trade was killing man. And man, in service of the Beast, gave one-sixth of his life and his labor to war and standing armies; and one-third of his life he gave to dissipation and drunkenness. This was the sixth era.

14. Jehovih called out to man to desist from evil; but man heard Him not. For the cunning of the Beast had changed man's flesh, so that his soul was hid as if in a cloud, and he loved sin.

15. Jehovih called unto His angels in heaven, saying: Go ye down to the earth once more, to man, whom I created to inhabit the earth and enjoy it, and say ye to man: Thus saith Jehovih:

16. Behold, the seventh era is at hand. Thy Creator commandeth thy change from a carnivorous man of contention to an herbivorous man of peace. The four heads of the Beast shall be put away; and war shall be no more on the earth.

17. Thy armies shall be disbanded. And, from this time forth, whosoever desireth not to war, thou shall not impress; for it is the commandment of thy Creator.

18. Neither shalt thou have any God, nor Lord, nor Savior, but only thy Creator, Jehovih! Him only shalt thou worship henceforth forever. I am sufficient unto Mine own creations.

19. And to as many as separate themselves from the dominion of the Beast, making these covenants unto Me, have I given the foundation of My kingdom on earth.

20. And all such shall be My chosen: By their covenants and by their works shall they be known henceforth on the earth as Mine, and shall be called FAITHISTS.

21. But to as many as will not make these covenants, have I given the numbers of the Beast, and they shall be called UZIANS, signifying destroyers. And these shall be henceforth the two kinds of people on earth, FAITHISTS and UZIANS.

22. And the angels of heaven descended to the earth, to man, and appeared before him face to face, hundreds of thousands of them, speaking as man speaketh, and writing as man writeth, teaching these things of Jehovih and His works.

23. And in the thirty-third year thereof, the Embassadors of the angel hosts of heaven prepared and revealed unto man in the name of Jehovih, His heavenly kingdoms; and have thus herein made known the plan of his delightful creations, for the resurrection of the peoples of the earth.

24. Not immaculate in this BOOK, OAHSPE; but to teach mortals HOW TO ATTAIN TO HEAR THE CREATOR'S VOICE, and to SEE HIS HEAVENS, in full consciousness, whilst still living on the earth; and to know of a truth the place and condition awaiting them after death.

25. Neither are, nor were, the revelations within this OAHSPE wholly new to mortals. The same things have been revealed at the same time unto many, who live at remote distances from one another, but who were not in correspondence till afterward.

26. Because this light is thus comprehensive, embracing corporeal and spiritual things, it is called the beginning of the KOSMON ERA. And because it relates to earth, sky and spirit, it is called OAHSPE.

THE VOICE OF MAN.

1. O Jehovih, what am I that I should supplicate Thee? Know I mine own weakness, or understand I the way of my thoughts? Thou hast placed before me most wonderful creations: They impress me, and my senses rise up in remembrance of the Almighty. Wherein have I invented one thought but by looking upon Thy works? How can I otherwise than remember my Creator, and out of Thy creations, O Jehovih, find rich food for meditation all the days of my life.

2. And yet, though I have appropriated the earth unto myself, I am not happy nor perfect withal. Misery and crime and selfishness are upon my people.

3. What is my weakness that I cannot overcome it? Or what is my strength that I succumb to the desires of the earth? I build up my belief and courage in Thee; but ere I know the way of my weakness, I stumble and fall. Am I made that I shall be forever a reproof to

myself, and a censure to my own behavior?

4. How shall I say to this man or that: Be thou pure and holy, O man! Are not my flesh and blood proof that man cannot be without sin? O this corruptible self, this tendency to fall from the right way! Thou, O my Creator, hast proven before my senses every day of my life, that Thou alone art mighty in purity and truth.

5. O that I had a starting point wherefrom to estimate Thy wonderful decrees, or could find a road in which I should never stumble! But yet, O Jehovih, I will not complain because of the way of Thy works. Thou hast invented a limit to my understanding, whereby I am reminded of Thee, to call upon Thy name. I perceive my own vanity; that whereas were knowledge mine, I should become less beholding unto Thee!

6. What am I, O Jehovih, without Thee; or wherein shall I find the glory of Thy creations but by the light of Thy countenance? Thou broughtest me forth out of sin and darkness and clothed me in light. I behold the smallness of myself in Thy great works. Thou hast bound me to travel on the earth, to sojourn with beasts and all manner of creeping things; nor given me one attribute wherein I can boast over them, save in the power of destruction. The high firmament placed Thou above me; the stars and moon and sun! I know Thou hast been thither, but I am bound down in a little corner of Thy works! I have not power to rise up to Thy distant places, nor to know Thy extended heavens.

7. Nay, I have not power to shape my own size and stature; but all things take form and dimension whether I will or no. In Thine own way are built the walls of the world; by their magnitude am I confounded; by the majesty of Thy hand appalled. Why have I vainly set up myself as the highest of Thy works? My failures are worse than any other living creature under the sun. I cannot build my house in perfection like a bird's; my ingenuity cannot fashion a spider's net; I cannot sail up in the air like a bird, nor live in the water like the fish, nor dwell in harmony like the bee. The half of my offspring die in infancy; the multitude of my household are quarrelers, fighters, drunkards and beggars; the best of my sons and daughters are less faithful than a dog! I go forth to war, to slay my brother, even whilst Thy wide earth hath room for all. Yea, I accurse the earth with starvation and sin and untimely death. O that I could school myself to boast not of my greatness; that I should be forever ashamed in Thy sight, Jehovih!

8. But I will make a clean breast of my iniquities; I can hide nothing from the eye of my Creator. Hear me then, O Father!

9. I took up arms against my brother. With great armies I encompassed him about to despoil him.

10. His widows and orphans I multiplied by the stroke of my sword; the cry of anguish that came out of their mouths I answered by the destruction of my brother's harvests.

11. To my captains and generals who showed great skill in killing, I built monuments in stone and iron. Yea, I inscribed them from top to bottom with their bloody victories.

12. And in my vanity I called out to the young, saying: Behold the glory of great men! These great monuments I have built to them!

13. And the youth of my household were whetted with ambition for spoil. The example of my hand made them train themselves for warfare.

14. To my colonels and generals I gave badges of gold. I called to the damsels, saying: Come, a great honor I give to you; ye shall dance with the officers of death!

15. And they tripped up on tip-toe, elated by the honey of my words! O Jehovih, how

have I not covered up my wickedness; how have I failed to make the flow of my brother's blood the relish of satan!

16. To my destroying hosts I have given great honor and glory. In the pretense of enforcing peace I hewed my way in flesh and blood.

17. I made an igneous fatuous, a kingdom. I called out to my people, saying: We must have a kingdom. I showed them no reason for it; but I bade them take up arms and follow me for patriotism's sake. And yet what was patriotism? Behold, I made it as something greater than Thee and Thy commandment: "THOU SHALT NOT KILL".

18. Yea, by the cunning of my words, I taught them my brother was my enemy; that to fall upon him and his people and destroy them was great patriotism.

19. And they ran at the sound of my voice, for my glory in the greatness of my kingdom, and they accomplished great havoc.

20. Yea, I built colleges for training my young men in warfare. I drew a boundary hither and thither, saying: This is my kingdom! All others are my enemies!

21. I patted my young men on the head, saying: Ye dogs of war! Great shall be your glory!

22. And their judgment was turned away from peace; I made them think that righteousness was to stand up for me and my country, and to destroy my brother and his people.

23. They built me forts and castles and arsenals without number. I called unto my people, saying: Come, behold the glory of my defenses which I built for you!

24. And they gave me money and garrisons, and ships of war, and torpedoes, shouting: Hurrah for our kingdom! We have faith in these things, but not in Thee, our Creator!

25. Thus I led them away from Thee. Their eyes I turned down in the way of death. By the might of my armies, I put away righteousness.

26. I covered the earth over with drunkards, and widows and orphans; to beggary I reduced them, but I whetted their pride by saying: Behold what great standing armies we have!

27. To the man that said: There shall come a time of peace, when war shall be no more forever, I mocked and said: Thou fool!

28. I know the counts against me, O Father. I cannot hide my iniquity from Thy sight. I have said war was a necessary evil to prevent a too populous world! I turned my back toward the wide, unsettled regions of the earth. With this falsehood in my mouth I stood up before Thee! Yea, I cried out as if for the righteous, saying: I war for righteousness, and for the protection of the weak! In the destruction of my brethren I stood as a murderer, pleading this excuse. Stubbornly I persisted in not seeing justice on the other side, whilst I cut down whom Thou hadst created alive. Above the works of Thy hand I raised myself up as a pruning knife in Thy vineyard.

29. Yea, more than this, I persuaded my sons and daughters that to war for me was to war for our Father in heaven. By my blasphemy led I them into ruin. And when the battle was over for a day I cried out: Behold the glory of them that were slain for the honor of their country! Thus have I added crime to crime before Thee, Jehovih; thus destroyed Thy beautiful creation. Verily, have I not one word in justification of my deeds before Thee!

30. O that I had remained faithful with Thee, Jehovih! But I invented Gods unto the glory of the evil one. In one place I called out to my sons and daughters,

saying: Be ye Brahmins; Brahma saveth whosoever professeth his name. In another place I said: Be ye Buddhists; Buddha saveth whosoever calleth on his name. In another place I said: Be ye Christians; Christ saveth whosoever calleth on his name. In another place I said: Be ye Mohammedans; whosoever saith: There is but one God and Mohammed is his prophet! shall have indulgence without sin.

31. Thus have I divided the earth, O Jehovih! Into four great idolatries have I founded them, and into their hands put all manner of weapons of destruction; and they are become more terrible against one another than are the beasts of the forest. O that I could put away these great iniquities which I raised up as everlasting torments to the earth. Verily, there is no salvation in any of these.

32. Their people are forever destroying one another. They quarrel and kill for their respective religions; setting aside Thy commandment, Thou shalt not kill. They love their own nation and hate all others. They set aside Thy commandment, Love thy neighbor as thyself.

33. They preach and pray in sufficient truth; but not one of these people practiceth peace, love and virtue in any degree commensurate with their understanding. These religions have not saved from sin any nation or city on the whole earth.

34. In vain have I searched for a plan of redemption; a plan that would make the earth a paradise, and the life of man a glory unto Thee, and a joy unto himself. But alas, the two extremes, riches and poverty, have made the prospect of a millennium a thing of mockery.

35. For one man that is rich there are a thousand poor, and their interests are an interminable conflict with one another. Labor crieth out in pain; but capital smiteth him with a heartless blow.

36. Nation is against nation; king against king; merchant against merchant; consumer against producer; yea, man against man, in all things upon the earth.

37. Because the state is rotten, the politician feedeth thereon; because society is rotten, the lawyer and court have riches and sumptuous feasts; because the flesh of my people is rotten, the physician findeth a harvest of comfort.

38. Now, O Jehovih, I come to Thee! Thou holdest the secret of peace and harmony and good will amongst mortals. Give me of Thy light, O Father! Show me the way of proceeding, that war and crime and poverty may come to an end. Open Thou the way of peace and love and virtue and truth, that Thy children may rejoice in their lives, and glorify Thee and Thy works forever.

39. Such is the voice of man, O Jehovih! In all the nations of the earth this voice riseth up to Thee! As Thou spakest to Zarathustra, and to Abraham and Moses, leading them forth out of darkness, O speak Thou, Jehovih!

40. Man hath faith in Thee only; Thou alone wast sufficient in the olden time: Today, Thou alone art sufficient unto Thine own creation. Speak Thou, O Jehovih !

BOOK OF JEHOVIH.

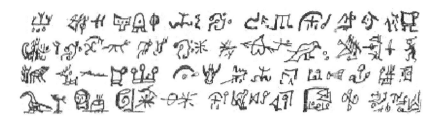

CHAPTER I.

1. ALL was. ALL is. ALL ever shall be. The ALL spake, and MOTION was, and is, and ever shall be; and, being positive, was called He and Him. The ALL MOTION was His speech.

2. He said, I AM! And He comprehended all things, the seen and the unseen. Nor is there aught in all the universe but what is part of Him.

3. He said, I am the soul of all; and the all that is seen is of My person and My body.

4. By virtue of My presence all things are. By virtue of My presence is life. By virtue of My presence are the living brought forth into life. I am the QUICKENER, the MOVER, the CREATOR, the DESTROYER. I am FIRST and LAST.

5. Of two apparent entities am I, nevertheless I AM BUT ONE. These entities are the UNSEEN, which is POTENT, and the SEEN, which is of itself IMPOTENT, and called CORPOR.

6. With these two entities, in likeness thereby of Myself, made I all the living; for as the life is the potent part, so is the corporeal part the impotent part.

7. Chief over all that live on the earth I made Man; male and female made I them. And that man might distinguish Me, I commanded him to give Me a name; by virtue of my presence commanded I him. And man named Me not after anything in heaven or on the earth. In obedience to My will named he Me after the sounds the wind uttereth, and he said E - O - Ih ! Which is now pronounced Jehovih, and is written thus:

CHAPTER II.

1. Jehovih said: By virtue of My presence created I the seen and the unseen worlds. And I commanded man to name them; and man called the seen worlds Corpor, and the unseen worlds Es; and the inhabitants of Corpor, man called corporeans. But the inhabitants of Es he called sometimes es'eans and sometimes spirits, and sometimes angels.

2. Jehovih said: I created the earth, and fashioned it, and placed it in the firmament; and by My presence brought man forth a living being. A corporeal body gave I him that he might learn corporeal things; and death I made that he might rise in the firmament and inherit My ethean worlds.

3. To es I gave dominion over corpor; with es I filled all place in the firmament. But

corpor I made into earths and moons and stars and suns; beyond number made I them, and I caused them to float in the places I allotted to them.

4. Es I divided into two parts, and I commanded man to name them, and he called one etherea and the other atmospherea. These are the three kinds of worlds I created; but I gave different densities to atmospherean worlds, and different densities to the etherean worlds.

5. For the substance of My etherean worlds I created Ethe, the MOST RARIFIED. Out of ethe made I them. And I made ethe the most subtle of all created things, and gave to it power and place, not only by itself, but also power to penetrate and exist within all things, even in the midst of the corporeal worlds. And to ethe gave I dominion over both atmospherea and corpor.

6. In the ALL HIGHEST places created I the etherean worlds, and I fashioned them of all shapes and sizes, similar to My corporeal worlds. But I made the etherean worlds inhabitable both within and without, with entrances and exits, in arches and curves, thousands of miles high and wide, and overruled I them with ALL PERFECT mechanism; and in colors and movable chasms and mountains in endless change and brilliancy. To them I gave motions, and orbits and courses of their own; independent made I them, and above all other worlds in potency and majesty.

7. Neither created I one etherean world like another in size or density or in component parts, but everyone differing from another, and with a glory matchless each in its way.

8. Atmospherean worlds I also created in the firmament, and I gave them places and orbits and courses for themselves. But atmospherean worlds I created shapeless and void of fixed form, for they are in process of condensation or dissolution, being intermediate in condition betwixt My etherean and My corporeal worlds. Of three degrees of density created I them, and I commanded man to name them, and one he called A'ji, and one Ji'ay, and one Nebulae.

9. But all of them are composed of the same substances, being like the earth, but rarified. Nor is there on the earth or in it one thing, even iron, or lead, or gold, or water, or oil, or stones, but the same things are in My atmospherean worlds. As I have given light to the earth so have I given light to many of them; and all such have I commanded man to call comets. And even so named he them.

10. And I also created atmospherea around about my corporeal worlds; together made I them.

CHAPTER III.

1. Thus spake Jehovih; by the light of kosmon proclaimed He these things amongst the nations of the earth.

2. Man looked upward in prayer, desiring to know the manner of all created things, both on earth and in heaven. And Jehovih answered him, saying:

3. The whirlwind made I as a sign to man of the manner of my created worlds. As thou beholdest the power of the whirlwind gathering up the dust of the earth and driving it together, know that even so do I bring together the a'ji and ji'ay and nebulae in the firmament of heaven; by the power of the whirlwind create I the corporeal suns and moons and stars. And I commanded man to name the whirlwinds in the etherean

firmament, and he called them vortices and wark; according to their shape called he them.

4. By the power of rotation, swift driving forth in the extreme parts, condense I the atmospherean worlds that float in the firmament; and these become My corporeal worlds. In the midst of the vortices made I them, and by the power of the vortices I turn them on their axes and carry them in the orbits I allotted to them. Wider than to the moons of a planet have I created the vortices, and they carry the moons also.

5. Around about some of My corporeal worlds have I given nebulous belts and rings, that man might comprehend the rotation of My vortexan worlds.

6. For each and every corporeal world created I a vortex first, and by its rotation and by the places in the firmament whither it traveleth, caused I the vortex to conceive the corporeal world.

7. A great vortex created I for the sun, and, within this vortex and subject to it, made I the vortices of many of the corporeal worlds. The sun vortex I caused to rotate, and I gave it power to carry other vortices within it. According to their density and position are they thus carried forth and around about the sun.

8. Think not, O man, that I created the sky a barren waste, and void of use. Even as man in the corporeal form is adapted to the corporeal earth, so is he in the spiritual form adapted to My ethereal worlds. Three great estates have I bestowed on man: the corporeal, the atmospherean, and the ethereal.

CHAPTER IV.

1. Man perceived the general formation of the world, and he prayed that his eyes might be opened for a sign in heaven; and Jehovih answered him, saying:

2. The clouds in the air I bring into view suddenly; by different currents of wind make I thus the unseen visible and tangible to man's senses. In like manner do I cause ethereal currents to bring forth a'ji and ji'ay, and nebulae, prior to making corporeal worlds.

3. In all the universe have I made the unseen to rule over the seen. Let the formation of the clouds stand in the view of man on earth, that he may bear witness to the manner of the unseen becoming seen.

4. Man perceived, and he prayed for a sign of duration, and Jehovih answered him, saying:

5. Behold the tree which hath sprung up out of the ground and fulfilled its time; it falleth and rotteth, and returneth to the earth. But lo, the wind, which thou seest not, never ceaseth to blow. Even so is the comparative duration of all things. Think not, O man, that corporeal things are annihilated because they disappear; for as a drop of water evaporateth and riseth in the air as unseen vapor, so do all corporeal things, even earth, and stones, and gold, and silver, and lead, become as nothing in the firmament of heaven in course of time.

6. Things that man seeth, created I with a beginning and an end; but the unseen I made of endless duration.

7. The corporeal man made I belonging to the seen; but the spiritual man made I as one within the unseen, and everlasting.

8. As the corporeal man beholdeth corporeal things, so doth the spiritual man follow upward the evaporated, corporeal entities of things. As corporeal things are tangible to

corporeans, so are es things tangible to the spirits of the dead.

9. As I cause water to rise upward as vapor, and take a place in the air above, let it be a sign and testimony of other places in atmospherea whereon dwell the spirits of the lower heaven.

10. As I made a limit to the ascent of the clouds, so made I a limit to the places of the different kinds of substances in atmospherea; the more subtle and potent to the extreme, and the more dense and impotent nearer to the earth.

11. According to the condition of these different plateaux in atmospherea, whether they be near the earth or high above, so shall the spirit of man take its place in the first heaven; according to his diet and desires and behavior so shall he dwell in spirit on the plateau to which he hath adapted himself during his earth life.

12. For I made the power of attraction manifest in all things before man's eyes that he might not err, that like should attract like made I them.

13. Man sought to know the progress of things. Jehovih answered him, saying:

14. Open thy eyes, O man ! There is a time of childhood, a time of genesis, a time of old age, and a time of death to all men. Even so is it with all the corporeal worlds I have created.

15. First as vapor the vortex carrieth it forth, and as it condenseth, its friction engendereth heat, and it is molten, becoming as a globe of fire in heaven. Then it taketh its place as a new born world, and I set it in the orbit prepared for it.

16. In the next age I bring it into se'mu, for it is ripe for the bringing forth of living creatures; and I bestow the vegetable and animal kingdoms.

17. Next it entereth ho'tu, for it is past the age of begetting, even as the living who are in dotage. Next it entereth a'du, and nothing can generate upon it. Then cometh uz, and it is spirited away into unseen realms. Thus create I, and thus dissipate planets, suns, moons and stars.

18. My examples are before all men. My witnesses are without number. I rise the tree up out of the ground; I give it a time to bring forth fruit; and then barrenness, and then death and dissolution. I prepare the new field with rich soil, bringing forth; and the old field that is exhausted, and man shall weigh the progress and destiny of a whole world.

19. Let no man marvel because of the size of the mammoth and the ichthyosaurus, for there was a time for them as there is a time for the infusoria of this day.

20. I have given thee a sign, O man, in the queen of the honey bee; because of the change of the cell cometh she forth a queen, even from the same manner of germ as the other bees. Be wise, therefore, and remember that the earth is not in the place of the firmament as of old. Let this be a testimony to thee of the growth, the change and the travail of the earth.

21. Nevertheless, O man, the seen and the unseen are but parts of My person; I am the Unity of the whole.

CHAPTER V.

1. Man perceived the magnitude and glory of the corporeal worlds. He said, How shall I speak of Thy great works, O Jehovih, and of Thy wisdom and power! Shall I open my mouth before Thee! I look upon Thy countless stars, suns and moons, spread out over the

heavens! The millions of years Thou hast rolled them on in the never-ending firmament! Processions in and out, and round about, of mighty worlds! By Thy breath going forth!

2. O Thou, All Highest! How shall I hide my insignificance! I cannot create the smallest thing alive! Nay, nor change the color of a hair on my head. What am I, that Thou has seen me?

3. Tell me, O my Creator, whence came life? This unseen within me that is conscious of being? Tell me how all the living came into life.

4. Jehovih heard the words of man and He answered him saying: Let a sign be given to man that he may comprehend se'mu. Thereupon Jehovih caused the jelly fish and the green scum of water to be permanently coming forth in all ages, that man might understand the age of se'mu, when the earth and the shores by the water, and the waters also, were covered over with commingled atmosphere and corporeal substance. And this substance was called se'mu, because by Jehovih's presence quickened He it into life, and thus made He all the living, both the vegetable and animal worlds. Not that se'mu is jelly-fish or the green scum of water; for the earth in this day produceth not se'mu abundantly; nevertheless the jelly-fish and the green scum of water are signs of that which was in that day of the earth.

5. Jehovih said: Because of My presence quickened I into life all that live, or ever have lived.

6. Because I am male and female, even in my likeness, thus made I them. Because I am the power to quicken into life, so, in likeness of Me thus, made I them, and with power to bring forth.

7. According to their respective places created I the living; not in pairs only, but in hundreds of pairs and thousands, and in millions.

8. According to their respective places and the light upon se'mu, so quickened I them in their color, adapted to their dwelling places.

9. Each and every living thing created I new upon the earth, of a kind each to itself; and not one living thing created I out of another.

10. Let a sign be upon the earth, that man in his darkness may not believe that one animal changeth and becometh another.

11. Thereupon Jehovih gave permission for different animals to bring forth a new living animal, which should be unlike either its mother or father, but he caused the new product to be barren.

12. Jehovih said: And this shall be testimony before all men that I created each and all the living, after their own kind only.

13. Such is My person and My spirit, being from everlasting to everlasting; and when I bring a new world into the time of se'mu, lo and behold my presence quickeneth the substance into life; according to the locality and the surroundings, so do I bring forth the different species; for they are flesh of My flesh and spirit of My spirit. To themselves give I themselves; nevertheless, they are all members of My Person.

14. As a testimony to man, behold the earth was once a globe of liquid fire! Nor was there any seed thereon. But in due season I rained down se'mu on the earth; and by virtue of my presence quickened I into life all the living. Without seed created I the life that is in them.

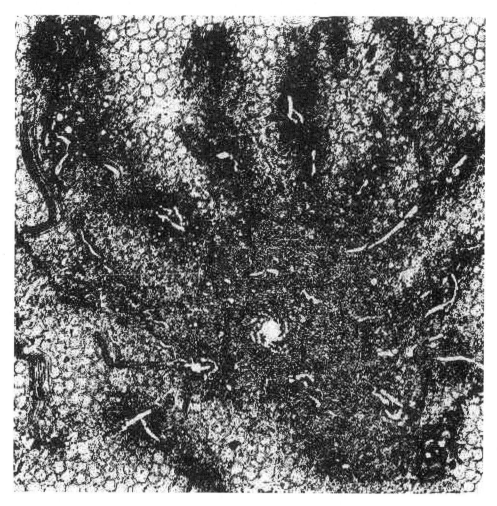

Plate 6. SE'MUAN FIRMAMENT.

Jehovih said : Behold, I caused all the living creatures to gestate in darkness. And this shall be testimony to the end of the world, that, when I created life on the face of the earth, she traveled in My se'muan firmament.

CHAPTER VI.

1. When man comprehended the earth he looked upward; and Jehovih saw him and knew the desires of his soul. So Jehovih sent his son Uz, and Uz spake, saying:

2. Hear me, O man; the mysteries of heaven and earth will I clear up before thy judgment. Thou art the highest, and comest to the chiefest of all kingdoms; from Great Jehovih shalt thou learn wisdom, and none shall gainsay thee.

3. Bethink thee, O man, of the magnitude of Thy Father's kingdoms and His places in the firmament. Save I take thee up to the heaven, thou canst not comprehend the places thereof.

4. Man then rose up in spirit and ascended into the firmament, for his spirit had crystallized into separateness; and Uz and Es ascended with him, speaking in the voice of the Father. And man beheld that each and everything in the firmament was orderly, and

26

still each to itself located. Then spake Es, saying:

5. Behold, O man! As a farmer soweth corn in one place, and wheat in another, and roots in another, and flax--everything in a separate place; even so doth Jehovih store the ingredients of which worlds are made--everything in its place--the substance of the iron in one place, the substance of the stones in another, the substance of the vegetable kingdom in another, and even so of the substance of the animal kingdom; and the oils and sand; for He hath places in the firmament of heaven for all of them. These that thou sawest are the a'ji and the ji'ay and the nebulae; and amidst them in places there is se'mu also. Let no man say: Yonder is hydrogen only, and yonder oxygen only. The divisions of the substances of His creations are not as man would make them. All the elements are to be found not only in places near at hand, but in distant places also.

6. When the Father driveth forth His worlds in the heavens, they gather a sufficiency of all things. So also cometh it to pass that when a corporeal world is yet new and young it is carried forth, not by random, but purposely, in the regions suited to it. Hence there is a time for se'mu, a time for falling nebulae, to bury deep the forests and se'muan beds, to provide coal and manure for a time thereafter. So is there a time when the earth passeth a region in the firmament when sand and oil are rained upon it and covered up, and gases bound and sealed up for the coming generations of men.

7. And man said: I am ashamed in Thy sight, O Jehovih! I looked upward and said, Behold the sky, it is nothing! Then I said: It is true, the corporeal worlds are made of condensed nebulae; but I saw not the wisdom and glory of Thy works. I locked Thee up in coincidences and happenings. Thy unseen world hath become seen; the unreal hath become the real.

8. O that I had been mindful of Thee! O that I had not put Thee afar, nor imagined laws and decrees. Teach Thou me, O Jehovih! How was the beginning of man? How was it with the first of the living that Thou broughtest forth?

9. Jehovih said: Have I not declared Myself in the past; in My works have I not provided thousands of years in advance? As I have shown system in the corporeal worlds, know thou, O man, that system prevaileth in the firmament.

10. To the tree I gave life; to man I gave life and spirit also. And the spirit I made was separate from the corporeal life.

11. Out of se'mu I made man, and man was but as a tree, but dwelling in ha'k; and I called him Asu (Adam).

12. I looked over the wide heavens that I had made, and I saw countless millions of spirits of the dead that had lived and died on other corporeal worlds before the earth was made.

13. I spake in the firmament, and My voice reached to the uttermost places. And there came in answer to the sounds of My voice, myriads of angels from the roadway in heaven, where the earth traveleth. I said to them, Behold! A new world have I created; come ye and enjoy it. Yea, ye shall learn from it how it was with other worlds in ages past.

14. There alighted upon the new earth millions of angels from heaven; but many of them had never fulfilled a corporeal life, having died in infancy, and these angels comprehended not procreation nor corporeal life.

15. And I said, go and deliver Asu from darkness, for he shall also rise in spirit to inherit my etherean worlds.

16. And now was the earth in the latter days of se'mu, and the angels could readily take on corporeal bodies for themselves; out of the elements of the earth clothed they themselves, by force of their wills, with flesh and bones. By the side of the Asuans took they on corporeal forms.

17. And I said: Go ye forth and partake of all that is on the earth; but partake ye not of the tree of life, lest in that labor ye become procreators and as if dead to the heavens whence ye came.

18. But those who had never learned corporeal things, being imperfect in wisdom, comprehended not Jehovih's words, and they dwelt with the Asuans, and were tempted, and partook of the fruit of the tree of life; and lo and behold they saw their own nakedness. And there was born of the first race (Asu) a new race called man; and Jehovih took the earth out of the travail of se'mu and the angels gave up their corporeal bodies.

19. Jehovih said: Because ye have raised up those that shall be joint heirs in heaven, ye shall tread the earth with your feet, and walk by the sides of the new born, being guardian angels over them, for they are of your own flesh and kin.

20. Fruit of your seed have I quickened with my spirit, and man shall come forth with a birth-right to My etherean worlds.

21. As I have quickened the seed of the first born, so will I quicken all seed to the end of the earth. And each and every man-child and woman-child born into life will I quicken with a new spirit, which shall proceed out of Me at the time of conception. Neither will I give to any spirit of the higher or lower heaven power to enter a womb, or a fetus of a womb, and be born again.

22. As the corporeal earth passeth away, so shall pass away the first race Asu; but as I pass not away, so shall not pass away the spirit of man.

CHAPTER VII.

1. Jehovih said: Let a sign be given to the inhabitants of the earth that they may comprehend dan'ha in the firmament of heaven. For even as I bequeathed to the earth a time for creating the living, and a time for angels to come and partake of the first fruits of mortality and immortality, so shall man at certain times and season receive testimony from My hosts in heaven.

2. And Jehovih caused the earth, and the family of the sun to travel in an orbit, the circuit of which requireth of them four million seven hundred thousand years. And he placed in the line of the orbit, at distances of three thousand years, etherean lights, the which places, as the earth passeth through, angels from the second heaven come into its corporeal presence. As embassadors they come, in companies of hundreds and thousands and tens of thousands, and these are called the etherean hosts of the Most High.

3. Not as single individuals come they; not for a single individual mortal come they.

4. And Jehovih gave this sign to man on earth; which is to say: In the beginning of the light of dan'ha, the spirits of the newly dead shall have power to take upon themselves the semblance of corporeal bodies, and appear and talk face to face with mortals. Every three thousand years gave Jehovih this sign on earth, that those who learned the powers and capacities of such familiar spirits, might bear testimony in regard to the origin of man on earth.

Jehovih said: And when it shall come to pass in any of the times of dan'ha that these signs are manifest, man shall know that the hosts of the Most High come soon after. Let him who will become wise, enumerate the great lights of My serpent, for in such times I set aside things that are old, and establish My chosen anew.

5. In the time of earth, when man was brought forth from mortal to immortal life, the earth passed beyond se'mu and the angels of heaven remained with corporeal man, but not in the semblance of mortals, but as spirits; and by virtue of their presence, strove to make man wise and upright before Jehovih. Upon the earth the number of such angels was millions. To these angels spake Jehovih saying:

6. Behold the work ye have taken in hand! It was commanded to you all, to partake of all the fruits of the earth save of the fruit of the tree of life, which is of the knowledge of the earth and heaven, lest ye lose your inheritance in etherea.

7. Behold, ye now have sons and daughters on the earth; by your love to them are ye become bound spirits of the lower heaven. Until ye redeem them in wisdom and power even to the sixth generation ye shall not again arise and inherit My emancipated heavens.

8. To which end ye shall be co-workers with one another in system and order. In My name shall ye become an organic body and known as the heaven of the earth, or lower heaven, which shall travel with the earth.

9. And I will allot unto you a Chief, who is wise in experience in founding heavenly kingdoms; and he shall appoint, from amongst you, officers, and messengers, and ashars, and asaphs, and es'enaurs and ye shall be numbered and apportioned unto your labor and places like unto My other lower heavens on other worlds.

10. And he who is Chief shall be called God of this heaven and the earth, unto his making bestow I them.

11. And God shall have a Council and throne within his heavenly city; and the place shall be called Hored, because it is the first kingdom of God in this firmament.

12. And God shall rule on his throne, for it is his; and his Council shall rule with him; in My name shall they have dominion over angels and mortals belonging to the earth.

13. And God shall appoint Chiefs under him who shall go down and dwell on the earth with mortals; and such Chiefs' labor shall be with mortals for their resurrection. And these Chiefs shall be called Lords, for they are Gods of land, which is the lowest rank of My commissioned Gods.

14. And God and his Lords shall have dominion from two hundred years to a thousand or more years; but never more than three thousand years. According to the regions of dan (light) into which I bring the earth, so shall be the terms of the office of My Gods and My Lords.

15. And God and his Lords shall raise up officers to be their successors; by him and them shall they be appointed and crowned in My name.

16. At the termination of the dominion of My God and his Lords they shall gather together in these, My bound heavens, all such angels as have been prepared in wisdom and strength for resurrection to My etherean kingdoms. And these angels shall be called Brides and Bridegrooms to Jehovih, for they are Mine and in My service.

17. And to God and his Lords, with the Brides and Bridegrooms, will I send down from etherea ships in the time of dan; by My etherean Gods and Goddesses shall the ships descend to these heavens, and receive God and His Lords with the Brides and

Bridegrooms, and carry them up to the exalted regions I have prepared for them.

18. And all such as ascend shall be called a Harvest unto Me, through My God and Lords. And the time of My Harvests shall be according to each dan, which is two hundred years, four hundred years, six hundred years, and five hundred years; and these shall be called My lesser cycles because they are the times of the tables of prophecy which I give unto My servants.

19. But at no other times, nor in any other way, shall My Harvests ascend to My emancipated worlds in etherea. Seven dans have I created for each and every dan'ha; and six generations of mortals have I given unto each dan.

20. The angels understood the commandments of Jehovih according to their knowledge in the etherean heavens; being heirs of other planets, and having died in infancy, and having matured in the es worlds; but they understood not the Creator according to the practice of the lower heavenly kingdoms. Wherefore their knowledge was incomplete.

21. Jehovih said: I condemn ye not because ye have become joint procreators with the asuans; for ye have done two services unto Me; which are to teach yourselves corporeal things, that ye may understand and sympathize with corporeans, and, secondly, because ye have caused the earth to become peopled with such as are capable of immortality.

22. Behold ye now what shall happen on the earth: such as are of your flesh and kin who cohabit together shall rise in wisdom and virtue; but such of them as cohabit with the asuans will bring forth heirs in the descending grade of life. The first shall bring forth heirs unto everlasting life; but the second shall bring forth heirs that shall go out in darkness.

23. In the dominion of which matters your God and Lords will instruct you, that ye may, by inspiration and otherwise, learn to control the behavior of mortals unto everlasting life. And that these labors be not too severe upon you, I created the dans and dan'has in the firmament, wherein ye may be relieved from the watch by other angels from other worlds coming to exchange with you.

24. This also do I put upon you: That to rule over mortals to virtue, by your own wills governing them in all things, is contrary to my commandments. For what honor hath any man if made to do a thing?

25. But ye shall give mortals of My light, leaving them to choose. Better is it for them suffer some than to grow up in ignorance of the stings of disobedience.

26. Behold, I make this a willing service on your part: because ye have bound your affections on the earth, to your own kin, ye willingly become guardian angels over mortals. Yet I made not a separate law unto you; as it is with you, so shall it be with the spirits of these mortals when they are born into the es world: They will also desire to become guardian angels over their mortal kin.

27. But these spirits, never having known My higher heavens, will be unsuitable for the office of ashars; they would be but the blind leading the blind.

28. To prevent which, God and the Lords shall provide these spirits in the first resurrection with places to dwell in; and with occupations and opportunities for education. For I desire them not to remain bound to the earth, but to rise up and inherit My etherean kingdoms.

29. And in this also shall ye be discreet in governing them, giving them the light of My heavens with some liberty to choose and to perfect themselves. Otherwise they would

only be slaves in heaven. According to their weakness or strength, so shall ye provide for these new spirits entering my es world.

30. Therefore such of you as are appointed by My God and My Lords as guardians over mortals shall be called ASHARS, and ye shall report to your respective Lords, according to the section of the earth where ye may be. Of many watches shall be the ashars.

31. And such of you as are appointed to receive the spirits of the dead into heaven shall be called ASAPHS, and ye shall report to your respective Lords and their kingdoms.

32. And the ashars shall make a record of every mortal, of the grade of his wisdom and good works; and when a mortal dieth, and his spirit is delivered to the asaphs, the record shall be delivered with him; and the asaph, receiving, shall deliver such spirit, with the record into such place in these heavens as is adapted to his grade, where he shall be put to labor and to school, according to the place of the resurrections which I created.

33. As ye shall thus become organic in heaven, with rulers, and teachers, and physicians; and with capitals, and cities, and provinces; and with hospitals, and nurseries, and schools, and factories, even so shall ye ultimately inspire man on the earth to the same things.

34. And mortals that are raised up to dominion over mortals shall be called kings and emperors. As My Gods and My Lords are called My Sons, so shall kings and emperors be called sons of God; through him shall they be raised up to their places, and given dominion unto My glory.

CHAPTER VIII.

1. Jehovih said: And God shall cause a record to be kept in heaven, of his dominions and his Lords. And he and they shall enjoin it upon their successors forever to keep a like record.

2. And in the times of my harvest a copy of these records shall be taken up to My etherean kingdoms and filed with My Orian Chiefs and Archangels in the roadway of the travel of the great serpent, for their deliberations as to the progress and management of the inhabitants of the earth and her heavens.

3. Think not, O ye angels, that the resurrection of your heirs, and their descendants that come up out of the earth, is an easy matter and of steady progress, devoid of mishaps and woeful darkness.

4. The angels under you shall become at times rebellious and defiant; disregarding your laws and decrees; and they shall desert your heavenly places and go down to the earth in millions and hundreds of millions. And they shall drive away the ashars, and then assume guardianship over mortals. But they shall develop no righteousness under the sun, but they will inspire mortals to war and destruction. And these angels will themselves take to war and evil on every hand within the place of your heavens.

5. With the foul gases of atmospherea shall they make weapons of war and places of torment. With these elements shall they make suffocating hells in order to cast one another in chaos.

6. And mortals who shall be slain in war shall be born in spirit in chaos on the battlefields; in chaos shall such spirits enter the es world. And they shall not know that they are dead, (as to earth life), but shall still keep fighting right and left.

7. And enemy shall take enemy, in these heavens, and cast them in the places of torment which they have built, and they shall not know peace nor wisdom.

8. And the work of your heavens shall become as nothing. And ye shall turn to, going about delivering hells and the spirits in chaos. And your labor shall be exhaustive; verily shall you cry out because ye came and peopled the earth.

9. This also have I created possible unto My creations; for both angels and mortals shall learn to know the elements of the heavens and the earth, and to know the trials of love and misfortune.

10. Nor have I made wisdom possible unto any man or angel that knoweth not My elements, and the extremes of evil and good which I created.

11. But in the times of great darkness which shall come upon earth and these heavens, lo, I will bring the earth into dan'ha; and my ethereans shall come in my name and deliver them.

12. And again for another cycle shall they be left with the lessons given unto them; but they shall fall again in course of time. But again will I deliver them; through my Gods and Goddesses will I cause them to comprehend the magnitude of My creations.

13. As ye travel from heaven to heaven in this atmospherea, even so shall ye inspire mortals to build corporeal ships, and sail across the oceans, that the inhabitants of different divisions of the earth may become known to one another.

14. And when the inhabitation of the earth shall be completed, and the nations shall have established civil communion around from east to west, in that same time will I bring the earth into the kosmon era, and My angel Embassadors, Gods and Goddesses, shall render up the records of these heavenly kingdoms.

15. Through them will I reveal unto mortals the creation of My worlds, and the history and dominion of My Gods and Lords on the earth, even from this day down to the time of kosmon.

16. And Jehovih caused the angels of atmospherea to assemble together and organize the first kingdom of of the heaven of the earth. And the place was called Hored, because it was the place of the first organic abiding place for the first God of this world.

17. And Hored was situated over and above the mountains of Aotan in Ughoqui, to the eastward of Ul, of that country hereinafter called the continent of Pan.

18. Thus endeth the inorganic habitation of the earth and her atmospherea.

END OF THE BOOK OF JEHOVIH.

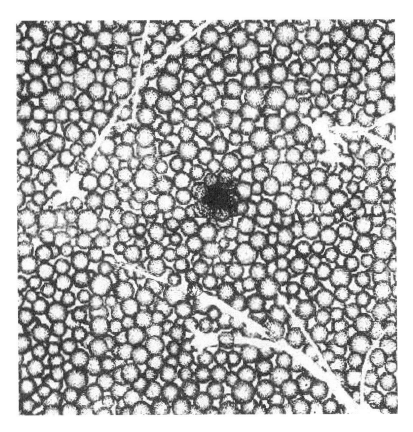

Plate 7. X'SAR'JIS,

or end of the se'muan age, that is, the time of the termination of creating animal life. Jehovih said: Behold, I quickened the earth with living creatures; by My breath came forth all the living on the face of the earth and in the waters thereof, and in the air above the earth. And I took the earth out of the dark regions, and brought her into the light of My ethereal worlds. And I commanded the living to bring forth, by cohabitation, every specie after its own kind. And man was more dumb and helpless than any other living creature. Jehovih spake to the angels that dwelt in His ethereal worlds, saying: Behold, I have created a new world, like unto the places where ye were quickened into life; come ye and enjoy it, and raise man upright and give him words of speech. For these will also be angels in time to come. (See Book of Jehovih, CHAPTER VI, verses 12, 13, 14, page 27)

BOOK OF SETHANTES, SON OF JEHOVIH.

FIRST GOD OF THE FIRST CYCLE OF THE EARTH AFTER MAN'S CREATION.

CHAPTER I.

1. In the beginning of the inhabitation of the earth, the angels of heaven assembled in Hored, a heavenly plateau resting on the earth.

2. And the archangel Sethantes was the wisest of them all, and he said unto them:

3. Behold, we have come from far-off heavens; by the voice of Jehovih came we to partake of the glory of the red star, the earth. Jehovih said unto us: Come ye and enjoy the new world I have created. Partake ye of all the fruits thereof, save of the tree of knowledge, which is the fountain of life. Partake ye not of this, lest ye die.

4. But the voice of the earth spake unto us, saying: Partake ye, for indeed Mine is the tree of everlasting life.

5. And many obeyed not the voice of the Father, and are now bound by the tie of life, which is in the blood.

6. And the voice of Jehovih came to me, saying: Sethantes, My son, behold, I gave into thy charge in My etherean heavens millions of angels, and thou has brought them to the earth, and they are fallen from their high estate. Go thou, deliver them.

7. And I said: What shall I do? And Jehovih said: Bring thy angel hosts to Hored, for there will I crown thee God of these heavens and earth for the redemption of angels and mortals. And it shall be a new heavenly kingdom from this time forth to the end of the world. For it is the time of the arc of Wan, and I will bring from etherea My high-raised Goddess, Etisyai, chief factor of Harmuts, and she shall crown thee in My name, GOD OF HEAVEN AND EARTH.

8. God said: When I had thus spoken in Hored before the angels of heaven, a great light, like a sun, was seen descending from the firmament above. And I commanded my es'enaurs to chant in praise of the Father and His works.

9. Meanwhile I had the angels of Hored numbered, and there were of them twenty-seven millions and six hundred thousand, and these were the same who were on an excursion in my charge when the voice of Jehovih commanded us to visit the earth.

10. The light above us descended fast toward us, like a ship of fire it came nearer and nearer, till we saw that it was wider far, than the place of Hored and all my angel hosts.

11. And it came to pass that when the great light had descended to the plateau of Hored there came forth out of the light one million archangels, from the arc of Wan in the Hosts of A'ji, in the orbit of Fow'sang in etherea, and they bore regalia and crowns from the Orian chief of Harmuts. Foremost of the archangels was Etisyai, and her brother Ya'tiahaga, commissioners from the etherean heaven.

12. When they came near me, Etisyai gave the sign of Jehovih's name, greeting, halting, and saying: All hail! In Jehovih's name, and in the love of Harmuts, Orian chief, we come to greet thee, first God of the lower heaven, belonging to the corporeal earth!

13. I said: All hail, O emissaries of Harmuts, Chief of Orian worlds! Come, O Etisyai, and thy brother and all this host! Come honor My throne, in Great Jehovih's name!

14. The archangels then came forward, saluting, and Etisyai said: In Thy name, O

34

Jehovih, I found here a throne!

15. And she caused to rise the form and substance thereof, and she ascended thereon, and Ya'tiahaga with her. And the other archangels formed a crescent in front of the throne, all of them bearing crowns or diadems, but they stood upright. And now the angels of the host of God took their places, that they might witness the testimony of Jehovih's commission, but the lights from the columns of fire, brilliant in all colors and shades and tints, baffled many of them from seeing plainly.

16. When all things were in readiness Etisyai, standing erect and brilliant like a star, raised her right hand, saying: JEHOVIH! ALL-WISE AND POWERFUL! IN THY NAME, THIS THY SON, GOD, I CROWN! FROM THE ORIAN CHIEF, HARMUTS, RAISED TO THE RANK OF GOD, AND BY THEE, O JEHOVIH, ORDAINED! HENCEFORTH TO BE KNOWN FOREVER IN THE EMANCIPATED HEAVENS AS THY SON ! PEACE! WISDOM! LOVE! POWER!

17. And now with her left hand she raised high the crown, so that all might see and bear witness, and giving the sign again of Jehovih's name above the crown, wherefrom a flame of light shot forth brilliantly. Thereupon she placed the crown on God's head, saying:

18. ARISE, O MY SON, THOU SON OF JEHOVIH! Instantly there arose from the millions of souls one universal shout: All hail, O Son of Jehovih! And God rose up, having the crown on his head, and the people cheered him lustily, for he was well beloved.

19. Etisyai said: Bring forth thy five chief Lords that I may crown them also. God then caused the five chief Lords whom he had selected to sit at the foot of the throne.

20. Again Etisyai raised her right hand, saying: O JEHOVIH! ALMIGHTY! FROM WHOM ALL GLORIES EMANATE! IN THY NAME, THESE THY SONS, I CROWN LORDS OF THE EARTH, AND OF THE WATERS OF THE EARTH! FROM THE ORIAN CHIEF HARMUTS! BY MY COMMISION DO I RAISE THEM TO THE RANK OF LORDS FOR KINGDOMS OF HEAVEN! PEACE! WISDOM! LOVE! POWER!

21. Then Etisyai took the crowns, which were handed her by the other archangels, and placed them on the heads of the Lords, saying:

22. ARISE, O MY LORDS, AND BE YE LORDS OF JEHOVIH FOR HIS GLORY! AND BE YE THE LORDS OF GOD, HAVING DOMINION OVER THE EARTH AND THE WATERS OF THE EARTH, IN LOVE, WISDOM AND POWER, AMEN!

23. The Lords rose up, having on their heads the crowns of Lords, and again the multitude saluted with great cheering. When the applause ceased Etisyai said:

24. My God and My Lords, give now the sign of Jehovih's name that His glory may be fulfilled. (For this was the oath of office.) (The sign is the circle twice cut. For further information see Emethachavah, Book of Saphah.)

25. And God and the Lords saluted Jehovih before the hosts of heaven. And they stood apart a little distance, and Etisyai said:

26. Behold the All Light, Jehovih, encompasseth me. My voice shall be His voice. By the glory of Faith in Him am I One with the Father.

27. And a fleece of golden hue descended from above and encompassed Etisyai around about, and she was like a central star with rays of light emanating. She was entranced by Jehovih. Through her the Creator spake, saying:

28. My Son, even God, I brought thee forth out of corpor, quickened into life everlasting. By faith I inspired thee to do whatsoever thou hast done. Faith gave I unto thee, as the tree whereon ALL PERFECTION is the fruit. By that faith within man that nurtureth the

I Am within Himself unto perfection, becometh he My son, doing by virtue of My presence. According to thy wisdom and love have I given thee strength; and by thy strength raised thee up.

29. Behold, this day have I given thee a kingdom in atmospherea, and made thee God before all the kingdoms of heaven. This place shall be thy place and Mine also. Here shalt thou dispense wisdom and laws, and appoint officers in My name and by virtue of My power.

30. And thy kingdom shall be like two kingdoms: One here with the hosts of heaven, and one on the earth, even over these thy Lords. For thou art the judgment seat and Creator of order over the whole earth, and in the heaven belonging to the earth.

31. Stretch forth thy hand, My Son, and clothe thyself in the golden fleece.

32. God made the sign, and then raised his hands upward, saying: Jehovih! Jehovih! By thy command I call upon Thee to array me in Thy golden fleece! Behold I am Thy Son.

33. And the archangels tossed up the raiment and regalia they had brought from their etherean arc in a'ji, and, by the faith that was in God, the substance flew to him and encompassed him around in raiment of the upper heaven.

34. Then Jehovih spake to the Lords, saying: As God hath built a kingdom in Hored, and reigneth over this heaven, and over ye and your helpmates, so shall ye build kingdoms on the earth, and ye shall rule over mortals in My name, teaching them of Me and My everlasting kingdoms in the firmament above. In testimony of my voice receive ye this raiment of silver and gold from My archangels.

35. The archangels then draped the Lords in shining raiment. And Etisyai came down from the throne, still entranced, saying:

36. Though, My Daughter Etisyai will rise up in the flame of fire, yet will I, even Jehovih, abide with thee, O God, and with ye My Lords, now and forever! And then Etisyai took God's hand and led him to the center of the throne, saying: Sit thou on this throne for it is thy Father's kingdom in the lower heaven of the earth!

37. When God sat down, the entrancement departed from Etisyai, and the Light of Jehovih went and settled upon God and the Lords. But Etisyai sat down at the foot of the throne, and thereupon all the archangels sat down also.

38. God said: Behold, she that is greatest maketh herself least of all. Arise, O Daughter of Jehovih, and enjoy my kingdom, for it is Jehovih's also. And God came down from the judgment seat and took Etisyai's hand and she rose up, whereupon God proclaimed the freedom of the hour. Thus was established the first throne of God in these heavens. And now all of the hosts mingled together, angels and archangels, joyfully.

CHAPTER II.

1. When the hour was ended, God again ascended the throne, and the marshals raised the signals of order, and the archangels went and stood in a crescent in front of the throne. Etisyai sat at the feet of God, and the splendor of her glory, unadorned, save with white and yellow drapery, shone through all the talents Jehovih had given her, the perfection of purity, wisdom, and love, the like of which only Gods had looked on!

2. God said: In Thy name, O Jehovih, do I now found the session of Thy kingdom in the lower heaven. As long as man and woman shall bring forth heirs unto Thee,

this kingdom shall not cease to glorify Thee. Let the Lords approach the throne.

3. The es'enaurs now sang, and in the meantime the marshals and escorts conducted the Lords before the throne. When they were in order, the music ceased, and God said:

4. Five great divisions of the earth there are, and I have ordained ye the five Lords thereof in Jehovih's name. According to the number of inhabitants on the earth's divisions, and your relative rank before heaven have I placed you. When ye have seated yourselves in your respective kingdoms, ye shall have each twelve messengers, whose duties shall be betwixt ye and me. Choose ye, therefore, your messengers, even this hour, that ere the resurrection of the archangels they may be confirmed and their registry borne to heaven above.

5. The Lords chose their messengers, and they were confirmed in the name of Jehovih, and the swift messengers, who ply with the upper heavens, made a record of their names and places. Thereupon God said to them:

6. According to your talents have you been chosen; according to your excellence will ye be promoted to wider fields of labor. May the wisdom. love and power of Jehovih be with you all, amen!

7. And now Etisyai signified that her time of departure had arrived.

8. God came down from the judgment seat, and standing one moment in sorrow, reached forth and took Etisyai's hand, saying:

9. Arise, O Daughter of Jehovih, and go thy way!

10. Etisyai rose up, pointing upward, said: My house is in the arc of Wan. Jehovih dwelleth with thee and me! My swift messengers shall come to thee at times. My love will abide with thee and thy Lords, and the harvest of thy resurrection. In Jehovih's name, farewell!

11. Etisyai then walked to the ship of fire; but ere she entered, she turned and took one more look at the hosts of Hored, and, then stripping from the frames, luminous drapery, cast it playfully over the en'enaurs, and quickly disappeared in the light.

12. The es'enaurs chanted, and the hosts of archangels joined in with them, and in that same moment of time the ship began to rise, and it was as thousands of columns of fire surrounding one majestic column, and the whole circle rising in spiral form, turning and rising, rising and turning. And when it was a little way up it seemed like an ascending sun; and then higher and higher, like a far-off star, and then it passed beyond the vision of the angels of Hored.

13. When order was proclaimed, the All Light began to gather around about the throne, covering over God and the Lords. Jehovih, through God, said:

14. Hear ye, for I abide also with these My Lords of the hosts of heaven.

15. The Lords said: What shall we do? And Jehovih answered: Summon all the angels to pass before the throne of God, one by one, that I may judge them. For as many as dwelt on any of My corporeal worlds of the fifth of the second rate shall abide in the kingdom of Hored, and their labor shall be with es'yans only; but all of the full of the first rate shall abide in the kingdoms of My Lords, and their labor shall be with corporeans.

16. The marshals then arranged the angels and they passed in front of the throne, and so great was God's wisdom that, in looking on the angels as they passed, he perceived the rates of every man and woman. And those destined for labor in atmospherea only, he caused to turn one way, and those for the earth, as ministering spirits with mortals, to turn

the other way; and when they had all passed, they were correctly divided according to Jehovih's commandment.

17. God said: Hear me, O ye Lords! Take your laborers and repair to your respective places on the divisions of the earth, and the waters of the earth. And ye shall be Lords with me, your God, for the glory of Jehovih. Whatsoever ye do on the earth will I ratify in heaven; whomsoever ye deliver from the earth will I receive in heaven. As ye shape and build up mortal man, delivering his spirit into my kingdom, so will I receive him and award him.

18. That your kingdoms may accord with me and Mine, I give you messengers sufficient, and they shall pass daily betwixt us: According to their proficiency and power to pass from place to place, so have I chosen them.

19. Let a record be kept within your own kingdoms, and these records shall be your own, to be carried upward with you in the next resurrection.

20. And yet, ye shall have a record jointly with me, separate from your own record, pertaining to your kingdom's relations with mine.

21. When mortals die and are born in spirit, ye shall receive them and enter them in your records as es'yans, signifying new born in heaven. And for these es'yans ye shall provide temporary abodes, where they shall tarry, some for a few days, and some for the space of one year or more. Of their numbers and conditions ye shall inform me, through the messengers, and I will send ships to bring them to My kingdom.

22. Ye shall appoint asaphs, whose office it shall be to receive es'yans from the ashars.

23. Whilst a mortal is alive on the earth, the ashars shall abide with him, guarding him in the name of the Lord, and in My name. But when he dieth the ashar shall deliver the es'yan to the asaph, saying: In Jehovih's name receive thou this new born spirit. He was My protégé; for the good or evil in him, charge thou to Me. And the ashar shall deliver up a record of the mortal life of the es'yan, and the record shall be kept within your own kingdoms.

24. And the asaph shall take the es'yan, saying: In Jehovih's name, receive I this new born spirit. He shall be my protégé according to the commandments of the Lord my God. He shall then take the es'yan to the place to receive it, where it will have nurses and attendants according to its requirements.

25. When ships come to your kingdoms, the asaphs shall deliver all the es'yans they have received, and My officer shall receive them, and bring them to My place in heaven.

26. When God had ended the instructions to the Lords, the Lords answered, saying: We will be thy Lords, O God, doing thy commandments, for the glory of Jehovih, our Father.

27. God said: To each of you have I given a great division of the earth, and each division shall be named after you, each in its place.

28. This, then, was the rank assigned: Waga (Pan); Jud (Asia); Thouri (America); Vohu (Africa); and Dis (Europe). And the lands were called after the names of the Lords and so entered in the books of heaven in Hored, by command of God in the name of Jehovih.

29. And the record of the Great Serpent showed the firmament of Tem'yi in the third circuit of c'v'wark'um and dan'ha twenty-four.

30. When all was finished the Lords went and sat down at the foot of the throne, and the es'enaurs chanted a hymn of praise to Jehovih and the entire multitude jointed therein.

31. When the hymn was ended, God rose up, standing amidst a sea of light, and raising up

38

both hands, said: O Jehovih! Almighty and everlasting! Help Thy servants in founding this Thy Kingdom for Thy glory! Peace, Wisdom and Power!

32. Then making the sign of Jehovih's name with his right hand, he came down to the foot of the throne, and taking the hand of Waga: Lord of Waga, he said: Arise, my son, and go thy way; and Jehovih will bless thee.

33. Waga rose up and stood aside, and then in like manner God raised the other four Lords and they stood aside also.

34. The marshals filed past the throne saluting, and after them the Lords, saluting also; and after them came the asaphs, and lastly the ashars; and the procession was under way, passing off between the pillars of fire with which God's laborers had ornamented Hored around about.

35. This was the beginning of the first kingdom in the lower heaven, and the first of the reign of the Lords on earth.

CHAPTER III.

1. And God appointed in heaven angel surveyors, to survey the earth and atmospherea; and astronomers, to note the place of the stars; and enumerators, to number the inhabitants of the earth and atmospherea, to grade them and apportion their places; and nurses and physicians, to receive the es'yans and administer unto them; and builders of heavenly mansions; and weavers of fabrics for covering the newborn, the es'yans; and builders of heavenly ships for carrying the inhabitants from place to place. And God appointed unto all of these, officers and teachers, according to grade appointed he them.

2. And when God had completed his appointments, the people were apportioned in heaven every one to his place, to begin the work allotted to them. And God called the asaphs, and he said unto them:

3. Go ye down to the earth, and bring to me the first fruit of the resurrection.

4. And the asaphs said: Thy will is our will, but what meanest thou by the first fruit of the first resurrection?

5. God said: The spirits of the dead. The asaphs said: The spirits of the dead. Who are they?

6. God said: When a corporean cometh forth out of his corporeal body, this shall be called DEATH.

7. The asaphs said: Who then are the spirits of death? And God answered them, saying: O ye that died in infancy, how can ye learn corporeal things! Go ye then to my Lord, Wagga, and he will show you.

8. The asaphs departed and went down to the earth, and the Lord, through the ashars, delivered unto the asaphs five hundred es'yans, and they brought them to Hored, before the throne of God. And God said unto them: Who are these?

9. The asaphs said: These are the first fruit of the first resurrection. Behold, we know now the beginning and the end of corporeality; the earth body of these es'yans was but a womb from which they are now delivered.

10. God said: Well done. Take ye these es'yans and feed and clothe them, for this is your labor.

11. The asaphs answered: Alas, we have tried them with all manner of food on which we

ourselves subsist, but they will not eat.

12. God said: Alas, O ye innocents! Ye feed on ethereal food; these es'yans must have atmospherean food, even as corporeans subsist on corporeal food. Go, then, fulfill this first resurrection; for as much as ye deliver them, so will ye be delivered in time to come.

13. The asaphs then departed, taking the es'yans with them. But in course of time they returned again to God, saying:

14. Behold, O God, we have gathered of the atmosphere of trees of all kinds, and of seeds and plants that grow on the earth, all most beautiful to our senses, and savory to the smell, and we gave these to the es'yans, but lo, they will not eat. Being alarmed, we again hastened to thee for information.

15. God said: O ye of little wisdom, knowing so much of heaven and so little of earth. Go ye back to the place whence ye brought these es'yans, and learn what manner of food they subsisted on.

16. The asaphs went back with all haste to learn in reference to the food. And in due time they came again before God, saluting, saying:

17. What shall we do, O God? Behold, these es'yans, whilst in the corporeal form feasted on fish and worms. How can we bring them the atmospherean part of these things?

18. God said: Even the last time ye were present ye said ye had gathered of the atmospherean part of trees, and seeds and plants growing out of the earth. Why, then, cannot ye gather of the atmospherean part of fish and worms?

19. The asaphs said: Alas, this difference have we observed: The trees, and plants and fruits emit delightful atmospheres, most nutritious to the spirit, but that which is emitted from the living fish and living worm is foul-smelling, being but the sweat and dead substance evaporating. What, then, shall we do?

20. God said: Go ye to the place where mortals kill fish and worms; and in the same time that mortals tear these things with their teeth, snatch from their hands and mouths the atmospherean parts of the food and give it to these es'yans. Remember, also, that little by little ye shall teach them to live on other kinds of food.

21. And as ye do by these es'yans, do ye also in after time to others, remembering that what men subsist on in corporeal life, is entailed on them in spirit for a space of time after entering atmospherea; and of like substance shall they be fed spiritually. The asaphs then departed.

22. On the third day thereafter, as above mentioned, the Voice of Jehovih came to God, saying:

23. My Son, behold what the asaphs have done in thy name thoughtlessly! They came to the fishery and did as thou badest, gathering food for the es'yans, and at their side stood the es'yans, saying: Why gather ye food for us? Behold, we are now strong in spirit; suffer us to gather for ourselves. And the asaphs said: It seemeth well; do as ye desire.

24. Thereupon, the es'yans went to the fishermen and fisherwomen, who were eating raw flesh, and the es'yans laid hold of the atmospherean part, and ate thereof a sufficiency. And then the asaphs said to them: Ye have feasted sufficiently; come ye away with us.

25. But lo, the es'yans engrafted themselves on the fishermen and fisherwomen, and would not depart. The asaphs, not knowing what to do, called on My name. Send thou, O God, quickly to them, those skilled in deliverance, that My es'yans be preserved unto everlasting life.

26. And God summoned those skilled in deliverance of engraftment, and dispatched them hastily with messengers to the place of the fisheries.

27. Jehovih said: From the trees, the fruits, the flowers, the grains and seeds, and roots that grow in the ground, have I created a ceaseless harvest going upward into the atmosphere, which shall be the sustenance of the spirits of men newborn in heaven. But whosoever feasteth on flesh on earth, shall not find spiritual food in heaven, but he shall return to the butcheries and eating-houses where flesh is eaten, and he shall feast on the atmospherean part thereof, before it is rotten. Be ye guarded of them, lest they engraft themselves on mortals, feasting on their feasts, and so go down to destruction.

28. After many days the asaphs came before God, saying: The physicians severed such as were bound, and we brought them away. Shall this be our labor day and night, to lead these es'yans about, finding them clothes and food? This have we observed, the more we do for them, the less they do for themselves.

29. Jehovih spake through God, saying: A nurse I provided for the newborn, but when he is grown I command him to provide for himself that he may be a glory in My kingdoms. By charity alone ye cannot raise man up; but be diligent to teach him to try continually to raise himself, for herein lieth the glory of manhood.

30. The asaphs said: If we leave the es'yans alone, they will return again to the fisheries and fasten themselves upon mortals, doing nothing but eating.

31. God said: Near the fisheries, but in atmospherea, go ye and fashion a colony, and it shall be your colony in heaven. Thither take these es'yans, not showing them the way of the fisheries. In the colony put ye them to work, weaving and making clothes and otherwise producing; but go ye for the food at the fisheries, and bring sufficient every day, giving only to them who labor, or to invalids and helpless ones. By this ye shall inspire them to labor, which is the foundation of the growth of the spirit; and in course of time they will not only care for themselves, but join ye in helping others, which is the beginning of the second resurrection.

32. Behold, this lesson have ye learned: that according to the diet and the habit of mortals on earth, so must ye provide their spirits when first entered in heaven.

33. Choose ye, therefore, of your own people a sufficient number to make all things required in a delightful colony, whether it be food and clothing, or nurseries, or hospitals, or place of worship, or place of dancing, and receive ye as many es'yans as may be delivered from the earth, raising them up in industry, virtue, wisdom, mirth, love, benevolence and adoration, and this shall be a new heaven unto you all.

34. Ye are My chosen, and an example colony of all the kingdoms I shall build in My heaven. The time cometh when the whole atmosphere around about the earth shall be filled with countless millions of angels born out of the earth.

35. Be swift in your labor; the people spring up from the earth rapidly into heaven, and every colony ye now found shall, in time to come, be a great kingdom, requiring experienced workmen. Whosoever laboreth most efficiently for Jehovih, him will I promote to wider fields.

36. Ye are as one of the corner-stones of Seffas, and his house shall embrace atmospherea and the whole earth. Words are already taking root in the mouths of mortals; and for tens of thousands of years will war reign; might against might; darkness against darkness. Hundreds of millions will be slain in wars on the earth, and their souls

be thrown into chaos. Even as ye beheld these spirits fastening on to mortals for food, so will spirits in chaos, millions of them, fasten themselves on the battlefields, still battling; or fasten themselves on mortals, obsessing them to madness and death.

CHAPTER IV.

1. So God established colonies in heaven for the reception of the spirits of mortals; and the colonies embraced the arts of healing, education, industry, drapery, manufactories, the building of ships, and all things required for the spirit, even as corporeal things are required by mortals.

2. And great labor came upon the hosts of God who founded these things, toiling day and night, receiving the es'yans and providing for them food and clothing. And many of the hosts of God lamented that they had come to the corporeal earth, and they framed songs and anthems of lamentation, and these they chanted even whilst at labor.

3. God was troubled that they should thus lament in the presence of the es'yans, and he called together the proper officers that he might rebuke them; but lo and behold, the light of Jehovih spake from the throne saying:

4. Rebuke them not, O My son. Did I not command them, saying: Behold I have created a new world; come ye and enjoy it, even the earth. And when they had come, said I not to them: Enjoy ye all the fruits of the earth, save the fruit of the tree of life, lest ye die. But corpor spake to them and they believed in corpor. Wherefore then shall they not lament? Do they not remember their former homes in etherea, and thus aspire to regain them?

5. But seek thou, O my Son, to make their lamentations a glory in the souls of the es'yans, that they may also aspire to a higher heaven.

6. The voice departed, and God perceiving the wisdom of Jehovih, commanded certain officers to collect many of the anthems and deposit them in the library of Hored, in heaven, and it was so done.

7. This, then, is after the manner of their lamentations, to wit:

8. Where is my home, O Jehovih! When I was happy and my feet wandered.

9. I dwelt with Thy hosts, afar! afar! Thy glory shining.

10. O the songs in Thy upraised kingdoms! when shall I rejoice in the music of my own house?

11. O those sparkling, running waters? O the pastimes and feasts of love!

12. Where is it, O Jehovih? It was my home in high heaven!

13. I fell, I fell in darkness! Wandering soul within me, that ledest me forth.

14. The gardens of Jehovih stood on every hand. O senseless feet to take me onward!

15. Into the darkness was I lured; sweet perfumes rose amidst the darkness.

16. Intricate in Thy glory, O Jehovih! I lost the way. I was lost!

17. The music of Thy spheres was shut out. I was environed in darkness!

18. Where is my home, O Jehovih? Why have I forsaken it?

19. Crystals, and high arches on every hand. Full, standing out, shining.

20. And the songs of my sweet loves! Such was my home and place of revelry!

21. I bartered them all away, wandering forth. Buried me in the opaque, in the dark!

22. O for my home in high heaven! Mirth, song, rest, and love, clear shining.

23. Thou, O Jehovih, hast given me sons and daughters. Out of this darkness my gems

were born!

24. O I will polish them up. Kin of my kin, I will raise them up!

25. Thy Goddesses in heaven above will come. In ships of fire descending!

26. My jewels shall enter and rise with me. We shall search for my home; the haven of rest!

27. I see Thee, O Jehovih, afar off. Higher than the highest of heavens!

28. O hasten, my home, and my rest! O ripen these, my precious diadems!

29. O take us to ethereal worlds.

30. But no one could repeat their numerous lamentations, for there were hundreds of thousands of them. And as the ethereans sang them, the es'yans, the new born, the atmosphereans, listened, longing listened, and looked upward.

CHAPTER V.

1. In the first year of Hored there were received into God's kingdom in heaven, one and a half million es'yans, men, women and children, born of the earth. And there were still left within the different divisions of the earth, with the Lords, three and a quarter millions of es'yans, being for the most part fetals.

2. In the first one hundred years there were born of the earth, one hundred and seventy million es'yans. Such then was the number of three generations of I'hins; which is to say, that in those days the number of the inhabitants of the earth (not including the asuans, who were not created to everlasting life) was fifty-four millions. And already had each of the Lords' heavenly places become large kingdoms.

3. In those days the period of five years was allotted to the es'yans as their time of infancy in heaven, requiring nurses and helpers, but some of them required many years more.

4. After five years the es'yans were taken from the nurseries, and taught by symbols and objects, the rudiments of education; and drilled in processions, and music and dancing and gymnastics; but every day they were required for a brief period to labor, some at weaving, some spinning, and some in transportation.

5. The voice of Jehovih directed God, saying: The structure of My Kingdom in heaven requireth it of thee, that thou shalt make all labor an agreeable exercise for the growth of the spirits in my dominions.

6. And God commanded the officers of the realm of Hored to lengthen the hours of labor, according to the age and strength of the spirits received up from the earth, and it was so.

7. Jehovih again spake to God, saying: In all labor thou allottest to those who have sprung up from the earth, freely give to them to do whatever they desire; but thou shalt not suffer them to return to their earth kindred alone, unattended, lest because of their love they engraft themselves, becoming bound to mortals. But when they have lived fifty years in heaven, thou shalt not only permit them to return to mortals, but thou shalt direct them to do so, for in this period they shall have no further desire for engraftment.

8. Again Jehovih said: As fast as thou canst appropriate the labor of earth born spirits to help in the resurrection of others, so shalt thou do in My name.

9. And even so did God and the Lords under him; and in the time of one hundred years, there were raised up to the second rate, twenty million souls, that had come forth out of the earth. And many of them comprehended the manufactories, the nurseries and schools

and hospitals in heaven to the full, and they were in many things alike equal to the requirements of their teachers.

10. The voice of Jehovih came to God, saying: It is well, My Son, to take a rest. Behold, thou hast toiled a hundred years, day and night, without ceasing. Thou shalt, therefore, appoint other officers, and spread out the kingdom of Hored to cover all the land of Wagga (the continent of Pan). And thou shalt appoint in My name thy most efficient officer to sit on the throne for a short space of time, for thou shalt travel and visit the five Lords of the earth and their kingdoms.

11. And thou shalt take with thee a thousand heralds, and a thousand messengers, and five thousand musicians. And thou shalt have a ship sufficient to carry thy host, and to be as thy house whithersoever thou goest. See to it, and set all things in order, and depart thou on a journey of one year.

12. And God called in the surveyors, who brought maps of earth and heaven showing the best places for extending the kingdom of Hored.

13. And God appointed fifty governors for the fifty places required, and he gave each of them five thousand men and women to accompany them. And when they were chosen God addressed them from the throne, saying:

14. According to the commandment of the Father are ye chosen; and by His command will I come to your respective places ere long, and bestow ye with all that is required for building up colonies in Jehovih's name. As ye witnessed the founding of Hored by the archangel Etisyai, so may ye understand that I will come to you all. Go ye forth, then, taking your hosts, and lay down the foundations for your cities. As ye have learned from me, go ye forth doing as I have done; and as ye do with a small colony, and a small city, so will I give into your keeping that which is greater when ye are prepared therefore.

15. When God ceased, the marshals led the way, and the hosts following their governors filed in front of the throne, saluting with the sign of Jehovih's name, which was answered by God's hands upraised. Meanwhile the es'enaurs sang in glory to Jehovih. Presently the hosts passed out and beyond the pillars of fire.

16. When all had quieted, God said: Let the builders of ships begin now and build a ship for me and my hosts, for the time draweth near. And let the graders choose from my laborers, who have toiled a hundred years, day and night, without ceasing, such as shall be my companions and hosts on my journey; according to their grade shall they be chosen.

17. And even so were they chosen and notified.

18. And God said: Whilst I shall be absent there shall sit on my throne, being God in my place, he who standeth highest in the grades. According to the transcendency of him who hath done the most for the resurrection of the es'yans, so shall be your God and my God.

19. And God commanded the graders to present before the throne the records, that the Council of Hored might determine the matter. And this was so done.

20. And Ha'jah, an etherean, was chosen. And God commanded them to send word unto Ha'jah, with an escort to conduct him to the capital.

21. In due time the escort brought Ha'jah into the palace of the kingdom of God, and God was sitting on the throne. With music they came in and filed in front of the throne, forming a crescent, with Ha'jah betwixt the horns.

22. God said: By command of Jehovih have I summoned thee thither, O Ha'jah. Long

before I have known thee, even on other worlds. Of all virtues in man which stand highest, which is, never to mention one's self, thou excellest all men in my kingdom. Thy labors for the general upraising of Hored excellest all others. For this reason thou art preferred, and by Jehovih chosen to be my assistant whilst I am here, and in my absence to be my very God in the Father's name.

23. Ha'jah said: This being the will of Jehovih, proceed thou.

24. God struck the gavel and the holy council rose to their feet. God said: In Jehovih's name I salute thee, Ha'jah, as God of Tek (See tablet Ah-iod'zan, Book of Saphah) to hold dominion in Hored. Come forth and receive thou my throne for the Father's sake. The marshals then conducted Ha'jah to the foot of the throne, and God came down and took his hand and led him up. And as they were going forth a light, as of golden fire, came down from the firmament above, sent by the kingdoms high exalted; and God and Ha'jah were covered around about and illuminated.

25. God said: By Thy Wisdom, Love and Power, O Jehovih, do I receive this Thy son on Thy Throne. Be Thou with him in Wisdom and Strength for Thy glory forever! Amen!

26. God raised up a rod, waving it, and rain came down from heaven. Ha'jah said: In Thy name, O Jehovih! Whereupon God stretched forth his hand unto Jehovih, saying: Give me a crown for Thy son, God of Tek, O Jehovih!

27. And there descended, as if a small star, far lengthened out, a light of gold and silver, and it settled on God's hand, and he fashioned it into a crown, and emblazoned it with the sign God of Tek, and placed it on Ha'jah's head, saying: In Jehovih's name, thee I crown, to sit on the throne in Hored during my absence.

28. Ha'jah said: Thy son, O Jehovih, shall fulfill Thy commandments in wisdom and love. May the Father, Creator of worlds, give this Thy son rest and comfort for the glories he hath wrought in Thy name! Amen!

29. The Council said: Amen! The es'enaurs chanted an anthem of praise to Jehovih. And God led Ha'jah forth and seated him on the throne, saying: Thou art God in my name and Jehovih's also. And since I now go down to the earth to sojourn for a season, thou shalt be known as God of both earth and heaven.

30. So God departed out of Hored and embarked on a ship, taking with him seven thousand men and women for his escort, beside a thousand es'enaurs and the crew of three thousand to work the ship.

CHAPTER VI.

1. And God went to the provinces of the governors of heaven dwelling on earth, whom he had appointed and sent forth; and as he himself had been commissioned by Jehovih in Hored, so did he install the governors on their seats.

2. And the governors were situated within Waga (Pan) at remote distances, but God sent messengers to them, notifying them of the time he would appear.

3. And the Lord being apprised of God's journey, established a protectorate in the Lord's kingdom in the city of Ul'oo, on earth, and went and joined the ship of God, and traveled with him throughout Waga, being present at the inauguration of the governors in these heavens.

4. To each and all the governors, God said: Remember that that which is given to my

governors pertaineth to things in heaven; for the Lord's matters pertain to earthly things, and to angels that labor with the corporeans. But ye are to attend to the es'yans, receiving them in heaven, providing them with places to sojourn, and in their helplessness supply them with food and clothes, and the rudiments of learning.

5. God said: Remember ye also, the time cometh when each of these governorships shall attain to an independent kingdom; and instead of being governors ye shall be raised as sub-Gods.

6. After God established the governors, the Lord persuaded God to visit his place in Ul'oo, and thence to go around about on earth and see the mortals with whom the Lord had to deal. And God consented, and the Lord sent messengers on before him, that the house of the Lord, which mortals had built, might be replenished and cleansed.

7. And the protectorate notified the ashars, and the ashars impressed mortals to go and cleanse and purify the house of the Lord. And so mortals fell to work and cleansed the place, and burned incense of sweet myrrh and hepatan, not even knowing they were fulfilling the command of the Lord.

8. When the ship of the hosts of God came to the city of Ul'oo, mortals saw it high up in the air, and they feared and ran hastily to consult the prophet of the Lord. And the prophet said: Behold, God appeareth in a sea of fire in the firmament of heaven.

9. And God caused the ship to be made unseen, that fear might subside on earth, and he descended with his hosts into the house of the Lord, and they went and touched the things mortals had built that they might perceive corporeally.

10. And the Lord gave a banquet, and the angels of God tarried four days, exchanging fellowship with the ashars, who ministered to mortals. And the ashars took the angels of God around about amongst mortals, both whilst mortals were asleep and awake, showing them all things.

11. And because of the presence of the hosts of God, mortals were aroused with new vigor to worship the Lord, rising early and going to the house of worship and continuing all day, and not one of them knew the cause thereof.

12. On the evening of the fourth day God commanded his hosts to prepare to renew the journey, and the ship was again illumed and set for its course.

13. God said: O Jehovih, who createth all, look down and bless Thy Lord! He hath from his high estate in etherea, descended to these poor mortals to lift them up. Already hath he toiled with them a hundred years. Three generations have risen up out of the earth, and they begin to glorify Thee in Thy kingdoms above the earth. Who but Thee, O Jehovih, can honor Thy Lord or know his sore trials! Behold, man groweth up out of the earth, saying: There is no Lord and no God. But his feet and his hands are guided every hour of the day. Yea, when he entereth the unseen worlds, they become seen; but he is helpless in a strange place. And Thy Lord provideth him and teacheth him Thy kingdoms. Thy Lord goeth from place to place on the earth. He findeth a corner and saith: Here will I build a city. He sendeth his angels forth and they inspire man on the earth to come and build a city. Yet when the city is built, man saith: Behold, there is no God and no Lord.

14. The Lord bringeth the corporeans together and guardeth them day and night; but man turneth away in strife and destruction. Then Thy Lord withdraweth his angels of the city because of its wickedness; and lo, the city falleth in ruins. But man knoweth not the cause. Yet Thy Lord toileth on, day and night, watching, guarding

and striving to lift man up out of darkness. O Jehovih, Father, bless Thy Lord and his hosts! Haste the time when man shall comprehend the foundations of Thy kingdoms!

15. The Lord said: O Jehovih, Ever Present! Hear the words of Thy God. He who comprehendeth the whole earth and the heaven of the earth, knowing no day nor no night. He dealeth with millions; his judgment is sufficient for all.

16. Glorify him, Thy Son, of heaven and earth. He fashioneth the homes of Thy Lords and Thy little ones in great wisdom. His love is the glory of all men; his strength fashioned after Thy foundations. Give swiftness and rest, and joy in Thy quickening to him, Thy God!

17. The mortals of the city of Ul'oo had gathered together to worship, and they were singing and dancing to the Lord, and the angels joined in the singing also. And God went and sat on the altar and illuminated it, so the mortals could see him. And the chief prophet came near the place of the Lord, and the Lord placed his hand on the forehead of the prophet, so he might speak in the name of God.

18. The prophet said: Behold me, I am the God of heaven and earth, and my words come out of the mouth of this my prophet. Keep holy the four days of the moon, for they are the Lord's days. (See ceremonies of Hi-dang, Saphah, and also Mas.) Do no evil, but strive for wisdom and to do good. And when ye are dead, behold, ye shall live, for I have places prepared for ye in my heaven. Rejoice and be merry, for the Lord liveth and reigneth.

19. When the prophet ceased, God rose up from the altar, and his traveling host also, and saluting the Lord in the name of Jehovih, disappeared in heaven above.

CHAPTER VII.

1. As mortals sail corporeal ships across the corporeal ocean, so sailed the ship of God in the atmospherean ocean. As a man having five sons sendeth four away to far-off countries and keepeth one at home, so did God with the five Lords bequeathed him by Great Jehovih.

2. And now had God departed from the foundation of Hored, in a ship, in heaven to visit his four far-off sons, the Lords of the four great divisions of the earth, who had to do with both mortals and the spirits of the dead, for the glory of Jehovih.

3. First to Jud, Lord of Jud, he headed his ship, running close to the earth, bounding forth, and sapping up fuel from the tall forests to feed the phosphorescent flame, running easy till the wild coast on the west of Waga was reached. Here halted he his ship, first God of the first Lords of earth, till his navigators told the distance of the wide sea before; then gathering fuel and substance from the rich growing lands, he stowed the ship to the full, he and his traveling host.

4. And God went in, commanding: Go forth, go forth! Forth into the sea of heaven! And on plunged the ship of God in the blue winds of the firmament, high soaring, above the black clouds sprung from the corporeal ocean. And the music of his thousand es'enaurs leaped forth in time and tune to the waves, plenteous and most defiant.

5. Jehovih looked down from the highest of all the heavens, His everlasting throne of thrones, saying: Onward! Onward! Tame the elements, O God! O man! The earth is thine, the air above is thine. Stretch forth thine arm and tame the elements I have made.

6. Onward sped the ship of God, by the force of wills matured; and from its hallowed

light displaying its purpose before other traveling Gods and men, in other ships cruising, on adventurous paths in Jehovih's wide oceans of splendor.

7. Merrily sang the crew, and danced, and sighted the wide expanse, premising of the scattering ships coursing hither and yon, in strange colors and marvelous swiftness.

8. On one side the rising moon, the setting sun on the other; beneath lay the black clouds and great corporeal ocean; and yet high above twinkled the stars and the planets of the Great Serpent on his long journey.

9. God came forth and surveyed the scene; and the power of Jehovih moved upon him. Then gathered around him his seven thousand loves and traveling companions. God said:

10. All Thy places are new, Great Jehovih! For thousands of years have I gazed on Thy matchless splendors, seen and unseen; but Thy glory groweth richer day by day. When Thy voice came to me, more than a hundred years ago, saying: Go, My son, I have a new garden planted; take some workmen and till the soil; I foresaw the long labor of the generations that would spring up out of the earth. I feared and trembled. I said:

11. How shall it be, O Jehovih? Shall the new earth be peopled over, and mortals run their course as on other worlds before? First, in wholesome love and worship and due reverence to the Gods, and then for ages and ages bury themselves in bloody wars? O lead me forth, Father! Jehovih! I will take Thy garden for a season, and fence it round with Lords, and wise kingdoms. And with Thy potent spirit hedge mortals on every side, that the earth shall bloom as a paradise for angels and men.

12. And Thy sons and daughters came with me, and engrafted Thy immortal kingdom.

13. How is it now? How compares my labor with that of other Gods on other worlds?

14. O ye archangels, Gods and Goddesses! Look down on the great earth! Jehovih hath filled my arms with a great load! I tremble on the immortal scales!

15. And God, transfixed, looked up into the swift-passing sky, for his voice reached to the thrones of etherean worlds whereon the Osirian regents reigned in all power. And down from admidst the stars shot a single ray of light engrossed with the adorable words: JEHOVIH'S SON! ALL HAIL! HAIL, GOD OF EARTH, JEHOVIH'S SON! GLORY! GLORY TO GREAT JEHOVIH, FOR ALL THOU HAST DONE!

16. Then upward furled the shining light till it faded midst the far-off stars. Anew the trumpeters and singers sent forth a strain of sweet music, spirited and sounding full of soul. And as the music glided forth across the waters, lo, other music, strange and welcome, came from the west lands to the borders of the ocean.

17. The ship was across the sea, and the hosts of the Lord had come to meet the God of earth and heaven. And now, saluting loud and long, the two ships drew to close anchorage. Presently the messengers interchanged, and in Jehovih's name greeted God and His hosts, who were old-time friends to the Lord and His.

18. God said: By Thy will, O Jehovih, let us take course for the Lord's kingdom and place of labor. And presently the two ships sped forth, close to the earth, conjoined in the music of anthems of olden times.

19. Far up into the heart of the country, where fertile lands and mountains and waters were close companioned to the asuan race, the ships led on till one pillar of fire, standing on a mountain side, proclaimed the place of the Lord, and here they halted and made fast the vessels, unseen by mortals.

CHAPTER VIII.

1. These chieftains had been long friends on other worlds, and pledged to join in an adventure on some new corporeal world, to raise up to Jehovih, sons and daughters. Now was it being fulfilled in the Lord and God remotely situated, and the time of this visit much looked forward to.

2. And so God and the Lord came forth, saying: In Jehovih's name! met at last! And they embraced and re-assured each other that it was really true, which they had talked of a thousand years before.

3. And then came forward all the hosts of God and the hosts of the Lord, knowing one another and saluting and embracing also. Thereupon they proceeded to the house of the Lord, which mortals had been inspired to build of wood and clay. And when they were within they joined in prayer and thanks to Jehovih, and they sang and danced, and rejoiced to their souls' content.

4. At sunrise the next morning the mortal priests and priestesses, led by a prophet, went into the house of the Lord, to pray and sing and dance as they had been taught by inspiration of the Lord, but many people lingered without, saying to one another:

5. I fear, I fear (ta hop)! For last night I saw lights in the house of the Lord, and I heard like singing and dancing before the altar of God!

6. Nevertheless their companions persuaded them, and they went in and sang and danced also.

7. After a time of rejoicing and of quiet the Lord said: Behold, O God, the follies of judgment, and the vain calculations of even Lords and Gods! We look upon the mature man, saying: Alas, he is stubborn in his own way; we cannot convert him. Then we desire the immature, saying: Him will I raise up in mine own way, and he shall not depart from my judgment. But we tire of his immaturity and slow growth.

8. God said: Hereon hangeth the highest testimony of The Person of Great Jehovih. The nearest blank of all the living created He man, purposely unlike all the rest and devoid of sense. Whereas, according to the order of the other animal world, a newborn babe should already be wise.

9. Jehovih said: All the living have I provided with certain paths to travel in; but man alone I created new out of all things dead and dissolved, and he shall grow forever. To the beast I gave an already created sense (instinct); to man I allotted angels. And even these have I provided with others above them; and yet others above them, forever and ever. Hence the first of man, the newborn babe, I created a blank in sense and judgment, that he may be a witness that even he himself was fashioned and created anew by My hand. Neither created I him imperfectly that he should re-enter a womb and be born over again. That which I do is well done, saith Jehovih.

10. The Lord said: Thou art wise, O God. The opposites prove Jehovih. Water runneth down hill, but man walketh up the hillside; the tree groweth up out of the ground whilst it liveth, but after death it falleth. Man standeth on the earth, but the earth resteth on that which is lighter than the earth. Jehovih saith: The life of the tree is of Me; the unseen that holdeth the corporeal earth in its place, is of Me.

11. And yet, O God, who can attain to know Jehovih? The mortal saith: When I am dead

and risen in heaven I shall see the Great Spirit; but he faileth, being still helpless, yea, as helpless in his place as he was helpless on the earth. Then he saith: when I am strong and wise, like Lords and Gods, and can traverse the wide firmament, then I will see Jehovih. But when he riseth and can shape his vessel through the whirlwinds of the vortices of heaven, and he is called Lord or God, lo, he findeth the arcs and the ethea standing before him still. More and more he is appalled at thought of the Great I AM who liveth still beyond.

12. He hurrieth down to the corporeal earth to teach mortals and spirits of Jehovih, and His endless worlds and exalted heavens. But lo, the darkness of men, they say: I see Him not; I hear Him not; I believe not in Him. He is but as the wind, going without sense; as the water goeth down the hill, so is He; He is dead. He is nothing.

13. And the Lord inventeth ways and means; yea, he teacheth man to pray and sing to Jehovih, that the sounds may lead his soul upward. The Lord telleth him to wear clothes and hide his nakedness from the Lord; and the Lord sendeth angels to award him for his good deeds. And the angels of the Lord lay plots and stratagems in man's pathway to stir him up. Yea, Jehovih gave man sleep, so that his corporeal-bound spirit might see and hear heavenly things. But man loadeth his stomach, and debaucheth on intoxicating smoke and drink till his soul is buried in darkness.

14. And the Lord crieth out in despair; How weak am I, O Jehovih, before Thee! I took upon me to be Lord over men on the earth, to learn my lesson in the government of worlds. But O Jehovih, I know I fail in Thy sight. What will Thy God say when he beholdeth my little good? What pity have the archangels for Thy struggling Lord of earth?

15. God perceived the sorrow of his friend, and he said: O Jehovih, who art Almighty, how keener has Thou made our sense of our own weakness, than those who look upon us! Thy Lord is my God in the glories he hath wrought out of such crude substance, and I sing to his praises and love. Lo I have looked upon the naked man and woman of this great land, crawling on hands and feet, with no thought but to eat, and I have seen them raised up by Thy Lord and his ashars, to walk upright and use words of speech and to wear clothes and skins to hide their nakedness. Yea, O Father, I have cried out with great joy, and I called aloud unto Thee, O Jehovih, saying: Who knoweth the labor of the Lord! Will man ever forget to sing praises to the Lord God?

16. But Jehovih said: I will keep some of the tribes of men in darkness, till the last days; for man in his conceit shall be confounded; for he shall perceive that the tribes of darkness cannot put away their own darkness. Yea, man shall bow down in reverence to My Lords in the early days of the earth.

17. Thus conversed God and his Lord, as they went forth to find the mortals that had given up the places of asu and come to live in villages and cities. Around about over the continent of Jud they traveled for many days and nights. And when God had seen all the work of the Lord, he said:

18. Behold it is good. Thy toil and seclusion away from the Lords of the upper heavens are severe, but thou art fashioning the love of millions, who shall bless thee.

19. Now whilst God sojourned hither, his hosts regaled themselves with the company of the ashars and asaphs in the kingdom of the Lord, and great was the love and rejoicing amongst them.

CHAPTER IX.

1. When God's visit was ended, and the hosts notified, the Lord gave a banquet that lasted two days and nights, during which the angels sang and danced and trumpeted before God. After that God and his hosts embarked on the ship in readiness to proceed on the journey; and the Lord went up to the ship to take leave, and his host went with him.

2. God said: When dan approacheth we shall meet again. May Jehovih prosper thy harvests till then!

3. The Lord said: That is another hundred years! O God, I almost live in a wilderness. I have not ten millions of souls, mortals and spirits!

4. God said: Thy kingdom shall be mighty when I come again. May it glorify Jehovih!

5.They embraced and separated! Each gave the sign of Jehovih's name. Upward raised the ship of God, with banners outstretched, and new ornamented by the Lord's angels. And now, taking course still west, sped on above the mountain tops, like a meteor hurled from heaven. Meanwhile the trumpeters gave forth the gladly solemn sound of the march of God.

6. But ere the ship had made half its journey, an approaching light came forth from the far west, radiant and laden with hosts from the Lord of Dis, and the Lord of the earth also.

7. When the ships drew near and halted, God called with a loud voice, saying: In Jehovih's name, all hail! I know my Lord cometh.

8. And thereupon the Lord answered: Hail to thee, O God, Son of Jehovih! And they turned the Lord's ship and lashed the twain together even as they sped on.

9. Now after they had all exchanged welcome and good wishes, the Lord said: Ere we go to my central throne let us survey the continent over which thy servant is Lord of land and water.

10. And God answered: Thy will be done, O Lord. And so they journeyed for many days, oft descending to the earth in places where the Lord's angels had begun colonies with mortals, impressing man with words of speech, and to live in villages.

11. And God saw that all he saw was good and well done. So they came to the throne of the Lord and halted and sojourned for sixty days.

12. And God and his hosts and the Lord and his ashars and asaphs were together in general reunion, praying, singing and dancing and reasoning on the endless works of Jehovih. But one book could not contain all that was said and done, and of the excursions made, and the visits over the plains and mountains, where in thousands of years hence man should live and build cities, and go to war and destroy them.

13. And the mathematicians foretold the great cities and nations that would rise up; how this one and that one would move to battle; how their great cities would fall in ruins and be covered up by falling nebulae, and by denuding mountains washing down upon them, so that even their remembrance should be lost. And yet, further on, the mathematicians foretold the coming of kosmon when the ruined cities would be discovered and their histories deciphered by the su'is of man in Great Jehovih's hand.

14. And now when all these things were estimated, the prophets and mathematicians went before God according to the commandments of the Lord, and they spake before God, Son of Jehovih, telling all these wonders.

15. When they had finished, God said: What is our service on the earth, O Lord? A few

centuries at most, and we will have risen up from the earth, taking our hosts with us to dwell in higher realms. But there shall be other Gods and Lords after us, to deal with mortals and spirits newly born. After awhile there shall be great warriors and great cities and nations; and they shall have Gods and Lords of their times who will dwell many a weary year, aye, century, in the darkness with man. After that again, even the Gods and Lords will be forgotten. And man will turn against Great Jehovih, putting to death his adherents, preferring idols of stone and metal, and spirits born of woman.

16. The Lord said: And yet further on, a brighter light adorneth the way: Great Jehovih's hand sendeth the traveling worlds into the light of kosmon, and new prophets arise gathering up the histories lost, and glorious plan of the Great Spirit over all. Yea, even thy labor and my ships will be seen by mortals of that day.

17. Thus they discoursed, reading the past and the future, and weighing the present; whilst angels less informed, gathered around to learn how worlds are peopled, and nations and cities destroyed; the far-off, and the near at hand, being as nothing in Jehovih's vast universe.

18. But the time came for God's departure, and he and his traveling host embarked, and the Lord and his angels drew around to receive God's prayer ere he left. And so after they had embraced and parted, God said:

19. Though I go away, my love abideth with you all. And now, O Jehovih, bless these my fellow-laborers, and make them strong to endure their great trials. Thine is the power and glory, O Father! Amen!

20. The ship rose up and the trumpeters gave forth: Glory to Thee, O Jehovih, forever and ever!

CHAPTER X.

1. Jehovih spake to God, saying: Steer thy ship to the south land, My Son, and visit thy Lord, who is God of Vohu. And God went as commanded, to the south, running close to the earth, over deserts and mountains.

2. But when they were a short way on the journey they were met by the Lord, who had been apprised of God's coming. And the ship of the Lord came also, and made fast to the vessel of God, and all the angels saluted and intermingled, having known one another hundreds of years, and some for more than a thousand years.

3. The Lord said: On our journey let us run through the valleys and the banks of rivers, for it is here that both asu and men dwell. And so they journeyed, surveying the earth as they sailed above. The country was mostly barren, not supporting man nor beast.

4. But by the river sides man dwelt, burrowing in the ground to avoid the heat by day and the cold by night. And they came to places where the angels of the Lord were dwelling with mortals, having inspired them to make villages and to hide their nakedness.

5. The Lord said: Behold, O God, only the unseen is potent over man. Could the beasts or the stones or the forest tell man to hide his nakedness, he would not; neither will he heed his brother's voice. Without experience man cannot be advised profitably to himself, for such hath Jehovih made him. Because man cannot discern angel presence, the angels alone can teach man and inspire him to new life. For they talk to him in his sleep, and show him what is for his own good. And when he waketh in the morning, he supposeth it was himself talking, and he is ambitious to obey himself. Patient and of long endurance

are the angels of the Lord.

6. God said: Will man ever know he hath been raised up? Will he be believing? Or will he, too, need go to some new world and raise up the first fruits thereof and toil his hundreds of years with naked mortals? O Jehovih, how wisely hast Thou shapen the labors of the believing and the unbelieving!

7. Lo, man cometh forth out of the earth, boasting of his unbelief, saying: Except I see with my own eyes, and feel with my own hands, I will not believe. But Thou, O Jehovih, hast fitted a labor for his eyes, and for his hands, to his heart's content.

8. And yet another man cometh forth out of the earth, being believing, and quickly he mounteth to the thrones of Thy exalted heavens. Great is the work of Thy Lord, O Father.

9. The Lord said: Who knoweth thy wisdom, O Jehovih! Who cannot perceive Thee in the foundations of Thy everlasting worlds? Thou hast provided nurses for the new earth; and out of this, Thy footstool, wilt Thou bring forth many, who will, in the far future time, be laboring as Thy Lord and his angels labor here. Of what expanse is Thy wisdom, O Jehovih!

10. Thus they conversed and journeyed forth till they reached the throne and place of the Lord. And here they made fast their ships, and they descended down to the city of Ong'oo, in upper middle of the continent of Vohu.

11. And the Lord now sent messengers to all the ashars in his dominions, appointing ten days of rest, and time for feasting and music, and dancing and worshipping Jehovih.

12. And so it came to pass that the angels of the Lord and of God held a reunion, being the first one for over a hundred years.

13. And then God went around about over all the continent of Vohu, inspecting the work the Lord had done, and he pronounced it good before Jehovih.

14. When God had rested the full time, he and his hosts entered the ship of God, and taking leave of the Lord and his hosts, departed on the journey, saluting the Lord with a thousand trumpeters in the name of Jehovih.

CHAPTER XI.

1. And now came the long journey across the ocean. God said: Great is Thy wisdom, O Jehovih, in the division of waters! Thy barriers provide nations against nations. A refuge hast Thou made beyond the waters, and the evil man cannot pursue. But greater still are Thy spirit oceans, O Father. The spirits of darkness cannot cross over, and the spirits of newborn peoples are not contaminated. Thou Far-seeing, Thou Bestower of thrift into the hands of Thy Gods and Thy Lords.

2. The master of the ship provided well for the journey; and presently the vessel of fire sped over the water, high above the clouds that cover the ocean. Onward to the west, bleak and desolate, through the spirit sea, unseen by mortals. On the far-off borders where the lands come to the waters' edge, the Lord of the land of Thouri stood, stationed in a ship, to welcome God to the great west lands.

3. And this was the land called by the angels in aftertime North Guatama, signifying the meeting of nations and the dawn of kosmon.

4. God came down out of the ship and stood on the land, and a light of etherean flame descended upon him, and Jehovih spoke out of the light, saying: Hear Me, O My Son! Hither have I brought thee. This land is the last of the circle, even as

Waga is the first. Behold, when the earth is circumscribed around about with such as choose Me, I will come hither with a great awakening light to the souls of men.

5. On this land will I finish the dominion of the Gods and Lords on earth, even as on Waga; through thee and thy Lords will I now lay the foundation for My kingdoms. On this land will I raise up a people who shall be the fulfilling of that which the I'hins of Waga profess; for My chosen shall come out boldly against all dominion save Mine, even Jehovih. Look over this land, My Son, and provide unto the time of kosmon.

6. My prophets shall foretell thee what shall happen; thou shalt look upon the mountains and strong standing rocks, and the thought of thy soul shall pierce them, and the impression thereof shall be as a written book before the races of men in that day. Neither shall they know the cause, but they shall come forth in tens of thousands, putting away all Gods and Lords and ancient tyranny, for My sake. Thy soul shall be My talisman, deep engraven in the land and water and mountains.

7. On this land alone shall not any Lord nor God be established by the sword, for it is My land, which I planned for the deliverance of the nations of the earth.

8. The hosts of both the ships came and joined in gleesome reunion after a hundred years' absence; and it came to pass that God traveled over the land and waters of the great west continent.

9. And all the places that the Lord had searched out, to the east and west and north and south, even to the farthest boundary, were revealed and recorded in the books of heaven.

10. God said: And thou, my Lord, shalt mark out the place of the dominion of Jehovih in the founding of His kingdom on earth. And a record of thy labors shall descend through the Lords and Gods that come after thee, even down to the time of the coming light of kosmon.

11. And the people who shall dwell here till that day, shall never be worshippers of any Lord or God, such as other people shall worship.

12. Let my seal be put upon this land, in the name of Jehovih, and to Him I consecrate it forever!

13. So, after that time, God rested from his labors, and the Lord with him. And the Lord prepared a feast and reunion for all the angels in his dominions.

14. And they thus assembled and sang and prayed and danced, and conversed on things long past and things of the future, re-assuring one another of their love and high esteem after the manner of mortals of this day.

15. When the banquet was ended, God and his traveling host, in due ceremony and order, took their leave. Thus God departed. And when the ship of God was raised up and under way, the voice of Jehovih came to God, saying:

16. Steer thy ship, My Son, around about over all the other lands and islands and waters of the earth. Go low down to the earth that thy recording angels may witness the affairs of men and all the places I created on the earth, and the waters of the earth.

17. Thus God visited all places on land and water, even where man lived not, as well as where he lived, and the angels made a record thereof in the books of heaven.

18. And the time of the journey and the visits of God to the places of earth and her heavens was one year and seven days; and his rest was completed. So he sent messengers to Hored, his heavenly kingdom, announcing the time of his coming. And he then set sail therefore.

CHAPTER XII.

1. When it was known in Hored that God was about to return, Ha'jah put all things in readiness for God's reception.

2. And there volunteered ten thousand musicians and five thousand bearers of banners, one thousand marshals and officers of the throne, and one hundred thousand receivers, to go part way and meet God and his companions.

3. And Ha'jah granted their prayers and they started at once, being the most majestic host that had as yet gone forth in the lower heaven.

4. And when they were a little way off, behold, God and his ship of fire approached in heavenly splendor. And the marshals met him and laid hold of the han'iv of the ship, whereon all the hosts did in like manner, save the musicians who sang and played.

5. When they drew near and entered Hored, Ha'jah broke down from his high estate, and left the throne, running to meet God as a child would run to its father. And when the multitude saw this, they also broke loose from decorous behavior and gave full vent to their outbursting love for God and his hosts. And all the people became as a tumult in rivalry of rejoicing.

6. In a little while God and Ha'jah turned and walked to the throne, ascending thereon; and Ha'jah took his place, and God sat on his right, and order reigned.

7. Ha'jah said: In Thy name, O Jehovih, I welcome back Thy First Son of earth to the kingdom Thou hast bestowed upon him, and Thy sons and daughters. As much as he hath glorified Thee, by his labor and by his wisdom and love, so do we honor him in Thy name and for Thy glory!

8. God said: In Thy name, O Jehovih, do I return to these, my loves! That I am returned I glorify Thee, O My Father. That Thou hast made them to rejoice, is the glory of my life.

9. And now a great light gathered up around the throne, so that many could not look thereon, and presently the power of Jehovih came upon Ha'jah, and the voice of Jehovih spake through him, saying to God:

10. This is again thy throne, O My Son! Thou shalt finish that which I have put upon thee. Thy people shall learn the manner of my kingdoms, and know that even as I make all, so do I rule over all.

11. Hang up thy traveling garb, My Son; dismiss thy traveling hosts and resume thy seat on the throne, for I gave it thee. The voice departed; Ha'jah rose up and stood aside, and the light fell upon God, and he resumed the throne and was hailed by the multitude in Jehovih's name.

12. God said to Ha'jah: Because thou hast prospered my kingdom during one whole year, thou shalt be my companion and assistant, with power and wisdom to superintend all matters not direct with my Lords.

13. Behold, this day have I set apart as a new day in heaven and earth; because on this day the sun taketh its course from the north line; and from this time forth it shall be called the new year's day. So shall it be, from this time forth, the day of the relief watch in Hored.

14. Hear my voice, O Ha'jah, and ye of the Council of the throne of heaven! That which I commanded shall ye proclaim throughout heaven and earth to all who serve me.

15. Because of the increase of the kingdom of Hored I will have the place enlarged; and

the Council shall no longer be called a Council, but Moeb, for it shall be an assembly over all councils below it.

16. And Moeb shall no longer deal with the affairs of individuals, even though they be Lords; but she shall have dominion with the cities and kingdoms of heaven, and with judgments and decrees.

17. But in all matters of less degree, this, my son Ha'jah, shall have dominion. And thou, O Ha'jah, shall build thee a house in Hored, near this throne, and it shall be thy house and the place of thy business.

CHAPTER XIII.

1. So God enlarged the place of Hored, and built one thousand more pillars of fire, enlarging the circle and otherwise making it a place of splendor. And God called together the recorders from the libraries of heaven, and caused them to select one hundred thousand new members for the house of Moeb (Parliament), choosing them from the highest on the lists. In this matter, God said:

2. Seek not the most learned, nor the most prayerful, for members; but choose ye such as rank highest in assimilating to Jehovih and to their fellows; for such are the first to become Gods and Goddesses. Jehovih saith: A strong man may do more good works than a weak one; and yet the latter may stand fairer in My sight. I open the way to the weak and the strong; to the learned and the unlearned.

3. God said: In all these matters, whatever man or woman hath put away self-desires for self's sake, serving the Father by laboring for others, is on the road to wisdom. And if the records show a sufficient time for growth in such man or woman, whereby these virtues become organic, then choose ye that person, for of such shall be Moeb.

4. So the laborers gathered from the heavens around about, agni, and built Moeb within, suitable for the members to be seated according to their rank; and when it was finished, on that same day, the recorders brought the new members, and they went into the temple to their respective places.

5. And when seated, God spake from the throne, saying: To Thee, O Jehovih, have I built the house of Moeb in Hored; and by Thy wisdom have I chosen the members thereof. To Thee, O Father, I dedicate this house, and it shall be Thy house. Give us of Thy light, O Jehovih, that we may not err.

6. A light descended from the heavens above and fell upon the members of Moeb, as a symbol of approval by the archangels; and presently the new members rose up, every one of their own accord, but the old members remained seated.

7. God said: Above your heads I make the sign of Jehovih's name, in a circle of fire, and the cross, and the leaf of life; for by it are ye sworn to the Father's labor.

8. Hear me, then, O my beloved: Ye are henceforth denied individual ministration with individuals, but ye are now become a unit with many, and with these must your labor and your love and your wisdom be in concert of action.

9. Henceforth must ye no longer say: What can I do for this man or that man, or this woman or that woman, or this child or that child? For this is individual labor; and on the earth such ministration belongeth to the ashars; and in atmospherea, such ministration belongeth to the asaphs. But ye shall minister to organic communities who are composed

of individuals. For there are communities for factories, and others for education, and others for treatment of the sick; and such communities exist both on earth and in heaven.

10. Ye shall divide yourselves into groups for this purpose, and every group shall have its special business in charge; and each group shall stand in Moeb as one member of Jehovih's judgment seat. According to your talents shall ye divide, and group together, choosing such department wherein each one hath the greatest wisdom and strength. Withdraw, then, and thus complete your groups according to the rates my proper officers will assign, and then return again into Moeb, and in Jehovih's name, take the seats allotted to you all.

CHAPTER XIV.

1. On the second day after the house of Moeb was completed, and all the members were in their respective places, Jehovih spake through God, saying:

2. Now is the beginning of the second resurrection. Even as the corporean putteth off the corporeal body, and is born a spirit, becoming the first resurrection, so are ye, putting away individual self and becoming an organic community, the beginning of the second resurrection.

3. As they of the first are for individual self, so have I bound them close on the face of the earth; as they survived on the earth on corporeal food, so have I made them to survive in the lowest heaven on atmospherean food. As Moeb hath risen above these conditions, so will I exalt the foundations of the house of Moeb higher up from the earth than Hored, and Moeb shall be the lower house of My kingdom.

4. The voice of Jehovih departed and God saluted Ha'jah in the name of the Father. And a great light enveloped the house of Moeb, and the es'enauers chanted a hymn of praise. Thereafter God arose and stood in the throne of Jehovih, saying:

5. Hear ye O all ye people of heaven above and heaven below, the house of Moeb in the beginning of the second resurrection is founded in Jehovih's name. Proclaim ye the words that have gone out of my mouth, to the east and west and north and south, and to the swift messengers of the arcs of the firmament above.

6. Glory, glory be to Jehovih! Boundless and Almighty Creator, Present, and full of love, wisdom and power, glory to Thee forever and ever, amen!

7. The house of Moeb chanted a proclamation. The swift messengers assumed their respective globes of light, and began to ascend in every direction, carrying the word to the exalted spheres.

8. And God crowned Ha'jah as the sub-God of Hored, and he was proclaimed to all the quarters of heaven and earth. And the history of his name exists to this day as Jah, amongst mortals.

CHAPTER XV.

1. Ha'jah said: With the exaltation of Moeb, so shall my places be exalted before Jehovih. Let the enumerators of the communities of heaven send representatives before me. The communities of manufacturers who produce food and clothes for the es'yans, the communities for hospitals and nurseries, the communities for education, the communities

for training messengers, and all other communities.

2. When the representatives came, according to the instructions of the marshals, and were before the throne, Ha'jah said:

3. The toilers shall not be always toilers; the physicians not always runners after the sick. Whosoever is proficient will I exalt. He that can walk shall no longer crawl.

4. Many are wise and strong, and some have passed beyond the boundary of self-desires for self-sake.

5. A child may not have self-desires, but then it lacketh wisdom and strength. A full grown man or woman may have wisdom and strength, but lack in the abnegation of self.

6. I will make every community a double from this time forth, and one shall be called Maga, and the other shall be called Minga. Maga shall be my promoted laborers, who are being prepared for the second resurrection.

7. And Maga's labor shall be in concert with Moeb, the house of Jehovih. But Minga's labor shall be as heretofore, even with individual affairs and the organizing of new places for the delivered es'yans, who are the fruit of the Lords and their kingdoms on the earth.

8. Let my marshals select judges to carry out these my decrees, in the name of Jehovih.

CHAPTER XVI.

1. From the founding of Hored until the instalment of Ha'jah, was one hundred and thirty years, and at that time the lower kingdom of heaven was fully organized according to the decree of Jehovih.

2. And the kingdoms of the Lords on earth were also fully established. And at that time the earth had passed into Hon'she, in the etherean space, where dwell the Osirian Shrevarhs, to whom the swift messengers from God had reported the condition of the earth's surface, with the tablets of Grade and Ingrade of mortals.

3. The Shrevarhs said: The earth hath not attained her fullness. The gases of her low regions must be purified to make more places for mortals.

4. So it came to pass there fell upon the earth, by command of the Shrevarhs, by the will of Jehovih, fire and brimstone and iron and phosphorous, and the shower thereof reached into the five divisions of the earth. But ere the fall thereof, God was apprised and he apprised the Lords, and they informed the ashars, and they impressed such mortals as were in rapport with heavenly things, and the chosen marched away from the places of destruction, so that not one perished.

5. But many of the asu'ans were consumed in the fire.

6. But God sent extra workmen, and surgeons and physicians, from heaven down, to such spirits as were falling into forgetfulness and dissolution, and commanded that they be engrafted on the surviving asu'ans for pity's sake; and this was accomplished through the Lords of the earth and their servants, the ashars.

7. At the end of two hundred years God enumerated the people in the lower heaven, and there were, besides the spirits of the Fetals (many of whom were doubtful as to everlasting life), two hundred and ninety-six millions of souls. Of this number there had been raised up to the grade of Brides and Bridegrooms to Jehovih more than thirty millions, who were the first of the earth's production.

8. And now was the sixth generation of the seed of the fallen angels delivered, and this

was the fullness of earth bondage for them.

9. God summoned the house of Moeb for the revelations of Jehovih on the first day of the first year of dan of Hon'she. And when they were thus assembled, and had chanted to Jehovih appropriate anthems for the times past, the All Light came upon God, and he said:

10. Behold, the time of dan of Hon'she is at hand. Ere three days pass by, the hosts from the etherean heavens will descend to accomplish the resurrection of my hosts to the regions whence they came two hundred years ago.

11. Summon my Lords of the earth, and my people of heaven; proclaim my words unto them.

12. Ye that peopled the earth with everlasting life, give ear; the harvest of the new year is ripened, it shall be gathered into the heavens above. Let my people rejoice, for the glory of deliverance is at hand.

13. There awaiteth, full of hope and love, in Osirian fields, hosts of angels and archangels, to receive these, the first fruits of the new earth.

14. Clothe them in quietness with the rays of light. Make ready; for etherean Gods and Goddesses are setting sail in the regions above to come and deliver us.

15. Proclaim my words in all places in the name of Jehovih. And add unto them, saying: And to as many as desire to ascend, come ye to Moeb, in the name of the Son of Jehovih!

16. Messengers went forth, both in heaven and on the earth, and proclaimed as had been commanded.

17. And on the third day there assembled in Moeb and Hored ninety million angels, to witness the descending and ascending of Jehovih's chosen. And the archangels of Hon'she sent a hundred thousand Gods and Goddesses to guard Moeb and Hored around about, to dispel and keep away the clouds and sunshine, so as to add glory to the scene.

CHAPTER XVII.

1. The Loo'is came before God, and having organized themselves into one community, so as to make it lawful to speak in Moeb, they appointed Ga'wasa to speak on behalf of the community. Ga'wasa said:

2. Hear me, O God, in the name of Jehovih! Thou hast ordained me according to the custom of heaven, to be a master of generations with mortals, and yet one generation is incomplete, wherefore I have come before thee. This day I have been summoned by Jehovih, through thy messengers, saying: To as many as desire to enter the next resurrection, come, for the time of harvest is at hand. Thus saith God, Son of Jehovih. Behold, now, another generation do I desire to dwell on earth.

3. God said: The places of heaven are open to all. If thou wouldst ascend now, do even so. If thou wilt tarry one generation, then thou shalt tarry two hundred years, for of such period will be the next harvest.

4. Ga'wasa said: In Jehovih's name, let my brethren pass before thee in judgment.

5. God said: Jehovih's will be done.

6. Ga'wasa withdrew and went and told his brethren what was said; and presently they came in and passed in judgment before God.

7. God said: Thou hast said, let me pass in judgment before thee! Hear me, then, for this

is my judgment: If thou ascend with thy work incomplete, thou wilt be the unhappiest of men. Remain, therefore, for a greater glory is within thy reach.

8. The Loo'is passed to the left, signifying their determination to tarry yet two hundred years more with mortals.

9. After the Loo'is, came others desiring to be adjudged by God, and to all who had incomplete work, God said: Remain! And they remained.

10. Besides these were seventy thousand ethereans eligible to ascend, who volunteered to remain with mortals another two hundred years. Amongst these were the five Lords and Ha'jah, and four hundred messengers belonging to Hored, and seven hundred women in fetal, in the western division of Hored under Waga.

CHAPTER XVIII.

1. Jehovih spake in the arc of O'wasti, in the Orian field of Hon'she, in the etherean heaven. Jehovih said: The time of the earth is at hand; the deliverance of her first-born will fall at your doors. Come forth, O My sons and daughters, receive ye them from My hand.

2. Onesyi, high aspiring Goddess of Hon'she, and the thousand counselors, gathered in a host of five millions of souls, emancipated, and to them the dignified Onesyi spake, saying:

3. Unlike all harvests heretofore delivered to us from other corporeal worlds, Jehovih sendeth us the first-born of the earth. Let us rejoice and glorify Him, O my beloved. Send forth to the boundaries of Hon'she and proclaim the hosts of earth upraised. Provide them with mansions and quarters, ye that remain at home. And ye that volunteer to go to the earth to receive them, come quickly.

4. Onesyi said: Swift messengers have just come to me from the arc of Wan; Etisyai will be there. She it was who bestowed Jehovih's crown on the first God of the corporeal earth. Her hosts, a million strong, go by the way of Tivyus, and pray we meet them in O'wea. And thou, Wistaw, shall sit on my throne. I will to the earth, to receive the thirty million newborn, the glorious gift of Jehovih.

5. Onesyi said: The young virgin earth hath given birth. O the joy of the firstborn! I will take with me a host of singers, a million strong. Their voices shall have power and sweetness to win the love and adoration of all the thirty millions. The glory of Jehovih's works shall shine so brilliantly upon them that all past trials shall be forgotten. Hasten, O ye Gods and Goddesses! Let down the curtains of fire! Here begins the play of Jehovih in the management of a new world!

6. Now gathered together men and women, long raised up in the emancipated heavens, whose wills were potent over a'ji and nebulae, and swift in appropriating what Jehovih had fashioned in the firmament. And they built a ship, the size of which was equal to the width of Hored, and filled it within with angels of the rank of Gods and Goddesses, many of whom had been brought forth into life before the earth was created, and whose native corporeal worlds had gone out of existence. And they let down curtains from the ship, and the curtains were like flames of fire, and they reached downward, equal to the breadth of the earth.

7. These Gods and Goddesses were as a unit in will, and potent and swift workmen, and

the ship was laden, and on her course through the vault of heaven. Past the a'jian fields of Che'wang she rode swiftly. Soon the hosts of the much-loved Etisyai were seen in a smaller craft, highly polished and swift, making way for O'wea.

8. Up goeth a shout of joy from millions of throats, then a song of delight; heaven is joyful in Jehovih's boundless dominions. And now the twain approach O'wea; and they slacken speed and near each other, nearer and nearer, till the ships touch and are joined by skilled workmen.

9. Forth leap the two Goddesses, Etisyai and Onesyi, and in no stateliness or ceremony, but like children in whom love is transcendent, they fly to each other's arms, amidst the outburst of joy from the countless throng. Yet onward moves the etherean ship, majestic and meteor-like, steadily taking course to the new earth.

CHAPTER XIX.

1. And now the evening of the third day had come, and God and his hosts in Moeb were hastening all things, to be ready for the great light that was to descend from high heaven.

2. The ninety millions of angels looked upward, watching for the dawning of the light, waiting and watching. And many a one who remembered Etisyai, of two hundred years ago, wondered if she would return in glory, like when she came and crowned God by Jehovih's command. Some were robing themselves in white, and hastening nervously, like a bride about to wed; some were half inclined to sorrow for leaving he earth and lower heaven, where they had toiled so long; and some were stately and by their presence said: Thy will be done, O Jehovih!

3. God ascended the throne, and Ha'jah came up and sat on his right hand; and the light of Jehovih shone upon them so that many newborn, especially of the es'yan spectators, could not look upon them.

4. God said: One dan hath come and gone; this harvest is but thirty millions.

5. Ha'jah said: Thy son, O Jehovih, hath shaped the destiny of a world. Great is his glory.

6. A light of golden hue gathered above the throne, and took the form of a triangle; and there was a graven image at every corner, the which, when read, was I-O-D; and it was in the character of Waga, bestowed by the Lord on the altars in the house of worship on earth, and its value was thirty-three millions, which was the exact number prepared for the emancipated heaven in etherea; and the thirty-three was the years of a generation of mortals.

7. God said: Jehovih is one; the living is one; inanimate corpor is one; and these three are the entirety. To teach mortals this, O Ha'jah, is to give wisdom to the earth. Take thou this triangle, O thou, Son of the Most High. And as long as Seffas endureth on the earth shall it be the bequeathed heirloom of heaven, descending from God to God that occupieth the throne.

8. Thereupon God stretched forth his hands, and the triangle became fixed and solid, and God hung it on Ha'jah's neck, adding: In the name of Jehovih, receive thou this jewel, as my parting testimonial. Remember that, when mortals are raised up to understand this symbol of three in one, then will kosmon begin to dawn on the earth.

9. Ha'jah said: O God, thou symbol of the three attributes, love, wisdom and power! Thou didst leave thy stately home, where thou hadst Gods and Goddesses for companions, and

come to the far-off earth, which was young and curtained round with poisonous gases, to guard the young and imperfect angels of other worlds in their wanderings forth, with thy wisdom, love and power concealed. Thou didst give them liberty and yet redeem them. Thou hast stretched forth thy hand over the earth and made it to yield souls to glorify the Creator. And yet in all the while thou hast never quoted thyself. O that this could be taught to angels and men! Who is it, that will not trip or mention himself, or make himself a manifested self?

10. This day I am to be crowned, to fill the place thou hast built up; but I falter and tremble like a child. Ha'jah burst into tears, and after a while he added: O Jehovih, why hast Thou laid Ha'jah's tears so close? Thou hast created love in my soul, and it hath grown to be a mountain. God, Thy Son, who hath been my tutor for a thousand years, and on many worlds, corpor and es, is now thrusting Thy glory upon me.

11. God said: Heed thou the earth and her heavens, for they are to be thine for one dan. And remember also, that though I ascend with my hosts to etherea, yet I have charge of this world until the completion of this cycle, two thousand eight hundred years: my archangels shall henceforth answer to thy prayers to Jehovih.

12. Suddenly a light came down from the firmament, like a new star, twinkling, with a halo extending wide on every side. All eyes were turned up, full of expectancy. Hushed and still, the ninety millions stood.

13. Presently the star assumed a brighter phase and spread its halo outward, with horns descending, like a crescent, such as is formed in sacred worship when a God standeth in the midst. Larger and brighter the light grew, and tremulous and waving like sheets of fire.

14. Then shot down toward Hored and Moeb three rays of light, piercing, and in advance of the central orb. And the three rays were red, blue, and yellow; but the crescent beyond was white, and it shone abroad over the heavens, so that the corporeal sun and stars in the firmament were invisible.

15. At beholding the majesty and grandeur of Jehovih's host of descending, millions of es'yans and clouded souls in the lower heaven, broke and fled; some ran and hid to avoid the threatening light. For such is the magnifying power of the etherean flame, that all dark thoughts and hidden evil lurking in the soul are magnified, and made so plain that even the dumb can read them through.

16. Millions of the ethereans on God's staff had seen such scenes before, and now stood in glee, firmly riveted by the joy within them. To them, a hundred to one, clung the newly raised from earth, who had never known any other heaven, save such as traveleth with the earth, around about the sun every year. From these there rose millions of whispers, saying: It is like a new death; like a new birth. Behold a man dieth on earth, and his spirit flieth off to another world. And yet now again it flieth off to still another world.

17. Quickly, now, came the three great rays, foremost projecting; and these were the orders of marshals from the a'jian fields of O'wea and Hon'she; the red lights represented A'ji, the blue lights represented O'wea, and the yellow, Hon'she. And there were of marshals one million, and they cast the curtains round about to cover all of Hored, the great kingdom.

Plate 1.
EARTH, LOWER HEAVEN, AND
ETHEREAN HOSTS DESCENDING

18. Chief of the marshals was Ah-jeng; and next to him were five sub-chiefs; and next to them one thousand tributary chiefs, who were masters of the ceremonies; and they came in the center of the descending three great rays of light, came swiftly and direct toward the throne of God. And the substance of the rays of light was like curtains of cloth, one end of which reached up to the now near approaching crescent sea of fire. 19. When the light was near touching on the pillars of fire surrounding Moeb, it slackened a little, and then more and more slowly. The chieftains leaped from the etherean flames and stood at the foot of God's throne, saluting in Jehovih's name. 20. God and Ha'jah stood up and answered the sign, then descended and went to the left and right of Ah-jeng, and they ascended, and Ah-jeng sat upon the throne, and the voice of Jehovih spake through him, saying:

63

21. Hold up your heads and rejoice, O my sons and daughters! Behold, I come in a flame of fire! I am here, and there, and throughout the place of heaven, boundless. I gather together and I put asunder the loves of mortals and angels. For they shall go abroad in My firmament and behold My glorious works.

22. Down to the corporeal world I descend and carry hence the loved, for they are Mine. I will make all people look up to My kingdoms. Down to the lower heaven I come in ships of light, curtained about with etherean mantles, and gather in My harvest of new births to higher worlds, more radiant. My hosts below shall look up and glorify My everlasting splendors.

23. I give the tear of grief and sorrow and pity; but, in its flowing forth, I come with holier light and power to stir up the souls of My people. For they shall learn to speak to their Father, who heareth and giveth ear, and is full of love.

24. My joy is in the birth and growing up of souls, and in the joy of their joys, and in the proclaiming of their adoration for My boundless universe.

25. I call to them in darkness, and they come forth; but they halt in the darkness, and I call again, and I send My higher, upraised angels to them, and they call also. Yea, I fill the sky with the splendor of My worlds, es and corpor, that I may stir man up to rise and enjoy the things I have made.

26. The voice departed, and Ah'jeng said: Behold the glory of the heavens, O my beloved, and the reward of the diligent in heart. Jehovih liveth and reigneth, the Highest and never to be reached, the Forever Beyond, and yet Ever Present.

27. O Thou Light of Light and Life of Life, how wonderful is the substance of Thy Creation! Thou hast given me light to behold Thy splendors, which are forever new. O Jehovih, Thou Past, Present and Future of one time, which is and was and ever shall be. Jehovih, Thou, Seen and Unseen and Potent, who hast from Thy very Self imparted a part to all the living! Who hast raised up these of Hored! Glory be to Thee forever and ever!

28. And now, by certain signs and signals, Ah'jeng directed the officers of his hosts to take possession of Moeb and Hored. And the marshals extended out around the place, and by their presence added new light to the pillars of fire.

29. The marshals were decorated with colored raiment and signs and symbols, denoting the places whence they came, and their rank as Gods, and the experience they had passed through.

30. When Ah'jeng ceased speaking, the music of the chosen band of descending angels broke upon the place; first, faintly and far off. The work of the marshals was in keeping with the time of the music; and as the music drew nearer and stronger, so also more and more of the number of marshals descended and filed off to their respective places.

31. Presently the advance of the horns of the crescent, and the cold wave of the falling sea of fire, swept over the lower heaven fearfully and of unquestionable power. By a signal from God, the Brides and Bridegrooms joined in the music of the archangels, and great was the glory thereof.

32. Betwixt the horns of the crescent was a star of wonderful beauty; and it came toward God's throne, reflecting countless rays of light, brilliantly and awe-inspiring. And as the star drew near, it opened on the advance side, as a shell is opened, and there, with arms entwined, sat Etisyai and Onesyi, Goddesses.

CHAPTER XX.

1. Ah'jeng stepped down and stood at the foot of the throne. Masters of the inner temple gathered about the star, and unrolled a carpet reaching across the threshold, and the two Goddesses stepped forth from the crystaled cushion within the star, and glided, as if on a ray of light, up to the judgment seat of Jehovih. Meanwhile the musicians, a million of voices, chanted: Glory, glory to Jehovih, Creator of worlds! Whose place magnificence is, and counterpart to endless time. The All, whose Great existence surpasseth the grandest thoughts of men and Gods! Whose worlds in splendor, are the scrolls on which His hands write with the souls of Mortals His Almighty Will, and Boundless Love!

2. And now did spread out, and round about the wheels of the great ship of fire; and all the millions of hosts, men and women (archangels and Gods and Goddesses), formed a mighty amphitheatre, in which Moeb, with his thirty-three million Brides and Bridegrooms of Jehovih, occupied the arena, themselves arrayed in white, but differently from the Redeeming Hosts from the etherean worlds.

3. In time to the music, without a word of command, moved the hosts; as one person moveth, they in unison moved; and each as a shining crystal in the place allotted, and void in nothing; and all so perfect, as if Jehovih had made each a special work of wonder to inspire men with reverence for the talents He had created withal.

4. In the same time the hosts were forming in place, so was the time of the music, and when the music ceased all was still. The throne was in the east, facing the west; the hosts of Moeb, who were the Brides and Bridegrooms of Jehovih, occupied the lower plane, and the ethereans surrounded them on all sides, raising higher and higher in the distance.

5. God and Ha'jah met the Goddesses at the foot of the throne. God knew Onesyi hundreds of years before in other worlds, and he remembered Etisyai, who had crowned him two hundred years ago. So also did Ha'jah know Etisyai and Onesyi. When they met they all saluted by touching the right hands; and immediately the Goddesses ascended to the centre of the throne, and God went on the right and Ha'jah on the left.

6. Etisyai and Onesyi looked hopefully on the Brides and Bridegrooms, but were passive. Presently the voice of Jehovih spake out of the light of the throne, saying:

7. Soul of My soul, substance of My substance, created I man. Out of My corporeal Self clothed I man. Out of My corporeal Self clothed I him with flesh and blood and bones. Man's spirit I gave from out Mine own spirit, ever present; and I quickened him to move on the face of the earth.

8. God and the Brides and Bridegrooms responded, being quickened by the All Light; Out of corpor I came, quickened by Jehovih's Ever Presence. By virtue of His Wisdom, Power and Love came I into the world; to Jehovih all glory is due forever!

9. Again Jehovih spake, saying: A time I allotted to man to grow, to attain wisdom, power and love; a time to rejoice and a time of sorrow; a time to beget offspring and know a father's care and love; in likeness of Me, to him gave I attributes of my attributes, that man might know Me and My Love.

10. Response: By the bondage of my love to my begotten, do I know my Father liveth and reigneth, and will watch over me forever!

11. Again the voice of Jehovih said: A time in the corporeal form I gave to man, that he might learn corporeal things, and to learn whence springeth the tree of life. From no self-

existence of his own made I man, but from Myself; and in the place I quickened him into life, I bound him for a season. But when man hath filled his corporeal life I provide death to deliver him into a new world.

12. Response: Beautiful is Thy Wisdom, O Jehovih, and far reaching. I was bound in the flesh even as a beast; likened unto the attributes of a beast was my judgment, struggling for things of the corporeal world. With horror I looked upon death; as a sore calamity did I value Thy cutting me off. But Thou deliveredest me into another world, preserving my judgment whole, bringing me to the heavens of my forefathers.

13. Then Jehovih said: In no time brought I man, newborn into the world, without a mother and a nurse and rich nourishment to feed him withal. Yea, I gave him angels to inspire him and lift him up; and I provided a Lord of the earth to manage his kingdoms and nations, and a God in heaven with a throne and judgment seat, that man in the angel world should be provided and wisely instructed in soul to comprehend the glory and harmony of my worlds.

14. Response: Bountiful, O my Father Above! From nothing that I knew of, Thou broughtest me into conscious being, and in my helpless days fed me with rich nourishment. Thou gavest me rulers and examples of government on the earth to discipline my soul to the order of men. And when I was born in heaven, I found God on his throne and a well-ordered haven of rest, with willing angels to clothe me and feed me and teach me the ways of Thy kingdoms in the firmament.

15. Again Jehovih said: When man hath fulfilled his time in the lower heaven, I prepare him by ample teachers for a higher resurrection. As Brides and Bridegrooms my hosts adorn them, and I come in a sea of fire. First was man wedded to the earth, by Me solemnized, and without man's knowledge. Then to the lower heaven was he wed, laboring with spirits and mortals.

16. The voice departed, and now Onesyi spoke, saying: Behold the Brides and Bridegrooms of Jehovih! When they were young they were wed first to the earth and then to the lower heaven, without their wills. Now they stand before the throne of God. In Thy name, O Jehovih, I command them to speak their wills.

17. Response: I put away myself for Thee, O Jehovih! Make me one with Thee. I put away the earth for Thy kingdom's sake, O Jehovih! Make me one with Thee! I put away Thy Lord and Thy God, O Jehovih, for sake of Thee! Thy Lord and Thy God raised me up and made me strong, but lo, the small spark of Thyself within my soul hath grown to be a giant, bowing to none but Thee, O Jehovih! O make me Thy Bride (Bridegroom), O Jehovih!

18. Onesyi said: The lame and the weak shall have a crutch, but the glory of the Father is to see His Brides and Bridegrooms walk alone. Whoever to Jehovih is wed, shall never more to this man nor that man, nor woman, nor Lord, nor God, nor to any person or thing, for self's sake, say: HELP!

19. Response: God and the Lord were my Saviors; without them I had never known of Thy exalted heavens, O Jehovih. Thy Spirit calleth me forever upward. Thy Lord and Thy God taught me to look upward; yea, they prayed for me. Now am I strong before Thee, O Jehovih! Henceforth will I pray to Thee only; but never for mine own benefit, nor for glory, nor for ease, nor for rest, nor for exaltation; but that I may be quick and strong and wise to do Thy will forever!

20. Onesyi said: Brides and Bridegrooms of Jehovih, ALL HAIL! ALL HAIL!

21. Response: Voice of Jehovih, ALL HAIL! ALL HAIL!

22. Onesyi said: To Jehovih and his everlasting kingdoms are ye wed forever!

23. Response: To Thee, O Jehovih, am I wed forever!

24. Onesyi said: To be one with him forever!

25. Response: To be one with Jehovih forever!

26. The voice of Jehovih said: They shall judge from My judgment seat; in them shall My Wisdom shine; for they are Mine forever!

27. Response: To consider Thee first, in all things, O Jehovih, shall I henceforth forever!

28. The voice said: Behold I have woven a crown for them; adorn them for My sake.

29. Response: I will have no crown, save that which is woven by Thee, O Jehovih! For thy sake will I wear Thy crown forever!

30. The voice said: Behold, they that were My sons and daughters have become My Brides and Bridegrooms; they are Mine forever!

31. Response: I am Jehovih's forever!

32. Onesyi said: Pass before the throne, O my beloved. The testimony of Jehovih awaiteth His redeemed. Ye shall dwell in the emancipated kingdoms forever!

33. And now the hosts of Brides and Bridegrooms passed singly before the throne of God; the whole thirty-three millions passed. And the es'enaurs chanted a hymn of glory, and there came down from the firmament above mists of yellow, blue and red; and the mists fell into the archangels' hands who stood about the throne, and by them was converted into crowns, the which were placed on the heads of the Brides and Bridegrooms. And on the crowns were the words: IN WAN BROUGHT FORTH; DELIVERED IN HON'SHE.

34. As the hosts passed in front of the throne, Onesyi said: By that which springeth out of the earth is the atmospherean fed and clothed; but the etherean draweth from the etherean worlds. Behold the crowns of the earth and of the lower heaven are but symbols of power, wisdom and love; but that which I bring from Jehovih's kingdom containeth real virtue.

35. And lo and behold, the Brides and Bridegrooms became as archangels by virtue of the crowns from Jehovih's hand.

CHAPTER XXI.

1. When the ceremonies were ended, Onesyi said: Soon, now, in the name of the Father will we rise and go a long journey; and that ye may be apprised and consorted in love, I proclaim the freedom of the hour in Jehovih's name.

2. And the people went and mingled with each other, rejoicing and saluting. And Ha'jah and God and Etisyai greeted one another, and the Lords came forward, and were also greeted; and then the marshals and the es'enaurs and all long-serving laborers. And lastly, all that had redeemed any man or woman from darkness to light, came also, and were saluted and duly honored.

3. And for the space of one hour all the angels indulged in revelry, reunion and fullness of heart; but no book could relate the thousandth part of the questions asked and love assurances expressed.

4. When the hour was ended, Onesyi signaled the proper officer, and he sounded the gavel thrice, whereupon all was hushed and still. Onesyi said:

5. As Jehovih bestoweth a newborn child, so also doth He take the father and the mother

away to the es world. As Jehovih sent Etisyai, my sister, to establish the lower heaven, so have I come by His command to bear hence this harvest to His everlasting kingdom. As a child bewaileth the loss of its father and mother, so will ye that remain bewail the loss of this rich harvest of archangels.

6. It is Jehovih's will that ye drink deep of the sorrow of parting, for by this bondage will ye be again reunited in the heavens still above. The progress of the soul of man is forever onward, and in steps and plateaux; and the glory of the resurrection of him that goeth before is equally great as is the sorrow of him that remaineth behind. But the love that bindeth together is as a chain outstretched across the universe; nor time nor distance shall prevail against the inventions thereof.

7. Swift messengers, well trained to course the vault of heaven, will pass between you, carrying the tidings of your soul's delight. And as Jehovih giveth summer to follow winter, and the winter the summer, so also shall the time again and again, forever, in which ye shall mingle and part; again labor together, but in broader fields, and again part for a season.

8. Behold the wisdom of Jehovih in placing far apart the places of the souls of men; for all things abiding near together equalize themselves. Even as there is glory in a new birth, so is there glory in death; as there is sorrow in death, so is there joy in resurrection. The time is now come when these that ye see, ye shall not see for a long season; but ye shall rejoice in this hour of parting, for they rise as Brides and Bridegrooms to Jehovih.

9. The es'enauers sang an anthem of praise in which all the hosts united, and great was the glory thereof. And now Onesyi arose, saying:

10. JEHOVIH, ALMIGHTY AND EVERLASTING! HOLY, HOLY CREATOR, RULER AND GIVER FORTH! LOOK UPON THIS THY SON, HA'JAH! O FATHER, IN THY NAME AND BY VIRTUE OF THY POWER IN ME VESTED, DO I PERPETRATE AND CROWN HIM GOD OF HEAVEN AND EARTH!

11. Ha'jah, now God, said: THY WILL BE DONE, O JEHOVIH! Then Onesyi turned to the five chief Lords of the five divisions of the earth, and bestowed them in like manner.

12. And Onesyi stretched forth her hand, saying: Give me a crown, O Jehovih, for Thy Son, God of heaven and earth! And there descended etherean substance into her hand, and she raised it up, and lo, it became a crown of great beauty, and she put in on God's (Ha'jah's) head. Then in like manner did she crown the Lords of the earth.

13. And Etisyai and Onesyi came down and sat at the foot of the throne.

14. God (that had been Ha'jah) came down and Waga and Jud with him, and stretching forth their hands, they said to Etisyai, Onesyi and Sethantes, the retiring God: Arise, O Goddess….. Arise, O Goddess…. Arise, O God…. and go thy way!

15. And they rose up and marched forth. The proper officers had already prepared the ship for its etherean journey; and soon as Etisyai and Onesyi had entered the central star, all the people that were to ascend went into the places assigned to them.

16. God (that had been Ha'jah) and the Lords returned, in tears, to the throne, and now the plateau of everlasting light began to ascend. Music sprang from every side, glorifying Jehovih and the magnificence of His bountiful worlds.

17. And those of the lower heaven were as the echo of the music above; and the light of the ascending ship of fire made all else as a shadow. But higher and higher it arose, in the form of a crescent, slowly turning on its upright axis, turning and rising, higher and

higher, and the music faded away in the distance.

18. In a little while the meteor-like ascending ship of heaven looked like a star, till farther and farther off it disappeared in the distance.

19. Thus ascended to the emancipated heavens in etherea the first harvest of angels born of the earth.

CHAPTER XXII.

1. God said: Arise, O Lords of my realm, and go to the kingdoms of earth, which ye received from Jehovih's hand; and may His wisdom, love and power be with you all!

2. And the Lords departed, they and their attendants, and went to their kingdoms over mortals.

3. And this was the beginning of the second dispensation of the first cycle of the Eoptian age of the earth. And the lower heaven was well established in habitations, angels and officers, and in all the requisites for the upraised souls of mortals.

4. And God dispensed laws and government after the manner of his predecessor, enlarging all the places according to the increase in the number of spirits rising up from the earth.

5. And the voice of Jehovih was with God; and as the first kingdom had been called Hored, so was the second called Hored, signifying the place of God.

6. And as it had been with the Lords of the earth in their places, so continued it with the new Lords, and they enlarged their places also, even according to the increase in the number of inhabitants of the earth.

7. And as it had been of old, that messengers went constantly from Hored to the Lords' places, so did they also continue to do; and by this means all the affairs of the lower heaven were kept in harmony, Lords and God.

8. And God ruled in Hored four hundred years, and Hored spread over all the lands of the earth.

CHAPTER XXIII.

1. When the time of God and his hosts was fulfilled, Jehovih brought the earth into dan of Eyon, in the arc Lais, whose angels descended in a ship of fire, and delivered God, his Lords and all the hosts under them who were prepared for the etherean resurrection. At this time there were in atmospherea six hundred and twenty-five million inhabitants. And the number of the second harvest was two hundred and eighty millions.

2. After the manner of the ascent of the first harvest, so was the ascent of the second harvest. And the place of the landing of the second harvest in the firmament of heaven was in Lais, and Bin, and the grade of the harvest was seventy-eight, being two less than the grade of the first harvest.

3. So the heavens of the earth passed into the care of succeeding God and Lords, who had been raised up and prepared therefore. And for the present there were no more ethereans dwelling in these regions.

4. Jehovih had said: They that come out of the earth shall be sufficient unto themselves. As a mother provideth for her child, so do I provide for the spirit generations of a corporeal world; but when they are mature in wisdom, strength and love, I command them to take the places of Lords and God in the management of my kingdoms.

5. So it came to pass after the ascent of the ethereans, the whole earth and its lower

heavens were under the dominion of such as had sprung up out of the earth. Hence it became a saying: The first was etherean rule; the second was atmospherean rule. For the earth had Lords who had been on no other world, and a God who had never been on other worlds.

6. And it likewise came to pass that the atmospherean rulers were more lenient and less tyrannical in their government than had been the ethereans. For as the ethereans had forbidden the es'yans, the newly dead, to return to their mortal kindred, even to the fiftieth year in spirit life, so, not so with the present Lords and God, for they indulged hundreds of thousands of es'yans for sympathy's sake to return to their mortal kindred. And these es'yans became not workers in heaven, either for others or for their own resurrection to higher regions; but they became idlers and vagabonds in the lower heaven, oft living with their mortal kindred till their mortal kindred died, and then in turn persuading such es'yans to do even as they did.

7. And God perceived, when it was too late, that his leniency had laid the foundation for disorganizing the kingdom of heaven; for the strolling idlers, knowing no other heaven, sowed the spirit of disbelief in the places of learning and industry in the lower heaven, persuading others that they were toiling to no good purpose.

8. They said: Behold, it was told us on earth there was a Jehovih! But we are in heaven, and yet we find him not. Now do we know of a truth there is no All Person. Come, then, let us seek ease and the rich viands that rise up out of the earth. A man liveth on the earth and dieth, and his spirit floateth around about, and there is no more of him. Why will ye serve the Lord? Why will ye serve God? Be free and live for yourselves instead of others.

9. Thus it came to pass t little by little the lower heaven began to fall from its high estate.

10. The third dan was six hundred years, and God and his Lords, having provided successors, ascended with their harvest to etherea. And the number thereof was four hundred and eight million Brides and Bridegrooms, and their grade was sixty-six.

11. The fourth dan was five hundred years, and the harvest was six hundred million Brides and Bridegrooms; and their grade was fifty-eight.

12. The fifth dan was three hundred years; and the harvest was two hundred millions; and their grade was fifty, which was the lowest grade capable of emancipation, or capable of surviving in etherea.

13. And now darkness set in and covered all the earth around. And from this time until the end of the cycle, which was three thousand years from the birth of man on earth, there were no more resurrections to the emancipated heavens.

14. The Kingdom of Hored was broken up and dissolved. The spirits loved not to labor and to learn according to Jehovih's plan, but returned to the earth-ornaments; and they were called DRUJAS, because they desired not resurrection.

15. And God and the Lords, and their officers and teachers, were without subjects and pupils. And mortals were beset by thousands and millions of drujas, so that the ashars were powerless to accomplish good inspiration.

16. At this time there were more than three thousand million angels in atmospherea, and for the most part, they dwelt on earth.

17. Thus ended the first cycle of the first heaven of the earth.

END OF THE BOOK OF SETHANTES, SON OF JEHOVIH.

FIRST BOOK OF THE FIRST LORDS.

BEING CONTEMPORARY WITH THE BOOK OF SETHANTES, SON OF JEHOVIH. THAT IS TO SAY, AS SETHANTES WAS GOD OF HEAVEN, SO IN THE SAME PERIOD OF TIME HIS LORDS HAD DOMINION ON THE EARTH, AND THIS IS THEIR BOOK, EVEN AS THE PROCEEDING ONE WAS GOD'S BOOK.

CHAPTER I.

1. In the beginning God created the heavens of the earth; and the Lord made man upright. And man was naked and not ashamed; neither knew man the sin of incest, but he dwelt as the beasts of the field.

2. And the Lord brought the angels of heaven to man; by his side took they on forms like unto man, having all the organs and attributes of mortals, for it was the time of the earth for such things to be.

3. And it came to pass that a new race was born on the earth, and these were called I'hins, because they were begotten of both heaven and earth. Hence it became a saying: The earth conceived of the Lord.

4. And the name of the first race was Asu (Adam), because they were of the earth only; and the name of the second race was I'hin (Abel), because they were capable of being taught spiritual things.

5. And the Lord said: Of all that live on the face of the earth, or in the waters thereof, or in the air above, that breathes the breath of life, man only have I delivered unto knowledge of his Creator.

6. And the Lord spake unto the I'hin, through his angels spake he to them, saying: Go hide thy nakedness, for it is the commandment of God.

7. And The I'hins were afraid, and they clothed themselves, and were no longer naked before the Lord.

8. And the Lord commanded the angels to give up their forms, and to be no more seen as mortals. And it was done. And the Lord said unto them: Because ye brought forth life, which is in flesh and blood, ye shall minister unto man for six generations on the face of the earth. And it was so.

9. And that man may continue to walk upright, ye shall teach him the law of incest, for man of himself cannot attain to know this.

10. Neither shall ye permit the I'hins to dwell with Asu (Adam), lest his seed go down in darkness.

11. And man was thus inspired of the Lord, and he walked upright, and prospered on the earth.

12. But after a season man became conceited in his own judgment, and he disobeyed the commandments of God.

13. And he strayed out of the garden of paradise and began to dwell with the asu'ans (Adams), and there was born into the world a new race called Druk (Cain), and they had not the light of the Father in them, neither could they be inspired with shame, nor of heavenly things.

14. And the I'hins were grateful to the Lord, and they gave sacrifice in burnt offerings. And they said unto the Druks: Go ye and sacrifice unto the Lord, and he will prosper you. But the Druks understood not; and they fell upon the Lord's chosen, and slew them, right

and left, taking their possessions.

15. And the Lord said unto the Druks: Because ye have slain your brethren ye shall depart out of the place of God; and that ye may be known to the ends of the earth I put my mark upon you.

16. And the mark of the Lord put upon the Druks was the shadow of blood, which, being interpreted, is WAR.

17. And the Lord God said: By this sign shall the tribes of Druk and their descendents be known unto the end of the world.

18. And woman, being more helpless than man, cried out with fear, saying: O Lord, how shall I bring forth unto thee, and not unto the sons of death?

19. And the Lord said: Because thou hast brought forth in pain, and yet called on my name, behold I will be unto thee as a shield and protector. For I will also put a mark upon the I'hins, my chosen, so thou shalt know them when they come unto thee.

20. And the Lord commanded the male I'hins, old and young, to be circumcised, that woman might not be deceived by the druks. And the I'hins circumcised one another, old and young; for it was the testimony of the Lord unto woman that seed of their seed was born to everlasting life.

21. And the druks (Cain) went away into the wilderness, and dwelt with the asu'ans and with one another.

22. God said: A boundary line will I make betwixt the tribes of druks and the I'hins; and this is the line that I the Lord God make betwixt them:

23. The I'hins shall labor and clothe themselves, and I will abide with them; but the druks shall wander in the wilderness, neither laboring nor clothing themselves.

24. And it was so.

CHAPTER II.

1. The time of the habitation of Asu was eight thousand years; and they survived two thousand years after the time of the birth of the I'hins, which is to say: Asu dwelt on the earth six thousand years, and then conceived of the chosen of God; and after that survived yet two thousand years.

2. And Asu (Adam) disappeared off the face of the earth.

3. And there remained on the earth the sacred people, the I'hins; and the carnivorous people, the druks.

4. The I'hins were white and yellow, but the druks were brown and black; the I'hins were small and slender, but the druks were tall and stout.

5. Now, because the druks had not previously obeyed the Lord, but went and dwelt with the asu'ans, there was a half-breed race born on the earth, called Yak, signifying ground people; and they burrowed in the ground like beasts of the forest. And the Yaks did not walk wholly upright, but also went on all fours.

6. God said: Because the Yaks cannot be taught the crime of incest, behold they shall not dwell forever on the earth. So also shall it be with the druks, save wherein they cohabit with the I'hins, whose seed is born unto everlasting life. But with the druks, and their heirs that spring from the Yaks, there shall be an end, both in this world and the next.

7. And the arms of the Yaks were long, and their backs were stooped and curved. And the Lord said: Because they are the fruit of incest, and not capable of speech, nor of eternal

life in heaven, the I'hins shall make servants of them.

8. And that they may not tempt my chosen to bring forth fruit unto destruction, they shall be neutralized in my sight. And the angels of God taught the I'hins to make eunuchs of the Yaks; of the males and females made the I'hins eunuchs of the Yaks, and took them for servants.

9. And the Lord said: The Yaks shall serve the I'hins, and build and sow and reap for them. And it was so.

10. The I'hins were disposed to live alone, but the Lord called them together, saying: Come and dwell together in cities. For it is meet that ye live after the manner of my kingdoms in heaven.

11. Build ye therefore unto the Lord your God; and my angels shall dwell with you, teaching you to sing and dance for the glory of your Creator.

12. And man built unto the Lord, and established worship on earth after the manner of heaven.

13. Now it came to pass that the druks came to witness the rites and ceremonies of the chosen, but they took no part therein, neither comprehended they the meaning thereof

14. And God said unto the I'hins: That ye may teach some of them of the Lord your God, build ye within the house of worship an image of me; in likeness of man build ye it. And I will manifest unto as many as are capable of everlasting life.

15. And the I'hins, men and women, with their servants, built images of stone and clay and wood unto the Lord, and stood them by the altars of sacrifice.

16. And in the time of worship, the angels of the Lord came and possessed the idols and spake therefrom, with audible voices spake before mortals.

17. And the druks inquired of the I'hins as to the cause thereof. And the I'hins said: Behold, there is a God in heaven, more subtle than the air of heaven. He it was that brought us forth out of darkness. He speaketh in idol that ye may know he abideth with his people.

18. The druks said: What saith he? The I'hins answered, saying: That whosoever hath attained to remember God is in the way of everlasting life.

19. The druks inquired, saying: How shall a man live forever? Behold, ye that believe also die!

20. The I'hins answered, saying: As the voice of the Lord is unseen but potent, so is there a spirit in man unseen and potent, which shall never die, but ascend to heaven to habitations prepared by the Lord.

21. And many of the druks pondered on these things, and their thoughts quickened their souls within them, so that they brought forth heirs unto eternal salvation.

22. And the Lord said unto the I'hins: Because ye have done a good thing, go ye abroad, by the roadsides and in other places, and build images unto me and mine, and my angels shall bestow gifts and signs and miracles.

23. And the I'hins covered the roadways of the earth over with idols of stone and wood and clay, and the angels of heaven descended to the idols and established thereabout heavenly kingdoms.

24. And when man came hither, and called on the name of the Lord, it was as a password for the angels; and they wrought miracles, and otherwise gave evidence unto man of the Unseen.

CHAPTER III.

1. And God gave commandments unto man, that the earth might be a place of rejoicing forever. And these are the commandments of the Lord God as given in that day:

2. Thou shalt strive to remember the Lord thy God with all thy heart and with all thy soul.

3. Thou shalt not kill man, nor beast, nor bird, nor creeping thing, for they are the Lord's.

4. Thou shalt build walls round about thy cities, that beasts and serpents may not enter and do thee harm. And if thy habitation be in the wilderness, thou shalt build mounds of wood and earth to sleep on at night, that serpents and beasts may not molest thee.

5. The I'hins inquired of the Lord, saying: If we build walls around about our cities, how shall we get in and out? How shall we gather our harvests of fruit and nuts and seeds of the field? How shall we ascend on the mounds which we build in the wilderness?

6. The Lord said: Behold, my angels shall teach you to build ladders and how to use them. And when ye go into the city at night ye shall take the ladders in after you; and when ye come out in the morning ye shall let the ladders down again.

7. And God's angels taught the chosen these things, and man provided the cities with ladders, and he provided the mounds with ladders also; according to the commandment of God were these things done.

8. And the I'hins prospered and spread abroad over the face of the earth; hundreds of thousands of cities and mounds built they, and they rejoiced in the glory of all created things. Neither killed they man, nor beast, nor fish, nor bird, nor creeping thing that breathed the breath of life.

9. And God saw that man was good and grateful in all things; and God called unto the angels of heaven, saying: Why are the I'hins good? For, as yet, they are ignorant!

10. And the angels answered, saying: Because thou saidst unto us: Go ye, as guardian angels, and inspire man to live without evil, even so have we administered unto the I'hins, guarding and inspiring them night and day.

11. God said: Why then, the I'hins have no honor. Except they learn of themselves to be good, they will be void of wisdom in heaven. For this reason ye shall withdraw a little, that man be tried as to his self-commandment.

12. And the angels withdrew awhile from the I'hins. And now it came to pass, that they had stored in their cities and on their mounds ample provision of food and raiment for the winter; but the druks followed not the example of the I'hins, for the druks stored up nothing.

13. And when the angels departed a little way, evil spirits came to the druks, and said unto them: Behold, it is winter, and ye are hungry. Go ye over the ladders and possess the stores of the I'hins.

14. And the druks plundered the I'hins; and evil spirits sat upon the I'hins also, and many of them were inspired to defend their stores. And war ensued; and it spread around about the whole earth.

15. And the I'hins besought the Lord as to why God suffered evil to come upon his chosen.

16. And the Lord said: Because ye depended upon me for all things, ye developed not yourselves. Henceforth shall man learn to face evil on his own account; otherwise he could not attain to the Godhead in heaven.

17. Two entities hast thy Creator given thee, that which is flesh, and that which is spirit. And the flesh shall desire earthly things; but the spirit shall desire heavenly things.

18. Behold, when the druks came upon thee for thy stores, thy flesh cried out WAR, and thy people fell.

19. Again have I come to thee to raise thee up; to make thee understand the spirit within. It is that, and not the flesh, which shall learn to triumph.

20. The I'hins said: Our people are scattered and gone; will they not mingle with the druks, and thus go out in darkness?

21. The Lord said: Behold there were druks who had learned a little from the images; now because thy people are scattered and gone, they shall go amongst the druks and teach the law of incest and the name of God, and they shall also begin to hide their nakedness.

22. So the Lord inspired other people besides the I'hins, to make and wear clothes, and they thus wore them.

23. And again the Lord brought the I'hins together in lodges and cities, and he said unto them: Henceforth ye shall live upon the earth as an example of righteousness. And your brethren who have mingled with the tribes of darkness shall no longer molest you, but be your defenders and protectors.

24. And there began to be a new tribe on the earth; and they were called I'huans, because they were half-breeds, betwixt the druks and I'hins. The I'huans were red like copper; and they were taller and stronger than any other people in all the world. And the Lord commanded the I'huans, saying:

25. Protect ye the I'hins, the little people, white and yellow; call them THE SACRED PEOPLE. For ye are of them, and ye are also of the Lord your God. And it was so.

CHAPTER IV.

1. About this time man began to use his lip and tongue in enunciating words, prior to which he spoke in the thorax.

2. And the Lord spake unto the I'hin, saying: That the labor of the Lord thy God may be remembered on the earth, go provide me a stone and I will engrave it with mine own hand, and it shall be called Se'moin (see first tablet, BOOK OF SAPHAH) because it shall be a testimony unto all nations and peoples, on the earth, of the first written language in all the world.

3. And the I'hins prepared a stone, and hewed it flat and then polished it smooth; and the Lord came down in the night and engraved it. And the Lord explained it; through his angels taught he the I'hins the meaning of the characters engraved thereon.

4. And the Lord said: Go into all cities in all the countries of the world, and provide ye copies like unto the tablet I have given. So it came to pass, the angels of heaven inspired the I'hins to make tablets and to read them, that the first language of the earth (Panic) might be preserved to the races of men. And it was so.

5. Now the I'huans partly obeyed the Lord and partly obeyed the way of the flesh; and they became warriors and destroyers; nevertheless they harmed not the I'hins, nor suffered harm to come upon them.

6. God had commanded the I'hins to make eunuchs of the Yaks, the monstrosities, and use them as servants; for the Lord saw that the Yaks were not capable of everlasting life

in heaven.

7. Now the I'huans also served the Yaks in the same way; but they disobeyed God in inflicting the neutral gender on their enemies whom they captured in war. And although they were themselves half-breeds with the druks, yet they hated the druks, and pursued them with vengeance.

8. In those days the relative proportion of the races of men were: I'hins, one hundred; I'huans, three hundred; druks, five thousand; Yaks, five thousand; and of monstrosities betwixt man and beast, three thousand; but the latter died each generation, for they had not the power of procreation amongst themselves.

9. And God saw the work of destruction going on (of the I'huans slaughtering right and left), and he sent the I'hins to preach amongst them, saying to the I'hins.

10. Thus say ye to the I'huans: Whomsoever is created alive, kill not, for it is the commandment of the Lord.

11. For in the time of your most success in slaughtering your fellow-man, ye are also peopling heaven with the spirits of vengeance. And they will return upon you, and even the I'huans shall turn upon one another; thus saith God.

12. But the I'huans understood not; believed not. And it came to pass that great darkness covered the earth. And man, save the few I'hins, gave up to wickedness all his days.

13. And the Lord's people worshipped and preached in the temples, and the Lord and his heavenly hosts manifested unto them; but all the other races of men heard not, would not come to learn of God.

14. And the Lord became tired in his labor, and He called his angels to him, and he said unto them: Behold, man on the earth hath gone so far from my ways he will not heed my commandments; he cannot hear my voice.

15. And your labor is in vain also. For which reason we will tarry no longer on the earth till man hath exhausted the evil that is in him.

16. So the Lord and his angel hosts departed away from the earth. And clouds came over the face of the earth; the moon shone not, and the sun was only as a red coal of fire; and the stars stood in the firmament as well in the day as at night.

17. The harvests failed; the trees yielded no nuts, and the roots on which man feedeth ceased to grow.

18. And the monstrosities, and the Yaks, and the druks, died off, tens of millions of them. And even yet they were not extinct. Nevertheless, the I'huans suffered less; and the I'hins not at all. For the Lord had previously inspired them to provide against the coming famine.

19. And the Lord bewailed the earth and the generations of man: I made man upright and walked by his side, but he slipped aside and fell, said the Lord. I admonished him, but he would not heed. I showed him that every living creature brought forth its own kind; but he understood not, believed not; and he dwelt with beasts; falling lower than all the rest.

END OF THE FIRST BOOK OF THE FIRST LORDS.

Plate 3. Asu.

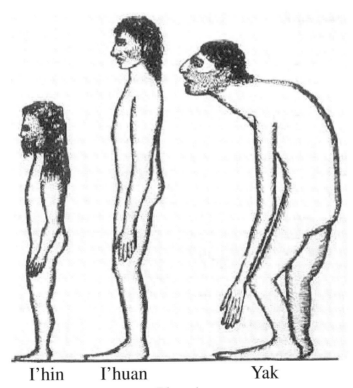

I'hin   I'huan   Yak

Plate 4.

BOOK OF AH'SHONG, SON OF JEHOVIH.

GOD OF THE SECOND CYCLE AFTER MAN'S CREATION.

CHAPTER I.

1. When God and his Lords of heaven and earth had lost their heavenly dominion, the swift messengers, that constantly ply through the atmospherean and etherean worlds, bore the report to Jehovih's kingdom in etherea.

2. The earth had passed the ji'ayan eddies at Shrapah, in the etherean roadway Hi-a-balk'yiv, and was heading for the eastern fields of Anakaron, having entered the dan'haian arches of Vehetaivi, where lay the great kingdoms of the Orian Chief, Hieu Wee, with his millions of Gods and Goddesses and high-raised ethereans.

3. Before Hieu Wee, came the swift messengers, fresh from the heavens of the earth, with their pitiful tales of woe that had befallen the inhabitants thereof.

4. Hieu Wee said: I behold the red star, the earth, O Jehovih! I have heard the tale of horror. What shall be done, O Father?

5. Then spake Jehovih, saying: Call thy tributary Chief, Ah'shong. Let him hear the will of Jehovih!

6. Then sent Hieu Wee for Ah'shong, who had dominion over the fields of Anakaron in etherea, through which lay the roadway where the earth was to travel for three thousand years.

7. And when Ah'shong came before the Holy Council of Hieu Wee's million Gods and Goddesses, the All Light fell upon the throne like a sun; and the voice of the Creator spake in the midst of the light, saying:

8. Hieu Wee, My son! and Hieu Wee answered: Here am I, Thy servant, O Jehovih!

9. Jehovih said: Behold the red star, the earth; she entereth the fields of Anakaron. She is dripping wet and cold in the ji'ayan eddies. Her God and Lords are powerless in the spell of darkness. Send thou thy son, Ah'shong, to deliver the earth and her heavens. For behold, I will bring them to his door.

10. Then spake Ah'shong, saying: Thy will be done, O Jehovih. Though I have been long honored in etherea, with many etherean worlds to command, I have not as yet redeemed one corporeal world and her heavens from a time of darkness.

11. Jehovih said: Go then, My Son, to the laboring earth and deliver her; but first appoint thou a successor for Anakaron.

12. Then spake Hieu Wee, who was older than the red star, who had seen many corporeal worlds created; had seen them run their course, and then disappear as such. He said to Ah'shong:

13. Send thou to Wan, and to Hivigat, in etherea, and get the history of the earth and her heaven; and obtain thou also an account of her harvests of Brides and Bridegrooms to Jehovih. And thou shalt call from my realms as many million etherean angels as thy labor may require, and with them proceed to the earth, and thou shalt have a line of swift messengers established betwixt this place and thine, and, by the power of Jehovih, I will answer thy prayers in whatsoever thou shalt need.

14. Then Ah'shong went back to Anakaron, his etherean kingdom, and before his Holy

Council made known Jehovih's will and his. And Ah'shong called for sixty million volunteers, to go with him on his mission; and they came presently: Some from Yohan; some from T'seing; some from Araith; some from Gon Loo, and from various other places in Anakaron; came in millions; came as many as Ah'shong called for.

15. So Ah'shong raised up a successor to Jehovih's throne in Anakaron, and he was installed and crowned according to the discipline of the etherean heavens.

16. And Ah'shong sent swift messengers into the former roadway of the earth to obtain its history; its harvests of Brides and Bridegrooms.

17. Then gazed Ah'shong toward the red star; and his sixty million volunteers also gazed, and watched her as she coursed along in the arches of Vehetaivi.

18. Thus Ah'shong, well skilled in the course and behavior of worlds, gathered together his millions of angels, trained in arduous enterprise and furtherance of Jehovih's will. Quickly they framed and equipped an Orian port-au-gon, and illuminated it with fire-lights and bolts. And these sons and daughters of Jehovih embarked and sped forth. A half a million miles, even on the outskirts of Anakaron, and they stood close above the earth, almost so near that the sweeping moon would touch the down-hanging curtains of etherean fire. And here they halted, that both mortals and angels belonging to the earth might behold and fear; for such Jehovih made man, by unusual sights, to become weak and trembling, to change him to new purposes.

19. Jehovih's voice spake to Ah'shong, saying: For three days and nights stand thou in the firmament that man on earth and in atmospherea may behold the power and majesty of My chosen in heaven.

20. Ah'shong said: On the fourth day, O Jehovih, I will cross Chinvat; on the fifth, descend toward the earth. Bring me, O Father, Thy messengers from the lower heaven. I will converse with them.

21. Jehovih sent the angels of the earth and lower heaven up to Ah'shong; disheartened they came, to know Jehovih's will.

22. Ah'shong said unto them: The Father's hosts are come from their high estate and glorious ease, to redeem these fallen heavens, and man on the earth. It is our labor to come in love to the helpless, and teach them how to sing in Jehovih's praise. Then the swift messengers answered:

23. In the All Person's boundless love, find thou recompense for thy holy words, most honored God. Down in darkness, long and earnestly, have the Lords of earth labored conjointly with heaven's God, whose kingdom fell. Alas, our God, who ministered over the lower heaven, is crushed and humiliated. The enemies of high heaven, exulting in their spoil of Jehovih's kingdom and His name, mock us, saying: Where now is Jehovih? Whence cometh the Higher Light? O ye Faithists in an All Person boundless!

24. But now thy high-shining sun, thy ship of etherean fire, maketh the sons and daughters of the earth and her heaven look, and fear, and tremble. And when thy Light appeared we made all haste in hope of succor. Our souls are more than filled with thankfulness; and in Jehovih's name, we will back and employ a million trumpeters to proclaim around the earth and heaven: JEHOVIH IS COME!

25. After due salutation the swift messengers departed; and Ah'shong made all things in readiness for his descent when the proper time should arrive.

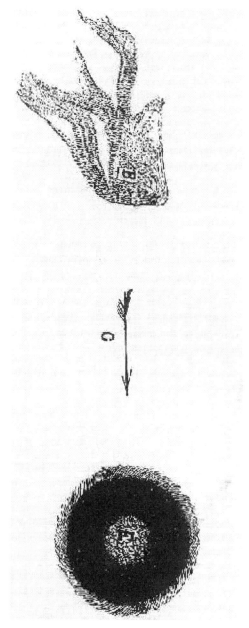

Plate 2.
Ethereans visiting the Earth.
A, Atmospherea; B, Ethereans; E, Earth;
C, Distance: 20,000 miles.

CHAPTER II.

1. Jehovih spake to Ah'shong, saying: On the evening of the third day shalt thou move thy etherean ship toward the earth. And when thou arrivest within an arrafon thou shalt halt for another three days, that thy magnificence may awe the men and angels of earth with

the power and glory of My emancipated sons and daughters.

2. Ah'shong proceeded as commanded, and when he came within an arrafon, halted for three days, and the magnificence of the scene overcame the stubbornness of men of earth and angels in atmospherea. Again Jehovih said:

3. Proceed again, My son, and when thou art within half the breadth of the earth, halt once more and make in the place thereof a plateau, and it shall be the place of thy abiding for the time of dawn, which shall be seven years and sixty days.

4. And from this time forth My etherean hosts shall not remain in atmospherea more than eight years in any one cycle. This, then, that I give to thee shall be like every dawn of dan, some of one year, some of two or three or four or more (years), as the time requireth.

5. And thou shalt dwell in thy kingdom seven years and sixty days, and the time shall be called the first dawn of dan, and the next succeeding shall be called the second dawn of dan, and so on, as long as the earth bringeth forth.

6. And the time from one dawn of dan to another shall be called one dan'ha; and four dan'ha shall be called one square, because this is the sum of one density, which is twelve thousand of the earth's years. And twelve squares shall be called one cube, which is the first dividend of the third space, in which there is no variation in the vortex of the earth. And four cubes shall be called one sum, because the magnitude thereof embraceth one equal of the Great Serpent.

7. Ah'shong proceeded again, and moved within four thousand miles of the earth, and the voice of Jehovih commanded Ah'shong to halt in the place, and found a new kingdom, using all things requisite to that end. Jehovih said:

8. Thy place shall be a distance away from the earth, that thy dominion be not disturbed by the confusion of the fallen angels thereof. So also, to as many as thou shalt redeem away from the earth and from mortal contact, the distance of thy kingdom will prevent them returning.

9. Ah'shong perceived, and he proclaimed what Jehovih had spoken to him. And the hosts cast out fastenings to the plateau, that the kingdom together with the etherean sea of fire might rotate with the earth and its atmosphere. Jehovih said:

10. Make strong the foundation of thy place, and erect ten thousand pillars of fire around about; and in every direction provide roadways and mansions; but in the midst thou shalt build the house of council, wherein shall sit thy host of dominion during dawn.

11. Ah'shong built the place as commanded by Jehovih, and when it was finished, Jehovih said: Thou shalt call the place Yeshuah. And it was so called, because it was a place of salvation. Again Jehovih said:

12. Choose now thy council, My Son, and also thy sub-officers, and when thou hast completed the list, leave in Yeshuah the sub-officers and proceed thou, and thy council of one million men and women with thee, down to the earth and heaven thereof, and cast thine eyes upon the inhabitants, for they are in distress. And when thou comest to the place of My Lords and My God, deliver thou them and bring them to Yeshuah, for they need rest. And as many of the I'hins in heaven as are capable, bring thou also away with thee, and give them into the care of thy people.

13. Ah'shong did as commanded, first selecting his council and his officers, and then he and his hosts proceeded to the earth as had been commanded.

CHAPTER III.

1. Up to this time the ancient names of the division of the lands of the earth had been maintained, and God and his Lords being driven from the place of Hored, which had gone into dissolution, dwelt part of the time in Waga and part in Jud and Vohu.

2. And God and the Lords had established three kingdoms, one in Waga, one in Jud, and one in Vohu; and within these kingdoms of heaven there were two hundred millions of redeemed angels capable of the second resurrection, and one hundred millions of es'yans and unlearned apprentices. Chief of the three heavens was Waga, and thither had God and his Lords congregated with their chief officers, as soon as the sign of the descending sea of Jehovih's kingdom appeared in the firmament above.

3. To God, Jehovih spake, saying: Make ready thy places, O My son, and thy Lords with thee. Behold, I come in a world of fire, and My faithful workers shall find rest and happiness.

4. Ah'shong will redeem thy sons and daughters; yea, he will girdle the earth about with new, etherean light and great power.

5. Call together thy people, O God, and bid them rejoice and make merry, for the time of deliverance is at hand.

6. Then God communicated to the Lords, and they again to others, the words of Jehovih; and at sight of the sign in heaven, the faithful began to rejoice and to gather together in their respective places. But of the unbelieving angels dwelling on earth, and with mortals, and in other abodes, of whom there were hundreds of millions, this is what happened:

7. They were overcome by the sight of the ship of fire in heaven above, and in fear fled in all directions. And by their great numbers, in the presence of mortals, caused mortals also to fear and flee in search of some secure place. And many of these spirits of darkness came beseechingly to be admitted into the kingdoms of the Lords, whither they had been invited for hundreds of years, but would not come.

8. But God and the Lords encompassed their places about with walls of light and would not receive the unbelieving. God said: Till such time as Ah'shong shall arrive, let order be maintained within my kingdoms. So it came to pass that for six days and nights the fear that prevailed on earth and in heaven was such as had never been before since the earth was.

9. And God and the Lords brought their es'enaurs out, and they sang and danced before Jehovih. And on the approach of Ah'shong's hosts, with his musicians and heralds, and the great multitude, arrayed in shining raiment, even God and the Lords were overcome by the splendor and magnificence.

10. They sat down on the improvised throne, and the etherean marshals approached and divided, first into single columns, then double, then quadruple, and so on till the fifty thousand marshals had enclosed all sides, save the east, where was an open space through which Ah'shong came, attended by his chief counselors, of which there were five thousand. After these came the council of one million, inter-broken here and there with groups of thousands of es'enaurs, who were chanting hymns of praise to Jehovih and his kingdoms.

11. The lower heaven above the continent of Waga and parts of Jud and Vohu was illuminated by the hosts of Ah'shong, the like of which had never been in atmospherea

before. Nor was there any more work being done on earth or in heaven, because of the fear and great stirring up.

12. But now Ah'shong approached before the throne of God and the Lords, saluting with the sign of the second degree of Jehovih, saying: In Jehovih's name and by His Power, Wisdom and Love, am I come to give you joy.

13. God said: In Jehovih's name, all hail! Ah'shong, chief of Anakaron, all hail! And God went forward to the foot of the throne and received Ah'shong, whereupon the Lords came forward saluting also. The es'enaurs ceased singing, and Ah'song proceeded to the throne and sat thereon, and God took off his own crown and gave it to Ah'shong, and also gave him the triangle, which was called the heirloom of the heavenly kingdoms of earth, bestowed by command of Jehovih.

14. The All Light was abundant around about Ah'shong, and the voice of Jehovih spake out of the midst thereof, saying: Inasmuch as these things are done in My name prayerfully, and in faith, so do I dwell with you all. My Son shall wear thy crown, O God.

15. Behold, I am come in might and swiftness, for it is the spring time of the earth. My Son, Seffas, is afoot on the earth; he hath stirred up the earth-born. But I will establish anew My light in these heavens.

16. Have I not said: I brought the seed of everlasting life to the earth? I gave God and his Lords to teach mortals and spirits of My glories in the upper heavens. And I commanded that they that come up out of the earth should be My God and My Lords in these realms.

17. Ye were installed by My hand, and have done a good work. Think not that I curse because Hored and Moeb are fallen! Knew I not beforehand that these things would be? Behold, I have provided all My works so that man should be forever making new things. Had Hored stood, there had been no heaven to rebuild on earth in this day. How, then, could My newborn Gods learn? Think not that I come to teach with Mine own labor; I provide My people that they shall teach one another.

18. What is so conceited as man? And yet I bring him into life the dumbest of animals. Man prideth himself in his power and wisdom. I send the drought, the rains and winds, the weakest of My members, and they show man he is nothing. So also do My Gods and Lords of the lower heaven become conceited of their power and wisdom; but a turn of a word, and their heavens fall. Thousands of millions of souls turn from order and high estate into confusion and anarchy. Thus do I confound men and angels, and in their seeming misery lay the foundation for an everlasting good. The voice ceased.

19. Ah'shong said: In the name of Jehovih, I announce my presence over earth and the lower heaven.

20. The marshals said: ALL HAIL! AH'SHONG, GOD OF HEAVEN AND EARTH! Proclaim him in Jehovih's name.

21. Hardly had these words gone forth when the voice of the entire hosts joined in proclaiming: ALL HAIL! O GOD! SON OF JEHOVIH!

22. Ah'shong, now God, said: Thy crown shall be my crown, for under this shall Jehovih's power triumph; otherwise people would say: Behold there is no virtue in Jehovih's crowns. So, he placed it on his head and rose up and saluted the retired God and Lords, saying to them:

23. I have a place for ye; and it is called Yeshuah. Retire thither with my proper officers, and partake of rest and the freedom of the place until I come also. But the retired God and

Lords said: We pray thee, put us to labor. Whereupon God (Ah'shong) said:

24. Jehovih's sons must not be humiliated; how, then, can ye labor under me? Were ye not Jehovih's God and Lords.

25. They perceived, and, after due salutations, were provided with an escort of five hundred thousand men and women; and they departed on their way to Yeshuah.

26. God (Ah'shong) said: Let M'ghi come before me, and Bing-fo and Nest. They shall be my Lords of dawn in Jehovih's name.

27. The three came and stood before the throne. God said: I announce the presence of Jehovih's Lords of the earth. The marshals said: ALL HAIL! O M'GHI and BING-FO and NEST, JEHOVIH'S LORDS OF EARTH!

28. These were also proclaimed by the voice of the assembled hosts. God said: In Jehovih's name, go your ways, O Lords of earth.

29. Whereupon the Lords crowned themselves and at once departed, saluting reverently.

30. God said: Bring the atmospherean marshals before me. They were brought and stationed in front of the throne. God said: Glory be to Thee, O Jehovih! I have looked upon Thy sons and daughters who have withstood a great darkness, but retained faith in Thee. In Thy name, and by virtue of Thy power, do I deliver them. Let him who is chief, answer me: How many angels are prepared for the second resurrection?

31. Sawni, chief marshal, said: Two hundred millions. God said: Retire thou and thy companions, and gather together Jehovih's harvest of souls, and I will send them to Yeshuah.

32. The atmosphereans were then duly arranged as commanded, and God called a hundred swift messengers and one thousand etherean marshals, and they provided abattos; and the hosts, prepared for the second resurrection, departed for Yeshuah, as commanded.

33. God said: I have now remaining my etherean hosts and the atmosphereans in darkness. Of the latter, let them remain as they are for three days, for I will travel around the world, and my etherean hosts with me, observing mortals and spirits in their places and habits, that I may the better judge them and provide accordingly.

34. So God and his etherean angels provided an abattos, and they embarked and started on their journey, traveling imperceptibly to mortals.

CHAPTER IV.

1. The Council of Yeshuah, of which there were one million members, was formed in groups, and these again represented in groups, and these in still other groups. Consequently, a group of one thousand had one speaker, who became the voice of that thousand; of these speakers, one hundred had one voice in council; and of these, ten had one voice before God, and he was the voice of the whole, and Jehovih was his voice. Thus was the whole council represented in all its parts. And this was the manner of proceeding, to wit:

2. God commanded the subject; the council deliberated in thousands, and each speaker became aware of the voice of his group. Then these speakers assembled in hundreds and deliberated, and they again centered into one voice; and each ten of these had one voice before God. Thus it came to pass that the decrees of God were both the wisdom of men

and of Jehovih. Hence the saying: When God said this, or God commanded that, it was the word of Jehovih expressed by men and angels.

3. After God and his hosts visited the earth and the lower heaven, they returned to Yeshuah and sat in council on the affairs of mortals and atmosphereans.

4. God said: Behold, the heavens and earth have become like gardens grown foul and rank, producing nothing. I have come with a pruning knife and a consuming fire.

5. God said: I withdraw from the druj and the druk the beneficence of Jehovih's chosen; I leave them destitute. Who can approach the beggar with wisdom, or the king with inspiration to be good? A drowning man will try to swim; but the reveler in lust must perish before his soul can learn Jehovih.

6. Better is it to labor with a child from infancy, and thence to maturity, to teach it aright, than to strive with a score of conceited adults, and fail to redeem one. Who is the mocker of charity more than they that give to such as can help themselves but will not? Wisdom and uprightness of heart are but bread. Preach not to unwelcome ears; are sermons of wisdom to be forced into men's souls?

7. Blessed Jehovih! He made hunger, and so men love bread. Without hunger they would not eat. A wise God driveth home to man's understanding his helplessness in spirit when Jehovih is denied.

8. Pursue the earth, O my beloved; bring hence all light. Pursue the lower heaven of the earth also; bring hence all light. I will leave the earth and heaven in darkness one whole year. They shall cry out; their conceit in the dumb wind shall fail.

9. Have not the spirits of heaven despoiled Hored and Moeb? Do not evil spirits and evil men say: Behold, there is enough! Let us divide. But they produce not. They are devourers; living on others' substance. The Great Spirit made man to exert; by exertion groweth he in wisdom and strength.

10. They seek ease and comfort; helpless and more helpless they fall; they are on the road to everlasting destruction. Happy is the God who can arouse them.

CHAPTER V.

1. God said: Blessed is the surgeon's knife; its burn is the capital of health regained; but yet a fool will cry out: Hold! hold! enough! thou inflicter of pain!

2. Who hath an eye like Jehovih? His whipping-posts are on all sides, but there is a clear road between them. Yet man followeth it not.

3. Withdraw all good men and good angels, and there is no person left; they would not be half made up. A man without an arm or a leg is but part of a man; a man without perception of the All Person is a deformity in soul. He seeketh a home for his own ease and glory; but the Son of Jehovih seeketh to find the severest labor that will profit his brethren.

4. Yeshuah shall be my homestead; hither will I bring the fruit of heaven below; hither build my training schools. Seven years shall be my service; and they shall learn the ways of etherea. Build me a house of brotherhood and fill it with willing pupils sworn to labor. I will make them Gods and Lords with power and wisdom.

5. Behold a man maketh a factory and turneth out fabric for sale. I make a college and I turn out sons and daughters of Jehovih, to give away. Bring me such material as will

stand in warp and filling; Jehovih's fabric shall endure forever. Search me out the seed of I'hin, and house them with care, for they shall redeem the earth-born after I ascend to the Father's kingdom.

CHAPTER VI.

1. All the first best angels of atmospherea were brought away from the earth and housed in Yeshuah, being placed at school and in factories new made in heaven. These were I'hins.

2. The second first-best spirits were brought also, but placed in hospitals and nurseries.

3. Of those who had advanced to receive the second resurrection, God said: Build an etherean ship and take them to Theistivi, in etherea.

4. So it came to pass there were two hundred millions raised to the second resurrection, of the grade thirty-five. Theistivi lieth betwixt etherea and Seven A'ji, which is the lowest of the etherean heavens next to an atmospherean abode.

5. God said: Two qualities have I left in Yeshuah, first and second. These shall be the new kingdom after I am ascended. From these I will raise up a God and Lords, and they shall rule over the lower heaven and the earth; and they shall bequeath to others after them to rule in like manner.

6. Thus was founded the second light of Jehovih on the fruit of the earth. God's etherean hosts became as a training school to raise up a God and Lords and marshals and es'enaurs, and all other officers, and men and women, for a lower heaven. God said: Yeshuah shall not approach nearer the earth; nor shall it be as Hored, where spirits of darkness might easily approach.

7. One hundred millions of spirits did God and his Lords and fellow-laborers bring from the earth to Yeshuah, and they were placed in a brotherhood apportioned in the places suited to their talents. And God divided the time of study, and of recreation, and of music, and of discipline, marching, and so on, suited to all the people; and it was a place of order and glory.

8. For without discipline there is nothing; and discipline cannot be without ceremony; nor ceremony without rites, and forms, and established words. Is it not a foolish soldier that saith: Behold I am wise! I need no discipline nor manual of arms. What more is he than one of an untutored mob?

9. God said: As I drill them in heaven to make them a unit, so give ye to mortals rites and ceremonies, that, coming into heaven, they go not back to their old haunts and fall in darkness. Whatever tendeth to harmonize the behavior of individuals is of the Father; the opposite tendeth to evil. Better is it that men march to the sound of one monotonous word, than not to march at all; the value lieth not in the word, but in bringing in unison that which was void. A fool saith: I need not pray, there is no virtue in words. But his soul groweth up at variance with Jehovih. Neither is there more virtue in the prayer or the words, than in marching (sacred dance) before Jehovih; for whatever tendeth to unite men in one expression of soul in harmony, is Jehovih's.

10. Sacred dances and rites and ceremonies were established in Yeshuah in the name of Jehovih; and the new heaven became a place of delight.

11. God said: Teach my chosen to labor hard and wisely; and to dance with energy, and to

sing with strength and fullness of soul. For what more is there in any man or woman than to learn to put forth? And what more pitiful thing is there in heaven than a man or woman who hath but dragged along?

CHAPTER VII.

1. When all the first best spirits of the lower heaven, and such as dwelt with mortals, were taken away and domiciled in Yeshuah, there were left only druj (spirits of darkness) on the face of the earth. For one whole year God left the earth void of Jehovih's light.
2. Mortals loved more to commune with the spirits of their kindred, who knew little of heaven, than they did with ethereans who were wise and holy.
3. God said: What man or what woman have ye found who saith: Come ye angels of Jehovih, tell me wherein I can do more good works, for I thirst, and am hungry to serve Jehovih with all my wisdom and strength in doing good to my fellows?
4. Rather do they turn away from such, and drink in the tales of the strolling druj, and so wrap themselves in darkness. For this reason shall they find darkness in heaven and earth; and they shall be as one who is sick and broken down in conceit.
5. When the year of darkness was ended God sent pruners around about the earth and in the lower heaven of the earth. Two millions of pruners sent he forth, saying to them: Find all the evil spirits dwelling with mortals, whether they be fetals or familiars, and gather them into one place. Then find the spirits and fairies who have taken up caves and waterfalls on earth as their abode, and bring them to the same place. Then find the idiotic and chaotic spirits who dwell on battle-fields, and bring them to the same place. Then find the lusters, who dwell in old castles and ruined cities, and in houses of evil, and when they are going out for raids on mortals, seize them and bring them to the same place.
6. The ethereans went and collected all the evil spirits and the spirits of darkness belonging to the earth, and brought them to a place in atmospherea, and there were of them nine hundred millions.
7. God said: Prepare a ship suitable to transport them to Hudaow, in Ji'ya, and there provide them a kingdom to themselves, giving them a God and Lords and proper officers to discipline and educate them for Jehovih's kingdoms.
8. Thus were they removed, and the earth and its lower heaven were purified from evil spirits by the decree of God in Yeshuah, in the second year of the first dawn of dan.

CHAPTER VIII.

1. In the second year of Yeshuah, God (that is Ah'shong) caused to be established in his heaven all requisite places of learning and industry, whereby and wherein es'yans might be educated to good works, and to a general knowledge of Jehovih's kingdoms (universe), and there volunteered a sufficient number of ethereans as teachers and practisers of work for all that was required.
2. God said: Now that the earth and heaven are purified from evil, my Lords shall deliver the es'yans to the asaphs, and enjoin them to deliver in Yeshuah, which I have established a short distance from the earth as a barrier against their returning to mortals. Jehovih said:

Suffer not the blind to lead the blind.

3. And it was so; at the time mortals died, their spirits were taken by the asaphs to Yeshuah; and to make this an acceptable labor to the es'yans, God said: Tell my Lords of the earth to teach mortals by inspiration and otherwise of my kingdom, Yeshuah.

4. And it so came to pass through the Lords and the ashars, that is, the guardian spirits with mortals, that the name, Yeshuah, was established on the earth. God said: In the time of kosmon, men shall say: Whence came the name of heavenly things? But Yeshuah shall lie hid away, and Jehovih will in that day stretch forth His hand and disclose all.

5. But mortals were thick in tongue, and could not say Yeshuah, and they said I.E.Su; hence came the name of many men, Iesu, signifying, without evil, which is the ultimate salvation of the soul.

6. Jehovih spake through God, saying: The time of the end of dawn cometh, and My emancipated sons and daughters shall return to their places, taking the resurrected with them. But that the earth and lower heaven may not be left in darkness, provide ye a God and Lords and marshals and messengers, and all other officers, to rule and teach in My name.

7. From the born of earth shall ye make them, and they shall hold office for two hundred years, and four hundred years, and six hundred years, according to the atmospherean cycles.

8. Suffer not My etherean hosts to remain longer than dawn, either on the earth or within atmospherea, for I shall take the earth into dark regions in order to build it up to a higher state for the time that cometh after.

9. The voice departed. God said: Let the voice of the council deliberate on this matter, and speak before the Father. For I will provide also a heaven in the ancient place of Hored, and it shall be called Bispah, for it shall be a place of reception for the spirits of the dead preparatory to their being brought to Yeshuah.

10. In course of time there were raised up many of the earth-born, and God selected them and appointed them to fill the places; and he founded Bispah, and officered it according to the command of Jehovih. After God established rites and ceremonies, and processions and dances, with sacred words, in Yeshuah, he commanded his Lords to give the same things to mortals, and they so fulfilled all that was designed from the beginning.

11. In the seventh year of dawn God commanded his council to select another God and Lords, and other officers; and the council proceeded after the manner of the ancients, selecting the most learned and the purest and holiest; according to their rank in Godliness chose they them, and a record was made of these matters and deposited in the library of Yeshuah.

12. So it came to pass that God called in his own Lords of the earth, and sat apart the first day of the new moon as the day on which he would consecrate the God and Lords, his successors; and he called the day Mas, the name of which endureth to this day of kosmon. Furthermore, God established the moon's day (mas) on the earth as a time of consecration. (And this is the origin of saying mass).

13. When the chosen were in place before the throne, God said: By command of Jehovih are ye brought before me, His Son; in His name will I consecrate ye to the places commanded of Him.

14. The marshals then conducted him that ranked highest up to the seat of the throne. God

said:

15. In the name of Jehovih, and by His Power, Wisdom and Love, do I ordain thee God of heaven and earth. He that receiveth from my hand receiveth from my Father, who raised me up.

16. The initiate said: All power cometh from the Father. All wisdom cometh from the Father. All love cometh from the Father. In His name and by virtue of His commandments through His Son, receive I all that is put upon me, for His glory, forever!

17. God then said: Give me a crown, O Father, for Thy Son! A scarlet light descended from above, and God reached forth his hands and wove it into a crown and placed it on the initiate's head, saying: God of heaven and earth, thee I crown. And now shalt thou receive also the sacred triangle, which is the heirloom of the Gods of earth. And he hung it around his neck, adding: And since there can be but one God on earth or in this heaven, I herewith uncrown myself in Jehovih's name and salute thee, O God, GOD OF EARTH AND HEAVEN!

18. Ah'shong now stood to the right, and God, who was ordained, went and sat on the throne, and there descended red and blue lights from above, enveloping him completely, and he was quickened. He said:

19. Let the initiates for Lords of earth approach the throne of the Most High Jehovih!

20. The five Lords came forward. God said: Join hands and receive ye from the Father. By virtue of the Power, Wisdom and Love of Jehovih, vested in me, receive I thee as the highest chosen; and I proclaim thee Lord of earth, in Jehovih's name! Accept this crown from heaven above, the like of which cannot be woven from earthly things; by its power shalt thou remain in accord with Yesuah and the kingdoms above.

21. God fashioned the crowns and then crowned them Lords of the five divisions of the earth. God said: Retire thou aside and choose thy messengers and officers, and after ordaining them, depart to the kingdom prepared for thee. The Lords said:

22. In Thy name, O Jehovih, do I accept that which Thou hast put upon me. With all my wisdom and strength and love will I serve Thee, O my Father, Jehovih!

23. The Lords retired; and the es'enaurs sang, more than a million of voices in concert!

CHAPTER IX.

1. Now had the time come for the end of the first dawn of dan after the creation of man. And this was known in the etherean heavens, where lived countless millions of Jehovih's sons and daughters emancipated. And, as might be expected, they determined to descend from all sides to witness the labors of Ah'shong, and to receive his works as a profitable lesson for their own future on other new worlds.

2. Consequently, there began to appear in the firmament far-off stars, approaching; and these were the etherean ships in remote places, where the name of Ah'shong had been known for thousands of years. From all sides they came, growing brighter and brighter, larger and larger.

3. Ah'shong spoke to his companions, saying: Make ready, O my beloved. My friends and your friends are coming. Put our ship in order. Light the pillars of fire and spread out the sails, shining, that they may be glorified in Jehovih's name.

4. The proper persons accomplished these things, and to the eastward of Yeshuah the

etherean ship of Ah'shong was anchored; and so great was the size thereof that there was room for the ethereans of Anakaron and upward of three hundred millions of the redeemed of earth besides.

5. Ah'shong said: When our friends arrive, we shall join them and make an excursion round the earth, discovering its rank and glorious promises; but as to the nine hundred millions of drujas which I sent off to Hudaow, in Ji'ya, we shall pass thither on our way to Anakaron.

6. Brighter and brighter grew the descending stars, the etherean ships from far-off worlds; and larger and larger, till in majesty they neared Yeshuah. Ah'shong then came down and sat at the foot of the throne, according to the custom of Gods. God came down and took him by the hand, saying: Son of Jehovih, that maketh thyself the least of men, arise, and take thy hosts, and embark in Jehovih's ship, going whithersoever thou wilt. Ah'shong rose up. The es'enaurs and trumpeters played and sang. Then Ah'shong said:

7. One more love have I in the world, O Jehovih. I go from Yeshuah, but my love remaineth. To thee, O God, will I look back in hope and love, for thou wert raised by me. And to thy Lords what less could I say? Yea, and to all the hosts I leave within these realms.

8. Ah'shong touched God's right hand, and then saluting, with the third sign of emeth to Jehovih, departed, and the marshals conducted him off to the ship.

9. Ah'shong and his etherean hosts rose up in curtains of light; and presently the ship was loosened from its anchorage and floated upward, and all the angels entered into it; and the sails were spread out, and the mantles suspended on every side, till the whole vessel, with its thousands of masts and arcs, looked like a world on fire. The inhabitants of Yeshuah feared and trembled for the mighty works of the Gods and Goddesses; and yet, as the es'enaurs on the departing ship chanted, more than a million of voices, the Yeshuans sang with them, amidst their tears, with souls overflowing, with awe and love and admiration.

10. And in this same time the descending stars of other Gods and Goddesses, the etherean ships from far-off worlds, were drawing nearer and nearer; and, on every side, the firmament was as if alive with worlds on fire.

11. Presently they came, first one and then another of the ethereans, and they made fast to Ah'shong's ship, until thus more than five hundred were united into one mighty vessel, and yet so near to Yeshuah that all could be seen.

12. And when they had united there were countless millions of angels thus in close proximity, many who had known one another for thousands of years; and some who were older than the earth, and knew its history. And these had companions as old as themselves; and they were ripe in experience with corporeal earths, stars and suns in other regions of Jehovih's kingdoms.

13. So great was the wisdom of these Gods and Goddesses that to come within the earth's atmosphere was sufficient to enable them to read all the souls and prayers of mortals, and all the thoughts and desires of the spirits of the lower heaven belonging to the earth. To each and all of them the voice of Jehovih was ever present, and their power was like unto their wisdom.

14. Jehovih hath said: To the corporean I have given power to hear one or two things at the same moment of time; but My Gods can hear intelligently tens of thousands of men speaking at the same time. Yea, they can find a way to answer them also.

90

15. When the ships were ready for departure, Ah'shong said: Let us pass low over Yeshuah, and ye shall hear and see those I have founded in a new heaven. His companions said: Jehovih's will be done. Thereupon they proceeded; and after they had visited Yeshuah they descended to the earth, and round about the places of the Lords; and when they had seen all, and heard the explanation, from those with Ah'shong, of the state the earth was in, and of the heavens of the earth, they rose higher and higher, and sailed toward Anakaron, whither Ah'shong had invited them for repast and social intercourse.

16. Thus departed the ethereans from the earth and atmospherea. This, then, was the beginning of the cycles of dan; and the first dawn was closed and past.

17. And the earth Gods, that is, the Lords, who were now called Adonya, were such as had been brought forth out of the earth. And God, who had dominion in the atmospherea of the earth, was also an earth-born; and so were all the angels in atmospherea the product of the earth.

18. And in Jehovih's name were the Lords and God appointed and crowned to rule in their respective places, and they thus became the instruments of Jehovih for His glory.

19. Jehovih said: Whoever serveth Me, in My name, is My son, or My daughter. The Light of My Judgment falleth upon them sufficient for the time and place. Inasmuch as ye honor them, ye honor Me also. Through the flowers of the field I express Myself in color and perfume; through the lion and mastodon I express Myself with power and voraciousness; through the lamb and the dove I express myself in meekness and docility. Through man I express Myself in words and actions; and all men, the wise and the ignorant, are channels of My expression. Some have thick tongues and poor speech, nevertheless they are My babes, My sons and daughters.

20. Jehovih said: After the Se'muan age I gave to the earth from My etherean heavens sons and daughters, and they abode with mortals for three thousand years. And My ethereans established loo'is on the lands of the earth; and they commanded the loo'is, saying to them: Your office is to lead mortals by inspiration to dwell together, man and woman, as husband and wife; and in such adaptation that their offspring shall rise higher in wisdom, love and power, than the father and mother.

21. Jehovih said: I will confound the wise man in the latter days; for he shall not discover why man and woman lived not indiscriminately, as the beasts. Yea, I will show him that they who profess Me are led by Me, that they who deny Me go down to indiscriminate communion. Out of My works, shall the lessons of the early days of the earth show the presence of My hand from the beginning. By My loo'is was man and woman inspired to raise up such sons and daughters as would glorify Me and My works; by My loo'is have I maintained My foothold amongst mortals.

22. Such as could comprehend Me, having faith that My presence in Person should ultimately triumph for the highest and best, I commanded to be called FAITHISTS. Since the beginning, have I kept a thread of this line inhabiting the earth and her heavens.

23. At the end of the second cycle there were in atmospherea six thousand million angels, who were for the most part in darkness; not knowing who they were, or where they dwelt; nor knowing nor caring whether there were other heavens or not.

24. And now began wars in atmospherea; thousands of angels against thousands, and millions against millions.

25. For the possession of sections of the earth, and the mortal inhabitants thereof, went forth these millions of warring angels. And it came to pass that mortals also fell to war; and, by the obsessing angels, were made to destroy their own cities and kingdoms.

26. And the attractions of this great wickedness caused other angels of heaven to desert their schools and factories, and descend down to mortals.

27. Thus again were the kingdoms of God and his Lords set at naught; the harvests of Brides and Bridegrooms had long since ceased to be.

28. The first harvest was two hundred years, and the number of Brides and Bridegrooms was six hundred millions, of grade ninety-two.

29. The second harvest was two hundred years, and was eight hundred million angels, of grade eighty-nine.

30. The third harvest was six hundred years, and was two thousand million angels, of grade eighty-three.

31. The fourth harvest was five hundred years, and was twenty-three hundred million angels, of grade seventy-four.

32. The fifth harvest was three hundred years, and was six hundred million angels, of grade sixty-two.

33. The sixth harvest was four hundred years, and nine hundred million angels, of grade fifty-one.

34. And this was the last harvest; for none were of sufficient grade to abide in the etherean heavens.

END OF THE BOOK OF AH'SONG, SON OF JEHOVIH.

SECOND BOOK OF LORDS.

OF THE SECOND CYCLE, BEING COTEMPORANEOUS
WITH THE BOOK OF AH'SHONG, SON OF JEHOVIH.

CHAPTER I.

1. In the beginning man was naked and not ashamed; but the Lord raised man up and bade him hide his nakedness, and man obeyed, and was clothed.

2. And the Lord walked by man for a long season, showing him the way of resurrection; and man was obedient, depending on the Lord for all things.

3. And the Lord said unto man: Behold, I have walked with thee, and taught thee; but by my indulgence thou hast neglected to put forth thine own energy.

4. Now I am going away from thee for a season, that thou mayst learn to develop thyself.

5. But lest thou stumble and fall, I leave with thee certain commandments, and they shall be a guide unto thee and thy heirs forever.

6. Hear thou then the commandments of the Lord thy God.

7. Thou shalt love thy Creator with all thy mind, and heart, and soul, all the days of thy life.

8. And thou shalt love thy neighbor as thyself.

9. Because thou wert born into the world without covering, thou shalt clothe thyself.

10. Then inquired man of the Lord: Behold, thou hast shown the ass what is good for him to eat, and the fish, and the serpent, and the lion; every living creature; but man only hast thou not shown?

11. The Lord said: Of everything that groweth up out of the ground that is good to eat give I unto thee, and they shall be food for thee.

12. But of all things of flesh and blood, wherein is life, thou shalt not eat.

13. For thou shalt not kill.

14. Man inquired of the Lord: Thou has shown the males and females of all the living the times and periods to come together; but man and woman hast thou not shown?

15. The Lord said: Thou shalt learn from the beasts, and birds, and fishes, that the female during gestation is in keeping of her Creator.

16. Thou shalt also respect the times of woman.

17. Man inquired of the Lord: Thou hast shown the bird how to build her nest, and the carnivore how to scent the subtle track of his prey, and the spider to weave his net; but as to the manner of man's house, or as to herbs that are good or are poisonous, thou has not shown man.

18. The Lord said: All the instinct that is in the bird, or beast, or fish, or insect, or creeping thing, was created with them, but man was created blank; and yet man shall attain to more subtle senses than any other living creature.

19. Man inquired: How shall man attain to these?

20. The Lord answered: Serve thy Creator by doing good unto others with all thy wisdom and strength, and by being true to thine own highest light, and all knowledge shall come to thee.

21. So the Lord left man for a season to himself; and man so loved the earth and whatsoever ministered unto his ease, and to his flesh desires, that he fell from his high estate. And great darkness came upon the earth. And man cast aside his clothes, and went naked, and became carnal in his desires.

CHAPTER II.

1. The Lord went abroad over the earth, calling: Come to me, O man! Behold thy Lord is returned!

2. But man heard not the voice of the Lord; for, by man's indulgence, the spirit of man was covered up in his own flesh.

3. The Lord sent his loo'is (masters of generations, angels next in rank above guardian angels, i.e., ashars) to the I'hins, and they raised up heirs unto the Lord; by controlling the parentage of the unborn brought they into the world a new race of men, of the same seed and blood as of old, and these heard the voice of the Lord.

4. And the Lord said unto man: Because thou kept not my commandments thou hast brought affliction upon thyself, and thy people, to the farthest ends of the world.

5. Now will I raise thee up once more, and deliver the tribes of men from darkness into light.

6. And the Lord delivered man into wisdom, and peace and virtue; and the earth became as a garden of sweet smelling flowers and luxurious fruit.

7. The Lord said: How sayst thou, O man? Shalt thou still have a keeper?

8. And man said: Behold, I am strong and wise. Go thou away from the earth. I understand thy commandments.

9. The Lord inquired: Knowest thou the meaning of, Love thy Creator? And man said: Yea, Lord; and to love my neighbor as myself; and to do good unto others with all my wisdom and strength. Yea, I have the All Highest Light. I am wiser than the ancients. Behold, I want no Lord nor God; I am the highest product of all the universe.

10. The Lord said: I will try thee, O man; I will go away for a season.

11. So the Lord departed once more. And man had nothing to look up to, so he looked at himself and became vainglorious. And the tribes of men aspired to overcome one another; war and destruction followed.

12. Man forgot his Creator; he said: No Eye seeth me, no Ear heareth me. And he neglected to guard himself against the serpent (corporeality); and the serpent said unto him: Partake thou of all things, for they are thine.

13. And man gave heed, and, lo and behold, the race of man descended into utter darkness. And man distinguished not his sister or mother; and woman distinguished not her brother or father.

14. And God beheld the wickedness of man, and he called out, saying: Hear my voice, O man! Hear the voice of the Lord!

15. But because of the darkness of man he could not hear the voice of God, his Lord.

16. And the Lord sent his angels down to man that they might appeal to man's understanding.

17. But the angels loved darkness also, and strove not to lift man up out of darkness. And the Lord was of no more avail amongst mortals, and he departed away from the earth. And man became on the earth as a harvest that is blighted and rotted because of its rankness.

END OF THE SECOND BOOK OF LORDS.

SYNOPSIS OF SIXTEEN CYCLES.

BEING FORTY-EIGHT THOUSAND YEARS; COVERING A PERIOD FROM THE CREATION OF MAN DOWN TO THE SUBMERSION OF THE CONTINENT OF PAN, CALLED BY THE ANCIENTS,

THE FLOOD, OR DELUGE,

WHICH WAS TWENTY - FOUR THOUSAND YEARS B.K. , SELECTED FROM THE RECORDS IN THE LIBRARIES OF HEAVEN.

CHAPTER I.

1. First, the earth plieth in a circuit around the sun, which circuit is divided into four arcs called spring, summer, autumn and winter.

2. Second, the sun, with his family, plieth in a large circuit, which is divided into one thousand five hundred arcs, the distance of which for each arc is about three thousand years, or one cycle.

3. During a cycle, the earth and her heavens fall in the etherean regions of hundreds of etherean worlds, where dwell Jehovih's high-raised angels, whose Chiefs have to do with the management of worlds.

4. During the time of a cycle, the earth is therefore under the control and management of such of Jehovih's angels for the resurrection of man of the earth.

5. At the time of the creation of man, the earth was traveling in the arc of Wan, where dwell thousands of Orian chiefs, with thousands of millions of high-raised angels.

6. The Holy Council of Orian Chiefs, through the Wisdom and Voice of Jehovih, appointed one of their number, Sethantes, to take charge of the earth, and to people it with immortal beings, during its travel in Wan.

7. The rank and title of Sethantes, thus raised up by Jehovih, Creator of worlds, was, FIRST GOD OF THE EARTH AND HER HEAVENS.

8. And Sethantes came with millions of angels, who had been raised up from other worlds previously, and he accomplished his work, and was known as God.

9. Sethantes was, then, the first God of the earth and her heavens, and his place was within the arc of Wan. And during his cycle of three thousand years, he raised up from the earth fifteen hundred million Brides and Bridegrooms to Jehovih.

10. After Sethantes came Ah'shong, sub-Chief in the realms of Hieu Wee in the Haian arc of Vehetaivi. And during the cycle of Anakaron, also three thousand years, Ah'shong raised up from the earth a harvest of two billion two hundred million Brides and Bridegrooms.

11. The third cycle was under the dominion of Hoo Le, surveyor of Kakayen'sta in the arc of Gimmel, and his harvest was three billion seven hundred millions.

12. The fourth cycle was under C'pe Aban, Chieftainess of Sulgoweron in the arc of Yan, and her harvest was four billion eight hundred millions.

13. The fifth cycle was under Pathodices, road-maker in Chitivya in the arc of Yahomitak, and his harvest was six billion four hundred millions.

14. The sixth cycle was under Goemagak, God of Iseg, in the arc of Somgwothga, and his harvest was seven billion nine hundred millions.

15. The seventh cycle was under Goepens, God of Kaim, in the arc of Srivat, and his harvest was nine billion three hundred millions.

16. The eighth cycle was under Hycis, Goddess of Ruts, in the arc of Hohamagollak, and her harvest was nine billion four hundred millions.

17. The ninth cycle was under See'itcicius, inspector of roads in Kammatra, in the arc of Jusyin, and his harvest was ten billion one hundred millions.

18. The tenth cycle was under Miscelitivi, Chieftainess of the arches of Lawzgowbak, in the arc of Nu, and her harvest was ten billion eight hundred millions.

19. And now the earth was full of people; all the continents and islands of the earth were inhabited by man; nor was there left any wilderness wherein man did not dwell.

20. But the generation of man had fallen from thirty-three years down to twelve years. And man and woman were at maturity at seven years old; and not many lived above thirty years; but they were prolific; many of the mothers bringing forth two score sons and daughters, and from two to four at a birth.

21. And man dwelt in peace, and the earth was tilled, and brought forth abundantly of everything that was good for man to eat, and to clothe himself. And there were in those days great cities of hundreds of thousands of inhabitants; thousands and thousands of such cities, and in all the five great divisions of the earth. And man built ships and sailed over the ocean in all directions, around about the whole world. By the angels of the Lord was he taught and guided in all things. And man had books, both written and printed; and the young were taught in schools, a knowledge of the sun and moon and stars, and of all things that are upon the earth and in the waters thereof. This was therefore called the first period of civilization on the earth.

22. Now, for the most part, all the people had become I'hins, small, white and yellow. Nevertheless there were ground people, with long arms, who were large; but they dwelt by themselves, and their food was of all manner of flesh, and fish, and creeping things. The ground people were brown and black, and they lived to be two hundred, and even four hundred years old.

23. Jehovih said: In the early days I raised up I'huans, and I gave them certain commandments, amongst which was, not to cohabit with the druks lest they go down in darkness. But they obeyed not My words; and lo and behold, they are lost from the face of the earth.

24. Because the I'hins have become a spiritual people and have prospered in peace and spirit, behold, they have degenerated in the corporeal body. They yield abundant harvests for My etherean realms, but they are like untimely births.

25. Now will I bring the earth into a'jiyan fields and forests for a long season; for I shall again reproduce the I'huans; and the time of a generation shall be thirty-three years. For my harvests shall be of fruit that is mature and full of ripeness.

26. And Jehovih brought the earth into new regions in the etherean worlds, and covered it over with a'ji, east and west and north and south.

27. And it came to pass that many of the I'hins lost the generative desire and, so, brought not forth many heirs. But the brown people burnt with desires, and they laid hold of the I'hin women when they went into the fields, and forced them, and thus brought forth again the I'huan race, the copper colored, strong and bright and quick.

28. Accordingly the eleventh cycle, which was under Gobath, God of Tirongothaga, in the

arc of Su'le, brought forth a harvest of six billion seven hundred millions.

29. The twelfth cycle was under F'aiyis, Goddess of Looga, in the arc of Siyan, and her harvest was two billion six hundred millions.

30. The thirteenth cycle was under Zineathaes, keeper of the Cress, in the arc of Oleganaya, and his harvest was one billion two hundred millions.

31. The fourteenth cycle was under Tothsentaga, road-maker in Hapanogos, in the arc of Manechu, and his harvest was only six hundred millions.

32. The fifteenth cycle was under Nimeas, God of Thosgothamachus, in the arc of Seigga, and his harvest was only forty millions.

33. The sixteenth cycle was under Neph, God of Sogghonnes, in the arc of Arbroohk, but he failed to bring forth any harvest.

CHAPTER II.

1. God, that is Neph, said: Hear my prayer, O Jehovih! The earth and her heavens are gone down in darkness.

2. The I'hin hath been destroyed off all the divisions of the earth save Wagga.

3. More than thirty thousand million angels are gathered on the surface of the earth, and they are too low in grade to be delivered.

4. What shall Thy God do, O Father?

5. Mortals are descending in breed and blood; only as diseased vermin do they inhabit the earth.

6. Their cities are destroyed, and they dwell after the manner of four-footed beasts.

7. The inspiration of Thy God and his angels can no longer reach them.

8. When they die and enter these heavens they are as festering sores on one another, thousands of millions of them.

9. For three thousand years have I labored with them, but the abundance of their darkness outmatcheth Thy God.

10. What shall I do with them, O Father! How shall Thy God deliver so great a carcass of death?

11. But Jehovih answered not the prayer of God; left him to consult with other Gods in the higher heavens.

12. But in etherea, Jehovih spake to His Orian Chiefs, saying: As I try mortals, so do I try angels; as I try them, so do I try My Gods. Forever and forever do I keep before them the testimony of AN ALL HIGHER.

13. Now it had come to pass on earth that the time of a generation of mortals had risen from twelve years to eighty years. And there were many who lived to be three hundred years old. And they had become very large; twice the size of men of this day. But they were without judgment and of little sense. Hardly knew they their own species. And they mingled together, relatives as well as others; so that idiocy and disease were the general fate of the tribes of men; and they were large and strong and prolific.

14. This then that followeth is the grade of declension in the heavens of the earth; that is, after Kishalon had changed the period of generation from twelve years into the upper grades, to wit:

15. Abner, seventh dawn of dan, enduring three thousand two hundred years in Hastaf,

etherean a'ji seven, Hoe'tan, grade ninety-nine.

16. Enseeni, Goddess of Marsef, etherea, dan of Gem, enduring three thousand years, grade ninety-three.

17. Boaz, God of Hom, Orian field, dan of Josh, enduring two thousand seven hundred years, grade eighty-eight.

18. Da'ivi, Goddess of Wowitski in a'ji thirty-six, dan of Ruth, enduring two thousand nine hundred years, grade eighty-two.

19. Lia'mees, Goddess of War in Broek, dan forty, Orian field, Semsi, enduring three thousand years, grade seventy-seven.

20. Divi'yas, God of Hut in Habak, ji'ya twenty-two, Neth, enduring three thousand one hundred years, grade sixty-nine.

21. Roa'yis'yis, Goddess of Tamak, Bent, one of Hud'du'owts, enduring three thousand and seventy years, grade sixty-one.

22. Yij, Chief of Orian field, Lud in Goo, dan seventy-four, enduring two thousand six hundred years, grade fifty-eight.

23. Gul'yaniv, Chieftainess, Orian field, Ob'Low in ji'ya forty, enduring three thousand four hundred years, grade fifty-one.

24. From this time onward there was found no grade in the roadway of the solar phalanx (great serpent), sufficiently dense for the angels of the heavens of the earth.

CHAPTER III.

1. Jehovih moved upon the etherean worlds; in the wide regions where traveleth the great serpent. His voice went forth, and amongst the counselors, the high ruling chieftains of the exalted kingdoms in the firmament, He spoke, saying:

2. Hear me, O ye Chieftains! Be ye far-seeing in My traveling worlds, and alert to My words. Behold the red star, the earth, hath attained her maturity! As a daughter cometh forth in the prime of life, so standeth the young earth in her glory. For fifty thousand years hath she played her part as an ornament of heaven and a harvester of bright souls for My exalted regions in the firmament.

3. Gather together, O ye Orian Chiefs, and ye etherean Goddesses; and ye that dwell in the roadway of the great serpent. Call ye a council of My everlasting rulers of worlds; and of them that plant my a'jian gardens and My ji'ya'an fields; and of them that whirl My nebulous vortices in the firmament.

4. The voice of Jehovih extended across the wide universe, and those who were high raised in the management of worlds heard and comprehended.

5. And there assembled in the etherean gardens of Senaya, near the roadway of the solar phalanx, millions of Jehovih's highest; and the place was as a park larger than a hundred times the earth; and round about on every side lay the crystalline borders of etherean worlds. And when they were assembled, Jehovih spake out of the light inherent, saying:

6. Sixteen times have my etherean hosts redeemed the earth and her heavens from darkness into light, and yet ere the end of a cycle she falleth again, and her atmospherea with her. And now it hath come to pass that her heavens are filled with thousands of millions of spirits that know not Me and My emancipated worlds. Speak, O ye Gods and Goddesses.

7. Thereupon Sut'Loo said: O Jehovih, I have heard; I have beholden. Too prolific is the earth, the young daughter of heaven. Too prolific is the red star of the firmament.

8. Next spake Ka'wha, saying: Thou hast spoken, O Jehovih! Too prolific is the rich earth, O Father. Her mortals are overpowered by her atmospherean hosts. Her people build up cities and nations for a season after dawn, but soon they are over flooded by fetals and drujas, and the mortals devour one another as beasts of prey.

9. Chi'jong said: Her people have tilled all the soil of the earth and covered it over with cities; but where are they? Her people have been learned in the matters of heaven and earth, but their knowledge is dissipated by the dread hand of war.

10. Dhu'itta said: Her people become wise in a day, but on the next they are fools. One generation becometh skilled in books and in knowledge of the sun and moon and stars, and in the mathematics of corporeal things; but a generation followeth, and lo, her people are cannibals again.

11. Gaw'zin said: I have heard, O Jehovih! I have witnessed, O Father! The red star is too prolific. She is like a garden too rich! Her products are overgrown, and they fall down and doubly enrich the soil again, to reproduce an imperfect giant stalk that is barren. So are her sons and daughters; they run all to earthly substances.

12. Loo'wan said: Great Spirit, I have heard, I have seen. We gather the earth's harvests for Thee, O Jehovih, but they are small. We gather the earth's harvests of dark spirits, O Jehovih, and they are ten times larger. Behold, there is no balance between them.

13. Thus spake the Gods and Goddesses, till thousands of them had spoken. After that the voice of Jehovih spake, saying:

14. Ye are blessed, My sons and daughters. How can ye bequeath the administration of the earth and her heaven to the earth-born, till she is made suitable as a gift from My hand? Now hear Me, O My sons and daughters: Five great divisions of the earth have I made, and they have all been inhabited over and tilled by mortals. Yea, on all the divisions of the earth have there been great cities and nations, and men and women of great learning.

15. And as oft as they are raised up in light, so are they again cast down in darkness, because of the great desire of the spirits of the dead to return back to the earth. These druj return to mortals and fasten upon them as fetals or as familiars, and inspire them to evil. Go now to the earth, O My beloved, and find the division of the earth where most of these druj congregate, for I will uproot their stronghold; I will break them from their haunts and they shall no longer carry My people down to destruction.

16. And now the council deliberated, and after a while caused the records of the earth and her atmospherea to be examined, and they discovered that the heaven of the land of Wagga (Pan) was beyond redemption because of the great numbers of the spirits of the cannibals and of the multitude of fetals. It was as if a disease in the flesh be healed over externally, leaving the root of the disease within. So was Wagga and her heaven; the redemption of the cycles remained not with her, but evil broke out forever in a new way.

17. So Jehovih said: Now will I prune the earth and her heaven. Behold, the division of Wagga shall be hewn off and cast beneath the waters of the ocean. Her heaven shall be no longer tenable by the spirits of destruction, for I will rend the foundation thereof and scatter them in the winds of heaven.

18. Go ye, therefore, down to the earth and provide nets and vanchas for receiving the

spirits of darkness, and for receiving the spirits of mortals who shall perish in the waters. And provide ye a place in My exalted heavens suitable for them; and ye shall wall them about in heaven that they cannot escape, but that they may be weaned from evil. 19. And when ye are come to the earth and its heavens, acquaint My God and his Lords with My decree. And say to them: Thus saith Jehovih: Behold, behold, I will sink the land of Wagga beneath the waters of the ocean, and her heaven will I carry away to a place in My firmament, where she shall no longer engulf My people in darkness. And Jehovih saith: Go thou, O God of heaven, and thou, O Lord of Wagga, down to My chosen, the I'hins, and say to them: Thus saith the Great Spirit: Behold, behold, I will sink the lands of the earth beneath the ocean, because of the evil of the spirits of darkness. Hear Me, O My chosen, and heed My commandments: Fall to, all hands, and build ships in all places, even in the valleys and on the mountains, and let My faithful gather together within the ships, for My hand is surely stretched over the earth.

20. And ye shall also proclaim unto the earth and her heaven that from the first, even in the ancient days, I proclaimed My three worlds unto all people, which are: My corporeal worlds and the lower heavens that belong thereto, and My etherean heavens which are in the firmament above. And I said: The first glory is of the earth, whereon is paradise when man obeyeth My commandments; and the second glory, which is greater than the first, I created for the spirits of the dead, but I bound the lower heaven to the earth that it might travel therewith, that the communion of the dead with the living might add a glory unto both. But the upper heaven I made the highest of all glories, and I filled the etherean firmament with countless worlds of their kind for the dwelling places of those that rose in the third resurrection.

21. And I sent from the exalted heavens down to the lower heavens, and to the earth, also, My holy angels, over whom I appointed Gods and Lords in the majesty of My dominions. And they came proclaiming these things in My name, teaching both mortals and spirits how to live that they might rise and inherit My illuminated worlds.

22. And because man was without knowledge, My Gods and Lords appointed certain masters of generations (loo'is), who were ethereans of great wisdom, to abide with mortals and inspire such marriages as would best promote spiritual growth from the start. And there came forth amongst all people certain ones capable of sar'gis and su'is, and they heeded the commandments of My Gods and Lords, forsaking evil and striving to serve the spirit, choosing Me above all things. Wherefore I chose them also, and called them I'hins.

23. For as much as they commenced putting away self and serving Me whilst they were yet in corpor, so were they not born in the spirit world before their full time. And even so are others not of full birth who have not in the corporeal form begun to triumph in spirit over their own flesh.

24. Jehovih said: Go forth, O my sons and daughters, and prune my vineyard.

25. Beseech My God of the earth and his Lords with him, to gather together all the angels of the earth, from east to west and from north to south; to the land of Wagga bring them.

26. My etherean ships of fire shall surround Wagga on every side. And I will cut loose the foundations of the earth, at the borders of the ocean and the mountains of Gan, nor shall any prop or corner-stone stay My hand. And I will send rains and winds and thundering; and the waters of the great deep shall come upon the lands; and the great cities shall go

down and be swallowed in the sea.

27. And the rich valleys of Mai, with her thousand cities, shall be rent with the madness of men and women fleeing before the waters of the ocean. And women and children shall fall by the way and be drowned; and men shall go down in the water and rise not.

28. And the wide plains of Og, with her thousand cities, and with the great capital of Penj, and the temples of Khu, and Bart, and Gan, and Saing, shall sink to rise no more. And in the deluge, the air of heaven shall be filled with the screaming and wailing of millions of mortals going down to destruction.

29. I will rescue them from darkness; I will carry them to a'jian regions which I previously created for spirits of darkness; and I will appoint over them Gods and Goddesses to teach them of Me and My kingdoms.

30. And the earth and her heavens shall take a new start amongst My habitable worlds.

31. Thus have I provided labor for My high-raised angels in the places I created, saith Jehovih.

END OF THE SYNOPSIS OF HEAVENLY RECORDS.

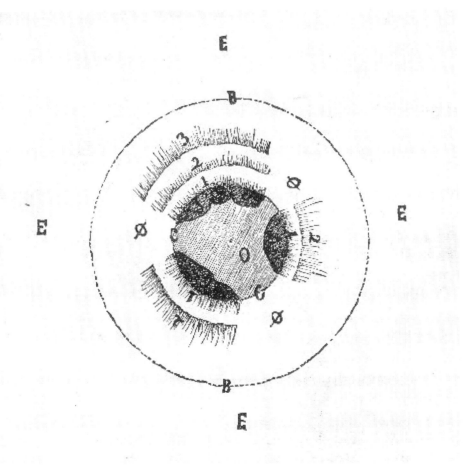

Plate 5.

E, Etherea; B, periphery of the earth's vortex. This line was called by the ancients the Bridge Of Chinvat. All within this area is called Atmospherea. The center is the earth, 1, 1, 1; O, the ocean. 1's, 2's and 3 represent different atmospherean plateaux. The O, O, O, with a line through it, represents atmospherean oceans.

101

BOOK OF APH, SON OF JEHOVIH.

BEING THE HEAVENLY RECORDS OF APH, SON OF JEHOVIH, AND OF HIS COMPANION, NINYA, DAUGHTER OF JEHOVIH, AS PERTAINITH TO THE SUBMERSION OF THE CONTINENT OF WAGGA (AFTERWARD CALLED PAN, SIGNIFYING EARTH). AND THIS PERIOD WAS COMMONLY CALLED THE DELUGE, OR FLOOD OF WATERS.

CHAPTER I.

1. In the time of the world twenty-four thousand years before the kosmon era, the great serpent (solar phalanx) being in the arc of Noe, in the etherean heavens, and of the Sum of Howt and ji'ya eighty-seven, the earth and her heavens were in great darkness. But the spirit of Jehovih moved upon His high-raised God, Aph, in etherea, to consecrate new dominions on the earth and her heavens. Aph said:

2. I, Aph, Son of Jehovih, God in the arc of Noe, in Sum of Howt, in etherea, came to hada, heaven of the red star, in Jehovih's name. In His wisdom, power and love, manifested in mine own resurrection, to become companion to Gods and Goddesses and Orian Chiefs on the thrones of high heaven, proclaim:

3. To the atmospherean spirits of the earth, and to the spirits of the first, second and third resurrections, abiding on the earth, or near thereto, either with mortals or without; to their God and Lords, and to their Savior, and to all holy ones by Jehovih raised up for the redemption of men and angels:

4. In the arc of Noe came to me the voice of Jehovih, Creator of worlds, saying:

5. I am the All Highest! My service extendeth forever. I go not, but I am afar. I come not, and yet I am near. My voice is in all places. The light of the soul of man heareth Me. I speak in the vine that creepeth, and in the strong-standing oak.

6. Hear the voice of your Creator, O ye angels of heaven. Carry ye the wisdom of My utterance down to mortals. Call them to the glories of the heavens and the broad earth. Behold, My voice is in the rocks, and in the wind that bloweth, and in all things that have not tongues.

7. Show them My suns and stars in the firmament above; for they are My written words. My voice proceedeth in the space of heaven; the wise angels of My exalted places hear the sound going forth. Hearken to My speech, O ye spirits of the dead; proclaim Me, O ye Gods and Goddesses.

8. They look for Me as they look for things; they hearken for my voice as for a man's voice. And they find Me not, nor hear that which I have spoken. Yet none can efface My words; My wisdom endureth forever. Behold, I come not as a sound to the ear; My voice hieth into the soul from all sides.

9. Teach them, O ye angels; they look not in the right way; their ears are turned after loud claps and noises. They cry out: Alas, I hear not the voice of Jehovih; He hath not spoken; His voice hath no man heard; He is the All Silent, and dumber than the things He created.

10. They have turned away from My God and My Lords; in conceit and darkness have they shut themselves up. They have peopled the air of the earth about with spirits of darkness, the drujas of men of darkness and cannibals. Their fetals float back upon them; like devouring vermin they burrow deep in pollution.

11. Remember them, O God, My Son, and ye, My Lords of earth. Have no pity, but be as

a surgeon's knife upon them. Thou hast told them, O God: Jehovih liveth and reigneth: His voice standeth the All Highest. But they have mocked thee and thy Lords, and turned away after iniquity.

12. They are fearful lest they believe in My Person and My voice; of their own gabble they have no fear. They criticize Me and My God and My Lords; but they own that they know Me not. They suppose My exalted heavens are without order and discipline. My captains they ignore, and the teachings of My holy ones are criticized by men of straw.

13. Have they not said: Who is God, that I should adore? And the Lord, that I should hearken? But I turn their eyes to the armies of the earth; to the general and the captain. Then they say: Ah, our affairs on earth are officered and disciplined; we reverence our highest, great captains.

14. Shall they turn God away, and the Lord? What shall the Creator do to please them? Is not the name of My general (God), and my captain (Lord), My own creation? Who found the name of God and the name of the Lord? Why are they not pleased with My Gods and My Lords?

15. Hear me, O ye etherean Gods and Goddesses; they desire not wisdom and resurrection. Their love lieth in darkness. To eat, to sleep and to devour are the delights of their souls. The first lesson of life they have not learned; the first heaven of the earth is to them the All of the created worlds.

16. Hear My judgment upon them, O ye, My holy angels, and long risen. For I have raised them up again and again; I have founded lower heavens for them that they might learn; but they fall the moment My Gods leave them alone.

17. Now will I carry away their heaven and earth, and they shall be seen no more forever. But the drujas and fetals shall be carried to Hautuon and cast into walls of fire. And they shall be divided up into groups; kin shall be torn away from kin, and friend from friend, and mother from daughter, and father from son; for they are become as absorbents, sucking one another continually.

18. And the walls of fire shall go up around them without ceasing, and they shall not escape. And they that guard them shall keep them from one another, that they shall do no evil. Neither shall they sleep nor rest, but be stirred up and made to know that they are alive, and can exist independent of fetal (sucking).

19. Hear my voice, O God, and command thy Lord to proclaim on the earth. Have I not made an example before mortals? Behold the carrion that rotteth in the field. Is it not the feast of the hyena, the wolf and the buzzard? Do not worms come to life therein and turn to and devour the carcass that brought them forth?

20. What more is the earth (Pan) to these spirits of evil and darkness? What more is their first heaven than a place of perpetual devouring? Have they not made it a place of everlasting destruction? They visit their evils upon mortals; the young child cannot escape them, nor the middle-aged, nor the old man nor old woman.

21. The heavenly kingdoms founded by Gods and Lords have become pest houses for drujas and fetals; there is no place left for founding the upright and virtuous in heart.

22. Are my Gods and Lords servants to an evil world? And shall they find only rottenness to deal with? Now have I answered in the firmament of my holy sons and daughters. I have called them from remote places in heaven to witness the work of My hand. For as I made the earth and its heaven, so rule I over it to the same end for which I created it.

23. When they are short of My measure, I lengthen them out; when they run foul, I prune them to My own liking; for they are mine. Behold, the fool hath said: Jehovih hath made a failure! Behold, the Creator created a world for a certain purpose, but it run foul of His mark!

24. Hear Me, O God, and through thy Lords answer thou him in his conceit. Did I not quicken man into life in Mine own way? At zero created I him, and I said: Two roads have I made, O man. One leadeth to everlasting light; and the other to everlasting darkness.

25. Now have I shown him the darkness; it is My witness, whereby man knoweth My word is All Truth. Wherefore, then, should I not create the world, and man, and angels, that they go down in everlasting darkness? Is it not by darkness and pain I push man forward? Yea, the conceited man would fail himself but for the failures I set up before him. Wherefore, then, have I not created wisely?

26. Have I not a right to do Mine own way? Are not all things Mine? If a man die in the corporeal part, is he a failure? How else could man rise to My etherean worlds? Open his eyes, O My God and My Lords. He was not, and I created him. He presumeth to look into My plans and judgments; by his little learning he exalteth his conceit and pretendeth to know all things.

27. I cause the grain to grow in the field, and the day before it is ripe I send wind and rains and destroy it utterly. I bring forth man with shapely limbs and strong arms, but in the day of his prime I cut him down. I gave the passion of love to the mother, but I take away her first-born.

28. Know I not that first of all things, man shall be taught to know My power, and after that My wisdom? Have they seen the places of the dead, and hell, and destruction? Teach them, O God; for their ultimate resurrection is My glory and My delight.

29. Shall man of earth say: The Creator was angry, and so sent the land beneath the ocean? He hath not wisdom to comprehend that this day I cast out hell and destruction. The druj is his love, and, as vampires, they feed on each other to the ruin of both.

30. But I know what is for their own good; and My decree hath gone forth.

CHAPTER II.

1. I, Aph, Son of Jehovih, high dwelling in the etherean worlds, and oft trained in the change and tumult of corporeal worlds, answered Jehovih, saying:

2. Father of Worlds; Jehovih, Almighty! Thy Son and servant hath heard Thy voice. Behold, my head is bowed, my knee bent to rush forth with a thousand million force to the suffering earth and hada.

3. Hear me, O angels of the earth's heaven; from Jehovih's everlasting kingdoms, I speak, and by His Power reveal! Again His Voice coursed the high heavens along where angels dwell, older than the earth. Jehovih said:

4. Hear Me, O ye Chieftains, of Or and of Oot, and in the plains of Gibrathatova. Proclaim My word to thy hosts of swift messengers of Wauk'awauk and Beliathon and Dor, and they shall speed it abroad in the a'ji'an mounds of Mentabraw and Kax of Gowh.

5. Hear My voice, O ye Goddesses of Ho'etaivi and of Vaivi'yoni'rom in the etherean arcs of Fas and Leigge, and Omaza. Proclaim My decrees of the red star and her heavens in

the crash of her rebellious sides, for I will harvest in the forests of Seth and Raim.

6. Hear My voice, O ye H'monkensoughts, of millions of years standing, and managers of corporeal worlds! I have proclaimed the uz and hiss of the red star in her pride and glory. Send word abroad in the highway of Plumf'goe to the great high Gods, Miantaf in the etherean vortices of Bain, and to Rome and to Nesh'outoza and Du'ji.

7. Hear Me, O ye Orian Kings and Queens of thousands of millions of Gods and Goddesses: I have spoken in the c'vork'um of the great serpent of the sun! A wave of My breath speedeth forth in the broad firmament. The red star flieth toward the point of My whetted sword.

8. Proclaim My voice in the Orian fields of Amal and Wawa; let the clear-tongued Shepherds of Zouias, and Berk, and Gaub, and Domfariana, fly with all speed in the road of Axyaya, where first the red star's vortex gathered up its nebulae, millions of years agone, and on the way say: Jehovih hath decreed a pruning-knife to a traveling world.

9. Shout it abroad in the crystal heavens of the summering Lords of Wok and Ghi and M'goe and Ut'taw; call them to the red star speeding forth. Lo, she skippeth as a lamb to be shorn; her coming shock lieth slumbering low. Let them carry the sound of My voice to the ji'ay'an swamps of exploded worlds, boiling in the roar of elements, where wise angels and Gods explore to find the mystery of My handiwork.

10. Tell them I have spoken, and the earth and her heavens near the troughs in the etherean seas of My rich-yielding worlds. I will scoop her up as a toy, and her vortex shall close about like a serpent hungry for its prey. Proclaim it in Thessa and Kau and Tin'wak'wak, and send them to Gitchefom of Januk and Dun.

11. Hear Me, O ye Kriss'helmatsholdak, who have witnessed the creation of many worlds and their going out. Open your gardens and your mansions; the seine of My fishing-pole is stretched; countless millions of druj and fetals will fall into My net. My voice hath gone forth in Chem'gow and Loo and Abroth, and Huitavi, and Kuts of mas in the wide etherean fields of Rod'owkski.

12. Haleb hath heard Me; Borg, Hom, Zi and Luth, of the Orian homestead, and Chor, whence emanate the central tones of music, from Goddesses older than the corporeal worlds. To them the crash of worlds is as a note created, and is rich in stirring the memory with things long past.

13. I have spoken, and My breath is a floating world; My speech is written in the lines where travel countless millions of suns and stars; and in the midst of the etherean firmament of the homes of Gods. Let them shout to the ends of the universe; invite them in My name to the hi'dan of Mauk'beiang'jow.

14. Around about in the place of the great serpent send swift messengers with the words of My decree; bring the Lords and Gods of Wan and Anah and Anakaron and Sith.

15. Call up Ghad and Adonya and Etisyai and Onesyi and the hosts of the upraised, for the past time of Jehovih's sons and daughters in the high heavens draweth near.

CHAPTER III.

1. O ye angels, of hada of the red star; and thou, O God, and ye Lords, upraised and mighty, with hosts, countless, and quick answering the thoughts of mortals, hear the words of Aph, Son of Jehovih:

2. When I was in the Orian arc of Noe, and the red star passed the Utswowldayark, in the etherean group of Vorh, the voice of Jehovih came to me, saying: Go thou, My Son, deliver the earth. Take with thee all whom I may send.

3. And I examined the records of the stars of heaven, and of the earth; and the accounts of Jehovih's harvests, and I perceived the bondage and labor of the red star were of the seventh magnitude in the advance of habitable worlds.

4. When His voice called the legions in high heaven, from every side, and below and above the earth, there moved myriads of shapely stars, which were ships of fire, coursing the firmament, whereon rode the Gods and Goddesses called by Jehovih to the labor of earth and hada.

5. Closing in on every side they came, and nearer and more compact, and brighter, with sparkling pillars of fire, and down-swaying curtains of light, till all the space around about the earth was hedged in with this army of Jehovih's etherean ships of fire.

6. Again I heard the Father's voice, saying: O Aph, My Son, My holy one, hearken to the voice of Jehovih, Creator of Gods and Goddesses:

7. Behold, I sent My Son, Neph, to the red star, with wisdom and power. Long hath he been gone; long struggling with the black darkness of men and angels.

8. As a valiant soldier rusheth into the heaviest part of battle, and forgetteth himself in desperate contest, but ceaseth not to struggle on against all odds, even so for three thousand years hath My God, Neph, hoped to save the whole limbs of the earth (the continents).

9. From My holy place have I watched the battle for everlasting life; but the too prolific earth contributeth more to the corporeal than to the spiritual man. And I bring My legions to the rescue of My valiant Son, Neph. Send thou to him, O Aph, My Son. Proclaim to him and his Lords, and to his ethereans, My just decrees. Aph said:

10. And I sent swift messengers down to hada, informing Neph, Son of Jehovih, of the march and presence of Gods, and of the decree of the Father; and I added thereunto, saying: O Neph, Son of Jehovih, come hither, bringing thy hosts with thee.

11. Presently Neph answered me in Jehovih's name, saying: O Aph, Son of Jehovih, I come! My prayers are answered. All praise to the All Highest!

12. Then we saw, making ready in hada, preparatory to ascending, the ship of Neph and his faithful hosts; and that which was seen from my place was also seen by the myriads of Jehovih's vessels surrounding the earth. And my place became as a central throne to which the hosts now made speed, swift and orderly.

13. And in the time they came, also rose up the ship of Neph from hada. Meanwhile, my ship rested on the borders of Chinvat, in the School of Hein, and from the moon seven agus.

14. Again the voice of Jehovih came to me, saying: My Son, make fast thy ship, for thy place shall be the head of the army of My hosts. And let thy consorts extend in a line from thy place down to the earth, for this shall be the delivery of them whom I shall cut off.

15. So I made fast, and my messengers hastened to the concentrating forces of heaven, informing the etherean groups on Jehovih's ships of His commandments. And now came Neph; his ship rose up, filled with his long-laboring hosts. And I greeted him and said unto him: By the power and wisdom of Jehovih, the continent of Wagga is to be cut loose and submerged, and her heavens carried away. Return thou to the earth and bring all the

spirits of darkness from all the divisions of earth and heaven to Wagga, that I may carry them away. Then Neph and his hosts viewed the imposing scene and returned back to the earth.

16. Quickly, now, the ships of fire formed in line, extending from my place down to hada, where rested Neph and his Lords of the earth, whose hosts extended to all the divisions of land and water, embracing the various heavenly kingdoms previously built by the Lords.

17. And in the line of the etherean ships were stationed the plateaux of rank; and the hosts of Gods and Goddesses took their places according to the rank of wisdom, power and love manifested in the etherean departments whence they came, with the two Orian Chiefs at either extremity.

18. And I divided the line into sections, each with two hundred and fifty ships, and there were one thousand sections. And every ship was contracted ten thousand fold, which was the force required to break the crust of the earth and sink a continent.

19. Along the line I stationed sentinels and talisman, and messengers, without number, so that Jehovih's voice and His sons' voices could traverse in a moment of time to every part. And after that I formed the tube of transit, which extended in front of the ships, and from the earth to beyond Chinvat; and I filled it with the earth's atmosphere to the extreme, whither it joined Io'sank, whither I determined to deliver the drujas and fetals of such as were to perish in the ocean of the earth.

20. For every ten sections I appointed one hundred marshals and one God, and for every ten Gods one Chief in Emuts; according to their rank in the heavens whence they came, so appointed I them. These, then, are the Chief Emuts, to wit:

21. Agar, of the order of Achav, Son of Jehovih, in Bowitch, from the corporeal star Godad, raised in Ben of a'ji, seventy, of seven hundred thousand years inhabitant of Gon.

22. Hoe'ghi, Son of Jehovih, Marsh'wan of Hadom and Ag, nebulae four and Petrath; swift messenger of Jun, of the corporeal star Alanx, of one million two hundred thousand years inhabitant of Roth'wok in Jois.

23. Fist'humitaivi, Daughter of Jehovih, ji'ya'an Oods'lon in Kaih; Goddess of Ine; Goddess of Ad; Governess of Wal'wal, of the corporeal star Ter'wig, and of the plains of Exwer and Gohen, in the etherean arc of Labis, of one million three hundred thousand years.

24. Hi'ata, Daughter of Jehovih, and nurse of Hue'enbak, in fifty-seven, a'ji, of the corporeal star Heats, a milkmaid, Goddess of Luf, Goddess of the plateau of O'banf, in etherea, rank ninety, and of two millions of years inhabitant of Nud and Ix.

25. Gon'leps, Son of Jehovih, God of Ney, God of Aper, God of Don, God of Mu, God of Reau; physician of Bo, and of Ir, and of Jan'er; marshal of Kute and Oblin of Sharar, in etherea, of the a'ji'an field of Do; of seven hundred thousand years inhabitant of On'lof and Pick'tus.

26. Neo, God of Lun and Hintaya; God of Mors, and of Thespune; Master of Peh and Savior of Woh'haggai, a'ji plain seven, and risen from the corporeal star Se'etiyi, and inhabitant of Sirne one million seven hundred thousand years.

27. Sicci, Goddess of Nu, in Loots and Rab; Goddess of Bad; Goddess of Ture; Goddess of Red, a'ji twenty, from the corporeal star Ith'mule, inhabitant of Suga one million of years; inhabitant of Ranna one million two hundred thousand years.

28. Listiac'ca, Goddess of Man; Goddess of Hirze; Goddess of Som and Nye; Weaver of

Olt'bak and Agimus. Rank ninety, raised on the corporeal star Mem; inhabitant of Das'sawig and Gabriomety two millions nine hundred thousand years.

29. Tussica, Goddess of Kol; Goddess of Lowst and Wittawhaggat; Goddess of Du'e'jhi and Loo of Maggatza; Goddess of Ep; Goddess Gek of Hennasshalonkya; Goddess of Tur in the ji'ay'an swamp of Dobbokta, fifty-five, raised on the corporeal sun Nitz, of the Serpent Tan, inhabitant of Tayay'hitsivi, two millions of years; inhabitant of Palla one million seven hundred thousand years.

30. Fiatisi, Goddess of Lubbuk; Goddess of Saran'ya, in Gowlolo; Goddess of Iz; Goddess of Serl; Goddess of Lok'low; Goddess Um of a'ji, seventy-five; Goddess of Wartz and Do'e'huitta; Goddess of Crayya; Goddess of Bak'hoo; Goddess of Teel and Ros'itz; Goddess of Mutz'mutz; Goddess of La'errets of Wouk'humhowtz; Goddess of Bil and Dusk'wan'guessel; Goddess of Ork'sa; Goddess of Unksoot; Goddess of Sl'huitta; Goddess of Shein; Goddess of Isa; Goddess of Ham; Goddess of Reikowow and Shuitit; Goddess of Daing and Gou'wok; Goddess of Faitta'zammel; Goddess of Zittayya'howb of the gardens of Zittayya'bauf in a'ji seven; surgeon of Hualla; surgeon of Bos; surgeon of Rappaya; surgeon of Lum'zon; nurse of Paigga of Semathais; nurse of Zid; nurse of Loo'see; nurse of Home; nurse of Briathath; Queen of Ouppa; Queen of Rog'ga, disciplinarian of Tuh; of Kaibbi'summak, of Tootz'mutz, of Bir'bir, of Ctenski, of Rivvia, of soon, of Hadab, of Fussohowtz and Ceres; raised on the star Planzza, swift messenger in Bal and Wawa'lauk five hundred thousand years; swift messenger in To'wakka and Runfwot five hundred thousand years; inhabitant of Terashash one million of years; inhabitant of the fields of Ni'jayay one million of years; inhabitant of Gun five hundred thousand years; maker of corporeal roadways five hundred thousand years.

31. So Fiatisi outranked all other Gods and Goddesses, and was special guest of honor to Aph, Chief over all the rest.

32. And the star of Fiatisi's etherean ship was stationed near the earth, that she might the better behold the deliverance of the spirits that were to be freed by the submersion of the land of Wagga; and of these spirits there were upward of twenty-four billion four hundred millions, of whom more than three billion were fetals and familiars and spirits in chaos.

CHAPTER IV.

1. Jehovih said: Aph, My Son, put a wall of pillars of fire around about the land of Wagga; plant them near, as a hedge is planted. For the false Gods and false Goddesses of hada, when perceiving their habitation going down into the water, will endeavor to escape to Jud and Vohu, and other countries.

2. But thou shalt not suffer one to escape; for they have migrated to this division of the earth because of its sumptuous productions, the better to feast their evil desires.

3. And thou shalt spread a net around the borders of Wagga, against the line of the ocean and to the high north mountains; and the net shall encompass the continent of Wagga, and it shall be to the height of a thousand miles, and in breadth, so that no spirit of darkness can escape and find the way abroad.

4. And when thou hast spread the net, thou shalt send to the large kingdoms in hada, and to the false kingdoms, a sufficient number of ethereans of great power; and thou shalt send down to the earth, to Wagga, a sufficient number of ethereans, that every mortal man and mortal woman, and every mortal child, shall have five to attend. And they that go to

mortals shall take with them birth-blankets a sufficiency; for in the time of destruction, when the mortals go down in death, thy servants shall receive he liberated spirits on the birth-blankets, and bear them to the atmospherean column of ascent. And hither shall thy hosts receive them and provide them with food and clothes, after the manner of es'yans.

5. But it shall come to pass that many mothers shall perish in the waters, with children in the womb, which live by fetal, as is proper in My sight, for so created I them.

6. Therefore, to all such fetals give special care, for they are without sin. And when the mother is dead corporeally, and the fetal also, bring hence their spirits, but together; and provide a volunteer angel of fetal power, and deliver the infant spirit to her to be nurtured until the proper time of weaning, and provide in the same place a home for the mother of the child, that she may inherit its love and mirth.

7. When the voice ceased, Aph, Son of Jehovih, looked about over the hosts as if in search of a sign that the time had come; but again Jehovih spake, saying:

8. In the misfortunes of a fallen world, created I food for the warm love of My etherean Goddesses. Behold them hereabout in millions; every one in hope of receiving a prize of that which was lost in darkness, to raise up sons and daughters, who shall rejoice in everlasting paradise. Think not that I gave the talent of love only to a mother for her child, and there the talent to end; for as the talent in its incipient age bindeth her soul to her child, so doth the same talent in My Goddesses overspread a helpless world.

9. Are they not as midwives and mothers to thousands and millions of souls being delivered from corporeal bondage into everlasting light? And who can number them? Here standeth a hundred millions come from Laygas; a hundred millions from Inopta; two hundred millions from Karduk; a hundred millions from Buchk; two hundred millions from Nin; two hundred and fifty millions from Luth'wig; a hundred millions from Pied; two hundred millions from Raig; fifty millions from Naivis; two hundred millions from Dak'dak, and two hundred and fifty millions from Od.

10. I spake in the etherean firmament, and they have answered Me. Yea, they come not as curiosity seekers, and with empty arms; but, behold them, arrayed with their thousands and millions of small equipments suited to the newborn! What thing is there under the sun they have not remembered to bring with them in some part, for regimen or drapery, to rejoice the souls of them that are to be cut off from corpor?

CHAPTER V.

1. Jehovih said: Now will I bewail thee, O earth. The glories of thy heavens that are past and gone shall be a lesson to the Gods. Thy place of Hored, once the place of the wisdom of My Son, Sethantes, upraised, behold it is measured and gone down. And Moeb is no more: Yeshuah is fallen. Where floated the plateaux of many resurrections, are now miring vampires and millions of souls that hear not and see not, but are forever burrowing deep in everlasting darkness.

2. The plateaux are broken up; the substance scattered and unorganized; nor is there a vestige left to show the glorious work of the Gods of the earth's past day.

3. Hear me, O ye Gods and Goddesses, for in beholding these deep miseries, the soul is quickened to retain great wisdom: Thus created I man; out of darkness created I him; and My holy angels taught him to walk upright and gave him My commandments that he

might advance to eternal light. But because man obeyed not the commandments of My God and Lords, he fell. Nevertheless, a few obeyed the commandments and fell not, raising up heirs for the glory of My heavens above.

4. Of such have I made an example on all the corporeal worlds I created; for those that fell not, became examplers before the fallen; for having faith in Me and My works they questioned not My wisdom and justice.

5. But of those that fell, this is the history: They first questioned My Person; next My Wisdom; next My Justice; next My Power. And after that proclaimed the folly of God and his Lords; whereupon they usurped to themselves to say: There is nothing higher than man. And they said of themselves: I am the highest.

6. Hear My voice, O ye Gods and Goddesses; for as out of a contrary wind I give a mortal sea-captain a wholesome lesson; or as out of a severe winter I give a corporeal farmer a lesson in providing for his household; even so, on the brink of a wicked world, give I ye a lesson on the management of My kingdoms. For from this time forth the earth shall not fail; nor her heavens above her. Wherein, then, shall not My Gods rule over her in wisdom and power?

7. Since many angels assumed they were the All Highest, they put aside the commandments, one of which was: To suffer not the spirits of the newly dead to return and dwell with their mortal kindred; for they, not knowing of the higher heavens, will teach falsely of Jehovih and His everlasting kingdoms.

8. And it came to pass that when one commandment was set aside the others were also; and it followed that the spirits of the newly dead, who were without knowledge of heaven, led mortals in their own way.

9. For they dwelt together and slept together, and in dreams and visions mortals judged themselves to be wise, not knowing they were obsessed in sleep; and for the desires of the flesh they found acquiescence in spirit, having no higher God or Lord.

10. And as one spirit returned and fastened itself on a mortal, so did another and another, till hundreds and thousands of spirits dwelt in one corporeal body, oft driving hence the natural spirit I gave in the time of conception; and these mortals knew it not; and they became void of direct purpose because of the confusion of soul, and they were worthless on the earth.

11. Jehovih further said: Henceforth for a long season shall it be on the earth that the spirits of the es'yans shall not be suffered to return and dwell with mortals. But the earth shall be encompassed on all sides with walls of emun, and with ashars to bear away the spirits of the dead in the hour of death.

12. But there shall come a time when mortals are capable of comprehending these matters, in which time their kindred spirits shall return at intervals from their holy labors in heaven, and see them and talk with them face to face.

CHAPTER VI.

1. And now Aph, Son of Jehovih, said: When the etherean hosts were arranged in due order, I called out to Thee, O Jehovih, saying: In Thy Strength and Wisdom, O Father, join Thou the heavens above and the earth below!

2. And the end of the etherean column that extended to Chinvat, on the border of the

vortex of the earth, was made fast by the pressure of Thy wide heavens.

3. Again I said: In Thy Strength and Wisdom, O Jehovih, join Thou the heavens above with the earth below!

4. And the end of the etherean column that extended down to the earth was made fast around the borders of Wagga, by the sea and the high mountains on the north.

5. Again I said: O Jehovih, deliver Thou the earth from evil, for Thy glory, forever!

6. And the vortex of the earth closed in from the extreme, and lo, the earth was broken! A mighty continent was cut loose from its fastenings, and the fires of the earth came forth in flames and clouds with loud roaring. And the land rocked to and fro like a ship at sea.

7. Again I said: O Jehovih, deliver Thou Thy heavens, which are bound as with a chain, to a rotten carcass.

8. And again the vortex of the earth closed in about on all sides, and by the pressure, the land sank down beneath the water, to rise no more. And the corporeans went down to death; and the fetals and familiars gave up the battle; neither had they whereon to stand, nor knew how to go to any place in all the heavens, but were lost and crying out for help.

9. And my hosts hastened in all directions with their birth-blankets, and received the druj and fetals and es'yans in millions and millions, and gathered them to the place of the fountain of light, whither I had provided atmosphere for them, and they were placed within. And their numbers were so great that even Gods had scarce seen the like before; and in order to attest before Thee, O Jehovih, I had them numbered, using the sections of the divisions of my Gods and Goddesses in order to do so.

10. And there were of druj and fetals sixteen billion six hundred millions, many of whom had lived on earth as fetals and druj for thousands of years, though many others of them were not capable of everlasting life. And of the first resurrection there were thirty-six thousand millions; and of the second resurrection there were three hundred and five millions. But during the last hundred years the earth brought forth none capable of everlasting life, save, indeed, the remnants of I'hins.

11. Now when the earth was delivered, and there was no escape for the spirits of the dead, nor no returning to mortals, I called out to Thee, O Jehovih, saying: Give me of Thy power, O Jehovih, and I will carry up all the plateaux of hell and the heavens of the buried continent! And Thy hand came as the blade of a sword, flaming like fire, and swept over the ocean of the sunken land, cleaving all asunder. And, lo and behold, the anchorage of my feet was cut loose, and the spheres of heaven at my command.

12. Thy voice, O Jehovih, came to me, saying: Descend thou, My Son, down to the floor of the resurrection, and take My Daughter, Fiatisi, with thee, and go into the midst of the place of ascension, for I will add unto thy glory the resurrection of all that thine eyes have beholden.

13. So I descended, and took Fiatisi, Daughter of Jehovih, with me; and when we were come into the place commanded, Thy power came upon the place, and it started upward; and soon thereafter it turned on its vertical axis and rose higher and higher, turning and rising; and we saw we were loose from the earth, and no longer rotated with the earth, but rose slowly upward, watching the earth rotating beneath us.

14. I said: Upward, O Jehovih! Upward, O Jehovih! Upward, O Jehovih! And all the hosts repeated the same words, for our wills and knowledge were as a unit, wherein we had strength in Thee, Our Creator!

CHAPTER VII.

1. Jehovih spake in the firmament, saying: Bring the newborn into the forests of Uk'loo and the ji'ay'an roads to the arc of Noe, in the etherean heaven of Hautuon; and when thou hast founded them on a world of their own, leave thou Gods and Goddesses with them to sort them and provide according to their necessities, for all things shall be provided unto them that they may attain to knowledge and individuality.

2. And when thou hast placed them, hasten thou with My Son, Neph, back to the earth, where I have labor with the ships of the I'hins. And they were thus delivered.

3. So I departed as soon as possible, taking leave of Fiatisi, thanking her for her assistance in this great deliverance; and I took with me Neph, Son of Jehovih, and other thirty thousand Gods and Goddesses, besides ten million ethereans who had had thousands of years' experience in heaven and on various corporeal worlds; and we came back to the earth, even to the ocean where the land had gone down.

4. And when I came to the ships in which the I'hins were escaped, finding the Gods who had them in charge, even as I had previously commanded, Thy voice, O Jehovih, came to me, saying: Bend thou the currents of the winds of heaven, O My Son; and shape the ships that they shall fall into groups; and thou shalt divide the groups, making four groups in all. And thou shalt drive the groups of ships before the winds of heaven, and bring them into the four different lands of the earth, according to its previous history and adaptation.

5. For in all countries shall My chosen begin the laying down of the foundation of My everlasting kingdom, and they shall never more be destroyed by the people of darkness, neither of earth or heaven.

6. So I divided my hosts according to the labor Thy commandments put upon me, making four divisions of them. And I said unto Neph: Direct them, O God, to such countries as Jehovih hath shown thee, for thou knowest all the earth; for, remember, thou art still God of earth.

7. I said: By Thy light, Jehovih, I desire two ships to go to the north land, which was not sunken, for they shall be a testimony in time to come. Let Thy Gods, therefore, shift the winds and drive two ships aside from the rest, and in that same time my messengers will go and lead the way to the north land, whither Thy Gods shall shape the winds of heaven.

8. Now, those in charge of the wind currents divided the ships and drove two of them off to the north land. And the Gods and angels turned the currents about and drove the four groups of ships in four different ways, according to the directions of God, Son of Jehovih; and the messengers of God led the way, showing the Gods and angels of the wind, the countries designated by Jehovih.

9. So it came to pass that in one hundred and fifty days' time all the ships of the Faithists were in the ports, and the people went ashore, in the different countries whither they had been taken. Again Thy voice, O Jehovih, came to me, saying: Behold, My people are few in the world, and lest they take the ships and sail about, and so get divided and lost, thou shalt send thy hosts down to the sea at night to sink the ships.

10. When I told God (Neph) what Thou hadst said, God said unto me: My angels shall inspire the I'hins to take all things out of the ships, and this night shall thy hosts fulfill the commandment of Jehovih. And so it came to pass; the I'hins took all their goods out of

the ships, not knowing they were inspired; and in the night I sent angels down, and they sank the ships.

11. And in the morning the I'hins beheld their ships had disappeared, and they said with one voice: Of a truth, I know I was inspired, for I would not rest till all the goods were taken out of the ships. Let us, therefore, build an altar unto the Lord, and sing and dance, because he is with us. And when God (Neph) saw that their souls were propitious for good works and miracles, he stationed his ashars (guardian angels) around about the altars, and sent other ashars into the country, and they gathered fruit which was growing wild, and brought it to the I'hins, casting it on the altars of the Lord, even whilst the people danced.

12. Thus did I fulfill the work Thou commandedst of me, O Jehovih, whereupon I surrendered my commission to Thy Son, Neph, God of heaven and earth.

CHAPTER VIII.

1. Neph, God of earth, said: Behold, O Aph, Son of Jehovih, by the power and magnificence of thy work am I bewildered in thy presence. Who can come so near the Almighty? Who but Jehovih hath attained beyond the power of thy soul? Who hath wisdom like unto thee, save the Great Creator? Thou hast stretched a line beyond the moon, and by thy spoken word crushed in the side of the great earth, as if it were nothing. Thou hast said: Arise! and a world moved at thy command! Yea, thou hast the love and esteem of millions of Gods and Goddesses.

2. And thou camest against the winds of the earth, saying: Turn ye hither or turn ye thither, and lo, the winds moved before thy words as an obedient child to its father's voice. Thou callest down the fire of heaven; it cometh at thy bidding; and thou sayst: O Jehovih, put thy hand under the heavens of the earth, and straightway a light and floor wide as the earth fly into the place of thy desire.

3. Now, behold thou hast said: O Jehovih, I surrender my commission; I have finished that which Thou commandest me to do. Wherefore, O Aph, my soul hath great sorrow. But because thou hast labored a hundred days and cleaned up the whole earth and her heavens, as one might sweep the floor of a house, I am bowed down in gratitude.

4. Then Aph, Son of Jehovih, said: O Jehovih, what have I done that Thy Son's love hath come to me? So far as I have become one with Thee, O Thou Everlasting Creator, so Thou showest me plainer and plainer that I am nothing. And yet Thy Son heapest praise upon me, seeing I am but as a figure moved by Thy hand. Shall a man lose sight of the Almighty!

5. Nevertheless, O Jehovih, who so weak in love as I, Thy servant? Because Thou hast quickened me in wisdom and power, so hast Thou made my love as a place that can never be supplied to the fill. How shall I find strength to leave this, Thy Son, on the far-off earth? Will I not glory in his love and great esteem; and yet know I not that I will repine because I have him not with me?

6. Hear me, O Jehovih, for I will measure Thy Son with swiftness. Scarce forty thousand years raised up to etherea, and yet Thou madest him God of heaven and earth. For three thousand years struggled he in the battle against evil and darkness; and the broad heavens in the etherean world looked on in sympathy and love and hope, because of his tenacity

and wisdom and power.

7. It was as one man fighting against a house on fire, and the place filled with helpless babes. And yet Thy God ceased not, nor once rested and said: It is useless; but forever renewed the battle in new ways and stratagems. As a light showeth better in the dark, so did Thy Son Neph, O Jehovih, move the souls of even Gods and Goddesses in Thy exalted heavens.

8. Then came Thy voice, O Father, saying: Go thou, O Aph, My Son, and deliver the earth. And, behold, the congregating of Gods and Goddesses! So eager to fly to the assistance of Thy honored Son!

9. And God (Neph) said: One favor, O Aph, Son of Jehovih, I ask of thee; which is that thou shalt tarry three days and honor the throne of God. For I will have it founded and ready; and my Lords shall have the honor of speaking to thee face to face.

10. Aph, Son of Jehovih, said: By Thy permission, O Jehovih, I will tarry three days and three nights with Thy Son, God of heaven and earth, and I will honor his throne and speak face to face with his Lords, that I may win their love.

11. In three days' time the kingdom of God was founded, and situated in atmospherea, near and over the land of Jaffeth (Chine'ya), but the plateaux extended with two wings, so as to embrace Shem and Ham (India and Egypt); and thither went the Gods, with their Lords and attendants.

12. Now, there were with God (Neph) two million spirits (earth-born) in the second resurrection, who had volunteered to serve another two hundred years for the founding of the new kingdom of heaven, and they were well learned in official capacity, knowing how to found plateaux, with factories, mansions, hospitals, nurseries, and all such places as are required in heaven for the newborn, so that God only had to say: Do ye thus, or so; and it was done, and without error.

13. And now, from the hosts of Aph, Son of Jehovih, there came before God half a million etherean volunteers who desired to remain two hundred years with God and his hosts.

14. God said to them: Behold, the earth hath passed Tryista, and it is no longer lawful for any but earth-born to hold the places of sub-Gods and sub-Lords and marshals; and since ye are from different stars raised, and from different etherean circuits, what shall I do that ye may be honored, and also profitable to yourselves in development?

15. Gaitivaya, chief spokesman for them, said: We desire to be laborers only. For what is two hundred years to us? We pray thee, appoint us not to the I'hins, for they are already advanced, but appoint us to the natives in the divisions of the earth, especially to those who speak but little, and who burrow in the ground. Neither do we desire a place in thy heaven, but we will abide with mortals, and in the first resurrection of those who are born in darkness.

16. God said: Thou shalt remain, and thy people with thee. For since thou hast volunteered to leave thy high estate and come and dwell for one dan on the lowest of all places, laboring for the blind and dumb, thou shalt be recompensed with the love of millions in time to come.

17. Then God departed, and Aph, Son of Jehovih, went with him, and they came into the midst of the kingdom of God, whereat they halted, and God said: Here will I build my throne; and inasmuch as Sethantes, in the olden time, called his place Hored, so will I call

my place Hored also, and on the earth it shall be called the Mountain of God, for it shall be my home.

18. So God stretched forth his hand to Jehovih, saying: Throne of Thy throne, O Father! And there came down from the heavens above a great light, and it settled around about in the midst of the place of God and Aph, Jehovih's Son; and presently the light gathered up of the atmospherean substance and made it shining and condensed, whereupon the attendants who do such matters brought and laid the throne of God, and thereafter fenced it around with pillars of fire, after the manner of Hored of the ancient days.

19. And God ascended and sat on the throne, and Aph also sat on the right hand of God, and the four Lords of the earth on the left hand; but the fifth Lord, Eolait, stood down at the foot. And he said: Behold, the division of the earth that was mine is sunk beneath the sea; how, then, shall I sit on the throne of God?

20. God said: Since thy labor hath been taken from thee, thou art as a parable on the newly dead; who have lost the earth, but have no place in heaven. Since the es'yan serveth a time through the proxy of others, so shalt thou in that which I will bestow upon thee. Know, then, thou shalt sit on my right hand, for thou shalt be my assistant and Vice-God during the time of my sojourn; and, after that, whatsoever thou wilt.

21. Eolait said: Thou hast honored me, O God! Jehovih's will be done! So God rose up, raising his hand, and said: O Thou All Light, crown Thou Thy Son Vice-God of Hored, for Thine Own Glory, forever!

22. And as the light of etherea descended into God's right hand, he shaped it into a crown and placed it on Eolait's head, with the usual ceremony of such rank in heaven. And Eolait came and sat on the right hand of God. And in that same time, Aph, Son of Jehovih, rose up, whereupon God and the Lords, and all people whatsoever, sat down, for the place was as if Jehovih had appeared in person. Aph said:

23. As a father is made to comprehend his own early life by looking on his infant son, so hast Thou, O Jehovih, forever raised up before my eyes the images of times and conditions long past. In these, Thy Lords, Thou hast called me back to the time and place when first Thou and Thy Son crowned me a Lord and a Vice-God over one of the divisions of my native star.

24. And my soul rose up to Thee in fear and prayer; for I understood how unmindful men and angels are of the labor of Gods and Lords, and prone to rate themselves as Chiefs of all created things. But Thy Voice, O Jehovih, came to me, saying: Complain not, My Son, against the self-conceit of men and angels, nor of their criticisms of My Gods and Lords; for to such boasters do I provide trials, which they perceive not till they are encompassed therewith. Suffer them, therefore, within thy dominions to grow in their own glory, for I have sufficient labor for them, either on earth or in heaven.

25. And I perceived Thy wisdom, and I applied it through my angels; and when my people rose to the first resurrection, and the second resurrection, behold, I knew where to place them that they might prove themselves all in all. And Thy light came upon me in my place, saying: As thou hast profited in the first lesson, so shalt thou comprehend the second, and even up to the etherean heavens.

26. Nevertheless, O Father, Thou sufferedest all things to harass me and perplex my soul; and I was filled with fear and reverence because of the great responsibility Thou gavest unto my keeping. So great were my tribulations and trials that I called out to

Thee in Thy holy place to remember all other Gods and Lords in Thy whole universe.

27. And Thou saidst: Hear the words of Thy Creator, thou, My God, My Son: For I created man to enter heaven as helpless as he entered earth life, and dependent on those above him, that he might comprehend the unity between high and low, strong and weak, light and darkness; and I placed him in My mills, wherein he should learn that, even as others grind for him, so should he grind for those beneath him.

28. For of what profit under the sun is it for My Lords to come down from their liberty and glory in My etherean firmament and become Lords over the grovellers in the flesh, or over the es'yans in darkness? Shall selfishness reign in heaven, and every one for himself? Have I not proved it on the earth that the love of doing good works unto others is all that insures a rich harvest of love in return.

29. Because they stoop from their high estate in order to promote My children which I created alive, are they not becoming the more one with Me? Even so is all exaltation in heaven; for as I stoop down to the dumb earth and water, and quicken them, making man, so have I stooped lower than can anything of all My universe. And they that do after My example, raising them up to make them have joy in life, are on the road to attain to all power and wisdom and love.

30. Aph, Son of Jehovih, said: I perceived Thy wisdom, O Father; and Thy power and wisdom came upon me tenfold. Then I sought forever after to go to the lowest and darkest places; but, lo, when I had grown in Thy judgment, Thou spakest again to me, saying:

31. O Aph, My Son, because thou hast found the key to unlock the doors to the highest heavens, behold, thou art too mighty for small labor. Come, therefore, with Thy Creator, for I have a whole etherean world at thy command, and thy wisdom and power are required at My hand.

32. And I obeyed Thy call, O Jehovih. And then again, after a season, Thou calledest me again, and again, and madest my labors to extend into many etherean worlds. But I loved to look back and glorify Thee for my first Lord-dom, and to treasure up the millions of loves I found in those days. And again, O Father, hast Thou blessed me to meet many millions of them in this pruning of the red star, the earth.

33. Now Thou hast called me to speak on the throne of Thy God of earth. Alas, thy God has said: O Aph, Son of Jehovih, come thou and honor my throne! Whereas, O Jehovih, I am the most honored of men and Gods because I have again opened my mouth before Thee and in Thy name. All glory be to Thee, O Jehovih, now and forever!

34. Then Aph, Son of Jehovih, sat down, and God signaled to the marshals, who proclaimed freedom for two whole days. Thereupon the Gods and Goddesses of Aph's staff filed past the throne, and after them came the hosts of God, and then the hosts of the Lords, for they all desired to pass near and look upon Aph, and receive the signal of his blessing.

35. And presently thereafter all the people joined in with the es'enaurs and sang a song of glory unto Jehovih, the All Highest. And when it was finished, the multitude turned to recreation and social intercourse.

CHAPTER IX.

1. When the time came, God called his proper officers, and they proclaimed his presence, whereupon the people came to order. And God said:

2. Even as it was before the submersion, so shall it now be, and ye shall fill the same places even as before, every one to the place provided. Nevertheless, from this time forth, all work in heaven and earth shall be new, and as if nothing had been. Let my Lords and their attendants, and their ashars, prepare for their departure; and from such other volunteers as have come into my kingdom they shall receive as they desire, and be assigned to labor suited to them, whether it be with mortals or with spirits in the first resurrection.

3. And to my marshals, messengers and asaphs: Hear ye the word of your God, which is that ye proceed throughout atmospherea, selecting and appropriating all suitable places for the spirits of the dead; and that ye apportion builders and workmen, and erect factories, and schools, and hospitals, and nurseries, and all other suitable places, adapted to receiving those of the first resurrection, as is done in all atmospherean heavens, and all who are thus received shall be called es'yans for the first five years; but after that they shall be called es'seans, signifying having separated from corporeal desire, being full residents of the es world. But those who will not become es'seans, being the spirits of druk-mortals and hard bound to the earth, shall be called druj, signifying wandering spirits of darkness and of evil; and those who engraft themselves on mortals shall be called fetals, signifying sucklings, and these names shall continue in heaven and on earth to the end of the world.

4. Wherein ye may perceive the fault of leniency of the Gods and Lords of old, be ye circumspect in these times; for never more shall the rod of water chasten the living earth.

5. When God thus completed all his commandments, and the people were ready to depart, the es'enaurs and trumpeters sang and played a hymn adapted to the new heaven and new earth; and when this was finished, Aph, Son of Jehovih, spake, saying:

6. Behold the light of the high heaven opens. Thy Son, O Jehovih, longeth for a great labor. I go on a journey farther than ten thousand suns. Fiatisi, Thy Daughter, O Jehovih, and Goddess of a thousand worlds, hath set apart to join two corporeal stars in a far-off heaven, whereon a thousand millions shall be delivered into spirit life in a single day. With her, by Thy Will and Power, O Jehovih, I go! But yet let not these, Thy Gods and Lords and all their hosts, surmise I will forget one single soul of all that are here. And when the next dan appeareth, behold, I will return to them to enjoy a portion of their sweet love. Aph is done.

7. And now the Chief descended and sat at the foot of the throne, and God, suffused with tears, came down and took his hand, saying: Behold, he who is greatest maketh himself least of all. Arise, O Aph, Son of Jehovih, and crowned IMMORTAL GOD OF THE ARC OF NOE, SON OF THE ALMIGHTY, arise and go thy way.

8. So Aph rose up, and shaking hands with God and his Lords, descended to the borders beyond the foot of the pillars of fire, and his hosts with him, being ten millions in number, where the proper persons had in readiness an ascending otevan with wings, wherein they all entered.

9. At a given signal the otevan started upward, but toward the east, and, swift as a shooting star, it sped forth, and presently disappeared in the distance.

CHAPTER X.

1. Jehovih said: Neph, My Son, God of earth, hear thou the voice of Thy Creator. For as

thou calledest on Me in thy sore hour of trial, so did I come to thee and deliver the earth and heaven through My son of the arc of Noe, in etherea. Remember now the upraised of Hautuon, heaven of darkness, in Uk'loo, in the firmament, for they are thine until the next dan appeareth on the earth.

2. God said: I have heard Thy voice, O Jehovih; but what shall Thy servant do? Behold Aph, Thy Arc-Son, hath left with the upraised children of darkness, Gods and Goddesses who transcend Thy servant so far in wisdom and power that he scarce can look upon them. How, then, shall it be with me, Thy servant?

3. Jehovih said: Nevertheless, the upraised children of darkness are thine own family, and the glory of thy house in heaven shall be the light thou shalt make manifest in them. Fear not, the Gods and Goddesses understand this matter.

4. Therefore, when thou hast put thy kingdom in order, and established the heaven of the earth in all its parts, and stationed messengers betwixt thy throne and the thrones of thy Lords on the earth, behold, thou shalt leave thy Vice-God to rule in thy stead for a season, and thou shalt go to Hautuon, in the etherean forests, for thou shalt be expected of them.

5. God said: Thy will be done, O Father. I perceive Thy wisdom and glory and justice. Now will I sojourn on my throne one year, and thou, my Vice-God, shalt relieve me whilst I go and visit my rebellious children in Uk'loo, where Gods and Goddesses are overseeing them.

6. The Vice-God said: Thy will be done, God of heaven and earth. So it came to pass that in one year's time God had established heaven in such good manner that he could control the affairs of angels and men into the way of everlasting life.

7. God informed his Council, which consisted of five hundred thousand ethereans, men and women, of the words of Jehovih, adding thereunto:

8. And for one year will I remain in Hautuon, that I may become known to them whom I have risen. But at the end of that time I will return hither, and bring with me such new volunteers as Jehovih may command.

9. It was known in heaven that God would leave at the proper time; and, to honor him in Jehovih's name, his hosts from far and near, to the number of ten millions, came to see him depart. And when God saw them, he proclaimed a day of recreation; and the people mingled together, and especially to re-converse on the matter of the deliverance of earth and heaven and the going down of Pan, as it had been.

10. On the following day, all hands being refreshed and assembled in order, according to the discipline of Gods, God spake from the throne, saying:

11. Hear the words of your God, and rejoice in the founding of a new heaven. Be wise in heeding that which I shall utter, and make yourselves steadfast in all proven things. Here are millions who stood by my side in the name of the Creator, in the days of darkness in heaven and earth. For three thousand years our battle lasted; and from out of the darkness behold our prayers went up to Him who is over all and above all.

12. And your God said: Surely Jehovih will deliver, when the vortex merges into Hi'dan; and ye all repeated the same thing; and the unity of our souls' desire reached up to the Orian Chiefs, Jehovih's mighty Sons and Daughters.

13. For as it is proven that a man in conflict with himself accomplisheth nothing, whilst he who is in harmony with himself is mighty wherein he ruleth himself to a good purpose; even so hath it been proven that the unity of many angels can, by force of their

own wills, control the place and proceedings of a world. And by your faith in this matter with your God, ye became a star of faith in Jehovih, which is the mastering of all things to His glory.

14. And they who were without an All Highest in Person, were without power, and of no effect, save to build up discord to our proceedings. Whilst those who assumed to be Gods and Lords, but ignored Jehovih, were not sustained, for having nothing higher than themselves, they rose only to themselves.

15. Which is manifested on earth, even as it was in those days in heaven; boasting of good works or of good prayers, but housing themselves about with the earnings of others. Did not these false Gods and false Lords set up self and worship it; and the fruits of their inspiration, and their slaves under them, were the angels they sent to rule over mortals, for the glory of their philosophy, wherein mortals also soon said the same things of themselves, which was: Behold, there is no God nor Lord of wisdom in heaven and earth.

16. Whereby the doctrines of the false Gods and Lords overturned even their own kingdoms, changing heaven into hada. But when the Light of Jehovih came, ye and your God and Lords were one with His voice. Wherefore ye have been preserved in victory. And now hath it come to pass that your God and Lords have established a new heaven and new earth for the glory of the Father. And he who labored so long in your love, now goeth to the other wing of the battle, where your brethren, toiling with those in darkness, will rejoice to hear of your fruitful labors.

17. Then God turned to his right, and said to Eolait, Vice-God of Jehovih: Because thou wert robbed of thy division of the earth, even whilst thou wert in good work, Jehovih hath bestowed thee well. Thou shalt, therefore, hold the triangle of the Gods of heaven until thy God returneth.

18. Thereupon God hung the triangle on Eolait's neck, saying: In Jehovih's name, ALL HAIL, GOD OF HEAVEN AND EARTH? The hosts repeated: ALL HAIL, GOD OF HEAVEN AND EARTH!

19. And God came down and sat on the foot of the throne, in the custom of Gods. And he who had been anointed came down and took his hand, saying: Arise, O God, and go thy way! And God rose up, and the two, with their marshals and attendants, went down by the borders, at the line of the pillars of fire, where the proper persons had a ship with mantles and curtains in readiness; and God and his hosts, even five hundred thousand in number, entered the ship.

20. Meanwhile the es'enaurs sang an appropriate anthem of GLORY TO JEHOVIH THE ALL HIGHEST.

21. At a given signal the ship started upward, amidst the applause of millions of angels assembled; and like a star it shot upward higher and higher, till it was seen no more.

CHAPTER XI.

1. The Council of Hored being still in session, God, that is, Eolait, ascended the throne. And the light of Jehovih fell upon God, so that he was well nigh obscured from sight, and the voice of Jehovih spake, saying:

2. Hear ye My voice; as by My Presence and of Mine Own Self I made each self, and gave thereto power of words, so am I in Light manifest by soul words to My etherean hosts. As to the Lords of earth, ye have provided ashars, and above them asaphs,

and betwixt all My kingdoms allotted messengers, so shall ye also provide for barbarians, familiar spirits, who shall be subject to the order of the ashars and their Lords.

3. I create alive all men, whether I'hins or barbarians, and your labor shall be not alone with My chosen, whom it is easy to save, but with those also who know Me not, and know not My es worlds. For, beside those destroyed by the flood, behold the earth is still covered over with men, women and children.

4. In the time of Aph ye received volunteers from Osi, in etherea; give them this matter in hand.

5. This was done, and they were divided up into groups, and the corporeans having been already numbered by the angels of heaven, the ethereans were distributed accordingly. And these again selected and apportioned familiar spirits to abide with the barbarians. And these familiar spirits were the fathers and mothers and friends who had recently died, but still sojourned in the first resurrection. So the officers provided places on earth for these spirits, and persuaded them to reappear before mortals in order to prove continued life; but the officers never showed themselves.

6. Jehovih hath said: Provide ye the way, but cause the familiars to do the labor. Neither shall ye make a familiar of the spirit of a young man or a young woman, lest they become fetals.

7. So it came to pass that a new department of heaven and earth was opened and set on foot during the absence of Neph, and in one year the matter was in prosperity.

8. At the end of one year God returned from the Hautuon Colony, bringing with him five millions of volunteers, being of the third resurrection. And, it being known in Hored when he would return, a great concourse of angels gathered together to receive him in honor, and to welcome the volunteers.

9. So that, when God's etherean star descended, the Vice-God, Eolait, proclaimed a recreation of ten days, which was to follow immediately after God should ascend the throne and regain his presence. And so, whilst the es'enaurs were singing, the star alighted, and the marshals and hosts of honor proceeded to the places, and received God, who at once ascended to the throne and saluted Eolait, Son of Jehovih, saying:

10. By Thy Will and Power, O Jehovih, Thy Son rejoiceth in the time of this proceeding. Eolait said: Welcome, God of heaven and earth. And he saluted with the sign of Jehovih's name, and was answered in like manner.

11. Without more ceremony, he took off the triangle of the Gods and placed it on God's neck, saying: In Jehovih's name, receive thou the gift of the ancient Gods.

12. Hardly had this been accomplished when the ship-star alighted in the floor of the Congress, before the Council, and near the altar of Jehovih; and the five millions of volunteers alighted, amidst the applause of the many millions assembled.

13. God, being reinstated, said: Let the marshals proclaim ten days of recreation. For we shall account to our especial loves how we found matters in Hautuon, and of the power of Jehovih manifested.

CHAPTER XII.

1. The voice of Jehovih spake through God, saying: Because a new heaven is established, and because the old hath been raised up, let signs be manifested, whereby men and angels in after times may know what hath happened. For it shall come to pass in later days that

men and angels may forget the flood and the purging of the earth. Bethink ye, O Gods and Goddesses, what shall be done?

2. Eolait spoke in behalf of the Council, saying: What shall we do, O Jehovih? And Jehovih answered, saying: Because I come near the earth in its early days, and farther off as it groweth older, men will say: Alas, the folly of the ancients! For I gave fear and faith as an heritage when men were weak in judgment; but, with the growth of wisdom, I take away fear and the substance of things not proven to the judgment.

3. Jehovih said: In kosmon, men and angels shall ask for proofs. One will say: How is it possible to relate the words spoken in the olden times? Another will say: How can it be proven that the old heaven was taken away?

4. Hear, therefore, the words of your Creator; and when one saith: Behold, in those days few men had the gift of words and speech, answer ye him, saying: Even so was it in heaven, and because they had not words, they could not be made to understand.

5. And another shall say: The Creator ruleth in large matters, but not in the small; and another shall say: Because the angels come in kosmon, so could they in the olden time. And ye shall answer them, saying: Who knoweth the plan for an earthquake, whether it be small or large before Jehovih? Is He not ever present? and do not certain conditions bring certain results? And they will answer: Yea.

6. Say ye: Give, then, a name to the Highest Cause beyond all research; and they will say: By the ancients called Jehovih. And they shall perceive that they have entangled themselves in a net. For if the condition of ignorance on earth begot ignorance in heaven, how could the light of heaven come afterward to the earth save from above? Since, then, the light of heaven came from above, who should invent the wisdom of a flood to come upon the speech of nations?

7. Give them, therefore, words in heaven and words on earth which are of matters of this nature, and make the sounds thereof sacred, so that it shall be proven in Jaffeth and Shem, and Ham, and Guatama, and in the heavens thereunto belonging. The voice of Jehovih ceased.

8. God said: Thou art All Wisdom, O Jehovih! Now have I a place for the new volunteers come from etherea. For this shall be their matter and business with the familiars who dwell with the barbarians. So, accordingly, were they allotted. And they were enjoined to sing to mortals the song of the flood; and they thus established its history to endure forever on earth.

CHAPTER XIII.

1. All things prospered in heaven for many years, nor were there great wars on earth, nor famines, nor epidemics. And the Lords of the earth had sufficient loo'is for all the Faithists, so as to control I'hin marriages to bring forth sons and daughters who would rejoice in heaven.

2. And as fast as they died on the earth, these angels were carried to heavenly places suited to them, where they were handed into the care of asaphs and entered as es'yans. But the Lords appointed no loo'is over the barbarians; and only commanded the ashars to watch for their spirits in the hour of death, and, if possible, to bring them to the organic places of God in Hored. And mostly they were so brought. This continued for many

years; but in course of time the familiar spirits aroused up the barbarians, and they began to have dreams and see visions, for their familiars talked to them during sleep. And when this became common, Jehovih said:

3. Behold, the time is come to appoint loo'is to abide with the barbarians. For herein will I reveal a great secret, which is that My chosen on earth cannot subdue it; for they are a harmless and defenseless people. Therefore, have I created the barbarian wisely; for he shall drive away and destroy all evil beasts and serpents; and the forests shall fall down before him.

4. For this purpose the loo'is shall select marriages with the view of raising up great kings and queens. But since, in the olden time, the kings depended on the prophets of God for counsel, and thus were advised against killing anything I had created alive, they quarreled; so in this time of the new heaven ye shall permit the kings and queens to consult the spirits of the dead with the talents I have given them.

5. This was done also; and the barbarians were attended by familiar spirits, many of whom took upon themselves any name pleasant to the ear, some of them calling themselves God or Lord, or after the name of some great king of the olden time. And these familiars, being stupid, supposed themselves to be such persons.

6. The result of their stupid impressions was to inspire the barbarians to believe they were attended by Gods or Lords, or by the spirits of kings or queens; and so they held up their heads and began to think. For as it had been said by the Gods of ancient times: Some are led by flattery, some by self-conceit, some by duty, some by love of righteousness; but there are others who can be led to self-improvement by persuading them they are chosen especially by some God or Lord, or the spirit of a renowned king or queen, to work wonders.

7. God said: There was a certain sick man who could not be cured by the physicians; so there came a foolish woman, seeing visions, and said to the sick man: To-morrow thou shalt be healed. God hath been trying thee; but thou hast proven thyself in soul, and thy God will withdraw the spell of thy infirmity; behold, thy God standeth by thee.

8. Now on the following day the sick man put forth his own spirit and rose up and was well; wherefore, it hath been adjudged even deceit may accomplish what truth could not. Suffer then the familiars to lead the barbarians on for a season, but be ye watchful at the proper time to appoint new spirits to be with them.

9. God said: Instruct the Lords that the time is now come to reveal to mortals, especially to the I'hins, the seven tetracts; for, as the ashars are withdrawn a pace, so shall mortals advance a pace.

10. Which is to say: These are the inheritances of all men born on the earth: ANASH, which is persistent stubbornness, by word or thought; ZIMMAH, wicked device; RA, delight in being bad; BELYYAAL, worthlessness; AVEN, vanity and self-conceit; DIBBAH, slander and reporting of evils; and SA'TAN, to be a leader, and especially to the delight of the other six entities.

11. These are the members of the Beast of all men and women under the sun; nor is any one without them in some manner or degree. Go ye, therefore, to the Lords and say to them: Jehovih hath set the beginning of the resurrection through Aph, His Son, Chief of the arc of Noe, to lay the tetracts on the shoulders of mortals.

12. The marshals of the Council provided messengers who were at once sent down to the

different divisions of the earth; for the tetracts were some of the words selected in heaven to be given as everlasting names, whereby, in after ages, the tribes of Faithists might be discovered; and they were given alike to the Faithists of Guatama, Jaffeth, Shem and Ham, who were the sons of the arc of Aph preserved on the earth in that day. For these words were provided in the Hebraic, Vedic and Algonquin languages, to be synonymous, till the coming of the kosmon era.

CHAPTER XIV.

1. The voice of Jehovih came to God, saying: Behold, the time draweth near when Aph, My Son, shall commit the care of Hored and her affairs to another God, for another four hundred years. This, then, is the commandment of thy Creator, O God: Hored shall advance to the second resurrection; but the first resurrection shall be established with My Lords.

2. And when the Lord hath a sufficient number of souls who are advanced to take the second resurrection, then shall they be brought to this, My holy place, where they shall be further prepared for the next resurrection.

3. This was accomplished; and heavenly kingdoms with thrones for the Lords, for the first resurrection, were established on the earth, and in the divisions of the Lords. So that there were allotted to these Lords' kingdoms thirty-three years for a resurrection, because thirty-three is the division of dan corresponding to one hundred dans to each cycle

4. Accordingly, every thirty-three years thereafter there was one migration of a group from the Lord's first resurrection to that of Hored, which was God's second resurrection. Whereby the light of dan fell on two hundred years, four hundred years, five hundred years, six hundred years and one thousand years, which became the base of prophecy for each cycle from that time forth for a long period.

5. God said: Close the gates of Hored, and from this time ever after only those of the second resurrection can enter. And it was so. And Hored was extended over Jaffeth, Shem and Ham to the second degree; but of Guatama this is the manner of her heaven: The Lord made two kingdoms, the first and second resurrections, and allotted the first to a proxy in his own name, but over the second he presided in person, teaching his people by proxy of God in Hored. For the distance of the sea lay between these heavens; and the access could not be made in the diminutive light of thirty-three. Nevertheless, the Lord and his attendants maintained an etherean ship that enabled him to cross the sea at intervals of eleven years.

6. Accordingly now, in the second resurrection, new colleges were established in heaven, and the spirits began the study of elements and illustrations in es and uz, and the process of travel and of carrying corporeal entities. And these spirits were at times, under ashars, taken down to mortals to assist in miracles and legerdemain. For the lessons in the second resurrection embraced the mastery of corpor in analysis and synthesis.

7. After the first year of God in Hautuon, he went therefore every eleventh year and remained one year of the earth's time; so that in two hundred years he made eighteen visits. Now on his first visit he brought back with him a certain number of volunteers, being of those raised by the arc of Noe; and the next visit he brought back twice as many as the first; and the next time three times as many as the second, and increasing for the

eighteen visits. And on the last visit it was estimated how many he had brought back in all, and the number was one thousand millions. And they were raised to the second resurrection, having been under the training of the Gods and Goddesses of Hautuon, under the direction of Aph, son of Jehovih.

8. And now that the time of dan was drawing near, and Aph should return to provide for the ascent of Jehovih's harvest, God looked up with a cheerful heart; for it was evident that by the expiration of the two hundred years from the submersion of Pan, many of the spirits delivered from the earth in that day would be prepared to take the second resurrection. Wherefore God prophesied, saying: Through Thee, O Jehovih, in another hundred years I shall have delivered them into etherea (Nirvana) as Thy Brides and Bridegrooms.

CHAPTER XV.

1. Jehovih spake in the light of the throne of God in Hored, saying: Behold, a star cometh!

2. The voice ceased, but God and his hosts knew the meaning, for it was the time of Aph to return and complete his deliverance of Neph and his hosts, and his Lords and their hosts.

3. So the Council were moved to look into the firmament; and the messengers who had heard the voice, and who were departing on their various missions, also looked upward, even as they sped forth to their places; and they proclaimed it in the places of all the heavens of the earth, and to the Lords and their divisions of the earth.

4. And the angels of heaven and those that abode with mortals were stirred up, and because of their contiguity to mortals, the latter comprehended that something unusual was near at hand.

5. The Council of Hored knew not how they should proceed, for the event was to surpass in magnificence anything they had ever witnessed.

6. God said: I have heard Thy voice, O Jehovih. I know a star cometh, and great shall be the glory thereof. Give me light, O Father. How shall Thy servant know the decorum of Orian Chiefs? Behold, I am as one abashed with obscurity in Thy wide universe!

7. Jehovih's voice answered, saying: Fear not, My Son. And let thy Council be strong also. Proceed at once to decorate thy people, preparatory to receiving the resurrection. And those who are to be My Brides and Bridegrooms clothe ye in white.

8. The whole Council heard Jehovih's voice, and they ordained officers to proceed throughout atmospherea and put in effect Jehovih's commandment. And the decorated angels, and those prepared as Brides and Bridegrooms for etherea, were ordered to form in companies near the throne of God in Hored; and the officers of companies were also provided with badges, whereon was inscribed an account of their labor on earth and in heaven, the number and nature of their charities and self-sacrifices for others' good, and their grade in purity and power and wisdom. And the privates were decorated with stars to illustrate the same things, in degree and number; and the stations of their file in Hored were provided in the order of music, rating them according to their chord and discord, and their social adaptability.

9. For these things were done before etherean judges, to whom Jehovih had said: Let the

people pass before you, and judge ye them, that being assorted and arranged they shall make one harmonious whole; for it is only by this they will have power to ascend and endure in My regions of light. There were one million of these judges, and they took up their stations in different parts of atmospherea, wherever the second resurrection had been established, every judge choosing a district for himself or herself, for they were both men and women.

10. And as the angels passed before them, the wisdom of the judges was so great they could comprehend all they had ever done, either on earth or in heaven. And by signals the proper officers were advised how to decorate and adorn all of them.

11. And as fast as companies of one thousand passed, they were provided with conductors, who took them to their places, which had been previously determined by the command of God.

12. Whilst this work was proceeding, lights began to appear in the firmament above; these were the marshals of the Orian fields in etherea, in their star-ships, making course for Hored, and their number was legion. But presently one brighter and more powerful than the rest made way from the western arc of Onah'yi, and it steered direct to God's throne, growing brighter and larger as it came. And when it entered past Chinvat, and was well within the vortex of the earth in the belt of the moon's orbit, its light spread across the whole atmosphere of heaven, and Hored was illumined, and the angels of Hored were stirred up with enthusiasm.

13. Not long the brilliant star delayed the suspense of the angel world, for he who sailed them was a God of millions of years, and by his wisdom attained to such mastery that the elements of earth and atmospherea gave way, as if appalled by a heaven on fire. Down came the star-ship whose majesty outweighed all ceremony, a very crown of magnificence, even to the arena of the Council of Hored. And he who came, attended by half a million, was Sue'ji, marshal for that which was soon to follow.

14. God rose up, saluting, and all the hosts rose up, whereupon Sue'ji ascended the throne, greeted by God and his Council, near at hand. Sue'ji said:

15. By thy will, O Jehovih! And God said: In Thy name, O Father, Creator! Welcome to Thy Son! And presently all the place was aglow with a golden light, which ranks first in heaven of all colors, and the voice of Jehovih descended on Sue'ji, and he said:

16. Well beloved, come! Long enduring, come! Of patience and steadfastness, My sons and daughters! Behold, I came in the darkness and delivered Mi, for she was of twins heavily laden. And the one dwelt with the mother, but the other I sent to nurse in Hautuon. And they are grown to maturity; a son and daughter twin.

17. Turn ye to Hautuon; lo, the twin cometh! She was the puny child; but look ye upon her, O ye Gods and Goddesses! Her thousand millions come as an avalanche of ji'ay'an worlds. Open your arms, O My beloved sons and daughters.

18. The voice ceased, and Sue'ji said: When the harvest of Hautuon arriveth, attended by the Gods and Goddesses who helped deliver the children of darkness, and who have changed them into beacons of light, behold ye, there shall be three days of recreation in atmospherea; for the hosts of Hautuon shall be shown their native world, whence they came; and they shall read the lineage of kin and condition whence they were rescued by Jehovih's sons and daughters.

19. But on the first day, behold, Aph, the Orian Chief, will descend in all his glory. And

on the fourth day all your upraised sons and daughters shall ascend into the etherean worlds, where there are in waiting, to receive you, millions of millions of souls, long since dwellers in Nirvana. Sue'ji ceased speaking, having given commands as to the stations of his marshals around about the earth and her heaven.

20. God sent his messengers, saying: Go ye to Wak'hah and say: God saith: My heavens have been numbered, and the account of my laborers rendered and recorded in the libraries of Hored. And of all the hosts who have labored with thy God, behold, thou, O Wak'hah, standest on the highest grade. Come, therefore, to the throne of thy God and be anointed God of heaven and earth for the next four hundred years, and as long after as Jehovih willeth!

21. The messengers, attended by one thousand marshals, departed for Adjun, the place of labor where Wak'hah dwelt, being a physician's nurse for es'yans and still-born mortal children and those killed by abortion. And they delivered the message of God, to which Wak'hah replied: Thanks, O Jehovih! Tell God I will come. But yet let me surmise: I have been all my life, now some thirty thousand earth years, trying to learn where I should be most serviceable to Jehovih and His sons and daughters. And when I judge that I have found it, lo, a summons cometh from another way, saying: Come thou hither. Wherefore it seemeth Jehovih forever hurrieth us onward, faster than our wisdom can discover the requirement. So the marshals provided an otevan, and Wak'hah was conducted before Hored, even to the foot of the throne of God, where he was saluted and received under a rod of water, according to his rank.

CHAPTER XVI.

1. Nearer and nearer came the visiting stars, the etherean ships from thousands of worlds, with countless millions of emancipated souls, dwellers in the Nirvanian regions of Jehovih. And when they reached the boundaries of the earth's vortex they halted a while, to form in rank and rank, that their glory might add to one another; and whilst they stood thus in the great vault of heaven, there opened on one side a gateway amidst the stars; and far beyond came a strange and mottled sun, swaying to and fro; and this was the great fields and forests of Hautuon letting loose the thousands of millions of the delivered earth.

2. God and his hosts saw it. And every soul burst forth one universal shout of applause. It was coming straight to Hored. And as it came nearer, the curtains and sails and streamers, made of yellow, blue and red fire, began to wave and surge, like a ship in a rough sea, but steadily holding course in the undulating elements. Presently could be seen guardian ships, thousands and thousands, traveling beside the laboring sun, the hosts of Hautuon.

3. And the guardian ships were themselves like stars, and carried millions of etherean souls who had been Gods and Goddesses on many worlds; and they formed wings for the Hautuon avalanche, to hold steady the course to the red star, the earth of mortals. And thus, in honored discipline, came the fleet of Jehovih's worshippers, who only two hundred years since, were but as vermin delving into darkness, and deep buried in death, as their only knowledge; to whom Great Jehovih and His exalted worlds were unknown.

4. Brighter and brighter grew that great waving sun, sailed by the immortal Gods, and larger and more imposing, till, when it entered the earth's vortex, it became as living fire,

large as the earth, and of brilliant colors, from black to adamant, and blue, and white, and purple, yellow, scarlet, pink, and of all shades; and living, and sparkling, with the broad curtains suspended, deep as the breadth of a world, and sails and flags that reached upward, high as the moon.

5. Midway in the vortex of the earth it halted, and the myriads of stars beyond now gathered in, majestically, from every side, till nearly around about the fabric of the earth's atmosphere was not a place but glowed with Jehovih's fire of heaven. Music, which rose from the throne of God a little while before, now ceased; for here was the play of elements in harmony, of which music is the same to the ear of mortals.

6. Hardly stood the kaleidoscope of splendors in one attitude, but moving, changing and forming by the decrees of the Gods and Goddesses; as a general on earth manipulates his armies, in the evolution of arms, so in majesty and splendor the marshaling stars forever evolved new and glorious changes stretching abroad over the whole firmament of heaven.

7. And now another gateway opened amidst the stars; and a cluster star was seen approaching from the southeast. It was as a star surrounded by stars, and brighter than all the others. This was the ship-star of Aph, the Orian Chief. At sight of which all souls in the firmament turned in pride and wonder. Swift and mighty above all the countless millions of Gods and Goddesses assembled had he attained in the play and management of worlds. And at sight of his etherean star, angels and Gods whispered: Aph! And the magic of his name, widely known in the Nirvanian fields of the emancipated heavens, spread abroad, till every soul uttered, APH! in all the regions of atmospherea and on the earth.

8. Nearer and nearer he came, nor halted at Chinvat, the boundary of the earth's vortex; but steadily, and with power, sailed on till his star stood in the doorway of heaven, and here halted as if to complete the immortal scene.

9. But a moment more, and all the avalanche of the glorious worlds around moved onward toward the earth, and surrounding it on every side, and the star of Aph making headway for Hored, even to the throne of God.

10. This was the morning of the third day in tide of dan, in which there were still four days left. But now the marshals took their parts; first, Sue'ji, Chief over all the rest, from the throne of God, cried out: All hail, O Aph, Son of Jehovih! And the words were caught up on every side, and uttered in one breath around the world. Yet nearer and nearer gathered in the great star-ships and sun of Hautuon, till even like a net they joined and filled the earth's atmosphere in the east and west and north and south, and below and above; on every side. And the words of the marshal: All hail, O Aph, Son of Jehovih! went like an echo over all the heavens.

11. Then Aph's fleet drew near, and he and his hosts alighted, and he ascended the throne, saluting, saying: All hail, O Neph, God of heaven and earth! And this was also uttered by the millions of hosts. Whereupon the signs and ceremonies of the Gods were briefly concluded, and a recreation of three days proclaimed. And the angels' hosts came forth out of their ships, or by the endless chain sped to any quarter of the earth they desired to visit. And for three days and nights the visitors dwelt on the earth and in the lower atmospherea; inspecting how the earth was made; its land and water; its mountains and valleys; its beasts of prey and beasts of burden; its birds and fishes; and above all, its mortal people and spirits who lingered about the earth, the great story tellers, who knew

no higher heaven. And then they surveyed atmospherea and the works of God and his Lords; their nurseries, hospitals, factories, schools and colleges.

12. And on the fourth day the marshals called order; and so great was the discipline of the hosts and the arrangement of the star-ships, that in a moment of time order reigned amongst all these countless millions of people.

13. Now, during the recreation, the Chiefs from many worlds, and Gods and Goddesses, mingled together, and exchanged their varied experience in the wide regions of Jehovih's universe, of the management of both corporeal and es'sean worlds, and of the cosmogony of etherean planets; and the surveying of roadways, and of turning worlds from their orbitic course, or changing their axic rotation, and of the deliverance of millions of souls into the ji'ay'an fields, and of the creation of new corporeal worlds and the dissolution of others, and the gathering together of the spirits disinherited, and of their final resurrection. Neither seemed there any end to Jehovih's universe, where such wonders go onward forever!

14. When order was restored, God commanded Wak'hah to rise to be anointed, and God said: In Thy name, O Jehovih, I anoint this, Thy Son, God of heaven and earth for the next four hundred years. Guide him in wisdom and love, O Father.

15. And God gathered from the abundance of eth'ic and made a crown and placed it on Wak'hah's head, saying: Hail God of heaven and earth, Jehovih's Son! This was shouted by the hosts. And then God took off the triangle, the sam'gan, the heirloom of the Gods of the red star, the earth, and God hung it on Wak'hah's neck, saying: Take this heirloom, the symbol of three entities in one, and wear it for the glory of the Great Spirit, Jehovih.

16. To which Wak'hah, now God, answered: Thy will be done, O Father, Creator and Ruler over all. And all on the throne stood aside, and God (Wak'hah) ascended the throne and sat in the midst, whereat the es'enaurs chanted, and the hymn sounded around the whole earth. Then Aph, Son of Jehovih, spake, saying:

17. In four hundred years, O God, I will come and deliver thee and thy harvest, and thy Lords and their harvest, for the glory of Jehovih, the Unapproachable Almighty! Amen.

18. And now Aph went and sat down at the foot of the throne, whereat God came down according to custom and took his hand, saying: Arise, O God, Son of Jehovih, and go thy way! And Aph rose up, saluting, and he and his attendants departed and entered his star-ship. The es'enaurs chanted, the trumpeters played, and the solemn MARCH OF JEHOVIH'S SEA OF FIRE sounded from heaven and earth.

19. The marshals now put the great works in order: Neph and his attendants were stationed on the right of Aph in a ship new built; next to him, the ships of his Lords and their attendants; after them, their marshals from the different divisions of the earth and atmospherea; next to them, the ships of the messengers; then the factors, then the nurses, then the physicians, and so on; and finally the divisions of earth-raised, who were now adjourned to the sun-avalanche, being of the same rank. And these comprised the harvest of Neph for Jehovih's emancipated realms; and the number of souls exceeded all other harvests raised up from the earth.

20. And now had come the time for the ascent, and Aph said: Give us of Thy power, O Jehovih! And his words were echoed in all places in heaven and on earth. The plateaux trembled and oscillated. Again Aph said: Of Thy power, O Jehovih! Arise, O Heaven! Arise, O Heaven!

21. And the plateaux of the sphere started from their foundations, and slowly moved back and outward from the earth. The es'enaurs played the march; the ethereans tore off strips of fabric and threw them down in Hored, and then formed flowers and leaves and perfumed them, and cast them out, to fall in the lower heavens.

22. Outward and outward the etherean world moved and moved, and then parted the breadth of the earth, and then rose slowly upward. Presently it turned on its own axis, and was as yet one entire world; but with its rotation the different stars began to individualize and separate, all save the harvest of Neph, which was the central figure, led onward and upward by Aph, Son of the Great Spirit.

23. Faster and faster rose the glorious scene, and more aweful, and sparkling with splendor! Nor could one from Hored scarce look upon the dazzling light. But higher it rose, and onward, toward its far-off destiny, till it disappeared in the firmament above.

CHAPTER XVII.

1. Now was the atmospherea like a new heaven stripped of visitors, and ready to resume labor after a glorious festival. So God at once dispatched all hands to their places, and the factories, schools and colleges, nurseries and hospitals, were once more alive with willing workers.

2. And Hored prospered in every department; and so also did the departments of the Lords on earth; and mortals also prospered under the light of the Great Spirit.

3. For four hundred years God reigned in heaven, and his Lords under him, and the second dan of Aph fell upon earth and heaven. So God appointed An'on as his successor. And now Aph and his attendants came to deliver God; his Lords and people prepared for their resurrection up into etherea.

4. And the number of Jehovih's harvest was one thousand million souls.

5. And God (An'on) reigned his time, and his Lords under him, and they were also delivered by Aph, but by proxy, and the harvest of Jehovih was eight hundred million souls.

6. And his successor, God of Hored and atmospherea, and his Lords, fulfilled their dan, and they and their harvests were delivered by the proxy of Aph also; and the number of souls delivered was six hundred million. And Jehovih commanded Aph to commit atmospherea and the earth to the successors of Ra'zan of Garowista, in Ems of the etherean phalanx of eighty Ar'doth.

7. And the next harvest of God and his Lords was two hundred million souls. After that the earth passed into the a'ji of Urk'stand for eight hundred years, and the light of the upper heaven was lost to earth and atmospherea; so there was no harvest for the etherean realms. And because of the darkness in atmospherea it began to fall in hada; and the seven entities of tetracts took root in Hored, and overspread the dominions of God and his Lords. And many in heaven rose up, and, proclaiming themselves Gods or Lords, obtained followers, some to the extent of three millions of souls.

8. And these false Gods made slaves of their followers, exacting service, and in lieu giving pitiful homes and regimen; and by the labor of their slaves embellishing their mansions and cities in hada.

9. Jehovih had said of old: Before mortals I keep death forever present that they may not

forget the change from corporeal to spirit life; otherwise they would dispute it possible in My hands for these things to be. But My resurrections in heaven are far apart, and the inhabitants thereof lose faith in those above them. Through faith is all power and glory attained; therefore have I exacted that angels cultivate faith in the next resurrection.

10. But during the last thousand years in atmospherea, there being no resurrections to etherea, many fell into disbelief of the emancipated heavens, and so sat about, building up heavenly kingdoms on their own account, and for their own glory. And in order to have exalted kingdoms they sent their slaves back to mortals to inspire them with the glory of their false God's kingdoms, that others in turn might become slaves also.

11. So confusion began in heaven again, and it reacted on mortals, through the angels' presence, and war and misery overspread the nations and tribes of men on earth. Thus ended the cycle of Aph's arc of Noe, which was three thousand six hundred years.

END OF THE BOOK OF APH, SON OF JEHOVIH.

THE LORDS' FIRST BOOK.

BEING COTEMPORANEOUS WITH THE BOOK OF APH, SON OF JEHOVIH, AND AS THE LATTER IS OF HEAVEN, SO IS THE LORDS' BOOK OF THE EARTH. FOR WHICH REASON ONE BOOK IS PLACED BEFORE THE OTHER.

CHAPTER I.

THE HISTORY OF THE FLOOD.

1. Hear me, O man, I am the Lord, the God of earth, Son of Jehovih! I am one of thine elder brothers. I, thy Lord, with my brother Lords and Gods, in the name of Jehovih, speak, saying:

2. Peace and patience be unto all men, that ye may comprehend my words, and bear witness that heaven and earth in every part is Jehovih's, and that all men and women are His sons and daughters, worlds without end.

3. As over mortal kingdoms, kings; as over empires, emperors; as over armies, generals; so hath Jehovih in his heavens crowned certain chieftains for times and places, and given to them certain names, whereby they have been proclaimed to men and angels, so that the discipline of heavens might manifest the glory and dominion of Jehovih.

4. In all time, honored in high heaven, and known to the people on the earth as Jehovih's Lord, Commander of heavenly light on earth, and Pacificator betwixt All Light and All Darkness, and entitled LORD OF EARTH and LORD GOD, so have I and my predecessors, and my successors, been handed down for thousands of years amongst mortals.

5. Whereas, if it be said: The King said thus; and generations after, if it be said, The King said thus; and all men know it was not the same man, but was nevertheless The King, so also proclaim I, the Lord, My predecessors and successors; for all of them were, and have been The Lord.

6. Wherefore I, the Lord, by virtue of my own authority, and in Jehovih's name, proclaim the light and the darkness of the past, for inasmuch as I have been exalted by the Father,

130

so are ye all in waiting for your turn in the heavens above to become Lords and Gods and Goddesses.

7. To draw your souls up in heavenly aspirations, to become one with the Father in righteousness and good works, sendeth Jehovih His sons and daughters, down to the earth, revealing the glory of His kingdoms in the etherean worlds.

8. But because of the darkness of man's soul, man setteth up to mock the words of his Lord, saying: How can I become a Lord, or a God? Behold, his word hath not been heard; none have written his speech?

9. Was it not so in all times on the earth? And because of this darkness amongst men, they have laid bare the iniquity of their own hearts. For out of the mouths of my chosen, who utter my words, come words of truth and love and wisdom and kindness, and the exaltation of virtue. But from those who deny me, come corruption, war, avarice, and the love of earthly things for self-sake.

10. Behold, they have quibbled about words and the meaning of words. One saith: How much of this came from the Lord, and how much from the prophet? Making of themselves mathematicians on a matter separate from the subject of the righteousness of their own souls, which lieth at the bottom of God's desires.

11. Are not all words at best but pictures and paintings of the spirit that findeth them? And whether the Captain (Lord) or his private (angel) carry the light to the prophet, what mattereth it to the man or woman who seeketh to serve Jehovih by doing good works?

12. Some have said: Behold, I have given all I had to the poor, and I rise early and visit the sick; and in the night I sit up with them; and I gather up orphans and helpless ones and make them so joyous of heart they thank Jehovih they are created into life. Now, verily, all men know that such behavior cometh from them that recognize my word, whether it come from the mouth of a babe or the pen of a fool.

13. Who, then, shall not find delight in the word of the Lord? Know they not that I am the same to-day, yesterday and forever? And in judgment why will they not perceive that my word cometh as well now as in the olden time?

14. Behold, I am not for one man only, nor for one woman, nor for one book; but wherever the light of wisdom and the desire for virtue and holy deeds shine, there will my speech manifest. Is not Jehovih wide as the universe, and immutable? And to be in harmony with Him, is this not the sum of all wisdom?

15. Therefore, if thy Lord, or thy God, hath attained to be one with the Father, and He come in dominion on the earth, with His millions of angels, who also know the higher light, and ye are inspired by them to do Jehovih's will, what discussion shall man have against heaven or its representatives?

16. I declare freedom unto all men in Jehovih's name, but with freedom I also give the experience of the Lords of earth. Suffer therefore my prophets on all hands to embellish the pictures of the past in their own way; and as far as the pictures fortify faith in Jehovih and His Works, and His Power and His Glory, be ye circumspect to desire nourishment therefrom. And rather than destroy that which is given in the name of Jehovih, go ye, and fall to work in like manner to build up His light in your own way.

17. Herein is wisdom, for they that strive for the light of my dominion shall receive my angels in my name; and by the words they find to express my commandments shall they be known to be of me.

18. All words came from the Lord your God; by him was man made upright on the earth. As the first race went down into the earth, the second man rose up by my angels, becoming like unto Lords and Gods, and capable of knowing good and evil.

19. But as the light of a full grown man differeth from that of a child's, so, in different degree, was the light of men; and those with the higher light were called Faithists (I'hins), because they perceived that Wisdom shaped all things and ruled to the ultimate glory of the All One; but those of the lesser light were called Cain, the druk, because their trust was more in corporeal than in spiritual things.

20. And the Faithists were also called the chosen people, because they chose God, who is Lord over corpor; but the Cainites, the druks, were classed as enemies of the Lord, because they sacrificed by means of war and death that which Jehovih made alive. And these two peoples have lived on the earth from the first, and even to this day.

21. And I, the Lord, Son of Jehovih, gave a certain commandment to man, saying: Thou shalt love the Lord thy God with all thy soul, thy wisdom and strength. But man had little strength in this matter; neither did I ask for more than he could give. And another commandment was: Thou shalt not kill; the which had man obeyed, there had been no war in the world.

22. In like manner gave I the light of heaven unto all men, but my enemies perverted my words in order to justify themselves in sin. For the Father so dwelleth in man that man can judge of truth and holiness. For if one man saith: The Lord said: Thou shalt not kill; and yet another man saith: The Lord saith, Thou shalt kill; then shall not any man mistake which is of the Lord in fact. For the Lord maketh not alive any man whom he desireth shall be killed.

23. Thus was my word perverted by man, and the little light which was not lost, man tried to obscure. Nevertheless, man multiplied and inhabited the earth over, building cities and nations and prospering in certain seasons in all things earthly. But as I came to the earth to develop the soul of man chiefly, and for his own ultimate happiness in the etherean worlds, I labored not with such as heeded me not, but suffered them to go on in their own conceit; and they became divided against one another, and war and pestilence and divers diseases came upon mortals, resulting in their further downfall.

24. And the spirits of those that denied me on earth, still denied me in heaven; and in their stubbornness and conceit continued to dwell with man on the earth. So that in the course of time the world was overrun by spirits of darkness, who knew not heaven. And it came to pass that my enemies slew my chosen on all hands.

25. In four great divisions of the earth, in Vohu, in Jud, in Thouri and in Dis (see SETHANTES, CHAPTER II, v.28) they left not one alive of the I'hin race. In Wagga (Pan) had I a remnant; and they were scattered far and near, and in separate places hiding away from their evil pursuers.

26. I had said unto them: Every living thing that groweth up out the ground shall be food for you; but of everything wherein is the breath of life, which is of blood and spirit, ye shall not eat. Who so sheddeth blood, wherein is life, by himself inviteth his own blood and spirit to the spoil. In likeness of God was man made heir of the earth and all things thereon.

27. Be ye fruitful and multiply; bring forth abundantly in remembrance of the Lord God of heaven and earth.

28. And I gave the circumcision as a measure of the boundary of my chosen.

29. But there were giants (druks) in those days and in time after that; and my chosen came unto them, and they bare children to them also. And their flesh became corrupt, so that vermin inhabited them from the time of their birth to the time of death. And they became rotten in the head with catarrh; and in the throat with ulcers and running sores; and in the lungs and joints with the poison of death. And their offspring that was born unto them came forth afflicted with the sins of their fathers and mothers, to linger in misery or to die in infancy.

30. And they thus peopled heaven with untimely births and with spirits of darkness, who, in return, came back and re-afflicted mortals.

31. And I said: I will destroy man from the face of the earth; for the flesh of man is corrupt, for by the eating of flesh and unwise cohabitation hath he corrupted his race upon the earth.

32. And I, the Lord, called unto my chosen, who were persecuted and hidden away in the valleys and mountains, even on the tops of mountains.

33. And I said unto them: Because ye have kept my commandments, come forth and hear ye the word of the Lord your God. And they came forth from their hiding places, thousands and thousands of them. And I sent my angels unto them, saying:

34. Say ye unto my chosen: This is the word of the Lord your God: Ye have found favor in my sight, for ye alone of all that is on the earth have kept my commandments; and ye have seen righteousness in the seed of your generations.

35. Go to, therefore, and build ships sufficient unto my chosen, and get ye within, where none can pursue or destroy.

36. For behold, I will bring a flood of waters upon the earth, even above the highest mountains; for I will destroy the corruption thereof, and purge it of all uncleanness.

37. Take ye, therefore, of all food that is good to eat, and gather it into the ships; for the flood shall remain a hundred and fifty days; and ye shall not come forth and find wherewith to eat.

38. And the angels of the Lord went to the Faithists in God and inspired them to build ships, both in the valleys and on the mountains; for two whole years builded they them, and then they were completed.

39. And the angels of heaven numbered the ships, and there were of them one hundred and thirty-eight. And the ships stood on the mountains and in valleys; nowhere near the waters stood one of all the ships that had been built.

40. And the earth stood in the arc of Noe in the firmament of heaven, in the place and grade of six hundred in the a'ji'an roads, twenty-four thousand years before kosmon.

41. And the Lord commanded the chosen to go into the ships; and they went in; and in the same day the gates of heaven and earth were opened.

42. And the earth rocked to and fro, as a ship at sea; and the rains fell in torrents; and loud thunderings came up from beneath the floor of the world. And the sea came up on the land; first upon the valleys and then upon the mountains; so that the ships floated on the waters.

43. But the land was swallowed up, valleys and mountains, and all the living perished, save the I'hins, who floated off in the ships.

44. And the Lord said: I numbered them that were saved, and there were twelve thousand

four hundred and twenty; and these were all that remained of the first race of man that walked on two feet.

45. Behold, I will carry them to all the divisions of the earth, and people it anew with the seed of my chosen.

46. And Jehovih blew His breath upon the ships of His sons and daughters; blew them about upon the ocean; blew them to the east and west and north and south.

47. By the will of God were the ships congregated into four fleets; thirty-four ships into each fleet, save two ships which were carried in a fleet to themselves.

48. The Lord said: I will name the fleets of my chosen, and their names shall be everlasting on the earth. And the Lord named them GUATAMA, SHEM, JAFFETH, HAM, and YISTA.

49. The Lord said: From these, my seed, will I people the earth over in all the divisions thereof. And that after generations, for thousands of years, may know the work of my hand; behold I give them a sign, which is my covenant to them and their heirs forever;

50. Which is my crescent, in the form of a rainbow; and whatsoever people bear this, my sign, shall be as a remembrance to me of my covenant. Nor shall they be destroyed from the inheritance which I have given unto them.

51. And the chosen looked out of their ships, and the sky was clearing; and a rainbow shone in the firmament; and by the light thereof the land was found, whither the Lord brought his people.

52. And in one hundred and fifty days from the beginning of the flood, the ships were brought into their respective places; as the Lord designed them, so landed they in the different countries of the world.

53. The fleet named Guatama was carried to the eastward, and the country whither it landed was also called Guatama. The Lord said: From this place shall my chosen spread out north and south. But they shall not inhabit the lands to the east or west as far as the sea; for they shall be testimony in time to come of this landing place from the continent of Pan.

54. God said: Suffer my people to bestow names to the places whither I lead them; for these names shall show in the kosmon era the work of my hand done in this day.

55. The fleet of two ships carried to the north was named Yista, which in the Wagga tongue was Zha'Pan, which is the same country that is to this day called Japan, signifying RELICT OF THE CONTINENT OF PAN, for it lay to the north, where the land was cleaved in twain. 56. And the Lord said to them: Behold, eight Hi'dan shall come and ye shall be as a key to unlock the labors of heaven; for of all people ye shall be reckoned the oldest in the world. And until I come and unlock the sea, ye shall remain an exclusive people from all tribes and nations.

57. Preserve ye, therefore, the names of my rites and ceremonies, and especially the names of land and water, and the firmament above, and the ships that plow the water, and all sounds whatever that man maketh in the throat and without the tongue and lips; for in the time of my glory on the earth ye shall also be glorified. Preserve ye also peace and righteousness and industry, for ye shall be a testimony in the later time of the presence of my hand and of the Great Spirit also. Thus was settled Japan, and it continueth to this day.

58. The fleet named JAFFETH was driven to the westward and north, and the country was

called Jaffeth for thousands of years thereafter, and is the same as is called Chine'ya to this day.

59. The fleet named SHEM landed to the south, and the country was called Shem for thousands of years afterward, and is the same as is called Vindyu (India) to this day.

60. The fleet named HAM landed south west, and the country was called the land of Ham for thousands of years, and is the same as is called Egypt and Africa to this day.

61. God said: Behold, my chosen shall manifest many signs and words common to one another in these different divisions of the earth.

62. They shall remember the flood.

63. They shall repudiate idols, but worship the Great Spirit, Jehovih.

64. They shall have the crescent.

65. They shall have the triangle.

66. They shall preserve the four days of the change of the moon as sacred days, and they shall be called mass (moon's) days.

67. They shall be circumcised.

68. They shall remember the seven tetracts: DIBBAH, the enticing evil; RA, the flesh evil; ZIMMAH, the joking evil; BELYYAAL, worthlessness; AVEN, vanity; ANASH, delight in destruction; SA'TAN, desire for leadership, which is the captain of death.

69. They shall have three great lights: OR, the All Highest; GOD, son of OR; LORD (Adonya), executor of heaven and earth.

70. They shall have three less lights: God's angels and lords; the prophets; the rab'bahs.

71. They shall have three representative symbols of light: The sun, the moon and the burning flame.

72. The Lord said: And my chosen shall use these lights and symbols, signs and seasons in all the divisions of the earth whither I have settled them.

73. And in the kosmon era I will come and show them the framework of my building which I raise up to the Almighty.

74. God said: Now was the world of one language and one speech; in all the places of my people spake they alike, man to man.

75. Nevertheless, in all parts of the earth there lived ground people, who were black and brown, and burrowed in the ground; and they had long arms and curved backs, and were naked and not ashamed, for which reason they were called DRUKS.

76. The Lord spake unto the chosen (the I'hins), saying: Behold the earth! I give it to you, to be yours forever.

77. Mingle ye not with the druks, for they are without understanding and are not heirs to everlasting life.

78. Now, many inquired of the Lord, saying: If these, having no understanding, be not heirs to everlasting life, how shall it be with our children who die in infancy?

79. The Lord said: This is a matter of the seed, and not of learning. Whosoever is born of my chosen shall inherit my everlasting kingdom.

CHAPTER II.

1. The Lord said: A wise physician amputateth a diseased limb and so preserveth the trunk to become healed.

2. Saw I not the rankness of the tribes of darkness, the druks; and that the proceedings of man would render the earth void?

3. What is all the world if it bring not forth heirs unto everlasting life?

4. Behold, I saw that my chosen had become exterminated, and on all the divisions of the earth save Pan. And I saw that they who had been their destroyers had in turn nearly exterminated one another.

5. And I saw that to bring the remnants of my people hither, they could again re-establish themselves and become the seed of a mighty people.

6. But, as for the land of Wagga (Pan), it was already in the throes of death. And the druks had become as a festering sore; and the spirits of the dead, tens of thousands of millions of them, would not quit their hold on mortals whilst life was on the earth.

7. And I sent my angels around about the whole earth, and gathered in the spirits of darkness; gathered them unto the land of Wagga.

8. And when my work was in readiness I raised up my hand, as a surgeon that would lop off a diseased limb, and I cleft asunder the continent of Pan and sunk it beneath the waters.

9. And my angels conducted my chosen out of that land, and not one of them perished.

10. I said unto the guardian angels whom I had given to man: In the lands whither I will take my people, let them build mounds and walled cities, with ladders to enter, after the manner of the ancients. In all the divisions of the earth, alike and like shall they build.

11. For in the time of kosmon their relics shall be testimony that the I'hin forerun the I'huan, the copper-colored, race in all the world.

12. So also will I, the Lord, provide in the kosmon era to discover the sunken land of Wagga, that mortals may comprehend the magnitude of the work of the Lord.

13. In those days the I'hins dwelt not alone, but in cities and villages; and they were clothed. And they tilled the ground and brought forth grains and seeds good to eat; and flax and hemp, from which to make cloth for covering the body. And their food was of every herb and root, and grain and seed, and fruit that cometh of the earth; but they ate not flesh nor fish, nor of anything that breathed the breath of life.

14. They toiled by day, bringing within their cities the fruit of their labor; and they slept within their cities, and on mounds, at night, that they might not be molested by beasts of prey and by serpents.

15. And every city had one rab'bah (head father), who knew the way of the Lord; by the rab'bah were the altars of the Lord built, and the times of the sacred days foretold.

16. And the rab'bah made records in writing on stone; the which they taught to their successors, and to whomsoever desired to learn of the Lord.

17. And the Lord abode with them; and they kept the commandments and multiplied exceedingly in all the divisions of the world.

18. Nor was there any war in any land under the sun in those days.

19. In three thousand years thereafter, behold, there were thousands of cities and hundred of thousands of inhabitants who had spread abroad over the lands of the earth.

20. And they had built ships and sailed abroad on the seas, and inhabited the islands thereof, north and south and east and west.

CHAPTER III.

THE SCRIPTURES OF THAT DAY.

1. God said: That my people may remain upright, behold, I give unto them and their successors forever, certain sacred words which shall be to them the bond of my covenant.

2. Seven degrees of sacred rites bestow I unto my people. And no man shall take the second till he hath learned all the words of the first; nor shall he take the third till he hath learned all the words of the second; and so on, shall man learn all my sacred words; from mouth to ear shall they be learned by every man and every woman of my people, saith the Lord.

3. Hearken, then, to the words of the servants of the Lord:

4. I will serve the prophets of the Lord my God.

5. Heal my flesh, O God (iod) (gau) and cure poison.

6. The Lord is my spirit (s'pe) unseen in the heavens.

7. He is all power, and wisdom and love and anger.

8. He can heal, and he can tear the flesh, and strike dead.

9. His prophets have his good grace; they can hear his voice and interpret him.

10. The Lord is my guardian; ten times a day will I remember him.

11. God who is Lord can stop blood; choke it up, O Lord.

12. He gave blood-stopping as a power of the prophet's hands.

13. Confound my enemies, O God.

14. The ashars (angels of the Lord) shield me.

15. I will honor the I'hins, the sacred people of God. They are my brethren.

16. This was the first lesson. The Lord said to his prophets: Go to the druks and cause them to sit on the ground in a circle, and stand ye in the midst, saying: Behold, O druk, the Great Spirit hath spoken; I have heard his voice. His words are holy words; whoever learneth his words shall have power over sickness and poison and the flowing of blood. And, if a woman, she shall become fruitful and have great rejoicing. Hold up your hands and repeat the words of the Lord.

17. And it was so, the prophets taught the words of the Lord, to wit:

18. Blessed be the name of the Lord. He can make me to be alive after I am dead, and this is all he requireth of me, to say: Blessed be the name of the Lord. In the morning I will say it; at noon I will say it; at night I will say it: Blessed be the name of the Lord.

19. I will wear clothes to hide my nakedness, because God requireth it of me.

20. I will not steal, nor speak untruth.

21. If my brother taketh what is mine, I will not be in anger, nor judge him; but I will lay the matter before the prophets of God.

22. I will do no violence, for it is God's commandment.

23. This, then, that followeth, was the third:

24. I will have but one wife, I will not go after other women whilst she liveth. (I will have but one husband; I will receive no other man whilst my husband liveth.)

25. I will suffer no man nor woman of poison (leprosy) to come near the oe'ugah (camp). In the Lord's name, I will drive them hence.

26. I renounce them; nor will I mingle therewith, for it is God's commandment.

27. The fourth commandment, that is to say:

28. I will forswear the hunt; but whatsoever cometh and is fit food for man to eat, I will kill it. I will take up fish in the name of the Lord, for they suffer no pain.

29. I will till the soil and gather roots to eat, and fibers of barks for clothing, and live like the I'hins, the chosen people of God.

30. I renounce murderers; nor will I marry with them, nor live as they live; they are the enemies of the Lord God.

31. I will curse no man, nor woman, nor child, for it is the Lord's commandment.

32. I renounce anger and all weapons of death; they are enemies of the Lord.

33. If a man injure me, I will lay the matter before the Lord's prophet, for his judgment is holy, saith the Lord.

34. If a woman entice me, I will go secrete myself and repeat the sacred words.

35. I will respect the times of woman, for she is the gift of the Lord to be man's helpmate.

36. When my wife hath a newborn child, I will do her labor for forty days, for it is God's commandment.

37. The fifth commandment, which is:

38. The four days of the moon are the Lord's; on those days I will not labor.

39. I will keep sacred the four days of every moon, and I will repeat the sacred words of the Lord thrice.

40. And when the prophets say: Behold, the Lord saith this is a sacred day; then will I keep that day holy, for the prophets hear the voice of God.

41. When the I'hins worship before the altar of the Lord, I will keep on the outer circle, for the I'hins are the chosen servants of God.

42. When the I'hins march forth, following the prophets, I will come after, for I will honor the Lord's chosen.

43. When the prophets say: Pitch the tents here, I will abide, for the prophets cannot err.

44. The sixth commandment, which is:

45. For the sick I will provide, and for the woman with a newborn child.

46. I will give, first to the I'hins, second to the druks, and lastly keep for mine own self.

47. To warriors I will give in time of sickness, but when they are healed, I will say: Go your way.

48. And if a man be sick of poison, or a woman sick of poison, I will go to the same. But before I go in I will say: O Lord, my God, in thy name I go in a dangerous business; come thou through thy ashars and protect me for thy sake.

49. For the Lord can encompass me around about, and I shall not receive the poison.

50. The seventh commandment, which is:

51. I will keep these holy words secret in the name of the Lord my God.

52. When the Lord commandeth, saying: Go here, or go there, or build here a city, or a house or an altar, then will I do the Lord's bidding.

53. Thus did the Lord establish laws amongst men; and because of the sacredness of the Lord's words, man treasured them and kept holy the commandments of God.

54. Now I, the Lord, reveal in this, the kosmon era:

55. My angels abode with the chosen in the days of the aforesaid sacred scriptures.

56. And when the words were repeated for the stopping of blood, behold, my angels compressed the veins. Not the words stopped the blood, but by the words mortals became in concert with my hosts.

57. And when a man went into the presence of dangerous diseases, repeating the sacred words, behold, my angels enveloped that man with my unseen blankets, and the man was protected from the disease.

58. Without such words, there could be no concert of action betwixt mortals and angels.

59. Think not that thy Lord taught a foolish thing; nor that the mumbling of words by my prophets were without wisdom and forethought by the Lord thy God.

60. Now in those days the Lord caused the rab'bah to make a wheel and hang it beside the altar. And the meaning thereof was: As this wheel is without beginning or end, so is the Creator. Whosoever turneth the wheel one round hath said: In thee, my God, I trust.

61. And the Lord made an image to stand at the extreme of the altar, whither only holy men and women might pass, and the Lord called the emblem Fete, signifying, BEYOND ME THERE IS NO APPEAL.

62. And the form of fete was a circle and an all light center, with four dark corners cut off. And the Lord explained the meaning, which was:

63. That there is a central light within man seeing clearly, but that the four dark corners of the world (ignorance, lust, selfishness, and anger) beset him on all sides.

64. And the Lord made an instrument and called it GAU, which was a triangle with a plumb line from the upper corner; and across the plumb line was a hollow reed for seeing through; and at the bottom end of the plumb line was a weight attached, which pointed to marks on the lower border of the triangle. And the Lord explained to the prophets how to use the gau for proving all things, even as to the height of mountains, and the velocity of running waters, and how to lay the foundations of the temples, that they might be square with the world. And the prophets on their part taught the I'hins, but with them the mysteries were kept a secret against all the world. Hence, in after time, came the saying: Even the wicked were compelled to employ the I'hins, and were thus beholden to the Lord.

65. In all there were two hundred and eighty signs and emblems and symbols and implements given by the Lord to his people; and when they were all completed the Lord taught the prophets the meaning; and these became the sacred language of mortals in all the divisions of the earth.

END OF THE LORDS' FIRST BOOK.

BOOK OF SUE, SON OF JEHOVIH.

BEING THE SECOND CYCLE AFTER THE FLOOD.

CHAPTER I.

1. Jehovih spake in the gardens of Atahavia, precinct of Sue, Orian Chief, in the etherean firmament, saying: Sue, My son, what of the red star, the far-off earth? Behold, her harvests are blighted; she is become barren in imparting immortal souls to My unending realms.

2. Sue heard the voice, and he said: In Thy name, O Jehovih, will I summon my Gods of Hoit and Izaracha.

3. Swift messengers departed; and Sue, quick-perceiving God of two worlds in the etherean Seamar, foresaw the importance of the coming red star. He said: This, with my Gods of Hoit and Izaracha, who will come in swift speed, shall be the second deliverance.

4. Then came Le Wing, God of Hoit; and presently, Sivian, Goddess of Izaracha, and they stood before Jehovih's throne. Sue said:

5. Jehovih hath spoken. Behold, the red star bringeth forth nor sons nor daughters more to Jehovih's realms. She is weak, unstrung, and out of tune, and cometh this way. And I said:

6. In Thy power and wisdom, O Jehovih, will I visit the red star! Six years I will stand on her soil, and course her heaven; and such potency give to her confused Gods and Lords as will make a thousand millions sing for joy. To accompany me, I have called you. Behold, I have charts and maps of her heaven and her corporeal parts; and a history of her, as yet, young adventures in the field of worlds.

7. Then spake Le Wing and Sivian, saying: To do Jehovih's will and thine, behold, we are come to thee. Give us to fulfill whatsoever thou wilt.

8. To the swift messengers Sue said: Ye have heard; go proclaim throughout my etherean worlds my will; and summon up from Ithyivius a hundred million skilled volunteers. When the red star shall cross the wing of Izaracha, we will go forth in power, and land on her troubled parts in a sea of golden light.

CHAPTER II.

1. In the Ariniisca of Portan of the etherean worlds and division of Hoit and Izaracha, flew the call of the Gods for volunteers, nor which a more welcome sound is not heard in high heaven to do Jehovih's will. And with the voice and call there rose up hosts from every quarter, and from every sub-division, till the complement stood ready for the great work. And yet so vast were the fields and arcs of Izaracha that the hundred millions chosen were as but a fraction compared to those left uncalled.

2. Coming near the throne of Sue in Aoit, the hundred millions formed in squares and stars, and the chosen God took his place to the head and front, looking to the low horizon, where rose the red star, the sick earth.

3. And now the builders who had measured the elements lying in the route toward the earth, formed their crescent ship of fire, and equipped it; and, with mantles and curtains and banners, created it a vessel of beauty and ornament as well as service.

4. Hardly was the ship completed when Jehovih's light encompassed it about on all sides, so that that which was beautiful before was now illuminated and sparkling and bright as a sun, and rich in golden colors; for of such kind was the ethe of the heavens hereabout created.

5. When Sue entered the ship, the voice of Jehovih came, saying: Another cycle came and is gone on the earth and her heaven, but still they fall to barrenness ere the succeeding dawn. Go now, O Sue, My Son, and a wider range give to the tetracts of both angels and mortals. Give a greater scope to tyrants, kings and queens on earth, and greater to the self-Gods and self-Lords in hada, and more responsibility.

6. Then all hands entered the etherean ship, singing and rejoicing, observed by countless millions come to wish them a haven of joy on their six years' visit to the corporeal earth.

7. Sue said: In Thy name, O Jehovih, and by virtue of Thy power in me vested, my hosts shall forth at my command. Cut loose, ye Gods, and thou, O ship, of heaven born, to the red star, the earth, be gone! And Sue stretched forth his hands and waved them, and lo, the mighty ship of heaven turned on its axis, cutting loose from the high firmament. And it turned, with its great curtains and banners sailing gracefully and swiftly through the blue ether.

8. The music of her es'enaurs swelled and rolled along on the spheres of many worlds unseen to mortals, where dwell countless millions of spectators viewing the marvelous speed and power and brilliant colors of the great ship. Faster and Faster she sped on, till nearing Chinvat, which now cut sharp in the fields and forests of Izaracha, over which was potent the name of Sue, the companion God and chiefest friend of Aph, Orian Chief, Son of Jehovih.

9. When the ship came to the bridge and halted, to take in the plan of the whirling earth, Sue said: A light! A light! Ye Gods! And at once, as high as the moon and bright as the son, the illumined ship stood, to overawe the self-Gods and warrior kings and murderers of the earth-born, whose plentiful souls in chaos polluted heaven.

10. For three days and nights Sue held his star-ship to the wonderful task of mastering by the marvelous scene. And then slowly he entered the vortex of the earth, but held his course, nor with the earth and her heaven; for he desired that both corporeans and atmathereans should witness the coming power. So slowly he came, but fifty thousand miles a day, that when the ship neared the disorganized Hored, the self-Gods and self-Lords fled and left their well-supplied kingdoms desolate, and down to the earth rushed in thousands, and with their hosts in millions, to hide or safely stow themselves from Agni's just hate.

11. But the true God and Lords stood firm in their depleted kingdoms, fearing naught, but in faith that this etherean ship was Jehovih's answer to their long cry for help from the heavenly spheres. And by their pillars of fire still standing, great Sue knew where to land in the lower heaven for safe anchorage. So to Hored he came, slowly, and toward the throne of God. And when he neared the place, his es'enaurs chanted and the trumpeters played; the sound of which music came to the ears of God and his hosts, and they were the hymns of more than a thousand years ago.

12. And God and his hosts sent up rockets and displayed the three primary colors, the sign of Jehovih's name; and God's es'enaurs joined in chanting with the hosts above. Presently the ship of fire was at the place of landing, and Sue, Jehovih's Son, cast out a ladder and

descended, with his hosts, the hundred million angels, led by Gussitivi, marshaless of the throne of Sue, in Izaracha.

13. Sue said: Hail, O God of heaven and earth! In Jehovih's name, I am come in power and wisdom. And God answered: Glory be to Thee, O Jehovih, that Thy Son hath come so far to bless Thy bewildered kingdom! Then they saluted with the signs of the sixth resurrection, whereupon God said:

14. In the name of the Great Spirit, come thou and honor my throne. So Sue went forward, and they greeted by shaking hands; and Sue ascended and sat on the throne, saying: Keep thy place, O God, for I am not come to displace thee or thy hosts of Jehovih, but to build up for His glory. Be seated, therefore, for I feel the light of the Father descending on my head.

15. Presently the All Light enveloped Sue, and the Father's voice spake through him, saying: Hear the words of thy Creator, My son, and rejoice because I have not forgotten thee and thy people. Behold, this is the hour of thy redemption from the trials of tetracts, which are run abroad in My dominions.

16. Was it not worse than this in the olden time? and I came with my hosts and delivered them. I created man in darkness and gave to him no judgment, that the creation of his own thoughts might be for his own glory, forever. But instead of beautifying his thoughts, he hearkeneth to tetracts and clotheth himself in clouds. The heaven I build for him he diggeth to pieces, and then buildeth his own, but only to be displeased and turbulent. Neither will he content himself with providing with his own hands, but searchest out My most dutiful sons and daughters, making slaves of them for his own exaltation.

17. Behold, I have afore time sent My sons and daughters to search out these traitors and self-Gods, declaring unto them that only by forsaking evil and practicing righteousness could they attain to My exalted kingdoms. Their evil places have I cast down, and rebuilt in honor and glory, that their own judgment might determine that virtue and good works are the sure foundation for happiness that will endure forever. But when I have raised them up in one cycle and made the lower heaven a paradise, alas, My ethereans have but gone away for a little while when the tetracts take root, and grow, and turn all things upside down.

18. But now will I build them up in a new way. Yea, I will appropriate the evil of their inventions to their own good in a way they dream not of. The false Gods and false Lords shall be arrested and brought before this judgment seat, and I will judge them by their own behavior and desires; neither will I torment them nor abridge their happiness. Send, therefore, My Son, thy marshals into the hidden places of these Gods and Lords, and say to them: Thus saith the hosts of heaven: Come, My Son, and inherit a kingdom in hada, in thine own way, for lo, there is room for all; but that thou art not left behind, come quickly to Hored.

19. And they will come, hoping to embellish themselves in the old manner. But My Light shall come in due time in Mine Own way.

20. The voice ceased, but Sue spake of his own account, saying: What Jehovih hath ordered, do ye. So marshals and priests were sent in all directions in atmospherea to gather in the false Gods and false Lords who had deserted their dominions in fear of the light of Sue's etherean ship. And after many days the false ones were brought to Hored; and there were of them seven thousand Lords and Gods.

21. Now when they were before Sue, Jehovih's Son, and arranged so that all could hear and see, even the whole Council beside, the Light gathered around about the throne, and Sue addressed them, saying:

22. Hear me, O men and women! I have sent for you, and ye are here. In this I am pleased. Know, then, that what I speak shall be in love and tenderness. Ye have deserted Jehovih's kingdoms, and it must be because it pleased you better than to remain. Is this not true? And ye also deserted your own false kingdoms?

23. For a little while they consulted together, and then answered, saying: Nay, it pleased us not to desert our own kingdoms; but we were afraid.

24. Sue said: Who think ye I am? They answered: A God from some far-off world, but where it lieth we know not. We desire to know who thou art?

25. Sue said: I am but a man; fear me not. But since ye feared, and so deserted your kingdoms, does it not prove that ye are not the All Highest? And do ye not perceive that, because ye had no All Highest, ye were divided and inharmonious?

26. Hear, then, that which I say, and consider my words: I want not your kingdoms nor anything ye have; but, that harmony may reign in heaven, I will give every one of you more than ye had, and add power unto you also.

27. Since ye behold I am come to Hored, the throne of the ancients, perceive ye not that whosoever accordeth with me is of my power also? Take, then, your kingdoms and be Gods and Goddesses, as ye assumed before, and I will anoint ye, and make ye as part and parcel of one united whole. Again they counseled together, and then answered:

28. Why shall we take our kingdoms? Our slaves have deserted us; our kingdoms are pillaged of all their value. Yea, our slaves have become wandering spirits, and are returned to the earth and are making their habitations with mortals. So that the people of earth are aroused because of miracles and wonders occurring on earth.

29. Sue said: What can ye say to these wandering spirits that will induce them to come up away from mortals? To which they answered: If we promise them provender and clothes and plenty of rest, they will come; but when we put them to labor, they will run away, having tasted of liberty.

30. Sue said: How, then, made ye slaves of them in the first place? To which they answered: We took them in the day their mortal bodies died, and they never saw nor knew any other place in heaven; so we appropriated them to our service dutifully.

31. Sue said: Know, then, this is my conclusion: First that ye shall all be made as sub-Gods to one confederacy, and your kingdoms shall be fair to look upon, and well supplied with all things needful.

32. Behold, there are on earth, with the barbarians, hosts of familiars and fetals; whoever, then, of you will go down to the earth and bring them away to Hored shall have them for his slaves; and, whoever bringeth the greatest number, will I award the greatest kingdom. And if it be that ye can find emissaries to work for you in bringing fetals and familiars away from the barbarians, then shall such labor be accounted to your credit. And ye shall station around about in the corporeal cities certain angels, whose labor shall be to receive newborn spirits on birth-blankets and bring them to your kingdoms also, for they shall be your slaves.

33. After that manner spake Sue; and the false Gods and Goddesses were highly pleased, and they divided themselves into certain districts over mortals and for the lower heaven,

and were at once sent off to labor in their own way, and they were named sub-Gods.

34. Sue said: These sub-Gods have much weight with the barbarians, because they advise them in war. But, behold, it shall come to pass when the sub-Gods have robbed the barbarians of their familiar spirits, the I'hin priests will have a greater weight with them.

35. And the sub-Gods will desire to find favor in my sight, and so, teach their slaves, the which will cause them to emancipate themselves in time to come.

CHAPTER III.

1. Jehovih spake through Sue, saying: Mine is a strong government, and everlasting. Hearken to the wisdom of your Creator, O My sons and daughters. Wherein have I not given liberty to all people? He that doeth aright, wherein is he not free? He that doeth awrong, wherein hath he liberty? Whoever endeavoreth to surpass himself, have I not shown him his limit?

2. I created man at zero, but for him to add unto himself forever. Liberty I gave him to add only that which perfecteth his own soul. Wherefore, if he eat poison, it taketh from him his body which I gave. Herein made I a boundary, both on earth and in heaven, which is to say, inasmuch as man accumulateth virtue, wisdom, patience, love, truth and pure words, he is free; because, in so doing, he followeth Me in My works. But he that seeketh to glorify himself in his possessions bindeth himself; because he is unlike Me, for I gave All, and thus made the universe.

3. Two states, therefore, have I created open to all men, both on earth and in atmospherea, which are, liberty and bondage. And man I made to choose that which he will; but that he might not err, behold, I send My emancipated angels to explain these things beforehand.

4. Even so are governments ordained by My holy ones, wherein ye may judge whether a government be of Me or against Me. For if it give liberty to all righteous works, and for the promotion of knowledge, providing teachers to the extent of the demand, it is of Me. But if the government maketh of itself a self, for which its aggrandizement is at the expense of My children's liberty, then is it against Me.

5. For I have not created a people to be to-day as were their forefathers, but provided them with perpetual growth in wisdom and virtue; wherefore the rising generations shall rebel against that which was well and good for their forefathers. All My governments understand this, whether on earth or in heaven. Whatever government accepteth not this rule, shall go down to destruction. For, as I have hedged man about with sentinels, such as pestilence, poverty and hunger, in order to awaken him to knowledge and industry, so have I hedged in all governments under the sun with sentinels, such as rebellion and assassinations, and war, and bankruptcy. As pestilence proveth man's disobedience to My commandments, so do rebellion and anarchy prove the disobedience of governments to the progressive spirit with which I created man.

6. The self-God saith: I will make a strong government; by armies and cruel masters will I bind the subjects of my dominions. And he draweth up a multitude of laws, and heapeth up books to explain the laws, and findeth judges to explain the books that explain the laws, and he saith: Behold how wise I am! Behold the great wisdom of my judges! Behold the great learning of my books! Behold my most perfect laws! Behold my armies that stand behind all, and in great power!

7. But lo, a star appeareth in heaven, and all his fabric goeth as a spider's web. For instead of choosing his Creator, Who is strong, he erected things that were as nothing.

8. Hear thy Creator, O My God, for through My Son I bequeath a new light to the lower heaven: For, as thou hast portioned to the self-Gods to take kingdoms, suffer them to hedge themselves about with a multitude of laws; but thou thyself shalt have no laws save the rites and ceremonies, which thou shalt adorn with music and processions.

9. And it shall come to pass that the dominions of the self-Gods will prosper for a season; and they will, for sake of self-glory, deplete the earth people of familiar spirits and fetals. But, in time after, their subjects will tire of the laws of the self-Gods, and hearing that thou hast no laws, save rites and ceremonies, they will come to Hored of their own accord.

10. Henceforth, then, shalt thou convert the nurseries and hospitals, and factories and places of education, into places of delight and recreation.

11. The voice ceased, but Sue said: Behold, a time cometh, in all the atmospherean heavens, when the discipline of former days must give way to something new; and such a time is now in this kingdom. It may be likened to a young child that hath been led by the hand for a long time, but now hath become strong of limb so as to walk alone.

12. For this purpose hath the earth been brought through the fields of Izaracha, and my hosts are come with music and wisdom. Hear, then, my decree, O God of earth, and thou shalt be the most blessed of Gods: Send thy messengers into all parts of atmospherea, proclaiming a recreation of ten days, of music and dancing and marching, with pageantry and feasting, to be in Hored in the first of the moon of Jaffeth.

13. The rest leave to the Father, for He will provide us in the time thereof. And whilst the time is coming, I will go around the earth with my hosts in my etherean ship.

14. God said: I perceive Thy wisdom, O Jehovih; in Thy decrees am I raised up with new wisdom and power. O that I could have devised a way for them before they fell so low!

15. Sue called the Council and his own hosts from labor to recreation for one day, and the people mingled together rejoicing; for of the ethereans with the hosts of Sue were many who had been earth-born, many thousands of years before, and their assurance of the emancipated heavens above had greater weight with the atmosphereans than anything that others could say. Then Sue and his hosts visited the earth and her heavens; and after that returned again to Hored.

CHAPTER IV.

1. When the time of the festival had come, there congregated in Hored, besides the etherean hosts, more than a thousand million souls, to witness and participate in the ceremonies. Sue said: Here is wisdom and folly; false Gods and their dupes; laziness and industry; swiftness and sloth. Yea, here is a world worthless before Jehovih.

2. And why? Simply for lack of discipline and harmony. Every one is for self, and none are producers for the general good. Alas, they are the same as mortals, but stripped of flesh. They are of no value to themselves. Now will I show thee, O God, that these hapless beings, with no joy in life nor hope of resurrection, shall become a great glory to the Father and His Kingdoms.

3. God said: Pity them, O Father! It is over a thousand years since they have been visited

by the higher heaven. Many of them are learned, but doubting if there be other heavens, save the plateaus of the atmospherea of the earth. Millions and millions of them have never seen an etherean. Alas, I fear for them.

4. Sue said: Fear not, O God. They are as mortar in my hands. Neither shall there be preaching to them, nor praying for them. They are tired of these things. But I will found a new light amongst them, and it shall speak for us. Hear me, then, and with the populace I shall be as One that is unknown. Call, then, thy es'enaurs, and thy trumpeters and harpists, and all the musicians belonging to thy kingdom and to the kingdoms of thy Lords, and let the procession begin.

5. For in all public matters those who are at the front, if wise, can lead on forever. Be politic, therefore, and shape the populace whilst the self-Gods are amazed at the immensity of the hosts assembled.

6. God did as commanded, and the people saw there was a head to the proceedings. Sue said: Send thy marshals and decorators to follow close after the musicians, distributing raiment to all who will follow in the procession. My etherean hosts are advised. They will stand by the way, and, with marvelous swiftness, provide the raiment. And all possible extravagant colors and fabrics, and hats and ornaments, shall be distributed, and gratuitously.

7. My hosts shall be arranged in plain white; and they shall march not, but be as servants and workmen. And when the atmosphereans have played and sung over all the boundaries of Hored, then shall My etherean band sing and play and start the dance.

8. All these things were done, and from the very start to the termination of the music there was harmony in every place and corner amongst the thousand millions assembled. Nor was there ever so extravagantly equipped a multitude in the earth's heaven. And, so completely captivated were the people, their enthusiasm was boundless. Then came the etherean dance, the which so far surpassed the capacity of the atmosphereans that not one could join in. Neither could they take part in the etherean music.

9. So the atmosphereans looked on, confounded by the excellence of that which was before their eyes.

10. Thus ended the first day's proceedings, which to describe in full would require a large book. So the people were called to refreshment. And the ethereans, still dressed in white, and as servants and laborers, provided the viands. For they had previously made convenience for a supply of material. And so easily and with such swiftness did they their work that now for the first time did the more learned of atmospherea begin to observe them with surprise and wonder.

11. Presently inquiries were made as to who they were and whence they came. For so Jehovih created man, that when of his own accord he admireth the excellence of his neighbor, he goeth to the extreme in praising him.

12. So God said: On the morrow shall a new entertainment be given, and new raiment and new viands for the feast. And the hosts shouted with great vigor and praise. Then the people mingled together to converse on all they had witnessed; neither comprehended they the object, save for pleasure only.

13. When the next day came the ethereans had been divided into groups, and the rites of the ancients and of the hosts of a'ji in Partha were announced, requiring extravagant toilets and millions of atmosphereans as assistants.

14. So great was their ambition to take part that only by promises of something in the next rites could the marshals make selections.

15. Sue, Jehovih's Son, had previously stationed signal bells at remote distances from one another, but connected them so that the sounds would answer quickly. And in the intervening places, extemporized forests and waterfalls were arranged; and near the middle space one thousand columns of fire were erected.

16. So, in the morning of the second day, when all these glorious scenes were completed, and the ethereans, still plain and in white, stationed about, the atmospereans were more confounded than ever, and more loudly shouting in their praise.

17. First came the birth-rites; then marriage-rites; then death-rites and the first resurrection; then the rites of harmony. And the play represented a million of ethereans who went to a corporeal world and followed it through its life, and to death and resurrection; its darkness and enharmony and terrible suffering in atmospherea; ending with a tableau of a great sun of light descending, to deliver them into everlasting paradise.

18. So grand was the spectacle, and so sublime the music and the spoken words, that the hosts of Hored wept, and laughed, and shouted, and prayed, as if their souls would break with joy.

19. Thus ended the second day, and so complete was the glorious work that every soul had sworn a solemn oath to forsake the earth and lower heaven forever. Then God announced for the third day, the display of etherean power.

20. And the people were so bewildered already that a child could have led the most stubborn of all. For thus Jehovih created man, who, having become much conceited in himself, turneth right about and maketh himself a submissive fool.

21. So, on the third day, the ethereans displayed their power over the elements of the atmosphere; making corporeal substances and dissolving them at pleasure; making light into darkness, and darkness into light. Weaving fabrics and making diadems and precious stones. Gathering viands from the essence of things evaporated up from the earth; founding plateaux and temples in heaven. Making ships and chains and musical instruments. And, lastly, the etherean marshals, with half a million ethereans, turned the winds and sent a heavy shower of rain down to the corporeal earth.

22. And all the while, the musicians of the hosts of Sue were discoursing music, the sweetness and grandeur of which surpassed the atmosphereans so far that they were as nothing.

23. So, because of the exhibition of great power and wisdom, the third day had changed the fortunes and aspirations of every man and woman in the lower heaven. And they were running hither and thither, pleading to be taken as apprentices or servants, pledging themselves to do anything required of them. Neither would they be put off, demanding that half of the next day should be given to initiating them as real beginners in the second resurrection.

24. Then God spake to them, saying: Ye know not what ye speak. Behold, I have commanded ye for hundreds of years to put away your fine raiment and sparkling gems, and to begin adorning your souls, so as to become Brides and Bridegrooms of the Great Spirit.

25. But ye would not, but strove continually to adorn yourselves, forgetting to labor for those beneath you. Behold, now stand Jehovih's Brides and Bridegrooms before you.

What is their worth compared to yours? Are they not plain? And are ye not decorated? 26. But millions of voices rose up, saying: We will do whatever thou commandest, O God. There is no God like unto thee. Then God spake, saying: Hear me, then, further: This is to begin the second resurrection: to put away your jewels and diadems and ornaments, and, above all things, to forsake self, and henceforth labor for others who are beneath you. If ye do this in a brotherhood, ye are already beginning the second resurrection. Neither is there any other road to wisdom and power. 27. Again the multitude cried out: We will do anything; we have faith. And God answered them, saying: Suffer, then, a few to be initiated on to-morrow; but be ye patient and of good judgment; slow to resolve, but firm forever.

28. So on the fourth day, in the morning, behold, more than a hundred millions of spirits had abandoned their showy raiment and stood arrayed in white, devoid of jewels and diadems, ready to be initiated and take the vows of the second resurrection, as above. And accordingly new music was prepared, and the procession and ceremonies so arranged that the greatest possible glory would be manifested.

29. Canopies were stretched overhead, and arches and columns on the borders of the march, decorated with flowers and vines; and amidst these, half concealed, were nestled the response singers, who were to speak for and with the initiates. But concealed from view, and afar off, were bells and explosives, which were the morning signals.

30. And the glad and solemn sound of the Immortal Voice came upon the souls of millions impatient to vow themselves to a new life; and God and his hosts welcomed them with great joy. So grand and imposing were the ceremonies, that, ere midday, another hundred millions came, robed in white, to be initiated also. Neither desired the people any other entertainment.

31. And so the initiations were continued on the fifth day; and yet another hundred millions applied, also robed in white. And this was continued on the sixth and seventh and eighth and ninth and tenth days. And, lo and behold, a thousand million angels had taken the vows of the second resurrection.

CHAPTER V.

1. After this manner were the words of the initiation, led by the etherean hosts, to wit:
2. God on the throne said: O E-O-Ih (Jehovih)! Almighty! Boundless!
3. Response: How shall I comprehend Thee, Thou Mighty One?
4. God: Thou Higher than All Gods and Lords!
5. Response: Who movest the universe, with power unlimited!
6. God: Creator and Controller of the corporeal worlds!
7. Response: In Whose hands the etherean firmament is like a fruitful garden, wider than the boundaries of time!
8. God: Whose members are All Space!
9. Response: Whose members are the All that is within place, beyond measure!
10. God: Thou, E-O-Ih! Thou Fountain and Terminus of all things!
11. Response: E-O-Ih! E-O-Ih! Of Whom all things are but parts, attuned to Thy will!
12. God: Thou All Person, O E-O-Ih! Incomprehensible!
13. Response: Who speakest in the Light! Whose voice is the progress of the universe!

14. God: E-O-Ih! Thou All Giver! By giving, Createth!

15. Response: What are Thy secrets, O Mighty One? O E-O-Ih, Everlasting, and Greater than Magnitude!

16. God: I see nothing in all the universe but Thee! All selfs are but fractions of Thyself, O E-O-Ih!

17. Response: Who hath not beholden Thee, O E-O-Ih? Thy Person is in the east and west and north and south! Below and above; far and near.

18. God: Who hath not heard Thy voice? Who hath not found Thy hand, that pusheth him along?

19. Response: Without Thee, O E-O-Ih, I go not; I move not. I set out to do things of myself, and fail utterly.

20. God: What is man before Thee, O E-O-Ih? He setteth up a kingdom, and it falleth as a house of straw.

21. Response: O E-O-Ih, how I have wasted my time! My buildings were lighter than chaff! My virtues were but bubbles, and they are burst and gone!

22. God: When will man learn to attune himself to Thee, O E-O-Ih?

23. Response: How can I put away myself, O E-O-Ih? Have I not said: I cannot put away mine own judgment?

24. God: Man saith: I will not put away my judgment! and lo, therein doeth he it!

25. Response: Have I not said: To protect myself is the first law, and to preserve mine own the highest law?

26. God: Man assumeth to protect himself, because he is without faith in Thee, O E-o-ih! And to preserve his own, which, in fact, is not his.

27. And here the Light fell upon the throne, and Jehovih spake out of the Light, saying:

28. I have called thee, O man, from thy youth up! My voice hath never ceased in thine ear. Who can come into life without Me? Who can measure his own footsteps? Behold, he treadeth on My ground. Of all that he is made, the substance is Mine.

29. The kingdoms of the earth and the kingdoms of Gods and Lords in heaven, what are they more than imitations of My works? Wherein they imitate Me well, I am with them in wisdom, love and power. Shall a man butt his head against a wall to prove he is greater than his Creator? Behold, I came in the ancient days, saying: Strive to become one with Me, and thou shalt rejoice that I created thee. Strive to set up for thyself, and thy vanity shall in time pierce thee as a two-edged sword.

30. Hear the love of thy Creator, O man! For I made thee with fondness for thy sons and daughters. Of love like Mine Own I gave thee a part. And as thou sendest to thy wayward son, beseeching him to return to thee, so do I bring My messengers from higher worlds to call thee. And, that thou mayst not mistake their higher place, I give them power and wisdom surpassing thee.

31. The voice ceased, and then the initiates said:

32. Henceforth I will serve only Thee, O E-O-Ih! Nor will I more think what shall become of me. For I know Thou wilt appropriate me wisely, O E-O-Ih!

33. Accordingly, as the stone is hewn and polished, so wilt Thou put it in the walls of Thy house.

34. My labor is to hew and polish and perfect mine own soul forever!

35. My soul shall become as a shining star.

36. My love like Thy etherean angels.

37. And plain my raiment, and clean, forever!

38. Nor more will I boast, nor speak untruth, forever!

39. Nor sloth attain me.

40. Nor vanity, nor self; nor will I talk of myself.

41. Nor criticize my brethren, nor my neighbors, for they are Thine, O E-O-Ih !

42. To do righteous works and lift up my fellows shall be my labor henceforth, forever!

43. Make me strong in Thee, O E-O-Ih!

44. And wise to do Thy will forever. Amen!

CHAPTER VI.

1. So great were the words and music of the ceremonies that the people were entranced beyond measure; the old and divided kingdoms, which were without unity and discipline, were now replaced by extreme sanctity and decorum.

2. Sue said: Hear me, O God, I will counsel thee further: Know, then, that the false Gods and false Lords have gone off to build up kingdoms of their own, nor know they what hath happened in Hored. Suffer them to proceed until they have purified the corporeans from familiars and fetals; but when they have finished, call thou another festival of all these people, and also send word to the false Gods and false Lords who deny Jehovih, the All Person, and they will come, bringing their slaves, having themselves adorned in extravagant raiment and jewelry. For they will expect, by their pageantry, to triumph over all other Gods and men, hoping to carry back with them millions of subjects.

3. God said: I perceive, O Sue, Son of Jehovih. So, God did as commanded, and sure enough, in course of time, the false Gods and false Lords stripped the barbarians of the earth of their familiars and fetals, making slaves of such spirits in heaven. And it came to pass that God gave another festival, and it was greater than the first, and there were present upward of three thousand million angels, who had become enlisted in righteous works.

4. This was the beginning of the third year of Sue; and his wisdom and power were now manifested all around the world, on earth and in heaven.

5. And this is what happened in reference to the false Gods and false Lords, who came to the festival, equipped in chariots and ships, and with banners and flags, and crowns and diadems, and such wonderful extravagancies, the like of which had not been in heaven since the flood. And each and every false God and false Lord endeavored to outdo the others in show and parade.

6. As might be expected, the first day of the festival neither won their applause nor censure. The second day they ceased to attract attention; for the thrift and purity and wisdom manifested in the countless millions of the second resurrection caused even children to receive more praise than the Gods and Lords with all their glitter and show.

7. On the third day one-half of the false Gods and false Lords cast aside their adornments and appeared in plain white, pleading to be initiated into the mysteries of the second resurrection. And on the day following, the rest of them came also, seeking like admission.

8. Whereupon the Light of Jehovih spake through God on the throne, saying:

9. Bethink ye, O ye Gods and Lords! What are ye doing? But as yesterday ye asked for kingdoms, desiring to be leaders and great workers, over and above your fellows.

10. And ye obtained your desires, becoming Gods and Lords over millions. And these became your dutiful subjects, and ye adorned your throne and your persons in great splendor.

11. Behold I gave a festival, and ye came as living witnesses of what self-made Gods and Lords could accomplish. And your dutiful subjects came with you to attest their loyalty and good faith in your wisdom and power.

12. Now have ye cast aside your crowns and high estate, praying to become workers amongst the host of men and women! Are ye not mad? And are ye not making yourselves the destroyers of your own subjects? For, behold, because of your abjuration of self-pomp and self-glory, all your subjects are cast aside in ignorance and misery.

13. With one voice the self-Gods and self-Lords answered, saying: Alas, O God! What shall we do? Our crowns we can give away; our raiment and jewels, and our thrones and kingdoms. But, O God, we cannot give away our subjects; they will not go. We have bound them to us; and we are bound to them because we accepted them. What shall we do, O God? The burden is more than we can bear!

14. God said: Be not disconsolate, O Gods and Lords! Ye have done a great work. Ye have rescued millions and millions of familiars and fetals. And even before ye applied for the resurrection, behold, most of your subjects had already deserted you!

15. Hear the judgment of your Creator, which is that when all your subjects and fetals are risen in wisdom and virtue and good works, so as to take the second resurrection, even on that same day shall ye be promoted. For only until then can ye have freedom of soul.

16. The voice ceased, and the self-Gods and self-Lords answered: Thou art just, O Jehovih. We will go to work amongst our poor and ignorant subjects, and make them comprehend Thy wisdom, power and justice.

17. For ten days the festival lasted, and then it ended. Thus were first established rites and ceremonies in the lower heaven as a power to work wisdom and virtue. And from that time ever after, music and marching and dancing were included in all ceremonies by the Gods and Lords of heaven.

CHAPTER VII.

1. In the fifth year of Sue he dispatched swift messengers to Opnetevoc, in etherea, saying: Thus saith Sue, God of two etherean worlds: Behold, I am sojourning on the earth, and, with the God of heaven and his Lords, have prepared one thousand million Brides and Bridegrooms for Jehovih's etherean harvest. Greeting to Nista, of Ho and Tow'en, Goddess; in the name of Jehovih, send an airavagna and complete the resurrection of the Father's Brides and Bridegrooms!

2. So it came to pass in etherea, the Goddess, Nista, provided an airavagna, an etherean ship, resolving to come as commander in chief. Sue advised God, saying: Make thou of this matter a great testimony in thy heaven. Send, therefore, thy messengers into all parts, and to thy Lords on the earth, inviting all people to be present to witness the ascent of Jehovih's Brides and Bridegrooms.

3. God did as commanded, and on the day of the appearance of Nista, daughter of

Jehovih, in her sun-ship, in the firmament, there were assembled in Hored countless millions of souls inspired of Jehovih.

4. Great was the rejoicing and the manifestations of delight when the sun-ship came in full view, descending, like a world on fire. And when she passed Chinvat and was fully within the earth's vortex, the enthusiasm of the people knew no bounds.

5. They sang, and prayed, and danced, and clapped their hands, as if mad with delight. Meantime the Brides and Bridegrooms had been arrayed in etherean white, and were now saluting those whom they were soon to leave.

6. Quietly the etherean hosts filled their part in the great play of the immortal resurrection; very Gods and Goddesses in demeanor.

7. Nearer and nearer came Nista in her sun-ship, slowly turning and descending, with ten thousand curtains suspended and waving; and ten times ten thousand banners and flags waving above and around.

8. And then slowly down, lower and lower, till the airavagna rested on the plateau of Hored, to the south of the Temple of Jehovih.

9. Gussitavi, marshaless to the throne of Sue, in Izaracha, with ten thousand deputies, went forward, and with open arms received Nista, Goddess descended, saluting with the sign of the star and square, having been warm friends two hundred thousand years in the plains of Oayad, in the etherean es'tu of Hi'dan, the spiritual center of the orbit of the great serpent when in Zagagowthaka.

10. The es'enaurs of both hosts were chanting, and the angels of the airavagna coming forth in hundreds of thousands, to be saluted by the previously trained Brides and Bridegrooms of Jehovih and by the hosts of Sue, the etherean laborers.

11. And when Nista came up to the throne, God and great Sue rose up amidst the light, now fast gathering as a mantle of brilliant fire over the place of council.

12. Sue said: All hail, O Nista, Jehovih's Daughter. God said: In Jehovih's name, welcome, O Nista. To which Nista answered, saying: By the Wisdom and Power of Jehovih, O my beloved!

13. And Sue and God parted, and Nista ascended and sat in the midst of the throne. After the ceremonies of salutation Nista said: Let the Brides and Bridegrooms of Jehovih approach the throne of God.

14. The marshals then ushered them to their places, a thousand millions, and the swift messengers bounded them on all sides, so that the responses should be uniform and as if spoken by one person. Whereupon Nista spake from the throne, and the Brides and Bridegrooms responded in the usual form of Gods and Goddesses, and then took the necessary vows and renunciations of the earth and lower heaven, according to Jehovih's commandments.

15. When the ceremonies were finished, God proclaimed one day of recreation, which was participated in joyously by upward of four thousand million souls.

16. So, on the next day, Nista and her hosts, with the thousand millions of Brides and Bridegrooms, entered the airavagna, amidst the cheers and weeping of millions of atmosphereans, who had never witnessed so grand a spectacle.

17. And then Nista, by the power of the Great Spirit, set her ship in motion; raised it up from the lower heaven; moved it upward by her command, saying: Arise! arise! Airavagna! By my will, arise! Embrace thou the realms of Great Jehovih!   Arise.

152

18. The es'enaurs and trumpeters were singing and playing; and those ascending threw down flowers and perfumes, and all manner of pleasant remembrances, to the countless millions below.

19. In a little while the airavagna disappeared in high heaven.

20. This, then, is what followed of Sue's ministration, to wit: When the end of dan'ha had come, that is, the six years, he delivered God and his Lords and another thousand millions of Brides and Bridegrooms, taking them into the extreme borders of Izaracha, where was assigned the a'ji'an field of Rus'tsoo with twelve etherean worlds.

21. And Sue left T-hi, as the anointed God of the lower heaven for the next four hundred years. And God (T-hi) anointed Lords for the divisions of the earth, the same as had been heretofore. And the earth and heaven prospered, so that in the dan following there were raised up two thousand million Brides and Bridegrooms.

22. From this time on there was a decrease in the etherean harvests for two thousand years, after which time there came great darkness on the earth and heaven belonging to it; and self-Gods filled all atmospherea. And, as for Lords, there rose up in every nation on the earth thousands and thousands, so that men and angels knew not if there were a true God or true Lord in all the universe.

23. Thus ended the cycle of Sue, being three thousand and two hundred years.

END OF THE BOOK OF SUE, SON OF JEHOVIH.

THE LORDS' SECOND BOOK.

BEING COTEMPORANEOUS WITH THE BOOK OF SUE, SON OF JEHOVIH. AS THE LATTER IS CHIEFLY OF THE ANGELS OF HEAVEN, SO IS THE LORDS' BOOK OF MAN ON THE EARTH.

CHAPTER I.

1. God said: I, the Lord, for my predecessors and successors and for myself, declare these things unto mortals:

2. The chosen of God, being called I'hins, because they were the fruit of both heaven and earth, were taken into all the earth in the protection of God, his Lords and angels, for the fulfillment of man on the earth for the glory of the Almighty.

3. And I, the Lord, a one-time mortal, with my holy angels, who had sprung from the earth in former times, walked with man to keep him upright in the way he should go.

4. By command of God, the angels watched over man, teaching man oft times unknowingly to himself in all good works and industry. By constant changes of watch did the angels relieve one another daily, weekly and monthly.

5. And in no time did the angels leave the I'hins alone, and without the light of heaven.

6. And whithersoever the I'hins went, there went the angels; and the angels often took on sar'gis, and were seen by man, even daily, and man talked with them face to face.

7. And the angels told man what was good for him; showing him the way of righteousness.

8. And man depended on the Lord and his angels for all things helpful to his

153

understanding.

9. Now when the earth was inhabited in many places, and there were thousands of cities and villages, the Lord said unto man:

10. Behold, thou hast made the earth the joy of the Lord; and now I give it into thy keeping. How sayest thou?

11. And man answered: It is well; I can keep the earth, and I shall rejoice thereon because it is the gift of God.

12. The Lord said: If I stay with thee, day and night forever, thou wilt not put forth thine own power and judgment.

13. Man said: Go thy way, O Lord.

14. Then the Lord withdrew awhile, taking his angels with him.

15. Now in those days there were ground people dwelling in the wilderness, who had not the light of heaven in them, neither could they be made to understand.

16. As one may discourse to an ox, and it heedeth not; so was speech to the people of darkness.

17. Nevertheless, in winter, when food was scarce, the ground people came to the cities of the I'hins, beseeching for food. And the I'hins, remembering the commandments of God, went out to them, treating them to everything good to eat.

18. Now, behold, the chosen were tempted by the people of darkness. And it came to pass that a new race was born on the earth, and they were called I'huans, after the manner of the ancient warriors that destroyed the chosen, before the flood.

19. These I'huans were copper colored and were capable of speech.

20. When God beheld what had happened, he called to the I'hins, saying: O ye that could dispense with the Lord! Gave I not unto you the mark of circumcision as a limit to the line of my chosen?

21. Hear me now in my prophecy: The I'huan shall be taught the name of Jehovih, the Great Spirit, and the plans of heaven and earth. And the I'huan shall inhabit the whole earth in time to come; and he shall have dominion over everything on earth, and in the waters on the earth.

22. And in time to come the I'hin race shall disappear from the earth; their like shall not be found on this my footstool.

23. The I'hins inquired of the Lord when these things should come to pass. The Lord said: In twenty thousand years.

24. The Lord said: From this time forth the I'hins shall not mingle with any other people on the face of the earth. This is my commandment. And whosoever violateth my word shall be cast out of my cities, and go and dwell with the barbarians.

25. Inasmuch as the I'huans are your heirs, and are capable of everlasting life, ye shall be unto them the light of my kingdoms. Teaching them peace, righteousness and mercy; but ye shall in no case suffer them to enter your cities and abide therein.

26. Neither shall ye raise a hand to do them harm. But if they come upon you in multitudes to take your stores, then shall ye depart out of that city, leaving the I'huans to take the goods and food for themselves.

27. For ye shall be an example of non-resistance for the sake of establishing the love of God in them.

CHAPTER II.

1. God foresaw that the I'huans should be separated from the druks, otherwise Yaks would again be born into the world.

2. And he said unto the I'hins: Behold, the I'huans cannot hear the voice of the Lord, therefore, go ye unto them, saying: Thus saith the Lord: If ye mingle with the druks your seed shall not inherit everlasting life, but go down in darkness.

3. And the I'hins went and told the I'huans the words of God. Nevertheless many of the I'huans broke the commandment. And, indeed, Yaks were again born into the world.

4. The I'hins said to one another: Are not these like unto those of the legends of old, who were made eunuchs and servants?

5. The I'huans inquired the meaning; and when they were told, they made a law unto themselves, making eunuchs and servants of both Yaks and the ground people wherever they came upon them.

6. The I'hins feared for the judgments of God, and they called out to him for a remedy.

7. But God answered them, saying: Because of the enmity betwixt these two races, behold, they will not marry. Suffer ye the I'huans to do in their own way. For of what profit is it to bring forth heirs that cannot inherit my exalted heavens? Because the tribes of darkness cannot be made to understand, behold their souls go out of being as a lamp that is burned out.

8. So it came to pass that the I'huans made eunuchs of the tribes of darkness; of both sexes did they thus; and they made slaves of them also.

9. The Lord said: The I'huans shall have laws of their own. Let my chosen go unto them and make laws for them, saying: Thus saith the Lord.

10. The I'huans shall be guardians over the I'hins, the sacred people; and through the I'hins will I bless the I'huans, and make them mighty.

11. Since it is not lawful for the I'hins to kill beast, nor bird, nor serpent, behold, their cities and mounds are invaded by all manner of evil beasts and serpents.

12. The I'huans shall slay all such evil beasts and serpents.

13. And they shall guard around about the cities and mounds, where abide my chosen.

14. Servants shall the ground people and the Yaks be unto the I'huan. And the latter shall cast their servants, that they shall not multiply on the earth.

15. Hear ye then, the law of God betwixt the I'huans, one with another.

16. Whoso doth an injury to his neighbor or to a stranger, the same shall be done unto him.

17. Whoso taketh from another, an equivalent shall he render two fold.

18. Whoso killeth a man, or woman, or child, shall be put to death.

19. Whoso marrieth his sister or mother, or his half-sister or half-mother, they shall all suffer death together.

20. Whoso oppresseth another shall be cast out of the tribe of his people.

21. He that blasphemeth the Great Spirit shall be put to death.

22. He that respecteth not the time of woman shall be put to death.

23. The fields have I given to the I'hins, but the forests and wilderness have I, the Lord, given unto the I'huans.

24. And it was so; the I'huans began to be carnivorous. But both the I'hins and the tribes of darkness ate neither flesh nor fish.

CHAPTER III.

1. In all the great divisions of the earth these things were; nor had one division of the earth much preference over another. But in the regions of summer weather, where the earth brought forth abundantly, the I'huans and ground people dwelt most numerously.

2. Though the I'hins dwelt in both the warm and the cold countries. For they clothed themselves; and built habitations. But the I'huans wore only a covering about the loins; neither built they any habitations. And they roved about far and near.

3. But the ground people traveled not; and they mingled with their own kin, bringing forth heirs of darkness.

4. The I'huans learned the laws and obeyed them; and they looked upon the I'hins as a sacred people, doing them no harm.

5. And it came to pass that the I'huans were a very prolific people; four times more prolific than the I'hins, or the ground people.

6. And they spread rapidly over the earth, in all the regions where the earth brought forth fruit and roots, and flesh, and fish, that were good to eat.

7. For two thousand years the I'huans prospered; and they became mighty in many countries.

8. But in course of time they began to war upon one another.

9. And for hundreds of years they descended lower and lower in darkness.

10. And they obeyed no longer the commandments of God. But they mingled with the ground people, bringing forth heirs of darkness.

END OF THE LORDS' SECOND BOOK.

BOOK OF APOLLO.

BEING THE HEAVENLY ADMINISTRATION OF APOLLO, AN ETHEREAN GOD.

CHAPTER I.

1. Apollo, Son of Jehovih, resident of Pti'mus, in etherea, and God of Suf'ad and Don'ga and Tah, in the South Province of Buru, Orian Chief, controller of vortices, said:

2. I, Apollo, once a mortal, proclaim: First, wisdom, peace and patience unto all men, and comprehensive judgment whereof I speak; second, to perceive the reason of things, as to what seemeth to have been, and of what cometh after.

3. For the Great Spirit is all Harmony and Perfection, abounding in time and in worlds to accomplish all possible imaginings; wherefore, be ye magnified in conception, not judging by the little understanding of mortals.

4. So that he that asserteth harmony being more to the order of Jehovih than that which is ill-formed or out of time, hath little reason to prove his assertion before a wise man. As one may assert that ripe fruit is nearer perfection than that which is green, which assertion is self-evident without proof, so, in the understanding of Gods in the management of worlds, are things past and present, not things past and present in fact, but more like the immature and the mature.

5. Since, then, man perceiveth that words, at best, are but slow and coarse representations of the soul's conception of things, how much farther distant lieth a God's wisdom beyond the reach of mortal understanding! Remember, O man, that couldst thou in a moment of time recollect all thou hadst ever learned thou wouldst be wise indeed. Wert thou in tune with thyself, such would be thy wisdom. To advance in such direction, whereby man becometh attuned, first with himself, then with his immediate surroundings, then with the magnitude of worlds, and then with Jehovih, so that he moveth, acteth, and comprehendeth harmoniously, is to become one with the Father.

6. Which condition awaiteth all men, and is called in high heaven, Nirvana, because, to him that hath attained it, things past and things to come are as an open book. He can look back to his own beginning in the world, and even beyond, and withersoever he directeth his eye, he can see and hear even as if the matter now were.

7. Marvel not, O man, that the Gods reveal the words and signs of things long since perished corporeally; the proofs he could give, thou couldst not understand, for the basis of spiritual entity lieth not within the measure of the corporeal senses. Nevertheless, Jehovih hath given thee comparisons; as a portrait of a man showeth his looks even after his corporeal body hath perished; and yet, the picture is but a representative. To the spirit, a corporeal body is but a representative, being a manifested production of a spirit.

8. As out of corporeal things a new thing is produced and born into the world, so out of Jehovih is born the spirit of man; neither leadeth the corporeal the spirit, nor the spirit the corporeal; but Jehovih doeth all. Think not, then, that when the corporeal body is dead and moldereth back to original elements, that in like manner the spirit of man will resolve itself back into Jehovih, for spirit is not bound by similar rules. As the corporeal body groweth by aggregating to itself, so not so groweth the spirit of man, but by the opposite, which is giving away.

9. Remember, O man, the more thou puttest forth thy soul to give light and wisdom to others, the more thou receivest; wherein thou shalt comprehend in the reason of things everlasting life to the spirit of man. So also, to him that desireth to comprehend Jehovih, let him describe the All Highest constantly. To him that desireth to comprehend the etherean worlds, the homes of spirits long risen in Nirvana, let him describe them. Fear not, O man, that thou shalt err; all the imagery thou canst devise is surpassed millions of times in the magnitude of the Father's kingdoms. Till thou canst shoot an arrow without striking the air, fear not for thy weak thoughts shooting amiss in Jehovih's worlds.

CHAPTER II.

1. I, Apollo, earth-born, of the continent Pan, submerged by Aph, the Orian Chief, by Jehovih's command, proclaim in the name of the Father, Creator of worlds, peace and wisdom unto all nations and tribes of men: First, against all vanity and self-conceit in the souls of men, wherein every cycle asserteth itself wise and great and learned, and the ancients, fools.

2. For the evidence of wisdom lieth not in learning one thing only, but in the adaptation of man to Jehovih and His works. In which measure, the modern and the ancient stand not upon their judgment in the matter, but by Jehovih's.

3. For if the ancient was not perfect in his place, neither art thou, O man, of this day. But before the Gods are all the ages adapted as Jehovih created them; judge not Him, for thy judgment is limited. That which was profitable to the soul of man, the Father revealed to the ancients; that which is profitable to the soul of man to-day, revealeth He this day.

4. For which reason I, His Son, am come to fulfill my labor, even as all men, in time, must complete that which hath been assigned them.

5. To rebuke vanity and self-conceit in them that perceive not wisdom in things long past, but applaud themselves without just measure before Jehovih. Wherein the Gods perceive their vanity, and pity them, hoping rather to exalt their minds, that they may learn to perceive the Father's hand manifested in all things.

6. Turn thine eyes inward, O man, and look at the spirit of things; make thyself as a God looking down on a new earth, where man hath been quickened into life and attained to strength and learning. Behold his palaces and temples; his work in stone and iron, and gold and silver; his knowledge of the sun and moon and stars; with written books to read; with clothes for the body and shoes for the feet. With great generals, and armies of soldiers; and with the land cultivated.

7. Are these civilized? And war abounding! By what right hast thou made thyself a judge, O man! Who hath measured the inhabitants of the earth and found them pure and wise? Do more people now live on the land in peace and happiness than in many of the cycles past? Because thou art different in many excellencies, thou shalt also remember that many great inventions are forgotten. The world hath been peopled over many times, and many times laid desolate.

8. Who hath been the chief enemy to man? Who is his chief enemy to-day? Is it not thyself? Think not, O man, that because a few people perceive the Higher Light the world is wise and good before the Gods. For in all ages there have been a few. Yea, to-day, there are a few more in number than in the ancient days. And this is the sum of the

enlightenment of the world.

9. Hear me, O man of earth, and ye angels of heaven: I proclaim harmony, symmetry and music. I am of the days of the fountain of these talents descending to mortals. I was as a shapely stone in Jehovih's edifice, and by hard toil a fashioner of the flesh mold of man and woman.

10. As the ear of one man heareth music, and he crieth out with delight: A tune! a tune! And as the ear of another man heareth music, and he cannot discern, and he crieth out: A noise! a hideous noise! Wherefore, then, shall ye not judge them, and say: The one hath an ear for music, and the other not? The one is one with the music; the other, being discordant himself, declareth there is no tune, but only noise. To which will ye give preference in judgment as to music?

11. Who hath not beholden Jehovih, the All Person? Who is it that crieth out: I behold Him not? No harmony, no symmetry, no music, no complete whole? And to which will ye give preference in judgment? Is not the judgment of the perceiver higher than he who perceiveth not?

12. This declare I of Jehovih, that in all ages there are many who perceive the All Person, and many who deny Him. If, then, the lack of an ear for music maketh a man dumb to a tune, is it not the lack of spiritual harmony that that causeth man to perceive not the everlasting presence of Jehovih, the All Person?

13. Hear me, O angels and men: Can a man learn to sing who heareth not the harmony of a tune? How much less, then, can man, or the spirits of the dead, harmonize with the Eternal Whole if they perceive Him not?

CHAPTER III.

1. I, Apollo, Jehovih's Son, proclaim an age when man on earth considered not harmony, nor symmetry, nor music, as Gods!

2. And Jehovih's voice came to me in the etherean firmament, and place of Pti'mus, saying:

3. Apollo, My Son, thou God of Su'ad, God of Don'ga, God of Tah, behold the red star, the earth, she cometh through thy dominions. Go thou to her with thy hosts, a sufficient number, and give her a new God, and call his name Apollo.

4. Behold, neither men nor angels on the red star comprehend the harmony of My works; and because of their own enharmony they deny Me, being blind to My Person. Go thou, My Son, and make them idolaters of harmony, symmetry and music, for a long season, that they may become organically attuned from the time of their birth upward.

5. I said: I perceive Thy wisdom, O Jehovih. And I called together a hundred millions of Thy sons and daughters, and told them what Thou hadst said. With one accord, they said: We have examined the red star since the time of Wan, and we perceive truly, the time hath come for thy labor, O Apollo.

6. I said: Send an oniy'yah to the heaven of the earth and deliver her God and Lords and all persons capable of the second resurrection. And say ye to God and his Lords: Thus saith Apollo, Son of Jehovih, and God of three etherean worlds: Greeting in the name of the Father, and love unto you all. For your glorious work I have assigned seven Teres and Don'ga. Thither gather ye your hosts, where is prepared a place of rest and comfort. The

earth and her heaven shall be left in darkness for thirty of her days, having neither God nor Lords.

7. So my legions departed for the earth in an etherean ship of fire, led by Tu'ain, Goddess of Proe'king, a place of great learning in the etherean mountains of Horatanad; and they delivered according to my decrees, and the earth was without a God and Lords for thirty days.

8. And the voice of Jehovih came to me again, saying: Hear thy Creator, O My Son, thou that sprangest from the land long since submerged, who has spanned many of My worlds, behold, the legions of Sue and his mighty resurrections are still preserved to mortals and angels earth-bound: Of the Gods and Goddesses who danced and sang before men; and of the uneven match betwixt spirits and Gods.

9. Profiting in this, the people of the red star have become rich in rites and ceremonies, and preferring the swift-footed to the slow, the nimble to the clumsy, the loo'is have well laid out the road to thy success.

10. So, I perceived beforehand how I should proceed when I landed in the lower heaven and her earth.

11. When the time came, I departed, still remembering my native star with well treasured pride. And that all things should express the labor Jehovih put upon me, my oniy'yah excelled in beauty all other etherean vessels that had ever descended to the earth.

12. How shall I comprehend Thy magnitude, O Jehovih? What is the journey of a God before Thee? We build a ship for a hundred millions, and are vain of its size and beauty; but when we launch out into Thy etherean realms, we fain would hide our faces in shame of our vanity. We sail through a thousand of Thy crystal worlds and talk of great distances, but the mirror of Thy boundless creation lieth still before us. We recall the red star, our native home, a single gem amidst the countless millions Thou hast cast into the universe, and we are speechless because of Thy Awful Extent.

13. Wherein hast Thou not excelled Thyself, O Jehovih! In one moment, we behold Thy Vastness; in another, Thy Microscopic Hand in the smallest ethe'ic wave, and in the spear of grass down on the swift corporeal stars. We applaud Thee for Thy handiwork, and yet ere our thoughts have overrun the smallest part, Thou turnest our eyes inward to the soul of things, an endless wonder.

14. How shall I comprehend Thy designs, O Jehovih? Thou drivest me back to the time Thy angels came and stood man upright, saying: Be thou a man; and be thou a woman! But they would not.

15. Again and again, Thy pitying hand stood them up, and Thy voice came, saying: Talk, O man! Come, thou shalt help to perfect thyself. But man was slow in perceiving wisdom; that which came to his flesh he loved.

16. I remember the earth, O Father! Men and women with long hair hanging down; and hands with claw nails, fierce and war-like. And hair in tufts and short-curled. Whose eyes were drawn down like a lion's, and mouth wide and falling open, like a dog that is tired.

17. Therefore Thou hast called me, O Jehovih; and I perceive Thy double purpose: For a man left alone would select and mate, and evolve to terrible war! And Thou storest here an idol to unfit him for cruel deeds.

18. So, from Thy etherean realms, wherein for fifty thousand years Thy Gods and Goddesses had trained me to comprehend the discipline of Thy created heavens, I came,

descending, down, down to the red star, where Thou first quickened me into being, that I might fulfill Thy mandates.

19. Thy hand took me up, Thy hand sent me down; I had learned not to fear; the tree of faith had grown in me; I knew the secret of All Power. As a mortal goeth into a dark cavern, where the air is damp and unacceptable to the nose, so came my hosts, O Jehovih, out of etherea into the vortex of the earth, the dull atmosphere.

20. Thy voice came to me, saying: Go around the earth with thy oniy'yah, My Son. Stir up the atmosphereans; they that know no higher heaven. Behold, they have mutinied against My God and Lords; have rejected My preferred wisdom. Their delight is in war and the deeds of mortals. As men on earth gather round to witness beasts in battle, so gather these countless millions of spirits to witness kingdoms of mortals in war, and fire, and plunder. And by their presence urge men to cruelty and cunning horrors.

CHAPTER IV.

1. Hear me, O man, and angels; from my words learn to be wise and deep perceiving. He who standeth in darkness, seeth not; the time of Jehovih, none can comprehend. In the Light should be the delight of all men. But who practiceth to his highest knowledge? Before my days, time was no nearer the beginning of the universe than now. There were men who believed that with death all would be ended to every man; and Jehovih sent angels to prove them in their folly; and though they saw them, and talked with them face to face, many would not believe.

2. And in the lower heaven they were the same; they would not believe in a higher heaven. And though ethereans came to them to prove them in their folly, and talked with them face to face, yet many would not believe.

3. I searched the disbelievers, to understand their souls; and I found they were begotten in enharmony. They prided themselves in their wisdom; but that that they called wisdom was as a serpent in the soul.

4. Jehovih spake to me, saying: Hear thy Creator, O My Son: In atmospherea thou shalt appoint ten thousand Lords, with ten thousand kingdoms; and the earth and the inhabitants thereof shall be divided between them.

5. And thou shalt build a new kingdom in heaven, and call it Gau, and it shall be thy judgment seat, with a Council of one hundred thousand men and women.

6. And all thy Lords shall be called Apollo! And they shall inspire men to make images of stone and wood. And the images shall have short arms and long legs; and nails instead of claws on the fingers, and well-formed mouths, with shape for motion of the cheeks.

7. And thy Lords shall find the loo'is who have been preparing these matters by birth; and the loo'is shall lead the angels around about amongst mortals, finding the most comely-formed men and women and young children. And when they have thus chosen them, they shall report the matter to the Lords, and they shall send ethereans to those mortals who are selected, and they shall be quickened by signs and miracles.

8. And it shall be proven before all the nations of the earth, and their kings and queens and governors, that the comeliness of the forms are pleasant in My sight, wherefore I come to them. And those who are thus selected shall sing and dance by entrancement; so that kings and queens shall be overcome by the achievements. And those that dance shall

be made to float in the air, and sail about in the dance.

9. For I will turn the judgment of man to beautify himself; and, in so doing, he shall learn to perceive beauty and harmony in My works.

CHAPTER V.

1. Think not, O man, the Gods always deliver the nations of the earth in a day or by miracles. They go to the foundation of a matter; they make man a servant to help deliver himself. They stir up the nations in rites and ceremonies first; then come after, and appropriate the rites and ceremonies. And the women look on, receiving the spirit of the matter in their souls, the which entaileth on their offspring that which is desired by the Gods.

2. With the hosts of high heaven, unseen by mortals, the Lords stir up the whole world. In one generation, behold, a new race is born. Man is unfitted for dangerous war, and no longer the delight of drujas hanging around. And the drujas, and the familiars, turn from the peaceful earth (to them stale and unprofitable in bloody entertainments), to find their own petty kingdoms broken down and gone.

3. Be wise, O man, and ye angels of earth! Hear the voice of thy brother, God of three worlds! I will tell thee a great secret: These are the words of thy Creator: Man and woman are pro-creators! Whom they beget, are theirs, saith Jehovih. Not for a day, but forever! Take heed of thy offspring, O woman! Take heed, O man! Wilt thou be entailed with druj, to pull thee down? Wilt thou choose offspring to glorify Jehovih?

4. Have not thy people boasted, O earth? Have they not said: O the poor ancients! What of them? Will they turn away from the idols of Apollo, and set up on their own account? Can the people hand down a name and models to live forever?

5. So I founded Gau in the place Hored had been, extending over Jaffeth, Shem and Ham; and the rest of the atmospherean heaven I divided amongst my ten thousand Lords and Lordesses, whom I selected and ordained in the manner of the ancients.

6. And the Lords established themselves in kingdoms, both on earth and in heaven. And they inspired kings and queens to erect images in the temples, and the images were given a name signifying Harmony, Symmetry and Music (Apollo). And the names varied in many countries, because of the languages of the people; but the significance was that these three entities comprised the All Light, the Creator, Jehovih!

7. And mortals were taught by the inspiration of angels how to make the images, for there were no corporeans sufficiently perfect for models.

8. According to the perfection of the images, so were they reckoned favored by Jehovih; and the sign of Jehovih's approval was manifested in the time of the sacred dance given by the su'is selected; which was, if the whirling dance caused many women to fall down by enchantment, then was Jehovih pleased.

9. Hear me, O man. The enchantment of the women was what the Lords desired, for the impression of the soul of woman shapeth the unborn child.

10. Wherefore, they worshipped blindly before the idols, not being sufficiently wise to understand how Jehovih was laying down the foundation for the coming race.

11. O ye of little wisdom, compared with the Lords of heaven! How ye are puffed up in judgment, not knowing the race whence ye sprang! Jehovih's Gods and Lords mold the

inhabitants of the earth as clay is molded in a potter's hand. They set them up and show them the way, and say to them: Go!

12. And mortals go on a little while, like a young child that tottereth and falleth. And again the Lords set them up; and man, in ingratitude, forgetteth and denieth his God.

13. The unseen angels lead man and woman together, and say: Marry! And they wed, and bring forth of the Lord. Then man inquireth: What meanest thou: Bring forth of the Lord? But his judgment is under a cloud; he flattereth himself that Jehovih created him, and then went away; and since then he hath been his own master!

14. O man, what is thy folly! How has thou found such cunning ways to put off thy Creator? What profit more hast thou to put Him away than to try and perceive Him in all things? Why wilt thou sing of man who is in darkness, and of the earth, which is but a fraction of the Great I Am? Hopest thou not for wisdom, so that guardian angels may go away and rest?

15. Why shall they stand over thee day and night, to keep away familiars and fetals and drujas? Who shall close thy mouth against falsehold, and thy lips against cursing thy Creator? Hopest thou not, O man, that a wiser age will follow? When shall man learn harmony, symmetry and music? Who will hire a musician that forever putteth his instrument out of tune? Why shall the Gods applaud men or angels who live not attuned to the All Highest?

16. Show me one who is as good as he understandeth to be; that liveth as wisely as his goodness desireth he should. He will understand my words; I can come to him and inspire him with great wisdom. He will comprehend the love a God hath over mortals; and the patience of the toiling Lords and angels.

17. Hear me, O man! I will answer thee a great matter: The angels of heaven who are good, labor for those beneath them. This is their work, day and night. Think not that they go away to idleness forever. To the etherean, industry becometh rest; to those who have attained to be Gods there is spontaneous growth forever. Remember this and be wise. To the atmospherean and to mortals, idleness of soul leadeth downward forever! Remember this also, and be wise.

18. Behold the rose and the lily; they are perfect in their order. Being one with Jehovih, they painted not themselves. Let thy soul practice with thy Creator, and thou shalt become one with Him, even His Son. Find thou the symmetry of flesh, the symmetry of the spirit; the harmony of music, and consider wisely thy behavior.

19. The star of Jehovih is within thy soul; feed it, O man, and thou, O angel of heaven, and it will grow to be a God! Rob it, or starve it, and thou shalt remain nothing. It is weak and dim in the vain; it is bright and of great power in him who forgetteth himself in laboring for others.

CHAPTER VI.

1. Jehovih spake in the light of the throne of Gau, saying: My Son, thou has set the temples of earth wisely, and thy ten thousand Lords have the voice of thy Creator. But, behold, this dawn of dan hath but five years and two hundred days. The five years are already gone. Call together thy etherean hosts, and they shall report to thee who shall be the successors to thee and thy Lords. I answered, saying: Thy will be done, O Father!

2. So I sent messengers around about the world repeating what Jehovih had commanded. And I added also: When the time of dan is completed, behold, my hosts shall assemble in Gau, from whence we shall ascend to our etherean worlds. Let my messengers invite all the people in all the kingdoms of atmospherea to be present. And these things were done.

3. Now, of the ten thousand kingdoms of the Lords of heaven and earth of that day, many of them held their places within the corporeal temples of worship, having spiritual thrones within them, where the hosts of angels assembled to counsel on the affairs of mortals, and to advise with them through the prophets and seers.

4. Neither was there a temple in all the world for consulting the spirits and Gods but what was usurped by my etherean hosts. So that when kings or queens came to consult the oracle on matters of war or personal aggrandizement, my hosts answered them not to their own profit, but with the voice of Jehovih.

5. So it turned out, that when the chief false Gods and false Lords were driven out of the corporeal temples, they lost interest in mortal affairs. And I classified them and made new kingdoms in the lower heaven for them, forming them into confederacies. And they, too, became earnest workers to establish themselves in harmony, symmetry and music. And at the end of the time of hi'dan there was not one false God nor false Lord in atmospherea.

CHAPTER VII.

1. Apollo said: Hear the decrees of Jehovih, O ye Gods and Lords: I, His Son, God of three worlds, speak! In my speech lieth the wisdom of Time; the evidence of fifty thousand years. Here is a great matter, O ye Gods; answer it, O ye Lords of heaven and earth: A child learneth from that which is around about; a man learneth from that which is around about; a God and a Lord learn from that which is around about. Neither can they acquire anything more, forever. Jehovih saith:

2. I have decreed the breaking up of old foundations; in new creations I provide food for the souls of Gods and men.

3. Apollo said: To condense and to expand; to expand and to condense, is this all? Who shall fashion a corporeal world by compressing ether? or, by standing still, expand his own soul? How long will they be entailed with idle desires, and self-ease, and self-glory?

4. Jehovih saith: When the lower heaven turneth into itself, it soon turneth downward, also. And its cast moldeth the earth-born. Look to it, O My sons and daughters, that ye preserve the high estate of heaven. Apollo said:

5. To be a God is not all; to be a Lord is not all; ye shall forever invent new stratagems in Jehovih's kingdoms. Your people shall be forever infatuated with continual surprises, or your kingdoms in heaven will go down.

6. Jehovih saith: Behold, I created man, and if he rest constantly, disease shall seize on his life parts. The kingdoms of men on earth that lack aspiration for the people shall bring destruction; to the kingdoms in the lower heaven, the lack of invented, new glories, shall breed up false Gods and false Lords.

7. Apollo said: To be a weak man, is nothing; to be a weak king, is nothing; to be a weak God, is nothing; but to be strong with Jehovih, furnisheth food for the kingdoms of men and angels. Think not, ye Gods and Lords, that to be a good God is easy, or to be a good Lord is easy, or to be a good corporeal king is easy. He who ruleth in heavenly kingdoms,

must forever furnish food for the souls of angels and men.

8. I, Apollo, Son of Jehovih, will give you a parable suitable for Gods and kings: A multitude go into a forest; one man goeth a little before the rest, and he calleth: Here! Here! Then he goeth a little further, and he calleth: Here! Here! And the multitude follow. Whereon, ye reason well, saying: If the leader go too fast for the multitude, they will not follow; and if he go not fast enough, they cannot follow. Wherein, of the last condition, anarchy ensueth, and new leaders are chosen.

9. And these conditions follow all peoples on earth, and in the lower heavens. But the glory of the emancipated heavens, in etherea, lieth in the development of every soul into ripeness and bloom, with none too fast nor too slow, but all as one, and one with Jehovih.

10. Is not this the testimony of the All Person: A ruler of a city; a ruler of a state; a ruler of a kingdom? Without a head to lead, and to govern, what people have been found? Without a God and Lords, and kingdoms in heaven, what angels are found? Strollers, beggars, drujas and vampires. He who setteth himself up against the king, what is he? He who setteth himself up against the All Person, what is he? Where is the fruit he hath brought to market?

11. His speech is cunning in denial; his arguments for liberty, the bait of hada. He crieth out, in justification of his mutiny: Liberty! Liberty! But he leadeth to inharmony and darkness. After that, he rusheth to the front, crying out: Follow me! follow me! I will lead to truth and light. And he himself becometh a God, but in falsehood, even as by falsehood he denied the true God.

12. A great fact declare I unto you, O Gods and Lords: A line lieth betwixt the man who hath too much opinion of his own, and he who hath no opinion at all. One is to be pitied, the other censured. Which, judge ye, do the Gods pity of these two, and which censure?

13. None could answer Apollo. So he spake further, saying: Pity ye him who hath too much opinion of his own; for of all men he standest the farthest from Jehovih. But the wise man and wise angel follow the median line betwixt the two. Herein lieth the harmony of a man's soul.

CHAPTER VIII.

1. Apollo, Son of Jehovih, said: In Jehovih's name speak I, Apollo, God of etherea. Hear me, O ye Gods and Lords; the power of the Father resteth in my soul; my words are of All Wisdom. Think of this great matter: The growth of love! As a man loveth his city and his country, what think ye Apollo hath forgotten? Have I not told it in etherea? I sprang from the red star, the earth!

2. Wherefore shall I not take pride before Jehovih? And hold up my head in etherea, where I have neighbors that sprang from other stars. Shall a man forget his love because he is a God? Nay, verily. When I was mortal, I loved my neighbors; when I entered the second resurrection, in atmospherea, I loved all the people of the earth; and when I rose to etherea, my love expanded to a thousand worlds. But, of all places, how can I make the earth and her heaven second in the love of my soul?

3. As a mother inventeth diversions and employment for her children, shall I not gather fruit from Jehovih's repositories to feed the atmospherean heavens? I came, and found ye in a dark forest, with briars and thorns; but, behold, now, O ye Gods and Lords! The

lower heaven hath become a paradise.

4. Let me recall the philosophies I have overthrown: The false Gods and false Lords said: It is well that there be war and destruction in heaven; otherwise, it would soon be too full! For they saw not the higher heavens; their arguments were framed in a dark corner. And, because of their evil inspiration, they gave mortals the same philosophy, saying: War is justifiable, lest the earth become too full. For these dark angels shut out from mortals the higher light of Faith in Jehovih. Justifying themselves in war, and the slaying of whom Jehovih had created alive; by their behavior, thrusting condemnation in Jehovih's face for what Jehovih had done!

5. Neither knew these mortal philosophers that they were under the inspiration of spirits of darkness; nor would they wait till the earth was full of people, to prove whether their philosophy was true or false.

6. For, as ye of heaven were given to deeds of darkness, your kingdoms reacted on earth, making druks out of men and women. From which have all these heavens turned from evil ways, and become as stars of glory in Jehovih's universe.

7. Think not that only great thunders and terrible stratagems can govern heaven and earth righteously; for, as one man, in an army, may cause a panic; or one brave man's upraised hand lead a nation on to victory, so can ye, O Gods and Lords, by wisdom, in the smallest of Jehovih's plans, rule over heaven and earth, for the glory of His everlasting kingdoms.

8. That which I declare unto you, go ye and declare throughout heaven; for the fruit of your teaching shall enrich the earth people, through their guardian spirits; and they shall, likewise, go about preaching amongst themselves.

CHAPTER IX.

1. When Apollo, Jehovih's Son, had finished his labor, the dawn of dan, God foresaw that his own resurrection, and his people with him, had come. So he sent his proper officers to the libraries of atmospherea, to learn who of all the etherean hosts should be selected to remain as God, and who as Lords, for the next four hundred years.

2. In twenty days the examiners returned and came before the throne of God, and the Council of Gau. Za'dukawaski, chief speaker, said: By the grace of Jehovih, Creator, we stand before thee, God of heaven and earth. We find, by the ancient precepts, adjudged wise in the foundation of atmospherea, one Gur, highest and most proficient of all the hosts of heaven, to be anointed God for the next four hundred years.

3. God said: I remember Gur, from Magel, in Sooftus, in etherea, God of Ra'yatuf and a'ji, seventy-two. Let the marshals go to him and acquaint him with Jehovih's decrees, in the name of God. And they shall provide suitable conveyance for Gur to come to Gau, according to his rate.

4. So the marshals, ten thousand in number, besides ten thousand musicians, went and brought Gur before the throne of God, coming in an otevan, prepared for the purpose, and adorned with one thousand pillars of light.

5. God said: I salute thee, O Gur, in the name of Jehovih, Creator. Behold Apollo!

6. Apollo stretched forth his hand, and Gur came and shook hands with him, standing by the throne. Gur said: That I have lived to see this day, O Jehovih, I am blessed indeed! Thy will, O God, and Jehovih's, be done!

7. God said: Behold, the dawn of dan is within thirty days to end, and all who choose, and are prepared for the third resurrection, shall be taken up to etherea. Besides thyself, O Gur, there are two hundred thousand ethereans who have volunteered to remain another four hundred years in these atmospherean heavens, and on the earth. From them thou shalt select one thousand Lords, and bestow them with kingdoms, over mortals. Two thousand millions of angels will raise up with me to etherea.

8. To thee, O Gur, I bequeath two thousand millions of atmosphereans who have been initiated in the second resurrection. And of the first resurrection, two hundred and fifty millions; and of fetals, three hundred millions; and besides these, the inhabitants of the earth (men, women and children) seven hundred millions.

9. God ceased speaking, and Gur said: Thy will be done, O Jehovih! Thereupon the es'enaurs sang, and the trumpeters played the MARCH OF APOLLO, JEHOVIH'S SON. Presently, the marshals and messengers filed before the throne; and a light of golden fire came down from etherea, cast out by the Gods of Helmatia, Orian arc of Tanaya, and it fell about the throne of God, so that many could not look thereon, because of the brilliancy.

10. God raised up, and Apollo by his side. God said: I stretch forth my hand unto Thee, O Jehovih! Behold Thy Son, Gur, God of Ra'yatuf, in etherea, an earth-born, forty thousand years inhabitant of Thy emancipated realms. By Thy power, and in Thy name, O Jehovih, I proclaim him God of heaven and earth, to bestow Thee and Thy kingdoms on angels and men! Be with him, O Father, Creator, that he may add unto Thy glory, forever! Amen!

11. God took off the triangle, and hung it on Gur's (God's) neck, saying: I now bestow thee with the heirloom of the Gods of the red star, the triangle of the ancients. And that thou mayest be still further honored, behold, one higher than I, even Apollo, shall weave a crown for thy head.

12. Apollo walked to the left hand, and raised his hand upward, and there came from unseen space a flame of yellow light, and lodged on his hand, and he turned it but half around, and lo, a crown with sparkling gems stood upon his fingers' ends. Apollo said:

13. Incomprehensible All Light! Weave me a crown for Thy Son, God of heaven and earth! And even whilst he spake, it was done, and he placed it on God's (Gur's) head. And God went and sat in the midst of the throne, saying: Throne of Thy throne, O Jehovih! All things are Thine! For my resting-place, to do Thy will, this shall be.

14. During the ceremonies, the music was timed accordingly; and when the new God was crowned, the multitude of a thousand millions applauded with great joy.

15. When all was quiet, God rose up from the throne, saying to Apollo and to him who had been God: In Jehovih's name, come and honor my throne! Accordingly, they both sat down on the right hand of God.

16. God said: In thirty days the dawn of dan will end. Let the marshals, through the messengers, proclaim the resurrection of two thousand millions to the etherean heavens on that day. Proclaim it in all the heavens of the earth; inviting all to come who can; for it shall be a day of the feast of glory. But say not to any one that there hath been a change of Gods, nor that great Apollo will rise also, lest sorrow come upon the people. The marshals then selected messengers, a great number, and sent them throughout the heavens of the earth, proclaiming the commandments of God.

17. God spake further, saying: For thirty days shall the Council deliberate on my ten

thousand Lords, selecting and allotting them; and I will crown them in the name of the Father.

18. Apollo then said: Now will I clothe myself in strange colors, that none shall know me, and during the thirty days I yet tarry, I will go around about the earth, that I may again look upon the star of my birth.

19. And he who had given up the throne said: Thy joy shall be my joy also. I, too, will again visit the star of my birth.

20. Accordingly, God said: Joy be unto ye twain, in Jehovih's name! Behold, I will throw a thick blanket over the throne, and ye shall change your attire, and when I withdraw it, ye shall walk forth unknown.

21. And this was done.

CHAPTER X..

1. So Apollo visited all the divisions of the earth, and the islands in the ocean; and his traveling attendants, companions and officers made a record of all things they saw, especially those relating to the corporeans; their manners, sizes, color, habits, education and procreative capacities; and the records were taken with them, to be finally carried to etherea in the coming ascent.

2. And Apollo and his companions then visited atmospherea, making like observations of the people in the first and second resurrections, recording the number and kind of nurseries, hospitals, factories, schools and colleges, together with the asaphs, teachers and physicians, nurses, and so on. And this record was also prepared so as to form a brief history of the earth's heaven.

3. On the twenty-eighth day, Apollo and his hosts returned to Gau, the place of the throne of God in the lower heaven. In the meantime, the word of God commanding the assembly for the ascent of two thousand million of Jehovih's Brides and Bridegrooms, had aroused the people of the lower heaven beyond measure; millions of them never having witnessed an ascent, nor, in fact, had seen an etherean adavaysit, a ship of fire.

4. On the twenty-ninth day, in the evening, a light was seen high up in the firmament, and to the north-west, brilliant, like a star of the first magnitude. Presently, it grew larger and brighter, and shot across toward the south-west firmament, and then began to ascend toward the earth, growing larger and brighter as it came.

5. The people of the lower heaven knew it was the adavaysit of the third resurrection, and they rejoiced before Jehovih, singing and praying. And now the marshals and proper persons for the purpose, commenced to form the groups of Brides and Bridegrooms of Jehovih. And the groups were arrayed in stars, crescents, squares and circles and ovals, being classified according to their rates in these figures; and the groups had banners, and signals of colored lights, according to their rank in love or intelligence, or good works, or other characteristic virtues.

6. And these groups were arranged into combinations, every combination representing the work done by a sub-Lord or sub-God. And these combinations were again formed into four divisions, representing the four great divisions of the earth, and the four Lords, Jehovih's Sons. So that when the whole two thousand millions of spirits were in due form, they characterized Harmony, Symmetry and Music, being the symbol

of Apollo, Son of Jehovih, God of three etherean worlds, brevet Orian Chief.

7. At midnight, the sea of fire, the adavaysit, reached Chinvat, the border of the earth's vortex, just beyond the orbit of the moon, and in size twice the moon's diameter. Here the ship halted for four hours, and then again began to descend, and rapidly, fearful to behold, becoming more scarlet within the vortex, but growing larger and definite in figure.

8. And, lo and behold, when the adavaysit drew near, it was in the form and figure of the groups of Brides and Bridegrooms of Jehovih. It had fifty thousand curtains, and one hundred thousand banners, and the hosts within the ship, seven millions of souls, bore each a streamer of phosphorescent light, of all colors, shades and tints, and arrayed in symbols of the name, Apollo.

9. Unlike all other etherean ships of fire that had as yet visited the earth's heavens, it was provided with openings in the bottom, five hundred thousand in number, which were the places of entrance and exit. And the openings were studded with crystals of ceaseless fire, of all conceivable colors, shades and tints, and sizes and figures, curves, circles, angles, crescents, and so on. And up within the openings, were the crystal and opaque chambers, provided for the heirs of the third resurrection. And yet, within these chambers, were the reports of the guardian angels, of the lives and good work heretofore done by every man and woman of all the two thousand million who were to ascend to Jehovih's higher heavens. But in all the records there was not recorded one evil thing, or dark deed, or selfish thought; for of these things the ascended hosts had long since purged themselves, till they were gems of the pure light of the Father of all. High up within the ship were the beams and net-work of timber and ropes and arches; and around about the whole ship was the photosphere of its power, so that the whole adavaysit was like a crystal ship within a globe of phosphorescent light; and yet, in fact, the ship was the true light, and the angels the light of that light, whilst the photosphere was really the shell of darkness made reflective.

10. This, then, was the size of the adavaysit; two thousand miles, east and west, and north and south, diameters; and seven thousand miles high. And the ship within it was one hundred miles, east and west, and north and south, diameters; and two hundred miles high.

11. As the earth is opaque, with a transparent vortex around it, so not so, but opposite, is the structure of an etherean adavaysit, being light and habitable within as well as without, like the etherean worlds in the firmament. As Jehovih maketh worlds, and sendeth them forth in the places of His firmament, so, in imitation of Him, His etherean Gods and Goddesses make adavaysits to traverse space from star to star, and from one etherean region to another. Great in wisdom and power are Jehovih's etherean Gods and Goddesses! Yet they, too, were once but men and women, with corporeal bodies.

12. Jehovih said: I have given power to spirits of the newly dead to clothe themselves from the atmosphere with corporeal semblances of flesh and blood; and, to My exalted atmospherean angels, I have given power to clothe themselves from ethe in forms of light. But, to My exalted etherean angels, I have given power to clothe their hosts with ships of fire, and otevans, and adavaysits.

169

CHAPTER XI.

1. Cventi, marshalless for the hosts of Apollo, with ten thousand marshals and fifty thousand respondents of ceremonies, made ready to receive the hosts of the adavaysits, commanded by Cim'iad, Goddess of Du'e'ghi, in etherea, Goddess of Noad and Rak, in ji'ya, thirty-eight, well known to Apollo, and to Phaeja, God of Norse, long residents of Um, in etherea.

2. Cim'iad was a small woman, dark, and of deep love, most jovial of Goddesses; and had long looked forward with joy to her pleasure of bringing so large a ship to deliver two thousand million of Jehovih's Brides and Bridegrooms into etherean worlds. And so, when the adavaysit was about to land in Gau, Cim'iad looked out from the clusters of central stars, the ornaments of the throne within the ship, to see the hosts who were assembled beneath, and joyously clapped her hands with delight, whereupon she was saluted by Apollo and Phaeja, and by God and his Lords.

3. Presently, the mighty vessel landed and anchored fast; and the ship of Apollo was moved up aside and made fast to the adavaysit. Meantime, Cim'iad came forth out of the ship, and was received in the arms of Cventi, marshalless of Apollo, and then proceeded to the throne of God.

4. All the while, the musicians had been playing and singing; and the music of the lower heaven was thus united with the music of the upper heaven.

5. God said: Welcome, O Daughter of Jehovih! Come thou and honor my throne, in His name!

6. Cim'iad said: By the grace and love of Jehovih, am I come, O God! And to thee, O Apollo, most wonderful of earth-born Gods, how can I express my boundless love! And to thee, O Phaeja, long-enduring Son of Jehovih, my soul is as a twin, for the glory of our Everlasting Creator!

7. Behold, I am come in Jehovih's name to wed these two thousand million Brides and Bridegrooms to Jehovih!

8. Phaeja said: Thy will and Jehovih's be done! And now they shook hands, as is the custom of Gods and Goddesses, and Cim'iad went and sat on the throne, saluting all the assemblage by making the sign of Jehovih's name with her right hand, which was answered by three thousand million spirits. And now the musicians played and sang the STARS OF JEHOVIH! Meanwhile, the All Light began to descend thick and fast on Cim'iad's head, so brilliant that many could not look thereon.

9. And Jehovih spake through Cim'iad, saying: I blow My breath upon a corporeal world, and man springeth forth into life, the highest of My created lights. In the womb of Mi, I fashion his spirit. When he is shapely and white, I deliver him. I open the heaven of suns, and warm his soul. Brighter than diamonds he cometh forth; male and female come they; as stars for My everlasting worlds. Dressed as Brides and Bridegrooms for My chambers of Light and Love. In My arms shall they be blessed forever; in My mansions rejoice forever.

10. The respondents said (being led by the etherean hosts): I am thy bride (or bridegroom), O Jehovih! My soul findeth love in Thee only, forever!

11. Thou, my Father, O Jehovih! I come to Thee to abide forever!

12. From Mi, my mother, the earth, who conceived me, I rise me up and go, forever.

13. All praise to Thee, O Jehovih! And to thee, O God of earth and heaven! And to ye, O Lords of the earth, praise forever!

14. Thy Lords, O Jehovih, raised me up. How can I render them joy for my stubbornness of heart! And Thy God, for my second resurrection.

15. How hast Thou made us brothers and sisters, O Jehovih! And given to me a higher world to abide in, forever!

16. O, Joy of my soul! To Thee am I beholden, O Father, Everlasting Creator!

17. Jehovih said: Behold Me, O Brides and Bridegrooms! I am the All that is Within All, and Over All. Members of My body are all things under the sun, seen and unseen, boundless, forever! I give them to you for your inheritance, forever!

18. Response: Who can give like unto Thee, O Jehovih! Not only gavest Thou myself, but sent Thy Gods and Lords to me to teach me how to live to enjoy Thy Fullness, forever!

19. I will rise to Thy immortal kingdoms, and learn the mysteries of Thy glory and wisdom, O Jehovih! And when I am strong, I will go forth to them who are beneath me, and raise them up, to rejoice, forever!

20. Jehovih said: Laborers with Me; helpmates and companions, forever! With ye I wed, from everlasting to everlasting.

21. Response: With Thee we wed, helpmates, forever! In the glory of Thy worlds, without end!

22. Jehovih said: Mine are All Harmony; All Symmetry; All Love; and will endure forever!

23. Response: When I was in darkness, I fed on hate, and anger, and war, and lust. But Thou hast taught me harmony, and symmetry, and love, and I shall indulge in them forever!

24. Jehovih said: Receive ye, My mantles and My crowns, O My beloved! The darkness is come and gone; the rain is dried up, and My flowers are blooming for you, My beloved!

25. Response: Glory be to Thee, My Creator and Preserver! All hail to Thy Wondrous Works, O Jehovih! In all my giving I cannot attain to Thee, forever! Thy Crown shall shine in my behavior, world without end! Amen! Amen! Amen!

26. Jehovih, Thou art mine, forever! Amen!

27. I am Thine, O Jehovih, forever! Amen! Amen!

CHAPTER XII.

1. The rites of the resurrection were completed, the whole of which would make a book, were the words written down; and as for the music, for which there were five hundred thousand singers and players, scarce a conception of it can be given to mortals. And when the light of the throne of God broke away a little, God announced six hours' recreation; whereupon, all the angels of Gau and of the etherean heavens, mingled together joyfully.

2. And after this (for, behold, the end of the dawn of dan had come), Apollo, mightiest of all, rose up, and waved his hand in the sign, IN JEHOVIH'S NAME! and stood aside from the throne of God. After Apollo, Cim'iad rose up, and gave the same sign; followed by Phaeja. And when these three stood aside, high raised, on the floor of the throne, so that all the assembled millions could see them, so hushed were all things, like as if Time had

come to an end.

3. Then filed in front the ten thousand Lords and Lordesses, they who had once been false Gods and false Lords, and, of the ancient times, arrayed in such gorgeous attire; now robed in plain white, and without ornaments.

4. The marshals opened the arches of the adavaysit, but yet not a soul moved from his or her place.

5. Then great Apollo, and Cim'iad, and Phaeja, came down and sat at the foot of the throne, more loved than all the Gods who had as yet visited the earth and her heavens.

6. God came down from the throne and took Apollo's hand, saying: Arise, O Son of Jehovih, and go thy way. Apollo rose up, himself in tears, and stood aside. God now took the hand of Cim'iad, saying: Arise, O Daughter of Jehovih, and go thy way. Next he raised up the long-tried Phaeja, when lo, both he and God burst into tears, and fell in each other's arms! Phaeja, of few words at most, was last to slack the fond embrace; and then he and great Apollo, and Cim'iad, light of heaven, broke loose and marched forth to the etherean ship of fire. God resumed the throne, blinded by his tears.

7. Now fell the mantles of Jehovih, and His crowns, on the two thousand million Brides and Bridegrooms. The awakening Light of the etherean firmament bespoke Jehovih's Awful Presence! The hosts moved with one accord, and presently entered into the adavaysit, amidst a shower of etherean flowers.

8. The marshals signaled, for the dawn was ended. The bright Cim'iad stretched forth her slender hand and arm to Jehovih, saying: By Thy Power, O Father, I command! Arise! Arise! Ad-av-ay-sit! Arise!

9. And the mighty vessel, and the vessel of Apollo, adjoined, arose up from Gau, rocking, rising, and moving to the music of a million trumpeters and singers, joined by the es'enaurs of the lower heavens. Higher and higher rose the etherean fire-ships, turning and rising, passing beyond the vortex of the earth, beyond Chinvat, out into the firmament of etherea, higher and higher, till all was lost in the distance.

CHAPTER XIII.

1. Jehovih spake in the light of the throne of God, saying: To the Council of Gau, heaven of My Heaven! Hear ye the words of your Creator, O My beloved: Sing songs to Apollo and his Lords; let my people rejoice; for the Glory of My Son is upon them.

2. From My kingdom is the Light and the Life; out of My Wisdom Apollo hath come. Sing to him, O ye Lords of heaven; let My angels rejoice in his name, for he shall abide forever.

3. Created I him for the glory of angels and men; in his idols and images shall My people behold the harmony of My beloved. With Mine Own hands, molded I the ankles and feet, and well-rounded thighs. Behold the arms of My Son, no longer than to the thighs, and with dimples, and small wrists.

4. His neck is straight and slender, and smooth and round, like the higin on an altar; and his shoulders like hewn stone, polished and tapering, like a woman's, who goeth not to war.

5. His instep is high; he can spring like a deer, swift as the wind. He sitteth not on his haunches all day, with his hands down, like a druk that is tired, waiting for food. He

fleeth to the plain and the forest on his swift feet.

6. Proclaim ye Apollo in heaven and on earth. He is risen! Higher than the sun is the Holy Begotten of Jehovih! Out of the Virgin Mi is he come, Holy; in symmetry and music, there is none like Apollo.

7. She was My betrothed from the foundation of the world; Spouse of your Creator, O God! Her name was Mi, Mother of Mine Holy Begotten Son.

8. They were without shapeliness before Me; they lolled about on earth; they lolled in heaven; on their haunches waited they hungrily.

9. The Virgin bowed down; for her first-born was the Redeemer of the world. In stone, and wood, and copper, and gold, and silver, is he stronger than ten cities; and wiser than ten thousand men.

10. He cometh to the young mother's dream, and shapeth her unborn, with limbs like a racer, and with long hair on the head. He standeth in the idol, and knoweth the Mother's prayer every day. Who calleth on the name, Apollo, calleth on the Father, Creator of all things.

11. Blessed are the Lords of Apollo; blessed are the sons and daughters of Apollo; blessed are they that bring forth in shapeliness like My Son, Apollo.

12. This mark have I put up before all women under the sun; the young women before marriage; and before the young men before marriage.

13. Choose ye of them in the likeness of Apollo; your heirs shall glorify your Creator.

14. Apollo is My judge; he sitteth on My right hand; swifter than an arrow is his judgment on a woman's first-born.

CHAPTER XIV.

1. Jehovih spake from the light of the throne of God, saying: Hear the words of your Creator, O ye Counselors of heaven.

2. They spin and weave and make clothes; they learn in the places of learning; neither do I condemn them.

3. But My physicians are tired; My nurses are tired; My teachers are tired. Be wise, O My Sons and Daughters. Who hath reformed a beggar by giving to him? What physician preventeth sickness by healing?

4. They bring forth in deformity on the earth, and ye must cure them in heaven. They squat on their haunches on earth, and they squat the same way in heaven, and ye must cure them.

5. Go ye to the root of the matter, O My beloved. Send ye down to the kingdoms of My Lords, and say to them: Thus saith Jehovih: Follow them, O My Lords! Double the number of ashars, double the loo'is; leave no young man alone; leave no young woman alone. Keep over them day and night; give them visions and dreams of Apollo. For I am concerted in heaven and on earth to remold the forms of the earth-born.

6. Jehovih said: Hear your Creator, O Gau! Make seven more plateaux for the second resurrection. Out of the idolatry of My Son, Apollo, will I beautify the inhabitants of the earth. And the cast and mold of men and of women shall become a great power.

7. Jealousies will overspread the earth; jealousies will rise in the first resurrection. Make seven more plateaux in the second resurrection, and sort the es'yans in the hour of birth.

8. God and the Council perceived; and so God appointed workmen, and fulfilled the commandments of Jehovih. And he established seven hundred tributary kingdoms of the second resurrection belonging to Gau.

9. These sub-kingdoms were provided with sub-Gods, second in rank below the Lords, of whom there were ten thousand who had direct supervision over mortals; and the Lords had every one a sufficiency of guardian angels, ashars, and loo'is, masters of generations, so that they could direct any required number to such mortals as they chose.

10. The Lords mostly established their heavenly kingdoms in the temples where mortals came to worship; and by inspiration, they established spirit chambers near the altars, where the prophets sat to learn the decrees of the Lord. Hither the loo'is came to receive their appointments over mortals, for the purpose of bringing about marriages acceptable before Jehovih.

11. The affairs of the sub-Gods were, however, wholly with matters in heaven, save when commanded by the Lords for special work.

12. And it came to pass that mortals, and the affairs of mortals, were directed and governed by the decrees of the lower heavens, and these again by the etherean heavens, which were of Jehovih direct.

13. So Jehovih changed the forms of the earth-born; but they became worshippers of Apollo; accrediting to one another Jehovih's perfection in them, according to the form and figure of the flesh. And because of the idolatry of the women for Apollo, their children were born of good flesh, and shapely; so that, in four hundred years, the hair on their heads grew long and straight, and men began to have beards. Neither considered any young man any virtue in a young woman so important as her form; nor did young women value any virtue in man so great as a well-molded form.

14. And when mortals died, and their spirits entered the first resurrection, half the labor of the asaphs, the receiving angels, was accomplished.

15. So God changed the es'yan period to three years, save for the heirs of cousins, and uncles, and aunts, which was left at five years.

CHAPTER XV.

1. So perfect was the way of heaven, that, at the end of four hundred years, God and his Lords, and his sub-Gods, had ready for the third resurrection, of grade eighty-eight, eight and a half thousand million souls for Jehovih's harvest.

2. So Apollo sent Adova, division Goddess of Reth, in Coak, in etherea, down to the lower heaven, to deliver God and his hosts. And they were thus raised up to etherea in a sea of fire, and made one with Jehovih.

3. In like manner, was the next government in the lower heaven and on the earth; and the next deliverance in dan was ten thousand million souls, of grade sixty-five.

4. In like manner was the next administration in the lower heaven and on the earth, and the deliverance was ten thousand millions, of grade fifty.

5. In like manner was the next administration on the earth and in the lower heaven, and the deliverance was ten thousand millions, of grade thirty-eight. So Apollo commanded these to be delivered in the a'ji'an fields of Oth, in Sanak and Orant, for they were unsuited for etherea.

6. In like manner was the next administration in the lower heaven and on the earth, and the deliverance was sixteen thousand millions; but they were of grade twenty-four. So Apollo commanded them to be delivered in the nebulous straits of Koppawotchiakka, for further development.

7. In like manner was the next administration in the lower heaven, but not so on the earth. For the kings and queens carried the idolatry too far, and mortals took to destroying ill-formed children and cripples, thus casting the ills of mortality into heaven. So there was no deliverance for the last dan of Apollo's cycle; and Jehovih received no harvest.

8. Thus ended the cycle of Apollo, being two thousand eight hundred years.

END OF THE BOOK OF APOLLO.

THE LORDS' THIRD BOOK.

BEING COTEMPORANEOUS WITH THE BOOK OF APOLLO, SON OF JEHOVIH. AS THE LATTER BOOK IS OF HEAVEN, SO IS THE LORDS' BOOK OF EARTH, FOR THE SAME PERIOD OF TIME.

CHAPTER I.

1. In the time of heaven known as the arc of Rupta and Mos, the Lord descended to the earth in a sea of fire, to the land of Guatama.

2. And the Lord spake over the land and over the waters, calling and speaking: Where are the I'hins, the chosen of the Lord? Speak, O man; come forth at the call of thy God.

3. Then spake man, answering to the call of God, saying:

4. More than a million; more than two, more than four millions, are thy people, O Lord!

5. The Lord inquired: Where are my people? Where is the place and boundary of the sacred people, the I'hins, whom I delivered in the time of the flood?

6. And man answered, saying: From the head of the Ca'ca'tsak, the mountain river of rivers (Amazon). In Thes'onka, wide as the ocean, and the mountain plains of Om (Mexico). To the great cities of O'wan'gache and Nathon; and Neshesh, and Tesumethgad, and Naphal; and Yeshuah, by the Lake Owane (Nicaragua), here standeth the tower of Rakowana, shining with copper and silver and gold. And by the river Raxaa and her lake, Jon'gan. And over the plains of Go'magat (crescent) and Takshan, where they build great boats with sails of cloth, and beams across. And to the north land of Uphsic and E'chaung, where beginneth the still river Eph'su (a canal), running to the wide oceans, Vid and Sajins (Lakes Superior and Michigan), where the I'huans dig deep down and bring copper and silver and lead in boats to the King of Avaya, I'huan monarch and good protector.

7. The Lord said: The greatest place of all thou has not named. Thine eyes have not seen, thine ears heard not. Search, therefore, and be wise. Man said:

8. I was ashamed before God, so I set out to get great learning to know of what the Lord spake. And I traveled one year to the north, and many moons to the south and east. And I found a rab-bah of great learning, both in books and spoken words; and not a few prophets of the Lord in the great cities. So I inquired, saying: Which is the greatest place

175

of the Lord's chosen? And, lo and behold, they answered even as I had answered the Lord. Then I came to the city of Ta'zuntqua, a place for the yearly dance in the valley of On-out-si, where the rab'bah's temple is covered with copper, polished; and I asked the same question. For the che'ba within me desired to make a record of all things valuable; but, alas, I got no other answer than the echo of my own words.

9. God said: Where are my chosen? Where is the greatest place of the I'hins? Thou hast shown me the I'huans, their great cities and kingdoms; their places of great learning. But the greatest of all, thou hast not shown.

10. Man answered: I know not, O Lord. Speak thou?

11. The Lord said: In amongst the I'huans are the I'hins, the little sacred people. The little cities in the suburbs of the large cities of the I'huans, these are the greatest cities.

12. Man inquired of God: How can that be? Behold, the I'huans are three to one, compared to the I'hins!

13. The Lord said: These that build temples of hewn stone, and cover them with polished copper, are not my people. These warrior kings, that fortify their cities with soldiers, are not my people. They are not great.

14. But these are my chosen, that live in mounds, and in cities with wooden walls, and clay walls. They are the greatest of all people. They dress not in gaudy colors, nor ornament themselves with copper and silver and gold.

15. They are the people of learning. They survey the way for the canals; they find the square and the arch; they lead the I'huan to the mines, where lead and copper and silver are buried. These are a great people.

16. Without them the I'huan could not build his own house; he could not find the level for a canal; nor provide the square of his temple. The I'hins are the greatest people.

17. My chosen have shapely legs and arms, and feet and hands; and their hair groweth long and straight, white and yellow.

18. The Lord said: Because the I'huan is of all shapes and sizes; and of all grades and judgment, even down to the ignorance of a beast, behold, he is bringing forth heirs of darkness.

19. Come unto the Lord, O ye that are chosen. Ye have built houses and temples for the I'huans, but of what avail are these things?

20. Behold, they are at war, tribe against tribe, nation against nation. They no longer hearken to my rab'bahs, the priests of my chosen.

21. Go to, now, ye shall build temples unto God.

22. Then the I'hins inquired the meaning of the word of God.

23. The Lord said: Long have I prophesied through my chosen, the I'hins. Now will I raise up prophets amongst the I'huans, the copper-colored race.

24. This is the temple ye shall build unto the Great Spirit and His kingdoms in haden.

25. Two peoples there are before my judgment, saith the Lord: The one that heareth not the voice of God, nor knoweth him; but the other people know me, and endeavor to obey my commandments.

26. And God was weary with laboring for the I'huans; for they went more after the way of darkness than light.

27. And the Lord called hence his guardian angels, leaving the I'huans alone for a season. And spirits of darkness came upon them and obsessed them.

28. And in that same time the Lord caused his chosen to display the mold of their thighs, and their short shapely arms. And the I'huans tempted them, contrary to law. So, it came to pass, that the I'huan women boasted of their conquests, bringing forth heirs of more shapeliness.

29. Now, in course of time, these heirs grew to be men and women; and, behold, they had the gift of prophecy, and of seeing visions and of hearing the voice of the angels of heaven. And they were called Ongwee-ghan, signifying, good shaped men.

CHAPTER II.

1. God said: Suffer not the Ongwee to dwell with the I'hin, lest the seed of my chosen be lost.

2. The Ongwees came suddenly into the world; came in the north and south and east and west; came by thousands and thousands. And they had long hair, black and coarse; but their skin was brown, copper-colored; and their arms were short, like the I'hins. Very proud were the Ongwees, they would not mix with the I'huans; and they dared not mix with the sacred people, because of the commandment of the Lord.

3. So, the Ongwee-ghan became a new race in the world, having all the symmetry of the I'hin, and the savageness of the I'huans. And, being feeders on flesh and fish, fell under the dominion of angels of the lower heaven, and they rejected the Lord God.

4. The Lord said: Even this will I appropriate for their own salvation in time to come.

5. So the Lord commanded the I'hins to give to the Ongwees laws, rites and ceremonies; and these things were done as commanded.

6. Then came the angels of the lower heaven, teaching the Ongwees the secret of making eunuchs of their enemies, the I'huans with the long arms; teaching them how to make spears and bows with arrows, and darts and fishing-hooks and nets; teaching them how to make fire by striking flint stones; teaching them how to cook flesh and fish to make them more palatable. And this was the first cooked food for man since the days of the flood.

7. The I'hins feared the Lord would visit a judgment upon the land, because of the Ongwees killing and eating flesh; but the Lord said unto them: Suffer ye the Ongwees to fulfill their labor; too full is all the land with beasts and serpents. Nevertheless, it shall come to pass that great destruction shall come upon the I'huans, and the ground people, and the Ongwees. Their great cities shall be destroyed, and the lands laid desolate; but I will rebuild them again with greater glory than in this day.

8. And so it came to pass, as the Lord had spoken through the I'hin prophets. In three thousand years the large and handsome race, the Ongwees, transcended the long-armed I'huans, the short-legged race.

9. God said: Hear me, O man! Understand the labor of the Lord thy God. Jehovih saith to the Lord: Go thou to yonder earth, and make man upright (on two feet). And the Lord accomplisheth it. Then saith Jehovih: Go yonder, and make man shapely on the earth. And the Lord findeth a way to do this also.

10. Forget not the Lord thy God; such labor will fall to thy lot when thou art long risen in heaven. Behold, there are millions of worlds, new coming into being every day. Expand thy judgment; make thyself comprehensive, that thou mayst fulfill in wisdom the glory of the Almighty.

CHAPTER III.

1. God said: Hear the word of the Lord, O man; be considerate in thy little wisdom of the magnitude of the labor of thy Lord.

2. Certain times and seasons are allotted by Jehovih for the development of new orders of men on the worlds He created. According to the times and seasons and condition of the earth, so hath the Lord thy God provided the race of man.

3. To raise man up, that he may comprehend the beautiful creation, and that he may be adapted in harmony therewith, is the glory of thy God.

4. Behold, I have spoken of the land of Guatama! Think not that as one division of the earth is made answerable to my will by a certain rule, that even so another division of the earth is provided in the same way. The Lord thy God findeth one place filled with beasts of prey and great serpents, which must be destroyed; and he provideth a race of men to accomplish this. And man is suffered by God to become carnivorous for a season.

5. In another country the Lord findeth drought and frequent famine; and he provideth man with knowledge adapted thereto. So also are there seasons to the earth, when man shall be changed from one condition to another; according to the progress of the earth, so God lifted up man for the glory of the Almighty.

6. Suffer not thy judgment to mislead thee as to a law of selection. There is no law of selection. Man hath no inspiration of his own to select and provide his progeny, neither in shapeliness nor judgment.

7. He marrieth because of the impulse of the flesh; nor careth he for the issue, whether they have long legs or short ones, or whether they become warriors or imbeciles. 8. And woman even careth less than man. Nevertheless, a time cometh upon the world, in a later age, when man and woman both consider these things, and somewhat govern themselves accordingly. But in such an era they are almost fruitless.

9. But in the early age of a world, man hath inherent but two impulses, to eat and to indulge in cohabitation. Neither considereth he what may result therefrom. And the Lord and his angels lead man, unknowingly to himself, to fulfill his times and seasons.

10. Now have I come to thee in kosmon to make plain the government of heaven upon the earth; and of thy God and his angels upon the race of man. Behold, in the time of Apollo, man in his present form was brought into being on the earth. The time and season of the earth was in that day come unto that end. Even as in this day thy Lord hath come to change man from a race of warriors to a race of peace; for now is the time and the season of the earth propitious to that end.

11. In the time of Apollo were the first prophets raised up from other than the I'hin race. In that day, the I'huan, the flesh-eating man, was first capable of hearing the voice of thy Lord understandingly. And thy God commanded man to remember the God of harmony, symmetry and music, and to build images of him in all the divisions of the earth.

12. Be most searching, O man; for thou shalt find, in this day and generation, the legends and history of Apollo in all the divisions of the earth.

13. And the word of his name, in all languages, hath the same significance.

14. Behold, as in Guatama, the Lord raised up seers, whom he instructed in the methods of slaying beasts of prey and serpents, in the same period of time raised up for the same purpose other seers in Shem, Ham and Jaffeth. And the names of the great slayers are

preserved to this day in the mortal histories of these countries.

15. Thus created the Lord a new race on the earth; and in all the divisions thereof, the new race came of the I'hins and the I'huans. According to the different countries where they dwelt, so are they found to this day. In which thy God provided all these people who are of pure blood to have no other God nor Lord than the Great Spirit, Jehovih.

16. Nevertheless, in the time of Apollo, this race was but a fraction compared to the hundreds of millions of I'huans and ground people and I'hins that dwelt on the earth. But the I'huans were at war for more than a thousand years.

17. They built great cities, and established mighty kingdoms, but as soon as built, lo, the wars laid them low or dissipated them.

18. God said: Now will I give to man a new commandment, which is, to go forth and subdue the earth; to slay every beast of prey and every serpent that cometh before him.

19. And of beasts of prey and of serpents, shalt thou not eat the flesh, nor the blood, which containeth life.

20. Neither shalt thou eat the flesh of the beast with uncloven foot; nor shalt thou eat swine's flesh.

21. But all cloven-footed animals I give unto thee, for food to eat. For in the day thou takest the place of beasts of prey, thou shalt also take to thyself to eat the flesh they would have eaten.

22. Then the Lord sent I'hin priests to circumcise the new race, the GHAN. And he commanded the Ghans to marry amongst themselves, promising to give all the world into their keeping.

23. And the Ghans began to wear clothes, after the manner of the I'hins; and the latter gave them rites and ceremonies, and taught them how to pray and dance before Jehovih.

END OF THE LORDS' THIRD BOOK.

BOOK OF THOR, SON OF JEHOVIH

BEING THE RECORDS OF THOR, APOLLO'S SUCCESSOR ON THE EARTH AND HER HEAVENS, FROM THE ARC OF MOS, TO THE ARC OF DAE, IN THE ETHEREAN HEAVENS, AND OF THREE THOUSAND TWO HUNDRED YEARS.

CHAPTER I.

1. Thor, Orian Chief of Don'ga, in etherea, God of Palla, Surveyor of Yorretz and Thassa, God of Galeb, Receiver of Saffer and Hoesonya, God of Wartz and Lo and Yisain, Counselor in the ethereal worlds Hituna, Ctaran, Seeing, Sethawan and Hababak, greeting:

2. In the Holy Council of Gods and Goddesses in Don'ga, the voice of Jehovih came to Thor, saying:

3. My Son, behold the red star, the earth; she courseth from Mos to Dae, and now draggeth in the swamps of Asath. Behold, thou shalt deliver her through thy dominions, three thousand two hundred years. Even now approacheth the dawn of Ghan.

4. Thor spoke before the Holy Council, on Jehovih's etherean throne, saying: Behold the young world, the earth, cometh our way. For three thousand two hundred years she will journey in the fields of Don'ga.

5. Then, the Holy Council deliberated on the matters of the earth and her heavens, and all other corporeal worlds that were to pass through Don'ga for three thousand years. And it was found that the dawn of dan would fall upon the earth first of all.

6. Then called Thor for the swift messengers that course the firmament in the regions of Apperwaith, the roadway of the earth's past history. And the swift messengers came and laid their report before the throne of Jehovih, as to what world the earth was, and the harvests of angels she had yielded up to the emancipated heavens.

7. When their reports were finished and deliberated on by the Holy Council, Thor, Son of Jehovih, said:

8. For further knowledge as to the present condition of this world, the earth, it is my command that Yathai, God of Gammotto, choose one million volunteers; and, in a airiata, proceed to the earth and her heavens to visit her God and Lords, and ascertain the condition of their angels and mortals, and report back in Don'ga.

9. So, Yathai, God of Gammotto, in etherea, was appointed for this purpose, and he provided an airiata, and took with him one million ethereans, and proceeded to the earth and her heavens, as commanded.

10. And Yathai came to the throne of God in Gau, in atmospherea; and God sent to his Lords an invitation to come also. And there came seventy and two of them.

11. God said to Yathai: Behold, the earth and these atmospherean heavens are full of false Lords and false Gods. Yathai inquired how many there were? God said: More than thirty thousand Gods and one hundred and sixty thousand Lords. Behold, in every great city on earth is there a false God or a false Lord, and he hath a small heavenly kingdom of his own, even on the earth. And the spirits of the dead of that place are his slaves, for his own exaltation.

12. And in many of these heavenly kingdoms there are wars and anarchy (hells), where the angels torment one another endlessly. Nor will these false Gods and false Lords and

180

their subjects admit that there are higher heavens than their own.

13. The spirits of the newly dead are captured and kept in ignorance of Jehovih and His vast creations; but made to bow in adoration and worship to the false Lord or false God. And these again, being in contiguity to mortals, inspire them to the same worship. Which fits them in time of death to fall as slaves into the dominion of him whom they worshipped.

14. The wars in heaven have inspired mortals to wars on earth; so that, all around the world, everlasting battles are going on.

15. And such as are slain on earth-battlefields are born in spirit in chaos, not knowing they are dead (as to the earth), and, so, they linger on the battle-fields, still battling imaginary foes.

16. All over the earth are these battle-fields covered with spirits in chaos and with the spirits of druks, and druj, and Yaks, and ground people, who know nothing more than the beasts in the field.

17. Return, therefore, O Yathai, to thy Orian Chief, Thor, Son of Jehovih, and say to him: The God of earth is powerless to rescue her angels and mortals from the great darkness upon them. And beseech him in Jehovih's name to come and deliver me and my kingdoms.

18. Yathai inquired as to the races of men on earth, and as to the times of their termination.

19. God said: In twelve thousand four hundred years the I'hin race, the mound builders, will come to an end. And in that day the Ghans will have triumphed over all the lands and waters of the earth.

20. When Yathai had obtained the required information, and also learned the localities of the divisions of the earth and her heavens, he departed in his airiata, with his companions, and visited all the chief places, and then returned to Don'ga, in etherea, before Thor, Son of Jehovih, to whom he reported all he had learned as to the condition of the earth and her heavens.

21. Then came the Light of Jehovih to Thor, saying: My Son, take thou a sufficient host of ethereans, and go to the red star and her heavens, and deliver them in My name.

CHAPTER II.

1. Thor called in thirty million volunteers; and he provided an avalanza, an ethereal ship of fire, in which they embarked for the red star, where they should remain four years and two hundred and thirty and eight days, which was called the dawn of dan, for Thor, of Don'ga.

2. Then outward, onward, through etherea, sped Thor and his thirty millions. Through the swamps of Asath. and the fields of Broddwuski; through the ethereal seas of Hoesonga, toward the arc of Mos, and thence to Chinvat, the boundary of the earth's vortex. Nor halted here, but sped onward in his ship of fire for Gau, the throne of God.

3. God and his Lords, being apprised of Thor's coming, had the capital in readiness for his reception. And they had beside gathered in all the angels of the second resurrection, and as many of the first as chose to come. In all, there were in Gau assembled nine hundred million angels, Fathists in Jehovih, Of these, not more than one million had ever seen an etherean, nor had they visited outward from the earth farther than the seventh plateau in

atmospherea.

4. Amongst these, even into the heavenly capital of Gau, alighted Thor and his thirty millions. And after due salutations, in the manner of Gods and Goddesses, a day of recreation was proclaimed from the throne of God; and thereupon the atmosphereans and ethereans mingled together joyfully.

5. Then ascended Thor on the throne of God, and he ordained as followeth, to wit:

6. One million constables to go to the false Lords and false Gods and arrest them, and bring them to Gau for judgment.

7. One million captors to possess the thrones and temples of the false Lords and false Gods, and hold them.

8. Eight million captors to gather in the angel slaves in all the hadan heavens.

9. Six million dispersers to overthrow and disperse the hells (heavenly battle-fields of spirits in chaos).

10. Six million physicians to disrupt fetals from mortals.

11. Two million founders of es'yan nurseries, for the spirits of infants and helpless ones, born into heaven before their full time.

12. One million founders of hospitals, for chaotic angels and others stricken in disease.

13. Half a million marshals; half a million messengers; and three million builders.

14. And when these had been selected by the proper officers, they were dispatched to their several places and duties.

15. Then Thor reorganized the Council of Gau for the period of dawn.

16. So, God and his Lords rested for a season, whilst Thor and his hosts delivered earth and her heavens.

17. In one year all the false Lords and false Gods and Goddesses were captured and brought to Gau; neither passed Thor judgment upon them until they were all brought in. And on this occasion, there were assembled in Gau millions of angels to witness the proceedings.

18. Thor said unto them: Perceive ye not that my power is greater than yours? How can that be? I have but thirty millions; and of you there are more than thirty thousand millions! Wherein, then, am I more powerful? Behold, I have arrested all your heavens and heavenly rulers. How it this? Whence my power?

19. Not one could answer Thor.

20. Then Thor said: My army is a unit. Yours are divided, one against another. Yea, each one was in anarchy.

21. This I declare unto you all: Jehovih, first of all; and His creations, which He hath given unto all His creatures.

22. To learn to master the elements of earth and heaven, this is the foundation for acquiring all power.

23. Because ye bound yourselves in heavenly places on the earth, ye rose not up to the places prepared for you. Answer me now: How standeth the world as to what is to come?

24. Many of the false Lords and false Gods answered after this manner: I fear to speak my mind, lest thou in anger cast me in hell.

25. Thor said: He who hath learnt to know Jehovih, and to serve Him, feareth nothing on earth nor in heaven. Fear is but the manifestation of weakness.

26. Speak, therefore, what ye desire; no harm shall befall you.

27. Then many of them said: This do I perceive, O God: There lie the earth and many heavens. The strongest mortals rule over the weaker; the strongest Gods rule over the weaker. Therefore, make me thy slave. I am content.

28. Then Thor said: A greater hardship give I unto all: I give you your liberty and freedom. Go, therefore, whither ye desire. I ask not one to serve me; but say unto you: Go serve Jehovih by lifting up whoever is beneath you.

29. They answered: Whither shall we go? We know not the way from one heaven to another, nor the way down to the earth. Thou sayest: Go serve Jehovih by lifting up such as are beneath us. Now, verily, we cannot lift up ourselves. Had we great riches, or power, or wisdom, then would we willingly do for those beneath us.

30. Thor said: Verily are ye Gods of darkness. I say unto you, wait not for any of these things, but go at once and serve Jehovih.

31. They answered: When we have first provided a way for ourselves, then will we serve Him.

32. Thor answered: Ye have spoken the darkness of all the world. I say unto you: Go serve Jehovih first; and after that come to me that I may see wherein ye lack in anything.

33. They answered: How can one serve Jehovih by lifting others up, if he have not clothes, nor food, nor habitation.

34. Thor said: It is well ye ask that question; but I say: Direct that question to your own souls; and, behold, the Father will answer you. Let that be the question ye ask yourselves every hour of the day; and watch ye for an opportunity to answer it by the labor of your own hands.

35. Then the false Gods and false Lords were dismissed from custody.

36. Thor commanded the light of the throne and of the pillars of heavenly fire to be raised to a higher grade. The false Lords and false Gods desired to flee because of the brilliancy of the light, but knew not whither to go.

37. Thor said unto them: Why have ye assumed to be Lords and Gods, since ye cannot even master the elements in the lower heavens?

38. i say unto you, the regions of Jehovih's universe are boundless. Let no one assume to do that which he cannot do; but, little by little, learn to master the elements surrounding him, and he will in time learn to traverse Jehovih's beautiful firmament, and be indeed a fit companion for Gods and Goddesses.

39. Then spake the false Lords and false Gods, saying: O that we had some one to teach us; some one to show us the way to learn!

40. Then Thor, perceiving they were in proper humor for resurrection, allotted unto them certain teachers and disciplinarians, and they were taken into educational colonies and put to work.

CHAPTER III.

1. Thor said: To induce men and angels to find the way of resurrection, this is the greatest of all teaching. Man saith: O God, raise up thy servant!

2. And the Lord saith: Hold up thy hands and I will lift thee up. But man will not. Man saith: Send wise and holy angels to me, O Lord, to guide me in righteousness and good works!

3. And the Lord saith: As thou asketh of God, even so do thou to thy fellows. But man will not.

4. As it is with man on earth, even so do we find it in hada.

5. To induce angels to develop themselves, by taking hold with their own hands, and by the exercise of their own talents, this is the work of Lords and Gods. To rule over them without their knowing it, so as to lead them in the right way, this is wisdom.

6. The first passion of man is to eat; the second, the sexual desire; the third, to make others serve him. And if he accomplish the latter, then is he indeed the prince of evil. For he then holdeth dominion to the hurt of others.

7. So, also, as man buildeth these habitations in his soul on earth, how vain his effort for happiness in heaven! To teach him to undo all his past, and to make full restitution unto others, this is the work of Gods and Lords over spirits of darkness.

8. Thor established two thousand educational colonies in atmospherea, besides innumerable places of manufacturing and building; teaching the angels of heaven how to provide habitations for those born of earth into spirit life.

9. In three years of dawn Thor had prepared for etherean ascension four thousand million Brides and Bridegrooms.

10. Now all this while the angels of atmospherea had been taught much in regard to the emancipated kingdoms in etherea; of the splendor and majesty and power of Gods and Goddesses there abiding.

11. Thor spake from the throne of God, before the Holy Council, saying: Send swift messengers to Betatis, Goddess of Terow, in etherea, greeting, and say unto her: Thus saith Thor, Jehovih's Son, Orian Chief of Don'ga: Come thou to the heavens of the earth; I have four thousand million Brides and Bridegrooms as Jehovih's harvest. Provide thou an airiata of great size and splendor, for its presence shall enchant my people.

12. The swift messengers departed. And proper officers at once set about making ready to receive Betatis. Others were sent into other parts of atmospherea with fire-boats to bring atmosphereans to Gau, that they might behold the glory of the higher heavens as manifested in the descent and ascent of the airiata.

13. All these things were accomplished; Betatis came in great splendor; and all the kingdoms and sub-kingdoms of Gau were filled with the thousands of millions come to witness the ceremonies.

14. This, then, was the size of Betatis' airiata: Diameter, east and west and north and south, two thousand miles to the borders of the photosphere, and nine thousand miles high. The ship, within the photosphere, was one hundred miles east and west and north and south, and was two hundred miles high. Of beams, the entire length, there were twelve millions four hundred thousand; and of uprights, two millions; but of the short beams and uprights, they were numerous accordingly. And there were a sufficient number of chambers within the airiata for every soul to have one; and besides these, there were halls and temples within, also suitable for music and other entertainments.

15. The colors, shades and tints, with mirrors, and with opaque ornaments, both movable and fixed, were provided in all possible ways, for ornament and for service, the like of which, for beauty, had never been surpassed in Don'ga. And when the whole airiata was completed, it looked like an oval globe of light, with a frame-work, transparent and opaque within, alternated so as to add beauty to every part. And it was fitted and equipped

for the third resurrection, having no storage places for atmosphere, or any thing in common with the lower heavens.

16. To add still further to its splendor, Betatis had her airiata ornamented with banners and streamers illuminated, so that at a distance, when seen descending, the whole vessel seemed like a sun surrounded on every side with movable stars and waving streams of light.

17. Amongst her hosts were one million trumpeters and players on harps; and two million singers.

18. In the midst of the forepart of the ship was the Holy Council chamber, with four million members. Above the Council chamber was the chamber of worship; and at either side were the halls for dancing and social reunion.

19. When Betatis' ship neared the atmospherean kingdom of God, millions of her hosts stationed themselves on the galley-beams and stay-lines, adding a scene of life to the ethereal ship of surpassing beauty.

20. With ballast had Betatis provided her ship, so that when she came within the earth's vortex she could stand where she desired whilst the earth and her heavens turned their axial course, that both mortals and angels might witness the brilliancy and glory of the works of Don'ga's chief Goddess.

21. And thus Betatis stood in her ship of fire, just beyond the plateau of Gau, whilst the earth and her heavens made one revolution.

22. The next day she descended into Gau, where God and his Lords, under direction of Thor, Jehovih's Son, had prepared their mighty audience.

23. When the ship was made fast, the chief marshal of Gau and of Betatis' hosts met and conducted Betatis up in front of the throne of God.

24. Thor said: In Jehovih's name, welcome, Daughter of Light!

25. Betatis said: Praise the Almighty! In love, am I come to answer thy prayer.

26. Then spake God, saying: Welcome, O Goddess! Come and honor my throne!

27. Then went Betatis forward in a flame of light, and was greeted after the manner of Gods and Goddesses. After which she sat in the midst of the throne. And at once the ceremonies of initiation for the Brides and Bridegrooms were accomplished.

28. Then came a day of recreation; and after that, Betatis and her hosts, together with the four thousand million Brides and Bridegrooms, entered her airiata and departed upward for the etherean heavens.

CHAPTER IV.

1. In the fourth year of dawn under Thor, Son of Jehovih, he received from the Holy Council in Buru, of Don'ga, in etherea, a dispensation from the Orian Chiefs, decreeing to the earth one hundred years' travail in vocent.

2. Thor called up Waak, God of Rhines, and said unto him: A sore travail hath Jehovih put upon these heavens. Go thou to Hey'loo and command him to provide an avalanza sufficient to deliver twenty thousand atmosphereans to the a'ji'an forests of Gonaya.

3. For the inhabitants of these heavens are too dark to endure the vocent of a hundred years, and would be precipitated to the earth and engage in fetalism.

4. Waak, God of Rhines, knowing the condition of the atmosphereans, proceeded at once

to Hey'loo, informing him of the decrees of the higher heavens, and of the command of Thor, Son of Jehovih.

5. Thor then sent word to his Lords and marshals, informing them also of his command, and, further, commanding them to bring from all parts of earth and heaven all the lowest grades of angels, to be concentrated in Gau, to which place the avalanza was to come for them.

6. Thor appointed Ti'See'inij, Goddess of Ares, to superintend the reception of the angels, and to arrange them for entrance into the avalanza; and he gave into her command, to assist her, five hundred thousand marshals and captains, and one million es'enaurs. And these she apportioned to their respective duties and places.

7. To accomplish all this, Thor allotted seventy-seven days (earth's time). And so wisely were carried out all the proceedings that, on the seventy-seventh day, the avalanza was on hand, and all the angels ready to enter therein.

8. Accordingly, these things were accomplished; the twenty thousand million angels were carried away on the avalanza, which was walled around on every side with pillars of fire, so that not one spirit could escape, even were he chaotic or imbecile. And Waak and Hay'loo had entire charge of the migration; and they proceeded upward and outward from the earth, seven diameters of the earth's vortex, which brought them into the forests of Gonaya, where they landed them.

9. Ti'See'inij, Goddes of Ares, had charge of the twenty thousand millions, and she had previously sent thither a sufficient force of angels, wise and strong, to provide for the reception.

10. So that, when the avalanza landed, all things were in readiness; and the angels were apportioned to different sections of the Gonaya forests, according to their development. And proper officers and teachers were provided unto them.

11. By Ti'See'inij were these things done. And she established a throne of a'ji, and provided a temple of Council, and all such things as are required in the government of a new colony. And, to reign after the expiration of dawn, she provided a God in Gonaya. She promoted to this one Hazedeka, a surveyor in Thalasia, the third heaven of Gau; and she gave him the title, GOD OF GONAYA, FOR FOUR HUNDRED YEARS.

12. Now, in reference to founding an a'ji'an habitation in etherea, this account is rendered unto mortals and angels of the lower heaven: Amidst the ethe'ic waves, the ethereans gather up the atomic elements floating therein, and, giving them axic motion, propelling them forth, aggregating the while, till, from a mite, it groweth as large as the whole earth, but is habitable within and without by the spirits of the dead, the angels.

13. Jehovih said: In likeness of the solid earth, and stars, and moon, that float in the unseen firmament, so made I atomic parts to all things, and made them to float in ethe. As the earth is to the air and the ether above, so is an atom of corpor to the ethe'ic solution.

14. Jehovih said: Think not, O man, there is but one member in My Person, and that different conditions and states of that one comprise My universe. The foolish man hath said, the blood is the flesh and bones, and that the flesh and bones are but a state of blood; but he seeth not that I make not flesh out of blood, but out of that that the blood carrieth. And in like manner carry I the corpor of My Person in the ethe of My Being.

15. Now, as to Thor, Son of Jehovih, after the departure of the avalanza, he provided a new God unto the earth and her heavens, and crowned him, and bestowed upon him the

triangle which had been handed down since the inhabitation of the earth by man.

16. As for the remaining time of dawn, Thor traveled around about the earth and her heavens, making records thereof, to be carried with him in Buru in the time of his ascent.

17. In consequence of the depletion occasioned by the resurrection of the twenty thousand millions to Gonaya, God and his Lords were greatly relieved of their burdens in Gau and on the earth.

CHAPTER V.

1. Peace and prosperity were established on earth and in heaven by the time of the expiration of the dawn of Thor. And now came the time for his own ascent, with his hosts, leaving the earth and her heavens in care of God and his Lords.

2. So Thor, Son of Jehovih, sent swift messengers to etherea, asking to be delivered; and asking for the deliverance of six thousand million Brides and Bridegrooms to Jehovih.

3. See We'ing, Goddess of Hotosk, in etherea, was appointed by the Council in Buru, to descend for Thor and his hosts, and his six thousand millions.

4. Accordingly, See We'ing built her ship and gathered in her hosts for the journey, her ten millions. This, then, was the make of her ship, which she named Harp, to wit:

5. The photosphere was flat to the north and south, but oval east and west; the openings were on the flat sides, with passages through. The crescent described a circle of three thousand four hundred miles, and the depth of the harp north and south was three hundred miles. The pillars of fire that ascended from the midst were one thousand seven hundred miles high.

6. The stars within the photosphere were provided with five points; and each star had one million chambers, one chamber being allotted as the habitation of one Bride or Bridegroom; and there were seven thousand of these stars.

7. The frame-work was crystalline, and opaque, and transparent, and of all possible colors, and shades, and tints. Now, besides the stars and their chambers, the base of the crescent was provided with a salon sufficient for one million musicians, and they were thus situated.

8. God had knowledge of the coming of See We'ing, and had commanded information to be sent throughout atmospherea, and to the Lords located on earth, inviting all who chose, to come and witness the ascent. And there came, besides the Brides and Bridegrooms, two thousand million angels; many not yet delivered from the first resurrection.

9. So it came to pass, See We'ing, Goddess of Hotosk, came down in her ship of fire, even to the foundation of Gau; came in great magnificence, and was received by Thor and by God and His Lords.

10. And she ascended the throne, and performed the marriage rite for the six thousand millions. And after that a recreation of one day was proclaimed in Gau, during which time the atmosphereans and ethereans mingled freely together.

11. On the day following, Thor accompanied See We'ing into her ship; and their hosts went in also, being nearly seven thousand millions. And then, amidst a rain of etherean flowers, See We'ing started her fire ship upward.

12. God and his hosts remaining in Gau saluted in the sign, JEHOVIH FOREVER! Which was properly answered by the ascending millions.

13. Then on its axis turned the great ship, rising and turning, higher and higher. And in a little while only an ascending star was seen, and then it disappeared in the distance. 14. Thus fulfilled Thor his great mission in dawn to the earth and her heavens.

CHAPTER VI.

1. Again the earth and heaven prospered for another season of two hundred years, and the next dan there were delivered five thousand million souls. And new Gods and Lords succeeded; and they also prospered, but not so well. The next harvest was four thousand million souls.

2. But, again, false Lords and false Gods began to set up kingdoms of their own, in heaven, and in the cities of mortals. And, lo and behold, every one called himself either Thor or Apollo. And the spirits who manifested in the temples, and for the oracles, all gave one of these names. And mortals who were obsessed, believed themselves to be the re-incarnation of Apollo or Thor; and the obsessing spirits so called themselves. Others, more intelligent, said: Have not the prophets foretold there was to be a second coming of Apollo? And are not these spirits, who appear through the sar'gis, the very person?

3. So great became the superstition of the nations of the earth, that in the fall of a leaf they found proof of the second coming of Apollo or Thor. Many of the spirits deserted the second resurrection, in heaven, and returned to the earth, to wait for information concerning the coming event, as they supposed, though there was no event coming.

4. Jehovih said: All corporeal worlds pass through the age of too much belief. As I gave to man judgment, that he might examine and weigh a matter, so runneth he into unbelief. Then My angels go to him and show him wherein he believed too little; but, lo, he goeth to the other extreme, believing all things, and not using his judgment.

5. God said: Why will not men and angels be patient, and wait till a matter is proven meritorious before they pursue it to extremes? The same sun shineth, the same stars stand in the heavens, and the earth traveleth steadily on her way; yea, her winds blow, her summers and winters come as in the olden time, yet man setteth up that a great wonder is near at hand. And no wonder cometh, and nothing new is near.

6. How shall I stay them, O Jehovih? Their desires for Apollo call down millions of spirits from my places of resurrection. And in trials and hardships they fall, and become suitable prey for designing false Gods and false Lords.

7. But there came no other salutation than the echo of God's own words. So God and his Lords bewailed the darkness of earth and her heavens.

8. But high up in the etherean heavens, came the Light of Jehovih; came the Voice of Jehovih, saying:

9. Hear your Creator, O ye Gods and Goddesses! Behold the magnitude of My works! I labor not for the profit of this man or that man; nay, nor for this people nor that people; nor for the inhabitants of one star and one heaven; but for the glory of millions of stars and millions of heavens.

10. Doth not one corporeal man bewail a shower of rain? and yet, his neighbor rejoiceth thereat. One man prayeth for sunshine, and another for shade. Think not that I labor for each one separately, but for the perfection of the whole. Wherefore, then, shall the God of earth and his Lords bewail the darkness that falleth on the earth in this day?

11. I have prepared places of darkness in the etherean firmament, and places of light; and My corporeal worlds must travel through them, for so I created them. And these places of darkness and places of light are as changes of seasons for My harvests.

12. Now doth the earth pass in deep darkness, for I fructify the races of men in new growth, corporeally, for things that shall come after. As they absorb from the a'ji of My places, in this age, so, also, do their souls become full of superstition and darkness.

13. Thus went the earth into great darkness during the last six hundred years of the cycle of Thor, and there was no harvest from her for the etherean heavens. But the spirits deserted atmospherea in millions and millions, and went down to the earth, to dwell with mortals, and to find places on the corporeal earth where to live.

14. And, save to the I'hins, the Light of Jehovih was shut out from men; thus ambition for improvement was at an end; they became as drones and vagabonds; and, when they died, their spirits continued to lie about in the places of their mortal life. And many of these spirits persuaded mortals to suicide, and they killed themselves by thousands and tens of thousands. Nor was there courage more amongst men to endure anything under the sun. They wanted to be with the spirits of the dead, to talk with them, to see them, and to be rid of earth trials.

15. Neither had the spirits that congregated on earth any knowledge of the higher heavens; nor could they impart knowledge as to where they dwelt, or how they employed their time, for, in fact, they did nothing useful to heaven or earth, nor even to themselves.

16. Thus ended the cycle of Thor; and it was three thousand two hundred years.

END OR THE BOOK OF THOR.

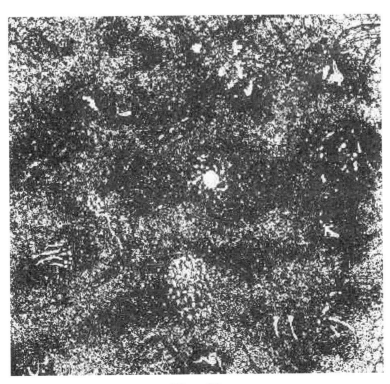

Plate 32.
THE EARTH IN A'JI.

THE LORDS' FORTH BOOK.

BEING COTEMPORANEOUS WITH THE BOOK OF THOR, CYCLE OF THOR, SON OF JEHOVIH. AS
THE LATTER BOOK IS OF THE HIGHER AND THE LOWER HEAVENS, SO IS THE LORDS' BOOK
OF THE LOWER HEAVENS AND THE EARTH, BOTH BEING FOR THE SAME PERIOD OF TIME.

CHAPTER I.

1. By altars and temples, and by idols and images, and by painted signs and engraved words, God foresaw that the knowledge of one generation could be handed down to the next. And though all these things are false in fact, as a written word is not a word, but an image of an idea which hath been spoken, so by symbols conveyed God the living truth.

2. God said: Behold, with my sacred people have I established myself in written words. Now hath it come to pass that all the races of men on earth shall be made to know me.

3. God commanded man to make stone and wooden images, and engravings also, of everything upon the earth; and man so made them according to his own knowledge.

4. God said: As every living creature hath a name, so shall the image thereof and the engraving thereof have the same name. And even so shall it be with all things on the earth, and in the waters thereof, and in the air above the earth; the image and the engravings shall have the same names, even as the real things themselves.

5. And God sent his angels down to man, to inspire him in the workmanship of images and engravings, and man thus accomplished the commandments of God.

6. And these were the first writings since the flood, other than such as were kept secret amongst the I'hins. And of this manner were the writings, to wit:

7. A picture of a man was a man; a picture of a tree was a tree; a picture of a bird was a bird; and even so was everything represented by its own name and image.

8. Then God said: When thou hast made the picture of a spear, behold it is a spear. And when thou desirest to show which way a man goeth, thou shalt add to the graven image the likeness of a spear; and the way it pointeth, shall show the way man goeth. Even so shalt thou express the going of everything on earth and in heaven.

9. Thus man made a written language, and in every region of the earth. By many men were these things done; according to the light of God upon them, so accomplished they the written languages of thousands of tribes of men.

10. God said: This shall be called the Panic language (Ah-ce-o-ga), because it is made of earthly images. And, in after ages, whoever desireth to find the first written words of man, shall have recourse to the pictures of all things on earth, and in the waters, and in the air above the earth.

11. God said: As in the olden time man named all things according to their own spoken words and sounds uttered, so in the days of Thor came the written words of everything on earth and in heaven.

12. When man had written the name of all things, *one* only had he not written, even the name of his Creator.

13. God said: Even that also shalt thou write. Then man inquired: O Lord, how can I find a word to express the Creator?

14. God said: Many tribes have I raised upon the earth, and, behold, they have all written the names of all things, save only the Creator. Go to, therefore, and write thou His name

also.

15. Man said: Alas, O my God! I know no name, save the names I have already made. If I could hear the Creator, or see Him, then could I write His name.

16. God said: Thou hast named the wind (wh-sh!), which thou hast not seen. Name thou thy Creator. And His name shall comprehend all things, far and near, seen and unseen.

17. Then man drew a circle and called it O, for it represented that which was without beginning or end, and which contained all within it. Then man drew a line cutting through the circle from east to west, to represent the light of the east traveling to the west. Then man drew a line from below upward, cutting the circle at right angles with the horizontal, to represent the one road of all things, from the bottom upward forever. The first line man called E, for it was the same as the wind speaketh in the leaves. But the second line he called IH, for it represented that unseen shaft that cutteth all things in twain.

18. And when man had completed the engraving, he called it E-O-IH!

19. God said: In this, thy symbol, thou hast found the way of a true square (true cross) and the four quarters of the world. (See tablet Se'moin, Book of Saphah.)

20. Keep thou His name and the image thereof a secret betwixt the rab'bahs and thy God. Neither shalt thou utter it aloud, for it is sacred upon the earth.

21. Betwixt thee and thy Creator standeth thy God, who is Lord of heaven and earth. Behold, I am the key of life and death; through me, thy Lord, shalt thou unlock all the mysteries of heaven and earth.

22. Neither shall my rab'bah, nor my prophets, call on the name of any spirit, save the Lord, who is God. The words I give corporeally I have recorded in heaven; neither can man alter my records and make them accord with that which is written above. But in the lapse of time I provide seers and prophets, to whom I can reveal to mortals the things of heaven.

23. This have I spoken to Jehovih for thee: Man shall measure Thy hand upon him; remember Thy eye upon him; seek for Thy wisdom within him; and be thankful for Thy good things before him; to consider the little good of them that deny Thee; the conceit of them that claim to be self-made; and the folly of uttering other glories than Thine, and yet to mention them not; for these are the attaining of wisdom.

CHAPTER II.

1. The Lord came down to man on the earth, and spake to man in two ways: By the voice, as man speaketh; and by the spirit, as soul answereth to soul.

2. The Lord said: The voice of man is air in motion; by the mouth of man cometh the word of knowledge.

3. But back of the voice; back of the air in motion; back of the mouth, which giveth voice, there lieth the soul, which it is that causeth man to think of speaking. And the soul lieth in the ocean of the Creator, Who is God of all.

4. The Lord said: That that speaketh to thy soul, O man, teaching thee wisdom and good works; reproving thee for thy faults, and enchanting thee with the glories of all created things, is the voice of thy Creator. And that is the road by which the Lord thy God cometh to thee.

5. The Lord said: Behold, man hath attained to written knowledge; now shall he have books, and learn to keep records, after the manner of the angels in heaven. Then God sent

angels down to man, speaking both by the soul and by the voice; in different places and to different rab'bahs, teaching them how to make books of skins, and of bark, and of cloth, for the graven words and images which he had taught man.

6. In these days the lands of Jaffeth and Shem and Ham were inhabited by millions of I'huans and Ghans; but the countries lying between them were inhabited by I'huans only.

7. And God spake to the people of Ham, saying: Behold, there are two other countries inhabited by kin of your kin, flesh of your flesh, and they are Ghans also. And they speak and write with Panic words, even as ye do.

8. And the Hamites inquired: How far are the two other countries? Where are they?

9. The Lord said: Gather together a thousand men and women, and I will lead you to your brethren, whose forefathers were also saved from the flood; saved by the sacred little people, the I'hins. Provide ye oxen and asses and all things requisite for a journey of four years, and I will lead you.

10. The Hamites obeyed God, and provided themselves as commanded; into two companies of a thousand each equipped they themselves, and started on their journey for Jaffeth and Shem.

11. Then spake God to the people of Jaffeth, saying: Behold, there are two other countries inhabited by kin of your kin, flesh of your flesh, and they are Ghans also. And they speak and write with Panic words, even as ye do.

12. The Jaffeth'yans said: How far are the two other countries? Where are they?

13. The Lord said: Gather together a thousand men and women, and I will lead you to your brethren, whose forefathers were also saved from the flood; saved by the sacred little people, the I'hins. Provide ye in all things requisite for a journey of four years, and I will lead you.

14. The Jaffeth'yans obeyed God, and provided themselves as commanded; into two companies of a thousand each equipped they themselves and started for Ham and Shem.

15. Then spake the Lord to the people of Shem in the same way, telling them of Jaffeth and Ham; and they also equipped themselves in two companies and started for Ham and Jaffeth.

16. Thus provided God these three separate peoples to go and visit one another, and all in the same period of time. And God said unto them, ere they started: Very fierce and savage are the I'huans who inhabit the wilderness on the way. Behold, they eat the flesh of both man and beast. But they will not harm the I'hins; therefore, O my beloved, on your long journey take with you two score of I'hins. Through the I'hins can the Lord your God speak all languages, even the language of the barbarians, the I'huans.

17. Leave all things in the hands of the Lord God.

18. So it came to pass, after a journey of four years, the migrants from each country came to the place of their destination. And by their written and spoken words knew they one another; and they called themselves the three children of the arc of Noe.

19. And the Lord said unto them in each of the countries whither they had come: Provide records unto the work of God; for these journeys shall be remembered to the end of the world.

20. And in all these countries there were made images of stone and copper, and engravings thereon of the children of Noc, and of the flood, and of the sacred tribes, Shem, Ham and Jaffeth.

192

21. God said: These shall be preserved as the first written names of these lands. And it was so.

CHAPTER III.

1. For two years the migrants tarried in the countries they visited; going much about, showing themselves, and relating a history of the country whence they came.

2. Thence spake the Lord to the migrants in their respective places, saying: Behold, the time is come for your departure. Gather together, O my beloved, and return to your own country, and there relate all the glories that your God hath shown you.

3. So they departed, and returned to their own respective places. And, behold, it took four years to accomplish the journey.

4. Now during the travel of the migrants the Lord spake to them every day; through the I'hin priests spake the Lord unto them.

5. The Lord said: Keep together, O my beloved. I will lead you; ye shall not be lost.

6. Nevertheless, the journey was so long that many lost faith, and were not heedful of the words of God. And some of them strayed off amongst the I'huans, the barbarians, and were lost.

7. Of the six thousand migrants, there were lost ten tribes; in all, three hundred and eighty-six people, men and women. Some were lost in one place and some in another.

8. God said: Sing ye songs of lamentations to my chosen who are lost, the Faithists in Jehovih. For this also shall become a matter of record to the end of the world.

9. Nevertheless, a time shall come when the Lord your God shall reveal the mystery of this day.

10. So, when the people had returned to their respective places, behold they all sang songs of lamentation for the tribes that were lost.

11. God said: I have shown you the far-off people; I have marked out the road. Keep the road open; keep the travel open between the great countries I have shown you.

12. Every eleven years shall one expedition start to the far-off countries. And, if perchance ye find my chosen, bring them home.

13. And on all the camping places of your journey shall ye build an altar to the Lord your God. In a circle shall ye build it; and the congregation shall sit in the circle thereof, but the priest shall sit in the midst. And, behold, I will speak in the mouth of my priest words of wisdom and comfort.

14. But, in all your journeys, keep aloof from the I'huans, the barbarians, the man-eaters. For they kept not my commandments; nor preserved they their seed through the circumcision.

15. But they mixed with the druks (ground people) and went down in darkness (barbarism).

16. Keep ye away from them, O my beloved; carry with you, on all your expeditions, I'hin priests, the sacred people, the mound-builders.

17. In your journeys ye shall encounter your brethren coming and going, who dwell in the far-off countries. That ye may distinguish them, keep secret the sacred password and the rites of my chavah (order).

CHAPTER IV.

1. Hear the word of thy God, O man, and be considerate in thy little learning; interpreting the records of the ancients rather by the spirit than by the word.

2. Wherein it was constantly commanded, in the ancient sacred writings, to avoid GOING DOWN TO DESTRUCTION, and they obeyed not the commandments of the Lord, behold ye the light of your God in this day.

3. For the I'huans, even before the flood, were in the first place born capable of everlasting life. But they mixed with the druks until the seed of the spirit of eternal life became exhausted, and they brought forth heirs incapable of self-sustenance in heaven. Hence it was said of them: They went down in darkness.

4. Now after awhile a new race of I'huans was brought forth, and they were at first capable of All Light and of everlasting life. But they also kept not the commandments of the Lord; but also mixed with the druks (the ground people), and they descended rapidly on the road of everlasting death (as a race).

5. But the Lord your God created the new race, the Ghans, capable of an upward inspiration.

6. And he gave unto them the same commandments, to preserve their seed from the races beneath them, lest they go down in darkness also.

7. To which end thy Lord gave unto them certain rites and ceremonies and pass-words, in addition to the circumcision, which would enable them to distinguish with whom they should mingle according to the commandments of God.

8. Behold ye then the testimony which I lay before you, that ye may perceive the wisdom of my ways: For it will be said by some that there is a law of evolution whereby man riseth from a lower to a higher state as the earth groweth older.

9. But I say unto you, there is no such law. Save but by the labor of thy Lord and thy God, through their angels, man riseth not upward; but he goeth the other way.

10. In which matter, behold, I have left many nations and peoples before you to this day, who are on the downward road. And ye have corporeal records before you, showing you that in times past, the same countries were inhabited by a higher race.

11. For thus Jehovih created man, to go as readily down the mountain as up it.

12. Behold, all resurrection cometh from above; all aspiration cometh from the Lord and his angels. For man, being in the flesh, goeth rather to the desires of the flesh than to the spirit.

13. As the light of the sun causeth sleep to pass away, so doth the light of Jehovih, through His Gods and Lords and angels, cause the soul of men to awake to the possibilities of everlasting life in the exalted heavens.

14. This also have I, thy Lord, proven in the world: that they who fall from the light of the Father, lose their symmetry and beauty of proportions.

15. Behold, in the time of Thor, man considered not the shapeliness of his spouse, nor the mold of her face, nor the clearness of her voice, nor her wit, nor conversational powers.

16. By all stratagems, and devices, and rites and ceremonies, have the Gods and Lords labored to make man mindful of the way of resurrection through the tree of life.

17. But even in this day, behold, the mother bartereth off her daughter to a rich man; and the man seeketh a spouse of wasted flesh for the sake of gold. And they bring forth heirs

of crime.

18. And man crieth out: He cannot be a good God that createth these!

19. But I say unto you, they keep not my commandments; they have gone astray in the wilderness.

20. Be wise, O man; from that which is before you, remember the times of the ancients, and the labor of the Lord your God.

21. In the beginning of the cycle of Thor, the Lord opened up many ways for the deliverance of the tribes of men on the earth; and man prospered in the way of God for a long season.

22. Then darkness came upon the races of men; millions of them returned to a state of savagery. And angels of darkness came upon the earth, verily taking upon themselves the semblance of corporeal forms, and dwelling with mortals, and engaging in practices whereof it is unlawful to write or speak.

23. So that, at the termination of three thousand years, the lands of the earth were covered with darkness.

24. And Jehovih cast a veil over the face of the sun, and it shone not in brightness for many years. (For these nebulous periods, see the latter part, God's Book of Ben)

END OF THE LORDS' FORTH BOOK.

195

BOOK OF OSIRIS, SON OF JEHOVIH

GOD OF LOWTSIN, AN ETHEREAN WORLD IN THE ARC OF SE'ING,
KNOWN IN THE HIGH HEAVEN AS OSIRE, SON OF JEHOVIH.

CHAPTER I.

1. Now came Osire, Son of Jehovih. To him, on his throne in Lowtsin, an ethereal world, where his reign a hundred thousand years had illumined many a corporeal star, came the Voice, Great Jehovih, Spirit over all, saying:

2. Osire! Osire: My Son: Forth from these immortal worlds, and grasp the perishable earth in its debauched flight; and proclaim, with uplifted rod, thyself The One, the commanding God. As an indulgent father treads softly by his infant son, guiding him tenderly, and with wholesome advice, so have I, through My Gods and Chiefs, the red star coaxed along for many, many thousands of years. But as a wise father turneth to his truant son, of later years, commanding, thou shalt or shall, so now do I, through thee, My Godly son, stretch My hand over the earth and her heavens.

3. Deep-buried she lieth, in anarchy, and by false Gods and false Lords, in war despoiling her heavens, and casting down on the troubled earth her millions of spirits of darkness, glutting themselves in crime. As driftwood, on a surging sea, now riseth high on towering waves, and quickly plungeth down in the roaring waters, to rise and fall, and repeat forever the ceaseless struggle, so do the spirits of the dead, of earth, rise in heaven to be plunged back again in unending toil and darkness, on the low earth.

4. Where toil and struggle My most holy God and his Lords, powerless to divert the terrible heedlessness of men and angels. Osire heard Jehovih's voice, and summoned swift messengers, well trained in the rise and fall of worlds, and bade them go to the red star, the earth, in masterly speed, a million strong, and survey the affairs of mortals and spirits, and quickly report back to Jehovih's throne, in Lowtsin, promising succor to God and his Lords of earth.

5. The swift messengers, with an arrow-ship, such as Gods, for speed and light work, use to accomplish Jehovih's will, shot forth through the ji'ay'an fields of darkness, midway between the Serpent's coils, and were soon deep hidden in the whirling atmosphere of the warring earth. Meantime, Osire called to council about Jehovih's throne, long-risen Gods and Goddesses, and told the Voice's words, that stirred his soul with compassion for those but recently quickened to life by the Creator's breath, who persisted in burrowing their souls down in hada, heedless of the call and persuasion of a loving God and Lords.

6. Jehovih's light overspread the Lowtsin throne of Osire, and curtained round the stars, the Gods and Goddesses, with the full history of the earth and her heavens, so that all were clear to comprehend His Almighty Wisdom. Yet not one was moved with haste to answer; for scenes like these were their daily deliberation concerning the countless millions of stars dotting the firmament. And then, slowly, one at a time, the speakers, each a representative of a thousand Gods and Goddesses, gave utterance to Jehovih's light from their respective seats.

7. And when the multitude had spoken, and Osire, charged with the wisdom of all, perceived from human souls how the light matched his own, as to him Jehovih spake, his first sphere of commandant God, stood plain before him. And then he rose up, and stood

in the throne of Jehovih, mantled in white, like one new illumined with a great change in his long life's administration.

8. To Gods and Goddesses, he spake: Give ear, for now the veil of the arc of Se'ing upraises before our hallowed shrine. As step by step, all things advance by Jehovih's will, and new roadways in etherea open up fields unexplored by traveling stars; so onward, step by step, our own endless realm takes the course of manhood in its giant strides. By you have the worlds of corpor and es been blessed for hundreds of thousands of years! Your busy scenes in an old routine change now to higher advent, and an Orian arc cometh anon.

9. As an oscillating star feedeth itself with a change of seasons, so hath Jehovih coursed the wave of His traveling Serpents to give our etherean realms an endless life, diversified by change of scenes and constant surprises, the glory of the soul.

10. As thus Osire, the Mighty, with a soul full of words, engraved by Jehovih's hand, discoursed on the glories awaiting the high worlds, where he and his brother Gods and archangels dwelt in the All Perfect, there came back, hastening, as with Omnipotence impelled, the swift messengers from the slow earth, with their etherean arrow-ship shooting like a meteor on fire. Then came Hagan, spokesman of the messengers, before Jehovih's throne, his mantle turned back, and his eyes radiant with sure knowledge, saluting in Jehovih's sign and name. He said:

11. O Osire, Jehovih's Son, and ye Gods and Goddesses, as the All Light gave Voice to our far-seeing God of Lowtsin, so stand I here to corroborate, in Jehovih's name. The day of sweet persuasion to the earth-born, and their countless angels down in darkness, is done. Lo, the race, the Ghans, planned by Jehovih from the foundation of the world, now standeth triumphant on the earth. As Jehovih led the I'hins in paths fortuitous, by gentle words and love, but left them not strong before the warring elements, so hath He created upon the earth the masters who shall subdue it, to the triumph of Gods.

12. Not like lambs are the Ghans, but lions untamed, born conquerors, with seed to learn and reason toward all things, faith in mastery, but not faith in Jehovih. As a man having two sons, the one low-strung and passionless, the other in ceaseless mischief and desire for havoc, because of the fullness within, so stand the twain, the I'hins and the Ghans, on the earth. And when they die, and enter heaven, the first, the I'hins, go like lambs, as they are directed; but the second, the Ghans, still full of inherent stubbornness and self-will, unheed the God and Lords, and mock at them. Back to the earth these well-formed and stately souls come, and set up heavenly kingdoms of their own, in darkness, and fain pursue with most relentless zeal their former enemies.

13. By their loud clamor and inspiring acts, they break up the weak Lords' kingdoms and despoil them of subjects, proclaiming heaven and earth free to all. Whereby, even hapless souls in the lower heaven have been persuaded to fly from the hospitals and nurseries back to mortals, and there fasten themselves as fetals, shutting up their eyes against all further light.

14. So, mortals have given themselves up to doing the wills of the spirits of darkness, making spoil and desolation a holiday.

15. We then came to God, Jehovih's Son, whose throne lieth in Gau, and he said: Take this message to Osire, Jehovih's Son, God of Lowtsin: Greeting, in the Father's name. Behold, the arc of Se'ing is at hand. Send thou, O God, a ship, and deliver my hosts, four

thousand millions. With that, and in due salutation, we hastened hither.

CHAPTER II.

1. Osire said: In the name of the All Light, I will have fifty millions of conquerors to do my will, on earth and in heaven. But first, send ye an es'elene, with suitable attendants, to deliver God, his Lords, and their hosts, the Brides and Bridegrooms of Jehovih. And leave ye the earth in darkness thirty days. Meantime, let my builders provide me a ship for my hosts; and let the heralds go abroad in Se'ing, announcing this, my decree.

2. Jehovih said: Think not, O man, I gave talents to men differently on earth, and there to end, making My exalted places to be even shorn and alike. Not so created I man; but as one on earth is mild, and leadeth on by smooth words and persuasive behavior; and as another, by quick perceiving and strong will, plungeth in headlong; even so carry I them onward in My high heavens, perfecting them in their bent, but with wisdom and love, till each becometh as a sun in his sphere.

3. Fear not, O man, that I have not labor for them in high heaven: I have worlds to be nurtured and coaxed at times; worlds to be pruned at times, and commanded; by most severe authority made to know that All Power lieth in Me, through My Gods and Lords.

4. For these exalted extreme Gods I have places in he firmament, and worlds numberless, whereon they dwell as stars in My heavens. Thither make I roadways for My traveling corporeal worlds, where lie My etherean fields of pasture, to glorify Me, and lead on the mortal born. So, now, to My commanding God, Osire, who ruled in Lowtsin most amiably, with equals, but was high-strung with impatience toward self-willed ignorance, I brought the undisciplined earth to feel his giant power.

5. Say'ah, scribe of Ctaran, thus described the scene: Osire had spoken; his word had gone forth. Heaven was stirred up; Gods and Goddesses knew that work was on hand, new of its order in this place in the firmament. the earth had sons, at last, worthy the will and service of Gods. Osire, impetuous and much-loved God of Lowtsin, was going to visit these earth-sons, and wash them clean, and put jackets on them.

6. Osire said: In written words will I set down explicit laws for these unruly false Gods, the Ghans, and give them bondage, like the people of other worlds. O that they had had discipline before, instead of sweet persuasion!

7. Say'ah said: When some Gods give command, the people move along; but when Osire decreed, the whole heaven of Lowtsin ran. And quickly, now, the mandates were filled; the ships were built, first, the es'elene, commanded by Yok, and equipped with five million souls, and started off in hot haste to the earth to deliver God and his Lords, and such Brides and Bridegrooms as were prepared for the resurrection. Next, the ship, Buer, an adavaysit, built for Osire and his hosts, fifty millions strong.

8. Osire said: That no adventure run foul, let swift messengers be stationed along the roadways; and they shall announce the proceedings of my Gods and Lords, and their whereabouts. And, even so, was the order of heaven executed. And time came, and passed, and the earth was stripped from her God and Lords, and on her, and her heavens, darkness reigned.

9. Then Osire left his high place, and with his hosts, aboard the etherean ship of fire, sat out toward the earth, at break-neck speed; for such was the disposition of this most

determined God. Nor halted he at Chinvat, the boundary of the earth's vortex, but sped on with banners and curtains flying, and most martial music to stir up the souls of his hosts to sudden tittle.

10. Down he came to the earth with his fire-ship, and sped round about it, to learn its weak and salient points; and next rose up a little to view the atmospherean spirits who had presumed defiance toward high heaven. In the place where Gau had been (whose God, a most holy one, had learned to rule by love for eight hundred years, and was unappreciated by the crude boasters, the unlearned druj), there stood now, castles and mansions of the false God, Utaya, round whom a million of sentinels armed for battle were stationed to protect him, the false, and do his will.

11. Hither came Osire, and over the battlements raised his ship, and brought it even into the arena of the Council of hada. Then, halting, bade his marshals proclaim his voice:

12. Come forth, O Utaya; behold my power! Thy sentinels stand appalled. I raised my hosts by higher law, and stand on my feet in thy citadel.

13. Utaya said: Strange and audacious God! From what unmannerly region hast thou sprung? Know thou, Gods should kneel outside my walls, and beg to know my will, for an audience. Then Osire determined to hear his arguments, and thus spake:

14. From Great Jehovih, I am come! I kneel to none save Him. To do His will in reverence am I come in power and majesty. But erst I demolish thy pitiful walls, and cast thee down, suppliant, to do my will, tell me wherein excusest thou thyself to turn from the exalted heavens, and build here a kingdom of slaves, for thine own glory?

15. Utaya said: O thou jester! Erst I demolish thee and thy ship, and enslave thy hosts as mine, I will, then, pacify thy worthless curiosity, that thou mayest hereafter know thy lesson well. But first, thou has mocked me for my slaves: what more are thy hosts? Hast thou not tampered with their too willing love by stories of thy unseen Jehovih, and persuaded them to suffer thee to lead them on to glory? Now I declare before thee, there is no Jehovih, no All Person! Hence, thy philosophy is founded on falsehood. The space is before us; the worlds are before us; there is nothing more. Let him who will, assume a kingdom; let him who will be a slave, be a slave. I am Apollo!

16. Osire said: When I shall have cast thee down, thou mightest say it was merely because it so happened that one was stronger than another. So, then, that thou mayest remember my words are more in wisdom than in blind force, hear me whilst thou canst, for it is not long that I can talk to such as thou: He who admitteth the universe moveth in harmony and discipline, already admitteth the All Person, Jehovih. He who denieth the All Person, Jehovih, denieth unity in all things. If all things are not in unity, then are all things divided, one against another. Whoever holdeth this, is a disintegrator; and whoever holdeth that all things are a unit, is a unitor. Wherefore, if there be greater strength in unison than in isolation, then therein hath unison won the battle and become the All Person.

17. Touching the matter of slaves: There is but One Master, and He ruleth over all; but it lieth in the power of each and every soul to attune himself with the All Person, which is freedom. Of such are my hosts. Thy slaves attune themselves to thee; they cannot rise higher than thou; my hosts have the universe for their model. Because thou canst not find the Cause of thy coming into life, why not say thou: A name I will call Him, and it shall be Jehovih!

18. And now began Utaya with a long discourse, the which Osire waited not to hear, but turned to his marshals, saying: Break ye down the walls of Gau, and raise me ten thousand pillars of fire. I will here rebuild Jehovih's kingdom. Let the es'enaurs chant, ALL HAIL TO OSIRE, GOD OF HEAVEN AND EARTH!

19. To which the astonished Utaya stood silently, as if to know if it were real, or but a frenzied dream, that any one should so unrecognize his power, now well established for three hundred years.

20. Out of the ship came the hosts, and without command, or waiting to know their parts, but every one in time to the music, taking place in the citadel. Osire strode forward, and by the majesty of his power, overturned the throne of Utaya, the false God, and heaped the rubbish aside. Then, stretching forth his hand, he said:

21. In Thy name, O Jehovih, and by virtue of Thy power, in me vested, do I here command the elements to do my will, and raise me a throne worthy of Thy Immortal Son! And with his voice, his hosts, in concert, quickly piled the adamantine seat, and hung it round with transparent tapestry, woven with the elements of silver and gold.

22. The while the laborers of Osire overturned the walls of Utaya's city, and set free his millions of slaves, even whilst Utaya's officers, panic-stricken, dropped on their knees, pleading for pity, or fled precipitously off to the earth. And Utaya, conjecturing the worthlessness of his stuff, compared to that which descended from the higher heavens, shouted and called in vain to his most steadfast zealots in time of peace and easy rule, beholding them, in thousands, vanquished without even a cruel deed or word.

23. Not long the fray lasted, for Osire's work was as if a man were overturning the toys of a child; and Utaya, to prove his faith in himself, stood sole spectator, unmoved from his tracks, but helpless, wondering what should come next. But now Osire, with no words of explanation or excuse, ascended the new throne and gave the sign, IN JEHOVIH'S NAME, which was answered by his mighty hosts; when, behold, from the vault of heaven above there descended mantles of light, matchless in brilliancy!

24. Utaya was himself illumined, and all his former evil deeds and cruelty stood out in huge black spots, quailing before the sea of light; for round on every side stood millions of souls, all pure and transparent, washed by the ordeal of time and holy works. But Utaya was not all evil, or short in owning an honorable adversary; and so, quickly comprehending his awful plight in the midst of Purity, first let fall a tear, the which, in pity, blinded him from witnessing further his dire humiliation; and next, with blubbering of a beaten school-boy, he cried out:

25. Enough! Enough! Thou God, Almighty! Take me hence, from thy dissolving fire! I was but wont to witness some great God's deeds, to find proof of mine own worthlessness!

26. But Osire was not new to such a situation, and proceeded with the affairs of heaven, appointing officers and laborers, and apportioning his High Council to do Jehovih's will, and so left Utaya to sweat a while in his own torments.

27. O give me relief, cried Utaya, thou God of heaven and earth! I consume, I burn in Purity's flame! For pity, turn down the consuming light!

28. Osire halted from his labors long enough to answer thus: All Light cannot cease for convenience of one man; clothe thyself, O false one, with robes of darkness, and hide thy cruel butcheries. Thou, that wouldst have made slaves of my hosts, should be of holier

200

metal than to plead for help. Behold, not one of thy slaves have I taken, or asked to bow in obedience. To the righteous, the worlds are free; only evil men and evil Gods quail before Jehovih's ceaseless fire!

29. Meanwhile, Utaya hustled close around himself his glittering robes, and pulled his flashing crown down over his scalded eyes, which worthless fabric but fed the fury of the All Light, from the throne of God, Osire's resting-place. The slaves of Utaya had fled, or lay piteously prostrate, speechless with fear and wonder. Over these the hosts of Osire watched, and hastily took them beyond the now rapidly rising pillars of fire, where they were housed temporarily.

30. Still the voice of Utaya rang aloud for help and pity; but to him none came. Then he saw that the prostrate victims fared better and were less conspicuous; so Utaya cast himself prostrate, along with the rubbish of his former throne. Whereupon Osire sent Yesta, sister of Atonas, Goddess of Opsa, in etherea, to rescue him, and mantle him around with balm from the upper heavens.

31. So Yesta and her band took Utaya hence, far beyond the boundaries of the new-laid Gau.

CHAPTER III.

1. Osire spake from the throne, saying: Proclaim it in the east and west, and north and south, there is a God in heaven! That which has transpired in Gau, go tell the false Gods and false Lords in hada, adding: Osire hath come!

2. Messengers started forth for every quarter of the world, inspired by the impetuous utterances of the commanding God. And so, half breathless, and in hastening speed, these young Gods and young Goddesses, the messengers, dropped in upon the Lordly defamers of holiness, and told the tale of the overturned Gau, where proud Utaya fell. And they, in manner and custom, inspired the false rulers to imagine even a worse calamity; and that much had been concealed out of deference to Utaya and other usurpers.

3. Osire called his Council and appointed new places, with new officers, having nothing in common with all past administrations of the Gods of earth and heaven. So far, these appointments were from his etherean hosts, and, moved by the fire of his own energy, quickly assumed their most honorable duties. Some to build, some to survey and lay out the course of streets, and places of habitations; and yet others to remove the old hospitals and nurseries, and make way for new ones, and for factories, and all requisites for the millions of souls now scattered and lost, or in dire confusion struggling in the outside darkness.

4. Whence rose a constant wail of fear and torment, strangely wild, compared to the glorious light fast spreading from the rising pillars of fire about the throne of God. Osire's hosts, fifty millions, attuned to harmony and precision, were proceeding fast with their labor, not one but knew his part and played close to the text in every motion, were yet in number as nothing compared to the thousand millions scattered in the gloomy darkness, wailing beyond the walls.

5. Here, a road! Osire would speak; or with his hand, command: An otevan to those hapless slaves! And, as if his hosts his thoughts had fashioned, his etherean workmen rushed to make his will omnipotent. No loss of time or space to inquire how the matter

should be done; for heaven's trained workmen have learned the power of knowledge braced to a single point, by which the elements stoop to do their wills. To learn this simple harmony, for all to be as one, what countless millions rise up from the earth, to be hurled back, discordant and powerless, before Jehovih's Sons and Daughters! 6. Yea, and kings and queens and potentates, high strung in unwarranted conceit, cast down to beg, beseechingly as a child. As a furious lion is tamed, worthless his giant power in the hands of man, whose strength by knowledge triumphs; so the ethereans from high heaven descend to humiliate first, and then to teach the false Gods and false Lords of hada.

7. Jehovih saith: What more, O man, have I put upon thee than to learn? And strewn thy path with lessons rich in happiness! To learn the elements, and master them; this it is to be a God or Goddess. And wherein one man is weak, let two or more unite; a simple thing, by which even the stars of heaven can be turned from their course.

8. Jehovih saith: Have I not said: The weakest king is he who hath the most soldiers; and the strongest nation, where none are required. How, then, may the false Gods, by evil deeds, fortify their thrones? Lo, My etherean hosts come unarmed, and by a breath blow away their mighty kingdoms.

9. And so it was in Gau; only one earth-day had come and gone since Utaya reigned over a hundred million slaves, who daily brought tribute up from the earth, to ornament this crown-like city; and now the dawn of another world stood supreme in the demolished kingdom.

10. What greater pity, most pitiful sight, than to see the former slaves still loyal to their deposed master, Utaya; coming to him in his banishment, fifty millions swearing terrible oaths of fidelity to him forever. For of such like, the Great Spirit created man, to even wed himself to misery, for zeal, in ignorance, to prove a most foolish love. And but for Utaya's guardians, his very slaves had smothered him, in desperate effort to manifest fidelity.

11. Then spake Yesta to him, saying: Raise thy voice against this unseemly crowd, and be commander still, at least to save thyself. Remember how Jehovih giveth this lesson to mortals, to say to evil: Away! For lo, to suffer first one and then another to fasten upon one's self, is crime great as a debauched passion unchecked. Bid them begone! For love of self, which is thy gift from Great Jehovih, be thou thyself! It will better them also!

12. Utaya, struggling, said: Alas, fair angel! These were my slaves! The hardest blow of all is their acknowledged love. The fire of the throne of Osire was tame to this. For hundreds of years, I gave these creatures pangs and wretchedness, and now they give me love. Poor idiots! I cannot drive them hence!

13. And so, sobbing, bowed Utaya his head, for such sudden great truths turned all his judgment into the darkness of his past deeds and wickedness, even whilst, crowding close on every side, the fifty millions kept up their ceaseless assurances of endless love. Nor was there any way open to flight from their ignorant jargon and foul breath. So, when Yesta saw how helplessly Utaya had given up, she raised her hand, saying: What shall I do, O Jehovih?

14. Whereat, the Light descended, and Jehovih spake through Yesta, saying: Flesh of My flesh created I man: from Mine Own Spirit gave I man a spirit also; and unto all men alike gave I all things in My worlds. But some men are not content with what I gave,

202

but ask for more, even that they may have their fellows for subjects. To these I have given in answer to their prayers. Behold thou, then, O man, why seekest thou to put away today even what, a day since, thou didst pray for? They are as good today as yesterday.

15. Thou hast said: Man can make himself whatsoever he will! So, thy Creator is worthless to thee. Love is the lightest of all burdens; if thou desirest not to carry their love, how didst thou carry their hate so long? Nevertheless, if thou desirest, thou canst put them away: They are thine; do as thou wilt.

16. Utaya said: How can I put them away? I cannot reason with fifty millions! Nay, before I persuaded a score, the first ones, so ignorant, would forget what I said. Tell me, then, thou Goddess, what shall I do to free myself from this great multitude?

17. Yesta said: Call not on me, but on thy Creator; and not to be freed for thine own good, but for wisdom to do some good unto them over whom thou hast long been a remorseless tyrant. These are a small curse to thee, compared to thine own judgment, for from thyself thou canst never flee. Thou shalt undo thy selfish deeds, which thou hast practiced so long. So, turn thou at once, and make oath to Him who made thee, that from this time forth thou wilt do good unto others with all thy wisdom and strength.

18. Utaya said: Alas, thy words are wise and holy, but I have no faith! I have not faith!

19. Yesta said: Say not this! Thy words are another bondage on thy soul. To say, I have no faith, is to imprison thyself away from All Light. Come, haste, or lo, I leave thee; for if thou profess not faith, why shall I longer labor with thee? Say thou: I have faith in Thee, O Jehovih! I can, I will raise up these I have cast down. Utaya wept, and thus answered: O that I had faith like unto thee! But for long years I taught myself that prayer to Jehovih was not required of one so great and strong as I. Alas, I smothered out the fire. And, amidst his sobs, Utaya fell prostrate at Yesta's feet.

20. Quickly, now, she raised her slender hand toward high heaven, saying: O Jehovih, by Thy power vested in me, I here encircle this, Thy prostrate child, with adamantine light! Down from above there came phosphorescent flames of light, and Yesta drew a circle round about, at which the multitude stood back and looked on in wonder and fear. But the surging mass beyond pressed forward, shouting: Utaya! Utaya!

21. Little by little, Yesta extended the light, and her assistants put up a structure to guard the place, so that in a little while it was like a miniature throne in heaven. Yesta then assumed the power, and so took command, placing helpless Utaya by her side. Meanwhile, her assistants sped through the multitude, making roadways, and selecting out the most intelligent of the former slaves, and making guards of them.

22. Yesta said to Utaya: Now will I give thee a lesson in righteousness; for thou shalt educate and develop all this host, thy former slaves, to thine own level, erst thou raise thyself one jot or tittle. Think not it is easy to assume to be a God or a Lord, or even a mortal king. They that make servants of others must also raise them up to be angels of light. Heaven is just, as well as bountiful. To whom Jehovih hath given bountifully, it is commanded he shall give bountifully. For hundreds of years thou hast had the service of these hapless creatures; so shalt thou now serve them by making them intelligent men and women. Yea, till the lowest of them are thine own equals, of whom thou canst be proud, and say before the Father: Behold, my sister! behold my brother!--thou, Utaya, shall not be free!

23. Utaya said: I perceive thy words are from the All Highest. This is justice! I perceive

now that whilst I rated myself supreme judge of right and wrong, I judged with partiality to myself. Yea, without an All Highest, I perceive there can be no justice in heaven or earth. O Thou All Light, how can I approach Thee! I have been feeding myself with an endless poison; my darkness was my fortress. Teach me the way, O thou angel of Light! Whatsoever Jehovih wills, that will I do, from this time onward, with all my wisdom and strength.

24. So Yesta restored order, and divided the multitude into many parts, and sent officers amongst them to select and assort them, so that as soon as Osire should decree asylums and schools for them, they could be taken to them.

CHAPTER IV.

1. Osire lost no time, but officered Gau and established his Council in hot haste, making Ote as temporary God on the throne, whilst he himself went forth to other regions, to conquer and overturn false Gods and Lords. Leaving, therefore, a sufficient guard and council, Osire, with a host of twenty millions, went westward in atmospherea, over and above the great central north lands, where was established Wotchak, a false God, with another hundred millions of slaves, to do his will.

2. Wotchak, having been advised by the messengers of Osire's approach to the earth's heavens, supposing Osire to be from some remote star, and not knowing there were etherean worlds in the firmament, had laid his kingdom round with new walls, and doubly fortified his throne, and gaudily attired himself and officers, in hopes to overawe the coming God.

3. To Wotchak came Osire, and waited not to be announced, nor halted for his sentinels, driving his ship straight up to the throne.

4. Halt! Halt! cried the astonished Wotchak. Who dares my throne profane, and all the rules of virtuous Gods set at defiance? Down from thy ship, and crawl on thy belly to thy sovereign God! Know thou, I am Great Apollo! But Osire deigned only to say: By what authority hast thou made slaves of Jehovih's sons and daughters, to augment thine own self-glory?

5. And, not waiting a reply alighted down before the throne, even while a thousand or more, well drilled, with him stood, in the form of a star, whereon the Upper Light descended in great brilliancy. Wotchak was frightened, and fled from his throne, and all his Council with him. Then spake Osire, saying to his hosts:

6. Suffer not this false God and his Council to escape. Encircle them round, and hold them, to know my will and the decree of Jehovih. Presently, the ethereans brought back Wotchak, who cried out: O, let me go! Take all, but let me go! What am I to thee?

7. Osire answered him, saying: Such hath been the history of these heavens. In ages gone, the usurping false Gods were suffered to go their way, leaving their former subjects helpless on the hands of the etherean hosts. That day is past. I am come to make such Gods know that their fate and responsibilities rest on the decrees of a Higher One, even the Creator, Jehovih. Behold, thou hast cast down and blighted a hundred million of Jehovih's children, making slaves of them, to do thy will. As thou wert the cause of their fallen state, from liberty to bondage, so, no, shalt thou redeem them to freedom, and wisdom and truth.

8. Whilst Osire spake, his proper officers let fall the light from the upper regions, the like of which Wotchak had never beholden. Presently, all things became transparent, and the enraged Wotchak, foreseeing trouble ahead, thus answered:

9. Accuse me not, thou audacious God! These, my Council, urged me hundreds of years ago to my course, and only for the favor they might remain my close advisors. I was their tool, and, if thou desirest justice, make them to feel the sting of repentant labor. Let them have my slaves. I want them not. I have been a most honest, upright God!

10. And now his counselors accused one another, and all of them heaping the blame on Wotchak. Lighter and lighter grew the etherean flames, from which there was no concealment; and all their former falsehoods and cruel words, and evil deeds, were unveiled, disclosing souls dark and hideous, with long-covered-up crimes, now made bare for the gaze of every eye.

11. The which scene brought the curious slaves, in millions, to witness it, and to reassure the suffering false God of their love and loyalty. And when Wotchak looked and beheld the abject wretches who claimed him as their worshipful God, he cried out: Enough! Enough! Unfeeling God! Thou art come in pretended right and peace; but, because of thy power, executest on me and my Council torments more terrible than I ever gave to slave of mine. Know thou, I am Apollo!

12. To which Osire answered: What are names to me! With that, Osire, by waving his hand, caused his hosts to cast aside the false God's throne, and all its glittering gems scatter abroad, relics for the multitude. And now three pillars of light shot up and stood beside Osire and his attendants, the which took all the strength and courage out of Wotchak and his confederates, and they crouched down at Osire's feet.

13. Osire called Itu, saying: Take them without, and hand them over to their slaves awhile. And Itu and his guard gathered them from the light and bore them hence. Quickly, now, Osire officered this newly-conquered place in heaven, and called it Autat, signifying, foundation of perishable laws. And on a new throne, appointed Luce as temporary God, giving him a council of one thousand ethereans. And now Osire drew the plans for roads, and temples, and schools, and hospitals, and nurseries, and all such other habitations as are required by spirits newborn, in heaven, leaving orders to have them completed by a given time.

14. Next, Osire ordered the divisions and selections to be made in the now scattered hosts of atmosphereans, and to have them all arrested and put into their proper places. These things he left in the charge of God, Luce, to be carried out.

15. Far out on the plateau, Itu and his attendants carried Wotchak and his confederates, followed by forty millions of his former slaves. There Itu left Wotchak and his people, and Itu and his attendants went aside to witness whatever should transpire.

16. At this stage, Osire departed with his ship and steered southward over the land of shem, coming to a place in the lower heaven called Vibrahj, signifying resplendent, where ruled the false God, Daveas, who had eight hundred millions of slaves, a thousand Lords, and ten thousand Governors.

17. And, even as Osire rushed in headlong upon the other false Gods, so came he with his fire-ship into the great city of Vibrahj, at this time the largest city of the lower heaven. Daveas had been warned by his sentinels, and so came to the front of his capital, just in time to see the fearless Osire alight on the piazza in front of the Council House.

CHAPTER V.

1. Osire said: In the name of Jehovih, peace be unto thee! To which Daveas replied: Nay, in the name of Apollo, who I am! How darest thou approach, save to crawl on thy belly? Four hundred years hath the honor of my kingdom been revered by all visiting Gods; but thou comest as a barbarian. Down, wretch! Erst I have thee bound and cast in prison!

2. Osire said: Why should I not come before thee? Behold, the Great Spirit created the whole universe for His Sons and Daughters. By what right hast thou usurped a portion? And whence thy authority to bid me kneel to thee? But if thou canst show me wherein thou hast one just claim to enslave these people, rather let thy argument run thither, for I am come in the name of the Father to liberate them, that they may be prepared for the second and third resurrections.

3. Daveas said: Think not that I have neglected to prepare for rebellious Gods like thou. Behold my millions of subjects! What is thy handful? Verily, I tell thee I have prisons large enough to hold thee and thy hosts. Neither flatter thyself that I am ignorant. For two hundred years I wrought in the so-called resurrections; I made myself a slave to the multitude, giving all my labor and time. Then I beheld my folly, and so built a third resurrection myself. This is, therefore, my lawful kingdom. Moreover, I tell thee to thy face, thou wretch, there is no higher heaven than mine. Neither comest thou from a heaven great as mine. But having great self-conceit, thou art come for mischief. I have heard of thee in other heavens! But now thou hast put thy head into the halter. Seize him, marshals! Seize him and his hosts! Cast them in prison!

4. Osire spake not, but raised his hand upward in the seventh sign, and suddenly his hosts casts forth sheets of light brighter than the sun. Daveas stood back affrighted, and his marshals fled. Presently, Osire, with a thousand attendants, stepped forth in flames of light, and went up into the capital and surrounded Daveas, the usurper, but touched him not. And now the ship was illumined, and lo, the sentinels of Daveas' Council broke and fled. Hereupon, Osire spake, saying:

5. Hand of Thy hand, O Jehovih; voice of Thy voice, overturn Thou this house and throne! And, behold, the light of the upper heavens rested in Osire's palms, and he smote the house and the throne, and they tumbled over as straw before a hurricane. Alone stood Daveas, the evil God, half speechless and half blinded by the great Light of Jehovih. Down! down! said Osire, to the walls and temples of the city. And his hosts concentrated at any point Osire's hand directed; and lo, everything fell and was scattered far.

6. Meanwhile, the officers of Daveas fled in all directions, save such as were overcome by the light, and these fell and were buried themselves amidst the rubbish.

7. Hold! Hold! cried Daveas. Give me air! I perish! I am a consuming fire! And he tossed his hands aloft; then cringed his face within his glittering robes. And now Osire called forth thunder and lightning, and sent shafts through, and over, and about the whole plateau of Vibrahj, and the din and roar confounded all the eight hundred millions of souls, so they ran no farther, but stood and waited, watching what should next befall.

8. Osire halted not, but went forward to a more suitable place, to build his throne. Jehovih! Almighty! he cried: Elements of Thy elements, O Father! Found here a throne for Thy Son! And even so, for whilst his words went forth, the elements rose to do his will, and there raised a most excellent throne, strong and adamantine, on which Osire

ascended. Daveas had fallen flat down, weeping and wailing; but Osire, by a motion of the hand, called Wang-te, a most enlightened archangel, with her attendants, to bear him hence, the which was quickly done.

9. Quickly, now, the place being cleared, the hosts of Osire fenced around a sufficient space for a city of a thousand million souls, with pillars of light, as brilliant as an arc in the etherean firmament. Hereat, Osire appointed Klesta, Dawn Goddess, and he gave her a council of fifty thousand ethereans. Outside of the walls of the pillars of agni were Daveas and his eight hundred million subjects, in dire confusion.

10. Wang-te, the archangel, said to Daveas: In thine own falsehood thou art favored to free thyself awhile, to organize a new kingdom, but in holiness, and return and command obedience from this smothering host. Behold, thou has taught them to believe thou art Apollo; say to them now: I am not Apollo! I have been false!

11. Daveas madly replied: Never! Jehovih and His kingdoms accursed be forever! Ye strange spirits, come from far-off kingdoms, to despoil and overturn the most righteous place in heaven! Are Jehovih and His servants destroyers! To which Wang-te replied: This is no time for argument; behold here these countless millions! If I withdraw from thee, and my attendants also withdraw, thou wilt be as one drowned amidst this sea of ignorance and horrid smells. Assume at once, for pity's sake, to purge thyself of thy life-long falsehoods and treacherous tyranny. Announce thyself as Daveas, as thou art, and I can save thee!

12. Daveas rudely thrust her aside, saying: Never! I acknowledge to none! If there be a higher heaven, I will ascend thither as I am, Apollo! Apollo! Wang-te said: Put me not off, in Jehovih's name! Remember what thou art, and of the little thou hast seen, how powerless thou art before Omnipotence! Thy fate is like that of all dictators, on the verge of a chasm of horrors. Daveas waited not to hear her further, but proclaimed aloud, Apollo! Apollo! and stood aside. And presently his former officers rushed to him, and with that came the sea of millions of spirits, unorganized, unwashed, unfed, frightened and mad, for love of the name Apollo, the meaning of which they knew not; and they became as a knot of serpents, entwined around the central figure, Daveas and his officers. And in the terrible brawl not one voice could be distinguished from another. And the outer extreme pressed inward, on every side, and presently the eight hundred millions were as a ball, a knot of darkness, with a dull and rumbling moan within, and fearful clamor on the surface, from which horrid smells issued in all directions.

13. Wang-te and her attendants hastened back to the throne of Osire, Son of Jehovih, to tell what had happened. Osire said: What shall I do, O Father? Then the Light of Jehovih came, and Jehovih spake, saying: Consider My Creation, My son. The young child I made to fall with few bruises; but the full-grown man falleth heavily. Shall I make a separate rule to favor kings and queens on the earth, and false Gods in heaven? Nay, verily. Behold, I will make of Daveas an example in heaven, and on earth, also. Because he hath spurned his own name, so will I make both angels and mortals to curse and shun the name, Daveas.

14. Osire said: Proceed ye with my kingdom, in the name of the father. Let Daveas rest awhile as he is.

15. At that, Osire departed, taking the remainder of his hosts with him in his fire-ship; and he went to a heavenly place to the westward, where was Seru, a false God, with

ten millions of slaves; and Osire destroyed Seru's kingdom also. Next, he went to a heavenly place in the north, where Raka, a false God, had seventy millions of slaves; and Osire destroyed his kingdom also, liberating his slaves, and putting a guard over Raka.

16. Thus went Osire throughout atmospherea, demolishing all the heavenly kingdoms of the false Gods, of whom there were, in all, seven hundred and eighty; but many of them had not a million of subjects. Thirty days, in all, was Osire engaged in destroying the evil kingdoms in the lower heavens, and then the work was finished.

17. Osire said to his hosts: For thirty days we labored in destroying that which was; now will we rebuild to Jehovih for another thirty days. Take the ship, therefore, to Vibrahj, for thither will I found my central kingdom. And after we shall have completed the work of starting the second resurrection on a sure foundation, then will we go down to the earth and overturn the kingdoms of the false Lords and men.

CHAPTER VI.

1. Jehovih said: Vibrahj shall be My place; thy throne, Osire, shall be My throne. Send sheriffs out into all the divisions of heaven where thou hast destroyed the evil kingdoms. And thy sheriffs shall arrest all the false Gods whom thou hast dispossessed, and bring them hither, that I may speak with them face to face.

2. Then spake Osire to the sheriffs, saying: Go ye out into all the divisions of atmospherea, and arrest and bring hither all the false Gods whom I have dethroned, saying to each of them: Osire, God of the lower heavens, commandeth my presence. Come thou, and hear the voice of thy Creator. But it shall happen that many will fear to come, because of the light, lest their evil deeds be seen; say to all such: The light will be lowered for a short space of time; come, therefore, quickly.

3. To all the knots, where the false Gods are enveloped, shall ye take umbrae, a sufficiency, that ye may release them. But leave ye with the knot a sufficient guard to keep them in their places.

4. The sheriffs went abroad, as commanded, being sufficiently provided with attendants and all things required for such adventures; and after many days the false Gods were arrested and brought before the throne of God, Osire, Jehovih's Son. And there were assembled, on that occasion, one hundred thousand archangels, of whom two thousand had risen to the rank of Gods and Goddesses, and thirty thousand to the rank of Lords and Lordesses.

5. Osire said to the false ones: Brothers, greeting, in the name of Jehovih! Nor shall ye fear, nor be expectant of torture or punishment. Though I come in All Power, my words shall be tempered with wisdom. But I can be no respecter of persons, nor swerve one jot or tittle from Jehovih's commandments.

6. The bondage of all men was in the Father; for, before ye were conscious individuals, Jehovih stretched forth His hand, and ye came forth from Void, which was your prison in which your selves had been as nothing.

7. In likeness of the Father, I came to deliver them ye had bounden; and through Him have I attained power to that end. So, in likeness of Him, also, I cannot bind you, or cast you in prison. Nay, my sheriffs have just delivered you from bondage, and I am now holding you free from the knots.

8. Most of ye are learned men of the second resurrection; but ye have used your wisdom

208

for self-glorification, being proud to call yourselves Gods; not to teach them of Jehovih and His kingdoms, but falsely teaching that your own kingdoms were the All Highest, thereby shutting out the true light from the unlearned.

9. Jehovih hath blessed you all with strong minds and handsome forms, whereupon, ye have each of you falsely proclaimed ye were Apollo. Think not that this matter was not known in high heaven. I have here the reports of swift messengers, which were brought to me in the firmament above. I came not in ignorance of what ye were doing; neither came I in weakness. More than a hundred thousand millions, who have been raised up to etherea from the earth and its heavens, stand at my side. Besides these, a million times as many ethereans, from other worlds; and above all of these, the Great Orian Chiefs; and yet beyond, and over all, Great Jehovih!

10. Have I not proved my power before you all? Did I go away in a corner and say: Come, I will show you my power? Nay, I came close to you all. As the Father first proveth power, so have I. After that, wisdom. That I may talk to you in wisdom, I had you arrested and brought hither. Hear me then, and remember my words.

11. In former cycles, the high Gods who descended to these heavens, finding false Gods, simply liberated their slaves, but put no labor of restitution on the false Gods. This was because the false Gods of those periods were too imbecile and unlearned. But the earth and her heavens have progressed to a higher state. And with progression cometh, also, responsibility. With learning cometh responsibility; and with wisdom, also.

12. Ye bound your subjects to your kingdoms; and ye perceive, now, ye cannot put them aside. Ye taught them your kingdoms were the All Highest; they must now be unlearned. Ye taught them that ye were the All Highest Gods! They must be unlearned in this, also. Ye put aside the ancient rites and ceremonies, wherein the name of Jehovih was used, teaching them to sing to you, only. They must be taught new songs, substituting the Great Spirit, to Whom none can attain, forever. Ye taught them to be unthinking, and contented as slaves; they must now be taught to think for themselves, and to labor for everlasting liberty.

13. And now, touching the law of the resurrection, remember ye, this is the same in all the created worlds; which is, that the spirit of man groweth by giving away of whatsoever the spirit hath to give. If ye have great learning, and ye give of it, then shall more learning be added unto you; if ye have goodness of heart, and gentle words, then, by giving this away, more shall be added unto you; if ye have craft in inventions or mechanics, and ye bestow of these talents unto others, then will more be added unto you. As the corporean man accumulateth corporeal things by not giving them away, not so accumulateth the spirit of any man.

14. For he who locketh up the light of the Father that is in him, cannot obtain more light; he who locketh up goodness of heart, cannot obtain strength of spirit. And without strength of spirit, no man can attain to the third resurrection. But, that men may learn to obtain strength of spirit, the second resurrection has been established in atmospherea belonging to all the habitable corporeal worlds.

15. The chief delight of man shall be, therefore, to find some way to impart his spiritual talents and strength, and to the greatest possible number of people. Think not that preaching to the ignorant is sufficient; but ye shall take hold with your own hands and show them how to accomplish. Yet not labor alone; for some are so created that ye cannot

inspire them without rites and ceremonies and music.

16. Nor shall a man, after having taught and raised up a few, say: Behold, what a good work I have done! But as long as he findeth a man, or woman, or child, who lacketh in anything, he shall feel to say: Alas, what I have done is as nothing in the resurrection of my fellows.

17. For the rule holdeth for all men alike, to desire exaltation, and everlasting liberty, and unlimited power; and unless ye are prepared to give even these unto others, then ye cannot attain them yourselves. Neither is it possible for man to turn away from responsibility; to whom the Father hath given, from him the Father requireth. Ye have had your kingdoms. Yea, and boasted of them. Your boasts have ascended to etherea. Will ye go thither and be asked: Where is thy kingdom? Shall it be said ye shirked from the care of them the Father gave into your keeping?

18. Bethink ye, O brothers! When the conscience of man turneth inward, there is still darkness slumbering in his soul. The etherean lights will burn him. He whose conscience no longer burned inward, becometh himself a brilliant flame of light. Through him Jehovih speaketh.

19. Osire ceased; and now a brilliant light descended around about the throne, and presently Jehovih spake through Osire, saying:

20. Times and half-times have I given to My corporeal worlds and their heavens. In a time have I made a full resurrection to those who aspire to My heavens above. Nor do I go away from any place I created, saying: Go thou alone for a season. But in a time I manifest a new light, for such, also, are My creations. Think not that I have given seasons to corporeal worlds only; I gave seasons to atmospherea, also.

21. Is not a summer on the earth half a time? And the winter half a time? And the two, one full time? So created I for atmospherea a time of four hundred years, and a half-time of two hundred years. And in seven times and one half-time created I one dan'ha.

22. I sent my Gods to teach these things since thousands of years; whereby My angels might know the times of My resurrections. Hath not a farmer knowledge of the resurrection of spring, when I cover the earth over with new-growing things which I raise up out of the earth? How much more knowledge should my angels have of my spring-times, in atmospherea, when My archangels come to gather in My harvests of emancipated souls.

23. I commanded My etherean hosts, saying: Go ye to the lower heaven and teach them there is no such thing as individual resurrection. And they came proclaiming My word, showing all people that any number of individuals were as nothing unless united, which is the salvation I provided unto all My worlds.

24. For I created progress to be in compact; nor gave I to any person individual salvation or resurrection. That men might learn the advantage of compact, I caused mortals to have corporeal languages, and to live in cities. That ye in atmospherea might learn the All Perfection of being one with one another, I gave you the second resurrection; teaching you, through My Gods and Lords, to abnegate self-aspiration, for self-aspiration is at the expense of others; but commanding ye to learn to assimilate with one another.

25. And I gave rites and ceremonies, amongst which was the oath of service unto Me and My kingdoms, and unto none other, wherein many bound themselves, which was, and is, the beginning of liberty. Touching which matter, I created types on earth and in

the lower heavens, that even the unlearned might understand Me and My works.
26. For to him that begetteth children gave I bondage, to them and to him conjointly. But this is a bondage that circumventeth not liberty in time to come, for they can ascend to heaven, and progress conjointly, better than alone. But some gave themselves up to love earthly things, such as houses, and money, and kingdoms, which things have no resurrection. Hence, such bondage holdeth the person after death to the thing he loved.
27. In type of which, many have set up kingdoms in the lower heavens, binding themselves to things that have no higher resurrection, which things belong on the plateau of atmospherea where I created them. But to them who have bound themselves to their fellows, saying: I am the salvation! it is like a young man saying to a maiden: Come, I will be thy husband. And she goeth to him in confidence. Here, then, is bondage; and she holdeth him as the way of her salvation. Wherein, not he alone can annul that which hath been united, nor yet they twain; for, by their bondage, I am also a party to the contract.
28. In which manner, they that assume kingdoms, professing to be Gods of salvation, and thus enticing My innocent ones unto themselves, become bound, not only to their subjects, but to the contract of deliverance unto salvation; for so, created I them.
29. The Voice ceased, and Osire said: If a man wed a woman with an evil temper, his glory lieth not in going away from her, but in teaching her to overcome her temper; or, if her husband be evil, her glory lieth not in going away from him, but in reforming him. Rather is it wise to accomplish whatever work Jehovih hath put in thy way, than to desert it for sake of personal comfort.
30. Nevertheless, there is a limit to all things, save Jehovih; and to the wise there is power to accomplish much that seemeth impossible at first. Hear ye, then, my judgment upon you, which is that:
31. Ye shall again assume kingdoms, and every one shall have all the subjects he had before. And ye shall be provided with places and thrones by my archangels, and with councils of my archangels also. And I will give to each and every one of you an assistant God, who shall sit on your right hand for four years, the time of this dawn, teaching how to teach, and what to teach.
32. My hosts will now conduct you to the places prepared for you, around which are erected walls of agni. And when ye are safely seated on your thrones, your former subjects shall be brought before you in groups, and adjudged to the labor, and to the schools, and such other places as are suited to them, according to their strength and talents.
33. And I pronounce it upon you, that ye shall deliver your respective subjects sufficiently for the third resurrection. Wherein, according to your zeal and faithfulness, will my hosts labor with you, to the end that Jehovih may be glorified in your harvests for the emancipated worlds. Attend, therefore, to give the sign, IN JEHOVIH'S NAME, and receive ye ordination from my hands, by the power and wisdom of the Great Spirit.
34. The sheriffs showed them how to make the sign, and how to stand before the throne; and then Osire said: By Thy Wisdom, and Love, and Power, O Jehovih, which rest in me, do I annoint these, Thy Gods, for Thy service, and for the exaltation of Thy kingdoms, forever! Amen.
35. The light was now becoming so brilliant that many of the newly-made Gods quailed before it. But the marshals conducted them, and they passed before the throne of Osire,

where they were crowned and arrayed as Gods of the second resurrection; after which they were again conducted before the Council, and saluted on the sign; and thence, to martial music, they were taken to the kingdoms prepared for them.

CHAPTER VII.

1. Who shall tell the story of the Gods of heaven! Their mighty kingdoms, overspreading he whole earth! Hundreds and hundreds, and thousands! Their libraries of records of valorous and holy deeds! A council chamber of half a million souls! Hundreds of departments; thousands! Here a board to select young students to the colleges of messengers. Another board to select students to the colleges of arts. Another to select students to mathematics. Another for prophecy. Another for great learning. Another for factories. Another for compounding and dissolving elements. Then come the departments of the cosmogony of the stars; then, of the ethereal worlds; then, the roadways of the firmament; then, a'ji and ji'ya, and nebulae; then, se'mu; then hi'dan and dan; then, the dawn of dan; then, histories of the heavens far and near; then, genealogy of thousands of Orian Chiefs; the creation of mineral, vegetable and animal kingdoms. Yea, but to enumerate the half of what cometh before a God and his council would itself fill a book.

2. Who, then, O Jehovih, shall venture to tell the labor and wisdom of Thy etherean Gods! How shall the second resurrection give up its mysteries? Shall Thy recorder follow the young student for messenger, and disclose the training put upon him? How, like a carrier dove, he is taught to go from place to place, but holding the message in his head? Then follow the student in another department, and make a record of how he is taught? And of the multitude of questions that come before the Council from far-off places. Then the rites and ceremonies, and the unending variety and magnificence of the music. Can a man describe a million men and women and children? A hundred millions! A thousand millions! Five thousand millions! Who hath seen so great a man, to do this! And yet this is but Thy lower heaven, O Jehovih!

3. A strange voice riseth up from the earth, saying: Have they anything to do in heaven? O ye Gods! And one half of the earth-born coming hither in infancy! And the countless millions who know little more than the beasts of the field! To be falsely taught that these unfortunates would skip off to paradise and possess great learning in the hour of death!

4. O that their understanding could be opened up to Thy kingdoms, Thou All-Extending Creator! That their eyes could look upon the greatness of even Thy lower heaven! To behold a thousand departments reaching as wide as the earth! And then the hundreds of thousands of branch departments, of hundreds of grades, adapted to every soul that riseth up from the earth.

5. O that they could look into the dark places in atmospherea! That they could see a million souls, plunged in chaos by terrible war! Crazed spirits, wild and battling! Not knowing they are dead! The ceaseless toil of a million nurses and physicians, laboring day and night with them! O the darkness upon them! O the glory of Thy exalted ones! Who is there, having seen the magnificence of Thy glories, will not bestir himself every moment to lift up his brother and point the way to Thy throne?

6. O that they could see Thy swift Gods of dawn! How they hear a hundred tongues at one time, and frame answers for all of them, and, by a motion of the hand, dispatch

messengers to fulfill the same in words! How they select officers, to know a hundred at a glance, and know where to place them; that every one shall fit his place! Who is there, O Father, can frame into words the proceedings of heaven, so that mortals can comprehend even a fraction of Thy great glories!

7. Shall a man light a candle and say it representeth the sun? How, then, shall they find the affairs of mortals comparable to Thy kingdoms? O, that they knew the meaning of the difference betwixt All Light and the darkness of man's judgment.

8. O that they knew Thee, Thou Central Sun of All Light! They have put away Thy Person, and they go in any direction. Thy Great Gods are but myths to them, because of the darkness of their souls. Behold, they look for a small man with a large sword! The power of great wisdom they know not.

9. That they could behold the coming and going of thousands of messengers, from far-off kingdoms, before the throne of Thy God! How he hath answered their matters suddenly! And the while heeded the voices of a thousand marshals! O that man knew the glory of Order! The power of Harmony!

10. They have seen a clock with a hundred wheels, and the eye of its maker overseeing its every part in motion, and they call it wonderful! But how can they know Thy Councils, O Jehovih? Thy millions? And Thy God on his throne, mantled in Thy Light, overseeing a whole heaven! What majesty of words can make mortals comprehend His wisdom, and power, and great labors!

CHAPTER VIII.

1. Thus Osire established Vibhraj, the resplendent heaven, with a thousand and eight hundred sub-kingdoms, in atmospherea, all under the commandments of the central kingdom. And then he established the roadways between them, and appointed seven hundred thousand messengers. After that he ordained proper officers for inter-communion; and the several sub-kingdoms established their places of learning and places of labor; their hospitals and nurseries, and their innumerable asaphs, the receivers of es'yans, the newborn spirits of the dead of earth.

2. Osire said: Behold, there is order in heaven. Now will I appoint a God to hold dominion two hundred years. For whilst the dawn of dan yet remaineth, I will assist him. Let the examiners search, then, amongst my hosts, from such as sprang from the earth, such one as standeth clear on the record, and chief in rank.

3. So the examiners searched; and after thirty days, they selected Konas; and when Osire was informed, he sent a thousand of his own attendants, in an otevan, and they brought Konas to Vibhraj, to Jehovih's throne. Osire said:

4. Greeting, in the name of the Father! Thou art chosen above all others; and, after the dawn of dan is ended, thou shalt be God of heaven and earth for two hundred years. Before the ascent of my hosts and of myself, behold, I will crown thee. Till then, thou shalt sit on my throne, and fill my place whilst I am absent.

5. I have now restored order in heaven, having given all the inhabitants a single purpose in concert, whereby their resurrection is surely founded. Now will I go down to the false Lords' kingdoms, on the earth, and to the mortal kings and queens, and restore order there also.

6. Konas said: Thy will and Jehovih's be done! I am exalted and rejoiced in what is

213

bestowed upon me. Make me strong and wise, O Jehovih, that I may glorify Thy kingdoms!

7. So, after due preparation, Osire departed privately, taking with him one hundred thousand attendants, going down to the earth and to the false Lords' kingdoms, in the cities and temples of mortals.

8. Seven days Osire spent traveling round about the earth, visiting angels and mortals, but telling none who he was, or what was his object; and then he halted his otevan, which had been built for the purpose, in the regions of the mountains of We-ont-ka-woh, in Western Jaffeth. He said:

9. We-ont-ka-woh shall be my headquarters for a season. Here, then, will I found the first Lord's kingdom for mortals; and inasmuch as mortals have made an idol of Apollo, so will I cast down Apollo, and make them know that I, Osire, am Lord of the earth. Then spake We'taing, saying:

10. Behold the glory of Jehovih from the first! In our journey around the earth, we have found the I'hins not idolaters, but still worshippers of the Great Spirit, Jehovih. But as to the half-breeds, who can understand them? They believe nothing; they believe everything. They ask the idol for rain, and for dry weather! For strength to slay the druks; for flesh to eat, and for famine to be visited on their enemies.

11. They are as living prey for druj to feast on; they invite the darkest of all evil. And to do their wills in return, the druj, the evil spirits, busy themselves inoculating the air with poison to kill their enemies.

12. Osire said: With the I'hins we have little to do; but as to the Ghans and the I'huans, they shall be converted into disbelievers of all spirits, save two, Jehovih and satan.

13. To accomplish which end, I will give them three figures: The signs of seasons, which shall represent the Creator in all the parts of the living; the sign of the sun, with motion and all life coming forth; and the hand of man.

CHAPTER IX.

1. Through Osire, Jehovih said:

2. I created man with a corporeal life, that he might learn corporeal things; but behold, the I'huans have lost all energy to acquire earthly knowledge, depending on their familiar spirits for information on everything. Thereby wasting their mortal lives in non-improvement. So that when they die, and enter heaven, they are easily made slaves of by evil spirits.

3. Better were it for them had they no knowledge of spirit life, that they might put to service the talents I created within them. See to this matter, O My sons and Daughters; for their desire for the presence of the spirits of the dead will draw fetals upon themselves, and they will go down in darkness, like the ancients.

4. The Voice departed, and then Osire said: Hear me, O brothers, O sisters; this is my commandment upon you, and to you to render unto your successors after such time as I shall call you for the resurrection:

5. Possess ye the temples and oracles, where the familiar spirits speak; neither suffer ye familiars to come more to kings, nor queens, nor governors, nor to leaders nor rulers of men; but take ye possession of all such, and answer ye the corporeans with corporean knowledge only.

6. And that ye may be as a unit unto mortals, give ye all the same name, even Jehovih, through His Son, Osire. For when ye answer at the oracle, or in the altar or temple, they will ask who the spirit is; and ye shall say: Osire, Son of Jehovih; doing this in my name and the Father's.

7. And when ye speak by entrancement, through the seers and prophets, also assert the same thing. And they will ask: Why has the Son of Jehovih come to us? And ye shall say:

8. Because ye are an idolatrous people, worshipping before stone and wood; whereby evil spirits take advantage of you, and rule you to your own hurt.

9. And they will reason amongst themselves, saying: How know we not, then, that thou thyself be not an evil spirit? And ye shall say: It is well that ye ask this, for I declare unto you, ye shall not worship Osire, but only Jehovih, the Creator. This doctrine, only, is safe. 10. Again they will say: Who is satan and his attendants? Ye shall answer: Whoever professeth any name save the Great Spirit, is of satan, which pertaineth to self.

11. Now whilst ye are thus reasoning with them, certain ones in the temples will be worked by the familiar spirits, writhing and twisting, and ye shall say to the next akin: Behold, I will tell thee how to cast out the evil spirit. Thou shalt say: I charge thee, in the name of Jehovih, to depart!

12. It shall come to pass they will do this, and at the time they use the words: In the name of Jehovih, depart! ye shall drive hence the familiars, thus proving the power of Jehovih greater than all spirits.

13. But that this matter may spread rapidly, and be valued highly, impart the name of the Great Spirit, in secret, not suffering them to speak it aloud. Choose ye, therefore, certain mortals, and ordain them through the king, and their labor shall be to cast out evil spirits.

14. It will come to pass in many places where ye dispossess the false Lords and their confederates, these evil spirits will inoculate the cattle and beasts of burden with poison, and they will die; and the evil spirits will show themselves to the dogs, and cause them to howl; and the evil spirits will obsess the swine, which are easily influenced, and the swine will appear drunk and foolish. All of which things ye shall prophesy to mortals beforehand, thereby attesting the wisdom of the Great Spirit.

15. After these things are accomplished, mortals will say further: Behold, thou Son of Jehovih, erst thou came, Apollo told us when to plant, and when to reap; when to bring the male and female cattle together; but now that we have put him aside, what shall we do? And ye shall answer them:

16. Come in the star-light, and I will give you the signs, that ye may know these things yourselves. And where ye speak in the oracle, or by entrancement, ye shall point out to them certain stars, and give them the names thereof; and certain groups of stars, with their names, also; and ye shall show them the travel of the sun, north and south, and give them a tablet of onk (zodiac), divided into twelve groups, with twelve lines coming from the sun.

17. And ye shall raise up priests by inspiration, and by entrancement, and through them illustrate the position of the sun in the signs of the zodiac (onk). And the priests shall explain these things to the unlearned, that they may comprehend of their own knowledge.

18. When these things are accomplished, ye shall inspire the I'huans to go to the I'hins and ask to be circumcised unto Jehovih; and the I'hins, also being under inspiration, will confess them and bestow them with the sign.

CHAPTER X.

1. When Osire had completed his instructions to his hosts, he sent messengers to Vibhraj, saluting, in the name of Jehovih, calling for one million more ethereans, who came presently; whereupon, Osire divided them into ten thousand groups, giving each group one or more of his attendants, whom he had instructed what to do. When all of them were in readiness for the work, Osire said:

2. Experience hath proven that to dispossess familiar spirits in one place, is but to drive them to another. It is wise, therefore, that in the same day ye make the attack in one city or temple, ye shall do so in the principal places all over the earth, giving the familiars no place to fasten upon. Let it be the sign, therefore, of attack, in each and every place, at the beginning of sunrise, on the morrow; and ye shall possess all the temples, and places of the oracles, and the cities, and the kings and queens, and rulers and leaders of men, driving hence, by stratagem or by force, all the false Lords, and all spirits professing the name of Apollo, or any representative spirit in the name of Apollo or Thor.

3. And immediately will mortals recognize that some change is going on in the unseen world; and they will go to the places of spirit communion, asking for Apollo to explain; and ye shall answer: Apollo is cast out! Hear ye the wisdom of the Great Spirit, Jehovih!

4. And thereafter, ye shall instruct them as I have commanded.

5. So it came to pass as Osire had decreed; the ethereans drove out the false Lords of the earth, and they banished the familiars of all the kings and queens and leaders of men. And the ethereans taught in the temples and oracles, and by entrancement, and by inspiration, even as commanded by Jehovih, through His Son, Osire.

6. But in all places the Great Spirit's name was made a secret; and it was commanded of mortals that His name should only be spoken in whisper, or low breath, because Jehovih speaketh to the soul of man silently. And these things were established; and this was the first universal teaching of the Great Spirit to mortals, save to the sacred people, the I'hins.

7. And Osire decreed: One Lord shall ye give to every city and oracle; but every Lord shall profess Jehovih, being His Son.

8. And this was also accomplished; and when the people consulted the oracles as to who the spirit was, the answer was: Jehovih, through His Son, Lord of earth (or God of earth). But it was made lawful to use the names, Lord and God, with audible words; and they were thus used and spoken of by mortals as the substitutive words, permissible in public, in place of the name, JEHOVIH. After this, the names LORD and GOD were worshipful.

9. Osire said: It is an easy matter to rule over the kings and queens and prophets, and all learned people; but not so easy to rule over the ignorant. Who, having been accustomed to worship Apollo through the idols, will long continue to do so; therefore, ye shall cause the kings to issue edicts prohibiting familiar spirits, and forbidding soothsayers and workers of magic; but teach ye mortals that these things come of satan (the evil disposition of men).

10. This was also done, according to the commandments; and now there was no place left for familiar spirits to obsess mortals. And these spirits distributed themselves after the manner of spirits of the olden times; some going into swine, and living with them; whereupon, Osire commanded his hosts to inspire the kings and queens to pass laws prohibiting the eating of swine's flesh, lest mortals become bound with fetals.

Accordingly, this law was established on the earth. Some of the dispossessed went into the forests to dwell, and some to the fountains and mists in waterfalls; others; who were depraved, dwelt in the fisheries and slaughterhouses; and still others, in the kennels, with dogs and cats. Nevertheless, there were many mortals who were dealers in magic and witchery, and these had an abundance of familiars. And when such mortals would die, the familiars would go to their sons or daughters; whereupon, it was said of them they inherited the gift of magic.

11. Osire, having overcome the evil spirits, now called a council at We-ont-ka-woh; and there came five hundred thousand angels.

12. Osire said: In Jehovih's name, will I now deliver them I have cast out; and ye shall labor to this end in conjunction with the Gods of atmospherea. Behold, I have had the familiars enumerated, and there are more than six thousand millions of them on earth. Ye shall go forth, therefore, into all the divisions of the earth, where they inhabit, and proclaim a great festival, to be held in We-ont-ka-woh, inviting them hither. And ye shall provide them conveyance, bringing them across the seas in suitable vessels. For, when I have them here congregated, I will destroy the ships, and they cannot return.

13. This was accomplished, and more than five thousand millions of spirits came to the festival, where were provided for them food, and also clothes of fantastic colors, to please the eye of the ignorant; and after they were provided in decency, they were entertained in music and dancing, they themselves being taught to take part. For seventy days the festival lasted, and every day varied from another; and the multitude became so intoxicated with delight, and withal, so broken off from their old habits and associations, that they forgot all about the ships and conveyances.

14. Osire spake to his Council privily, saying: Provide ye an airiata large enough for all these people. I will show you what shall happen! So, whilst the festival was going on, the proper workmen built the vessel, and its capacity was sufficient to carry all the multitude of spirits, besides a sufficiency of regimen for them on a long journey.

15. Now, after the festival had lasted seventy days, Osire proclaimed order, that he might speak to them. He said:

16. Brothers and sisters, in the name of the Great Spirit, greeting to you all. I am about to depart to a higher world. That ye might hear my voice, I proclaimed order. That ye may rejoice in my words, I speak in love and tenderness. My home is in a world far away. Where there is no suffering; no sorrow. And the spirit of my people is radiant with light. I would tell you of the beauty and glory of my home, but it would not be just to you. Ye would no longer be content to remain here. So I seal up my mouth.

17. Because ye suffered, and my soul was full of pity, I made this festival. The Great Spirit taught me how to make food and clothes, and to travel far, and be not afraid. All the people where I live can hear the voice of the Great Spirit. They learn all things by first learning to hear Him. His Wisdom supplieth every want.

18. It will be a long time before I come again; my heart of love will come back to you. The time of the festival is ended; your time is come to return to your old places. These Lords of yours, which you have had so long, may provide you.

19. Almost at once, when Osire began to speak, the people desired to go whither he would decree, and when he suggested for them to return to their former Lords, who were also present, they answered with a universal shout: Nay, never more with them!

20. Osire said: I perceive ye desire to go with me and my hosts. I have learned to understand the souls of people. But do ye understand me? I mentioned the great glories in my heavens; but I did not tell you that we worked to make them. Yea, we work every day. The Great Spirit made the tree to get its food and clothes without labor; but, behold, it hath no power to travel. Some things in the world labor not; but man, who hath neither feathers nor hair to cover his body, is provided with talents. Talents are the greatest of all gifts. The air and the ground provide the substance of fruit and foliage to the tree; but the spirit who hath talent can find the substance of fruit and foliage in the air, and gather it.

21. Lights of various colors were now being set up by the ethereans, and the place enriched with the most enticing perfumes.

22. Osire proceeded: By the cultivation of talent, all things are possible unto all men and women. With a sufficiency of talent, ye need no Lords or oppressive rulers. I mentioned the great beauties in my etherean home. Ye go to the spray of fountains, and disport yourselves in rainbows; but ye are in a small corner, at best, and the substances of your joys are in perpetual failure. Behold the sprays and bows made by my hosts! Hear the music played in the elements of their handiwork!

23. The hosts here overcast the entire multitude with the vapor of the air, converted into millions of kaleidoscopic pictures, and filled the place with the music of wind currents trained to tunes.

24. The hosts were overjoyed beyond measure. Again Osire said: Hear me yet further; the festival must cease. Ye forget, I told you I must go. My marshals will now conduct me and my hosts to my fire-ship. As for ye, my heart is broken. I know the toil and hardship put upon you. But if ye desire these things, they are yours.

25. The universal shout was: We will go with thee! Take us in your fire-ship. Teach us how to improve our talents!

26. Osire said: What will the Lords do? Shall they remain without subjects? But the false Lords answered quickly: We will also go with thee, and be servants to do thy bidding!

27. Osire said: When I am on the ship I will answer. So he departed, and went into the airiata, to the side of which his own fire-ship was made fast; and presently, he commanded all who chose to come aboard; and lo and behold, the whole of them, even more than five thousand millions, went in. Osire at once commanded the ascent; and thus he delivered them high up in atmospherea, where his proper officers had already provided a plateau of habitation for them; and the name of the plateau was Assan, signifying, no escape, for here Osire decreed to have them educated, and purged from evil; nor was it possible for them to return to the earth of their own power and learning.

CHAPTER XI.

1. In Assan, Osire appointed Sha'bon as God over the delivered hosts; and Sha'bon selected officers and teachers, and then divided the people into groups and sections, according to their development, and then erected schools, and nurseries, and factories, and put the inhabitants to work, feasting them plenteously with rites and ceremonies.

2. After Assan was duly organized, Osire departed, and went and sojourned in various kingdoms that had been established by his Lords.

3. And all the heavens of the earth were thus organized anew under Osire. And the whole time of organization was three years; but Osire spent the balance of dawn in Vibhraj,

perfecting it as the central kingdom of atmospherea. And lastly, he decreed the appointment of ten thousand Lords, to dwell on earth. Some at the temples of worship, or oracles; some within the cities of the Ghans; and he decreed for his Lords as followeth, to wit:

4. Ye shall not teach mortals of heavenly things, neither by inspiration, nor through the oracles.

5. Ye shall not suffer them to commune with the spirits of the dead, not even their own kin.

6. Ye shall not permit spirits to come to their mortal kin. And the spirits of those who die in infancy ye shall deliver to the asaphs in Vibhraj.

7. Ye shall not permit spirits to inhabit deserted houses; nor permit them to form habitations on the grave-yards, on the earth.

8. Ye shall not permit spirits to inhabit caves nor waterfalls on the earth.

9. Ye shall not permit spirits to obsess mortals, nor to speak through them by entrancement, save they be such spirits as ye appoint in order to carry out these, my decrees; or save they be masters of generation (loo'is), whom ye shall appoint over mortals for other purposes.

10. Ye shall control the selecting and appointing of guardian spirits over newborn mortals.

11. And all such guardian spirits shall teach their wards nothing of heaven near the earth, but inspire them that it lieth far away, and very high, from which place none return.

12. And the guardians shall also inspire their wards to consult God only, or his Lord, and to do this by secret prayer.

13. And that the Lord and God are all goodness, and all wisdom, and all love, and all power.

14. And that all evil cometh from tetracts, born with man's mortal condition.

15. And ye shall inspire mortals to acquire a knowledge of the sun, and moon, and stars, giving names unto them, together with their places in the firmament.

16. And give them temples for observation, and tablets for instruction.

17. For in all things ye shall direct man's soul to the acquisition of corporeal knowledge, causing him to look into corporeal things to find a reason for the behavior of all created substance.

18. And they shall not in any sense longer depend on the spirits for knowledge, nor truth.

19. For I am not laying the foundation for spiritual knowledge on earth; that must come after. For as Jehovih first gave to man a corporeal life, and then a spiritual life, so am I laying a foundation for a new race (the Ghans) on the earth. For from their kin shall spring the heirs of kosmon, who shall embrace both corporeal and spiritual knowledge.

20. But these shall rise in corporeal knowledge, and go down in it, suffering death in that which I now rain on the earth.

21. Ye shall teach them in truth; but they will in after generations contort your teachings into corporeal worship, prostrating themselves before the sun, and moon, and stars, going down in disbelief in not only the spiritual life, but in the Great Spirit, and His Gods and Lords.

22. And these things must come to pass on the corporeal world; nor is there any resurrection in the latter days, save these of this day go through the fall which I am

preparing for them.

23. For which reason, ye shall found corporeal knowledge in the stars, and name them, for these things will be testimony in kosmon, of the fate of the worshippers of corporeal knowledge, in the time of the Osirian cycle.

24. Wherein ye shall leave nothing undone that can be done, to make mortals put aside all spirituality, save to believe in the Great Spirit and a distant heaven; but make them pursue knowledge wholly corporeal.

25. For the labor of God and his Lords shall not always be to fetch spirits back to earth, to learn of corpor, for this is not Jehovih's plan.

26. A heaven shall be built up of corporeal knowledge, which shall have a base in the firmament of heaven, where spirits can be taught in time to come.

27. Fear not that man can be too unbelieving in spiritual things, in this age; Jehovih requireth even perfection in unbelief, in certain periods of time. And this is the founding of that era on the earth.

28. Do ye, therefore, these matters with all your wisdom and strength; and may the Light of Jehovih be with you, now and forever.

CHAPTER XII.

1. Osire, through his mathematicians, now furnished the Lords with maps of corporeal stars, and moon, and sun, and the position of the earth, with the sun-belt, and bestowed the names of animals upon them. Showed where the region of Cows was; the place of Bulls; the place of Bears; the place of Horses; the place of Fishes; the place of Scorpions; the place of Sheep; the place of Lions; the place of Crabs; the place of Death; the place of Life; the place of Capricornus; and marked the seasons, and made twelve sections (months) to the year, which was the width of the sun-belt.

2. And he placed the sun in the midst and made lines thence to the stars, with explanations of the powers of the seasons on all the living.

3. And he gave the times of Jehovih, the four hundred years of the ancients, and the half-times of dan, the base of prophecy; the variations of thirty-three years; the times of eleven; and the seven and a half times of the vortices of the stars, so that the seasons might be foretold, and famines averted on the earth.

4. When the tablets were completed and ready to deliver to the Lords, Osire said: Take these and bestow them on mortals, both through the oracles and by inspiration, making them sacred with the prophets, and seers, and priests, and their kings and queens.

5. And ye shall inspire them to build temples of observation, to study the stars; teaching by the gau and by the travel of the sun north and south, and by Cnest, and by dark chambers, that they may prove the Fichtus of Haak, for nothing shall be left undone or untaught whereby man's corporeal senses shall not prove adequate to a perfect corporeal life.

6. For this rule followeth on all corporeal worlds; that with the culture of the corporeal senses, man becometh vigorous, strong, and independent; and with the culture of the spiritual senses in corporeans, they become weak, sensitive and dependent.

7. In the first case, they ultimately become selfish and wicked; in the second case, they become impotent, and unadapted to corporeal life, and thus become extinct.

8. On all corporeal worlds, Jehovih hath provided these two seasons for every race He created; a season for the development of the corporeal senses, and a season for the development of the spiritual senses. To find the mean between these is to find kosmon, which lieth far in the future.

9. In this day, therefore, I give the matter into your charge, in the name of Jehovih, that you consider not the spirutual nature of the corporeans in any respect, leaving that matter to God and his sub-Gods, who will receive them at the time of their mortal death.

10. But ye shall teach them to fear no spirit, nor Lord, nor God; teaching them that by their own wills they can cast out the tetracts which assume to be spirits. Rather inspire ye them to be Gods and Goddesses themselves; and by their aspirations they will become large and powerful, and of fearless disposition.

Plate 65 .
ARIES. See book of Jaffeth.

CHAPTER XIII.

1. And thus was finished the dawn of dan, when great Osire had spoken, and to his God and Lords commissioned the harvesting of earth and heaven for another cycle. Order reigned in heaven and on earth, because a man, a God, had spoken. Men and angels had their eyes turned inward, to know of what capacity Jehovih had made them. And the earth and moon, and sun and stars, were shown in a new light to the sense of men; not to be shunned and despised, but glories given by the Great Spirit for useful purposes.

221

2. Jehovih had said: Some men I created to reason near at hand; others to speculate in far-off regions, with thoughts diverse and unlike in procedure. Think not, O man, that in high heaven such men become all alike; not so created I them, but to run in their various extremes forever!

3. Of the first, Osire, My Son, enthroned to give reason practice, came not a random period, but just when I had designed to sow the seed of unbelief broadcast over earth and heaven.

4. For such appeareth in all peoples under the sun; a season of belief; a season of unbelief. And with the believing is the practice of truth and love; and with the unbelieving is the practice of great research and learning, with cruelty and disputation.

5. Osire said: Send for my resurrection, O Jehovih; I have uprooted the evil of idol worship, the extreme that followeth too much belief. To Thy corporeal worlds I have opened man's eyes, and set a mark on man's souls, wherein man shall not come from earth to heaven, saying: Alas, I have no corporeal knowledge!

6. Jehovih said: To further man's ultimate glory, I have decreed the earth to ji'ay'an fields for three thousand years, in which thy fruit shall have its full growth.

7. Osire foresaw the times and places in the future road of earth and heaven, and that from his decrees would spring corporeal philosophy, the first of earth, whereto man should look back in after ages, saying: Thence sprang the Osirian system; thence the Asyrian races. Yet he looked further on, when men should become idolaters in disbelief of spiritual things, doing worship to the sun, moon and stars; and in very corpor profess to find the cause and foundation of all.

8. Jehovih said: Man shall search all things in order to find Me; but I gave this labor not to one generation of men, nor to those of a hundred, or a thousand years, but to cycles. For, when I come in kosmon, to found My kingdom on earth, man shall have the testimony of all speculation and philosophies before him, together with the fruits thereof. And he shall judge that which is good by the evidence of past practices.

9. High in the arc of Se'ing rose Osire's call, where millions waited, knowing the dawn of dan on the red star was near its end. Swift messengers told the story of Jehovih's work, through His Son, Osire; and, measuring the width of His harvest, laid the scheme at the feet of the reigning Goddess, Antwa. And she gave the word, Go, to her legions in waiting, who had moored an obegia, a float, a fire-ship, ready to proceed for the hosts redeemed by Great Osire.

10. And they cut her loose, amidst music and dancing, the obegia, five million souls aboard, commanded by Eticene, Goddess of Antwa's Garden, an etherean plain, where dwelt ten thousand million souls. A place of rest, for Gods and Goddesses to regale themselves with stories of redemptions of mortals on the countless stars floating in Jehovih's etherean veins.

11. Off to the red star, the earth, steered the obegia, the pride of Eticene, for the marriage festival of seven thousand million Brides and Bridegrooms, the yield of Osire's harvest for the upper kingdoms.

12. Meanwhile, Osire and his hosts, prepared in the usual way, waited the signal, the coming of Jehovih's light, within the earth's vortex. For strange it seemeth to Gods and men, everything in the firmament is upward; who leave a star, upward rise; who leave an etherean world for the stars, rise upward also, but call it downward, to suit the

understanding of mortals. So pierced the vortex of atmospherea, the obegia, and the hosts of Eticene. The Brides and Bridegrooms shouted with joy.

13. And the millions of guests, assembled to witness the awe-inspiring ceremonies, joined in applause.

14. Then down came the ship of fire, broad as a sea, with all her appurtenances in trim, and adorned in majesty, even to the floors of Vibhraj. And from the mantles of light came Eticene, to salute great Osire, in the name of the Great Spirit, and receive his contribution to the unchangeable worlds!

15. Osire, with his attendants, the archangels of Lowtsin, received Eticene under the Sign of Ormadz, Master Creator of Power, and then presented his delivered sons and daughters, seven thousand millions.

16. Whereupon, due ceremonies were proclaimed, and the Brides and Bridegrooms of Jehovih entered the obegia. Osire saluted God, who was ordained to be ruler of heaven and earth for the next two hundred years, and, with sorrow in his soul, departed, going into the obegia, the fire-ship, for a higher heaven, where waited millions of loves, calling to him to come home.

17. Then upward rose the mighty ship, commanded by the slender Eticene, the young Goddess of Antwa's Garden; her little hands stretched upward to Jehovih, her mighty faith, Commander of the elements.

END OF THE BOOK OF OSIRIS.

THE LORDS' FIFTH BOOK.

BEING COTEMPORANEOUS WITH THE BOOK OF OSIRIS, SON OF JEHOVIH. AS OSIRIS IS OF THE HIGHER HEAVENS, SO IS THE LORDS' BOOK OF THE LOWER HEAVENS AND OF THE EARTH, FOR THE SAME PERIOD OF TIME.

CHAPTER I.
OF THE HINDOO SCRIPTURES.

1. God apportioned certain of the earth for the tribes of Shem of the arc of Noe'chi, a heavenly place, seat of mountains, and Lords, All Wise, and from His Wisdom directed Hirto into His pastures.

2. Hirto, Son of Neph, born of an egg, descended out of the highest heaven. He was a most gracious Lord, and in deference to Om, smote against the rocks of heaven. So, when the egg was broken, one-half of the shell ascended, the other half became the foundation of the world.

3. The evil voice (satan) spake to the children of men, and polluted them. Whereupon the Great Spirit spoke in the firmament of heaven, saying: To Hirto, son of Neph, I bequeathed the tribes of Shem forever. For they have withstood Anra'mainyus, My everlasting enemy. So Hirto became Lord of Shem, and he banished Anra'mainyus down under the earth, where he busieth himself building fires for the furnaces of hell, whereof the smoke and flames come up through the earth and are called Agni (volcanoes), that his existence might be known to men.

4. Thus came Evil from Good; but that Everlasting Wisdom should prevail with mortals

223

and the spirits of heaven, All Light created Visvasrij (law, or natural law), as a creator to abide forever. Before this time there were two things in the world: Voidness was one, and Vachis was the other. Vachis vach, and the world was. So it came to pass that Voidness was divided into two parts, the seen and the unseen worlds.

5. The unseen spake in the wind three sounds, E-O-IH, and was called by mortals Eolin, God of the wind; so Eolin showed himself in three colors: yellow, which is the highest color; blue, which is the coldest color; and red, which is the warmest color.

6. Eolin said: Out of My three sounds, are all sounds made; out of My three colors, are all colors made. He was the All Master.

7. He said: Three worlds have I made: the earth world, which is for mortals; the all high heavens, which is for pure and wise angels; and the intermediate world, which resteth on the earth.

8. Eolin said: Three lights have I created: the sun, to rule the day; the moon, to rule the night; and the burning fire, for the use of man.

9. Three spirit lights created I: Ruch, which issueth out of My soul; Shem, which cometh from My Lords in heaven to the souls of men; and Vas, which cometh from the spirits of the intermediate world.

10. Eolin said: Three states am I in: Ghost, which is ever-present and unchangeable; Corpor, which is in places, like the earth and stars and sun and moon; and Motion, which is everlasting unrest. So am I, Eolin, Mightiest in three, in All Place and All Time.

11. When the egg was broken and the shell distributed, lo and behold, the se'mu of the egg had nowhere to rest, and being void of compact distributed in the void world and was not seen. Then Hirto, High Lord of the upper heavens, sent whirlwinds abroad, and they gathered of the substance of the egg and rained it down on the earth.

12. Uz, son of Eolin, ran quickly and turned Anra'mainyus' fires to the north, and Eolin touched the earth with his quickening hand, and straightway all the living were created.

13. So Eolin said: Thou, My first begotten Son, it shall be thine to keep forever. Neither shall there be any other God.

14. But it came to pass in course of time the evil voice (satan) encompassed the earth about with serpents that spake like men and angels, and the serpents made friends with All Evil, Father of Anra'mainyus; and the women of the tribes of A'su went and tempted the first men, the I'hins, whereby there was born into the world evil offspring.

15. Hirto, Lord of the earth, drove the first men out of the region of light, and sat high-born angels on the boundaries of Chinvat, at the gates of the upper heaven, to guard the tribes of Faithists ever after. Nevertheless, evil, being set on foot, soon overspread the earth. So Hirto rested his hands on his thighs, and swore an oath unto All Light that he would drown the world and all the living. And in answer to the Lord a seraphim, a mighty fire-ship, came down out of the sun region, opening the flood-gate of heaven with a sea of water, and all the people perished, save the I'hins, the sacred people, friends of the Lord of earth.

16. So the Lord took the hollow of his hand and lifted up his people, and gave them doves' wings, and they flew afar and came to the land where dwelleth the Lord, so it was called Shem as a proof to all the world.

17. In those days God was near mortals, so that, when an honest man spake, the Lord answered him. And Anra'mainyus was near also, and when an evil man spake an evil

voice answered him. For that reason the Lord singled out the purest and most virtuous of women; the wisest, strongest and most faithful, best of men, and married them, giving two women to one man, according to law. And the heirs of the wisest and most virtuous of men and women were wiser than their parents. And the Lord gave this secret to his people in the house of God, and they gave the knowledge to the chosen people.

18. Hirto said: For this reason, O my beloved, shall ye not wed with the druks, the dark people, that burrow in the ground, lest your seed be polluted, and your heirs go down to hell with Anra'mainyus.

19. But Anra'mainyus, evil creator of evil, went to the druk women; speaking to them in a dark corner, he said: Ye have of the root of Babao to make delirious; fetch it to the white people that came with doves' wings; fetch, and they will eat and get drunk. And when the young men are drunk, go ye to them, for they are my gift.

20. So, of them that came out of the arc of Noe'chi, was sin newborn; for the druks went in where they were drunk, saying: Lest the white people and the yellow people fall upon us, and our seed perish on the earth, make us of flesh and kin, bone and bone, blood and blood.

21. Hirto, the Lord God, saw into the darkness, and being compassionate, said: A great punishment will I visit on Anra'mainyus for this; his head shall droop in sorrow. But as for the I'hins, being drunk, I will forgive them. And as to the newborn people, they shall become the mightiest of all people in the whole world, because they came out of both darkness and light. The darkness in them shall battle all darkness; the light that is in them shall then master over their own darkness. But as for the druks, they shall go down in darkness forever.

CHAPTER II.

1. Shem had many tribes, who settled on the borders of the sea at Haventi and Gats; and the Lord (Hirto) dwelt with them, speaking through the chief prophet, Tah (Tae), who made a record on stone, and wood, and cloth, of the Lord's word, and these were preserved in the Valens (house) of God (Hirto).

2. And when Tah was old, and died, the mantle of the Lord's gifts fell on Tah's son; who also had power to hear the Voice; and he also kept a record of the Lord's words.

3. And then he died, and his son succeeded in the same way; and, because of this truth, the Lord called all of them by the sacred name, Tah, the order of which continued for a hundred generations. And it came to pass that the I'hins filled the country far and near with cities; and yet, in all the while, they killed nothing that had been created alive to breathe, on the earth, or in the water, or in the air above.

4. In the early days of the I'hins, the Lord spake through the chief prophet, saying: When the inhabitants of one city or tribe marry with those of another city or tribe, behold, it is but just that the names of father and mother be given to the offspring.

5. But men were in darkness in those days, and understood not God. So, accordingly, the inhabitants combined the names belonging to the neighboring tribes. That is to say, one tribe said, ut (wheat); another tribe, for the same thing, said, yat; and another tribe said, wat; and another, hoot; and so on. So, the after-generations said, utyatwathoot (wheat), and this was called the Yi-ha language; and so great were the number and the size of the words used, that the writings of the ancient prophets were lost, because none could

understand them.

6. The Lord spake, saying: Because I desired to preserve the genealogy of my chosen, ye have applied the law to things that are worthless in my sight. Ye have built a babble, a tower of words, so that your tongues are confounded one with another. Ye strove to reach to heaven with a multitude of words, but made food for hada (hades).

7. The Lord said: Come, now, into murdhan (a spirit circle), and I will deliver you. So the people sat in crescent, and the Lord came betwixt the horns, saying: Behold, ye are Tau, but I am the S'ri (Spirit). My word shall stand against all the world.

8. Hear, then, the commandments of God (Hautot). Because ye have built a tower of words, ye are confounded. But I come not in anger, but to deliver you. Neither will I write more, nor teach written words, for they are only folly, save to the learned.

9. By mouth-words will I teach, and ye shall repeat after me. And these shall be sacred words to the end of the world.

10. So the Lord taught orally in the temple, face to face with the people, and they learned the words and the meaning thereof.

11. And those who learned the best, the Lord named Ritvij, because he made them teachers over others. The Lord said: Because ye have confounded the language of the ancients, I will give you a new language, and it shall be vede (perfect), against all my enemies; nor shall any man more meddle with the words I give.

12. Hirto (Lord) said: Love thy Lord God only, and with all thy soul. Turn thy face away from the angels who come to thee; they are the emissaries of Anra'mainyus.

13. Hirto said: Love the sun and moon, and all things on the earth, for they are the Lord's gift. What is spirit? It flieth away; it is nothing.

14. Smite the druj (spirits) that prophesy. They are nothing but lies; they are Anra'mainyus' emissaries.

15. Learn to prophesy by the sun, and by the moon and by the stars. They tell no lies.

16. The Lord then gave the signs of the zodiac (the horses, and cows, and lions, and sheep, and birds) that rule upon the earth, and upon the winds of heaven, and on the heat and cold, and the sun, and moon and stars, and spring and summer, and fall and winter. But these things are here omitted in this book, because they are known in mortal histories to this day.

17. The Lord saith in this day, the kosmon era: Behold, O man, in the time of Osiris, I, the Lord, raised up many philosophers on the earth, and inspired them not only to fulfill the legends of the ancients, but also to write books of disputation, in order to turn man's mind away from the consultation of familiar spirits. After this manner did I inspire men to write, to wit:

18. Touching the matter of the egg, and also of Anra'mainyus, they appear never to have been proven, neither are they given on the authority of Hirto, the Lord of earth. It is reasonable to suppose that the Great Spirit divided up the worlds amongst His Gods and Lords, and that the earth (Bhu) fell to the portion of Hirto; whilst the stars, which are also worlds like this, fell to other Lords and Gods. But as for evil Gods, like Anra'mainyus, who hath ever seen one?

19. As for Hirto, the Lord, I have seen him myself, and so have thousands of other honest prophets. But when the Lord spake it was not about foolish stories, but to teach man how to live, that he might be happy himself and a glory to the Great Spirit. Neither did I ever

226

hear the Lord assert that he was more than the spirit of a man risen from the earth. In my opinion, therefore, the Lord is the captain over the earth, and over all other spirits. But even to know this, is not so great a good truth as to know how to do righteously. 20. Of all things, therefore, man should learn, especially of what he can see, and hear, and prove, rather than of spirits whom he cannot prove, nor find when he wanteth them.

CHAPTER III.

1. The Lord said: As a farmer planteth wheat in one field, and rice in another, and flax in another, so I, the Lord, inhabit the earth with the seed of man. Neither shall any wise man say: These things came by chance; that it so happened that one people settled in Jaffeth (China), another in Vindu (India), and another in Arabinya (Arabia). Such is the argument of my enemies, saith the Lord. Not perceiving wisdom in my work as it seemeth for a day, they fail to extend judgment into the thousands of years of my plans, and so, stubbornly, shut themselves up in ignorance, saying: There is no God.

2. For I foresaw the breadth of the earth, and that it should be subdued for the glory of man; and in the early days, I divided my armies with wisdom.

3. To Ham I allotted the foundation of the migratory tribes of the earth. And of the tribes of Ham, behold, I selected many colors of men; whereof I fore-ordained the name Ham to stand as a living testimony to the end of the world. For I foresaw that the time would come when the nations would look back for histories of my peoples, and I erected certain words and signs which should be testimony in the later times of earth.

4. Of all colors (black, white, yellow, copper, red and brown) were the tribes of Ham; nevertheless, they were I'hins (Faithists), having flat nails and short arms, and of such as desired to acquire knowledge. And I brought them to a country of sand fields and of fields of rich pastures interspersed, where lived but few natives, the dark people, with short hair. Neither omitted I even the hair of the head of man without providing testimony of my word.

5. Of the I'hins, I provided testimony in all the divisions of the earth, with long hair belonging to the tribes that worshipped Jehovih, that man of the kosmon era might perceive that the land whence they sprang is not above the water.

6. Behold, the multiple (Yi-ha) language of the tribes of Shem! Side by side with the tribes of Jaffeth raised I them. And, behold, the latter use the derivation of the Panic language to this day.

7. For I gave unto the tribes of these two different lands my ten commandments and ten invocations, to be not written, but spoken and taught from mouth to ear, to be sacred in the language given.

8. Wherein man shall perceive that the same stories of the egg, and of the origin of evil in the world, could not have been communicated by mortals.

9. For I locked up sufficient of the Panic language in Jaffeth as a testimony to be discovered in after years; showing that, unlike Ham and Shem, a mighty nation could retain one language for thousands of years.

10. For I foresaw that philosophers would try to prove that languages were of mortal origin, and that they would change according to the growth of knowledge amongst men.

11. Behold, I gave scriptures unto all my people, enjoining some to adhere to the text; and, so, I preserved the work of my hand.

12. The tribes of Ham were previously ordained with characteristics to make them love to emigrate westward; and the tribes of Jaffeth and Shem with characteristics to make them love to stay within their own countries. And the tribes of Guatama with characteristics to make them love to go eastward. For I set a boundary to the tribes of Guatama, that they should not reach the ocean on the east.

13. The Lord said: Having designed Ham for teaching the barbarian world of me and my dominion, I also prepared them that, through their seed, men and women should have hair neither straight nor short, but long and curled, and red, and white, and brown, whereby might be traced in after ages the genealogy of nations.

14. Now, in the midst of three great countries, Jaffeth, Shem and Ham, was the chief place of the I'huans, where they founded a new nation; and the Lord called them Parsi'e, signifying, warrior Faithists, because he created them as a shield, to guard his chosen, the I'hins.

15. The difference betwixt the I'huans and the Parsi'e was that the I'huans lived near and about the I'hins, but the Parsi'e'ans lived in a nation by themselves.

16. Nevertheless, they were all of the same blood and kin, being half-breeds betwixt the I'hins and the native druks; and they were large, and mostly of the color of new copper.

17. And because they were favored of the Lord, the Lord gave them separate laws, and commanded them not to mix with the druks; the which commandment they kept for more than a thousand years.

18. But, in course of time, the Parsi'e'ans were tempted by the druks, and fell from their high estate, and they became cannibals.

19. And the Lord sent the Ghans, to whom he delivered his oral scriptures, to travel in search of his people; and, lo and behold, ten tribes of the Lord's people were lost in the wilderness; and this was the country of the Parsi'e'ans, and that land was filled with wild goats. Hence came the name, LAND OF GOATS.

20. And the lost tribes, not being flesh-eaters, were at a loss for food; and they said: Come, let us live on goat's milk.

21. And they so lived for a long season, taming the goats, and keeping herds of them. And they roved about, driving their herds with them, for which reason they took the name of SHEPHERD KINGS.

22. And the Lord looked on them with favor, saying: These that call themselves shepherd kings shall have this country. Behold, out of the seed of these people, will I do mighty wonders.

23. The Lord said: What man can discover, I, the Lord, left for him to discover; what man could not discover, I, the Lord, taught him.

24. To the shepherd kings revealed I how to make leather out of skins; neither had man any means to make this discovery. The shepherd kings made bags of leather in which they carried milk, which was thus churned; and they made butter, which was the first butter made in this world.

CHAPTER IV.

1. God said: Without evil preserved I the I'hin race, as the foundation of my light, wherefrom I could reach forth to the tribes of darkness.

2. For I fore-ordained not to go within darkness to battle it, but to stand without, and give

an example of righteousness for man to look upon.

3. Neither planned I from the beginning that my chosen should labor without examples of cities and kingdoms of righteousness.

4. The evil man and evil priest, who are subjects to satan and his hosts, remain in evil, preaching righteousness without a city or kingdom of example. But my chosen go away by themselves and build their cities, as a testimony of their faith in the Father.

5. And they practice the fullness of my commandments by their lives toward one another.

6. To him who saith: THIS IS MINE, I have not spoken. To him who saith: MY HOUSE, MY LANDS, I have not spoken.

7. For inasmuch as these things belong to them, such men belong to such things, and not to me.

8. For illustration of which truth, I raised up separate from the world's people, the I'hins, who were my living examples of righteousness.

9. Think not, however, that the I'hins were the perfection of manhood and womanhood. They were not a developed race, nor righteous because of their own knowledge.

10. By the constant presence of my exalted angels, they were obsessed to righteousness, being restrained away from evil. They were my sermon before the tribes of druks and cannibals that covered the earth over; and, by virtue of signs and miracles, and by non-resistance, preserved I them.

11. For man of himself evolveth only to power in evil; wherefore, O man, thou shalt behold my dominion over the races of men, to work righteousness and good-will.

12. And my examples reached into the souls of the barbarians, so that, in after ages, I should prepare them to hear my voice, and to comprehend my commandments.

13. For it is the fullness of light amongst men, when, without my presence or the presence of my hosts, they shall understand virtue and knowledge, practicing them of their own accord. In which time men shall perceive that righteousness, and peace, and love toward one another, are the foundation of the happiness of the spirit, and the only light of its resurrection.

14. The Lord said: Think not that I came to one nation alone, leaving the others in darkness; I came not to one alone, but unto all the divisions of the earth. According to what was required for them at times, so held I my hand over them, and they accomplished that which was designed from the beginning.

15. It being not the will of Jehovih that man should be forever led, because, forsooth, his Lord saith; but that man should ultimately have the light of practicing good works organically, from infancy up.

16. The Lord said: A teacher that doeth all things for his pupil, also sacrificeth his pupil; he who teacheth his pupil wrongly, sinneth against the Father; he who teacheth his pupil not at all, is accessory to evil. So standeth the Lord, your God, over the children of men.

17. Behold, I have demonstrated that my chosen can maintain themselves unharmed amongst barbarians; also that by unrestrained marriages a sacred people is quickly lost amongst barbarians.

18. For man, witnessing terrible conflicts, should rather desire sons of strong limbs and arms and crafty minds, to do murderous work abundantly; from which condition he had no incentive to rise in gentleness and love, for the glory of the Spirit.

19. That I, your Lord, might show after-generations, first, that without my hand in the

work, no good nor peace could come amongst men; and, second, that only by a race of I'hins, as examples of my power, through signs and miracles, could the barbarians be reached for their own good.

20. Not only did I leave the ruins of my cities which had no gates of entrance, and houses without doors of entrance, that ye might have testimony of the race of I'hins, but I have shown you that only by such procedure could the barbarians be induced to a higher evolution.

21. Think not, O man, that I did not foresee the time when men should question whether the Great Spirit ever placed a Lord over the earth; and that man should say: Behold, there is no Lord and no God. For I foresaw these times, and provided angels to go in advance, to show, first, the evolution of the races of men from out of the lowest darkness; and, second, that the cause of the evolution came from the Great Spirit, and was directed unto righteousness; but had not been so, but for the Lord, your God.

22. For I left sufficient tribes unto this day, who dwell in darkness, even cannibals, as a testimony, that of themselves they possess nothing to cause a desire for evolution into knowledge, and peace, and industry, and love, and good works unto one another.

23. Will not man say: One people is raised up in consequence of the presence of their neighbor, and without a Lord or God, and the angels of heaven.

24. Now, behold, I have left savages at your door, and ye raise them not up, but destroy them. Showing you, that even your wisest and most learned have no power in resurrection. Neither have I left any way open for the resurrection of barbarians, save by examples of Faithists (I'hins), who shall practice righteousness and miracles.

25. And there shall rise up those who will do these things, and they shall succeed; and because of their success, they shall also be testimony of the I'hin race, in whom I laid the foundation for the redemption of the whole earth.

CHAPTER V.

1. Thus the Lord established the five peoples who were saved from Pan; and he commanded them to preserve Panic words in their respective countries, and they so preserved them, many of which exist to this day.

2. Here followeth, then, what became of these I'hins, to wit:

3. Those that came to Guatama survived twenty-one thousand years, and then became extinct.

4. Those that came to Jaffeth survived twenty-one thousand years, and then became extinct.

5. Those that came to Shem survived twelve thousand years, and then became extinct by amalgamation.

6. That that came to Ham survived twenty-one thousand years, and then became extinct by amalgamation.

7. Those of Guatama attained to one thousand large cities, and three thousand small cities, being more than four million souls. And they never had any king or queen, or other ruler, save the Lord, who ministered unto them through the city fathers. And they retained their sacred name of Guatama to the last; but the I'huans called them Oech'lo'pan, signifying, people of another world.

8. And in course of time they became diminutive, and desired not to marry. And there

came great darkness (ocgokok) on the earth, with falling ashes, and heat, and fevers; and so the Lord took them up to heaven.

9. Those of Jaffeth attained to two thousand large cities, and seven thousand small ones, being more than eight million souls. And they retained the name Jaf-fa, to the last; but the I'huans called them Tua Git, signifying, people of spirit light.

10. And there came a'ji on the earth, and it touched them with impotency, and they brought forth no more heirs; so the Lord took them home.

11. Those of Shem attained to six hundred large cities, and two thousand small cities, being more than two million souls. Neither had they any king, but served the Lord through the city fathers. And they retained their name, Shem, to the last; but the I'huans called them Sri-vede-iyi, signifying, people of the true light, woman-like. And impotence came upon them, and they disappeared, even as a drop of water in the sunlight, and no man knew when they ceased to be.

12. But hoping to preserve their seed to the Lord, many of them married with the I'huans; but their children became I'huans also, neither having the silken hair nor the musical voices of the I'hins, nor the light of the upper heavens.

13. Those of Ham attained to one thousand two hundred large cities, and three thousand small cities, being four million souls. But, being of mixed colors, they did not become impotent. But they broke the law of God more than all other Faithists, being of warm blood; and they mixed greatly with the I'huans. And they had no kings nor queens, serving the Lord only, through the city fathers. And they retained the name of Ham to the last, when they ceased to exist as a separate people, because of their amalgamation with the I'huans.

14. The tribes that went in the two ships to the north land (Japan), no man could draw the line, after a thousand years, betwixt them and the I'huans, for they mingled therewith, and were lost, as I'hins. Nevertheless, they redeemed the barbarians into wisdom and peace.

CHAPTER VI.

1. God said: In the time of Osiris, thy Lord provided for the light and knowledge, that had been with the I'hins, to be merged into the new races, the Ghans and I'huans. By the Lord and his angels was such foundation laid.

2. Before this time, the I'hins could not inspire the barbarians to make leather and cloth; nor could they inspire them to industries of any kind in the way of virtue and peace.

3. The Lord provided unto the inhabitants of the earth, oracle houses, wherein the Lord could speak face to face with mortals; through his angels, chosen for this purpose, did the Lord thus teach mortals.

4. Persuading them to industries, and peace and righteousness, after the manner of the I'hins.

5. Teaching them of the stars and sun and moon; showing them how to find the times and seasons of the earth.

6. Inspiring them to observe the stars, and to name them, which names are preserved to this day.

7. I have established landmarks, saith the Lord. What I do, man cannot do. I lift the barbarian up; he giveth over his cruel practices by my command.

8. I call him to the observation of the stars, and he heedeth my voice.

9. Behold, O all ye that say there is no Lord, I have left a remnant of the barbarians. Go try your hand. Let them that find the cause of the progress of man, to come of the earth, go raise up the barbarian.

10. I say to man: Go commune with the spirits of the dead, and man doeth it. I say: Come away from such worship, and fall down before the stars, and man doeth it.

11. Jehovih said: My Lord, My God, go thou; call man to one thing to-day, and let him worship it. And to-morrow call him to another, and let him worship it. For man shall fall down and worship everything in heaven and earth. By trying them shall man know them. For in the day of my glory, kosmon, man shall put away all worshipful things, save Me, his Creator.

12. The Lord God said: Through the worshipful talents man can be raised up. Even as to great learning, man will not pursue it till he first worshippeth it.

13. In the time of Osiris, the Lord named the stars in heaven after the legendary names of Gods and Lords. And the Lord taught not that man should worship them, but that he should learn their glory and majesty in the firmament.

14. But man forgot the Creator because of the wonder of His works. Even to this day man inclineth to view as substantial and real, things that are seen, and to reject the All Potent, which is Unseen.

15. This was the command of God (Osiris), for man should learn corporeal things as well as spiritual. And I, the Lord, carried away the spirits of the dead, not suffering man and angels to commune together. For heretofore they had done this, and so had, both, rejected the higher heavens.

16. Jehovih saith: It is not the plan of My heavens for the spirits of the dead to remain on the earth forever, engaging in mortal servitude and practices.

17. Behold, the way of My kingdom, is upward; rather shall man on the earth seek to rise upward, than that the angels of heaven go downward.

18. Hence the Lord carried away the spirits of the dead, and he turned man's judgment to learning the glories of the lower kingdoms (corpor).

19. And man advanced in great learning; both of the sun, moon and stars, and of all things on the face of the earth.

20. The Lord said: These signs have I given to man, that he may comprehend the cycles of his Creator. When spiritual research is chief amongst men, they advance not in science, nor art, nor inventions, that belong to the earth. But, when man is bereft of spiritual aspiration, he advanceth in corporeal knowledge, and inventions, and investigations.

21. These signs foreshow the changes being wrought on mortals by the hand of the Almighty, through His Gods and Lords.

22. God said: Behold, I raised up great kings and queens on the earth; and I gave them pageantry, and rites and ceremonies, after the manner of heavenly things. And these I made as an aspiration to the multitude, that they might learn to provide themselves with the luxuries of all created things.

23. For I desired not that man should become spiritual until the earth and all manner of savage beasts and serpents were subdued. Otherwise man had descended into impotence, and failed on the earth.

24. These testimonies have I left before thee to this day; that the spiritual man inclineth to shut himself up in seclusion and prayer; but that the Osirians go forth to work manfully.

25. The Lord established reciprocities between kings and queens in those days. And this was the manner thereof:

26. The central kingdom was called the sun-kingdom, and the others were called satellites. And the chief ruler was called THE SUN - KING, or KING OF THE SUN.

27. And the king maintained an observatory, for determining the times and seasons of the sun, moon, earth and stars. The name of the observatory was TEMPLE OF THE STARS (Oke'i'git'hi).

28. The Lord said unto man: Build thou a chamber unto God within the temple of the stars.

29. And man so built it. And the Lord chose seers, one for every STAR CHAMBER; and the seer sat therein, with a table before him, on which table sand was sprinkled. And the Lord wrote in the sand, with his finger, the laws of heaven and earth.

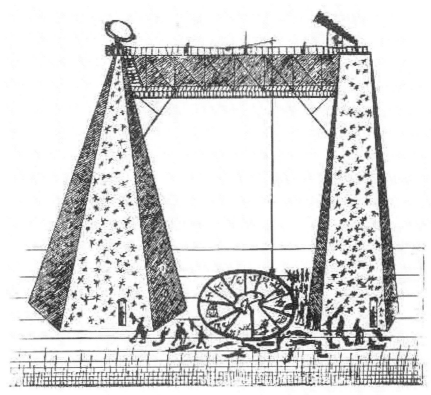

Plate 69.
STAR WORSHIPERS.

30. Thus gave God to man the names of the stars, and their seasons; and the seasons of the sun and moon and earth.

31. And the seer gave it to the king; and the king proclaimed the words thereof. And God gave man sacred days, for feasts and rites and ceremonies; according to the times of the moon and stars gave he them.

32. And the king, by command of God, caused the people to watch the stars and moon and sun, so they would know the sacred days.

33. The Lord said: I have days for planting, and days for reaping, and days for sailing of ships, and days for males and females. By the stars in the firmament, and by the moon's

changes, shall man learn to know my times and seasons.

34. So man took to learning from the stars and moon and sun, to ascertain the will of God.

35. And nowhere in all the world prospered man in the Osirian philosophy as in Parsi'e, and in Jaffeth (China), and chief of all were the shepherd kings.

CHAPTER VII.

1. Great became the wisdom of man in that day, and his power and glory were greater than had ever been in all the world. He established mighty kingdoms and sub-kingdoms, over the lands of Jaffeth, and Shem, and Parsi'e, and Arabin'ya.

2. He excelled in building temples and palaces; and in all manner of inventions; in fabrics of linen and silk, and wool and find leather; in writing books and tablets; in mathematics; in laws and reciprocities; in navigation, and in inland travel; in making thermometers and barometers, and magnetic needles, and telescopes and microscopes; in chemistry and botany.

3. Verily did the philosophers of those days know the mysteries of heaven and earth.

4. And man became no longer thankful to God and his Lords; but man became conceited, saying:

5. The Gods are fools! All things are Nature, and of growth. Man had become wise in spite of God and his Lords. All things evolve into higher states; it is the natural order. Neither is there any All Person, Jehovih! He is void, like the wind.

6. And God saw the conceit of man, and he said: Behold, he that I have raised up, turneth against me. Now, verily will I go away from man for a season, that he may learn wisdom. Behold, man shall also find that many of his fellows whom he raiseth up, turn against himself.

7. So the Lord departed out of the star chambers; and, lo and behold, the places were filled by the spirits of the newly dead, who knew not the heavens above nor the way of the Almighty.

8. And man inquired of them, thus: Behold, thou art now a spirit! Tell me, is there any God, or Lord, or Jehovih?

9. And the spirits, desiring to flatter man, and, withal, not knowing the heavenly kingdoms, answered, saying: Nay, there is no God, nor Lord, nor All Person, Jehovih!

10. So the kings issued edicts, commanding the people to no longer worship God, nor Lord, nor Jehovih!

11. But woe, for the judgment of kings and queens. Man, having inherent worship in his soul, ceased indeed to worship God and his Lords, and even Jehovih; but, instead, he took to worshipping the stars.

12. Now, the spirits manifesting in the temples, advised one thing through one seer, and another through another; for they were of little knowledge, and wholly unorganized.

13. So, presently, the kings took to war against one another. Anarchy ensued, and man fell to destroying all the glories he had made.

14. Thus again, after three thousand years, man went down in darkness; again fell under the obsession of drujas, and again became a barbarian.

END OF THE LORDS' FIFTH BOOK

BOOK OF FRAGAPATTI, SON OF JEHOVIH.

CHAPTER I.

1. In Horub, an etherean world on the borders of the arc of Aza, in the procession of Sayutivi, Cnod and Gorce, a region of light, of ten thousand earth years, and one hundred vesperes, where reigned Fragapatti, Orian Chief of Obsod and Goomatchala one thousand years; God of Varit, God of Lunitzi and Witchka, and Schleinaka, and Dows, thirty thousand years; Surveyor of Gies, roadway and trail of Fetisi, and Mark, seventy thousand years; Prim of Vaga, Tsein, Loo-Gaab and Zaan, forty thousand years.

2. Fragapatti said: To me Jehovih spake in the Council of Obsod, capital of Horub, where sat my million Gods, our throne itself an arc of light, and there came from the Almighty's throne a greater light, all brilliant, and, with it, the Matchless Voice. Jehovih said:

3. My Son! My Son! Go to the red star, the earth. She cometh thy way; her coat is red with mortal blood!

4. Fragapatti said: The Father saith: The red star cometh this way; her coat is red with mortal blood!

5. To their tables the Gods and Goddesses turned, to mark the time; and now, quickly, the whisper ran to the million ears: The red star! The earth! Ye recollect, it was the little star where Sethantes stood man upright, now agone some sixty thousand years. And Aph crushed in her walls, and pruned her to the quick.

6. And then they overhauled the earth's history, these Gods and Goddesses; measured her course to learn just when she would pass; and they found five years and fifty days would be her dawn of dan, her time to cross the arc of Aza. And as yet she roamed two hundred years away.

7. Fragapatti said: That this sudden light hath given such long warning, so, great work cometh anon. Let my swift messengers come; I will speak to them.

8. Then the marshals ushered in the swift messengers, saluting, before Jehovih's throne.

9. Fragapatti said: Autevat, my son, the All Light fell upon me, saying: My Son, go to the red star, the earth; her coat is red with mortal blood! Now, by her time, she standeth more than two hundred years beyond the boundaries of Horub. For this, I called thee and thy attendants. How long will it take thee to go thither and survey the earth and her heavens, and return hither?

10. Autevat, well trained in such matters, said: Of the earth's time, forty days. Fragapatti said: What number of attendants wilt thou require for so great a distance? And Autevat said: Twenty thousand.

11. Fragapatti said: Provide thee, then, all thou requirest, and go at once. And if thou shalt find the inhabitants of the earth suitable for sacred records, commission thou the God or Lords to send loo'is to raise up an heir for Jehovih's kingdom.

12. Autevat said: Thy will and Jehovih's be done. And, duly saluting, he and his attendants withdrew, and, coming to Gat-wawa, ordered an arrow-ship of twenty thousand gauge. In two days it was completed; and, during the time, Autevat had chosen his attendants. And so he departed, swiftly, like a ray of light, Autevat and his attendants, for the red star, the earth. To see what was the matter, that a God so far away as

Fragapatti was, could feel and know the flow of human blood!

13. For such is the all perfection of Jehovih's Sons and Daughters. Even mortals can sense things a little way off; but Jehovih's upraised Gods feel the breath of the stars, and know when they are disordered.

CHAPTER II.

1. Fragapatti and the Council were deeply engaged in the Sortiv of an Orian arc, through which the phalanx of Inihab and her constellation pass every thousand years; an etherean region where the star, Unhowitchata, was dissolved, some twenty days agone, and cut loose thirty thousand million bound spirits, wrapped in corporeality, by the chief, Avaia, and his band of etherean Gods, who had drawn largely on the inhabitants of Ful, a garden of Horub, in Fragapatti's dominions.

2. And Avaia had quartered the dismembered hosts near Sortiv, where the light of the arc fell sharply on them; to deplete which concourse, taxed the Gods for more help than was at hand. To remedy which, Fragapatti's hosts were extending the ji'ay'an fields of Uth and lowering the grade suitable to the spirits of darkness rescued from Unhowitchata, a prolific world, bringing forth imperfect human souls too abundantly for the quality.

3. And Inihab was near at hand, to pass the arc of Sortiv, with her hundred stars, many of them larger than the earth, to seventy of which the inhabitants of Horub would need go as redeeming Gods and Goddesses for the dawn of dan upon them. To apportion all of which, Fragapatti and his million Council had work on hand, so that not seriously the condition of the earth and her heavens weighed upon them.

4. But in forty days' time, or in such period as would be forty days on the earth, Autevat and his attendants, twenty thousand, with the arrow-ship of fire, returned from the earth and her heavens, speeding close to Obsod, where the marshals received them, and announced them to the Council. Fragapatti said: Let Autevat and his attendants approach the throne.

5. And Autevat went in, saluting, and stood before the Chief, Fragapatti. Autevat said: In Jehovih's name, and by His power and wisdom, am I here to proclaim of the red star and her heaven: First, then:

6. It is three thousand one hundred years since great Osire sowed the seed of mental culture amongst mortals, and it hath grown to be a giant, and a most merciless tyrant. To learn whereof I speak, even God and his Lords, to honor thee, O Fragapatti, gave me voice and word, and opened the libraries of their heavens, and accompanied me around about the earth, to all nations, tribes and wanderers. To me, the God of earth said:

7. Greeting to Fragapatti, in the name of the Father! And to thee, His Son! Take thou this record to Him, and His Council, in Horub. For I am powerless through my Lords and hosts against such odds.

8. God said: From the time great Osire ascended to his etherean realm, our heaven yielded ample harvests for one thousand five hundred years. And God and Lords succeeded in regular order for every dan put upon the earth.

9. But then came a change, for the a'ji'an fields pressed close on every side of heaven, and the souls of angels and mortals turned down to the gross earth. After which time, only such as were already within the second resurrection came and strove for the upper worlds.

10. These depleted the constant rise, and left our colleges, schools and factories vacant; for the hosts of es'yans, newborn from the earth, were stubborn in their much earthly learning, spurning wise counsel and association.

11. And there were born from the earth into atmospherea, millions and millions of spirits, who could not believe they were dead, but maintained they were confined in dark dungeons, howling and cursing day and night.

12. For the seed of corporeal knowledge had taken root in the I'huan race. They had learned the motions, names and places of the stars, the moon and sun; and from these, prophesied the affairs of nations and men. And duly marked out, with maps and charts, the destiny of things, according to the dates of corporeal births and movements, attributing the highest central cause to the sun and stars in conjunction.

13. And thus they cast aside all spirit, even Jehovih, reasoning, that if the sun made winter and summer, and grass to grow and die, so it ruled over animals and men. And so, the temples built to observe the stars, before which men once fell down and worshipped Jehovih, became the places of decrees to horrid deaths of all who taught of or believed in spirit.

14. And now rose a mighty nation on earth, of the I'huans, and called, Parsi'e, and they ignored the decrees of Gods and Lords to build no city larger than two thousand souls; forsooth, declaring the Lords and Gods to be but inspirations from the quickening power of the sun and stars, made dark and personal by the credibility of past ages.

15. And so, in representation of the solar phalanx, they built Oas, a sun city, which standeth to this day of a million souls, sworn to make it the central governor over all the earth, and all other places tributary and paying for its glory. And over Oas they made a king, and called him, KING OF THE SUN, to be to him and his heirs, successors forever.

16. And Oas was embellished and adorned above all other places that had been on the earth; the fame of which spread abroad over Jaffeth and Shem and Ham, betwixt which it lieth centrally. Its colleges became famous, and its observatories were of such magnificence that their roofs were covered with silver and gold. The mirrors and lenses and dark chambers within the towers were so constructed that the stars could be read as well in the day as at night; and the records of observation covered more than a thousand years, by men of great learning.

17. But now, alas, Oas aspires not only to be the central sun in knowledge, but in power and dominion, over the whole earth. And so, from her ample treasures, she sendeth forth armies to conquer and destroy, to gather and plunder, to build still greater her magnificence.

18. So Jaffeth and Shem and Ham run red with human blood, whereat, I raised my voice to high heaven, that Jehovih would send deliverance for the souls of men.

19. For of the millions slain, whose spirits still lie on the battle-fields in chaos, or madly fighting some unseen horror of hallucination, none can be persuaded to come to holier places in heaven; whilst hosts of them rush madly into Oas, to find even their souls accursed by mortals.

20. God said: So the heaven of the earth hath fallen to the earth, save the I'hins and the far-off I'huans, whose spirits my Lords gather in and prepare for the after resurrection. But amongst the Parsi'e nation, none more believe the dead shall rise, nor that spirit is; but that with the mortal death there is the end, to which the king hath made a decree that

never more shall man teach or preach of a heaven for spirits of the dead, nor proclaim a Great Spirit, a Creator.

21. Autevat said: In such manner God disclosed the affairs of earth and heaven, now dead-locked in everlasting destruction; which things, in fuller details, I with my attendants, beheld in every land and kingdom. And as we sat in Vibhraj, in the sacred circle, a light, a single star, appeared before us, even at the throne of God; and from its center the book of heaven fell, as if to send broadcast before mortals the plan and will of Jehovih, near at hand.

22. At this, God said: Tell me, Autevat, thou that travelest across the mighty heavens, and art stored with the knowledge of Gods ruling over other worlds, what is the signal of this light and sacred book? To which I replied: This, O God: The time hath come to earth to prove to mortals the things whereof the Gods and Lords have taught. History shall no longer be locked up privately with the chosen race, the I'hins; but it shall stand before both saints and sinners.

23. Thou shalt prove the resurrection before these stubborn kings, the slaughterers of men, that they may say, not as the I'hins, we believe the soul immortal, because handed down from the ancients, but because it hath been demonstrated before our eyes.

24. God said: How shall this be? To which I replied: Not I, great God, can tell, for that department is not in my keeping. But this much I know: Thou shalt send loo'is into the city of Oas, and they shall raise up a su'is'sar'gis of the fourth grade. All else leave thou till Fragapatti cometh.

25. God said: To reach the fourth grade, will require five generations, which shall spring from the I'hin race commingling with the I'huans. Go, then, O Autevat, to thy etherean home, before the Council of Obsod, to Jehovih's throne, and say to great Fragapatti: An heir to the light of resurrection shall be born ere the dawn of dan of Horub.

26. Autevat said: On learning these truths, I took my leave, and rose and came swiftly back to thy realm.

27. Fragapatti said: It is well. In the time of the next dawn of dan on the earth, I will take a resting spell in which to fulfill Jehovih's plan on earth and in her heavens.

28. So, saluting Autevat, who retired, Fragapatti proceeded with his Council in the affairs of other worlds, making a memorandum of the time and place the earth should near the plains of Horub, in the etherean worlds, some two hundred years yet to come.

CHAPTER III.

1. But the dawn came; and in the wing of Goomatchala, home of Fragapatti, Orian Chief in the etherean worlds high standing, came the Voice, Jehovih's word, saying: My Son! Behold, the dawn of dan neareth the border of Horub. The wailing earth, the red star, cometh apace. And God and Lords call out the name of My infant Son, Zarathustra.

2. Fragapatti rose up, hearing the Voice, and saw the time fulfilled, the two hundred years and more, for the coming world, the time for the revealed word to mortals. To Thee, O Jehovih! he said, Boundless! I come with my hosts, ten million strong.

3. Fragapatti went into the etherean Council of Gods and Goddesses. He said: The time hath come; the red star borders on the plains of Horub. Jehovih calleth!

4. Then the Council rejoiced, for the weighty matters of hundreds of etherean worlds

were settled for a space of time, with promised rest and recreation in corporeal fields. First spake Ad'ar, God of many worlds, a decreer of time in a'ji'an vortices, in the regions of Hispiain sons saying: O Jehovih, give to Thy Son, Fragapatti, five years' rest, the dawn of earth in dan. Only the earth and her heavens to deal with!

5. Next spake Fivaka, Goddess of three etherean worlds, the white-haired Wielder of the Scimetar of Bars, period of Os, Carbon fashioner for the arcs of Job and Sawl. She said: O Jehovih, Almighty! What shall be the prayer of Thy Daughter, Fivaka? What can her love devise for the rest and glory of our high God, Fragapatti, Orian Chief! Then spake Che'sin, marshal in chief for seven etherean worlds, small man, with flowing beard, brought forth from the star, Indr. He said: O Jehovih, make me contributor of my much love to the rest and glory of our Holy Chief, Fragapatti!

6. Thus spake ten thousand Gods and Goddesses of their love and high esteem for the worker, Fragapatti, rich in power and wisdom and love, above all etherean Gods in Horub.

7. Fragapatti said: Ten millions strong my hosts shall be. On the earth, and her heavens, during her dawn of dan, five years and fifty days, we shall have no other labor, thus making it as a holiday for Gods and Goddesses to redeem the fallen world!

8. Fragapatti had spoken. So the proper officers and workmen proceeded to their parts; and in seven days the Yattal announced the fire-ship, the beyan float, ready for the journey. Meantime, the selection of the ten million Redeemers had been made, and they came, every one like a brilliant star, to take their rooms in the monarch vessel.

9. Fragapatti made Huod Commander in Chief, and gave him ten thousand aides. For the curtains and tallij, he made Metrav, Goddess of Rook, Mistress to the Flowing East. And for the spires, he made Iata Mistress of Restless Morn. She was Weaver to Ga'ing, in Reth, four thousand years, and much loved, with black eyes, piercing. Of music, Fragapatti made Theritiviv conductor. She was Goddess of Helm, an etherean world in the roadway of Zi and Olus, four thousand years Mistress of Ne'alt and Exan; one time companion to Etisyai, the Vruiji, loved in Wan and Sangawitch, for her mirth in adversity. Of the trumpeters, Fragapatti made Boan conductor; he was God of Ixalata, now on leave of absence. For Chartist, he made Yan the Chief; he was Surveyor of Oatha, an etherean sea in the Orian arc of Wede and Hollenpoitchava, also on leave of absence during the red star dawn. Of the libraries, he made Hetta Chief Mistress; she was Goddess of Vitia in the Wails of South Eng; thirty thousand years Teacher of Imes, and ten thousand years Counselor of the Orian Chief, Erris, of the arc Wiamesse.

10. Besides these, Fragapatti distributed the minor offices of the float to such Gods and Goddesses whose most exalted states were the extreme opposite, that the great journey through etherea be the transverse of all serious purpose. And thus they started on their course, amidst the applause of thousands of millions of ethereans, wishing them love and joy on their mirthful cruise in furtherance of Jehovih's will.

11. Speeding swiftly across the swamps of Ull, where seven corporeal stars were dismembered a thousand million years ago, now set with a'ji'an fields, and forming nebulae; whereto they bring, at times, the drujas, the dark spirits of other worlds, that they may take on the semblance of corporeal forms to complete their neglected good works in times past; the ship rose freely, and then shot into the pastures of Ze, where Lepsa, God of the corporeal star, Tessa, four hundred years, feedeth seventy million es'yans, colonizing

them to truth and good works. Lepsa knew the float was coming, and so had called a thousand million spectators, to look on, knowing they desired to see great Fragapatti; and they sang and blew their trumpets, rejoicing; to which the Gods and Goddesses of the float cast out myriads of arc'ian flowers, and sweet perfumes, mementoes of love.

12. To Evul, now, the ship made way; where seven etherean worlds bordered in the arc of Nu, pastures of Elim, God of Ooh'sin, where congregated another host of two thousand millions, to see them pass, cheering with singing, and with trumpets and stringed instruments; and to this God, Elim, Fragapatti caused the banners of the float to salute on the sign, Jehovih's Name, being friends for ninety thousand years, and Elim answered him with a million posts of light, amidst the waving of innumerable banners.

13. Onward moved the float, the fire-ship, with its ten million joyous souls, now nearing the borders of Horub, the boundary of Fragapatti's honored regions, known for hundreds of thousands of years, and for his work on many worlds. Here, reaching C'vork'um, the roadway of the solar phalanx, near the post of dan, where were quartered five hundred million ethereans, on a voyage of exploration of more than four millions of years, rich stored with the glories of Great Jehovih's universe. Their koa'loo, their ship, was almost like a world, so vast, and stored with all appurtenances. They talked of going home! Their pilots had coursed the firmament since long before the earth was made, and knew more than a million of roadways in the etherean worlds, and where best to travel to witness the grandest contrasting scenes.

14. By their invitation, Fragapatti halted here a while, and the hosts interchanged their love, and discoursed on their purposes, rejoicing in the glories of Jehovih's everlasting kingdoms; and though they had lived so long, and seen so much, every one had new and wondrous works to tell of; for so great is the inventive power of the Great Spirit, that never twice alike will one find the scenes in the etherean worlds; radiant, differently; moving into everlasting changes, as if each one were to outdo the former in beauty and magnificence.

15. And then again they sped onward, now richly stored with the awe-stirring wonders they had just heard from strange travelers. Presently, now, the float neared the borders of Chinvat, the earth's vortex, just beyond the orbit of the moon. Here Fragapatti halted for a day, sending swift messengers down to the lower heavens, and to the earth, to resolve where he should anchor during dawn.

16. And, the next day, he ordered the lights lowered, and now slowly moved toward the rolling earth; down, down, till he reached the third grade of plateaux from the earth's surface, called Haraiti.

CHAPTER IV.

1. Jehovih said: Here, O My Son, Fragapatti! Here, in Haraiti, have I laid the foundation of thy kingdom. Make fast here the fire-ship, five years and fifty days.

2. Call forth thy hosts; build thou a throne of My throne; the voice of thy Creator is with thee. Fragapatti said: Throne of Thy throne, O Jehovih, here will I build. Haraiti shall be my headquarters for the dawn of dan. Come forth, O ye Gods of dawn! Come forth, O ye Goddesses of dawn! Hear the voice of the Son of Jehovih. Bow down, O ye heavens!

3. The ship was anchored, and the ten millions came forth and assembled in a living altar.

Fragapatti raised his hand, saying: Throne of Thy throne, O Jehovih! And the hosts raised their hands, and the elements took shape and majesty, raising into a throne brilliant as fire. Then Fragapatti ascended and sat on the throne, saying: Glory be to Thee, O Father, the Highest!

4. A light came down from the etherean firmament, and covered the throne over with a canopy, wide enough for five million men to sit under; and at the borders of the canopy, the ethereans, whose work it fell to, sat up columns of crystals, opaque and transparent, illuminated in all possible colors and shades and tints.

5. Fragapatti said: From Thy Council Chamber, O Jehovih, will I build to Thee forever! And now the hosts, Gods and Goddesses, held up their arms, lifting and casting in; and, lo and behold, there rose and stood the habitable Mouru, council chamber and capital of Haraiti.

6. Then to prayers all hands turned, glorifying the Father; then in singing with praise.

7. After which, Fragapatti said: In Thy name, and by Thy Power and Wisdom, O Jehovih, will I now establish heaven anew over the earth. My marshals shall now proceed down to the earth and command the presence of God and his Lords, and all such others as can endure this light. They shall hear my voice, and learn my decrees.

8. Ten thousand marshals, saluting, departed for the earth and regions below.

9. Fragapatti said: Meanwhile, I will appoint my High Council of the first house of Mouru, Gods and Goddesses of dawn. Hear me, then, in the name of Jehovih, the All Light:

10. Caoka, God of Airram; Ata-kasha, God of Beraitis; Airyama, God of Kruse; Pathema, Goddess of Rhon; Maidhyarrya, Mistress of Karyem; Gatha-Ahunavaiti, Goddess of Halonij; Rama-quactra, God of Veres; Vahista, God of Volu; Airam-ishya, God of Icisi, the Myazdas; Haptanhaiti, God of Samatras; Yima, God of Aom; Sudhga, God of Laka; I'ragha, God of Buhk-dhi; Elicic, Goddess of N'Syrus; Harrwaiti, Goddess of Haut-mat, in a'ji; Dews, Goddess of Vaerethagna; Wettemaiti, Goddess of Dyhama; Quactra, Goddess of AEgima; Ustavaiti, Goddess of Maha-Meru; Cura, Goddess of Coronea; Yenne, Goddess of Aka; Caoshyanto, God of Aberet; Rathweiska, God of Huri; Cpentas, God of Butts; Vairyo, God of Nuga-gala; D'Zoata and her brother, Zaota, God and Goddess of Atarevasksha; Ratheweiskare, God of Nece; Yatha, God of Ameshas, and Canha, God of Srawak.

11. Fragapatti said: O Jehovih, behold the glory of my house! I have chosen only such as have ruled over whole worlds. Was ever a God so favored, with such a Council! Was ever so great a light sent to so small a world as the red star?

12. Jehovih said: As I have created man to need relaxation at times, so have I carried the same conditions to be desired by My highest of Gods. Neither have I exalted any God so high but the most menial office is his glory. Neither shall the autocrat learn sympathy till he liveth with a beggar; nor the highest best man learn love and tenderness without taking a season in the depths of misery.

13. Fragapatti said: Shall the strong man forget he was once a child; can an Orian Chief forget he was once a slave; can he that is in the light forget them that are in the dark?

14. Mighty art Thou, O Jehovih! I came to the earth and her heavens to rest myself in Thy service; but Thou wert here before me; Thy voice riseth up to rebuke me; yea, I am still but a child to Thee!

CHAPTER V.

1. When Fragapatti had selected both departments of his Council, which comprised one hundred thousand souls, he said:

2. When a God espouseth a new kingdom, it is customary for him to create his own capital, and affix the boundaries of his lights and hall of audience; but when he hath Gods and Goddesses for his assistants, it is meet and proper for them to help in the buildings. In this case, I give into your hands to provide this realm.

3. Hardly had his words gone forth when the Gods and Goddesses stretched forth their hands unto Jehovih, and, lo and behold, the elements of the plateau took shape, and there stood the canopy of a new kingdom; then again they stretched forth their hands to Jehovih, and there came the walls of the house of heaven; and yet again they stretched forth their hands to Jehovih, and there came the floor and foundation.

4. And the house was called the House of Mouru, the place of the throne of Fragapatti, in the lower heavens. On the plains beyond the house, Fragapatti created a thousand fields and pastures; and in each and every one he created ten thousand mansions, and every mansion was capable of one thousand souls. With roadways from one to another Fragapatti created them, his hosts being the workmen, in the wisdom and power of Jehovih.

5. Whilst this work was going on, the marshals who went down to the earth returned, bringing God and his Lords with them, and also bringing with them twelve hundred thousand spirits of the second resurrection. Fragapatti commanded them to bring God and his Lords into the House of Mouru, and they were so brought.

6. Fragapatti said: In the name of Jehovih, I salute thee, O God, and thy Lords, and thy hosts.

7. God said: In Thy name, O Jehovih, am I, and my Lords, and my hosts, blessed with great joy. That thou, O Fragapatti, hast come to redeem the earth-born and the spirits of these heavens, is a joyful period in the time of worlds.

8. The Lords said: For ourselves and our hosts, O Jehovih, do we thank Thy Son, Fragapatti.

9. Fragapatti said: That thou, O God, mightst know my decrees, I commanded thee and thy Lords, and thy exalted hosts, hither. Hear me, then, and to whom I send thee, do thou my commandments, in the name of Jehovih: The time hath come when mortals on the earth shall begin their lessons in spiritual things proven, being themselves made part in the building of Jehovih's kingdoms.

10. Through thee, the present reigning God of the earth and her heavens, must be carried out the death and resurrection of thy chosen heir, Zarathustra; to prove, first, that man on the corporeal earth can live All Pure and without sin; second, that corporeal death belongeth to the earth-body of man, and not to the spirit; and, third, that after death, the same person can rise in spirit and appear to mortals, to be seen and known; after which, he shall show his final ascent toward the upper heavens, in the arms of his God.

11. Whilst this cometh upon thee in person to carry out, thou shalt also, through thy ministering angels, prove to mortals the advantage of virtue and truth over sin and darkness. For thou shalt cause also to be stricken in death two evil men who are all impure; and they shall suffer death at the same time with thy heir, Zarathustra; but these

shall not appear before mortals after death. For mortals shall hereafter be a testimony to one another of the reward of virtue, and the power of being one with the Gods, Sons of Jehovih.

12. But since all attestation by spirits can be set at defiance by the craft of philosophers, thou shalt not wait till after the death of thy heir, to teach the truths of the Father's kingdoms; but beforehand. Causing Zarathustra, whilst yet mortal, to write down rules of mortal life, and doctrines, and faith, and repentance, and praise of the Great Spirit; and of prophecy, and all manner of righteous gifts, and the power of miracles, and the triumph of the spirit of man over corporeal elements.

13. And when thou hast completed these things, thou shalt bring the spirit of Zarathustra to this House; but the druks who suffer death with him, thou shalt deliver in the usual way to the places prepared for their resurrection.

14. Tell me, then, how standeth thy heir; and ask thou of me whatsoever thou wilt, to assist thee, to carry out these, my decrees, and it shall be granted unto thee.

15. God said: Zarathustra hath attained his twentieth year, and comprehendeth the destiny put upon him. He is pure and wise, with faith and gentleness; but he is larger and more powerful than any other man in the world. He is instructed, both in the spiritual and corporeal senses, having a knowledge of the books of the ancients, and of writing and making tablets.

16. Fragapatti said: Five years shalt thou have in which to complete thy labor. Depart, therefore, to thy place, taking with thee such of thy Lords and hosts as thou mayst require. I will appoint a thousand messengers to travel betwixt thy place and this, that every day thou shalt ask for this or that, it shall be granted unto thee. To which God replied:

17. I will go now and cause Zarathustra to write a book of wisdom, and give him prophecy over the kings and nations and tribes of men. What I do shall be proven to thee in Mouru. Thus saying, God withdrew a little, and selected his Lords and such other assistants as he desired; and, after this, Fragapatti granted a day of recreation, in which time the ethereans were made well acquainted with the conditions of mortals and of the thousands of millions of spirits still lingering in the first resurrection, and in darkness and chaos.

18. On the next day God and his hosts departed for the earth, well attended by thousands of volunteers from the etherean sojourners of Haraiti.

CHAPTER VI.

1. Fragapatti said: The voice of Jehovih cometh to me, saying: My Son, appoint thou an assistant chief to sit on thy throne, and go thou around about atmospherea, taking surveyors and inspectors with thee; for thou shalt see with thine own eyes the condition of thousands of millions of spirits in hada.

2. Fragapatti said: In Jehovih's name, I announce Athrava my assistant, God of Mouru. There was great rejoicing in the Council at this. Then came Athrava forward, and ascended Jehovih's throne and sat on the right hand of Fragapatti. Etherean lights fell upon the place from every side, and Fragapatti gathered from the elements and made a crown for Athrava, and crowned him.

3. Officers and workmen were sent to build a conveyance for Fragapatti, and for such

attendants as he might take with him. So, the next day, Fragapatti chose his companions, thirty thousand, making Verethragna speaker, and he and they departed for their inspection of hada and the earth.

4. His ship was built without lights or curtains, so they might travel unobserved. First he inspected the plateau of Haraiti, which, prior to this, had never been inhabited; and he found its distance from the earth was equal to ten diameters of the earth; and its east and west and north and south diameters corresponded in size to what the earth would be were it that volume; that is to say, the superfice of the plateau was five hundred and twenty-eight thousand miles in every direction. And in the ratio of the number of mortals on the earth, this plateau would inhabit five hundred and twenty-eight thousand million souls. And yet this was not the thousandth part of the number it could sustain, in fact, within and without.

5. Fragapatti said: Such is Haraiti, O Jehovih. And yet there have been, till now, no spirits to come and inhabit it! Who can survey Thy works, O Father! Who shall fear for the limit of Thy handiwork!

6. Verethragna said: And yet we shall find in the lowest hadas spirits huddled together like bees in a hive. And yet wherefore, O Chief, for is it not so with mortals also? They cluster together in cities and tribes, warring for inches of ground, whilst vast divisions of the earth lie waste and vacant!

7. Fragapatti said: Is this not the sum of the darkness of mortals and of spirits in the lowest realms---. They know not how to live? A spider or an ant is more one with the Creator than these!

8. Next they visited Zeredho, six diameters of the earth distant. Here they found a colony of two thousand million spirits, that had been founded by Osire three thousand three hundred years before. But not the same people, but such as came up from the earth afterward. They had a God named Hoab, an atmospherean from the earth, two thousand one hundred years. And he was upright and wise, and of good works most excellent; but knowing nothing of etherea, had no ambition to rise thither. And his content had visited itself on the colony, and they were contented also.

9. Fragapatti said: To remain here forever, is this the extent of thy desires, O Hoab? And Hoab answered him, saying: Yea, Master. What more is life than to reach the highest place and remain there? To which Fragapatti said: Is this the all highest? And Hoab said: Yea, Master. Any place and condition is the all highest, if man make it so. None can attain higher than I; no people higher than my people. We are freed from the earth and hada; and we desire not to return thither, nor to go to any other place.

10. Fragapatti said: Let us walk a little, that I may see thy kingdom. Hoab consented, and they walked along, seeing the inhabitants lying at ease, some amusing themselves weaving threads of light, then unraveling them and weaving them over again; others playing with crystals and lenses and opaque and transparent elements, but not doing anything for another; nor, in fact, needed they, for all were capable of doing for themselves. Now, after they had traveled a while, Fragapatti said: Hast thou not, O Hoab, a desire to return to the plateaux below thee, where the inhabitants are in misery and darkness, and bring them into thine own realm? To which Hoab said:

11. Nay, Master. Let them shift for themselves. Even if we helped them up they would be thankless. Nay, my doctrine is: Man is the all highest of all things. The elements are

dumb; the worlds are many and wide. Let man choose a corner for himself, and there settle forever. Fragapatti asked: Because a man chooseth a corner, is it necessarily his own? Hoab said: Our place was bequeathed us by our forefathers; of course it is ours, and to remain so forever. Neither suffer we any other spirits to settle in our dominions. Being far away from the rest of the world, we are not much molested.

12. Fragapatti said: How came ye hither? Hoab said: Long ago there came a God hither, named Osire, bringing six thousand million drujas up from the earth. With them he founded a colony here; with factories, colleges, hospitals, and all things necessary to enlighten the people, giving them ample teachers. In course of time, many of the inhabitants migrated away from this place, and it was almost depleted of its people. But the Gods below this sent new supplies of inhabitants, of which we are the second and third installments; so we inherited the place with all its factories and educationals, and other places.

13. Fragapatti said: As ye were raised up by the Gods of other places, would it not give ye joy to raise up others, who are still in darkness? Hoab said: Nay, Master. We are pure and refined; the atmosphere of drujas is unpleasant to us. They would vitiate our own happiness, besides entailing toil and responsibilities upon us. We cannot mix with any people but the refined and holy. We take care of ourselves; let others do the same, and all will be well.

14. Fragapatti said: Who thinkest thou I am, and my people with me? Hoab said: Visitors from some far-off realm, who are either discordant with yourselves, or bent to meddle in the affairs of other peoples. We have had visitors before, and we never grieved when they left us. To which Fragapatti replied:

15. Thou art strong in thy philosophy. Had no nation or people such ambition as this, there would be no content in the world. To be satisfied with one's own self and behavior is to be a God in fact. Hadst thou nothing to fear from immigration coming to thy shore, or to fear from some new philosophy undermining thy long-established convictions, thou mightst indeed be the happiest of Gods, and thy people the happiest of people.

16. Hoab said: True! Thou perceivest wisely. O that there was nothing to fear; nothing to dread, forever!

17. Then Fragapatti said: And I declare unto thee, Hoab, that that condition can be attained. For I have seen kingdoms in heaven so fortified. And wert thou and thy people prepared to receive the sacred secrets pertaining thereto, I would most willingly unfold them before thee. Hoab said: Thou art a wise God; tarry thou and teach us.

18. Fragapatti said: I am now on a journey, and cannot remain longer; but, on one condition, I will return hither and disclose these matters, so that never more shalt thou fear for immigration into thy country, nor for any philosophy which any man or God may teach: Exact a promise of secrecy from all thy people. Hoab said: It shall be done.

19. And Fragapatti and his hosts withdrew, and departed out of that plateau, promising to return when notification had been served on his people. But Fragapatti inspected the whole superfice, and found it capable of educating and providing for ten hundred thousand million spirits; whereas, there were but two thousand millions in Hoab's kingdom; and they inhabited only a small corner of the plateau; nevertheless, Hoab laid claim to the whole.

20. After this, Fragapatti descended to the next plateau, the first grade plateau above the

earth, called Aoasu, signifying, land and sky world, for the first spirit life after mortal death. Aoasu hath its foundation on the earth, and it undulateth with mountains and valleys, like the earth, having seas over the corporeal seas. And the outer superfice of Aoasu is from twenty to a hundred miles above the earth's surface; and it is habitable within and without, after the manner of all spirit worlds. But the first resurrections were within it and on the earth surface; and the second resurrections, mostly, on its superfice; though all atmospherean plateaux are also made for the second and third resurrections. On the roadway betwixt Aoasu and Zeredho, next ascending, it was that Osire established Vibhraj, which was now so depleted of its people that Fragapatti halted not to examine it, but proceeded to Aoasu direct.

21. Here lie the mountains of Morn and Eve, and mountains of the Moon and Sun and Stars; chief of which groups are:

22. Ushidaho, Ushidarena, Erezifya, Fraorepa, Ezora, Arezura, Tudae, Bumya, Doitya, Raoidhita, Mazassavao, Autare, a place of light, inhabited by Hura, Lord of Vouta; Ereasho, Vata-gaiko, a place of Uz, signifying torments, because of its darkness.

23. This group of mountains is ninety miles higher than the earth mountains of Jaffeth. South of these are Adarana, Aayana, Isakata, Somya, Kanaka-tafedrhao, Vahra, and the double mountain, Hamanakanna; eight ranges of the round mountains, Fravanku; the four peaks, the Vidwaana.

24. These extend over the earth mountains of Shem, and have an altitude above the earth of one hundred miles. These are the oldest inhabited spirit worlds, since the submersion of Pan, whose spirit worlds were carried up to a higher heaven, which hath since been called Haraiti.

25. Extending east and west lie the group called the Red Men's group: Aezaka, Maenaka, Vakhedrakae, Akaia, Tudhakkae, Ishvakhaya, Draoshisvao, Cairivao, Nanhusmao, Kahayuyu, Autarekanhae, Karayaia, which were the first places in heaven for colonizing the spirits of the I'huan race.

26. The next group lieth to the west and south, which are: Gichindava, I'huana-Varya, Raegamna, Akaya, Asha-cteambana, Urinyovadidhkae, Asnahovao, Ushaoma, Utsagaerenao, Cyamakhama, Cyamaka, Vafrayaotso, Vafrayao, Vourrusha, and Uasoakhao.

27. To the south of this group are the Towering Eagles, which are: Ijatarra, Adhutuvavata, Ceptimavarenao, Cpentodata, Asnavoaya, Kairogakhaivacao, Tauraiosa, Baroyo, Barocrayama, Fraayapoa, Udrya, Usayaokhava, Raevao. All of which groups were named by the Gods and Lords of the intermediate worlds during the time of the Yi-ha language amongst mortals, being named after the amalgamation of the tribes of I'hins, every syllable, in former ages, being one tribe, whereof the Gods have made this testimony to endure from before the time of Fragapatti and Zarathustra, wherein it may be proven to mortals and spirits that this division of the spirit world was revealed to man at the time language was carried to its highest compounding.

28. Besides these mountains in the lowest heavens, there were four thousand others, the names of which were duly registered in the libraries of heaven, by Thor and his sub-Gods; but more than two thousand of them were uninhabited, owing to the fact, that Jehovih had not as yet created a sufficient number of people for them. But the mountains here mentioned above were those, chiefly, where, at the time after Apollo, the false Gods and

false Lords sat up kingdoms of their own; and the names of the mountains are also the names they espoused unto themselves.

29. Fragapatti said: Alas, these heavens! Who can measure the vanity of men and angels, that cut loose from the Great Spirit, endeavoring to set up kingdoms on their own account! Their places perish; sorrowful histories! Behold these vagrant spirits, strolling about, or hiding amidst the ruins! Ashamed of their rags, and nakedness! Prowling around; millions of them; hundreds of millions!

30. Verethragna said: I thank Thee, O Jehovih, that I am once again amongst the lowest! Keep me, O Father, amidst this darkness, till I shall never again forget the lowest of my brothers and sisters. I behold Thy Wisdom, O Jehovih! But for these cycles of time, in the dawns of which Thy ethereans can come down to witness the bounden in hell, they would themselves forget the horrors. O that Thou wilt not suffer me to rest till I have helped to raise them up to know Thee, and to be a glory within Thy works!

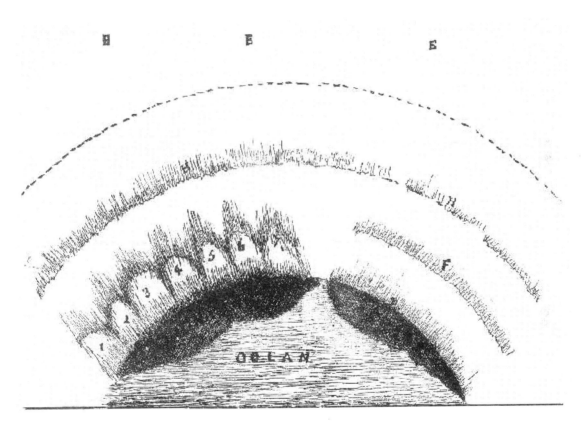

Plate 10.

ETHEREA.

E, E, E, Etherea. All that lieth between the dotted line and the earth is atmospherea. H, Haraiti, highest lower heaven, founded by Fragapatti. F, Zeredho, second highest lower heaven founded by Fragapatti. 1, 2, 3, 4, 5, 6, 7, third lowest heavens founded by Fragapatti. These seven were called the Seven Heavenly Mountains, and known by the name Aoasu. (See Vedas.)

CHAPTER VII.

1. Fragapatti surveyed Aoasu in all the Morn of East Birth, and his officers enumerated the spirits, and recorded their condition, and then he called his conductors, saying:

2. I have measured the Morn of the East Birth; take me now to the Setting Eve of Death.

3. So the ship, with its passengers, was raised a little, and started for the west, running low over the regions lying west of Ham, Shem and Jaffeth. Fragapatti said:

4. I perceive, the plan of the Gods on this star was to complete its inhabitation by going westward. For this reason, I will see where they designed to have the Eve of Death and the birth of the Father's kingdom on the corporeal part.

5. When they came to the Atlantic Ocean (Uzocea), they raised their ship still higher, and sped across for the regions inhabited by the I'hins and I'huans.

6. Arriving thither, they came to Ipseogee, a region in the lower heaven where Hapacha, Lord of the I'hins, had a kingdom of seventy million souls, many of whom were I'huan spirits. Here Fragapatti halted, and made fast his ship, remaining seven days. And Hapacha received him and his hosts, and entertained them. And during the time of their sojourn, Hapacha sent his otevan out around over all the heavens belonging to Guatama, north and south, taking the surveyors and inspectors of the hosts of Fragapatti into all inhabited places, so they could complete their records.

7. In the meantime, Hapacha conducted Fragapatti throughout his kingdom, exhibiting the factories, schools, colleges, hospitals, and all such places as belong to the second resurrection.

8. Fragapatti said to Hapacha: In thee and thy kingdom I am well pleased. Thou shalt hear from me ere many days. At present I must depart. So Fragapatti told not who he was, nor what was his mission; but gathering together his hosts, departed, still going westward, until he completed the circumference of the earth.

9. Now will I again go around the earth, said Fragapatti, and inspect mortals and their kingdoms. So, his conductors now run the ship just above the lands, being guided by messengers familiar with the earth and with all the habitable places. And they zig-zagged their course, going into all kingdoms and into all large cities, and into forests and plains, determining the condition of the earth, and its capabilities, as well as the conditions of mortals and their capabilities.

10. And when Fragapatti had completed this latter inspection, he returned to Mouru, in Haraiti; and the whole of his absence was seventy-seven days.

11. And all the records obtained on the expedition were immediately filed in Mouru, where the High Council and all others who chose could read them. And on the third day thereafter, Fragapatti resumed the throne of Jehovih, and was prepared to found anew the kingdoms of atmospherea, and also those of earth; to overthrow or set aside what was not good; and to raise up both mortals and spirits who had proved themselves worthy.

CHAPTER VIII.

1. This, then, is the manner of the House of Mouru: Fragapatti would announce the subject; then, rank and rank, according to exaltation, the representatives of hundreds and of thousands would speak on the subject. When all had spoken that desired to, or whom

Fragapatti asked, then Fragapatti would pronounce in the name of Jehovih. And these were the decrees. For example:

2. Fragapatti said: What shall be the divisions of the earth, and who the Lords thereof? And when the House had expressed, then Fragapatti said: In the name of Jehovih, these shall be the divisions of the earth, to wit: Jaffeth on the east and north, by the sea and to the ice regions, and on the west to the mountains of Oh'e'loo, which shall be called the first division.

3. To the east and south, water and water, and to the west, the highlands of E'zar; and its name shall be Shem.

4. The south land shall henceforth be called Arabin'ya, encompassed by the sea. And north of this, the first country of the brown red race shall be called Heleste, bordering on Shem and Jaffeth on the east, and extending half way to the sea on the west.

5. Uropa shall be Goddess of the west part, and it shall be called after her. And the two great west lands shall be called North Guatama and South Guatama. And all the islands of the earth shall be called Oce'ya; and the waters of the earth shall be called Oce'a, signifying, in likeness of the earth and sky.

6. For the seven divisions of the earth there shall be seven rulers of the rank Lord God; and for South Oce'ya, one ruler of the rank Lord; and for North Oce'ya, one ruler of the rank Lord; and for Japan (Zha'pahn), one ruler of the rank sub-God.

7. Hear me, O ye Gods and Goddesses: Who I shall proclaim from amongst you shall reign during dawn of dan only, but shall raise up a successor in your own name, and in Jehovih's name, to the same rank, to hold dominion two hundred years, the next succeeding resurrection.

8. Fragapatti said: I proclaim, in the name of Jehovih, Ah-oan, Lord God of Jaffeth; Yima, Lord God of Shem; E'Chad, Lord God of Arabin'ya; Gir'akshi, Lord God of Heleste; Uropa, Lord Goddess of Uropa; Yaton'te, Lord God of North Guatama; Kow'anea, Lord God of South Guatama; M'wing'mi, Lord of South Oce'ya; Ots'ha'ta, Lord of North Oce'ya; and Soo'fwa, sub-God of Japan.

9. Approach the throne, O ye Lord Gods, and Lords, and sub-God, that ye may be anointed in the name of the Father, and duly crowned with the emblem of All Light.

10. First came the Lord Gods; and they stood before the throne of Jehovih, now illumed brilliantly, in gold and white. Fragapatti said: By Thy Power and Wisdom, O Jehovih, which rest in me, do I these, Thy Lord Gods, anoint and bestow to Thy kingdoms, for Thy glory. Amen! Receive ye of this fire, for it is His anointing with power and wisdom, that all men and women and children, mortals and spirits, coming under your dominion, may rejoice in their Creator, rising forever. Amen!

11. The Lord Gods responded: May I glorify Thee, O Jehovih, in the kingdom Thou hast bestowed upon me! In Thy name I receive this fire, for it is Thy baptism with power and wisdom. Whomsoever Thou hast entrusted to my dominion will I cause to rejoice at all times, and to rise up forever in Thy numberless kingdoms!

12. Fragapatti said: And to you I bequeath, in the Father's name, power to exalt successors, that ye may also bequeath to your successors power for them to exalt successors also; and so on, till the next dawn of dan from the etherean kingdoms, for of such manner shall be the dominion of the Gods and Lords of earth, and her heavens, for a long season hereafter.

13. The Lord Gods responded: Thy power, O Jehovih, do I accept, to exalt a successor to me in my dominions, with power to bequeath the exalting power to his successors after him, till the next etherean dawn of dan.

14. Fragapatti said: Crown of Thy Crown, O Jehovih, do I weave of Thy golden light, for these, Thy exalted Sons and Daughters; and with my hand, in Thy name, crown them. Be Thou with them, now and forever. Amen!

15. Then Fragapatti gathered of the light present, and fashioned crowns for them, and they came forward to the foot of the throne, and he crowned them. So also, at the time they said: I receive Thy fire! there came down from above a stream of light, bright as the sun, and settled upon them.

16. And now they sat down at the foot of the throne, in ancient custom, and Fragapatti came down from the throne, bringing attendant Gods with him; and they took the hands of the newly-anointed Gods, and rose them up; and Fragapatti said: Arise thou, O Lord God, and go thy way. Jehovih is with thee. Then they stood aside, a little way off.

17. Then came forward the two Lords. Fragapatti said: O Jehovih, by Thy power and wisdom in me vested, do I appoint and announce these, Thy Lords, to their divisions of the earth; and with my hands, and in Thy name, weave I a crown for each of them, and crown them Lords of Thy light, for Thy glory. Amen!

18. Hear me, O Lords; that which I bestow in the name of the Father, and ye receive, ye shall also bestow in the name of the Father upon your successor at the end of this dawn of dan. Though a Lord God hath dominion, first, with mortals, and, second, with the first heaven in his division which resteth on the earth; and though a Lord hath dominion with mortals only, and with such ashars as minister unto them, ye twain are made Lords of far-distant islands, where ye shall determine many things in your own way, often being Gods also, which I also bequeath unto you, and your successors forever.

19. The Lords said: What thou hast put upon me, O Jehovih, I will do, with Thy power and wisdom, for Thy glory, forever. Amen! I receive Thy crown with praise and thanksgiving, and will bestow it in Thy name upon my successor, bright as I now receive it.

20. Fragapatti then laid the crowns upon them, and they sat at the foot of the throne, also. Then Fragapatti took them by the hand, and raised them up, saying: Arise, O Lords of Jehovih, and go your ways.

21. And when they stood aside, Soo'fwa came forward. Fragapatti said: In Thy name, O Jehovih, and by Thy power in me vested, do I this, Thy Son, crown sub-God of his division of the earth and its heavens. Of Thy light I crown him, and bestow him with a rod of water and rod of fire, that he may have dominion in Thy name, and for Thy glory. Amen!

22. Hear me, O God: Thy duties make thee both Lord and God; but thy second resurrections shall be removed at short intervals, as thou shalt be hereafter informed. But thou shalt have power to appoint assistant Lords to be with thee, in my name, and the Father's. And thou shalt also exalt a successor after thee, with power to his successor also.

23. In Jehovih's name, receive thou this crown of yellow light, for it is the emblem of the oldest habitable country above the waters of the earth! And may the Father be with thee, now and forever. Amen!

24. He also sat at the foot of the throne, and Fragapatti raised him up, even as the others,

saying: Arise, O God, and go thy way. So he stood aside. And now the es'enaurs sang and chanted, and the marshals led the way; and the newly empowered Gods departed out of the House of Mouru. And there had been provided for them, already, a vessel sufficient to reconduct them back to the earth; and they entered the vessel, and, amidst the flying of banners and the music of the trumpeters, they sped forward, and were soon out of sight.

CHAPTER IX.

1. The hosts of the second resurrection were now conducted to the mansions previously created in Haraiti by Fragapatti; and they were provided with teachers and occupations, according to their development.

2. Fragapatti said: The marshals in chief will now send the builders of the fire-ships before me; I will speak to them. Now when the builders had come, and duly saluted before the throne, Fragapatti said:

3. Go build me an avalanza capable of carrying three thousand million angels, with as many rooms, capable of descent and ascent, and east and west and north and south motion, and prepare it with a magnet, that it may face to the north, whilst traveling.

4. The builders saluted, and then withdrew, and went and built the vessel. And it was two hundred thousand paces east and west, and the same north and south; its height was one thousand lengths, and the vesture around it was a thousand paces thick; and it was provided with etherean curtains, two hundred thousand; and with four hundred thousand banners, of all possible colors and shades and tints. Besides these were fifty thousand small flags and streamers. The floor was woven in copy of a spider's net, extending from the centre outward, and with circular bars at crosses; and the frame-work within was constructed with one million uprights, the entire height of the vessel; and yet across these were twenty millions of bars; within the whole, were the rooms and halls, and places for musicians.

5. When it was completed, the builders notified Fragapatti. He said: Athrava, come thou and sit on the throne. I promised to go and see Hoab and his colony, in Zeredho, when he should send me word regarding certain matters. Behold, messengers have notified me, and Hoab desireth to know how he can establish his colony, that he may never more fear to be annoyed by other Gods and angels.

6. Let fifty thousand musicians enter the ship with me, besides a sufficient number of captains and officers to manage the ship. The marshals at once made the proper selections, and took them to the ship, when they all entered, Fragapatti with them, and they departed.

7. So, Fragapatti returned to Zeredho, the second highest lower heaven, of which the ambitious Hoab, with his colony, desired to be sole occupant forever.

8. Hoab was waiting to receive him, having aroused up a sufficient number of his indolent subjects to maintain the semblance of a heavenly Council. But what a surprise! He had expected only a small vessel, with a few attendants. And now, when he beheld the magnificence of the avalanza, and the majesty of the band of musicians, so far transcending anything he had ever seen, he feared, and was awe-stricken.

9. Fragapatti approached slowly, but with Avom lights, and when the ship was near at hand, the hosts aboard cast out hundreds of thousands of perfumed ovaries, which

exploded with beautiful colors, filling the atmosphere around about with the most delightful perfume. Finally the avalanza came to anchor, and Fragapatti, without any ceremony, alighted, taking a thousand attendants with him, and came directly up to Hoab, who was abashed somewhat on account of his shabby appearance.

10. Fragapatti said: Friend and brother, peace and joy be unto thee and thy house! To which Hoab replied: All hail, great Chief! Happiness attend thee and thy hosts! And were it not that I had previously discovered thou wert a philosopher like myself, I would apologize for the vast difference betwixt the respective appearances of our hosts. But ye are welcome all the same!

11. Fragapatti said: A mere incident of conditions, most noble God. Thou art aware, when children go on a holiday excursion, they attire themselves in their best; so it is better that I find an apology than that thou shouldst.

12. Hoab said: Nay, Chief, there is a philosophy in this matter which hath worried me of late: A thousand years ago my colony was ambitious to retire itself in grandeur, and to build fine ships and go on excursions, also. Five hundred years later, they ceased building ships and going on excursions, saying: What is the use? Latterly, they are all utilitarians, doing just as little as possible. In fact, many of my subjects deny themselves comforts, on the plea that they can do without them.

13. Fragapatti said: Thou rememberest, when I was here before I said to thee that without contentment no people had attained to peace; and thou didst acquiesce. Why, then, shouldst thou not rejoice that thy people have thus subdued ambition and curiosity? Hast thy mind, in so short a time, lost its contentment? Thou knowest I came hither to impart to thee and thy people the great secret, that ye may so fortify yourselves that ye shall never fear for Gods or angels molesting you.

14. Hoab said: Hear me, O Chief: If my people lose all ambition for rites and ceremonies, and dancings, and excursions; and keep constantly striving to deny themselves of everything save what necessity calleth for; and if that necessity becometh smaller and smaller, where will be the end? Will not all inspiration die out? For, to tell the truth, since my people have given up rites and ceremonies, and prayers and singings, they have also given up rejoicings of soul, and are becoming like a dead people.

15. Fragapatti said: Then thou wouldst seem to prove that to hold on only to the useful in life would ultimately end in suicide to the state, to the family, to the individual, and even to the soul?

16. Hoab said: Many of my people are too lazy to clothe themselves; and because of shame, they seek secluded places, as they say, to live as they please. Do not such people commit suicide against the state? Hath a man a right to withdraw himself from his fellows, saying: It suiteth me better? We have been told that in the first age of mortals, they had no ambition to live together, being void of all talents, and that the Gods inspired them to language and to society, giving them rites and ceremonies as an inducement to make them harmonious and attractive to one another.

17. Fragapatti said: How shall I account for the difference betwixt thy arguments now and the other time I was with thee? Thou desiredst me to believe that thou and thy people were the highest, best, happiest of all people in the heavens. Why this change?

18. Hoab said: Thou didst promise me thou wouldst teach us some way of protection against being molested by other Gods and spirits from other kingdoms. Since then I have

reasoned on the subject, and I perceive that if such a state of security could be given to my people, they would wander off into isolation, and even forget language and judgment. How, then, was it, thou toldest me thou hadst been in heavens where such a state of seeming impossibility existeth.

19. Fragapatti said: Let not arguments sway thee, O Hoab. But rather, examine proofs for thyself. I mistrusted that my statement to thee was too extravagant to be believed without evidence. Behold, then, what I have done: I brought a vessel large enough for all thy people, desiring that ye go with me to my kingdom, new founded in Haraiti; and if thou shouldst find any further desire, at the end of a few years, I will take thee and thy people to still another kingdom, in a far-off world. After that, and thou desirest it, I will provide the same conveyance back to Zeredho, with power to rule over it to thy heart's content.

20. Hoab said: Fairest of Gods! I feared, indeed, thou hadst come with the same old story; to worship the All Light, the Unknowable Nothingness; with foolish ceremonies and rites, and prayers, and songs of praise; which, however good for the ignorant and superstitious, are worthless to a God as enlightened as I am. This thou perceivest with thine own judgment. Gladly will I go with thee, and I will persuade as many of my people as possible to go also. Thou art the first God that ever came to our heaven, that wanted not to circumscribe our liberties, which neither I nor my people can tolerate.

21. These things were then communicated to the people of Zeredho; and after a few days they gathered together, and went into the avalanza, every soul of them. Fragapatti signaled the commander not to go directly to Haraiti, but by way of Utza, one of the hells in the Aoasu mountains, inhabited by thousands of millions of spirits in darkness, many of whom knew not who they were, nor had they names, being infants, idiots, and chaotic and foul smelling.

CHAPTER X.

1. When they came to Utza, Hoab cried out: What do my eyes behold! As I live, here are people who once belonged to Zeredho, mine own heaven! By what strange law left they my kingdom to come and dwell in these torments?

2. Fragapatti caused the avalanza to halt, that information be obtained. So he called the druj, and there came thousands of them, ragged and drunken. Hoab knew many of them, and he said: Know ye who I am? And they answered: Yea, Hoab, God of Zeredho. Again spake Hoab, saying: For what reason left ye my glorious kingdom to come and dwell in this hell of iniquity?

3. They answered, saying: Alas, that we left, indeed! But since it is so, it is so. Hear us, then, O Hoab, this is the reason: Even as mortals oft leave Purity in order to revel in sin. More reason we know not.

4. Then spake Fragapatti, saying: Jehovih saith: I have given man many talents. Because the roadways are not open for their growth, he plungeth into darkness. Think not that ye can draw a line, and say: O man, thou shalt not do this, or thou shalt do thus: for ye are powerless to hold him, whom I created to go forward. And if he find not a way to go forward, he will turn and go backward.

5. The drujas said: Yea, master: Zeredho did not fill our souls; we were thirsty for amusement and lightheartedness. We heard no voice but Utility. We sheared off all

ornament and diversion, and art, and, finally, even music. We fain would hear from Zeredho, to know if they have not ceased to talk, and perhaps to live, because, forsooth, Utility hath spoken!

6. And they laughed, and frolicked about like idiots and fools, mingling with harlots, and thieves, and liars, and drunkards.

7. Fragapatti caused the ship to move on a while, and then halted, and called other drujas, and questioned them in the same manner, and received answers of the same character.

8. Again they moved onward, and the same was repeated; finally, they came to a place where all was darkness and noise and confusion, where they even heeded not the ship, nor the calls made to them. Then spake Fragapatti to Hoab, saying: Hath it been proven to thee that man cannot stand still? Hoab said: It is true. This matter cometh close home to me. I perceive now that had I not come out of Zeredho, I had not witnessed these things, nor had I seen Zeredho as I now see it.

9. Fragapatti said: Be not hasty against thine own philosophy, for I will show thee thine own wisdom by and by. So they traveled seven days in hell, the lowest division of hada, where there was neither government, nor order, nor truth, nor virtue, but torments and wailings and cursings.

10. Fragapatti said: Thou hast seen that these many people know not their own darkness.

11. Hoab said: Is it not true, O Chief, that no man knoweth his own darkness? Who, then, is safe? Who knoweth he is not on the downward road?

12. Fragapatti said: Thou hast said man is the All Highest. But doth it not come home to us all, as to the ancients, that to do good with all our wisdom and strength, and have faith therein, that we are on the road to the All Highest?

13. Certainly thou hast proven, said Hoab, that Zeredho is not the All Highest, for it cannot retain its people. Even hell hath prevailed over her. And doth not hell prevail over all self-righteousness, and over riches and kingdoms and empires? If, therefore, hell prevaileth, is not hell the most powerful? And if the most powerful is not hell, therefore the All Highest? The ancients were happy in ignorance, for in believing in an All Person, a Creator, and that they should ultimately see Him, they had an object in view. But with the growth of wisdom, we find we cannot realize such a Person, and so have no object in view ahead of us. Thereupon, we recoil upon ourselves, and all is dead.

14. Fragapatti said: Hath man no lesson from the past? In the ancient times the Gods persuaded mortals to make stone idols and worship them. And they were sufficient until man attained more knowledge. Again came the Gods to mortals, inventing a large man-God in the sky, persuading them to worship him. He was a sufficient God till man learned to commune with angels; and the angels contradicted that philosophy. But hear me, O Hoab, have we not a lesson in this, which is, that we must ever have an All Highest Person so far ahead that we cannot attain Him? If this be true, when we have surpassed a Person whose figure and condition we can comprehend, is it not incumbent upon us to create within our own souls the thought of an All Person beyond our comprehensibility?

15. Hoab said: It seemeth so. But how canst thou teach thy soul to think of an All Person beyond man's comprehensibility?

16. Fragapatti said: For a basis to reason from, let us consider the etherean, the atmospherean and the corporeal worlds to constitute His body; and the motion therein and thereof, the manifestations of His Power and His Wisdom. Since, then, we ourselves have

these things in part, we find, also, we have another attribute embracing all the others, which is combination concentrated into one person. Shall we not, then, give to Him, who embraceth all things within Himself, combination concentrated into one person? Otherwise, He is our inferior, which cannot be. Therefore, being ourselves persons, are we not mere offshoots from the All Person? Otherwise, we could not have attained personality. Doth not a child take its personality because its mother was a person? Can man have an entity save he receive it from an entity? Could man be a person, save he sprang from a Person?

17. Hoab said: Thou art a great light, O Chief! Verily, hast thou unfolded a universe before me! Yea, there must be an All Person! O that I had seen this philosophy before!

18. Fragapatti said: Be not infatuated, O Hoab, with sudden appearances. For were I to show thee, first, what it is to believe in an All Person, Whose magnificence surpasseth the universe itself, and then that man can attain to be one with Him, even as a note in music is one within a tune, I would so far enrapture thy soul that thou wouldst do naught but listen. Let us, therefore, suspend our research awhile, that we may devise some resurrection for this hell of suffering millions.

CHAPTER XI.

1. The avalanza was so constructed that the words spoken by Fragapatti and Hoab could be heard by all who chose, of whom there were two thousand millions on board. And when Hoab expressed conviction, the same sentiment seized upon the whole assembly; whereupon, Fragapatti raised his hand, saying: By virtue of Thy power, O Jehovih, will I illume this hell!

2. And by Fragapatti's will there was created a sudden light, so brilliant, none present, save the ethereans, could look upon him. Hoab bowed down, and hid his face, and Hoab's hosts were overcome with fear, prostrating themselves on the floors of the avalanza.

3. Fragapatti said to the swift messengers: Go at once to Mouru, greeting, and say that Fragapatti demandeth, at once, one thousand million etherean volunteers, for signal centers in Aoasu's lowest hells, bringing rods of fire and water.

4. The swift messengers departed hastily. Fragapatti then commanded that the avalanza be anchored for a day; and he and many of his hosts went out into hell, where the spirits were weeping and wailing, and cursing, or lying in drunkenness and lethargy. Many of them were naked and foul smelling; and hundreds of thousands of them, having had diseased corporeal bodies whilst on earth, had now carried with them into hell the substance of their corruptions, even the rottenness of plagues and consumptions, and of other diseases it is not even lawful to mention.

5. Fragapatti said: By Thy Power, O Jehovih, shall a wall of fire encompass these people about. They shall not escape. For were they to return to a nation of mortals, they would inoculate them unto death. Fire, O Jehovih, fire! Thou All Purifier!

6. And he cast his hands outward and upward, in majesty, and there rose up walls of fire on the face of the mountains; and the light thereof fell into the valleys of Ugh'sa, the pit of hell. To the east and west and north and south, Fragapatti turned, saying: A wall of fire! a wall of fire! And he, himself, shone as a sun, united with the Eternal All Creator, Whose voice was power to wield the elements to His will.

7. Presently, there were hemmed into one field more than five hundred million drujas, who, by the sudden transformation, were roused up to desperate wildness, with bated breath, running hither and thither, first one way and then another.

8. And yet there were other millions of them, so low and stupid and crazed, that the others ran over them as if they were but a heap of rubbish, death!

9. Then Fragapatti went to Hoab, saying: For pity's sake, come thou and help me, and persuade thy hosts also.

10. Hoab said: O friend, and brother, do not mock me! Thou hast undone me entirely. I am nothing. My hosts are nothing. For pity's sake, temper thou thine own light. It pierceth me through!

11. Fragapatti said: Shall I not send thee back quickly to Zeredho, with thy hosts? Hoab said: My wish is nothing; my will is nothing! Thine and the Great All Power's will be done. Fragapatti said: If ever thou hadst faith in thy life, I charge thee now quickly to summon it to thy soul, for Great Jehovih is with me now, and but ask and speak in faith by the Creator, and it shall be granted unto thee. Speak quickly, whilst yet the power holdeth upon me: Shall I put on a thousand-fold more light? Say thou: In Faith I will endure all, for the glory of Jehovih! Give me, or fire or torments, or whatsoever Thou wilt, O Jehovih!

12. Hoab trembled, and then strained in every part, and at last suddenly sprang up facing the light, melting in the flame of fire; and he said: I will endure all, in faith of Thee, O Jehovih! Give me, or fire or torments, or whatsoever Thou wilt. Henseforth I will do for Thee, forever!

13. Presently, his spirit took the crystal form, and the victory dawned upon his soul. A smile, denoting knowledge of All Holiness and Majesty gleamed in his countenance! The light began to retract and to reflect from his face, brilliant and sun-like. He had conquered and won! He said: Thanks, O Jehovih!

14. Fragapatti said: Quick, now, seize the goal; go forth practicing thy light for others, and it will grow, giant-like. And Hoab was strong in faith, almost mad with the delight of such wondrous change; and he rushed forth, commanding, in the name of Jehovih, raising up hundreds and thousands, even as he had been raised, crystallizing.

15. All one day and one night they labored, and all the ethereans with them; and they rescued, and divided, and sub-divided the spirits of darkness into grades and sections. And many of the spirits belonging to the hosts of Hoab were thus raised to the second resurrection, with light and power.

16. But of the hundreds of millions of spirits in the torments of hell none were as yet raised even to the first resurrection. But they were stirred up and routed out of lethargy; and the supplies for their drunkenness were cut off by the walls of fire, created by Fragapatti, which went up day and night, without ceasing.

17. And Fragapatti stationed sentinels with power near the walls of fire, commanding them to cast in the elements of ughs and brimstone, so that the suffocating smell would prevent the drujas from escaping.

18. On the second day, millions of ethereans, with rods of water and rods of fire, came from Mouru, in answer to Fragapatti's commandment. And when they had arrived before him, and had saluted in the sign of Jehovih's name, he said unto them: Behold, I have established one signal center in hell. It will require a thousand more centers before we

have broken them up and delivered them. From the rank of DAS the marshals shall select from amongst you ten thousand to remain in this center and complete the work I have laid out.

19. So the marshals selected from the ethereans of the rank of DAS ten thousand. Now the das are such as have attained to power with the rod with water, and the rod with fire, but not with the hand, like the ranks above them. They go amongst the denizens of a signal center with the two rods, casting water with one and fire with the other. And the hosts of spirits in darkness run for them, like cattle for salt; and the das thus discover and assort them; for the lowest spirits go for the rods with water, and the highest for the rods of fire. Because the lowest spirits dread the light; and because the highest desire to be rescued from the lowest.

20. On the second day, therefore, the das began work; and there were baptized with water many millions; but with fire only one million. The latter were then taken without and beyond the walls of fire, and colonized, and clothed, and fed, and guardians placed over them, preparatory to the nurseries, hospitals, schools, factories, and such other educationals as belong in the lowest heaven.

21. On the third day the das went through the same labor again, and again many millions were baptized with water, and but two millions with fire. The latter were also taken without and beyond the walls of fire, and colonized in the same manner as those of the previous day.

22. Such, then, is the labor of the das in hell, baptizing and selecting; and it continueth until all the people are taken without and beyond the walls. The last taken are, therefore, the lowest grade, and the first taken are the highest grade. But the last are usually so low in knowledge and ambition that they move not of themselves, but are bestowed in nurseries and hospitals, to be cleansed from their foulness, and to be healed of their infirmities.

CHAPTER XII.

1. Fragapatti caused the ship, the avalanza, to be moved to other black mountains, deep buried in revolting crimes and misery; wherein no one with God-like power had ventured in for hundreds of years. Again he called down Jehovih's fire, and raised walls, impenetrable, high on every side, affrighting and stirring up the self-condemned with frenzied fear. And they ran, all polluted with foul thoughts, which had clothed them about with foulness terrible, and oaths and curses and imprecations against all righteousness.

2. And Hoab, too, now a very sun, desperate to do overwhelming good things, even more a thousand times than in his self-ease of other days he refrained from dark company lest he be polluted, now rushed in headlong to the very worst and foulest. Proclaiming Jehovih and active work to stir them up; and by his quick and unmistakable zeal proving his soul's connection with the Almighty's Power.

3. After Fragapatti and Hoab rushed in, hundreds of thousands of ethereans did so also, laboring for the Father's kingdom; with flames of fire cutting loose the demons' grips of torture on the helpless, and hurling them separate. None could escape because of the walls around, now seething with the choking smell of brimstone; and must needs fall prostrate, before the crystallizing lights thrust at them, weeping and wailing.

4. All day long, and all night, Fragapatti and Hoab, now a powerful worker, the which Fragapatti had previously seen would be the case, and the etherean hosts, rested not; but waded into the hell of death. Turning them to the right or to the left, the miserable, devouring wretches, brothers and sisters of mortals and spirits, now engulfed in their own depravity, and by their desperate desire for sin, holding millions of the moderately good as officers of torture, in order to gratify their horrid love of witnessing horrors. Into groups and series they roughly selected them, as a starting point for the das that were to come after, and more carefully divide them.

5. Then Fragapatti called the das and put them to work with their rods of water and rods of fire, making stations beyond the walls of fire, where the naked, trembling, rescued sufferers and drujas were housed and fed, restrained by guardians of ample strength and foresight. For of such nature is the low man and low woman, that love of evil in time delighteth to feed itself in evil more than in good, and will even turn against benefactors, and spurn good offerings.

6. Of whom Jehovih saith: As by fire the dross of metal is burned and cast out, leaving that which is pure; so created I the righteous with light from My countenance, to burn out the dross which the wicked nestle into their bosoms. Wherein, man shall perceive that it is the dross that healeth Me and My chosen. Go, then, deliver the wicked in hell, and make them clean with water and with fire, and ye shall find a star in every soul. And as many of these as ye deliver, so is your glory in My etherean kingdoms.

7. For each deliverer is as a sun around which these stars congregate, and they magnify one another forever. And when these stars have grown, they also go and do in like manner; for it is of such that My exalted ones are in the highest heavens, whom ye call Gods and Lords, and justly so, because of their supremacy.

8. Thus went Fragapatti through the lowest regions of Aoasu; for forty days and nights labored he and his hosts, and he broke up the regions of hell, and cast out the souls of the tortured, thousands of millions of them. Neither was there left any place standing in all the lower heavens where evil held dominion.

9. And there were established in those regions around about, two hundred thousand colonies, comprising the evil ones who had been rescued. But the very lowest, who knew not anything, who were: some, infants who died at the time of birth; some, infants of drunkards, who came to the lower heavens with the intoxicating liquors or smoke of their mother's debauchery; some, very young abortions, slain by their mothers and fathers; some, chaotic, killed in wars, who were mad and crazed, howling and screaming and fighting, of whom there were nine hundred millions: these Fragapatti had brought away from all the others, putting guardians over them for the present.

10. Then he called together the crew of the avalanza, and all the hosts of Hoab, and Hoab himself; and when they were duly in order, Fragapatti extemporized a throne and sat on it; and thus he spake, saying:

11. Without Thee, O Jehovih, man is nothing. Nor can he stand upright, nor hold up his head, nor his soul after he is up, save but by Thee. When he cutteth himself off from Thee, he falleth like a limb of a tree that is severed.

12. He goeth about boasting: There is no All Person. But his words are as a severing knife, and he knoweth it not. He setteth up his judgment, saying: Thou wert good for fools, O Jehovih; but as for me, Thou art a foolish encumbrance!

13. Yea, he saith: Who hath seen Jehovih! And he laugheth because of his cleverness. He saith: What stood Jehovih upon when He created the worlds? How long slept He before He created? He saith: What a foolish Creator! He created sin and death! He saith: Who knoweth the size of His head; the length of His arm; the place He liveth; or who hath heard His voice!

14. He saith: Verily, there is no All Person; no All Highest; no Light. This is the second downward stage, and in the third, he saith: A curse upon Faith! A curse upon all things! A curse upon myself! And then cometh hell and her horrors to swallow him up.

15. But thou art near, O Jehovih! Thy hosts traverse the universe. In Thy name they come, and Thy power and glory are with them. In their majesty they encounter all evil; they cast out hell and its prisoners.

16. Then Fragapatti turned to Hoab, saying: Speak, O Hoab. Nine hundred millions of dead, that are still sleeping in death, lie at our feet. These regions are unsuited for their treatment; whither shall we take them? Or shall we, because they are so dead, leave them to shift for themselves.

17. Then rose Hoab, saluting, and tears were in his eyes. He said: Mighty art Thou, O Jehovih! Lo, I was on the verge of an everlasting fall! I was on a steep precipice, but saw not. With blinded eyes I walked about. I lost Thy countenance. My family became strangers to Thee, and we were following close after, to become strangers to one another!

18. Yea, I was ungrateful before Thee. I forgot that Thou createdst me. I forgot that all the joys I had ever had were bestowed by Thee; and that by Thee I had been made capable to appreciate mine own enjoyment. And then I raised up my voice against Thee, and turned Thee out of the world.

19. Yea, I chose a corner and appropriated it for my own ease and glory. I said: To keep other Gods and angels away from my lands, this is all I desire. But Thou wert mindful of me, O Jehovih! Thy voice sounded in the heavens above, and Thy Son came down in Thy glory. He beheld my vanity and my weakness, but he rebuked me not. Yea, I told him I loved not to go to those beneath me and raise them up. I said: Let them shift for themselves!

20. Now am I rebuked in mine own words! Now have I cast myself out of hell. Behold, I said: Zeredho shall be a place for me and my people forever! None shall come hither to make us afraid or to annoy us. And Thy Son said to me: I can teach thee and thy people that ye shall never more fear to be annoyed by the low or by the evil-minded; nor shall ye fear for Gods or angels to come and inhabit Zeredho!

21. Thus spake Thy Son, O Jehovih! And he hath given us the secret. We no longer fear that others will encroach upon Zeredho. Behold, Zeredho is Thy place, O Jehovih. These unfortunates, these drujas, are Thy children. They shall go to Zeredho. I fear not pollution now, nor do my hosts. We will wade into this filth, like scavengers into a filthy street, and we will make these children like shining stars in Thy firmament!

22. Yea, O Jehovih, nothing more can make us afraid! We have nothing; we have nothing to lose. We are Thy servants, now and forever!

23. Then spake Fragapatti, saying: Behold the size of my avalanza, O Hoab! If thou wilt but take the measure, thou shalt find it is just the size and build to take thee and thy hosts and these drujas. Think not that this matter so happened, for I sent beforehand, and had all these unfortunates enumerated, and thy people enumerated also.

24. When Hoab perceived this great wisdom in Fragapatti, and comprehended the care that had been used to accomplish so much, he made no reply at first, but, looking at him, burst into tears. Presently, he said: By Thy Power and Wisdom, O Jehovih, will I, also, lift my fellows up out of darkness and misery!

CHAPTER XIII.

1. Then Fragapatti sent swift messengers to Mouru, relating all that had been accomplished, giving, also, the names of the generals and captains over the newly established colonies redeemed from Utza, in the Aoasuan mountains, so they might be registered in the libraries of Haraiti. And Fragapatti established a line of messengers betwixt the colonies, and also from the colonies to Mouru, and selected and appointed the messengers, to hold office during dawn.

2. And when the affairs of this region of the lower heavens were completed and in working order, Fragapatti was ready to ascend with the mad and dumb drujas rescued from hell. Accordingly, the proper persons fell to work and carried them into the avalanza; being obliged to blindfold them because of the light. Nor did the drujas cease wailing and crying with fear and pain and craziness. But because of the multitude of infants, Fragapatti had previously provided five hundred thousand women of fetal, that the infants might be redeemed to everlasting life.

3. Sixty thousand physicians had Fragapatti aboard, and they fell to work right and left, resuscitating and restoring to consciousness the unfortunates. And of the hosts of Hoab, not one was there but went to work, willingly, as nurse and helper.

4. Now struck up the es'senaurs with music, thirty thousand of them, but soft and gentle as a breath of wind, carrying the tones around about the ship, even as an endless echo, calling and answering from all possible directions, a continuous and enrapturing change, as if near, and as if far off. So that the uninformed knew not whence the music came, nor how it was produced.

5. All these things were set to working order just as the great avalanza was ready to start. Then Fragapatti went into the ship, being almost the last one to enter. Already was the light gathering bright and dense about him, his head almost hid in the brilliancy of the halo. And then he called out:

6. Arise! Arise! In Jehovih's name, upward rise! And as he spake, behold, the avalanza moved with his will, for all the hosts joined in the same expression, and presently started upward the great fire-ship; leaving the burning walls and signal centers flickering below, so that even hell overthrown shone with great grandeur.

7. Fragapatti spake to Hoab, saying: When I took thee and thy hosts from Zeredho, I promised to take thee to Mouru, the capital city of Haraiti, my kingdom. Now thou desirest me to go with these drujas to Zeredho. I will ask thee now, thinkest thou that thou couldst plan their salvation, and restore them to light?

8. To which Hoab replied, saying: I perceive that of myself I can do nothing but go down hill; or, at best, keep on a level road. As I now comprehend All Light, there is no one thing in all the universe that can rise of itself; but, by the external pressure of other things, all tend downward, even man. To attain to be one with Jehovih is the beginning of the resurrection of the individual; but he who hath attained power to resurrect others is strong

indeed. There are many who spasmodically resurrect others, but, alas, how few can keep them resurrected! Not only must he have the Light of Jehovih within himself, but power to make others obtain the Light for themselves. Alas, I am weak!

9. Fragapatti said: Understand thyself, O Hoab. Be not deceived, nor short in faith to accomplish; for herein lieth the key to all Wisdom and Power. Suffer not thyself to go to the other extreme, saying, man of himself can accomplish nothing. To teach a child this, is to hew off its legs and arms. To teach it that it can accomplish, is to make it giant-like and effective.

10. Hoab said: I perceive thy wisdom, O Chief. How, then, shall we find a line by which we can train this economy? If we inspire them not with faith to accomplish, they will accomplish nothing; if we teach them they are dependent on Jehovih for all things, and that Jehovih doeth all things, and that no man can change his own destiny, that he is moved as a machine, then we will make nonentities of our people. On the other hand, if we inspire them that they can accomplish, it will grow upon them, and, finally, they will believe that they do all, and Jehovih nothing. This was the mire my other kingdom ran into.

11. Then spake Fragapatti, saying: Thou perceivest that reason cannot solve the matter. Let us, then, suspend the subject, and I will take thee to Mouru and her kingdoms, and we may obtain facts more pertinent than opinion or reason.

CHAPTER XIV.

1. Upward rose the avalanza with its contrasting assemblage of the souls of Light, and with the souls of darkness, the drujas, the holy es'enaurs chanting anthems of praise and thanksgiving, whilst the drujas were engaged in _____ or cursing everything in heaven or earth, or in weeping and moaning, or in stupor, dull as if dead.

2. Fragapatti had previously sent swift messengers to Athrava and the Holy Council of Mouru, where had descended the Light of Jehovih, Whose voice came upon them, saying:

3. Lo, my hosts come in the avalanza; prepare ye to inhabit them, thirty millions. Choose ye from My ethereans and My atmpublic who shall receive the hosts of the avalanza, the nine hundred millions in darkness. Go ye, therefore, to the borders of the sea, Che-wan, near the cross-roads, Tse-loo, where I have created the plains of Hoo'e'tse-gam, ample for their resurrection. And ye shall provide them houses and hospitals and nurseries, suitable for them to dwell in, being ready, when the avalanza cometh, to deliver them.

4. Athrava and the Holy Council had responded to this, and the swift messengers in turn had informed Fragapatti of the place prepared. Accordingly, the avalanza was landed in Hoo'e'tse-gam, where the thirty millions were in waiting to receive them, disciplined by Ardi'atta, Goddess of Zhei, in etherea, first of the seven le'tas in Gom. And they had ten thousand trumpeters, besides other players, four thousand and two hundred.

5. Ardi'atta had provided the pastures in green and in red and brown, but the green she had laid near Che-wan, where the avalanza would land; hence, it was called, Hoo'e'tse-gam, signifying, green for the newborn. Consequently, the drujas were delivered from the avalanza on an open green plain, neither dark nor light, suited to the diseased in mind.

6. Fragapatti knew Ardi'atta, for her former kingdom in etherea lay in one of his own

provinces, and it was easy for him to commune with her at a distance, and without messengers. So, even before the avalanza landed, he said unto her:

7. I will cast the drujas on the green fields, and as fast as thou and thy hosts can resuscitate them to consciousness, they shall be selected and carried into the houses and nurseries thou hast provided for them.

8. Thus was the avalanza discharged of the drujas, for the present in Haraiti, to receive treatment prior to being carried to Zeredho. And Ardi'atta and her hosts took charge of them, although more than four millions of Hoab's hosts, also remained with them, as volunteers, to assist in the redemption.

9. Then Fragapatti directed the ship to be steered for Mouru, whither it arrived in due season; and there were in waiting to receive him more than one thousand million souls, and they had provided musicians, one million players and singers, so that far and near it was like a sea of music.

10. When Hoab looked upon the beauty and magnificence of the scene, and especially the discipline, his soul was filled with thanks to the Great Spirit, so that he could scarce speak. And when he mastered himself a little, he said: O Chief, Fragapatti! How could one so exalted as thou art come to me in Zeredho! Every hour am I rebuked by myself because of my former vanity.

11. Fragapatti said: To learn not to speak of one's self, nor to think of one's self, whether praised or rebuked, is this not the right road to Jehovih? Hoab said: It is true. Therefore, the opposite, is going on the wrong road.

CHAPTER XV.

1. When the avalanza was made fast, and the hosts come forth, many of the Zeredho'ans, fearing the brilliancy of the lights of Mouru, were permitted to go and dwell a little way off; but the others, led by Fragapatti and Hoab, entered the capital city, and came before the throne of Jehovih, greeted by Athrava and the Holy Council.

2. Athrava said: In the name of Jehovih, O Chief, greeting: And to thee, O Hoab. Come ye, and honor the throne of Mouru.

3. Fragapatti said: Greeting to thee, Athrava; and to ye, most Holy Council, in the name of our Father! Hoab said: Greeting, in Jehovih's name!

4. And then Fragapatti and Hoab went forward and ascended the throne, and sat on the left hand of Athrava. At once the Light from the etherean worlds began to fall upon the throne, and even upon the whole Council, and the light was golden yellow,   the most sacred color, and brilliant. Hoab had never seen such before, and was overwhelmed with fear and delight; but many of his hosts were obliged to hide their faces.

5. Presently the light condensed over the throne, even whilst three thousand millions looked on, till like a very sun it stood above Fragapatti's head. And then came the Voice of the Almighty, Jehovih, out of the midst of the light. Jehovih said:

6. Hear the words of thy Creator, O man! I, Who created the corporeal and the es'ean worlds! Behold the works of My hands! Who can find a place where I have not created!

7. Think not that I cannot also create a voice and words. For is this not easier than to create a man who shall create words. Behold My corporeal suns amidst My corporeal star-worlds! Behold My etherean suns amidst My es'sean worlds.

8. I made corporeal darkness, and I made corporeal light. I made spiritual darkness, and I made spiritual light. But I am the Light of light. I am the Word of words.

9. As the wisdom of man inventeth words, so doth the light of My Light come in words to them that can bear My Light.

10. Behold My wisdom, O man, in creating souls out of the substance of corporeal darkness! Thus can their souls hear Me and not be afraid. But to them who become pure souls, I come openly. Their throne becometh My throne! Their voice becometh My voice. Their hosts look upon My throne, and My light shineth before My people.

11. Hear, then, thy Creator, O Zeredho. Thy people called to me in their darkness, but I came not. Thy hand was upon them. Thou hadst said unto them: Behold my wide countries; my mountains and valleys; my bright rivers and refreshing winds. Come ye; they are yours to keep forever!

12. And because thy hand was upon them, they were beset with darkness; they could not find their way out; neither beheld they more the glory of My kingdoms. Yea, thou wert as a wanton going after My chosen, and thy voice luredest them away from Me!

13. But I spoke in Nirvana, high above, in My thrones of light. And My Sons and Daughters heard My voice. I said unto them: Lo, the red star and her heavens are fallen in darkness! Go ye to them and deliver them into a new resurrection.

14. Had I not spoken in the ancient days, saying: Inasmuch as ye raise up them that are beneath you, so will I send them who are above down to you, to raise you up also.

15. But they forgot My words; neither strove they more to raise up them that were in the hells below. And I said unto My Nirvanians: Go ye to Zeredho, for she hath enticed My holy ones away from Me. And ye shall give them a parable of compensation openly, and they shall come before My Light and hear My voice. For ye shall take them to hell and cause them to deliver the drujas, through the light of My countenance; and thereafter shall ye bring them to Mouru, that I may speak with them face to face.

16. Hear the commandments of your Creator, O ye Sons and Daughters of Zeredho, for that which I give unto ye shall be inviolate. Which is, that ye shall have dominion over the earth and her heavens for two hundred years, commencing at the close of this dawn of dan.

17. And thou, O Hoab, shall be God over all the rest, and thou shalt be anointed with power to raise up successors with power and wisdom. Be wise, O My children, and profit ye in the wisdom of My etherean hosts whilst yet the dawn of dan remaineth.

18. The Voice ceased. Then spake Athrava, saying: In Thy name, O Jehovih, do I suspend myself from Thy throne till it be the will of Fragapatti and Thy will also. And he rose up and stood aside. Then Fragapatti went and sat in the midst of the throne.

19. Fragapatti said: I proclaim three days' recreation to the Holy Council, and to the city of Mouru. Behold, my people shall mingle together as brothers and sisters, rejoicing in the Light of the Father. Be ye joyful, singing and dancing. The ascent to Jehovih's kingdoms may be likened unto a ladder with steps, and not an even plain, and ye shall call this the first step in the resurrection of the earth's heavens in this dawn.

20. The hosts then mingled together, greeting and rejoicing, for the Zeredho'ans had long desired to see the ethereans now dwelling in Mouru; and the ethereans were equally desirous of seeing the atmosphereans. Consequently, there was great rejoicing and merriment.

CHAPTER XVI.

1. When the time of recreation was ended, Fragapatti ascended the throne of Jehovih, and signaled to the marshals to proclaim order and labor; and, at once, the vast multitude took their places; and, in the same instant, the es'enaurs discoursed music, with anthems, the which, when finished, was the signal for business, heavenly. Fragapatti said:

2. Again am I about to depart, and again to leave the God of Mouru, Athrava, with you. And Hoab, and such of his hosts as I may choose, shall go with me. For, according to the rank and glory of Gods, I must now deliver Hapacha and his kingdom of Ipseogee, raised up from Guatama.

3. Thereupon, Fragapatti descended to the foot of the throne and sat down; and Athrava, God of dawn of Mouru, came down and took him by the hand, in ancient manner, and said: Behold, thou hast honored my throne, and the time of thy departure is upon thee. Arise, then, O God, and go thy way.

4. And Fragapatti rose up and stood aside, and signaled for Hoab to go and be raised in the same manner; the which he did, becoming wise in the behavior of Gods toward one another.

5. The marshals had filed fifty thousand attendants, besides ten thousand es'enaurs, and, at a signal from Fragapatti, marched forth out of the capital, followed by the hosts of Hoab and one hundred thousand ethereans.

6. And when they were once beyond the lights of Mouru, behold, some of the hosts of Hoab rejoiced, because they were better pleased to be where there was less light. Yet there were seven hundred millions of them who rejoiced not, but rather loved the light more.

7. Then Fragapatti said: It is well that not all are of one mind. The seven hundred millions who love the light more, shall be my traveling companions to Ipseogee. Because they are strong in light, I have work for them. But the others shall be taken back to Zeredho, whither I will also come in due time.

8. And after they are settled in Zeredho, behold, I will send a God to them, and they shall found a new kingdom, in Jehovih's name. Let all hands, therefore, enter the avalanza, following me.

9. At once the hosts entered the ship, and Fragapatti gave the word to be off, and they sped forth direct for Zeredho, led by swift messengers who well knew the nearest route and the lightest places. And the route taken was through the sea of Foo'witchah and the Oram of Haiti.

10. Hardly had they gotten under way, when the light of the upper heavens began to descend on Hoab, whose excitement, from the wondrous scenes, made him propitious to the change; and, feeling the buoyancy of the light, he thus held forth, saying:

11. How could I forget Thee, O Jehovih? Or Thy purposes observe, and deny Thy designs? How saw I not that at my quickening in my mother's womb, I was the farthest from Thee? And yet, even then, Thy breath was upon me!

12. And when Thou hadst fashioned me and badest me walk upright, Thou didst send Thy angels to me, saying: Behold, Thy Creator liveth. Life of His Life thou art; flesh of His Flesh created he thee. And He gave thee thyself in proof of Himself.

13. In the earth was I conceived; housed up in darkness; of Thyself built up; nor was I of

myself anything under the sun.

14. And Thou createdst the honey-bee, and bade him speak to me for mine own benefit. He said: Behold me, O man! I am a worker. In a community I live with my brothers and sisters. I shut my eyes to things sour and bitter, and I store my house with sweet provender only. Soul of man, hear me! I am the voice of thy Creator. Behold the harmony of mine house, and the provision I make for my newborn!

15. And Thou createdst the ant, and bade him speak to me for mine own benefit. He said: Behold me, O man! I am a worker. In a community I live with my brothers and sisters. Soul of man, hear me. I am the voice of thy Creator. Behold the industry of mine house, and the burdens we bear jointly into our stores.

16. And Thou createdst the spider, and bade him speak to me. He said: Behold me, O man! I am one with thy Creator. By the spirit of things I move; by the geometrical figures of the unseen worlds I build mine house. Think not that I reason or take lessons from other spiders; I take no lessons; I move by the spirit within me, and it moveth in concert with the spirit of things without. Hear me, spirit of man! There are two ways to knowledge before thee; one is by the soul of things, and one by reason.

17. And Thou heldest up before mine eyes continually that the unseen ruledest over the seen. Then I became vain before Thee, O Jehovih! I said: When I am dead, and born a spirit, then will I see the unseen, and cannot err more.

18. But lo, my folly in Thy sight! When I was risen in spirit, I saw the spirit of things; but, alas, the soul laid still beyond. And to me the soul was now the unseen cause, and ruler over the spirit.

19. Again Thy holy ones came from the etherean worlds, speaking to me, saying: And yet beyond the soul cometh Nirvana.

20. Now have I beholden Thy crystal spheres, and Thy matchless glories. Yea, I look into this sea of Foo'witchah, whither I had often gazed before, seeing nothing then; but now, beholding ships laden with Gods and Goddesses from Thy Nirvanian fields, in higher works and worlds moving.

21. And Thy Fire stirreth me to the soul, to expand to the mastery of these atmospherean heavens. O that I could vent the hallowed glory Thou hast bestowed upon me! O that I could thank Thee for the happiness I have because Thou createdst me!

22. O that I could open up the souls of men to behold Thy wondrous works, and the majesty of becoming one with Thee, Thou Almighty, Jehovih! O that they would hear me and believe! O that they would not turn away from Light! O that they could learn to glorify Thee every day, for the little Light and little joy they receive! How like Gods and Goddesses would they become in Thy kingdoms.

23. But they harbor discontent; they discourse on the little they have received from Thee. Like the canker-worm, that groweth to devour, they feed their sorrows by recounting them over and over. For pain they cry out; and for disappointment they weep. Yea, they feed their own darkness with darkness, and in the end forget Thee, Thou All Light!

24. Hoab ceased, but gazed at the coursing ships in the atmospherean heavens; whereupon Fragapatti said:

25. Behold Thy wisdom, O Jehovih! Whom Thou wouldst make strong, Thou hast made to feel adversity's sting. For the emergencies that lie ahead, Thou plannest Thy Gods to run near the cliffs whereon millions perish.

26. Who can attain to know Thy wisdom, O Jehovih! Who can comprehend the millions of millions of Thy Sons and Daughters! And yet Thou knowest every one, and carriest them by a breath, so gently they feel Thee not, nor know Thee. To a very hair's breadth Thou takest them; and in the time of desperation, Thy hand cometh to the rescue of the righteous.

27. Man saith: Now will I fortify myself with riches and houses, and all manner of possessions; adversity shall not come upon me; I have more faith in my possessions than in Jehovih. Mine is a kingdom I can see; but Jehovih is afar off.

28. But Thou art suffering him, in his vanity, to go away from Thee for a season. Sooner or later Thou bringest him in with a short turn; either on earth or in heaven. And he goeth down as an example to hundreds and to thousands that envied him.

29. Thou hast set up the poor man in faith; he toileth day and night; he is weary and sore; he crieth out with hunger; his rags are a shame to him; but he remembereth Thee, O Jehovih! In Thy praise he singeth a song in his soul every day. To do good unto others is his great delight.

30. And Thy hand reacheth down to him in time after; his soul is like a giant. Thou hast planned him for a very God in heaven!

31. The spark of faith that was in him he nurtured, and it became as a mighty tree that fell not down before the blast. The good he received he exalted, and it fructified and grew as a harvest in rich soil; and he stood mighty in all places.

32. In Thy praise are his songs, and they endure forever; his psalms are the voice of Thy loves; and the multitude of Thy people remember him, whilst all else are cut down and destroyed. Thy work hath a sure foundation; Thy Wisdom standeth before man's wisdom; not one hath found a failure in Thy word, as it speaketh to his own soul.

33. Thy labor is from the subtle and unseen; Thy footstool the cause of causes. But the vain man looketh to Thy object; he turneth Thy ways upside down; he maketh the cart to push the horse. And Thou sufferest him to drink to the fill of his own vanity; and when he runneth himself into torments, Thou findest a way to reach him and bring him home to Thee.

34. Great is his glory when he findeth Thee; his voice becometh the love of Thy loves forever! For Thou hadst shaped him as an example, and given him scope to run his extreme, for his own glory. Yea, Thou hadst planned him for one of Thy great workers, that would not go down afterward.

CHAPTER XVII.

1. On the way to Zeredho, Fragapatti and his hosts in the avalanza were joined by a ship of a thousand million explorers from the north regions, a thousand times farther than the north star, of the seventh magnitude of light, even three higher than Fragapatti. Ctu, the Chief in command of the expedition, greeted in the sign, JEHOVIH'S NAME, the which Fragapatti answered; and by certain signals the ships approached and made fast, the es'enaurs of the twain singing and playing the same anthem, five millions of voices, and half as many trumpeters.

2. Then Ctu came near to Fragapatti, saluting, and the hosts stood in line, so they might hear what was said. So, after due ceremonies, and acquainting each other who they were,

whence they came, and such like, then spake Ctu, saying: I see thou hast thy ship ballasted with a north magnet?

3. Fragapatti said: This is but a five years' dawn, and I teach my hosts how to ballast that they may the better read the maps and roadways and stars and suns. Of these, my hosts, five hundred millions have become capable of being delivered into etherea, save in cosmogony. I am providing them, that when they shall have ascended, they may not be lost in the etherean worlds, or be dependent on others.

4. Ctu said: What is the length of this serpent? Fragapatti said: Seven and one-eighth Hoitumu. And he asked Ctu what distance he had come from his home; and Ctu said: One million four hundred and twelve thousand eight hundred and thirty and two Hoitumu!

5. What time hath thy journey yet before thee? Ctu said: Five hundred thousand years! Then Fragapatti inquired how many star-worlds Ctu had so far passed on his journey, and Ctu said: Twenty thousand star-worlds we have passed, some smaller than this red star, and some ten thousand times larger. Some of them yet liquid balls of fire, some newly crusted over, some with atmosphere and water and earth and minerals not yet separated, but boiling, seething, whirling; some firm and just entering the age of se'mu; and some old and worn out. And one we passed which had become barren as to living creatures; and the God, through whose pastures it passed, dissolved and dissipated it before us, having invited thousands of millions of guests to witness the scene.

6. Of atmospherean worlds we have passed more than ninety thousand; some of them larger than the vortex of this red star, and capable of giving homes to a million times a million of inhabitants; and yet, on many of them, there were no people.

7. Thus they discoursed on the size and wonder of Jehovih's kingdoms; but their numbers and descriptions only the Gods themselves could comprehend, they were so vast; and when they had about concluded, Ctu remarked:

8. The mortal desireth to become a spirit; then his ambition is to become an etherean; next, an Orian; next, a Nirvanian; next, an Oe'tan, and then to travel in the surveys of magnitudes. But those ahead still call to us to hasten, because the glories ahead are still more surpassing in magnificence! Who, then, can approach the Unapproachable, All Highest! He Who fashioned the plan of all creations! Who is there that is not swallowed up with devotion and awe of Him Who is Ever Present, that extendeth beyond all limit, our Father, Jehovih!

CHAPTER XVIII.

1. When they drew near Zeredho, Ctu, with his ship and hosts, withdrew, duly saluting, and they sped on their journey. But Fragapatti halted on the borders of Zeredho and landed seven hundred millions of his hosts, the others remaining aboard.

2. Again the avalanza put forth. Fragapatti said: Now will I visit Yaton'te, Lord God of North Guatama, and see what he hath accomplished, and perchance he will accompany us to Ipseogee, to see Hapacha, my well-loved God of the West Wind.

3. Now, when they came to the sea of Ctevahwitich, they rose the avalanza fifty thousand miles, for the benefit of Hoab and his hosts, for here lieth the roadway of Tems, whither pass countless numbers of fleets filled with students in the dismembered warks belonging

to the earth.

4. Here the students learn the process of condensation, and the process of dissolution of meteoric stones and small planets, such as a mortal could walk around one of them in a day. On the outer extreme of this sea, the nebulae is in constant waves, where the vortices play, condensing and bursting, like whirlwinds on the earth or corporeal ocean.

5. Here Fragapatti explained, saying: In this thou shalt behold the wisdom of Jehovih, and the uniformity of His works. Here lieth the first belt away from the earth capable of having nebulae condensed into meteoric stones. All nebulae lying nearer than this to the earth's surface is either attracted to the earth or repulsed from it. Compute, therefore, the distance of this belt from the earth, together with its density, and thou shalt find that it is the same distance that the wark belts are, with the stars in the firmament of the size of the earth, and of its density and velocity. The first wark belt of the sun is, therefore, the place of its nearest planet; the second wark belt is the place of its next nearest planet, and so on; and these wark belts are all graded in distance accordingly as I have spoken.

6. Jehovih hath said: Two ways have I created for My mathematicians to prove My works; one is, to measure that which is near at hand, in order to determine that which is far off; the other is, to observe that which is far off, in order to determine that which is near. For, since man could not measure the wark belts of this world, I provided him with means to determine the wark belts of the sun, so that he might the better comprehend his own world.

7. That man might find still further evidence of the earth's wark belts, I created the nearest one with different densities, so that not every year on earth would be alike as to heat and cold. And in certain cycles of dan I condense the first wark belts so that the sun seemeth to mortals as if in eclipse. For it is upon this belt that My cycles of dan'ha give either light or darkness to mortals spiritually.

8. Let man compute My times for his own profit; I created the first wark to gain in rotation faster than the earth, one year for every eleven. So that when the wark hath made twelve of its own years, the earth shall have completed eleven years.

9. Fragapatti caused the avalanza to be driven in amidst a forest of whirlwinds, to illustrate and to explain, so that the hosts might observe. He said: Thou shalt perceive now, that such stones as are condensed beneath the apex fall to the earth, whilst those ascending frequently rise toward the lighter plateau and explode, to be attracted back within the wark belt. This belt compareth unto the cloud belt near the earth. Thither the wind currents make rain-drops and snow-flakes; here the currents make the first nebulous formations that come under the name corpor.

10. Whilst Fragapatti was thus discoursing, the avalanza rocked to and fro, and many of the people perceived now, more than ever, the knowledge and power required by angels and Gods, to contend successfully with the elements. But the beauty and grandeur of these fountains, these fire-spouts, and whirlwinds on fire, together with the roar and whistling of the flying stones, so enraptured Hoab and his hosts, they could do naught but look and wonder at the glory thereof.

11. For seven days and seven nights did Fragapatti and his hosts travel in this wark belt, observing and studying these miniature worlds, creating and dissipating; and on the eighth day the avalanza was lowered beneath the currents, and they sailed direct for the kingdom of Yaton'te, Lord God of North Guatama, piloted by messengers well acquainted

with the course. But not being in a much frequented roadway, they encountered few ships or processions of other Gods.

12. Yaton'te had been apprised of Fragapatti's coming, and had accordingly notified his kingdom, and summoned seventy of his Lords to his capital, which was named after himself. So Yaton'te commanded his otevan to be put in order and lighted, and having provided five hundred es'enaurs in addition to his crew, together with his Lords and ten thousand attendants, went forth to the borders of Hagak, a thousand miles, to meet Fragapatti.

13. But, lo and behold, the otevan was only as a small boat is to a ship, when compared to the avalanza. And, accordingly, when they approached each other, Fragapatti caused the front of the avalanza to be opened, and at this place the otevan entered within the walls and was made fast. And the hosts of the otevan came out and were received with great joy by Fragapatti and his people.

CHAPTER XIX.

1. A thousand miles north of the northern line of the sun on the earth, in the middle betwixt the east and west front of North Guatama, and from the earth upward, and without intervening space, five hundred miles, had Yaton'te founded his kingdom, and hither it was that Fragapatti came to see him. Five hundred miles westward lay Ipseogee, extending north and south two thousand miles, where reigned the good Faithist, Hapacha, styled God of the West Wind.

2. After the avalanza reached Yaton'te's capital, and the hosts duly landed in the lower heaven, Yaton'te ascended his throne, and after due ceremonies of welcome and thanksgiving, and with music rendering praise to the All High, Yaton'te proclaimed recreation for three days and three nights.

3. Then spake Fragapatti to him, saying: I am glad of this, because I desire to hear the story of thy adventures, and of thy success in this kingdom, for thy record must also be my record, to be taken with us, at the end of this dawn, to heaven above. Hoab and his hosts shall also hear thy words.

4. Yaton'te replied: What I have done, I have done. Nevertheless, he who hath built great kingdoms may find little to admire in a small one.

5. Fragapatti said: I have seen old men who doted more on a grandchild than on a large family they had bred themselves. And is it not a wise provision of our Creator that He bestowed us with such means as enableth us at all times to live over again our past history in the young? Every hour we find a new way open to remind us of our follies in youth; and also a new channel in which to behold Jehovih's Wisdom.

6. Yaton'te said: If a man convert his neighbor from evil into good, two great things are accomplished, the triumph of the man and the reformation of the neighbor. If on the other hand a man fail to convert his neighbor from evil to good, two misfortunes have transpired, which are, the disappointment of one and the loss of glory to Jehovih. It is a strong man that can recount his own failures and say he glorifieth the Father because thereof.

7. Fragapatti said: How shall we measure magnitudes, O Yaton'te? Hath not a mortal, that hath delivered one druk into light, as great a glory as a God that delivereth hundreds of

thousands? Is not the one as great in magnitude as the other? According to our worthiness in righteous persistence, no matter what our limit is, is not this the greatest glory? Jehovih gave to man, to first learn to deliver himself in the All Highest. He who can do this is a great ruler. And in the next time Jehovih giveth him to rule over a small kingdom, perhaps a drunkard, or a wanton, or even over his own family, to righteousness. He that doeth this is a great ruler. Is not, then, man's persistence in righteousness the whole glory of his kingdom?

8. Yaton'te said: The Father knoweth! To try, and to try, and to try; this is the sum of the good a man doeth. And yet what man is there in heaven or on earth but can find an apology for the good work he accomplished? Doth not the poor man say: O, if I had this, what great good I would accomplish? And the rich man maketh the same speech, and the king also. And yet Jehovih hath given a kingdom to each and every one of them. But he who can say: I have done all I could, according to my strength and wisdom, rateth amongst the highest of men and Gods.

9. Hear me, then, O Fragapatti; and thou mayst best understand; suffer thyself to forget all the light of high heaven, and to be in a place of darkness, where three thousand million spirits are vagrants, scattered far and wide on the corporeal earth. Such was Aoasu in this kingdom; but the spirits congregated not together in hells, as they did in the east, for they had no association; no Gods, nor Lords. They were perpetual migrants, save such as dwelt with the druks as familiars.

10. And as to the spirits of those that died in infancy, they were taken by the spirits of their fathers and mothers, or others, and cared for until they also gained sufficient knowledge to serve them as vagrants, and there was the end.

11. And strange to say, all these spirits were without clothes or drapery of any kind, and devoid of shame; neither were they good or evil, nor had they desire for, or knowledge of, a higher heaven, being content to rove about, to sleep, and to eat. And they had a thousand languages; or, at least, a thousand different kinds of signs and utterances, which they had acquired on earth, but lost and mixed up so that neither Lords nor Gods could converse with them.

12. Thus I surveyed them and found them, before I built this capital, for which reason I came thus centrally amongst them. Know also, O Chief, that I traveled amongst them with music and with fire, and gaudy apparel, in hope to gain their aspiration; but, alas, they neither smiled nor frowned on my fine shows, but vacantly gazed at us, or even fell asleep whilst our otevan was paraded before them.

13. Then I came hither and built this capital, and founded Jehovih's throne, whereon thou now honorest me. And then I sent to them, here and there, presents of gaudy attire, in hope to inspire the multitude through the few; but, alas, those I attired soon divested themselves of their clothes, preferring nakedness. Thus ended my second failure.

14. After this, I sent a hundred thousand preachers to them, to portray the greater glory of a higher heaven. But, alas, they heeded not, or, if heeding, in a day would forget all that had been told them. And thus ended the third failure.

15. Then we held a holy council, imploring Jehovih for light and power; and His voice came upon me, saying: Go to their loves, My Son; go to mortals. Begin thou with es'yans.

16. Then I commanded my hosts to go and live for a season amongst mortals; and they brought the es'yans to Yaton'te, under guard of the asaphs. And the next of kin followed,

270

desiring to remain. And I said unto them: Behold, my place is fair, and my people are clothed. Save ye be clothed also, ye cannot dwell with us, nor shall ye more look upon your next of kin, whom I have taken for myself.

17. And for love there came many mothers and fathers, and brothers and sisters, belonging to the recent dead; and they suffered themselves to be clothed; and these were the first in my kingdom.

18. Again I called my hosts together, and I said unto them: A thousand Lords I must have. I will divide North Guatama amongst my Lords, and they shall dwell with mortals, having a sufficiency of ashars to give one to each and every mortal, man, woman and child. And whether by natural death or by war, it mattereth not, the es'yans shall be brought to my kingdom.

19. This I accomplished, providing nurseries and places of entertainment for such as were brought hither. But, alas, the tens of thousands of spirits who thus came because of their kin, and accepted clothing for sake of remaining, had little talent to talk, or even desire for anything.

20. At the next holy council the Light came to me, saying: Hear the voice of thy Creator, O My Son; because thou hast been diligent in striving for the resurrection of My children, I am come to thee. Behold, I created man naked, and with shame, as the foundation of industry. But because this people followed, in the Osirian age, the abandonment of spirit communion, whilst they were yet mortal, they lost the light of My countenance.

21. Neither canst thou inspire them to industry, save through clothing the body; but, first of all, thou shalt make them ashamed of nakedness; otherwise, there is no higher resurrection for them.

22. Then I inquired of the Creator how I should teach them shame. He said: Of themselves, to themselves, for themselves, thou canst do but little. But thou shalt inspire them through mortals.

23. Every plateau shall be a thousand miles in breadth every way, save the lowest, which shall be two thousand miles, with a rise of one degree, so that the plateaux shall extend from the earth up to thy kingdom, like a stairway, one plateau higher than another.

24. And thy Lords shall provide for the lowest, and for the second lowest plateaux, subjective entertainments, subjective teachings and subjective things in general. Neither shall there be anything real on these two plateaux, save the inhabitants and their food, and the mirrors and lenses, and machinery for producing subjectives.

25. And the lower plateau, being on the earth, shall be provided as a mirage, having everything spiritual in appearance, as they are corporeally on the earth. And it shall be provided with forests and lakes and rivers, and with all manner of animals and birds and fish, and of whatsoever is suitable food for mortals. And the lowest plateau shall be called Hochedowa, signifying, happy hunting ground.

26. And thou shalt send word to thy Lords, saying: Thus saith thy Creator: Behold, I have created a good place, and called it Hochedowa. Teach ye this to mortals, by inspiration and otherwise, saying also to them: Go tell one another, for, after death, the soul shall go thither in great delight. And ye shall say unto them: Save ye wear garments to hide your nakedness, ye shall not enter Hochedowa.

27. Yaton'te said: When the lowest plateau was made habitable, covering a large portion of North Guatama, the Voice came again, saying: Through thy Lords, My Son, thou shalt

possess all mortals, every man and woman and child, suffering not one of the drujas to come near them.

28. And, behold, I will send upon the land in many places, great droughts, because of the construction of thy plateau, and these wandering spirits shall not find sustenance, save but through thee and thy Lords. And as fast as they come, thou shalt oblige them to be clothed or draped about the loins; but thou shalt show preference to all such as wear ornaments.

29. Yaton'te said: This much have we accomplished, O Fragapatti: The foundation of my heavenly kingdom is broad and sure, but as yet I have few subjects to show thee.

30. Fragapatti said: Behold, I will take two days of rest, and then I will inspect thy places. Proclaim, therefore, recreation for two days.

CHAPTER XX.

1. When the recreation was ended, Yaton'te called his council together, and he sat on the throne, and Fragapatti and Hoab sat on his left hand on the throne, also.

2. The Voice of Jehovih came to Yaton'te, saying: Behold, O My Sons and Daughters, this heaven and this land shall not be like any other place; for hither shall rise in time after, they that shall begin the founding of My kingdom amongst mortals. For in the lands of the east, and the heavens of the east, I have given them Lords and Gods before whom they fall down and worship. But in this heaven, and this land beneath it, shall not be given any Lord, nor God, nor any person born of woman for their resurrection.

3. To this end have I created this subjective heaven and her plateaux, and they shall endure till the dawn of kosmon, and the overthrow of war and mortal kingdoms. From this throne will I come in that day, through My Chiefs, and reveal the histories of My kingdoms. And I will radiate outward, around about from this heaven, until My kingdoms encircle the whole earth, and until the earth's heavens are Mine also.

4. And whether the I'huans be mortals or spirits, ye shall not here teach them to worship any one, save the Great Spirit.

5. For a question will arise amongst mortals in the beginning of kosmon, as to whether mortals are ruled by the angels of heaven. And I will prove it before them that in this land all Gods and Lords and Saviors shall be cast out, and mortals shall become worshippers of the Great Spirit, being ruled to that end by the inspiration that shall descend from this heaven, through the spirits of the I'huan race. And they shall know that I, Jehovih, alone rule over all, and within all My works.

6. Be wise, My Sons and Daughters, for as ye now find little aspiration amongst the hosts of wandering spirits, so will the same lack of aspiration be manifested in the beginning of kosmon, amongst mortals. The Voice ceased.

7. Yaton'te called Et'seing, his assistant God, saying: Come thou and sit on the throne. I will go now for forty days with Fragapatti and show him all my works. And I will go also with him to Hapacha, God of Ipseogee, after which I will return hither.

8. Et'seing came and sat on the throne, duly saluting, having been anointed and crowned previously. Then rose up Fragapatti to speak, perceiving that the great multitude desired to hear him. He said:

9. In what they have done I am well pleased, O Jehovih. Through Thy voice I selected them, and they deserve neither praise nor censure, being Thy servants. Thou hast wisely

chosen them, for in this dawn I perceive the foundation of that which will reach mortals in the third dan'ha that cometh after. And because Thou hast chosen this place, O Father, great is the responsibility of these, Thy Lords, and Thy Lord God.

10. Because they have supplicated Thee, Thou hast guided them, and they cannot err. Because their work hath been slow, they have great honor in patience and persistence. May Thy Wisdom, Power and Love continue with them, for Thy glory, now and forever. Amen! Fragapatti ceased, but the light became brilliant above his head; and the Voice came out of the Light, saying:

11. More shall they concern themselves in a righteous foundation of My kingdom, than in a multitude of conversions and resurrections. For the standard of their Lords and Gods, and their successors, is of more value than tens of thousands of redeemed who are of little wisdom and strength. For the latter will be raised up afterward.

12. The Voice ceased, and Fragapatti came down from the throne, followed by Yaton'te and Hoab. The es'enaurs chanted, ALL HAIL, GREAT JEHOVIH'S POWER! HIS LIGHT THE IMMORTAL VOICE! And when the Gods advanced to Ctius, they halted, standing abreast, and then filed in front of the throne, saluting in the SIGN OF OHM, and were answered by Fragapatti. Lastly came the marshals of the traveling hosts; and when they had passed, the Gods followed after, thus passing out of the capital to the place of the ships of fire, followed by the inhabitants of Yaton'te.

13. Thus they entered the avalanza, with music and cheering; and thus they departed, first to survey the kingdom of Yaton'te, and then go to Ispeogee.

CHAPTER XXI.

1. After Fragapatti had examined the places of the asaphs and of the physicians, and such other places as belong in the lower heavens, he descended to Hochedowa, the land of delusion, the happy hunting ground, in order to witness the games and tournaments, which were so far maintained by a great expenditure of labor on the part of the ethereans, for teaching by subjective illustrations. Jehovih said:

2. As mortal children can be taught by objective illustration, so have I created My es worlds capable of a similar process subjectively. My rules are not man's rules; nor are My worlds illustrated as man illustrateth. Behold My rainbow, which is a subjective illustration to mortals of a bow without the substance of a bow. But man bendeth a stick, and saith: Behold, a bow! And he holdeth it in his hand; but Mine he cannot touch.

3. I gave to mortals to teach their sons and daughters many combinations by the use of objects; that they should know a circle, a square, a triangle, or learn to compute numbers by the use of objects. Inversely in the same way I created subjective means for the spirits of the dead, that they might be taught and amused with My works.

4. To corporeans I give corporeal eyes and corporeal ears, that they might attain to wisdom on the earth; but to a few I give su'is, that they may see and hear things spiritually.

5. To the spirits of mortals who die in infancy, I give spiritual eyes and spiritual ears; but without cultivation they hear not corporeal things, nor see corporeal things. But to such spirits as have fulfilled an earth life, I created them to see and hear after death the matters of both worlds.

273

6. Nevertheless, there are many spirits in heaven who have not fulfilled either a spiritual or a corporeal life, and they can see but little and hear but little; for which reason I commanded that they should be called drujas, signifying, spirits of darkness.

7. And I sent My Gods and My Lords, saying to them: Go ye to the spirits of darkness, for they neither see nor hear heaven nor earth, and are wandering about indifferent even to their own nakedness.

8. And ye shall create mirrors and lenses, and optical illusions and delusions, and provide games and entertainments for them, so that their understanding may be opened up for the glory of My kingdoms.

9. When the avalanza arrived at Hochedowa, it was lowered and made as an observatory, in order to witness what was going on, and yet so provided that it could be moved about from place to place.

10. And they witnessed the heavenly tournaments and games; the boating and fishing and hunting, and all other entertainments representative of what these angels had been engaged at in mortal life; and yet these things were but subjective, and not real.

11. But it came to pass that many drujas were restored to memory of earth-life; restored to seeing and hearing, and, in fact, to know they had entered another world; illustrating to their dull senses that it was possible for them to learn to see things, and to hear things, understandingly.

12. Nevertheless, there were within these regions hundreds of millions of angels so stupid as to be void of form and expression.

13. Jehovih had said: When a man hath fainted, thou shalt arouse him, by calling his memory to things past. And when the druj in heaven hath seen who he is, and his place also, thou shalt show him symbols of things past, and thus awake him.

14. Jehovih had said: Behold, O man, thou art the chiefest glory of My creations. Neither created I any animal that walketh on land, or flieth in the air, or swimmeth in the water, or that crawleth on its belly, with desire for spiritual life, nor with capacity to accumulate spiritually. But to thee only, O man, have I given power to aggregate the spiritual entity.

15. For My animals, I bestowed like a vessel that is full of water; no more can be put into them; and also, when the vessel is destroyed, the water runneth back to the ocean. I quickened them into life by Mine Own hand; but when I take away My hand, lo, they are gone back into dissolution. As a drop of water hath no power before the sun, but evaporateth and is seen no more, so is the spirit of all the animals I created before the light of my countenance. But to thee, O man, I gave power for everlasting life.

16. Nevertheless, as a man may take a drop of water and put it in a vial, and keep it for a long time, so have I given to My exalted angels power to take the spirit of a fish, or of an animal, suddenly dead, and reclothe it with the semblance of a body, for a season; but yet it is only a subjective existence. And, even as a man letteth a stone out of his hand, and it falleth to the ground, so, when My angels let go their hands on My spiritual animals, their spirits fall into the sea of My body, and are seen no more. Even so, also, but in less degree, created I the trees, the grass, the moss, and all vegetable things that grow on the face of the earth. And I gave to My exalted angels power to take the spirit out of a tree, or a bush, or a plant, and to carry it away and reclothe it with corporeal substance. But to My exalted Gods I gave power to do the same things, not with one plant only, but with whole forests, and with animals, and fishes, and serpents.

And when they do these things in atmospherea, they are called subjective heavens.

17. Wherefore it came to pass in the ancient days that when spirits of darkness returned to mortals, they told them that heaven was like unto the earth, with everlasting life unto all animals as well as to man. Turn not away from such spirits, O man, but learn from them that thou mayst not tarry long in My bound heavens, when thou becomest a spirit also.

18. For if thou settest thy soul to feed on animals, and to dwell with them, the Gods cannot deliver thee to My emancipated heavens, till thou hast served thy time in the lower heavens. One great light have I bestowed unto all men, that they may progress forever. Though the waters of the ocean rise up and make clouds; and the clouds fall down as rain and run to the rivers, and thence back into the ocean, a thousand times, ten thousands of times, yet that water hath not progressed. Neither have I given progress to a stone, nor to a tree, nor to an animal; but to man only have I given progress.

19. Be wise, O man, and tie not thyself to things that progress not, nor set thy soul upon them, lest they become a bondage to thee in the next world. But for the druks, I have created heavens midway betwixt light and darkness, subjective and objective, that they may be redeemed.

20. Fragapatti also visited the Washa'wow'wow, the great hunting fields; and the place of tournaments, the Se'ka'to'si, where thousands and tens of thousands of drujas were being amused, and instructed, and awakened to their condition and to their possibilities. And when Fragapatti and his hosts had seen the beauty and grandeur of this lowest of heavens, and made a record of the affairs, Yaton'te said:

21. Now have I shown thee, O Fragapatti, the foundation of a great house, even my kingdom, which is Jehovih's. I am at thy service, to go whithersoever thou mayst desire. Then spake Fragapatti, saying:

22. I desire to descend beneath, even to the earth's surface, and survey the plains, and rivers, and lakes, in the regions where the Father's kingdom will be founded. Let my mathematicians compute the time, and these things shall also be recorded in the etherean libraries, for benefit of the angels of that day.

23. The mathematicians computed the time, and then Yo'tse'putu, the chief, said: Eight thousand nine hundred years! So Fragapatti caused the avalanza to be lowered down to the earth's surface, and he coursed the land over, east and west and north and south, and when he saw it was a fair country as to land and water, he said:

24. Behold the Wisdom of Jehovih in the foundation and plans for inhabiting and subduing the earth. And yet, eight thousand nine hundred years! O what innumerable millions on the earth will go down in darkness ere that day! Here the Light will fall! Here the beginning of the death of Seffas! Yet Thy Hand, O Jehovih, is over all.

CHAPTER XXII.

1. Fragapatti sent messengers to Hapacha, God of Ipseogee, apprising him of the visit. So, Hapacha hastily called in his Lords and captains and fathers, preparing a time of recreation, and also preparing suitable reception and entertainment.

2. And Hapacha provided in this manner: First, one hundred thousand musicians, formed in eight parts of a circle, with eight intervening spaces. With each group he provided one thousand marshals, and they stood in front of the musicians, with eight intervening spaces

also. Next within, he provided places for the messengers, of whom there were three hundred thousand. Then next came the asaphs, of whom there were one million; next came the ashars, of whom there were two millions; next, came the nurses and physicians; next, the teachers in factories and schools and colleges; and of all these there were fourteen millions six hundred thousand.

3. Of the grade first above the es'yans there were twenty millions; of the second grade, which was the highest, there were thirty millions; but no es'yans were present.

4. In the midst of the circle was the throne of Hapacha, now extended so as to accommodate his Lords. To the south of his throne were the seats of the captains of the hosts. In a crescent were his counselors, of whom there were one million.

5. Hapacha having thus called them together, and having explained to but few of them the purpose, now addressed them, saying:

6. By the Wisdom and Power of Jehovih I speak before you. That which I say is not of myself, more than of the faith I have in Jehovih, of which faith ye are likewise blessed.

7. Since our youth up we have been advised by the guardian angels, their Lords and God, to be firm in faith in Jehovih above all things. For it was declared to us, in the olden times, that there was a higher heaven and a lower heaven, and that through faith in the Father we should all ultimately ascend and dwell in His Holiest Kingdoms.

8. For which reason ye have been steady workers since your mortal lives have been put away; even for this kingdom, raising up many, and causing them to rejoice in everlasting life. But as it has been promised ye beforehand that the Gods above us would surely come and deliver all who are prepared for the next resurrection, even so, to this day, cherish ye the hope for wider fields of labor, where ye may overtake your kindred and others who have become wise in Jehovih's light.

9. The time of that resurrection is near at hand for many of you. Our Father hath brought this heaven into a lighter region, that ye may be prepared for that still greater light beyond. And because of the new light that is with us, ye have beholden that many of the I'huan es'yans have deserted our nurseries and gone back to the earth, for they love the darkness of earth more than they love the light of heaven.

10. My Lords have sent messengers to me from various parts of the earth, saying to me: As much as they have deserted your places in heaven, even so much have the es'yans returned to mortals in great numbers. And it hath come to pass that great manifestations of spirit presence are now common to men and women and children on earth.

11. Many of these es'yans, falling in with drujas, have adopted their roving habits, denying that there is any higher heaven, honestly believing they will have an opportunity to re-incarnate themselves and dwell again in mortal form. Knowing no higher heaven than the earth, and, knowing no happiness save in the indulgence of lust, they appear to mortals, and marry in manifestation, falsely pretending to be the kin of the living.

12. Which sign forerunneth the approach of a new dawn of dan near at hand. Being thus doubly armed in prophecy, your God called you to witness the words and proceedings of Fragapatti, who is on his way hither, accompanied by Yaton'te, God of Yaton'te, Creator of Hochedowa.

13. For more than six hundred years have many of us labored in this field, and our harvests for Gau have been the most esteemed of all the resurrections contributed by the Lords of earth. To comport with our dignity, I have commanded the builders of otevans to

have in readiness, representing these harvests, a vessel for my Lords and their attendants, and my chief marshal, to go part way and meet our visitors, bearing the sign of the triangle, and of fruit, and the altar.

14. Hapacha then gave instructions in full; and, presently, the receiving hosts departed in the otevan, with music, rejoicing, being cheered by the hosts remaining. In the meantime, Hapacha caused the house to be put in order.

CHAPTER XXIII.

1. Fragapatti had previously visited Hapacha, but told not who he was, save that he was God of Lunitzi, in etherea; consequently, Hapacha, now knowing that Fragapatti was coming, mistrusted not that it was the same person, but expected to see one coming in great pomp and glory. For he had heard of the wonders Fragapatti had already accomplished in the eastern heavens, particularly the breaking up of the hells of Aoasu and the deliverance of the tortured inmates.

2. Thus came Fragapatti to Ipseogee in his avalanza, displaying neither lights nor curtains; coming with the receiving hosts within his vessel, anchoring near the throne of Hapacha.

3. Presently Fragapatti came down out of the ship, Yaton'te and Hoab with him, also the marshals, who were on the left, the receiving hosts being on the right. Hapacha's en'enaurs struck up, PROCLAIM JEHOVIH'S NAME, O YE LORDS AND GODS! and the hosts of the avalanza joined in singing, and with trumpets and harps and triangles, knowing the symbols of their kingdom, and great was the glory of their music.

4. When Fragapatti approached the throne, the music ceased. Hapacha said: Who cometh here? and he made the ancient sign of Jehovih's name. Fragapatti said: A Faithist in Jehovih; and he gave the countersign. Whereupon, Hapacha said: In His name, welcome brother, and welcome to thy hosts also. May His love and wisdom be manifested in me and my people during your sojourn with us.

5. Fragapatti said: Jehovih is All Wise. He fashioneth some men as suns, and out of their souls the light extendeth into the far-off spheres. Coursing these vast fields at certain times and seasons, He sendeth swift messengers from His most exalted heavens. And these messengers, passing through both light and darkness, with their great wisdom, scan the distant kingdoms where mortals and angels dwell, and quickly catch from the guardian hosts, and from the scenes around, the brightest, best stars, and carry the record to the reigning Gods above. And when these Gods descend to the regions and places of these immortal gems, they go visit them.

6. Even so, O Hapacha, standeth thy record in the higher heavens. And when the Father called me to visit the red star and her heavens, I looked over Jehovih's messengers' reports, where was set thy name, radiant with love and fire. So to thee I made haste and came, unknown, because as yet unproved in these heavens; and thy much worth, and the amity of thy hosts, won my love. I told thee thou shouldst hear from me soon, and so thou hast. Behold, Fragapatti is before thee!

7. Hapacha said: Blessed, O Jehovih! Come thou, O Fragapatti, and honor my throne, in the name of the Father! And come thou also, O Yaton'te, and thou, O Hoab! And they went up and sat on the throne, and Fragapatti sat in the midst.

8. Again the es'enaurs sang and played, and during the singing the light of the

upper kingdoms began to envelop the throne. Then spake Fragapatti, explaining:

9. Hear me, O all ye people, and be ye attentive to my words:

10. Because ye have been faithful from the first, ye are become the light of the earth, and of this heaven, and inasmuch as ye have maintained your altar and times of sacrifice, there have been maintained in the upper heavens altars and sacrifices in conjunction with you.

11. Whereby ye have been blessed in hearing the Voice in all the darkness through which the earth and her heavens have passed.

12. As the Father hath given voice betwixt mother and child, though they be distant from each other, so, in like manner, do Jehovih's kingdoms, which are in sympathy in righteousness and love.

13. As ye behold the light gathering about this throne, think not that I bring the light, nor that it is sent to me in person. There is a cord betwixt me and my etherean kingdoms, and I am one end thereof; the other end is the throne in etherea. When I sit in the midst of this throne, behold, it is also illuminated by the higher heavens.

14. Think not that my heavens are the highest of all, for such, the All Highest, can never be attained. Nevertheless, my heavens are connected as with a cord to them above me, and they to others still above, and so on forever, upward, upward! The All Highest conceived of, is called Jehovih; and no matter how long it descendeth, still the Voice is His Voice.

15. That ye may hear Jehovih's Voice, I will now set my sun above the throne.

16. Fragapatti ceased, and a light most brilliant, in the figure of the sun, settled above his head back of the throne. Many could not look upon it because of its brightness. Presently Jehovih spake out of the Light, saying:

17. Rejoice, O Hapacha, in the name of thy Creator! Sing thy songs of delight, and let thy people hold up their heads. Behold, I have watched over thee and thy hosts; in My promises have ye fulfilled the dawn of My Light!

18. Three thousand years are as one day in My sight. Yesterday I said: Sit ye here, stand ye there, for to-morrow I come again. And this was my commandment for thousands, and tens of thousands of years.

19. But others remembered Me not; in the night they went down, as a child that falleth asleep. And when I came on the morrow, behold, they had not awakened. But I roused them up, and showed them My great Light.

20. Again I said to them: Three thousand years are as one day in My sight. Sit ye here, stand ye there, and remember Me. To-morrow I come again. But lo, they went down in sleep; they remembered not Me, their Creator.

21. But thou, O Hapacha, hast maintained the watch all night long. Thou art the first of Gods who hath kept this kingdom whole from dawn to dawn. Thou art the first of Gods who hath kept My kingdom safe in the lower heavens till the morrow came.

22. Now have I come to thee to deliver thee and thy kingdom to Haraiti, whither thou shalt tarry till the close of dawn, when My Sons and Daughters shall bear thee upward to My emancipated worlds; and thy hosts shall go with thee.

23. The Voice ceased. Then spake Fragapatti, saying: For three days will I tarry here; two days shalt thou have of recreation, but on the third day thou shalt appoint thy successor, and I will then again speak before thee and thy people.

24. Hapacha then proclaimed two days of recreation, and the hosts mingled freely together, those of the avalanza coming out and rejoicing with the Ipseogee'ans, and great was the glory of those two days.

CHAPTER XXIV.

1. Hoab rejoiced not; and he alone of all the people assembled, was burdened in soul. He said: Jehovih! Thou hast rebuked me, and I am cast down. Thou hast shown me Thy Son Hapacha, one of Thy Gods in the lowest of heavens. And Hapacha, Thy Son, hath maintained his kingdom unto Thee till this dawn of light hath come.
2. Yet Thou gavest into my keeping a kingdom far higher than this, even Zeredho; and I went down, as a child that falleth asleep. My kingdom forgot Thee; my people ceased to sing songs unto Thy name. We buried ourselves in darkness.
3. And Thou hast chosen me to be the next succeeding God of earth and her heavens! How shall I fulfill Thy commandments? How shall I know the way to choose Gods and Lords under me who will be steadfast and zealous?
4. As he thus communed with Jehovih, Fragapatti said unto him: Through faith are all things accomplished; without faith, all things are uncertain. He who saith: I know Jehovih liveth and reigneth, hath said wisely. But he who saith: I go forth in Thee, O Jehovih, for I know Thou wilt accomplish, hath said much more. For his words maintain the power of the Father in him.
5. When the morning of the third day had come, Hapacha called the hosts from recreation to labor; and the es'enaurs chanted a hymn of rejoicing; and, after that, Hapacha said:
6. To Thee, O Jehovih, are all things committed, even as from Thee they came forth. Thy Voice is ever upon all men, but they hear Thee not. Thine eye is observant of all men, but they believe it not. To teach men these simple things, is to make Gods of them. To open up their understanding, to find Thee, to know Thee, and to realize Thy Ever Presence, to become one with Thee, this is the labor with Thy Gods, and Thy Lords, and Thy holy angels.
7. In Thy name have I raised up one who is to succeed me in this, Thy kingdom. From Thy Light shall Thy Orian Chief weave a crown for him. With mine own hands will I crown him unto Thee and Thy kingdom.
8. The marshals now brought forward, Penoto, of Caracas, highly learned in discipline, and he stood before the throne of God. Thereupon Fragapatti rose up, saying:
9. Without a key-note a number of instruments cannot be attuned to harmony. Without a faith in an All Highest Person, neither angels nor mortals can live in harmony.
10. Individuals may be strong, but many in concerted action comprise the Father's kingdoms.
11. Neither angels nor mortals can assimilate of themselves; but all can assimilate with the Father, every one perfecting himself differently. Such persons are then assimilated to one another.
12. Whoever serveth his own conception of the All Highest, making himself a servant thereto, is on the right road; and, in the plan of the universe, will drift into an association adapted to himself.
13. Many such, becoming a unit, are powerful over the elements surrounding them.

Disbelief in an All Highest Person is caused by weakness of spirit, resulting from disease or from pre-natal sin, or by laudation of one's own self. Such persons cannot harmonize, because each one is his own self-esteemed all highest. They are without power, without unison and without sacrifice, accomplishing little good in heaven or on earth.

14. Think not that darkness belongeth only to the earth and the lowest heavens; there are those, who rise to the second resurrection, and then fall into unbelief, and then fall to the first resurrection, and afterward become wandering spirits. And some of them even fall into hell, which is belief in evil and destruction being good; and yet others become drujas, engrossed in the affairs of mortals, and in lust, teaching re-incarnation; and they finally become fetals and vampires on mortals.

15. Whoever hath attained to the height of his own ideal, is on the precipice of hell; but he who, finding the God of his forefathers too small for himself, and so, inventeth one much higher, is a great benefactor. A fool can ridicule the ancient Person; his delight is to pull down; but a wise man furnisheth a greater Great Person. To pull down the All Person, is to pull down His people.

16. To try to make a non-appreciable Person out of Jehovih is to make one's self the opposite of a creator. To learn to create, to invent, to cast one's spirit forth with power to congregate and make, is to go on the right road.

17. To learn to pull down, to scatter, to annul, to disintegrate, to set things apart from one another, to find evil instead of good, to find folly instead of wisdom, to expose the ignorance of others instead of finding wisdom in them; even all these follow after the first inception of disbelief in the All Person.

18. And since, from disintegration of the compact betwixt the Creator and His children, the cord of communication is cut off with the exalted kingdoms in etherea, they have indeed double grounds for disbelief; nor can they comprehend how others can be believers in an All Person, much less have Faith in Him.

19. And the same rule applieth to communities and to kingdoms as to individuals, in regard to the fall consequent in unbelief in an All Person. For a community becometh One Person; a kingdom in etherea becometh One Person; a kingdom in the lower heavens becometh One Person; a kingdom on earth becometh One Person; each and every kingdom being a single figure-head of many parts, which is the perfection of each and every individual.

20. Hence, as a single individual can cut himself off from the Father, so can a community, or a kingdom, and so go down to destruction.

21. The strongest, best man in the community is he who laboreth most to perfect the unit, that is, the Person of the community; the strongest man in the kingdom is he who laboreth most to perfect the Person of the kingdom; the strongest man in heaven is he who laboreth most to perfect the All Person of heaven.

22. The weakest of men is the opposite of these; he laboreth to show there is no All Person in anything; verily, he is already falling away from the Father. Yea, he accuseth himself, for he saith: I neither see nor hear an All Person, nor believe I in one.

23. It is a wise man who, finding he is going into disbelief too much, correcteth himself. And he is not less wise, who, finding he believeth too much, and hence, investigateth not at all, correcteth himself.

24. It was said of old, first, testimony; second, belief; third, faith; and fourth, works; but I

declare unto you that, with the expanse of knowledge, testimony must be strengthened. For in the olden times, angels and men could be commanded to believe, and they believed.

25. Herein have many of the Lords and the Gods of the lower heavens erred; for they furnished not to those beneath them the necessary testimony comporting with the advanced knowledge in heaven or on earth. A God shall be swift in devising food for meditation; for angels, as well as mortals, without an advanced teacher, are as well off with none at all.

26. It was said of old that a God taught the people on one of the stars to believe Jehovih lived in a straw, and they rose in wisdom, and harmony, and unity. Then, afterward, another God came and taught them there was no Jehovih, because, forsooth, He could not live in a straw; and the people fell into disbelief and inharmony and disunion. Which, then, of these, was the better God?

27. Yet I declare unto you, they were both necessary. For without a habitation and a figure, the Great Spirit cannot be taught to either angels or mortals in the first place. The labor of the Gods is to lead the people upward, step by step, until they learn to be Gods and Goddesses themselves.

28. On this earth, mortals were taught through stone and wooden idols; and afterward by engraved images. In some of the mixed tribes it will be necessary to teach them incarnated Jehovih in mortal form, and by sympathy for his sufferings, teach them to follow his spirit up to heaven. But all these subterfuges should be set aside in the kosmon era.

29. This heaven, more than any other heaven of the earth, will be regarded by the etherean kingdoms. Beneath you, even on this part of the earth, will mortals first espouse the Father's kingdom.

30. Of all things, let your labor be first of all to sow the seed of belief in an All Person, the Great Spirit. As ye now sow, and build Jehovih's kingdom in your heaven, so, in the coming of the kosmon era, will the same teaching take root in the souls of mortals.

31. Nor shall ye, under any circumstances, permit Gods or Lords or Saviors to be established as worshipful beings, either in these heavens or on this part of the earth. For this land is dedicated by Jehovih for the overthrow of all idols, of God, and Lord, and Savior, and of everything that is worshipped, save Jehovih, the Great Spirit. Neither shall any of these idols be established with effect in these heavens or on this land. But be ye most circumspect to establish Jehovih, the Light of light, the All Person, in the souls of angels and mortals.

32. Fragapatti ceased, but signaled for Hapacha to ordain Penoto, God of Ipseogee. Hapacha rose up, saying: Penoto, Son of Jehovih! Thou hast been chosen to be God of Ipseogee for six hundred years, and even after, if Jehovih so will. Thou hast passed the examination, and standest above all others.

33. Thou hast been favored with much traveling in heaven; and, for thy benefit, many swift messengers from the emancipated worlds, have explained to thee the dominions of the Great Chiefs.

34. He, through whose fields this world is now traveling, hath stood up before thee. He hath spoken to thee and thy people. Heed thou his words, and thou shalt be one with his kingdoms in wisdom and power.

35. By proxy I have visited the etherean worlds; thou hast not. By being one with this Chief, thou wilt inure to All Light, and soon thou shalt visit his places by proxy also.

36. And at the end of six hundred years, thou and thy harvest will be called for by the etherean hosts. Be thou ready for them! And erst thou depart, thou shalt raise up one sufficient to take thy place, and thou shalt bestow him.

37. Penoto said: Thy will and Jehovih's be done! That which is given me to do, will I do will all my wisdom and strength, so help me, O Jehovih!

38. Hapacha said: By virtue of Thy Wisdom, Power and Love, O Jehovih, vested in me, do I this, Thy Son, ordain God of Ipseogee for the period of six hundred years. Be Thou with him, O Jehovih, and may he and his works glorify Thee forever! Amen!

39. Penoto said: Which I accept and covenant with Thee, O Jehovih, for Thy glory forever. Amen!

40. The es'enaurs now sang, Thou Light and Person, approved and sung on high, Jehovih! Our God Hapacha; Jehovih Thou hast called him! Welcome Penoto! Thou, alone, Jehovih remainest forever! Glory, glory be to Thee, O Thou Creator!

41. The light gathered brilliantly over Fragapatti's head, and when the music ceased, the Voice of Jehovih spake out of the Light, saying:

42. In the first days I blew My breath upon the lands of the earth, and man became a living soul. Then, in the second time, I moved My hand upon the earth, and man went forth in power.

43. Thus near hath My Voice approached the earth. Be ye steadfast in My commandments. The time shall surely come, and in the third season, when My Voice shall be heard by mortals.

44. The Voice ceased, and then Fragapatti took the light in his hands, as one would take fine flax, and he turned it about thrice, and, lo, a crown was woven, most brilliant, but of a reddish hue. He said:

45. Crown of Thy Crown, O Jehovih, have I woven for Thy Son, God of Ipseogee. And he handed it to Hapacha, who said: And in Thy name, O Father, I crown him, second God of Ipseogee, six hundred years. Be Thou with him, O Father! Amen!

CHAPTER XXV.

1. It being now the end of the fourth day, Fragapatti commanded the hosts to embark in the avalanza; and the marshals conducted them in, taking, first, the sons and daughters of Ipseogee, being sixty millions; next the Zeredho'ans, ten millions; and then Fragapatti's attendants, being most ethereans, five millions.

2. When those were abroad, Fragapatti and Hoab and Yaton'te and Hapacha rose up, and after making the sign of the Setting Sun, went down and sat at the foot of the throne.

3. God, that was Penoto, went down and took Fragapatti's hand, saying: Arise, O Chief! The Father calleth. Fragapatti rose up and stood aside. Next, God raised Yaton'te, and he stood aside; and then he raised Hoab, and he stood aside. And now came the greatest trial of all--. He took Hapacha's hand, saying: Arise, O God, Great Jehovih calleth thee! Go thy way and His.

4. But they both burst into tears, and fell into each other's arms. Hapacha said: O Father! Penoto said: His will be done! And now the light gathered brilliantly over

the scene; Fragapatti moved forward, then Yaton'te, then Hoab, and next Hapacha!

5. Penoto resumed the throne. The es'enaurs chanted, and the fire-light of the higher heavens descended over all the place. Like a sweet dream, the scene closed. Fragapatti and his hosts were gone.

6. Like a bee that is laden with honey, flying from a field of flowers to its home, so returned Fragapatti with his avalanza laden, to Haraiti, swiftly through the vault of heaven, a shooting star in Jehovih's hand.

7. Athrava, God of Haraiti, and assistant to Fragapatti, knew that the avalanza was coming; and that Hapacha and his hosts were aboard; and he determined to provide a glorious reception.

8. So, for the space of a thousand miles, he caused pillars of fire to be erected, in two rows, so that the avalanza should pass between them; and near the pillars he stationed trumpeters and harpers, one million, divided into one hundred groups. And they were so arranged, that when the avalanza passed them, they could come aboard.

9. Now during the absence of Fragapatti, many of the spirits who had been rescued from torture and madness in the hells of Aoasu had been restored to consciousness, more than one hundred and fifty millions of them.

10. Of these, Athrava said: Clothe ye them in most gaudy apparel, and let them be the bearers of perfumes and flowers, and torches, as presents for the I'hin hosts of Hapacha. And the lights shall be lowered at the place of landing, to make it acceptable to those newly raised, who are aboard.

11. Athrava said: As for Mouru, within the walls of light it shall be rated seven; but when Fragapatti hath ascended the throne, it shall be raised to nine. And in those days, nine, in Haraiti, was fifty per cent of the capacity of endurance in the plateau.

12. Jehovih hath said: If they raise the light, it will be more acceptable to My etherean hosts, for they have dwelt a long time near the earth, and are thirsting for etherean light. But yet consider ye, here are thousands of millions of atmosphereans who cannot endure the etherean light, but delight in a lower per cent. See to it, then, that the walls of light protect My hosts in the dark on one side, but raise ye the grade to nine within.

13. Athrava said: There shall be flights of stairs leading over the walls of Mouru, and they shall be white and illumed on that day, which will be sufficient for dividing the people according to the light suited to them. The I'hins with Hapacha will go over the walls, for they entered their corporeal cities in the same way; besides, they are capable of enduring the light; but the I'huans with Hapacha will desire to remain without. For them prepare ye a place of delight and rest.

14. But in regard to the ethereans Athrava gave no orders, for they were capable of perceiving all necessary things, and without instruction.

CHAPTER XXVI.

1. When Fragapatti entered the Road of Fire with his avalanza, where Athrava had stationed the musicians and groups of furlers, the hosts aboard broke loose from all bounds of propriety, so great was their delight, and they shouted and sang with the trumpeters with most exalted enthusiasm. Many of them entered the Orian state, and not a few, even the Nirvanian. And they became even as Gods and Goddesses by their own

entrancement, seeing, hearing and realizing, even to the third rate above the Brides and Bridegrooms of Jehovih!

2. These were but spasmodic conditions of light, from which they returned in course of time, being able to give descriptions of their visions. For Jehovih so created man, with spells of clearness far in advance of his growth, the which, he having realized, he returneth to his normal condition, to prepare himself constitutionally.

3. Along the road, on either side, were mottoes and sayings peculiar to the hosts of Hapacha, and to mortals of Guatama. When Hapacha saw these, he said: How is it possible? Whence derived these Gods this information? But the light came to his own soul, saying: The wise and good sayings of men below, are born by Jehovih's swift messengers to realms above. Hoab stood near by, and heard what Hapacha said, and Hoab said: How can men and spirits be inspired to wise and good sayings? Who had thought to erect such signboards on the road to All Light! And yet what darker deeds are done, when the soul of man findeth curses and evil words to vent his awful sins, and walls himself around with horrid imprecations! The which to face in after time and be appalled at the havoc of his own deadly weapons. How few, indeed, comprehend the direful thrust of hateful words, imagining them but wind, to pass away and be seen no more, but which are placarded on the signboard of heaven, as his fruit sent to market! The poison dealt out of his mouth to his brother man! A man throweth a spear, deadly, but it falleth on the earth and lieth there; but words and sayings are more potent, scoring deep in the soul of things. Fair, indeed, is it with thee, O Hapacha, and with thy hosts also, with yonder pure scroll to enter Haraiti!

4. As fast as the ship passed the lights, the etherean musicians came aboard, being anxious to meet Hapacha and his hosts, especially the I'hins, and to congratulate them on being the first harvest from the lowest heaven at the end of a cycle. And strange to say, there were just twice as many as Sethantes had prepared in the first dawn on earth. Fragapatti called the swift messengers belonging to the Roads of Gon, in etherea, and he said unto them: Go ye to Sethantes, whose fields lie in the Roads of Gon, and say unto him: Greeting, in the name of Jehovih! The earth hath reached Obsod and Goomatchala, home of Fragapatti, who sendeth love and joy on behalf of sixty millions, first harvest of h'ak, grade sixty-five.

5. Of these messengers, four hundred departed, leaving a reserve of eight hundred, who continued on the avalanza.

6. The drujas, who were arrayed in gaudy attire, withdrew a little from the landing, fearing the light. When the ship drew near the walls, and was made fast, the marshals of Mouru came to the front, two millions, as an escort to conduct all who chose over the ascending stairs.

7. And so great was the faith of Hapacha's hosts, that over fifty millions of them passed within the sea of fire, singing: GLORY BE TO THEE, O JEHOVIH! CREATOR OF WORLDS!

8. Seeing this great faith in them, Athrava commanded red and blue lights, to favor them; and there was not one of the whole number that quailed, or turned from the light. And now was beholden, to many of them, their first view of the glories and powers of Gods and Goddesses. Mouru was illuminated in every part. The structure of the temple, its extent and magnificence in conception, with its hundreds of thousands of mirrors and lenses, its transparent and opaque crystals, translucent and opaque circles and arches,

hundreds of millions, the which, when viewed from any one place, was unlike when viewed from another place, as if each position were striving to outdo the others in beauty and perfection. So that, were a person to walk for a thousand years in the temple, he would every moment see, as it were, a new palace of surpassing grandeur.

9. And so wonderfully was it arranged that the faces of one thousand millions of people could be seen from any place a person might be; and yet all these people constituted a part and principle in the building, being as jewel stones, created by Jehovih for the ornamentation of His celestial abodes.

10. Hoab, always quick to speak, said: O that angels and mortals would strive to make of themselves such jewels as these! Hapacha spake not, being overwhelmed with the beauty and magnificence. Yaton'te said: When thou art on the throne, Fragapatti, I will leave for the kingdom of Yaton'te: Here, then, I will take my leave. Fragapatti shook hands with him, saying: Jehovih be with thee!

11. So Yaton'te remained where he was, but Hoab and Hapacha continued on with Fragapatti. All eyes were turned to them, and especially to Hapacha, whose persistence in faith in Jehovih had won the lower heavens to Wisdom and Love. And as they moved toward the throne, great Athrava rose up, smiling, holding out his hands to receive them. Next, and back of Athrava, were the five Goddesses, Ethro, of Uche and Rok; Guissaya, of Hemitza, of the Valley of M'boid, in etherea; Si'tissaya, of Woh'tabak, the one-time home of Fuevitiv; Ctevi, of Nu, Porte-Auga; and Rinava, of the Swamps of Tholiji, in South Suyarc of Roads, near Zuh'ta and Hitch'ow, in the South etherean vault of Obsod.

12. And the Goddesses also rose up with extended hands; and now, because of the brilliancy of their presence, the throne became a scene of hallowed light, and threads thereof extended to all the Council members, and by these were radiated outward so that every person in the Temple of Jehovih was connected with the throne, which made every spoken word plain to all.

13. Athrava said: In Jehovih's name, welcome, O Fragapatti! And thy hosts with thee! The Goddesses repeated the same words, and they were echoed by the entire audience. Fragapatti said: In Thy name, O Jehovih, am I delivered to my loves. Be Thou with us, O Father, that we may glorify Thee! Receive ye, O my people, Hapacha, Son of Jehovih, who rose up and stood in the dark all night long, in faith in Jehovih. Behold, I have delivered him in dawn, and his hosts with him.

14. And now there appeared, rising like a new sun, Jehovih's light beyond the throne, reddish tinged, emblem of the Western Light, in honor of Hapacha. And it rose and stood above Fragapatti's head in great brilliancy. Then spake Jehovih out of the Light, saying:

15. With My breath create I alive the earth-born child; with My hand quicken I the newborn spirit; and with My Light illume I the soul of My Faithist. Behold, I dwell in the All Highest place, and in the lowest of created things; whoever findeth Me, I find also; whoever proclaimeth Me, I proclaim in return. Hapacha, My Son, Savior of men! of My Light shalt thou be crowned!

16. The Voice ceased, and now Fragapatti advanced to the midst of the throne, and took of the light and fashioned a crown, and placed it on Hapacha's head, saying: Crown of Thy Crown, O Jehovih, crown I Thy Son! In Thy Light shall he be wise and powerful, with Love to all Thy created beings, henceforth, forever.

17. The Goddesses then received them, and after due ceremonies they all took their seats,

Fragapatti in the midst of the throne. Arthrava resigned at once, during the stay of Fragapatti. The es'enaurs now chanted: GLORY BE TO THEE, O ALL LIGHT; THE PERSON OF EVERY KINGDOM HIGH AND LOW; WHO HATH BROUGHT OUR BROTHERS AND SISTERS HOME!

18. By natural impulse of thanks, Hapacha's hosts, fifty millions, rose up and responded, singing: TO THEE, O JEHOVIH, HOW SHALL OUR SOULS FIND WORDS! THY SON'S AND DAUGHTER'S LOVE, HOW CAN WE RECOMPENSE? MAKE US LIGHT AND CLEAR, O FATHER! SPOTLESS BEFORE THEM AND THEE!

19. But the anthems were long, and sung with brilliancy, rejoicing and responding, millions to millions, as an opera of high heaven.

20. When the music ceased, Fragapatti said: With the close of dawn of dan, these hosts shall be received as Brides and Bridegrooms of Jehovih, and ascend with us to the regions of Goomatchala, in etherea. The apportioners will therefore divide them into groups in Haraiti; with etherean teachers to prepare them. That this may be accomplished, I proclaim one day's recreation, to assemble on the next day in order of business.

21. The marshals then proclaimed as had been commanded, and the hosts went into recreation, the ethereans rushing to Hapacha's atmosphereans with great glee, every one desiring some of them.

CHAPTER XXVII.

1. When they were called to labor, Fragapatti said: For the convenience of my own hosts, the light shall now be raised two degrees. In which case it will be well to permit the hosts of Hapacha to retire to the fields of Hukaira (in Haraiti), where Athrava hath already a place and teachers for them.

2. Accordingly, the conductors now removed Hapacha's hosts, save about one million who resolved to endure the light. The es'enaurs chanted whilst these arrangements were being carried out, and when they were accomplished the music ceased.

3. The chief marshal said: Swift messengers, who are waiting without, salute Jehovih's throne, and His God, and pray an audience. Fragapatti said: Whence come they? And what is the nature of their business?

4. The marshal said: From the Aoasu'an fields of Howts. Their business is of the Osivi knots. Fragapatti said: On the sign of Emuts, admit them, greeting from God, in the Father's name.

5. The marshal withdrew for a short while, and then returned, bringing in one thousand swift messengers, of whom Arieune was Goddess. She advanced near the throne to the left. Fragapatti said: Goddess Arieune, Greeting to thee, in Jehovih's name! Proceed thou.

6. Arieune said: Greeting, in love to thee, Fragapatti, and to all thy hosts. I hastened hither from the fields of Howts, section twelve, on the one-time plateau and place of Hored, where are a thousand millions in knot, since many days. This I reported to the Lord God of Jaffeth, Ah'oan, whose forces are all employed, and he sent me hither.

7. Fragapatti said: It is well. Thou art at liberty! Hoab, canst thou untie the knot? Hoab said: I have faith to try. To which Fragapatti replied: Athrava will go with thee, but do thou the labor. Choose, therefore, thy hosts from my ethereans, and have a vessel made sufficient, so that if thou findest it advisable to bring them away, thou canst do so. Retire, then, with the captain of the files, and make thy selections, and, in

the meantime, give commands for the vessel to be made, and put in readiness for thee.

8. Hoab said: With Jehovih's help I will deliver them. And he saluted, and, with the captain of the files, he withdrew and made his selections, choosing five millions in all, of whom half were physicians and nurses. In the meantime he had the proper workmen build a vessel of sufficient capacity and strength, as commanded by Fragapatti. And in seven days' time everything was completed, and Hoab commanded his hosts to enter the ship, and he and Athrava went in also; and presently they were off, being conducted by the Goddess Arieune, in her arrow-ship, to the place of the knot.

CHAPTER XXVIII.

1. The Goddess Arieune slackened the speed of her arrow-ship to suit that of Hoab's vessel; so, onward together they sped in a direct line, propelled as a rocket is propelled, by constant emissions from the hulk; the which expenditure is manufactured by the crew and commanders, skilled in wielding Jehovih's elements. For as mortals find means to traverse the ocean and to raise a balloon, so do the Gods and spirits build and propel mightier vessels through the firmament, betwixt the stars and over and under and beyond the sun.

2. And when the ethereans, highest raised in the most subtle spheres, send their ships coursing downward in the denser strata of a corporeal world, their ready workmen take in ballast, and turn the fans, and reverse the whirling screws to match the space and course of travel; for which purpose men learn the trade, having rank and grade according to proficiency. Many of them serving a thousand years' apprenticeship, becoming so skilled in wielding the elements, and in the knowledge of the decrees of density, that thousands of millions of miles of roadways in heaven are as a well-learned book to them.

3. And, thus conversant with Jehovih's wide domains, they are eagerly sought after, especially in emergent cases, or on journeys of millions of years; for so well they know the requirements, the places of delight, the dangers of vortices and of eddies and whirlpools, that when a God saith: Take me hither, or yonder, they know the nearest way and the power required.

4. For, as Jehovih hath made icebergs on the corporeal ocean, dangerous to ships; and heavy currents of trade winds, and currents in the oceans, so are there in the etherean firmament currents and densities which the well-skilled God can take advantage of, be it a slow trip of pleasure, or a swift one on urgent business to suffering angels or mortals.

5. And, be it God or Goddess, dispatched by a higher Council, to a distant place suddenly, he, or she, must be already acquainted with navigators sufficiently to know who to choose; and, likewise, understand the matter well enough to lend a helping hand if required. For oft the navigators have not swift messengers to pilot them; and yet a short journey of fifty thousand miles may require as much skill as a million, especially in descending to a corporeal world.

6. Hoab knew, and he managed well. Following close on the arrow's trail till they neared the ruined plateau, and then, amidst the broken currents, Arieune dropped alongside, perceiving Hoab's less wieldy vessel, and made fast. She said to Hoab:

7. Behold, we are near the place. Then Hoab asked: How foundest thou a knot in such a wasted country? Arieune answered him:

8. When Jehovih created women, He gave to her two chief attributes, curiosity and solicitude for others. So, passing here, surveying the place where the first heavenly kingdom was, I remembered it had been said that Aph left some island places where once a colony in heaven had been built, and I halted to examine it. A moan and terrible sound greeted me! I heard the Osivi knots, as I had oft heard others before.

9. We landed and made fast, and presently went about searching, led by the sad, sad noise. Then we came to the great mound, the knot, a thousand million drujas bound in a heap! Wailing, muffled, moaning as if all the heap of them were in the throes of death, but could not die!

10. Being myself powerless to overcome such fearful odds, I took the bearing of the regions where I should find the nearest God; and so, having measured the knot, I set sail as thou hast heard.

11. Hoab said: Every day I behold Thy wisdom, O Jehovih! In a new light Thy wondrous judgment riseth up before me. Who but Thee, O Father, had seen the fruitage of Curiosity made perfect in Thy daughters? From the little bud seen in mortal form, to the overscanning of Thy heavens by such Goddesses!

12. As thus Hoab discoursed, they arrived at a suitable landing-place, where they made their vessels fast, and then hurried to the knot. Without much ado, Hoab walled the knot around with low fire, leaving a gateway to the east, where he placed a thousand sentinels. One million of this army he stationed outside of and beyond the walls, and these were divided into groups of selectors, guardsmen, physicians, nurses and bearers, and manufacturers of fire and water. The selectors were provided with rods of fire and water, and the guardsmen with shields and blinds.

13. Then Hoab stationed another million betwixt the knot and the gateway, and these were stationed in four rows, each two rows facing, and but two paces apart; so that betwixt the rows it was like a walled alleyway. And the other three millions Hoab caused to surround the knot on every side. Each and every one of these was provided with a fire lamp, which they held in the right hand. And when all things were thus in readiness, Hoab commanded the attack to begin. And at once the attackers thrust their fire lamps in the face of of the druj nearest by, and, seizing them with the other hand, pulled them away. The druj do not all relinquish their grip in the knot at the sight of the lamp, but often require to be nearly burned and stifled with the light before they release their hold. Neither cometh this grip of evil, but of fear.

14. The knot is nothing more nor less than a mass of millions and millions of spirits becoming panic-stricken and falling upon their chief, or leader, who becometh powerless in their grip, and is quickly rolled up in the midst of the knot.

15. And when the deliverers thus begin at the exterior of the knot, peeling off the crazed and moaning spirits, they hurl them backward, where they are caught by the seconds, who, in turn, hurl them into the alleyways, where they are again thrust forward till past the gate in the wall of fire. From the time, therefore, that the druj receiveth the thrust of the fire lamp in his face, he is not suffered to linger, but is whirled suddenly from one to another, so quickly he cannot fasten to any person or thing. For were they to fasten on even the deliverers, first one and then another, soon a second knot would result. Because of which, to untie a know of a thousand million crazed angels is not only a dangerous proceeding, but a feat of unusual grandeur to be undertaken by five million ethereans.

16. To provide against accident, Hoab appointed Athrava to take charge of the delivered after they were beyond the walls; for Athrava had been long practiced in such matters, thousands of years. So Athrava divided and arranged the drujas into groups, placing guardians with fire rods over them; and in some cases taking the groups away and walling them around with fire also.

17. Now by the time five hundred millions of the knot were released, some of the external, delivered groups, began to tie themselves into knots. And when Athrava saw this, he said unto Hoab: Behold, they are becoming too numerous for my hosts. I have not sufficient guardians. Hoab said:

18. Then will I cease awhile, and, instead of delivering, come and assist thee. Accordingly, Hoab suspended the battle for a time, and together they labored with those without, untying the small knots and arranging them in safer ways, placing a greater number of guards over them.

19. This done, the es'enaurs struck up lively music, starting dancings and marchings; for such is the routine of the restoring process practiced by the Gods. Then come the nurses with cheerful words, with mirth and gaiety, following one diversion with another in rapid succession. But to the raving maniacs, and to the stupid, and to the helpless blind, the physicians now turn their attention.

20. Again Hoab and his army fell upon the knot, pulling the external ones away and hurling them out, but not so rapidly, having fewer deliverers, for he had bequeathed an extra million to Athrava, outside the walls. And after another three hundred millions were delivered, Hoab ceased again, and joined with Athrava to assist and divide and group them in the same way. And he bequeathed another million of his army to Athrava, and then again resumed the attack on the knot, and thus continued till he reached the core of the knot, having untied the whole thousand million drujas, gradually lessening his own army and enlarging that of Athrava.

21. And when Hoab came to the core of the knot, behold, he found Oibe, the false God, who falsely styled himself Thor, the etherean. And in the midst of the knot they had jewels of rare value and stolen crowns and stolen symbols, and rods, and holy water, and urns, and incense, and a broken Wheel of Jehovih, a broken triangle of the Gods, and, in fact, a sufficiency of things whereof one might write a book in the description. Suffice it, a false God and his kingdom had collapsed, and he fell, crushed in the glory of his throne. And there were with him seven false Lords, who were also crushed in the terrible fall.

22. Oibe and his Lords, from their confinement in the knot, were also crazed and wild with fear, screaming and crying with all their strength, even as were all the others, like drunkards long debauched, delirious and fearful of imaginary horrors, which have no existence. Or as one's hand, long compressed, becometh numb, so that when the pressure is taken away it still seemeth not free. So would not Oibe nor his Lords believe they were free, but still cried, calling for help.

23. At this time there came from Ah'oan, God of Jaffeth, a messenger with forty companions, and with five hundred apprentices; and the messenger's name was Turbe, an atmospherean, three hundred years, grade two. Greeting from Ah'oan, in Jehovih's name! Turbe said: To whom shall I speak; to whose honor this deliverance credit, save Jehovih's? Athrava said:

24. To Hoab, a Zeredho'an disciple of Fragapatti, who is sojourning in Mouru, capital of

Haraiti. And Athrava further asked Turbe his name, whence he came, and especially if he knew about this knot before, and the history of its cause? To which Turbe replied:

25. From Ah'oan this I have learned: Some four hundred years ago, one of the sub-Gods, named Oibe, because of his modesty and bird-like fleetness, was promoted by Samati, who is now commissioned master of the I'huans by Fragapatti. This, whom Hoab hath delivered, is Oibe, the one-time faithful sub-God of honorable purposes. His kingdom prospered for two hundred years, and his name and fame spread throughout all these heavens, and even down to mortals, who were inspired by his admiring spirits to make images of birds (oibe or ibis), and dedicate them to Oibe.

26. He became vain of the flattery, and, losing faith in Jehovih, finally came out in unbelief, saying there was no All Highest, save as each and every God chose to exalt himself. Within his dominions, which numbered nearly a thousand million angels, were a score or more of Lords under him; to the wisest of whom he began to preach his views, looking to personal laudation and glory.

27. In the course of a score of years, the matter culminated in Oibe and a few of his favored Lords proclaiming a new kingdom, styled, THE ALL HIGHEST KINGDOM IN THE ALL HIGHEST HEAVEN! And the title he assumed was, THOR, THE ONLY BEGOTTEN SON OF ALL LIGHT! THOR, THE ALL LIGHT PERSONATED! THOR, THE PERSONAL SON OF MI, THE VIRGIN UNIEVRSE!

28. Thus Oibe cut loose from the true God and his kingdoms; and he immediately walled his kingdom around with a standing army; promoting seven of his most efficient admirers as Lords; and others as generals and captains. And at once he sat about enlarging and enriching his throne, and his capital, which he called Osivi, and known as Howts on the true charts.

29. In the course of one hundred years his kingdom became a place of two thousand million souls. His chief city, Osivi, was the richest and most gaudy city that had ever been in these heavens. The streets were paved with precious stones; the palaces for himself, his Lords, and his marshals and generals, were built of the most costly jewels with pillars, arches and chambers of the most elaborate workmanship, and of the most costly material.

30. Oibe became a tyrant; and, save his Lords and a few favored friends, none were permitted to approach the throne but by crawling on their bellies, and even under guard. Nor were they permitted to raise their eyes upon him, save at a very great distance. And all his subjects were his slaves, in fact, though under progressive discipline. These slaves were sent far away into atmospherea, or else down to the earth, to gather tribute for the glory of Thor (Oibe) and his favorites; nor did these slaves mistrust but they were working for Jehovih, believing that he lived in the capital, Osivi!

31. At first, Thor educated and otherwise improved his slaves; but, finding them less obedient in consequence of knowledge, he finally destroyed all the heavenly schools and colleges, and resolved to keep his subjects forever ignorant. Consequently, the wiser ones deserted him, save his officers, and his angels were without knowledge, knowing nothing, save that they had to work for Thor forever!

32. In addition to ignorance, Thor kept his subjects forever in fear of himself, forever threatening them with terrible punishments if they ceased to pray to him as the only personified All Light, Jehovih. And in the course of time, his people forgot all aspirations for any other heaven or any other God. Many of these were deputized to dwell with mortals as guardian spirits, persuading mortals to worship Thor and Ibis, threatening them

with being turned into serpents and toads after death if they obeyed not these injunctions.

33. Thus ruled Thor, the false, for four hundred years in Osivi; neither was it possible for Samati to send an army of sufficient strength to overcome such a kingdom. But a change finally came. A light descended from the higher heavens six generations ago; and, according to the legends of old, it was ominous that the Gods of higher worlds would intercede.

34. So, Samati, taking advantage of this, sent emissaries to Thor, otherwise Oibe, and solicited him to give over his evil ways, and re-establish Jehovih. Thor, the false, sent back word, saying: When I was a child, I was taught to fear Jehovih, and I feared Him. After long experience I have discovered there is nothing to fear in all the worlds. If there be any Jehovih, He is without form or person or sense! I fear Him not! I revere Him not! My heaven is good enough for me and my Lords. As for my subjects, let no man, nor God, nor Lord, meddle with them.

35. Samati, who was the lawful God of all these heavens and of the earth, thus perceived no way to reach Thor's slaves, for the slaves were too ignorant to desire anybody or thing save Thor. Nevertheless, he sent word the second time to Thor, this time saying: Thy kingdom is even now destitute of intelligent people sufficient to protect thee in case of panic. If a comet, or any sudden light, or the passage of an avalanza through thy dominions should take place, thou wouldst surely find thyself overthrown in a knot. Thy subjects look upon thee as the All Highest; they will surely rush upon thee.

36. Thor sent the messengers back with an insulting answer. Thus the matter stood till after Ah'oan's appointment as God of Jaffeth and her heavens, which at once cut off Thor's emissaries to mortals, and confined him within his own kingdom. At this time, Samati was commissioned to establish the word of God amongst mortals, but he communicated Thor's position to Ah'oan.

37. Ah'oan sent embassadors to Thor, the false, beseeching him in the same manner to give up his personality, and return with his kingdom to Jehovih, promising him the best of assistance. To this, Thor, the false, replied, by the messengers, saying:

38. Ah'oan, thou usurper! If thou desirest favors of me, thou shalt approach me as all Gods and angels do, by crawling on thy belly before me. Encroach thee not one jot or tittle on my Most High Kingdom, or I will banish thee back to thy miscreant regions with stripes and curses!

39. Ah'oan was surprised, but perceived that till trouble came upon Oibe nothing could be done for him. So the time came; Jehovih suffered him to go the full period of self-glory. Thus Oibe fell!

40. Turbe ceased, and Athrava said: O Jehovih, when will man cease to fall? Thou hast proclaimed Thyself in all places, high and low; Thy Gods and Lords and countless angels have proclaimed Thee! Thou alone art the pass-word to all the universe! Thy name hath a thousand exalted devices to win the souls of mortals and angels from darkness to light, and yet they turn away from Thee, Thou Creator of suns and stars and countless etherean worlds! And they set up themselves as an object of worship! O the smallness of Gods and men! O the vanity of Thy little children!

41. Thou hast said to mortals: Go not into the marshes, for there is fever; build not large cities, for there is sin; go not after lust, for there is death! But they go in headlong, and they are bruised and dead!

42. To those who are risen in heaven, Thou hast said: Remember the lessons of earth, lest ye fall! Remember the fate of self-conceit, lest ye be scourged. Remember the king and the queen of earth, how they become bound in heaven, lest ye also become bound. 43. But they will not heed; vain Self riseth up in the soul; they behold no other God but themselves in whom they acknowledge wisdom.

CHAPTER XXIX.

1. Hoab heard the story of Turbe, and he said unto him: Since I have heard these things, I am resolved to bind Thor, the false, and his Lords, and send them with thee to Ah'oan! Turbe said: This would be my delight. Because Thor insulted Ah'oan, it would be well for Ah'oan to restore him to his senses.

2. Hoab said: Tarry, then, a little while, and my physicians shall bind them, that they do no harm in their madness, and I will have them delivered into the boat. So, the proper persons bound up Thor and his Lords with bands of cord, for they were wild and delirious; and after that, they were put into Turbe's boat, ready to be carried away. Hoab said to Turbe:

3. Greeting to Ah'oan, in the name of Jehovih. And say thou to him that, according to the laws of these heavens, a false God, or false Lord, who hath led the people away from the Father, shall, after his deliverance, be made to re-teach the truth to his deceived subjects; neither shall he be promoted higher or faster than the lowest of his former subjects. For which reason, after Ah'oan's companions have restored Oibe and his Lords to soundness of mind, he and his Lords shall be again bequeathed with their own kingdoms. In the meantime, I will in this same plateau begin the establishment of a new kingdom to the Father out of these crazed drujas.

4. Turbe and his companions then reentered their boat and set sail at once for Ah'oan's kingdom; Thor, the false, and his Lords, wailing and crying with fear, knowing not any man, nor woman, nor child.

5. Hoab now turned his attention to the hosts of panic-stricken drujas, who were constantly forming themselves in knots, and yet being as rapidly severed by the ethereans. To Athrava he said: How more helpless is a deranged spirit than a mortal! They float on their own wild thoughts. At one time they fly from us before the wind; at another they run together, or upon us, like molten gum, and we cannot keep them off.

6. Athrava said: Behold the wisdom of the Father in creating man in a corporeal body! What a glorious anchorage for a young, or a weak, or a deranged spirit! What a home a corporeal body is! How better we could manage these crazed ones were they thus provided!

7. Hoab said: Which showeth us the way we must proceed to restore them. Since we cannot create corporeal bodies for them, the Father hath given us power to provide them subjectively for a time being.

8. Thus proceeded Hoab and Athrava: First walling the place around with fire, so none of the druj could escape, and then dividing them into thousands of groups, by means of fire also; then creating subjective bodies for them, to which they bound themselves willingly, and which prevented them from fastening to one another.

9. (This is what drujas call re-incarnation in another world.) And whilst they were thus

provided temporarily by their teachers, and governors, and nurses, many of them imagined themselves to be kings and queens and high priests, and even Lords and Gods!

10. For more than a hundred days, Hoab and Athrava labored in the above manner; and the physicians and nurses and es'enaurs labored to restore the minds of the people; and they mastered the adversity, and had them well-nigh all restored and disciplined when messengers came from Fragapatti, greeting, saying:

11. Behold, the dawn of dan is passing swiftly, and I must yet visit the Lord Gods in the different heavens of the earth. It is therefore my decree that Athrava return to Mouru and resume the throne; and that Hoab return also, and join me as my student and companion on my journeys. Send these, my commandments, to Ah'oan, greeting, in my name, and he will provide a Lord to rule over the delivered knot of Osivi.

12. So, Hoab and Athrava were relieved by a Lord appointed by Ah'oan, and his name was Su'kah'witchow, an atmospherean pupil of Samati, of four hundred years, and of great resolution and proficiency. So Hoab provided Su'kah'witchow with a throne, and left four millions of teachers, nurses and physicians with him. And with the other million, Hoab and Athrava departed for Mouru, in Haraiti.

13. Now as for the cruisers, the swift messengers with Arieune, as soon as the knot was safely untied, and Oibe and his Lords bound and delivered into Turbe's keeping, to be sent to Ah'oan, they departed, having recorded the proceeding in Arieune's diary.

14. Fragapatti, having heard of the success of Hoab in delivering the knot, determined to honor him on his reception at Mouru. Accordingly, Fragapatti sent heralds out into Haraiti, proclaiming a day of recreation, and inviting as many as chose to come to Mouru to receive Hoab. The proper officers provided musicians, flags, banners and fire-works, suitable for the enjoyment of hundreds of millions of the inhabitants of Haraiti. Others provided reception boats, one thousand, to go part way and meet Hoab's ship.

15. So it came to pass, when Hoab returned to Mouru, he was received in great honor and majesty, and in lights of unusual splendor.

16. Fragapatti afterward said of this matter: I had policy in this; Hoab was to be the next God of earth and her heavens. And whatsoever would win the love, the admiration and awe of his unlearned subjects would contribute to their resurrection.

CHAPTER XXX.

1. So for one day there was great rejoicing in Mouru; and when it was ended, and the people retired to their respective places, the lights were raised for business.

2. Fragapatti said to Athrava: Come thou and resume Jehovih's throne. As for myself, I will go now and establish another habitation in Zeredho; and after that I will visit the Lord Gods of the divisions of the earth.

3. And when I have completed these labors, it will be near the end of the dawn of dan. See to it, therefore, that all who wish to prepare for the third resurrection be duly notified.

4. And now, when Fragapatti had risen up from the throne, swift messengers were announced from Sethantes, the inhabitor of earth. The marshals were commanded to admit them; and presently the swift messengers came in, greeting in Jehovih's name. They said: Sethantes sends love to Fragapatti. When the resurrection of this dawn is come, Sethantes will visit Mouru. And he will also bring with him Onesyi, first deliverer of

Brides and Bridegrooms of the first harvest of the earth.

5. When the message had been thus delivered, there was great rejoicing in the capital. Fragapatti thanked the messengers in the Father's name, and after that, the swift messengers withdrew.

6. Presently, Fragapatti withdrew also, taking Hoab and Hapacha with him; and when they departed out of the capital, and came to the avalanza, the marshals had the accompanying hosts assembled, ten millions, and so they entered the ship, and, amidst music and rejoicings, they departed, going direct to the kingdom of Yima, Lord God of Shem and her heavens.

7. Yima had been notified of their coming, and had had a piedmazr (a row-boat) made, in order to go and meet them. The piedmazr was sufficient to carry ten thousand musicians, thirty thousand rowers, and two hundred thousand travelers; and such were the numbers who embarked on her to meet Fragapatti.

8. Three years had now elapsed since Yima set out to establish the Father's kingdom in the heavens of Shem; and, save through messengers, little was known in Mouru of Yima's labors. Fragapatti had said of him: Yima liveth with the Voice; he cannot err.

9. In the seventh diaphragm of the east Apie, the vessels met, and Fragapatti opened the lower division of the avalanza, and took in Yima's boat and crew and passengers, amidst music and rejoicings. And, after due ceremonies, Fragapatti caused the avalanza to proceed, conducted by Leaps, one of Yima's messengers, and they proceeded rapidly until they arrived at Astoreth, the capital of Yima's kingdom in atmospherea, first grade, and resting upon the earth.

CHAPTER XXXI.

1. After Yima's appointment by Fragapatti, he had come to these regions; and, finding great darkness upon both spirits and mortals, he besought Jehovih, to know the cause and cure thereof.

2. The Voice of Jehovih came to Yima, saying: Whether spirits or mortals, they seek rather to obey their own self-desires than My commandments. Behold, I sent them Apollo, and he gave them intercourse betwixt the two worlds, angels and mortals. And for a season they held up their heads and remembered Me and My kingdoms.

3. But presently, they turned everything upside down, and built on their own account. I had shown them that by industry and perseverance they could attain to knowledge and power. But because mortals discovered that prophecy could come from the spirits of the dead, they ceased to perfect themselves, and they grew up in idleness.

4. The angels loved not to labor, to achieve My exalted heavens, being contented with the lowest. And they likewise fell in darkness, forgetting Me and My higher places above.

5. I called out to My Son, Osiris, saying: Go thou down to the earth and her heavens, and build them up, in My name. Yea, thou shalt wall them apart, that there shall be no communion betwixt the two worlds, save to My chosen.

6. And Osiris came, and fulfilled my commandments; to mortals he provided them that no spirit could come to them; and, as for the spirits that infested the earth about, he drove them away and colonized them, and he cut them off from the earth. And for a season, mortals prospered under My judgments; and they sought to improve the talents I created

withal.

7. But again have they confounded My judgments and perverted My laws. Every man on the earth hath a philosophy of his own; every spirit in these heavens hath a philosophy of his own. And there is no uniformity between any of them. Hear Me then, My Son; thou shalt not teach as Osiris did, nor yet as Apollo, but pursue a mean betwixt the two.

8. Thou shalt select them, permitting certain spirits to return to mortals, and permitting certain mortals to attain su'is and sar'gis, and to see and commune with spirits. But thou shalt provide them in judgment; making the process of inter-communion a secret amongst mortals. For in this thou shalt shut off the drujas of heaven and the druks on earth.

9. Behold, My Son Samati will come this way; labor thou with him and Zarathustra. Into God's hands have I given my decrees; he shall build on the earth. Build thou in heaven. As he buildeth for mortals, build thou for the spirits of the intermediate world. But keep thou open the doorway to My holy places in the heavens above.

CHAPTER XXXII.

1. Yima inquired of Jehovih, and the Voice answered him, saying:

2. Go thou from place to place in these heavens, and prove thy power. To the ignorant, power is antecedent in gaining the judgment; after power, wisdom. The fool saith: What canst thou do that I cannot? But when he seeth the power that cometh from My hand, he openeth his ears and eyes. To teach men and angels to unite, how have they not failed on all hands!

3. Mortals have said: It is good to be good, but it is not practicable. They have said: It is wise to be wise, but wisdom runneth in a thousand roadways; every man for himself.

4. The angels of these regions have said: It is good for us to unite into kingdoms; to have Gods and Lords; but who can unite us? Shall we sell our liberty to one person? But they will not unite; they dwell in inharmony. Every one taketh the earnings of another; the profit of one is the injury of others; they are barren of united good.

5. Jehovih said: One kingdom may have many good men and many good women, but be of no good as a kingdom. I measure not the individuals, but the entire household. I judge the virtue of a kingdom by its combined harvest delivered unto My keeping.

6. When a kingdom is aggregating to itself more wisdom and virtue, the amount of its increase is My harvest. When a kingdom cannot retain its own members, it is falling away from Me. The uprightness of its few is as nothing in My sight. The secret of the power of a kingdom lieth in its capacity to aggregate in My name and obey My commandments.

7. For a hundred days Yima went through the lower heavens, displaying the miracles of the upper heavens; and his hosts, many of whom traveled with him, enlisted pupils, particularly collecting the spirits of young children. And in a hundred days he had many millions of spirits, abracadabras, mostly helpless wanderers.

8. With these he repaired to Astoreth, and made ready to found his kingdom. Jehovih spake to him, saying: Fear not, My son, because of the helplessness of thy subjects. He who would start a new kingdom is wise in choosing none who have hobbies of their own. Whosoever goeth forth in My name, I will be with him.

9. Yima inquired of Jehovih who should be appointed assistant God, and the Voice answered: Thulae. So Yima appointed Thulae; and he made Habal chief marshal of the

capital.

10. Again the Voice of Jehovih came to Yima, saying: Thou shalt appoint unto Shem one hundred Lords, and they shall have dominion over mortals. Hear thou the Voice of thy Creator: Through My Son, Zarathustra, will I establish temples to My Lords and Gods; and thou shalt so provide thy heavenly kingdom, that thy Lords shall inhabit the temples, communing with the rab'bahs, who shall be called God-irs; but the communion betwixt spirits and mortals shall be known only to the God-irs, and to the sub-priests under them. But mortals shall be left to believe that these fathers have attained to spirit communion by great purity and wisdom.

11. Likewise, when drujas manifest to mortals, it shall not be countenanced but as a mark of evil, raised up against truth.

12. And when thou hast established thy kingdom, thou shalt cut off the supplies of the drujas, so they will become borrowers from thy people. In this manner, they will in time consent to labor.

13. Yima then appointed one hundred Lords, who became as the roots to the tree of heaven. The Aoshoan Lords were:

14. Ithwa, Yaztas, Micros, Jube, Zarust, Hom, Paoiris, Vadeve, Niasha, Cope, Drhon, Yus'ak, Cood'ayay and Thracton.

15. The Thestasias Lords were: Kashvre, Tusht, Yain, Amesh and Amesha; Armait, Wai'iv, Vahois, Vstavia and Comek.

16. The general Lords were called Ashem, with voice; that is to say, Ashem-vohu, Lords in chief, given for the kingdoms of the Sun, in the land of Shem. They were: Shnaota, Zathias, Mutu, Aoirio, Kaeshas, Cter'ay, Shahkya, Thraetem, Gahnaetobirischae, Habarshya, Paitis'gomya, Huiyus, Hakdodt, Anerana, Tibalath, Kever, Darunasya, Hors, Maidoyeshemo, Runnas, Gayomoratischi, Ba'ahraya, Zartushta, Kai'boryawich-'wich'toe'benyas and Cpitama. And Yima made these twenty-five Lords controllers of the Voice, with mortals, to take the place of Samati after the death and ascension of Zarathustra, for which reason they were called the Ashem-vohu. (See the Vedic Scriptures.)

17. The Lords of farmers and herdsmen were: Gaomah, Hoshag, Tamur, Jamshed, Freden, Minochihr-bani and Hus.

18. The Lords of sea-faring men were: Thaetas, Mirh-jan, Nyas, Khaftras, Thivia, Agreft, Ardus'lor, Tanafar, Avoitas, Marganesiachta, Hoakastanya and Vartuan.

19. The Lordesses of births and mothers, the Hotche'che, were: Kaviti, Way'huts, Howd, Anechorhaite, Juveas, Wisseta, Hopaeny, Ctnevirchow, Aivipohu, Cadhan, Hucrova, Dion, Balkwoh and Gamosyi.

20. The Lords of buildings were: Irathama, Haira'thracna, Heidas, Hutu, Coy'gaga, Haira-Wahti, Vivi'seeon, Muta'hagga, Kaoyas, Macyo, Aims, Hodo, Trusivi, Verecopagga and Suyi.

21. The Lords of time-keeping, who had dominion of the change of watch, were: Copurasastras, Vaitimohu and Howitchwak.

22. Jehovih spake to Yima, saying: In this day will I bless thy labor. Because mortals have ceased to believe in immortality, they have shut off the intercourse with drujas. For which reason thou shalt establish pure communion with thy pure Lords, and none other.

23. Yima sent his Lords to their several places, and every Lord took with him a thousand

attendant angels. Yima said to them, before they departed: See to it, O ye Lords; in your several places stir the people up. And wherever ye find kings or queens or generals surrounded by spirits that urge them on in their affairs, cut off those spirits, leaving the mortals destitute of inspiration, and their kingdoms and armies will become disorganized and helpless.

24. And whenever (the mortals) Samati and Zarathustra come to a city, go ye also, laboring with them. And when Zarathustra holdeth up his hands and saith: O Father, Light of Thy Light! gather ye of the substance around about, and shield him with a wall of fire. And if Zarathustra say: O Father, Ormazd, give Thy children food, then shall ye cast down, from the air above, fish and fruit.

25. And if a king or a captain raise a hand against Zarathustra, gather ye about him and shield him. And if a man draw a sword against Zarathustra, catch ye the blade and break it to pieces.

26. Jehovih spake to Yima, saying: The time will come when the present mortal kingdoms will fall. But the followers of Zarathustra, who will succeed them under the Zarathustrian law, shall be protected, even, as ye, during dawn, protect Zarathustra.

27. For which reason, thy Lords shall raise up other Lords to take their places after the ascent of this dawn. And it shall come to pass that All Light and All Truth and All Success shall come to mortals through the priests (rab'bahs), who shall succeed Zarathustra. But as for the kings of great cities, who will not accept My Light, they shall go down in darkness, and their kingdoms shall fall to pieces.

28. Yima having established his Lords, now turned his attention to the heavenly kingdoms of hadas.

CHAPTER XXXIII.

1. Jehovih said to Yima: Thou shalt separate the spirits, the partly light from the wholly dark. Build thou, therefore, a throne and a plateau sufficient for three thousand million souls; and because there are more females than males, thou shalt call the place of thy throne Astoreth. And when thou hast provided a house for thy Council, thou shalt send forth selectors, who shall bring unto thee as many as choose to come; and these shall be the foundation of thy kingdom.

2. Yima proceeded as commanded by the Father, and presently he had congregated around about Astoreth a sufficient number to establish places of amusement, places of worship, and places of learning. Again the Voice came to Yima, saying:

3. Because thy kingdom is attractive, thou art flooded with idlers, who are of no profit to any person in heaven or earth. To keep them away, thou shalt wall thy kingdom around with pillars of fire. For thus have I created man, that to whom putteth him away he will return with zeal. Because thou shalt make thy labors seclusive, they will run for thee.

4. And when they come to thee, thou shalt bargain with them for righteous behavior erst thou feedest them. And when thou hast thus gathered in all who come in this way, thou wilt not yet have the half.

5. But those who are left will be without judgment, and thou shalt take possession of them, and bestow them in colonies. And thou shalt rank them. The lowest of all shall be the first rank; those who come after the pillars of fire are built shall be the

second rank; and those who come with the selectors shall be called the third rank.

6. And thou shalt divide thine own hosts; those who go with thy Lords down to mortals as guardian spirits shall be called ashars, and they shall bring the spirits of the newly dead and deliver them to thy hosts in heaven, which hosts shall be called asaphs.

7. And the ashars shall drive all spirits away from mortals, save such as are appointed by thee or thy Lords. For above all things shalt thou seek to become controller over mortals, to the end that they become Faithists in Me and My dominion.

8. Yima then divided the spirits of heaven according to the commandments of the Creator. After that he took possession of the wandering spirits of darkness, whether they were on earth or in heaven, and he had them taken into places prepared for them. And he provided them with physicians, nurses and teachers, and they were made to understand they were dead as to their earth bodies, and that they must give up the earth.

9. After this, Yima established places of learning in heaven, and places of labor, teaching the angels to clothe and feed themselves by their own industry.

10. Again the Voice of Jehovih came to Yima, saying: Behold, My Son, the lower heaven hath reached Scpe'oke. It is, therefore, the time in which angels of the first grade be taught to build heavenly mansions.

11. Yima commanded the teachers and the superintendents of factories to prohibit the spirits from returning to mortals, save by permission. Yima said:

12. It is wiser to inspire mortals to rise in heaven after death than to have them ever drawing the angels down to the earth. And my Lords on the earth shall labor to this end also. So Yima taught new inspirations, both in heaven and on earth, which were that the angels of the dead should build homes in heaven for their kindred, and that mortals should be taught that there were mansions in heaven ready for their souls after death.

13. Yima said: Mortals becoming founded in this belief, will not so readily become wandering spirits after death.

14. Whilst Yima was thus building in heaven, his Lords, with their attendant spirits, were manifesting on earth, as had never been before since the foundation of this world.

15. The temples of the stars were broken and thrown down by the spirits; the iron gates of the cities were taken off and carried into the forests; the palaces of kings and queens were unroofed, and the stones of the walls of the palaces were hurled from their places; even to the foundation, one stone was not left upon another; and these things were done by the spirits of heaven.

16. And men and women and children were carried in the air by the angels, and unharmed. The household goods were carried out, and the food of the tables stripped off, even as mortals sat down to feast, and they were made to behold the food going away; with their own eyes beheld they these things.

17. And mortals were made to see visions and to dream dreams of prophecy, and to have unusual powers. And in many places the spirits took on sar'gis, and walked about amongst mortals, being seen and felt; and they talked audibly, explaining to mortals the dominion of Yima and his Lords.

18. In all things that Yima and his hosts did in heaven, his Lords worked in harmony with him in their labor on the earth. Nevertheless, there were also vagrant spirits on earth who belonged not to the kingdoms of heaven, but who made manifestations on their own account; and they were given to lying, and to flattery, and to evil generally. Yima, little by

little, cut off these evil spirits, and took them away to his colonies, and disciplined them.

19. Such, then, were Yima's labors when Fragapatti came to see him, to honor which occasion, Yima had proclaimed recreation in Astoreth, and invited his Lords and captains and others to be present and take part in a season of enjoyment.

CHAPTER XXXIV.

1. On the arrival of the avalanza, the es'enaurs of Astoreth, and the trumpeters of the colonies, sang and played, being joined by the hosts aboard the vessels. And when they ceased, Thulae, assistant God of Astoreth, commanded the marshals to receive the hosts, foremost of whom were Yima and his attendants, preceded by his traveling marshals and harpers, the latter being five thousand females, led by We'aytris, Goddess of Foes'ana, in etherea. After these came the marshals of Fragapatti, ten thousand; then the swift messengers, ten thousand; then Fragapatti, on whose left was Yaton'te, and on whose right was Hoab. And these were followed by the musicians, and then came the hosts in general.

2. Yima ascended the throne at once, but Fragapatti and his hosts halted in the arena, within the circuit of the altar. Next beyond these were the guards of the lights; and still outside of these were the Crescent Members of the Council.

3. Yima said: In the name of Jehovih, I welcome thee, O Fragapatti, Chief of Obsod and Goomatchala, to the throne of God! In His Wisdom and Power I would have thee honor Astoreth by taking possession, in the Father's name!

4. Without replying, Fragapatti walked alone to the throne, saluting on the sign of HIGH NOON, which Yima answered IN THE SETTING SUN! Yima stood aside, and Fragapatti ascended and stood in front of the middle of the throne. He said:

5. Into Thy possession, O Jehovih, receive Thou this, Thy Throne! Hardly had Fragapatti spoken, when a light, bright as the sun, settled above his head, and a Voice came out of the midst of the light, saying:

6. To thee, My Son, and to thy son, and to thy Gods and Lords, and to all who follow them in My name, do I bequeath this, My Throne, forever! Whosoever becometh one with Me, shall not only hear My Voice and receive My Power, but also inherit that which he createth out of My creation.

7. Jehovih's Voice continued, saying: Whosoever looketh upon My works and saith: Behold, I cannot cope with these elements! is short in faith and wisdom. For I have not created in vain, that either mortals or spirits cannot control My elements in their respective places. They shall improve the talents I have given them.

8. I made the earth wide, and filled it with many things; but I gave man a foundation, that he might attain to the mastery of land and water, and minerals, and of all the living. Yea, I gave him a corporeal body to practice with, and as an abiding place for the assistance of his own soul.

9. And I created atmospherea wider than the earth, and filled it with all manner of spiritual things, and with the substance of plateaux; but I gave also to the spirits of the dead, talents, the which can attain to the mastery of all things in atmospherea.

10. Whoever hath attained to these things is like a traveling sun: My light is upon him; he prepareth the place, and My Voice cometh out of the Light thereof. Let My Sons and

Daughters stir themselves up; where they are gathered together in My name, there am I also. My hand is upon them; My Power becometh one with them, and My Voice is possible in their midst. The Voice ceased.

11. There were many present who had not previously heard the Voice of All Light, and because of the brilliancy they were blinded for a while, but presently restored. Fragapatti then said: Hoab and Yaton'te, come ye and sit on the throne. And they went up and sat on the throne; and in the same time the es'enaurs chanted, HAIL TO GREAT JEHOVIH'S VOICE! HIS SONS AND DAUGHTERS, OF THOUSANDS OF YEARS, ARE RETURNED ONCE MORE TO THEIR NATIVE STAR, TO PROCLAIM HIS BOUNDLESS GLORY!

12. Fragapatti said: In the Father's name, I proclaim a day of recreation; to resume labor at the sound of the trumpet in the east. And now the hosts mingled together freely, being buoyant with cheerfulness. And during the recreation, millions of ethereans went out into the plateau, visiting the places of learning, the factories and hospitals, and such places as belong to the lower heavens.

13. On the next day, at the call of the trumpet, the people resumed their places, and after the music, Fragapatti said: To Thee, O Thulae, will I speak in the name of Jehovih. Thou art chosen by the Father to be assistant to Yima, Jehovih's Son, during this dawn, which is near its end, and after that thou shalt be Lord and God of these heavens and of the earth beneath, for two hundred years.

14. Because thou art wise and good, the Father hath raised thee up, and great is thy glory. That thou mayst have strength and power, thou shalt in thy reign be called Yima, also; for the time hath now come to the earth when mortals must learn to know the Lords and Gods who rule over them.

15. During two hundred years will the earth be traveling in my Orian field, Goomatchala, and thou shalt be one with me in thy dominions. Whatsoever thou shalt require at my hand, I will send to thee. Thou shalt, therefore, keep thy place in order; and if thou needest a'ji, I will send it; if thou needest dan, I will send it.

16. Be less concerned about the spirits in thy heavens than about mortals on the earth. Mortals must have sufficient a'ji, that the race become not extinct; they must have a sufficient dan, that they become not as beasts. For which reason, every eleventh year thou shalt number abracadabra (See tablet, BOOK OF SAPHAH) and supply my swift messengers with the lists thereof. And I will bring the elements of Goomatchala to bear upon thy labor profitably to the Father!

17. In the next place, be thou careful of too much leniency toward the spirits in the first resurrection. Suffer them not to abide with mortals as teachers. Remember thou that mortals so love their dead kindred, they would even deprive them of heavenly education for the sake of having them around about them. Remember, also, that the spirits of the recent dead, who are entered as es'yans in all good heavens, so love their mortal kindred, that they would seek no higher heaven than to linger around about them on the earth. Which habit groweth upon them, so that in two or three generations they become drujas, worthless to themselves, knowing little of the earth and less of heaven.

18. Be thou firm, therefore, in holding dominion over the es'yans, permitting them only to return to mortals under guard; and especially preventing them from teaching other than the Ormazdian religion.

19. After this, thou shalt be circumspect in Astoreth: remembering that it is the part of a

God to provide his kingdom for the development of all the talents Jehovih hath created withal. For thou shalt so commingle labor and recreation, and rest and learning, that each and every one is of equal attraction.

20. And whether thy commandments be for angels or for mortals, thou shalt, first of all, and last of all, inspire them to faith in the Creator, and to follow the little star of light He hath given to every soul. Fragapatti ceased.

21. Jehovih said: I have drawn My crescent and My altar. Whoever would hear My Voice and heed My commandments, let them hearken to the forms and ceremonies that shape the soul of things. I am Order; I am Stateliness without severity; I am Love without passion; I am Wisdom by suggestion, and without dictation; I am the most Silent, but most Powerful; I am the Least Seen, but Always Present when asked for.

22. And now, since the people knew Fragapatti was about to depart, the proper officers arranged matters, so that all could pass in front of the throne to receive his blessing. Accordingly, the es'enaurs commenced singing, and the procession began. The master of the lights of the Council lowered them, and Fragapatti lowered his own lights, and came down and stood at the foot of the throne, covered with light drapery, which fell down to his feet.

23. His hands he held upward, waving gently; and he created drapery and perfume, and wreaths of flowers, and bestowed something upon every soul that passed, of whom there were more than a thousand millions!

24. And when the procession had all passed, Fragapatti sat down at the foot of the throne. Then came down Yima and took his hand, saying: Son of Jehovih, arise and go thy way, and the Father be with thee! So Fragapatti rose up and departed, and Hoab and Yaton'te and Yima and Thulae with him; and Yima left Hi'etra, Goddess of Me'Loo, on the throne of Astoreth.

25. So they entered the avalanza, and, with music and rejoicing, departed on their journey. And Yima conducted them throughout his dominions, both in heaven and on earth. For many days Fragapatti thus dwelt with Yima and Thulae; and after he had inspected their labors, and his recorders completed their record, which was to be afterward taken to etherea and deposited in the libraries of Fragapatti's dominions, Yima took leave, and his piedmazr was discharged, and he departed for Astoreth, whither he arrived in due season. But Fragapatti proceeded to the dominions of Ah'oan, Lord God of Jaffeth and her heavens.

CHAPTER XXXV.

1. The Voice of the Creator was with Ah'oan from the time of his landing in these lower heavens. And Ah'oan chose from his hosts a Council of ten thousand, and they sat in a living altar; and the Voice directed him to build a capital and a throne, and call the plateau thereof Sang'hi; the which he did.

2. And when it was completed, Jehovih said to Ah'oan: Thou art My Lord and My God; the labor of thy hand shall endure on the earth and in heaven. Whatsoever thou buildest, I will build, for thou art of My holy place. Make thyself an otevan, and go around about in thy dominions, and inspect all things, making a record of the same, which shall be deposited in the libraries of these heavens, that angels and mortals, in after ages, may read

them.

3. Ah'oan made an otevan, and traveled as commanded, making a record, and preparing also a place of records, in Sang'hi, where these things were deposited; of which these words are a brief transcript. That is:

4. Heaven was without order or organization, save one kingdom, ruled over by Oibe, who falsely styled himself Thor, the only begotten Son of Jehovih.

5. The spirits of these heavens are mostly of the first resurrection; nevertheless, there are millions of them who believe they are not dead; and for the greater part, these are in chaos, still lingering on battle-fields or in the places where they were cut off from the earth.

6. In many places there are spirits who set up colonies, trying to provide themselves with homes and clothing, and to found heavenly abodes; but they are forever overrun and pillaged by drujas.

7. With and around about the people of Jaffeth there are more than two thousand million angels who know not how to get away from the earth. Of these, millions of them are fetals, making themselves as twin spirits to mortals. These spirits oft show themselves to mortals, but are believed to be doubles; but the spirits thus bound know not themselves who they are, or whence they came; neither can they go away from the mortals to whom they are bound, and on whom they live.

8. As for the mortals of Jaffeth, they have cities of warriors, huge and fierce. The earth of this region hath been in a'ji thirteen hundred years.

9. After Ah'oan had thus discovered the condition of things, he returned to Sang'hi, and they sat in Council, and Jehovih said to Ah'oan: Forty Lords shalt thou appoint to dwell on the earth; and to each Lord thou shalt give ten thousand assistants. And these Lords shall go down to the earth, and drive away the drujas, and take possession of the kings' and queens' palaces, and of the temples of the stars; and they shall obtain control over the captains and generals of armies, and blind their judgment, and lead them astray, so that they will be powerless in war and destruction.

10. And when Samati, God of Zarathustra, traveleth in Jaffeth, thy Lords shall go with him, with a sufficient number of angels to accomplish successfully all that Zarathustra professeth in My name. And thy Lords shall shield Zarathustra around about, that no harm come to him; and when enemies pursue him, thy Lords shall lead them astray or detain them till such time as will enable Zarathustra to escape. For in this dawn shall My word be established on the earth, to perish not forever.

11. And when thou hast thus established thy Lords, thou shalt colonize thy heavens, giving them seventy colonies; but Sang'hi shall be the central kingdom. Thou shalt choose from amongst the atmghereans one who shall be thy assistant God, who shall sit on thy throne during thy absence.

12. And thou, and thy Holy Council, shall instruct thy assistant God in such manner that, when this dawn is ended, he shall become God, in My name, of Sang'hi, for the next succeeding two hundred years.

13. Ah'oan informed the Council of the words of Jehovih. And Ah'oan appointed the forty Lords, as commanded; also appointing an assistant.

14. These, then, were the Lords appointed, to wit: First, to have control over the WORD OF GOD on earth: The; Seung-bin, Go-ma-git, Ben-hong, She-ang, Bog-wi, Ah-tdong,

Mwing-wi, Ah-tchook, Gonk-boy, Yuk-hoh and Ahwotch.

15. Second, to have control over the palaces of kings and queens, and temples: Mina, Ahchaung, Ahyot, Yowgong, Ohonto, Yongwe and Ahma.

16. Third, to have control over armies and kingdoms: Kear-ak-a, Geeouh-young, Bi, Gwan-gouk, Gee-ooh-young, Sam-sin and Deth.

17. Fourth, to have control over sea-farers: Shopgee, Agan-ha, Rax and Lo.

18. Fifth, to have control over mothers and births: Songheng, Someconc, Yahiti, Ogne-ka-was and Hoah'ava.

19. Sixth, to have control over marriages: First, the loo'is in general, and then: Ahsam, Oanis, Yotsam, Ivitgom and Sap-sang.

20. So Ah'oan sent his Lords to their several places, with their assistants. And after that he began the colonization of the angels in his heavens. And in one year he had raised up from Jaffeth more than a thousand million, and prepared them with houses, hospitals, nurseries and factories, and all such things and places as are required in hada.

21. In the second year he delivered another thousand million, more than half of whom had to be taken away from the earth by force. And these he also housed and provided with teachers and overseers in like manner.

22. So by the time Samati, God of Zarathustra, was prepared to travel in Jaffeth, visiting the kings and queens, the Lords of Ah'oan had so far banished the drujas that they were powerless to prevent the decrees of the Father's word. And when Zarathustra went into Jaffeth, behold, the Lords of heaven were with him, and God of the Word was with him, and the kings and queens of earth were powerless before him.

23. And when Zarathustra went to a city, and, being inspired by God, said: Fall down, ye walls! behold, the angels of heaven rent the walls, and they fell. And when Zarathustra said: Come forth, ye spirits of the dead! behold, the Lords seized the drujas and held them up so that mortals could see them. And when Zarathustra said: O Ormazd, give Thy children food! behold, the angels had previously provided fish and fruit, which they let fall upon the people, the time and place being previously arranged betwixt them and God of the Word!

24. Thus did Ah'oan's dominions extend down to mortals; thus became the word of Zarathustra Jehovih's Word to mortals.

25. And now Fragapatti, Chief over all, was coming to inspect the labors of his Lord God, Ah'oan, and of Samati. Ah'oan had sent commands to his Lords, and to their assistants, to return to Sang'hi and remain three days in recreation. And Ah'oan commanded the captains of the colonies of heaven to come, and to bring with them as many of their pupils and subjects as possible.

26. And it came to pass that when Fragapatti's avalanza came to Sang'hi, there were assembled upward of two thousand million souls to witness the pageantry and proceedings. Ah'oan had provided the means and facilities that these things should be magnificently carried out.

CHAPTER XXXVI.

1. Never in these heavens had there been such pageantry and display as when Fragapatti's avalanza entered Sang'hi; never so many musicians, two millions, distributed to lend so

great an effect to a procession.

2. Of this matter, Ah'oan said: By the pageantry and the music were my hosts of delivered drujas made to realize the glory of the upper heavens; by the glory of those three days' recreation did I shut out the attractions of the lower world. My people were entranced with delight; they were born for the first time into the kingdom of heaven!

3. Ah'oan said: But the greatest glory of all was when Fragapatti honored the throne of Sang'hi. Jehovih cast a sun upon the place; and the Voice spake from the Light, so that all the multitude saw the Light and heard the words of the Father! And when Fragapatti rose up and stood in the midst of the throne, the Light was so great that millions of the people fell down because of its glory.

4. The lights were lowered to suit the newly born in heaven, and the people of etherea mingled with the atmosphereans, diverting, explaining and inspiring them with the magnitude and glory of the higher heavens.

5. After the recreation, and when the multitude were in order, Fragapatti spake from Jehovih's throne, first, to Es'pacia, Daughter of Jehovih, assistant Goddess to Ah'oan, who was to succeed him after dawn. To her he said: Es'pacia, Daughter of Jehovih, hear thou my words; I am one with the Father, and in His name salute thee. Behold, from this time forth the Father's Word shall dwell with mortals.

6. It shall become anchored to the earth, never to depart; though it may be mutilated and perverted, yet His hand is over it, and it shall not fail. As a mother delighteth in the first spoken words of her child, so shall we all take delight that the Father's word hath become engrafted on the earth. Before this time, the Word was with the I'hin tribe, but locked up in secret. It could not be maintained on the earth, but by locking it up in secret, with a people prepared as seed for delivering all the races of men. But now the Word is delivered openly to mortals.

7. If the spirits of the lower heavens know not the Father's Word, they can be hereafter taken down to the earth and there taught His commandments. Prior to this time, the angels of these lower heavens had no Word at anchorage; they constantly fell in darkness, and pulled mortals down with them. Behold, the Word is now engraved, through our Sons, Samati and Zarathustra; it cannot be lost.

8. Thou hast been exalted first Goddess of these heavens, and Lordess of this division of the earth, to maintain the light of this dawn, to angels and mortals. Thou shalt first of all labor to protect the Word to mortals; to all the priests and cities of Zarathustra thou shalt appoint the wisest of thy angel hosts, to protect them and to maintain the Word.

9. But to such mortals as deny the Word, and to such as seek to destroy the Word, thou shalt lend no assistance, but leave them either without angels, or with only such as will lead them into failure. Maintain thou thy hosts in the temples of worship, where they worship the Great Spirit.

10. Throughout Jaffeth thou shalt inspire mortals to hang the wheel of the altar in country places, by the roadsides. And when mortals pass the places, they shall turn the wheel, in remembrance of the Creator. For which reason thou shalt station at each and every one of these altars angel sentinels, who shall have messengers to thy throne. And when a mortal passeth the wheel and turneth it, and is afflicted with sickness, thou shalt send angels to him to heal him. But if hc turn not the wheel in remembrance of the Father, and yet be afflicted with sickness, thy sentinel shall not send to thee, nor shalt thou send angels to

heal him. Nevertheless, the wheel and the altar shall cause men to think; and if, after a disbeliever hath passed the wheel and not turned it, and he be afflicted with sickness, and he repent and go back and turn the wheel, then shalt thou send to him in haste and heal him, that he may proclaim abroad what the Creator hath done for him.

11. For as much as thou carriest out these decrees of All Light, so shalt thou remain united with my heavens above, which are united with those above, which are united with the Creator. And wherein thou shalt lack in power or wisdom, ask thou the Father, and I will answer thee in His name.

12. Fragapatti then spake to the Council, which was after the manner of his words in Astoreth. After that he walked down to the foot of the throne, where the marshals had provided a place for the people to pass before him, even as they had done in Astoreth. Accordingly, when the musicians began singing and playing, the people marched before him, and by the waving of his hands, he created drapery, and flowers, and wreaths, and gave to all the people something, even though there passed before him two thousand million angels!

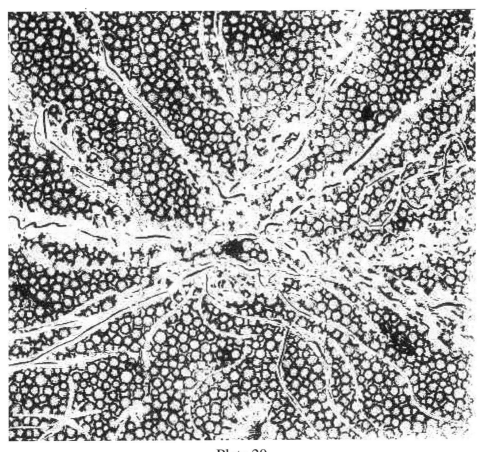

Plate 20.

THE EARTH IN THE CROSS-ROADS OF HORUB.

Jehovih said: In Horub I delivered My first Holy Book to mortals, through My Son, Zarathustra. After that I carried the earth in darkness, that it might be perfected for the generations of men to come afterward. Thus provided I the nations which I delivered through Capilya, Moses and Chine.

CHAPTER XXXVII.

1. So, Fragapatti departed, and sailed for Hi-rom, the heavenly kingdom of E'chad, Lord God of Arabin'ya and its heavens.

2. E'chad had also the Voice of Jehovih with him, and could not err. After his appointment to this division of earth and heaven, Jehovih commanded him, even as He had Ah'oan, to make an otevan and visit all the places, and make a record, before he established his kingdom. And these things E'chad did, taking thirty thousand companions with him, being surveyors, inspectors, recorders and numerators, and of such order as are required in preliminary examinations of the earth and lower heavens. Besides these, he had also his hosts of musicians, his heralds and messengers.

3. Forty days he spent in this labor, and then the record was completed, of which E'chad had two copies made, one for his own kingdom in etherea, and one for the heaven he was about to found. Of these records, which are everlasting in heaven, the numerators estimated one thousand million and eight hundred thousand spirits, wandering about, mostly on the earth, many of them falling into forgetfulness and dissolution. And many of them had forgotten who they were, and had no remembrance of once having lived mortal lives. Millions and millions of them had forgotten their speech, and were dumb. Millions of them lived with mortals as fetals and familiars, depending upon the spiritual part of the food mortals drank and ate for their own existence. And yet other millions of them pursued evil for evil's sake, inspiring mortals to war, for the delight of seeing them destroy one another, and of persuading mortals to suicide, and to all manner of wickedness.

4. In the region of Gavies there were four hells, in which there were sixty million souls in torments, tormenting one another in perpetual horrors, especially males and females doing what is even unlawful to mention. And these tormentors would bring es'yans, fresh from the earth life, and cast them into their hells for these wicked purposes. For even as mortals delight in vengeance, so can the talent grow until its feast lieth in the fruit of hell; neither desire such spirits to have even their own torments lessened; nor could they of themselves escape were they to try.

5. E'chad would fain have rushed in and delivered these hells, but Jehovih said unto him: Go thou first and establish Hi-rom, with suitable habitations, and then return and deliver these hells, and thou shalt have places for them. So E'chad established Hi-rom, and appointed the Holy Council of one hundred thousand men and women. Sa-ac he made chief marshal; and he appointed Geth'ya his assistant God. Jehovih said to him: Sixty Lords shalt thou appoint to thy division of the earth; and they shall dwell in the principal cities of Arabin'ya, and have dominion over mortals. And each and every Lord shall have ten thousand ashars to do their commands.

6. These, then are the Lords appointed by the Lord God, for Arabin'ya, to wit: First, to have dominion over the revealed Word: Tsdasag, Bachar'Raab, Nathan, Neshu, Dath, Shephat, Gaon-ay, Cha'ya and Zeker.

7. Second, the loo'is in general; but for special masters of generations: Achuzeh, Chata, Galah, Dayyan, Aphsi, Ishsah, Basar and Goi. Third, for destroying evil cities, and for protecting good ones, and for building new ones: Atsil, Sherngoth, Matshebah, Achime, Amos, Ahio, Yat-gaab, Zer, Howdawitch, Beodi, Machal, Yay-baoth, Ammah, Fakir,

Cephets, Bachre, and Hiv-iv.

8. Fourth, to abide on earth with rab'bahs (priests) and shield them in danger: Machaveh, Emul, Ashshaph, Alcmosum, Lai-awotch, Trivi-yab, Herivir, Beli-gib, Barat'ay, Shav'ya, Tir and Bowd-wahtal. Fifth, to inspire to inventions: Kartum-mim, Moses, Beged, Chakasat, Mih-gad, Jagri, Hen-di, Sru, Amothes and Benguda. Sixth, to have control over altars and temples: Atman, Krit and Anach.

9. In addition to these, the Lord God appointed censors of Hi-rom and her colonies in heaven; and the ashars appointed over mortals as guardians were directed to which colony to take their es'yans, where were stationed the asaphs, the receivers.

10. As soon as E'chad had these matters completed, he descended into the four hells with his otevan, taking with him three million angels to help him deliver them. And when he arrived at the place, behold, the power and light of Jehovih was upon him! And he surrounded the four hells with his hosts of angels.

11. Fire of Thy Fire, O Jehovih! he cried; give me here walls of fire, to inclose these suffering hells! And in the line of his hosts there fell from the firmament above sheets of fire, and he walled the places around in such brilliant flames and suffocating flames that not one of the inhabitants of hell could escape.

12. And E'chad and his hosts fell upon them, right and left, building fires in pillars and walls, blinding to the drujas, so they fell flat down and hid their faces. And they marched through and through the four hells, until all the inhabitants were fallen prostrate before them, crying out. And they were all naked, men and women; and only the recent victims were ashamed.

13. E'chad said: Fall to, now, and deliver those who are ashamed, making a place beyond the walls of fire; but wall ye the place around also, and then clothe and feed them. So E'chad's hosts delivered those who were ashamed. Again E'chad called out: Begin now in sections and deliver the others into prisons, surrounded by fire, suffocating, so they cannot escape. And let not the light cease to fall upon them that will not be clothed. Better is it that they lie prostrate than to display themselves nakedly. But as fast as they will accept and wear clothes, and cease cursing, deliver ye them into genial lights.

14. For six days and six nights E'chad labored in delivering the four hells, and on the seventh day they were all delivered. And there were amongst these drujas three and a half millions in chaos, spirits who had lost their minds by the torments that other spirits had bestowed upon them. These E'chad had placed in his otevan and sent to Hi-rom, to be treated by the physicians.

15. But E'chad and many of his hosts remained with the groups of the delivered, further preparing them for resurrection. And now E'chad had them inspected, and he further searched the es'pe of the earth to establish the origin of these hells, and as to who they were. This, then, is the substance of the history of that matter, to wit:

16. In the lower country of Arabin'ya, on the earth, there had been a tribe of I'huans of hundreds of years, who had attained to thirty cities, chief of which was Os'nu, which was the capital over all the rest. Os'nu was ruled over by Che-muts, a king of great wisdom and power in his youth; but, after subjugating all the large cities of Arabin'ya, he became a tyrant and a man of wickedness.

17. Being learned in the earth, and moon, and stars, he drew to his palace other men, and not a few women, of great learning, and, together, they resolved upon obtaining from the

I'hins, the sacred people, the secrets of their miracles and religion. Up to this time all the people in the world respected the I'hins, neither denied them in anything, for they were the forefathers and foremothers of the I'huans.

18. Che-muts, the tyrant, said: Because from our youth we have been taught to revere the I'hins, we have become superstitious regarding them. Now it is evident that they have some other means (than consulting the stars) of prophecy. It is my command, therefore, that the different cities of I'hins be seized, and the people put to death, offering succor only to such as reveal their secrets. With their gifts of miracles and power of prophecy, I can march successfully against Parsi'e, Jaffeth, and Ashem, and I shall become king of all the world. And ye that help me in this matter, instead of having merely cities to rule over, as ye now have, shall have kingdoms with many cities.

19. The learned men acceded to this, and, shortly after, the king's people fell upon the I'hins, pulled down their flimsy walls, putting them to flight or slaying them outright, offering no salvation save they would reveal their secrets, and give themselves up to marriage with the I'huans.

20. Hab-bak, a chief rab'bah of the I'hins, went to see the king and expostulate. He said unto Che-muts: Behold, my people are older than this country. Our wisdom cometh not as other men's, but through marriage. How can we reveal? We are born vailed. No other people are thus born. How canst thou obtain the secrets of the womb? Besides this, we are sworn before our birth by our fathers and mothers to secrecy in our religion.

21. Thou desirest us to intermarry with thy people. I foresee thy aims. Thou hopest for the gift of prophecy, which, if given to evil men, would give them all power. But know thou, O king, he that desirest prophecy for such purpose can never obtain it. Prophecy cometh by the other road.

22. If my people intermarry with thine, it is simply the loss of mine. If thou hadst our pass-words and our signs, they would avail thee nothing, being born as thou art. According to our number, we pay thee thy just tribute. I pray thee, then, to change thy decree and suffer my people to remain as they have, thousands of years!

23. Che-muts, the king, said: Why call ye yourselves I'hins? Hab-bak said: Because we are Faithists in One Great Spirit. The king asked: What is the secret name of the Great Spirit? Hab-bak said: I can only repeat that name under certain rules; otherwise I will lose my power of prophecy. Besides, if thou knowest the name, it would be worthless to utter it. To whoever uttereth His name not in faith, it is void. Whoever uttereth His name for earthly gain or earthly glory, uttereth in vain also. Of what value, then, would the name be to thee, even if I violated mine own oath and revealed it to thee?

24. The king mocked him, and had him seized and taken to the lions' den, of which all kings and rich people, in those days, had one or more, as a place for casting in their disobedient servants. And when Hab-bak was at the lions' den, the king again offered to save him if he would reveal even the name of the Great Spirit, hoping that by its utterance he could also heal the sick, restore the blind and deaf, and especially prophesy. Hab-bak said: Though thou mayst cast me in, and I be devoured, suffer me beforehand to prophesy concerning thee and thy kingdom. Yea, I will even prophesy concerning myself. Hear thou, then, my words:

25. Thou hast sought to destroy my people, who are, compared to thine, only as one little finger to a man's whole arm. In Os'nu thou hast hundreds of thousands of people, and in

other cities tens of thousands, and tens of thousands; so many that one man in his whole life could not number them. Yet, as to my people, what are they? Not more than ten thousand altogether. Hear thou, then, my words: Not one thousand of my people canst thou destroy. Neither will my people raise a hand in self-defense.

26. But thou wilt cast me into the lions' den, and I will be devoured. And this little hat, without a brim, will come out of the lions' den, and it will be a mighty power for thousands of years. It will be red with my blood, shed because I am faithful to the Great Spirit in my oath. And it will be restored to my people, and it shall be called The Scarlet Hat! And in the day that it is carried in the streets of Os'nu, thou wilt be slain by thine own people.

27. The king laughed, saying: A prophecy often causeth fools to carry it out. With that, he gave the executioners the sign, and they pushed Hab-bak on the trap, and cast him into the den, where there were thirty lions. And they fell upon him and devoured him. And his hat was colored red with blood; and some of the people, who were superstitious in regard to the I'hins, procured the hat and went about repeating the prophecy of Hab-bak, and the multitude were anxious for some pretext to justify themselves in destroying the tyrant. So, presently, the city was in riot, and the people fell upon the king and slew him, and also slew the learned men and women who were his counselors and subsidiaries.

28. In the libraries of heaven it is recorded as followeth, to wit: Because of the cruelty of Che-muts, king of Os'nu, on earth, thousands and tens of thousands of people had been put to death; and because they died in anger, and because of the injustice, their souls went into torment in hada, and they came and incensed the king to greater wickedness, in order to have him slain. And it so came to pass that Che-muts, chief king of Arabin'ya, was slain by his own people, and the king's counselors were slain with him.

29. And when their spirits were delivered from their mortal bodies, the drujas fell upon the king's spirit, and the spirits of his counselors, and bore them off to a foul-smelling place in hada, and cast him and them in, and the drujas went in after them, beating them. Whereupon it became known in hada there was a newly-started hell, and other spirits brought other victims there and cast them in. And the drujas went around about on the earth, in Arabin'ya, finding whomsoever they hated, bringing their spirits into hell, beating them and otherwise punishing them, until these four hells became the habitation of sixty millions of souls.

CHAPTER XXXVIII.

1. When E'chad had discovered the history of these hells, he searched and found the king's spirit, and also the counselors, but, alas, they knew nothing, being in chaos, or more like one in a troublesome nightmare, from which there is no awakening.

2. But E'chad appointed physicians and nurses for them, and it was three years before they began to awake; but yet at the time of Fragapatti's visit they were not sufficiently restored to know who they were, or, if knowing one moment, would forget in the next moment. Yet it was not many days after the deliverance of the hells that E'chad had the inhabitants removed to Hi-rom and the colonies thereof.

3. E'chad having been informed by heralds that Fragapatti was coming, sent word to his Lords and to his generals and captains, and superintendents of schools, and of factories,

and of hospitals, to come to Hi-rom and enjoy three days' recreation, bringing as many atmosphereans as they could with them.

4. So Fragapatti came, and the hosts of E'chad, and there was great rejoicing for the space of three days; during which time Fragapatti visited all the places and labors of E'chad, having records made thereof, to take with him to etherea at the end of dawn. Now at the end of the three days' recreation, the trumpet in the east called the Council to labor and the hosts to order. Fragapatti sat in the midst of the throne, E'chad next him, and then Hoab and Yaton'te, and then Thulae and Es'pacia and Geth'yo, and others of lesser rank.

5. A light immediately gathered above the throne, but, this time, deep scarlet, with white border. Fragapatti said: Thy Voice, O Jehovih, be upon these people! Whereupon, the es'enaurs chanted a hymn, and after that the Voice of Jehovih spake out of the light, saying:

6. Whosoever raiseth up My children, do I raise up with Mine own hand. To whomsoever uttereth My words in wisdom and truth, do I speak from My judgment seat. Because ye have come down from your exalted kingdoms in the upper heavens and raised up the drujas of these heavens, so come I from My All Highest Holy Place to raise you up. As ye have prepared to found My Word with mortals, so prepare I here in Hi-rom a heavenly place of delight.

7. Was I not with the I'hins since the creation of man on the earth? And wherein they have been faithful unto Me have I come in great security. Now, behold the earth rose up against My chosen and sought to destroy them, but they failed utterly. And when they cast My faithful servant into the lions' den, yet would he not violate his oath, even though he suffered death. And I stretched forth My hand and took His hat, red with blood, out of the lions' den; and I gave power unto the hat. And into the far-off country of Jaffeth will I take the title of KING OF THE SUN, and bestow it upon Ya'seang, and neither Arabin'ya nor Parsi'e shall endure in holiness.

8. Behold, I give you a new sign, in addition to the triangle, and it shall be the sign of Hi-rom (scarlet hat) from this time forth, signifying, FAITH EVEN UNTO DEATH.

9. The Voice ceased, and Fragapatti turned to the red light and stretched forth his hand and took thereof, saying: OF THY SCARLET, O JEHOVIH! GIVE UNTO THY SERVANT A HI-ROM, AS AN EMBLEM OF THIS HEAVEN! And he fashioned it into a hat without a brim, and laid it on the throne. Presently a swift messenger, from without, desired admittance before Fragapatti, and he was permitted to come. He said:

10. Greeting to thee, O Fragapatti, Son of Jehovih! And by the love of E'och, God of Tshi, in Ude, grade six, am I sent before thee in Jehovih's name. Behold, one Hab-bak is without, who was the wearer of Hi-rom!

11. Fragapatti said: Admit him, and bid him approach the throne of God. The swift messenger retired, and presently returned, bringing in Hab-bak, faithful unto death. And he went up to the throne, and Fragapatti took the scarlet hat, saying: Second only to Jehovih's crown, with Hi-rom, cover I thy head in the name of the Creator! And he placed it on Hab-bak's head, and the light of it was so great that hardly any but ethereans could look upon it.

12. Then Hab-bak said: By this, Thy Power, O Jehovih, will I go now and deliver unto everlasting light the king's soul, of him who slew me. And I will restore the Council also. For they will remember the scarlet hat, and it will be as an anchorage for their

310

crazed minds to rest upon! So Hab-bak saluted on the sign of the triangle and departed.
13. And now was come the time of departure for Fragapatti and his hosts. So he instructed Geth-yo, and bade him travel with him. Then Fragapatti instructed the Council, which was after the manner of his instruction to the preceding Councils. And then he descended to the foot of the throne, and the marshals caused the people to march before him. And Fragapatti created flowers and drapery and ornaments, and gave to every one something as they passed, though there were more than a thousand million souls!
14. And when they had all passed, and resumed the places assigned them, Fragapatti sat down at the foot of the throne in ancient custom, and E'chad descended down to him, taking his hand; and he said unto him: Arise, O Chief, thou Son of the Most High, and go thy way! Fragapatti rose up and departed, followed by the Gods and Goddesses officiating, and they all went into the avalanza and departed, going to the kingdom of Gir-ak-shi, Lord God over Heleste and her heaven.

CHAPTER XXXIX.

1. When Gir-ak-shi arrived at his division of the earth and heaven, the Voice of Jehovih came to him, saying: My Lord and God, hear thou the Voice of thy Father. In thy division I have no I'hins left upon the earth, and the place is like a field without seed. The I'huans have degenerated also, by marrying with the druks. And thou art come to this, My farm, where it is grown up full of weeds and thistles.
2. Look about thy division, and thou shalt find no loo'is, nor ashars of any avail to righteousness. Consider, then, what shall be done, that both mortals and spirits may be made to know Me and My kingdoms.
3. Gir-ak-shi found the mortals of Heleste to be barbarians, many of them naked, or at best clothed with the skins of animals to keep them warm in winter. Some of them burrowed in the ground, and some lived in houses made of bark, and leaves and grass. And their food was mostly fish and flesh. Their cities were numerous, but small, and every city spake a different language.
4. Their weapons of war were clubs, and spears, and bows and arrows, but they had neither iron nor copper, and used stone for cutting.
5. Gir-ak-shi said: What incentive can I give such a people, that will raise them up?
6. Gir-ak-shi then surveyed his heavens, but alas, there were no kingdoms, no organizations, no societies. As mortals lived and died, so continued their spirits around about in the same places. Procuring subsistence in the same way, but spiritually; and often taking part in mortal wars and hunting, seeing and hearing through their mortal kin's eyes and ears.
7. Gir-ak-shi said: What incentive can I give such angels, that will raise them up?
8. If I tell the mortals to till the soil and make clothes of flax and wool, my words will be interpreted as folly, or as implying hardships. If I tell the angels there are higher heavens, more beautiful, my words will be disbelieved. If I tell them that all growth dependeth upon exercise and labor, they will decline to grow. Have I not seen rich men and rich women in other countries whom I told that, in order to rise, they must learn to labor? But they heeded me not.
9. Jehovih said to Gir-ak-shi: Thou hast more than a thousand million drujas in thy

department. The mountains and valleys and forests are filled with them, roving about. As thou wouldst entrap birds by rich bait, so thalt thou gather together all thou canst of these drujas. But as to thy mortals, thou shalt call famines into certain places, and thus drive them to observe the Unseen Cause of things.

10. Gir-ak-shi called together his hosts, millions and millions. He said unto them: Form ye, in sacred circles, hundreds of thousands, and go to the places I will point out, and invoke the higher heavens in Jehovih's name. Cast ye a famine here; and a blight in the animals of the forest. Into the water cast ye imbrele, that the fish may die. Make mortals stop and consider.

11. Let the ashars go, then, and find the most prophetic amongst mortals, and make them prophesy concerning the famines and the blight. Make ye their prophets objects of worship; then I can rule the inhabitants of the earth through the prophets.

12. Concerning the angels, Gir-ak-shi said: Five heavenly places will I build for the drujas. One shall be called Monk, one Acha, one Troy, one Be-yome and one Hellen. Five Lords shall be my Lords to rule in my heavenly divisions: Ki-liope, Lord of Monk; I'tius, Lord of Acha; Foebe, Lordess of Troy; Liriyi, Lordess of Be-yome, and Co'ye, Lord of Hellen. These shall be heavenly places in the mountains, pure and delightful.

13. And ye shall make them places of feasting and sporting for one whole year; nothing that can be done to make them attractive for drujas shall be left undone.

14. Into five divisions, half a million each, shall my hosts be selected and apportioned; whose mission shall be to go around about throughout Heleste, bringing in drujas to my five heavenly places.

15. As for myself, I will build a plateau in these mountains, the Aguaadica, with a Council of half a million. Let my Lords stand aside, and I will apportion to each of them their attendants; by the star-lights that fall upon them shall they be known and come forth.

16. The Lords stood aside, in different places. Gir-ak-shi then cast stars until the three millions were selected. After that Gir-ak-shi proceeded according to the Voice of Jehovih; and he conducted his hosts to the places the Father commanded.

17. After they were all placed, Gir-ak-shi chose his own Council, and built a plateau and a throne to Jehovih on Mount Aguaadica; and when he considered the wisdom of the manner Jehovih had directed him to thus lay a foundation for so great a work, he soliloquized, saying: O Jehovih, will these drujas ever understand the manner of Thine armies? Will these mortals ever understand the proceedings of Thy Lords and Gods?

18. For one year the hosts entertained and fed and clothed the drujas sumptuously, and they won them away from the earth; won them to the kingdoms prepared for them. And then Gir-ak-shi commanded the founding of schools, factories and hospitals in heaven; and he appointed ashars and asaphs, and began the resurrection through his Lords. And by the fourth year he had colonized in his heaven nearly all the drujas, giving them sufficient recreation to restrain them from returning to the earth.

19. For a long time prior to Fragapatti's coming he had it proclaimed, giving invitations to them to be present. This he communicated to Fragapatti, through messengers. So, Fragapatti, knowing the grade of the place, determined to come in gaudy colors, and with sufficient music, very loud, and for the manifestation of power.

20. To match which, Gir-ak-shi had his people attire themselves in the greatest gaudy colors; for in such manner do the unlearned judge of the glory and possibilities of high

heaven.

21. So, it came to pass, Fragapatti's avalanza descended from above like a sea of fire, but decorated in thousands of ways with banners, flags, curtains and such other ornaments as would convey the idea of greatness to the minds of the es'yans. On the other hand, Gir-ak-shi had decorated his place and kingdom and throne, Aguaadica, in the most extravagant splendor. And he and his Lords, and his captains and generals, and his holy Council, were arrayed majestically.

22. In addition to these things, Gir-ak-shi had provided a feast, which was to succeed the ceremonies; and, after the feast, there were to be divers entertainments. But of these matters, who knoweth the thought of Jehovih! How hath He not provided ingenuities to bring the dark soul to understanding!

23. Gir-ak-shi said: To teach mortal teachers how to teach the barbarian, O Jehovih! To teach Cold-Awe to impart Warm-Mirth, O Jehovih! Shall they build a prison and decorate the convict in fine clothes, and bid him take his ease, beholding the virtuous working for him, O Jehovih! Will they ever learn Thy power in resurrection, O Jehovih!

CHAPTER XL.

1. Fragapatti and his hosts remained thirty days with Gir-ak-shi, and great was the enjoyment of the people; and then Fragapatti departed, going to the kingdoms of Uropa, first Goddess of a barbarian division of the earth. The Voice of Jehovih had been with her from the first, but there were but few corporeans in her division, and only six hundred million angels, mostly drujas.

2. Nevertheless, Jehovih said unto Uropa: Thou shalt found here a kingdom in My name, and it shall become mighty in heaven and earth. Uropa said: What is the first best way, O Jehovih? Jehovih answered, saying: As for the drujas, thou knowest. But as for the corporeans, behold, they have neither copper nor iron, but use stone. Send, therefore, of thy hosts of ashars, five hundred who are well skilled in the art of inspiring mortals, to Arabin'ya; and thou shalt cause fifty men to migrate into thy lands. And the fifty men shall be such as are skilled in mining and working copper and iron.

3. And thy ashars shall inspire them to go to the mountains and find the ore, and then to work the same, to make tools of, and to make implements for hunting and fishing.

4. So Uropa sent angels to Arabin'ya, and they inspired fifty men to go to Uropa, and find copper and iron, and work it. And in the space of four years, behold, there had gone out of Arabin'ya not less than twenty thousand men. And the ashars inspired them to marry with the druks and half-breed I'huans. And in this way a new people of higher light was born into Uropa's division.

5. In Zeigl Uropa build her heavenly kingdom and founded the city of Oitch. Five hundred thousand angels were her holy Council, and fifty thousand captains; and of ashars, two millions, partly ethereans and partly atmosphereans.

6. Her heavenly kingdom was of the kind and manner of Gir-ak-shi's, and her administration in the same way. And in four years she had rescued nearly all the drujas in these regions of atmospherea. So when Fragapatti came to see her, she provided entertainments after the same manner as did Ger-ak-shi, having all her hosts present.

7. After this Fragapatti visited Kow'anea and his heavenly kingdoms, and also his earth

divisions. Next Fragapatti visited M'wing'mi and his heavenly kingdoms and earth divisions. Next he visited Ots'ha'ta and his places, and then Soo'fwa.

8. With all these Lords and Gods Fragapatti spent many days, examining and recording all the labor done; and he spake before them all, so that his voice was heard by nearly all the people in the lower heavens. And so great was the work accomplished by Fragapatti with any one of these Lords or Gods, that were a history thereof written it would require the whole lifetime of a man to read it. Nor is it possible with earth words to describe the beauty and glory of a single one of these recreations in his travels.

CHAPTER XLI.

1. The close of dawn was near at hand. Fragapatti returned to Mouru, the heavenly kingdom of Haraiti, in atmospherea, richly stored with a knowledge of the earth and her heavens. The capital was illuminated, and the decorum of the higher heavens prevailed.

2. Already were there assembled more than four thousand million angels prepared for the third resurrection. Fragapatti sent word to his Lord Gods, and to his Lords and Gods, and to Samati, God in inherent right up to the end of dawn. And he notified all of them of the day and hour when he should accomplish the resurrection.

3. And then Fragapatti called his swift messengers, whose labor is with the thrones of Jehovih in etherea. He said: Behold, the dawn of dan is near the close. The Brides and Bridegrooms of Jehovih will number ten thousand million souls. Two divisions will I make of grades fifty-five and seventy, for the forests and plains of Goomatchala. This ye shall communicate to Hoseis, Goddess of Alawatcha, on the road of Affolkistan, saluting in Jehovih's name, and of His Son, Fragapatti, Chief.

4. The swift messengers saluted, and then departed. Next he called the messengers for the kingdoms below, and of these messengers there were twenty thousand, divided into twelve groups, and they had been previously apportioned to certain divisions of heaven and earth.

5. To them Fragapatti said: To the Lord God of each division, and to the Lords and Gods, and through them to the officers under them, greeting, in the name of Jehovih! Appoint and anoint the successors in Jehovih's name; and when your kingdom is in order, appear ye at the throne of Mouru, for the resurrection of my hosts is near at hand. Provide ye ships and such vessels as are suitable, and bring, as visitors, from your kingdoms and most holy places, as many atmosphereans as desire to come, that they may witness the ceremonies and the ascent of Jehovih's Sons and Daughters.

6. And these commandments were carried unto all the divisions of the corporeal earth and her heavens. Fragapatti then said unto Athrava: Thou shalt receive the Brides and Bridegrooms. As for myself, I will go down to the earth and receive God and Zarathustra, and they shall be borne in mine own ship even unto this place, and thence to etherea.

7. In all places on earth and in heaven the spirit inhabitants were stirred to the utmost. In Haraiti there were already more than four thousand colonies, and every one had thousands and thousands eligible to the third resurrection, who would depart in the coming ascension. Of these there were persons of every occupation, and they were perfect in their order, belonging to groups and series of groups. And now the captains and generals were re-organizing them into phalanxes; and the Gods again organizing the phalanxes into

kingdoms.

8. Zeredho sent her contributions to Haraiti, four hundred million souls. The Lord Gods were making their groups in their own several divisions, to be further organized after arriving at Mouru, the place whence the final ascension would take place. Some of these had a thousand millions of their own resurrection, including whom they had previously sent to Haraiti.

9. Fragapatti sent special messengers to God, Samati, to learn the day appointed for Zarathustra's death; and he further allotted to Zarathustra three days in hada, in which to preach to mortals by the inspiration of God, and appointed the fourth day thereafter as the time of his ascension from the earth.

10. And now, when all these matters had been put in shape, Fragapatti ordered the assembling of the sacred circle of the Holy Council, Sons and Daughters of the Most High. The lights were raised, and only Gods and Goddesses could remain in sight of, or near the throne of Jehovih. Fragapatti commanded Hoab to stand in the midst of the circle, facing the judgment seat.

11. Fragapatti said: Hear the words of thy Creator, O Hoab. I called thee up out of the ground, and with Mine Own spirit quickened I thee into life. From thy youth up I have followed thee day by day. I have called out to thee from My holy hill; with a woman's tenderness came I after thee. When thou didst try to run away from me, I followed after. Yea, I called My Son, high raised in My everlasting kingdoms, and I said unto him: O My Son, run thou quickly, for Hoab, My well-beloved, runneth away from Me. Go thou and bring him; for he is my Chosen.

12. He shall be My God of the red star; her heavens shall bow down before him. I will raise him up and anoint him with My holy fire; his countenance shall shine like a sun in My firmament.

13. And Fragapatti, My Son, overtook thee in thy flight; with great cunning he captured thee unto My labors. And thou hast raised up thy voice and glorified Me; thine arms have been bared to the harvest; thy fruit is a song of glory.

14. Have I not given thee experience in all things? Even to the precipice of hell made I thee to walk and fall not. The darkness of everlasting death I made to encompass thee; in the hour of thy despair I came to thee and raised thee up.

15. Have I not great profit in thee, My Son? My countless millions cry out in all places; they behold Me not; they know not of Me and My heavenly places. Like a troubled sea that knoweth no rest, the voices of mortals and angels forever cry out: There is no light!

16. Wherefore, then, was I not wise in thee, O Hoab? I made thee of strong limb, and with arms that reach far; thy judgment I fashioned for the great multitudes.

17. I say to the bird, the young bird with feathers: Fly! And it goeth away. I say to man: Go forth, in My name! But he looketh around. Again I say to him: Go forth! But he turneth to his neighbor for his opinion. Again I speak, calling: Come to Me! But he standeth wondering. Again I say: Come! But he saith: By and by. Again I say: Come! He replieth: I have not all light! Again I call, and he saith: Alas, there is nothing!

18. And he goeth down in darkness; he curseth Me and accuseth Me of errors! He preacheth My shortness, but in his words cutteth himself off from Me. In the foul-smelling place of his darkness, My holy angels cannot come; he burroweth himself in stubbornness that is blind and deaf.

19. But I blow My breath upon the earth and the stars; I drive them into new roads in the firmament of heaven. Into the dwelling-places of My high Gods I drive them as chaff before the wind. And when the light of My heavens hath cleared away the darkness, I send My Gods with great power.

20. To this end have I raised thee up, O Hoab. My shield is upon thee; thou shalt wear the triangle of the red star; two hundred years shalt thou hold dominion over the earth and her heavens. In My name speak, O Hoab!

21. Then spake Hoab, saying: Thy Voice is upon me, O Father! My limbs are weak; my hands tremble like an old man that is palsied. Behold, I have sought in vain to find anything perfect in me; I am as a trumpet that is bruised and split; there is no harmony or power within me.

22. Thou first gavest me a wife and sons and daughters to rule over and to raise up for Thy glory, but I failed utterly. My wife saw not with my eyes, nor heard with my ears, nor judged with my judgment; we were like two instruments, broken and out of tune. As for my sons, they went astray, like sheep without a herdsman; my advice was as weak to them as the shadow is to the tree. And my daughters went away from my love, and chose young men, even before my eyes.

23. Then I cried out unto Thee, saying: O Jehovih, why gavest Thou me a kingdom? Behold, it is scattered and gone! Then I went down into the grave in sorrow. But Thy hand raised up my soul in heaven; and Thou gavest me another kingdom. But my people would not see through my eyes nor hear through my ears. Then I sought to know if my eyes were not wrong, and my ears wrong, and my judgment wrong.

24. And I turned about, like one who is lost in a forest, and shutteth his eyes as to the direction of the sun, going by the sound of a multitude of tongues. And my kingdom drew a boundary around itself, and shut out all light. But Thy Son came and delivered me and my people.

25. Behold, I was as weak as a child; in my weakness Thy light came upon me. Never more shall I desire others to see through my eyes, or hear through my ears, or judge by my judgment. Thou hast healed me of my infirmity, O Jehovih. Only by one Eye can things be seen through; by one Ear can things be heard through; by one Judgment can things be judged.

26. Thou hast said: Go forth in My name! I will go, O Father! Thou hast said: Thou shalt have dominion over the earth and her heavens! This will I accomplish also, by Thy Light and Power, O Jehovih!

27. Then spake Jehovih through Fragapatti, saying: Accept the earth, O Hoab, My Son, My God! It is thine to keep and to rule over! Accept atmospherea, O Hoab, My Son, My God! It is thine to keep and to rule over!

28. Hoab said: I will be Thy Son, O Jehovih! I will be Thy God, O Jehovih! From Thee I accept the earth to keep and to rule over! From Thee I accept the earth's heavens, to keep and to rule over! Again Jehovih spake through Fragapatti, saying:

29. What thou doest henceforth do thou in My name, for it is of Me and is Me in thee!

30. Hoab said: What I do henceforth do I in Thy name, O Jehovih! For I know it is Thee in me that doeth all glorious things!

31. Jehovih spake through Fragapatti, saying: With Mine Own hands weave I a crown for thee My Son, My God of the red star! I place it on thy head for the glory of My kingdoms,

which are endless in number and full of holiness! Wear thou My Crown, for it is with Wisdom and Power!

32. Then Fragapatti's hands were waved about by the Great Spirit, and a crown was woven and placed on Hoab's head, and it was brilliant and white, studded with countless millions of gems. Hoab said: Crown from Thy hand, O Father! I accept it and wear it, emblem of Thy kingdoms, endless in number and full of holiness. I know that Thou wilt ever be with me in Wisdom and Power! I will glorify Thee forever! My kingdoms shall glorify Thee forever!

33. The chief marshal now conducted Hoab to the throne of Jehovih, which had been previously vacated, and Hoab sat in the midst of the throne. In the meantime, the es'enaurs chanted a hymn of glory. Hoab then said: Fragapatti, Son of Jehovih, Orian Chief, come thou and honor my throne in the name of the Father. Then Fragapatti went to the throne and sat thereon. Next Hoab called up Athrava, then Hapacha, and then other Gods and Goddesses.

34. And now, whilst the Council held, Fragapatti said: Behold, the time of the death of Zarathustra hath come. Be ye here, and I will go quickly down to the earth and receive God and him, and the hosts of God and his Lords.

35. So Fragapatti departed, and sailed swiftly down to Parsi'e, on the earth, and came to the place of meeting of the corporeans who had charge of the Holy Word. And it was on the morning of the fourth day after Zarathustra's death. For three days and nights his spirit had been preaching to the Faithists, explaining the kingdoms of Jehovih.

36. So Fragapatti called unto God, saying: Behold, my Son, thy labor is done. In thee have I great delight. Behold, my ship lieth by the river; my lights are raised for the everlasting thrones! God (Samati) said: It is finished! That that thou didst put upon me I have done! Behold, here standeth Zarathustra, my Son.

37. Zarathustra was then taking leave of his corporeal friends, for his soul was fast becoming illuminated. Yea, he had looked up and beheld the ship of All Light, and he knew now the Voice of the Father.

38. So Fragapatti went and took Zarathustra in his arms, saying: Come, my beloved. Thy home is yonder! So, they went into the ship of fire and ascended to Mouru.

CHAPTER XLII.

1. And now the Lord Gods, and Lords and Gods, began to arrive in Mouru. The marshals, and their officers and workmen, had extended the landing-places for the hosts of ships; receivers had been appointed and allotted their various places. Heralds and messengers had been provided with places of announcement; and lines of intercommunion had been laid, so that the words of heralds and messengers could be heard by all the millions in waiting.

2. Be it known, O angels and mortals, such is the glory of Jehovih's works that, stand where ye will, His kingdoms are always seeming above. As ye of the earth look upward and behold the stars, so they that live on the stars look upward to see the earth. If, therefore, ye were receiving messengers from the stars, it would seem to you that they came downward; but to them, as if they rose upward, even until near the landing-place, when it would be downward to them also. Because the feet of a mortal or the feet of an

angel are on the foundation of his place, and because his head standeth in the opposite way from his feet.

3. First came Ardi'atta, Goddess over the spirits that had been delivered out of the hells of Aoasu by Fragapatti and Hoab, housed in Zeredho and Haraiti. And with her, her successor, Gaipon, manager of the hosts. Ardi'atta brought one thousand and three hundred millions of souls in her ship, mostly visitors who had been delivered out of hell. Besides these, were twenty millions raised to light, clothed as Brides and Bridegrooms of Jehovih. These latter were the harvest of Ardi'atta, and in her charge. The receivers of her ship stationed it in its place, and then the receivers of her hosts conducted them to their places.

4. And now came E'chad, Lord God of Arabin'ya, in his ship, with more than four thousand million souls, half of whom were Brides and Bridegrooms. His ship was received by the proper officers, and stationed in its place; and his hosts received by the proper persons, and conducted to their respective places. With the Brides and Bridegrooms E'chad entered the south wing of the capital; and E'chad's successor was with the visiting hosts. When E'chad entered before the throne, Fragapatti saluted him on the sign Jehovih's Rest, and E'chad answered in The Glory of Evening!

5. Before the hosts of E'chad were landed and placed, there came Ots-ha-ta, Lord of North Oceya, with his successor, in a ship of thirty millions, of whom Ots-ha-ta had two million Brides and Bridegrooms. His ship was received and stationed in its place; and his hosts received and assigned to their places.

6. In the meantime, Kow'anea, God of South Guatama, came in his ship, with his successor, bringing seven hundred million souls, of whom Kow'anea had sixty million Brides and Bridegrooms. And they were received by the proper officers and assigned to their places.

7. Hardly had Kow'anea landed, when Yaton'te came, with his successor and his hosts. Yaton'te's ship was the most beautiful of all that had yet arrived. His hosts were four thousand million souls; but of Brides and Bridegrooms he had but thirty millions. Him Fragapatti saluted on the sign of Star of the West, and Yaton'te answered in the sign of the Golden Circle! He and his hosts were then assigned their places.

8. Now came M'wing'mi, God of South Oceya, and his little ship was laden with four hundred million souls, and he had three million Brides and Bridegrooms. His ship was received and stationed in its place, and his hosts received and stationed in their places.

9. Next came Soo'fwa, God of Japan and her heavens. His was the most brilliant of all the ships, and he had three thousand five hundred million souls aboard, of whom two hundred millions were Brides and Bridegrooms. His ship was received and stationed, and his hosts also; and when he entered before the throne, Fragapatti saluted him on the sign of Before the Ancients! And Soo'fwa answered him in the sign of Little Star!

10. And now the most loved of all came, Uropa, Goddess of the barbarians! Her ship was the swiftest and best trimmed, and she brought one thousand million souls, of whom she had eighty million Brides and Bridegrooms as her harvest. When she entered before the throne of Jehovih, leading in her Brides and Bridegrooms, Fragapatti saluted on the sign, Persistent Fire! And Uropa answered him in the sign, Jehovih's Trust!

11. Now came great Ah'oan, Lord God of Jaffeth and her heavens. His ship was the largest of all, and he brought five thousand million souls, of whom nearly two thousand

millions were Brides and Bridegrooms. When he came before Jehovih's throne, Fragapatti saluted him on the sign, THE POWER OF LOVE! Ah'oan answered him in the sign, EVERLASTING LIFE!

12. And now the ship of Gir-ak-shi came in, bringing a thousand million souls, of whom eighty millions were Brides and Bridegrooms.

13. Besides there were seventy and six other Gods, from departments of the grand divisions of the heavens, bringing, some five million souls and some even twenty millions. And there were Lords of islands and Lords of small places on the earth, who had also come in small ships, bringing, some five and some ten million souls. And all these Gods and Lords had Brides and Bridegrooms according to the place and number and condition whence they came. And they were all received and stationed in their proper places.

14. Thus there came to Mouru upward of thirty thousand million atmosphereans that had sprung up from the earth by Jehovih's will; and of these there were ten thousand millions and eight hundred million spirits prepared as Brides and Bridegrooms unto the Great Spirit. Besides these, there were the hosts of Fragapatti, the ethereans, ten millions, mostly Gods and Goddesses, and these formed the inner sacred circle of the Holy Council. Next to these were their successors, ten millions, who were to be the Holy Council of Mouru after the ascension. And next outside of these were stationed the Lord Gods and their attendants, behind whom stood their Brides and Bridegrooms. Next stood the Gods and their attendants, and Brides and Bridegrooms; and then the Lords, their attendants, and their Brides and Bridegrooms.

15. And next outside of these stood the successors, the Gods and Lords, with their attendants; and yet behind them, their visiting hosts. And within and amongst them all, the musicians, the marshals, messengers, swift messengers and heralds were assigned their respective places. But so vast was the multitude of angels, and so great the glory, that one might look thereon all day and not even see the millionth part; nor is it possible for corporeal words to convey but a crude picture of the magnificent scene.

CHAPTER XLIII.

1. God, that is Samati, said: In my hands gavest thou the red star and her heavens, O Jehovih! As an emblem of Thy first three worlds, and of the first, second and third resurrections, Thy Sons, bestowed upon me the triangle. Behold, the time of my reign hath come to an end. With Thy holy harvest Thou callest me to a higher world.

2. But Thou hast raised up Thy Son, Hoab, who is of great Wisdom and Power in Thee. He shall be Thy God and Thy Son in the places I have been. To him, in Thy name, O Father, I bestow the triangle, symbol of Thee and of Thy created worlds, and of the individuals thereof. By my parting with it is the end of this dawn recorded; by Hoab's reception of it is his dominion begun.

3. God then took off the triangle and hung it on Hoab's neck, saying: I salute thee, God of earth and heaven! Immediately the es'enaurs chanted, HAIL TO THEE, O GOD, SON OF JEHOVIH!

4. Now during the time of the arrival of the hosts of Gods and Lords and their resurrections, there were to be seen, high in the firmament above, two stars, like twins,

319

descending. These were the avalanzas of Hoseis, Goddess of Alawatcha, coming to receive the Brides and Bridegrooms of Jehovih, to take them to the etherean realms prepared for them by the Orians of the higher heavens.

5. Her avalanzas were descending by the road of Affolkistan, and coming swiftly. Now betwixt the glory of these lights, and the ceremonies in Mouru, one knew not where best to look, for the awe and grandeur on every side was overwhelming. And not less to move so vast a host were the es'enaurs, the singers, and the far-off trumpeters. There stood also the great multitude of Brides and Bridegrooms, arrayed in white, like a vast sea of white, more than ten thousand millions!

6. But not long the waiting was, for so the Gods time their labors that every adventure fitteth to another. The twin stars grew and grew in size, till, like two suns descending, they seemed as wide as the borders of Haraiti! And whilst the multitude thus gazed and watched, Fragapatti rose in his place on the throne and called out, saying:

7. Behold, the time hath now arrived for the brotherhood of Gods and Lords to be bestowed upon the earth and her heavens. As the earth is divided into many sections, so have I bequeathed on the earth many Lords, to hold dominion over mortals; and yet over all of these have I chosen and appointed one God.

8. For in this manner were the first heavenly kingdoms of the red star founded by Sethantes, Son of Jehovih. In the history that followed since his day, it hath turned out that first one Lord and then another lost power in his kingdom, and finally, even the Gods were powerless to rule angels and mortals to righteousness.

9. That ye may henceforth be strong, like the heavenly kingdoms on other worlds, I now decree Diva, in the name of Jehovih! And God and his Lord Gods and his Gods and Lords of divisions, shall comprise the Diva; nor shall any other person be eligible to the order, neither of this world nor of any other world; male and female shall be the members of Diva.

10. And he who is God, who was Hoab, high raised from Zeredho, shall be Div over all the rest. Nevertheless, the name Div shall be used by all the members of Diva, when abiding in their several dominions. But no other person, neither on earth or in heaven, shall be entitled to the rank of Div.

11. And the Diva shall meet thrice every earth year, and in this capital, Mouru, to render unto one another the matters of their several dominions; and when the meetings take place, each and every Lord and God, and Lordess and Goddess, shall be present and fulfill these, my commandments.

12. And when the members are thus assembled, Div only shall have the title of Div; and the members shall salute him as Div, Son of All Light. And the meetings of the Diva shall be private; nor shall any person be eligible to be present in Diva, save the novices who may be in preparation to become Lords and Gods by succession. But none of the novices shall be entitled to speak in Diva.

13. And each and every member of Diva shall report his department, as to whether in need of assistance, or his capacity to provide emigrants to other plateaux, and such report shall be made in person before Div; and when all the reports are given in, then shall Div render judgment thereon, giving to or exacting from any one or more of the dominions, according to the Voice of Jehovih.

14. And the judgments of Div, Son of All Light, shall be called Divan law, from which

there shall be no appeal. And the Lords and Gods shall carry these decrees down to mortals, in their several dominions, rendering them unto the God-irs on earth, whereby mortals through the Rab'bah shall receive communion from the All Light.

15. In the time of the assembling of Diva, swift messengers shall be present and witness all the laws that shall be passed; and immediately thereafter shall such swift messengers depart from Mouru and come to the etherean kingdoms in the roadway of the earth and her heavens, and render the same unto the nearest Orian Chief, or other etherean God, Son of Jehovih.

16. To the end, therefore, that my commandments shall be in the name of Jehovih, let God and Lord Gods, and Gods and Lords, and Goddesses and Lordesses, approach the Father's throne, that I may bestow them according to the rites and ceremonies of the Gods of other corporeal and atmospherean worlds.

17. The marshals now conducted all of them, save God, before the throne: First, Thulae, then Es'pacia, then Geth'ya, and so on, until the hosts of the dominions were before Fragapatti. And then God (Hoab) rose up and faced toward the west. Fragapatti said:

18. In Thy name, O All Light, do I create a Diva unto the earth and her heavens; and this, Thy God, I anoint as Div, with power to him to anoint his successor in like manner. May Thy Voice and Judgment be with him forever! And these, Thy Lord Gods, and these, Thy Gods and Thy Lords, and these, Thy Goddesses and Thy Lordesses, do I anoint as members of Diva; and to each and all of them give I power in Thy name to appoint successors after them for Thy allotted seasons. May Thy Wisdom and Power be with them forever. Amen!

19. God said: In Thy name, O All Light, do I accept the Diva. And, on behalf of my Gods and Lords, proclaim Thy Divan Power unto heaven and earth.

20. The others responded: We will fulfill thy decrees, O All Light, now and henceforth, forever. Be Thou with us in wisdom and strength for Thy glory!

21. Fragapatti then extended his hand upward, saying: Inqua git s'ang, of Thy Inqua git s'ang, O All Light! (Dominion within dominion, give me Thy symbol, O Jehovih!) And there came out of the light before the throne a substance, and Fragapatti seized it and formed therefrom, first, a hollow ball, and within it another ball; and second, two interlocked triangles; and he gave to each of the Diva a pair, that is, a ball within a ball and a triangle; and he said unto them:

22. Behold, O Jehovih, Thou didst call me from my high place in heaven, saying: Go thou to the red star, the earth; her soil is wet with human blood! Her heavens are dead; My harvest is nothing! And I came and delivered Thy Word to mortals; in blood gave I it, and then washed clean the whole earth. And I gathered together Thy lost children in the lower heavens, and have raised them up with power. Whereof, in token of Thy Light that was within me, have I become one within Thy labors, and I have raised up Gods and Lords in Thee also; that one perfect thing may be within another, after the manner of Thy created worlds, this, Thy holy sign, do I bequeath unto them, to be theirs and their successors' forever!

23. So Fragapatti bestowed the Lords and Gods, and his labors were finished.

24. In the meantime, the sun-ships of Hoseis drew near and landed, both to south and west of Mouru, and so mighty and full of grandeur were they, the thousands of millions looking on were breathless in awe and wonder. Then descended out of the fire-ships the

marshals of Hoseis' hosts, of whom there were thirty millions aboard. And they spread a frowas from the ship even to Jehovih's throne, and Hoseis alighted from the ship and walked briskly forward on the frowas, and Fragapatti and his hosts went and received her, and conducted her to the throne.

25. And now, after due ceremonies betwixt the Gods and Goddesses, Athrava rose up and said: To thee, O Hoseis, Goddess of Alawatcha, in the name of Jehovih, do I bestow the Brides and Bridegrooms of heaven and earth. They are the harvest of Samati, God of the division of Haniostu, his Lords and Gods through the Orian Chief, Fragapatti, for the Father's emancipated heavens!

26. Hoseis said: Brides and Bridegrooms of Jehovih, in His name receive I you, to deliver unto the All High Worlds.

27. And then Hoseis and Athrava proceeded in the ceremonies in the usual way, and were responded to by the ten thousand million Brides and Bridegrooms.

28. When the ceremonies were finished, the time of the ascension was at hand. So Fragapatti and Hoseis, accompanied by their Gods and Lords, went down to the foot of the throne and sat down, and God, that had been Hoab, sat alone in the midst of the throne. The es'enaurs then sang a hymn on THE MARCH OF JEHOVIH'S WORLDS! When it was concluded, God went down and took Fragapatti's hand and Hoseis' hand, saying: Arise, O Son, and thou, O Daughter of Jehovih! The Father calleth! Go your way! Fragapatti and Hoseis rose up, and then all the Gods and Lords rose up.

29. Hoab, that is God, fell into Fragapatti's arms! And when they had embraced, God withdrew and returned to the throne. Fragapatti saluted him on the sign, FAITHIST, and God answered him in the sign, FOREVER! Whereupon the hosts followed after Fragapatti and Hoseis, and entered the great avalanzas.

30. Fragapatti gave his own avalanza to Athrava and his attendants, and they took from it the magnet and made it rotary also. And when they were all aboard, Hoseis commanded the ascension, and the mighty fire-ships rose up, turning and rising.

31. Fragapatti created flowers and drapery, and cast overboard sufficient, so that all the twenty thousand millions remaining had every one some memento. In a little while the resurrection was complete; the sun-ships rose higher and higher; passing the earth's vortex and entering etherea, going to the kingdoms prepared for them by the high-raised Sons and Daughters of Jehovih!

END OF THE BOOK OF FRAGAPATTI.

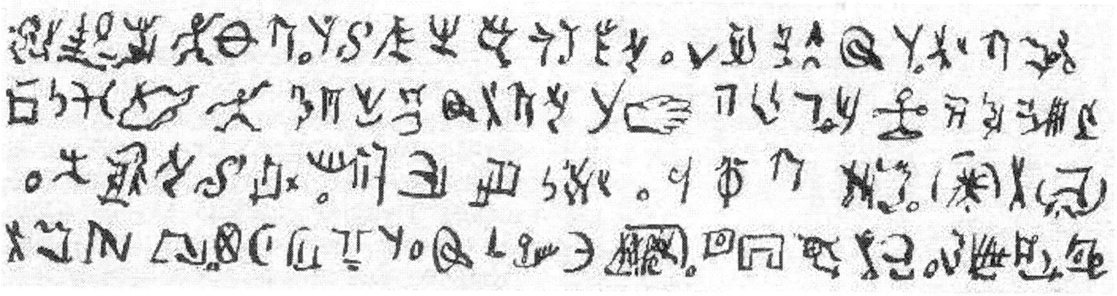

PLATE 13.

THE SIGNATURE

BOOK OF GOD'S WORD.

BEING COTEMPORANEOUS WITH THE CYCLE OF FRAGAPATTI, SON OF JEHOVIH. AS THE UPPER BOOK IS OF HEAVENLY THINGS, SO IS THE LOWER BOOK OF THE EARTHLY ADMINISTRATION OF GOD FOR THE SAME PERIOD OF TIME. AND IT IS CALLED THE BOOK OF GOD'S WORD, BECAUSE IT IS OF THE FIRST DESCENT OF GOD TO THE EARTH TO ESTABLISH HIS WORD WITH MAN. THROUGH ZARATHUSTRA, A MAN OF PAR'SI'E, CAME GOD TO THIS END, EIGHT THOUSAND NINE HUNDRED YEARS BEFORE THE KOSMON ERA.

CHAPTER I.

1. Hear My word, O man, saith I'hua'Mazda. Perceive My utterances in things that have been and that will be. Remember the lapse of time; open thy understanding to the substance of the affairs of the ancients.

2. Quibble not on names, saith I'hua'Mazda. Nor on places, nor words. All places are My places; all words, My words; all names, My names. All truth is My speech. All fact is My voice. By My commandments shall all the nations of the earth be made to know Me and My works.

3. The Master of the I'huans, Samati, High God of heaven, whose home was in Mount Vibhraj, a heaven created in heaven, a thousand miles high.

4. I'hua'Mazda said: How shall they know me, I, Holy Mazda? They are sealed up; their souls blind as death. Behold, the king, high ruler of Oas, king So-qi? Valorous with a strong sword. So-qi! So-qi! I call, but he heareth not. I go to the temple; it is closed against God, I'hua'Mazda!

5. Where are the altars of thy God? The place of the holy dance. So-qi heareth not. None can hear the Voice of I'hua'Mazda. Angels and Gods are scouted.

6. O man, canst thou measure swords with thy Creator? O that thou couldst open the curtains of heaven, and see! What is thy little learning? Shall a chick that is not hatched discourse on the philosophy of life?

7. Behold, O man, I have told thee that the natural senses cannot understand spiritual things. But I will reach thee; thou vain city, Oas. Thou, king So-qi! Thy sword shall fall from the hilt; thy mandates be as a breath blown away.

8. Hear me, O man, saith I'hua'Mazda: I opened the door a little, that thou mightst learn a little about the stars. And now thou art puffed up; vain boaster of thy knowledge, thou slammest the door in the face of thy Master!

9. Thou hast gone in darkness; a driveler to familiar spirits; lazy and longing to die. Then I said to thee: Behold, it is a good world; go, then, and be wise. Quickly thou wert changed; bewailing the stupidity of the ancients. What better art thou? Because I delivered thee from darkness, thou killest my prophets.

10. I'hua'Mazda said: I make thee free, O man, but thou deniest My person. When I suffer thee to fall in bondage, thou criest: O God, my God! When I deliver thee into freedom, thou goest with a sword and spear to lay thy fellows in death.

11. Hear, me, O man, what I have done for thee, saith I'hua'Mazda. Of A'su I cleft a rib and stood it up, saying: Be thou a man, upright in likeness of thy God. And My Voice made thee; what thou art, but was not, proveth I am. I said: Save thy seed, O man. I'hin stood aloof from the Asu'ans, and was holy; but thy brother, dwelt with them and brought

forth unto destruction.

12. Be admonished, saith I'hua'Mazda. I smote the earth and broke it as an egg is broken; for I would cut loose the bound in heaven. Then all the tribes of men cried out: There is a Mazda! An All Power Unseen!

CHAPTER II.

1. In those days when an army captured a large city, slaying the people, they carried back the spoil to So-qi, king of Oas, capital of Par'si'e, and received rewards according to the amount of plunder. The wars were between the different nations of I'huans. The sacred people, the I'hins, had nothing; they were unmolested.

2. I said: Whosoever lieth up treasures in this world, shall find no peace! But ye have built so great a city, ye hope nothing can break it down. Now I will show thee, O king: thy city shall prove the weakest of cities. I will raise up one man out of the seed of the I'hins; and, Oas, the mighty city, shall fall before his hand.

3. I'hua'Mazda, God of heaven, sent certain loo'is, highly learned angels, to look around, and afterward he called them and asked what they saw? They said: Work! Work! Ihua'Mazda said: Work it shall be! Go ye, holy masters of generations, down to mortals close around the city of Oas. And search ye out seed of the I'hin race, and by inspiration lead them to the fairest daughters of I'hua, in the city of Oas; and they shall be tempted, and anon a quickened fruit shall ripen in the city, sons and daughters. Again go ye to the I'hins, and by inspiration bring others and have them tempted by the improved fruit. And yet again repeat this method, and in the sixth generation ye shall raise up a son having the gifts of su'is and sar'gis, and ye shall call him Zarathustra.

4. The loo'is, the angels who were guardians over mortals for such purpose, went and accomplished what had been commanded by God. And the child's mother's name was Too'che, and the father's name Lo'ab. Too'che was su'is born herself, and was by Sa'moan, an angel, obsessed before she conceived, and during the time of maternity not suffered to wake from her unconscious trance. And by the loo'is, her soul was oft taken to high heaven to behold its glories, and then to return and inhabit her own body. Thus, the child was born of All Light, and in that same day the obsession fled, and Too'che proclaimed within the city that no man was father to the child, but that she conceived from All Light, believing, because unconscious in gestation.

5. The learned men cast the horoscope, but found nothing in the stars to alarm the kings, or worthy of credence to the maiden's story. The loo'is went before God, saying: Behold, a child is born, capable of All Light. Then spake God, saying: I will come; go ye and lead the way.

6. When yet the child nursed, I'hua'Mazda spake through the child, whilst its own spirit slept. Then again came the learned men, chief of whom was Asha, son of Zista, learned in a thousand stars and all living creatures, and in the bones of animals no longer living. So Asha spake to Too'che, saying: Canst thy suckling talk? Whereupon God answered him, saying:

7. Not the child, but I, even I'hua'Mazda. Think not, O man, these small lips utter words prompted by this child's soul. I am come to stay the cruel hand of war; to make man know there is an Unseen Master. Behold, this child hath no sex! He is an Yeshuah (Iesu), a

324

passionless birth.

8. To which Asha said: Can it be this woman hath a man hidden under her cloak, and hopes to evade the just punishment of the king! O, thou harlot! That toldest a shameful tale of conception without a man! Thy lies are now added to others to make good the first. Out of the city, wretch! or thou shalt be stoned to death, and thy child with thee!

9. Too'che made no answer, save with a flood of tears. Then spake I'hua'Mazda, saying: Hold thy hand on these lips, and perceive thou how I gesticulate with these little hands. Yea, take thou the little form in thine own arms.

10. Then Asha feared, but fain would hide his fear, and so took the child, whilst I'hua'Mazda spake, saying: O man, that thou couldst behold the spirit, and would temper thy judgment down to patience and wisdom!

11. Asha said: If it be in truth thou art the Mazda of the I'huan race, why hast thou come in so questionable weakness? What can a child do? Wieldest thou a sword with these little hands? I had hoped to see a God come in stronger shape, and in majesty of a thousand angels, winged, and in flames of fire!

12. I'hua'Mazda said: My wisdom is not man's wisdom; my weapons, not arrows and sharp swords. What is great in man's judgment is as nothing to me; what is as nothing to man, I will make great, for I shall overturn this mighty city. Because I am come in peace and love, the city shall be divided, man against man, and bloody war run riot in this walled kingdom.

13. Asha said: To what end art thou come? For if it be true thou art a God born in this questionable shape, thou hast some motive more than to overthrow the town. I charge thee, then, most precocious youth, tell me what thy purpose is, that justice may be done?

14. I'hua'Mazda said: The cities of man are as nothing in my sight; I come to teach man of other worlds, and that the souls of the righteous shall live forever; I come to deliver man from darkness into everlasting light.

15. Asha said: Thy words are wisdom, or else my sudden surprise hath unfitted my judgment. I will go now, that I may reflect on this wonder. To-morrow I will come again. Keep this matter quietly. For if it be known that I, of so high estate, have talked in temperance on spiritual things, I will be doomed to death.

CHAPTER III.

1. When Asha had gone, I'hua'Mazda spake to Too'che, the virgin mother, saying: Take thou thy child away and hide thyself, lest the king have thee and thy child put to death. So Too'che departed with her child, and hid away in another part of the city.

2. Now Asha went direct to So-qi, the king, and related what had transpired. When he had finished, the king said: According to the histories of the ancients, when a God appeared amongst mortals, there were signs and miracles. Thou hast told me only words. Go, therefore, again to the child and say: The king desireth a miracle.

3. Asha returned the next day, but lo and behold, woman and child were gone, and not one of the neighbors knew whither. Asha said: If I go before the king with this story, he will have me slain as an inventor of lies. So he returned not to the king.

4. But where Too'che and her child dwelt, there came a maker of songs, by name Choe'jon, and he spake to the virgin, saying: Where is the child? She answered: He

sleepeth in the rack of hay; I will fetch him. So she brought the child from its bed of new hay, fetching straws with its mantle, neither had the straws roots.

5. I'hua'Mazda spake through the child whilst its own spirit slept, saying: I came to thee, O Choe'jon; I brought thee hither, for thou shalt frame songs about the virgin's babe. Choe'jon was frightened, but nevertheless, he said: Can it be true, in this enlightened age! A miracle! Shall I talk to thee,O child? Then I'hua'Mazda said:

6. Behold, thou speakest not to the child, but to I'hua'Mazda. Take these straws to thy writing-box and plant them in new earth, and in one day they shall grow and bear ripe wheat. So Choe'jon departed and planted the straws, and in one day, they grew and bore ripe wheat.

7. Choe'jon had sung his songs before the king, and so had permission of the court; and he went and told the king of the miracle. The king said: The philosopher, Asha, told me about this child, and I sent him for a miracle, but he returneth not. Thou hast come and said: Behold, a miracle! What value is a miracle, save to those who witness it? Shall thy king take a thing in belief only? Is not belief the fruit of darkness? Go, therefore, again to the child and bring it before me, that I may see with mine own eyes.

8. Choe'jon returned to the place, but, lo and behold, virgin and child were gone; neither knew the neighbors whither. But she was concealed in another part of the city. And now there came before her one Os'shan, who was weeping because of the apparent death of his son. To him I'hua'Mazda spake, saying: Weep not, O man; I have healed thy son and also given sight to thy daughter.

9. Os'shan trembled at such words coming from the lips of a child, and he ran away, finding of a truth his son was healed, and his daughter restored to sight. In his joy he returned to the place, but the virgin and child were gone. Os'shan was hostler to the king, and capable of audience, and so he went and told the king of his good fortune.

10. The king said: Asha, the philosopher, told me a fine story of this child, but when I sent him for information, he returned not. Then came Choe'jon, the maker of songs, telling me what he had witnessed. I sent him to have the mother and child brought before me, but he returneth not. Now thou comest with a miracle, such as were told in the dark ages. Go thou, therefore, and search the city over till thou findest this wonder, and bring it before me.

11. On the next day another man, even the king's brother's son, came before the king, saying: This day I have seen such a wonder as would have been marvelous in the days of angels and Gods. Behold, a little child hath spoken to me such words of philosophy as made me tremble. And yet, O king, thou knowest I am no coward. My house is hung with a hundred scalps. Ay, and this child already proclaimeth itself Zarathustra in communion with the God, I'hua'Mazda! To me it said: Why killest thou the sons and daughters of thy God? Think not that thy multitude of scalps are a glory before heaven. Behold, I am stronger with my little finger than So-qi, thy king.

12. So-qi, the king, said: It is enough. Save this mother and child be brought at once before me, that I may behold the truth of these wonders, every male child in Oas shall be cast into fire. The king's brother's wife had a child, and the son's wife had a child, and they foresaw that the decree of the king touched them closely; so there went forth many, searching for Too'che and Zarathustra.

13. But the spirit, I'hua'Mazda, directed the mother to go beyond the gates, and led her far

off into the Forest of Goats, where the tribes of Listians lived by fishing and hunting, and on goat's milk. I'hua'Mazda talked to the virgin, saying: Twenty years shalt thou tarry in the forest, fearing naught, for thy God will provide for thee. And when thy son shall be larger and stronger than other men, behold, thy God will manifest for the redemption of the races of men who are hunted and slain for the glory of the kings.

14. So it came about that the virgin and her son dwelt in the Forest of Goats until Zarathustra was a large man and of mature years, and his stature was equal to three ordinary men; nor could any number of men lay him on his back. But because of his gentleness like a young goat, the tribes of the forest called him the Lamb of God, signifying, strength and good-will.

CHAPTER IV.

1. When So-qi, the king, issued the decree to have Zarathustra found and brought before him, otherwise all the male infants of Oas to be slain, the Lords sent travail on the king's wife and on the king's daughter, wife of Asha, the philosopher, and the two women gave birth that day to two sons, a month before their time, but nevertheless unto life and strength and beauty. Now, according to the laws of Oas, a king could not rescind or change his own decrees, for he had assumed the position of infallibility, whereupon he had doomed to death kin of his kin, flesh of his flesh.

2. Accordingly, after search had been made in vain to find Zarathustra, the king repented of his decree, but knew no way to justify a change of commandment. Asha, hearing of this, came out of concealment, saying to himself: Now will I go to the king and hold him to his decree, even demanding that he slay me also. So Asha came before So-qi, and after saluting, said: O king, I have heard of thy strait, and am come to thee that I may counsel thee.

3. The king was angered, and he said: Asha, my friend, hear thou thy king: Thou camest before me, relating a marvelous story regarding an infant son of the virgin who saith she never knew a man. Now, according to the laws of the City of the Sun, any man stating for truth that which he cannot prove, is already adjudged to death. Shall not the law be fulfilled, because, forsooth, thou art near me in blood?

4. Asha said: Most assuredly, O king, the laws must be carried out. Are they not the all highest? For it followeth that man being the all highest person, his laws, above all else, must never be set aside. Therefore, thou shalt have me slain. Think not I am come before thee to plead an excuse, in order to save myself; rather let all men perish than that the king's decrees go amiss.

5. The king said: Thou art wise, O Asha. The laws cannot err, for they are the standard by which to judge all else. And he who hath risen to be king standeth by nature the infallible highest of all things. History hath proven this. But yet hear me, thou who hast wisdom from the movements of the sun and moon and stars: The king, being the all highest, how can he be bound? Cannot he decree new decrees forever?

6. Asha said: I will not deceive thee, O king! I know thou art arguing not for me, but for thine own infant son, and for thy daughter's infant son. Neither have I come before thee in prowess, though I love life. But here is the matter: If thou change one law, thou admittest that all laws made by man may also need changing; which is to say, wisdom is folly.

How, then, shall the judge, judge any man by the laws? Is it not setting up error in order to find truth?

7. The king said: Thou reasonest well. Methought this morning, in my walk in the market gardens, when the soldiers were spreading the scalps of their enemies in the sun to dry, whether or no, in ages to come, the weaker nations and tribes of men might not attempt to justify their right to life. And were the kings to admit fallibility in their decrees and laws, no man can foresee the end; for even slaves and servants and women will raise up against the laws, and claim their right to life. Wherein, then, would the earth be large enough for all the people? Yet, wherefore, O Asha, cometh this heart-ache of mine against killing mine own son?

8. Asha said: What are thy sympathies, O king? If thou wert to justify the escape of thy child's death for sympathy, would not my wife and my children justify their sympathy in desiring me to live? Nay, sympathy is the enemy of law and justice. It is the evil in our natures that crieth out for evil. The laws must be maintained; the decrees must be maintained; the king's word must be maintained. No man must suffer his judgment to go higher than the law, or the decree, or the king.

9. Asha said: This is the City of the Sun. If this city goeth back on its own laws, what will not the tributary cities do? Will not they also begin to disrespect the laws, or say: Perhaps the laws are in error? This will come to anarchy. To one purpose only can a great city be maintained. To divide the purposes and judgment of men is to scatter to the four winds the glory of our civil liberty. Was it not disrespect of the laws, combined with superstition, that caused the nations of ancients to perish?

10. The king said: What shall I do, O Asha? My son hath smiled in my face!

11. Asha said: Thou shalt send me and thy son and thy daughter's son, and all male infants to the slaughter's pen, and have us all beheaded and cast into the fire. Otherwise, it will come true what the infant Zarathustra hath said: Behold, my hand shall smite the city of Oas, and it shall fall as a heap of straw.

12. Think not, O king, I am superstitious and fear such threats; but this I perceive: Suffer the laws to be impeached, and every man in Oas will set up to interpret the laws to be wrong and himself right. And thy officers will rebel against thee on all sides, and the glory of thy kingdom will perish.

13. After the city had been searched for thirty days, and the virgin and child not found, the king appointed a day for the slaughter, according to his former decree; and there were ninety thousand male infants adjudged to death, the king's son among the rest.

14. Whilst these matters were maturing, the Lord went to Choe'jon, and inspired him to make songs about Zarathustra, the infant that was stronger than a king. And also songs about the decree of death to the ninety thousand infant sons of Oas. And the beauty of the songs, together with the nature of these proceedings, caused the songs to be sung in the streets day and night; and the songs, in satire, approved of the horrors, so that even the king could not interdict the singing.

CHAPTER V.

1. When the day arrived for the slaughter of the male infants, not more than a thousand mothers appeared at the place of execution with their infants, the others having risen in

the night previous and departed out of the gates, upward of eighty-nine thousand mothers.

2. When the king went to the place of execution, having set apart the day as a holiday, and not finding but a thousand infants present, he inquired the reason, and, having been told, he said: Can it be that mothers love their offspring more than they respect the decrees of the king? Asha was standing near, having stripped himself ready for execution, and he answered the king, saying:

3. Because they love their offspring, is it not the love of the flesh? And doth not the law stand above all flesh? In this matter, then, because they have evaded the law, they have adjudged themselves also to death.

4. Then came Betraj, the king's wife, bringing the infant. Betraj said: Here is thy son, O king, ready for the sacrifice. Asha reasonest well; there must be an All Highest, which never erreth; which is the law of the king. Take thou my flesh and blood and prove thy decrees. What! Why hesitate? If thou swerve one jot or tittle, then shalt thou open the door for all men to find an excuse against the law. Doth not the sun blight a harvest when he will? Yea, and strike dead our most beloved? Art thou not descended from the Sun Gods? Who will obey the laws if thou, thyself, do not?

5. The king said: Behold, it is yet early morn; let the officers go fetch all who have escaped beyond the walls, and both mothers and children shall be put to death. Till then, let the proceedings be suspended. Now there had congregated a vast multitude, anxious to witness the slaughter; and when the king suspended matters, there went up cries of disappointment. And many said: When a thing toucheth the king, he is a coward.

6. The king returned for his palace, leaving Asha standing stripped for the execution. And the multitude cried out: More is Asha like a king than So-qi. Let us make him king. King So-qi! We will not have a sheep for a king! And none could stay them, or be heard above their noise; and they ran after the king and slew him with stones, and they made Asha King of the Sun. And there was not one infant slain according to the decrees.

7. God saith: Think not, O man, that things happen without a cause, or that all things are left to chance. In my works I go beforehand and plan the way, even more carefully than a captain lieth siege to a city. Before Zarathustra was born I sent ashars to choose out my personages. Think not that Asha made his own arguments; but by virtue of the presence of my ashars, whom he saw not, he spake and behaved in my commandments, not knowing it. And even so was it with the king's wife; my angels also inspired her to speak before the king. And those that fled out of the city, were inspired by my hosts of angels.

8. God said: Yet with the king's decree I had no part, for I foresaw he would do this of his own will; and with the multitude in slaying the king I had no part, for I saw they would do this on their own account. Neither would the multitude hear my voice, even though I had spoken to every man's soul; for in them tetracts were the ascendant power.

9. God saith: The multitude slew the king because he had gone so far from me he heeded me not. And I made Asha king, because he came so near me my power was with him through my ashars.

CHAPTER VI.

1. During the infant age of Zarathustra, God manifested no more through him; but he sent Ejah, one of his Lords, to be with Zarathustra, day and night. And Ejah taught the infant

wisdom in all things, but showed himself to none else.

2. When Zarathustra was half grown, the Lord began to manifest through him, giving signs and miracles and prophecy before the Listians who lived in the Forest of Goats. This forest was of the width in every direction, save the east, of forty days' journey for a man, and in all that region there were no houses, the inhabitants living in tents made of bark and skins.

3. The Lord inspired Zarathustra to teach them to build houses, and tame the goats, and to live in cities, and otherwise subdue the earth through righteousness; the chief center of their habitations being on the river Apherteon and its tributaries. And it was from these inhabitants that sprang in after years the migrants called Fonece'ans, signifying, out of the mountains. Nevertheless, these people were I'huans, but because of the cruelties of the Par'si'ean kings, they fled and lived in the forests.

4. The Lord said to Zarathustra: Behold the people who fly from the kings! I have made them kings over goats and over the beasts of the fields.

5. And from this time forth the Listians styled themselves shepherd kings. And Zarathustra taught them of the Lord, that man should have dominion over the beasts of the forests, but that no man should hold dominion over his neighbor. Consequently, every man of the Listians styled himself a king, and every woman styled herself a queen.

6. Again the Lord said to Zarathustra: Go thou, my son, whither I will lead thee, and thou shalt find a people sacred to the Great Spirit. So Zarathustra wandered beyond the Forest of Goats, and came to Hara'woetchij, to the south of the mountains of Oe'tahka, where were three large cities and twelve small ones, inhabited by I'hins.

7. And the Lord had been with the I'hins, and foretold them Zarathustra was coming, so that it was proven on both sides. The Lord said to the high priest: Thou shalt suffer Zarathustra to come within the walls of the cities, for he is pure.

8. So Zarathustra went in, and, in the time of worship before the altar of God, the Lord appeared in a great light and commanded the high priest, saying: Behold, I have brought my son to thee. Him shalt thou anoint as a priest according to the I'hin laws; and thou shalt teach him the rites and ceremonies of the ancients.

9. Accordingly Zarathustra was made a priest and was otherwise accepted as an I'hin, and bestowed under the rod with water and with fire. And he also taught the sacred words and the art of writing and making tablets; and of weaving cloth and making clothes from flax.

10. Seven years Zarathustra remained with the I'hins, fasting and praying, and singing and dancing before the Lord. And then the Lord commanded him to return through the Forest of Goats, the which he did, teaching before the Listians whithersoever he halted for a rest, and the Lord was with him, working miracles.

11. At the end of another seven years the Lord said to Zarathustra: Behold, the dawn of light is come! Thou shalt, therefore, bestow thy mother with thy people, and I will lead thee to the city of thy birth. Zarathustra said: Tell me, O Lord, of the city of my birth?

12. The Lord said: It is a great city, but it shall fall before thy hand; for I'hua'Mazda hath turned his favor away from its kings.

13. In two days' journey Zarathustra came to Oas, and entered into the city, but he brought no provender with him. Now, it was a law of Oas, that all strangers coming into the city, should bring provender as a testimony of fidelity to the laws and to the king. So, when he came to the inner gate, the keeper asked him for provender; but Zarathustra answered

him, saying:

14. Naked I came into the world, and Ormazd asked me not for provender. Is thy king greater than the Creator?

15. The keeper said: I know not thy words; shall a servant explain laws? To which Zarathustra said: Thou art wise; neither shalt thou suffer for disobedience in letting me pass. The Lord will give thee food.

16. When he had spoken thus, there fell at the feet of the keeper an abundance of fruit, and the keeper feared and stood aside, suffering Zarathustra to pass in. The keeper not only told the people of the miracle, but ran and told the king, likewise. This was Asha, who had reigned since the death of So-qi; and Asha no sooner heard of the miracle than he imagined the person to be the same whom he had seen in infancy.

17. Asha, the king, sent officers at once to find Zarathustra, and bring him before the court. But the Lord knowing these things, inspired Zarathustra to go on his own account; and he went accordingly before the king, even before the officers returned.

18. The king said: Who art thou? and for what purpose hast thou come before the king?

19. Then spake I'hua'Mazda through Zarathustra, saying: I am I'hua'Mazda, God of the I'huans. He through whom I speak, is Zarathustra, whom thou sawest in his mother's arms. We twain are one. I have come before thee, O king, because of two reasons: thou hast sent for me; and I desire to use thee.

20. The king said: Speak further, stranger, that I may approve of thy words.

21. In the time of So-qi, said I'hua'Mazda, I made thee king of Oas, and from that day to this my ashars have been with thee and heard thee oft praying privately for information of the infant thou sawest; for it resteth heavily on thy judgment whether or no man be immortal. Sit thou with me this night privily, and I will show thee So-qi's soul.

22. Asha said: Thou wert to smite the city and it would fall. Behold, it standeth! Yet I desire not to stand in my own light. Then Zarathustra spake on his own account, saying: Fear not, O king, for this philosophy. As thou wouldst bend a straw, so do the Gods wield the nations of the earth. The city will fall ere six years pass, and thou shalt be reduced to beggary, and yet thou shalt be happier than now.

CHAPTER VII.

1. When night came, the king sat privately with Zarathustra; and I'hua'Mazda cast a light on the wall, and the soul of So-qi came and appeared before Asha. So-qi said: Knowest thou who I am? And Asha said: Yea, So-qi.

2. So-qi said: True, O king, the soul is immortal! And then it disappeared. Asha said: It seemeth to be So-qi. And yet if it were he, would he not have called me, Asha, instead of, O king? Then spake Zarathustra, saying: Call thou for some other spirit? Asha said: Suffer, then, the soul of my wife to appear.

3. Again the light appeared, and the soul of Asha's wife inhabited it, and he saw her. Asha said: It is, indeed. And then she disappeared. Asha said: Had it been she, she had spoken. Zarathustra said: Call thou for another spirit. Asha called Choe'jon, the songster, who looked like no other man under the sun. And Choe'jon also appeared; and even sang one of the songs about the slaughter of the infants.

4. Asha said: It was like Choe'jon; but had it been he, he had surely mentioned the

miracle. Then Zarathustra said: Call yet for another spirit. And Asha called, and another appeared; and thus it continued until twenty souls of the dead had shown themselves, and talked with him, face to face, and every one had related things pertinent to themselves.

5. Then spake Zarathustra, saying: To-morrow night shalt thou again sit with me. Now, on the next night, twenty other spirits of the dead appeared and spake face to face with the king. But yet he believed not. Then spake I'hua'Mazda through Zarathustra, saying: What will satisfy thee, O man? For I declare unto thee, that spirit is not provable by corpor, nor corpor by spirit. There are two things; one groweth by aggregating, and the other groweth by dissemination, of which All Light is the highest. As by darkness light is known, and by light darkness known, similarly diverse are corpor and spirit known.

6. I'hua'Mazda said: Thy generations, O king, have been long bred in unbelief in spirit, and unbelief is so entailed upon thee that evidence is worthless before thee. Who thinkest thou I am?

7. Asha said: Zarathustra. Then Zarathustra asked him, saying: Who thinkest thou I am?

8. Again Asha said: Zarathustra. To which I'hua'Mazda said: Because thou seest with thine eyes this corporeal body, and heareth with thine ears this corporeal voice, so dost thy corporeal judgment find an answer.

9. But I declare to thee, O king, there is a spiritual judgment as well as a corporeal judgment. There is a spiritual man within all men, and it never dieth. The spiritual man, which is within, is the only one that can discern spiritual things. It is the only one that can recognize the spirits of the dead.

10. Then Asha said: How shall I prove there be not some element belonging to thee personally, that is as a mirror, to reproduce a semblance of whatsoever is within thy thoughts?

11. I'hua'Mazda said: What would that profit thee if proven? And what profit if not proven? Hear me, then, for this is wisdom: There are millions of souls in heaven that are in the same doubt thou art now in, not knowing that they themselves are dead. Especially those slain in war and in unbelief of spirit life.

12. The king said: Who, then, sayest thou, thou art? I'hua'Mazda said: First, there is Ormazd, Creator, Who is over all and within all, Whose Person is the Whole All. Then there are the unseen worlds in the sky; then this world, and the stars, and sun, and moon. After them, mortals, and the spirits of the dead.

13. Hear me, O king; because the dead know not the All High heavens, the Ormazd, Whose name signifieth Master of All Light, sendeth His exalted angels down to the earth as masters and teachers, having captains and high captains, that their labor be done orderly. The highest captain is therefore called I'hua'Mazda, that is, master voice over mortals and spirits for their exaltation.

14. Know, then, O king, I, who speak, have thee and thy city and thy country within my keeping. I am come to stay man's bloody hand. And through Zarathustra will I reveal the laws of Ormazd; and they shall stand above all other laws. Because thou art the most skilled of men, I made thee king; because thou hast seen that man must have an All Highest Law, I have come to thee. Yea, from thy youth up, and during thy long life, I have spoken to thy soul, saying: Asha, find thou the All Highest: Asha, thou shalt have a strange labor before thou diest! Asha, thou, that hast attained to the measurement of the stars, shalt find a Power behind the stars!

15. The king said: Enough! Enough! O stranger! Thou turnedst my head with wonders. I scarce know if I am living or dead, because of the mastery of thy wisdom. Alas, my kindred are dead; my friends are fools! I have none to tell these wonders to. All thy days shalt thou live in my palace, and whosoever thou demandest for wife, shall be granted unto thee.

16. I'hua'Mazda said: Till I come again to thee, O king, keep thine own counsel. For the present, I must return to the forest. Give me, therefore, of thy choicest ink and brushes and writing cloth, and send thou two servants with me. Asha said: Suffer thou me to be one of thy servants, and I will abdicate my throne!

17. I'hua'Mazda said: I shall need thee where thou art. Thus ended the interview with the king. The next day Zarathustra returned to the forest, to write the Zarathustrian laws.

CHAPTER VIII.

1. These, then, are the Zarathustrian laws; the I'hua'Mazdian laws; which, being interpreted into the English language, should be described as GOD'S WORD, transcribed from the libraries of heaven by the will of Jehovih!

2. That is to say:

3. Zarathustra said: Interpret to me, O Holy One.

4. I'hua'Mazda said: O Pure One, All Pure! Hear thou. I will interpret; write thou.

5. Zarathustra wrote. Then spake I'hua'Mazda to Zarathustra, the All Pure!

6. First, Ormazd was, and He created all created things. He was All; He is All. He was All Round, and put forth hands and wings. Then began the beginning of things seen, and of things unseen.

7. The first best highest place He created was the All Possibility. And the second best highest place He created was the All Good. With Him are all things Possible. With Him are all things Good.

8. Ormazd then created the first best of places, the longest enduring, the Airyana-vaja (etherea), the highest of good creation.

9. The third best created places created Ormazd, which was Haraiti, a high heavenly good place, a Home of Fragapatti, a Creator Son of the heavenly Airyana-vaja, a rescuer of men and spirits from Anra'mainyus, the evil of blood and bone.

10. The fourth best created places created Ormazd, the Creator, which was Gau, the dwelling-place of Sooghda, of heavenly shape and straight limbs and arms, and ample chest, full of music.

11. Out of Mouru, of the regions of Haraiti, came the Voice, created by the Creator Ormazd; came to I'hua-Mazda; and now cometh to thee, Zarathustra, thou All Pure.

12. Fifth best place created the Creator, the Bakhdhi, with lofty standards.

13. Then came Anra'mainyus, the Black Doubt, the Sa-gwan, sowing seeds.

14. After that, the Creator created Tee-Sughi, the reason of man, and turned his eyes inward, that he could see his own soul.

CHAPTER IX.

1. Came to Zarathustra, the All Pure, the voice of I'hua'Mazda, by the hosts of Haraiti: Hear me, O Zarathustra; I am I'hua'Mazda. Hear thou of thy Creator, who created all

created things.

2. These are the chief first best places created: First, the earth and the air and the water, and all the living that are on them and in them.

3. Out of darkness, void! Waste, and nothing was, as seeming nothing. And shaped He, the Creator, Ormazd, the shape of things.

4. The living that live; the living that are dead; the first of all that breathed, created the Creator, Ormazd.

5. With legs or wings, or hair or feathers, or naked; to crawl or walk or fly, created the Creator, Ormazd, all the living.

6. To all to live a life; a right to live and die, out of the life of Ormazd gave He them life and death.

7. Then asked Zarathustra, the All Pure, inquiring of I'hua'Mazda, saying: To whom else hast thou these things spoken?

8. I'hua'Mazda said: Since, a million! Before, a million! To more than a thousand millions. Then asked Zarathustra: Tell me one; of one, to one to whom thou hast revealed? And then answered I'hua'Mazda: To Vivanho, the first of men who had words; the first of women who had words. In the first best created days of pure men and pure women I came, I revealed. Then Zarathustra, the All Pure, said:

9. To be all pure; to be all good; to be all wise; to be all holy; to do all good works; what are these?

10. I'hua'Mazda said: These are to hear my voice, O Zarathustra. Then Zarathustra said: To be all bad; to be all foolish; to be all evil thinking; to do evil works, what are these?

11. I'hua'Mazda said: These are not to hear my voice; these are Anra'mainyus, O Zarathustra! Then Zarathustra inquired, saying: Is not the, --- not to hear thy voice, a person? Is the, --- to hear thy voice, a person?

12. I'hua'Mazda said to Zarathustra, the All Pure: Anra'mainyus was a person; but he is dead: Vivanho is a person, and he liveth to all the holy, to all the good, to all the wise. But to all the evil, to all the bad, to all the foolish, Anra'mainyus is not dead.

13. Then inquired Zarathustra, the All Pure: Whence came All Good; whence came all evil? Who is All Good; who is all evil? Then answered I'hua'Mazda to Zarathustra, saying: Thou perceivest now, all evil must have a name; All Good must have a name. Without names, no man could talk. Behold, I will write for thee, O Zarathustra, thou All Pure. The mark I make first, thou shalt call the All Good, the Creator, the Master, the Light! Here, then, have I made a circle and a cross and a leaf. (For these characters with explanations, see Tablet Se'moin, BOOK OF SAPHAH, verses 8 and 9. -Ed.)

14. I'hua'Mazda said to Zarathustra, the All Pure: Whoever looketh upon this mark, whoever seeth it, seeth the Name of All Names, the Creator. Whoever maketh this mark, writeth the name of the All Good; whoever pronounceth this mark, pronounceth the name of Ormazd, the All Master.

15. Then made I'hua'Mazda a circle, and painted four dark corners in it, and called it Anra'mainyus, the Uh-druk, the opposition to All Truth, and All Light, and All Good. And I'hua'Mazda explained to Zarathustra.

16. And, behold, there stood within the circle of evil, the name of All Good, the cross, and it was light, and the corners were black. I'hua'Mazda called this mark FATE, explaining to Zarathustra, the All Pure, saying: These three marks embrace all the created

334

creation; hence, the name of the third one is Fate, from which there is no escape, nor separation, forever.

17. Zarathustra inquired of I'hua'Mazda, saying: Is evil, evil; is good, good? I'hua'Mazda said: Evil is evil to man, but evil is not evil to Ormazd. Good is good to man; but good is not good to Ormazd. Only two conditions are before Ormazd; not evil, nor good; but ripe and unripe. To Ormazd, that which man calleth evil is unripe; to Ormazd, that which man calleth good is ripe.

18. I'hua'Mazda went on explaining, saying: For sake of understanding, O Zarathustra; for sake of not confounding, thou shalt call evil, evil; and good, good. Hear me, then, my son:

19. Without green fruit, none could be ripe; without evil none could be good. So Ormazd created all creation, and called it good; but lo, and behold, there was nothing to do. All things moved not; as if dead, all things were as nothing.

20. Then Ormazd blew His breath outward, and every created thing went into motion. And those at the front were called All Good, and those at the rear were called all evil. Thus created the Creator the Good Creation and the Evil Creation; the I'hua'Mazda and the Anra'mainyus.

CHAPTER X.

1. Then spake I'hua'Mazda to Zarathustra, the All Pure, saying: Thus thy Creator created all things; and the time of the creation was as a time, and a time, and a time, and without measure.

2. I'hua'Mazda said unto Zarathustra: Thus are the created creations; thus were the created creations; thus shall ever be the created creations. The Light of all light is Ormazd; He the Soul of all souls. These are the things seen and things unseen, created by Ormazd, thy Creator: Mi, the Mother Almighty: Then is Voice, the Expression of things, the All Speech, the All Communion, created by Ormazd, thy Creator, and by Mi, the Almighty Mother, a virgin never before conceived, and this was Vivanho, the Son.

3. I'hua'Mazda said to Zarathustra, the All Pure: Behold me, O thou, Zarathustra! Here I make one straight line; and now I make another straight line, and now another, all joined.

4. Then Zarathustra answered, saying: Thou hast made a triangle: What is the meaning, O I'hua'Mazda? Then answered I'hua'Mazda, saying: Three in one, O Zarathustra: Father, Mother, and Son; Ormazd, the ghost of all things; Mi, the seen and unseen, and Vivanho, the expression of things.

5. I'hua'Mazda said unto Zarathustra: These three comprise all things; and all things are but one; nor were there more, nor shall ever be. Nevertheless, O my son, each of these hath a million parts, a thousand million parts, ten hundred thousand million parts. And every part is like unto the whole; thou, O Zarathustra, also. For thou hast within thyself those three attributes, and no more. And each and all created things have these three attributes in them. Thus Ormazd created all the living creation; brothers and sisters created He them, in likeness of himself, with three entities embraced in one; which are, first, the ghost, the soul, which is incomprehensible; second, the beast, the figure, the person, which is called individual; and, third, the expression, to receive and impart.

6. I'hua'Mazda said unto Zarathustra, the All Pure: To receive and to impart; what else

hath man; what more desireth he? Then I'hua'Mazda made a picture of a cow, and a picture of a horse, a strong male horse dashing forth. And he asked Zarathustra, saying: Which of these signifieth receiving; which of these signifieth to impart? And Zarathustra perceived.

7. I'hua'Mazda said unto Zarathustra: To be negative is to be a cow; to be positive is to be a horse.

8. Zarathustra inquired of I'hua'Mazda, saying: How many words are there, that can be written words! Thou hast now written many wise words, full of meaning. How many more words are there? Then answered I'hua'Mazda, saying: A thousand words and ten thousand words would not be all; but ten times ten thousand hundred thousand, and those are all the words created.

9. Then Zarathustra, the All Pure, said: Write me down all the words, and explain the meaning of them to me, that I may go before the world teaching All Truth, so that men will no longer be in darkness.

10. Then I'hua'Mazda wrote down tens of hundreds, and thousands of words, and explained the meaning. After that, Zarathustra sat in the bushes for thirty days and thirty nights, neither eating nor drinking nor sleeping. And then I'hua'Mazda revealed the secrets of heaven and earth to him, and commanded him to write them in a book; the which he did; and this was the first book, the Zarathustrian law, the I'hua'Mazdian law.

CHAPTER XI.

1. By this authority then, I, Zarathustra, by the power of I'hua'Mazda, reveal the created creations.

2. Ormazd created a good creation. First, the land and water and firm things; out of the unseen and void created He them. Second, the lights, heavenly; and the heat and the cold everywhere. Third, all living animals, and fish and birds. Fourth, man and woman.

3. Then spake Ormazd through His Son, Vivinho, saying: Speech! Voice! Words! and man and woman were the only talking animals created in all the created world.

4. Ormazd then created death, Anra'mainyus; with seven heads created He him. First vanity (uk), then tattling (owow), then worthlessness (hoe'zee), then lying (ugs'ga), then incurable wickedness (hiss'ce), then evil inventions for evil (bowh-hiss), then king and leader (daevas).

5. Ormazd then created association (clans) by words bringing men together, Haroyu.

6. Ormazd then created habitations (oke'a). And then He created dwelling-places for the Gods, with four good corners and four evil corners, created He them, Varena.

7. And Ormazd created sustenance for the living and the dead, haoma. Then He created the boon of rest, for the weary, haraquaiti. After that he created sweet-smelling and rich-growing pastures, Urva.

8. And Ormazd created combination, which is strength, chakhra. Then power to receive knowledge, haden'amazd.

9. Ormazd then created the holy day (rak). Then He made the four signs of the moon, Uk'git, E'git, Ki'git and M'git, for all holiness.

10. And He said: Six days shalt thou labor, O man; and worship on the seventh, because they are the moon's times.

11. Then Ormazd, the Creator, created the power to live without kings; like the I'hins in

the east, and the name of this power He created was Ranha.

12. Then spake I'hua'Mazda to Zarathustra, the All Pure, saying: To attain to Ranha; how to attain to Ranha; this, then, is the holy Mazdian law:

13. Ormazd shall be King, and thou shalt acknowledge no other. He shall be thy All Highest love forever, and above all other loves.

14. Thou shalt disown all other rulers, and kings, and queens, and Lords, and Gods.

15. Thou shalt not bow down in reverence save to Ormazd, thy Creator.

16. Thou shalt covenant thyself to thy Creator every day, and teach thy children to do so also.

17. Thou shalt keep holy the four moon days, for they are the change of watch of the Gods and angels over them.

18. Thou shalt not kill what thy Creator created alive.

19. Thou shalt love thy father next to thy Creator, and obey his voice, and honor thy mother, because she brought thee forth by the will of thy Creator.

20. Thou shalt not suffer thy desires to lead thee after woman.

21. Thou shalt not take that which is another's.

22. Thou shalt not be vain, for nothing is thine.

23. Thou shalt not speak untruth.

24. Thou shalt not talk of thy neighbor behind his back, for Ormazd heareth thee, and the angels will go tell thy neighbor's soul what thou hast said.

25. Thou shalt not be idle or lazy, or thy flesh will become weak and bear down thy soul.

26. Thou shalt not envy, nor harbor hatred against any man nor woman nor child.

27. Thou shalt not reprove any man nor woman for their evil, for they are the Creator's.

28. Thou shalt reprove thine own child, and teach him the right way.

29. Thou shalt not lie with thy wife during pregnancy.

30. Thou shalt not take to wife any of thy kin, save beyond the fifth generation.

31. Thou shalt not take to wife a woman of unclean habits.

32. Thou shalt not commit the self-habit.

33. Thou shalt not desire of thy neighbor more than thou wouldst give.

34. Thou shalt fast one day of the fourth moon all thy life, neither eating fish nor flesh, nor bread nor fruit; nor anything but water shall enter thy mouth.

35. One whole year of thy life thou shalt dwell with the poor, live with the poor, sleep with the poor, begging for alms for the poor.

CHAPTER XII.

1. I'hua'Mazda said unto Zarathustra, the All Pure: Three castes have I made; the first are the I'hins, sacred above all other people, because they keep my commandments; second, the I'huans, more powerful created I them than other people, because by them I will subdue the earth; and third, the druks, the evil people, who will not learn.

2. I'hua'Mazda said to Zarathustra, the All Pure: Remember the caste of men; keep thy blood in the place I created thee; nor shalt thou marry but in the caste I created thee.

3. I'hua Mazda said: A thousand castes I created among the I'huans: The king, the doctor, the magician, the priest, the farmer, the bearer of burdens, the messenger, swift-footed, and for all other occupations under the sun. Each and all within their own castes created I them; nor shall they marry but in the caste I created them.

337

4. Zarathustra responded to I'hua'Mazda, saying: I will keep thy commandments. Thy seventy commandments, and seven hundred and seven thousand.

5. I will preserve sacred the castes thou hast created, O I'hua'Mazda. And I will teach these holy truths to my children; to my servants, and unto all men.

6. Then I'hua'Mazda wrote all the commandments, as hereabove, and he stooped down and kissed the books, which were of stone and of cloth, saying: This is my holy book. Take it, O Zarathustra, thou All Pure, and go thou forth into all the world, teaching it, and explaining it.

7. Then Zarathustra, the All Pure, stooped down and kissed the book, saying: This is thy holy book, O I'hua'Mazda. I take it; and I will go into all the world, teaching it, and explaining it.

8. Thus was completed the first sacred, most holy book created for mortals. And Zarathustra rose up from his writing, tall and handsome, inquiring of I'hua'Mazda, saying: Whither shall I go first, O master?

9. Then answered I'hua'Mazda, creator of the Ormazdian law, the Zarathustrian law, saying:

10. Take my holy book, the Ormazdian law, the Zarathustrian law, first, to Asha, king of the I'huans, king of Oas, the City of the Sun. Him have I prepared for thee and thy work since the day of his birth; since the day of thy birth, the day I spake to him in thy infancy.

11. Then went forth Zarathustra, strong in faith; and he came to Asha, the king. And the king said unto him: Thou hast tarried so long! Behold, I have cast the horoscope a hundred times, a thousand times. I have proved all the stars in heaven and named them, and made maps of them. And I have measured the power of one star over another star; and the powers of the stars on this world, and the powers of the sun and moon.

12. Yea, I have sent into the great cities of the east, to men of great learning; and to the south and north and west, to men of great learning. And then I sent to the kings of Jaffeth and of Shem; to Bow-gan-ghad; to Bing-thah; and to the great city of Huug-sin, where the great philosopher, Ah-tdong, liveth. And from all of these I have obtained great wisdom.

13. Hear me, then, O Zarathustra; I will speak to thee as if thy philosophy were true; but yet I believe it not: First, then, in all the stars there is nothing but lies; neither mattereth it if a man be born under this star or that star! I am old now and have observed thousands of men, yea, kings and queens, as to whether the stars rule over them, and I declare unto thee that the philosophy of the stars is nothing but lies. Yea, I have searched in mine own self, and I find I am often doing things contrary to my first intentions; but as to the cause, I know not.

14. This also have I discovered; there is one kind of causes that lie with individuals; and there is another kind of causes that lie with kings and kingdoms; but, yet, I perceive that each and every man is bound in his own channel by something stronger than himself. To find the cause of this, I have searched to the extent of all the stars in the firmament, but found not the truth.

15. Now I ask thee, in the name of thy Gods, if thou canst prove this matter to thy king?

16. Then answered Zarathustra, saying: Through my hand hath I'hua'Mazda written a most holy book, explaining many philosophies. This book have I brought unto thee, according to the commandments of my God; read thou it.

17. Then the king took the book and read it; and on the next day Zarathustra came again

before the king. The king said: Thy book saith thus and so, but it proveth little. Thy God asserteth he hath done thus and so, and that he created thus and so. First of all, then, I know not if there be a God; second, if there be a God, I know not that he cometh to thee; and third, if he come to thee, and he be a just God, why he cometh not to me. And yet, after all this, for I doubt not thy wisdom will give sufficient answers to these questions, if it be true there are Gods unseen that rule over us, and spirits of the dead that come to us, persuading our souls unconsciously to ourselves, what mattereth it whether we try or not, to obtain truth and wisdom? Shall not all things be left to the spirits and Gods and Lords? Knowest thou not that the ancients believed these things? 18. And yet what of the ancients? Were they not in darkness, and addicted to horrid rites and ceremonies, and murders, and savagery? With our wisdom of disbelief in their religions, have we not attained to great cities and empires? Behold our thousands and tens of thousands of large cities! And do they not all have just reason to be proud? For there is not one city but that its walls and gates are adorned with thousands of the skeletons and skulls of serpents and lions, and the scalps of druks. 19. Then spake I'hua'Mazda to the king, speaking through the voice of Zarathustra, saying: Hear thy God, O king, and be considerate of my words. There are two births unto all men; the first is from the mother's womb, and the second is from the corporeal body. Prior to the first birth, the will and power of the child is nothing as to shaping its own destiny. But prior to the spiritual birth, which is the mortal death, the man hath much to do as to shaping his future destiny in the next world. 20. I declare unto thee, O king, that the corporeal man is, therefore, but half accomplished as to his real life. He is but half his own master; but half the controller of his place and behavior in the mortal world; nevertheless, he is the first half, the first chooser. Think not that spirits and Gods rule men as if they were slaves or toys; for another power also lieth over man, which is neither spirits nor Gods nor stars, nor moon nor sun; but the corporeal surroundings that feed his earthly desires.

21. This is the Ormazdian law; not the corporeal stars, or corporeal earth, or corporeal moon, or corporeal man, ruleth over the spirit; but the subtle, the unseen to mortals, is the cause and ruler of all things.

22. Asha said: O that I could believe this! O that I knew this were true! O that the unseen worlds could be opened up to my understanding! For I perceive there is more power and virtue in thy philosophy than in my decrees. But touching thy book, O Zarathustra, answer thou me this: Who do the people in the world belong to, if not to me, the Sun King? Are not the people mine?

23. I'hua'Mazda said: All belong to Ormazd. Is it not here taught that man shall acknowledge obedience and worship to Ormazd only?

24. Asha said: I so perceive. Answer me this, O Zarathustra: To disown the king and the king's kings; will not this bring anarchy? For will not the rulers declare thy doctrine robbeth them of subjects? To which I'hua'Mazda suffered Zarathustra to reply. He said:

25. Is it not hard for a man not to have the privilege to choose his own master? Behold, they are now impressed into war; yea, thou keepest standing armies, trained in the labor of death. And this for the glory of the Sun Kingdom. Now hear me, O king, for I am now speaking on my own accord, and no God is speaking through me. And I declare unto thee, I have attained power to go in soul into the unseen worlds and behold with mine own eyes

how it is with the souls of the dead. And I declare unto thee there are great torments for the wicked. I have seen them in hell, with walls of fire going up around them day and night; suffocating fires of brimstone, from which they cannot escape. And those slain in war, both those that are for the king, and those against the king, are equally cast into ceaseless torments, and even kings and queens with them, where all are wailing and gnashing their teeth, and cursing; and in their madness, doing wickedly unto others with all their might.

26. The king said: If it be that thou canst go into heaven and hell, it must be true thou canst go to places on the corporeal earth in the same way. Prove thou this to me, and I will believe all thou hast said. Then Zarathustra said: Tell me whither I shall go, that I may convince thee, O king?

27. Ashar said: Go thou to the tower of the horoscope and find the words on the calendar.

28. Then spake I'hua'Mazda, saying: Have I not said, spirit cannot be proved but to spirit! Have I not said I am I'hua'Mazda; and Zarathustra hath said he is Zarathustra. But this thou canst not see. Behold, thou shalt witness now thine own craft. Here returneth Zarathustra.

29. Then spake Zarathustra, saying: Thou saidst to me: Go to the tower of the horoscope and find the words on the calendar. Lo, I have been there, and am already returned before thee. These, then, are the words of the calendar: To-ka, Seis, ctvai tnong, biang loo-sin-gooh wotchich; an porh, an oot, an dhi, an git.

30. Asha said: This is true. But how shall I not determine that thou gatheredst not the calendar from my heart? For I had the knowledge in my heart since sunrise. Then answered Zarathustra, saying: Try me once again; yea, thou shalt ask me for some toy of thine, and I will go fetch it.

31. Asha said: Behold, when I was a boy I let fall into the river betwixt the cliffs, at the outer wall, a golden case; go, thou, bring it.

32. Then spake I'hua'Mazda: Two conditions belong to all men, belief and unbelief. They are as seeds, planted in the soul of men whilst he is yet in his mother's womb; and when he is born forth into the world, they begin to grow within him. If man favor one only, it will grow at the expense of the other. Because of unbelief in man, he searched after truth and knowledge; but because of belief in man, he findeth happiness; but the latter may lead to stupidity, and the former to cruelty. It is a wise man, therefore, that keepeth these two talents evenly balanced.

33. Now even whilst I'hua'Mazda spake, the long-lost golden case fell at the king's feet, and it was yet dripping with water. The king examined it, and then exclaimed: This is true. And yet, if there be spirits and Gods, how shall I determine which one brought this? May it not have been an evil spirit as well as a good one?

34. Then spake I'hua'Mazda, saying: Have I not said: I will show thee thine own craft in finding some other reason than the right one?

35. Asha said: O ye Gods, cannot ye heal me of my unbelief? My judgment showeth me I am diseased in my heart. O that my mother had been a believing woman before I was born! Tell me, O Zarathustra, or I'hua'Mazda, whoever thou art, for I perceive thou art not like any man under the sun, tell me what I shall do, that I may become thy servant?

36. I'hua'Mazda said: On the morrow at sunrise I will come to thee, with Zarathustra, and I will tell thee many things.

CHAPTER XIII.

1. When the time had come, on the morrow, the king said: I have not slept. All night I was as one burnt with a fever; for thy wondrous words and thy miracles have well nigh turned my judgment upside down.

2. I'hua'Mazda said: Because a man cannot understand a thing, shall he cry out, MIRACLE! Now I declare I have done no miracle; nor hath Zarathustra. Yet to mortals these things are miracles! If so, is not a man a miracle to himself? Is not procreation a miracle?

3. This, then, I have found, O Asha, what man is not accustomed to, he calleth a miracle; after he hath seen a matter frequently, he calleth it natural law. What man hast thou found that comprehendeth the first cause of anything under the sun?

4. Why, then, shall man waste his time in unprofitable research? Is it not wiser that man labor to raise his fellow-men out of misery and darkness, than to gratify his own personal desire for great learning?

5. The king said: Thou reasonest well. And yet, what learned good man hast thou found who will not say: Yea, to do good is a pretty philosophy! And there endeth his aspiration. What, then, can I say, or what canst thou say, that they words will not be barren of fruit?

6. I'hua'Mazda said: Thou art this day king of all the world; nor is there any other kingdom but payeth thee tribute. Whatsoever thou desirest is as a law unto all other kingdoms. For that reason am I come unto thee. Yea, thou wert born to this end. Hear, then, the voice of thy God, and thou shalt do that which is good for thy soul and good for all other people.

7. Asha said: Almost am I tempted to accede to thy wishes ere thou hast revealed; but yet hear thou the voice of thy king; what matters it to me about the good of other people? Even if it be proven that great men have souls that live after death, it is not yet proven that the druks have souls also. If they have souls, then heaven must be a stupid place indeed. For thou hast not shown me that man obtaineth wisdom by dying, nor is it reasonable that he should do so. Rather tell me, O Zarathustra, how I may get rid of the world; for of what use is life at most?

8. I'hua'Mazda said: Because thou rejoicest not in thy life, thou perceivest that thy philosophy is deficient, and not that the world is. For I will yet prove to thee that thou art overflowing with happiness. To believe the things I reveal and have faith therein, is to become happy. Then the king answered him, saying: To believe, there is the matter. I declare unto thee, there is not a grain of belief in my heart. How, then, can it grow?

9. I'hua'Mazda said: He who can say, I can think of an All Highest, hath the seed of everlasting life in him. He who liveth the all highest he can; he who thinketh of the All Highest; he who talketh to the All Highest; he who trieth to perceive from the standpoint of the All Highest, quickly transcendeth belief and becometh a very God in faith. He becometh master of himself, and feedeth himself with happiness, even as men feed themselves with bread.

10. Asha said: What wouldst thou have me do? To which I'hua'Mazda said: With the people thou hast greater authority than a God, greater than miracles. Thy decrees are all powerful. Thou shalt have a copy of this book written on stone and cloth, one copy for every sub-kingdom in thy dominions. And thou shalt send it to them with a sword and a

serpent, saying to them: Receive ye this book, for it is a Holy Book, the ALL HIGHEST LAW! the I'hua'Mazdian law, the Zarathustrian law, the Ormazdian law. And it shall be a rule and guide unto you and your kingdom forever. And every king in the KINGDOM OF THE SUN shall serve one year in living with the poor, carrying the alms-bowl for sacrifices unto Ormazd.

11. And when thou hast sent this decree forth into all the world, thou shalt thyself give up thy kingdom; and thou shalt give to the poor all thy gold and silver and cases, and all thy treasures whatsoever, having nothing left unto thyself but the clothes that cover thee. And thou shalt go and live with the poor, carrying the alms-bowl thyself in the streets of Oas. And of the food thou gatherest in the bowl, thou shalt give the choicest parts to the poor, saying: THIS IS THE SACRAFICE OF THE MANY GIVEN UNTO THEE; EAT YE OF IT, FOR IT IS THE VERY BODY AND BLOOD OF ORMAZD, OUR FATHER IN HEAVEN! But the poorest of all that is in the bowl shall be thy portion.

12. At the end of one year, thou shalt go about preaching the Ormazdian law, commanding the cessation of war and the abandonment of evil, and the acceptance of righteousness.

13. The king said: What canst thou promise me if I do all these things? Then I'hua'Mazda suffered Zarathustra to answer him: He said, NOTHING! Did the Creator ask this, before He made the world? If thou desirest to approach thy Creator, do thou like unto Him. Nor is it my place, nor the angels' place, nor the place of God, to promise thee anything. Thou art not my servant; and thou shalt serve only the Master, All Light (Jehovih).

14. And as I have taught thee, so shalt thou go and teach others, explaining the Ormazdian law.

15. Asha said: Do the Gods in heaven give rewards for good works and sacrifices done on earth? Zarathustra said: He that doeth good works and maketh sacrifices unto Ormazd hath his reward. For it is by this means that the soul of man becometh strong, and especially strong for the first and second resurrections in the next world.

16. Asha said: To be with thee, O Zarathustra, and feast on the wisdom of thy words, I would make any sacrifice. Wilt thou go with me amongst the poor?

17. I'hua'Mazda said: Nay, thou shalt go alone. And for company thou shalt pray to thy Creator, and make songs of praise unto Him, nor think no more of thyself than as if thou wert dead.

18. The king said: It is said of mad-men that they think they are not mad. How, then, am I to know but I am mad? Will not the world so adjudge me if I obey thy commandments? And cannot the world judge me better than I can judge myself? It was said of the ancients that Sughdha obsessed old men and weak-hearted women; and it was for that reason Osiris came and slew him. If there be Gods in heaven, as thou sayest, mayst not thou have come to slay Osiris.

19. I'hua'Mazda said: Thou art a great multiplier of arguments; but in all thy speech I have seen nothing that planned the resurrection of men from darkness into light. And is not this the All Highest that man should aim at?

20. Asha said: I am done. Thy judgment is greater than mine. All thou hast commanded of me I will do. From this time forth I will serve only Ormazd, the Creator. Thy God, O Zarathustra, shall be my God. Thy ways shall be my ways. Henceforth I will argue forever on the side of the Creator. And touching all matters, I will first ask myself what I shall say

that would be like thy God would say it; and what I shall do that will fulfill the Ormazdian law.

CHAPTER XIV.

1. Asha, KING OF OAS, the City of the Sun, KING OF THE SUN, ruler over the whole corporeal world, owner and possessor of all mortals, men, women and children, COMMANDER OF ALL FLESH, descended from the SUN GODS thousands of years, and whose forefathers were the fathers of all living creatures, HIGHEST OF MEN, and by whose good grace the inhabitants of the earth are permitted to live, and whose decrees are the standard of all things, MAKER OF JUSTICE AND MAKER OF TRUTH, and whom none dare question, and on whose word the sun and moon and stars bow down, greeting:

2. To the kings and queens of the east and west and north and south, over all the cities in the world, rulers in the temples of the stars (observatories), slayers of dragons, and slayers of lions, and slayers of tigers, and of men and of women and of children and serpents, honored in the golgothas, and by millions of cowering slaves, owners of thousands of wives, and whose boats sail in lakes of mortal blood, and whose crowns are honored by ten thousand men slain every year, sworn on the flesh of the thigh, whose words are life and death; and most obedient to the SUN KING, I command:

3. First, that there is an Ormazd, Creator, Person! Whose Soul is in all the world, and in all things in the firmament above; Who is Father; Who is the Light of light, Creator of darkness and men, Who is forever The Going Forth; Who is Cause of causes; larger than all things seen and unseen; the Power of all power.

4. Second, I'hua'Mazda, His Only Begotten Son, born of the Virgin Mi (the Substance Seen). Pure and All Holy; Master of Men; Person of Word; Essence of Ormazd revealed in Word; SAVIOR OF MEN; Holder of the keys of heaven; through WHOSE GOOD GRACE ONLY the souls of men can rise to Nirvana, the HIGH HEAVEN:

5. Third, Zarathustra, A man, All Pure, conceived by a Virgin, and born wise, being one with I'hua'Mazda, who is one with Ormazd. Of Whom the word saith: Doeth He without miracle. THE RAISING OF THE DEAD; HEALING THE SICK BY LAYING ON OF HANDS; WHOS WORD OF COMMAND BRINGETH FORTH RIPE WHEAT, FULL GROWN, IN A DAY; and doing all things that the ancients accredited to the Gods as miracles, but which the Ormazdian law showeth to be NATURAL LAW TO ANY ONE WHO IS ALL PURE, and who draweth power from Ormazd, the Creator, and His holy angels.

6. Fourth, A Book, holy and sacred, revealed by I'hua'Mazda to Zarathustra, the All Pure; and written on stone and cloth, revealing All Wisdom, which is styled, the Ormazdian law, the I'hua'Mazdian law, the Zarathustrian law, which is the All Highest Law in All the world, approved by ASHA, I, THE KING OF KINGS!

7. Fifth, by ten thousand learned scribes in my command, written a copy of The Holy Book, and herewith sent with commands by the KING OF THE SUN! That this book shall be the All Highest law in all my sub-kingdoms, and that all my kings shall believe it and command the same of their slaves. Nor shall any man stand up against this, my decree, and live; nor shall any man alter one word or sign in this Holy Book; nor disbelieve one word it containeth.

8. And my kings and sub-kings; and my queens and sub-queens, shall obey all the

commandments, even as I obey them; nor shall any man, or woman, or child, question these things, as to whether they be the All Highest, or whether there be error in whatsoever cometh from my hand; for by my decree they are made All Truth!

9. For I was raised up to the High Estate by Ormazd, for this purpose; and not one in the whole world hath power like unto me.

10. And ye, to whom these holy words come, shall make oath on a serpent and a sword to obey these, my commandments, now and forever.

11. Thus did Asha send officers to carry the books he had made to the kings and queens in the east and west and north and south; and they that he sent were men of great learning, and of the highest caste; and they took with them serpents and swords, and gave them as commanded, exacting an oath from all who received them.

CHAPTER XV.

1. When Asha, the king, had thus completed the labor of making the books, and of sending them as commanded by I'hua'Mazda, he sent for Zarathustra, for further counsel as to how he should abdicate the throne according to the Highest Light. And when I'hua'Mazda was before him, even before Zarathustra had yet come, Asha said: Here cometh that quickened thought again! Behold, I sent for Zarathustra in order to ask certain questions, and lo, my heart answereth me!

2. Yea, I have nothing to do with what is not mine own! Now, whilst he thus framed his own answer, Zarathustra came and said unto him: Thou desirest counsel in regard to abdicating thy throne? Behold thou, I'hua'Mazda hath been to thee even now, saying: What hast thou to do with that which is not thine own!

3. Asha said: I have heretofore said: That that speaketh to my heart, what is it? Now according to thy wisdom, that that speaketh to my heart is I'hua'Mazda? How shall one know it to be so! Zarathustra said: If a man ask the All Light in reference to his own affairs, and for his own concerns, then receiveth he an answer from the tetracts; but if he ask the All Light in reference to what he shall do for others, to render the highest good unto them, then is the answer from I'hua'Mazda. I declare unto thee, O Asha, he is a dark man indeed to whom the Creator speaketh not every day.

4. Asha said: What, then, shall I do in a matter like this? As yet, all the world belongeth to me. Presently I shall deliver it to itself; shall I not provide a ruler for them?

5. Zarathustra said: Why, then, thou wilt be bound to give them one as good and wise as thyself, otherwise thou wilt cheat them! Furthermore, doth not the Ormazdian law say: Thou shalt not have any king but thy Creator?

6. Asha said: I so perceive. What then, shall I go away saying nothing? Then answered I'hua'Mazda, saying: Thou shalt do more than this; for thou shalt give liberty to all men, and proclaim unto them, commanding that they shall obey the doctrines of the Holy Book, serving no master but the Creator. And when the people are completely broken up by thy decree, thou shalt go away, leaving thy throne and thy capital to whatsoever may come to them.

7. Asha said: I perceive. That which hath been given me to do, I will do. Behold, I will bestow freedom on all the world; and with my alms-bowl go about begging. Heaven must be just, and it is right that I should have the experience of the poor as well as

of the rich. How else would I ever become sufficiently wise to be a God in heaven?

8. Yet one thing, O Zarathustra, and I will ask thee no more questions; thou hast said I must pray to Ormazd: Now, behold, I never prayed in my life! Who will teach me to pray?

9. I'hua'Mazda said: Let thy lips utter thy holiest desires, and let thy soul seek constantly for new expressions magnifying the wisdom, love and power of Ormazd, the Creator.

10. Neither shalt thou take a thought in regard to rules of prayer; the rules are for the unlearned. He who inventeth a new prayer to Ormazd every day of his life hath done wisely indeed. For the glory of prayer is the strengthening of one's own soul to perceive the Higher Light.

11. Prayer is not given in order to change the decrees of Ormazd, but to change one's own self for the better. Yet he who repeateth words of prayer as a parrot repeateth, improveth himself but little.

12. Asha said: If a man think a prayer, and use no words, is it well with him?

13. I'hua'Mazda said: It is well with him; but it is better to add words also. It is well for Ormazd to think a universe, but better to create it. To begin to learn creating, thou shalt use spoken words; the perfection of creating is to have the words bear fruit. He who omitteth words of prayer will in time omit prayer also, and his soul tendeth to barrenness.

14. A vain man saith: I have no need to pray; Ormazd knoweth my soul! Why, then, shall not the field say: I shall produce no harvest, because Ormazd knoweth my capacity! I declare unto thee, O Asha, the secret of all spiritual growth lieth in giving out the spirit: He who would grow in wisdom, must give wisdom; he who would grow in love, must give love; he who would grow in power of spirit, must give out power of spirit.

15. Bethink thee, then; if thou prayest silently, thy power goeth weakly to thy audience; but if thou prayest with words, openly, thou givest to thine audience of thy fruit; and, for this glory, Ormazd provideth thee abundantly.

16. When thou shalt go with thy bowl to feed the feeble, and old, and helpless, and blind, thou shalt teach them prayer and confessions; and thou shalt absolve them that are depressed because of their sins, that they may rejoice in their own lives.

CHAPTER XVI.

1. So Asha, being converted, gave up all he had on earth, and went and lived with the poor, carrying the alms-bowl for one year, preaching and praying for the poor. And it came to pass that at the end of the year he had thousands of followers.

2. And he built altars for them, teaching them to worship the Creator; to restore the mark of circumcision; to be upright before men; to labor for the helpless and distressed, and to do not to any man that which they desired not to be done unto themselves.

3. And these people took the name of Zarathustrians, in contradistinction from the Parsi'e'ans. Nevertheless, they were the I'huan race, and the Ghans.

4. And because of their religion, they could not own property, neither houses, nor lands, nor cattle, nor beasts of burden. Many of them gave themselves into servitude to the Parsi'e'ans, but many of them lived on the contributions brought by converts who had had great possessions.

5. Now it so turned out, that when Asha abdicated the throne, there were many aspirants

to his place, and the Council of the Sun was puzzled to know whom to select, that peace might remain in Oas; but they finally made Hi'ya'tseing king, because he was a great warrior, having bestowed to the city's walls and gates more than ten thousand skulls, from the refractory tribes adjacent.

6. Hi'ya'tseing assumed the titles of his predecessors, chief of which were King of the Sun, King of Kings, and King of Oas, the central city of all the world; and sent his proclamations to the chief cities of Jaffeth and Shem and Ham, commanding earth, water and fruit to be sent to him from every place under the sun. And he stipulated certain presents that must be sent to him every year, amongst which were thousands of subjects (slaves).

7. Hi'ya'tseing was a man of great learning, and had traveled far and near, and he knew the people and the lands of the earth, and he knew the different products of the different lands, and the number of peoples in the great cities of the world, and the number of warriors belonging to the different sub-kings under him. Besides these things he knew the stars and their places, and the groups of cows, and horses, and bulls, and bears, and lions, and fishes, and serpents, even as they had been taught in the Hyartien period amongst the ancients.

8. Hi'ya'tseing said: The Fete hath made me king of all the world; hence, it is right that I am king. He said: It is evident, because Asha abdicated the throne, that man must have a religion. He said: Because I know all the rites and ceremonies of the ancients, I will give man a religion on my own account. He said: Because Asha commanded the Zarathustrian religion unto the far-off kingdoms, then are Asha and Zarathustra my enemies. He said: Let my officers arrest Asha and Zarathustra and bring them before me. I will make an example of them.

9. And on the day that Asha was arrested, behold, the year of his carrying the alms-bowl was ended. Asha and Hi'ya'tseing had known each other for many years. When Asha was before the king, he said: I have nothing in all this world; why, then, hast thou arrested me? The king said: Because thou gavest away thy possessions, thou art the most dangerous of men. I have decreed thee to be put to death. Art thou prepared?

10. Asha said: Yea, O king. And yet, because of our long acquaintance, I ask of thee one boon, which is, that I may be put to death according to the Panic rites which were before the flood? And if, perchance, it be proved to thee there is a God with power to release me, and he so doeth it, then shall not thy hand be raised against me? The king said: Thy boon is granted.

11. Accordingly, a wheel of uh'ga was built and Asha was bound upon it, the king having appointed a guard to watch him till he should die. But because of the king's fear that the test might be tampered with, he caused the yogernot (jaugernot) to be set up in his private piazza, with the uh'ga facing the Gate of Lyons, so that his private attendants might also watch. (See plate 11.)

12. Great was the wailing and crying of the people when it was known that Asha had been decreed to death. The city of Oas became as a house of mourning and madness, and it was divided against itself, some for Asha and some for the king.

13. Because Asha was old, and thus in view of the king all day, the king repented, but he had no power under the laws to set aside his own decree. And when the sun went down, the king went before Asha, saying: Behold, thou hast been six hours on the

wheel, and yet thy God hath not come to release thee. This is a great torture, and I weep for thee. If thou wilt, therefore, slay thyself with a sword, I will have thee taken down?

14. Asha said: I declare unto thee, O king, I have no pain. Whether it be my madness, or whether it be the Gods favor me, what mattereth it, since I suffer not? Nor have I a right to slay myself, since I created not myself alive. Moreover, if it be the will of my Creator, Ormazd, that I die on the wheel, then it is just. If it be not His will, then will He release me. Therefore, O king, I am content.

15. The king said: This indifference cometh of madness. And thy madness hath affected the City of the Sun. Have thy way, then, and die!

16. The king returned into his palace, but on the next morning he came again, making the same proposal, and receiving similar answers. And at night he came again, repeating his offer, and again being refused, determined to come no more.

17. Now on the night of the third day, Asha felt the power of I'hua'Mazda coming upon him, and he said unto the guard: Behold, this night I shall be released! See to it, therefore, as to whether the thongs are well fastened. For, if it so turn out that the Father release me, then will ye stand before the king accused of conniving at my release. Accordingly, the guard re-examined the fastenings, and sent word to the king of what Asha had said. And the king replied: Nay, if he be released, then will I know of a truth there is a God; neither shall one man of my guardsmen stand accused.

18. This they told to Asha, and Asha said: I say unto you, not only one shall stand accused, but all of you. And there were of them one hundred, being two watches of fifty each; but it being the change of watch, they all heard, and they laughed in derision.

19. And behold, in that same moment of time, the thongs fell off, and I'hua'Mazda delivered Asha down from the uh'ga. And the spirit of I'hua'Mazda was in Asha, nor was Asha himself, though knowing to the things done through him.

20. I'hua'Mazda said: Go ye and say to the king: Behold, Asha is delivered by the power of his God. Then the guardsmen said: It is not morning; the king sleepeth.

21. I'hua'Mazda said: I say unto you, the king sleepeth not, but is joyful in drinking wine with his courtiers. They went, then, and told the king, finding, of a truth, he slept not. And the king commanded them to bring Asha before him, which they did.

22. Hi'ya'tseing said: What profit have my guardsmen in releasing this old man? Behold, it hath been said that thou, Asha, hadst gold and silver hidden away. I know now of a truth thou hast bribed these guardsmen to set thee free. For which reason, every man of these guardsmen shall be put to death, and their skulls mounted on the walls of Oas, and their skins tanned for leather. Away with them, ye marshals; bind them till the rising sun, and at that hour hew off their heads, as I have decreed.

23. And now as for thee, thou old hypocrite and destroyer of liberty! What sayest thou?

24. Asha said: According to thy promise I should now be free. There was no stipulation in thy decree that I should not bribe thy guardsmen. Behold, then, my wisdom! Have I not revealed to thee that thou canst not trust any man?

25. The king said: Thou art the wisest of men. I had hoped to hear thee say thy God released thee, and I had here twelve swordsmen to hew off thy head. But because thou hast shown me great craft, thou shalt live for a season, but only on condition that thou shalt leave Oas and never return.

26. Then spake I'hua'Mazda through Asha, saying: Thou hast decreed the guardsmen to

death at sunrise! Now I declare unto thee, O king, not one of them shall die as thou hast decreed. But I, I'hua'Mazda, will deliver them. Think not that I am Asha; I am not Asha, but a spirit, the God of the I'huans. Neither will I spirit away thy guardsmen by a miracle, but by natural means, and will I show thee that I am mightier than all kings.

27. The king said: It cannot be that there are Gods or spirits. Is man's judgment nothing? These things were suited to the dark ages. They affrighted men to justice, and so far served a purpose. But in this enlightened age man shall know justice and wisdom of himself.

28. Whilst the king yet spake, I'hua'Mazda caused the attending spirits to assume mortal form by the curtains of Arizzi, back of the king, and they made a noise, so that the king turned to look, and lo and behold, he saw them. He feared, not knowing but they were evil persons concealed, and he said: Robbers! murders! And he drew his sword and thrust at them; but they vanished! He said:

29. Verily art thou a devil, O Asha! And he thrust his sword at Asha, but it fell from the handle. He said: Ye Fetes! Kill him! kill him! And whilst he was thus puzzled, Asha walked forth out of the palace, nor would the king's guards lay hands on him.

CHAPTER XVII.

1. When Asha went away from the king's palace, Zarathustra met him, and they went together to the prison where the guardsmen were confined, prior to execution on the morrow at sunrise; and there came four hundred of the converts of Asha, and, when they stood around about the prison, Zarathustra said unto them:

2. Stand ye in the altar (crescent) of the living God, for his power is upon me, and I will deliver this prison! And the keeper of the prison, and also his attendants, woke up, and came with spears, saying: Disperse! disperse! Or, by the King of the Sun, ye shall die!

3. Zarathustra said: Art thou greater than I'hua'Mazda? Thrust, then, thy spear against my breast. The keeper did so, saying: Thy size is nothing to me, thou boaster! But, lo, the shaft was broken in a thousand pieces, neither touched the blade against his garments. Seeing which, the other spearsmen feared, and Zarathustra walked up to them and took their spears from them.

4. And the Zarathustrians stood in the form of a living altar, and Zarathustra laid his hands against the front wall of the prison, saying: In thy wisdom and power, O I'hua'Mazda, deliver thou this prison! And, behold, the front wall opened as a door openeth, and the prisoners came out unharmed.

5. Zarathustra said: On the morrow the king will decree to death every Faithist within the city. Go ye, therefore, whilst it is yet night, and command all my people to rise at once and depart out of the city, and I will lead them to a place of safety. So that same night the Faithists fled beyond the walls.

6. And it came to pass that on the next day, when the king heard what had transpired in regard to the prison, he decreed to death every Zarathustrian found within the city, even as prophesied by Zarathustra. But they were already gone, and were in the Forest of Goats, and there were of them four thousand six hundred and thirty, men, women and children.

CHAPTER XVIII.

1. I'hua'Mazda spake to Zarathustra, the All Pure, saying: Explain these things to my people, for they shall not dwell in darkness nor in fear. Zarathustra said: What shall I tell them, O I'hua'Mazda?

2. I'hua'Mazda said: My people are united; my people are delivered out of the evil city. To themselves, of themselves, and by themselves, have I delivered them, as a separate people.

3. I found an easy way to unite them; I went not by a dark road. This is no miracle, but the manifestation of Faith in the All Light.

4. Take them further away from Oas; far away in the forest. And since Asha is an old man, and learned above all other men, he shall be the ara'ba over them.

5. I'hua'Mazda said: But as for thee, O Zarathustra, thou art young and strong. Thou shalt choose fifty men from amongst my people, well learned and strong, full of vigor. And they shall be thy companions; and thou shalt visit the large cities of Jaffeth and Shem and Ham. For four years shalt thou travel, delivering the Zarathustrian law; but at the end of that time thou shalt return to Oas, and to this people, my first chosen.

6. And behold, after that, Asha shall go with thee to Oas, and thou shalt raise thy hand against the city, and it shall fall.

7. Zarathustra then explained these things to the people, and thereafter took them to the valley of Yan'she, by the river Witch'owitch; and he divided them into three large cities and four small ones, after the manner of the I'hins, the sacred people, white and yellow.

8. And he gave them fathers (rab'bahs), and made Asha chief father over all the others. Thus was founded the Zarathustrian religion; the I'hua'Mazdian law, the Ormazdian law, the Zarathustrian law.

9. And Zarathustra chose fifty men, well learned, and vigorous, not old; and they departed, to establish the Zarathustrian law in the cities of the east and south. I'hua'Mazda led them forth, speaking to Zarathustra, the All Pure, telling him whither to go, and directing him in the nearest roads, over the mountains and plains, and across the rivers. And wheresoever they went, I'hua'Mazda provided them with beasts of burden, and beasts to ride on, converting their owners to the Ormazdian law, who gave them all things required.

10. The first large city Zarathustra came to was Tse'gow, on the plains of Jo'ab, high walled with wood and stone; and when he came to the gate thereof the keeper demanded his name and business, speaking in another language, and Zarathustra understood him not. Then came I'hua'Mazda, answering the keeper in his own tongue, saying:

11. I am a servant of the Creator, Ormazd; I come to prove immortal life before the king. Send, then, to thy king, and he will admit me and my people. So the keeper sent to the king, who commanded that Zarathustra come before him.

12. And when he and his attendants were thus before the king, the king said: Art thou he of whom the King of the Sun hath spoken? And what is thy business with me? Thy king, even the king of kings, is mad. Then answered I'hua'Mazda, saying:

13. Zarathustra, of whom the Sun king spake, is before thee. I am here to prove to thee many things pertaining to what is written in the Book of holies. But ere I utter many words, I pray thee, that thy son, Ha'sing, and thy wife, Hi'ti'us, and thy daughters, Peutu,

349

Zoo, He'in and Zabee, be also present.

14. The king said: How knowest thou the names of my people? And I'hua'Mazda said: Here stand guardian spirits, ashars, and they speak to me. Chief amongst them is Ay'ay, thy grandfather, who slew himself; and next to him are thy kinspeople in spirit, Noa, Wess, Lut, Gan'ce, Mith'ce, Nim'och, Wo'huin, Ruks and Pa'stcue.

15. The king was concerned, for many of these had been slain in wars, nor knew he how Zarathustra discovered their names. So he sent for his wife and son and daughters, and they all went into an inner chamber, Zarathustra with them. Then spake I'hua'Mazda to the king, saying:

16. Think not that Asha is mad because he hath given up all he had and gone to live with the poor. The Gods call all men mad who do otherwise, especially rich men, and kings, and rulers. For such men set value on things that they cannot retain but during earth life at most. Asha setteth value on that which will last forever. I would that all men would do as Asha hath done.

17. Because of unbelief in the Great Spirit, man hath set himself up as the All Highest, and his trade hath become war and destruction. I came not to persuade thee to give away thy kingdom nor thy riches, nor yet for any glory or profit to myself. I speak for the hosts being slain, tribe against tribe, city against city; I speak for the millions of spirits in darkness, who dwell on the battlefields.

18. I'hua'Mazda thus gained the attention of the king, and, meanwhile, the angels who accompanied him took on forms, looking like mortals; and presently, the king and his family looked about and saw them, and were frightened; and the king drew his sword, saying: Who have entered thus, uncalled! But as he advanced, behold, the spirits disappeared. The king was amazed. I'hua'Mazda continued, saying:

19. Concern not thyself because the spirits show themselves; neither call thou these appearances miracles. Spirits are always present; but because they thus clothed themselves with corporeal parts, thou hast for the first time seen them. Whilst thou was quiet, they came; with thy sudden passion they disappeared.

20. The king said: Will they come again? Then answered I'hua'Mazda, saying: Since thy wife and thy daughters are frightened, why should they appear again? Yet hear thou me, O king! Since thy youth up thou hast been prepared for this. Thy wife is half-breed with the I'hins, the sacred people. The I'hins were preserved by the Gods to this end, for they are as the leaven, prepared for the resurrection of all the races of men. Because of this great virtue in thy wife, the spirits of the dead can show themselves before thee.

21. Whilst I'hua'Mazda thus spake, the angels again assumed sar'gis, and there were present several spirits whose mortal lives had been cut short by the king's own sword. Chief of these was Awetakeytha, one time king of the city of Tse'gow.

22. The sar'gis spake to the king, saying: Think not that I am dead, O king! I am not dead, save in the corporeal part. As by thy sword thou didst cut me off, so by the sword shalt thou be pierced through. Next spake Too'Sain, another sar'gis, saying: Till thou art dead, O king, and thy soul cast into hell, I will not cease to torment thee! Next spake Ghon, another sar'gis, saying: Before yesterday I brought venom from rotten flesh, and inoculated thee in the breath of thy mouth! Thou shalt cough blood and foul-smelling corruption! Next spake Owd, saying: I am come from the land of the dead, O king, with the torments of hell for thee! Then spake We'Seay, a sar'gis,

saying: I am thy first wife; why slewest thou me? Was not the world wide enough?

23. Thus the spirits continued to speak, suffered by I'hua'Mazda to manifest their evil desires and passions in their own way; nor did one spirit appear who had a single good word of cheer for the king. Then the king spake, saying:

24. Go away, spirits, or devils! I will see no more! And, with that, he swung his sword about fiercely; but when he quieted a little, I'hua'Mazda spake to him, saying:

25. I declare to thee, O king, the air is filled with the spirits of the dead; and because they were slain by thee, they lie in wait for thy soul, when thou shalt die. Think not that by slaying a man thou art rid of him; only the corporeal part is within thy power. The soul never dieth. Ormazd is just. Whom thou hast injured, thou shalt restore.

26. The king said: If a man be a bad man, and I kill him, is it not a great good? I'hua'Mazda said: To kill him is a great evil. Thou shouldst convert him to good. The king said: But if he belong to me? Then I'hua'Mazda said: No man belongeth to thee. The same Creator created all men; from Him are all men created; and they belong to Him.

27. The king said: But I have possession of them. They are mine. If thy Creator is stronger than I, let Him take them. I'hua'Mazda said: To take them from thee would be no honor; but for thou to deliver them is thine own honor.

28. Now whilst the king's mind was thus engaged, the angels fell to work to demonstrate their presence and power, in some unusual way; and, accordingly, they cut loose the tapestry about the walls, and let it fall to the floor, and with great explosion. The queen and her daughters rose up and fled.

29. The king was angered, and thrust his sword at Zarathustra; but, lo, it broke into a hundred pieces, and yet no part touched Zarathustra. I'hua'Mazda said: Save thou repent of thy evil ways, I will withdraw my holy angels from this house, and thou shalt bear witness that ere the morning sun appears, this palace shall not be left standing.

30. But the king was hardened. So, when I'hua'Mazda perceived there was no repentance in the king, he withdrew the Lord and his ashars, abandoning the palace to evil spirits, but he sent guardian spirits to inspire the queen and her daughters to flee from the house that night, and they so fled. And the spirits of darkness went to the king's enemies and inspired them to go against the palace; and they so went, and destroyed it.

31. The next day, Zarathustra went about in the city, which was in great tumult, and I'hua'Mazda spake through him to the people. And in one day he received more than a thousand followers; and when the king saw this, he decreed Zarathustra to death, offering a reward to whoever would slay him.

32. The next day he preached again before the people, and received great addition to his followers; and then the king ordered his soldiers, of whom there were ten thousand, to fall upon Zarathustra and his people, and destroy them. But I'hua'Mazda had prophesied this to his adherents beforehand, and had advised them to flee. And many escaped before morning; but there were also many who were still within the walls when the soldiers came upon them.

33. I'hua'Mazda stretched his hand upward, saying: Fire of Thy fire, O Father! Give me here a wall of fire! And there rose up a wall of fire betwixt them and the soldiers; and the latter, seeing this, turned and fled, crying out: Shri! shri! --signifying spirit.

34. Thus Zarathustra led them out of the city, and not one man or woman or child was injured. But it came to pass that the deeds done through Zarathustra were greatly

exaggerated in relating them, so that people who had not yet seen him believed the world was about to come to an end.

35. Thus the king lost all discipline over the city; and the people lived without law or order; robbing one another, or destroying whatever stood before them.

CHAPTER XIX.

1. Zarathustra called his fifty companions before him, saying: Because these people are delivered from the tyrant, they will become his enemies. A people long oppressed, love vengeance. This would thwart the Ormazdian law. Take them, therefore, away from the city, dividing them into groups amongst yourselves, and I will send angels, capable of interpreting languages.

2. I'hua'Mazda said: Behold, a God cometh not to accomplish at random. Nor cometh he to one man only, in order to overthrow the evil of a whole world. Ye have been prepared for this work since the day of your birth. My angels have been with you, and ye are a part of my army. Now this shall happen to you, after ye have divided these people, and conducted them into the forests: ye shall begin to speak with new tongues, and these people will understand you. And ye shall build altars of worship to Ormazd, teaching these people songs and prayers and dancing, explaining to them the Ormazdian law.

3. Zarathustra said: Wait not for me to come, nor for the voice of I'hua'Mazda, but do ye in faith as I have commanded, and the Voice will be with you.

4. So, those who fled from the anarchy of the city, were led away, half a day's journey, and there encamped. And the companions of Zarathustra, who were styled Inquas, were entranced, and comprehended the language of the people, and could talk with them understandingly.

5. So they built altars to Ormazd, and taught the people worship, and caused them to take an oath not to kill any man or woman or child, nor beast, nor bird; nor any animal created alive. And they bound them on the oath taken under the thigh, to eat only fruit and nuts and roots and bread, according to the Ormazdian law. And they divided them into families of tens and families of hundreds, and of a thousand, giving them one rab'bah for each, according to the Zarathustrian law.

6. But Zarathustra returned into the city, and I'hua'Mazda clothed him about with fire, at night, and with clouds in the daylight, so that the people could behold his power, and no man dare raise a hand against him.

7. Then he commanded the people to gather together all the skulls on the walls, and the scalps that were hung about the houses and on the poles; and they were taken away and burned. And as for the soldiers, he disbanded them; and thus, the king was rendered helpless, left to stroll about, cursing.

8. And Zarathustra advised the people to go out of the city and live; and they so went forth by thousands, beginning new lives. After that, Zarathustra left the place; and at once it was filled with drujas, and they went to the druks and inspired them to fire and plunder. And it came to pass, in not many days, the great city of Tse'gow, with all its temples, and towers, and palaces, was reduced to a heap of ashes.

9. Zarathustra went before the people, hundreds of thousands of them, speaking by the voice of I'hua'Mazda, saying: I hear certain ones saying: Whoever setteth value on earthly

things, above heavenly things, it is good for him to have fire and destruction. All things come of the Father, Ormazd, or by His permission. When He withdraweth His hand from a wicked city, evil spirits rush in.

10. Ye have said: Who are evil spirits? Why doth not Ormazd destroy them? I say unto you, evil spirits are both yourselves and the dead. Whom ye have slain in passion, still live to torment you in spirit. Ye had their skulls hung on the gates and walls; your temples of science were portaled with the scalps of your enemies. The spirits of these people still live, though their bodies be dead, and they obsess you to deeds of wickedness.

11. This is the Ormazdian law; when a man is dead, ye shall either burn the body, or bury it in the ground, that the spirit be not troubled. But ye bound them in spirit; Tse'gow was an eye-sore in the sight of them that were slain for its glory. They delighted to see it destroyed.

12. More than ye have lost by the fire, these spirits have gained ten-fold; for now the Gods can deliver them in heaven. For which reasons, I declare unto you that it is a great good that Tse'gow is destroyed. The world is large; the lands are very wide. Kill no man, nor woman, nor child. They are Ormazd's.

13. Neither shall ye build large cities; they are a curse on the face of the earth. Neither shall ye live alone, for such become bound to self; but dwell in families of tens and hundreds and thousands. Hath not the Father given you an example in the I'hins? They kill not, nor take that which is another's; nor are given to lust, nor war, nor quarrelsomeness.

14. The Voice said: Where is the king's wife, Hi'ti'us? Where is Ha'Sing, the prince? And the princesses, Pentu, and Zoo, and He'in, and Zabee? The multitude answered: They are gone!

15. After that the Voice said: I say unto you, they were gone, but they are returning. Presently they will be here. They shall speak before you. And sure enough, presently the king's wife and son and daughters, came. Hi'ti'us said: Behold, Tse'gow of Oas is burned. Who hath seen the king? He'in and Zabee, the princesses, were very young girls, and they cried for their father. He had slain himself, cutting his bowels across with his sword.

16. I'hua'Mazda spake through Zarathustra, saying: Come thou, Hi'ti'us, and stand on the rocks so that all can see, and bring thy children. She came and stood beside Zarathustra. And now the Voice said: Let these bear witness whether the dead do not live in spirit?

17. Hi'ti'us said: With my own eyes have I seen the spirits of the dead; with my own ears, heard them talk. My children shall hold up their hands if these things be true. The children held up their hands. Again Hi'ti'us said: Where is my husband, the king?

18. Whilst they were yet standing on the rocks, lo and behold, the ghost of the king rose up before all the people, and He'in and Zabee cried out: Here is my father! Then spake I'hua'Mazda, saying to the soul of the king: Knowest thou that thou art dead? The soul of the king spake loud, so that all could hear him; he said: No, I am not dead, but I have done a foolish thing, I cut my bowels across.

19. Then Hi'ti'us said: I fear, indeed, the king is dead, and this is his spirit. He looks strangely! I'hua'Mazda said: There is no cut. Thy belly is unharmed. But the spirit persisted, saying: I thrust my hands in the hole, and yet thou sayest, there is no wound! Thou art mad! I remember thee; it was thou who broughtst back these phantom enemies to torment me!

20. I'hua'Mazda said: What enemies seest thou? The spirit answered: All I ever slew; a thousand or more! Away, ye torments! Ye mockers! I will thrust you through.

21. The soul of the king then stamped and raved, for he saw the spirits of the dead; but the audience saw them not, though they saw him, for he was in sar'gis form.

22. I'hua'Mazda said: I say unto thee, O king, thou art dead, and risen from the dead. Couldst thou but awake to this fact, thou wouldst be risen in spirit. Neither canst thou be delivered till these, thy enemies, are also delivered. Then answered the spirit of the king, saying: I banish thee from the city of Tse'gow! Nor shalt thou ever return, under penalty of death!

23. I'hua'Mazda said: I tell thee, O king, the city of Tse'gow is destroyed. Verily is there not one house standing in all the place! The soul of the king answered, saying: Thou tormentest me! Thou madman! Thou assertest lies in the face of facts! Begone, wretch! O that my belly were not cut across; I would at thee with vengeance!

24. I'hua'Mazda withdrew the sar'gis, and the king could not be seen; nevertheless, his spirit continued cursing and raging all the same. The queen, Hi'ti'us, comprehended the matter fully, and her heart was heavy with sorrow.

25. I'hua'Mazda said to her: Remember the faith of thy forefathers, the I'hins. Be thou strong in the Ormazdian law, and these sorrows will pass away. Nor is there anything in heaven or earth can satisfy the soul that is short before the law. To her that can say, I live the all highest, happiness hath a sure foundation.

26. And, whosoever perceiving the dead are in torments, let them pray for them, singing anthems unto the Father. Intercede ye with the All Light, to bestow them with peace. Think not that because of your prayers the All Light runneth with haoma, to feed the spirits of the dead. But this I declare unto you, that, by peace and joy in your devotions to the Father, the spirits are thus reclaimed to virtue and exaltation.

27. These things will I show unto you yet this night; be steadfast and hopeful in Faith, and, when the evening hath come, I will again call up the spirits of the dead before you.

CHAPTER XX.

1. Because of the destruction of Tse'gow, there were hundreds of thousands of people rendered homeless and destitute, and groups were surging about in all places, crying out for food, or for some needful thing. I'hua'Mazda said to Zarathustra, the All Pure: The ill-fortune of mortals is the good fortune of the righteous Gods; but the good fortune of mortals is the glory of the evil Gods. Think not that because Tse'gow is burned, and the people hungry, the Voice of the Father is out of place. Now is the time they will give ear. By the loss of earthly treasures, the soul seeketh for that which will endure forever.

2. Go thou, therefore, O Zarathustra, and I will go with thee; and criers shall be sent out, calling the people to the valley of Tsoak'ya this night.

3. So it came about, when night set in, Zarathustra came before the people, and there were tens of thousands of them. I'hua'Mazda spake to them, explaining the Ormazdian law.

4. When he was done speaking, he took Hi'ti'us, the king's widow; her children, and forty others, and made a crescent of them; and he stood betwixt the horns thereof. And to his left and right were many of his companions. Thus prepared, Zarathustra sang a song, such as the I'hins had taught him in his youth.

5. And the drujas were ushered into the crescent, taking on sar'gis, the king amongst the number. And the spirit of the king was softened, for they sang peace to his soul and joy forever; and presently, he awoke from his craziness, and remembered he was dead; and he rejoiced in Zarathustra, and applauded him before all the people. And likewise the spirits of darkness who were with him did in the same manner.

6. Zarathustra said: Behold, I have not come in a dark age. Ye shall not worship any man born of woman, nor call him sacred. One only, Who is Ormazd, the Creator, is Master over all the world. Hear ye now my voice unto Him!

7. Zarathustra stretched his arms upward, full of energy, and I'hua'Mazda spake through him, saying: Light of Light, O Father, hear Thou Thy Son! With thy Almighty hand bless Thou these faithful sufferers! Hardly had these words been spoken, when there fell from the air above, fish and fruit and grains and roots, and all things good to eat, more than sufficient to feed the famished people for three days; and there were more than thirty thousand of them.

8. And all this while the sar'gis of the king looked on, and beheld what had been done; and he cried out with a loud voice: Blessed art Thou, O Ormazd! O that I had known Thee! O that I had sought to find Thee! Hi'ti'us, my wife! And my blessed babes! Swear ye to the king, ye will proclaim the I'hua'Mazdian law, forever! Swear it! Give me joy! Swear! swear! swear!

9. Then Hi'ti'us and the children held up their hands as directed by I'hua'Mazda, swearing a solemn oath to maintain the love of Ormazd and the Zarathustrian law, forever. After these, there came thousands and thousands of others, who also swore in the same way. I'hua'Mazda then took away the sar'gis, and the spirits could not be seen by mortals.

CHAPTER XXI.

1. On the next day Zarathustra appeared before the multitude, and I'hua'Mazda spake through him, saying:

2. I came not in an age of darkness, but of light and knowledge. I am not here to proclaim miracles; I serve the Father, whose Son I am.

3. In heaven above there are two kinds of spirits; those who serve the earth and those who serve the Father. If ye serve the earth ye shall be ministered unto by the spirits of the lower heavens, who are bound to the earth. If ye serve the Father, ye are ministered unto by the spirits of the higher heavens.

4. Because ye were united in prayer last night to the Father, His holy angels brought ye food. His harvests are over all the earth; His fields are broad. It is not just that He also gather it and bring it to you. To be just to Him, go ye and bring forth out of the fat earth wherewith all ye need, rejoicing in Him. Cease warring; kill not anything He created alive, that runs on the ground or flies in the air. And no flesh save fish, which is without blood, and is cold in life, shall enter your mouths.

5. In the morning, when ye first awake, pray to the Creator, Ormazd, praying after this manner: Glory be to Thee, Thou All Light! Because Thou hast created me alive; I will strive with all my might to be upright before Thee; I have faith Thou createdst me wisely; and I know Thou wilt show me the right way.

6. Make my eyes sharper to see into my own soul than into all else in the world, I will

discover its dark spots and wash them clean. Seal Thou up my eyes from the sins of others, but magnify their goodness unto me, that I may be ashamed of my unworthiness before Thee.

7. This day will I run quickly to the distressed and helpless, and give them joy by some deed or word. Seal up my tongue against slandering any man, or woman, or child, for they are of Thy creation, and of Thine Own handiwork.

8. What Thou feedest me with, sufficient is it for the day thereof; complaint shall not escape from my mouth. Quicken me all day, O Ormazd, with this, my prayer, that I may become a glory in Thy works. Amen!

9. I'hua'Mazda said: Touching prayer, remember, that to utter words, but to practice not, is of little value. He that is true to his own light is strong in soul; to be false to one's own light is to put out the eyes and stop up the ears. He that would rise in heaven, let him begin to rise on earth. The resurrection lieth in following the All Highest Light one already hath. He that doeth not this, is a fool to ask the Father to raise him up. Hell fire is his boundary in the next world.

10. Because Ormazd sacrificed Himself, He created all things. By sacrifice for the elevation of others doth a man begin at the beginning of approaching Ormazd. This is resurrection, in fact.

CHAPTER XXII.

1. I'hua'Mazda called together those who swore allegiance to the Zarathustrian law; and he separated them from the others, and there were in ten days thirty thousand professed followers.

2. Nevertheless, I'hua'Mazda spake to Zarathustra, saying: Of all these, only one in ten will remain long in faith. And to establish the tenth firmly is more valuable than to have ten times as many who understand not what they profess. Zarathustra asked: How can a tenth be made firm?

3. I'hua'Mazda said: Long ago I told thee to go and live with the I'hins. Zarathustra said: I understand. I learned the Wheel of Ormazd from the I'hins. Then said I'hua'Mazda: Make thou a Wheel of Ormazd. (See BOOK OF SAPHAH, tablet Semoin, E-O-IH, and Eloih. --Ed.)

4. Zarathustra made a wheel, and hung it slanting, facing the sun at high noon. Then I'hua'Mazda explained to the people, saying: This is a symbol of the name of the Creator, Ormazd, the All Light Master! Put it in the place betwixt the horns of the crescent, for it is sacred; it is the Sign of the Altar; it is called the Altar. Let the Faithists go with me, and I will explain.

5. They carried it to the meeting-place and faced it in the same direction. And when the people stood in a circle around it, I'hua'Mazda said: The name of this place shall be Harel, and the name of the wheel shall be Altar. Behold, then, ye have already sworn an oath under the thigh, in the custom of your forefathers, but ye shall now renew your oath on the Altar of Ormazd, and His Holy Book.

6. I'hua'Mazda then administered the oath unto many, wherein they covenanted to turn from evil and strive to do good; and each and every one turned the wheel once round, as a witness before the Father. When they had all covenanted, I'hua'Mazda said: Ye shall make many wheels, and carry them along the roadways, and wherever one road crosseth

another ye shall fix an Altar; and ye shall dedicate the wheel to the Creator.

7. And whoever passeth that way afterward shall halt and remember his Creator; and he shall renew his covenant, to turn from evil and strive to do good; and in testimony before the Father, he shall turn the wheel once round.

8. Thus was established the sacred wheel of Zarathustra amongst the I'huan race.

9. I'hua'Mazda spake to Zarathustra, saying: What is the most potent thing? Zarathustra said: The eye is the most potent. The eye is most to be feared; the most desirable. The eye of man can go away from man; his hand cannot go away from him, nor his foot. Man's eye can go to the mountains; to the clouds, the moon, the sun and the stars.

10. I'hua'Mazda said: If the eye of man is his most potent instrument, what then? So, Zarathustra made a picture of an eye, and placed it over the altar. Whereupon I'hua'Mazda made the people covenant anew, but this time to the I'hua'Mazdian law, the Ormazdian law. Whereupon they said: I know Thine eye is upon me night and day; nothing is hidden from Thy sight, O Ormazd!

11. And I'hua'Mazda commanded them to place a picture of an eye over the altars in all places of worship.

12. Then came the first night of the new moon, and Zarathustra went into the place of worship; and a great multitude also came in. So I'hua'Mazda said: This is mas night for the spirits of the dead. That the widow, Hi'ti'us, may have joy this night, I will sing and pray for the spirit of the king. And, afterward, for all spirits who are in darkness.

13. When they sang and prayed, the spirit of the king came in sar'gis, and talked to Hi'ti'us, and to others. And, after that, the spirit of the king prayed and sang with I'hua'Mazda. Thus was established the first night of the new moon as moon's night (mass) for the spirits of the dead, and it was demonstrated before the living.

14. I'hua'Mazda taught through Zarathustra for forty days and nights; teaching the Zarathustrian law, the Ormazdian law. And thousands and thousands of people were converted unto righteousness; and these were called disciples (ga'spe Zarathustra) of Zarathustra.

15. Zarathustra inquired of I'hua'Mazda what was the best, most potent thing for the generations of men. Then answered I'hua'Mazda, saying: The best, most potent thing for the generations of men is to teach the very young child the ever presence of the All Potent Eye, which sees into the body of mortals, into the behavior of mortals, and into the soul.

16. Zarathustra inquired concerning very young children. Then I'hua'Mazda answered, saying: In three days and five days and seven days the rite of circumcision for the males, and piercing the ears for the females. And, when they are old enough, they shall be consecrated on the wheel.

17. Zarathustra said: To consecrate, what is that? Then answered I'hua'Mazda: To profess the All Highest, the Creator, Ormazd. And from that time forth the young child shall pray to Ormazd every night before going to sleep, and pray every morning as soon as awake to Ormazd, renewing its covenant and acknowledging the presence of the All Potent Eye.

18. Zarathustra inquired concerning children who were not thus provided. I'hua'Mazda answered, saying: Such children may live, or they may die. If they die, they fall into the care of the drujas and become drujas themselves; but if they live, they will grow up liars and druks, killing and stealing.

19. Zarathustra inquired concerning a consecrated child, if it die? Then I'hua'Mazda

answered: If a consecrated child die, its soul is received in heaven by the consecrated spirits of Ormazd. It is then taken to a place of all good, a place of delight.

20. When these things were explained to the disciples, the mothers brought their children before Zarathustra; and I'hua'Mazda consecrated them on the altar, and they were baptized with water and fire, and given names by the rab'bah.

Plate 11.
UG-SA or UH-GA.

CHAPTER XXIII.

1. Zarathustra, the All Pure, inquired concerning protection against imposters. To which I'hua'Mazda answered, saying: Prove all things on the altar. If a man come before the people saying: Behold, I am a prophet! and he teach strange doctrines, he shall be tied on the wheel with his face toward the sun at high noon. And if he be a true prophet, the spirits who dwell by the altar will set him free. But, if he be not released on the third night, the wheel shall be carried out into the forest and stood up by the bushes. And if he be an imposter the wild beasts will come and devour his flesh.

2. Zarathustra inquired concerning the wheel afterward. I'hua'Mazda said: When an imposter hath perished on the wheel, behold, the wheel shall be no longer used as before. But the disciples shall cut away the rim of the wheel, and cast it away, for it is useless. But the cross-bars of the centre of the wheel shall be retained, for it was on the bars that he was bound, and the cross of the bars is sacred; and it shall be hung in the place of worship, for it is a true cross. (See Se'moin, Book of Saphah, as to the origin of the true cross. Look for symbol, Fete. --Ed.)

CHAPTER XXIV.

1. Zarathustra inquired concerning the government. To which I'hua'Mazda replied, saying:

2. To the All Pure disciples there is no need of government, save to do the Will of Ormazd. But no people are all pure; no people are all wise. Two kinds of government created the Creator; the first is His Own, the Government of Ormazd; the second is the government mortals have amongst themselves.

3. Zarathustra inquired if government did not abridge liberty. I'hua'Mazda said: The Ormazdian government giveth liberty; so far as man's government partaketh after the Ormazdian government, it giveth liberty also.

4. Zarathustra inquired: What is the best, most potent, man's government? To which I'hua'Mazda replied: This is the best, most potent, man's government: First, there shall not be more than two thousand people, so that they can know one another; and no city shall be larger than that.

5. The oldest, wisest, best man shall be the chief rab'bah; but the families of tens and families of hundreds within the city shall have each, one rab'bah, being the oldest, wisest, best man.

6. These rab'bahs shall be the government of the city. They shall have a government house, and it shall be the place of decrees.

7. Zarathustra said: How shall they make decrees, that the decrees pervert not liberty? I'hua'Mazda said: Ask not this, O man! He who crieth out constantly for his liberty is a selfish man, he is a druk. Save a man be willing to sacrifice his liberty somewhat, for the public good, he is unworthy before Ormazd. To find the amount of sacrifice, this is the business of the decrees.

8. Zarathustra said: How, then, shall the rab'bah proceed? I'hua'Mazda said: When they are seated, the chief rab'bah shall announce the subject; neither shall any other rab'bah announce the subject. But if a rab'bah have a subject, he shall state it beforehand to the chief rab'bah.

9. After the subject is announced, then shall all the rab'bahs speak on the subject; but they shall not speak against one another; each one declaring his highest light.

10. When they have all spoken, then shall the chief rab'bah speak his highest light, which he gathereth from the others in the first place, but which is afterward illuminated by the Light of Ormazd, and this shall be the decree.

11. Zarathustra inquired concerning the laws betwixt cities. I'hua'Mazda spake to Zarathustra, the All Pure, explaining the Ormazdian law. He said: A city is a family of one. A small village is a family of one; for which reason is a city called Ir. And every city shall have one God-ir, who shall be the oldest, best, wise man. The God-irs shall meet in council to consider what is good for all the cities jointly. For some cities are situated for flax and wool, some for iron, and some for copper, and some for ships.

12. Zarathustra inquired concerning the Council of God-irs. I'hua'Mazda answered him, saying: The God-irs shall choose the oldest, best, wise man amongst them, and he shall be called God-ir Chief. And he shall sit in the east in the Council chamber, and he shall present the subjects, after they have been told him by the other God-irs. And when he hath presented a subject, all the members shall speak upon it. And after they have all spoken, then the God-ir Chief shall speak, and his words shall be the decree, which shall

be called the Zarathustrian law, because the All Light dwelleth with the Chief, and he cannot err. This is the Ormazdian law, the I'hua'Mazdian law, the Zarathustrian law.

13. Zarathustra said: Of a walled city (giryah), what is the Ormazdian law? I'hua'Mazda answered, saying: To the I'hins, walled cities; to the I'huans, cities without walls. To the cities of the druks, walls. This is the kingdom of I'hua'Mazda; they that have faith, why shall they build walls? They shall not hoard up gold and silver; none will rob them. After Zarathustra, two people will live. One shall be the people of this world; the other shall be the people of Ormazd. The former shall strive for earthly things; the latter for spiritual things. And there shall be no affinity betwixt these two people. From this time forth, the Zarathustrian people, who have faith in the Father, shall not have walled cities (save the I'hins, the sacred people). But this world's people, having no faith in the Father, shall have faith in stone walls; whereby ye may know which are righteous in my sight.

14. Zarathustra inquired concerning the smallest of cities. I'hua'Mazda answered him, saying: The smallest city is a man and his wife and children. And even as the people in a large city are one with one another, so shall a man and his wife and children be one with one another.

15. And as a large city must have a head father, so shall a small one. Whatsoever hath no head is nothing.

16. Zarathustra said: In the government of a large city, the fathers speak on a subject, and after them, the head father decreeth.

17. I'hua'Mazda said: Even so shall it be in a family of husband and wife. The wife shall speak first, and the children next, if old enough; and after that the father shall decree. That which is a good law for a large city, is good for a small one. As the kingdoms in heaven are governed, so shall be the kingdoms on earth.

18. Zarathustra inquired concerning a bad husband and a good wife, and a bad wife and a good husband? I'hua'Mazda spake to Zarathustra, the All Pure, saying:

19. Who knoweth what is good and what is bad? Are not all men to give themselves as sacrifice to the Father, and all women also? If a good woman is not willing to sacrifice herself to a bad husband, after having sworn to Ormazd, then she is not good, but a lover of herself. A good woman hath no self to serve. Because her husband turneth out bad, shall she also? Is it not good for her in the place Ormazd provided? Shall she set up her judgment against the Father's?

20. There be men of evil, and of passion, who abuse their wives. Knoweth not every damsel this? For this reason, if she commit herself to her husband in the name of the Father, He heareth her. And He establisheth His kingdom in her house. And that man and woman have no longer themselves to consult as to their desires; for if the Father desireth her to leave her husband, or the husband to leave the wife, He taketh one of them to heaven. Think not that He changeth as the wind, or boweth Himself to please the caprice of man or woman. Rather let the good wife, with a bad husband, say to Ormazd:

21. Because I was vain, Thou hast rebuked me, O Father. Because I sought to change my condition, Thou hast shown me I knew not what was good for me. Yea, thou hast shown me the folly of my judgment before Thee, and I will profit in turning to Thy Will. I will not more open my mouth in complaint. Though I be scourged with stripes, and made ashamed of my household, yet will I glorify Thee. The city Thou hast founded in me, will I begin at the foundation, and build up as a holy city, in Thy name.

22. And she shall say to her husband, who beateth her: Because the Father gavest thou to me, I will rejoice and sing in thy praise. Before I sleep at night, I will ask His blessing upon thee, and in the early morning, and at high noon. Though thou mayst hate me, yet will I do so great good works for thee, thou shalt love me. Though thou mayst kill me, yet will I go into heaven and build a house for thee.

CHAPTER XXV.

1. Zarathustra, the All Pure, divided the people, leading his followers away from the others, taking them into good places of delight. After that, he looked back with compassion, and he said to I'hua'Mazda:

2. What of them who will not accept the Ormazdian law? I'hua'Mazda answered him, saying: Behold, thy arms are full! Let the dead have dominion with the dead. Not only this generation, but many that come after thee, will not be alive to the Ormazdian law.

3. Zarathustra apportioned his people into cities and villages and families, but over the whole of them he appointed Yus'avak as Chief, one of his companions who came with him from Oas.

4. And when Yus'avak was established, Zarathustra and his companions traveled further, and came to the city of Ne'ki'ro, kingdom of Aboatha, king of twelve generations through his forefathers, whose title was, ABOATHA, SON OF UZZA, SON OF NIMROD, SON OF THE HOUSE OF TUS'IANG, WHO IS DESCENDED FROM BEFORE THE WORLD WAS !

5. Ne'ki'ro was a walled city, but the Zarathustrians gained entrance without paying tribute, because the law thus favored strangers. Aboatha, in his youth, had traveled amongst the Parsi'e'ans, and knew the language; and when Zarathustra was before him, speaking in the Oas'an tongue, the king inquired his business, and how long he purposed staying, stating, moreover, that he had received the tablets of the Ormazdian law, with the interpretations, from the King of the Sun, Asha; and that he had desired to see Zarathustra.

6. Zarathustra said: I came to establish the Ormazdian law. In the name of the All Light will I blunt the edge of the sword and the spear. Until I have fulfilled the commandments upon me, I shall tarry within thy city. Of things thou hast read in the holy book I am come in the Person of I'hua'Mazda.

7. The king said: My city is not so large; I have more scalps and skulls, for the size of my city, than any other king in the world. But know thou, O man, I am a philosopher. Many of my people are also learned people. Hear thou me, then, and if thou hast a greater philosophy than I have, I will not only bequeath to thee the public skulls and scalps, to be thy treasures forever, but I will also give my skull and scalp into thy hand, as the most valuable treasure in the Jaffeth'an empire.

8. Zarathustra said: Though thou settest great value on skulls and scalps, because they are the product of labor, yet they are of no value to me, nor to the Father in heaven. Neither have I any philosophy for thee, or for the Father's begotten. To accept His will; to be servant unto Him, by doing good unto others, comprise the whole of the law, by which all men may be made to rejoice in their creation.

9. The king said: Think not that I am as other men. I am not as other men. In the first beginning of all things, there were SEVEN and NINE things. I was one of them. By division,

we created all there is in heaven and earth. Seven thousand and seven millions, and nine thousand and nine millions of times, have I divided myself. One-seventh and one-ninth of all there are of created things is my very self. Tell me, then, hast thou as great a philosophy as this?

10. Zarathustra said: O the folly of men before Thee, O Ormazd! They run after that which flattereth self, seeing their fellows going down in death, and they raise not their hands to lift them up! I tell thee, O king, thy poorest slave that bringeth out of the earth food for two men, hath a greater philosophy than thine! He that can rule over his own self-conceit, that speaketh not of himself, giveth a better philosophy of himself than thou hast. He who hath not yet risen from his mother's breast, hath more treasures to give than thou has obtained with all thy philosophy. Ere three days have passed by, the city's skulls and scalps will be burned to dust. Nor will thy philosophy avail thee to stay the hand of I'hua'Mazda.

11. The king said: Proposest thou with this handful of men to battle with my army? Zarathustra said: I have spoken. There is no value in discoursing with any man who hath an opinion to establish, nor is man's opinion of value to raise up the souls of men. Bring thou, therefore, thy army, and command them to fall upon me and mine!

12. The king said: Thou hast no weapons; think not that I battle with men who use their tongues, like women!

13. Zarathustra said: Why boasteth thou? Thy soldiers will turn and flee when thou bringest them against me!

14. The king turned away then, and ordered his officers to bring soldiers, and dispatch Zarathustra and his companions, and to hang their skulls and scalps on the walls. Zarathustra and his companions went into the king's garden, and formed in an altar. When the sun had set, and evening came, the king's soldiers, more than ten thousand, came upon them.

15. I'hua'Mazda had great power, because of the faith of Zarathustra, and he spake with a loud voice, saying: Light of Thy Light, O Ormazd! Build me here a wall of fire! And behold, there fell from heaven curtains of fire, till a great wall stood betwixt the two peoples; nor would one soldier throw a spear or sling a stone; and many of them broke and fled.

16. When the king saw the power of Zarathustra, he feared for his kingdom; and not deciding at once what course to pursue, he went into his palace. Then came Zarathustra and his companions out of the garden, but the light extended up above Zarathustra's head like a pillar of fire. I'hua'Mazda spake to some who were nearest, saying:

17. Run quickly and call the soldiers back, saying to them they shall be my soldiers, and I will give them the weapons of the Creator. So, the messengers ran, and brought many of them back. I'hua'Mazda commanded them to gather the skulls and scalps from the city walls, and from the gates, and go and burn them, and the soldiers did these things.

18. The next day after they were consumed, I'hua'Mazda began to preach, explaining the Ormazdian law; and he received many followers. The king had tried by all means to gather his soldiers together, but no one obeyed him. After that Zarathustra went to him, saying: If thou art one-seventh and one-ninth of all things, who thinkest thou I am?

19. The king said: They say thou art a very Creator! But, as to my opinion, thou art only a magician. Thou canst not do anything real; for which reason, I hoped thou wouldst come

before me. Know, then, thy end hath come! With that, the king struck at Zarathustra; but the king's sword was broken into pieces, and of non-effect.

20. The king had two trained chetahs, large as the largest lions, and he ordered them to be unloosed and set upon Zarathustra. And it was done; but, lo and behold, the chetahs came and licked his hands. But the king was hardened, and would not believe. I'hua'Mazda called the king to come near, and he came.

21. He said unto the king: I am not thine enemy, but the enemy of evil; I come not to take thy kingdom. In a few days I shall leave this place. So, thy kingdom would be worthless to me. And yet I come to establish another kingdom, which is the Father's. I come to overthrow sin and wickedness, and to build up that which is good. And in so doing, it shall be known amongst men that the soul is immortal.

22. Rather would I see thee and thy people alive and full of joy, than to see them dead. Thou hast said thou understandest the Ormazdian law; perceiving there is also a king's law.

23. The king's laws are for the earth-world; to punish the wicked and reward the valorous; the Ormazdian law is for the Zarathustrians, who need no kings. Thy subjects are for war and plunder; but the subjects of the Great Spirit are for doing good, and in love and mercy. And have I not shown thee that the Ormazdian laws are the stronger of the two? Yea, a hundred fold. It is wiser for thee to espouse the stronger law. Thou hast gathered certain treasures, boasting of thy treasures' value. Because thou hast made a law of exchange for skulls and scalps; how sayest thou? Maketh thou them valuable? Because a man bringeth a skull to thee, thou givest him bread. Now I declare unto thee, values consist not in the rate of exchange betwixt men. Shall a man gather a heap of stones, and say: Behold, they are valuable! Or iron, or gold, or copper, and say: Behold, they are valuable! A piece of bread is valuable, or flax, or wool.

24. Because man hath set value on things not valuable, he buildeth in falsehood and death. Ormazd alone is valuable; the man who hath the most All Light, hath the greatest valuables. For by the Light of the Father all righteous things can be obtained easily. Whilst I'hua'Mazda was yet speaking, the spirit of Zarathustra went abroad, and, with ten thousand other spirits, brought fish and fruit, and let them fall around about the place. The people ran and gathered them up for food. The king made no reply at first, for he was encompassed about with evil spirits, who were angered with I'hua'Mazda and his proceedings. Presently the king said:

25. Because I am transcended by thee, it is no longer useful for me to live. With that, he cut his belly across, and fell dead. And Zarathustra commanded that the king's body be laid straight for three days; and it was done; and there came thousands of people to look upon the king, and witness that he was dead. And they saw of a truth that the bowels were gushed out of the wound, and that there was no breath in him.

26. So I'hua'Mazda suffered the spirit of the king to live three days in torments, and then he called his disciples around him, saying: Now will I raise the king to life, and it shall be testimony in Jaffeth.

27. And Zarathustra pushed the bowels back into the belly, and drew the place shut, saying: In Thy name, O Father, heal I this man's body, as a testimony of Thy Wisdom and Power! And when Zarathustra had drawn his hand over the belly twice, it was healed. And then Zarathustra said: O Father, as by Thy spirit Thou didst quicken into life this,

Thy child, in his mother's womb, restore Thou him to life!

28. And the king was healed, and restored to life before the people; and he awoke and looked about, and then rose up. He said: Even now I was dead and in hell, and I saw millions of the dead, and they were in hell also. And there went up around about them fires of burning brimstone, and none could escape.

CHAPTER XXVI.

1. When the king was restored, he was as another man, having su'is, and believing with a full conviction; and he asked Zarathustra what now he should do that he might escape the fires of hell after death.

2. I'hua'Mazda spake through Zarathustra, saying: Think not what thou canst do to escape hell fire, for that would be laboring for self. Think what thou canst do to save others. For which reason thou shalt practice the Ormazdian law. One year shalt thou dwell with the poor, carrying the alms-bowl, according to the Zarathustrian law. After that thou shalt preach the I'hua'Mazdian law, of the denial of self for the good of the city, teaching the turning away from earthly things, and striving for spiritual things, having faith in Ormazd.

3. The king said: All these things can I do, yet one thing I cannot do, which is having faith in Ormazd. If He be a Person, and created all the creation, is He not the foundation of evil as well as good? If He heretofore created evil, or by incompetence suffered it to enter into creation, may He not do so in after time, even after death?

4. I'hua'Mazda said: When a potter hath a pot half made, sayest thou it is an evil pot? Nay, verily, but that it is not yet completed. Even so are all men, created by Ormazd. Those who are good are completed, but those who are evil are unfinished work. But the Creator also gave to man knowledge, that he might see himself in the unfinished state, and the Creator gave to man power and judgment, that man might turn to and help complete himself, thereby sharing the glory of his creation. The man that doeth this is already clear of hell fire; he that doeth it not shall not escape.

5. The king inquired concerning animals, to which I'hua'Mazda answered, saying: Animals are of the earth creation, and are completed in the place of their dwelling. Neither hath any animal aspiration to make itself better or wiser, that it may contribute to the creation. And some men have no more aspiration than an animal serving the beast (the flesh-man) only. Only the torments of hell can stir them up.

6. When I'hua'Mazda explained the Ormazdian law, the quarter of which is not here related, the king comprehended, whereupon he took the vows on the altar, and under the eye, according to the Zarathustrian law. So when those people were restored, Zarathustra left one of his traveling companions with them, as God-ir in Chief, and Zarathustra departed, taking his other companions with him.

7. Whereof it is recorded in the libraries of heaven, showing that the next city kingdom was likewise delivered, and the people became Zarathustrians.

8. And again Zarathustra departed, and came to another city, which was overthrown and delivered also. Until it came to pass that Zarathustra overthrew and delivered twenty and four cities and kingdoms in Jaffeth.

9. After that he departed to the upper lands of Shem, where he also overthrew and delivered many cities and kingdoms, establishing the Zarathustrian law. For two whole

years he labored in Shem; and so great was the power of Ormazd upon Zarathustra that all the cities and kingdoms of Shem threw off the bondage of the Sun Kingdom of Parsi'e. 10. After that Zarathustra traveled toward Ham, which was called Arabin'ya. But in those countries Zarathustra had not so great success, because the people were not learned in books, nor in the stars, nor tablets. Nevertheless, Zarathustra delivered many cities. 11. So I'hua'Mazda said to Zarathustra: Go back, now, to thine own country; and thou shalt overthrow yet seven cities and seven great kingdoms; and after that thou shalt return to Oas, and it shall fall before thy hand, that the prophecies of thy childhood be fulfilled. 12. So Zarathustra returned to Parsi'e and went to the seven great cities and kingdoms, and overthrew them; and many of them were destroyed utterly by fire and by war; but Zarathustra delivered the faithful and established the Zarathustrian law with all of them. 13. And now he returned to his native city, Oas, according to the commandment of I'hua'Mazda.

CHAPTER XXVII.

1. In those days, Pon'yah was king of Oas, and, by title, KING OF THE SUN; KING OF THE MIDDLE WORLD; KING OF KINGS; MIGHTIEST OF MORTALS; OWNER OF ALL HUMAN FLESH; RULER OF THE EARTH, MASTER OF LIFE AND DEATH!

2. For nearly four years had Zarathustra been absent, and the effect of his preaching in foreign lands had been to cut off the paying of tribute to the City of the Sun. For which reason, Pon'yah, king of Oas, had sworn an oath under his own thigh to pursue Zarathustra, and have him slain.

3. Accordingly, the king had equipped many different armies and sent them in search of Zarathustra; but I'hua'Mazda led Zarathustra in a different way on the one hand, and sent spirits to inspire the soldiers to go another way. Consequently, none of the armies sent to capture Zarathustra ever found him. When he was heard of in one city, and the soldiers came to that city, he was gone. And so it continued, until now Zarathustra had returned to the very gates of Oas.

4. Because Zarathustra was the largest man in the world, he was easily known; and from a description of him, even those who had never seen him, would know him the first time they laid their eyes on him.

5. Asha had continued with the Zarathustrians; but in consequence of the persecutions of the kings of Oas, they had been obliged to retire further into the forests and plains and unsettled regions, where roved the Listians, the wild people. To these the Zarathustrians were friends, and the Listians came in great numbers, and dwelt near about the Zarathustrians.

6. After Zarathustra had completed his travels, he returned to the Forest of Goats, in the first place, to meet his followers, and to rejoice with them for the great light I'hua'Mazda had bestowed upon them. So, when Zarathustra returned to them, there was great rejoicing; and there were present Zarathustra's mother, and many of the Listians who knew him in his childhood.

7. After many days of rest and rejoicing, I'hua'Mazda came to Zarathustra, saying: Behold, the time hath now come to go against the city of thy birth. Take Asha with thee, and I will cause Oas to fall before thy hand.

8. Accordingly, Zarathustra took Asha and returned, as stated, to the gates of Oas; but he was known at once; and when he demanded admittance, he was refused, because the king had previously decreed his banishment and death, there being an offer of reward to whoever would destroy him and bring his skull to the king.

9. The keeper of the gate, whose name was Zhoo'das, thought to obtain the reward, and hit upon the following plan, saying to Zarathustra: I know thee; thou art Zarathustra, who art banished under penalty of death. I have no right to admit thee within the city, nor have I a desire to witness thy sure death. But if thou wilt secrete thyself, till the change of watch, when I am absent on the king's reports, thou mayst take thine own risk. But if I admit thee, I will also be put to death.

10. Zarathustra said: As for myself, I fear not; but I would not have thee put to death on my account. Where, then, can I secrete myself, till the change of watch?

11. Zhoo'das, the keeper of the gate, said: Within the chamber of the wall. Go thou, and thy friend with thee.

12. So Zarathustra went into the chamber of the wall, and Asha went with him. And now, when they were concealed, Zhoo'das called his wife and said unto her: Be thou here, walking back and forth, that they who are concealed will think it is I. And I will run quickly to the guards, and they shall come and seize Zarathustra, for whom the reward is offered.

13. And the keeper's wife came and walked back and forth; and the keeper ran quickly and brought the guards, one thousand men, with spears and swords and war clubs and slings and bows and arrows, and they surrounded the place of the chamber on all sides. And then spake Zhoo'das ironically, saying: Come forth, Zarathustra, now is the change of watch!

14. And Zarathustra and Asha came forth and beheld what was done. Zarathustra said to Asha: The Light is upon me. Go thou with me. No harm shall come to thee. But now is the time come in which I shall fulfill what hath been prophesied of me in my youth.

CHAPTER XXVIII.

1. So Zarathustra suffered himself to fall into the power of the Sun King; and the soldiers caused him and Asha to march in their midst to the place of the skulls. And there came thousands and tens of thousands of people forth to witness the proceedings; for at this time there were many who were in sympathy with Zarathustra, as well as many against him.

2. And in order to stay the multitude, the captain of the army called out many soldiers in addition to those who made the arrest. Others ran to the king's palace, carrying the news of his arrest, and the place he had been taken to.

3. The king said to the heralds: Though this man shall die, it is fit that proper judgment be rendered against him, as an example before all men. Go, therefore, to the executioners, and command them to bring Zarathustra into my presence, that I may adjudge him to death according to law.

4. This was accomplished. Zarathustra was brought before the king, who accosted him, saying:

5. By thy behavior thou art accused before thy king, and I adjudge thee to death. But

that thou mayst be as an example before the world, I will render my judgments before the heralds, who shall proclaim my words unto all who desire to witness thy death.

6. First, then, thou wert ordered for arrest by my predecessor, and thou deliveredst not thyself up to my soldiers; neither could they find thee. For which thou art adjudged to death.

7. Second. Without permission from the KING OF THE SUN, thou hast traveled in foreign lands, sowing seeds of disallegiance against the CENTRAL KINGDOM. For which thou art adjudged to death.

8. Third. The KING OF KINGS offered a ransom for thy head, and the king's soldiers were disappointed in finding thee. For which thou art adjudged to death.

9. Fourth. In thy youth thou threatenedst to overthrow the city of Oas, the CITY OF THE SUN and failedst to make thy word good, thereby being a teacher of lies. For which thou art adjudged to death.

10. Fifth. Thou hast cut off the foreign tribute to the rightful OWNER OF THE WHOLE WORLD! For which thou art adjudged to death.

11. Sixth. Thou hast revived the doctrines of the dark ages, teaching of spirits and Gods, which things cannot exist, because they are contrary to nature, and contrary to the laws of the KING OF THE WORLD! For which thou art adjudged to death.

12. Seventh. Thou hast taught that there is an unseen Creator greater than thy king; which is contrary to reason. For which thou art adjudged to death.

13. Eighth. Thou returndst to Oas not openly, but as a thief, and hid thyself in a chamber of the wall. For which reason thou art adjudged to death in the manner of thieves, which is the most ignoble of deaths.

14. Therefore, I command the executioners to take thee to the den of thieves and cast thee therein; and on the morrow, at high noon, thou shalt be hung up by thy feet along with the thieves, where thou shalt be left hanging till thou art dead.

15. That my judgment may appease thy best friends, what sayest thou against my decrees?

16. Zarathustra said: All the charges thou hast made against me are true this day; but ere to-morrow's setting sun I will have disproved some of them. To-day thy kingdom is large; in two days I will be dead, and thou wilt be dead; and this great city will be destroyed. Yea, the Temple of the Sun will be rent in twain, and fall as a heap of rubbish.

17. The king laughed in derision, and then spake to Asha, saying: Thou art an old fool. Go thy way. So, Asha was liberated, and Zarathustra was taken to the den of thieves and cast therein. And the den of thieves was surrounded by the dens of lions that belonged to the king's gardens. And a bridge passed over, and, when the prisoners were within, the bridge was withdrawn. And no prisoner could escape but would fall a prey to the lions, which were fed on the flesh of the persons executed according to law.

CHAPTER XXIX.

1. During the night, Pon'yah, King of the Sun, bethought him that perhaps he might obtain the secrets of Zarathustra, as regards his powers with uz, and he sent him the following message, to wit: If thou wilt reveal the secrets of thy power to thy king, thy life shall be spared; and if thou wilt prostrate thyself before the King of Kings, saying: There is none higher! thou shalt have five cities to rule over all thy days.

2. To which Zarathustra sent back the following reply, to wit: Zarathustra hath no secrets to reveal; neither desireth he five cities, nor one city, to rule over. To-morrow I shall die, and on the following night thou also shalt die. And yet, erst thou diest, thou shalt see the temple of the stars rent in twain and fall down; and the city of Oas shall fall and rise no more; and Ya'seang, in Jaffeth, shall become KING OF THE SUN, and his dynasty shall stand thousands of years.

3. The king was surprised at such an answer, and so angered that he smote the messenger with his sling, and he fell dead, and the king ordered his body to be cast into the den of lions.

4. It was near the middle of the night when the body was brought, and Zarathustra, being tall, saw above the wall, and he called out, saying: Cast not the body into the dens with the lions; for I will call him to life in the name of Ormazd. And the men laid the body down by the outer wall, and Zarathustra said: He that is standing by the body shall lay his hand upon it, for the power of life is through life.

5. And the man laid his hand on the flesh of the man's body betwixt the neck and the back, and Zarathustra said: The words I say, say thou also: LIFE OF THY LIFE, O ORMAZD! Restore Thou this, Thy Son, to life!

6. And, lo and behold, the man awoke to life, and opened his eyes, and presently rose up; and Zarathustra bade him depart out of the city. Now the arrest and condemnation of Zarathustra had caused thousands of people to assemble around about the prison; and they beheld the man restored to life; and some of them went with him out of the city. And all night, after that, Zarathustra healed the sick, and restored the blind and deaf, by calling over the walls in the name of the Father.

7. When it was near sunrise, the next morning, the place of the executions was crowded with spectators. Many of the Zarathustrians believed that Zarathustra would liberate himself by the power upon him; and on the other hand, the king's people, especially the learned, desired to realize his execution, for they denounced him as an imposter.

8. The latter said: If he be the Master of the I'huans, let him prove his powers whilst he is hanging by the feet.

9. It was the law of Oas to keep twelve executioners, representing twelve moons, and at sunrise every morning they put to death whoever had been adjudged to death the previous day. Now, there were in prison with Zarathustra two thieves, condemned to the same ignoble death. And they were weeping and moaning! Zarathustra said to them: Weep not, nor moan, but rather rejoice. He Who gave you life is still with you. He will provide another and better home for your souls.

10. Behold, I weep not, nor moan. They who put us to death know not what they do. Rather should the multitude pity them than us. Ye shall this day escape from the tyrany of Oas.

11. Zarathustra preached till high noon, and when the light fell on the top of the temple (of the stars) the twelve executioners entered the prison and bound the prisoners' hands together behind their backs; then with another rope they tied the feet, bringing the rope up the back of the legs and passing it betwixt the arms; and they carried the end of the rope up over a beam and down again; and the executioners seized the rope and pulled upon it. And they swung the bodies of the victims high above the walls and made fast, leaving them hanging there.

12. Thus was Zarathustra hung betwixt two thieves; and whilst he was yet alive a bolt of light fell upon the temple of the stars, and it was rent in twain, and fell to the ground. And when the dust rose it was as a cloud that magnified itself, till the air of the whole city was choking; and there came another bolt of light, and, lo and behold, the walls of the city fell down, and Zhoo'das perished in the chamber of the wall.

13. The multitude ran for the king; and when they brought him out of the palace, another bolt of light fell on the palace, and it was crumbled into dust. The king called to his guards, but they obeyed him not, but fled; and so, the multitude slew the king.

14. The learned men then went down to the place of executions, and Zarathustra was not yet dead; but the two thieves were dead. And Zarathustra said unto the learned men: Now will I give up my body, and behold, ye shall say I am dead. Let the executioners then take down my body and cast it into the lions' den, and ye shall witness that they will not eat of my flesh. And some shall say: Behold, the lions are not hungry. Thereupon shall ye cast in the bodies of the two thieves, and lo, the lions will fall upon them and eat their flesh.

15. Then shall the learned men say: Behold, Zarathustra's virtue laid in different flesh. Now I declare unto you, these things are not of the flesh, but of the spirit. For angels shall gather about my body and prevent the lions from tearing my flesh. Of which matter ye shall prove before the multitude; for in the time the lions are devouring the flesh of the thieves, the angels will go away from my body, and, behold, the lions will return and eat of my flesh also. Whereby it shall be proved to you that even lions, the most savage of beasts, have spiritual sight, and are governed by the unseen world, even more than man.

16. When Zarathustra had thus spoken to the learned men, he spake to the Father, saying: Receive Thou my soul, O Ormazd! And his spirit departed out of the body, and in that same moment the whole earth shook and trembled, and many houses fell down. So they cast the body into one of the dens, wherein were seventeen lions, but they fled from the body. Then the executioners cast in the bodies of the thieves, and, lo and behold, the lions fell upon them instantly.

17. And when the angels went away from Zarathustra's body, the lions returned to it and ate also. And the keepers turned in other lions, and all the flesh was eaten. And the multitude ran and brought the body of Zhoo'das and cast it in, and the lions ate it also. And next day they cast in the king's body, and the lions ate of it, and were appeased of their hunger.

18. Now when it was night, some of the Zarathustrians gathered together at a neighbor's house; and Asha was present, and they formed a living altar in order to pray for the soul of Zarathustra, and for the two thieves, and for Zhoo'das, and, lastly, for the king. And now, came the learned men, saying: Why have ye not, during all these years, notified us of these things? Behold, Zarathustra is dead! Asha said:

19. Have I not carried the alms-bowl publicly, proclaiming them from day to day? And the learned people said: Pity, old Asha! A knave hath dethroned his reason! Now I declare unto you, it is the same now as in the olden time; the learned men are farther away from the Father than are those devouring lions. Ye look into the corporeal world for light, and truth, and power, but are blind to the spirit, which underlieth all things. I declare unto you, whether it be heat or light, or disease, that floateth in the air, or growth that cometh out of the air, in all things it is the unseen that ruleth over the seen. And more powerful than heat and light, and life and death, is Ormazd, the Person of all things.

20. Till ye have learned this, I can explain nothing that ye can comprehend. And yet, to know this, is the beginning of the foundation of everlasting happiness.

21. Whilst Asha was thus speaking, behold, the soul of Zarathustra came and stood before them, and he was arrayed in the semblance of his own flesh and color, and in his own clothes. And he spake, saying: Fear not; I am the same that was with you and was hanged and died, whose flesh was devoured by the lions; I am Zarathustra! Marvel not that I have the semblance of a corporeal body, for its substance is held together by the power of my spirit. Neither is this a miracle, for the spirits of all the living hold in the same way, each its own corporeal body. As iron attracteth iron, the spirit learneth to attract from the air a corporeal body of its like and measure.

22. Then inquired one who was present: Where are the two thieves? To which Zarathustra said: As steam riseth from boiling water, without shape or form, so are their souls this hour. For this reason was I sent into the world by the Father. Let him who would become controller of his own spirit unto everlasting life, learn the Ormazdian law, seeking to grow in spirit, instead of living for the things of this world.

23. Behold, there are here present Lords of the Hosts of Heaven, who are Sons and Daughters of the Most High Ormazd, the Creator. They will now gather together and reclothe the thieves, and show you of what like they are. Presently the two drujas, the thieves who were hanged with Zarathustra, stood before the people in sar'gis, and they raved, and cursed, and moaned; but they were blind and dumb as to the place. Then Asha inquired of them, as to who they were and what they wanted, but they only cursed him, and added that they were to be hanged.

24. Asha said: Behold, ye are already dead, and your spirits risen from the earth! To which they replied by curses against the king. And now the Lords of heaven sat up the spirit of the king, but he knew not that he was dead, and he cursed also; whereupon the spirits of the thieves fell upon him with evil intent, and all the people beheld these things. But the Lords of heaven took away the sar'gis, and the drujas could not be seen more by mortals.

25. Zarathustra said: As in the earth they were angered and dumb, they cling to the earth. For which reason ye shall sing anthems and pray for them three mornings at sunrise; three high-noons, and three evenings at sunset. Do ye this also, henceforth, forever, for three days, for all your kindred who die, or who are slain.

26. And ye shall utter only words of love for the dead; for whosoever uttereth curses for the dead, bringeth drujas upon himself. In your love and forgiveness do ye raise them out of the torments of hell. And inasmuch as ye raise up others, so doth Ormazd raise up your own souls.

27. One who was present asked how long a spirit lingered around about? To which Zarathustra said: Some for three days, some for a year, some for a hundred years, and some for a thousand years! Until they have wisdom and strength to get away. But after three days ye shall no longer desire the spirit of the dead to remain with you; rather shall ye say to Ormazd: Deal Thou with him and with us in Thine Own Way, O Father; we are content. Better is it for the spirits that ye call them not back from the higher heavens down to the earth; better for you is it, that ye remember them high up in paradise; for these thoughts will enable you to rise after ye are dead.

28. Remember that All Light answereth everything in heaven and earth after its own

manner: If ye kill, ye are answered in torments sooner or later: If ye utter falsehood, ye are answered in falsehood: If ye curse, ye will be cursed in return: If ye hate, ye will be hated: If ye seclude yourselves, ye will be excluded: If ye keep evil company in this world, ye will be bound in evil company in heaven: As ye seek to become a leader of men, remember that they whom ye rule over will be your burden in heaven: If ye teach not, ye shall not be taught: If ye lift not others up, none will lift you up: For in all things the same rule applieth in heaven as on earth, for it is a continuation in spirit of that which is practiced in the flesh.

CHAPTER XXX.

1. On the following evening, when the Zarathustrians were assembled for prayer and singing, the soul of Zarathustra again appeared before them in sar'gis, teaching the Word of Ormazd. He said:

2. Two people there are on the earth: the one is engrossed in the affairs of the earth; the other in the affairs of heaven. Better is it for ye to be of the latter. The fool will say: If all people are engrossed with the affairs of heaven, then who will provide on the earth? Such is the argument of all druks. Fear not, therefore, for the earth people becoming short of votaries.

3. So also will it be said of celibacy. The druks will say: If all people become celibates, then will the race of man terminate. Wherefore, I say again unto you, fear not, for there will be plenty left who are full of passion, and are unmindful of the kingdoms of heaven.

4. Let all who can, live for the Higher Light; the lower will ever be supplied sufficiently.

5. Even as ye find two peoples on earth, so also do two peoples exist in heaven. The one followeth the Highest Light, and ever riseth toward the highest heavens. The other followeth the affairs of earth, and riseth not, and hence is called druj. The latter engageth in sensualism, and quarrels amongst mortals, inspiring them to evil and low desires.

6. One present asked: How shall we know one another, whether we be of heaven or of earth? Then Zarathustra answered, saying: Seek to know thyself; thou art not thy neighbor's keeper. Search thine own soul a hundred times every day, to know if thou practicest the All Highest according to thine own light. Neither shalt thou find excuses for thy shortness; nor reflect overmuch on past errors, but use them as inspiration to perfect thyself henceforth.

7. Another one present asked: How of thieves, and falsifiers, and murderers? Zarathustra said: The man who serveth himself only is worse than any of these; there is no resurrection in him. But if a man cease his evil way, and practice virtue, he is on the right road.

8. A falsifier is like one with a clean gown on, that goeth about casting filth upon it; he soileth his own spirit.

9. A thief is worse than an overburdened beast; he carrieth his stolen goods not only in this world, but in heaven, to the end of his memory.

10. A murderer is like a naked man, who is ashamed, and cannot hide from the multitude. When he is in heaven, his memory of the deed writeth in human blood a stain on his soul, which all others see.

11. Another one asked: According to the I'hua'Mazdian law, the highest, best men forsake

the world, laboring to raise up the poor and ignorant, reciting prayers and anthems; taking no part in the affairs of people who are engrossed in the matters of earth; who, then, shall be the government of the wicked? To which Zarathustra answered, saying:

12. When there are not sufficient men and women for such purpose, there will be no wicked to govern. With all thy preaching, that the highest life is celibacy, there will be plenty left who will marry; with all thy preaching that the highest, best man will not be a leader of men, nor a king, nor a governor, yet there will be plenty left who will fill these places, even though they beheld the walls of hell opened up to receive them.

13. Another one asked: If the Zarathustrians separate, and live by themselves, what will be their power to do good amongst the evil? To which Zarathustra said:

14. As the highest heavens send Lords and masters down to mortals, so shall the Zarathustrians send emissaries amongst the wicked, preaching the truth, and citing the example of the Zarathustrian cities (communities).

15. For above all philosophy that man may preach, practice holdeth the highest place, and is most potent. See to it, therefore, that ye practice the Ormazdian law toward one another in all things. Avoid men of opinion; men of learning; who have pride therein; men of argument; men who quibble for proofs in improvable things; men who wish to be known as wise men; men who deny; men that can see defects in everything, and have nothing good to offer in place thereof.

16. Shun the disbelieving man, for he is diseased, and may inoculate thee; the flatterer, for he is purchasing thee; a woman, for woman's sake; or a man, for man's sake; company, for company's sake; for all these imply that the Creator is less in thy sight, and not so well loved.

17. One asked concerning spirits. To which Zarathustra said: For the affairs of earth, consult the spirits of the earth, the drujas; for the affairs of everlasting resurrection, consult thy Creator, and His holy spirits will answer thee in His name. And to whichever thou hast made thyself companion, there will be thy abiding place after death.

18. See to it that thou becomest not inveigled by drujas, for spirits can assume any name and form; but weigh their words, whether they be wise, and according to the Ormazdian law. If they teach not the higher heavens, but profess a long life in the lower heavens, consider them by their words. To flatter thee, they will profess to remember thee in another life; and to please thee, say thou wert a king, and hath had many successions of lives on the earth.

19. But of what value under the sun is such philosophy? But to rise up, away from the earth, and from the lower heavens also; it was for bestowing this word unto men that I was sent into the world. It is to teach you to know the Father's upper heavens, and the way to reach them, that His words were given unto men.

20. As it was in the olden time, so will it be again ere another generation pass away. Drujas will teach that the spirits of the dead go into trees and flowers, and inhabit them; and into swine, and cattle, and birds, and into woman, and are born over again in mortal form. Argue not with them; their philosophy concerneth not thee. Whether they be in darkness or in light, judge thou by the glory and beauty of the heavens where they live. If their words are of the earth, they belong to the earth; if they are servants to false Gods or false Lords, they will preach him whom they serve. But these matters are nothing to thee; for thou shalt serve the All Highest, the Creator. In this no man can err.

372

21. And in regard to the heaven, whither thou wouldst desire to ascend after death, magnify it with all thy ingenuity unto the All Highest Perfection. People it with thy highest ideals for thy companions. Then see to it that thou makest thyself a fit companion for them also. If thou do this with all thy wisdom and strength all the days of thy life, the Father will be with thee, and thou shalt be a glory in His works.

22. Thus preached Zarathustra after his resurrection from death; for three days and three nights preached he before his disciples; and Asha wrote down the substance of his words, and they were preserved unto the generations of Faithists from that time forth. And the words were called the Zarathustrian law, the I'hua'Mazdian law, the Ormazdian law. And they were the first heavenly words given on tablets and skins and cloth, and in books, to mortals, save what words were given in secret to the tribes of I'hins, of which the different nations of the earth knew nothing of their own knowledge as to what they were.

23. On the morning of the fourth day, when the disciples sat in crescent, which was called the living altar of God, Zarathustra again came in sar'gis. He said: Behold, the time hath come for me to rise out of hada, where I have dwelt for three days.

24. The Gods who were with me all my earth life are gathered together even here, and there are millions of them. Just near the river yonder standeth the boundary line of a heavenly ship of light! It is wider than the eye can see, and higher than the eye can see! A million of angels are singing in that ship! And there are great Gods and great Lords in it. So bright, mine eyes dare not look on them. They are all Sons and Daughters of the Great Spirit.

25. The drujas are all run away now. Their foolish gabble is hushed, gone! It is as if another world came alongside, so majestic that this one was lost. Above, high, very high, yonder! Something like a sun illumes the ship of fire! I know it is He Who hath come for me. I go now! Whither I go I will build for you all.

26. And thou, O Asha! The Gods have thrown a mantle of light over thee! A chain reacheth from thee to Ormazd! Asha was overcome, and fain would have gone to the spirit, Zarathustra. The latter said: Stand thou, and I may kiss thee! So, Zarathustra kissed Asha, and departed.

END OF THE BOOK OF GOD'S WORD.

BOOK OF DIVINITY.

WHICH DESCENDED TO THE EARTH AND BECAME KNOWN BY THE NAMES, DIV, AND
DIVA AND THE DIVAN LAWS. BEING GOD'S LABORS IN ATMOSPHEREA (HADA), FOR A
PERIOD OF THREE THOUSAND AND ONE HUNDRED YEARS, DURING THE PASSAGE OF
THE EARTH FROM THE ARC OF LOO TO THE ARC OF SPE'TA, IN ETHEREA; AND ON THE
EARTH, FROM THE TIME OF ZARATHUSTRA TO THE TIME OF ABRAHAM AND BRAHMA.

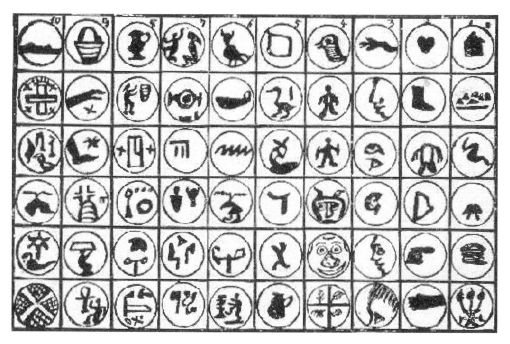

Plate 14.

THE DIVINE SEAL.

CHAPTER I.

1. God, Son of Jehovih, said: By virtue of mine own authority, and in the name of Jehovih, Creator of all things, peace and comprehensive judgment be unto angels and mortals.

2. That ye may be taught from the little that has been demonstrated in the world, of governments and principalities being manifest on earth, that similar organic bodies exist in the heavens belonging to the earth.

3. Which heavenly places and governments were the cause and forerunners of good governments manifested amongst mortals.

4. Jehovih said: He that is chief of a government on earth shall be called king, but he who is Chief of My heavenly government shall be called God. And it was so.

5. I, who am God in mine own behalf, for the enlightenment of the world, declare the Glory and Wisdom of Jehovih above all things on the earth or in the heavens above.

6. Wherein Jehovih provided that no man could be a king forever, but must give way to a successor, even so, in His heavens, provided He also unto His Gods and Lords for successors at certain periods of time.

374

7. That the way might be open for the everlasting resurrection of all men, whereby all who choose may, in time, become also Lords and Gods for the countless worlds that now are, and shall yet be created.

8. Jehovih said: I blow My breath outward, and, behold, all things are created. They go away in disorder, but they come back to Me orderly and in organic companies. And every individual member is like a tree, bloomed in perfection in every branch.

9.Jehovih said: These companies, returning to Me in all their glory, are marshaled in decorum and discipline by My Gods, for such is their labor.

10. Jehovih said: The labors of My Gods shall be chiefly in atmospherea (hada). Nevertheless, My Gods and Lords shall not only labor with the spirits of the dead to teach them organic discipline and harmony, but they shall provide unto mortals that they also may learn the system and glory of My creations.

11. In the time of Fragapatti, in the dawn of the cycle of Loo in heaven, Jehovih commanded the founding of an organic Congress for His God and Lords, and His Lord Gods.

12. And Fragapatti thus created the organic body, and named it, the Diva, making God the Chief thereof, with the title, Div, even as is known to this day in the sacred books of mortals.

13. Jehovih said: In the early days of a world I give the races of man (on the earth) a despot to rule over them. But in time after I give them representative governments with many voices, having a right to help make the laws. Even so do I provide unto the hadan heavens. In the early days I provide a God who shall be dictator and governor in his own way. But in after times I provide a parliament in heaven, wherein My God and My Lords shall jointly consult together in framing laws for angels and mortals. And these shall be called Divan laws.

14. Jehovih said: Behold, My God and Lords and sub-Gods shall teach the same things in the different parts of the earth and these heavens. I will not have one Lord teaching one thing in one place, and another teaching the same thing differently in another place.

15. Jehovih said: My God and Lords shall provide comprehensively, so that all peoples, on earth and in heaven, may be drawn toward Me in harmony and discipline.

16. God said: I, God of earth, being made Div, by Jehovih's will, through His Son, Fragapatti, heard the Creator's voice, saying:

17. Div, My Son, proclaim thou the Ormazdian law, and the I'hua'Mazdian law, and the Zarathustrian law.

18. God said: This, then, is the Ormazdian law: Ormazd, the Creator, displayeth His creations, which He created. He set the stars in the firmament; these are the words of the book of the Almighty. He made the earth-substances of the earth, and all the things thereon and therein. These are the words of the Creator, Ormazd, the Jehovih.

19. The substances of things going and coming forever; creating and dissolving from one shape into another, these are the Ormazdian law, the Jehovih'yan law. By virtue of His presence these things speak (impress) upon one another forever. What these things speak upon the soul of man, write upon the soul of man, these are man's knowledge, acquired by the Ormazdian law, the Jehovih'yan law. What these things speak upon the souls of angels, write upon the souls of angels, these are the angels' knowledge, acquired by the Ormazdian law, the Jehovih'yan law.

20. God said: This also is the Ormazdian law: Perpetual growth. As a man, being brought forth out of what was not an entity, thereby becoming an entity, this is brought about by the Ormazdian law.

21. With capacity in man for life everlasting; with capacity to acquire knowledge and power forever, and never attain to the Almighty. As a road, whereon a man may run in full liberty forever, and never come to the end thereof; rejoicing on his journey, this is the Ormazdian law.

22. As the actions of corporeal substances produce light; as light is the expression and speech of certain corporeal changes, so is Ormazd, the Master Light, the Creator, that which illuminateth the soul of man, making man conscious that he is; making man express his impressions. This is the Ormazdian law, this is the Ever Presence that terminateth not forever.

23. Though worlds come into being and go out of being (as such), yet Ormazd remaineth; He is the Forever; and within Him are all creations created. These are the Ormazdian law, the Jehovih'yan law.

24. God said: This, then, that followeth, is the I'hua'Mazdian law: The school of knowledge, kept by God and his Lords, for teaching mortals and angels.

25. Wherein certain discipline and words are necessary to cause the congregating of men and angels, to dwell together and to travel onward forever, in harmony and rejoicing.

26. Behold, a great multitude was in disorder and confusion, and unhappiness resulted. Then came order and discipline, and the multitude were harmonized and filled with rejoicing. This that accomplished it, was the I'hua'Mazdian law.

27. Jehovih had said: Behold, I create man with the possibility of becoming a creator under Me. The first lesson of creation I give into man's hands, is, that he shall create harmony and affiliation within himself and with his neighbors, that the many may become in concert, even as one man.

28. God said: Such was the Ormazdian law; to create man with the possibility of becoming a creator under Jehovih (Ormazd). But wherein man and angels, through their God and Lords, began to make, to create, harmony and discipline; this was the I'hua'Mazdian law.

29. As the manual of arms is to soldiers, making them a unit in motion, so is the I'hua'Mazdian law in making and teaching peace and order and unity amongst mortals on earth and angels in heaven.

30. By the I'hua'Mazdian law are the heavenly kingdoms in hada maintained; and by the same law are great kingdoms and nations on earth built up. The discipline of God and the Lords, through their ashars, in ruling over mortals, for the comprehensive benefit of the whole; this is the I'hua'Mazdian law. It is called the I'hua'Mazdian law because God and his Lords, through their ashars, keep guard and rule over all good mortals and angels for their own exaltation in the heavens above.

31. God said: Here followeth then the Zarathustrian law: The bestowal of words to mortals, of the dominion of God and his Lords: The making of all good mortals joint heirs and members of the same heavenly kingdoms, wherein God and his Lords and their Holy Council in heaven devise and administer laws for the ultimate resurrection of all men.

32. The revealed word of heaven, to mortals; this is the Zarathustrian law.

33. The word was with God, and God became the word; this is the Zarathustrian law.

34. For the word being established through Zarathustra became the life of God in flesh, being perpetual to the end of the world.

35. For though Zarathustra be forgotten, and the words of his mouth remembered not on the whole earth, yet the Zarathustrian law (the revelations of God to man) became everlasting in the souls of mortals from that time forth, forever and ever.

36. For man to know of, and to desire to become one with the All Highest, this is the Zarathustrian law. Nor mattereth it through what name he striveth, even so he strive to know the will of God.

37. When a king desireth soldiers for his army, he sendeth recruiting emissaries, calling: Come ye, join the armies of the king. Even so, but for peace and righteousness, sendeth God his Lords and holy angels down to mortals, saying: Come ye, join the kingdom of God. And when they come, behold, they use certain rites and ceremonies, with words and sacred days: The name of these rites and ceremonies and the words revealed by God, these are the Zarathustrian laws. For they are the initiative, by which mortals become joint workers with God and his Lords.

CHAPTER II.

1. God said: Be attentive, O man, to the voice of thy Lord and his angels; be patient, that thou mayest understand the dominion of thy God, and add glory unto the Almighty.

2. The Div was the chief, and the Lords and their officers comprised the Divan Congress, of the period of time whereof this book pertaineth.

3. And such mortals of that day, who joined in the armies of God, were represented by the voice of guardian angels through their Lord, according to the nation or place represented.

4. And the ashars reported to their Lord, as to the conditions and places of mortals, and as to the conditions and places of angels also, and the Lords spake thereon in the Diva.

5. And the Div decreed laws and governments, unto mortals and angels, according to what was best for them.

6. Jehovih said: I am the Light and the Life; behold Me, I am Ormazd. When I shape My thoughts into words, behold, I am I'hua'Mazda; I am the word. When the words of My kingdom are registered with mortals, behold Me; I am the Zarathustrian law. I am three in one.

7. Even so have I given unto thee, O Div, and to My angels and My mortals; for ye three shall be a unit in the furtherance of My kingdoms.

8. Behold, your labors shall be henceforth called Divinity (Divan). And whoso falleth under your inspiration shall be called Divine (Divas).

9. God said: Consider, O man, the wisdom of thy God, to perceive what is feasible to thine own judgment, and be thou far-reaching with thine own members.

10. The Div decreed: To carry birth rites down to mortals; to teach mortals when their children were born to consecrate them to Diva, under a rod with water, after the same manner es'yans were baptized in heaven. With rites and ceremonies, and words, according to the Zarathustrian law, the I'hua'Mazdian law, the Ormazdian law.

11. God said: In the time of the baptismal of mortal children, behold, my Lords appointed ashars unto such children, to keep them in the way of the Almighty.

12. This was the first Divan (Divine) law.

13. The Div decreed: To establish wedding rites and ceremonies with words and processions, in order to bind firmly monogamic marriages, according to the Zarathustrian law, the I'hua'Mazdian law, the Ormazdian law.

14. God said: In the time of marriages, behold, my Lords appointed new ashars unto man and wife, whose duties were to minister unto them as unto a small kingdom, for the glory of Jehovih.

15. This was the second Divan (Divine) law.

16. The Div decreed: To establish funeral rites and ceremonies, with words, according to the Diva, that is, the Zarathustrian, the I'hua'Mazdian, and the Ormazdian law.

17. This was the third Divan law.

18. God said: In the birth rites; in the marriage rites, and in the funeral rites, recording angels of the Lord were present; and afterward, they reported these things to my kingdom in heaven.

19. And all such mortals as carried out these rites and ceremonies, with words, were named Zarathustrians. Nevertheless there were many others, who, not being capable of the inspiration, stood aloof from me and my kingdoms.

20. Jehovih said: I blame not My God and My Lords that their love ran more to the favor of such mortals as became Zarathustrians, than to such as rejected God and his Lords. Neither do I censure God and His Lords for favoring their chosen in building cities, nations and empires, leaving such other mortals as were enemies to perish in their cities, kingdoms and nations.

21. God said: Ye who are one with the Divine law, are free from the law; but they that reject me and my kingdom are bound by the law.

22. Of the first three Divine laws, God said: These are the sacred words decreed to mortals: By father or mother: I bestow this, my child, to be a good Zarathustrian, according to the Diva. And in marriage: By the Bride and Bridegroom: I bestow myself to this my mate, a good Zarathustrian, according to the Diva. And in sacrament previous to death: I confess, with repentance, I, a good Zarathustrian, unto Thee, O Ormazd; and to Thy Lords of the heavenly hosts of Diva.

CHAPTER III.

1. God said: Behold, I come to reveal what was done in heaven, that thou, O man, mayest understand the cause of things being done on earth.

2. These Divan laws were made in heaven, and by the Lords of that day, through their angels, given to mortals, whereby mortals became a manifestation of heavenly things.

3. Here, then, followeth, to wit:

4. If a man be not too weak he shall confess to all the Lords with repentance. On the other hand, if he be too weak to utter words, than shall the priest confess him by holding the right hand whilst he saith the holy words. And whilst this is being done, the ashars shall provide a sufficient number of spirits to receive the newborn, and bring him to the place in heaven that hath been previously selected for him.

5. The third Divan law also decreed as followeth: If the es'yan be a Zarathustrian, and his kin in heaven be drujas, he shall not be taken to the heaven where they are; nor shall

his kin be permitted to see him for thirty days. But after thirty days in his own place in heaven, his kin, if drujas, may be permitted to see him, but only under guard.

6. The fourth Divan law: If the es'yan be a Zarathustrian, and his kin in heaven belong to the organic heavens, then he shall be taken to them, and his abiding place shall be with them for a season.

7. The fifth Divan law: If the es'yan be a Zarathustrian, his spirit shall not be suffered to remain longer than three days and three nights about his mortal kindred. And then he shall be taken to his place in heaven, and given into the keeping of the asaphs, who shall explain all things to him.

8. God said: Whilst the mortal priest is reciting prayers after death, in the morning, at noon, and at sunset, the ashars shall assemble in the same house, along with the newborn spirit, and join in the singing and praying, for it will pacify the spirit and restore him to know what hath taken place. And this shall be called the sixth Divan law.

9. God said: And the same law shall apply in the case of a Zarathustrian woman as with a man. In the case of a Zarathustrian child, that died in infancy, the Div decreed:

10. The seventh Divan law: The child of a Zarathustrian being too young to speak, shall not make confession, even through the priest. The mortal priest shall say: O Thou Master Light! Behold, my child is dead! Receive Thou its little, tender spirit! Take it to Thy heavenly place of delight! And the ashars shall take the young es'yan to a place suited to it, and deliver it to the asaphs; and the asaphs shall examine it, and, if it require fetal, they shall provide it in heaven, if possible. But if it be too young, then the asaphs, with a sufficient guard, shall take it back to its mortal mother, or to its mortal father, or to its brother, or its sister, or other near kin, or to whomsoever the asaphs find most advisable. And the spirit child shall be put to bed every night with its fetal mother, or fetal father, that its spirit may draw sustenance sufficient to grow into everlasting life. But the asaphs who have it in charge shall bring it away in the morning to its place in heaven. But in no case shall a Zarathustrian spirit child be left to fetal with a contentious mortal woman, nor with a drunken mortal man.

11. God propounded: If a Zarathustrian be dead, and his spirit many years in a place of heavenly delight, and then his mortal wife die, and she be not a Zarathustrian?

12. The members of the Diva all spake. Then God decreed the eighth Divan law, which was: The spirit of such a woman shall not be suffered to go to the place of her husband. For thirty days she shall be kept in a place suitable for her. After that she may visit her husband under guard; but until she accept the Ormazdian law, she shall not dwell with the husband, in heaven, nor with her children, in heaven. And if she have mortal children, she shall not be permitted to see them, save under guard.

13. The ninth Divan law was the same, wherein a Zarathustrian woman whose husband was not a Zarathustrian; for he was bound by the same law, and thus kept separate in heaven until he accepted the Ormazdian law.

14. God propounded: If a Zarathustrian have a wife who is not a Zarathustrian, and she have an untimely birth, whether by accident or abortion, what then of the spirit of that child? On this, all the members of Diva spake, and after that, God decreed:

15. Such spirit shall not be brought to heaven for a season, but shall be fetaled on its natural mother or father, day and night, until the full nine months are completed, and then it shall be delivered with due ceremonies by the ashars. After that it shall

be fetaled the same as in the seventh Divan law. And this was the tenth Divan law.

16. The eleventh Divan law: If a Zarathustrian attain to maturity before he die, his spirit shall be es'yan two years. And during this time he shall be attended by not less than two asaphs when he goeth away from his heavenly home; and the asaphs shall teach him the mode of travel, the manner of knowing localities, both on the earth and in the first resurrection. And they shall teach him the varieties and kinds of food suited to the highest best education of a spirit. But when he traveleth with his companions of his own heavenly group, then the asaphs of the group shall go along with him and them. And, during the two years, he shall be provided from the stores in heaven with food and clothes, and he shall not labor to provide himself with anything.

17. The twelfth Divan law was in reference to the same spirit, which was: At the end of two years the asaphs shall deliver him, and such of his group as are prepared, into the department of first instruction, and his name shall be entered in the library of that department of heaven as ENTERED APPRENTICE, IN THE FIRST RESURRECTION. Here his first lessons shall be as to making clothes and providing food for himself and others. And he shall be entitled to participate, if he so desire, in the recreations of the entered apprentices, such as music, dancing, marching, painting, or other arts.

18. The thirteenth Divan law was in reference to the same spirit, which was: Not less than two years shall he serve as entered apprentice, and longer if his proficiency be not sufficient for advancement. But when he is advanced, he shall no longer be called entered apprentice, but a CRAFTSMAN. And he shall be taken to a place suitable, where his labor will contribute to the heavenly kingdoms. And his recreations shall entitle him to instruction in both corporeal and es'sean knowledge, and their correspondence. As a craftsman he shall serve seven years.

19. The fourteenth Divan law was in reference to the same spirit, which was: The craftsman's examination being completed, he shall then return to labor in the nurseries in heaven, becoming assistant to the asaphs. And during this period he shall report himself at the roll call. And his teachers shall take him with them down to mortals and teach him how to see and hear corporeal things. And they shall also explain to him fetalism and the obsession of mortals by drujas, that he may understand the cause of lying, and of stealing, and of tattling, and of conspiracies, and of murders amongst mortals.

20. The fifteenth Divan law was of the same spirit, which was: After he hath served three years as nurse-assistant to the asaphs, he shall be promoted to the hospitals in heaven, as assistant to the physicians. And they shall teach him the restoration of spirits in chaos, and crazy spirits, and deformed spirits, and of sick spirits, and of spirits afflicted with foul smells, that cannot clean themselves, especially of the spirits of women who produced abortion on themselves, or suffered it to be done unto them, and of monomaniacs, and all manner of diseased spirits. And the physicians shall take him with them when they go down to mortals to remove fetals, and he shall learn how they are severed, safely to both. And they shall take him to the battle-fields, where mortals slay one another, whose spirits are in chaos, or are still fighting, and he shall assist in bringing them away from the corporeal place, and also learn how to restore them, and where to deliver them when restored. And if there be knots in any region near at hand, the physician shall take him to the knot, and show him how they are untied, and how they are mastered and delivered. And if there be any hell near at hand, the physicians shall take him thither and teach him

how hell is delivered and its people restored. For ten years shall he serve as assistant to the physicians.

21. The sixteenth Divan law was of the same spirit, which was: Having fulfilled the part of assistant physician, he shall be promoted to the full rank of Nurse. And in that department he shall serve ten years, which completeth his emancipation in that order, and thereafter any and all the nurseries of the lower heavens shall be free and open to him, and he shall go to whatsoever one he desireth, save when specially commanded for a certain work by his Lord, or by the God of his division.

22, The seventeenth Divan law was of the same spirit, which was: Having passed a satisfactory examination by his Lord, or his Lord's attendants, he shall be promoted to the full rank of Physician. And in that department in heaven he shall serve fifty years. And then his emancipation in that order shall be complete. And all the hospitals in the lower heavens shall be open to him, and he shall choose whichever of them he desireth as his place of labor, unless specially required by his Lord, or by the God of his division.

23. The eighteenth Divan law was of the same spirit, which was: He shall now pass an examination by his Lord or his Lord's deputy, and if he prove himself in a knowledge of the structure of both the corporeal and spiritual man, he shall be registered as Entered Factor, and he shall serve twelve years in forming and making fabrics for raiment, and for other useful and ornamental purposes.

24. The nineteenth Divan law was like unto the eighteenth, save that his labor shall be gathering and transporting food for other twelve years. And the twentieth Divan law was like unto the nineteenth, save that his labor shall be the wielding of large bodies, and of carrying the same long distances.

25. The twenty-first Divan law of the same spirit, was: He shall now enter the Creatif as an apprentice. Thirty years shall he serve in the Creatif, learning how to create. And the twenty-second Divan law was like unto the twenty-first, save that he shall dwell in Uz and serve twelve years in learning Uz.

26. The twenty-third Divan law of the same spirit was: He shall now enter college, and serve according to his talents, from five to forty years, learning measuring, and distances, rotations, velocities, magnets, corporeal and es'sean; currents of vortices; roadways in vortices, and how to measure vortices by their spiral force; how to find the center and the periphery of vortices. And if he serve the full term of forty years, he shall have the freedom of the eighteenth, nineteenth, twentieth, twenty-first, twenty-second and twenty-third commandments; and all such places shall be forever open for him. And if he choose to go into any of them he shall do so, unless especially ordered to some other emergent place by his Lord, or the God of his division.

27. The twenty-fourth Divan law of the same spirit was: He shall now enter architecture as an apprentice, and learn the building of heavenly mansions and cities; and he shall serve eight years, and be promoted to build judgment seats and thrones, and serve sixteen years more.

28. The twenty-fifth Divan law of the same spirit was: He shall now be eligible to the School of Light and Darkness, and learn the relative power of attraction and propulsion belonging to them; and his education here shall embrace practice and experiment; and he shall serve seventy years for the full course. After which, if he be proficient in creating light and darkness, he shall be emancipated from the twenty-fourth

and twenty-fifth Divan laws, and all such places shall be open and free to him forever.

29. The twenty-sixth Divan law of the same spirit was: He shall now serve twenty-four years in building and propelling heavenly boats, and small ships. And the twenty-sixth Divan law was of like kind, which was: That he shall now travel fifty years in atmospherea, and on the earth, and on the oceans of the earth.

30. This completeth the primary education in the first resurrection.

CHAPTER IV.

1. God said: For the spirit of a Zarathustrian who hath completed his primary education, what then? On which all the members spake. After that Div decreed:

2. He shall serve two hundred years as an apprenticed loo'is. He shall become proficient in the knowledge of procreation of mortals. Learning to prophesy what the off-spring will be, according to the parentage; to become wise in discerning how the es of a living mortal governeth the flesh, to good or evil; how the es of a mortal controlleth the sex and ultimate size and health and strength of the offspring.

3. To learn which, the loo'is shall take him to thousands of mortals, and he shall make a record of what he hath under observation; and when such mortals have offspring born unto them, he shall make a record thereof; and he shall observe the character of the birth, and the foundation of the child, together with what conditions surrounded the mother of the child. And he shall follow that child till it hath grown up, and also married, and begotten a child, or children, and so on to the sixth generation. This is the twenty-eighth Divan law.

4. Div decreed: After he hath served two hundred years he shall be examined by his Lord, or his Lord's deputy, and if proficient in prophesying to the sixth generation, he shall be entered as an ashar on a list of four twelves for every moon's change. But the forty-eight ashars shall not be ashars to more than one hundred and ninety-two mortals, unless otherwise specially allotted by the Lord or God in dominion.

5. For four generations, of one hundred and thirty-three years, shall he serve as an ashar. And he shall learn to have dominion over his mortal protégés night and day, not suffering them, however, to know his presence. To accomplish which, he shall begin with his protégés in their first infancy; remaining with them whilst they sleep, talking to the spirit of the mortal, teaching and persuading. This was the twenty-ninth Divan law.

6. Div decreed: Having served as ashar, the full term of ashar, he shall be entitled to examination by his Lord or deputy. But herein beginneth a new examination; which is, that the examination pertaineth to his protégés, as to what kind of fruit he hath sent to heaven, the grade of his es'yans being the standard. This was the thirtieth Divan law.

7. Div decreed: Having passed the examination as ashar, he shall now be promoted as asaph, where he shall serve sixty-six years. Here again his examination shall be not of himself but of the harvest of his department. This was the thirty-first Divan law.

8. Div decreed: His examination being complete, he shall now receive emancipation for all preceding departments and decrees; and he shall have his choice in all places he hath passed, unless otherwise specially detailed by his Lord or God of his division. This was the thirty-second Divan law.

9. Div decreed: He shall now be entitled to enter the CHAPTER OF THE PRIMARY SOUL. His

first lessons shall be in colors and sounds both of corpor and es. First, beginning with gray of not more than three combinations; and when he hath mastered these, he shall have four, then five, then ten, then a hundred, and so on, until, when any combination of colors is placed before him, he can instantly perceive every color, shade, tint, and the velocity of light, and its force (actinic) emanating. And he shall pursue this study until he can create in es the counterpart of anything in corpor, or create in corpor the counterpart of anything in es. And of sounds he shall proceed in the same way; first, learning a combination of three, so that when his teacher produceth any three sounds together, he can hear them and determine the exact velocity of wave. Then he shall begin with four sounds (notes), then five, then ten, then a hundred, and even a thousand, the which, even though made in the same instant, he shall detect every one, and the velocity and force of each. This was the thirty-third Divan law.

10. Div decreed: He shall now begin the practice of combining and creating color by sounds, and sounds by colors, both in corpor and es. His teachers shall make explosions with light, and explosions without light, and by his eye and ear only shall he be able to determine with what elements the explosions were made. This was the thirty-fourth Divan law.

11. Div decreed: He shall go far away from the explosions, and when the waves come to him, even though he heareth not the explosion, he shall be able to determine, by the waves, of what substance the explosion was made, and whether in light or darkness. And, if in light, what colors were manifested. This was the thirty-fifth Divan law.

12. Div decreed: He shall now receive instruction in the sounds of conversation. First, his teacher shall cause him to hear two people conversing at the same time, missing nothing that is said; then three, then four, then five, then ten, then a hundred, and then a thousand, but no greater number in this department. This was the thirty-sixth Divan law.

13. Div decreed: He shall now analyze the waves of voice, wherein he cannot hear the sounds thereof. His teacher shall station him in a certain place and cause him to read the waves of light and sound that come to him, so that he knoweth not only the words spoken, but the kind of person speaking or singing. This was the thirty-seventh Divan law.

14. Div decreed: His teacher shall now cause him to read the waves of light and sound emanating from two persons talking at the same time, whom he cannot hear, and he shall understand not only the words spoken, but the kind of persons speaking. Then, he shall read the waves in the same way for three persons, then four, then eight, then a hundred, and even a thousand. This was the thirty-eighth Divan law.

15. Div decreed: Then he shall be taken to a distance from a battle-field, where mortals are in deadly conflict, but he shall not be sufficiently near to hear the sounds; but when the waves come to him, he shall read them and know the number of the men in battle, the kind of weapons in use, and the cause of contention. This was the thirty-ninth Divan law.

16. Div decreed: He shall now be promoted to be a messenger between Lords, and between Lords and Gods. This was the fortieth Divan law.

17. Div decreed: For one hundred years he shall serve as MESSENGER, and at the end of that time his Lords and Gods shall render his record, and promote him to be marshal. And hereupon the emancipation of all the preceding decrees and departments shall be open to him, to choose whatsoever he will, save on such time and occasion as specially required

by his Lord or God. This was the forty-first Divan law.

18. Div decreed: For two hundred years he shall serve as marshal, and under as many as forty Lords and Gods, and in as many as twenty heavenly kingdoms. This was the forty-second Divan law.

19. Div decreed: He shall now be promoted Lord, and have dominion over a city or nation of mortals, and over the spirits belonging to that city or nation. This was the forty-third Divan law.

CHAPTER V.

1. God propounded: If a man die, and be not a Zarathustrian, what then? All the members spake, and then:

2. Div decreed: Inasmuch as he accepted not the Zarathustrian law whilst mortal, he is unsuited to the highest exalted places of delight. For all official preference shall be to the Zarathustrian. This was the forty-fourth Divan law.

3. Div decreed of the same spirit, who not being a Zarathustrian: His education shall not run to the Lord-head, nor to the God-head. He shall not be a column in the Father's building, nor of the arch-stones of great strength, but he shall stand as a plain brick in the wall.

4. Div said: I am not created God to merely serve my time, and there an end. I am to look far ahead as to who shall be Lords and Gods over the earth and atmospherea.

5. Div propounded: What, then, shall be the course of a spirit who was not a Zarathustrian? And this was made the forty-sixth Divan law: He shall be delivered to the asaphs, who shall enter him in the nurseries as an es'yan, where he shall remain six years, learning the elementary powers and expressions.

6. Div decreed the forty-seventh Divan law: The same spirit shall then be apprenticed in manufacturing and general labor, where he shall serve twelve years, unless previously instructed in these things whilst mortal.

7. Div decreed the forty-eighth Divan law: He shall now enter school and learn surveying and measuring without instruments, and determining the kind of emanations that rise up from the earth, their altitude and density; and he shall learn exploration and enumeration in both corpor and es; the building of piedmazrs and otevans; the constructing of arrow-ships, and all other vessels used in the heavens to carry things from place to place. And he shall serve thirty years in these things.

8. Div decreed the forty-ninth Divan law: He shall now be promoted to restoring, nursing and caring for the drujas who are being rescued by the captains, generals and Lords; in which service he shall be for thirty years. But in both the forty-eighth and forty-ninth Divan laws it was afterward decreed: Whatsoever service he did in mortal life, in these respects, shall stand to his credit two-fold in spirit.

9. Div decreed: If he now acknowledge and practice faith in the Great Spirit, he shall be promoted to the College of Creation, and taught to create light and darkness. After this, he shall be taught to sar'gis flowers and trees and clothes, and to take elementary lessons in music and expression, in which branches he shall serve fifty years. And then, he shall be entitled to examination, and if he can withstand the third grade of light, he shall be ranked Bridegroom of Om. This was the fiftieth Divan law. The fifty-first thus provideth:

10. If he doth not yet comprehend faith in the All Person, he shall be granted freedom to all the places where he hath served, and he shall be emancipated from all Lords and Gods, and from all labor and education, and honorably discharged, to pursue whatsoever he desireth in any place in heaven or earth. Nor shall the Lords nor Gods take more notice of him than due respect and honor.

11. Whereupon, Div, Son of All Light, spake, saying: This also shall be part and parcel of the Divan law, which is to say: Of the latter class rise the false Gods and false Lords, that oft set up kingdoms of their own in atmospherea. They shall not rise above the second resurrection.

12. The Voice of Jehovih came to God, saying: Without the disbeliever in spirits, mortals could not find courage to smite serpents; without false Gods and false Lords the lowest drujas would never be put to work. They who cannot be risen by persuasion, may be aroused by less scrupulous masters, who make slaves of them.

CHAPTER VI.

1. In the twelfth moon of the Diva the Voice of Jehovih came to Div, saying: That My Lords and My Gods may not err, thou shalt promulgate the foundation of the Divan law. God perceived, and in the name of Div he decreed:

2. Hear me, O Gods and Lords! This is the foundation of Divan law: The decrees of God and his Lords, his Lord Gods, his Gods, and his Lords; not singly, but by all members, and ratified by the Council of Diva under Div, Son of All Light. That is to say:

3. A kingdom in heaven riseth or falleth by Divan law; a kingdom or nation on earth riseth or falleth by Divan law. The virtuous are rewarded and exalted by Divan law; the wicked are cast into trials by Divan law.

4. But this is not Divan law: Man to be created and live; to live a time on earth, then die and enter heaven: These are done by the Ever Presence, the All Light, the Creator, and not by the Diva.

5. This is Divan law, to wit: To assist man out of darkness into light; to give security to the helpless; to raise the souls of man to everlasting light; to minister unto the needy; to deliver them that are in pain; to teach man to desist laboring for himself; to teach him to labor for others.

6. But this is not Divan law: For seed to grow; for a tree to grow; for a spider to weave its web; these are done by the Ever Living Presence, the All Master, Creator!

7. This is Divan law, to wit: To regulate the affairs of angels and mortals, for their ultimate resurrection; to lay the foundation for harmony in community; to gather together the inharmonious, and put them in tune.

8. But this is not Divan law: To provide the earth with life, or to hold it in its place; to build the place of the higher or lower heavens; to provide corpor or to provide es; these things are by the Ever Personal Presence, the Creator, and shaped and molded by His hand through the Chiefs of the higher heavens.

9. This is Divan law: To bring together in marriage wisely for the child's sake, and for the joy of all.

10. But this is not Divan law: To give desire to marriage, or desire for marriage; these are from the All Person, the Master Light.

11. This is Divan law: When a man walketh along, to take him by the hand and bend him to the right or left.

12. But this is not Divan law: For the man to go forth; this he doeth by the Ever Presence, Jehovih, the Ormazd.

13. A carpenter buildeth a house, but he built not the logs nor the stone. The Diva buildeth kingdoms in heaven and kingdoms on earth, and shapeth them for usefulness and beauty; and when they are old and out of sorts, the Diva abandoneth them, and they fall to pieces. Nevertheless, Ormazd provided and provideth the wherewithal for the whole.

14. Div decreed: This also shall ye promulgate in heaven and earth, lest angels and mortals worship Div and Diva. For though the Diva appoint mortal kings, yet mortals shall not worship Div (Divinity).

CHAPTER VII.

1. In the sixth Diva, Div decreed: The Divan law shall be the higher law; and ye shall give to mortals a law copied after it, and the mortal law shall be called the lower law.

2. One of the members of Diva said: If a mortal judge, being in judgment between certain men, by which law shall he judge? On this matter the members spake at great length.

3. Div then decreed: He cannot discern the higher law but dimly; the lower law he can read plainly in a book. He shall therefore judge by the lower, but by the highest interpretation. And then Div on his own account said:

4. For the priests of the Zarathustrians, who have carried the alms-bowl and lived in all things pure, being celibates, serving the Creator, Ormazd, only, going about doing good, they have the higher law, the Divan law, within their hearts; they shall judge by it. Nevertheless trouble cometh not into any of the worlds by those who strive to do aright, but by those who evade. The time shall come when the judge shall not interpret according to the higher law; he will strive to hide justice in a corner, using words to conceal his own perversity. It is by such men and such angels that heaven and earth will be blighted in coming time.

5. For, as through Zarathustra, God's Word hath been established on the earth; and since words themselves perish and are supplemented by new words, the time shall come when the higher law will fall, as a house on sand. For there are no words that are everlasting, and that are understood by all men alike; words themselves are but as husks that surround the corn. Men in darkness quibble on the husks, but discern not the fruit within.

6. Jehovih spake to Div, saying: Man buildeth a house, and it perisheth. Succeeding generations must also build, otherwise the art of building would perish. Better the building perish, than the art of building. I created all men to labor and to learn. What less requireth My Gods and angels? Because language melteth away, the language-makers, that is, My Lords and ashars, have constant employment of delight.

7. Div said: Foolish men run after a language that is dead and moldered away; but the wise seek language to express the spirit of things. The latter is under the Divan law; the former is bound as a druk. And herein shall ye be circumspect; because mortal judges, who judge by the lower law, are bound in words.

8. Copies of these Divan laws were given to mortals through the Lords and ashars, either by inspiration or by words spoken in sar'gissa. And in Jaffeth and Shem and Arabin'ya

mortal kings decreed mortal laws and revelations, based on the Divan laws, and on the Zarathustrian laws.

9. Div propounded: A man and woman in mortal life were as druks, being filthy, and idle, begging from day to day, and yet they had born to them many children. And the children were alike lazy and worthless, being beggars also. Now in course of time, the man and woman die, and in time after, the children die also, and none of them are yet entered into the first resurrection in heaven, being beggars still and dwelling around their old haunts. What of them?

10. The Lords all spake on this subject, and after that Div decreed: Such spirits shall be reported by the ashars to the Lord, and the Lord shall send a captain with sufficient army to arrest them, and bring them away from the earth, and enter them in a colony for such purpose. This was called Divan act, the first.

11. Act, the second: For thirty days such drujas shall be clothed and fed. If by this time they manifest no inclination to labor, but are still lazy, they shall be removed into another region, where food can be obtained only by exertion.

12. Act, the third: This law shall apply also to mortals; through the ashars shall they be inspired to migrate to cold and unproductive regions. Div said: Herein hast Thou wisely planned, O Jehovih! For all Thy places in heaven and earth shall be subdued, and made to glorify Thee!

CHAPTER VIII.

1. The Diva met thrice every year in Mouru, and enacted many acts, after the manner herein before related; and the number was so great that all the spirits in heaven and mortals on earth, were fore-planned, from before birth until they became Brides and Bridegrooms in heaven.

2. And heaven and earth became as one country, with one king, who was God; and his word ruled over all. And the Lords' kingdoms prospered, and the kingdoms of the sub-Gods and Goddesses; the like of which glory had not been since the earth was created. And there were rites and ceremonies, and recreations, and games, and pageantry on earth and in heaven, so great that one might write a thousand books thereon, and yet not have told the tenth part.

3. So, after God had reigned one hundred and ninety years, he descended from his heavenly place, and went about in all the Lords' dominions, and the sub-Gods' dominions in the lower heavens, that he might rejoice before Jehovih in the great good works he had done.

4. And in all the heavenly places there was great rejoicing before God; and the singers made and sang hymns of rejoicing; and trumpeters and harpists proclaimed the glory of Jehovih's Presence.

5. So God had the people numbered, that the Gods of the etherean worlds might send in dan for the great resurrection. And the number of Brides and Bridegrooms to Jehovih would be sixteen thousand millions!

6. After that, God directed his fire-ship to run close to the earth, that he might survey mortals and their kingdoms. And he visited all the great nations of earth, to the south, and north, and east, and west. And now his soul cried out with great sorrow! The great

peoples of the earth were turning celibates!

7. And the Voice of Jehovih came to him, saying: God, My Son, Hoab, why sorrowest thou? And God answered, saying: Behold, the earth is not peopled over; the plains and mountains are not subdued; the wilderness is filled with beasts of prey; the Zarathustrians are running into the same line as the I'hins; they kill nothing; they live for the soul only. And since they have learned the bondage of the lower heavens, they will not marry and beget offspring.

8. Again Jehovih spake to God, saying: Call not down a'ji nor ji'ay, My Son! Fear not. In ten years, behold, I will bring the earth into dan, and thou shalt bring thy harvest into My emancipated worlds.

9. So God sorrowed no more; and on his return to Mouru, and in the next following meeting of the Diva, he propounded: If a husband and wife have a child born unto them, they both being Zarathustrians: What then? When the members had spoken,--

10. Div decreed: They shall have rites and ceremonies, that the ashars of the order of Zarathustra may be appointed unto it. What the ashars do in spirit shall the corporeans do in corpor. And this was the first supplemental Divan law.

11. Through the commandment of the different Lords, the ashars assembled in the house of a Zarathustrian at the time of the birth of a child, and these spirits baptized the child with a rod, sprinkling water on its head, after the manner of selecting victims who have been delivered out of hell. And by inspiration the angels induced the mortals to go through the same ceremony, having a priest to perform with the rod, which had been dipped in water.

12. Div decreed: A baptized child showeth it hath sprung from the Zarathustrians, and it hath inherent in it high possibilities. And if it die in infancy, it shall be received not with the children of druks in heaven, but in such place as will enable the parents, after death, to visit it with delight. This was the second supplemental Divan law.

13. So it became common on the earth for mortals to have their children baptized in infancy, that in case of death they should be taken to a place of delight, and not fall into the power of drujas, the evil spirits.

14. Div propounded: If a young man, who is a Zarathustrian, and a young woman, who is also a Zarathustrian, and both every way obedient to the Ormazdian law, and to the I'hua'Mazdian law, what shall be the rites and ceremonies of marriage for them? On this all the members spake, and after that,--

15. Div decreed: They shall be married by a rab'bah, with kin and friends present. The rab'bah shall say: Ormazd hath united you forever; live ye in peace and love on earth, and ye shall dwell together in a heavenly place of delight after death. What Ormazd hath joined, no man can separate forever. And whilst the mortal ceremony is being performed, the ashars and spirits akin shall have rites and ceremonies in the same house, and this shall be called the beginning of a new heavenly kingdom. This was the third supplemental Divan law.

16. Besides these, there were passed a hundred and eight supplemental Divan laws; and they comprehended all things in life and death of mortals, and all things pertaining to the resurrection after death. And so great was the power of the Zarathustrian religion on earth that war ceased, and the tribes and nations dwelt together in peace. The people ceased to build large cities, and ceased striving for the things of earth.

17. But they learned little, save rites and ceremonies, and prayers, and singing hymns of praise unto Ormazd, and to his Gods and Lords, and to Zarathustra, the All Pure. Thus ended the dominion of Hoab's reign in heaven and earth, the like of whose greatness had never been surpassed.

18. So Jehovih brought the regions of dan, and sent seven ships, and delivered God and his harvest of sixteen thousand million angels into places of delight, the Nirvanian fields of Niscrossawotcha, in etherea.

CHAPTER IX.

1. Then God bewailed the state of the earth, because man ceased to love anything thereon. His whole mind and heart were set upon heavenly things, and the earth was becoming like a neglected farm grown up with weeds and briars. So Jehovih answered God's prayers, saying: Behold, I will bring darkness around about the earth on every side. See to it then, My Son, for not only will man desire of the earth, but the angels in thy high heavenly places will forsake them, and go down to the earth.

2. So it came to pass, Jehovih brought ji'ya upon the earth, and it was in a state of darkness for four hundred years, and the sun shone not, but was like a red ball of fire, and mortal beings were without lights and shadows.

3. And men's minds and hearts took after the nature of the corporeal world, losing sight of Ormazd and His heavenly promises, and they bethought them of the desires of earth, and of the pleasures of flesh-life. Now during ji'ay there fell perpetual atmospherean substance on the earth, and it was of the nature and kind of substance of which the earth is made, but atmospheric, and this is that which is called ji'ya.

4. And the plateau of Haraiti and Zeredho were driven down to the earth and near the earth; and the belt of meteoris was moved nearer by thousands of miles, and meteoric stones fell in many places upon the earth, like a rain shower, but burning hot, and with suffocating smell. And the affairs of mortals were changed; they built new cities, and became great hunters, applying the wisdom of their forefathers to the matters of the earth.

5. And the heavenly places of delight were broken up and descended to the earth; and the angels were cast upon the earth, turning away from faith in Ormazd, seeking joy in the affairs of earth. And God and his Lords were powerless unto righteous works, either with mortals or angels. But man and woman became prolific, and they grew large, and full of resolution and power.

6. The Voice of Jehovih spake to God, saying: Maintain thou thy kingdom; and thy Gods and thy Lords under thee shall also maintain their kingdoms. Nor suffer thou My people to be discouraged with My works.

7. Because I have sent darkness upon the earth to benefit mortals in mortality, so have I also given My heavenly hosts lessons in My es worlds. Nor shall they call this a judgment upon them, nor say, I do these things in anger, nor as punishment, nor for benefit of one to the injury of others.

8. Because thou wert guided by My voice and My commandments in bestowing the Divan law, behold the strength and wisdom of thy pupils! For inasmuch as they learn to master the elements I created in atmospherea, so will they become triumphant in My etherean worlds.

9. God perceived, and he and his Lords and sub-Gods fortified their kingdoms on all hands, and provided assistance to their colleges, factories, hospitals and places of education, in order to maintain the angels who had sought resurrection.

10. Nevertheless, it came to pass, many angels believed a new order of light was coming on the earth, wherein the earth would become the all highest abode for angels and Gods. Others having lived two or three hundred years in atmospherea, and never having been in etherea, began to disbelieve in the higher heavens, and finally to disbelieve in Jehovih, also.

11. And in two hundred years later, God and his Lords lost influence and power with both angels and mortals. And the latter took to war, and the angels who had ministered unto them became wanderers and adventurers, without organization, and cared neither for truth nor wisdom, but flattered mortals for their own glory.

12. And the kings and queens of the earth built temples for their familiar spirits, who assumed the ancient names of Gods and Lords. Now, when the next arc of dan was near at hand, God enumerated his upraised hosts, and there were prepared as Brides and Bridegrooms for Jehovih's higher heavens twelve thousand millions.

13. And because it was less than the number of his predecessor, he cried out unto Jehovih, bewailing his weakness. And Jehovih answered him, saying: Bewail not, My Son! Thou hast done a great work. Neither ask thou that thou mayst remain another dan, for the next will not be so fair a harvest. So God grieved no more, but bestowed his kingdom on his successor; and his Lords did likewise, and so did his sub-Gods and all other persons having protégés. And God called together the Brides and Bridegrooms of Jehovih; and the latter sent down from etherea five great ships of fire, and delivered God and his hosts into the emancipated worlds.

CHAPTER X.

1. In the twelve hundredth year after Fragapatti, in the east colony of Haraiti, one Ctusk, a former Lord of Jehovih's host, renounced Jehovih, the Creator, and falsely proclaimed himself Ahura, the All Master; and he took with him three Lords of grade eighty-eight, and twelve sub-Gods of grade sixty-four, and one thousand six hundred students of eight hundred years' resurrection, none of whom were less than grade sixty, and were sufficient to pass as Brides and Bridegrooms. And these students took with them thirty-six thousand teachers, factors, and physicians, and nurses, all of whom were upward of grade forty.

2. And Ahura appropriated to himself one colony of one hundred and ten million angels, together with the colleges, schools, factories, and all things whatsoever belonging therein. And the three Lords took their kingdoms, and by annexation made them part and parcel with Ahura's kingdom. Now these three Lords' kingdoms comprised the largest habitable places of mortals in Vindyu and Jaffeth, and the greatest heavenly places of angels in the first resurrection.

3. And Ahura divided up the regions he thus obtained, making confederate heavenly kingdoms, sufficient in number to give place of dominion to his Lords and Gods, and to make sub-Gods out of all the one thousand six hundred students. And after that, Ahura numbered his people, and there were in his heavens more than three thousand million souls!

4. God sent messengers to Ctusk, who had assumed the name Ahura'Mazda, inquiring, admonishing and inquiring: My Lord, whom I have loved, whom by mine own hand was crowned in the name of Jehovih, why hast thou deserted the Father's kingdoms? Wherein hast thou had cause to complain against Jehovih? Wherein, against me, thy God? O my son, my Lord, say not thou hast gone so far thou canst not return! What canst thou ask of me that I will not grant unto thee? Nay, even judge thou me, and if thou desirest all the heavens and the earth in my place, I will abdicate unto thee, and become thy lowest servant, or whatsoever thou wilt put upon me.

5. Ahura returned this answer, to wit: Because I have nothing against thee, I have alienated myself and my kingdom from thee. I desire not thy kingdom, nor even mine own. Behold, I looked upon thee, and thou wert pure and holy. I looked upon the kingdoms of heaven, and the kingdoms of earth, and they were impure and unholy. Then came certain brother Lords to me, most wise Lords, and they said: A less pure God, a less holy God, would be more efficient. So, I was persuaded to my course.

6. God replied to this, saying: Behold, we have a Diva! Why spakest thou not thus before me, face to face? And thy three great Lords were also Divans; and they were silent on the matter likewise. The Div would have decreed whatever was all wise. Because I was in darkness, I saw not thy thoughts, nor thy Lords, and ye have heaped shame upon me. How shall I send my record to etherea? Shall I say, Behold, certain Lords consulted clandestinely, and then concluded to overthrow the Creator? And, forsooth, they have gone and set up a kingdom of their own, calling it the All Highest.

7. Hear me yet, and I will endeavor to speak wisely unto thee. Thy messengers notified me some days since that thou hadst repudiated Jehovih, saying: There is no All Highest Person; I can make myself high as the highest! And thereupon, thy messenger gave me a map, saying: Behold thou, here are the boundaries of the kingdom of Ahura'Mazda, the All Sufficient High God!

8. I looked over the map, and beheld its great extent; and I surmised to myself: He is a great God that can rule over all that! For I knew thee and thy education, which is as great as any Lord's in atmospherea. And thou knowest thou canst not control even a plateau! Canst thou raise thine hand and stay the a'ji, or the ji'ya, or the nebulae! Scarce canst thou change a single current of wind; nor canst thou cast a drought on any land. And yet thou knowest there are Gods who can do these things by a motion of one finger! How darest thou, then, proclaim thyself an All Sufficient High God!

9. But I will not rebuke thee, for I desire thy love and thy help. I would win thee by any sacrifice I can make. Behold, there is great darkness in heaven and on earth. Wherein I may be short, I will rebuke myself in after ages. I pray thee, then, return thou to me, and make exactions upon me and my kingdoms. With thy loss, behold, Diva is broken up. With thy dismemberment of heavens, others will follow. Alas, I will not look upon even that which my soul seeth. I plead for thy love and for thy assistance. Nevertheless, if the All Highest Light, for the All Best Good, showeth thee that thou art right, come not to me! I know the Great Spirit will sustain me, even though my soul is well nigh crushed to pieces by the loss of so fair a love.

10. To this Ahura replied: How came the thought to me to do as I did, if it be not the wisest, best course?

11. God replied: Because of the long reign of ji'ya, thou wert inoculated with darkness;

even as a mortal, on a rainy day, loseth his patience to be wise.

12. Then Ahura sent the following, to wit: I have been patient in mine answers; but now I will speak plainly. First of all, thou art All Pure, and Most Wise, above all other Gods. For more than two hundred years I have been a faithful Lord unto thee and thy kingdoms. At first the Great Light came to thee, and a voice came out of the light! Then I feared, and was awe-stricken. Because I believed thee so near the Creator, thine every word and act were to me worshipful.

13. At last I rebuked myself, saying to myself: Fool! Givest thou worship to man born of woman! Remember thy Creator only!

14. But the times changed; ji'ya fell upon heaven and earth. Our glorious kingdoms were cast down by the great darkness. Then I reasoned, saying to myself: Behold, when we were in light, Jehovih's Voice spake unto us. When the darkness came, the Voice came not. We sat in the Diva, in the altar circle, praying for light from the Father, but it came not. And I said: More we need the Voice in darkness than in light. For a hundred years we saw not the light of the Voice, nor heard the Voice speak. Thou hast said thou heardst in thy soul! Who is there in heaven or earth that cannot say as much?

15. In my soul I no longer believe there is an All Person. There are great Gods, a thousand times greater than I; but there is the end! Yea, some of those great Gods may have cast the ji'ya upon us. But that is not my matter. There is room for thee and thy people. Here is room for me and my people.

16. Jehovih spake to God, saying: Answer thou not Ahura more. Behold, I will interpret him to thee: He will even yet persuade angels and mortals that it was he who inspired Zarathustra. But he seeth it not himself. Suffer him, therefore, to go his way; neither take sorrow to thy soul. Have I not, from the lowest to the highest, given unto all men even that which they desired? Behold, I can use even bad men in the far future!

17. Jehovih said: For a long season Ahura will strive to walk upright, but because he hath cut Me off, he will also cut himself off in time to come. Behold, a mortal man striveth for riches honorably, and when he is rich, his riches cut him off from Me by the ruin he casteth upon his competitors. Nor can he extricate himself. Even so will it be with Ahura: His kingdom and his sub-kingdoms, and his multitude of officers will cause him to enslave hundreds of millions of drujas, and they will draw him into a vortex from which he cannot escape.

18. So God answered Ahura no more; but nevertheless, his heart was full of sorrow. Now, when the time of the meeting of Diva came, God foresaw that not more than one-half of them would be present, and he feared the questions that might come up.

19. But Jehovih said unto him: Fear not, My Son; for even though many more leave thee, yet shalt thou preserve the Diva to the end of this cycle. So it came to pass that Jehovih stilled the tongues of all the Gods and Lords of the Diva in reference to Ahura, even as if they had never known him. And Ahura sent quizzers to different Gods and Lords afterward, to learn what action the Diva had taken in his case. But when he was told that he had not been mentioned, he became angered, and he swore an oath that he would build the largest of all heavenly kingdoms.

20. Because of the great darkness on heaven and earth, God sent hope and promise into all the kingdoms, urging his Lords and his sub-Gods to maintain faith, not only in themselves, but within the hearts of their respective inhabitants. Now, from the time of

the secession of Ahura to the next dan would be three hundred years, and God knew this, though the multitudes in heaven and earth knew it not. And God commanded great recreation and extensive labors in order to prevent further dismemberment. But in the course of a hundred years many were carried away by the extravagant stories told about Ahura's kingdoms being places of great delight, and of ease and idleness.

21. Ahura's Lords said unto him: Thou shalt adorn thy kingdom; thy throne and thy capital, Ctusk, shall be the largest and most ornamental of all places in the universe; and our sub-kingdoms shall be places of great delight. And Ahura was persuaded, and so began self-glorification, and his Lords with him.

22. And in another hundred years Ahura had withdrawn and annexed unto him in heaven the following provinces, with their sub-Gods: Etyisiv, with seventy million souls; Howwak, with one hundred million souls; Hyn, with twenty million souls; D'nayotto, with eighty million souls; Erefrovish, with one hundred and ninety million souls; the whole of the kingdom of Gir-ak-shi, six hundred million souls; the whole of the kingdom of Soo'fwa, with eight hundred million souls. And all of these confederated in the lower heavens, making the kingdom of Ctusk, with Ahura as MAZDA IN CHIEF, the central kingdom.

23. The Diva was by this reduced to seven members, but these remained faithful. And God kept up the standard of resurrection for yet one hundred more years. And then Jehovih sent a region of dan to heaven and earth, and the Most High heavenly hosts descended in fire-ships and took God and his harvest up to Jehovih. And with all the misfortune that befell God and his Lords, there were, nevertheless, six thousand million Brides and Bridegrooms to Jehovih raised up to the higher heavens.

24. Now, when the etherean hosts came for the resurrection, knowing the darkness upon the lower heaven and the earth, they sent otevans, with heralds and trumpeters around the earth, proclaiming the resurrection at hand, and asking all who chose, to repair to Mouru, in Haraiti. And the word was whispered throughout Ahura's kingdom: What! Then, of a truth, there must be higher heavens than this! Alas, had we been faithful till now, we had been Brides and Bridegrooms! So potent was this disaffection for Ahura, that five of his Lords broke membership, and re-affiliated with God and his kingdoms.

25. And thus matters stood when God's successor came to the throne.

CHAPTER XI.

1. The next dan was five hundred years, and God and his heavenly kingdoms prospered before Jehovih. But as to the Lord's kingdoms on earth, and as to mortal kingdoms and empires, not much light was manifested in them.

2. Ahura, who had thus falsely taken, and was known by, the name of Ahura'Mazda, established Lords to rule over mortals. And these Lords were in direct opposition to God's Lords; for the latter taught the higher heavens and the All Person, Jehovih, or Ormazd, according to the language of mortals. But Ahura's Lords taught only one heavenly kingdom, which was Ahura's, called Ctusk, the All Holy Highest Heaven.

3. God's Lords inspired mortals to everlasting resurrection; Ahura's Lords inspired mortals to Ahura's kingdom, and there the end. And since mortals had built temples for their priests (rab'bahs), who were gifted with su'is, the spirits congregated in the temples,

and oft appeared in sar'gis, teaching openly their several doctrines. And the ashars that labored for Ahura extolled the glory and the delight of Ctusk, and the wonderful majesty and power of Ahura. But the ashars of God's hosts inspired and taught of the Great Spirit, Unapproachable.

4. For five hundred years were God's hosts confronted with this opposition; and it came to pass that mortals, especially in Vindyu, were divided into two great classes of worshippers. And just before God's successor came into dominion, he propounded the matter in Diva; whereupon all the members spake at great length. Afterward, Div decreed:

5. Whatsoever is worshipped, having comprehensible form or figure, is an idol. He that worshippeth an idol, whether of stone or wood, or whether it be a man or an angel, sinneth against the Creator. This was given unto all of God's Lords, and by them to the ashars, and commanded to be taught to mortals by inspiration and otherwise.

6. When the time of dan came there were seven thousand million Brides and Bridegrooms raised up to Jehovih's emancipated worlds, and the succeeding God and Lords came into dominion under more favorable auspices, but which were not to continue long.

7. The Diva had extended to fourteen members; and God's Lords had succeeded in securing kingdoms in the principal parts of Jaffeth, Vind'yu and Arabin'ya. On the other hand, the emissaries of Ahura, the false, had been most active in extending the kingdom of their idol. Ahura was most cunning with the last Divan act: Instead of interdicting it, he altered it, so it read as followeth, to wit: Whatsoever is worshipped, having comprehensible form or figure, is an idol. He that worshippeth an idol, whether of stone or wood, or whether it be a man or an angel, sinneth against the All Highest, who is personated in Ahura'Mazda, the Holy Begotten Son of all created creations!

8. And next, Ahura, determined to found a second heaven, decreeing to his emissaries as followeth, to wit: Behold Gir-ak-shi, the heavenly region belonging above the lands of Heleste! Thither will I build a new heaven, greater than all other heavens, save Ctusk. And when Gir-ak-shi is well founded, I will people it with many millions of mighty angels, Gods and Lords. And my hosts shall descend to the corporeal earth, to the lands of Parsi'e and Arabin'ya, and they shall obsess mortals day and night, and inspire them to go to Heleste, where they shall build great cities and kingdoms unto me and my hosts.

9. And when these things are fulfilled, behold, I will send my hosts to Uropa, and build there also heavenly kingdoms and mortal kingdoms; and when these are established, behold, I will send into other countries, one after another, until my heavenly kingdoms embrace all places, and until all the earth is mine.

10. For I will be God over all, and ye that labor with me shall be my Lords and sub-Gods forever. And my kingdoms and your kingdoms shall be bestowed with glories and ornaments, the like of which never was. Neither shall the Gods of other worlds come against me or mine to carry away my people. They shall no longer flatter them, calling them Brides and Bridegrooms to Jehovih, a thing, none can see or comprehend.

11. And Ahura and his emissaries set to work to carry out these decrees, and in two hundred years they had inspired the Parsi'e'ans and the Arabin'yans to emigrate by tens of thousands to the land of Heleste, which was inhabited by druks and wanderers, full of wickedness. Ahura inspired his immigrants to fall upon the native druks, and destroy them. Wherein had come to pass that which Jehovih spake in Mouru, saying:

They who cannot be risen by persuasion may be aroused by less scrupulous masters.

12. For whilst Ahura's hosts were slaying the druks of Heleste by tens of thousands, God's heavenly hosts were receiving their spirits and conducting them away to other atmospherean regions.

13. These, then, were the divisions of mortals on earth at this time: First, the I'hins, who were the original Faithists. And they were capable of prophecies and miracles to such an extent that all other people called them the sacred people. Neither did the great warriors of other nations and peoples molest them. The I'hins lived secluded and separate from all other people. Nevertheless, they were the seed of everlasting life on the earth, and the foundation for raising up prophets and seers unto other peoples. Even as the mother of Zarathustra was of the I'hins, so was it with all men and women born into the world with su'is and sar'gis. For being near Jehovih, they had faith in Him, and Him only. The second race, equally ancient, was the druks, the barbarian hordes, incapable of inspiration, save for their stomachs' sake. And though they were told a thousand times: Behold, ye have a spiritual body! they understood not, cared not, and forgot it a moment after. And though it were said to them: Behold, there is a Great Spirit! they heard it not, nor understood, nor heeded the words. The third race was the I'huans, born betwixt the I'hins and the druks. To this race, in its early days, a commandment was given by God not to marry with the druks, and they had maintained that law amongst themselves by the sign of circumcision. This, then, was the first beginning of persecution against Faithists in Jehovih.

14. When Ahura usurped his heavenly kingdom, and appointed guardian angels over mortals, he determined to leave nothing undone in order to overthrow the doctrine of Jehovih, the All Person. So he decreed as followeth, to wit:

15. Since, by the mark of circumcision, they have pride in being Faithists, I will not have circumcision. After the third generation (one hundred years) whosoever hath this mark upon him is my enemy. He shall be pursued, and no profit shall fall to his lot. Suffer not little children to be maimed for my sake; rather let them be circumcised in heart.

16. And Ahura put no restriction upon his mortal followers marrying, and it came to pass that those druks not slain in Heleste married with the worshippers of Ahura.

17. And about this same period of time Jehovih brought the earth into a light region for two hundred years. And when the Diva was in session, Jehovih's Voice spake to Div, saying: Let My Sons be not cast down because of the sins of Ahura; rather be ye wise and appropriate from his wickedness that which will be good in the end. For as it was not lawful for My people to marry with the druks, behold, Ahura hath made a law on his own account against circumcision, and it shall come to pass that by their sins even druks shall be raised up to learn of Me and My kingdoms.

18. And it came to pass that a fourth race rose up in the world, and it was mongrel, being dark and short and less noble. The I'huans were red, and brown, and tall, and majestic; the I'hins small, and white, and yellow. And Jehovih put these marks upon His peoples that the races might be read in thousands of years.

19. Ahura perceived this. One of his Lords said unto him: Behold, the marks of su'is are written! Then Ahura sought to disprove Jehovih in this. He said:

20. Behold, there are two senses to all men, the es and the corpor. When one is in abeyance the other acteth. This is su'is. Call together thy companions, and find a remedy; for I will prove all things in heaven and earth.

21. For fifty years Ahura and his hosts tried by other means to have born into the world a great prophet and seer, but failed. Ahura said: I know the way of the loo'is: They decoy the I'hin men to go with the I'huan damsels. But I have sworn there is no Jehovih; how, then, shall I go to the sacred people? And, after all, such a prophet might prove treacherous to my kingdom. So Ahura commanded his emissaries to weigh the matter for other fifty years, and then to solve the problem.

22. So Ahura's emissaries inspired thousands of experiments to be made, whereby a prophet or seer could be made amongst the mongrels. And Jehovih suffered them to discover that by pressing down the front brain of infants they could be made capable of su'is. And infants were strapped on boards, and another board strapped on the forehead to press the head flat; and every day the head-board was strapped on anew, tighter and tighter, until the forehead, which holdeth the corporeal judgment, was pressed flat, and the judgment of the brain driven up into light-perceiving regions at the top of the head. (See Che-guh and Took-shein, BOOK OF SAPHAH)

23. Ahura thus raised up prophets and seers, and they were willing instruments in his hands. And he sent into all the divisions of the earth tens of thousands of angels, teaching this to mortals, thus laying down the foundation for his grand scheme of reducing heaven and earth into his own kingdoms.

24. Jehovih spake in the Diva, saying: Even this permit ye. The druks will heed more what one of their own people saith as a seer, than if the same thing were said a hundred times over by an I'hin.

CHAPTER XII.

1. The next resurrection was six thousand million souls, and God and his Lords and his sub-Gods had maintained the Diva, and maintained all the orders of heaven, and the divisions and kingdoms, save what had confederated with Ahura and his kingdoms. And God and his Lords had preserved their colleges, schools, factories, hospitals and nurseries, and their standard in the temples with mortals. And of mortals who remained Faithist, that is, the I'huan race preserved in purity, God, his Lords and ashars held command for the glory of Jehovih.

2. But of the mongrels, who were multiplying fast on the earth, Ahura, his Lords and ashars held command. But alas for the grade of Ahura's hosts in heaven! In less than one thousand years he had abolished his colleges and schools, save what pertained to acquiring a knowledge of the earth and atmospherea. He taught not his people to look higher for other worlds, and herein he began the work which was in after time to be his own downfall.

3. Jehovih had said: Whoever provideth not a philosophy for the endless acquisition of knowledge, dammeth up the running waters I have made. Suffer Ahura to teach what he will; the time will come when he will be obliged to find an outlet for My created beings. And rather than acknowledge Me in My Person, he will profess to send souls back into earth to be re-incarnated.

4. Ahura's heavenly kingdoms numbered more than six thousand million souls, and half of them were little better than drujas, being slaves to certain masters, doing whatsoever they were bidden without knowing, or desiring to know, the reason therefore.

5. As yet there were six hundred years to pass before another dawn of dan, in which God, his Lords and their people had faith that Jehovih's hosts would come from on high to help deliver heaven and earth out of darkness.

6. On the other hand, Ahura, although having been taught the cycles in his early education, spread the word abroad in heaven and earth, that there were no cycles; that, as things are, they had been, and would continue to be.

7. So, as much as God's hosts prophesied a coming light, Ahura and his hosts prophesied that nothing of the kind would come. Ahura, moreover, sent the following order to his Lords, to be taught in heaven and earth, to wit: Am I not he who inspired Zarathustra, the All Pure? Spake I not to him, face to face? Are not all created things mine own? Who, then, knoweth but I will light up the world again? Behold, I am the Personation of Ormazd, Who was VOIDANCE, but now is Me, Ahura'Mazda. In Me only is life and death and resurrection. Whosoever calleth: Ahura'Mazda, Ahura'Mazda! is mine, and within My keeping. Suffer not thy judgment to be warped by prophets who hope for impossible things.

8. In the sixth dan and the eightieth year, Ahura's numberless heavenly kingdoms began to be disturbed by his sub-Gods' lack of advancement, and so, sixty of them congregated together and appealed to Ahura, saying;

9. In reverence to thee, O thou All Highest God! Many hundreds of years have we served thee. And we have paid thee tribute whenever thou requiredst of us. We have helped to adorn thy capital, Ctusk; with diamonds and pearls we have laid thy streets. Thy mansions have we built with precious gems. And as to thy throne, what one of us is there but hath contributed to glorify it before thee. Yea, in all things have we been most loyal and tributary to thee.

10. Nor are we unmindful of our own wisdom. We remember thy arguments of old. Thou didst say to thy God: Behold, thou hast long promised we should be raised to more exalted kingdoms, but, behold, two hundred years have elapsed, and there is no advancement. This thou didst use as an argument for seceding from thy God's kingdoms. Behold, now we have served thee and thy kingdoms more than a thousand years. We come to thee to know wherein we can now serve thee that thou mayst exalt us into kingdoms commensurate with our wisdom and power?

11. To this Ahura replied, saying: Most humble and well-meaning Lords and sub-Gods, why came ye not before me, face to face? Why have ye consorted in private? Was not my capital, and before my throne, the proper place for your argument? Had ye suggested any way whereby advancement was possible unto you, I had answered your demands.

12. But his Lords and sub-Gods came not before him, but sent this answer, to wit: As thou promisedst us advancement provided we served thee, so promised we our ashars, and our marshals and captains. Now they come to us, saying: For hundreds of years have we served; give us preferment. But we have nothing to give. Think not, O God, that we are unwise, or that we hunger and come begging; or that diadems, or gems, or costly thrones, would satisfy us. We know what thou hast to give--promises! We know every corner of thy vast kingdom, and that all places are full, and that thou canst not exalt us. Wherefore, then, shouldst we have spoken before the throne in Ctusk? Would not our voices but breed mischief amongst thy other Gods and Lords? Rather let us err in our proceeding, bringing just punishment upon ourselves, than that we should injure thee and

thy kingdoms. Hear us then, O Ahura'Mazda:

13. Whence the desire for endless advancement if this heaven be all? If a little knowledge giveth power, wherein is not great knowledge desirable. We have destroyed our great colleges, saying: Higher than we, ye must not go. Remember thou, O Ahura, we were students under the Faithist's God and Lords when thou secededst; and thou said unto us: Behold the long training of your course; a curriculum of a thousand years! Come with me; I will give you kingdoms at once.

14. So we came to thee, and we were suddenly puffed up with great pride. Behold now, we look abroad and the same stars shine upon us. We have not visited them. We know not how to go so far. The countless etherean worlds lay beyond ours. We are told that they are habitable. We know not. We have no knowledge enabling us to get away from these heavens; save, indeed, back to the filthy earth.

15. To this Ahura replied, saying: It is plain to me ye are beside yourselves. This heaven is good enough. If there be higher heavens, let them come or stay. I go not to them. But, in truth, with your present convictions, I would be an unwise God not to grant you dismissal from my kingdoms.

16. This ended the matter, and the sixty sub-Gods then deliberated on their course, and finally sent to God, in Mouru, the following address, to wit:

17. In reverence to thee, God of the Faithists in Jehovih: We have had sub-kingdoms, and know our rank is beneath thine. But we are reaching outward and onward; to thee we submit our cause. First, then, there are sixty of us, of the rank of sub-Gods, and we hold seven hundred million subjects. Disaffection hath risen betwixt ourselves and Ahura'Mazda, from whom we are alienated. But whether we shall unite our hosts into a new kingdom of our own, or affiliate with some mighty God, that is our question?

18. What preferment canst thou give unto us if we turn our subjects over to thee?

19. God answered them, saying: Brothers, hear me patiently, and consider my words. First, then, I am not God of the Faithists, nor of any other people, but God of the locality which was assigned me by the Father, through His Son. Neither can ye give your subjects unto me; for by my service to Jehovih I can have nothing, and, least of all, my brothers and sisters.

20. In the next place, I can give you no preferment; I have nothing, neither to give nor to sell. Wherein the Father giveth me wisdom and power, I impart them unto others. Besides, until ye have also learned to know that ye have nothing, neither subjects nor jewels, also desiring nothing, save wisdom and strength to impart to others, how hope ye to gain admittance into my places of learning?

21. And lastly, since ye have kingdoms of your own already, raise ye them up, and thus prove unto me your just merit.

22. To this the confederated Gods replied: What meanest thou? That Gods and angels must labor for others than themselves forever, and receive nothing therefore?

23. God answered them: Even so; save and except ye shall receive an abundance of happiness, and it will endure forever! Here the matter ended for two whole years; and the sub-Gods understood not the plan of Jehovih's kingdoms. But their kingdoms were out of sorts, having no head; and hundreds of thousands of their subjects were deserting them and returning down to the corporeal earth, becoming wanderers and drujas.

24. Finally the sub-Gods again appealed to God in Mouru, inquiring as followeth,

398

to wit: Is not a God a God, whether he be for another or for himself? Behold, we have helped to build up Ahura; he is a mighty God! If we affiliate with thee, we will labor to build thee up also. Yea, we will adorn thy throne and thy great heavenly city. But since we have been sub-Gods we desire not to enter thy service as menials and servants. What, then, shall we do, that both thee and ourselves may have honor and glory?

25. God answered them, saying: Ye cannot serve me; I have no servants. Serve ye Jehovih only. Behold, we are all brothers, being Sons of the same Great Spirit. As for building me up, sufficient is it for me that He who created me will build me up according to my just deserts. As for adorning my throne, ye can only bring substance to it from the lower kingdoms, which I desire not. Why will ye adorn the heavenly city of Mouru? Behold, it is but a resting place on the great journey to the kingdoms of endless light. In a few hundred years, at most, not only I but my hosts will rise from this place to return not to it forever.

26. And lastly, to be a self-God, as is Ahura, is to own all things possible, and hold on thereto; to be a God as I am, is to own nothing, and to retain nothing; but to be forever giving away all one receiveth. Said I not to you before: Begin with your own hosts and exalt them. Inasmuch as ye asked for subjects, behold, the Father gave unto you. Think not that He will suffer ye now to cast them aside or barter them off. Nor shall ye suffer them to become wanderers, nor to return back to the earth as drujas. As much as ye raise up the kingdoms that have been entrusted to you, so will ye also be raised up.

27. Nevertheless, if ye desire to affiliate with Jehovih's kingdoms, the way is open unto you; and your first labor would be, to gather together all your own hosts, and to labor amongst them, teaching them wisdom, strength and individuality equal with yourselves; and when the lowest of them is so risen, then can ye enter the kingdoms of the Father. As ye have had the profit of your subjects for hundreds of years, return ye now unto them service for service. Jehovih is Justice!

28. The sub-Gods made no answer to this for awhile, but Jehovih moved upon their hearts, and they perceived wisdom and justice, and they repented, bitterly bewailing the loss of the thousand years in which they had espoused kingdoms. But they had neither power nor learning sufficient to extricate themselves; so they petitioned God for more light. Whereupon, God affiliated them, and appointed Vishnu Lord unto them and their hosts.

29. And Vishnu took three hundred thousand teachers, captains, physicians, nurses and laborers, and went to them in Maitraias, a heavenly place to the west of Vindyu, and there established a Lordly division, with messengers in connection with Mouru, in Haraiti. And Vishnu sent his captains with sufficient forces, under command of the sub-Gods, to arrest such as had become wandering spirits, or had returned to the earth as drujas. And whilst these were on this duty, Vishnu organized his Lord-dom, and this was the first Lord-dom established in heaven, which is to say, as mortals on earth have military stations, so was the Lord-dom of Vishnu.

30. Jehovih's Voice had spoken to God in Diva, saying: Behold, the time is coming when the sub-kingdom of Ahura, the false, will begin to revolt. And they have thousands of millions of slaves who will strive to go back to the earth to dwell with mortals. They dwell in darkness, and thou shalt not suffer them to regain the earth, lest the races of men go down in darkness, even as before the submersion of Pan.

For which reason, thou shalt establish a Lord-dom, and raise a sufficient army to shield the inhabitants of the earth. And thou shalt make Vishnu thy Lord in My behalf.

31. When it was known in Ctusk, the heavenly place of Ahura, that sixty sub-Gods, with their hosts, had affiliated with Jehovih's kingdoms, general disobedience to Ahura was manifested by the remaining sub-Gods, of whom there were yet more than eight hundred, who had within their dominions upward of two thousand million angels, all slaves, and with light of no other heavenly place than the small precinct where they had been kept in drudgery hundreds of years.

32. The Voice of Jehovih came to God, saying: My Son, take advantage of the seed of disaffection in Ahura's kingdom. Send thou an otevan of great power throughout the heavenly kingdoms. And thou shalt put trumpeters in the otevan, and they shall prophesy the dawn of dan within two hundred years.

33. God perceived, and he had his workmen build an otevan of great power; and he provided trumpeters, and sent them forth, saying to them: Ten years shall ye travel in the heavenly places around about the whole earth, prophesying: In less than two hundred years, Jehovih's etherean hosts are coming. Prepare ye for the resurrection; His kingdoms are open for the weary; His Lords and Gods will give you rest!

34. Ahura summoned his Council of false Gods, hoping they might invent a remedy to counteract so great a prophecy. And he and his Council sat forty days and forty nights in their heavenly capital; but there was no high light amongst them, merely each one giving his opinion. But at the end of forty days Ahura resolved upon the following method, to send a prophecy of his own.

35. Accordingly, he had an otevan built, and sent trumpeters forth with these words, to wit: I, Ahura'Mazda, Only Son of the All Nothing Presence, personated in My Very Self, proclaim from My All Highest Heavenly Judgment Seat! Hear My words, O ye Gods, and tremble! Hear Me, O ye angels, and fall down! Hear Me, O mortals, and bow down to My decrees. Behold, I sent My fire-ship, prophesying that in less than two hundred years I would come in a dawn of dan! But ye obeyed not; ye were defiant before Me! Then I swore an oath against all the world! Ye shall know My power! Then I came down out of My holy, high heaven; and I am already come. Now is the dawn of dan! I send My trumpeters first; after them come my lashers and enchainers, whose captain is Daevas, whose God is Anra'mainyus. I will have Mine, and I will give druks and drujas by thousands and tens of thousands over to everlasting torments.

36. Ahura's Gods had become acquainted with him, during the hundreds and hundreds of years, and they no longer trembled at his commandments. In their hearts they knew he could not do what he professed; they knew his prophecies were vain boastings. Yea, his very trumpeters believed not what they proclaimed.

CHAPTER XIII.
JEHOVIH PREPARES A WAY FOR THE BIRTH OF ABRAM, PO, BRAHMA, AND EA-WAH-TAH.

1. In the one hundred and eightieth year preceding the dawn of dan; that is to say, two thousand nine hundred and twenty years after Fragapatti and Zarathustra, Jehovih sent swift messengers with six thousand etherean loo'is from the Nirvanian fields of Chen'gotha in etherea.

2. And the swift messengers brought these words with them, to wit: Greeting to thee, God of the red star and her heavens, in the name of Jehovih! By the love and wisdom of Cpenta-armij, Nirvanian Goddess of Haotsaiti, we speak in the Father's name. Peace and joy be unto thee, O God, and to thy sub-Gods and Lords, and Lord Gods and Goddesses. One hundred and eighty years of darkness will now come upon thy kingdoms. And then the darkness will go away, and dawn will be in the places thereof. And in the time of darkness, behold, the nations of the earth will go down in great darkness.

3. But the light of the Father's Presence will not be destroyed. A little seed shall endure amongst mortals. That that seed may be propitious to the labor of thy Goddess, who will come in that day, she sendeth herewith two thousand etherean loo'is for Vindyu; two thousand for Jaffeth, and two thousand for Arabin'ya.

4. And thy Goddess decreeth that thou shalt appoint unto these loo'is one of thy Gods, high raised, and he shall go with them, and his labor shall be with them.

5. And the business of this, thy God, and of these, my loo'is, shall be to raise up heirs and followers, who shall be grown to maturity when I come. For through these that they raise up will I deliver the Father's chosen out of the afflictions that will be upon them in that day.

6. To this God replied: In the name of Jehovih, greeting and love unto Cpenta-armij, Goddess of Haot-saiti. I receive thy loo'is with joy, and I appoint unto them my favored God, Yima, God of a thousand years' tuition, namesake of Yima, son of Vivanho, the Sweet Singer.

7. So the swift messengers, with due ceremonies, left the six thousand etherean loo'is and then departed. And God sent messengers to Yima, commanding him to come to Mouru at once, deputing his assistant God to take his place and to retain it until dawn. So Yima appeared presently before the throne of God, and the latter instructed him in all that had been commanded from on high. And Yima sent word to his former kingdom for a thousand of his attendants, and they came also. Meanwhile, Yima conferred with the loo'is, who explained to him what all they required. And after this they provided a piedmazr, and descended to the earth, to Jaffeth and Vindyu and Arabin'ya.

8. And Yima stationed his piedmazr midway betwixt the three countries, in the first plateau above the clouds, and called the place Hored, in honor of the first heavenly kingdom on the earth. And when he had founded his place and named it, he sent word to God, Jehovih's Son, who gave him five hundred messengers, mostly college students. And God gave them, to return, heine currents, so the ethereans could be supplied with regimen of their own order.

9. Yima made the watches twenty-four hours, changing at dawn of sunrise every morning, half on and half off. And he called in all ashars from the regions of mortals where he designed labor; and when they had assembled in Hored, he thus addressed them, saying:

10. Behold, it is yet one hundred and eighty years till dawn of dan. In that time Cpenta-armij, Goddess of Haot-saiti, situated in the Nirvanian fields of Chen-gotha, will come in the Father's name, and with wisdom and power!

11. But until that time, alas, great darkness will be in heaven and earth, especially in these regions. And it shall come to pass that the mongrels, the worshippers of Ahura'Mazda, will triumph in these lands. They will build great cities and kingdoms, and they will rule over the I'huans to great injury. But the druks (aborigines), will be redeemed to

everlasting life during this period; for the mongrels will wed with them, and their progeny will be capable of receiving light, even in mortality.

12. But these mongrels will be great savages, nevertheless, and there will be cannibals all over these three great lands. And they that are slain in battle will be cut up and put in vessels with salt, and their flesh will be thus preserved for food.

13. But because the I'huans, the Zarathustrians, will not war, they will be enslaved by the mongrels, save such as escape to the forests. And betwixt celibacy and torments, the Zarathustrians will have great suffering and bondage, and many of them will be discouraged and lose faith in the Creator.

14. But that their seed may be preserved and delivered out of bondage, ye shall raise up many who are capable of su'is; and in the time of dawn they shall be rescued from their enemies. Behold, here are present etherean loo'is who will go with you throughout these lands and survey the people, and provide also for such great lights as shall lead the people.

15. After Yima thus instructed the ashars in a general way, he handed them over to the loo'is, who divided them into companies of thousands, and each and every loo'is had one company of ashars. And when this was completed they departed out of Hored, going to their several places.

16. And in eleven days thereafter, behold, a'ji began to fall on heaven and earth. The belt of meteoris gave up its stones, and showers of them rained down on the earth, and the sun became as a red ball of fire, and remained so for one hundred and sixty-six years. And the peoples of Arabin'ya and Vindyu and Jaffeth fell from holiness; the Zarathustrians gave up celibacy by hundreds of thousands, and married, and begot children in great numbers; many women giving birth to twenty and some even to five and twenty children. And some men were the fathers of seventy children, and not a few even of a hundred. And the Zarathustrians, even the Faithists with the mark of circumcision, went and married with the mongrels, and they with the druks, so that the foundations of caste were broken up.

17. So great was the power of a'ji that even the I'hins oft broke their vows and lived clandestinely with the world's people, begetting offspring in great numbers, not eligible to enter their sacred cities. And yet mortals saw not the a'ji; saw their cities and temples as it were, sinking in the ground; but they sank not; it was the a'ji falling and condensing.

18. Jehovih had said: What I give that groweth the corpor, inspireth man to corpor; what I give that groweth the es, inspireth man to es. And in the days of a'ji, neither angels or men can enthuse mortals with spiritual things, only they that are organically grown in spirit can withstand.

CHAPTER XIV.

1. Jehovih said: When a'ji cometh near a dawn of dan, let my loo'is be swift in duty; far-seeing in the races of men. I not only break up the old foundations of temples and cities in those days, but the foundations of the abuse of the caste of men. My Voice is upon the races of men. To-day I say: Preserve ye the caste of men; marry ye thus and so, every one to their own line. For I perceive it is wisdom. To-morrow I say: I will have no caste, for the races are becoming impoverished in blood; marry here, marry there! And I give them a'ji, and their desires break all bounds, and I raise them up giants and strong limbed.

2. But in those days my loo'is shall fly swiftly and with great power, that a seed may

be preserved unto Me and My kingdoms. I come not for one race alone; but unto all men; as by My Spirit created I them all alive, so is My hand over them to all eternity.

3. And when the shower of a'ji is over and gone, I send My high-raised Gods and Goddesses to gather together My flocks, and to proclaim unto them anew My Wisdom and Power. And those that have been selected and preserved by My loo'is are the foundations of My new order.

4. Ahura took advantage of the age of darkness to sow disbelief in Jehovih broadcast over earth and heaven, and to gather in his harvest for the glory of his own kingdom. And when war and murder and lust were thus reigning on earth, Ahura decreed to his Lords, and they again to his ashars, and they again to mortals: That all that was required of any man or woman was not celibacy, nor carrying the alms-bowl, nor any sacrifice whatever; but by saying prayers to Ahura'Mazda, and to his Lords, and to wish them hither with praise was all sufficient; that on the third day after death they would ascend and dwell in Ahura's paradise. Nevertheless, such was not truth, for Ahura's emissaries caught the newborn spirits, and made slaves of them, commanding them to gather regimen and substance for the glory of Ahura's heavenly kingdoms.

5. In the fortieth year before dawn, the Voice of the Father came to God, saying: Mouru is becoming inhabitable; Haraiti shall be moved into the earth; Zeredho shall be no more. Go not to Ahura with this prophecy; he hath denied My Voice; he will not hear. But I will take the foundations of Ctusk from under him, and it shall go downward into the earth.

6. But thou, O God, My Son, I forewarn; for thy kingdoms and thy upraised sons and daughters shall be preserved through the darkness. They shall become My Brides and Bridegrooms; I will prepare a place for them in great glory.

7. Call together the Diva, and I will speak before them, and My Voice shall be proclaimed throughout all these heavens, save in the heavens of Ahura, where My Voice shall not be proclaimed.

8. So God called the Diva, and they came and sat in the sacred circle, and the light, like a sun, gathered above God's head, saying: Come up above Haraiti; behold, I have broken up meteoris; I have fashioned a new plateau in the firmament above; whereon are all things plentiful for heavenly kingdoms. Come thither with thy Lord Gods, and with Thy Lords and Gods, and I will show thee. And when thou hast seen, thou shalt possess the place and begin its inhabitation, taking thither thy hosts of thousands of millions.

9. When the Light ceased speaking, it took wing and rose upward, and Div and Diva rose also and followed after; and thus Jehovih led them to the plateau; hence it was called Craoshivi, signifying, THE LIGHT HATH CHOSEN.

10. And God and his sub-Gods possessed the place, and laid the foundation for habitation; and after that he and his Lords and Gods returned and counseled on the manner of removal.

11. At this time there were four thousand million Faithists belonging to God's kingdoms, most wise and upright, full of purity and good works. But God and his Lords, and Lord Gods, had not sufficient power to remove so many angels, especially as many of them were yet below grade fifty, and hence gravitated downward more than upward. So, after due counsel, God decreed to build an avalanza capable of two hundred thousand, and to begin with the highest grades.

12. And God foresaw of his own wisdom that he should render unto Vishnu and his Lord-

dom an all sufficient force to protect the mortals of Vindyu and Jaffeth and Arabin'ya, which were soon to be flooded by the hosts of Ahura being cast down on the earth. Accordingly, he sent for Vishnu, and when Vishnu was before the throne of God, the latter told him all the words Jehovih had said in regard to Ahura and his kingdoms, to be precipitated to the earth; and told him about the new plateau, Craoshivi, whither the light had conducted them. And he further commanded Vishnu to return again to his own place, Maitraias, and survey the dominions, and estimate what force he should require in order to protect the mortals of those three earth divisions.

13. Vishnu replied: As to the latter part of thy commandment, O God, I have already accomplished. For I feared these things might come to pass, and I provided accordingly. The number I will require of and above grade eighty will be six hundred millions! For I must have at least one angel for each and every mortal.

14. God answered him, saying: Thou shalt have eight hundred millions! Whereupon, Vishnu took leave and returned to his own place, Matraias. God immediately sent forth selectors with power; and they went into all the colleges and factories, and other places of Jehovih's kingdoms, and selected out the eight hundred million angels required by Vishnu, and God sent them to Maitraias as soon as possible.

15. Of the six hundred million angels taken to Maitraias, who had been subjects to sub-Gods, besides a hundred million that had strayed off, becoming wanderers and drujas, Vishnu found thirty millions above grade fifty, and these he appropriated at once, to work in concert with the sub-Gods in building schools, colleges, factories, and all such required places for the elevation of man. When he had thus established order, he called together the sub-Gods and said unto them:

16. Think not that I am about to leave you; I am not about to leave you. But ye are not mine to keep; nor are ye hosts of mine. Ye asked for them in the first place, and Jehovih gave them to you. I have restored order; the time is now come when one of you must be chief captain over all the rest, and he shall apportion you according to his highest light. Choose ye, therefore, your captain, and I will give him a judgment seat and badge of office, and ye together shall comprise a Council. For I will make this a kingdom when the majority hath passed grade fifty.

17. The sub-Gods deliberated for eight days, but, perceiving the responsibility of leadership, not one of them would accept the place. So they came before Vishnu, saying: We pray thee, release us, and raise thou up another person, and he shall be our captain.

18. Vishnu said: A certain man and woman married, and they prayed Jehovih for offspring, and he answered their prayer, and they had many children. And now, when they beheld their responsibility to the children, they said unto the Great Spirit: We pray Thee, give the responsibility to some other persons. What think ye of them?

19. Now I say unto you, Jehovih heard their first prayer, but not the second. If I serve Jehovih, how, then, shall I answer your prayers and appoint another person in your stead? It is a wise man that rusheth not into leadership and responsibility; but he is a good man, indeed, who, having gotten in, saith: Now will I go ahead in Jehovih's wisdom and power with all my might. The Gods who are above us come to such a man and help him! Go ye, then, once more into Council, and appoint a chief captain.

20. Hardly had Vishnu said this, when the sub-Gods perceived what was meant by the higher light, and the whole sixty held up their hands, saying: I will serve Thee, O

Jehovih! Give me whatsoever thou wilt!

21. With that, Vishnu commanded them to appoint the one with the highest grade. This they did, and it fell upon Subdga; and accordingly, Subdga was made captain in chief of Maitraias, with rank sixty on the first list. So Vishnu created a judgment seat for Subdga and gave him a badge of office. And the other sub-Gods were made captains of divisions, and numbered according to their assignment, and none of them were humiliated before their former subjects, but became trainers and disciplinarians in new fields of labor. And their former subjects were no longer called subjects, but hosts, and they were liberated in all things, save with no liberty to return to mortals.

22. Hardly had Vishnu these matters settled, when the hosts, eight hundred millions, came as the guard and shields of mortals. These Vishnu organized, making Maitraias the central throne over them; and he divided them into companies of one million, and gave to each company one marshal and one thousand messengers. And the marshals again sub-divided their hosts into thousands, and numbered them, and to each thousand he gave one master, with his quota of messengers.

23. Next, Vishnu divided the three great countries, Vindyu, Jaffeth and Arabin'ya, into as many parts as he had appointed marshals; and the lands were mapped out, cities and towns and country places, and each marshal was assigned his place. And there was made a record of these things, with the maps and divisions, and the names of the marshals and masters; and it was registered in the libraries of heaven.

24. So Vishnu's hosts were sent to their places and commanded to give daily reports of their labors, which were to be carried by the messengers to Vishnu.

CHAPTER XV.

1. In Mouru, God and his officers were using all their strength and wisdom to provide for the removal of his hosts to Craosivi. The demand for builders, surveyors and carriers, with power, was so great that God determined to send trumpeters through the kingdoms of Ahura, the false, asking for volunteers.

2. For this purpose he sent twelve otevans in different directions, some even going through the city of Ctusk, Ahura's capital, and they proclaimed aloud what they wanted. And it came to pass that in less than one year the otevans gathered out of Ahura's kingdoms seven million angels capable of grade seventy, who were able to fill the places required.

3. This was the most damaging blow of all to Ahura's kingdoms, for he thus lost the wisest and most powerful of his people. And this news went like fire before the wind. His sub-Gods began to revolt against him, claiming their own kingdoms. Many of them openly preached in their heavenly places against him, accusing him of falsehood and of being a mere pretender, with little power.

4. Nevertheless, he had great power in the name Ahura'Mazda, for he was believed in heaven, to be the same God, even I'hua'Mazda, that inspired Zarathustra. And mortals also, living and dying in this belief, could not be convinced otherwise. And when their spirits left their mortal bodies, Ahura's angels took them to the heavenly city of Ctusk, where they beheld its glory, shining and magnificent. And they took them in sight of Ahura's throne, but not near it, and they were obliged to crawl on their bellies a long distance even for this purpose. And the throne was kept radiant with perpetual fire. Then

they were made to re-crawl their way back again, until out of the city. After that it was said unto them: Behold, we have shown thee Ahura'Mazda's heavenly city and the glory of his throne. Himself thou canst not behold till thou hast performed the service which is required of all souls entering heaven. Nor canst thou come again to this city, most brilliant, majestic, till thou hast served under thy Lords and masters thy allotted time. After that thou shalt come here and dwell in peace and rest and happiness forever!

5. And these spirits knew not otherwise, nor would they believe, if told; and they thus willingly made slaves of themselves hundreds of years, carrying provender, or doing drudgery to certain masters who were again serving the Lords and the sub-Gods, going through the same rites and ceremonies in heaven as they were accustomed to on earth.

6. But Jehovih provided for all things, wiser than the wisest Gods. He created His creations with a door on every side, full of glory and freedom. Out of earth and atmosphere conjoined, He created animal and vegetable kingdoms. And He created the trees of the earth and the flesh of animals out of these two things, the dust of the earth and the air of heaven.

7. With this possibility created He them; that in death their corporeal elements should go to their respective places, where they belong. But this possibility created the Creator, that in the death of a vegetable and in the death of an animal, when the atmospherean part flieth upward, that it should carry with it a small possible part of the dust of the earth, and it thus doeth His bidding.

8. With this possibility created He His creations: that the earth giveth away of its substance into atmospherea hundreds of years; and the fields become barren, and produce not; and certain animals become barren and produce not, and their races go out of existence. And He created man subject to the same forces; and when the earth is in the giving-off period, behold, man ceaseth to desire of the earth; he crieth out to his Father in heaven for the light of heaven.

9. With this possibility created the Creator the earth and the heavens above the earth: a time for the earth to give off its substance, the which flieth upward hundreds of years; and a time for the earth to receive from the atmosphere, surcharged from the regions far away, an addition of substance, for hundreds of years. And when it is thus receiving, it is called the time of a'ji, because that which falleth (condenseth) is aji.

10. When a'ji cometh upon the earth, the drujas come also. The days of the darkness of earth are their delight; their harvest is in the rich falling a'ji; it suiteth their laziness and their inclination to bask about. They become in those days like an over-fed animal; and to their masters, the false Gods, they become worthless, for they derive their sustenance without labor. A'ji is their delight; but they are also like a foolish man drinking wine with delight, who continueth till his delight turneth to madness. So the drujas feast and disobey their masters; and then they become boisterous and unruly, full of disorder and evil intent, defiant, believing themselves to be Gods and Goddesses. Like a beggar with a pocket full of money, who lacketh discipline and determineth to glut his passions to the fill, so is it with the drujas in the time of a'ji.

11. Thus Ahura counted without Jehovih; in his heart he had conceived great power in his kingdom; but the long a'ji told upon his heavenly places seriously. His sub-Gods no longer paid him tribute, to support in ease and glory his five millions of heralds, his five millions of musicians, his five millions of ceremonious paraders, giving

and providing for them constantly new costumes and new palaces and new decorations.

12. So, first one and then another of his sub-Gods revolted; and Ahura was powerless to enforce obedience, for so dense was a'ji that whoever Ahura sent forth only reveled in sumptuous feastings. And it came to pass that, in years after a'ji sat in, when over six hundred of Ahura's sub-Gods had dissolved all connection with him, and of the two hundred yet remaining, who were situated close about Ctusk, Ahura's heavenly place, not ten of them could be relied upon in emergency.

13. At this time Ahura resolved upon regaining his lost dominions, and it was like a man having lost heavily at the games, resolving to win all or lose all. Accordingly, Ahura set his workmen to building parade ships, fifty thousand. He said unto his remaining sub-Gods: Behold I will traverse the heavens in such magnificence and glory that all angels and mortals shall fall down and worship me. And surely, too, this time of a'ji must come to an end; and in that day I will remember those that have been faithful unto me. And I will also remember, with a curse, those who have been unfaithful to me.

14. For fourteen years the workmen were building Ahura's fleet, and yet they had built but thirty thousand ships. For so great was the desertion of his skilled men that failure met him on all sides. But with these thirty thousand ships Ahura determined to travel throughout all the atmospherean heavens.

15. Accordingly, he called together his heralds, five millions; his musicians, five millions; his masters of ceremonies, five millions; his masters of rites, five millions; his marshals, ten millions; his captains, twenty millions; his generals, three millions; his Lords, one million, and of his sub-Gods, one hundred and fifty, with their attendants, twenty millions; his bearers of trophies, ten millions; his light makers, ten millions; his waterers, ten millions; his torch-bearers, five millions; his body-guard, thirty millions. Besides these there were the bearers of banners, the proclaimers, the road makers, the surveyors, the directors, and so on, more than fifty millions. And yet the traveling hosts, one hundred millions, and waiters for them, one hundred millions. In all there were upward of four hundred millions of spirits that went within the thirty thousand ships, and the ships were not full.

16. And the ships traveled in the form of a pyramid, but not touching one another, and yet fastened together. And the base of the pyramid was four hundred miles wide every way, and four hundred miles high. And the belt of light around the pyramid was a thousand miles in diameter every way; and it was ballasted to run within fifty miles of the earth's surface.

17. Thus sat out Ahura for a whole year's cruise in atmospherea; and wherever he went he proclaimed himself thus: Ahura'Mazda, the Creator! The Only Begotten Son of the Unknowable! Behold, I come; I, the Creator! I have come to judge heaven and earth! Whoever is for Me I will raise up to Nirvana; whoever is against Me I will cast into hell.

18. The pyramid reflected light in its travel; and Ahura's emissaries on earth used this as a testimony that all things were about to come to an end; the earth to be cast out, and heaven and hell to be filled up with spirits, each to its place, according to its obedience or disobedience to Ahura'Mazda.

19. On the other hand, Ahura's revolted sub-Gods laughed at him; and, as for the over-fed and debauched drujas, they mocked at him. So it came to pass that when Ahura visited his revolted sub-Gods in their kingdoms, instead of regaining their allegiance, he was sent on

his way with hisses and groans. And yet never since the earth and her heavens were, had there been such great show and pageantry.

20. Before Ahura had visited half the kingdoms in atmospherea he foresaw the futility of his project; the probable downfall of his own mighty kingdoms began to break in on his heart. Enthusiasm for his name was on the wane, and all his magnificence had failed to restore him to what he had been.

21. Now, whilst he was absent from Ctusk, the capital of his kingdoms, he had deputed Fravaitiwagga to reign in his stead, and to maintain the order and glory of his throne. Fravaitiwagga was a deserter from God's Haienne colony in Haraiti, where he had been educated two hundred years, and was expert in primary surveys and buildings, but impatient for advancement beyond his capacity. He had now been with Ahura three hundred years, learning little, but feasting and frolicking, being a great flatterer of Ahura, and given to long speeches and flowery words.

22. Whilst Fravaitiwagga was on the throne, and after the departure of Ahura on his excursion, there came to him one Ootgowski, a deserter from Hestinai in Zeredho, who had been in Ahura's service a hundred and fifty years, but banished from his heavenly place by Ahura on account of gluttony and drunkenness, since which time he had been a wandering spirit, dwelling sometimes in one kingdom and then in another, and oft visiting the earth and gaining access to the oracles, and even to mortal priests, where he represented himself, sometimes as Ahura'Mazda, sometimes as God, sometimes a favorite Lord, sometimes Fragapatti, and Thor, and Osire, and, in fact, any name he chose, issuing decrees and commandments to mortals, then flying away to return no more.

23. Ootgowski came to Fravaitiwagga and he said unto him: Greeting to thee, O God, in the name of Ahura'Mazda! Behold, I am sent to thee in great haste by our Creator, Ahura; who commandeth thy presence in the province of Veatsagh, where is held a mighty Council with Ahura's re-affiliated sub-Gods. What preferment Ahura'Mazda hath fashioned for thee I know not. To this Fravaitiwagga answered as followeth, to wit:

24. Who are thou, and from what kingdom? And above all, why art thou come without heralds and attendants? To this Ootgowski answered, saying: Behold me! Knowest thou not me? I am Haaron, God of Sutuyotha! Who else could come so quickly? Who else but I runneth fearlessly unattended betwixt the kingdoms of the Gods?

25. Fravaitiwagga had been drunk many days, and was so dazed with the pretentious Ootgowski that he took for granted that he was indeed Haaron, a great friend to Ahura. Fravaitiwagga called his Council together and appointed Semmes to be God in his stead; and so Fravaitiwagga departed in an arrow-ship, with messengers, for Veatsagh, which lies in an entirely different direction to where Ahura was traveling.

26. Semmes, the deputized God of Ctusk, was faithful to his office for four days, and then proclaimed recreation until the trumpet call from the throne. And in this interval the debauchee, Ootgowski, obtained access to the floor of the inner chamber, and seduced Semmes to accompany him, carrying off all the costly gems and jewels of the throne! And when without the capital, they embarked with their plunder in an arrow-ship to some unknown region.

27. For many days the members of the Council waited for the trumpet call, but not hearing it, resolved to learn the cause. And after diligent search, not finding Semmes, but discovering that the throne had been plundered of its valuables, they were thrown

into great confusion. In two days after this the throne was destroyed, the Council divided and gone, and the heavenly city of Ctusk turned to riot and plunder.

28. And there were in Ctusk and near about, upward of four thousand million angels with no God, nor leader, nor any head whatsoever. Thus it came to pass that Jehovih took the throne from Ahura, as had been prophesied.

29. And whilst this was going on, Ahura was away with his pyramid fleet, being discomfited wherever he went. But in two hundred and twelve days after his departure on his journey, messengers came to him and told him what had happened in Ctusk.

30. Ahura gave orders to sail at once for his capital; which was done, and his pyramid fleet hastened with all possible power. Suffice it, in a few days he was back in Ctusk, a witness to the rioting and plundering going on. But the majesty and splendor of his fleet quieted the people, and restored order for the time being; nevertheless he was without a throne and without a Council.

CHAPTER XVI.

1. During the fall of a'ji, God decreed to his Lord Gods, to his Gods and Lords, and Goddesses, as followeth, to wit: As ye have gathered of the rising atmospherean part of the living earth-substance, so shall ye now turn for your regimen above. It is in heaven now like unto the waters of the earth. When it raineth not, mortals go to the well and fetch up water out of the earth; but when it raineth they go not to the well for water, but set out vessels, and the rain filleth them.

2. So, in the times of dan and half dan and quarter dan, our hosts bring their regimen up from the earth. Wherein ye have many employed as laborers. Behold now, a'ji will rain down upon us sufficient and more than sufficient regimen for one hundred and eighty years. Suffer not, therefore, your laborers to fall into idleness, for this will lead to mischief. But immediately put them to other occupations; suffer them to have no spare time.

3. The mathematicians discovered there would fall no a'ji in Yaton'te, nor on the lands of Guatama. So, God sent from several divisions in the heavens laborers for those regions.

4. Two heavenly kingdoms, Gir-ak-shi and Soo'fwa, of Heleste and Japan, grieved God more than all the rest. For these had become strongholds for Ahura, who had pursued the warfare on earth till in those two great divisions all the Faithists, the Zarathustrians, had been put to death. And the mortal kings of those countries had issued laws commanding all people to be put to death that professed the Great Spirit, Ormazd (Jehovih). And the law had been carried out effectually.

5. So God bewailed Soo'fwa with lamentations. He said: O Japan, my beloved, down stricken! How can I restore to thee mortal seed? Thou art afar; no man on thy soil heareth the Creator's voice! How can I carry her; she lieth down with cold feet.

6. Whilst God lamented, the voice of the Father came to him, saying: Hear Me in My wisdom, O My Son. I will not suffer Ahura to go thither. Withdraw thy guards from the evilest of men. Suffer him to go his way. Ahura shall be brought home before he visiteth Soo'fwa and Gir-ak-shi.

7. God perceived; and he sent messengers to the guard over Ootgowski, saying to them: When ye come to the guard, even to the captains, ask permission to speak to Ootgowski. And the captain will permit. Whereupon, ye shall say to Ootgowski: My son, thou camest

hither, saying: Put a guard over me, for I am obsessed of Satan with the seven horns (tetracts). And God appointed a guard over thee. In this day, behold, God sendeth to thee, saying: I will no longer guard Ootgowski. For his glory he shall enter the kingdoms of Jehovih and become a worker for righteousness' sake.

8. When the messengers had said this much to Ootgowski, the latter said unto them: God is wise; I volunteered to have myself put under guard, but I am tired thereof. Say to God, his Lords and sub-Gods, I will come to Jehovih's kingdoms and work, for righteousness' sake. But yet a little while I desire rest and travel. So Ootgowski was granted freedom purposely, and of his own accord he went and destroyed the foundations of Ahura's throne, as hath been told. And Ahura thus hastened home without completing the travel of the heavens.

9. Jehovih said: What mattereth a name? Let them call the Creator Ahura'Mazda, and call Ahura'Mazda the Creator. Since He hath not shown Himself in a ship, or in the figure of a man, behold, thy inspirers shall teach His Ever Presence.

10. God perceived, and a record of the name was made and entered in the libraries of heaven. And God looked abroad and saw that the same thing was even so in Gir-ak-shi and Heleste. And God entered this also in the libraries of heaven. And the reading thereof, translated, is as followeth: In the land of Celeste, the highest, most sacred name of the Great Spirit, the Creator, was decreed by God to be Mazda; and the same thing is decreed of Japan.

11. Hence it was known from that time forth that the origin of the word Master, as applied to the Creator, sprang from those two countries only, and from no other division of the earth. Of this matter, God said: In thousands of years this word shall be testimony to mortals of the war in heaven of this day, which reached not to the heavens of these two lands. And it was so, and will continue forever!

12. So God had no footing in Japan nor in Heleste, nor had he sufficient power to establish a God or Lord in either country, or in the heavens belonging to them.

13. And when Diva assembled, God propounded this matter, on which the fourteen members spake at length. And then Div decreed: To the swift messengers in attendance, and through them to the etherean Goddess, Cpenta-armij, deploring of Diva in Jehovih's name: Two heavenly kingdoms and two corporeal divisions have walled themselves about in idolatry. A'ji hath yet six years, and dawn twenty-six.

14. In thirty days thereafter the star-ship, Gee'onea, from Haot-saiti, in etherea, made its appearance in the heavens above, first observed on the borders of the bridge Chinvat. God sent immediately a swift-rising Ometr to meet the star-ship and conduct it to Craoshivi, whither he had gone with one of the transports, with two hundred millions, well selected, to found a new city in heaven. Suffice it, in three days' time the star ship landed in Craoshivi with one million laborers provided to endure till the coming dawn.

15. After due salutations, Os, chief Captain of the ethereans, said unto God: In Jehovih's name am I come to possess the heavenly places, Soo'fwa and Gir-ak-shi, and their lands, Japan and Heleste. This work must be accomplished before dawn; before the coming of Cpenta-armij. Send thou, therefore, thy messengers who know the places, that I may conduct my hosts thither to labor.

16. God then gave messengers to Os, and the latter departed and went to the kingdoms named; and it so happened, by the wisdom of Jehovih, that this took place at the same

410

time that Ahura had returned and found his capital and throne demolished. Hence Ahura was powerless to interfere with the labor of Os and his hosts.

17. So Os divided his forces and possessed both Soo'fwa and Gir-ak-shi, together with the divisions of the earth thereunto belonging. And Os possessed the corporeal temples of worship, and the places of the oracles, and all places for consulting spirits. And he taught not the name of Jehovih, nor of the Great Spirit, nor of the Father; for none of these would be received. But this he taught; thus he extolled; thus inspired OF THE MAZDA, THE CREATOR; OF THE VOICE THAT SPAKE TO ZARATHUSTRA, THE ALL PURE. To goodness and good works; to self-denial and love; to justice and truth; of mercy and obedience to the all highest light in the soul.

CHAPTER XVII.

1. But even Gods fail at times. For by failures do all persons learn there are higher powers. Only Jehovih never faileth.

2. In the last month of the last year of a'ji, even whilst God, Jehovih's Son, and his Lord Gods, and his Lords and sub-Gods, were proud of heart that they should carry the earth and her heavens through safely, they met sore trials. This, then, is what happened: A comet came within the earth's vortex, and was drawn in, even as floating drift is drawn within a whirlpool in a river. The substance of the comet was condensed, and fell on the earth in mist, and dust and ashes. And the earth, and the heavens above the earth, were in darkness twelve days, and the darkness was so great that a man could not see his hand before him.

3. And during those days of darkness there were more than four score hells founded within Ahura's heavenly regions, and he himself was cast into one of them, and he was walled about by more than three thousand million angels; pilfered and stripped of all he had. And his remaining sub-Gods were also bound in hell and robbed of all they had.

4. And presently the spirits ran for the kings' and queens' souls (of them who had been tyrants on earth), and they caught them, and brought them and cast them into hell also, taking vengeance on them with stripes and foul smells. And hundreds of thousands of spirits went and gathered foul smells and cast them into hell, and surrounded the hells on every side with foul gases, so that none could escape.

5. So desperate became the madness upon them, that even the tormentors rushed in, making a frolic of madness. And whosoever had ever had an enemy on earth now ran for him and caught him in hada and brought him; and others helped; and they took and cast him into the torments of hell. And those who had been slaves hundreds of years to Ahura and his Gods, now caught every one they could lay hands on, and dragged them into hell.

6. As soon as God's messengers came and told him what had happened, God sent all his available forces to overthrow the place if possible. Vishnu, full of hope and courage, sent one-half of his forces to God's assistance, thereby risking the guardianship of the three great mortal kingdoms, Vindyu, Jaffeth and Arabin'ya. And God sent messengers to the heavenly kingdoms of North and South Guatama, saying to the Gods of those places: Behold, Ahura, the false, is involved in torments; his hosts are upon him, three thousand millions! Send all above grade seventy at once. To Uropa he sent also, saying the same thing, and adding thereto: Alas, my little wisdom in sending off a thousand million of mine own hosts to Craoshivi at such a time!

7. Craoshivi was the new plateau, difficult of access, and it was scarcely possible to recall his hosts in the time required. And God summoned the Diva, that they might sit for the Father's Voice; and the members came and sat in the usual way, and Jehovih spake unto God, saying:

8. Peace be unto Thee, My Son! Neither regret thou that thou sent thy most exalted hosts to Craoshivi. Did not I lead thee thither? And I said unto thee: Possess this place, and send thou thy hosts hither. Neither grieve thou because I sent the nebulae and the darkness of that time. Is it more to thee to behold these things, than for mortals to witness the spring floods that wash away the summer's coming harvest?

9. To learn to provide against contingencies, this is wisdom. Yet not All Wisdom is in man's heart, nor yet with My Gods. How canst thou perceive how it is with Ahura's soul, whether this hell be good or evil unto him in the end?

10. If thou behold My sudden power, how much more must not Ahura feel it? Yet thou shalt deliver him out of hell; by thy hosts shall he and his sub-Gods be delivered. But far greater shall be the torments of his own soul, than what his drujas can heap upon him.

11. Then God inquired of Jehovih, saying: What is the best, most perfect way, to deliver Ahura and his subjects out of hell?

12. Jehovih answered him, saying: Whom he hath despised, send; whom he hath ill-treated, send; whom he hath humbled, send. And when thy Lords and Gods are come to the place, let these, his abused enemies, take the hand of thy Lord or thy God, and they shall call out to Me in the name, Ormazd, the which name Ahura hath tried to destroy for the glory of his own. And at the sound of the name, Ormazd, thy hosts shall cast burning light into the faces of the drujas, and thus scatter them away till Ahura be released; and he shall witness that he hath been released through the name, Ormazd.

13. God sent E'chad, and Ah'oan, to deliver Ahura out of hell, and they labored four years in accomplishing it, and then Ahura was free, and his hosts were divided into groups of tens of thousands, and hundreds of thousands; and God appointed generals and captains over them. Save and except eight hundred million drujas that escaped from hell and through the guards' fires, and descended back to the earth, to torment and to deceive mortals.

14. So it turned out that Vishnu failed in some degree to save the nations of the earth from the approach of evil spirits. Jehovih spake to Vishnu, comforting, saying: Because thou hast helped to deliver Ahura, thou shalt not take sorrow to thy heart. What are eight hundred millions to thee? So Vishnu grieved no more.

15. Now during the time of the deliverance of Ahura, no less than six knots had been tied in hell, and in one of these Ahura and his sub-Gods had become bound, so there was no escape for them. But the outer and extreme knots were untied first, and as fast as the delirious spirits were rescued, they were carried without and beyond the firewalls and placed under guard.

16. Thus in sections was Ahura's hell cast out; and when the deliverers came to Ahura and his confederates they were all, save Ahura, in a state of chaos, frenzied with fear. But Ahura was not beside himself, though in serious fright. Ah'oan, Lord of Jaffeth, spake to him, saying: In the name of God, and of Ormazd, I have delivered thee. How is it with thee?

17. Ahura said: I am done! I am nothing! One God alone can do nothing. Do with me

whatsoever thou wilt. I am thy servant.

18. Ah'oan said: Nay, be thou servant to none save Ormazd, thy Creator. His name is the watch-word and the power in all the high heavens. By his name thou shalt become one amongst Godly companions.

19. Ahura said: But thou must torment me first! Ah'oan said: Wherefore? My work is not to cast down but to lift up. So it is with all of Ormazd's Gods. Behold thou here, even thy sub-Gods, and such as thou hast in times past evilly used! See, they hold up their hands in prayer to Ormazd for thee!

20. And is this not the way of knowing angels and mortals, whether they be of the Creator? If they pull down, they are not His. If they slander or torment, or speak evil of one another, or give pain, they are not His. How, then, shall I not do good for thee and restore thee to thy kingdom?

21. Ahura said: Give me anything, but give me not my kingdom again; for of all torments this is the worst. Ah'oan said: Wouldst thou evilly treat them that had been thy subjects? If so, thou art not of the everlasting resurrection. Ahura said: Nay, I would see them not forever! I would hear them not, know them not forever. If, therefore, thou wilt do me good instead of evil, I pray thee take me afar off, and alone, that I may meditate forever on the horrors I have passed through.

22. Ah'oan said: Hear me now, once for all, and I speak in the name of God and of the Great Spirit, Ormazd: Because thou hast served thyself and compelled others to serve thee for nearly two thousand years, thou hast become blind to the Ormazdian law, which is: That thine own peace and happiness can only come by making restitution to thy servants, and by lifting up those whom thou hast cast down. How can I deliver thee away from them? I may take away thy person, but I cannot deliver thy memory. No man can be delivered from himself.

23. One way only is open for thee, which is under the Ormazdian law; which is, that thou shalt take thy kingdom again, and deliver it unto righteousness, intelligence and good works. Serving Ormazd by doing good unto them whom the Creator gave thee. Many of them have served thee more than a thousand years; wouldst thou now cast them off without recompense?

24. Ahura said: Thou art just, O Ormazd! I perceive the wisdom of Thy Gods, and the bondage of men. Take me, O Ah'oan, put me in a way to carry out this great light.

25. Ah'oan said: Hear thou thy sentence, in the name of Ormazd, the Creator; which is, that thou shalt be taken to a place of safety, which E'chad shall select; and thither shall thy best, most exalted people be taken, and put to work and to school, and in nurseries and hospitals; and thou shalt go about amongst them, teaching and encouraging them in industry and righteousness, for Ormazd's sake. And when thou hast certain ones disciplined in this way, thou shalt receive another installment of thy people, and they shall be disciplined in the same way. And then another installment, and so on, until thou hast all thy kingdom.

26. And that thou shalt be successful, these, my Lords, and generals, and captains, shall go with thee and labor with thee and thy hosts. And thou and thy people shall have no ornaments; and your raiment shall be white-gray, alike and like, teachers and pupils, save when especially ordered otherwise by God and his deputies.

27. And when thou and the majority of thy hosts have risen above grade fifty, thou shalt

be crowned in the name of Ormazd, and thy kingdom shall have a throne, and thou shalt be one amongst the united hosts of the higher heavens. Till then, go thou to thy labors diligently, and may Ormazd abide with thee in wisdom and power.

28. Ahura said: Thou art just, O Ormazd. I will henceforth, forever, serve Thee with all my wisdom and strength!

29. And then E'chad and his attendants led the way, and the marshals and generals and captains brought Ahura's hosts, the first installment, and they went to a place called Ailkin, a heavenly place capable of seven thousand millions, and there they founded the new colony for Ahura.

30. But Ah'oan and his hosts continued their labors in delivering the hells, until they delivered the four score and placed all the spirits under guard and discipline.

CHAPTER XVIII.

1. Thus drew to a close the cycle of Fragapatti, being three thousand and one hundred years. And at this time there were but few people on earth or in heaven but were capable of everlasting life, even the druks and drujas also.

2. Jehovih spake to God, saying: Now shalt thou enumerate earth and heaven, as to all that I have created capable of everlasting life; and of My harvests since the habitation of the earth, when man first walked upright. And thy numbers shall be entered in the libraries of heaven, to remain forever.

3. So God called together a council of mathematicians, and they numbered mortals and angels, and recorded their labor in the libraries of heaven, where the wise men of heaven and earth may read the records.

4. In Fragapatti's cycle were born alive ninety-two thousand millions. Of these ninety percent were born to everlasting life. Ten percent went into dissolution, as a drop of water evaporateth before the sun and is seen no more.

5. In Osiris' cycle, ninety-one thousand millions. Of these eighty-seven percent were born to everlasting life. Thirteen percent went into dissolution and were seen no more.

6. In Thor's cycle, eighty-eight thousand millions. Of these eighty-five percent were born to everlasting life, and fifteen percent to dissolution.

7. In Apollo's cycle, eighty thousand millions. Of these seventy-two percent were born to everlasting life.

8. In Sue's cycle, eighty-seven thousand millions. Of these sixty-two percent were born to everlasting life, and thirty-eight percent went into dissolution.

9. In Aph's cycle, sixty-six thousand millions. Of these fifty-four percent were born to everlasting life, and forty-six percent went into dissolution.

10. In Neph's cycle, before the submersion of Pan, one hundred and twenty-four thousand millions. Of these twenty-one percent were born to everlasting life, and seventy-nine percent went into dissolution.

11. And this comprised one-sixth of the people that had been created alive on the earth since man walked upright; that is to say, three thousand six hundred and seventy-eight billions.

12. But in the early days of man only a small percentage were born to everlasting life; and, first of all, only one percent.

13. And God gave thanks unto Jehovih, the Creator, because all the races of men on earth were now capable of everlasting life.

14. Of the hells and knots springing out of hada since the days of Wan, this was the proportion, to wit:

15. In the cycle of Fragapatti, two hundred and seventy-six hells, of average duration, thirty years. Involved in these hells, two thousand million angels. Sixty-four knots, of average duration, two years. Involved in these knots, one thousand million angels.

16. In the cycle of Osiris, three hundred and eighty-nine hells, of average duration, four hundred years. Involved in these hells, seven thousand millions. Two hundred and twelve knots, of average duration, three years. Involved in these knots, three thousand millions.

17. In the cycle of Thor, five hundred and ninety-one hells, of average duration, six hundred years. Involved in these hells, nine thousand million angels. Four hundred and thirty-six knots, of average duration, six years. Involved in these knots, four thousand million angels.

18. In Apollo's cycle, seven hundred and forty-two hells, of average duration, eight hundred years. Involved in these hells, ten thousand million angels. Six hundred and four knots, of average duration, twelve years. Involved in these knots, five thousand millions.

19. In Sue's cycle, twelve hundred and seventy-three hells, of average duration, one thousand years. Involved in these hells, thirteen thousand million angels. One thousand and five knots, of average duration, thirty years. Involved in these knots, eight thousand millions.

20. In Aph's cycle, three thousand five hundred hells, of average duration, two thousand years. Involved in these hells, twenty-eight thousand million angels. Two thousand knots, of average duration, fifty years. Involved in these knots, twenty-five thousand millions. And these were the numbers of spirits cast into hell and into knots, from the submersion of Pan to the end of the cycle of Zarathustra; but at the dawn of each and every cycle, both the hells and the knots were delivered by the etherean Gods. Save in Fragapatti's cycle, when they were almost entirely delivered by the atmospherean God.

21. Prior to the submersion of Pan, commonly called the flood, more than half the people entering the first es world went into hells and into knots. And in all ages of the world there have been thousands and millions of spirits who delight in hell for certain seasons, even as is manifested in mortals who delight in debauchery, and vengeance, and war. Nor is a hell widely different, as regards the spirit, from what war is amongst mortals. And as mortals of this day glorify themselves and their generals and captains for the magnitude of their havoc in war, so in the olden times, in atmospherea, there were great boastings and laudations for such as inflicted the greatest torments and horrors in hell.

22. As mortals of the druk order oft leave their evil ways for a season, and become upright and virtuous, loving decency and righteousness, and then break away and indulge in a season of debauchery, so in the es world hath it been with millions and thousands of millions of angels. In one day the teachers and physicians were rejoicing before Jehovih because of the steadfastness of their wards to righteousness; and in the next day were left to deplore the loss of hundreds and thousands who had broken faith and gone off for indulgence's sake in some of the hells. And these had to be rescued, persuaded, threatened and coaxed back again and again to the nurseries and hospitals, or to the factories and colleges.

415

23. Neither knoweth any one, save Jehovih, the labor and fretting and anxiety that were undergone by the teachers and physicians, and Lords and Gods, who had such drujas in charge. For even as it is beholden on earth that men of great learning and high estate oft fall, becoming lower than the beasts of the fields, so in heaven were there hundreds of thousands, and even millions, oft high raised in the grades, that would stumble and fall into the lowest of hells, and even into the knots.

24. So Jehovih brought the earth and her heavens into another dawn of dan, in the arc of Spe-ta, in the Nirvanian roads of Salk-watka, in etherea.

25. Now, up to the last, God and his Lords maintained the Diva; and mortals somewhat understood the matter, that there were certain Divine laws in heaven that ruled over mortal kingdoms and empires. So that the words Div, and Diva, and Divine rights, began to be realized as a concerted power in heaven greater than man's power.

END OF THE BOOK OF DIVINITY.

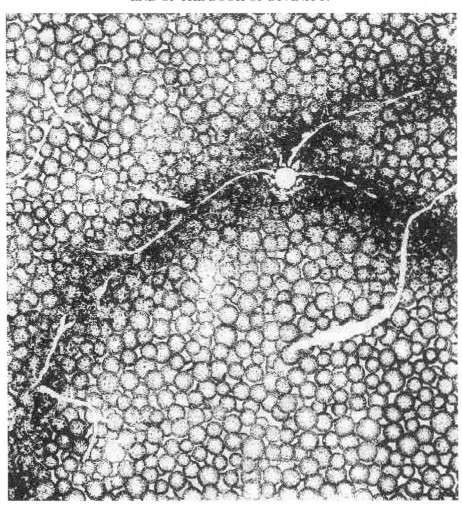

Plate 18.
THE EARTH IN OCGOKUK.

Jehovih said: Out of the etherean mountains of Ocgokuk I brought the earth, prepared for My four Sons: Abram, Brahma, Po and Eawahtah. And I numbered the earth at one hundred, for it had attained to fullness.

416

BOOK OF CPENTA-ARMIJ, DAUGHTER OF JEHOVIH.

BEING OF THE FIRST DELIVERANCE OF GOD'S CHOSEN PEOPLE.

CHAPTER I.

1. Jehovih spake to Cpenta-armij, Goddess of Haot-saiti, in Nirvana, in the arc of Spe-ta, Commander of the South fields of Abarom, in the Orian Plains of Bilothowitchieun, of a reign of two hundred thousand years; Surveyor for Otsias, ten thousand years; Leader of the Oixan, seventy thousand years; Captain of Geliyas' roadways, in the forest of Lugga, twenty thousand years; Founder and Ruler of Isaas, thirty thousand years; Trencher of the Haigusets swamps, four thousand years; Goddess of Nor, Goddess of Eunigi, Goddess of Poutu, each ten thousand years, saying:

2. My Daughter, behold, the red star and her heavens come thy way. She will cross the arc of Spe-ta, four years and thirty-two days' riding. Open thou thy fields in Abarom, and give her forty years' indulgence, for this is the first of her deliverances.

3. Cpenta-armij answered, saying: I see the red star, the earth, O Jehovih! Like a wandering ship in a wide ocean she cometh through my fields, the young earth, traveling on, carefully, in the roads of Salkwatka. Hath she so soon, but little more than sixty thousand years, overcome her enduring knots and torturing hells?

4. In Thy Wisdom and Power, O Jehovih, I will go in person to this corporeal world, and encourage her God and Lords for the excellent labor done.

5. Jehovih said: Call thy Council, and proclaim from My throne the FEAST OF THE ARC OF SPE'TA. Then Cpenta-Armij called her High Council, a hundred millions, Sons and Daughters of Jehovih, and she ascended to her place in the midst of the throne of the Great Spirit.

6. And there were present: Obed, God of Oise, in Embrahk; Gavaini, Goddess of Ipthor, of the Solastis Plains; Ab, First Shriever of Riv-Seing; Holon-ho, God of Loo-Gam; Raisi, Goddess of Esdras; Wish-tse, God of Zuth, in Ronega; and all these Gods and Goddesses were above a hundred thousand years raised in etherean realms, and knew the earth before inhabited by man.

7. On a visit to Cpenta-armij were: Owks, Orian Chief of Maiter-lan, fifty thousand years, Marshal of Wiski-loo, thirty thousand years, God of Tunsin, in the Tarps Roads, ninety thousand years; and See-wah-Gon, Chieftainess of the Orian arc of Su-los, two hundred thousand years, Mistress of Aftong, in the Plains of Bel, three hundred thousand years, Pilotess of Lu-wow-lu, one hundred thousand years, Goddess of Eune, in the Mountains of Gem-king; and Ha-o-ha, Founder of Ogee, of Siam, of Wick-a-wick, and the twelve Nirvanian Old-tse, in Lo-owtz, Eli-hagam, together with their traveling hosts, each five millions.

8. Cpenta-armij said: For Thy glory, O Jehovih, I proclaim the FEAST OF THE ARC OF SPE'TA. And these, my visiting hosts, shall enjoy the four years' deliverance of the red star and her heavens!

9. Then responded Owks, and then See-wah-Gon, then Ha-o-ha, speaking at great length, and rejoicing for the invitation. And they related many adventures on other stars in the time of the arc of deliverance, the arc of Spe-ta, and with what Gods and Goddesses they

journeyed, and what Chiefs and Chieftainesses.

10. So Cpenta-armij spake to her chief marshal, saying: Send thou heralds to the builders, and order me an airavagna capable of five hundred millions, and of speed, grade sixty. After this thou shalt select from my attendants one hundred millions, and after that three hundred millions of the Egisi.

11. With these, and with my visitors, I will start for the red star in twenty days. The proper officers attended to these things, and whilst they were moving about, behold, the red star, the earth, rose up in the far-off place, the roadway, and the es'enaurs saw it, and they chanted:

12. What is yonder? The red star, Jehovih! Thy breath hath spoken. Thy voice, the silent motion. O Thy endless power, Jehovih!

13. Around about her, close; what is that filled with angels, thousands of millions! Wondrous are Thy works, O Jehovih, and measureless. She rideth around the sun, two hundred and seventy million miles.

14. It is her atmosphere, traveling with her; its boundary, Chinvat. How fearfully hast thou created, O Jehovih! And the magnitude of Thy places! That little red star is a world, O Father! And the thousands of millions of angels, why do they stay in such heavens, O Jehovih!

15. Then the trumpeters afar off answered: She that spinneth round the sun, the red star, the earth, a new world, a generator of the souls of men. The Gods have called her, but she will not hear. Her atmosphere is full of angels struggling for the earth. But Thy hand is upon them, O Jehovih. Thy trumpeters will line the roads of Salkwatka.

16. Then sang the es'enaurs: How lovely are Thy works, O Jehovih! Too lovely are Thy places, O Jehovih! Too lovely is the red star, the earth, O Jehovih! Thy children love it while in mortal form; after death too much they love it, O Jehovih!

17. The pipers answer for Jehovih from the Wide East: O so little to love, made I the earth, the red star. I gave her poisoned weeds and vines and grasses; millions of death-dealing serpents. Then I created poisoned marshes and terrible fevers. In sore travail, and full of misery, created I man on the earth, that he should turn and look upward for a holier place.

18. Then sang the en'enaurs: Too lovely createdst Thou Thy atmospherean heavens, O Jehovih! Thy bounden heavens that travel with the red star, the earth. The spirits raised up from the mortal earth find too much to love in Thy lower heavens, O Jehovih!

19. The pipers again answered for Jehovih: My lower heavens created I full of darkness and evil possibilities. A place for madness created I it; a place for lying and deceit; full of hell and torments. To drive man upward; to blow My breath upon him, to lift him up, as one lighteth the fire by blowing.

20. Cpenta-armij spake from Jehovih's throne, saying: What is the deliverance of man? Is it from his mother's womb? Is it from his corporeal body? Is it from the corporeal world and her atmosphere? Three births hath the Father given unto all men. In the first, man hath nothing to do, as to his shaping or time in his mother's womb. In the second he hath a little more to do as to directing his course during his mortal life; but for the third, for the higher heavens, he must work for his own deliverance.

21. Cpenta-armij said: Three kinds of earth deliverance for man created the Creator; First from his mother's womb, coming crying, blank and helpless; second, from the tetracts

(earthly passions and desires), serious and full of fear; third, from the enemies of the Great Spirit. This is the Feast of Spe-ta.

CHAPTER II.

1. Cpenta-armij said: I looked afar, and saw the earth and her heavens traveling on. I listened to the voice of mortals! A merchant counted over his gains; he said: This is heaven! A drunkard quaffed a cup of poison; he said: This is heaven! A wanton said: This is heaven! A general, red with blood, counted the badges on his breast; he said: This is heaven! A tyrant, rich in toiling slaves, said: This is heaven! Then a vast multitude, all smeared with the blood of war, pointed to a field of mortals slain, and said: This is heaven! A farmer stretched wide his arms, toward his great possessions, uncultivated; he said: This is heaven! A little child with a toy said: This is heaven!

2. Then spake Jehovih, saying: None of these canst thou convince to the contrary. They are not ready for deliverance.

3. I listened to the voice of spirits, the angels traveling with the earth. A wanderer, going about, with nothing to do, said: This is heaven! An obsessor of mortals and of other angels said: This is heaven! The fairies, the butterfly angels, the triflers, that forever look in crystal waters to behold their own forms, said: This is heaven! The rollicking, deceiving angels, went and inspired mortals to falsehood; these angels said: This is heaven! Vampire angels, that nestle in the atmosphere of mortals, largely living on their substance, said: This is heaven! Evil angels, obsessing mortals for murder's sake, to make mortals burn houses and torture helpless creatures, said: This is heaven!

4. Then spake Jehovih, saying: None of these canst thou convince to the contrary. They are not ready for deliverance.

5. Again I listened to the sounds coming from the far-off earth. And I heard the prayers of mortals. The king prayed for his kingdom and for himself. The general prayed for success in war. The merchant for great gains; the tyrant for great authority.

6. Jehovih said: Only the earth can answer such prayers.

7. I listened again for the prayers of mortals; they had great afflictions, dire diseases, and famines, and wars; the merchants were bankrupt, and there was great suffering, and they prayed for deliverance.

8. Jehovih said: Shouldst thou deliver them they would return to their old, evil habits. I say unto thee, the merchant shall be bankrupt; the king shall fail; the general be overthrown; the healthy shall be sick for a season. Save they know My power, they cannot learn; save they feel affliction, they will not help one another. Shall a man say: O Jehovih, come Thou and heal the sick? Shall he not first of all recognize My will and know My power?

9. To give money to the drunkard, what good is that? To give wealth and earthly prosperity to them that acknowledge not Me, is to set them against Me. To give healing to the fevered, is to teach them that I have no power in the unseen air. Answer not thou the prayers of these.

10. I listened once more to the prayers of mortals. And they were such as lived according to their highest light; they purified the flesh by pure food, and by bathing every day; and they went about doing good constantly, hoarding up neither clothes, nor silver, nor

gold, nor anything earthly. And they purified their thoughts by putting away the evil tongue, and the evil eye, and evil ear; and many of them were bound by the kings, and the tyrants, and the laws of mortals; and some of them were sick. And they prayed, saying: Great is my affliction, O Jehovih. I know that in Thy sight I am justly punished.

11. But hear Thou my prayer, O Father! Make me strong, that I may carry heavy burdens for the weary; give me liberty, that I may go about helping the poor forever. Give me wisdom, that I may uncover Thy glories before men.

12. Jehovih said: Go thou, My Daughter, and deliver them. They are ready for deliverance! Answer thou the prayers of such.

13. Then I called my hosts together, five hundred millions, in the Nirvanian heavens in Haot-saiti, in etherea, the highest heaven. And we entered into the airavagna, as, swelling high on every side, the music of millions cheered us on. Upward, high up, shone the glimmering red star, whereon now our steersman pointed the fire-arrow, to shoot meteor-like across Jehovih's pathway, and thitherward turned our buoyant souls, saluting our starters with a happy good-by!

14. Arise! Arise! By my vested power in thee, O Jehovih, shall the elements fall before my will! Arise; onward! To the red star, speed on! Airavagna, upward, on!

15. Thus spake Cpenta-armij, her voice mellow and sweet, but so tuned to the spheres it could be heard the breadth of a world. And Jehovih, with whose power and will she had learned to be as one, by long experience and studying submission to His will, lent a willing ear and strong hand. Out shot the flames, the buoyant force manufactured by less skilled workmen learning the trade of Gods, where whirled the million screws of fire, propelling, till the mighty ship reeled, and turned, and rose from its foundation, with all its joyous hosts aboard, shouting loud, and singing praise to Him who ruleth over all. Then turning round and round, slowly, spiral like, the great secret form and force of vortices now first revealed to man, to show the plan of worlds, and how holden in their places and moved in universal harmony and endless creation, the great airavagna began her course in the roadway of Salkwatka, in etherea, shooting toward the red star, the young earth.

16. Nearing first the Oixanian Spars of Ochesu, where were gathered near the road ten million spectators to see the Goddess pass in her ship; and their banners waved, and their music burst forth most exhilarating; the which were answered by the airavagna's cheering hosts and sailing streamers. She halted, to salute in honor, the Goddess Yuetisiv, and then upward shot a thousand miles suddenly.

17. Again onward, turning the breadth of the road, a million miles, to the right, to salute Vultanya, Goddess of the swamps of Ailassasak, where stood by the portico of her heavenly palace seventy million pupils, in their thousandth year of tuition, to receive the passing blessing of the Orian Chieftainess, Cpenta-armij. And thither, but a halt, as it were a nod, and downward on their heads Cpenta-armij sent a shower of newly-created flowers from the sphere above, and in turn heard their chorus rise joyfully, in as many million words of love and admiration.

18. Still onward, upward sped the airavagna, her hosts viewing the scenes on every side, here most, the richest part and most glorious places of Salkwatka. Where the etherean worlds, rich in the glitter of swamps shining on the countless rainbow arches and crystal pyramids, afford an extensive view of the new Orian boundaries of Oteson's broad

kingdoms. Here course the thousands of excursionists from the measureless regions of the Huan lights, where are to be seen a million varieties of fire-ships, of sizes from ten miles across to the breadth of a world, in unceasing travel, in tens of thousands of directions, onward in their ways, every several one a history of millions of years, and of thousands of millions of souls, and every soul rich in the knowledge of thousands of worlds.

19. By music alone, some their ships propelled, the vibratory chords affording power sufficient in such high-skilled hands, and the tunes changing according to the regions traversed. Others, even by colors made in the waves of sound, went forward, carrying millions of angels, every one attuned so perfectly that his very presence lent power and beauty to the monarch vessel. And downward and upward, and east and west, and north and south, and of every angle and course; such were the traveling regions of Wellagowthiij, in the etherean fields of Oteson.

20. And of the million ships, with their tens of thousands of millions of spirits, who so great a Goddess, like Cpenta-armij, could turn her well-learned eyes on any one, and know its home regions, and from what Orian pastures sailed; or perhaps Nirvanian rivers! Or, like her visiting friends now with her, great Owks, and See-wah-Gon, and Ha-o-ha, that with her stood side by side, reading the coursing fleets, and relating to one another who they were, and the great Chiefs aboard, with whom thousands of years ago they had been together taming some rambling star and quieting its disturbed vortex, or perhaps surveying a roadway many millions of miles through an a'ji'an forest.

21. And the while the airavagna was shooting on in the hands of her proper officers, every one to his part and all the hosts in varied amusement; for such is the labor of the high raised in heaven, labor itself becometh an amusement of great relish. Coming then to the Crossings, near Bilothowitchieun, where was a small colony, ninety million etherean weavers, superintended by Cpenta-armij's ward, Hoewuel, God of two thousand years, who knew she was coming his way, and had lighted the roadway a hundred thousand miles in honor thereof, she turned the airavagna and cast the streamers and banners, saluting. Here again Cpenta-armij sent down to her beloved sons and daughters, for every one, flowers and keepsakes; and on every flower was written the history and mission to the earth and her heavens. And then again the airavagna upward rose and sped on.

22. Thus in Jehovih's wide universe went forth the Goddess, the Chieftainess, Cpenta-armij, went toward the red star; passing through ten thousand varieties of etherean worlds and roadways in the ji'ay'an fields and forests of high heaven, seeing millions of etherean ships going hither and thither, every one knowing its own mission and field of labor, whilst the highest raised Gods and Goddesses could exchange courtesies with the fiery vehicles, and speak them, to know whither bent, and for what purpose.

23. Then rising high; here on a level lieth the earth, here the boundary of her vortex, Chinvat; just beyond the sweep of the moon; halteth here to view the rolling earth, her land and water; and her atmospherean heavens, the sojourning place of the newly dead, and of such as have not aspired to rise to holier heavens.

24. Quickly, now, Cpenta-armij taketh in the situation, and ordereth on the airavagna, which now taketh a downward course, steering straight toward the habitable earth. Slowly now, turning slowly, and descending; viewing all the regions on every side in the great vortex, she spies the plateau Craoshivi, the place of God, new founded.

25. And to her companions and to her hosts quickly Cpenta-armij, of the Nirvanian

Chengotha, explaineth the place; and, stretching forth her slender hand, itself most like a stream of fire, she crieth out: Behold my anchorage! Here bring my ship and make fast, where riseth now the voices of my weary God and his Lords, of me so long expectant. In Thy wisdom and power, O Jehovih, I will raise them up!

CHAPTER III.

1. Jehovih spake to God, ruler of atmospherea and of the earth, saying: Well done, O My Son! The beginning of the end of thy trials is at hand. I have spoken in the highest heavens, in My etherean worlds; in the gardens of Haot-saiti, near the arc of Spe-ta, to My Daughter, who hath attained to One with Me, a Nirvanian in the regions of Chen-gotha, the holy Cpenta-armij.

2. Her ship, an airavagna, with five hundred million ethereal deliverers on board, hath started on the road Salkwatka, swiftly bound to thy regions, to thy new plateau, Craoshivi.

3. Send thou word to Yima to come, and to Vishnu, and to Os, each to come in rank, attended by ten millions, grade above seventy, with es'enaurs, and marshals, and captains, and generals, to come to Craoshivi.

4. And send thou invitations to thy Diva to come, and to thy sub-Gods, and to thy Lord Gods, and to thy Lords, in all the divisions of heaven and the divisions of the earth; and to bring of their people all above grade fifty. And to thy marshals give thou a list of all who will be with thee in Craoshivi on that day. And thy marshals shall apportion and divide and arrange all thy hosts thus assembled in Craoshivi, according to grade, approaching thy throne in four lines, east and west and north and south, and thy throne shall be the extreme east.

5. And in the center of the cross shall thy marshal provide space sufficient for the hosts of Cpenta-armij to land her airavagna, and to disembark. But at the extreme boundary of the lines of thy hosts thou shalt draw a circle, and thither shall thy light makers erect pillars of light, making the circle as a wall of light; and, as the diameter of the circle is to the distance down to the earth's surface, so a tenth thereof shalt thou make as the summit of the apex of the canopy of thy capital chamber, for the Holy Council of thy Goddess, Cpenta-armij.

6. God said: Thy will be done, O Jehovih! And thereupon God sent word by his messengers, as commanded by the Great Spirit; sent invitations to all the Gods and Lords of heaven and earth, commanding them to come to Craoshivi.

7. And the Lord Gods, and Gods and Lords, thus notified, appointed substitutes to rule in their places. And they made otevans, every one suitable to the number of angels he was to take with him, and they embarked and rose up from their several places in atmospherea and the earth, and, being guided in their courses by such experts as had learned the way, they came to Craoshivi, where they were received by the chief marshal of God and his officers, and allotted their several places, according to their respective grades. But as the plateau was above grade fifty in the earth's vortex, so there were no angels of less grade than fifty amongst all the hosts assembled.

8. And Jehovih commanded God to number the angels thus assembled in Craoshivi, and there were seven thousand millions, and nine hundred and seventy-five millions, and eight hundred thousand, officers and all.

9. And the day and the hour of their assembling, when they were numbered, was the self same time that Cpenta-armij's fire-ship arrived at Chinvat, when her light burst in full view to the hosts of God in Craoshivi. And they all beheld her coming; saw the manner in which a Chieftainess cometh to the lower heavens. And because of the great glory before them, they burst forth in a song of praise to Jehovih, the seven thousand millions.

10. Jehovih spake to God, saying: Ascend thy throne, My Son, and allot the Council and thy officers to their place, for quickly now, behold, My Daughter will descend. And when she cometh. My Voice will be with her for the years and the days of the dawn of dan.

11. So God caused his Council and his marshal and his Diva to take their places and be in readiness for the emancipated Sons and Daughters. And presently the descending star grew brighter and larger, larger and brighter, till like a sun she shone abroad over all the plateau of Craoshivi.

12. In awe stood the Gods at sight of the sublime spectacle; for the light of the airavagna was brilliant, and unlike all the lights of the lower heavens, and new to nearly all the people.

13. Nearer and nearer descended the ship of light, till soon the music of her hosts descended down to those beneath, who, awe-stricken and buoyant with delight, burst forth, entranced with the glory thereof, singing, by the force of Jehovih's light upon them, the same glorious anthem.

14. And now the marshals spread the way, for close at hand came the airavagna, over the bows of which Cpenta-armij shone like a central sun, and with her, her visiting hosts, Owks and Ha-o-ha and See-wah-Gon; so, but for Cpenta-armij holding out her taper hand, the hosts below had hardly known which of the four great lights Jehovih had sent. Presently the curtains swept across the high pyramid of the capital, and then the transparent blankets and crystal frame-work; and now shot down the anchors, three hundred thousand; lower and lower, slowly came the mighty ship, till her screen-work, from which the anchors hung, touched the very floors of the capital; and, all radiant with holiness, before God and his hosts stood the ethereans, the glory of the most high heavens.

15. The attendants then quickly spread the homa; the masters of arches opened the floor and sides of the airavagna, and there, seated or standing, was ready the central part of the etherean Council chamber, even as if the throne of God had been built for it. Then came forth the Chieftainess, Cpenta-armij, accompanied by Owks and Ha-o-ha and See-wa-Gon, and arriving before the throne stood, waiting for the salutation and the sign.

16. God, still sitting on the throne, said: Daughter of Jehovih, Chieftainess of Haotsaiti, in the name of the Father! And hereupon he gave the sign ARC OF SPE'TA.! Cpenta-armij and her three companions saluted in the SIGN OF THE CIRCUIT! Which was the highest compliment any God of the earth had ever received.

17. Cpenta-armij said: By Jehovih's command am I before thee, O God. In Love and Wisdom and Power am I come. Behold, My Voice is His Voice, Creator of Worlds!

18. God said: My throne is founded in Jehovih's name. Come thou and honor it, and bring thy most high Gods and Goddesses with thee.

19. They went forward then, and all the Gods and Goddesses, and Lords and Lordesses stood up, saluting by shaking hands; and then Cpenta-armij went and sat in the midst of the throne. Meanwhile, the es'enaurs chanted a hymn of thanksgiving.

20. Cpenta-armij, being under the Voice of Jehovih said: For joy created I man and woman; for seasons of labor and seasons of recreation. Be ye mirthful before Me, and jubilant toward one another, in remembrance of My creations. And when I call you to labor, behold, My hand will move upon you for the furtherance of My kingdoms in their resurrections.

21. Hereupon the multitude broke off from their places and stateliness, and commingled together joyfully. And all that were on the throne came down and went into the multitude, saluting and rejoicing.

CHAPTER IV.
OF THE BIRTH OF PO, ABRAM, BRAHMA AND EAWAHTAH.

1. For two whole days Cpenta-armij left the people in recreation, but on the third she ascended the throne, and lo and behold, even in that same moment of time, a light spread abroad over all the place, so that the people comprehended indeed what was meant by Jehovih's hand being upon them. And they all resumed their places, whereupon Jehovih spake through Cpenta-armij, saying:

2. Whom I brought with Me from Haotsaiti shall be My Council during dawn; but the portals shall remain open on every side.

3. Who are not of My Council are not bound unto these, My labors, and the same shall go and come as they choose, remembering the call of their respective Gods.

4. For know ye all, that whoever aspireth to Me shall come to Me; but the nearest way for many is round about. Ye being above grade fifty are already more to Me and for Me than against Me or from Me, and in equal degree are cast upon your own responsibility. For such is the light of My kingdoms, from the first to the highest: To the child, no responsibility; to grade twenty-five, one quarter; to fifty, one-half; to seventy-five, three-quarters; but to the emancipated in My etherean realms, responsibility not only to self but to all who are beneath.

5. Wherein My highest worlds are responsible for the lowest, being bound unto one another through Me for the resurrection of all.

6. In this day am I come to deliver My Gods down to the earth, to walk on the earth with mortals, raising them up in My name.

7. They who shall be raised up in Me, even though still of the earth, shall be holden alike responsible for all who are beneath them; for with My light and power before them, and doing in My name, they that are beneath them will hold them, not only on the earth, but in heaven, for their labors and words.

8. The Voice departed, and then Cpenta-armij spake in her own behalf, saying: Once around earth and heaven will I now travel, seeing with mine own eyes and hearing with mine own ears, even as is commanded of me by the Father; that I may know of mine own knowledge the condition of mortals and of the spirits who dwell both with them and in the lowest heavens. He who is still your God shall abide with you, and on this throne, until I return.

9. Cpenta-armij then descended and sat at the foot of the throne, and Owks and Ha-o-ha and See-wah-Gon with her, whereupon God went down and took her hand, saying: Arise, O Goddess, and go thy way. And then he raised up the other three in the same way, and

they saluted and stood aside. Now, as soon as God raised them up, the All Light settled upon him, and he again ascended the throne, and sat in the midst. Then spake Cpenta-armij, saying to God:

10. Jehovih hath commanded the raising of a voice in four divisions of the earth; what is thy light, O God? God said:

11. In Jaffeth I have raised up a man named Po, an Ihuan of the I'hin side, of grade ninety-five. In Arabin'ya I have raised up a man named Abram, an I'huan of the I'hin side, of grade ninety-five. In Vind'yu I have raised up a man named Brahma, an I'huan of the I'hin side, of grade ninety-nine. I Guatama I have raised up a man named Eawahtah, an I'huan of the I'hin side, of grade ninety-five.

12. The loo'is who have accomplished this labor are still with their wards, but are apprised of thy coming. Behold, I send with thee messengers who will answer thy commands.

13. Hereupon, Cpenta-armij, with her hosts, departed, and entered an otevan which God had had previously prepared for her; and she took with her one million attendants, going straight down to the earth. And first of all to visit mortals and mortal kingdoms, kings and queens, temples and oracles, and then to see Po and Abram and Brahma and Eawahtah, all of whom were sufficiently illumined to see her and to know she was the Person of the All Voice.

14. Next after these she visited all the heavenly kingdoms belonging to the earth, going first to the heavenly kingdom, belonging to Japan, thence to Ah'oan, of Jaffeth, thence to E'chad, and so on until she saw them all.

15. After that Cpenta-armij returned to Craoshivi, making a circuit sufficient to examine all the plateaux below the belt meteoris.

16. Now the whole time Cpenta-armij had been gone was thirty and two days. Whilst she had been absent, God extended the receiving grounds of Craoshivi twelve thousand miles in breadth toward the south, and founded sixty colonies. For even now were, and would be, for the four years to come, ships arriving daily with hundreds of thousands of angels who were being prepared for the degree of Brides and Bridegrooms to Jehovih, ready for the third resurrection.

17. Messengers had arrived in Craoshivi daily from Cpenta-armij, so that God knew when she would return. And accordingly he had prepared all things in readiness, and she was received in the name of the Father, in due ceremony.

18. And Cpenta-armij ascended the throne of God and sat in the midst, and a light like a sun settled around about her. Her companions, Gods and Goddesses, now sat not near her, though on the throne to the right and left. Whilst they were taking in their respective places, the es'enaurs were chanting anthems, and the awe and majesty of the scene were magnified to the utmost.

CHAPTER V.

1. When the light fell upon Cpenta-armij, the Voice of Jehovih spake through her, saying:
2. In thee whom I made God over the earth and her heavens I am well pleased; by My hand hast thou raised them up; through thee have I maintained the Diva even unto this day.

3. Thou shalt have honor in My exalted heavens because thou art the first in Spe-ta; but thou shalt crown thy glory by descending to the earth and walking with mortals for the term of four years, even with My Son, Brahma. And when thy time is completed, I will come and deliver thee and Brahma.

4. In My name shalt thou raise thy voice and establish Me amongst men; and I will be with thee in Wisdom and Power. Take thy attendants and proceed to thy labor; in whatsoever thou desirest of Me, call, and I will answer, for I have messengers who shall labor betwixt us.

5. God then saluted, and withdrew. Next came Yima, and to him Jehovih spake, saying:

6. Being one with God, thou shalt labor even as he laboreth; and thou shalt descend to the earth, even to My corporeal Son, Po, who hath been prepared in My name, and with him shalt thou walk the earth four years. And thou shalt speak in My name, establishing Me amongst mortals, to the end that My chosen shall be delivered into My kingdoms. For thou shalt lead them away from the mortal kings, and teach them to know Me as their only King.

7. Take, then, thy attendants and go to thy labor, and at the end of four years I will appoint a successor to thee, and I will deliver thee into My etherean kingdoms.

8. Yima then saluted and stood aside. Next came Vishnu, renowned for his labor in Vind'yu and her heavens. To him Jehovih said:

9. Being one with God, thou shalt with him fulfill the completion of Spe-ta in My name. To which end thou shalt descend to the corporeal earth, even Arabin'ya, and dwell thereon for the period of four years, with My corporeal Son, Abram. With Abram shalt thou walk and sojourn day and night, speaking and laboring in Me as fully as My very Self. And thou shalt deliver My chosen away from the kings' peoples, teaching them to have no king but Me, their Creator. To Abram shalt thou reveal My name, JEHOVIH, and establish it in secret, with due rites and ceremonies. And at the end of four years will I appoint a successor to thee; and thee will I deliver into My emancipated worlds. Take, then, thy attendants and depart to thy labor, and I will be with thee in wisdom and power. Vishnu then saluted and stood aside.

10. Next came Os, sent by the etherean regions of Haot-saiti to deliver the kingdoms of Japan and Heleste and their heavens, but who was now relieved by the Divan successor. To Os Jehovih spake, saying:

11. In honor of thy volunteering in the days of darkness for the relief of God and his kingdoms, I now create thee God of the first Spe-ta of the red star, and crown thee with Mine Own hand.

12. And, lo and behold, even with these spoken words, a light descended in the form of a crown and settled upon his head. Thereupon Jehovih said: In which I have made thee a lawful Div with corporeal power.

13. And thou shalt descend to the corporeal earth, even to Guatama, and walk with My Son, Eawahtah, whom the loo'is have bred for My Voice, for the term of four years, sojourning with him day and night, gathering together the remnants of My lost tribes, and establishing them in faith of the Great Spirit, in My name, Egoquim, suitable to the utterance I have created them.

14. And at the end of four years I will appoint a successor to thee; and thee I will restore into My etherean worlds. Take, then, thy attendants and depart to thy labor, and I will be

with thee in wisdom and power.

15. Then Os saluted and stood aside, and the Voice departed; then Cpenta-armij, on her own account, said: This hour, even now, I dissolve the Diva with honor and glory unto them. The kingdoms ye ruled over shall be my kingdoms during dawn; in the Father's name I assume them and their affairs. Peace and love and wisdom and power be with you all, amen.

16. The four inspiring Gods then departed, and in the outer circuit of Craoshivi they had in waiting, which their attendants had prepared beforehand, each one an otevan fully equipped and ready, into which they embarked, with their attendants, fifty thousand each. The musicians then saluted them, even as they moved off, severally, in direct lines for the earth.

17. Cpenta-armij then lowered the light a little, and her three visiting companions, Owks, Ha-o-ha and See-wah-Gon, sat near her on the throne, even before her etherean Council, five hundred millions.

18. Cpenta-armij said: I have visited the earth and her heavens, even her heavens on her very surface. By the power vested in me, I relieve from duty all Lords and Gods, and sub-Gods, and sub-Lords, on the earth and in the heavens of the earth. This my messengers will communicate to them, commanding them, in my love and wisdom, which are one with the Father, to come at once to Craoshivi, that I may honor them and apportion them for the third resurrection, which will occur in four years.

19. To the Lord-dom, Maitraias, founded by Vishnu, I appoint and allot Yugsaesu Lord, with thirty millions of my etherean hosts, to be chosen by himself. Let Yugsaesu come before me! Yugsaesu then came before Jehovih's throne, and Cpenta-armij said unto him: Repair thou unto Maitraias, taking thy hosts with thee. And when thou art come to the place, possess it in Jehovih's name, and order it after the manner of a Lord-dom, providing sub-kingdoms unto thy place as may be required.

20. And thou shalt have dominion over all angels that are already with the plateau of Maitraias, or such as may be hereafter sent to thee from the other heavenly divisions and from the earth. And thou shalt provide thy kingdom unto the service of the Father, chiefly to prevent angels returning to the earth to obsess and pollute mortals. For thou shalt find hundreds of millions of them who have no aspiration but destruction. Many of them were slain in wars on the earth, and are still seeking vengeance, and if escaping to the earth, obsess mortals to burn cities, and to murder, and to all manner of wickedness.

21. Thy labor, O Lord, is not to reform them or teach them, for I shall appoint and allot others to that end; but thou shalt labor wholly and entirely to prevent the return of Maitraisans to mortals. And that thou shalt be strong before them, thou shalt draw from all other heavenly kingdoms, which I shall found, a sufficient guard to enforce my commandments.

22. For four years shalt thou labor in this matter, and thou shalt also raise up one with thy Lord-dom, to be thy successor after thee. Take, then, thy hosts and go to thy labors, and the Father will be with thee in wisdom and power.

23. Yugsaesu then made his selections from Cpenta-armij's hosts, and they came and passed before Jehovih's throne, saluting, and then withdrew and went into a ship which had, likewise, been prepared for them by the proper persons, whose labor lies in that matter; and, having saluted with music, they departed, Yugaesu and his hosts, rejoicing.

24. Again Cpenta-armij spake, saying: Behold, the time is now come upon the earth when I will divide and allot unto each of its several great divisions heavenly kingdoms accordingly.

25. To Japan, because she is a remnant of the submerged continent, I establish a heavenly kingdom, and it shall be called Suasu.

26. To Jaffeth, because she has preserved much of the first language, I establish a heavenly kingdom, and it shall be called Hi-jee-tse.

27. To Vind'yu, because she is the most advanced in holiness of all the earth, I establish a heavenly kingdom, and it shall be called Vri-mij.

28. To Arabin'ya, because she is the foundation of Jehovih's migratory hosts who shall go forth around the earth, I establish a heavenly kingdom, and it shall be called Paradise.

29. To Heleste, because she was rescued from darkness by Os in time to meet this arc, I establish a heavenly kingdom, and it shall be called Spe-ta.

30. To Uropa, because she was first founded by a woman, I establish a heavenly kingdom, and it shall be called Himmel.

31. To South Guatama, because she is the least inhabited of all the great divisions of the earth, I establish a heavenly kingdom, and it shall be called Ahden.

32. To North Guatama, because she is the ground on which the circumscribing of the earth by the different nations shall take place, where the revelations of heaven and earth shall be made to man, I establish a heavenly kingdom, and it shall be called Kosmon.

33. To all the South Islands, I establish a heavenly kingdom, and it shall be called Flue.

34. To all the North Islands, I establish a heavenly kingdom, and it shall be called Sin-yot.

35. Hereupon the light of Jehovih overspread Cpenta-armij, and His voice spake through her, saying: To My ten heavenly kingdoms which I have made through My Daughter, behold, I choose ten Lords, and My ten Lords shall go to the kingdoms I apportion unto them. In My name shall My Lords build unto Me ten heavenly places of delight, for the spirits of the dead that rise up from the earth.

36. And My Lords shall establish in My kingdoms places of learning and places of labor; places for the sick and helpless angels that arise up from the earth, that My Lords shall raise them up, to know Me and the glory of the worlds I have created for them; inspiring them to perfect themselves in wisdom and purity and power, that they may arise and inherit My etherean heavens.

37. And My Lords shall appoint ashars unto mortals at the time of their corporeal birth; and the said ashars shall be appointed in watch and watch, that they may relieve one another, having a time of labor and a time of rest. And My Lords shall so appoint My ashars that each and every ashar shall have a hundred changes of labor with a hundred different mortals, in order to learn all the varieties of men and women I have created. And the number of ashars shall be equal to the number of mortals dwelling on the earth.

38. And My Lords shall appoint asaphs to reside in heaven, sufficient in number to receive the spirits of all who die on the earth, which they shall receive from the ashars in My name. And the asaphs shall take such angels, thus received, and place them in the regions My Lords shall have prepared for them, where there shall be sufficient of teachers and nurses and physicians in My heavenly places to administer unto them.

39. And My Lords shall provide discipline to the spirits thus received, who shall be trained according to the Divan law which I established through My Gods, which shall

extend beyond the es'yan even to the thirtieth grade.

40. And My Lords shall provide for them that have attained to the thirtieth grade to be sent in suitable ships to this place, Craoshivi, and deliver them to My daughter, Cpenta-armij, and to her successor, God or Goddess, who shall have dominion over the whole earth and her heavens.

41. For behold, it is the nature of man on the earth to go after earthly things instead of heavenly; and it is the nature of the es'yan to strive for the earth instead of My higher heavens. Be ye guarded, therefore, to lay a foundation to prevent angels and mortals from going downward; to provide inspiration to make them desire to ascend to My holy regions.

42. The Voice now departed, and Cpenta-armij spake on her own account in Jehovih's name, saying:

43. Whosoever I call, let them come before Jehovih's throne, for they shall be the Lords whom I shall anoint for the heavenly kingdoms I have established:

44. Le-tzoo, Lord of Suasu, a heavenly place over Japan.

45. Oe-wah, Lord of Hi-jee-tse, a heavenly place over Jaffeth.

46. Loo-gam, Lord of Vri-mij, a heavenly place over Vind'yu.

47. Ha-kappa, Lord of Paradise, a heavenly place over Arabin'ya.

48. Jes-Sie, Lordess of Spe-ta, a heavenly place over Heleste.

49. Yo-han, Lord of Himmel, a heavenly place over Uropa.

50. Hinot-tse, Lordess of Ahden, a heavenly place over South Guatama.

51. Ami, Lordess of Kosmon, a heavenly place over North Guatama.

52. Horam, Lord of Flue, a heavenly place over the Southern Islands.

53. Puetse, Lordess of Sin-Yot, a heavenly place over the Northern Islands.

54. All the angels named came before Cpenta-armij when called, and they now stood abreast Jehovih's throne, whereupon the All Light overspread the place, and the Father's Voice spake through Cpenta'armij, saying:

55. Ye are My Lords and Lordesses, by Me raised up and allotted your places. For four years shall ye labor, even to the end of this dawn; and ye shall provide successors to take your places after you. And herein lies your greatest glory and Mine. For they that succeed you shall hold dominion two hundred years. And they in turn shall provide successors after them, and so on, for these successions shall continue till the arc of Bon.

56. With Mine own hand weave I crowns, and crown you severally for my kingdoms!

57. When these words were spoken, the now fast gathering light, of a variety of colors, took the shape of ten separate crowns, and descended on the heads of the Lords and Lordesses. The Voice ceased, but Cpenta-armij spake on her own account, in Jehovih's name, saying:

58. My Lords and Lordesses, go to your labors in the love, wisdom and power of the Father, and He will be with you; and ye shall be a glory in His kingdoms. Choose ye, therefore, each and every one ten millions of my hosts, who shall go with you to your places, to be afterward exchanged or divided, as I may direct. That ye may choose in order, he who was first appointed shall choose first; the second next, and so on until ye have your chosen.

59. All these Lords and Lordesses were of the Higher Light, and knew beforehand, and had in like manner already chosen their attendants, so that at a given signal the multitudes

429

thus chosen rose up and came before the throne, forming ten groups of ten millions each. And they at once formed in line and passed before Jehovih's throne, saluting in the sign, BIRTH OF SPE-TA ON THE EARTH, and Cpenta-Armij answered in the sign, JEHOVIH AND THE LOWER HEAVENS.

60. Cpenta-armij said: For the glory of this scene, I bequeath a day of rest, that my hosts may witness the departure of the fleets of Jehovih's Lords and Lordesses. At once the hosts joined in a mighty chorus of thanksgiving and praise; and they went without and saw the ships laden with the joyous crews; saw them set their great fleet in motion; sang and shouted to them in Jehovih's love, for the glory of His high heavens.

CHAPTER VI.

1. In the beginning of the second year of Cpenta-armij in Craoshivi, messengers came before Jehovih's throne, saluting, and greeting from Ctusk, who now lived under the name, Ahura, and submitted the following communication, to wit:

2. Ctusk, who hath become Ahura, a servant of Jehovih, and is now God of Ailkin by just judgment of Jehovih, desireth audience with the Most High-Raised Cpenta-armij, Daughter of the Great Spirit.

3. To this Cpenta-armij answered: Greeting, in love to my brother, Ahura. By the Grace and Power of Jehovih, come and see me, bringing thy attendants. Now, after the lapse of a few days, Ahura came to Craoshivi, attended by one million, escorted by music, and proclaimed according to the discipline of the higher heavens, with heralds and trumpeters. And Cpenta-armij's hosts received Ahura and conducted him and his hosts within the capital chamber; and Ahura went before Jehovih's throne, saluting on the sign, SECOND PLATEAU, and Cpenta-armij answered in NIRVANIAN ROAD, SALKWATKA. She said:

4. In the name of the Great Spirit, Whose Daughter I am, I welcome thee in love and high esteem. I know all thy past record, and do look upon thee as the foundation of one of Jehovih's brightest suns. Long have I desired that thou shouldst petition to come to see me; and much desired I to see thee and greet thee in the Father's name.

5. Ahura said: O thou Most High Chieftainess, of hundreds of thousands of years, how can I stand before thee? I know thou hast seen many truants in thy day, and watched their course thousands of years. Thou canst see before me all that awaiteth me and mine; the past and the future are as an open book before thee. That I have stood before thee and looked upon thee, I am blessed above all things since the day of my birth.

6. Behold, the hand of the Great Spirit hath appeared before me; I comprehend the only road that leadeth on to everlasting resurrections; I know that the ONE ALL PERSON must ever stand as the key-note for angels and mortals. Without Him, a man is as a ship without a rudder; the seas around about him drive him to ruin in the end. Blessed is he who hath had the experience of this in an early day of his life. Nervous and full of fear is he who hath been tried two thousand years!

7. Then spake Cpenta-armij, saying: I perceive thy desires, O Ahura! I understand why thou art before me. Thy wisdom is great indeed. Thou perceivest that thy plateau is in the second removal from the earth. Thou fearest that some of thy hosts will forsake Jehovih, and usurp kingdoms of their own, even as thou didst in time past. Thou desirest me to raise thy plateau farther away from the corporeal earth.

8. Ahura said: If it be Jehovih's will, even for this purpose am I come before thee!

9. Now came a great light, bright, like a sun, and settled over the throne, enveloping the Goddess, Cpenta-armij, and Jehovih's Voice spake out of the light to Ahura, saying:

10. My Son, My Son, why hast thou so little faith! Behold, I am with thee even as with this, My Daughter. All thou lackest is faith. Go thou back to thy plateau and raise thou it thyself. My Daughter shall come to thee, and show thee, and thou shalt not fail. To have faith in Me is to be one with Me; to lack faith in Me is to be far removed from Me.

11. Ahura said: O Jehovih, teach Thou me how to begin to have faith. To find the beginning, there is my stumbling block!

12. Jehovih said: By trying Me, there is the beginning. By learning to know thine own power in Me; and to know My power in thee; this is the sum of all power and wisdom. By the lack of faith in Me, man setteth up himself; by the lack of faith in Me, the self-assuming Gods build kingdoms for themselves.

13. The failure of man is proof of My power; the failure of all kingdoms is proof of the lack of faith in Me, whereby My power is manifested over them. First, after the abjuring of self, cometh the constant manifestation of power through faith, the example of which holdeth the multitude to Me and My works.

14. Inasmuch as thou hast suffered fear in thy soul for a relapse in thy kingdom, thou hast opened the door for disaster. Have I not proved this on earth? --wherein the faith of a captain leadeth his soldiers on a victory, and his lack of faith breaketh them down in weakness. Think not, O Ahura, that My examples are less with My Gods.

15. If, therefore, My Daughter should come to thy kingdom and raise it up, behold, she would lessen thy hosts' faith in thee. For which reason thou shalt return to Ailkin, and proclaim to thy people that thou wilt raise thy plateau. And though millions of them will consider it vanity, and beyond thy power, behold, I will provide unto thee that thou shalt not fail.

16. Ahura said: I perceive Thy Wisdom, O Jehovih! That which Thou hast put upon me, I know I shall accomplish through Thee. The Voice departed, and Cpenta-armij spake on her own account, saying: Thou shalt proclaim a day for this great work; and thou shalt send invitations to me and my hosts, and to my Gods and Lords, Goddesses and Lordesses. Send thou, therefore, thy surveyors and inspectors, and determine whither thou wouldst raise thy plateau, and thou shalt be provided from my hosts whatever assistance thou mayst need.

17. Ahura then saluted, and he and his hosts departed without the capital chamber, where they rested awhile in recreation with the etherean hosts, and then they entered their ship and departed, and returned to Ailkin. After which Ahura appointed the day for the resurrection, and sent messengers throughout atmospherea, proclaiming what he would do, inviting Gods and Lords, with their attendants, to come and spend the day with him.

18. Jehovih spake to Cpenta-armij, saying: Send thou thy mathematicians to estimate the grade of Ahura's plateau; and send thy surveyors to the place he hath chosen, that thy hosts may know the power required; and provide thou from thine own hosts, privily, suitable stationers that Ahura shall not fail. For, in time to come, Ahura shall be one of My greatest of Gods.

CHAPTER VII.

1. Ahura immediately on his return to his kingdom set about accomplishing this great labor.

2. Now there were with Ahura many who had been sub-Gods and were captains and generals under him whilst he was in rebellion against Jehovih and His kingdoms; and when they heard of the proclamation they said within their souls: What, is it possible Ahura is at his old games? For they knew not his concert with the kingdoms above, and so believed not in his power.

3. Jehovih moved upon Ahura, and induced him to send numerators and graders throughout his kingdom, to take the measure of those who had faith, and of those who had no faith; and of those who had neither faith nor non-faith. And these Ahura graded and numbered, so when the time came he should know where to place them. Then he numbered the unlearned and dumb; and then the enthusiastic; and he graded them and arranged them also.

4. When he had this much accomplished, there came to him one Anuhasaj, a former sub-God, and he said to Ahura, privily: I love thee, Ahura, and for that reason come before thee. Thou shalt meet only failure and disaster in thy undertaking. How many times, in thy mighty kingdom of Ctusk, didst the All High fail to come to thee?

5. Ahura said: Because of thy love I rejoice in thee; but because of thy lack in faith I deplore thee. How long will it be before angels and mortals understand the Father and His kingdoms? Behold, in the days of Ctusk I labored not for Jehovih, but for myself and my exaltation, and for the exaltation of my kingdom for mine own ends. Hence the All High came not to answer my prayers. Now, in this matter, I am doing that which is not for me, nor for my kingdom for mine own sake, but for the Father's sake only. And I know He will not fail me.

6. Anuhasaj said: Hath it not been from the time of the ancients till now, that certain ones say that by prayer and faith all things are possible, assuring us, moreover, that by such are all things accomplished in earth and in heaven? And yet, who hath not witnessed more failure than success? I do not desire to discourage thee, O Ahura, but I know so well the lack of faith on the part of all men, and that to get one's self weaned away from self is the weakest talent in the soul. And, for which reason, too, it is ultimately the greatest glory. But this would seem to me expedient: To have Cpenta-armij and her hosts do this resurrection for thee.

7. Ahura said: Even thine every thought have I already fulfilled. And through the Chieftainess came the Father's Voice, commanding me to do this resurrection on mine own account.

8. To this Anuhasaj made no reply, but in his soul he was not free from the tetracts, being jealous that Ahura had advanced him in obtaining the Father's commands. But Ahura perceived it not, and he said unto Anuhasaj: The hosts of Ailkin have been numbered, and there are four thousand millions and five hundred millions. And within the grades above es'yan there are one hundred and seventy thousand schools, two hundred and thirty thousand colleges, four hundred thousand factories, and two hundred thousand hospitals.

9. Behold, on the day of resurrection I shall have the Han-od-wotcha recreation for my hosts. Let this, then, be thy labor, to have the matter proclaimed throughout Ailkin.

Anuhasaj said: By Jehovih's leave and thine, I am satisfied.

10. Thus ended the matter, and Ahura remembered afterward, that Anuhasaj had not answered positive acceptance, and so Ahura feared, and, to make doubly sure, called Evasan, and committed the same charge to him.

11. Now when the time came, lo and behold, Anuhasaj fulfilled not his part, but Evasan did; and Evasan, moreover, came to Ahura, bringing answers from all the departments.

12. In the morning of the day of the resurrection, Ahura sent for Anuhasaj and inquired concerning the matter. Anuhasaj said: Nay, I issued not thy proclamation nor thy invitation; for I reasoned on the matter, saying to myself: If the resurrection be a failure, then would it indeed be better that the ignorant know not of it.

13. Ahura said: To do well one's own part; is this not the highest? Anuhasaj said: It is the highest. Even so have I done that which seemed the highest in mine own sight.

14. Ahura said: The resurrection was not for thee nor for me, but for the hosts. For thou hadst previously admitted that the resurrection of this plateau was the highest, best thing to be done. Because it seemed impracticable in thy sight, thou wert not justified in withholding thy hand. Thou shouldst have striven to accomplish that which was for the universal good, not even whispering thy distrust to any one. Then, had it failed, thine own soul had been clear. For which reason Jehovih came to me, and I was so admonished to depute Evasan in thy stead, and he hath fulfilled my commands.

15. Anuhasaj made no reply, but went away in displeasure, and for the present the matter was dismissed.

16. Ahura had sent invitations to the Lords of all the divisions of the earth, asking them to come, bringing their attendants with them. Of these the following came, to wit: Oe-wah, Lord of Hi-jee-tse; Ha-kappa, Lord of Paradise; Loo-gam, Lord of Vri-mij; Jes-Sie, Lordess of Spe-ta; Ami, Lordess of Kosmon; Horam, Lord of Flue; and Puetse, Lordess of Sin-Yot, each bringing one million attendants, besides hundred of thousands of visitors of lower grade.

17. Cpenta-armij, with her visitors, Owks, and See-wah-Gon, and Ha-o-ha, and five million attendants, and five and thirty million visitors, from Craoshivi, came in an avalanza made for the purpose.

18. The place of removal which Ahura had decided to inherit was in the second belt below meteoris, known in atmospherea at that time as Vara-pishanaha, which laid betwixt the land of Vind'yu and the star-region known as the HORSE AND COW AND CALF PASTURES, a heavenly place, uninhabited. From Ailkin to Vara-pishanaha was fourteen hours in grade twenty-five, which was the average of Ahura's hosts; but its enlargement in the upper belt would be as fifteen to nine.

19. Cpenta-armij and her hosts were the first to arrive in Ahura's dominion; for she had determined that nothing should lead to failure in Ahura's enterprise. Through her advice Ahura stationed water-bearers the entire distance of travel, lest, in the excitement, the drujas might run into knots or riot. For such is the nature of darkness, both on earth and in the lower heavens: the low delight to dwell in a city, or near a place of filth, if companionable, rather than go to a place of isolation where improvement is possible.

20. Jehovih had said to Ahura: Suffer not thy drujas to know thou wilt remove them so far from the earth; confide thou only with the wise in reference to thy destiny. Cpenta-armij had said to Ahura: Provide thy drujas a holiday in parade, with rites and ceremonies. And

Ahura perceived how the matter had to be, and he apportioned eighty millions of his hosts to provide parades, rites and ceremonies for the drujas of his hosts, and of these drujas, ranking below grade five, there were one thousand millions and two hundred millions, being such angels as knew not the left hand from the right, nor could remember to count five from one day to the next. And yet the next thousand million, rating below grade twelve, knew so little more, they were scarcely wiser than beasts in the field.

21. Cpenta-armij, seeing these, exclaimed: O Jehovih, how long must Ahura labor with these in order to raise them to grade ninety-nine! O that they who set themselves up as Gods knew what lay before them! O that leaders of men knew! O that mortal kings and queens knew the bondage that they lay down for themselves! What a work in the lower heavens for them before they can ascend! And yet, O Jehovih, Thou art just. Some one must labor with these unfortunates. It is well that man aspireth to be king, and Lord and God.

CHAPTER VIII.

1. When they were assembled for the resurrection, the thousands of millions, Cpenta-armij went and stood at the right hand of Ahura, and next to her stood Owks; and on the left hand stood See-wah-Gon and Ha-o-ha, and the Voice of Jehovih fell upon Ahura, saying: Extend My lines to the four corners of the world; give into My labor the highest grades.

2. Accordingly, the marshals drew the line on the plateau, and the hosts of etherea stood equally toward every corner, arranged in phalanxes of ten millions each; each having the form of a quarter of a circle; leaving the lines of power from center to circumference, and the distance thereof was equal to the width of Vind'yu on the corporeal earth. And the center of the plateau was high raised, so that Ahura stood on the highest place, which laid near the Capital of the Council.

3. Now it so happened that the jealous Anuhasaj stood twelfth on the east line, being the thirteenth from Ahura's left hand. Cpenta-armij said to Ahura: Behold, the line is shattered. Ahura said: I feel nothing; how sayest Thou, The line is shattered? She answered him, saying: He who doeth Jehovih's work must deal as Jehovih dealeth. Only those who are in concert with thee must labor with thee. Otherwise thy best endeavors will be thwarted. Ahura said:

4. O thou far-perceiving Goddess! In my much love and sympathy I admitted Anuhasaj to the lines. He hath been my best friend. Cpenta-armij said: Thou shalt know but One Friend, Jehovih.

5. Ahura perceived, and he now felt the shattered place, and he sent his chief marshal to Anuhasaj to bring him from the rank. And when Anuhasaj was before Ahura, the latter said unto him: Because thou servest thyself, thou shalt not stand in line; behold, there is but One to serve, even Jehovih. Anuhasaj said: A joy upon thee and thy scheme. Because thou art powerless, thou hast singled me out as an excuse before these Gods and Goddesses!

6. Ahura made no answer, but spake before Jehovih, saying: Give me strength for Thy Children's sake, O Father! Behold, I have cut loose the foundations of Ailkin; with high extending cords I have bound her to Vara-pishanaha. By virtue of Thy power in me I will

raise her up. In Thy name, let my hosts in will command: ARISE! UPWARD! ONWARD! O AILKIN! ARISE, UPWARD, ONWARD, O AILKIN! ARISE, UPWARDS, ONWARD, O AILKIN!

7. With the third enunciation, which came from the thousands of millions in concert, behold, the plateau moved from her foundation; turned a little, then slowly, upward arose. Loud shouted all the inhabitants of that heaven; with their own universal will the Great Spirit stretched forth His hand and raised up the heavenly continent. Even as with His hand He toucheth a corporeal continent and sendeth it beneath the ocean, so raiseth He His heavenly places toward His emancipated worlds. Yea, because of His Spirit upon His people, they desire it risen; with them and Him, ALL IS ONE.

8. And now, the Gods, with unbroken will, held their places as it were a day for the corporeal earth, and not a God or Goddess from the single purpose in thought strayed a moment of time and no distracting thought intervening; for such is the will and mastery of Gods over their own thoughts. Even then, to keep up the concerted force joyously, those who had the drujas in charge sat the games and tournaments going, with racing and music, such as should leave not one idle moment for all the hosts of Ailkin, nearly five thousand millions.

9. Upward and onward rose the great plateau, making straight course for Vara-pishanaha. Ahura stood in the eyes of the unlearned populace as the greatest and most masterly of all the Gods. One alone, even Anuhasaj, stood a while transfixed with disappointment and chagrin, even hoping some mishap to Jehovih's proceedings. And finally, he went wandering about, sore and out of sorts with all righteousness.

10. Thus was raised the heavenly place, and no longer called Ailkin, but Vara-pishanaha, home of Ahura and his hosts. And now, when they were securely established in the place, and the Gods and Goddesses broke from line, they all came greeting to Ahura. And, even in the same moment of time, a messenger came from God, who was with Brahma on the corporeal earth, bringing to Cpenta-armij the following commandment, by proxy, to wit:

11. In Jehovih's name, give thou a throne and crown to Ahura for Me, and in My name. I promised him thus!

12. The light came upon Cpenta-armij, and Jehovih spake through her, saying: Behold the work of My hand, O Ahura, My Son! In the substance of heaven fashion I thee a throne and high-raised capital. And with Mine own hands weave thee a crown. From this time forth thou shalt be My God, and I will abide with thee.

13. Whilst the words were being spoken, the throne rose up before Cpenta-armij's hand, and a high-raised capital came and stood over and about the throne. And there descended from the heavens above bows of light and color, which in Cpenta-armij's fingers were shaped and woven into a crown which alighted on Ahura's head. And there went up from the hosts a universal shout of praise and thanksgiving. Then broke in the trumpeters, seven millions, and after they prayed a while, the es'enaurs chanted, THE CONCERTED HOSTS OF JEHOVIH.!

14. Thus was founded Jehovih's heavenly kingdom, Vara-pishanaha; thus established Ahura his dominions where rebellion and secession were cut off forever. And Cpenta-armij gave to Ahura a thousand messengers, and opened a roadway to Craoshivi. Ahura ascended his throne, and the Gods and Goddesses saluted him, GOD OF PARA-PISHANAHA, and they and their attendants departed to their several places.

435

CHAPTER IX.

1. In the third year of dawn Jehovih spake to Cpenta-armij, saying: Gather together the officers of thy traveling hosts, and take with thee thy companions, and go visit all the Lords and Lordesses of the earth, of thy appointing. And let thy recorders make their accounts of the affairs of the earth and her heavenly kingdoms, that they may be taken to, and entered in, the libraries of the Nirvanian kingdoms.

2. Also shalt thou set thy collectors of Brides and Bridegrooms to work in Craoshivi; and give to thy collectors otevans, that they may also visit thy Lords' kingdoms and collect all the angels prepared for the next resurrection, and bring them to Craoshivi, where they shall be classified. For in the coming resurrection thou shalt provide twelve avalanzas, and those who are raised to the etherean heavens thou shalt cause to be divided according to their grade and rate, and have them delivered into regions suitable to their advancement.

3. During the time prior to this, the Lords had contributed largely to Craoshivi, and already there were upward of twenty thousand million angels capable of taking the third resurrection. The departure of Cpenta-armij on this visit was important, for it involved the selection of the next succeeding God of earth and heaven, who should sit on the throne during her absence. At this time, the reigning God was with Brahma on the earth. To him Cpenta-armij sent messengers, acquainting him with the commandments of Jehovih.

4. God answered through his messengers, saying: Greeting, in the name of Jehovih, to Cpenta-armij, His Daughter, Chieftainess! The reigning God deputeth thee, O Goddess, to make the selection in his stead, to be crowned at the termination of dawn. And now, accordingly, Cpenta-armij sent forth her examiners, to search after the highest, best, most learned of all that had been raised up of the earth, capable of the God-head. For sixty days her examiners were at work, and on the sixtieth day, in the evening, they had completed the search. And it fell upon Thale of Peola, of corporeal birth, five thousand years.

5. Thale, a tiller of the soil in corpor, born in spirit in Yueson, ninety years; five years in es'yan; thirty years in factories; in the nurseries, ninety years; in the colleges, one hundred and eighty years; projector, seventy years; surveyor, sixty-five years; measurer, two hundred years; entered an etherean airavagna, and traveled seven hundred years; returned to the lower heavens of the earth and was Lord in six successions for each of the chief earth divisions twelve hundred years; was called by Onavissa, Goddess of Ni-ya-ag-ag-ha to clear the roads of Chenshaya, beyond Chinvat, where he labored six hundred years. Returned again to the earth and her heavens, and served as captain and general four hundred years; served as marshal seven hundred years, under four different Gods and Lords; and the balance of the time traveled as messenger and swift messenger. Of the rates in a thousand, he was nine hundred and ninety-nine. And he knew the whole earth and her capabilities; could read a thousand million voices at the same time, and interpret them and answer them, and had even created plateaux. He knew the atmospherean heavens, habitable and uninhabitable; the roadways; the oceans and nebulous regions; knew the ascending and descending ethe; knew the power in the different rings of the earth's vortex; knew the cevorkum, and its times and places.

6. Cpenta-armij sent a delegation of one million angels to wait on Thale and bring him before the throne at Craoshivi, sending them in their private otevan, and under the

guardianship of her chief marshal, with this commandment:

7. Thale, of Peola, greeting to thee, in the name of Jehovih, Who commandeth thy immediate presence at the throne in Craoshivi. Of all the honored in these heavens, thou standest first on the list, and art appointed by our Father the next succeeding God, through His Daughter, Chieftainess of Haotsaiti. In my stead thou shalt sit on the throne whilst I complete my labor in dawn; after which thou shalt be crowned, of the earth and her heavens, Jehovih's God!

8. Cpenta-armij knew Thale, for he had sojourned in Otsias, in etherea, three hundred years, where she had been Surveyor ten thousand years. So when he came before Jehovih's throne, Cpenta-armij was rejoiced to meet him in person; nevertheless, she first saluted in rank, saying:

9. My brother, welcome in the Father's name, and joy be unto thee. Jehovih hath called thee to this throne; thou shalt be one of the pillars of His everlasting temples. What I put upon thee in the Father's name, thou shalt consider from Him.

10. Thale said: Before Thee, O Jehovih, I bow to Thy decrees, which come through Thy High-Raised Daughter, Chieftainess of Haot-saiti. I accept whatsoever is given me to do, that will raise up man to rejoice in his creation. By virtue of Thy power in me, O Jehovih, I know I shall not fail. May Thy Light be upon me!

11. Cpenta-armij now raised the light to the highest atmospherean grade, and said unto Thale: Approach Jehovih's throne, O my brother, and hold up thy hands toward High Noon, as the symbol of the highest light, for as the sun is to the earth and atmospherea, so is Jehovih to the soul of man and to the etherean worlds.

12. Thale stepped on the foot of the throne, and the marshal stood at his side. The whole Council were seated, and sweet music rose from the es'enaurs, and added to the solemn scene. Thale then faced the place of High Noon in the temple and held up his hands, saying: I am in Thy Will, O Father!

13. Jehovih spake in the light over Cpenta-armij's head, saying: Thale, My Son, Thou art My God, and thou shalt have dominion over the earth and her heavens for two hundred years. Whatsoever thou shalt do shall be of Me and My doing. Thy word shall be My word; thy labor My labor. And thou shalt have Lords and kingdoms, and all manner of heavenly places; and all of them shall be My places through thee.

14. And at the expiration of thy service, thou shalt raise up a successor to thee, who shall be worthy of thee and Me. And he shall likewise have dominion in Me and in My places; and likewise raise up a successor to come after him, and so on until the next dawn of dan. Be thou joyful in dominion; My worlds are places of delight, and mirth, and peace, and love, and righteousness, and good works.

15. The Voice ceased, and then Cpenta-Armij spake on her own account, saying: He who will crown thee will come at the end of dawn; till then thou shalt hold dominion in the RED HAT in remembrance of the FEAST OF THE LIONS. Approach the Judgment Seat, my brother, and I will give to thee in Jehovih's name. With that, Cpenta-armij gathered from the colored rays of light a substance light as ethe, and made a red hat and put it on Thale's head, saying: Sit on the throne in remembrance of the FEAST OF THE LIONS, that I may be honored of thee, and rejoice before my hosts.

16. Thale then sat down on the throne, and the Council proclaimed in the sign, LION'S DEATH! Thale answered in the sign, DOMINION OF THE LAMB! Thereupon Cpenta-armij said:

Council of Jehovih, hear my voice. A new God have I raised up unto my labor. And thou, O God, hear my voice. A new dominion have I given into thy keeping.

17. For one year I shall now visit my Lords and Lordesses in the first plateaux of the earth, for it is a part of my labor for the Father. And when I shall have finished with them, I shall return to my present reigning God of the earth, who is with Brahma, and I will deliver him and Brahma, and return again to this kingdom, whence the etherean resurrection will take place.

18. Provide ye accordingly in all things, even as I would were I here; and number the Brides and Bridegrooms one hundred and sixty days in advance, and send swift messengers to etherea, to the Nirvanian fields and forests in Chan-us-hoag, and thence through Salkwatka to Haot-saiti, in the etherean Abarom, finding six regions, suitable for grades from sixty to ninety. And ye shall send greeting to my sister, Chue-in-ista, Goddess of Oambuyu, asking her to deliver us.

19. Thus saying, Cpenta-armij, and Owks, and See-wah-Gon, and Ha-o-ha took leave, and in their own proper way departed out of Craoshivi, and in the airavagna descended to the lowest plateau, and so visited the Lords of the lower kingdoms.

CHAPTER X.

1. The Lords and Lordesses gave not much labor to Cpenta-armij; for they had long been high-raised Gods and Goddesses in other worlds, and knew their parts well. But to each heavenly place Cpenta-armij sent her heralds in advance, and the Lords and Lordesses in turn sent receiving escorts to meet the airavagna. And when the Chieftainess arrived, she was asked in the usual manner to honor the throne, and she thus sat on all the thrones, ruling in very person, and in her presence the Voice of Jehovih spake in the Light before the assembled COUNCIL OF THE HOSTS, and it was thus fulfilled in the ARC OF SPE-TA that the Voice had circumscribed the whole earth.

2. And when Cpenta-armij was about to depart from each heavenly place, she always descended to the foot of the throne of the Lord, and sat thereon; and the Lord went down and took her hand, saying: Arise, O Goddess, and go thy way; the Father calleth thee! And then would she arise and depart to another Lord or Lordess, in like manner.

3. Cpenta-armij took with her three thousand angel scribes and recorders; three thousand angel artists; three thousand angel geologists and mineralogists, besides many others; whose trade was to make reports of the lands of the earth, and the waters of the earth, and the air above the earth, with pictures thereof.

4. Jehovih had said to Cpenta-armij: Thou shalt make reports of the land and water and air of the earth; and of all the living thereon and therein, with pictures thereof; two copies shalt thou make; and when the end of dawn is come, thou shalt take the two copies with thee in thy ascension to My etherean worlds. One copy shalt thou put on record in the library of Haot-saiti, and the other copy shalt thou send to the Hyperiis Council of the United Chiefs and Chieftainesses, for their own deliberation.

5. For the Hyperiis Council shall determine from this, thy report, what is good for the earth; as to whether she shall be changed in her course, or broken up and divided; or whether she needeth a'ji or dan; and they shall send out road-makers to that end, or send vortices against her vortex, to break it or rule over it, according to My light upon them.

6. Besides these, Cpenta-armij had a thousand recorders, whose business it was to prepare reports of the Lords' kingdoms, and of the factories, colleges, nurseries, hospitals, the hells, if any, and knots, if any; to record the grade and number of spirits in each heavenly place; to record the earthly kingdoms, and kings and queens and their subjects, their occupations and grades, and their rate of corporeal life age. To record the percentage of familiar spirits with mortals; the fetals, the drujas; as well as the ashars and asaphs; and the temples and oracles in use by mortals; the altars and places of worship. To record the number of I'hins still inhabiting the earth; the number of pure I'huans, who worshipped only one Great Spirit; the druk order, who always have idols or saviors, and are given to war.

7. One full moon of four quarters remained Cpenta-armij with each one of the Lords of the earth; and then she departed, going into all the habitable places on the earth, and in the heavens that rested on the earth. In ten moons she had completed her labor with the Lords of the first resurrection; had witnessed the manner in which the Lords sent away the upraised to Craoshivi, to enter the second resurrection. And her scribes and recorders had completed their labor also.

8. And now the Chieftainess sent her airavagna back to Craoshivi, with her visitors, Owks, See-wah-Gon and Ha-o-ha. But for herself she had a piedmazr build; and, taking ten thousand attendants, besides the workers of the boat, she descended on to the very earth, to visit the four Gods, in the four great divisions of the earth; with Wah-tah; with Brahma, with Abram, and with Po. With each of these she spent twelve days, and then she departed and went to Maitraias, the heavenly place, the only Lord-dom of the earth, where ruled Yug-sae-su, with thirty millions. Here she remained twelve days also; and the inhabitants gave a tournament and festival.

9. After this Cpenta-armij departed for Craoshivi, for the end of dawn was near at hand.

CHAPTER XI.

1. In the Council of Craoshivi the Voice of Jehovih came to Cpenta-armij, saying: Behold, the time of thy sun and stars riseth in the Road of Salkwatka. The red star neareth the fields of Abarom; Great Oteson hath filled the sinks and slues of Yosawakak; thousands of millions of My Sons and Daughters behold the Feast of Spe-ta.

2. Hear thou thy Creator, O Cpenta-armij! For thou shalt spread broad the table of My hosts; such like as hath never been before in Haot-saiti. And thou shalt send Obed, God of Oise; Gavaini, Goddess of Ipthor; Ab, Shriever of Riv-Seing; Raisi, Goddess of Esdras; Wish-tse, God of Zuth; Harava, God of Yon-yon; Vraga-piet, Goddess of Zoe; and Loo-chung, God of Ata-bonaswitchahaha. And thou shalt send for the Gods and Goddesses of the Plains of Cnoe-Chang; and for the Gods and Goddesses of the Chi-ha-wogo Roads; and for all the Gods and Goddesses in their own Nirvanian fields; and for the Great Chief, Shoo-lo, of the Roads of Jinihassij, and for all the Gods and Goddesses in his dominions in My etherean worlds.

3. And yet thou shalt remember of thine own knowledge many Gods and Goddesses; and thou shalt charge thy companions, Owks, and See-wah-Gon, and Ha-o-ha, to sit in Council with thee, that ye may remember whomsoever of Chiefs and Chieftainesses, of Shrievers and Gods and Goddesses, that may be delightful:

4. And thou shalt command them in My name to meet in the Feast of Spe-ta, for it is the first in this, My new world. Make way for them; make place for them, O My Daughter! Make wide the roadways in My lower heaven; make My Holy Feast glorious.

5. Cpenta-armij said: Too wide are the dans of earth; too far apart and cumbersome, O Father! More than two thousand millions and four thousand millions will be my harvest unto Thee, O Jehovih! Great is Thy wisdom in Spe-ta; the time for the beginning of quarter ascensions, fifty years.

6. Thy Gods and Goddesses, O Jehovih, and Thy Chiefs and Chieftainesses, will bind up these loose heavens into wholesome discipline. I will send my swift messengers into Thy far-off etherean worlds, and bring Thy Sons and Daughters to Thy Feast.

7. Cpenta-armij sent off into the wide heavens, high beyond the earth heavens, invitations to tens of thousands of high-raised Sons and Daughters of the Great Spirit. Then she called her surveyors and table-makers before Jehovih's throne, and said unto them:

8. The end of dawn is near at hand; I will give a feast, a very great feast. Go ye and survey the ground from Craoshivi to the Lakes of Oochi-loo, in etherea, and for the length thereof make ye a width in the form of Fete; and the road of the Fete shall be sufficient for the passage of twelve avalanzas abreast; and the depth of the Fete shall be as from the surface of the earth unto Chinvat. Within twelve sios of Abarom, and of the height of the circuit of Bilothowitchieun shall ye carry the border flames; and the flames shall be of double currents, going and coming, that the food of the feast may be brought from any region suited to the high-raised grades.

9. And the arc of the feast shall encompass the whole earth, and extend outward to the belt of Craoshivi, and then downward in two lines, east and west; and the downward lines shall be like the feet of a compass, one stationary and the other movable. And the light that extendeth from the arc down the movable line shall rest on the delivered hosts of Abram, and it shall bear upon his people, that they may hereafter draw Light direct from the Father's throne in Craoshivi; and it shall move westward and be as an inheritance of Jehovih's light upon His corporeal sons and daughters.

10. But the line that standeth in the east shall be a base line and center, whither shall descend the Father's light upon the delivered sons and daughters of the hosts of Brahma and Po. And because of the arc of Spe-ta upon them, they shall remain in their own divisions of the earth.

11. And for the deliverance of the harvests of the quarter, the high-raised horns of the arc shall stand to the four quarters, east, west, north and south.

12. Jehovih then spake through Cpenta-armij, saying: For I will illume the horns thereof, and My new world, the earth and her heavens, shall rest in the light of My Roads forever. That no man, having My examples before him, can misunderstand Me.

13. Behold, it is given to a child, only one lesson a day; and to a youth, two lessons a day; and to a mature man, many lessons a day; so, in the early creation of man, I give few lessons; then in the youthful age of the race, many more lessons; but when the race hath attained to full manhood, behold, I lay My light at their feet, that they may take My lessons every day.

14. In one time I send the angels of the dead to lead man up to a knowledge of Me and My places; but when man hath attained to think for himself, I set up my arc of Spe-ta; and it is as a candle in the firmament of heaven, wherefrom My Light falleth upon the soul of

440

My people, without any interpreter, save Mine Own Voice.

15. For which reason, when one of My worlds hath attained to Spe-ta, I come to deliver them from kings, and queens, and priests, and angels, and it is as the maturity of a son in his father's house, when he inviteth his neighbors and spreadeth a feast.

16. Open wide thy places, O Cpenta-armij! A great joy is upon My etherean worlds; My high-raised Sons and Daughters shall have great glory in the earth and her heavens. Behold, I have proclaimed Myself in the words of mortals; four high-raised sons have learned to know their Father in heaven.

CHAPTER XII.

1. Cpenta-armij said: Who can understand Thy models, O Jehovih! Who cannot understand Thy models, O Jehovih! Thou hast shown to mortals the food of the flesh, and the source of the substance of the blood. As a symbol before them of Thy es'sean worlds and Thy es'sean peoples, Thou hast created Thy corporean members; to receive and to impart, but this is not all. Thou createdst poison, to show man that that which receiveth not, and imparteth not, is death.

2. Most wisely, O Father, hast Thou provided the degrees of subsistence unto all Thy creations: To the corporean, corporeal food; to the atmospherean, atmospheric food; to the etherean, ethe'ic food. Wide will I spread my tables, O Jehovih. Thy Gods and Goddesses, and Thy high-raised Chieftains, shall sit at the Feast of Spe-ta.

3. The Chieftainess sent swift messengers into the regions of etherean worlds, near the Roadway of the Great Serpent, five hundred thousand swift messengers. Down to the atmospherean regions she sent messengers to the Gods and Lords, her laborers, ten thousand messengers. To her invited guests she privileged each one million attendants.

4. Next Cpenta-armij sent fifty thousand arrow-ship makers in the regions of Cventagma, in the etherean Itis, to prepare ceremonial salvers and connecting rods, so that all the thousands of millions, being united, could hear the Voice of Jehovih from her throne, movable, in her airavagna. Twelve counterparts to these she sent down to the lowest heavenly regions, so the All Light should pierce the corporeal earth.

5. And now, when her well-skilled workmen, of tens of thousands of years' experience, had saluted and gone off to their respective labors, the Chieftainess spake before the Council, saying: Because of my arc upon the earth and her heavens, the Light of our Father will forever remain with mortals and in the hadan fields. But, behold, even as a young man, coming to maturity, goeth away on his own account, in great hope and self-conceit of his powers, to meet many misfortunes and great darkness, so will it be with the earth and her heavens after Spe-ta. Because I plant my arc in these heavens, and say to the Gods thereof, Ye are free! Behold, there shall rise numerous false Gods of great power. And as a young man going forth is puffed up with conceit, so will the atmospherean Gods believe they know all things, and so bring great darkness and misery upon their kingdoms and upon themselves.

6. But the Light of my arc shall stand; shall grow like a small seed planted; and in time to come, both angels and mortals shall understand that there is but ONE ALL LIGHT, a very center, to Whom all Gods are but as small diadems. As a young man of the earth must have experience of his own to realize his own shortness, so must even the Gods of these

lower heavens be left to run with a loose rein, for the glory of Jehovih, and for themselves in final deliverance. For which reason, hereafter, the bondage of the discipline of the God and his Lords shall be as nothing. Only hells and knots shall they longer cast out with fire and water; only by persuasion, and the example of practice, shall they hold dominion in their respective places.

7. As in the early days, a king ruleth with a rod and with tyrannous laws; and as, in a riper age, the king and his armies give way to a power vested in the people, so shall my arc be the giving of the lower heavens, and the earth beneath, into the keeping of themselves. But my arc, which is the foundation of the Father's upper kingdoms within the lower heavens, shall stand forever.

8. I go, now, on my journey down to the earth, in my airavagna, to receive and deliver my four Gods, Os, and Vishnu, and Yima, and Ela-elia, God in Chief.

9. Thus saying, Cpenta-armij descended to the foot of Jehovih's throne, and the light fell upon Thale, and he rose up from the throne and descended, taking her hand, saying: Arise, O Goddess, and hear thou the Voice of thy Father, Creator and Ruler! Behold, thy labor on the earth and her heavens is near the end; and because of thy steadfastness, I am honored in thee, My Daughter.

10. Whilst thou art delivering My Gods, behold, I will be with thee, and whatsoever thou desireth of Me I will give unto thee. My Sons and Daughters shall receive the visiting hosts from the high heavens, and allot them places in the feast; and My Sons and Daughters shall receive and adorn My Brides and Bridegrooms; and My trumpeters shall proclaim Me in My works, from the surface of the earth to the farthest places in Salkwatka. Yea, My Light-makers shall plant the staff of My holy fire in the throne of Craoshivi, and the foot thereof shall pierce the earth in the land of Vind'yu, to receive and deliver My earth Son, Brahma.

11. Go thou, O Chieftainess, Holy one, of Great Wisdom and Power; it is the Voice of thy Father!

12. Cpenta-armij stood aside, and then said: To ye, my beloved companions, Owks, and See-wah-Gon, and Ha-o-ha, when the staff of the Father's light hath descended to the earth, come ye then to me quickly in my arrow-ship of fire, for it shall be a signal betwixt us that in that hour I will raise up my Gods from the corporeal earth; and I will open the earth and bring forth the bodies of my son, Brahma, and his wife, Yu-tiv, whose youngest son holdeth the leaven of the Osirian law. And I will have there assembled the hosts of my ten Lords, and I will deliver into their hands, for their successors, the fulfillment of the Divan laws.

13. Her companions responded: In Jehovih's wisdom and power, we will be there.

CHAPTER XIII.

1. The Light of Jehovih now spread over Haot-saiti and lined the Road of Salkwatka, in etherea, extending from the Orian Banks of Loo-che-wan to the Oixanian Spars of Ochesu. The Cross Roads, Chi-ea-wha-chong, and the plains of Sha-tumatz, were as seas and worlds of crystal fire. And in the piercing light, the old-time Gods, of millions of years agone, sped forth in awful majesty, in answer to the prayers of Cpenta-armij.

2. And there rose over the earth and her heavens, farther than Chinvat, a trident arc, broad

442

as a world, of shimmering light, the countless rays of ethe, as mortals see the glimmering air in a summer's day; but the ethe was of every color, hue and tint, reflective and brilliant, the clear soul of things separate, the very breath of Jehovih. It was the beginning of the form of the arc of Spe-ta, the deliverance of the earth and her heavens into a new condition; to give, to bestow it upon itself, ratified by the ceremony of a festival for the Gods and Goddesses of that neighborhood, hundreds of millions of miles around about!

3. Meanwhile, their high-raised companion, Cpenta-armij, known and loved in hundreds of etherean worlds, was down on the low earth, laying the corner-stone for Jehovih's everlasting kingdom, whereon should fall, presently, from out the arc of Spe-ta, a shaft of fire, the feast for the purified Chieftainess, who had for four years subsisted on the coarse provender of the lower heavens!

4. And, touched by the hand of Immortal Light, was Brahma, long trained to look toward Jehovih; for his angel wife rose upward, leading his vision toward a realm amongst the Gods and Goddesses, whom he beheld in countless numbers receiving her most royally. Thus gazing on the glorious scene, the great man in soul came forth, leaving his corporeal part stretched on the ground. And Cpenta-armij and God took him; received the soul of Brahma, and held, in obedience to the sacred purpose, his place in the sacred circle with mortals three days.

5. Then, on the fourth, the Chieftainess signaled her swift messengers; and they touched the currents along, till they ran high beyond the earth's vortex, where the stationed Gods of etherea fastened on the ethe'ic wave, extending to the great arc over all.

6. It was the signal for the shaft of light; of which mortals have a weak and coarse symbol in the electric currents which tear things unmeaningly and without judgment; but the ethe'ic current is not so small and purposeless, but mighty, and a tool from Jehovih's fountain of All Power, with skill, and learnedly directed by such high-raised angels as have had millions of years of experience, who know well what prayers deserve an answer from the Immortal spheres.

7. And Cpenta-armij's name, and word, and wisdom, had long been in fellowship with mighty works on many worlds; and her well-trained thought, so tuned to the Creator's purpose, kept ever in concert with the ethe'ic foundation of the place and administration of thousands of Gods and Goddesses.

8. And when the signal shot upward, and the shaft of light began to pierce the earth's vortex, making way for Craoshivi, it was also the signal for Owks, and See-wah-Gon, and Ha-o-ha, to fly instantly for their arrow-ship and make all speed for Cpenta-armij; the which they did now, even as a flash of light darteth forth, guides and directors of Jehovih's flame to the grave of Brahma and Yu-tiv.

9. As Cpenta-armij, standing by her ship, saw the shaft descending, she flew forth to the center of the circle; her hand pointing to the graves, she said: There, O Jehovih! Come forth, O earth! Earth, in Jehovih's name! 'Tis I command!

10. And down fell the bolt of light, piercing the new disturbed ground, rich with mortal tears, and thus made powerful to the soul current; and as a breath of wind would move a heap of feathers, so did the light, by the wave of Cpenta'armij's hand, blow the earth away, and lift up the buried forms of two dead lovers, Brahma and Yu-tiv, and marched them full before the mortal audience, newly animated, and lovingly, hand in hand, triumphant over death.

11. Then spake Hog, the youngest mortal son, an Osirian in belief, seeing the resurrected forms: It is, it is! The very Brahma! And Yu-tiv! My father and mother!

12. The great Brahma, now quickened in Cpenta-armij's arms, and God's, spake from Jehovih's throne, a few words, to the loving sons and mortal concourse, then took final leave. Cpenta-armij seized the folds of the shaft of light, as a mortal would the ropes and canvas of a toy ship, and wrapping the earthly part of Brahma and Yu-tiv about securely, then wheeled in line her own ship and raked in the etherean current from high heavens.

13. Tossing up her hand, the known signal to the great workers in the trident arc above, the exchanging currents of the traveling flame began, and now raised up the whole etherean hosts and the bodies of Brahma and Yu-tiv, the which had not raised a mile before they were etherealized, scattered and gone, and the souls of the two sweet loves in cognizance and fellowship with the millions of Jehovih's Sons and Daughters now swiftly making way for Craoshivi.

14. Cpenta'armij's work was done. In the arc of light and companionship of her compeers, the feast was open, and the thousands of millions in rapport sat along the series of tables, hundreds of millions of miles, to relish soul food brought from more than a thousand worlds.

15. Meanwhile, God, to finish his labors, resumed his throne in Craoshivi, just in time to receive the twelve avalanzas sent from Yuckowts' factories, in Abarom, in etherea, to receive the four and twenty thousand million Brides and Bridegrooms in Jehovih's name, who were to take the degree of third resurrection and be raised beyond the earth's vortex and emancipated in the etherean realms of Hoat-saiti.

16. Chue-in-ista, Goddess of Oambuyu, chief commandress of the fleet, having been apprised of the number of initiates, had prepared twelve thousand rings, a thousand for each avalanza; and the fleet in turn was in a ring, and the ring extended sufficiently wide to encircle the holy capital and throne in Craoshivi, so that when it had descended to its place, God and his officers, and the Holy Council of heaven and earth, now thirty million members, were in the center of the audience. On every side, far as the eye could see, stood the Brides and Bridegrooms of Jehovih, arrayed in spotless white, fearless before the Light and ceremonies.

17. When the fleet landed, Chue-in-ista, the commandress, came forth from the east, facing God on the throne. She said: Thy voice, O God, hath called the name of Jehovih. Behold, I am His Daughter, sent by Him to know thy will and Holy Desires ?

18. God said: Behold, I am His Son! Thou art my Sister! Hear me, then, in our Father's name. I have here a harvest of four and twenty thousand million angels brought up out of the earth, pure and holy, for Jehovih's emancipated kingdoms.

19. Chue-in-ista said: In His name let them answer before me, that I may witness their wisdom and power sufficient to dwell in All Purity. My Father and I are one; my hosts have crossed the Nirvanian pastures; they no longer feed on substance rising from below, but on the Light emanating from etherean realms above.

20. God said: I know Thou hast provided me, O Jehovih!

21. Then here responded the hosts of Brides and Bridegrooms, saying: By Faith I know I am safe in Thy kingdoms, O Jehovih. Take me to Thy emancipated worlds; give me scope and power and wisdom for greater works.

22. Then followed the full ceremony in the usual way of the third resurrection; and when

it was completed, the which had been witnessed by Cpenta-armij and other Chieftainesses and Chiefs above, who were at the feast of the arc of Spe-ta; and when God had said: O Jehovih, give me crowns for Thy Sons and Daughters, Brides and Bridegrooms for Thy etherean worlds! there were cast down by Cpenta-armij and her hosts, four and twenty thousand million crowns; and they alighted on Jehovih's Brides' and Bridegrooms' heads.

23. And now God turned to Thale, who was to be his successor for the next two hundred years. God said: In Jehovih's name, to thee I bestow the crown of earth and her heavens. And to thee also do I bequeath the triangle, symbol of these regions and the inqua, and the trident, the latter being new in these worlds, and symbolical of the arc of Spe-ta; and the interpretation of the trident shall be The Three Lights, Jehovih, His Son, God, and the Star in the mortal soul, emblem of resurrection.

24. Thale said: In Thy name, O Jehovih, will I be God of earth and her heavens till the next rise of dan! Be Thou with me, O Father!

25. Thereupon, he that had been God laid the crown and jewels on Thale, saying: Hail, O God of earth and heaven! Hail, O God of earth and heaven! Hail, O God of earth and heaven!

26. Thus ended the ceremonies. He that had been God descended to the foot of the throne and sat down; and then God, who had been Thale, came down and took his hand, saying: Arise, O God, and go thy way! And he rose up and prepared to depart, for now had the ceremonies lasted one full day.

27. Cpenta-armij, seeing it was finished, signaled the hosts for the close of the festival, and with her airavagna passed over and above the fleet, and gave Chue-in-ista, the commandress, the sign, whereupon the ascent began. The tens of thousands of millions of angels entered their respective places. The music of the es'enaurs and of the trumpeters sounded, and resounded, to the distance of a hundred worlds.

28. Upward rose the fleets; downward fell the showers of flowers and perfumes to those left behind. Higher and higher the great world of lights; higher and higher, till soon they passed beyond the earth's vortex, the boundary Chinvat.

END OF THE BOOK CPENTA-ARMIJ, DAUGHTER OF JEHOVIH.

FIRST BOOK OF GOD.

BEING COTEMPORANEOUS WITH THE BOOK OF CPENTA-ARMIJ, DAUGHTER OF JEHOVIH. AS THE UPPER BOOK RELATETH TO THE HIGHER HEAVENS, SO IN LIKE MANNER DEALETH THE FIRST BOOK OF GOD WITH THE LOWER HEAVENS AND WITH THE EARTH, FOR THE SAME PERIOD OF TIME. FOR WHICH REASON THIS BOOK IS PLACED BELOW THE OTHER. THIS BOOK TREATETH FULLY OF THE FOUR GREAT PERSONS CHOSEN BY GOD, NAMELY: PO, OF CHINE'YA, INSPIRED BY THE GOD YIMA; BRAHMA, OF VIND'YU, INSPIRED BY THE GOD DIV; ABRAM, OF PARSI'E, AND AFTERWARD OF EGUPT, INSPIRED BY THE GOD VISHNU; AND EA-WAH-TAH, OF NORTH GUATAMA, INSPIRED BY THE GOD OS. AND THESE INSPIRATIONS WERE FOR THE SAME PERIOD OF TIME, KNOWN IN THE KINGDOMS OF HEAVEN AS THE TIME OF THE ARC OF BON. THESE FOUR GODS WERE THE CHIEF DIVAN GODS OF THAT DAY, HA'CHUE BEING DIV IN CHIEF.

CHAPTER I.

1. The Creator of creations: Out of Whom are all voices: Of Whom are all things in semblance. From Him and in Him these utterances. By His Gods and Lords and high-raised angels and mortals.

2. Into Whose dominion gave He the earth for the glory of Jehovih, Whose God came and walked and talked with such as had been prepared for the deliverance of His chosen.

3. For the four preserved divisions of the earth gave he four Sons of holy light and power for the voice of God and his Lords:

4. Po, of Jaffeth; Abram, of Arabin'ya; Brahma, of Vindyu, and Eawahtah, of Guatama, whose records are everlasting on the earth, which are testimony that these men were raised up by the Father for His Own glory, and for the deliverance of men.

CHAPTER II.

THE FIRST CHINESE BIBLE. BEING OF PO, AN IESU, CHOSEN BY GOD FOR THE CHILDREN OF JAFFETH.

1. These are the generations of the line of Light from the time of Zarathustra:

2. Shu sa, Gwan, Loo, Sam, Dhi Jo, Wee, Him, Gow, See, Wing, He Wen, Tse Kong, Lam Ne, Moo Yow Tine, Luts, Hime, Mai Se, Hong, Ghee, Wan Ghee, Tse Loo, succeeding one another.

3. All the foregoing were seers and prophets of God (Light), having the Voice from their youth up, and were each in turn a shield and guardian unto the chosen of God (Faithists).

4. God (Light) said: With Tse Loo, behold, the Voice was lost. But I called aloud on the face of the earth, and my Light spread abroad.

5. And there came a woman of Che Song, named Ha-se, an I'hin, through whom the Voice was regained.

6. Ha-se had seven sons and seven daughters, all of whom heard the Voice, and saw the Light.

7. And God divided the fourteen sons and daughters, one from another, and sent them in different ways.

8. These, then, are the tribes than sprung of them: King, Si, Gwe, Loo, Hi-Gah, Hi-se-Gua, Yo, Ha Fung, Ne, Hi Lam, Se'ing, Yuth, Lo, Jon, Ying'e and Ho Lun Gow.

9. From the line of Ha Fung sprang Enam-jo and Ze'zoo (half I'hin). From Ying'e sprang No'e and Yu Laim; also Yu'tse and He-ah. And God commanded the He-ahns to dwell

toward the south, and they so dwelt.

10. From the line of King descended the We Yah-ho; and they lived toward the north and made fellowship with the Foe-Sim, who were I'huans by blood, and also followers of the Zarathustrian law under the name Sa Sin, having rab'bahs whom they called bah, the same as to this day.

11. From the tribes of Foe-Sim sprang Han; and from We Yah-Ho sprang Hi and Te-Wing'e; both of which tribes had the Light and the Voice.

12. And all the north regions of Jaffeth dwelt in peace and happiness.

13. And God looked upon them and blessed them in all things.

14. Nevertheless, it came to pass that the tribes of Han forgot the commandments of God; and Le Han, a mighty chieftain, rose up amongst them, and re-established the Osirian doctrines; that corporeal knowledge should stand higher than the Ormazdian law.

15. Han usurped the central throne of Jaffeth, calling himself Han, King of the Sun. And so Han gave himself up to getting knowledge, and to enforcing knowledge upon the people.

16. Han issued the following decree: Han, King of the Sun! Behold, there is one sun and his satellites. There shall be but one kingdom, with satellites.

17. Behold me, I am the sun king! I will put away all other doctrines and learning. Let all the world bow down to me!

18. Han was asked: Shall a man not worship the Unseen? He answered: Better is it to worship a stone, which thou canst see.

19. Han said: Worship not in words, but in works; worship not in prayer, but in doing righteously. What is prayer but crying to one's own weakness?

20. If there be an Unseen Light, He will do His own way. What is the use of praying to Him? Rites and ceremonies to Him are the expression of folly. Rites and ceremonies to our forefathers are excusable. If their souls continue to exist, the rites and ceremonies may give them good pleasure.

21. So, Han abolished the worship of Jehovih (Light) and His God and Lords.

22. God looked down from his holy hill in heaven, and he said: It is well; let Han have dominion. Behold, Han enraptureth the multitude with his new doctrines, remembering not that these doctrines were tried thousands of years before.

23. God prophesied through his prophet Ze-wing'e, saying: Hear me, O Han, and all ye people of the whole world. I prophesy by the Voice and Light (God and Jehovih); I know my words are true words; by words the soul is bent; by not praying to the Unseen, the Unseen will be forgotten. By the abolition of rites and ceremonies to the Gods, the Gods will be forgotten. Man will rise up in self-conceit against his Creator, saying: Behold me; I am the highest of all things; my judgment is the greatest of all wisdom. And the tribes of men will aspire to establish opinions as fundamental doctrines. War and destruction will come upon the nations!

24. Han would not heed the prophecy of God. Han established what was called The First Han Dynasty, and it overspread the land of Jaffeth from center to circumference.

25. And there came of the laws of Han great persecution against the Faithists, the worshippers of Jehovih (Light).

26. Han said: Try them by the food they eat; and whoso refuseth to eat fish or flesh shall suffer death. Neither shall any man nor woman have favor in the courts, who holdeth

sacred the life of a cow, or a horse, or a dog, or any other animal on the face of the earth, or in the waters, or in the air above the earth.

27. So, the Faithists, the followers of the Zarathustrian law, were outlawed, and were tortured and put to death on every hand. And it had come true as prophesied by Ze-wing'e.

28. God said: Behold, they have not only forgotten the Creator, and denied His Person in words, but in behavior also. For they no longer hold sacred anything He created alive, even man.

CHAPTER III.

1. From Ze-wing'e, God raised up prophets for seven generations. Ze'wing'e begat Do Tse, who begat Yin, who begat Hi Ne, who begat Lan Se'ang, who begat Dhi Hsotch'e, who begat Ho Lon, who begat Po, who was an iesu in birth.

2. When Po was yet very young, the voice of God came to him, saying: Be steadfast in the doctrines of thy forefathers, eating neither fish nor flesh; thy God will not only preserve thee alive, but thou shalt gather together the scattered tribes of Zarathustrians, the Faithists, and re-establish them in this great land.

3. In those days many of the Zarathustrians were celibates; and the king saw his people being reduced by war, and he made a law against celibacy, commanding all men to marry, and all women to bring forth children, or be put to death.

4. When Po was grown up, God said to him: Behold, thou canst not fulfill the law, for thou art iesu-born. But I will fetch thee a wife like unto thee, who is also barren, but ye twain shall be blessed with three children, and thou shalt call them Wan-le, Toghan, and Tse Loo.

5. And it came to pass that a woman of Hong Ge, with three adopted children, escaped from the tyranny of Dhi'wan, fleeing for the southern tribes of HiSeeGua and Yo, and Gwan Goon; and with her, Po wed, and he named his wife Ah T'dowh Jee.

6. Po was twenty years old when he married, and he went with his wife and three children to the country of Heng'a Di, which name signified brother land, and he labored at scutching flax and hemp.

7. And God came to Po, saying: What is the extent of thy fidelity to the All Highest Light?

8. Po said: I will obey him in all things.

9. God said: Wouldst thou sacrifice thy three sons, if commanded by thy Creator?

10. Po said: They are the Creator's, not mine. How dare I sacrifice that which is another's?

11. God said: Thou art wise; thou knowest the Ormazdian law.

12. Then Po asked: Who art thou? Who is this that cometh upon me silently, asking questions?

13. God said: Go thou, visit Hi Seiang, the philosopher, and question him.

14. Hi Seiang was governor of the south province of Heng'a Di, and was, withal, a man of great learning.

15. Po came to him and questioned him, saying: What is this that asketh us questions? Why do we question and answer ourselves all day long?

16. Hi Seiang answered: Are we not two selves? Do we not discourse within ourselves like

448

two selfs?

17. Po said: Which, sayest thou, is the superior self, that which questioneth within us forever, or that which is forever answering?

18. The governor said: That which asketh questions must be the superior self.

19. Po said: Who is it?

20. Hi said: It is nothing, it is something. Po answered him, saying: It appeareth to me, these two selfs are two different persons; one belongeth to the flesh, the other to the Creator. Because this questioning self is the same one that seeth and heareth Gods and angels.

21. Hi said: What sayest thou? God and angels?

22. Po replied: God and angels.

23. To which the governor took exception, saying: Dost thou too defy the law?

24. Po said: What I see I see, what I hear I hear. Something external to ourselves made us, and ruleth over us.

25. The governor asked: Have we not rid the world of superstition? Why dealest thou with doctrines that were in the dark ages? I tell thee there are two things only in all the universe; the unseen firmament, and the corporeal worlds that float therein. Their action and reaction on each other produce what we call life, which is but an effervescence that cometh and goeth, and there is the end. The laws are right. Han hath done a good thing in abolishing the doctrines of the ancients.

26. Whilst they were yet talking, God sent a blaze of fire into a bush standing nearby, and a voice spake out of the flame, saying: Who, then, sayest thou I am? For verily I am!

27. The governor saw the light, and beheld that the bush was not burnt; and he also heard the voice. But God suffered him to be hard of heart, and Hi said: Behold, thou comest to me, knowing I am a philosopher, and thou castest thy spell in the bush, like a magician. I am master of a thousand books, and am registered as a man of great learning. Thou hast offended me.

28. Po said: Why accusest thou me? For is it not just for me to accuse thee of casting the spell? I cast it not.

29. Again did God appear and speak, saying: Accuse thou not this, my son, Po. Thou shalt labor with him. Behold, I give into thy keeping the country of Feh; for even this hour hath died Moo Gwon. The tribes of Ghan shall be gathered together in Feh and Heng'a Di.

30. Hi Seiang, the governor, was astonished at the words of the Light; and he sent a servant, to ascertain if Moo Gwon was dead; and it turned out to be true, though the distance was a day's journey each way.

CHAPTER IV.

1. Hi Seiang, the governor, sent for Ah Sin to come and investigate the nature of Po. So, when the three were together, God wrote in the sand the word TE-IN, and it was as if a flame of fire pierced the ground.

2. Po said: From this time forth Te-in shall be the name of the tribes who have faith in the Creator only. Because he alone hath written it.

3. Ah Sin said: How canst thou distinguish betwixt that which is written by the spirits of

the dead, and that which is written by the Creator?

4. Po said: Light cometh in light; darkness cometh in darkness.

5. Hi Seiang asked: Sayest thou, thou canst see the angels and the Gods?

6. Po said: I see the angels, but the Gods I cannot see. Angels are like ourselves; but the Gods are as a flame of fire.

7. Now, whilst they were thus discoursing, a light in the form of a triangle came and rested on Po's head, and the word Te-in was inscribed on the sides of the triangle.

8. The governor said: What signifieth this? And Po, being under the influence of the light of God, said:

9. Call me Te-in; I am the Father (rab'bah, or bah) over all the living. I write in the sand, and speak in the mouths of my seers and prophets. He that ye call Po is My Son, begotten for the deliverance of My chosen out of the bondage of Han and his satellites (sub-kingdoms).

10. Behold, My people are imprisoned and tortured; persecuted and abused. And ye twain have kingdoms taxed for the glory of Han in his unrighteous work.

11. Provide ye also triangles, and espouse Me, and I will deliver your kingdoms also.

12. Hi Seiang and Ah Sin both desired some pretext to throw off the yoke of the Han dynasty, and now lent willing ears to the instruction of Po and the Voice (Te-in).

13. Accordingly, the learned men of these provinces were called together, to learn of God, through Po, the mysteries of earth and heaven, and especially as to the great monarchy.

14. When these Councils were assembled, God cast his light upon Po, and they all saw it. And the words Po spake were called GOD'S WORDS (Vede'or). Word by word learned they the wisdom of God, repeating them over and over, which was called LEARNING BY THE MOUTH, being in contradistinction from learning by books and tablets.

15. God said: Great trials will come upon My people. The kings will seek to destroy the doctrines of the Lord thy God (Te-in).

16. For which reason ye shall not write nor engrave My words until I come in judgment of the world.

17. These, then, that follow, are the sacred laws given through Po, by God (Te-in):

18. Seek to bring forth heirs that will be a glory to thy Creator.

19. Marry not because of the impulse of the beast (the natural man), but consider thine own spirit and the spirit of thy spouse.

20. Shut not up thyself in celibacy, but multiply and adorn the earth.

21. Thy Creator provided milk for the infant; but with the coming of the teeth, thou shalt provide for their service also.

22. Feed thou him according to the Ormazdian law. To make him a warrior, give thou him fish and flesh. To make him patient and strong, with docility, remember the camel and the ox, feeding on the herbs that grow on the earth.

23. Ne-gwon asked: Was not celibacy the highest of all laws? Is it not so now?

24. God said: There are times for all things. In the days of Zarathustra celibacy was the first of laws. In those days man was not ready for God's laws. Yet thou shalt not call the one law higher than the other.

25. The fullness of earth knowledge requireth marriage, yet the bondage after death holdeth the spirit of man for six generations to his own heirs. By celibacy, a man's soul is not bound after death (by the love he beareth his children) to linger about the earth, and

he may ascend quickly into paradise.

26. The man or woman that is weak, or deformed, or blind, or deaf, or with running sores, or with hidden sickness, shall not marry, nor bring forth heirs. Nor shall man take sorrow to his soul for this; for it is the testimony of the Father that his race is emancipated from the earth.

27. Thou shalt keep sacred the Panic language; nor shall these, my holy words, be given in any language till my time is fulfilled on the earth.

28. Thy sons at the age of eleven years, and daughters at the age of nine years, shall begin to learn maxims. And at that same time they shall be consecrated to the Creator and committed to His service. And of the sixth law this is made a part, to wit: Teachers in public shall be celibates; children who decide that they will become teachers, or priests, or priestesses, shall take the vows of celibacy. For such persons are married to the Great Spirit; and they shall be as Gods and Goddesses, knowing no more love to one person than another.

29. Remember that they who marry, are chosen by Ormazd to raise up offspring for the glory of heaven and earth; and they shall dwell together in peace, love and harmony.

CHAPTER V.

1. The wise shall rule over the foolish, but to raise them up.

2. The rich shall apportion their riches for the benefit of the city.

3. The poor shall reverence the rich and take counsel from them.

4. Behold, I have given many gifts unto my people: the woman to give suck; the very strong man to carry burdens; the wise man to oversee the city; the learned man to explain the ancients; the prophet to hear my voice; the magician to hear the voice of angels; the physician to heal the sick; every several one gave I good gifts.

5. Thou shalt not covet another man's gifts, but be wise in discovering thine own, and using them for the benefit of the city.

6. Neither shalt thou covet another man's riches, nor anything that is his. What more is a rich man than a watch-dog? Behold, it is his matter, whether he fulfilleth my commandments.

7. According to every man's gifts do I require of him, as to what he can do for the people of his city.

8. To the poor man, my exactions are lighter than a straw on a camel's back.

9. For the ignorant man, and for the very young child, I provided the wise and rich as Gods to raise them up. As they minister unto them, so do I bless them for their labor.

10. What they do corporeally for the resurrection of those beneath them, so do I answer them in spirit in my resurrections in the heavens.

11. Thou shalt not marry but once; neither shalt thou look after any other partner all the days of thy life.

12. The husband shall be the master of the house; but when he is not present, the wife shall be master.

13. Seven castes have I made for my chosen: The first are the prophets; the second, such as have the highest genealogy; the third, the rab'bahs and priests; the fourth, the nuns (spe-e-su); the fifth, physicians; the sixth, the rich; and seventh, the very poor.

14. Each and every caste shall remain by itself; all of them are worthy before me, and are equally my children.

15. Thou shalt not kill, for food to eat, anything that breathes the breath of life.

16. Thou shalt love to search for thy Creator in all things on the earth, in the earth, in the waters, and in the air above the earth.

17. Thou shalt love to search for all that is good in thy neighbor; but to excuse all the evil that is in him.

18. Thou shalt keep the sacred days of thy God, and cause all thy people to rejoice in the delightful creations of thy Creator.

19. Thou shalt obey the prophet of thy God; and be obedient to the father (rab'bah) of the city. Next to these, thou shalt honor thy father and thy mother, and pay reverence to thy grandfather and grandmother.

20. In the house (temple) of thy God, remember that all men are alike; for even as death layeth the high and the low alike, so stand my people in the house I have built.

21. Thou shalt respect the opinions of all men; for even thyself may be in error.

22. Thou shalt speak but little of thyself or anything that is thine; for all others have a history also.

23. Thou shalt make thyself compatible unto others in all righteousness.

CHAPTER VI.

OF CITIES AND GOVERNMENT.

1. To re-instate the Zarathustrian law, the largest city shall not exceed two thousand souls; and the smallest shall be ten families. Save they are celibates, in which case a city may be as small as eight souls, having one rab'bah or priest.

2. The best, highest learned man, who shall be a celibate, shall be the priest and ruler of the city; and the sins of the people of the city shall be upon his head. But if it be a large city he may choose one, or as many as six priests, to rule with him; and in that case the sins of the city shall be upon them.

3. When a matter cometh up, the priest shall call whom he will to speak thereon; and when they have spoken, he shall decree by his highest light, and that shall be the law without repeal, save by himself.

4. It shall be lawful for the governor, who is the chief priest, prior to death, to repeal all his laws; so that his successor shall make new laws. For no man shall be bound after death by his own laws, in which case he could not come back and repeal them.

5. But as regardeth the laws a governor or chief priest maketh whilst he ruleth over a city, and over all persons whom he hath ruled during his life-time, he shall be responsible for them, both in this world and the next. For if a priest or governor maketh a law of darkness, and his people live by that law, their souls will be in darkness in the next world through his fault, and he shall answer to them in the soul world for what he hath done in this.

6. Wherein the manufacture of copper or iron, or other things, require more than two thousand people, there shall be another city, with five breadths of the first city between them. And the government of the second city shall be like unto the government of the first. But in no case shall there be more than four cities near about in the same country.

7. Ye shall neither hire nor be hired; neither amongst yourselves nor with the king's peoples. Nor shall ye have servants nor masters, for all shall be alike servants to Ormazd only.

8. Sin-wah inquired: Was it not taught in the Zarathustrian age to respect the caste of men according to the number of their servants? And whether, according to the descent of men, they were born of parents who had risen above servitude for many generations?

9. God said: The old law was for the olden time. It was a good law to improve the breed of men for special trades and learning. And that law hath fulfilled its purpose. The physician hath found great cures; and he knoweth all the parts of the flesh and the blood. The miner knoweth the different kinds of stone, and the metals in them, and how to extract them. The farmer knoweth grounds and the yield thereof, and what they will best bring forth. The spinner and weaver have found the best of fibers for paper and for cloth. And so hath it come to pass in all departments; by the Zarathustrian law of caste have they perfected these things sufficient unto the requirement of man.

10. For which reason ye shall teach all things unto all; and they shall work with their own hands at all industries; remembering that the highest, best, most perfect man is he that can do all things.

11. Jon-Le inquired: Since a man dieth in a few years at most, why shall he strive to learn things that pertain to the earth?

12. God said: All learning is as a gymnasium to the spirit. Knowledge is the strength of the soul.

13. Ye shall teach all things unto your sons and daughters, perfecting them in the talents created withal. First, to useful labors; second, to learning; third, to music and art, in sculpture and painting; fourth, to mining; and fifth, to perfectness.

14. And ye shall intersperse labor and learning with recreation, not only in rites and ceremonies, but in harmless games, as in dancing, racing and playing, old and young.

15. Cultivating joyous hearts, for these are outspoken words of glory to the Great Spirit.

16. Every governor, and priest, and rab'bah, shall provide for a successor; after the light of the Counsel of the All Highest shall they be chosen.

CHAPTER VII.

1. Hi Seiang became converted to the doctrines of Po as taught by God, who was called Te-in in those days in that country.

2. Ah Sin and Hi Seiang and Tse Gow entered into compact to throw off the dominion of Han, and so notified him. Han thereupon declared war against them. And he pursued them cruelly, laying waste a great country.

3. Po and his followers were thus driven toward the south; and on their way they gathered up the Faithists of the tribes of He-ah.

4. Now it came to pass that Han's success in war was so great that he concentrated not his armies, but caused them to scatter in different ways. And behold, he went so far that the barbarians fell upon his armies and destroyed them. And Han himself perished by the blow of a barbarian woman.

5. In the fourth year of the inspiration of Po, he returned and possessed the countries of Feh, Heng'a Di and Se Lov, and he reinstated Ah Sin and Hi Seiang as governors.

6. Hi Seiang called a council of thirteen kingdoms of Jaffeth, and after seventy days' deliberation Hi Seiang was made ruler over Jaffeth, receiving the title, KING OF THE SUN.

7. And he established the doctrines of Po by law, changing the name of All Light, to Te-in, signifying God. And he stopped all persecution against the Faithists; and he prohibited idol worship.

8. And Po traveled east and west, north and south; teaching and displaying miraculous things. And God was with him at all times and places.

9. Gathering together the chosen; explaining and practicing the commandments of God (Te-in).

10. And man ceased to worship all idols and Gods and saviors; worshipping the Creator only.

END OF THE FIRST CHINESE BIBLE.

CHAPTER VIII.

THE FIRST FONECEAN BIBLE.--BEING OF ABRAM, A MAN
CHOSEN BY GOD FOR THE CHILDREN OF ARABIN'YA.

1. Out of the hosts of Parsi'e, who were of the people of Shem, who were since the days of the flood, came Abram, a man chosen by God, in the arcs of Spe-ta and Bon, for the deliverance of the Faithists of Arabin'ya. God said: Because they have not raised up one out of the sons of Ham, thy name shall be, henceforth, Abra-Ham, and it shall be testimony in thousands of years of my records in the libraries of heaven.

2. And it came to pass that forgers and deceivers, not having the fear of Jehovih before them, falsely gave the interpretation of the meaning of the words of Abra and Ham, not knowing (in thousands of years) that in so small a matter He would display the truth and glory of His revealed word.

3. God led Abram away from He-sa, his native place, where he was a maker of baskets, and took him to the ancient land of Ham, which had been destroyed by druks, before the flood, as the name signifieth; whereafter God surnamed him Abraham, and made him chief rab'bah over the Faithists of Arabin'ya.

4. These, then, are the generations of the line whence came Abram, that is to say: Of Shem and the seventy tribes, first going forth beyond the mountains of Owatchab-habal, Tur who settled in Parsi'e, and his descendants Raf-bak, and his descendants Goe, and his descendants Wawa, and his descendants Sadr.

5. In Sadr the line was lost, but through his daughter Bar-bar regained through the I'hins in the land of Goats, where the Listians lived, having fled from the tyranny of the kings of Oas.

6. From Bar-bar was descended Egount, from him Dir, from him Wow-sha, from him He-lial, from him Rac-ca. And here the line ran by female heirs, beginning in Rac-ca's daughter, Hess, from whom was descended Gil-gil, from whom was descended Thussa, from whom was descended She, from whom was descended seven generations in su-is; and it was lost in We-ta-koo, but regained again through I'hin seed, and appeared in Re-both, and again su-is extended through these generations: Arfaxad, Sala, Eber, Peleg, Roo, Sa-rug, Na-hor and Terah; but in Terah the line was lost, but regained by I'hin seed, from whom sprang Geth, from whom sprang Choe, from whom sprang Gus, from whom

454

sprang Ra-bak, from whom sprang Ya-shem, and by I'hin seed sprang Ti-lot, and by I'hin seed Shi-ar, and by I'hin seed Shir-ra, from whom descended Na-hor the second, from whom sprang Abram.

7. Abram was of pure blood, an I'huan; and the light of su-is had been with his forefathers and foremothers since the flood, and he was large and red, like new copper, and had black hair and long beard, fierce to look upon; but his soul was gentle as a woman's.

8. Abram could see without eyes and hear without ears, knowing things by the light of God which dwelt in him. Wherefore God chose Abram to gather together the Faithists in Arabin'ya and the adjacent countries, even as he had appointed Po in Jaffeth.

9. In those days there were great kings and men of great learning, and they had books of learning and instruments for measuring things far and near.

10. And Abram knew these things, for he had been a servant in a king's family where learned men and women congregated. And so, knowing the power of God was upon him, he ran away in his youth, and lived amongst the Listians, who made baskets and trinkets in the forests, which they sold to the king's peoples.

11. God spake to Abram, saying: Fear not for men of learning; neither grieve thou for the learning in books. When they are forgotten, thy words and thy labors will overspread the world.

12. And God lived with Abram, teaching him and working miracles through him. And it came to pass that the Listians in their rambles, selling wares, told the slaves of the kings about the wonders of Abram.

13. And the slaves fled from bondage and went into the wilderness in search of Abram. And when they came before him, he spake unto them, day by day, as they came, saying:

14. Why have ye come? I called you not! And when they could not answer, Abram said unto them: God brought you. Man of himself doeth nothing. Search, then, the records of your generations; for ye are descended from the Faithists of old.

15. And they searched, and found not one had came but was descended from before the time of Zarathustra.

16. Abram said: Think not that God cometh to one man alone; when he provideth a voice he also provideth ears and hearts. Because ye have been faithful unto him, he calleth you to deliverance from your enemies, who are God's enemies also.

CHAPTER IX.

1. When there had come to Abram in She-a-do-wan four thousand five hundred souls, God spake to Abram, saying: Come, now; I will lead thee and thy people into another country.

2. So Abram led them thence and came into Lower Howd-Lutz. And it came to pass that in the next year after they departed out of She-a-do-wan a famine came upon the land and the enemies of God were cut off, and could not pursue Abram and his people.

3. After this it was that Abram was called Abraham, and he built altars of worship and altars of sacrifice, according to the commandments of God.

4. Now it came to pass in the early days of Abraham, he told his brothers that the light and power of God were with him; and, though others believed in Abraham, yet Lot, Abram's brother, and Lot, Abram's nephew, believed not in Abraham, saying of him: He

was born naturally, and is wise of his own judgment.

5. God said to Abraham: Behold, it is an easy matter to commune with spirits, but to judge righteously of them is not so easy. For which reason thou and thy wife, and one hundred picked men, shall go and visit Sodom and Gomorrah in the valley of Siddim.

6. And Abraham and his people went as commanded by God, and visited the cities of Sodom and Gomorrah; and God spake privily to Abraham, saying: I will destroy these cities, for they are as hells for evil spirits; but Lot shall escape for thy sake.

7. And when they came to Sodom, behold, angels walked amongst the people, and the people knew they were angels, but cared not for them. And there were laws made by Bera, king of Sodom, regarding the behavior betwixt angels and men.

8. And Abraham, being pressed by the presence of God, said unto his people: Behold, there are angels that love to dwell in lust, and to partake with mortals; to eat with them, to lie down with them, and to partake in all ungodly pleasures.

9. God, through his angels, rained down fire and brimstone on Sodom and Gomorrah, and they were burnt and destroyed. Lot, the elder, escaped, and went and lived in a cave.

10. Now, after Abraham and his people were returned to Jireh, his camp, and it was night, God said to Abraham: Be thou steadfast, and show thy people that they may understand my words.

11. And whilst they were yet praying before the altar, God withdrew from Abraham, and suffered the evil angels, who had followed them from Sodom and Gomorrah, to draw near about the altar. And one of the angels clothed himself in a great light, and with a crown, and with sparkling gems, and he appeared, so all the multitude of people could look upon him.

12. Abraham said: Who art thou? And the spirit said: I am thy God, ruler of heaven and earth! Abraham said: I am thy servant; what wouldst thou? And the spirit said: Thou shalt take thine only son, Isaac, and thy hosts who were with thee at Sodom and Gomorrah, and go with me whither I will lead thee, for I have a great work for thee.

13. Abraham said: Whatsoever thou puttest upon me to do, that will I do.

14. So in the morning Abraham and his son Isaac, and the hosts who had been with Abraham to Sodom and Gomorrah, assembled together. And Abraham spake, saying: Whither, O God?

15. The spirit answered, saying: Take sticks and a fire-brand and come thou to the summit of yonder hill, for thou shalt restore the rites of burnt offerings. So Abraham told what God had said, and they started, and Isaac carried the bundle of willows, such as basket-makers use, saying: This will light the large pieces; but what wilt thou burn for an offering, O Father? And Abraham said: God will provide.

16. And when they ascended to the place, Abraham gathered logs and heaped them up, and Isaac placed the willows.

17. Then spake the spirit, saying: What shall a man love above all things in the world? And Abraham said: God. And the spirit said: For which reason thou shalt offer thine only son, Isaac, as a burnt offering. And it shall be testimony before thy people that thou wilt obey God even to the sacrifice of thine own flesh and kin.

18. Abraham said: Show me that thou art God, that I may not err, for I have been commanded not to kill.

19. And the spirit departed away from Abraham, perceiving that he knew the higher law.

And Isaac was grieved at heart, for he desired to witness what a sacrifice was. And the people, seeing a ram near at hand, went and caught it, and slaughtered it, and sprinkled the blood on the sacrifice, and they lighted the fire and roasted the flesh, and took it and gave it to the poor.

20. And Abraham called the place Jehovih-Jireh, and they returned to the camp; and Abraham, being moved of God, spake before the people.

CHAPTER X.

1. Abraham said: This testimony declare I unto you, whereof witnesses are of your own brethren, that even the chosen of God can be deceived by evil angels; for they can take any name and form; and, having no fear of God before them, declare falsehood for truth and darkness for light.

2. And, as ye have seen, the evilest of cities, even as well as the purest, may be the abiding place of angels.

3. For which reason ye shall not seek signs and miracles, for these may be of evil spirits, even to the showing of their bodies and of conversing learnedly. It is not in the power of man to know by words and signs, or by oaths or promises, what is truth.

4. One thing hath the Father created withal, which is His Own Light. Wherefore be ye believing toward men and angels; and wherein they teach ye according to Jehovih, which is life unto all, and happiness unto all, without sacrifice to any, they are holy.

5. If man or angel say: Visit the sick, and administer to the distressed, follow his advice, for it is of the Father.

6. But if man or angel say: Do thou thus, and thou shalt have profit, or glory, or applause, obey him not, for he adviseth for thyself and not for the brotherhood of men. He is not of God.

7. For spirits will come in disguise of your fathers and mothers who are dead, professing love and profit to you. Believe them not, save they teach you to sacrifice self for the good of others.

8. The wicked in heart, having profited in herds, and in gold and silver, say: Behold, God hath blessed me! But I say unto you, they are cursed, and not of God. Hath he here gathered you together because ye were rich? Ye were slaves, and in poverty; sick, and in bondage. And he came and delivered you. Be ye like unto him, and he will abide with you.

9. If a man come, saying: Behold, this is my coat; give it me! Thou shalt say: Prove thyself as to who thou art. But if a man come to thee, saying: Thy herd has gone astray; thou shalt not say to him: Prove thyself as to who thou art. But go thou, and see after thy herd.

10. If a spirit say: Behold, I am thy father, say to him: It is well; what wouldst thou? And when he answereth thee, consider if his words be of God. And if his words be not of God, which are for the glory of the Creator, thou shalt challenge him to prove himself.

11. As God is captain of heaven and earth unto all righteous souls, so is there a satan who is captain over evil spirits.

12. And inasmuch as the kings' peoples have not faith in the Father, their souls fall a prey to satan and his hosts.

13. Let not any man flatter himself, saying: Behold, I have joined the Faithists (Israelites); my soul shall escape hell. For in that day and hour God may be putting him to the test, to see if his heart be for good works and holiness. For as ye profess God, ye are doubly bound to practice godliness in your behavior toward men and angels.

CHAPTER XI.

1. When Lot the younger escaped out of Sodom, he halted in a small city called Ben-ah, and tarried there whilst Sodom and Gomorrah were being consumed with fire; and because he was saved, he called the place Zoar, because he was a worshipper of the doctrines of Zarathustra, who was called in the Fonecean language Zoa-raastra. And the place was called Zoar for more than a thousand years.

2. When Lot departed out of Zoar, there went with him two tribes, and there were born of the house of Lot, offspring to the two tribes who accompanied him, and these became the nations in after years known as Moabites and Ammonites, who were of the Foneceans, as their names show, and they followed the doctrines of Zarathustra.

3. In former years God appeared to Abraham in a dream, and said unto Abraham: Thou shalt be a father to many peoples.

4. When Abraham awoke he told Sarai, his wife, and she was troubled, being barren, and she prayed God for Abraham's sake.

5. Now it came to pass that Hagar, Sarai's maid, had a son, and called his name Ishmael; and Sarai was jealous of Hagar, and abused her during pregnancy. And the Lord spake to Abraham, saying: Because of the hatred betwixt thy women, Hagar's son will be as a wild man; his hand shall be against every man, and every man shall be against him.

6. Abraham said: How, O God? And God said: I told thee thou shouldst be a father of many peoples, and thou toldst Sarai, thy wife. Now Sarai became vain in her desires for offspring, and, in her eagerness, she opened the door of thy house to satan, and hence this matter is upon thee.

7. Go, therefore, my son, and reconcile thy women. And Abraham told Sarai what God had said. And Sarai inquired of Abraham, saying: Before God, tell me, is Ishmael thy son? And God shall judge betwixt us. Abraham said:

8. Teach me, O God, to answer Sarai, that I may reconcile them. And God said: Behold, thy Creator is the Father of all the living.

9. And when Abraham told Sarai God's words, she cried in sorrow and repentance, saying: Thou art wise, O God! For what matter is it to me, since I know that Ishmael is thy son, and Hagar is thy daughter?

10. And Sarai went to Hagar and said: O my sister, I have sinned before the Lord, my God. I saw thy son, and knew God gave him, but I turned against mine own soul, and loved not thy treasure.

11. Hagar said: Saidst thy God that Abraham was father to my child? And Sarai said: Nay, O Hagar. Hagar said: Neither said I thy husband was Ishmael's father.

12. So they were reconciled, and by right of the beginning of Abraham's nations, Ishmael was Abraham's son before God, but not in the flesh.

13. Sarai had a son, and he was called Isaac, because he was born of Sarai after she had passed the time of child-bearing.

14. And when Hagar beheld that Sarai bore a son, Hagar became jealous for Ishmael's sake, and she wept before Abraham. Hagar said:

15. I am an Egyptian woman, and I left my people for thee. Behold, I am not favored of thy God. Abraham said: Have I not been as a father to thee and thy son? Yea, when all people reviled thee because thou hadst a child in maidenhood, laying it on me, I denied thee not nor justified myself before the king's people, suffering these things for God's sake, and thine, and thy child's.

16. Complain not, then, against my house, nor my wife, nor my son, Isaac; all things are of the Creator. And Hagar was pacified for a season, but afterward returned to grief and jealousy, and finally resolved to depart away from Abraham's house.

17. Then said Abraham to Hagar: The matter lieth with thee. And I give thee, according to the custom of the Egyptians, a jug with water, and bread and blankets.

18. So Hagar persisted, and Abraham provided her, and she departed, taking Ishmael with her, and she went into Par-an and dwelt there.

19. In those days Arabin'ya was divided into many kingdoms, some having one city and some two, and some as many as six cities. And they were constantly at war one with another, and the victors always changed the names of the kingdoms. The largest and most powerful always called itself the Sun Kingdom, after the manner of the Parsi'e'ans (Persians).

20. In the Sun Kingdom dwelt men and women of learning, and they had tablets and books and maps relating to heaven and earth, which books, maps, and tablets were kept in a library, the summit of which building was used as an oracle for consulting with the spirits, called Lords of heaven.

21. For which purpose, a man or woman, whose head had been flattened in infancy, sat by a table covered with sand, whereon the spirits wrote with the finger. And the person so communing with the spirits was called AEjin in the Egyptian language, and was in rank next to the Sun King. Now, no matter what wars took place, the library, the temple of the oracle and the AEjin were sacred, and never suffered harm even betwixt enemies.

22. The kings kept scribes whose business was to write and to translate, and to keep the records of the kingdom. Besides these, there were gatherers of news, who held the second rank of scribes.

23. Now when Abraham and his people came into Arabin'ya, especially into Egupt, the matter was entered in the records of the different kingdoms, with especial reference to Abraham's professing to hear the voice of God, for he had not a flat head, and moreover, had good judgment of his own, quite unlike the AEjins in the temples.

24. But because Abraham gave no counsel as to war or to earthly gain, he was not favored by any of the kings, and was suffered to go his way unmolested.

25. When Sodom and Gomorrah were destroyed, the kings' people heaped the blame of it on Abraham's head, and there rose up enemies against Abraham in those regions.

26. And they also accused him of attempting to burn his son Isaac as a sacrifice to his God, after the manner of the heathen of old.

27. And they accused Abraham of being the father of Ishmael, by his servant-maid, and of driving Hagar and Ishmael away to Par-an after he tired of her.

28. And these accusations, and many more of like wickedness, were heard of by the news gatherers, the scribes, and they wrote them down, not knowing of a truth what they were

doing before God; and so, their records were entered into the libraries of the kings of Arabin'ya, especially of Egupt.

29. Abraham perceived these matters, and he wept before God, saying: Alas, O God, would that I had great learning and could write my record truthfully before men! God answered him, saying:

30. Thy faith being in Jehovih, it is well with thee. In thousands of years, one Ezra shall send his scribes into these countries to gather news, even as do the kings of this day. And his scribes shall translate from these records, with all their errors and falsehoods, and Ezra shall publish the matter as the history of THE DELIVERANCE.

31. Abraham hearing this of God, bowed down his head and wept, saying: Thy will be done! And God comforted him, saying: I am the Light and the Life!

32. The God of heaven and earth will come afterward and render the records of thy life, which are not dead, but of life everlasting. Since, then, thy people shall be honored by even that which shall come from their enemies, how much greater will be their glory when God of heaven speaketh for thee and them!

CHAPTER XII.

1. Abraham inquired of God concerning the peoples of the kings and of the Faithists. And God said: Whoever I lead to thee shall be thine; thou shalt henceforth be father to all men and women and children that are thine. And they shall be thy family. But all other peoples shall not be thine; nor shalt thou be to them a father nor a prophet. Neither shalt thou make laws for the kings' peoples; nor laws betwixt thy people and them. Of thine own people shalt thou be, and for thine own people shalt thou be forever.

2. Nor shall thy people have anything in common with the kings' peoples, nor with any other people under the sun. Nor enter into treaties, nor alliances, nor in any way whatsoever. Both thy labor and the labor of thy people are for Jehovih, through the Lord thy God.

3. But touching the intercourse betwixt thine and the kings' peoples, be circumspect to the value of a fraction in buying and selling, to give the full value. Neither suffer my chosen to accept presents, or otherwise to become obligated to other peoples, for it is the law of thy God. For it shall not be said by the kings' peoples: Behold, I made them!

4. For I say unto thee, neither kings nor rich men make the people of thy God.

5. Whosoever would give thee gifts, let him quit his people and come and dwell with my people in person and spirit. I cannot be put off with money and with gifts, like a peevish child or a wanton woman.

6. Shall a man say: Here are gifts for thy God, he is a good enough God! But as for my soul it is too good to give to thee or thy God.

7. Neither shalt thou suffer thy people to marry with the kings' peoples, for the same reason. But whosoever will marry my daughters, let him come and dwell, first with my people, proving that he hath forsaken all the idolatrous gods for Jehovih's sake. It shall be the same of thy sons; if they desire strange damsels or wives, they shall first bring them to dwell one year amongst my chosen.

8. Abraham inquired concerning government. And God said unto Abraham: To teach people to dwell together in peace, order, harmony and love; being disciplined to these,

what more is required? Government belongeth to the kings' peoples.

9. Abraham said: That I have spoken before thee, O God, teach thou me, for I am as one in the dark cellar groping about? Behold. my people are unlearned!

10. God said: Who is learned? I say unto thee, he who knoweth the stars and the rocks, and the mountains and valleys, and all that is living and dead, and the tongues of the ancients, but knoweth not the Creator, is unlearned. But he that knoweth the Creator is learned indeed.

11. Better is it that thy people dwell in tents and under trees; and their children roll on the ground, and die not, but grow strong in person and in spirit for the glory of the Creator, than to dwell as the kings' peoples, in magnificent cities, and in lust and death. Before thy God, thy people are a most learned people.

12. Abraham inquired of the Lord concerning servitude. And God answered him, saying: There is but one Master, even Jehovih; thy people shall be His servants only. But all people have loves; a damsel saith to her lover: I will be thy servant, and he marrieth her. A man saith to another: Thy judgment is greater than mine; I will be thy servant. And the man taketh him in love to work for him.

13. Therefore, for convenience sake, thou mayst say, master and servant. Nevertheless, my chosen shall not, in fact, have either masters or servants, for the one shall not have authority over the other but by love and free consent.

14. Abraham asked concerning the products of labor. God said unto Abraham: Even as I have said of servants and masters, so also is it of the productions that come out of the earth. Nothing belongeth to any man, for all things are Mine, saith the Creator.

15. Nevertheless, for convenience sake, thou mayst say: This is his product, or that is such an one's product. But still he holdeth it only by his Creator's consent.

16. Let all men render unto the Creator His creations, for they are Jehovih's. After that, Abraham said: Some men grow flax, and some wool, and some corn; but the seasons bring forth not alike unto all. Others spin and weave; and others make butter and cheese. And yet this happeneth also: One man is strong, another weak; one riseth with the sun and toileth all day; another sitteth on the bank, fishing.

17. Now when the products are brought in, lo and behold, there are no two that are equal.

18. And God said: Every man's matter is betwixt him and his Creator. According to diligence and industry He rewardeth them in the end. He that perceiveth this, knoweth his heavenly Father; he that perceiveth it not, dwelleth in darkness.

19. Abraham said: Shall the lazy be rebuked, and they that shirk be upbraided?

20. And God said: Nay. Let all thy people bring their products and cast them before thee, saying: This is my sacrifice unto Jehovih; distribute thou it. And if some bring not anything, neither rebuke them nor pity them; they are the sons and daughters of thy God. And if some decorate themselves with fine raiment, or jewels, censure them not; thy God searcheth their hearts.

21. Abraham asked concerning lands. God said: Consider thy God. Did I go to the king and to the rich man and say: Give thou me thy sons and daughters? Nay, but I went to them that were despised by the rich, and by the king, and I said: Come ye! and they came.

22. And when thou wert come hither, did I say: Take thou the king's lands, or the rich man's? Nay, but I led thee to that which was neglected and waste in the eyes of the kings' peoples, and I said: This is thy inheritance.

23. Sufficient is it for thee and thy people to buy burying-places for the dead, which shall not be disturbed. But of all other lands, neither buy nor sell.

24. And after thy people have improved a place, and a king cometh against thee, saying: Either by purchase or by battle, I will have this land; thou shalt say: Nay, neither by purchase nor by battle, shalt thou inherit that which is Jehovih's. But if thou desirest the land, then will I give it thee without money and without battle.

25. And it shall come to pass upon my chosen that they shall be driven from place to place, whither I will lead them; and they shall make the waste lands to bloom like gardens, and the deserts to yield ample harvests; for they shall dig wells, and till the soil, and prove unto the nations of the earth the glory of thy works.

26. And they shall be cut down and driven away, and scattered, but I will come and gather them together. Their places shall be inherited by idolaters and worshippers of strange gods, who will build mighty temples. But my people shall not build in stone, nor wood, nor iron, that shall endure; for they shall go from place to place, proclaiming me and my works; but where they have been, there shall be nothing left on the earth to show their labors.

27. But when I have taken them across all the earth, and they are scattered as dust before the wind, and no man can say: Here is a nation of the children of Abraham, lo. I will raise up my voice for them, even I, the God of heaven and earth. And in that day the idolaters and worshippers of strange Gods will be on the wane; their temples of stone and mortar will still be standing.

28. But a voice shall go up from the whole earth, even from the far-off nations of the earth, saying: What of them who laid the foundations of the temple of ONE GOD, EVEN JEHOVIH! Who were the sons and daughters of Abraham! O that mine eyes could have beholden the Faithists of that!

CHAPTER XIII.

1. When Abraham's wife was getting old, her ears were opened to hear the voice of God. And God said unto her:

2. Concerning thy son, Isaac, hear thou thy God, even the God of Abraham: My labors are not for a day, nor without judgment.

3. Behold, in the land of Es-seth, the place of thy husband in his youth, have I built for many generations concerning the seed of my people. For which reason thy son Isaac shall take a wife that shall inherit my voice.

4. Before the time of thy husband's father's father, I sent my angel from heaven, saying: Go thou and raise me up an heir to hear my voice, for I will dwell for a season with the children of men.

5. And my angel fulfilled his part, and I have come and talked with thee and with thy husband face to face. And even in like manner can I talk to thy son, Isaac, and he can hear me also. And Isaac shall raise up heirs to my voice through his wife, to whom he is not known in this day.

6. Sarai told Abraham what God had said to her; and so Abraham and Sarai went to the altar which Abraham had built, and they prayed alone; and God came and spake, saying: What would ye?

7. And Abraham said: Concerning our son Isaac's wife? And God said: Because of the blessing of Sarai, thy wife, who hath been upright all her days, I will give her comfort in her old age.

8. Send thy servant to the land of thy fathers, and I will send my angel with thy servant, and he shall come to a maiden who shall be Isaac's wife. So, Abraham called his servant, who was overseer over his goods, and he said to him: Equip thyself with camels and asses, and with servants, and with jewels I will give thee, and go thou to Syria, the land of my fathers, and bring a damsel hither, who shall be Isaac's wife.

9. The overseer said unto Abraham: Alas me! How shall thy servant choose a wife for thy son? Or, if choosing, how shall he induce her to come so far? Abraham said: That which God hath commanded of me, I have told thee, save that God saith: My angel shall go with thy servant, and he shall not err.

10. So the servant of Abraham, in fear and trembling, equipped himself with ten camels and twenty asses, and with thirty servants, taking presents and goods, and departed, and the journey occupied two and twenty days. And all the while the overseer reasoned upon what he should say, for he had misgivings that he was on a fool's errand.

11. Nevertheless, he prayed to God that he might do his own part wisely. So when he came near Abraham's father's people, the angel of God spake in his heart saying: She that cometh with a pitcher on her head shall be Isaac's wife. Say thou to her: Wilt thou give me a drink? And she will say: I will give thee a drink, and also draw water for thy servants, and for thy camels.

12. And the overseer looked, but saw no damsel, and he marveled; but presently he saw many damsels, one of whom had a pitcher on her head; and his heart failed him till she came near, and he said: Give me a drink? And she gave him a drink and said unto him: Thou art a stranger: pray thee, I will water thy camels and give drink unto thy servants.

13. And she so gave as she said; and when she had finished, the overseer said unto her: Who art thou? And she answered him, and he perceived she was Isaac's niece by Abraham's father's second wife, but of no blood kin. And then she asked the overseer who he was and whence he came; and he told her, even from Abraham, whose servant he was. So she invited him to her people's houses, and she ran ahead with joy to tell who had come so far, bringing word from Abraham.

14. Now when the camels and asses had been fed, and straw spread for the travelers to lie upon, and when the repast was spread for them to eat, the overseer rose up, perceiving the way of God, and he said: Till I have spoken, eat not, but hear ye the words of God. So he related the object of his visit as commanded by God, and in reference to the angel of God, and the words that came to him.

15. And when he had finished, the power of God came upon the damsel, whose name was Rebecca, and she rose up and spake, saying: Isaac shall be my husband, and I shall be his wife, for I know this matter is of God!

16. So it came to pass after some days, Rebecca departed from her people, and by her faith in God came to Abraham's home, and Isaac took her to wife, and Sarai rejoiced before God because of the light of his kingdom through Abraham's heirs.

17. And God said unto Abraham: Divide thou thy people into families of tens, and families of hundreds, and families of thousands, and give to each family one rab'bah, and yet to all of them together one chief rab'bah. And make thou thy will, and appoint thy son

Isaac and his heirs by his wife Rebecca to be thy successor, that My voice may remain with My chosen.

18. And Abraham made his will and did in all things as God commanded; and he further made the rab'bah officers in the rites of Emethachavah, and communicated to them the sacred name of the Creator (E-O-Ih), and the plans of the upper and lower heavens, the dominion of God and the dominion of satan, which were kept secret with the rab'bah.

* * * * * * * * * * * *

19. God said: Behold, there is a time to clear up all things, present and past: Were Abraham father to Hagar's son, Ishmael, and had he been true to the law of sacrifice amongst the heathen, then, Ishmael, being first-born, would have been chosen for the burnt offering.

20. In which matter the Ezra Bible is shown to be false before Jehovih, in regard to Abraham and Ishmael and Isaac, and the burnt offering also.

21. Which words were not my words, nor the words of my angels, but the words of the Eguptian record.

END OF ABRAHAM'S HISTORY, AND OF THE FONECEAN BIBLE.

CHAPTER XIV.

THE FIRST BIBLE OF VIND'YU. -- BEING OF BRAHMA, A MAN CHOSEN BY GOD FOR THE CHILDREN OF VIND'YU. GIVING AN ACCOUNT OF BRAHMA BECOMING AN IESU; OF HIS LABORS AND HIS RESURRECTION AFTER DEATH.

1. These are the races of Brahma: Gons, Shone, Gamma, This, Ram, Zerl, Mex, Shriv, Vat, Eun and Delta, each a thousand years. Of Gamma and Delta, in the upper country (Wa-wa-o-gan), were born Gu-sem and Hagu by Gamma, and by Delta, Yots, Rammus, Borgl, Otesiv and Riv. Gamma was of the fourth descent of Git-ow; and Delta the third descent of E'wangga.

2. The ascending caste of light in the lower country (Ho-jon-da-tivi) was by Ram, first; then Zerl, migrants from the land of Ham; then Shriv, then Vat, then Gons and Eun, the half-breed druks; then Shone, and then This.

3. Jehovih, who by the Brahmins was called Ormazd, sent His light to the earth world once for every hundred generations. And the light fell upon His sons, prepared from before their births by the angels of Ormazd. Of the times before the submersion of Pan, each cycle was called one man, and the length of his life three thousand years.

4. But of the times after, Ormazd commanded the nations of the earth to be rated as a man, and it was so. Ormazd said: That man may not be confounded, thou shalt number Osiris with the generations that believe not, save in the sun; but of the Zarathustrians, their number shall be as those who survived in the darkness of his cycle.

5. Which were: Zarathustra from the races of Shone and This; and of Zarathustra, Haman; of Haman, Wonchakaka, who begat Zoar, who begat Theo, who begat Andassah, who begat Mur, who begat Romsat; these were tribes of the Zarathustrian order, who rejected idols, Lords, Gods, Saviors, kings, queens, and all other rulers on the earth or in the heavens above the earth, save Ormazd, the Creator. And in Him had faith that to do

righteously, and practice good works, made the best, nearest perfect man.

6. The Light by the Voice was lost in the sixth hundredth year after Zarathustra, but regained in Romsat by the I'hins, whence came the tribe Lo-jon, who begat Thonegalahogreif, who begat Subinij, and from him to Wowthutchi-subinij, which were forty-four generations, the Voice always came to the chief rab'bah.

7. In Chusa-king the Voice was lost, but again restored by the I'hins, whose heirs were called Wah-sin-chung, who begat Avar, who begat Irigavagna, who begat Ben-haoma, from whom was descended thirty generations, the chief rab'bah of whom could hear the Voice.

8. Ben-haoma numbered the Faithists of his day, and there were of them four thousand, men, women and children, and all other nations and tribes in Vind'yu were idolaters.

9. Through the descendants of Romsat the Voice was again regained by the I'hins, through a tribe called Shriviyata, who begat Them-saga, who begat Friavamargalum, who bred with the I'hins and begat Thace, who begat with the I'hins Anu, who begat the I'hins Maha, who begat with the I'hins Brah, who had both voice and power from the Father. And he was called Brahma because of his great wisdom.

10. The angels of Ormazd had prophesied, saying: Out of thy seed shall come one called BRAHMA, who shall have su'is with power. Things that were revealed to Zarathustra have been lost, but shall be recovered in Brahma.

11. Romsat had prophesied, moreover: With the coming of Brahma is the end of the I'hin race in Shem (Vind'yu).

12. God spake in kosmon, saying: Let no man say: With Brahma, or with Abram, or with Po, or with Eawahtah, was the beginning of the doctrine of One Spirit. For since man walked upright on the earth, behold, I have said unto him: Thou shalt have but one God, even the Creator. And in the cycles of my times I have raised up many who have comprehended my words, but others constantly put away the I AM, and raise up idols instead.

13. But let all men understand who and what, is meant by the terms, Po, and Abram, and Brahma, and Eawahtah, which is, that though I walked the earth with these, teaching and speaking through them, yet none of these were idolized by men. For the nations of the earth, in the time of these four men, comprehended that they were not Gods, but men through whom, and to whom, I, even God, had spoken.

14. Brahma said: Have all men stars? Behold, since my childhood up, I have had a star above my forehead.

15. No man could answer Brahma. They said: Brahma is foolish, with all his wisdom.

16. Brahma asked the star: Who art thou?

17. God said: I am thy star; I am the light of the second heavens.

18. Brahma asked: What is thy name, O star, thou mysterious light?

19. God said: Call me Ormazd; I am the same light that spoke to Zarathustra in the olden time.

20. Brahma asked: Who art thou, O Ormazd, thou voice of light?

21. God said: With one only shalt thou commune, thy Creator; one only shalt thou worship, He who made thee alive.

22. Brahma said: Why hast thou taken up thy abode above my head?

23. God said: Attain thou to be one with thy Creator, in wisdom, and goodness, and

purity, and thou shalt answer thine own questions.

24. Then Brahma applied to the rab'bah, the Zarathustrian priests, and he learned abnegation of self, and the rites and ceremonies of the ancients.

25. When Brahma was grown up, God said to him: Arise on the morrow, my son, and I will lead thee into another country, where thou shalt marry, and settle down for a long season.

26. Brahma said: Peaceful have been my slumbers, and joyous my wakeful hours all my life. I have made labor a pleasure, and I give all I have to the poor, doing Thy commandments with all my wisdom and strength.

27. From my youth up I have killed not any living creature of Thine that goeth on the earth, or swimmeth in the waters, or flieth in the air. Neither ate I of anything that had ever breathed the breath of life; and I have been most abstemious in plain food and water only, according to the Zarathustrian law. Hear Thou me, O Ormazd; for I will break my soul unto Thee, and hold nothing back.

Ormazd said: It is well.

28. Brahma said: Woe is me, if my soul turneth toward woman! Was I not wed to Thee, O Ormazd? Was I not Thy Bridegroom from my youth up?

29. Why, then, protectest not Thou me unto Thyself? Ormazd said: In times past I raised up many an iesu, and they were without flesh desires all their days.

30. Such men could not perpetuate the earth; they were good for their day. Zarathustra was an iesu. My Light is now for them that can perpetuate. All things are possible in my hands. Grieve not, nor smother out any talent I created unto the pure in flesh.

31. Brahma said: If I love a woman, O Ormazd, may I not lose my love for Thee? Ormazd said: By faith in Me thou shalt triumph by the road I marked out for thee, since before thou wert born. Arise, then, O Brahma, and follow thy star. I will lead thee.

32. Brahma said: Can there be another way than by celibacy? Can a married man serve Ormazd?

33. So, Brahma traveled, and came into the country of Etchoyosin, where lay the mountains of Talavitcha, under King Tyama, who had enforced the Zarathustrian religion with sword and spear, and with chains and death, being himself sole interpreter.

34. When Brahma came to Au'watcha, he halted to inquire the way to the high priest's house, that he might be absolved for twenty days in Tyama's kingdom, according to law, paying the price as apportioned for strangers.

35. In answer to his summons, there came to the gate, the damsel Yu-tiv, fairest of women, draped, also, to go before the priest for confession. Brahma inquired of her concerning the priest and the tax. Yu'tiv informed him, and, moreover, said: I am going thither, and shall delight to lead thee to the place. So Brahma went with Yu-tiv, and when they were gone a little way she said unto him: Whence camest thou, and what is thy mission? Peradventure, I may serve thee. Behold, I see a star above thy head!

36. Brahma said: Seest thou a star? Now I say unto thee, there is an old legend that the pure in heart, looking upward, oft see their own paroda, and think it belongeth to another. Yu-tiv reassured Brahma that she saw the star, whereupon Brahma took heart and said:

37. Yea, I have a star, and the Voice of Ormazd cometh to me at times. For some years I strove to be a priest, for I saw the wickedness of the world, and, moreover, the tyranny and tortures of the church (ha'oke), and my soul cried out for the oppressed who had faith

in the Great Spirit more than in the priests. And Ormazd came to me and said: Brahma, my son, forsake thy studies, and take thy broad-axe, and go and hew logs. Behold, I will come to thee some time, and thou shalt bless the earth.

38. So I gave up my studies and became a hewer of wood, living abstemiously day and night, and praying and striving with all my soul and with all my strength to purge myself of all earthly thoughts. So I grew, as thou beholdest, to be a large man of great strength. But, alas, evil overtook me; my soul desired a woman. And I cried out unto Ormazd, saying: Why hast Thou put this matter upon thy son? Lo, I strove to be wedded to thee only; I shut my eyes to all the earth, but thou hast suffered me to fall. Rescue thou me, I pray.

39. Then spake Ormazd to me, saying: Behold, I have revealed my word through such as have no earth desires; but that time is past. I will now prove unto the nations of the earth that I have power in directing the flesh, that heirs may be born unto me. Arise, therefore, and go whither I will lead thee, for thou shalt take a wife and raise up seven sons, and I will deliver my edifice (church), unto liberty.

40. So I rose up and walked after the light of my star; thus far have I come, but how much further I must go I know not; but I will go to the end of the earth if Ormazd require it of me.

41. Yu-tiv said: I pity thee, O man! One so holy should never with woman wed. To win such a man's love, the best of women would forget her God! To bear thee one child, instead of seven, a woman would cleave the earth in twain. It would be like peopling the world with Gods and Goddesses.

42. O promise me, stranger, thou wilt turn from such unholy desires. I know not what moveth me past all modesty thus to speak to thee, but before Ormazd, Creator of heaven and earth, erst thou camest to my father's gate a voice spake in mine ear, saying: Quickly, thou, put on thy robes for confession, and hasten to the priest.

43. I tell thee, O man, to save thee, the angels of Ormazd came to me. It is true that two can see more than one.

44. Brahma said: Who are thou, O woman? Yu-tiv said: A weaver of mats; no more. My father liveth in yonder thatch; my mother's soul ascended to heaven, giving me birth. She was of the I'hins. From place to place my father and I have been driven; all the ills of earth are written on my soul. And the rudeness of men; the light-heartedness of women! By day and by night my soul crieth out for the miseries of the earth. O the sins of the earth! O the death of little infants! O the trials of the poor! O the suffering of the sick! O the anguish of the imprisoned! O stranger, stranger, stranger! People not this world more!

45. Let us turn our souls upward; to Nirvana; to the regions of endless paradise! To the voices of angels and Gods! To wisdom that erreth not; to music never discordant! To love that never separateth! Never!

46. Brahma said: Now I beseech Thee, O Ormazd, that I may never marry! But because Thou hast raised up here so fair a woman, and withal so wise, give me leave that I may dwell near at hand!

47. Then spake Ormazd, out of the midst of the voices of their stars, saying: Hold up thy hand, O man! Hold up thy hand, O woman! And they held up their hands, and Ormazd said: I am the Father, and ye are My children. That I may have joy, dwell ye near together.

48. Now after this, Brahma and she proceeded to the priest's house and made their

sacrifices, and returned and came to Yu-tiv's father's house, and the father's name was Aliegan-is, called Ali. And Yu-tiv told her father all that had happened, but Brahma said little. Ali said: What the All Light doeth is well done. My house is ample. Brahma shall sojourn so long as he desireth.

49. Brahma said: Of mine own accord I am not master of many words. When it pleaseth Ormazd to speak with me, I will raise my voice. Then Yu-tiv spread mats and provided food, and sat it before Brahma, and he ate; and after that they said prayers according to the laws of the king, and then retired to sleep.

CHAPTER XV.

1. When morning came, Brahma and Yu-tiv rose early, and came and spake together, in joy greeting, and they were moved to shake hands, though such a proceeding was not according to the fashion of the country, save betwixt relatives. And it came to pass that they were much together during the day, and in the evening they walked together, but touched not one the other.

2. Now on the second day, when they walked together, they held hands. And on the third day they joined arms. And on the fourth day they kissed each other. And after that they were only separated at night when they slept. But it came to pass that they were so delighted with each other that they sat up nearly all night, so as not to be separate.

3. And all the while they neglected not their devotion to Ormazd; but finally they sat up all night, sleeping not, save in each other's arms.

4. Yu-tiv said: Since we sit up all night, it is wiser to sit on mats than on stools. Brahma said: It is wiser. So they provided mats, half raised and half spread down, for a season, and finally laid the mats full length, and they laid down together. More than that, history saith not.

5. But Brahma followed his trade in that country, and it came to pass they had a son born to them, and his name was Whe-ish; and in time another son, and his name was Vus, and then Git-un, and Vede, and Oos, and Sa-it.

6. Now after they lived together as man and wife, the voice of Ormazd came not to Brahma; though the angel of Ormazd remained, and at times talked to both Brahma and Yu-tiv, his wife. Now during all the time, until after the birth of the sixth son, Yu-tiv had faith in Ormazd, and was a Faithist in her whole heart. But during all these years she had only communion with the angels, and withal had suffered many hardships in common with Brahma.

7. And their love abated not one jot or tittle, and Yu-tiv believed in her husband, and encouraged his aspirations. He had said to her ten thousand times: I know Ormazd will come; through me will He deliver the Faithists out of bondage.

8. And she believed in him; and believed these things would come to pass, and believed her sons would have the Voice of the Creator with them also. But after the birth of the sixth child, Yu-tiv lost faith in the Father! She said: All my life I have been in error. There is no All Person. There is no Voice, save the spirits of the dead. And they know little more of heaven than we. The Creator is dumb, like the wind; His voice is like the wind, it speaketh nothing.

9. And after that, she ceased to use the name Ormazd, or Father, but said, Eolin, after the

manner of the ancients. And Brahma ceased more to speak in presence of Yu-tiv of the coming of Ormazd to himself; and he also adopted the name Eolin, signifying, like the wind, void of shape or person.

10. Whilst this state of unbelief was upon them, they had another child born to them, and they called his name Hog, signifying, FACT, or without inspiration; an animal that rooteth in the ground.

11. Yu-tiv weaned Hog when he was three years old, and, on the day following, the voice of God came to Brahma, saying: Brahma! Brahma! And Brahma said: Here am I, O Eolin. And the Father said: Be thou faithful another eighteen years! I shall be with thee to the end!

12. Brahma was so delighted, he ran home and told Yu-tiv, but she rejoiced not; she made no answer. Silently she looked upward for a long while, and then she said: Eighteen years! Hog will be twenty-one. And thou and I will be old.

CHAPTER XVI.

1. For eighteen years more God spake not to Brahma, but Brahma remained faithful, and Yu-tiv was full of hope. But when the time was fulfilled in Ormazd's own way, He came with renewed light, which was on the twenty-first birthday of Hog.

2. Whilst Brahma and his family were seated on mats, eating breakfast at sunrise, lo, a light, as of a sun, came within the hut, and passed over Brahma's head, and then disappeared. And out of the void, in the space above their heads, came these words, to wit: From this time forth the twenty-first birthday shall be the time of maturity for man. Be ye watchful for the voice of Ormazd; He is Ever Present!

3. And all of them saw the light and heard the words, save Hog, and Hog, having been begotten in unbelief, neither saw the light nor heard the voice. And when they all had exclaimed: Behold the light! Hear that voice!--Hog thus spake before them:

4. For many a year ye have prophesied this should come to pass when I should reach my twenty-first birthday. For the love ye all bear me, I know ye would not put a joke upon me; but I am seriously grieved that ye say: Behold the light, and hear the voice! For I say unto you, these things are not in reason, and cannot be so. But in much hope and faith and belief, all of which ye have cultivated for years, ye suffer your imaginings to stand for realities.

5. Now whilst Hog thus spake, the light came again and stood over Brahma's head whilst one might count twenty; and the Voice said: Blessed art thou, O Brahma; blessed thou, O Yu-tiv! These things had to be fulfilled. I preach not by reason alone, but provide living examples! (In his old age Brahma had attained iesu!)

6. Again all of them saw and heard the manifestation of Ormazd, save Hog, and he saw not, and heard not what came of the Spirit. Hog said: Have I not eyes good as the best? Show me a hair that I cannot see; let fall a mite that I cannot hear. Then Whe-ish, the first-born, answered him, saying:

7. First, my brother, I greet thee with my love, for thou art the fairest and best of all the great born sons of this God and Goddess, our father and mother. And I appeal to thee in thy great wisdom, how have we all imagined the same light at the same time and place? And greater yet, how have we imagined the same spoken words? Hog replied:

8. How can my answers cope with one who hath wisdom like unto thee, O my brother? Thou hast confounded me; but yet I understand not wherein thou, and ye, my most loving brothers, can see and hear things that I cannot. Have we not all the same parts, so like unto one another that our neighbors scarce distinguish us? And above all, we are all the same fruit from a father and mother, the holiest and wisest of created beings.

9. Now spake Yu-tiv saying: I am before Thy judgment, O Ormazd! That which I have done, I have done! Deal Thou with me for my great unbelief; I have sinned against heaven and earth. Even whilst Thou quickenedst into life within my womb this star of everlasting light, lo, I put out his eyes and stopped up his ears against Thee. The unbelief of my soul penetrated the walls of my womb and shaped the fruit of my holy husband into a man of darkness. O Ormazd, why was Thy daughter born!

10. Hog said: O thou Goddess, mother! Weep not, but rejoice for the glory of my birth. That thou and my holy father, a very God amongst men, brought me into life, my soul is boundless in rejoicing. I declare unto thee, O mother, I am not in darkness, nor am I blind and deaf. If there be another world, what mattereth it to me? The glories of this one are boundless. And if there be a Great Light and a Voice, what are they to me! Thou hast so filled my every vein of blood with thy warm love, and with the sweet love of these, my holy brothers, and with the wisdom of my father, God of men, that I know nothing but to rejoice and to invent praises and thanks to you all, with all my wisdom and strength.

11. And now the Light gathered within the soul of Brahma, and he was as one with the Father. Ormazd, the Creator, then spake through Brahma, saying:

12. I created the earth not to be despised, as do the Zarathustrians through the hearts of monarchs and priests, but that it should be the glory of man. This was the Zarathustrian law, but, for sake of profit, and bondage, and evil, they have perverted My doctrines and bound up My peoples. They profess Me, even Ormazd; but they have turned My commandments and My doctrines upside down.

13. I came through Zarathustra and delivered them that called on Me in faith; and they became My chosen for a season; but they suffered evil to usurp their hearts; they squandered My substance in building temples and providing a superabundance of priests and priestesses. They raised up the sword and spear for me; by blood and death they established kingdoms and called them by My name, Ormazd!

14. The spirit of My Voice they put aside; but the words they retained, and added earthly meaning thereto. Whereby they proclaim darkness for light, and light for darkness. And the poor and distressed that worship Me in truth and spirit have learned to hate the words established. For which reason they are persecuted, and bound, and taxed, and despitefully used.

15. Yea, they that would kill not because of their natural love to Me and My created sons and daughters, they impress into service of war, taking them from their kindred, saying to them: Come away from peace and kill! Be thou a slayer of men; be a soldier of death for the glory of the king.

16. I commanded them, in the olden time, to kill not at all. My words were plain. But the kings commanded the priests to interpret My words round about, whereby war might be justified.

17. I commanded them against taking that which was another's. My words were plain. But the kings commanded the priests to interpret the meaning, so the kings could exact tribute

for their own glory. And so they levy wheresoever and whensoever they will, saying: For the defense of the king and the country!

18. Thus have they perverted My commandments from beginning to end. But I declare unto you, that in My sight, to kill one man, I will hold him accountable who doeth it; and ten times accountable if he kill ten men, and a hundred times for a hundred. They shall not hide death and murder from My sight by the word war.

19. Neither shall they excuse stealing by levying tax for the king or the country's protection. For by their own evil, hath it come to pass that they talk about protection. Have I made a law that one king or one country shall protect itself against another? Seest not any man that these doctrines come of the flesh and not of the spirit?

20. They profess to be Faithists in Me. But straight away they go and build fortifications of earth, and stone, and wood. And they that know Me in spirit and truth, perceiving I am wrongly interpreted for evil's sake, being such as rebel in their souls against these iniquities, they seize and impress for their lifetime as slaves, or, if refusing, they kill them.

21. And they that work such wickedness say: Behold, we have the Zarathustrian law, the I'hua'Mazdian law, the Ormazdian law; ours is the holy, the revealed word. Let no man raise up his voice against these truths, or he shall surely be put to death!

22. But I looked down from My holy heavens and saw, and Mine ears heard; and I cried out in My soul for the evils of the earth. I said: Behold, I will go and deliver them that have faith in Me in spirit and truth. And I went over the lands of the earth, but I found no man in whom My light could shine. And I called My holy masters of generations, My angels high raised in heaven, and I said unto them: Come ye and dwell on the earth many generations, and by inspiration raise ye up one in whom My light shall shine, for I will surely deliver My people.

23. Now I declare unto you who are assembled, the time is at hand, and ye are all so many parts in My work. Even through My angels named ye these sons; according to their names, so will I establish My kingdom.

24. Suffer, therefore, Vede to write down the words I have spoken, for lo, he hath learning and memory provided to that end. Be ye watchful, when I come again!

25. Jehovih (Ormazd) ceased, and Brahma woke as from a trance, though he had heard all that was said. So Vede remembered the spoken words, every one, and he wrote them down on cloth prepared for that purpose. And this was the beginning of a new name of a people on the earth, though they were Faithists in fact, and nothing but Faithists; but they were called by their neighbors sometimes Vedans and sometimes Brahmins.

CHAPTER XVII.

1. The next morning, at sunrise, Jehovih came again, speaking through Brahma, saying:

2. As I prepared a way for My voice, be ye wise in laboring to show this light unto all peoples. Neither take ye sorrow to your souls for the latest born, even Hog; for he is also in My keeping, and his wisdom shall be the glory of the earth.

3. For is not all fact interpreted by each and every man from the light of his own standing place? Wherein error cometh into the world by the darkness of men, in not perceiving rightly the things I have created. Behold, one man seeth the forest with reference to its

value in logs; another for splints for mats; another for shade to lie in; another for its solitude; and they all alike see by what dwelleth in them, but they see through their own several windows.

4. Consider, then, the injustice of man that saith: Ye shall see as I see; hear as I hear; or who saith: This I have proven for a truth, and that for an untruth; or who saith: Behold, we are many witnesses, and we attest.

5. Whilst Jehovih was thus speaking, His angel appeared and stood in the doorway of the hut, and all save Hog looked and saw the angel, and witnessed the color of the angel's hair and eyes, and the clothes he wore. And they pointed, saying in a whisper: Behold, an angel of heaven!

6. Then spake Jehovih, illustrating, saying: Whilst yet no one hath spoken, let one at a time privily describe to Hog the appearance of My angel in the doorway.

7. Accordingly, they all, save Brahma, told Hog all that pertained to the angel, and they accorded one with another. And Jehovih said: Speak thou, My Son, Hog. Hog said:

8. To whom shall I speak? For, be Thou my very father, or, of a truth, the Creator, I know not. God said: Who sayest thou the Creator is? Hog said: Even as the wind; the great void; without person, or shape, or sense.

9. God said unto him: For which reason I say unto thee, because of the unbelief of thy father and thy mother, whilst thou wert in thy mother's womb, thou art as thou art. This have they attested unto thee thousands of times since thou wert weaned. And they have also attested to thee as often, that during the bringing forth of thy brothers, they were in the fullness of faith in Jehovih (Ormazd).

10. Thou wert born of the earth, and can only see with earthly eyes, and hear with earthly ears, and can reason only with earthly reason. Hog said: Then of a truth I shall go down to earth and there shall be no more of me; but these, my sweet brothers, and this Goddess and this God, my very father and mother, shall inherit everlasting life?

11. God said: I would place two eggs before thee, with the birds within them nearly hatched; now with one thou shalt open the shell a little, and the young bird seeth out, but the other thou leavest closed. Sayest thou one bird will have much advantage over the other when they are hatched? Or that one shall not live, because, forsooth, it saw not through the shell? Such, then, is thy way to everlasting life. Of thy darkness will I make light that will reach unto millions. Thy sacrifice is the sacrifice of a very God amongst Gods.

12. Hog said: Because of Thy great wisdom, I fear to speak in thy presence. But thy words come out of his mouth who is the sweetest and holiest of created beings. Therefore I take courage in mine argument.

13. Now, behold, they have all described the angel in the door; alike and like have they described it in all particulars. And the wisdom of thy words goeth to the bottom of things, not like the words of man, but faultlessly. Thou hast made me to behold I am bound as with iron hoops, and must go my way all my days. Against this I complain not; for I perceive it is not within my judgment to know even myself, as to what is good for me or not good for me. This, however, thou hast shown me. I was molded as I am; I am as I am. If I have faults, they are not my faults. Neither are they of my father or my mother; for the cause of their unbelief at that time lay not with themselves, but with thee.

14. God said: Thy words shall Vede also write down; the glory and the wisdom of the

earth shall come out of thy mouth. The manner of my edifice shall be shown unto the inhabitants of the earth. Thou hast seen the king's temple and how he buildeth it. For the fine posts he sendeth his best hewers into the forest, and they choose the straightest and strongest trees, and fall them and hew them, and polish and engrave them, and the posts are set up in the front as strength and ornament. But as to the walls of the temple, the king calleth not the best hewers, but the choppers, and they also go into the forest to fetch logs, not the straightest and handsomest, but whatsoever their axes come upon. And their timbers are put in the walls with mortar and withes. And the temple is completed to the king's will.

15. Jehovih said: Of such like is My heavenly edifice; I send not winter to please one man, nor summer; nor the rain. I consider in what way I shall induce men to raise up one another and to be considerate. Through Me, thy father and thy mother and thy brethren, and all Faithists that come after these, My doctrines, learn to consider the unbelief of mortals, and the impossibility of one man seeing through another man's eyes.

16. For as I have raised you up a house in love, one to another, so will I show the wisdom of disbelief, and its necessity on the earth.

17. The foremost of all lessons is that all men shall have liberty; and no man's judgment be binding on another's; for all do not see alike, nor can they understand alike.

18. That ye shall be alike considerate to them that see not My light, or My Person, even as to them who are born in su'is; for they are of the same flesh and blood, and their spirits have they even from the same Creator.

19. For in the evidence of the past and of the present it is before you, that men endeavor to enforce their doctrines by saying: BEHOLD THE WORD OF ORMAZD! THUS HATH HE SPOKEN! AND I AM HIS PRIEST! BOW DOWN YOUR HEADS!

20. Whereas, man shall not bow down, but hold up his head and rejoice. They that seek to enforce Me are My enemies.

21. Nor have I said of this man or that: Hear ye him, for he is Truth. Shall the Creator make one greater than Himself, and thus cut Himself off? And yet the kings and the priests of this day assume this in Ihua's name. And the mothers and fathers of many have become discouraged because of their great hardships; and they bring forth heirs that have eyes but see not, ears but hear not.

22. God said: In the days of Zarathustra, I came to deliver them that had faith but were in bondage; to-day I am come to prove three worlds unto men, and to teach them how they shall bring forth heirs with eyes to see, and with ears to hear spiritual things, with liberty unto all men.

23. First, of the earth and its fullness; second, the intermediate world of spirits, where all shall sojourn for a season; and, third, the Nirvanian worlds beyond Chinvat, where lieth unending paradise for the pure and wise.

CHAPTER XVIII.

1. On the next morning, at sunrise, God spake again to Brahma, saying:

2. Consider the fruit of the earth, and the pasturage in the fields. The male and the female feed on the same grass; the one yieldeth milk, the other is for the yoke; neither can any man change these creations.

3. What man shall say to another: Feed thou on this; or on that? But they take of them that are born in darkness, and raise up priests! The food for the flesh, or even fasting, cannot bring su'is. The air warmeth the earth, and not the earth the air. The spirit enlighteneth the corporeal part, and not the corporeal part the spirit.

4. Light is the freedom of all; to know this is the beginning of wisdom. Nevertheless, without suffering, some that are bound would not know they are bound, or, if knowing, would not desire freedom.

5. At this time, Hog, the youngest born, was greatly moved, whereupon God bade him speak.

6. Hog said: O that I could believe these things! O that I could see! O that I could hear! O the misery of my darkness! O the horrors of the suspense of not knowing a matter! Bitter is my soul, and full of anguish! O the madness of this hour upon me!

7. Wherein, O Wisdom, forgottest Thou the time of my begetting, to let me spring up as an offensive weed in such a garden of paradise!

8. And he bowed his head and wept; and then spake Yu-tiv, his mother, that brought him forth. She said: I perceive Thy light, O Father, but I cannot bear it. Thou didst unlock my members to bring forth these seven Gods! Never woman on the whole earth brought forth so rich a harvest; but yet my soul is tortured to the very center! O that the light of my soul could be transferred to this God of men! And she also wept.

9. Now spake Sa'it, saying: Next nearest am I to thee, O my sweet brother, Hog. No love lieth so fondly to thee as mine. And as to thee, Yu-tiv, my Goddess mother, thou hast most wisely named me ABUNDANT. For in our love hath Ormazd provided us equal to the highest of Gods. Because I have witnessed that this purest and best of brothers cannot see spiritually, my soul is mellowed toward all the world. Yea, my outstretched arms shall receive the darkest of men, and my soul shall go up in praise of Ormazd forever!

10. Oos spake next; he said: Most wisely am I named SPACE; for it hath pleased Ormazd to show me the breadth of His Creations. What belief or unbelief is there that He hath not provided a glory for it! Because my sweet brother, Hog, has been thus blessed with darkness, he shall be guardian unto me in earthly wisdom all my days. In my faith I know it is well with him; yet in my love I would that he could see as we all see!

11. Then spake Git-un, whose name signified TIME. He said: Behold, I am the fourth born, and, as it were, in the middle. Whose love is so delightfully hedged about as mine! Who so surrounded by the Light of heaven and earth! At one end behold my father, God of men; the very voice of heaven and earth; interpreter of the Creator's words! At the other end, the best, sweetest brother ever created on the earth, with all the wisdom of men and angels. O the glory of this hour! O the delight to be with these Gods, and with Yu-tiv, Goddess of women!

12. Then Vus, the second born, spake. He said: Wherein shall I glorify Thee, O Ormazd, and not glorify myself! I am full to overflowing with delight for the love of these, my brothers, and father, very Gods! But for Yu-tiv I have more than love. I perceive through my own sweet mother how the different castes of men are made! O mother, how nearly a righteous woman dwelleth with the Creator!

13. Whe-ish said: To rank one's thoughts and desires ever high; would not this deliver the world? Vede said: To know the truth and ever speak it in love and kindness, would not this deliver the world and establish Ormazd?

14. Now woke Brahma from his trance, and he spake, saying: To find the Father; to know Him; to reveal Him; these are all, and for His glory only.

15. Now again spake God, saying: Wiser than all the rest is Brahma. Who of ye all hath not spoken of himself or herself? Who hath uttered a word of praise or of thanks, and left out self? Judge ye, then, what is required of men that my spirit may find utterance through their lips.

16. Then the Voice departed for that day; and the angel of God appeared in the door, so all save Hog could see him. The angel said: That ye may see the spirits of the intermediate world, come ye at midnight and sit in the sacred circle in the grove of Ebon. We will appear in sar'gis.

17. Hog heard not the angel, but the others told him what the angel said. Accordingly, at midnight they sat in circle in the grove of Ebon.

CHAPTER XIX.

1. And the angel of God appeared in the midst of the circle, in sar'gis, and talked with them face to face. And Hog said unto the angel: Of a truth, I know thou art not mortal, and yet thou hast the semblance of flesh, and limbs, and arms, and a very body, and art clothed withal, and thy clothes are like mortal clothes.

2. Now I tell thee face to face, I believe thou art no angel of the dead, but a very reflected self-substance, produced out of the substance of my father. How sayest thou? The angel answered, saying:

3. Mortal words cannot convince thee; neither the words of a spirit. Behold, I will show thee a friend of thine who is dead. With that, the angel showed the spirit of Hog's friend who was dead, and the man's name was Aara-acta; and so Hog said unto him:

4. Thou art a very counterpart of him I knew. What is thy name? The spirit answered: Aara-acta! I tell thee, O Hog, these things are true. I am the spirit of thy friend; yea, I am that very friend. Hog said: Where dwellest thou? Where hast thou been? Art thou happy? Hast thou visited all the heavens?

5. The spirit answered him, saying: I dwell on the earth even as before death; around about. I am happy; the glory of my present world surpasseth the earth. I have not visited the highest heavens. I am only as yet in the first resurrection. Up above us there are heavens where all the people are Gods and Goddesses. I cannot go there; they are too white. The spirit then disappeared, and Hog said:

6. What I have seen I have seen; what I have heard I have heard. Yet I believe not that I have seen a spirit nor heard one. A spirit must in reason be thin and subtle and air-like.

7. Then spake the angel of God, saying: How shall I please this man, O Ormazd? This day I showed myself in the door of the hut, thin and subtle and air-like, and he saw me not, nor heard me. Who can find a way to open this man's soul to Thy Wisdom, O Ormazd?

8. Now spake Yu-tiv: Great is the glory of Thy angel, O Ormazd! Heavenly are the spirits of the dead. Welcome, O ye angels of heaven! Then spake Whe-ish, saying: Even the lowest of heavens hath great glory! O the delight to dwell in such a paradise! Then Vus spake, saying: Such wisdom and truth! What are Thy kingdoms, O Father, when even the first heaven hath such glory. Git-un said: Because I have lived to behold these things, I will proclaim Thy wonders, O Ormazd, as long as I live! Vede said: Truth is Thy

mightiest work, O Ormazd! Oos said: How wisely hast Thou framed Thy worlds, O Ormazd! Even Thy lowest of angels are a delight of my soul! Next spake Sa-it; he said: Give us of Thy abundance, O Ormazd. Open wide the gates of the lower heavens. I will take Thy angels to my arms and rejoice forever!

9. Brahma then came out of his trance, though he had heard and seen all. He said: Whoever cometh that can make me better, and show me how most to benefit Thy world, him, O Ormazd, send Thou unto me. And, lo, first of all, Brahma was answered! A light, bright as a sun, stood in the midst of the circle, and it was higher than the clouds, and displayed a staff on which was a banner of gold and silver; and on the banner, stars clustered to spell the words, Love, Wisdom and Power!

10. Presently the scene changed, and the angel of God said: He that spake last (Brahma) hath been answered first, because his words reached to the Fountain Head. Wheresoever ye send your prayers, there are ye answered. To which end I will now open the gates of the lower heavens, and ye shall witness what ye may.

11. The angel withdrew all the lights around about, so that great darkness might be upon the circle. Presently, Yu-tiv started as if affrighted somewhat. Then Vus sprang up, saying: What was that? And then another started, till presently all but Brahma and Hog were wild and startled, whispering: What do mine eyes behold! O that foul smell! O that vulgar touch! And then one screamed; and another, and another, until all broke and fled, screaming and crying out in fear and distress; flying in the darkness of the grove, frantic; almost dead with fear!

12. Hog ran not; saw nothing to fear; heard nothing to dread; felt nothing to make him ashamed.

13. And his father, Brahma, ran not, nor was afraid, and the twain called to the rest, pleaded, coaxed and called in vain; could not stop them; could not find them in the darkness. They returned to the hut, Brahma and Hog; saw the torches burning brightly, and came in and found Yu-tiv and her sons huddled together in each other's arms, white and pale as death.

14. Hog asked the reason. Yu-tiv said: Sh___, are they gone? Sh___, keep them away! Then spake Vus, saying: O my brother, ask not what we saw! Ask not what we felt, and what felt us! These things would not be lawful to mention! Say no more, in heaven's name! The air of heaven is full of demons (druj).

15. Now spake Vede, saying: Alas, O my father, I dropped the holy book, the Veda I am writing. In my fright I let it fall. It is not sized yet, and should it rain ere morning, the holy words will be lost! And not for a thousand worlds would I go back to the grove this night. Oos said: Nor I, for a thousand worlds! Whe-ish said: For all the gold and silver in the world I would not go there this night.

16. So they all spake save Hog, and with all the love they bore for Ormazd's words, nothing doubting they were His very words, not one would venture amongst the evil spirits they had seen, to recover the book.

17. Then spake Brahma, saying: For many generations Ormazd hath labored for this; I will go myself; I know He will protect me at all times and in all places. And Brahma rose up to depart; but then spake Hog, saying: Nay, father; thou art old; I am fresh and young, and withal, know there are no spirits but in the imagination of men. I will go alone!

18. Nor will I bear a lantern nor a torch; nor will I whistle nor sing. I will confront all the

476

evil spirits of hell and their captains. I will recover that book this night though I scrape every leaf from Ebon grove! And mark ye, too, I will return unscathed; nor will I see nor hear a spirit the while I am gone. So, Hog and Brahma only were fearless.

19. With that Hog departed, and after a while he returned, rejoicing, bringing the book; and he said: I neither saw nor heard a spirit, and I declare unto you, that none of you saw nor heard them, for there are none. By the extreme bent of your minds, these imaginings seem real. And as to the great Light, with the words, Love, Wisdom and Power, which I also saw, I say unto you it is some emanation from this, our holy and most loved father. How oft have we heard him use those same words! And as to those figures that talked, and had the semblance of men and women, even to their garments, I say unto you all, they emanate from the same source, even from our father, even Brahma.

20. Now spake Yu-tiv, saying: O happy unbelief, my son! O that I had been born as thou! O that I had never seen such sights as I saw this night!

21. Then said Oos: O happy brother, our youngest born! Would that I were like unto thee! O the vulgarity of those hands that came upon me this night!

22. Vus said: O that I had never known the unseen world! O that I had been born in darkness like unto thee, our most favored brother!

23. After that manner they all spake deploringly of their gift of su'is; and when they had thus spoken, the angel of God spake through Brahma, saying: Whilst it is yet night, I speak. With the dawn, at sunrise, is the Father's Voice. Hear me, then, briefly, expecting not much wisdom, for I am not long born in heaven.

24. Two great men created the Creator, the Faithist and the unbeliever; the one who hath passed through the trials of the flesh, and attained to the Father's Voice; for in becoming one with the Father, he no longer standeth in fear of anything in heaven or earth. The glory of constant resurrection is before him forever.

25. All men who have not attained to this may be likened unto a man going up a slippery hillside, who oft riseth high, but suddenly slideth low. They glorify themselves for their own light and wisdom and good gifts, rejoicing for self-sake for the glories that have fallen upon them. But they are cowards.

26. Nevertheless, the Creator created a great man amongst these; and such is the unbelieving man. He hath neither gold nor silver, nor house nor land; and he is without spiritual sight or spiritual hearing; but his glory is in understanding his own understanding.

27. He it is that subdueth the forest, and tameth the beasts of the field to man's service. He goeth alone in the dark, fearing naught. He followeth not the course of any man, but searcheth for himself; the priest cannot make him believe, nor can the angels of heaven; none can subdue his judgment. He beholdeth the glory of the earth and of manhood. He calleth to the multitude, saying: Why permit ye others, even priests, to think for you? Arise, O thou, and be a man! Arise, O thou, and be a woman!

28. He inspireth of the earth and for the earth; through his arms are tyrants and evil kings overthrown. Through him are doctrines and religions sifted to the bottom, and the falsehood and evil in them cast aside. Yea, who but Ormazd could have created so great a man as the unbeliever?

29. And these two men, the Faithist and the unbeliever, do mostly all the good that is done in the world; the one laboreth at the top of the hill, calling upward; the other

laboreth at the bottom of the hill, pushing upward.

CHAPTER XX.

1. On the next morning, at sunrise, Ormazd spake again through Brahma, and Vede wrote down the words; and on the succeeding morning, in like manner; and so continued for forty days; and in forty days, behold, the Veda was completed; the holy words of Brahma were written.

2. God said to Brahma: Go now, and preach my gospel unto whosoever will hear; proclaiming liberty to all who will follow thee. I will be with thee to the end. And thou shalt take Yu-tiv, thy wife, and all thy sons with thee, even Hog, the youngest born.

3. So Brahma went forth preaching by day, and exhibiting the spirits of the dead by night. But to the chosen he spake at dawn, in the early morning, the time the All Light was upon him. And his sons also preached and explained; and Yu-tiv explained to all women how it was with her when pregnant with her sons. Only Hog preached not; neither opened he his mouth before the populace as to his unbelief. In his soul he said: These things may be true, and if they be true, it is well. If they be not true, still the believing of them, by the populace, worketh righteousness and goodness. With all my philosophy, I cannot move the multitude to righteousness. But my father maketh them as a flock of sheep; they cease from evil, and they practice good fellowship. Therefore, I will stand by my father to the end.

4. When Brahma came near a city, he halted outside the walls, that according to law the kings could not stay his voice. And the multitude came out of the city to hear him, and many returned not; but remained with Brahma and his sons in their camp. And when Brahma moved to another city they went with him. And in a little while the hosts of Brahma were as an army of thousands.

5. And not a few of them were men and women of wealth, and they cast their treasures at Brahma's feet, saying: Take thou this trash, and give me of everlasting life instead. But men of learning came not to Brahma; neither came the priests, nor kings, nor magicians, nor consulters of oracles.

6. God said: Take thy hosts and establish them in families of tens, and of twenties, and of hundreds, and of thousands, and give thou a head father unto each and every family. And thy people shall be a people unto themselves, having nothing in common with the kings' peoples.

7. Behold, my angel will go with thee, and show the waste lands, such as the kings' peoples desire not; and thou and thy people shall possess the lands and dwell together in love and wisdom, doing good to one another.

8. So Brahma did as commanded, and he established the mountains of Roam, and the valleys in the mountains of Roam, and his people dwelt there, in all six thousand eight hundred and twenty, men, women and children.

9. And there came to Brahma a certain captain-general of the army of King Syaythaha, of the West Kingdom of Vind'yu, wherein lay the city of Gowsehamgamrammus, of a million inhabitants, and he said unto Brahma:

10. In the name of the king, mightiest of men, Syaythaha, am I before thee, O Brahma. Behold, the king sendeth thee gold, silver and copper, saying: Brahma is good! Brahma

shall give me the blessing of heaven!

11. Brahma answered the captain-general, saying: Brahma saluteth the king, mightiest of men, Syaythaha, in the name of Ormazd, the Creator, in love and in these wise words, that come to the soul of Brahma. Brahma sendeth the king's servant, even the captain-general, back to the king, with his gold, silver and copper, saying: Deal thou with thy Creator and not with men! The Great Spirit holdeth all blessings in His own hands. Give him thy treasures!

12. The captain-general departed and returned with his gold, silver and copper to the king, and told the king Brahma's words. The king was pleased with the wisdom of Brahma, but withal felt rebuked and sore at heart. So Ormazd suffered satan to possess the king for a season; and the king resolved to destroy Brahma and all his people. And he commanded the captain-general to assemble together fifty thousand men, with arms, ready for battle. And when they were thus prepared, and started on their journey, which would require seven days, the king bethought him to inquire of the oracle as to his best mode of success.

13. Now the angel of God had taken possession of the oracle, and yet the magi knew it not, nor did Syaythaha. So the king came before the sand table, and the spirit wrote these words: He who hath become one with Ormazd is mightier than an army. Take off thy crown, O king, mightiest of men, and thy golden robes, and all that is fine and fair to look upon, and clothe thyself in the poorest of garments, even as a druk that wandereth about. But thy crown and thy costly robes, and thy raiment, fine and fair to look upon, put upon thy body servant. And ye twain shall go in advance of the army, even before Brahma.

14. And thou shalt witness that man who professeth to labor for the poor will fall on his belly before the man of riches and power. And behold, O king, thou shalt feel justified in destroying him that falleth before the crown and robes, knowing he is a hypocrite.

15. The king was pleased with this, and he fulfilled all that was commanded of the oracle; and when he came near Brahma's camp, a man came before the king's servant, saying: Behold, O king, command me as thou wilt! And he prostrated himself on the ground before the king's servant. Whereupon the king, dressed as a druk, came to him and said: Who art thou? And the man answered: Begone, beggar! My matter is with the king! (For he mistook which was which.)

16. The king ordered the man to be seized and taken away and put to death; and the advance guard fell upon the man and slew him with war clubs. And when the man was quite dead, behold, Brahma came, and the king, nor none of his advance guard, knew him. And Vus and Whe-ish were with their father, and the three came and stood by the dead man. Brahma then took the king's hand, saying: Thou that art in the garb of a druk come hither, for thou hast flesh and blood unto holiness. Lay thou one hand on on the dead man; put thine other hand on my head, for I will prove Ormazd before thine eyes. Behold, thou who hast tried to kill Brahma, killed another person!

17. And when the king's hands were placed, Brahma stood by the head of the dead man, and his two sons by the heart; and Brahma said: In Thy name, O Ormazd, and by Thy power in me, return thou to life, O man! And arise! Arise! Arise!

18. And behold, the man was brought to life, and rose up and stood before the multitude.

19. The king trembled with fear, and the guard stood aback, amazed. And, as for the servant arrayed in the king's garb, he cast aside the crown and robes, and fled into the forest.

20. Brahma said unto the king: Here standeth the angel of Ormazd, and the angel saith thou art the king in disguise, and, moreover, that he, the angel, commandeth thee here for this purpose, saying to thee in the oracle: He that hath become one with Ormazd is mightier than an army!

21. The king said: This is true. I swear before Thee, O Ormazd, henceforth I will wear such garments as these I have on, and my life shall be given to Thy service. Let who will, take my kingdom and all I called mine.

22. So Syaythaha joined Brahma's hosts; and with Syaythaha came his brothers and their sons and daughters. And, those that came, cast into a heap, whatsoever goods or moneys they had, and the head fathers of the families divided and distributed the same according to their best wisdom. And Brahma's people, by commandment of Brahma, called themselves not Brahmins, but Vedans; that is, Truth-followers.

23. In those days the language of the kings of Vind'yu, and of men of learning, was All-ao, signifying, Out of all that is good. But the Vedans were the unlearned, and their language was imperfect, and of many meanings for every spoken and written word.

24. And God foresaw the liability to corruption of the Brahmin religion, and he spake to Brahma, saying: Behold, I have given thee seven sons, six of light and one of darkness. Thy six sons of light shall establish each one a school amongst my chosen, and teach my scriptures by word of mouth. And all that henceforth become rab'bahs shall be capable of repeating every word of the Veda by heart. And, in after ages, if the plates and the books of my holy religion are destroyed by war, it mattereth not. The substance of thy labors shall live.

25. Then did Brahma's sons as commanded, each and every one becoming a teacher. And again God spake to Brahma, saying: Arise, and go where my angel will lead thee, taking thy wife and thy son, Hog, with thee. And thou shalt travel yet two years from place to place, and then return thither, for thy labor will be completed.

CHAPTER XXI.

1. The place thus founded by Brahma was called Haraoyo, and his people, at this time, extended in seven cities and thirty villages, and possessed all the country of Roam, which had been uninhabited hundreds of years. And the Vedans cultivated the lands, living on fruits, roots, and on bread made of wheat grown in the fields; but they ate neither fish nor flesh, nor anything that had breathed the breath of life.

2. Brahma and his wife, Yu-tiv, and his youngest son, Hog, departed from Haraoyo, accompanied by seven disciples, and went forth under the direction of the angels of Ormazd, to preach and explain the Veda, carrying one book with them. And they went first to the north-east, through the kingdoms of Haomsut, and Ali-oud, and Zeth, and Wowtichiri; thence westerly to Hatiqactra, where the tyrant, Azhi-Aven, had built a temple of skulls, after the manner of the ancients. Azhi kept six dens of lions, for devouring his condemned slaves. So, because of oppression, the kingdom of Azhi was profitable unto Ormazd. From Hatiqactra Brahma obtained three thousand followers.

3. And when Brahma had seven thousand followers, the angel of God directed him to the plains of Cpenta-armaiti. And here he established his people, dividing them into families and villages, and appointing priests unto them. And Cpenta-armaiti became known over

all the world from that time after.

4. After this the angel directed Brahma to go to the south-west, through the kingdoms of H'spor and Vaetaeyo, and Aramya, and thence to Dacyama, to the city of H'trysti, where Ormazd had a host of one thousand already inspired to join Brahma.

5. And now the angel directed Brahma to take his hosts to the mountains of T'cararativirwoh, and establish them; the which he did. And behold, the time of Yu-tiv and of Brahma was near an end, for they were grown quite old.

6. The angel said to Brahma: Great hath been thy labor. Very great Yu-tiv's! Where in all the world is such a woman? From the day thou first beheld her! For the glory of thy sons! And in her age to follow thee, walking so far!

7. Behold, O Brahma! Yu-tiv is weakening fast. Rise up and take her back to Haraoyo! The mountains of Roam are calling her! And thy faithful son, Hog, strong and tall. Take him back with his mother. Haraoyo is calling.

8. Brahma went and looked at Yu-tiv; and his soul spake within him, saying: O Ormazd, have I not forgotten her, in Thee! The mother of my Gods! O her proud young soul when first I saw her! Alas, I see, she is tottering and feeble!

9. Brahma went nearer to Yu-tiv, and she spake to him, saying: O Brahma, thou God of men! I know not if my eyes are turning dim. But O, I have had so strange a sight, even toward the high sun. It was myself I saw, rising, going upward! The earth going downward! Then I called: O Ormazd! Not alone! Behold, my God is yonder! Let me back to Brahma! Then I thought the Creator brought me back and said: Go thou quickly and see thy godly sons in Haraoyo, for thy time hath come!

10. Brahma said: My angel saith: Go thou back to Haraoyo, thy labor is nearly finished. For this reason I came to thee. It is well, therefore, for us that we return, taking Hog with us.

11. So Brahma, and Yu-tiv, and Hog, with five remaining disciples, departed for Haraoyo, which lay three days' journey for a man to walk, and they knew not how Yu-tiv would go, for she was worn to the last step, and, above all, her shoes were worn out, and she had only pieces of cloth to her feet.

12. And whilst they were deliberating, having only gone a short distance, Hog perceived, going in another direction, a score of soldiers, mounted on horses, and they were leading a number of spare horses with them. Then the soul of Hog spake within him, spake to himself, saying:

13. Behold, my father hath made many converts in his day, made good men out of bad ones. And he hath ever refused money, and gifts, and presents. Now, wherever justice liveth I know not; but many of the rascals who became followers of my father were conscience-stricken with ill-gotten gains, and, finding that my father would not receive their stuff, they tried me, and behold, my pockets are full of gold and diamonds. In truth, it may have been a very devil prompted me; but I am supposed not to know the higher light but to know the lower. Of myself and for myself I want not these things. If they belong to Ormazd, it followeth I should not keep them. Therefore, if I give of gold or diamonds to those soldiers, they will give me a horse for my angel mother to ride on. Who knoweth but by the way of those soldiers is the nearest road for this gold to find its way to Ormazd?

14. So Hog went away and purchased a horse, and brought it to his mother, saying:

Behold, a man hath given thee a present in the name of Ormazd, but forbiddeth thee to retain it save to ride to Haraoyo, whither thou shalt sell it and give the money to the poor.

15. Yu-tiv said: A good man he was, and wise, for only on his own conditions could I have accepted the horse. Accordingly, Yu-tiv was mounted on the horse, and they proceeded on their way, going slowly, for Brahma was also near the end. And after seven days they arrived at Haraoyo, where they were received by Brahma's sons, and by all the multitude of disciples.

16. But owing to Yu-tiv's deep love for her sons, and being worn out withal, and having witnessed the glory of righteous works fulfilled through her husband and her sons, the strain was too much for her corporeal parts. And they brought straw and stretched her along, and a bundle of straw under her head. Then she spake, saying:

17. First to thee, O Ormazd, my blessing, because Thou createdst me alive, to enjoy Thy glories. Next, O Brahma! My husband, my blessing on thee, God of men! Thou hast taught me the fullness of earth and heaven! O the glory of having been thy wife!

18. Then she called Whe-ish and said: O my son, my first born! My blessing on thee. Because I have watched thee from the hour of conception, I have had the wisdom of creation demonstrated before me. O the joy when first mine eyes beheld thee; I am going now, to prepare a place in heaven for thee!

19. And, after that, Yu-tiv blessed all her sons, and coming to Hog she said: My blessing on thee, O my latest born, God of men! To all my other sons I have told my love, but to thee my soul so overfloweth, I am as a dumb woman. Thou hast been a very God in all thy ways, and believest not in Ormazd; nor in heaven nor angels! For which reason I look upon thee as the highest of all creations. Thou art good for goodness' sake; wise for wisdom's sake; happy in finding a way to master all unhappiness!

20. And these were Yu-tiv's last words; she shut her eyes. She was dead! So they took her body, and robed it in white, and buried her in the forest of Roam.

CHAPTER XXII.

1. On the day of Yu-tiv's death, Brahma said: Sing no songs; pray in silence only. Let her soul be in quiet with Ormazd.

2. On the second day Brahma said: Pray in whispers; praise in whispers, the best, good deeds of the dead.

3. On the third day Brahma said: Burst forth a song of praise to Ormazd; extol the virtues of the dead.

4. On the fourth day Brahma said: In song and in prayer bid the dead arise and go onward, upward!

5. Thus they put Yu-tiv in the ground on the fourth day; and then they went and sat in the sacred circle and sang and prayed for her soul to go on to Nirvana (paradise). And when they had finished, a light came down in the midst of the circle, and an angel in white appeared. It was Yu-tiv; the soul of Yu-tiv in the glory of Ormazd, the Creator!

6. Then spake the angel Yu-tiv, saying: Out from the head of the corporeal body the spirit is born; and angels stand around; on a spirit blanket receive they the spirit of the dead. One day, in quiet, they keep the spirit, teaching it to reconcile and understand. On the second day, the spirit heareth the prayers of the earth-people coming upward; and on the

third day, the spirit understandeth death and birth of spirit.

7. And on the fourth day, when ye sang: O Goddess, arise from the dead! The Father calleth thee from on high! Arise, O Goddess, and go thy way! Then was my spirit free from the earth; resting in the arms of Gods and Goddesses, who had come from on high to receive me. Thus, O my beloved, on the third day is the first resurrection; and to the holy, the second resurrection beginneth on the fifth day. After the fifth day call ye me not back again! My labor lieth yonder! I must build houses for you all. Thus Ormazd sendeth me on before! If it be his will for me to return to you at times, I will return. His will above all; this is the greatest wisdom.

8. Whe-ish, her first-born, asked: What of the angels of the intermediate world, O mother? Then answered his angel mother, saying: They were shown to us in Ebon grove! Alas, some of them do not begin the resurrection for a thousand years!

9. Then came the angel Yu-tiv over, near Hog, her latest born, whom she loved so well. She said: Canst thou see me, my son? Hog answered: Nay, I see only a glimmering light faintly; I hear a voice, but it soundeth not like my mother's voice. Yet, if it be that there is a soul that liveth after death, and if of a truth, thou art the very spirit and soul of her who brought me forth, be thou not unhappy because of my unbelief. As for myself, I am happy because thou broughtst me forth in unbelief; neither would I of my own will be any other way. Whether our eyes be blue or black, or whether we are tall or short, or whether we are believers or disbelievers, even as we are created, and to fill our place in doing good unto others with all our wisdom and strength, is this not glory enough?

10. Yu-tiv said: O thou wisest of men! In the day thou art born in heaven, thou shalt not linger long in the intermediate world, but be crowned a very God indeed! Here endeth my labors with the earth, O ye, my beloved. An otevan waiteth by the way for me to ascend; the Gods and Goddesses are calling me! Farewell, my beloved! Farewell!

11. And now the music of heaven descended, and even whilst the mortals sang, the very gates of heaven opened, and the angel Yu-tiv rose upward in a sea of fire!

12. But behold, the love of great Brahma was too much for him! His eyes raised upward after the ascending light, and his soul burst within him. He fell down and stretched himself on the cold earth! He, too, was dead.

13. Then burst the mighty hearts of Brahma's sons. The whole earth shook with the wail of Gods. The wind, the air above the earth, stood still, and the forest of Roam shuddered as if the earth were bent in twain. Then wailed the sons and daughters of Haraoyo. Though no man uttered it, yet all knew that great Brahma was dead.

CHAPTER XXIII.

1. The angel of God came in the sacred circle and stood in the midst. He said: Greeting, in the name of Ormazd! In His name I speak before you. First, then, who of all that was dearest to Brahma, he or she, shall arise!

2. And lo and behold, there arose every man, woman and child, more than ten thousand. The angel said: By the side of Yu-tiv shall ye, his most beloved, bury his body. On the third day after his death, even at the hour of his death, shall ye bury him. And around about the grave shall ye sit thrice a day, morning, noon and night, for one hour, singing and praying for the soul of Brahma, for two days.

3. And behold, on the evening of the second day ye shall behold the graves of both Brahma and Yu-tiv opened, and their very bodies will come forth, and Brahma shall speak with you face to face. The angel then disappeared.

4. And the people did as commanded; and they sat watching around the graves in a circle, at a distance of ten paces therefrom. And the brothers favored Hog above all the rest, that he might be converted. And it came to pass, when the sun had been two hours set, there descended into the midst of the circle a light, bright as the sun, so that the multitude held their hands before their eyes; and so bright was the light that even the graves could not be seen, and the graves were burst open.

5. And in the space of a moment of time, the light was lowered, so all could look therein; and, lo and behold, Brahma and Yu-tiv, arm in arm, stood in the midst of the circle, even with their flesh and bones and their burial robes.

6. Brahma said: Have ye faith in the Creator; with Him are all things possible. He is the All Master of all things. Accept ye not, forever, any God, or Lord, or Savior, or priest, or king, but Him, the everlasting All One, the Person.

7. Practicing good works unto all men; abjuring self in all things; and Ormazd will dwell with you and in you forever.

8. Then Brahma and Yu-tiv came near Hog, that he might see clearly. Hog said: Art thou truly Brahma, my father; and thou, too, Yu-tiv, my mother? Yu-tiv spake not, but Brahma said: I am thy father, even Brahma. To practice the highest light a man hath; that is all that is required of any man.

9. Hog said: Of a truth it is my father! Of a truth it is my mother!

10. Brahma said: We are blessed! This is the first belief; to believe in the spirit surviving the corporeal body; the second belief is to learn the All Person. After this cometh faith.

11. Hog said: Thou hast proved the first; but as to the All Person, I cannot understand.

12. Brahma said: As I and thy mother have revealed ourselves to thee, and so proven ourselves, so in due season will Ormazd reveal Himself unto thee.

13. And these were the end. Brahma and Yu-tiv rose up in the sea of fire, smiling and waving their hands in love to those beneath, higher and higher, till they disappeared in the sky.

14. Then went the people, and witnessed that the graves were open and the bodies gone. They filled up the places, and set a post inscribed: TOMB OF BRAHMA AND YU-TIV, GOD AND GODDESS.

END OF THE HISTORY OF BRAHMA.

CHAPTER XXIV.

THE FIRST BIBLE OF GUATAMA (AMERICA).-- BEING OF EAWAHTAH, A MAN CHOSEN BY GOD FOR THE CHILDREN OF GUATAMA.

1. In Guatama, in the Middle Kingdom, by the sea of So-ci-a-pan, came down from heaven, Gitchee, the Creator, the World-Maker, Manito! With silence, speaking in the soul of things. He said: Speak, O earth! Have eyes, O earth! Have ears, O earth! Behold Me, your Maker!

2. The earth answered him, not with words, boasting, but raised up man!

3. Man said: Here am I, O Gitchee! The Creator looked, and lo and behold, the I'hins of Guatama stood before Him, the little people, white and yellow. Gitchee (God) said: Because thou hast answered Me in faith, O earth, thy ong-wee (talking animals) shall be called I'hin. Thus was named the first talkers; men with mouths for words; ears for words.

4. Then Gitchee (God) called the I'hins together, and said they were good; even the handsomest of all created creations. And He commanded them to marry, male and female, and beget heirs.

5. And they obeyed God's commands; but the dumb earth cast clouds upward, and blinded the ways of the I'hins, and they strayed away from the mounds, and came to black druks, which speak not; have no words; being dumb like the black mud of the earth where they burrowed.

6. In the darkness of the earth the I'hins mingled with the druks, and lo and behold, a second born speaking animal (ong'wee, or Indian) stood upon the earth, tall, and red, and strong, swift and handsome. Gitchee (God) said:

7. I blame thee not, O I'hin! I saw the darkness; saw thy straits! But never more shalt thou dwell with druks, nor with the new red-born, those with faces like new copper. Call them I'hua; for they shall be protectors over My chosen, the I'hins, forever. The I'hua shall drive away the baugh and mieu and great serpents, and all man-slaying beasts; for I will make mighty nations out of the seed of the I'huans.

8. The first I'huan's name was O-e-du, and his wife's name was Uh-na; and they begat Owena and Dan and Shu-sa, but they had no more heirs. At a time soon after, the second man, whose name was Ka-Ka-och and whose wife's name was Wees, begat Somma, and Pan-ah, and Kac-ak, and Ku-bak, and Jessom.

9. And these were the first tribes of I'huans in the land of Guatama (after the flood), and they dwelt together, marrying and begetting offspring, dwelling in peace. And the I'hins taught them in all things, so they became an honor on the earth and a glory unto the Creator; but they were mixed so together that one tribe had no preference over another. So, by commandment of God, they were called the tribe of Oedukakaooh, of the middle kingdom, Waneopanganosah (Central America).

10. In the valley of Owak, by the river Ho-e-jon-wan, Gitchee (Jehovih) created another tribe called Bak-Haw-ugh, and to the north of them, in the mountains Mein-how-an-go-to-bah; and their tribes commingled, and Gitchee (God) named them, Bakhawugh-meiuhowangotobah.

11. Jesson, son of Rakaooh, married Wepon, daughter of Bakhawughmeiuhowangotobah, and they begat Sto-gil-bak, and he begat Kom, and he begat See, and she married Ban, son of the tribe Rakaooh, and Ban's first-born son's name was La-ban-a-see.

12. And Labanasee was born in su'is of the second order, and could hear the voice of the Creator, Gitchee, the Great Spirit. And the Voice remained with Labanasee during his life-time, which was one hundred and twenty and five years, when he died. And the Voice descended to Labanasee's son, Hootlabanasee, who lived one hundred and one years, and he died, and the Voice descended to his son, Hatapanagooshhootlabanasee; and thence to his son after him, named Arapanseekasoodativhatapanagooshhootlabanasee.

13. Thus were represented the eighteen tribes of Gitchee's chosen amongst the I'huans who should become everlasting heirs to the Voice.

14. And God said unto Ara: Arise and go forth; my hand will steer thee. So Ara rose up

and departed by the hand of the Creator, and came to the valley of Owg, broad and sweet-smelling, full of health-giving food and air and water. And there came with Ara into Owg one thousand men, women and children; and they built a city and called it Eftspan, signifying place of beauty.

15. And these took the name of the tribe of Ara, the which name survived one thousand seven hundred and fifty years. And their people were tens of thousands.

16. After the tribe of Ara lost the Voice, there was raised up Sho-shone, of the tribes of Sto-gil-bak. And Gitchee raised His hand before Sho-shone and pointed the way, and Sho-shone departed out of the country of Tabachoozehbakkankan and came to Owg, and took to wife Hisam, daughter of Ooeguffanauha, and they begat E-a-ron-a-ki-mutz, a son of great beauty and strength, a swift runner.

17. And the voice of Gitcheemonihtee (Son of Jehovih) came to Earonakimutz and remained with him during his natural lifetime, which was ninety years. And to his son, Fassawanhootaganganearonakimutz, and thence to his son, Monagoamyazazhufassa-wanhootaganganearonakimutz.

18. And Monag inhabited the regions of the plains of Yiteatuazow (Arkansas), and his people became mighty in cities and agriculture. For four thousand years the Voice of the All Father remained with the regular succession of the heirs of Monag, but their names and their cities' names became so long that no man could speak them or write them.

19. So Gitchee (Jehovih) raised up Honga, son of Ab, of the tribe of Oedu, of the land of the Middle Kingdom. And Honga went into the mountains of Ghiee (Rocky or Eagle Mountains), sloping to the east.

20. Gitchee (God) spake to Honga, saying: Thou shalt take Oebe for thy wife; out of thy seed will I raise up a greater tribe than all other tribes; and thy first-born son shall have thy name; and thy son's son shall be called Honga also; and thy son's son's son, and so on forever. For I am wearied with the burden of names; thy Great Creator hath spoken.

21. Then asked Honga, saying: What if I have no son, but only daughters? Or of my son or my son's son, they cease to have a son, but only daughters?

22. Then spake Gitchee, saying: The wife's first daughter. So it came to pass, in course of time, Honga married and begat heirs; and the Voice of the Great Spirit remained with the tribes of Honga, and it came to pass that he who heard the Voice, who was always the chief high prophet for the tribe, was called Hoanga; but the peoples themselves were called ong'wee, the same that hath endured to this day, and is called Indian.

23. And the generations of Honga were called, --first, Honga; second, Honga; third, Honga; and so on. And this was the beginning of the counting of time in Guatama. Neither knew any man the number of generations before the time of Honga the first.

24. And the land became full of cities, from the east to the west, and from the north to the south, and the people dwelt in peace, tribe with tribe, the world over. Then came the God of evil, I'tura (Ahura), sowing evil in the temples and on the altars. Yea, with a false tongue and cunning came he, before the prophets, stealing their eyes away, stealing their ears away, holding up his hand, saying: It is the Great Spirit's hand.

25. And I'tura obsessed the nations and tribes of men to worship him; infatuating them with the stories of far-off countries, and the glory of kings and queens. And he set on foot a war of plunder; brought ten thousand times ten thousand evil spirits to aid and abet mortals in war.

26. And I'tura, the God of evil, taught mortals to flatten the head, to make prophets, and, lo and behold, the land of Guatama became a land of seers and prophets and conjurers, seeking evil for sake of evil; consulting the spirits of the dead for war and for earthly glory in blood and death.

CHAPTER XXV.

1. These, then, were the principal kings of that day: Lanoughl, king of Eboostakagan, a city of tens of thousands, in the valley of Aragaiyistan. Lanoughl was the son of Toogaoogahaha, who was the son of Eviphraiganakukuwonpan, who was the son of Oyoyughstuhaipawehaha, who built the canal (oseowa) of Papaeunugheutowa, which extended from the sea of Hoola'hoola'pan (Lake Superior) to the plains of Aigonquehanelachahoba (Texas), near the sea of Sociapan, where dwelt Heothahoga, king of kings, whose temple was roofed with copper and silver. Of ten thousand boats (canoes) was the canal, extending along, carrying copper and silver from the north regions to the cities of the valley of Hapembapanpan, and to the cities of the mountains of Oaramgallachacha, and to Ghiee, home of Honga the first, the mightiest of red men.
2. Next in power to Lanoughl was Tee-see-gam-ba-o-rakaxax, king of the city of Chusanimbapan, in the plains of Erezehoegammas (Central America), with twelve tributary cities extending along the river Akaistaazachahaustomakmak, to the mountains of Nefsaidawowotchachaeengamma.
3. And the third king in power was Chiawassaibakanaizhoo, of the city of Inuistahahaha-cromcromahoesuthaha, and to him were tributary seven and twenty cities and their kings.
4. Chiawassaibakanalszhoo was the son of TenehamgameralhuchsukzhaistoMaipow-wassaa, who was son of Thusaiganganenosatamakka, who built the great east canal, the Oseowagallaxacola, in the rich valley of Tiedaswonoghassie, and through the land of Seganeogalgalyaluciahomaahomhom, where dwelt the large men and women, the Ongewahapackaka-ganganecolabazkoaxax.
5. The fourth great king of Guatama was Hoogalomarakkadanapanwowwow, king of the city of Itussakegollahamganseocolabah, which had seventeen tributary cities of tens of thousands of people. And his kingdom extended from sea to sea in the Middle Kingdom (Panama). Here was the temple of Giloff, with a thousand columns of polished mahogany, and with a dome of copper and silver. And within Giloff dwelt the Osheowena, the oracle of the Creator, for two thousand years.
6. The fifth great king was Penambatta, king of the city of Liscararzakyatasagangan, on the High Heogula Ophat (Tennessee), with thirty tributary cities of tens of thousands of inhabitants. Here was situate the school and college of great learning, the Ahazahohoputan, where were taught tens of thousands of students. Penambatta was learned, and had traveled far, devoting his life to imparting knowledge. He had six thousand attendants, besides six hundred and forty officers.
7. The sixth great king was Hoajab, son of Teutsangtusicgammooghsapanpan, founder of the kilns of Wooboohakhak. Hoajab's capital city was Farejonkahomah, with thirty-three tributary cities, of tens of thousands of inhabitants, of the plains of He'gow (South-eastern Ohio).
8. The seventh great king was Hiroughskahogamsoghtabakbak, and his capital city was

Hoesughsoosiamcholabengancobanzhohahhah, situate in the plains of Messogowan-choola, and extending eastward to the mountains of Gonzhoowassicmachababdohuy-apiasondrythoajaj, including the valleys of the river Onepagassathalalanganchoochoo, even to the sea, Poerthawowitcheothunacalclachaxzhloschistacombia (Lake Erie). Hiro had forty and seven tributary cities of tens of thousands of inhabitants.

9. Betwixt the great kings and their great capitals were a thousand canals, crossing the country in every way, from east to west and from north to south, so that the seas of the north were connected with the seas of the south. In kanoos the people traveled and carried the productions of the land in every way. Besides the canals mentioned, there were seven other great canals, named after the kings who built them, and they extended across the plains in many directions, but chiefly east and west.

10. These were: Oosgaloomaigovolobanazhooegollopan, and Halagazhapanpanegoochoo, and Fillioistagovonchobiassoso, and Anetiabolalachooesanggomacoalobonbakkak, and Ehabadangonzhooeportalicha-boggasa-megitcheepapa, and Onepapollagassayamganshun-iatedoegonachoogangitiavatoosomchooibalgadgad, and Hachooaolagobwotchachabakar-axexganhammazhooelapanpan.

11. In those days the kings and learned men put their hearts to work building canals and finding places and roadways for them, and herein laid the great glory and honor of man at that time.

12. And God (Gitchee) perceiving the virtue and wisdom of men, sent His angels to teach man the mystery of canal-making; to teach man to compound clay with lime and sand, to hold water; to teach man to find the gau, the level, and the force of water. The angels also taught man to make pots and kettles; to burn the clay in suitable shape; to find copper ore and silver ore, and gold and lead for the floors of the oracle chambers, clean and white shining, suitable for angels.

13. And they taught man how to soften copper like dough; how to harden copper like flint rock, for axes and mattocks for building canals; taught man how to work the ore in the fire and melt it; and how to make lead into sheets, like cloth.

14. Taught man to till the soil and grow wheat and corn; taught the women how to grind it and make bread. Taught the hunters how to slay the lion and the tiger and the mastodon, the HOGAWATHA, THE ROOTING ANIMAL OF WISDOM.

15. Besides all these inhabited regions there lay another country to the far west, fifty days' journey, the land of Goeshallobok, a place of sand and salt, and hot, boiling waters. And this region was a twenty days' journey broad, east and west, and fifty days' journey broad, north and south.

16. In the High North lay the kingdom of Olegalla, the land of giants, the place of yellow rocks and high spouting waters. Olegalla it was who gave away his kingdom, the great city of Powafuchawowitchahavagganeabba, with the four and twenty tributary cities spread along the valley of Anemoosagoochakakfuela; gave his kingdom to his queen Minneganewashaka, with the yellow hair, long, hanging down. And the queen built temples, two hundred and seventy, and two adjacent to the spouting waters, where her people went every morning at sunrise, singing praise to Gitchee, Monihtee, the Creator.

17. South of Olegalla lay the kingdom of Onewagga, around about the sea of Chusamangaobe hassahgana-wowitchee, in the valley of Mauegobah, which is to say, CONSECRATED PLACE OF THE VOICE, a kingdom of forty cities. Here reigned for twenty

generations the line of kings called Wineohgushagusha, most holy and wise, full of manliness and strong limbed. On the eastward of the lake lay the Woohootaughnee, the ground of games and tournaments, where came tens of thousands every autumn to exhibit their strength, carrying horses and oxen, and running and leaping, running races with the trained aegamma. And to the strongest and the swiftest, the king gave prizes of handsome damsels, with straight limbs and shapely necks, proud, who loved to be awarded handsome, mighty husbands.

18. Next south lay the kingdom of Himallawowoaganapapa, rich in legends of the people who lived here before the flood; a kingdom of seventy cities and six great canals coursing east and west, and north and south, from the Ghiee Mountain, in the east, to the west mountain, the Yublahahcolaesavaganawakka, the place of the king of bears, the Eeughohabakax (grizzly). And to the south, to the Middle Kingdom, on the deserts of Geobiathaganeganewohwoh, where the rivers empty not into the sea, but sink in the sand, the Sonagallakaxax, creating prickly Thuazhoogallakhoomma, shaped like a pear.

CHAPTER XXVI.

1. I'tura, God of evil, dweller in hell, looked over the broad earth; saw the land of Guatama, the mighty races of I'huans. And his mouth watered, like a lion's when a lamb standeth before him. I'tura called his legions, tens of thousands of drujas, devils from the regions of hell: Come, he said, I have found a rich feeding place. Behold, I will make my kingdoms wider; spread out the walls of hell and gather in this great harvest of innocent souls.

2. Then came I'tura's hosts of evil, ten times tens of thousands, for such is the nature of spirits and men; call for ten thousand to do a righteous work, and only a hundred come; call for ten thousand to do an unholy work, and behold, ten times ten thousand come. They said to I'tura:

3. How shall we do? Where strike in? And I'tura, wise in wickedness, said: Go to the temples, the places of shining copper and silver, to the oracles, and obsess them, every one. And when the kings and the learned men come to consult Gitchee, my deadly enemy, assume ye to be Him, and answer them with lies and all manner of unprofitable speculation; turn them upside down; make them curse Gitchee; make them ask for I'tura. And when madness cometh on them, follow ye them to their sleeping couches and whisper in their souls that their neighbors are their deadly enemies. Incite them to war and to all manner of deeds of death; and when they overturn each other's kingdoms and houses, and their dead lie like ashes over all the land, gather ye in their distracted spirits to fill my mighty kingdom with Gitchee's harvest!

4. Then answered the hosts of I'tura (who was known in heaven as Ahura): Most mighty God, what are thy prizes, for the souls of men, for souls to extend thy heavenly kingdom?

5. I'tura answered, saying: According to the number of subjects any angel bringeth me, so will I exalt him to be a captain, or a general, or a Lord, or a God, and he shall have a sub-kingdom in my heavenly regions, with thousands of servants to do his bidding.

6. With that the evil God and his evil spirits fell to work, night and day; and lo and behold, the fair land of Guatama was overspread with human blood. Fell war spread along throughout all the mighty kingdoms; kingdom against kingdom; city against city;

man against man.

7. And the holy temples were pulled down or burnt; and the canals broken and wasted; the cities on fire, and the fields laid desolate. Neither grew there any grain; the grinding mills of the women were silent, like the dead stretched over all the fields!

8. Into the forest, afar off, fled the women with the children, hungry, weeping, starving. And the cities went down; the nations went down; the tribes of men were broken up; only remnants here and there remained. And where had been great and mighty peoples, lay only heaps of ruins, past the power of man to rebuild.

9. Then looked down from the highest heaven, the Creator, the Great Spirit; saw the work of desolation; saw I'tura at his bloody work.

10. And the Great Spirit cried out with a loud voice, so that the earth and heaven shook with the power of His voice; sifted all things, as a woman sifteth meal. And He found one grain of corn not ground by the God of evil, found Honga! The tribes so fast sworn to the Great Spirit that the evil Gods' and evil spirits' words rolled off and took no hold on them.

11. The Great Spirit saw the tribes of Honga, they that stuck most to the I'hins, the sacred little people, white and yellow, oft marrying with them, thus preserving the stock to the Hand and Voice. And He called loud and long:

12. Honga! Honga! Honga! The Creator would not be put off with silence; called again: Honga! Honga! But He heard only His Own Voice resounding far; knew His mighty Power! Again He called: Honga! Honga! Honga!

13. In the first call, I'tura and his evil hosts ran away. In His second call, it was like spring-time, after heavy winter. And in the third call, it was like budding summer. And there came up a sprout of the seed of Honga, an I'huan; taller than any other man with a bright shining face of copper; shining as if all the destroyed temples glistened in his broad head.

14. And he spake, saying: Here, O Great Spirit, here am I! And the Great Spirit said: Who art thou, My Son? And he answered: I am Son of the Creator. Then asked the Great Spirit: Of what tribe? And he answered: My flesh is nothing; my genealogy is of the spirit. Of the I'hin my mother; of the I'huan my father.

15. Then said the Creator: For which reason, I name thee Eawahtah, spirit and flesh even balanced, best of men. Come thou with Me; walk along with Me; thou shalt re-instate the tribes of men; deliver them out of darkness; make them worshipful.

16. Eawahtah said: I am Thy servant, O Great Spirit. What shall I call Thee, that the tribes of men be no longer distrustful? Then answered the Creator: Call Me after the wind, O Eawahtah!

17. Eawahtah said: How after the wind? The Great Spirit said: Come with Me, My Son. Then Eawahtah walked along and came to a place where the wind blew in the leaves.

18. The Creator said: Tell Me, My Son, what saith the wind in the leaves? And answered Eawahtah: E! Then the Creator took Eawahtah to the big sea water, and asked: What saith the wind in the water, My Son?

19. And Eawahtah answered: Go! Then took the Creator Eawahtah to the high crags, the rocks above the clouds, piercing, where the wind whistled; and He said: What saith the wind, My Son? And Eawahtah answered: Quim!

20. And the Great Spirit said: Call Me Egoquim, O My Son. I am three in One; the earth, and all that is in the earth and on the earth, and all the stars and moon and sun; they are

one of My members. And the air above the earth, the Atontea, is another member of My Person. And higher yet; in the high place above the air, is the ether; the great penetrator; and that is the third member of My Person. I am everywhere, far and near; all things thine eye seeth; all things thine ear heareth are of Me and in Me.

21. Whatsoever is one with Me hath no hard labor. Behold the flowers of the field; I color them. Behold the ant and the honeybee; I lead them; the bird I teach how to build.

22. Man alone is stubborn, setting up ways of his own. O that he could learn to be one with Me! To move and labor with Me! Then spake Eawahtah, saying: Holy Egoquim! I will go and teach man, give him Thy words; make him understand.

23. Egoquim said: For that labor called I thee forth, made thee tall and handsome, with strong limbs, and broad shoulders. Come, then, My Son, I will go with thee; into all the lands; amongst all the scattered tribes; thy voice shall be My Voice. So near thee will I stand, when thou openest thy mouth to speak, fear not, I will give thee words; thou shalt not err.

24. Eawahtah inquired: What shall I say; how teach the sons and daughters of men; give me a synopsis?

25. Egoquim answered Eawahtah, saying:

CHAPTER XXVII.

1. One Great Person, even Egoquim, Creator and Ruler over all in heaven and earth.

2. Him shalt thou have and no other God, nor Lord, nor idol, nor man, nor angel, to worship, forever!

3. Him shalt thou love above all things in heaven above, or on the earth, or in the waters of the earth!

4. And thou shalt teach him to thy children, and command them to teach Him to their children, and so on forever!

5. And thou shalt swear against all other Gods, and Lords, and idols, to serve them not forever! And the same to thy children, and to their children after them, forever!

6. And this is the first Egoquim law.

7. And thou shalt deal unto all men, and women and children, as justly and as kindly as to thine own mother, out of whose breast thou wert fed when thou wert helpless and of no strength.

8. Teaching this to thy children, and to their children after them, forever.

9. And this is the second Egoquim law.

10. And to the sick and helpless; to the stranger and the man that cometh afar; to the widow who is destitute; to the child that hath no father; thou shalt be both father and mother to them; and take them into thy house and feed them; and give them skins and cloth to wear; and if they be lost, thou shalt go with them and show them the way.

11. Commanding these things unto thy children, and to their children after them, forever!

12. And this is the third Egoquim law.

13. And thou shalt not tell lies; nor speak falsely against any man, nor woman, nor child; nor break thy word of promise, even though death come upon thee to induce thee otherwise. Unchangeable as the setting and rising sun shall be the word of thy mouth!

14. And thou shalt command this to thy children, and to their children after them, forever!

15. And this is the fourth Egoquim law.

16. And thou shalt not take and possess that which is another's; nor suffer thy children to do so, nor their children after them, forever.

17. Which is the fifth Egoquim law.

18. And thou shalt respect the times of woman; and when she is bearing unto thee, thou shalt not lie with her; nor give her heavy labor, nor angry words, nor fret her; but be obedient to her, doing whatsoever she asketh thee to do, for it is her time, and she is thy queen.

19. Teaching this to thy young men and to thy young women, and to theirs that come after them, forever; for their young are begotten of Me, and I will have them shapely, and strong, and brave!

20. Which is the sixth Egoquim law.

21. Thou shalt labor six days, but on the seventh day it is the moon's day, and thou shalt not labor, nor hunt, nor fish, but go to the altar of thy Creator and dance and sing before Me; and sit in silence to hear My words, which I speak into the souls of men, and of women and children.

22. Teaching this to thy children, and to their children that come after them, forever.

23. Which is the seventh Egoquim law.

24. Thou shalt restore the rites and ceremonies of Choe-pan and Annubia-pan on the part I swear thee which thou shalt not restore; which is: Thou shalt not flatten the head to make a seer, a Haonga, to drive the judgment of the brain away to the prophetic regions.

25. Teaching these things to thy children, and to their children after them, forever!

26. Which is the eighth Egoquim law.

27. Then rose up Eawahtah, Son of Egoquim, saying: I am Thy servant! Lead Thou me, for I am going in Thy name, even to the end of the world!

28. When thus spake Eawahtah, Son of the Great Spirit, a Light came over him, dazzling, brilliant, lighting the way, showing him the way.

29. And so great was the spirit on Eawahtah, that when he came to the river, he rose up like an angel, sailed over and landed safely on the other side.

30. Neither knew he whither he was going; knew not the places of the scattered, destroyed peoples.

31. And the angels of Egoquim went before him; went into the forests and valleys, calling to the souls of the suffering, starving, dying, saying to them in their despair:

32. Egoquim, the Mighty, is coming! His Son! Behold Him! He holdeth the keys of Yaton'te, the heavenly hunting ground. Come forth from your hiding! Come forth, O My beloved! It is your Heavenly Father calling.

33. And the women heard! The little children, with sore, bleeding feet! The proud, brave men gave ear! They said: Why do we fight? Why do we destroy? It was a wicked God! He called himself the Savior,--the wicked monster, I'tura!

34. Then came Eawahtah; came first to the kingdom of Took-shein, and to his queen, Che-guh, in the land Anagoomahaha, the flat-heads. Told them all the words of the Great Spirit, Egoquim.

35. Then spake Took-shein, saying: To me the Great Spirit hath spoken; told me all the words thou hast. I know all thou hast said is true. Then spake Che-guh, saying: To me spake Gitchee, the Great Spirit. True are all thy words, O Eawahtah. By thee will all the

scattered tribes be gathered together. Many tribes will there be of the red man; Egoquim will be the center, the Mighty Spirit!

36. Then spake Eawahtah, saying to his good host and hostess: Your place shall be the centre; from your place I will shoot out around about, always returning, bringing in followers.

37. Whilst they thus talked, a Light came above them. Look, said Took-shein: It is the hand of Egoquim! Look, said Che-guh: It is the Voice of Gitchee! Then spake Eawahtah, seeing more clearly, raised up expressly: It is a ship of fire coming down from heaven! I hear the voices of the angel of Egoquim, the Mighty!

38. Then Eawahtah went and stood betwixt Took-shein and Che-guh, holding their hands, so the Voice of Egoquim could speak plainly; so he could hear.

39. Then spake Egoquim, saying, speaking out of the ship of fire:

40. Yea, My beloved! I am with you! Behold, My worlds are wide and many. When My back is turned, evil Gods come to steal My children; tell them lies to win them; tell them they are My Sons come to save them!

41. Hard is the fate of those that worship one God only; but they are Mine. I look around at times; I set the evil Gods flying. Be of strong heart, O My beloved! Many races will come and go on these lands. But the red man shall possess it: inhabit it far and near. Then shall come another evil God (Christ), to flay and destroy My sons and daughters, to cover all the lands over with pure blood. Then will I come again and rout the evil God, raise up My sons and daughters, full of glory.

42. From far over the water will I bring their kindred (Jews), who worship none born of woman; a wise speaking people. A people that war not; who kill not off weaker nations. I will come in the Mohawk (Tenonachi), and the Mohegan (Hoochiquis); My hand shall reach around the earth in that day. I will chase away all Gods and Saviors born of woman. Only the Great Spirit shall all men worship.

43. Go forth, My son; build wide My foundation; in this land will I found My earthly kingdom.

44. Then upward rose the ship of heaven; and Eawahtah buckled on his traveling slippers; bade good-by to Took-shein; filled his pockets with the bread of Che-guh; kissed her hand good-by, and started.

45. For many years traveled Eawahtah, over all the regions of Guatama; teaching, gathering together, swearing the people ever after to be firm to the Great Spirit: made them swear solemn oaths that never more would they listen to any God save the Creator; made them swear they would never be caught by another cunning Savior, like I'tura, whose people delight in war.

46. Into villages gathered Eawahtah the frightened tribes, and taught them writing and engraving; taught them the secret name of the Great Spirit, Egoquim; and explained to them the moon, how to keep the seventh day for worship.

47. The Creator saw the great work of Eawahtah; saw the people gathered together in tens of thousands of places. Then spake the Creator to Eawahtah, saying:

48. Forty mighty nations shalt thou found, O My son; and every nation shall be an independent nation; but all the nations shall be united into a brotherhood of nations, as ONE mighty people, and that one shall be called O-pah-E-go-quim, signifying ONE. For when I come in kosmon, My people shall have many states, like unto thine, and their

combination shall be called UNION, signifying ONE. Build thou a model for them, O Eawahtah. For, though when they come they shall overthrow thy people in the earth, the angels of thy holy ones shall come and purge them of their Savior, and make them clean in My sight.

49. Then Eawahtah made the nations; united them into one mighty people, and called them the nations of Opahegoquim. And they planted the country over with corn-fields, and dwelt in peace.

END OF EAWAHTAH'S HISTORY.

Plate 15. TOOK-SHEIN   Plate 16. CHE-GUH

CHAPTER XXVIII.

1. God said: Be wise, O man, in the words of thy God. My records come not up out of the ground, nor from the books of mortals.

2. I open my heavenly libraries, and find my living sons and daughters who once trod the earth.

3. Their light I recast down again to mortals in a stream of fire, and lo, my words are rewritten.

4. Search thou for the evidence of my footsteps on the earth; find the people who stand by the Creator, the All One, God of All! Who can shake their faith, or feed them with thy story of a Savior born of woman?

5. Hearken to the voice of the millions of Chine'ya and Vind'yu, and the remnants of the Algonquins! Their bibles are a power to this day. Their people are appalled at the work of

494

thy bloody sword.

6. They will not fall down and worship as thou decreest; they know that Jehovih is mightier than thou.

7. Be thou considerate of all the races of men, and their doctrines and rites and ceremonies.

8. Behold, I raise up the nations of the earth in mine own way. According to the times and conditions of mortals, so do I deal unto them from my heavenly kingdoms.

9. Thou hast tried on all my people, to convert them, but hast failed utterly. Behold, I come now with a new book; and they will accept it from my hand.

10. Herein do I prophesy to thee, beforehand, that thou shalt witness in time to come, that I, God of heaven and earth, have spoken.

11. Nor shalt thou say: Man of himself progresseth; and that such and such would come of a natural order.

12. I say unto thee, man progresseth not, save by me, through my angel hosts in heaven.

13. In testimony of which I have left many peoples before thee, for hundreds of years. Thy natural order is laziness and uncleanness. Wherein thou art quickened in spirit, behold, it is the heavens upon thee that stirreth thee up.

14. Thou shalt not mistake the teaching of thy God; which was manifested the same in the ancient days as in this day: Which is, to worship thy Creator only; to bow not down to any other God nor Lord; to love thy neighbor, and to do good unto others with all thy wisdom and strength, having faith in the Almighty!

END OF THE FIRST BOOK OF GOD.

BOOK OF WARS AGAINST JEHOVIH.

OF GOD'S LABOR IN ATMOSPHEREA. -- CONTAINING AN ACCOUNT OF THE ESTABLISHING ON THE EARTH THE NAMES: LORD GOD, AND DE'YUS, AND DYAUS, AND DIETY AND TE-IN, AND SUDGA, AND OSIRIS, AND BAAL, AND ASHTAROTH. COVERING A PERIOD OF TWO THOUSAND FOUR HUNDRED YEARS; THAT IS, FROM THE TIME OF ABRAHAM, AND BRAHMA, AND PO, AND EAWAHTAH, TO THE TIME OF MOSES, AND CHINE, AND CAPILYA. THIS BOOK OF GOD PERTAINETH TO BOTH, THE EARTH AND LOWER HEAVENS, AND CONTAINETH AN EXPOSITION OF THE LABORS OF THE ABOVE FALSE GODS, AND THEIR FALL AND ENVIRONMENT IN HELLS, ALL SAVE BAAL AND ASHTAROTH.

CHAPTER I.

1. Jehovih spake to God on the throne, in Craoshivi, saying: These are My divisions in the cycle of My Daughter, Cpenta-armij: Two hundred years; four hundred years; five hundred years; three hundred years; four hundred years, and six hundred years; after which I shall send dawn. Five successors shalt thou have, and their reign shall be according to the divisions I have made.

2. Forty years' indulgence in a great light have I allotted to thee, My Son; so thou shalt perfect all the orders of Lords and Lordesses in the lowest lower kingdoms of these My heavens. Neither shall it be dark during my reign; and thy labor shall be productive of a great harvest for My etherean worlds. For which reason thou shalt prepare to reap in fifty years, and again in fifty years, and again in fifty years, and again in fifty years. And for each reaping, behold, My daughter Cpenta-armij will send to thee ships of deliverance for all thou mayst have prepared as Brides and Bridegrooms.

3. And behold, I give a new law unto thee; which is, that thou shalt cause thy Lords to deliver unto thee for thy kingdoms all whom they have raised to grade fifty, in advance of thy reapings, in divisions of time like unto thine.

4. And thou shalt call together to thy capital thy Lords from all the divisions of the earth, once every reaping; and ye shall sit in COUNCIL OF DIV for seven days each time, and ye shall constitute MY HOLY ELEVEN; nor shall the Div be larger or smaller than eleven during its life-time. And the Div shall make laws relating to the affairs of each of the heavenly places, to make them harmonious, one with another, and these shall be called DIVAN LAWS.

5. God inquired concerning the light and darkness of the cycle. Jehovih said: The first division shall rate seventy; the second, fifty; the third, forty; the fourth, eighty; the fifth, thirty; and the sixth, twenty.

6. God inquired concerning the Lord of the Lord-dom. Jehovih answered him, saying: Because he is not a teacher, he shall not be eligible to the rank of Div. But he shall have the benefit of all the decrees, and all the kingdoms of My other Lords; for he is the earth's body-guard, and a beneficent unto them.

CHAPTER II.

1. When the Diva were assembled, God propounded the duties of the Lord-dom. On which the members spake at length, and then God decreed:

2. First: The Lord God of Maitraias not having, from this time forth forever, force to enforce: Permission to use violent force, neither by fire nor water, save in hells or knots.

496

3. Second: By the ARC OF SPE-TA: By the decree of the Most High: The Lord God of Maitraias is bound by the same rule as the Lords of the lowest heavens; whose walls and pillars of fire are abolished, save on special occasions; whose respective kingdoms are open and free for all spirits above the es'yan grade.

4. Third: The Lord God of Maitraias' times and successors shall be the same as the Diva: The stations of the hosts of the Lord God shall be according to the heavenly realms of the Lords, with Maitraias as the Lord-dom in chief.

5. Fourth: The hosts of the Lord God shall be distinguished from ashars and asaphs by the name MISHM, but of a single one the name shall be MISH-AH. And their leaders shall be called captains and generals.

6. Fifth: The labor of the Lord God shall be to prevent drujas returning to the earth to dwell with corporeans; to capture drujas on the earth and carry them off to the nearest Lord's heavenly place, and there deliver them. Force by violence or without consent being abolished, the mishm shall devise stratagems, by games and tournaments, or otherwise persuasively.

7. Sixth: The mishm shall not arrest fetals, nor infants, nor the wards of ashars, nor spirits in chaos on battle-fields; for these labors belong to the Lords and their hosts.

8. Seventh: Where there are companies of millions of drujas, and the Lord God hath not a sufficient number of mishm, the Lord God shall summon the nearest Lord for help, and it shall be given unto him.

9. Eighth: In no case shall it be the labor of the Lord God to teach the captured drujas, nor to house them, nor to provide them with schools and factories, nor hospitals, nor nurseries, for these labors are the Lord's, to whom the Lord God of Maitraias shall deliver them.

10. Ninth: To prevent the establishing of heavenly kingdoms by self-constituted Lords and Gods, otherwise false Lords and false Gods; the Lord God of the Lord-dom of Maitraias shall be the central head, in conjunction with all the Lords of the lowest heavens; and his voice shall be the rule and guide as to the manner of such labor.

11. Tenth: The Lord God shall have one hundred thousand messengers; and he shall determine their stations and routes of travel.

12. This was the first section of DIVAN LAW in the heavens of the earth.

CHAPTER III.

1. In God's heavenly place, Craoshivi, Jehovih said: For My chosen on the earth, of Abram, and Po, and Brahma, and Eawahtah, provide thou in Craoshivi; for they shall not tarry in the lowest heavens.

2. And for the infants of My chosen, who die in infancy, suffer them not to be engulfed in hada, but bring them also to the place of My God.

3. The Diva then decreed: Lines of roadways from the earth up to the kingdom of God for such transport, and appointed officers and laborers to prevent the spirits of God's chosen from falling into the hands of the drujas, and to bring them to Craoshivi. The Diva said: On the third day after the death of a mortal, his spirit shall be borne to the home of God. And it was so.

4. But as to the heathen, the Diva decreed: The labor of the Lords of all the divisions of hada and of the earth shall be with the undelivered sons and daughters of the earth and her

heavens; but in no case shall they labor more with the Faithists; for the Faithists, mortals and spirits, come under the higher law, which is of Jehovih, through His Son, God of Craoshivi. This was the second section of the Divan law.

5. And herefrom rose the saying: The believers go to God, but the unbelievers go to his Lords; they that live the higher law on earth escape hada. And after some years the Diva passed the law, according to the saying, and called it the third section of the Divan law, and it was so promulgated throughout heaven and on earth.

6. Now it came to pass in course of time that some corporeans, who belonged not to the societies of Faithists of any of the tribes of Jehovih's chosen, became believers in the All Person, and that to live by the All Highest light was the fulfillment of the Divan law. And they joined not the Faithists, nor followed the rites and ceremonies.

7. God propounded this in Diva: Where shall the spirits of such be delivered? Behold, even on the earth they have delivered themselves away from the druks; shall we now suffer them to fall into the kingdoms of mixed company in hada?

8. Upon this the Diva decreed: A separate kingdom shall be prepared for them that believe, who have lived isolate, and who know not the rites and ceremonies. This was the fourth section of the Divan law. The fifth was like unto it, but explanatory, which was:

9. To have faith in One Great Person, the Ever Present Spirit, Creator and Ruler, is well; but to have such faith, and yet not committing one's self to an association of brethren of like faith, proveth such lack of discipline as requireth beginning at the fifth grade in the es'ean world.

10. The sixth section of the Divan law provided: The name for the kingdom for them that profess faith in the Great Person, Jehovih, but are without practice, shall be called Me-de, and its place shall be in the first remove from the earth.

CHAPTER IV.

1. Jehovih spake to God, saying: Because thou hast founded Me-de thou shalt make Me-de-ci laws; and thou shalt send thy surveyors down to hada and to the earth also, and they shall choose a heavenly place for thy new kingdom. And thither shalt thou go and create a plateau and holy place and capital, and provide a throne for it.

2. And when thou hast completed thy work thou shalt call to the throne a sub-God, who shall rule in thy place with wisdom, and power, and love, in My name.

3. But since many of My chosen forget Me and so apostate themselves, thy sub-God shall also receive their spirits, and his kingdom shall be their kingdom till they are purged of their sins.

4. God spake in the Council of Craoshivi, relating what Jehovih had said to him, and the Council then ratified the commandments of Jehovih. And there was selected one A-chung-le, and made sub-God of Me-de, with the title Anubi, signifying mediator, and judge of grades.

5. God said: Anubi shall have a badge, and a pair of scales; with mine own hands will I invest him. And, accordingly, the place, the kingdom, the person, and the badge of office were duly established by God under the commandment of Jehovih through his kingdom of Craoshivi. And the term of office was made to correspond with God's and his Lords'.

6. Thus was put upon the throne in the heavenly place, Me-de, Anubi, who had been

A-chung-le, an angel of a thousand years in the colleges of Jehovih, most wise and full of love, and industrious withal.

7. Again Jehovih spake to God, saying: From this time forth My colleges shall be in Craoshivi; from this time forth My schools and primaries shall be in the kingdoms of My Lords. The Diva afterward made this another section of the Divan law.

8. So God and his Lords removed all his colleges and places of great learning to Craoshivi; but the schools and primary educationals were left in the dominions of the Lords, their heavenly places.

9. Now, during the dawn of dan, four etherean Gods had sojourned on the earth, walking with four mortals, namely: With Po, of Jaffeth; Abram, of Arabin'ya; Brahma, of Vind'yu, and Eawahtah, of Guatama. And the four Gods preached through these four men, explaining Jehovih and His kingdoms; and the angels of Jehovih inspired many followers unto them. For four years these Gods dwelt on the earth, and then ascended into the upper regions.

10. Jehovih spake to God concerning the matter, saying: For four years I bestowed My light in Person on the corporeal earth, and then I departed; for it is well that men and angels learn to be self-raising. For which reason I left four substitutes, Lords of heaven, on the earth, with My four peoples whom I delivered. And I commanded these My substitutes to abide upon the earth for forty years, in order to indulge My chosen in a surety in My creations founded in corpor.

11. Provide thou unto them; for My substitutes are ethereans; and thou shalt have their places filled by atmosphereans from the highest grades.

12. The Diva then made a section of the Divan law, providing for the four who stood highest in the grades in Craoshivi to take the places, to dwell with the Faithist in the names of the Great Spirit; and the names given were: To Jaffeth, Te-in; to Arabin'ya, Jehovih; to Vind'yu, Ormazd; to Guatama, Egoquim; according to the languages, and to the capabilities of mortals to pronounce words.

13. The Diva then made another section of the Divan law, which was the title to be given to the four angels thus provided to bestow the Voice of Jehovih on mortals, and the title was O-yra; that is, O the High Heaven; and Y, going to; and ra, the earth.

14. The twelfth section of the Divan law provided that each O-yra should have ten thousand attendants; angels from above the eightieth grade, from the colleges of Craoshivi, and their attendants were to sojourn on the earth with the Faithists as inspiring spirits and protectors.

15. The thirteenth section of the Divan law made the terms of office for the O-yra eleven years each; and the same for their attendants.

16. The fourteenth section of the Divan law explained the duties of the O-yra and their attendants, which were: that the O-yra should reside with the chief rab'bah or high priest, and be his inspirer; being with him day and night; and by virtue of his presence make the chief rab'bah know the voice of the All Highest. And the attendants first in rank were to dwell in the same way with the ordinary rab'bah, and for the same purpose. And the other attendants were to dwell with the multitude in like manner, and for the same purpose. And each O-yra was to have a heavenly place in the mortal temple, where he could meet his attendants in Council in reference to the Faithists and their affairs.

17. The fifteenth section of the Divan law made the O-yra and his attendants the heavenly

kingdom for the ashars of the Lords who dwelt with mortals.

18. The sixteenth Divan law provided for the O-yra to increase the number of his attendants, according to the increase of the number of Faithists in each of the four divisions of the earth.

19. Such, then, were the chief of the Divan laws made in heaven in the cycle of Cpenta-armij, during the first two hundred years. And all the kingdoms of atmospherea were established and officered; and all the people in these heavens became organic as soon as passing the es'yan age. Nor was there any dissatisfaction amongst any of the Gods, or Lords, or other officers, or in any of the colleges, or hospitals; and never since the foundation of the world had there been such prosperity in the resurrections of the inhabitants of heaven.

CHAPTER V.

1. And the harmony of heaven reigned on earth; war ceased amongst men on all the divisions of the earth. And man began to esteem wisdom, and truth, and virtue, and industry. The inspiration of the angels set man to imitating the affairs of heaven. He built schools and colleges, nurseries and hospitals, and factories for silk cloth, and linen cloth, and cotton cloth, and for paper; and factories for making glass, and leather; and factories for smelting iron, and copper, and silver, and gold.

2. Three great peoples sprang upon the earth within two hundred years; in Jaffeth, in Vind'yu, and in Arabin'ya; and a fourth great people were overspreading Heleste in every quarter. And the kings of Heleste were sending emigrants by thousands and thousands into Uropa.

3. The Lords sent ashars of great wisdom to dwell with mortals, to teach them by inspiration in regard to all knowledge; to teach them to spin and weave finely; to teach them the seasons, the times of the earth, and moon, and sun, and stars; to observe them with lenses, as had been the case in the cycle of Osiris, but was lost on the earth. Yea, the spirits of thousands of years previous were brought back to the earth, to reveal to mortals the lost arts and sciences.

4. By night and by day these angels remained in the presence of mortals, and by virtue of their presence spake unto the souls of men, and made them to understand.

5. And the Lord God of Maitraias restrained the drujas of heaven from coming back to afflict mortals or lead them astray. He guarded the earth around about on all sides, so that, in heaven, the Lords and the Divan hosts, in mirth, styled him THE SAVIOR OF MEN!

6. Jehovih rebuked them, saying to God: They that sow in mirth oft reap in sorrow. But even the Lords, with all their wisdom, saw not what was in store for their successors.

CHAPTER VI.

1. The O-yra, the four angels with their thousands of assistant angel hosts, dwelt on the earth, with the Faithists; inspired them in peace, and rites, and ceremonies; inspired them in prayers, and psalms, and sacred dances; dwelt with them day and night; talked to their spirits when they slept; led them by inspiration to happy marriages, that they might beget offspring capable of the Voice.

2. And in each of the four countries the Faithists became as bands of brothers and sisters.

And there came to them from the kings' peoples tens of thousands, and joined them, living as Faithists, casting their wealth into the rab'bah's hands, for the benefit of the poor.

3. In two hundred years there were in Jaffeth three million Faithists. In Arabin'ya there were two million Faithists. In Vind'yu there were four million Faithists. In Guatama there were one million Faithists.

4. But the Faithists were mostly poor people, and inhabited many far-apart regions.

5. But the kings' peoples were rich, and had large cities, an abundance of elephants, and horses, and camels, and asses, and cheetahs.

6. The Faithists had little learning as to books and instruments for measuring the stars, and moon, and sun; they derived their knowledge from the angels of the Lords. The Faithists' knowledge pertained mostly to perfecting the soul; but the knowledge of the kings' peoples pertained mostly to earthly matters, and to the gratification of self.

CHAPTER VII.

1. The Anubi's labor on earth was to win the disaffected of the kings' peoples into association; and as far as possible bring them to the rites of Faithism.

2. Anubi sent tens of thousands of angels into all the regions of the earth. By inspiration and otherwise these angels established the rites of Anubi.

3. By these rites even kings were converted to Faithism and the full ceremonies of the brethren.

4. And by the same means were the Maichung, of Jaffeth, made into Faithists; and by the same rites were the Effins, of Vind'yu, converted into Faithists, adopting all the rites and ceremonies of Emethachavah afterward.

5. And it came to pass in course of time that there were no suffering poor in all the world. The Faithists had gathered them all up and made brethren of them; and the contributions to the Faithists by the kings' peoples rendered all the people comfortable.

6. For the degree of Anubi any one (who desired to learn heavenly things) was eligible. The rites and ceremonies were in dark chambers; and the angels of heaven, clothed in sar'gis, took part therein. And the angels taught mortals by the voice the mysteries of spirit communion; how to sit in circles and in crescents; taught the four dark corners, and the four bright sides; taught them how to ascertain from what grade in heaven the spirits came; how to keep off evil spirits; how to attract righteous spirits; taught them how to develop in su-is and sar'gis; the secrets of falling water; the application of lotions to the skin, that would make poundings and rappings.

7. The second degree taught the people of the Great Spirit and His secret names; taught them His high holy heavens, where all is rest and happiness forever. Whoever took the second degree had to live one year with the poorest of the poor, going about soliciting alms, reserving only the poorest of things for himself. And if he found a person naked he must take off his clothes and give them to that person. Men and women alike served the same conditions.

8. The third degree taught the dominions of God and the Lords, and the place of their abiding, and the irrespective labors in heaven. And the members must learn the names of the God or Gods, Lord or Lords, and the Divan laws; the words of salutation; the anthems; the prayers; the praise; the positions of utterance; the orders of marching; to

write sacred names; the secret of begetting pure offspring, and the key to the two preceding degrees.

9. The fourth degree taught the arrangement of the heavens; the places of the sun and stars and moon; the places and grades of the unseen worlds; the localities of the lower and higher heavens; the places and dominions of false Lords and false Gods; the places in hada, and of hells and knots; of familiar spirits, and also of fetals, both the harmless and the destructive vampires, that live on mortals and in swine and cattle, that induce mortals to eat flesh food for that purpose; the key to the place of the north star; the position of the earth's vortex; the vortices that move the corporeal worlds, and hold them in place; and the rules for building temples and pyramids, with their spirit chambers.

10. Besides this there was the fifth degree, which reached the secret of life in the flesh; the power of will and how to use it far and near; how to rule over others without their knowing it; to cast spells; to enter the prophetic state; to estimate numbers without counting; to find proportions and distances without measuring; to forecast the time of things; to find the weight of things without weighing; to find the power of the capstan before it is made, and of the lever and screw; to find the friction of things before they were moved, in order to know the power required. The fifth degree was called the degree of prophecy; and the place of initiation was called the college of prophecy.

11. In this degree the angels came in sar'gis and taught these things orally, and mortals initiated thus learned them. But no one could take the fifth degree without having become proficient in all the four preceding degrees, and without the recommendation of the rab'bah (or priest) who had charge of the college.

12. And such was the wisdom of God that only Faithists could receive the degrees, save the first degree; and, therefore, the greatest knowledge of the earth was kept in secret with the Faithists. And the kings' people, even the richest and most powerful, were beholden to the sons and daughters of the Faithists. To build a palace or a temple, or an aqueduct or canal, or a ship or any great affair, the kings and the kings' people were obliged to employ Faithists of the fifth degree to superintend the work.

CHAPTER VIII.

OF ANUHASAJ; WHO BY TREACHERY, BECOMETH LORD
GOD, SECOND IN RANK TO GOD, SON OF JEHOVIH.

1. Jehovih spake to God in Craoshivi, his heavenly place, saying: Behold, I have given great light to the earth and her heavens hundreds of years; and My Gods and Lords are becoming conceited in their own power and wisdom to rule in heavenly places.

2. Now will I try them for a season, by sending them a'ji'an darkness; for My Gods and Lords must learn to master the elements I have created in the firmament.

3. So Jehovih brought the earth and her heavens into a dark region for a season.

4. Anuhasaj, a one-time sub-God under Ahura, the false, was cast into hell, and then delivered out of hell, whereupon he repented, and became a Faithist in heaven; serving many years in holy works in Ailkin, a heavenly place of great wisdom.

5. And it came to pass that Ailkin was raised into a new heavenly place, called Varapishanaha; and in the removing, behold, Ahura ordered Anuhasaj from the line because of his inharmony. And Anuhasaj suffered himself to become angered.

6. Satan (self) said unto Anuhasaj: Who art thou, that one of less wisdom ordereth thee?

Anuhasaj said: Alas, I am a fool, and without will to assert myself.

7. For many years Anuhasaj became a wandering spirit in heaven, going from kingdom to kingdom, doing nothing; and at times descending to the earth, observing the kingdoms of the earth.

8. Satan came again to him and said: Hear thou my voice, and thou shalt triumph over all other Gods. Anuhasaj said: What shall I do? And satan said: Go thou to Ahura, who offended thee in presence of the Chieftainess, Cpenta-armij, and say to him: O God, I crave thy forgiveness. Thou wert right, and I was wrong. I have repented most bitterly. Now I come to thee, with faith in Jehovih. Him will I serve forever. Turn me not off, O Ahura; remember thine own one-time shortness; and the high Gods above thee accepted thee.

9. Satan continued: Ahura will delight in thee and take thee at thy word. And thou shalt enter Vara-pishanaha, asking for the lowest of places; practicing humility in all thy behavior. But be thou fruitful in making acquaintances with such as shall serve thee afterward.

10. Satan continued: And whether it be fifty years, or a hundred, or two hundred, bide thou thy time. But the time shall surely come when thou shalt be exalted; and thou shalt solicit and accept a place in the dominions of the Lord God in the Lord-dom of heaven and earth, Maitraias.

11. Satan continued: And whether it be one hundred years more, or two hundred years, it mattereth not to thee; but thou shalt finally attain to the Lord-dom, and be duly installed and crowned Lord God of heaven and earth.

12. And when thou art thus exalted, thou shalt seek to have appointed such Lords to the ten divisions of earth as are thine own special friends. And it shall come to pass that the whole earth and her heavens shall be thine, and thy title shall be Lord God, and all people on earth and in heaven shall be thy servants.

13. Anuhasaj said: Thou art the wisest of Gods, O satan. All thou hast advised will I do; neither shall any one in heaven or earth know my designs.

14. And it came to pass in course of another hundred years, Anuhasaj was promoted on the staff of the Lord God, the guardian, where he served the Lord God one hundred and seventy years. So the Lord God named Anuhasaj for his successor.

15. So God came from Craoshivi and crowned Anuhasaj Lord God of heaven and earth; with great pageantry and display, God gave him a throne and placed him upon it. And from this time forth Anuhasaj was known and saluted as Lord God, which is the first rank below God.

16. The Lord God said unto satan: Who first shall I bring into my favor? Satan said: Thou shalt first bring into thy favor Anubi, MASTER OF THE SCALES OF HEAVEN, and when thou hast this to thy liking, thou shalt call him THY SON and SAVIOR OF MEN!

17. The Lord God said unto satan: Who next shall I bring into my favor? Satan said: Thou shalt next bring into thy favor the ten Lords of the heavenly kingdoms of the earth. And when thou hast them to thy liking, thou shalt exalt the chief one of them to be above the rest; and him that thou exaltest thou shalt call Osiris, for it is a name loved on earth and in heaven.

18. Satan said: Thou shalt re-establish thy Lord-dom and call it Hored, and it shall be the central kingdom of all the heavens belonging to the earth.

19. And Anubi shall send the spirits of his department to thy heavens; and Osiris and all the other Lords shall send the spirits of their departments to thy kingdom. And in no case shall any more spirits be sent to Craoshivi; for all people in heaven and earth shall be taught that thy kingdom is the All Highest Place; and that thou art the All Highest God, even the Creator of all things; and all angels and mortals shall be thy servants.

20. Then went the Lord God to work earnestly, but slowly and surely. The Lords of all the divisions of the earth were his special friends, and of such kind as would willingly do his bidding. And they were learned and of high grade of heavenly experience of more than a thousand years.

21. And the Lord God told no one in heaven or on the earth of his designs; gave no sign or token in his behavior that would make messengers or swift messengers look at him to read him; and he passed for the meekest and holiest of Gods.

22. But the time came at last for which the Lord God had labored hundreds of years; and he gave a festival in his heavenly place, inviting the Lords and captains and generals and marshals, whom he knew would willingly do his bidding.

23. And they came even as the Lord God had planned, and it was a time of great joy. And when the feast was ended, then spake the Lord God before them, spake as one moved in sorrow to do a solemn duty for the sake of Jehovih.

24. The Lord God said: O my brothers, hear the words of your Lord God! Behold, I have charge of the Lord-dom of heaven and earth, I am as a guardian that standeth by a corn-field to see the corn grow unmolested. My experience is not of a year, nor of a hundred years, but of thousands of years.

25. In Jehovih's name I speak before you; for the love I bear for the souls of men and angels. I belong not to the Diva as do ye Lords; my voice findeth vent in the fullness of the Father in me.

26. Who is here that hath not seen great decline, during the last hundred years, in these heavens, in the faith of angels in the All Person? Speak then, O ye Lords; and if ye have hearts for more energetic service for the Father and His kingdoms, now let your tongues have full liberty, as becometh Gods.

27. Anubi said: thou art wise, O Lord God. God of Craoshivi layeth the blame on a'ji.

28. Then spake Hi-kas, whose heavenly place was over Jaffeth, he said: My Lord God and my Lords, before your wisdom I bow. I am but as a child in heaven, little more than a thousand years. My tongue should be silent before you, my long experienced Lords. Hear me though in my little wisdom, and pity me for it.

29. To the east or west, or north or south, all things grow, in heaven and on the earth; I have seen no greater wisdom than this. One thing groweth not, the Diva. Behold, the Diva made laws hundreds of years ago, and they were wise laws in the time they were made. Ye and I, all of us, are bound by the old Divan laws. The laws have not grown.

30. Gods older than I am, and Lords also, tell us that the All Light is a Person and hath Voice; and moreover that long ago He spake to high-raised Gods, saying: These things, shall be thus and so.

31. I appeal to your judgment, O my Lord God and My Lords, was that not a wise doctrine for the ancients? For on this authority angels and mortals fell down and worshipped Him they saw not. And they were obedient to do the will of their masters and teachers on this self-asserted authority of a Person no one had seen!

32. Which is to say: It is wiser to worship Him we know not, and cannot comprehend, and is therefore as nothing before us, than to hearken to the words of most wise Gods and Lords.

33. If to worship that which we are ignorant of is the highest of worship, then the fool is the greatest of worshippers. For he is ignorant of all things. And by virtue of this reason, he who is the wisest must be the poorest of worshippers. And of a truth, is it not so, both in heaven and on earth?

34. With the acquisition of knowledge, they all put away the Unknowable; the ignorant are devout worshippers. Shall we hold our tongues, saying: Wh-ce, Wh-ce! The ignorant must not know the truth; the whole truth!

35. To do this, are we not hypocrites? Some have come to us from far-off regions, saying there are more delightful heavens, much higher! Why, then, shall we not all run away and leave this?

36. My Lord God, and my Lords, these heavens are good enough, if improved. The earth is good enough, if improved. We want larger kingdoms and more adorned thrones in our heavens and on the earth.

37. Next spake Che-le-mung, whose heavenly kingdom was over Arabin'ya. He said: My Lord hath spoken soul words. With knowledge, what more need angels or mortals? What value to them is it to say: Beware! The Unseen heareth and seeth? Or, halt and consider the Divan laws?

38. My Lord God, for the wisest and best and most honest to assume dominion, this I have not seen. Thy kingdom should be the largest and most adorned of all kingdoms. And thou shouldst have, to labor with thee, Lords with kingdoms greater than all Craoshivi. Cannot our Gods and our Lords make these heavens the greatest of all regions in the universe? Shall we and our people forever run off to etherea in search of higher heavens? And not improve our own? To exalt a place by going away from it, who hath seen this done?

39. Arc-wotchissij spake next: his heavenly kingdom was over Vind'yu. He said: O that I had not struggled so long to put away wisdom like this! All that hath been spoken I have understood. But I curbed my soul; I thought I was alone in such reason. Now, so suddenly, I have not words well schooled. I speak little, lest I trip myself up afterward. It is the joy of my life to listen to such wise arguments. Another time I will say more.

40. After him spake Baal, whose heavenly kingdom was over Heleste and the south end of Jaffeth to the sea, a young Lord of great promise. He said: How shall one of my inexperience speak before such Gods as are here! But because ye have touched upon a matter dear to my soul, my words will forth. I have seen all these heavens, and even Craoshivi, waning for hundreds of years. Our kingdoms are like old women, resigned to routine, living, but dead.

41. We have the same rites and ceremonies as the ancients; parades and salutations and anthems sung for thousands of years; and to whom? A figure-head that is void of shape and person and sense. Who is here that hath not deserved honor more than such a being? My Lord God hath labored two thousand years! I have seen him in Vara-pishanaha for more than a hundred years, stooped to the vilest labor, over bad-smelling drujas, teaching them, washing them!

42. The Lord God should have a kingdom wide as the earth, and a million attendants to

do him honorable parade. And when he goeth forth he should have hundreds of thousands of heralds and trumpeters to proclaim he is coming. We need such. We need wider fields and more pomp and glory in our heavens; and kingdoms with great capital cities, and thrones arrayed in splendor.

43. Then rose Ashtaroth, assistant to Baal, and Lordess of the East Wing of his heavenly place. She said: Here are other Lordesses, can speak wisely. As for me, my words are few. The ancients have taught us to be plain in all things. And we have made our heavens like orchards stript of leaves and blossoms. As fast as angels are made bright and useful, they are persuaded to become Brides and Bridegrooms to Jehovih, and fly off to remote worlds. Our own beloved earth, that brought us forth, together with her heavens, are thus forever stript of the most valuable fruitage and ornaments.

44. We all know that atmospherea is extensive enough to contain all the angels the earth will bring forth in millions of years! I appeal to thee, my Lord God, and to ye, most wise Lords, are not these Brides and Bridegrooms hoodwinked by the tales of the etherean Gods? And by the parade and pageantry of the marriage ceremony? And by the fire-ships, and pomp and splendor of the marshals, and trumpeters, and music, and the high-raised Gods?

45. Behold, we have here one who can invent all these glories, even our Lord God. He should have such a heavenly place of splendor that the Brides and Bridegrooms would fly to him instead of the far-off heavens.

46. After this manner spake the Lords and Lordesses, and when they had all spoken, there rose up Anuhasaj, now lawfully anointed Lord God. He said:

CHAPTER IX.

1. Most wise Lords, in words ye have done me great honor. There let the matter end. I perceive what any one can understand, which is that the center of the heavens should be here. The heirs of the earth and atmospherea, why should they be carried off to other heavens? Sufficient is it for us that we cultivate our own. I am not competent for so great a work. Rather shall ye choose from amongst yourselves the highest, best, wise man, and make him your God. I will be his servant to do whatsoever he putteth upon me.

2. I have traveled far, and took the measure of many worlds. I declare unto you there are no glories in the far-off worlds, but what can be built up in these heavens, and even on the very earth.

3. Hear me then and judge ye, not for my fitness, but for my unfitness, and so dismiss me save to make me your servant.

4. Send not off the highest raised angels, but make these heavens suitable unto them.

5. Make this kingdom the All Highest heavenly kingdom; and make your God the highest of all Gods, even the Creator. Him shall ye surround with a capital city, a heavenly place paved with diamonds and most precious gems. And his throne shall be the most exalted, highest of all glories. To which none can approach, save by crawling on their bellies. Yea, such majesty shall surround your God as becometh a Creator; and such newly-invented rites and ceremonies, dazzling beyond anything in all the worlds!

6. The rites and ceremonies should be carried to the highest. Without rites and ceremonies a people are as a dead people; they are as an army without discipline. In fact, discipline is void without the formalities of rites and ceremonies. To not have these is to have every

one do for self, which is the dissolution of all union. Baal hath spoken wisely on this; we need new rites and ceremonies, adapted for the highest grades. We shall no longer bow to a God we know not, a scattered substance wide as the universe!

7. Because ye have spoken, I am pleased. Because ye have come to my feast, I am delighted. To be with one's own loves, what is greater than that? It hath been said, man shall love all alike; but I say unto you that that is impossible. We have our preferences, and we delight to come together. Who shall say us nay?

8. And yet, my Lords and Lordesses, shall we not deliberate on these things? And council with our best loves upon it; for such is the construction of the mind that it oft seeth better through others' eyes. And, above all, shall we not mature the subject to know if in our own souls we are sincere, doing all things for the good of heaven and earth, and not for ourselves.

9. Ye know how Ahura's kingdom prospered until he began to work for his own glory; let us not, then, fall into his errors, but from his errors learn to avoid similar ones. And now, since the time of the feast is ended, and our respective kingdoms waiting us, I declare the assembly dissolved. Arise, then, my Lords and Lordesses, and go your way. And whatsoever ye may have on this matter, desiring to commune with me, do ye even so through messengers, which ye already have.

CHAPTER X.

1. Satan went to all the Lords and Lordesses in hada, and said unto each and every one: Thine shall be exaltation without labor; because thou art wise, others shall serve thee; and great shall be thy glory. As thou hast witnessed the rites and ceremonies, in Craoshivi, of the high-raised Gods, even so shall it be with thee. Behold, the heavens of the earth shall become the brightest and most glorious of all heavens. Be thou patient, enduring anything, for thou shalt surely, in time to come, be second to none, the highest of Gods!

2. And thy name shall be sung in the ceremonies, and shall be honored even in the far-off heavens. It shall be said of thee, thou art amongst the youngest of Gods, that by thine own self-will mastered all things so suddenly that even the oldest of Gods stood appalled at thy daring.

3. Be thou patient, and seeming most humble, and bide thou thy time; thou wert born to be a leader even amongst Gods. Be secret; disclosing naught.

4. Satan said to Anuhasaj, even Lord God: Be thou dignified, and by thy much-professed love, like a father unto all the others. And it shall come to pass that they will thrust these great dominions upon thee.

5. Now whilst these matters were with these Lords, behold, in far-off Craoshivi Jehovih spake to God on the throne, before the Council of Jehovih's Son, saying: Because I indulged thy Lords and Lordesses in prosperous places, they are becoming forgetful of Me.

6. For so I created man, in prosperity he idolizeth himself. He saith: Behold me! What great things I can do: Yea, I am wise; I perceive the nothingness of the Creator! And he buildeth to his own ruin. I created life and death all around him, that he might learn My power ere he quitteth the earth. And hada I made wide, with a place of ascent and a place of descent. Upward I placed My holy lights, saying: Come! Downward, I made darkness, saying: Beware! hell lieth hither! But they plunge into misery headlong.

507

7. God said: What have they done, O Jehovih? Jehovih said: They are laying their heads together to rebel against the manner of My everlasting kingdoms. Summon thou the Diva before thee, and bid them speak outright as to what they desire.

8. God sent messengers into all the divisions of the lowest heavens, to the kingdoms of Jehovih's Lords and Lordesses, as the Father had commanded, summoning them to Craoshivi. On the other hand:

9. Satan spake to Anuhasaj, the plotter of the mischief, saying: Lest God in Craoshivi get wind of this matter, and so set at naught thy long-laid plans, send thou to him, saying: Greeting, in love to thee, Son of Jehovih, God of the heavens of the earth. From the light before me I am resolved to resign the Lord-dom. Search, therefore, and provide one in my place.

10. Satan continued, to Anuhasaj: Send thou to thy Lords and Lordesses, saying: Greeting in love to thee, Lord of Jehovih. I foresee that many will desire me to take the place of God of the earth and her heavens. Seek thou to relieve me of this, and choose one less radical, that thou mayst the more fully endorse him. Behold, I am about to resign the Lord-dom, and desire to see thee.

11. The Lords and Lordesses received the two communications at the same time; and they severally laid the matter before their Holy Councils; and great was the excitement therein. That which had been planned to be in secret was thus made public in all the hadas in a day, before thousands of millions!

12. At once the Lords and Lordesses hastened to Anuhasaj's capital; and they were each attended by ten thousand attendants.

13. Now when they were assembled, perceiving that God in Craoshivi knew of the matter, they were by their own shame further incited to disobey the Divan summons, and at once proceed to founding a consolidated kingdom, with Anuhasaj at the head. Anuhasaj made believe he desired not the Godhead, and only agreed to serve provided they installed him with oaths of fidelity. And this they did.

14. So, after a session of three days, Anuhasaj was elected and enthroned in Hored, a new heavenly place, and crowned Our God of the earth and her heavens, the Very Lord God in Jehovih. Thus he became a false God.

15. But they crowned him not with the true crown, for that was with God in Craoshivi; but they made one, creating it in the sacred circle. But since he could not be crowned by those beneath him, they were in a quandary how to proceed. Then satan spake to Anuhasaj, saying: Command them to lie on their bellies in token of submission to thee, and say to them: Lay the crown at my feet, and I will stand with my head bare; and when ye have prostrated yourselves, I will command the crown in my own name to rise up and lie upon my head; and if it so rise, then know ye of a truth our work is the highest, best work.

16. Anuhasaj then repeated this to the Lords and Lordesses, and they laid them down on their bellies, each being anxious to show fidelity, in hope of exaltation. And when they were down and saw not, Anuhasaj, having not power in Light, said: Crown of these most holy, wise Lords and Lordesses of heaven and earth, arise thou and lie on the head of him who shall have dominion on earth and in these heavens!

17. And thereupon he stooped down on the sly, and with his own hand raised it up and crowned himself, and commanded the Lords to rise up. And lo and behold, some of the

Lords and Lordesses said they saw with the second sight of the soul, and that the crown rose of its own accord, being under the will of the circle!

18. And they clapped their hands, saying: ALL HAIL, OUR GOD! ALL HAIL, OUR GOD! ALL HAIL, OUR GOD! Proclaiming him in the east and west and north and south.

19. He responded: THE LORD, YOUR GOD, REIGNETH! Peace be unto you. Behold, the heavens and earth are mine; be ye steadfast unto me, and ye shall be glorified in my name. Ye that have been Lords and Lordesses shall be Gods and Goddesses, with great power and with mighty kingdoms. As I foresaw this, so have I provided for you beforehand. In this very time and place will I crown you and apportion you with great glory. Yet think not that this is the last; it is but the first, and temporary until the new heavens are founded with broader boundaries.

CHAPTER XI.
OF THE DEITY, ALIAS, DYAUS, ALIAS DE'YUS, ALIAS DEUS; ORIGIN AND POWER IN THE HEAVENS AND ON EARTH.

1. Anuhasaj said: I, the Lord, your God, being the All Highest, through your choice, decree, for sake of harmony and concert in our labors, the establishment of a De'yus.

2. As the Craoshivians have had a Diva (Divinity), so will I have a De'yus. And by virtue of mine own authority I proclaim ye, my Lords and Lordesses, as the holy members thereof.

3. As the Diva hath been taught in these heavens, so also be the De'yus, whereof I assume the chief head.

4. As the Diva had laws, so also shall our De'yus; and they shall be promulgated on the earth, and taught to mortals as the laws of De'yus (Deity). Therefore by my own voice I dissolve the Diva of heaven; and it shall not be from this time forth forever. And whosoever of ye being members thereof, shall this day resign the Diva, and send word to the ruler of Craoshivi, for his benefit, and for his kingdom's benefit.

5. And the ruler of Craoshivi shall continue in his own place and kingdom; for it is his.

6. And the ruler of Vara-pishanaha, called Ahura, shall continue in his own place and kingdom, for it is his.

7. First, then, I take unto myself Anubi, the Lord loved by you all, and he shall be my associate, and his title shall be MASTER OF THE SCALES OF HEAVEN, for he shall determine the grades of the spirits and send them to their respective departments. On earth his title shall be SAVIOR OF MEN, SON OF DE'YUS.

8. Second, thou, Hi-kas, shalt be RULER OVER JAFFETH and its heavenly kingdom; and thy title shall be TE-IN, and of the first rank of GOD OF THE EARTH.

9. Third, thou, Wotchissij, shall be ruler over Vind'yu, and her heavenly kingdom, and thy title shall be SUDGA, and of the first rank of GOD OF THE EARTH.

10. Fourth, thou Che-le-mung, shalt be ruler over Arabin'ya, and her heavenly kingdom, and thy title shall be OSIRIS, and of the first rank of GOD OF THE EARTH

11. Fifth, thou, Baal shalt be ruler over Heleste and her heavenly kingdom, and thy title shall be BAAL, and of the first rank of GOD OF THE EARTH.

12. Sixth, thou, Ashtaroth, shalt be ruler over Parsa, and its heavenly kingdom, and thy title shall be ASHTAROTH, of the first rank of GODDESS OF THE EARTH.

13. Seventh, thou, Fo-ebe, shalt be ruler over Uropa and her heavenly kingdom, and thy

title shall be Fo-ebe, and of the first rank of Goddess of the Earth.

14. Eighth, thou, Ho-jab, shalt be ruler over Japan and her heavenly kingdom, and thy title shall be Ho-jab, and of the first rank of God of the Earth.

15. After that the false God made appointments for the other divisions of the earth and their heavenly places, and after that he said unto them:

16. All my Gods and Goddesses shall have thrones in their places, and holy councils and attendants as becometh Gods of the first rank. And every one shall have a capital city, with subsidiaries according to the number and place of their spirits and mortal subjects.

17. And every God and Goddess shall manage his or her own kingdom in his or her own way; but every one shall nevertheless be tributary to my kingdom, according to the exactions I put upon him or them.

18. That ye may resign the Diva, and choose your assistants, before being crowned, I declare a day of recreation, to assemble at the trumpeter's call.

19. Hereupon the hosts relaxed from duty and made their resignations of the Diva, and sent them with messengers to God in Craoshivi, but not one of them mentioned the new state of affairs resolved upon. On the next day, at the trumpeter's call, they assembled again; and Anuhasaj said unto them: Come ye with me, and I will show you the place of Hored and its boundaries; for it shall not be my kingdom alone, but yours also, for my kingdom shall be the kingdom of your kingdoms.

20. And they entered an otevan, and, coming in the fourth belt below meteoris, in the sign of the twelfth arc of Chinvat; and Anuhasaj said: From this time forth this belt shall be called Hored, and it shall be my place forever. It shall be the central kingdom of all the earth's heavens.

21. And the multitude said: Hail, Kingdom of Hored, the holy hill, place of the Most High God! And it was known thereafter as the belt of Hored, hill of God. It was a three-quarters belt, and the base thereof was ten thousand miles from the earth, and the summit was fifteen thousand miles high; habitable within and without. And its ascending rank in grades was twenty, that is, it was easily habitable by spirits that attained to that grade; being above the grade of infants and drujas, and above the region of hells and knots, save in cases of great panic. Now, from the first place of Hored, where Anuhasaj crowned himself, which was the eastern base of the hill, to the place for his capital city, he made a roadway and called it Loo-hored, and it was the only opened roadway to the kingdoms below.

22. So it came to pass Anuhasaj had two capital cities; and the first was called the City of the Gate of Heaven, that is, Anubi; and the other was called the Place of Everlasting Rest, that is, Sanc-tu. Anuhasaj said to Anubi: Behold, the City of the Gate of Heaven shall be thy place. And thou shalt determine the rate of all souls who desire to enter the Place of Everlasting Rest. Thou shalt be judge over them. And whosoever is not for me shall not enter, but shall be cast into the kingdoms of hada. And those that are for me, thou shalt send unto me.

23. And thou shalt have a Holy Council of one hundred thousand; and of examiners thou shalt have one million. And thy capital shall be guarded on every side but one, with pillars of fires, so that none can pass but by the Gate of Heaven. And of guardsmen thou shalt have seven millions, divided into seven watches, one for each day. Of messengers betwixt thy place and mine, thou shalt have ten thousand; but betwixt thee and the Gods

and Goddesses of the lower kingdoms, thou shalt have five hundred thousand. But, of thine own choice, shall be the number of es'enaurs, trumpeters and marshals, and thy attendants also.

24. And all Gods and Goddesses coming to me, or sending messengers to my holy place, shall come through thy city, even through the Gate of Heaven; and they shall come according to certain rites and ceremonies which I will give unto thee. Come, therefore, and receive thy crown.

25. Thus was crowned Anubi; and after him were crowned the other Gods and Goddesses; and Anuhasaj bequeathed to each one his own kingdom, according to the custom of the ancients. And when these matters were completed, he again spake before them, saying: Behold the example I have made before you; even before I provided myself for mine own kingdom I have given unto every one all things required. It is meet and proper, therefore, that ye contribute unto me and my place workmen and materials, that I may build in great glory also.

26. For, as I am exalted, and my kingdom made glorious, so have ye whereof to preach gloriously to your inhabitants of the place in store for them. Thus, did Anuhasaj put Gods and Goddesses under obligations to himself, and they acquiesced in his proceedings, saying: Nay, we will not only contribute man and women for this purpose, but we will labor with our own hands for the space of twenty days, helping to build the capital city, and to open roads, in all directions.

CHAPTER XII.

ANUHASAJ, THE FALSE GOD, DECLARETH HIMSELF AGAINST JEHOVIH.

1. Anuhasaj never established the De'yus as projected at first, but took the name De'yus (Dyaus) upon himself, and became known in the heavens by that name. When he had thus established Hored in its entirety, he gave a feast to the Gods and Goddesses; and after it was ended, previous to their departure, he spake before them, saying:

2. The time of duty is now upon you, and upon me, the Lord your God, also. Be ye then solicitous of these things I speak of, that in the everlasting times we may be brethren, and there shall be no other Gods, but ourselves forever.

3. Behold, I have given into your hands to manage your own kingdoms in your way; for which reason I can no longer say, do ye this, or do ye thus and so, for my affairs are in mine own kingdom. But wherein I have wisdom I freely impart, and the choice is yours, whether ye will follow my advice or do otherwise, for ye are of equal rank with me. And, moreover, my kingdom is dependent upon you, and not yours upon mine. Hear ye then my words as if I were but one in a Council with wise Gods:

4. To overturn Jehovih and his dominions on the earth and in these heavens will be your first labor. And whenever corporeans embrace Him, calling themselves FAITHISTS IN THE GREAT SPIRIT, or FAITHISTS IN JEHOVIH, or FAITHISTS IN ORMAZD, or by any other name signifying the ALL LIGHT, or UNSEEN, or PERSON OF EVER PRESENCE, ye shall pursue them, and destroy them off the face of the earth. To do which ye shall use the oracles, or prophets and seers, or magicians, or inspiration; and ye shall set the kings and queens of the earth to war upon them, and spare them not, man, woman or child.

5. And of spirits of the dead who fall into your respective kingdoms, being Faithists,

bring them before Anubi and his hosts, and he shall send them into regions of darkness, saying to them: Behold, ye have your Jehovih! And Anubi shall place guards over them, and they shall not know where to go, but will cry out in their darkness.

6. Whereupon they shall be sworn into servitude in Hored to the Lord your God forever, and become slaves within your kingdoms.

7. And ye shall teach both mortals and spirits that Hored is the All Highest heaven, and that it is the place of the All Highest God, even De'yus. For them to attain which, ye shall exact servitude of them in your heavens accordingly as ye may desire.

8. In the rites and ceremonies, both in your heavens and on the earth, shall ye enforce the exchanging of words signifying Great Spirit to words signifying Lord God, who is of the form and size of a man, declaring of a truth that I sit on my throne in judgment of the world, for it is mine, and ye are one with me.

9. And all songs of praise shall be changed; and prayers and beseechings to your God, instead of Jehovih, or Ormazd, or the Great Spirit. For both mortals and angels shall be made to know that He is my enemy, leading my people astray. And as to the prophets and seers on the earth, who will persist in preaching or singing to the Great Spirit, ye shall incite torture and punishment and death unto them.

10. And whether I be De'yus, or God, or the Lord God, or the All Perfect, me only shall they worship, forever. And my place, Hored, shall be the sacred hill of God forever! And none shall approach me but by crawling on their bellies; for I will so exalt my lights that none can stand before me.

11. When the Lord God had finished his discourse, the other Gods responded in love and adoration. Thus ended the feast, and, according to the rites in other heavens, the Gods and Goddesses went and sat at the foot of the throne, and De'yus came down and took them by the hand, one at a time, and raised them up, saying: Arise, O God, and in my name, and wisdom, and power, go thy way. Thus they departed.

12. And as to the earth, great havoc and persecution were visited upon the Zarathustrians and Israelites, being put to death by hundreds of thousands.

CHAPTER XIII.

1. Swift messengers coursing the heavens, from far-off etherean worlds, bound for destinations remote, passed over the regions of Hored; and the high-raised travelers felt the discordant plots of satan's Lord God and his hosts, thus bent to overthrow the Great Spirit's happy world. And so they sent word of it to Cpenta-armij, through whose fields the great serpent moved along. And her Most High Council, one with the Creator, cast about to know the cause and treatment of the dastardly outrage.

2. Then spake Jehovih to His Daughter, Chieftainess, saying: The Lord God was duly honored in My name, and swore before Me to serve faithfully, forever, by his highest light. Hold thou him to his purpose, and bind him in the world he hath assumed to rule for his own glory. And to his fellow-God, conspirators against Me, Who brought them into being, give thou them full sway to destroy My worshippers. Let them raise the name of their God, and bait mortal kings and queens to glut themselves in the havoc of My chosen, the Faithists.

3. The earth neareth her greatest corporeal growth, and these self-assuming Gods shall

build monuments through their mortal emissaries, in the greatest divisions of the earth: Temples, and pyramids, and oracle-palaces, which shall stand thousands of years as testimonies of the audacity of Gods and Saviors. To honor whom, the Lord God hath sworn to make angels and men suppliant slaves in heaven and earth.

4. For I will use the corporeal temples and pyramids they shall build on the earth at the expense of My chosen, as testimony, in coming ages, of the oppression in the hadan-heavenly kingdoms of these self-Gods. Till which time I cannot teach mortals of the vanity of the lower heavens, save in the deserted ruins of their moldering monuments.

5. For in kosmon, mortals shall know that even as the earth hath been a place of foolish sacrifice to persons born of woman, so were My heavens debauched in that day by similar oppression and cruelty.

6. Let him who is falsely crowned Osiris, build in the Osirian field, and him who is proclaimed De'yus, build in the hadan field, for the time shall come when these testimonies shall be required in the sum of earth and heaven.

7. For I will show them that without an All Highest Person there is no resurrection for angels or men. Of which they that are slaughtered, ten thousand millions, and bound by the Lord God, shall swear, in kosmon, the fall of all things save Me.

8. Down to the lower heavens, to God in Craoshivi, sent Cpenta-armij swift messengers, with the words of Jehovih, comforting to God and his hosts, as to the wide plans on which the Father lieth the destinies of worlds. And God received them, and now comprehended why, alas, his Diva came not, nor answered his call but by resigning.

9. But God, the true ruler of heaven and earth, now saw how the prosperity of the indulged heaven had made bad men out of most holy Gods, even as prosperity on the earth closeth up man's eyes against his Creator, making him an egotist in self, and vociferous as to Jehovih's shortcomings, according to man's views. And God remembered how he had prayed for the continuation of the light in heaven, which Jehovih granted him; and he repented now, saying:

10. O Jehovih, why said I not: Thy will be done; let darkness come! Had I not seen on the earth how night must follow day, and winter after summer; that I must need pray for endless light in a heaven where Thy sons and daughters are as yet but babes in the time and course of worlds? Mine own judgment should have shown me that spells of darkness should follow seasons of light in Thy lower heavens. For, then, had these half-tried Lords and Gods stopped to consider ere they rushed into so mad a scheme.

11. God called together the Holy Council in Craoshivi, and told them of the words of the Creator, through His High-Raised Daughter. Then the Council spake, all who chose, and the thirty millions listened. And, meanwhile, messengers fresh from Hored, the seat of rebellion, came in, bringing full news to Craoshivi of the proceedings of the Lord God, alias, De'yus, and his self-Gods and Goddesses.

12. When the full particulars had been related, and the Council had spoken upon it, then the light of Jehovih came upon God, and God said:

13. In the name of our Father, I will speak to these Gods and Lords and acquaint them with Jehovih's words. Yea, I will entreat them to return even as they were.

14. Then God, overwhelmed by the terrible adversity of the heavens entrusted to his keeping, as in a small degree the captain of a merchant's ship, far out at sea, meeting with a mishap of broken masts, stripped to the bulk, and rudder gone, powerless to save,

feeleth the burning shame of incompetence before mariners, so God, before the High-Raised Chiefs of the etherean worlds, must helplessly view his shattered kingdoms.

15. With great sorrow God sent word to De'yus and his Gods, of Jehovih's warning; and he plead for them to return, as a father pleadeth to a wayward son. Off went the messengers swiftly; and God, even though long schooled to adverse trials and suspensions, burned with impatience for his messengers to return, hoping that his sweet pleadings might yet reverse the scenes.

16. Then came back the messengers, empty handed! Not one of the truant Gods had deigned to answer him. And God wept, scarce believing his messengers, that so great an insult could be heaped upon him, who had done nothing whereof any one could complain. Then Jehovih came and spake to God, saying: Weep not, My Son! He who followeth his highest light from day to day, great is his glory; and in whatsoever he loseth he shall regain a thousand-fold. Behold, I will bring love to thee that thou knowest not of: Remember thou, as this season is upon the earth and her heavens, even so do I send a season like unto it upon all My worlds.

CHAPTER XIV.

1. In course of time, word came to Ahura, in Vara-pishanaha, of the proceedings of the Lord God, now styled De'yus, and of the revolt of all the lowest heavens in one fell swoop. And Ahura remembered his own shortcomings, thousands of years ago, and the terrible bondage that came upon him in the end. And he knew De'yus, who had been a sub-God under him hundreds of years, under the name Anuhasaj, who had tried to break the lines in the arc of Spe-ta, in the resurrection of Ailkin.

2. So Ahura prayed to Jehovih, before the Holy Council in Vara-pishanaha, to know what he should say or do in the matter, or if nothing at all. Jehovih answered him, saying:

3. My Son, thou art no longer a child. Address thou the Lord God, or not address him, as seemeth fit in thine own eyes. Behold, I suffered thee to try the same road, that thou mightst understand Me and My kingdoms.

4. Thereupon Ahura determined to send word to De'yus, in his own name, and in his own way. Then, then, is what he sent, to wit:

5. To Anuhasaj, my one-time sub-God, greeting to thee in justice and wisdom. Wert thou inexperienced I would treat thee with respect. But thou knowest thou art false. And because thou art false, thou shalt reap in falsehood.

6. Behold, the day shall come when thy Gods will desert thee; for such is the tree thou hast planted in thy kingdoms. This rule holdeth on earth and in all the heavens. Can that which is unborn, restrain its own birth? Or that which is not quickened into life, restrain the Creator's hand?

7. So also is it of him that soweth for self; he shall reap a harvest of selfs. And thy Gods will be for themselves, and thy marshals, and all thy hosts; every one pulling in an opposite way.

8. Not suddenly will these things come upon thee; for thou shalt have a mighty kingdom and great honor and glory, such as no other God before thee hath had in these heavens. And thy people shall be jealous to serve thee, striving with all their might to outdo one another in worshipful obedience to thee. And thy name, even the names De'yus and Lord

514

God, shall stand for a season the highest on the earth of all names that have ever been.

9. And yet the time shall come that thy names shall be cast out of earth and heaven. Even the deeds that thou shalt do shall be the means of making thy names execrable.

10. Think not, O my Lord God, that thou wilt deal righteously, and keep thyself holy. Behold, I, too, was a revolted God that sat up a kingdom for mine own glory. And, in the time of the beginning thereof, I was most resolute to practice righteousness in all things.

11. But the surroundings overcame me; for as I was allied to self, so selfish officers under me beset me on all occasions, and I was forced to find new places and new glories for them, or, by their grumbling, they would sow my fields with mutiny. I was powerless in the great kingdom I built up. Thou knowest the result.

12. Thinkest thou the larger thy kingdom, the greater will be thy power to avert thy fall? My experience was the opposite of this.

13. I admonish thee in wisdom and justice; I know thou art doing these things not for the raising up of the fruit of the earth, but for thine own aggrandizement and glory. And I say unto thee, the time will surely come when thy Gods will do the same things against thee. And in that time the wise and learned and truthful will fly from thee, but the drujas and slaves will not leave thee; but thou shalt be environed with them, and cast into hell.

14. Thou shalt heap misery upon millions of thy subjects, but thou shalt not escape the hand of justice: Thou shalt reimburse them every one. Thou hast cast thy net in shoal water; thine own feet shall be tangled in the meshes thereof.

15. Behold, I, too, once craved a great heavenly kingdom; now I weep day and night because I have it. And thou, too, shalt experience the time of scalding tears, to be rid of that which thou cravest even now.

16. Yet, how else shall the dumb be raised in heaven? Who else shall minister to the wandering spirits that overspread the earth? And the evil drujas? And the lusters, and foul-smelling? Shall I say to thee: Go on, thou self-presuming Lord God, the Great Spirit hath a rod in pickle for thee!

17. Yea, He answereth the ambition of men and Gods sooner or later; in a way they think not of, He bringeth them up with a round turn.

18. Thou art like a man desirous of great bulk, that shutteth up the pores of the skin of his flesh; thou seekest to shut up the course of the heavens that riseth out of the earth, upward forever. And as the one choketh up with a foul smell, and dieth, so shall it be with thy kingdom. Behold, the way of everlasting light is outward; onward, away from the corporeal world; but the way of darkness is toward the earth.

19. Sayest thou the spirits of the dead shall not rise away from the earth? And, in their ignorance of the higher heavens, become guides to mortals!

20. Behold, thou hast traveled far; and thou struttest about, saying: It is enough; I, the Lord God, have traveled in the far-off heavens; stay ye at home, and work for me forever, that I may be glorified!

21. Wilt thou say: I, the Lord God, I, De'yus, am the only Son of the Void! Behold, by kingdom lieth in a little corner! Come and worship me, the Lord God, and ye shall see me on my throne!

22. Or wilt thou say: The impersonal space, senselessness, by accident fructified itself in corporeal substance, and became me, the Lord God, in size of a full-grown man, and then I created all the creations! Wherefore let men and angels fall down and

worship the man, De'yus, who dwelleth in Hored, a ripple in the lowest heavens!

23. I profess not love to thee, Anuhasaj, but justice toward them beneath thee. For thou shalt hoodwink mortals, and even angels of little experience, to believe thou wert the very Creator; but thy Gods know thee as to who thou art, and the Gods above thee know also. All thy days at most have been but two thousand and seven hundred years! And the time shall come upon thee that thou shalt be forced by thine own fault to assert thou wert the very Creator, whose worlds have run thousands of millions of years! Who can carry so great a falsehood as this! And not carrying it, it shall fall down on thee and on thy people, and take root and spread abroad till thy place and thy Gods' places are the foundation of nothing but lies.

24. For the rule holdeth in all places, high and low, that according to the seed sown so shall be the harvest, whether good or bad. Nor can any man or God alter this rule, or bend it to the right or left.

25. If it be Jehovih's decree that some one shall make the name of God, and Lord God, and De'yus, execrable on earth and in heaven, it may be well that thou hast put thyself into the yoke to that end. Yet I would not have thee so, could I prevent it.

26. Thou wert one time my sub-God, and I remember thee well; thou wert young and full of promise. My judgment spake to me of thee, saying: A sub-God, to be proud of for thousands of years! But my judgment was not Jehovih's. My love for thee was early nipped in the bud. For thou wert forever talking of thyself. Thou madest thy neighbor Gods sick by forever relating thy experiences and thy prophecies as to what thou wouldst do.

27. And when Jehovih encompassed me about in mine own evil, thou didst tantalize me because I had not followed thy advice. Now I repeat unto thee, I could not follow any one's advice. And thou, too, shalt be environed about, and be unable to follow any one's advice. For such is the bondage of the Godhead, save we cut ourselves loose, making Jehovih the Head and Front, and ourselves His servants. For the God should not only be the greatest in his kingdom, but the most menial servant of his people; forever throwing off responsibility, and forever urging his subjects not to idolize him, but Jehovih! Forever showing them that their God is nothing more than themselves; that they must stand alone, and become, not slaves to their God, but independent beings full of manliness, having faith in the Great Spirit only.

28. By which the God bindeth not himself nor his people; giving full sway to the love of liberty in every soul, but in tenderness and love that harmonize with Jehovih's proceedings.

29. Now when thou camest back to me, after I was delivered out of hell, and my kingdoms raised to Vara-pishanaha, thou didst profess to understand these things, and of a truth, to love this philosophy. And thou didst pray fervently to Jehovih, repenting of thy former ways, taking part in the rites and ceremonies.

30. Then I opened my heart to thee. My much love for thee, as when I first knew thee, returned upon me a thousand fold. In joy and in tears I fell upon thee, and I praised Jehovih that He had sent me so sweet a love.

31. In each other's arms we repented, and we swore our mutual love forever. Then we both saw the way of Jehovih clear, and He made us strong and wise, full of rejoicing.

32. And we fell to, hand in hand, laboring with drujas, dark and most foul, teaching them

day and night, forever repeating to their stupid minds. And when we were both well nigh exhausted thousands of times, and we slacked up, and withdrew for a short spell, we rested in each other's arms!

33. Then we reasoned and philosophized on the plans and glories of Jehovih's works; hopefully watching signs of progress in our wards. O the glory of those days! O the richness of thy wisdom and love to me in those days of darkness! For a hundred years we toiled thus, and I was blessed, and my people were blessed by thee, thou star of our love.

34. When we raised them up, my wards, four thousand millions, were lifted a small way up out of darkness, and our far-off Goddess, Atcheni, needed one who was great, like unto thee, to travel in other regions. And I parted with thee. My soul was as if divided in twain.

35. For hundreds of years thou traveledst and became rich in knowledge; but not to return to me, to my bursting heart! What more can I say? Thou art in my place, and I am in mine; but Jehovih is with Wisdom, Love, Truth and Fidelity, for these are his abiding places.

CHAPTER XV.

1. De'yus replied not to Ahura, God of Vara-pishanaha, but sent the messengers away without a word. And satan came again to De'yus, saying: Send word to thy Gods to be firm, for this day hath Ahura and the God of Craoshivi beset them to return to Jehovih's worship.

2. De'yus feared nevertheless, so he inquired of satan what was the best great thing he could do. Satan said: O Lord, my God, this is the best thing thou canst do: For all the Divan laws destroyed, make thou De'yus laws instead. Why shalt thou follow in the footsteps of the ancients?

3. The Lord God said: Yea, yea! I will not be bound by the laws of the ancients, but I will have laws of mine own, and they shall be called the LAWS OF THE LORD GOD.

4. Satan (self) said: These, then shall be thy words, O Lord God, which shall be the laws of De'yus, to wit:

5. I, the Lord God, have made self-preservation the first law.

6. Thou shalt love the Lord thy God with all thy soul, thy heart and mind.

7. Him only shalt thou worship now, henceforth and forever.

8. Thou shalt not worship Jehovih; He is void; He is nothing.

9. Nor shalt thou worship any idol of anything, on the earth or in the heavens of the earth.

10. Whoever worshippeth anything save me, the Lord God, shall be put to death.

11. Behold, I am a God of justice and truth; I am a God of anger; vengeance is mine.

12. I have a gate at the hill of Hored; my guardians are cherubims and seraphims, with flaming swords.

13. Whoever raiseth his arm against me shall be destroyed; to do my will is the sixth law.

14. Whosoever putteth the mark of the circumcision on a male child shall be put to death.

15. Neither shall any man do evil for evil's sake; nor by violence oppress any man, woman or child.

16. Whoever exalteth me on earth, him will I exalt in heaven.

17. Whoever overthroweth other Gods, save the Lord God, who is the De'yus of heaven and earth, him will I exalt in heaven.

18. Now it came to pass that these decrees of the false God were established on the earth. And the names Dyaus became paramount to all other Gods in Vind'yu and eastern Parsi'e; and the name Te-in, in Jaffeth (China), and the name Lord God, in Arabin'ya (Egypt). And these peoples had now a new sacred book given to them. And yet all of these names represented only angel only, Anuhasaj, a one-time mortal.

19. Prior to this the Faithists on earth were taught non-resistance; to ignore leadership; to return good for evil, and to dwell together as brethren.

20. But now, because of the decrees of Anuhasaj, alias De'yus, Faithists were led astray, becoming warriors, and aspiring to become kings and rulers.

21. Nevertheless, many of them still called themselves by names signifying Faithists, but changing their belief from the Great Spirit to a God in shape and figure of a man, with attributes like a mortal.

22. And mortals in these countries made images of cherubims and seraphims, having flaming swords; and images of Anubis holding a pair of scales; the same as is made to this day, and called JUSTICE.

23. In addition to these earthly decrees, Anuhasaj, alias the Lord God, made heavenly decrees betwixt his own kingdom and the kingdoms of his Gods. The chief decrees were: That, for the first one hundred years, all angels borne up out of the earth shall fall into their respective divisions, and shall belong as subjects to my Gods, to be appropriated by them in their own way.

24. That after the hundredth year, my Gods shall deliver to me one-tenth of their subjects of the highest grades.

25. De'yus made two hundred laws in reference to the kingdoms of his Gods, as to their boundaries and ornamentation, providing great pageantry and countless numbers of heralds, staff-bearers, musicians, and players of oratory (theatricals), besides innumerable servants and decorators, so that the pageantry might be in great splendor.

26. When he had completed these forms and system of government, he sent an invitation to his Gods to again feast with him, that they might ratify his laws and receive them.

27. And it thus came to pass that the laws of De'yus were ratified and accepted by the Gods; and they went away rejoicing, returning to their respective kingdoms, where they fell to work at once to provide themselves in their glory.

CHAPTER XVI.

HEREIN IS REVEALED THE MANNER IN WHICH THE GODS CARRIED OUT WHAT HAD BEEN PREVIOUSLY STATED.

1. Thus was established the CONFEDERACY OF SELFS; that is, the false Lord God, and his false Gods, were as many kingdoms united into one; yet every god was secretly sworn unto himself, for his own glory.

2. From the time of the beginning of the revolt until it was completed as a confederacy was sixty and four days, and the number of inhabitants in these heavens at that time was eight thousand millions, men, women and children. And they are well-ordered, in nurseries, and hospitals, and schools, and colleges, and factories, and in building ships, and in surveying and in road-making, and all such other occupations as belong in the lower heavens, objective and subjective. Four thousand million of these were presently sent to Hored, to De'yus.

3. De'yus at once set about the work laid out, and issued a decree commanding the destruction of all otevans and other vessels plying to the upper plateau, Craoshivi; and commanding the seizing and destroying of fire-ships or other vessels that might come from the upper regions down to the lower. De'yus said: My people shall not ascend to other heavens. I have made the earth and this heaven sufficient unto all happiness and glory. Whosoever buildeth a vessel, saying: I will ascend; or if he say not, but my judges discover him, he shall be cast into the hadan region, prepared for im. And if a man or a woman preach in my heavens, and say: Behold, there is a higher heaven, that person shall be cast into hell, as my son judgeth.

4. And I, De'yus, command the locking up of all the books in the libraries of my heavens that in any way teach of Jehovih or Ormazd, or of heavenly kingdoms above mine or greater. For I, the Lord God, will have but one kingdom, and I will draw all people into it to abide with me forever.

5. And my Gods, and my marshals, and generals and captains, shall take their hosts and go around about the regions of Hored, and make a clean roadway, and cut off all connection with the outer kingdoms. And they shall place in the roadway around my heavens a standing army, sufficient to guard my kingdom and my Gods' kingdoms forever. And no man-angel, nor woman-angel shall pass outward beyond my roadway forever.

6. These things were carried out, save as to the libraries. But there were destroyed four thousand otevans and other ascending ships; and of the places for manufacturing ships for the outer heavens that were destroyed, more than seven hundred. And there were thus thrown out of employment seven hundred millions, men and women! And many of these were compelled to go to Hored, where they were assorted as to grade, and put to work, beautifying the capital and Council house and palace of the Lord God, the false. Others were impressed into the standing army, being allotted seasons and years.

7. After the outward extreme of hada was thus secured in every way, De'yus turned to the interior. He said: Now will I hide away text-books in my heavenly places, as relate to higher kingdoms and to Jhovih; for from this time forth He is my enemy and I am His. Upon my own self have I sworn it; the name of Jehovih and Ormazd shall be destroyed in heaven and earth; and my name, De'yus, even the Lord God, shall stand above all else.

8. For sixty days, the armies of destruction traversed the lowest heavens, high and low, far and near; and they hid away many of the records, and books, and maps, relating to the higher atmospherea and to the etherean worlds beyond; and in sixty days the work of destruction was complete in these heavens, and there was nothing left within sight to prove or to teach the higher heavens, or of Jehovih, the Ormazd.

9. The Lord God, the false, said: Let my name and my place, even Hored, be replaced instead of those destroyed, for I will make the name De'yus to rule in one-half of the world, and the name Lord God to rule in the other half.

10. The inhabitants of heaven and earth shall know where to find me, and shall behold my person, and witness the strength of my hands. Yea, they shall know my pleasure and my displeasure, and serve me in fear and trembling.

11. And the books in the schools and colleges of these heavens were thus made to rate De'yus and the Lord God as the All Highest, Most Sacred, Most Holy.

12. When these things were established thus far, De'yus gave a great feast, and brought

into his companionship all the valorous fighters and destroyers that had proved themselves great in fulfilling his commandments. In the meantime, the laborers and officers in charge had extended and beautified the palace and capital of the Lord God in Hored beyond anything ever seen in these heavens. So that at the time of this feast, the place was already one of magnificence and glory. And the order, and temper, and discipline of the officers and servants, more than one million, who had charge of preparing and conducting the feast, were so great that the assembled Gods and great generals, and governors, and marshals, and captains, for a long while, did nothing but ejaculate applause and astonishment.

13. Besides these, De'yus had provided receiving hosts, fifty thousand, and of es'enaurs and trumpeters half a million, and proclaiming heralds one hundred thousand; and the latter, when conducting the distinguished visitors into the presence of De'yus, proclaimed them, amidst the applause of the Holy Council, such honor surpassing anything that any of them had ever witnessed.

14. The substance of the feast, being above grade twenty, which was above the animal region, was, consequently, of vegetable and fruit es'pa from the earth, previously brought by trained shippers and workers, for this especial occasion. But there was no es'pa of flesh or fish present on the tables; but an abundance of the es'pa of wine, and this was called NECTAR (su-be).

15. The walls of the chamber of the feast were ornamented with sprays of colored fire, and from the floor of the chamber there rose upward innumerable fountains of perfume, which were also es'pa brought up from the earth, and forced up in the fountains by more than one million servants, impressed into service from the regions of shippers, which had been destroyed previously.

16. At the feast, with the Lord God and his Gods, there were in all one thousand two hundred guests; and the feast lasted one whole day, and the Gods and guests ate and drank to their hearts' content, and there were not a few who felt the intoxication of the rich nectar.

17. When the feast was ended, De'yus, through his marshals, signified that he would speak before them; and when quiet was restored, he said: What greater joy hath any one in a matter than to make others happy! Because ye served me, doing my commandments, behold, I have served you. My feast hath been your feast; my substance have I given unto you, that ye may rejoice in the glory I have received from your hands.

18. Yet think not that the Lord, your God, so endeth this proceeding: I will not so end it. I have commanded you here that I may honor those that deserve honor from me, your God. My Gods have also great exaltation in the labor ye have done in my heavens, for my heavens are their heavens, and yours also. Because ye have destroyed the ascension, the most worthless and foolish of things, and cleared away the rubbish of my heavens, ye have also prepared a place for endless glory for yourselves.

19. For which reason, and in justice to you, I have appointed this time to promote you all, according to your great achievements. Nor shall ye fall back on my promotion, resting in ease; for I have a greater labor for you, as well as greater honor and glory.

20. Behold, I have commanded the earth and her dominions; and ye, my Gods, shall subjugate her to my name and power. And ye that have proved yourselves most valiant in heaven shall be their chosen officers to go down to the earth in my name, with millions of

my heavenly soldiers, to plan and fix the way of mortals unto my hand. As ye have cast out the names Jehovih and Ormazd in heaven, even so shall ye cast them out on the earth.

21. Remember ye, I am a God of anger; I have declared war against all ungodliness on the earth. Whoever worshippeth the Great Spirit under the name Jehovih, or Ormazd, shall be put to death, both men and women. Only little children shall ye spare, and of them shall ye make slaves and eunuchs and whatsoever else that shall profit my kingdoms.

22. Whether they have an idol of stone, or of wood, or of gold, or of copper, they shall be destroyed. Neither shall it save them to make an idol of the Unseen; for such is even more offensive in my sight than the others. For will I leave alive one Faithist on the face of the earth.

23. To accomplish which, my Gods shall select ye who are of my feast; according to their rank shall they choose; and when ye are thus divided and selected, ye shall receive badges from my hand, and repair with my Gods to the places and service they desire.

24. And when ye are come down to the earth, ye shall possess yourselves of the oracles and places of worship, driving hence all other angels, and Gods, and Lords, and familiars. And when mortals come to consult the spirits ye shall answer them in your own way in order to carry out my commandments.

25. And when ye find prophets and seers, who accomplish by the Unseen, who have with them spirits belonging to the kingdom of Craoshivi, ye shall drive away such spirits and obsess the prophet or seer in your own way. But if ye cannot drive hence the Ormazdian angel, then shall ye go to the depths of hell in hada and bring a thousand spirits of darkness, who are foul and well skilled in torment, and ye shall cast them upon that prophet until he is mad. But if it so happen that the prophet or seer be so protected that spirits of darkness cannot reach him, then shall ye send evil spirits in advance of him to the place he frequenteth, and they shall inoculate the place with virus that shall poison him to death.

26. But if a prophet of Jehovih repent and renounce the Great Spirit, and accept De'yus, or the Lord God, then shall ye drive all evil away from him, and put a guard around about him, for he shall be my subject in time to come.

27. And whether ye reach a king of the earth by means of the oracles, or through prophets and seers, or by obsession, it mattereth not; but ye shall come to him by some means, either when he lieth asleep or is awake, and ye shall inspire him with the doctrines and the love of the Lord your God. And he shall rise up in great war, and pursue all people who do not profess De'yus, or the Lord your God; for he shall be as an instrument in your hands to do my will.

28. When De'yus ceased speaking, the Gods immediately made their selections, and the generals and captains were thus allotted to new places. And now the attendants carried away the tables of the feast, and the Gods, each with his captains and generals, faced toward De'yus, and formed twelve rows; whereupon De'yus conferred badges, as previously promised.

29. De'yus then departed to the Council chamber, and took his seat on the throne. The guests, and Gods, and Councilors, entered the south gate, and went and stood in the midst of the floor of the chamber; whereupon the Lord God saluted them, WARRIORS OF GOD, and they embraced in the SIGN OF TAURUS, signifying, TO ENFORCE RIGHTEOUSNESS, for the image of a bull was one of the signs above the throne. (And this was called the EDICT OF THE BULL.)

30. These, then, are the names of the Gods and Goddesses, with their generals and captains, that were empowered in heaven to go down to the earth to subjugate it unto the Lord God, the false, that is to say:

31. The Gods were: Anubi; Hikas, now called Te-in; Wotchissij, now called Sudga; Che-le-mung, now called Osiris; Baal, Ashtaroth, Foe-be, Hes-loo, He-loo, Orion, Hebe and Valish.

32. Their generals were: Hoin, Oo-da, Jah, Knowteth, June, Pluton-ya, Loo-Chiang, Wah-ka, Posee-ya-don, Dosh-to, Eurga-roth, Neuf, Apollo-ya, Suts, Karusa, Myion, Hefa-yis-tie, Petoris, Ban, Ho-jou-ya, Mung-jo, Ura-na, Oke-ya-nos, Egupt, Hi-ram, T'cro-no, Ares, Yube, Feh-tus, Don, Dan, Ali-jah, Sol, Sa-mern, Thu-wowtch, Hua-ya, Afro-dite, Han, Weel, Haing-le, Wang-le, Ar-ti-mis, Ga-song-ya, Lowtha, Pu, Tochin-woh-to-gow, Ben, Aa-ron, Nais-wiche, Gai-ya, Te-sin, Argo, Hadar, Atstsil, E-shong, Daridrat, Udan, Nadar, Bog-wi, She-ug-ga, Brihat, Zeman, Asrig, Oyeb, Chan-lwang, Sishi, Jegat, At-ye-na and Dyu.

33. Their captains were: Penbu, Josh, Yam-yam, Holee-tsu, Yoth, Gamba, Said, Drat-ta, Yupe-set, Wag, Mar, Luth, Mak-ka, Chutz, Hi-rack-to, Vazenno, Hasuck, Truth, Maidyar, Pathemadyn, Kop, Cpenta-mainyus, Try-sti-ya, Peter, Houab, Vanaiti, Craosha, Visper, Seam, Plow-ya, Yact-ta-roth, Abua, Zaotha, Kacan-cat, Hovain, Myazd-Loo, Haur, Abel, Openista, Isaah, Vazista, Potonas, Kiro, Wiska-dore, Urvash, Ashesnoga, Cavo, Kalamala-hoodon, Lutz-rom, Wab, Daeri, Kus, Tsoo-man-go, and Le-Wiang.

34. Besides these, were one thousand officers of lower rank; and now, when they were sealed as to rank and place and allotment, they withdrew; and De'yus gave a day of recreation that the Gods with their officers might make the selections from the multitude, as for their private soldiers.

35. And in one day's time the armies were made up, two thousand million angels, and they departed down to the earth to destroy the Faithists and the names Jehovih and Ormazd, and establish De'yus, otherwise the Lord God, the false.

CHAPTER XVII.

1. God, in Craoshivi, bewailed heaven and earth. He said: Great Jehovih, how I have failed in Thy kingdom! Behold, Thou gavest into my keeping the earth and her heavens, and they have gone astray!

2. Jehovih said: Behold the plan of My government; which is, to come against nothing in heaven or earth; to seize nothing by the head and turn it round by violence to go the other way.

3. Though I am the power that created them, and am the Ever Present that moveth them along, I gave to them to be Gods, like Myself, with liberty to find their own direction.

4. I created many trees in My garden, the greatest of which is the tree of happiness. And I called out unto all the living to come and dwell in the shade of that tree, and partake of the fruits and its perfumes. But they run after prickers and they scourge themselves; and then, alas, they fall to cursing Me, and accusing Me of shortness in My government.

5. I confined them in their mother's womb for a season, showing them there is a time for all things. But they ran forward hurriedly, desiring speedy happiness and wisdom, without halting to observe My glories by the road-side.

6. I said unto them: Even as I have given liberty unto all My people, so shall ye not impress into your service your brothers and sisters. But the self-assuming Gods make slaves of their fellows; they build roads round about, and station armies of soldiers to prevent My newborn from coming to My most glorious kingdoms.

7. They go down to the earth and inspire kings and queens, and rich men, to do the same things. And they portion out to their servants, saying to them: Serve ye me, and I will do for you. They little think that their servants will become as thorns, and stones, and chains, and spears against them in the far future. They build up a justice of their own, saying: As much as my servants labor for me, so will I render unto them. But I have said unto them that no man shall serve another but for love, which shall be his only recompense.

8. The king and the queen of the earth, and the rich man, shut their own eyes against Me, thinking by that means I cannot see them; they flatter themselves that in heaven they will give the slip to their servants. But I sowed a seed of bondage in My garden, and I said: Whosoever bindeth another, shall himself be bound. And behold, when they are risen in heaven, their servants and their soldiers come upon them; their memory is as a troubled dream that will not away from them.

9. Nevertheless, with these great examples before them, still there are angels in hada that have not profited therein. For they say unto themselves; I will build a great kingdom in heaven; I will become the mightiest of Gods; millions of angels shall serve me; I will shut out the Great Spirit and His far-off heavens; I will wall my place around with an army of soldiers, and with fire and water.

10. As a libertine stealeth an unsuspicious damsel to abuse her; and, in time, she waketh up to the matter but to curse him, so do the false Gods steal upon the inhabitants of My places and carry them into bondage. But the light of My understanding dwelleth in the souls of My little ones; it waiteth for the spring sun; and it will spring up and grow into a mighty tree to accuse these Gods.

11. God inquired concerning warfare?

12. Jehovih said: I answer all things by good. To the good at heart I give good thoughts, desires and holy observations. To the perverse of heart I hold up My glories and the beneficence of virtue and peaceful understanding. To them that practice charity and good works unto others, laboring not for self, I give the highest delight. Though they be pricked in the flesh with poverty and wicked persecutions, yet their souls are as the waters of a smooth-running river. Amongst them that practice evil, and destruction, and war, I send emissaries of benevolence and healing, who have plenteous words of pity.

13. These are My arrows, and spears, and war-clubs, O God: Pity, gentle words, and the example of tenderness. Soon or late, these shall triumph over all things in heaven and earth.

14. Behold, these wars in hada and on the earth will continue more than a thousand years. And the inhabitants will go down in darkness, even to the lowest darkness. For which reason, thou and thy successors shall provide not hastily, as if the matter were to change with the wind. But thou shalt organize a new army of deliverers for My Faithists, and it shall have two branches, one for the earth and one for hada. And the business of thy army shall be to rescue My people from them that seek to destroy them. And as to the spirits of the dead who were Faithists on the earth, provide thou means of transportation and bring them to thy new kingdom, which thou shalt call At-ce-wan,

where thou shalt provide a sub-God, and officers, and attendants, hundreds of millions.

15. And in At-ce-wan, thou shalt provide the sub-God all such places and nurseries, hospitals, factories, schools, colleges and such other houses and places of instructions required, in the kingdoms of My Lords in hada.

16. And when thou hast this matter in good working order, thou shalt speak before thy Holy Council; in My name shalt thou say to them after this manner: Two hundred thousand hath Jehovih called; by Him am I commanded to find them; and they shall be wise and strong and without fear. For they shall be angel-preachers in Jehovih's name to go down to Hored, the place of De'yus, the Lord God the false, and to the kingdoms of his Gods; and their labor shall be to preach and proclaim the Father and His glories in the etherean worlds.

17. And my preachers shall not say one word against the Lord God nor his Gods; but rather the other way; by majesty of Jehovih's love, be loving towards them and their officers and subjects. For by this means shall my preachers have peaceful dwellings in these warring kingdoms; and thus their voices shall have great weight. For the greatest wisdom of a great diplomatist is not to be too opposite or too vehement, but conciliating.

18. Jehovih said: And thy preachers shall travel constantly in the lowest kingdoms, teaching and explaining My boundless worlds, sowing the seed of aspiration with the wise and with the ignorant, and especially with the enslaved.

19. And to as many as become converted, and desire to ascend to Craoshivi, thou shalt say: Go ye to the border of your kingdom, whither the Father's laborers have a ship to take ye to His kingdom. But thy preachers shall not go with them to excite suspicion or hate, but continue on preaching and inciting the slaves to ascend to higher and holier heavens.

20. Then God, of Craoshivi, fell to work to carry out the commandments of Jehovih. And his Council labored with him. At-ce-wan was established and Yotse-hagah was made the sub-God, with a Holy Council of one hundred thousand angels, with a thousand attendants, with fifty thousand messengers. He was provided with a capital, and throne, and with ship-makers and builders of mansions, one million angels.

21. After that God and the Council of Craoshivi organized all the armies as commanded by Jehovih. And there were in these armies, all told, seventeen hundred millions, and two hundred and eight thousand five hundred and sixty, all of whom were above grade fifty, and some as high as ninety.

22. And it so turned out that these organizations were completed and in working order two days prior to De'yus and his hosts beginning their war on the earth. But the Faithist angels were distributed mostly in hada and the regions above. So that whilst De'yus' hosts of two thousand millions were gone down to the earth, there were of Faithist angels for the same place but four hundred thousand, save the ashars who were in regular service.

CHAPTER XVIII.

OF THE BATTLES OF THE GODS FOR THE DOMINION OF THE EARTH AND THE LOWEST HEAVENS; AND THESE WERE CALLED BATTLES OF A THOUSAND YEARS.

1. De'yus was no slow hand; not a dull God. He had two thousand seven hundred years' experience, and his soul quick and strong in mighty works. He rushed not in without first measuring the way, most deliberately and in great wisdom.

2. At first he felt his way along, to humor the populace, doing as if by proxy Jehovih's

commands, till safely fell into his dominion and power his flattered Gods and officers, then boldly launching forth: I, the Lord God, command!

3. The very audaciousness of which overtopped his friends' judgment, and made them believe for a fact that De'yus was the foremost and greatest, mighty God. To do whose will, and reverently applaud his name, was the surest road to home laurels.

4. To win great majesty to himself, and after having sworn to havoc the whole earth in order to establish the name De'yus, and Lord God, he called to his side his five chiefest friends: the Gods, Hikas, falsely named Te-in; Wotchissij, falsely named Sudga; Che-le-mung, falsely named Osiris; Baal, and Ashtaroth. And thus in dignity De'yus spake to them:

5. It is well, my Gods, ye stand about and see the battles; but let your generals and high captains go forth and mingle in the bloody work. In your kingdoms be constantly upraising your magnificence, and in times sallying forth to the earth valiantly, as when kings and queens and prophets are to win a victory, or be plunged into mortal death, to show how your august presence turned the tide of battle. Then hie ye back in dignity to your thrones, leaving your officers and inspiring hosts to go in the game of mortal tragedy.

6. Then spake Osiris, falsely named, saying: To exalt thy name, O De'yus, thou Lord God; and to persuade mortals that thou, of all created beings, can stand in Hored, and by thy will control the victory to whomsoever applaudeth thee and praiseth thy name, be thou to me the bond of my solemn oath, so will I lose or win battles on the earth accordingly as they shall honor thee and despise the Great Spirit, or any other God or Lord.

7. Then Te-in, also falsely named, said: To keep mortals in constant war for a thousand years; to teach them that battles are won or lost according to the loudest call and praise to thee, O De'yus, under thy thigh will I be as an oath renewed from everlasting to everlasting.

8. Sudga, the false, said: By all my parts, to shape the arms and legs of the unborn in comeliness, shall my legions drum into the ears of enceinte women a thousand years, swearing them to thy name, O De'yus; or, if refusing, to curse with crookedness all their progeny. And when these mothers sleep, my legions shall find their souls in their dreams, and give them delight or torment, accordingly as they, when awake, applaud thee, my most might Lord God.

9. Baal said: To overturn the oracles of Jehovih, and to make the prophets and seers receive and announce thy name, O'De'yus, thou Lord God of heaven and earth, have I already sworn more than ten thousand oaths.

10. Ashtaroth said: The work of my legions shall be to deal death to thy enemies, O De'yus. To them that raise the name Jehovih, or Ormazd, or Great Spirit, my legions shall carry foul smells to their noses whilst they sleep. And for thy enemies, who may win a battle against thy people, my legions shall carry inoculation from the rotten dead; in the air shall they carry the virus to the breath of them that will not bow down to the name, Lord God!

11. De'yus answered them, saying: So spoken, so shall these things be; I, the Lord your God, command. Send forth your generals and high captains thus decreed; to each and every one sufficient armies to make patent these, our high resolves. Into three great armies shall my legions be divided for the earth battles: one to Jaffeth, one to Vind'yu,

and one to Arabin'ya and the regions lying west and north. Of the latter, thou, Osiris, shalt have chief command; and thou, Baal, and thou, Ashtaroth, ye twain, so linked in love and one purpose, shall be the earth managers to Osiris' will. For your efficient service, behold, I have given you these high-raised generals and captains: Jah, Pluton-ya, Apollo-ya, Petoris, Hi-ram, T'cro-no, Egupt, Ares, Yube, Ali-jah, Afro-dite, Ar-ti-mis, Ben, Aa-ron, Argo, Atstsil, Nadar and Oyeb, besides Peter, Yact-ta-roth, Haur, Abel, Said, Josh and Wab, who shall be the conquering spirits to play on both sides in battles, urging stubborn mortals on to religious feud till both sides fall in death, or till one, to me and my Gods, boweth down in fear and reverence. And they shall sing their names in mortal ears day and night, and teach them to live in praise of the Lord, your God, the De'yus of heaven and earth, and to be most daring in the overthrow of Jehovih, most hated of Gods.

12. To thee, Te-in, another third of my legions is committed, to deal with the land of giants, and urge them on in the same way, to greatness or to death, doing honor and reverence to me and my kingdoms. High raised are thy generals: Wah-ka, Ho-jou-ya, Oke-ya-nos, Thu-wowth, Haing-le, Gochin-woh-to-gow, and Eurga-roth, besides Yam-yam, Hi-rack-to, Kacan-cat, Isaah, Lutz-rom and Le-Wiang, and others of high grade and power.

13. And to thee, O Sudga, in like manner have I given another third of my legions to play battles with mortals for a thousand years. Like Osiris and Te-in, to set mortals up in war, and move them one way and then another, and thus plunge them into each other's bloody arms and death. That they may learn to know of a truth they are but machines and playthings in the hands of angels and Gods; that they are worked like clay in a potter's hand, till they cry out: Enough! I will bow my head to God, who is Lord over all, great De'yus. Yea, more, I will fight for him and drink even my brother's blood, if De'yus but prosper me and mine in slaying Faithists, fool-worshippers of Ormazd, the Unseen and Scattered Wind. To him, in likeness of a man, with head, and legs, and arms in boundary and size of a man, sitting on a throne in Hored; to him, the great Lord God, will I ever bow in reverence.

14. And thou, O Sudga, shalt play war in Vind'yu, with the most, highest learned people of the earth. For which purpose thou shalt have these, my high-raised generals and captains: Asij, Gaeya, Naiswichi, Samen, Yube, Sol Mung-jo, Don, Hefa-yis-tie, Lowtha, Daridrat, Udan, Brihat, Bogir, Eshong, Weel, Vanaiti, Plowya, Vazista, Kiro, Cpenista, Visper, Cpenta-mainyus and Urvasta, and many others, most determined to rescue the earth from the dominion of far-off Gods.

15. De'yus continued: Go forth, ye Gods, and in majesty build your thrones; in great splendor ornament your high places, that even the magnificence shall be as a million preachers' tongues proclaiming the heavens' well-chosen Gods. And as fast as mortals fall in battle, gather the spirits of the dead into groups, not suffering them for pity's sake to lie in chaos, but bring them to your kingdoms in easy riding ships. And when thus housed, apply your physicians and nurses diligently, to restore them to their senses and new condition; and when they wake up in heavens, beholding the great glory of your thrones and kingdoms, initiate them by solemn rites and ceremonies to sworn servitude to yourselves and to me, your Lord God, to inherit such bounteous kingdoms.

16. And as ye shall thus despoil those of earth, to make them know my power and yours, so shall ye pursue those newly-arrived in heaven, to make them swear solemnly against

Jehovih, the Great Spirit, the Ormazd, and against all other Gods; but if they stubbornly refuse, though in heaven, even as they did on earth, take them before my son, Anubi, who shall further examine them; but if still they refuse, Anubi, with his strong guard and brands of fire, shall send them down in hell.

17. I, the Lord God, have spoken; my commandments are gone forth in heaven and earth; whosoever praiseth and glorifieth me, with everlasting service for the exaltation and glory of my kingdoms, shall enter into everlasting happiness; but whosoever will not bow down to me shall be cast into everlasting torments.

CHAPTER XIX.
OF THE HOSTS OF OSIRIS, THE FALSE.

1. Now sallied forth the captains, generals, and well-disciplined hosts of hada, the angels of De'yus, bent on independence to the earth and heaven from all other rulers save the Lord God, and to establish him forever. Foremost of the three mighty divisions was Osiris' army, of more than a thousand million angels, going boldly forth to cover the great lands of the earth, Arabin'ya, Parsi'e and Heleste.

2. In the front, dashing madly on, was Baal, and next him, his assistant Goddess, Ashtaroth, followed by their first attendants and high exalted officers. Some of whom displayed great maps of mortal cities and cultured lands, where the peaceful worshippers of Jehovih dwelt, hundreds of thousands. And the lists of altars and temples to the Great Spirit, where the righteous came daily and deposited their earnings and products as sacrifices for benefit of the weak and helpless. And the wide fields, where toilers brought out of the earth, religiously, wheat, and flax, and cotton, and barley, as gifts from the Great Spirit. And the canals, filled with boats, carrying produce, and fruit, and cloth, in interchange, one district with another. And the mounds and tree-temples of the I'hins, the sacred people, small, white and yellow; the forefathers and foremothers of the great I'huan race, the half-breeds, betwixt the brown burrowers in the earth and the I'hins.

3. Over these maps, and charts, and lists, the generals and captains discoursed as they descended to the rolling earth; most learnedly laying plans to overturn Jehovih's method, and build up De'yus, the God of Hored.

4. Osiris himself, to display such dignity as becometh a great God, halted in his heavenly place, and now head-quarters of the belligerents. And so rested on his throne, with his tens of thousands of messengers ready to answer his summons and bear his will to the remotest parts of his mighty army, and to bring him back news in return of the nature of the proceedings. And betwixt Osiris' and De'yus' thrones another long line of messengers extended, a thousand angels, high raised and resolute, suitable to travel in the ever-changing atmospherean belts of great velocity.

5. Beside Baal, on the downward course to the earth, but a little behind him, woman-like, was Ashtaroth, with her thousand attendants, all accoutered to show their high esteem for their warring Goddess. By the oft-changing wave of her hand, her part of the army had learned to know her will, and most zealously observe her commands.

6. And now, on every side, farther than the eye could see, the thousand millions rushed on, some in boats, some in ships and otevans, and others in single groups, descending. As one can imagine an earthly kite sufficient to carry its holder high up in the wind, so, reversed, and single-handed, hundreds of thousands flew toward the earth by ballast flags,

the most daring of angels.

7. Toward the earth they came as if on a frolic, full of jokes and loud boasting, sworn and swearing to forever clear the earth of Jehovih's worshippers. Many of them, long trained in schools and colleges and factories, in heaven, only too glad for a change of scenes and labor, and all promised by their superiors that now they were to take their first lessons in becoming Gods and Goddesses. Of whom thousands and thousands hoped for some daring deed, in order to gain sudden promotion.

8. To the east and west, and north and south, Baal and Ashtaroth spread out their armies, wide as the three great lands they had sworn to subdue unto the Lord God, who, of woman born, was the most presuming son the earth had yet brought forth. And to alight on the earth, to flood the temples and altars with so great an abundance of spirits as would drive Jehovih's ashars into disastrous confusion, and vanquish them, was the theme and project. To be foremost in so great a work was the temptation of promotion, which caused them on every side to strive with their utmost speed and power.

9. The which Jehovih foresaw, and so spake to God in Craoshivi, warning him; whereof due observance of the danger had been communicated by messengers to the managing angels in the altars and temples of worship. And these again, through the rab'bahs and the oracles, had spread abroad amongst mortals the threatened dangers, cautioning them.

10. Thus Jehovih's angels fortified themselves, through the faith of mortals, and held on, bringing together their scanty numbers, knowing well that by Jehovih's law they must not resist by arms, but only through words and good example, high-toned by faith in the Father over all.

11. Down, down, down on these, on every side came the destroying hosts, the thousand millions; with oaths and loud clamor rushing for the altars and temples; flying suddenly to the holy arcs; in hundreds of thousands of places, shouting:

12. Avaunt this arc! Avaunt this altar! Avaunt this temple! Ye Jehovian usurpers, begone! In the name of the Lord our God! We command!

13. But alas, for them, every arc, and altar, and temple to Jehovih was invincible. There stood His angels, so strong in faith, unmoved and majestic, that even the assailing spirits halted, overawed. And as they stood a moment, contemplating whence came so great majesty, to be in such common place, the Jehovians made this reply:

14. To none we bow in adoration but Great Jehovih! Whose Very Self contributed to make us what we are, His servants in doing good unto others with all our wisdom and strength! In Him we stand to shield His helpless ones by virtuous peace and love harmonious. Wherefore, then, come ye in arrogance, demanding our wards to service of your God, born of woman?

15. The Osirians said: Fly, O sycophants! Ye that bow down in fear and trembling to One hollow as the wind, and Personless. Too long have earth and heaven been cajoled by far-off foreign Gods, who come hither to win subjects for their kingdoms' glory, by that pitiful tale of an Ever Presence Over All, Whom none have seen nor known. Begone! Give us these earthly anchorages! To build in unit, earth and heaven, to rule ourselves by Gods we know and reverence!

16. The Jehovians said: Is this your only power? By threats and commands? O harmless words, in mockery of truthful Gods! No good works nor promises, save to exalt the self of earth and hada, and glorify your masters, born only equal with yourselves. Why not

rush in and carry us off, ye that are a thousand to one, and by your deeds prove the great source whence ye draw your power?

17. The Osirians said: To give ye a chance of liberty, to save ye from the Savior's judgment, Anubi, who shall cast ye into hell, we hoped to find your willing departure in peace. Behold ye, then, we will wall this altar around and shut off the attendant ashars with mortals, and flood the place with drujas, to obsess them to total madness. If, then, ye love your wards as ye profess, abandon all to us, for the glory of De'yus, whose son is Osiris, our commanding God.

18. The Jehovians said: Words! words! words! At first no explanation, and only your command. Now, forsooth, an argument! And presently ye will withdraw, deceived in what your commanding Gods told you would result. We tell you we will not hence, save by our superiors, Jehovih's, rightly raised to precedence.

19. The Osirians said: For which reason, behold our Lord God, who was honored in the title through Jehovih's hand; whom ye should obey according to your oaths.

20. The Jehovians said: Till such time the Lord God put aside Jehovih, we were his; but when for his self-glory he denied his Creator, his false position freed us from his obligations. To obey him now, would make us false to Jehovih, and forever weaken us in reaching the Nirvanian kingdoms.

21. But now the clamoring angels, Osirians, in the background crowded forward menacingly, and the tide rose to the highest pitch. The morning sun was dawning in the east, a most wonderful assistant to Jehovih's sons in time of battle; and their messengers brought from the fields and country places many ashars who had been on watch all night with sleeping mortals. The Osirians saw them coming; knew the turn, one way or another, was at hand! But by the audacity of the Jehovians, one to a thousand, were kept looking on in wonder till the sun's rays pierced their weapons and melted them in their hands.

22. First one and then another of the Osirians, then tens and hundreds and thousands, turned away or looked about, discomfited, like a host of rioters attempting to assault a few well-trained soldiers, and, becoming affrighted, turn and flee harmlessly. So Jehovih's sons and daughters won the victory in the first assault, save in rare instances, one in a hundred, where the Osirians triumphed and got possession.

CHAPTER XX.

1. And over all the lands, east and west and north and south, of Arabin'ya and Parsi'e and Heleste, stood the discomfited Osirian angels, in groups, tens of thousands, unseen by mortals, and considering how best to proceed to overthrow Jehovih and His worshippers.

2. Meantime, messengers and map-makers bore the disastrous news to Osiris, who in turn sent word on up to De'yus, the self-Lord God, who now, through Osiris, his most favorite God of power, sent these commands:

3. When night is on and mortals sleep, my hosts shall fall upon the ashars, the guardian angels, and drive them hence, obsessing every man, and woman and child, in these great divisions of the earth. What care I for the altars and temples and oracles and arcs? Possess ye the mortals before the morrow's morning sun. Hear ye the command of De'yus, The Lord your God, through his high-raised son, Osiris!

4. And the well-stationed messengers plied all day long to the near and remote parts of the assaulting armies, giving De'yus' commands. And ere the sun went down, the whole

thousand millions knew their work, and were wheeled in line, to march with the falling darkness, and pounce furiously upon the ashars of Jehovih.

5. But the true God, in Craoshivi, had been warned by Jehovih's Voice of the course of events, and he had sent his messengers with all speed down to the earth to warn them of the enemy's designs that night; the which they accomplished none too soon, for, already, when they had completed their most exhaustive work, the sun had dropped below the west horizon.

6. So, at the midnight hour, the terrible approach began on all sides; and to each and every spirit there came enemies, in tens, and hundreds, and thousands, shouting: Begone, thou Jehovian fool! The Lord our God and his son, Osiris, command! Away from thy sleeping mortal ward, or by the voice of God we will cast thee, bound, at Annubi's feet, food for hell! Begone!

7. Each Jehovian answered: To Great Jehovih I am sworn! Though ye bind me and cast me into hell, by the Great Spirit's hand I will free myself and come here again and teach His sacred name. And repeat forever my peaceful mission to raise up this heir of Jehovih!

8. Again the threatening adversaries stormed, and wondered whilst they stormed, that one alone stood so boldly in face of such great odds and flew not away at once. And every ashar laid his hand on the sleeping mortal in his charge, for by this his power was multiplied a thousand-fold, and raising up his other hand, thus addressed the All Highest: By Thy Wisdom and Power, O Jehovih, circumscribe Thou this, Thy sleeping heir, that whosoever toucheth the mortal part shall cut himself from off Thy everlasting kingdoms!

9. And, with the words, a circle of light fell about the place, bewildering to the assaulters, who, having once halted, opened the way to their own cowardice to recoil within them, a most valiant warrior against unrighteous deeds. Whereupon, a war of words and arguments ensued, till again the morning sun rose upon the almost harmless assault, and left the Osirians discomfited and ashamed.

10. Though not in all places, for in some extremes they waited not for words but rushed in and laid hands on the mortals, gaining power sufficient to hurl clubs, and stones, and boards, and stools and tables about the house, and so roused, wide awake the mortal occupants. Who, seeing things tumble about by some unseen power, were quickly up and frightened past composure. Some hurried off to the rab'bahs, some to the oracles and temples, to inquire about the trouble betwixt the ruling Gods.

11. And in these few places, when once De'yus' spirit-soldiers gained possession, they fastened on in thousands, even quarreling as to who had most honor in the hellish work. And yet not one of the ashars in all the lands was seized or borne away.

12. And now, in the time of the rising sun, the messengers of the Lord God flew hastily to Osiris' kingdom, where he sat on his throne, expecting news of an overwhelming victory. And when they told him of the most pitiful failure, save in so small a degree, Osiris raved and swore: By my soul, I swear an everlasting curse, but I will fill all the hells in hada with these fool-hardy ashars! Yea, even though I go down to the earth in person, and with Baal and Ashtaroth go from house to house throughout the world!

13. Osiris again sent word to De'yus, who was of vast experience, and not so hasty; a wiser God, and better acquainted with the tides in mortal energy to serve Jehovih. So De'yus sent back word to this effect: To rest the soldiers three days, that the surveyors might measure the stature of mortal faith, and so make the third attack more successful.

And with these words concluded, to wit:

14. Because of the long spiritual peace amongst mortals, there must be many grown to intellectual disbelief in an All Highest. For groveling down in the earth to measure the rocks, and to study the habits of worms and bugs, for generations, their seed hath brought forth many skeptics, believing nothing of spiritual kind, but rating high their own judgment. With these, for lack of faith in Jehovih, the ashars are powerless to ward off my soldiers. Mark them out in every city and in all the country places, and again at mid-hour of the night, fall upon them, crowding away Jehovih's ashars.

15. Besides these, find ye the ignorant and superstitious amongst mortals, who are lazy and of lustful desires, for by their habits the ashars have little power in their presence. Mark these also, and, at midnight, fall upon them and possess them.

16. And go ye amongst the rich, whose sons and daughters are raised in idleness and pleasure; whose thoughts seldom rise to the heaven; for with them the ashars are also weak to protect them, who are most excellent subjects to spirits fond of sporting pleasures. Mark ye them, also, and at midnight fall upon them, driving hence the ashars.

17. Abandon ye the altars and arcs and temples and oracles, and all the strongest, most zealous Faithists, for the present. Save such few as still flatten the head and are dull in judgment, whom ye shall also possess.

18. Thus prepared Osiris and Baal and Ashtaroth for the third assault on Jehovih's angels. And their millions of groups were kept in constant drill, ready for the work. The first fire and flush of boasting was already gone from them, save of a few, and the serious aspect of a long war stared them in the face.

CHAPTER XXI.

1. Thus laid the three great countries, Arabin'ya, Parsi'e and Heleste, of which Parsi'e was mightiest, peopled with very giants; lofty-bearing men and women, of red, copper colored; and with an abundance of long black hair; high in the nose and cheek bones; with determined jaws, and eyes to charm and command; mostly full-blooded I'huans, half-breeds betwixt the I'huans and the burrowers in the ground, the brown people, dull and stupid. The Parsi'e'ans were a proud race, built up in great comeliness by the God Apollo, whose high-raised office was to fashion the breeds of mortals into noble forms. Foremost in all the world was Parsi'e in all great deeds, and in men of learning, and in ancient wars. It was here great Zarathustra was born and raised for Jehovih's Voice and corporeal words. Here the first great CITY OF THE SUN was built, Oas, whose kings aspired to rule all the world; and great riches amongst men were here first tolerated by the Gods.

2. A strip of Parsi'e'an land cut betwixt Jaffeth and Vind'yu, and extended to the sea in the far east; but the great body laid to the west, covering the Afeutian Mountains, still plentiful in lions and tigers and great serpents. In these mountains came the I'huan hunters to catch lions and tigers to fight in the games, where men oft, unarmed, went into the arena, and fought them with their naked hands, choking them to death before applauding multitudes. From these mountains the hunters supplied the private dens of kings and queens with lions, whose duty was to devour thieves and other prisoners, according to mortal law.

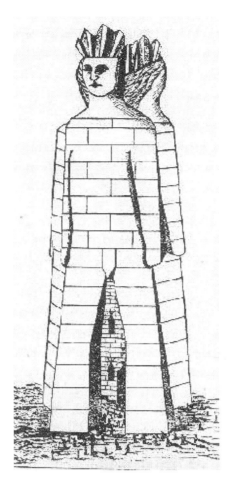

Plate 92.

GALL.

3. And oft these traveling hunters dwelt with the sacred little people in the wilderness, the I'hins, whom Jehovih had taught to charm even the great serpents and savage lions and tigers to be their friends and worshippers. And herefrom sprang a people called Listians, who, living mostly in the forests, went naked, to whom the I'hins taught the secret of CHARMING AND SACRED HAND POWER, who worshipped Jehovih, owning no man nor God as master, for which the Great Spirit named them SHEPHERD KINGS, for they ruled over flocks of goats, which supplied them with milk, and butter, and cheese, and wool for cloth for crotch-clothes, the only covering they wore.

4. These Shepherd Kings, the Listians, lived in peace, wandering about, making trinkets, which they oft exchanged with the inhabitants of cities and the agricultural regions. One-fourth of the people of Pars'ie were Listians, who were well guarded by Jehovih's angels. And these were such as De'yus meant to obsess for future use in terrible wars, but the other three-fourths lived in the fertile regions of Parsi'e, the lands of which were rich in yielding ample harvests. The cities were filled with mills, and factories, and colleges, and common schools, free for all people to come and learn; and altars, and temples of worship, and oracle structures, made without windows, so Jehovih's angels could come in sar'gis and teach His Holy Doctrines. Besides which were temples and observatories for

532

studying the stars, which were mapped out and named even as their names stand to this day. And next to these were the HOUSES OF PHILOSOPHY, in all the cities; where great learned men undertook to examine the things of earth, to learn the character and property thereof. And whether of fish, or worm, or stone, or ores, or iron, or silver, or gold, or copper, they had learned to read its worth and nature. And of things dead, no longer living on the earth, and of strange stones, and of skins and bones of animals, their houses were well filled, for benefit of students and visitors. It was these that De'yus meant to have his armies possess, body and soul, for his own glory, knowing that by their researches in such matters for many generations they had strayed away from Jehovih. For such is the rule pertaining to all children begotten on the earth. If the father and mother be on the downward road in unbelief, the child will be more so; but if on the upward way, to glorify an All Highest, the child will be holier and wiser than its parents.

5. In olden times the Gods had inspired the Parsi'e'ans to migrate toward the west and inhabit the lands of Heleste, also a country of giants, but less given to rites and ceremonies; and they carried with them three languages: the Panic, of Jaffeth; the Vedic, of Vind'yu, and the Parsi'e'an; and because they used the same sounds, mostly, but different written characters, a confused language sprang out of these, and was called Fonece, and the people thus speaking were called Foneceans, that is to say: We will use the same sounds, but take to our judgment to use whatsoever written characters we choose. Hence, Fonece is the first and oldest of mortal-made languages; and this was styled in heaven the period of the emancipation of mortals from the dictatorship of angels in regard to written signs and characters and words. Jehovih had said: In that respect man on earth hath advanced enough to stand alone; and it was so, for, from that time to this, neither Jehovih nor his angels have given any new language or written characters to mortals. And all languages that have come from that time onward, are but combinations and branches, and amalgamations and malformations of what existed then on the earth.

6. The Helestians were rich in agriculture, and in herds of cattle and goats, both wool goats and hair goats; for it was in this country that the angels first taught man how to breed the goats for hair or for wool, accordingly as he desired. And these people were also mostly worshippers of Jehovih, and had many altars and temples; dwelling in peace, and loving righteousness.

7. Arabin'ya had four kinds of people within her regions: The I'huans, the Listians, the I'hins, and the brown burrowers in the ground, with long noses and projecting mouths, very strong, whose grip of the hand could break a horse's leg. The brown people, though harmless, were naked, living mostly on fish and worms and bugs and roots; and they inhabited the regions of the great river, Tua. Over these people, to subdue them and destroy them, Osiris allotted his great angel general, Egupt, servant of De'yus. Egupt called the region of his allotment after himself, Egupt, the same which is corruptly called Egypt to this day.

8. In the time of Abraham this country was called South Arabin'ya; but when, in after years, the great scholars entered the records in the kings' libraries, the later names were used, being written in the Fonecean language and not Eguptian, which was the language of the unlearned.

9. But the chief part of all the people in Arabin'ya were I'huans, of color and size and figure like the Parsi'e'ans, being also the offspring of the I'hins and the brown earth-

burrowers, the hoodas, from whom they inherited corporeal greatness, even as from the I'hins they inherited holiness of spirit. But the flat heads had mostly disappeared from Arabin'ya.

10. And here were thousands of cities, great and small, even as in Parsi'e and Heleste, and they had colleges and houses of philosophy, even like Parsi'e, besides thousands of public libraries, which supplied books freely to the poor, who came here to be taught in the sciences, and in the arts of painting and engraving and sculpture, and in astronomy, and mathematics, and chemistry, and minerals, and assaying, and in the rules for inventing chemical combinations. But the Listians were the only people who dealt in charms and the secrets of taming serpents and beasts by virtue of the hand, and by curious scents, prepared secretly. And the Listians maintained the fifth rite in the resurrection, whereby, on the fifth day after death, the soul appeared in mortal semblance to his living people, and advised them lovingly, after which he ascended in their burning incense going to Jehovih!

11. Of such like, then, were the people over whom De'yus, named Lord God, had set his thousand millions, to subdue them for his own glory. And thus it came to pass, Jehovih spake in Craoshivi, saying: The time shall come when angels and mortals shall know of a truth that the Lord God is a false God and a vain-glorious usurper. For I will leave one race of I'huans on the earth, in Guatama, even till the era of kosmon. And men and angels shall see and understand that man of himself never inventeth a God in figure of a man born of woman. And that only through the inspiration of My enemies, who build kingdoms in hada for their own glory, hath any people ever fallen from My estate to worship a God in image of man.

CHAPTER XXII.

1. And now came the third assault of Osiris' legions of angels, inspired to desperate madness by the harangues of their generals and captains. And every mortal was marked out, and his degree of faith in the Great Spirit known, so the destroyers knew well where to strike effectively.

2. At midnight again came the Osirians, rushing on, and by force of numbers laid their hands on many mortals, millions! Held fast, and hurled missiles furiously about the sleeping apartments, to rouse from sleep their mortal victims, who, to wake and see no cause for the whirling stools and tables, and the terrible noises and blows in every corner of their houses, sprang up affrighted, and lost as to know what to do. In many places the angels of De'yus spake audibly in the dark, saying: There is but one God, even the Lord your God, great De'yus, on the throne of Hored. Bow down in reference before him, or destruction and death shall be your doom!

3. The Osirian angels, gloating in their much success, now filled every house, where they had fastened on, and made all such places head-quarters for their captains and generals and thousands and tens of thousands of angel servants, who were proud and boastful, most hilarious in knocks and hideous noises about the house walls.

4. In many instances the ashars, the guardian angels, were overpowered and crowded off, for because of the small faith and little spirituality in the mortals captured, their power was weak and scattered.

5. But not in all cases had the Osirians won, but were in hundreds of thousands of families overcome or baffled till the rising sun, which drove them off, leaving the Jehovians still victorious. But sufficient was the glory unto Osiris and his legions, wherefrom messengers were sent to De'yus speedily, with most exaggerated tales of the victories won.

6. In Parsi'e there fell this night twelve hundred thousand men, women and children into the clutches of the hosts of De'yus, the Lord God, the false. In Arabin'ya the fallen victims numbered two millions; and in Heleste one million and a half! But not yet had the captured mortals realized what had happened; they only knew frantic noises, and flying missiles disturbed them all night long. Many rushed forth to the oracles and altars to learn the cause, and to know if, in truth, the angels of heaven were at war; if God had come, as had been told in the old legends, to afflict mortals. The learned acknowledged not the cause to be angels, but sought for cracks in the wood, or concealed persons, or cats, or dogs. The which excited their disbelieving souls so they proclaimed before all men each special wonder, a hundred times magnified.

7. The unlearned believed in the angels thus suddenly come upon them; and cultivated their coming, and hearkened to their words, to put away Jehovih and accept De'yus; or otherwise, after death, their souls would be weighed by Anubi, and, for lack of faith in the Lord God, instead of Jehovih, cast into everlasting hell.

8. And such mortals, willing tools to follow spirits' advice instead of Jehovih's light within their own souls, were led through the Anubian ceremonies, but malformed by substituting words to glorify De'yus, and Osiris, his so-called son.

9. But the philosophers searched deeper, to find if, of a truth, the soul were immortal; and if it be a very truth that the souls of the dead come thus back, setting at defiance nature's laws, as they called the common things about them? What, then, were the sum and substance of the created worlds, and ultimate end, the all highest place for man?

10. The which the Osirian angels answered, explaining that the first heavenly place was hada, wherein were many hells; and that the all highest heaven was Hored, where the Lord God sat on his throne in great glory. And around him on every side were thousands of millions of angels who had attained to everlasting peace, with nothing more to do but to bow and sing praises unto their God forever!

CHAPTER XXIII.

1. Not many more days passed, till Osiris called together his legions and gave them four days' recreation and a great feast, heavenly. And after the feast was over, he thus spake from his temporary throne on Mount Agho'aden, that is, a place in the sky over the earth mountains of Aghogan, in Parsi'e; complimenting them, saying:

2. In the light and power of life and death I speak! Greeting, in De'yus' name, highest of Gods! In his love, to glorify you all for your great victory, this feast was spread, and my voice upraised in your praise.

3. First, to thee, Baal, wise and powerful amongst Gods, for thy great energy and glorious success, do I bestow the Sign of the Sacred Bird, Iboi, to be thine forever. And next, to thee, Ashtaroth, the Goddess that never tireth, or is without a stratagem, for thy glorious success I bestow thee with the fete, the circle and the true cross, to be thine forever.

4. To thee, Hermes, most unflinching of generals, second in rank to Lord, for thy victories won, I bestow the Inqua. To thee, Apollo-ya, I bequeath a bow and arrow, for thou shalt break the bonds of the creed of circumcision, and tempt mortals to wed by no law but by the impulse of the heart. For as the Faithists have been bound by their sign to marry not outside their own people, so shalt thou teach the opposite; for by the cross of the breeds of men, they shall be broken off from Jehovih.

5. To thee, Posee-ya-don, I bestow a model ship, for thou shalt have dominion over sea-faring men in all these divisions of the world. To thee, He-fa-yis-tie, I bestow a forge and tongs, for thy dominions over mortals shall be with the workers of metals and weapons of war.

6. To thee, Pluton-ya, I bestow a torch and brand of fire, for thou shalt rule over mortals for the destruction of cities and houses, to whomsoever will not bow down to De'yus as the highest God. To thee, Ura-na, queen of the es'enaurs, the very stars of my armies, I bestow a quill and staff, for thou shalt have dominion over the songs of the earth, inspiring mortals to sing praises unto the Lord our God.

7. After this manner Osiris went through the list, bestowing and assigning medals, and signs, and symbols, and emblems upon the generals and captains, and exalting many of the privates for daring deeds done, and for victories. And then Osiris allotted to the generals and captains tens of thousands of spirits especially adapted to their respective work; and he placed Baal and Ashtaroth as chiefs over them. Next Osiris organized a new division of angels, an army of one hundred millions, distributed into one hundred parts, and called this army See-loo-gan, signifying spirits who travel about amongst mortals in systematic order, to measure them as to how best they can be used for the glory of the heavenly kingdoms; and to possess them, or hand them over to be obsessed, as may be deemed profitable.

8. At Pluton-ya's request, Osiris made his selection for him, and then further explained, saying: To thee, all privilege in thy line. If thou find fire not well suited to destroy a city, even though thousands of mortals be obsessed at the same time to fire it, then shalt thou suffer thy spirits to carry virus and inoculate mortals unto death; or to fill the city with epidemic air, well poisoned, throwing mortals into fevers so they shall die. For in all cases, whether Baal or Ashtaroth, or any of thy superior officers, say to thee: Destroy thou that city, or this city, or that family, or this family, or that man or this man; thou shalt so fall upon the man or place as commanded, and accomplish it.

9. And now, with due ceremonies, and with excellent music, the assemblage was commanded back to the earth to resume work. And Osiris' messengers bore the news to De'yus, well exaggerated, extolling the fidelity of Osiris to the highest.

10. From this time forth no masterly raids were made by the Osirians, but they improved the well-adapted times to give to mortals an abundance of wonders in angel manifestations; the which bait mortals caught at eagerly. And they were, for the most part, easily persuaded to follow angel advice, and so fell to work and built temples, and established oracles of their own; obliterating the doctrine of the Great Spirit, and substituting the words: The Lord God, and De'yus, and Anubi, his holy Son and Savior and Judge of the world; and Osiris, God's commanding Lord of the earth. And mortals traveled about throughout all regions, preaching and explaining spirit communion, and establishing the Anubian rites and ceremonies, but never using the names Great Spirit or

Jehovih, save but to deride and accurse. The rites taught virtue, and love, and truth, and the acquisition of knowledge, but taught not peace, but war, which was maintained to be justifiable if done for the glory of the Lord, or for the Lord God, or for the Son, the Savior, Anubi, whose sign was a pair of scales, and who was sometimes called Judge, and Keeper of the Gate that led to the upper heaven, Hored.

11. Wherefore it came to pass that the mortal adherents of Osiris began to war on the Faithists and take their possessions. And inasmuch as the Faithists, by their pledges to Jehovih, dared not resist by weapons of death, but only by walls around their cities, and by stratagems, and by running away, the Osirians had easy victories in most instances.

12. In ten years the Osirians began to build great cities, after the manner of the ancients; and to gather in their plunder taken from the Faithists.

13. And Osiris, and Baal, and Ashtaroth, through their angel hosts, chose from amongst mortals the largest and strongest, most war-like, and by means of the oracles, declared them kings and queens, and instructed them in building palaces and having thrones, after the manner of Lords and Gods. And directed mortals how to make themselves powerful by organization and obedience to the kings and queens, who were recognized as adopted sons and daughters of the Lord God.

14. Now it came to pass, in course of time, that in consequence of the great abundance of angel manifestations, mortals sought by this means to obtain knowledge of heaven and earth, and especially in regard to the end of man.

15. And the Osirian hosts, being the only angels engaged in the matter of establishing De'yus, answered them, saying: The life and the end of man are to glorify God, who is Lord of heaven and earth.

16. And the mortals pressed the matter further, asking: Who is God? What are the worlds? Whence came all things? How were the creation and the Creator?

17. For an answer to these questions, Osiris sent messengers to the Lord God in Hored; whereupon De'yus called a Council of his God and Lords, to meet in Hored, to solve the matter, that a uniform answer might be given unto all the divisions of the earth.

18. In the meantime, and before the Council assembled, the self (satan) of De'yus spake to him, saying: If thou admit a Creator save thyself, thou art undone. For is this not the point whereon hang the power and dominion of Jehovih? The Lord God inquired of satan, saying: Why spakest thou not of this before? Behold, the Great Spirit signifieth everywhere. But I am only as a man, small, compared to the size of the worlds!

19. Satan said: It mattereth not; thou shalt say thou wert the Creator of heaven and earth.

20. De'yus said: But this is not truth? When thou persuadest me to assume dominion of earth, thou saidst: Be thou Truth in all things. How, then, shall I say, I created heaven and earth? Satan said: When Osiris hath come before thee, say thou to him: Who hast thou found amongst mortals to be the greatest and wisest, best su'is? And when he telleth thee, say thou to him: Osiris, my son, him thou sayest is the greatest su'is shalt thou inspire in person. And thou shalt cause him to write answers to the questions of mortals, that the learned and the ignorant alike may know me and my kingdoms. Behold, before my time both heaven and earth were void as to a Godhead, save to the servants of Jehovih. And because they were void in this respect, thou shalt persuade thy seers to know I created them from voidance unto mine own glory.

CHAPTER XXIV.
OF THE JAFFETHAN ASSAULT.

1. Anuhasaj, alias the Lord God, had said to Te-in, the false, to whom he gave in charge Jaffeth and her heavenly places: In the self same time that Osiris and his hosts fall upon the divisions of the earth, even in that day and hour shalt thou and thy hosts fall upon Jaffeth (China), possessing the temples and altars, and places of oracles, where they serve the Great Spirit under the name Ormazd, and thou shalt subdue them to me under the name Joss, who is and ever shall be Ho-Joss of heaven and earth.

2. So Te-in, the false, with his thousand million warriors sped forth, downward, to the earth, wide spread his army, to cover the whole of Jaffeth, in hope to capture it suddenly. And even as Osiris plunged into the temples and oracle-houses, and about the altars, in the dead of night, to drive away Jehovih's guardian angels, so, like him, and even worse, Te-in was baffled and repulsed, and saw the morning sun arise upon his shame in total failure. And then he, too, with his mighty legions, went stalking about, all day long on the earth, waiting for the next night's assault on sleeping mortals, and to receive new orders from the Lord God, as to the next proceeding.

3. Then came the second night, and Te-in went in, with his army, furious because of the last night's cowardly failure. And to the sleeping mortals, men, women and children, hied them with oaths and loud boastings, threatening Jehovih's angels with the tortures of hell if they did not instantly resign all unto Ho-Joss, the all highest ruler, dweller in Hored.

4. But faithful stood the Jehovians; laid their hands on the sleeping mortals, and became all powerful against the terrible odds, and held them in abeyance again, till the sun arose and scattered Te-in's hosts, ashamed and sulky, in most pitiful defeat. Of which news Te-in now, most painfully, sent to his commanding God.

5. To him, even as to Osiris, De'yus sent word to next attack the houses of the men of learning, the unbelievers; and the ignorant, the superstitious; to abandon, for the present, the arcs, and temples, and oracle-houses, and the Faithists, firmly sworn. De'yus said: Send thou thy numerators and mathematicians; and measure and mark all mortals in Jaffeth, as to the vulnerable points, and map their localities; and when thou hast completed this work, set apart another night for an attack upon them. And thy hosts shall fall not upon the Faithists who are firm in the Great Spirit, Ormazd, but upon the weak and disbelieving, the skeptical and much learned philosophers, who are weak in spirit, and thou shalt not fail.

6. So Te-in enumerated the Jaffethans, as commanded, marking them as to their vulnerable points, whether in disbelief in spirit, or if given to lust, or to hasty passions, or to telling lies, or to stealing, or to murder, or to hypocrisy, or to desire for leadership. And before the time of battle, Te-in knew the grade of every mortal in Jaffeth. And he called his generals and captains before him in his heavenly place, Che-su-gow, over the Chesain Mountains, twenty miles high, showing them the lists and maps.

7. Take these, he said, and distribute them before my mighty armies, and ere tomorrow night they shall learn every mortal's place and quality; and in the night my legions shall rush upon the places, laying hands on the sleeping mortals, thus gaining power; and they shall hurl missiles, with terrible noises, through the houses of the sleepers, and so arouse them to awake and behold the war of heaven carried to their homes.

8. The generals and captains took the lists and maps, and had millions of copies made of them, and then sent them into all the regions of De'yus' militants; and besides sent proclaimers, millions and millions, with terrible oaths against the Great Spirit, but who extolled the magnificence of De'yus to the utmost; appealing to their love of independence, and to their power to cast off all other rulers forever, save Ho-Joss.

9. And now, when the night of battle came, the infuriated angel warriors of Te-in marched in lines, millions strong, toward the sleeping mortals. Spread abroad their great armies, covering the land of Jaffeth from east to west and from north to south. Over Glang'e'loe, the CITY OF THE SUN, were sent thirty millions of Te-in's warring angels, sworn to objurgate the people of great learning, alive or dead, and scatter the angels of Jehovih, or bind them and cast them into hell. Over the city of Pen Goo were Te-in's hosts, twenty millions; and over the cities of Tsee, and Wung, and Ha-tzo, and Ne King, and Zoo Wun, each twenty millions of Te-in's angels of war.

10. Besides these there were millions and millions stationed over the great valley of Wan, and in the mountains of So-Jon. In the plains of Wow Gan were stationed seventy millions. Five millions were allotted to each of the following cities, to wit: Sum Conc, Ah-gee, Ah-sin, Chang-ha, Gee Oooh-young, Gwan Gouk, Na'tji, Yuk Hoh, Ah Tosh, Ah Koan, Chaung, Shon, Nufow, Zow, Lin, Gee Bak, Ow-wa, Tdong, King-do, Ghi Sam, Seung, Chog, Doth, Jawh, Bing-Tah, Gha, Haih, Hung, Wing-tze, Ni Am, Ah Sam and Zow-lin.

11. In the mountains of Witch How Loo were stationed eighty millions, laying for the Listian breed of men. On the borders of the sea, for sea-faring men, and for their wives and children, were one hundred and ninety millions of Te-in's angel soldiers, ready for the assault. Besides these there were tens of thousands of smaller armies, stationed in the small cities and country places, waiting for the signal.

12. Now, in this age, Jaffeth had attained to great wisdom in many things, especially save in war, in which her people were as babes. More than half her people were Faithists, followers of Po, worshippers of the Great Spirit. And they practiced peace and dwelt in communities. Even many of the cities were in families of tens, and hundreds, and thousands, but nowhere more than two thousand. And the city families were after this manner, that is to say: The manufacturers of cloth of wool, one family; of cloth of linen, another family; of cloth of silk, another family; of leather, another family; of paper, another family; of transportation, another family; and so on, till all departments were full; and of these combinations there were cities of fifty thousand, and a hundred thousand, and two hundred thousand inhabitants. And in the country places there were small cities, whose people tilled the soil and gathered the fruits of the earth, and they exchanged goods with the manufacturers who dwelt in large cities.

13. The government was by priests, one for each communion family, and the priests, who were called Wa-shon, were the receivers and distributors of goods, and they ministered in the temples and at the altars of worship in the name of the Great Spirit, Ormazd, sometimes called Po-e-tein, and sometimes E'O'lin, and by other names also.

14. Besides the schools and colleges there were HOUSES OF PHILOSOPHY, and HOUSES OF PROPHESY, and HOUSES OF ASTRONOMY, thousands and thousands.

15. The Jaffethans were large, being I'huans, with one degree more of the brown people's blood in them than the Parsi'e'ans. Nor in all the world was there, at that time, so strong a

people, and clean and jovial, high aspiring, with great gentleness. And because the land was tilled and made to bloom on every side, the angels named it the FLOWERY KINGDOM; and because the people reveled in song, and poetry, and oratory, they were called, LAMBS OF THE GREAT SPIRIT IN THE FLUSH OF SPRING TIME.

16. And these things were well known to De'yus, and to Te-in, the false, and to hundreds of millions of the assaulting angels, sworn to subdue them to Ho-Joss or to everlasting destruction.

17. But because of the power of Jehovih with the most faithful of the Faithists, the arcs and temples of worship had stood unharmed by the satanic raid. Equally so the Te-ins failed to overpower the Great Spirit's guardian angels. So now, after due preparation, the time came for another contest, this time upon the least Jehovih-like of mortals.

18. On the other hand, the true God, Son of Jehovih, sent word from his throne in Craoshivi to the guardian angels dwelling with these mortals, so unmindful of the Father's care. He said: Come defeat, or disaster, or terrible darkness, overpowering your utmost strength, still struggle ye, in the name of Jehovih. The true Faithist knoweth nothing impracticable, but doeth his utmost for his highest light, though failure stare him in the face.

19. For once distrust of weakness entereth the human soul, the man slideth backward down the hill of faith; whilst he who will not consider results, save to serve Jehovih right on, fail or not, riseth, even though his project fail.

20. With this and no other word from Jehovih, the Faithists stood about their weak and helpless wards on the low earth, waiting for the thousand million Te-ins. But not in any lengthened suspense, for when the sun stood with the widest part of the earth between, the midnight hour, the militants came rushing on, with oaths most hideous, and by their dense flood of numbers reached the sleeping mortals and laid hands on them.

21. Then, with joy run to madness because of triumph, sent hurling round about appurtenances in the dwellings. And, in many places, with audible speech thus held forth in the dark to the affrighted mortals:

22. From Sanc-tu I come, to lie in the dust every mortal born that will not bow down in reverence to Ho-Joss, ruler of worlds. Give ear, O man; the anger of heaven's Creator is let loose upon a disobedient race!

23. And then, to give semblance of truth to the words, the angel intruders let fly such knocks and poundings that they moved many a house on its foundation, and roused the mortals, panic-stricken, to find the cause, or to hasten them quickly to repentance and prayers.

24. But not all was their victory; for the Jehovians firmly held the power in hundreds of thousands of places. And yet the Te-ins had a wonderful victory.

25. Te-in quickly sent word to De'yus, exulting, and exaggerating the victories won. And in turn, De'yus congratulated him and his army, his thousand millions, who, now anchored on the earth, and with mortals, frolicked about in all regions.

26. And in Jaffeth, in course of time, the same questions arose as in Arabin'ya; questions from mortals to the spirits; as to the destination of the soul of man; as to the origin of things; as to the heavenly places? And Te-in in turn sent word on up to De'yus, in Hored, as to what answer should be given. It was thus, that he, too, was summoned to Sanc-tu, in Hored, to meet with Osiris, and Baal, and Ashtaroth, and Sudga, subduer of Vind'yu.

CHAPTER XXV.

OF THE VIND'YUAN ASSAULT.

1. Sudga, the false, sent by De'yus to overturn the Great Spirit's dominion in Vind'yu, and to establish the highest heavenly place, Urvatooz, was wiser than Osiris or Te-in in his wicked work. For he permitted not his army, his thousand millions, to rush on for the places of worship and for the oracle-houses. But most deliberately halted his forces in Haroyu, the lowest heavenly place over the mountains of Vivrat, in Vind'yu, three miles high and broad as the earth, and a commanding situation.

2. Whence, in a sure way, he sent his measurers on ahead down to the earth, to measure mortals, as to their weakness and strength in faith in Jehovih (Ormazd), and other rulers, heavenly; to map them and mark them, and to number them.

3. Great was the peace and beauty and glory of Vind'yu in that day. Her rivers and canals coursed the country over, and her industrious sons and daughters, two hundred millions, were, in the eyes of the angels, the pride and glory of the earth. Hundreds of thousands of her people were prophets and seers. And so abundant was spiritual light amongst the people, that even those who had learned but one language could understand and speak other languages with people from remote parts; words and sentences they had never heard; even when first meeting strangers. Like the inhabitants of Jaffeth, as to government and industry, mostly by the exchange of goods, and not by buying and selling, lived the Vind'yuans. This was their weakest point, as to an assault.

4. Sudga said to his generals and captains: Only by confounding the languages of these people can they be broken up and subdued. Behold, they are becoming as Gods; knowing and understanding in advance of the words spoken. What, then, is their greatest liable shortness, save we confound them suddenly in the meaning of words? Fall ye upon them, and possess them, and obsess them, all who are easily captured. Get ye a foothold here and there in the first place; and in their commerce cripple them.

5. Sudga said: It is a strong city that maketh all kinds of goods; it is a weak place indeed that dependeth on another, which is far off. Such people are easily tripped up. Behold, I will teach these people that I am the militant before whom every knee shall bow; or, in failing to win them thus, I will set city against city, and country place against country place; all against one another, for which their superabundant languages will furnish excellent material.

6. Sudga opened the door at night for his hosts to fall on the weakest of mortals, as to faith in Ormazd, Who had become as a stale story to hundreds of thousands of men and women. In Vind'yu had woman risen in knowledge, higher than the highest of women in other parts of the world. In the HOUSES OF PHILOSOPHY and HOUSES OF SCIENCE women were foremost, as to men, and skeptical as to the Ormazdian power.

7. On rushed Sudga's legions; and even as Osiris and Te-in won in the third assault, so now Sudga in the first. And, he too, sent word to De'yus, and exaggerated beyond all bounds of truth, as to his victories. Nevertheless, his hosts were sufficiently anchored on the earth to claim an everlasting victory for De'yus and to establish his name.

8. And here, also, after a few years, the questions came from mortals, asking thus: Behold, ye cut off the heavens of the ancients, the Nirvanian regions beyond Chinvat. Ye

teach us that De'yus is the ALL HIGH RULER. What, then, is the all highest for man? How came the worlds? Whence came man? How was the creation created?

9. To answer which Sudga sent to De'yus for instructions. And De'yus sent to Sudga, even as to the other Gods, an invitation to meet in Hored, to hear the words of the Lord God, to learn his commands.

10. Thus invited, thus went the five great warrior Gods before De'yus, taking with them each his ten thousand attendants, besides thousands of trumpeters. De'yus had a good feast prepared for them; he had sent receivers forth to meet them and conduct them to Sanc-tu in great splendor.

CHAPTER XXVI.

1. Great was the feast, the pomp and parade and glory, in Hored, when De'yus' victorious Gods and their companions and attendants came in answer to the summons of Anuhasaj, alias the Lord God. The trumpeters of Hored were stationed along more than a thousand miles on the heavenly roadways, and in turn the trumpeters and heralds of the visiting Gods extended in advance of the Gods themselves an equally great distance.

2. All the way were the roads lined with flags and banners, and millions of spectators, the same who had formerly been in schools and colleges in heaven, but were now emancipated from the restrictions of self-improvement, and used as applauders, to sing and shout praises to De'yus (Dyaus) for his own glory.

3. The table of the feast was private and in secret, and only prepared for the Gods and their close companions, one hundred all told, but the serving host numbered more than one million souls.

4. Whilst at the feast, De'yus said to Osiris: Speak thou of thy exploits, and of Baal and Ashtaroth and their valorous legions.

5. Then Osiris explained the nature of the earth countries, and of the battles and incidents, well exaggerating the last result. After Osiris had finished his story, De'yus said to Te-in: Speak thou of thy exploits, and of thy generals and captains, and of thy valorous legions.

6. Whereupon, Te-in displayed the maps of the earth regions where he had been, and his battles, and final success, also much exaggerated. And now, after he had finished his story, De'yus said to Sudga: Speak thou of thy generals and captains and thy valorous legions.

7. Then Sudga explained the earth region where he had fought and won, extolling his generals and captains, and his hosts, well exaggerated also.

8. When they had all finished their hilarious accounts, and applauded one another in sufficient zeal, in that same time the feast of eating and drinking was ended also. Whereupon Anuhasaj rose up and said:

9. I now declare the feast ended. Let the tables be removed. Behold, I will speak from the throne, in private, before my five Gods only, save mine own marshals. But unto all others I declare a time of recreation and sport, to be called again to duty when I have finished with my Gods, of which my marshals will inform the trumpeters, who shall sound the call.

10. Speedily, now, the attendants took away the tables; and the hosts all withdrew, save

the Gods and De'yus and his marshals. Whereupon De'yus ascended the throne, and then spake, saying:

11. I, the Lord your God, who am De'yus of heaven and earth, declare unto you, my Gods and earth rulers, in mine own name, and with love abounding:

12. To declare my doctrines and creations before you; that all the earth may be subdued alike unto me and mine forever.

13. To surpass not mine own age in my doctrines, nor to explain my axioms. But to surpass the understanding of mortals sufficiently unto their knowledge of earthly things, and so appease their curiosity, as to the questions they put to ye, my Gods.

14. Neither will I bind myself as Ahura did; for I will not explain who I am, save that man is in mine own likeness; nor when the beginning of things was.

15. This heaven I created; and ye also bear witness that I have established the earth in me, through your valorous deeds.

16. I, who am your God, look not to matters of a day, or a year; my times are as one time, for from this time forth forever this heaven and earth are mine, time without end.

17. In which ye behold days and years and the generations of men on the earth pass rapidly. Who, then, shall think seriously of the inhabitants that now are yours and mine?

18. Behold, the earth is fruitful; a thousand years are but as one day; and there shall spring up out of the earth thousands of millions of souls newborn. For them are my answers shaped, more than for such as now are.

19. In the beginning I created this heaven and the earth (unto mine own name and glory). For they were void and without order; darkness was upon them. Whereupon I moved upon them, saying: Let there be light; and there was light. And I drew a line betwixt darkness and light (for they had worshipped the void instead of me).

20. Wherefrom I declare this the morning and evening of the first day. And I have divided those that were void, and established my firmament betwixt them, even as land betwixt water and water.

21. And my firmament is heaven, and I have made it to be over such as were void, like water.

CHAPTER XXVII.

1. Osiris, being commanded of God to speak, said: Give us one day, O De'yus, that we may digest this matter.

2. Thereupon the Lord God gave them one day; and on the next day, when they were assembled, the Gods ratified every word De'yus had spoken. And it was called the morning and evening of the second day.

3. Again De'yus spake, saying: Let the waters of the earth be in one place, and the land appear unto itself, for it was so. And I saw that the earth was good (and that heaven might reign thereon). And I saw that the earth brought forth grass, and trees, and fruit, and seeds, everything after its own kind; and I said: Behold, they are good. (Neither attributed I evil unto anything on the earth, or in the waters, or in the air above. But I separated the light from darkness; this was the substance of my creation).

4. Again Osiris asked for a day, that the Gods might weigh the words of the Lord God; and this was the evening of the third day. And God gave them a day; and when they were

again assembled, De'yus said:

5. Let there be Gods in the firmament above the earth; and they shall separate the darkness from the light of the earth (that man may know me and my kingdoms).

6. And my Gods shall teach signs and seasons, and days and years, forever, unto the sons of men. And I made myself to rule the light of the world; but Osiris I made to rule the darkness of the world, which is the earth, my footstool.

7. Again De'yaus gave the Gods one day, to weigh the matter of his words, and to ratify them; which they did. And this was the morning of the fourth day.

8. Again De'yus said: Let the waters of the earth bring forth abundantly the moving creatures that live; and let the fowl fly above the earth in the air of the firmament. For they are good. Let them be fruitful and multiply, every living creature, and fill the air above the earth, every creature after its own kind. Wherefore my blessing is upon them.

9. Again the Lord God gave his Gods a day to weigh his words and ratify them, which they did; and this was the morning of the fifth day. And then De'yus said: And now, my Gods, let us make man in our own fashion; and in likeness of ourselves, let them have dominion also, but over the fish in the waters, and the fowl in the air, and over the cattle, and over the earth, and over every living creature upon the earth. And ye shall go to them and say to them: In our own likeness are ye created, male and female, and God's blessing is upon you. Be ye fruitful, and multiply, and replenish the earth and subdue it; and have dominion over the earth, and the fishes, and fowl, and every living creature on the earth, for they are yours forever! And behold, ye have every herb, and seed, and fruit, which is on the face of the earth, and the roots that grow in the earth, and they shall be your food. But of whatsoever hath breathed the breath of life man shall not eat.

10. Again De'yus gave the Gods a day of rest, in order to weigh the matter and ratify it; and this was the morning of the sixth day.

11. And again De'yus spake, saying: The Lord your God said unto thee, Osiris; and to thee, Te-in; and to thee, Sudga: Search thou amongst mortals for one high in su'is, for when I announce my doctrines, thou shalt go to such mortal and cause him to write my words, saying: Such are the words of the Lord, thy God. In answer to which I bid ye all now speak before me.

12. Osiris said: According to thy commandments have I searched and have found Thoth the highest man in su'is, and he dwelleth in Arabin'ya.

13. Then spake Te-in, saying: In like manner, also searched I, and found Hong, in my division of the earth, the highest man in su'is; and he dwelleth in Ho'e'Sin.

14. Then answered Sudga, saying: Even so have I accomplished in Vind'yu, and I have found one Anj-rajan.

15. De'yus said: To these mortals go ye and give my doctrines in your own ways; according to the language of mortals, and their capacity to understand. Neither bind I you to my exact words, nor limit you, save that that I have spoken shall be the foundation.

16. Thus, then, endeth the feast; and behold, it is the seventh day; for which reason I sanctify it and declare it a day of recreation.

CHAPTER XXVIII.

1. On the following day the Gods departed, with due ceremonies, after the manner they came, and returned to their kingdoms, and thence down to the earth, each one to his own

division.

2. And each of the three Gods went to his own chosen mortal (who had power to see and hear spiritual things). And the Gods possessed them by their presence, and inspired them to write the words of Anuhasaj, alias the Lord God, word for word; and they were so written, alike and like, in the three great divisions of the earth. And copies of them were made and filed in the libraries, and in the houses of philosophy of mortals.

3. But when these matters were thus entered, in answer to the queries of mortals, as to the origin of man and his destiny, they were not deemed sufficient by the learned men. Many of them said: The Lord God hath evaded our questions.

4. Then satan came to each of the three Gods who had the matter in charge, and he said unto them: Consult with one another as to what shall be done. So Osiris sent messengers to Te-in and to Sudga, asking them to come to Agho'aden, his heavenly place, for consultation. And, in due course of time, Te-in and Sudga came to Osiris, to his throne, where they were received in great honor and glory. And presently Osiris' marshals cleared the place, so the interview was private, for even the marshals stood afar off.

5. Osiris said: What shall we do without a Creator in fact? I know not if my judgment be beside itself, for it is said they that lose their reason are the last to discover it. The time was when De'yus, our much-loved Lord God, said: Whilst ye labor on the earth for me and my kingdoms, behold, I will reciprocate in all things. Neither shall ye ask for aught but it shall be granted unto you.

6. Hear me then, O my brothers, in my complaint; mortals have asked us, to know the origin of man, and his destination; and to know the cause of good and evil. These things I submitted unto our Lord God, in Hored, to learn his will and decree.

7. Thereupon he sent messengers to me announcing a feast, on which occasion he would answer the questions of mortals satisfactorily. Ye and I went to the feast, and De'yus hath furnished us with something, which is nothing. For mortals can also perceive that what the Lord God hath said is one and the same thing that was said by the Gods through Zarathustra; and, moreover, that the questions are still unanswered.

8. De'yus is my friend, and I desire not to press him further on the subject; and so I have called you, to learn of you how ye managed the same issues?

9. Te-in said: Before our heavenly kingdoms were confederated, Anuhasaj professed that he would announce himself the head and front of all created creations. Shall we say his courage is less? And so excuse him?

10. Sudga said: When he should have said: I created man in mine own image, behold, he hath weakly said: LET US MAKE MAN! Is it not clear, then, that he shirketh from the responsibility, and desireth ourselves commingled in the pitiful story? Hear me, then, my brothers; I am asked how I have answered the issues with mine own division, and I say unto you, I have been in the same quandary, and have not answered them at all.

11. Te-in said: Neither have I. But that we may be justified in so doing, behold, the Lord God said unto us: I bind you not to my words, nor limit you, save that that I have spoken shall be the foundation. Now, it is clear, that if we admit that sin is in the world, we must find a way to justify the Lord God, whose servants we are. If he be not justified, then is sin justified.

12. For mortals perceive good and evil understandingly; but to justify a good God for permitting evil is not an easy matter. For in the breath we praise him, we must praise his

works; of which sin is apparent; and in the same breath that we condemn sin, how shall we glorify De'yus? For have we not proclaimed him the foundation of all things; the head and front, before creation was created? Was not this our battle-cry, to urge our angel warriors on to overthrow Jehovih? And hath not our loud-praised Lord God said: LET US MAKE MAN! A child should have more courage than this!

13. Sudga said: It is plain we all understand these issues, and perceive, also, what is required of us. For since De'yus hath left us liberty to add to his doctrines, according to our own judgment, is it not well that we agree upon a doctrine, even as De'yus professed prior to the confederacy? And thus give it to mortals?

14. Osiris said: This is wisdom, O my brothers. To make our Lord God the Creator, we must account unto him all things, both good and evil. Wherefore we shall give two masters to man, the one being the serpent, the earth, the lowest inspirer; and the other the voice of our Lord God.

15. Sudga said: My brother hath spoken wisely. And yet, is the term two masters the wisest term? For in declaring the Lord God the highest, we must make him master over the earth also.

16. Te-in said: Why shall we not adopt the E'O'LIN of the ancients, substituting the words Lord God? And make a commandment over man, forbidding him hearkening to the serpent, lest he be led away from the Lord God, and throw the cause of sin upon man, for violating the Lord God's commandment.

17. Osiris said: Most wisely spoken, my brothers. For by accusing man, through the serpent, we clear the Lord God unscathed.

CHAPTER XXIX.
THE OSIRIAN BIBLE OF EQUPT, AND VIND'YU, AND CHINA.

1. On the following day the three false Gods, Osiris and Te-in and Sudga, wrote their account, each in his own way. And when they were read, Osiris' stood clearer than either of the others'; but nevertheless, Te-in's and Sudga's had much of merit. So it came to pass Osiris' account was adopted, with interpolations from the others'.

2. This, then, is the completed report, to wit:

3. These are the times of earth and heaven when created; the time the Lord God created them. And the Lord God formed man out of the dust of the earth, and quickened him through his nostrils with the breath of life, and man became a living creature.

4. And God caused mists to rise up from the waters, and spread over the earth, and rain upon it. And he caused trees and herbs to grow up out of the ground; everything that is pleasant for the sight and good for food. Thus out of the ground the Lord God caused man to come forth, being of the earth, of the land of Eden (Spe-a).

5. To dress the land and keep it pleasant, the Lord God commanded man, saying: This shall be thy labor, in which thou shalt be perfected unto everlasting life. Of all things in the land of Eden mayst thou freely take and enjoy.

6. And man prospered on the earth for a long season; and he was naked and not ashamed. And God planted the tree of knowledge in the land of Eden, and he said unto man: This tree have I planted; partake thou not of it, for it pertaineth to life and death.

7. And God called the name of the first man A'su (Adam). And the Lord God caused man to name all things on the earth, and in the waters, and in the air above the earth, and whatsoever man called every living creature, that was the name thereof.

8. And the Lord God caused A'su to fall into a trance; and an angel of heaven came and stood by his side. And the Lord God drew from the flesh, and from the bones, and from the blood of A'su, and thus made woman, and brought her unto A'su.

9. And the Lord God repeated his commandment unto woman, saying: Thou shalt sojourn for a season on the earth, and cleave unto A'su, for he is thy husband, and thou art his wife; and thou shalt partake of all things on the face of the earth, save of the tree of life, which is of both good and evil, for in the day thou eatest thereof thou shalt surely die.

10. But because of the serpent (the earth) of the woman, she hearkened unto him, and he said unto the woman: I say unto thee, in the day thou eatest thereof thou shalt have thine eyes opened, and shalt become as a Goddess, creating offspring.

11. And the woman was more easily persuaded than man, for she had confidence in the serpent; and they partook of the fruit thereof; and, of a truth, their eyes were opened, and they beheld their nakedness.

12. And presently they heard the Lord God walking in Eden, and they hid themselves in the bushes. And the Lord God said: Where art thou, A'su? And A'su said: Because we heard thee walking, we hid ourselves, for we were naked.

13. The Lord God said: Who told thee thou wert naked? Hast thou eaten of the tree whereof I told thee thou shouldst not eat? A'su said: The woman thou gavest me to be with me, led me, saying: Behold, it is good fruit; and we ate thereof.

14. The Lord God said: Woman, what hast thou done? And the woman answered, saying: The serpent beguiled me. And the Lord God said unto the serpent: Because thou hast done this, thou art accursed, and thou shalt not rise up from the earth, but return to dust whence thou camest.

15. Unto the woman the Lord God said: Because thou hast conceived, thou shalt have great sorrow; in sorrow bring forth children; thy desire shall be to thy husband, and he shall rule over thee. And I will put enmity betwixt the serpent and thine offspring; and the flesh shall call one way, which is unto earth, but the soul of man shall call unto me, the Lord God. And though the serpent bite, yet man shall bruise him, and subdue him.

16. And God taught man to make coats of skins and be clothed. And the Lord God said: Lest man partake further, becoming as one of us, he shall go out of Eden, where I created him. So he drove man out of Eden backward, and gave him cherubims to hold him on every side, to preserve unto man the tree of life, that man might not only fulfill the spirit, but the flesh also.

17. When Osiris had gone thus far, Sudga interposed, saying: If we say, Becoming as one of us, will not man say: Behold, there are more Gods than the Lord God?

18. Te-in said: Because De'yus said: Let us make man, shall we not use us in this instance?

19. Osiris said: Hear me, my brothers, yet further; for I previously found a way out. For I have divided the Lord from God; that is to say:

20. And the Lord God said: Because man hath learned good and evil, I am as twain unto him, for I am Lord of the earth and God of heaven. And that which is on the earth is the Lord's, and that which is in heaven is God's.

21. And A'su called his wife's name Eve (We-it), for she was the fountain of all men. And Eve brought forth a son, Cain, saying: I have begotten a son from the Lord. And she brought forth another son, Abel. And the first-born was begotten in darkness, but the second of the light of the Lord. And the Lord had more respect unto the second, Abel, than unto the first, Cain.

22. In course of time Cain brought of the fruit of the ground and offered it unto the Lord. And Abel brought for the Lord, as his offerings, the firstlings of his flocks. And Cain perceived that the Lord had more respect for his brother, and Cain was wroth, and his countenance fell.

23. And the Lord said unto Cain: Why art thou jealous? If thou doest well, shalt thou not be accepted? And if thou doest not well, sin lieth at thy door.

24. But Cain would not be reconciled (because of the darkness in him), and when he and his brother were walking in the fields, Cain turned upon Abel and slew him.

25. God said: Behold, darkness is between men; the son begotten in darkness falleth upon him begotten in the light. And it shall come to pass on the earth from this time forth that the righteous shall be persecuted by the unrighteous.

26. And the Lord said unto Cain: Where is Abel, thy brother? And he said: I know not. Am I my brother's keeper? The Lord said: The voice of thy brother's blood crieth out unto me from the ground: Now art thou accursed from the earth, for it hath opened to receive thy brother's blood from thy hand. In my sight thou shalt be a fugitive and a vagabond upon the earth. And because thou hast shed blood, blood shall not cease to flow from thy sons and daughters forever.

27. Cain said: O Lord, my punishment is greater than I can bear. For I am become the first foundation of all the wars on the earth; for thou hast hid thy face from me; and it shall come to pass that every one that findeth of me in them shall be slain also.

28. And the Lord said unto Cain: Whosoever slayeth thee or thine, vengeance shall be upon him seven-fold. And the Lord wrote upon Cain's forehead the word Asugasahiben, signifying, BLOOD FOR SAKE OF SELF, a mark, lest any finding him might kill him.

29. And from this time forth Cain lost the voice of the Lord, because he went off into Nod (darkness). And Cain took a wife and begot heirs unto himself after his own manner, and they were called Cainites, and the heirs after them were called the tribe of Cainites, which survived him nine hundred and ten years, after which they were divided into six and twenty tribes. (And the name Cain was lost. But the people survived, and are known to this day as THE WORLD'S PEOPLE.)

30. And We-it bore another son, Seth, in place of Abel, whom Cain slew. And after these came the generations of men, good and evil. And the Lord God said: Behold, I created man without sin, and I gave him warning, that he might remain holy on the face of the earth. But woman hearkened not to my counsel, but to the serpent, and sin came into the world. Therefore shall woman bring forth in pain all the generations of the earth.

31. Thus it was that the Lord God created man; in the likeness of God created he him.

32. And the sons of Cain were called tribes, even unto this day, but the sons of the righteous were sons of God; wherefore it was said of old: Behold the sons of earth and the sons of heaven.

33. And the Lord said: Shall I not accord to myself to choose what I will? For this right I gave to man also. And from that time after the sons of God were called God's chosen.

34. And it came to pass that man multiplied on the face of the earth; and the tribes were mightier than the sons of the Lord God, and the wickedness of man became great in the earth, and the desires of his heart were evil continually.

35. And the Lord God repented that he had made man on the earth, and it grieved him at his heart. And the Lord God said: I will destroy man whom I have created; nor will I spare beast nor creeping thing in the place I gave.

36. Behold, I will bring a flood of waters upon the lands of the earth, and I will destroy all flesh wherein is the breath of life. But my covenant is with my chosen, who shall not be destroyed by the flood of waters.

37. And God's sons in Noe took with them pairs of the living, of beasts and birds, according to the commandments of God, to keep the seed alive on the earth.

38. And when the earth was six hundred years in Noe, the flood of waters was come upon the earth. And for forty days and forty nights the rain fell, and the fountains of the sea came up on the lands of the earth. And man and beast alike, that drew the breath of life, died, for the land was no more.

39. But the heirs of Noe suffered not; and the ships of the arc, whither the Lord had concealed them, rode upon the waters. And God made a wind to pass over the earth: and the fountains of the deep were stopped, and the rain of heaven restrained, and the ships of the arc borne upon dry land.

40. And the Lord God said: Behold, I will build a new earth and a new heaven. For these, my sons, have proven their faith in me. Neither will I again destroy the tribes of men because their hearts are set on evil. And the Lord God swore an oath by the bow of the arc, saying: This is the token of the covenant which I have established between me and all flesh that is upon the earth. And by the sons of Noe was the whole earth overspread, and the Lord blessed the earth, and said: Every moving thing that liveth shall be meat for man; even as the green herb I have given. But flesh with the life thereof, which is the blood thereof, shall men not eat.

41. For surely your blood of your lives will I require; of every beast will I require it; at the hand of every man's brother will I require the life of man that feedeth on living flesh and blood.

42. And whosoever sheddeth man's blood, by man shall his blood be shed; for in my image made I man. And ye, be ye fruitful, and multiply, and bring forth abundantly in the earth, and inhabit it, for it is yours for perpetual generations.

43. Thus ended the words of Osiris. Te'in said: Because of flesh blood, thou art wise, my brother. Sudga said: Hereon hangeth the glory of our enterprise. For man being less restrained than in the Divan laws, will accept the new readily.

44. After this, Osiris prepared a book of generations of men on earth; and these were the substance of the doctrines of De'yus and his Gods. And Osiris and Te-in and Sudga departed, and came down to the earth, to their mortal wards, and by virtue of their presence inspired they their wards to write them in mortal words, according to the languages in the places where they lived. And they were so written by these seers; and copies of them were made and put on file in the libraries of the records of the kings and queens of the earth, in Arabin'ya, Jaffeth and Shem. And these became the bible of that day.

CHAPTER XXX.

1. Now, after the three false Gods, Osiris and Te-in and Sudga, had revealed these things to mortals, they sent messengers to the Lord God, praying audience with him, that they might disclose to him what they had done. Anuhasaj, alias De'yus, therefore, appointed a time of meeting, and the Gods came before him and made their report. After which De'yus said:

2. In all ye have done I acquiesce; neither have ye said aught that I would not have said, save that I desired not to laud myself with mine own mouth. And thus ended the matter, as to how mortals were taught to worship the names Lord and God, and Lord God, and Ho-Joss, and Joss, and De'yus, and Deity, and Dyaus, and Zeus, and various other names, according to the languages of the people of Jaffeth, and Vind'yu, and Arabin'ya, and Parsi'e, and Heleste. And thousands of millions of angels of the Lord God and his Gods, who were sent down to mortals, inspired them and taught them the same things through seers, and prophets, and magicians, and through other people, also, by dreams and visions.

3. And mortals were taught the secret of spiritually going out of their own corporeal bodies, and returning safely; and in this state they were taken subjectively to the kingdom of the Lord God, where they beheld him even as a man, sitting on a throne; and they saw the great glory of his kingdom, and beheld the worshippers, millions of them, glorifying De'yus, the false Lord God. And these persons became preachers on the earth; enthusiastically stirring men up on every hand to draw the sword and spear and sling to go forth in battle, to overthrow the doctrine of the Great Spirit and establish the De'yus.

4. And it came to pass that they thus accomplished the will of the Lord God in all these divisions of the earth. The Jehovians, being non-resistants, were powerless before them. Kings and queens on the earth accepted these doctrines, and they marshaled their armies in all directions to establish the Lord God, who had said unto them: As much as ye exalt me and my kingdoms, so will I exalt you. As I behold, ye are become wise and powerful to rule over many on the earth, so will I give unto you large kingdoms in heaven.

5. And the false Lord God and his false Gods prospered in earth and heaven, as to themselves and their kingdoms, hundreds of years, nine hundred years, and at this time the Faithists of the earth were reduced to a small fraction of people, mostly hid away, as sheep from wolves.

6. But in nine hundred and fifty years, behold, the worshippers of the Lord God, the false, began to quarrel and fight amongst themselves. Even as by blood they had established him, so by blood were the kings and queens of the earth overthrowing one another.

7. Because of the warfare, schools, and colleges, and houses of philosophy, were wasted away; the factories for spinning and weaving were destroyed, and the lands not tilled.

8. And now of the heavenly kingdoms of Anuhasaj and his Gods, this is what occurred, to wit: They had accumulated twenty-eight thousand millions of spirits, all of whom were servants to De'yus and his Gods. For the most part they were below grade ten, whilst three thousand millions were below grade five, which is helplessness.

9. Jehovih had so made men and angels that, whosoever had learned to abnegate self and to labor for the good of others, was already above grade fifty, and his ascension should be perpetual thereafter; whilst they that were below grade fifty, who had not put away

self (satan), should gravitate downward, toward the earth. Wherein it had come to pass that the false Lord God and his false Gods were burdened with their kingdoms.

10. And though they were adorned to the utmost, having vast cities for their heavenly capitals, with millions of attendants, and millions of musicians, who were forever inventing new and wonderful music, and playing and singing, millions and millions in concert, with millions of trumpeters, near and far off, to fashion echoes beautiful to the ear; and though they had decorators forever inventing and changing their thousands of millions of flags and banners, and the ornaments for the pageantry; though they had millions of heavenly cities, built with heavenly precious stones and gems of splendor, and with roadways and streets paved with heavenly diamonds and pearls; and though they had tournaments, heavenly, and games, and rites and ceremonies, prostrations and salutations, without end, with great ships, heavenly, capable of coursing atmospherea in journeys and excursions, ships to carry hundreds of millions of angels, whose chief occupation was to sing and chant the glory and power and dominion of De'yus and his Gods; yea, though a large book could not contain a description of the thousandth part of their wonderful glory, yet each and every God began to see coming danger.

11. Jehovih had said: Two precipices have I left open for testing man's strength, and they are: great prosperity and great adversity.

12. And behold, satan came upon them in the guise of a good friend. First, he went to Anuhasaj and said unto him: Thou greatest of Gods! Who is like unto thee? Behold, I came to thee in the beginning, and told thee what to do, even to stretch forth thine hand, and heaven and earth should be thine forever, for thine own glory. And lo, it hath come on finely! Thou hast routed Jehovih and His hosts in heaven and earth; they are as a remnant skulking away. Hear me, then, O De'yus, for I will not only praise thee for what thou hast accomplished, but I will chide thee for thy failings.

13. De'yus said: Wherein have I failed, O satan? And satan answered, saying: Thou art too honest for thine own good; too pure for thine own benefit; too unsuspecting as regards thy Gods. Being thyself honest, thou hast easily attributed honesty unto others, and they have taken advantage of thee.

14. Anuhasaj said: How? Satan answered, saying: In the first, thou saidst to thy Gods: Maintain ye your schools, and colleges, and factories, and otherwise prepare the spirits of the dead unto resurrection. And as fast as they arrive at grade thirty, send ye them to my kingdom, that Hored may be glorified forever. But lo and behold, thy Gods used the angels as slaves, to build up the glory of their own kingdoms. They have suffered their heavenly places of education, for the most part, to be scattered and gone. Neither have they inspired mortals to instruction, as I warned thee at the first. And mortals have thrown aside their schools and colleges, and their places of art, and have become riotous, and given to gross living, and there is no resurrection in them. Which matters show thee that, soon or late, all the spirits of the earth will be of no grade at all, but as fetals and vampires to live on mortals.

15. De'yus said: Why are mortals become gross livers? Satan answered him, saying: Behold, in thine own revelation to mortals thou saidst to them: Partake not of fish, nor flesh, nor blood, for food, nor of anything that breatheth the breath of life. And now, behold what came to pass: Thy three Gods, whom thou hadst elevated and trusted, fell to and made other revelations, wherein they said: Partake of fish and flesh; for they desired

to please mortals. And lo, it hath come to pass that man not only warreth for thee, but he warreth to the right and left, for it is in his blood, after the manner of beasts that feed on flesh. Thy Gods had no right to give this law unto man without first consulting thee, to know thy will and pleasure.

16. Anuhasaj said: Alas, it is true. What shall I do? Satan said: Thou shalt call thy Gods before thee and chide them in thine own way, and command them to go down to mortals and re-establish learning and industry, instead of war. Anuhasaj said: Even so shall they come and receive my reprimand. They shall know of a truth that I am the Lord their God.

17. Satan went to the other false Gods, every one separately, saying unto each: Hear me, O thou wisest of Gods, who shouldst in fact be at the all highest Godhead in heaven, because of thy great wisdom and integrity. Behold, I came to thee at the first and foretold thee how thy kingdom should become great and glorified; and even so hath it come to pass. When thou puttest forth thine hand to do a thing, it is done; for thou wert born into life different from all others, and for the highest of glories. And because of thy greatness, behold, all the Gods of heaven are jealous of thee and fear thee, all of which thou knowest of thine own knowledge. Now, whilst I accord this unto thee, I will also chide thee for thy shortness.

18. For, because thou art honest thyself, thou believest the same of others; wherefore thou art cheated and ill-used on all hands. In the first while, thou didst send thy highest grades to the Lord God, to be his; yea, thou hast robbed thine own kingdom of its finest and best subjects for the glory of De'yus. And who is De'yus more than thou? Is he not a coward? for he feared to give his own doctrines to mortals; but he abridged his words till they were worthless. And thou and thy fellow-Gods made his doctrines up in full for him! Yet thou servest him as if he were thy superior.

19. The false God said: Alas, it is true, with all my wisdom I have acted like a fool. Because I was too honest and pure for De'yus and his Gods, they have taken advantage of me. What shall I do? Satan said: I told thee at the first, that the time should come when thou shouldst rise to be higher than all other Gods. Behold, the time is near at hand when thou shalt strike the blow. Thou shalt not only have thine own kingdom, but the kingdoms of thy companion Gods; and even De'yus shall be tributary unto thee and thine.

20. The false God said: What shall I do? And satan answered, saying: De'yus will scent the danger to his kingdom, and he will summon his Gods for consultation. Be thou ready with thine answer unto him and them; not hastily, for such is the manner of the weak; but most deliberately, in high holiness of purpose, for the good of mortals and spirits.

21. Thus alike and like spake satan unto all the false Gods; and they nursed the planted seed; held it in the light and shade to see it grow, till it became the very giant of each one's understanding.

CHAPTER XXXI.

1. In course of time Anuhasaj called the meeting of his Gods in Hored, and Osiris and Sudga came; and great were the pageantry and show that day; and the pomp and glory and splendor of Sanctu; with thousands of millions of trained slaves, with their dashing officers of high rank. For at this time it was nearly seven hundred years since even generals and high captains could come into the presence of the Lord God, the false, save

by crawling on their bellies, even for miles.

2. And in and around about the heavenly house of the capital were erected fifty thousand pillars of fire, kept forever going by the labor of his slaves, some of whom stood in their tracks laboring at one thing for more than a hundred years, without change of watch, or rest, being threatened with hell, and being too impotent to believe otherwise. None could walk upright to the throne of the Lord God save his high Council, his high marshals, and his Gods, and Anubi. And none else were permitted to look upon him, under penalty of being cast into hell.

3. At first his Gods came to feast with him once a year, for more than a hundred years; after that, for awhile, once in six years; and afterward, only once in fifty or a hundred years; and then only by special command.

4. So it came to pass that the coming of De'yus' false Gods was an occasion of rejoicing and glory to upward of twelve thousand million inhabitants of the kingdom of Anuhasaj. For, far and near, they were extra clothed and fed, and granted freedom for the time being.

5. On the last occasion referred to, the Gods were received by hundreds of millions, called the receiving hosts, in fire-ships of great size and brilliancy, and thus conducted up to the roadways of the court, nearer than which the receiving hosts dared not approach. There the Gods were met by De'yus' high Council and high marshals, and with them entered the area and walked up to the high arch of the capital, which led into the place of the throne of the Lord God. When inside of the Arch, the Council and marshals parted on either side, and, with the head bowed, chanted an anthem of praise to De'yus. The Gods also bowed with respect and friendship, and walked in the midst directly toward the throne.

6. When they were near at hand, the vice-Gods, on either side of De'yus, rose up, saying:

7. In the name of the Lord God of the heavens of the earth, who come here, upright, and as Gods?

8. The Gods responded: Behold, we are sons of the Lord God, great De'yus, and of a truth are we Gods! We demand audience with our Godhead, for the glory of our kingdoms and his.

9. De'yus said: Peace, O my vice-Gods! I do recognize these, my brother Gods. Greeting, in the name of heaven and earth.

10. The Gods responded: Greeting unto thee, O Lord God, mightiest of Gods. In thy mighty name, De'yus, we salute thee worshipfully, to know thy will and pleasure, that we may serve thee in wisdom, and power, and love.

11. De'yus said: Welcome, O ye Gods; the freedom of Sanc-tu is at your hands. Behold, I will clear my palace, that we may privily, and most holily, consult together for the good of angels and mortals.

12. Thereupon De'yus gave a signal for all his officers and attendants to retire beyond the Arch, the which they did. And now that the ceremony of reception was over, Anuhasaj came down from his throne and greeted the Gods cordially by clasping hands, after which they all sat down on the foot seats of the throne; and there were present De'yus, and Osiris, and Sudga, and no others within hearing; for Te-in had not come.

13. And for a while they talked together like long-separated friends; and lo and behold, the satan that was within each one of them began to fail him as regardeth reproving the others. For even the smothered seed of love which the Great Spirit had given them began

to swell up, as if about to burst forth a mighty power. So the time passed on, and none dared approach the subject of his soul and resolution.

14. Till at last, De'yus, the most schooled in satan's cause, put an end to their old-time stories and trivial conversation; he said:

15. So much have I loved you both, and am now moved by your august presence, that with all my majesty and power I am weaker than a young child: who will unconcernedly reprove its own father. Or more I am like an old man that, in the absence of his child, findeth cause to quarrel with it; but on seeing it return, breaketh down utterly, and turneth from his previous grieving to an outburst of manifest love.

16. Osiris said: What can move thee to this seriousness, O De'yus? For even as thou hast spoken, so hast thou uttered the sentiment long heavily lain on my heart. But which now, in reverence to thee and thy great kingdoms, causeth me to melt down like snow in a summer's sun. Pray thee, go on!

17. Sudga said, As I live, ye twain, so far my superiors as before whom I am nothing, have spoken the very sentiment of my soul. Pray ye twain, go on; for so great is my love unto you, your most extravagant wish shall be answered by me, though I labor a thousand years to accomplish it.

18. Thereupon De'yus sweetly told his tale, even as satan had taught him. And then he bade Osiris speak his mind, and also Sudga speak his; which they did, even as satan had taught them their parts. When they had finished, De'yus, much surprised by their pitiful tales, even as the others were at his, thus spake:

19. My Gods, how easier it is to find fault with the state of affairs than to find a remedy. I have seen such as find fault with their neighbors, or with the kingdom, or ancients, and yet turned and accomplished the same faults themselves. We all do know that one of the complaints we had against the old Divan laws was their bondage over the Lords and their dominions, holding them to the letter. Whereupon, when we confederated, it was to give independence to each and every Lord to rule his own heaven and division of the earth in his own way. And this was granted unto all my Lords and unto me and my kingdom likewise. And behold where it hath harvested! In the fullness of my soul I gave you certain doctrines to give unto mortals, chief of which was to make my names worshipful on the earth. But I bound you not, saying: Do ye this, and no more. But I said unto you: Here is the substance of the foundations of my doctrines. Go ye unto mortals and teach them these things, adding or abridging according to your own wisdom.

20. And this ye accomplished, and added thereunto the temptation to mortals to become carnivorants, whereby the grades have fallen woefully. And now ye find fault with me for exacting a certain number of slaves annually of a certain grade; complaining that your own kingdoms are becoming flooded with drujas.

21. Osiris said: Hear me, O Lord my God, for I have labored for thee and thy kingdoms many a hundred years. Nor are my words in passion, but well considered; wherein, therefore, if I err, I ask no excuse on account of hastiness. First, then, that our confederation was founded to make a mighty kingdom, heavenly, having dominion over mortals on the whole earth; of which kingdom thou wert to be the chief and greatest glory, and ourselves second. To all of which our songs to this day bear testimony. But, as for songs or testimonies in the libraries of heaven, that our confederacy was founded chiefly to get rid of the Divan laws, I have not seen nor heard of one.

554

22. Sudga said: What I have done is done. I was commanded to a division of the earth, to subdue it unto De'yus, and I have so accomplished it. I have listened to your complaints, but neither hath offered a remedy. Ye twain are higher in rank and wisdom than I; when ye have spoken to the purpose I will also speak. For my part, I am thankful there are no Divan laws to bind me.

23. De'yus said: The remedy lieth in overturning the cause of the falls in the grades. For sake of glorifying themselves, my Gods have suffered places of learning and industry to fall to pieces, both in heaven and earth. There be such as give glory unto charity, and unto rites and ceremonies; but I say unto you, my Gods, INDUSTRY AND LEARNING stand higher than charity or rites and ceremonies; especially so standeth industry that yieldeth profitable support.

24. Osiris said: Where, O Lord my God, lieth the difference betwixt that which is written or spoken? In thy opening words thou hast even now reiterated the bondage of the Divan laws over the Lords. And in the next breath thou sayest: I command you to re-establish the places of learning and industry.

25. Sudga said: Are not written laws less arbitrary than spoken ones? for we see them beforehand, and are not, therefore, shocked by the sudden audacity.

26. De'yus said: In either case is it not true that the highest in power and mightiest in the plans and arrangement of his kingdoms must either take jibes and insults from his inferiors, whom he hath lifted up and made what they are, or otherwise fall broken-hearted on the loss of their love and worship? For on all hands we behold, alas, beneficiaries are apt to turn like venomous serpents, and strike, even though the blow would send themselves into destruction.

27. Osiris said: That is most especially true, O De'yus, where the highest kingdoms owe their glory and greatness to those that have been subsidiary and built them up. None are so slow to see their danger as they that are exposed to it. There be such who, holding high places, if but their slaves knew who they were and how deceived, would bind them in knots and cast them into hell.

28. Sudga said: But in such cases is it not better, O my wise brothers, that the highest who have been raised up by the toil and industry of others, that labored to have them glorified, turn from their own glory and selfish ends, and divide up their ill-gotten kingdoms, and bestir their lazy carcasses by sending assistants to those that have them in their power?

29. De'yus said: Most wisely spoken, both my Gods. But how shall we teach apes and monkeys to know their masters? They crook their tails and squeal, imagining themselves great monarchs. Whereas, were they cut off from their masters, they would come to grief most ignominiously, or be the foremost plunged into torments.

30. Osiris said: Thou wisest of Gods, is it not most strange, wonderful, how better we can see others' shortness than our own? Nor are we much quicker to find a way to save them, which we oft could do were they not self-conceited fools, than to guard our arms, so that when they show the least sign to do us wrong, we inwardly swear within our souls to hurl them into hell.

31. Sudga said: O my loves, it is a sad reflection, when we survey mighty kingdoms at their quarrels, knowing that, if either dare lift a hand to destroy, we ourselves hold the key whereby they can be, both, stript of their highest subjects and their greatest glories, and left in the ruins of their own evil concocting. But the wise abide their time, and oft are

fortified when others know not of it.

32. De'yus said: My most wise Gods, ye have spoken great wisdom. I will weigh your words and be governed accordingly. For your most holy visit I am honored above all I deserve.

33. Osiris said: Words cannot express my reverence for thy spoken words, O De'yus.

34. Sudga said: I am bowed with sorrow to leave the place of so much wisdom, love and power.

35. And now Osiris and Sudga stepped backward, four paces each, but separate from each other, with their heads still bowed. By a signal, the vice-Gods re-entered and stood beside the Gods, and then all, with heads bowed, raised their hands and saluted in the sign CENTRAL SUN. De'yus answered them on the sign MUSIC OF THE SATELLITES.

36. Slowly now, and with measured step, to low sweet music, backward, the Gods and vice-Gods crossed the area and passed the Arch, where the vice-Gods left them and returned within. But the Gods were now met by the high Council and high marshals and conducted to the entrance gate, where they left them, and they were received, Osiris and Sudga, by their hosts and reconducted to their ships, with great pomp and honor, and they at once set sail for their own heavenly kingdoms.

37. Now, in this whole proceeding, the Gods were all surprised that Te-in came not, nor, by messenger or otherwise, answered the summons; nor could one of them imagine the cause.

CHAPTER XXXII.

1. Te-in, whose heavenly kingdom contained three thousand million angels, being informed when Osiris and Sudga were gone to Hored, satan said to him: Now is thy time, call thy Council together; proclaim thyself God of heaven and earth, mighty in all regions, the Central Kingdom of the Eternal Heavens! Choose from amongst thy Council the highest grades, and make them Lords under thee. After which thou shalt renew the battles in Jaffeth, on the earth.

2. Te-in said: Why on the earth? Satan said: Behold, Jaffeth must be subdued to one nation of people, and this shall be thy footstool, and thy heavenly kingdom's head-quarters. After which thy Lords shall proceed to the lands of Parsi'e and Arabin'ya, and inspire the inhabitants thereof to another central kingdom, and when mortals are thus subdued to limited numbers, thou shalt have but few to deal with in order to make thyself God of the whole earth.

3. Te-in said: Thou art wiser than all Gods. Behold, my way is clear.

4. So on the day of De'yus' meeting with Osiris and Sudga, even the same day, Te-in severed the bonds betwixt his heavenly kingdom and all others, and he chose twelve of his highest grade in the Holy Council, and made them Lords of the earth; but he allotted no portion of the earth to any one alone. He said:

5. I will not give them kingdoms; this is the strongest way; to keep every thing in one's own hands.

6. Te-in, then, through his Lords, whom he sent down to the earth, made Kan Kwan mortal king of Jaffeth, with the title, KING OF THE WORLD, AND SUN, AND MOON, AND STARS! And the Lords caused Kan Kwan to build an oke'spe, where he could receive the

commandments of Te-in, the holiest, all highest ruler of heaven, as to what he should do in order to subdue the earth unto himself.

7. Te-in said: And, my Gods, say ye to Kan Kwan when the earth is subdued unto himself: Behold, I will also come down and dwell in the temples he buildeth for my Lords. And when the king goeth forth and subdueth a place unto himself, he shall immediately build a worshipful temple and dedicate it to me and my Lords, whose names ye shall give alike and like in all places. For I will not confuse mortals with a multiplicity of heavenly Lords. And the king shall show unto the people that there is but one High Ruler in heaven, whether he be called Ho-Joss or Joss, or Po-tein, or Te-in, and that I am the Person. But in no case shall the king suffer the worshippers of the Great Spirit to remain alive upon the earth.

8. Te-in said: My Lords, take with you, each, one million angels, strong and cunning in war; twelve millions are sufficient, for ye shall not scatter them about, but keep close in the neighborhood of war and of the king. As when a fire burneth, beginning from a spark and spreading outward till a city is consumed, so be ye concentrated and potent. This is the whole art of power. And whilst mortals sleep, your angels shall come upon them and give them dreams and visions of glorious success, make them see themselves in the heat of battle, rushing through the jaws of death unscathed, whilst their manly arms slay about them on every side their enemies by the score in flowing blood. For when these mortals awake and remember their dreams, they will be well whetted up for the valorous work. But as to those that are to be conquered, let your angels go to them whilst they sleep, and give them dreams and visions of horrid deaths; make them see the heat of battle and themselves overpowered on every hand, and, pierced with sword and spear, they fall, dying in great agony. For when such mortals wake up and remember their dreams, they are half conquered already.

9. Te-in said: My Lords, ye shall inspire the king to be merciful and gentle; and when his soldiers come to a place to subdue it, they shall send truce-men before them, inquiring: Who, say ye, shall be the ruler? And if the people answer: We are Kan Kwan's slaves, they shall not be slain.

10. Te-in said: My Lords, amongst mortals, what is righteousness? Now one Lord said: Rites and ceremonies. Another said: To worship thee, O Te-in. Another said: To follow the doctrines of the ancients. Another said: To purify one's self. Another said: To do good with all one's might. Another said: To practice truth. Another said: To harm no man.

11. Te-in said: Not one of you knoweth righteousness. Behold how you stand: The doctrines of the ancients were their own, and they are as dead. To put on a dead man's clothes, will they make the wearer like the dead was?

12. Rites and ceremonies are what show-men train their horses with, to run or leap, or lie down, to please their masters.

13. To purify one's self! What is that? A mortal man's body cannot be purified, for it is rotten at best.

14. To do good with all one's might! Who knoweth the meaning of that? To cut off a crushed foot to save a man's life: Give him pain in the cutting, even whilst he is suffering. Then it is well that some men's heads be cut off for their own good. Yea, even nations extirpated. Let him that doeth, then, do with all his might. See ye not that in this, that before one attempteth to do good, he is his own judge, judging by his own judgment?

15. To practice truth! What is that? The Jehovihians say: Jehovih is All Truth. But Jehovih is nothing, scattered as the wind. Then truth is nothing. Who hath found a man but saith: To see as I see, is to see the truth; to see as thou seest, is to see falsely? A man told lies knowngly, and practiced them, and he was all truth to himself, for he was a liar. Therefore, he practiced truth.

16. To worship me is unrighteousness instead of righteousness. To worship Joss is unrighteousness; to worship the nondescript Jehovih, is unrighteousness, and to worship Po is unrighteousness also. Behold this matter: The large trees in the forest were smothering out the small ones; and the small ones said: We praise you, giant oaks, for the many blessings we have received; be merciful unto us! The large trees laughed at them, and they died. Is this not Jehovih? Is this not the Gods? For all mortals, at best, are but as unhatched eggs; and when they are dead, their souls are as hatched chickens, for the Gods to play with, and to use in their own way.

17. Te-in said: Teach ye this to mortals; and tell them, moreover, to choose what God they will; and if it be me, then I will labor for them; if it be not me, then am I against them. This, then, is righteousness: Reciprocity betwixt Gods and mortals; reciprocity betwixt mortals themselves; to war for opinion's sake in order to develop in steadfastness; to help the helpless, to feed and clothe the stranger, and to worship the father and mother.

CHAPTER XXXIII.

1. Te-in's Lords and their angels departed out of Che-su-gow, Te-in's heavenly place, and descended to the earth on their mission; and this is what came of it, to wit:

2. Kan Kwan was the son of Kwan Ho, a flat-head; but Kan Kwan came of the converts to the Brahmin priests, and so had not his head flattened. But because su'is and sar'gis had been long in their family they descended to Kwan all the same. And he could see and hear the angels and their Lords; hear all the words spoken to him, a most excellent thing in a king, when drujas are restrained from observing him.

3. The Lords guarded Kan Kwan on every side, day and night, and Kwan being stupid, because of the flat heads of his parents, he was well suited to carry out all that was commanded of him. So he at once announced himself with all his titles, and sent heralds hither and thither to proclaim him and let all peoples and kings know that he was coming to subdue them unto himself.

4. Kwan issued this decree, to wit: Kan Kwan, king of the world, and of the sun, and moon, and stars, I command! I, son of the sun, son of Te-in, behold! There is but one ruler in heaven, Te-in! There shall be but one on earth, Kan Kwan. Bow your heads down! I come! Choose ye: to bow down, or to die. One or the other shall be. When the world is subdued to me, I will war no more!

5. In those days there were many great kings in Jaffeth, and their kingdoms were in many places far apart. Betwixt them, in a sparse region, in the Valley of Lun, lay the city of Ow Tswe, and this was the small kingdom of Kan Kwan, known for a thousand years.

6. When the other kings heard of Kwan's proclamation they laughed. And this is the vanity of mortals, for they heed not the power of the Gods over them.

7. So Kwan started with an army of four thousand soldiers, men and women, with spears, axes, scythes, swords and slings, and bows and arrows; and he marched against Tzeyot, a

city of a hundred thousand people; and here ruled king Cha Ung Chin, with twenty thousand soldiers. Cha Ung Chin laughed. He said to his captain: Send thou a thousand women soldiers and kill Kwan and his army; they are mad, they know not what war is.

8. The captain went forth to battle, but he took beside the thousand women soldiers a thousand men soldiers. But lo and behold, Kwan and his soldiers knew no drill, but they ran forward so strangely that their enemies knew not how to fight them, and they fled in fear, save the captain and a hundred women, who were instantly put to death. But not one of Kwan's army was killed.

9. Cha Ung Chin was angry, and he sent ten thousand soldiers against Kwan's ragged army; and when the battle was begun, the angels cast clouds before the hosts of Cha Ung Chin, and they thought they beheld hundreds of thousands of soldiers coming upon them, and they turned and fled also, save five hundred, who were captured and instantly slain, men and women.

10. Cha Ung Chin said: It is time now I go myself. My laziness has cost me dear. On the morrow I will lead thirty thousand pressed men and women, and make it a day of sport to slaughter Kwan's army. So the king sent his marshals to select and summon his soldiers during the night. Many were too frightened to sleep; and those that slept had such visions and dreams that when they awoke they were as persons nearly dead.

11. Cha Ung Chin, next morning, sallied forth out of the city to battle, going before his army. When he saw the pitiful army of Kwan, he said: Of a truth, the world is going mad! That such fools have courage is because they know not what a battle is. With that he rushed forward, faster and faster, calling to his soldiers. But they stretched out in a line, after him, for they trembled from head to foot, remembering their dreams.

12. Presently Kwan and his army started for them, not with orderly commands, but screaming and howling. Cha Ung Chin's soldiers took panic, broke ranks and fled in all directions, save one thousand, including King Cha Ung Chin, who were captured and instantly slain.

13. And on the same day Kan Kwan went and possessed the city, Tzeyot, commanding obedience and allegiance of the people. And on the following day he set twenty thousand men to work building a temple to Te-in, pulling down other edifices for the material thereof. Nor had Kwan a learned man in all his army; but the Lords with him showed him how to build the temple, east and west and north and south, and how to make the archways and the pillars to support the roof; and the sacred chambers and altars of sacrifice. Of brick and mortar and wood built he it, and when it was completed it was large enough for twelve thousand people to do sacrifice in. And it was, from first to last, forty days in building.

14. Besides this, Kwan put another ten thousand men and women to clearing houses and walls away, and making new streets in many ways; so that at the time of the first sacrifice the city of Tzeyot looked not like itself; and Kwan gave it a new name, Lu An, and commanded all people to call it by that name, or suffer death.

15. Kan Kwan made the people go and do sacrifice to Te-in in the temple every morning; enforced a day of rest for each quarter of the moon; enforced worship on the part of children to their fathers and mothers, the father taking first rank.

16. Then Kwan made them pray for those who were slain in battle. And these are the words he commanded them: Te-in! Father of Life and Death! Who feedeth on suns and

stars! Whose refuse is mortals. In thy praise I bow my head. For thy glory I lie on my belly before thy altar. I am the filthiest of things; my breath and my flesh and my blood are rotten. Death would be sweet to me if thou or thy soldiers would slay me. For my soul would come to thee to be thy slave forever.

17. Behold, my brothers and sisters who fought against thee are dead, and I glorify thee because thereof. We have buried their rotten carcasses deep in the ground, good enough for them.

18. But their spirits are lost and wild on the battle-field, howling about. O Te-in, Father, send thy spirits from Che-su-gow, thy heavenly place, to them, to help them out of darkness. And we will ever praise thee, our mightiest, all highest ruler!

19. When they made the sacrifice they laid down on their bellies, certain ones prompting them with the words which Kwan received from the Lords.

20. After this, Kwan appointed them a governor, Ding Jow, who was the first governor of a province in Jaffeth, after the order of governors as they exist to this day. Which is to say: As a Lord is to a God, so is a governor to a king. And this was the first of that order established by the Gods of hada. Prior to this a like government had been given by Jehovih to the Faithists; even as it had been given in its purity to the pure, so was it now given in its crudity to the crude.

21. Jehovih had said: Independent kingdoms shall not exist side by side; nor shall one be tributary to another; but there shall be one whole, and the lesser shall be parts thereof, not over nor under them, but as helpmates. The wicked will not see this now; but their own wickedness will bring it about in time to come. And it was so.

CHAPTER XXXIV.

1. Kan Kwan again went forth to conquer and subdue, going to the southward, to Ho-tsze, a large city having five tributary cities, ruled over by Oo-long, a king with two hundred wives and thirty thousand soldiers, men and women, well disciplined.

2. Kwan's army was now seven thousand strong, but without discipline; and with no head save himself. And on his march through the country he compelled the farmers to embrace the Te-in religion, under penalty of death.

3. Now when he had come near Ho-tsze, he sent an order for the king to surrender, even after the manner as at the city he had already conquered.

4. Oo-long laughed when told of the kind of company that had come against him, and he sent only women soldiers, eight thousand, to give him battle. When the armies were near together, the Lords said to Kwan: Send thou a truce, and beseech thine enemy to surrender under penalty of death; for the angels of Te-in will deliver them into thy hand, and not one shall die.

5. A truce was sent, and lo and behold, the whole of Oo-long's army surrendered, and made oaths of allegiance to Kwan, and not one was slain. Oo-long, when informed of it, said: Now will I go with all my army and slay this ragged king and all his people, and also my eight thousand who have surrendered. So he marched to battle with twenty-two thousand soldiers. Kwan's army was scattered about the fields. Oo-long said to his captain: Go, thou, tell this foolish king to set his army in line of battle; I desire not to take advantage of a flock of sheep.

6. The captain started to go, but ere he reached the place, he fell down in a swoon, for the angels overpowered him. The king saw his captain fall, and he cried out to his army: It is enough! My army have never seen such fools, and know not how to battle with them. Come, I will lead!

7. At that, he rushed on, followed by his thousands. Instantly, Kwan's army set up their screams and howls, and ran forward in every direction, and lo and behold, Oo-long's army broke and fled, save one thousand two hundred who were captured, Oo-long amongst them; and they were instantly slain. But of Kwan's army only one man was killed.

8. The Lords sent messengers to Te-in in his heavenly place, informing him of Kwan's success. Te-in returned this commandment: In what has been done I am well pleased; but suffer not your mortal king, Kan Kwan, to win so easily hereafter; but let him have losses, that he may not forget me and my Lords and my hosts of angels. Place ye him in straits, and cause him to pray unto me; and his army shall pray also. And when they have thus sacrificed, deliver him and his army from their straits, and make him victorious for a season.

9. Kwan entered the city of Ho-tsze without further opposition, and possessed himself of it. At once he caused thirty thousand laborers to fall to work building a temple to Te-in. Another twenty thousand he caused to pull down houses and make other streets, more beautiful. In twenty-eight days the temple and the streets were completed; and on the twenty-ninth day the sacrifices commenced, and all the people were obliged to swear allegiance to Kwan and to Te-in, or be slain. And on the first day there were slain four thousand men and women (worshippers of different Gods, but for the main part the Great Spirit) who would not take the oath.

10. After that, none refused, and so Kwan gave the city a new name, Tue Shon; and he appointed So'wo'tse governor, and commanded the tributary cities to come under the yoke.

11. After that, Kan Kwan went forward again to conquer and subdue; and the Lords of heaven and their twelve millions of angels went with him and in advance of him, preparing the way. And the news of his success was spread abroad amongst mortals also, well exaggerated; so that the inhabitants of cities far and near feared him.

12. The Lords suffered Kwan to conquer and subdue yet three other large cities without loss to his army; and lo and behold, Kwan began to think it was himself that possessed the power, and not Te-in.

13. The next city, Che-gah, was a small one, of fifty thousand inhabitants. Kwan inquired not of Te-in (through the Lords) as to how to make the attack, but went on his own judgment. Now there ruled over the city a woman, Lon Gwie, a tyrant little loved, and she had but four thousand soldiers, and Kwan had seven thousand.

14. Kwan, arriving near, demanded the place; but the queen answered him not with words; but had her soldiers in ambush, and thus fell upon Kwan's army, and put one-half of them to death; and yet the queen suffered small loss. Kwan, not finding his Lords with him, fled, and his remaining army with him. But the Lords urged the queen to pursue him, and she again fell upon them and slew another half, and crippled hundreds more. But the queen suffered small loss.

15. The Lords then spoke to Kwan, where he had escaped, and said unto him: Because thou wert vain and rememberedst not me, who am thy heavenly ruler, Te-in, I have

labored to show thee that of thyself thou art nothing. Then Kwan prayed to Te-in, saying: Most mighty ruler of heaven and earth, thou hast justly punished me. I pray thee now, with good repentance, in the bitterness of my shame. What shall I do, O Te-in? I am far from home, in a strange country, and my army is well-nigh destroyed. All nations are against me; a sheep is safer in a forest with wolves than I am in these regions.

16. The Lord said unto Kwan: Now that thou hast repented, behold, I, Te-in, will show thee my power. For thou shalt gather together the remnant of thy army and turn about and destroy the queen and her army, or put them to flight and possess the city.

17. Kwan, on the next morning, being inspired by his Lords, prepared for battle, though he had but seven hundred men. On the other hand the Lords and their angels appeared in the dreams and visions of the queen's army, saying to them: The queen is deceived and led away into a trap. Kwan will be joined in the morning by fifty thousand men. Prepare, therefore, to die to-morrow.

18. On the morrow, then, on the queen's side, the soldiers related their fearful dreams to one another; and hardly had they finished the matter when Kwan's army came upon them. And the angels, more than fifty thousand, took on sar'gis, seeming even like mortals. At sight of this, the queen's army were so frightened they could not flee, save a few, but nearly the whole army surrendered, throwing away their arms and lying down.

19. Kwan and his army fell upon them and slew them, more than four thousand, who were rendered powerless by the angel hosts with them. Kwan then went into the city, doing as previously in other cities, establishing himself and Te-in.

20. Such, then, was the manner of Te-in, the false, of establishing himself in Jaffeth. Hear ye now of Sudga, of Vind'yu, and her heavenly kingdom.

CHAPTER XXXV.

1. Sudga, the false God of Vind'yu and her heavens, whose heavenly kingdom contained more than three thousand million angels, on his way home from Hored, said to himself: Two things I am resolved upon: to proclaim myself CREATOR AND RULER OF HEAVEN AND EARTH; and to change the name of my heavenly place and call it AHL-BURJ, THE MOUNTAIN OF THE CLOUDS.

2. Satan spoke to Sudga, saying: Thou all highest God, hear me. In the land of Vind'yu, down on the earth; and in the heavens above the land of Vind'yu; what God hath labored like unto thee? Thou didst establish De'yus, for nearly a thousand years in these regions. Thou possessest by right that name, and thou shalt call thyself De'yus and Sudga; and thy heavenly place shall also be Hored, because, forsooth, it is also a heavenly mountain.

3. Sudga said: Most wisely said, O satan.

4. And so it came to pass that Sudga at once fell to work moving his capital and throne, and to founding his new place. And he also chose twelve Lords, saying to himself, after the manner of Te-in: Though I will have twelve Lords to rule over mortals, yet will I not give to any one of them a certain division of the earth for his.

5. And when Sudga was thus founded in his new heavenly place he called his Lords about him and said unto them: Go ye down to mortals, to T-loyovogna, who hath a small kingdom in the Valley of Hachchisatij, in Vind'yu, for I will make him king of all the earth, even as I am ruler of heaven. And by obsessions and otherwise ye shall lead him

forth to conquer and subdue.

6. Precede ye him in his journeyings, and cause mortals to fear him, that they be easily overcome. Twelve million angels I allot to you as your army, nor shall ye return into my presence until ye have made T-loyovogna king of Vind'yu. After that I shall bestow you according to merit.

7. The twelve Lords, with their twelve million angels of war, departed for the earth, and came to Varaja, the city where lived and ruled T-loyovogna, and they covered the regions around about, even beyond the Valley of Hachchisatij.

8. T-loyovogna was the son of Hucrava, who was the son of Han Cyavarat, who was the son of Aipivohu, sacred in su'is to the Gods and Lords of heaven. So T-loyovogna talked with Sudga's chief Lord, who said unto him: Behold, thou shalt proclaim thyself king of all the world; for I and the hosts of heaven are with thee.

9. T-loyovogna said: Alas, mine is the weakest of kingdoms; I have not a thousand soldiers. Other kings will laugh at me. But the Lord answered him, saying: What are mortal kings in the hands of De'yus, he who was Sudga? I say unto the nations of the earth: Go down! and they fall. I say: Rise ye up! and they rise. Man looketh to stone and clay and water for great power; but I that am unseen am greater than all the lands and the waters of the earth, for I rule over them, and over heaven also.

10. I will have but one king on the earth; and as I rule the angels of heaven, even so shalt thou rule mortals, and establish thee and me forever! For thy heirs, and their heirs after them, shall have dominion over every kingdom and country in the world.

11. T-loyovogna said: I fear thee, O De'yus; I know thy power. But how can a king go to war without soldiers? Or an army without arms? The Lord answered him: Send thy proclamation unto kings far and near, commanding them to bow down unto thee. And presently I will come unto thee and lead thee forth, and thou shalt conquer and subdue them, and not a hair of thy head shall be harmed.

12. T-loyovogna did as commanded; and some days after his proclamation had been sent unto the nearest kings, all of whom knew him well, he mustered his army of seven hundred men and one hundred women. And they that had neither spear, nor sword, nor scythe, nor bow and arrows, took clubs, and clappers, and pans, to make noise with, and others took lanterns.

13. The first city they approached was Abtuib, ruled over by Azhis, who had an army of four thousand men and one thousand women. When near the place, T-loyovogna sent his demand for the surrender of the city. Azhis answered him not, but said unto his army: Go ye and surround yonder fool, and destroy him and his army.

14. Now, behold, the night came on, very dark, ere the attack was made. And the Lord said unto T-loyovogna: Command thy soldiers to light their lamps. T-loyovogna said: I fear, O Lord; for will not lamps expose us unto death? But the Lord said: Light the lamps! So when the lamps were lighted the enemy began to march as if to surround them, some going one way and some the other.

15. And the Lord's angels made lights also, to the left and to the right, so that the enemy, in order to surround the lights, kept extending in two lines, away from each other. Presently, they judged by the lights that there were tens of thousands of soldiers come against them. Suddenly, now, T-loyovogna's army sounded their pans and kettles, and set up furious howls and screams; and in the same time the angels of heaven cast stars of

light in the midst of Azhis' army, and they became panic-stricken and fled in all directions, save three hundred who were captured and put to death. Then T-loyovogna sent one hundred men into the city and captured Azhis and slew him. After this, T-loyovogna entered the city and declared the place his.

16. And whilst it was yet night, thousands and thousands of the people came and prostrated themselves before T-loyovogna, swearing allegiance. And in the morning of the next day he proclaimed himself king; and he impressed thirty thousand men to build a temple to De'yus; and yet other twenty thousand to change the streets, and otherwise beautify the place. In forty days the temple was completed, and was large enough for eight thousand souls to do sacrifice in at one time. T-loyovogna compelled the people to prostrate themselves on their bellies and pray to De'yus, whose home was in Ahl-burj, a high heavenly place, a mountain above the mountains.

17. After this T-loyovogna changed the name of the city of Savazata, signifying, first fire-place; and he appointed to rule over it Vistaqpa, to be governor, with right to bequeath it to his son after him.

18. For Sudga had said: To concentrate power, this is the greatest. There shall be but one heavenly ruler, and his Lords shall be his helpmates. Even so shall there be but one king, and his governors shall be his helpmates in the same manner.

19. T-loyovogna then marched forward, to conquer and subdue another city; which he accomplished also, and changed the name, appointed a govrnor, making all the people swear allegiance to himself as king, and to Sudga, the De'yus, as heavenly ruler, creator of worlds.

20. In this way, even after the same manner as Kan Kwan in Jaffeth, did T-loyovogna proceed in Vind'yu, from city to city, conquering and subduing. For the Gods, Te-in and Sudga, had oft conferred together on this subject previously, and had long experience in manipulating mortals in their games of life and death, nor did mortals mistrust the power over them.

21. Hear ye next of Osiris and his Gods, Baal and Ashtaroth, whose heavenly kingdoms contained more than twelve thousand million angels.

CHAPTER XXXVI.

1. When Osiris, the false God of Arabin'ya and her heavens, left De'yus, in Hored, the self (satan) that was in him, spake to him, saying: Osiris, thou art a fool! Thou deservest to be ground to dust! Behold thy wisdom and power, and yet thou cringest to thy inferiors on every side. Wert thou not made as well; and withal, as masterly in making others bow down to thy will and decrees? What more is required for Gods or men, than to make slaves of others, to do him honor and reverence? Then Osiris said:

2. Thou truest of Gods. O that I had struck out from the first for myself! But I will amend my time. When I am in my heavenly place I will send to the earth to my laboring Gods, Baal and Ashtaroth, to come to me, and I will make our three kingdoms into one, and mine shall be chief. And I will offer emoluments to the best, highest grades in Hored, thereby drawing from De'yus his best fruits and flowers, and I will send to him some two or thrcc thousand millions of my superabundant drujas.

3. Accordingly, when Osiris arrived at Agho'aden, his heavenly place, he sent messengers down to the earth to Baal and Ashtaroth, summoning them at once to his presence. And they came, being attended, each, with ten thousand companions, besides heralds, musicians and trumpeters.

4. Osiris had made great preparation for them. His receiving hosts, one million, were newly adorned for the occasion. The roadway, for three hundred miles, was illumed with pillars of fire. The Holy Council, half a million, were in extra session. The laborers, four thousand millions, were granted a day of rest. So that when Baal and Ashtaroth entered the heavenly capital, it was a magnificent scene, and as if in fact Osiris, the false, was a mighty God.

5. Great were the ceremonies and salutations between the Gods, as also with the generals, captains, marshals and others; to describe which a whole book might be written and yet not mention one-half.

6. After the reception, Osiris proclaimed an extra day of recreation to Agho'aden, and in the meantime he and Baal and Ashtaroth retired to a private chamber beyond the throne, to the east, to consult on the matters of heaven and earth.

7. Osiris said: My brother and sister, ye are my loves; the worlds are all vain else! De'yus is the most selfish of Gods, and unreasonable. He said to me: Thou shouldst keep up the grades! Now, behold ye, his own grades are broken down. As I and other Gods send him contributions in subjects, so remain such subjects; no more education for them in Hored. Then he complaineth and assumeth to dictate. And this for De'yus' glory. Not a word for lifting angels or mortals up out of darkness.

8. Baal said: A most unreasonable God. Saidst thou not to him: O that I had the power and means thou hast! What great good I would do!

9. Ashtaroth said: This I have found before, the greater power a God hath, the less he doeth for others' good. As for my part, what good can I do? I have scarce two thousand million slaves, all told! O that I had a kingdom like De'yus! But what proposest thou, O Osiris, thou far-seeing God?

10. Baal further said: Ashtaroth, thou wise Goddess, thou hast expressed mine own soul. Mine own kingdom is but little larger than thine; I am a very helpless God indeed. But once I reach De'yus' means, my soul's delight will be to fill all the heavens full of schools and hospitals! But speak thou, Osiris, whatsoever thou hast resolved is wise. As for myself I have been two thousand years trying to put myself in good position first, so I could help others.

11. Osiris said: To cut loose from De'yus; this is wisdom. To send drujas into De'yus' kingdom, is greater wisdom. To establish Agho'aden as the all highest heavenly kingdom, with myself at the Godhead, and ye twain to be my sole Gods of the earth, is the greatest wisdom.

12. Baal said: As I swear, thou hast spoken at last what I have for five hundred years hoped to hear thee say. To thee am I sworn forever. Put thou upon me whatsoever thou wilt.

13. Ashtaroth said: Now am I blessed above all Goddesses! What I have heard thee speak, is what I would have spoken.

14. Osiris said: It is enough then, this I proclaim, and on our crossed hands we swear: AGHO'ADEN, ALL HIGHEST HEAVEN! OSIRIS, SON OF THE ALL CENTRAL LIGHTS! THE MOST HIGH

GOD! HIS ONLY SON, BAAL, RULER OF THE CORPOREAL EARTH! HIS ONLY DAUGHTER, ASHTAROTH, RULER OF THE CORPOREAL EARTH! FIDELITY AND UNION FOREVER!

15. Thus they swore themselves into the Godhead. And on the next day Osiris sent messengers to De'yus, in his heavenly place, informing him of what had been done, and adding thereto: But thou, De'yus, I cut thee off from these earth regions. Get thy supplies whither thou canst. Adversity doth a proud soul some good.

CHAPTER XXXVII.

1. Osiris said to Baal and Ashtaroth: Go ye down to the earth to subdue it; and your first labor shall be in Arabin'ya, and Parsi'e, and Heleste; after that ye shall fall upon remote parts and subdue them unto ourselves also. But go ye not as other Gods, to destroy mortals, for we want them to propagate and make subjects for us. Nor pursue ye them, tribe against tribe, putting them to death if they worship not Osiris or Baal or Ashtaroth. Nay, not even the worshippers of the Great Spirit, save of such, whose spirits we cannot catch at time of death; them destroy.

2. But suffer mortals to worship as they may, and if they worship the Creator, say unto them: It is well. If they worship Ahura, say: It is well. If De'yus: Yea, it is well; for all of these are but one person, who is Osiris, whose high heavenly place is Agho'Aden. Thus teach them.

3. This also shall ye do: Re-establish places of learning, teaching the Osirian law; cause to be rebuilt, houses of philosophy, oracles and temples; and in all such places where mortals come to consult the spirits, provide ye such spirits who shall answer through the oracles for benefit of our dominions.

4. It was ourselves that gave the name Lord God to the Arabin'yans; it was ourselves that gave the name De'yus to Parsi'e and Heleste. Let us not waste ourselves away undoing what hath been done, but appropriate it to ourselves.

5. Such, then, was the basis on which these three Gods set out to establish heaven and earth. Osiris gave to Baal and Ashtaroth, in addition to their own kingdoms, twelve Lords each, to labor with them in the earth department; and every Lord was allotted one million servant soldiers, to be under the Lord's jurisdiction.

6. With this, Baal and Ashtaroth returned to their heavenly kingdoms on the earth, and at once set about their labors. First, by inspiring mortal kings and queens to build the required oracles. And the kings and queens thus inspired impressed tens of thousands and hundreds of thousands of their subjects to do the building.

7. And in seven years' time there were built in Parsi'e and Arabin'ya four thousand altars for the sacred dances; seven thousand temples of sacrifice, four hundred and seventy oracle temples, and thirty-one sar'gis temples, where the Lords took on corporeal forms and reasoned with mortals; especially on the stars and moon and on the earth; teaching the philosophers the four motions of the earth: axial, oscillaic, orbitic and vorkum; the plan of the hissagow, and the cycles of the earth; the cycles of the sun; and the cycles of the sun's sun; the north star-belt therein, and the vortices that move them all.

8. And the inhabitants of Arabin'ya and Parsi'e and Heleste began again to prosper, and became mighty. But after many years, behold, Baal and Ashtaroth rebelled against Osiris, and seceded from Arabin'ya. And this was the end of the heavenly confederacy founded

566

by De'yus. As for the far-off Gods in other divisions of the earth, they seceded at the time Osiris and Te-in and Sudga did. And from this time on, no more spirits were sent to the Lord God, the false, the author of the name De'yus.

9. When Baal and Ashtaroth seceded from Osiris and resumed their own kingdoms, behold, in all the divisions of the earth, every God was for himself and his own kingdom. But between Osiris and Baal and Ashtaroth a triangular war ensued in reference to the boundaries and divisions of the lands of the earth.

10. Now, therefore, since the self-Gods had become the beginning of a new order of dominion in heaven and earth, every one in his own way, it is profitable to leave them for the present, to be resumed afterward. Hear ye, then, of De'yus, the false Lord God; and of God, the true Son of Jehovih:

CHAPTER XXXVIII.

1. After the meeting between De'yus and Osiris and Sudga, when De'yus was left alone, he thus reasoned: Since Sudga and Osiris have thus left me uncivilly amidst a most disgusting quarrel, it must follow that on their arrival home they will secede, taking their kingdoms with them. Well, it will be well; I will the more warmly bind my fellowship to Te-in, and we twain shall overthrow Sudga and Osiris, and take all their spoils.

2. While De'yus thus soliloquized, messengers came from Che-su-gow, Te-in's heavenly place, bringing this word: Greeting to thee: our Lord God: Te-in hath seceded, and taken both his heavenly and his corporeal dominions unto himself. With an army of two hundred million angel warriors he is walling his heavenly kingdom around on every side; none can pass or repass without his permission.

3. Before De'yus recovered from his surprise, behold, other messengers came from Sudga's heavenly place, saying: Greeting to thee, our Lord God: Sudga hath seceded, taking with him his heavenly kingdom and his earth dominions, Vind'yu! With an army of two hundred million angel warriors he is walling his heavenly kingdom around on every side; none can pass or repass without his permission!

4. De'yus said: So alike and like! Then these rascal Gods had this planned beforehand! Presently other messengers arrived, saying: Greeting to thee, our one-time Lord God of heaven and earth! Osiris and Baal and Ashtaroth have seceded, taking their heavenly kingdoms and their mortal dominions with them. I, Osiris, have spoken. Thy higher grades I will draw unto myself; my lower grades I will banish unto thee!

5. De'yus said: Well, it is well. I will now make stronger the other heavenly divisions unto me; and the earth divisions, too long neglected by me; Uropa, Guatama, North and South, and their heavenly places.

6. But whilst he thus soliloquized, behold, messengers arrived from these places, also announcing their secession in like manner. Then De'yus was silent for a long while, considering. But satan came to him, saying:

7. Darkness cometh unto all the great, for by this the light is made to shine brighter. Now, since all access to the corporeal earth is cut off, and since all thy supplies for food and raiment must come up from the earth, it followeth that thou shalt lower Hored, thy heavenly place, nearer to the face of the earth. The which accomplished, thou shalt send ten thousand millions of thy warrior angels against these rebellious Gods and despoil

them of their dominions, and cast them into hell, and repossess thou the whole earth.

8. De'yus said: It is true! My way is clear. These rascally Gods know not how foolishly they have exposed themselves. Hored is wide enough to cover them up. And by fire will I chase the drujas upon them, ten thousand million strong; flood them with such foulness that their kingdoms will go to pieces under them and suffocate them in the horrid stench.

9. De'yus then called together his vice-Gods, and his Holy Council, and his highest-raised officers; and he related to them what had occurred, and his plans ahead. But that he might the better deliberate and gain their acquiescence, he granted a day of recreation to meet on the following day at the trumpet call.

10. But lo and behold, on the day of recreation, no less than seven hundred millions of his highest grades left him and Hored, and descended to the heavenly kingdoms of his former Gods, some to one and some to another, whilst a few of them descended to the earth to found small kingdoms of their own. Danger was already staring Anuhasaj in the face.

11. Accordingly, he at once chose his officers, and set them to work, but owing to their lack of knowledge in such matters, only small sections were bound and lowered at one time, at which rate a hundred years would be required to accomplish the work. Hereat, De'yus' heart began to fail him. The prophecies of the higher Gods, that he and his kingdoms would be ultimately broken up and cast into hell, began to show signs of realization fearful to contemplate.

12. Anuhasaj had no time for war, but must now use every stratagem in his power to prevent dismemberment in his own kingdom. In these straits a good fortune came to him in a ji'ay'an harvest falling in all the atmospherean heavens, compressing and falling, so that his lowest grades were provided with sustenance from above, and they were pacified.

13. Jehovih had spoken to Cpenta-armij, in her far-off etherean worlds, saying: Behold, the earth, she entereth now the ji'ay'an fields of Tu'e'vraga, in My high roads, Loo-sutsk. A little while will I feed the self-Gods of the lower heavens, and lead them on to know My power.

CHAPTER XXXIX.

1. Jehovih spake to God, His Son, in Craoshivi, saying: Prepare thou, for the fall of ji'ay in atmospherea. The earth and her heavens enter Loo-sutsk, seventy years in the rates of seven hundred; forty years in five hundred; twenty years in a'ji! Be thou advised; for Craoshivi shall fall to thirty, and Hored be buried in the earth. Call thou My Son, Ahura, and reveal My words!

2. So God, in Craoshivi, advised his High Council, and also sent messengers in haste of Vara-pishanaha, to Ahura, and acquainted him. After this God propounded in Council: Anuhasaj, what can Craoshivi do for him? Thereupon the members spake at great length, more than a thousand of them.

3. So God decreed: A commission to wait on Anuhasaj and inform him of his danger, and offer to succor and save him. This that followeth is the message thus sent, to wit:

4. To thee, O Anuhasaj, greeting in Jehovih's name, and by our love assured. Thou art adjudged to be in perilous condition. Behold, one hundred and thirty years' pressure will fall on the heavens of the earth; Craoshivi will go down to the depths of hada. Reach up thy hands, and I will come and save thee and thy kingdom. Wilt thou withdraw thine

armies and permit the resurrection of thy lowest grades?

5. Anuhasaj answered this in these words: Who art thou that thus assaileth my peaceful kingdom? Thou pretended son of the Void Nothingness? Call thou on me as becometh one with thy small kingdom, and if thou need help for thyself, or for thy paupers, I will give unto thee!

6. Thereupon God returned this answer, to wit: Be thou patient with me, O brother: If it be that I am proved to be in darkness, and thou in the light, I will make thee ample amends. If on the other hand I be in the light and thou in darkness, I will say naught that would wound thee. If thou wilt apply thyself diligently to solve the place of the earth and her heavens thou wilt find in truth the coming pressure whereof I told thee. Think not that my words are spoken at random, but try them by prophecy and by mathematics.

7. As to the coming danger, it is an easy matter to estimate. A thousand years ago, when thou first established thyself and thy heaven, Hored possessed an average grade above fifty, all told. And there were four thousand millions of them.

8. In two hundred years thou hadst six thousand millions, and the grade was raised to sixty-five. In the next two hundred years the number was nearly doubled, but the grade had fallen to forty. And in two hundred years later the inhabitants had nearly doubled again, but the grade had fallen to twenty-eight. In the next two hundred years, the increase in numbers was at the same rate as the decrease in the grade.

9. Now behold, thy twenty-eight thousand millions, more than half of whom are in Hored, are below grade ten. And when thou didst first possess Hored, a ten grade could not survive thereon. Think not that some accidental thing will raise so great a weight.

10. Look into this matter, as to what thou hast done! Thou hast persuaded thy hosts not to look up to Jehovih and His kingdoms, and lo, they incline downward to the earth. Yea, they have already filled the earth with war and destruction.

11. Thou shalt not hope to throw these things on thy Gods, for they will turn against thee and accuse thee. At present they are content to found kingdoms of their own. But they will also come to an end. Because they have seceded from thee, let it be evidence that all the highest grades will follow in the same way.

12. As for Craoshivi, her lowest grades are above fifty, and therefore self-sustaining; her highest grades are ninety-nine and her average eighty-eight. And hundreds of millions of these are such as my Lords have rescued from thy bondage; others, such Faithists on the earth as thy false Gods put to death for refusing to bow to thee. And have they not proved it is better to suffer death than to renounce faith in Jehovih? Otherwise they had now been within the company of thy slaves, toiling in darkness.

13. Yea, my kingdom is made up of those that were despised and abused; and of those that thy Gods slew in war, chaotic and mad. For my asaphs followed thy cruel wars and gathered in the spirits of the slain, whom thou wouldst not have. Thou callest them poor still. Why, so they are; they are washed white as snow; and because they have been taught to keep on casting aside all accumulation, save knowledge and goodness of heart, in which they are rich indeed.

14. They would come to thee now in pity to take thy people by the hand and deliver them away from thee and darkness. And if thy slaves be not delivered away from thee, they will surely, soon or late, turn upon thee and cast thee into hell. I pray thee, therefore, assume thou conversion to Jehovih, and cast thy kingdom upon Him whilst thou mayst. For I

have the power and the means to deliver thee and thy slaves. Yea, I will give thee a new name, and hide thee away, that they cannot find thee. And thou shalt be one with my in my holy place.

15. To this Anuhasaj made no reply, and so the matter remained.

CHAPTER XL.

1. In Vara-pishanaha Ahura had now toiled nearly two thousand years with his people, who for a great part had been drujas, but were now high in the grades. Of them, more than two thousand millions had been raised into light; had become Brides and Bridegrooms to Jehovih, and had been delivered into the etherean worlds.

2. But Ahura suffered not his dominions to be depleted, but did after the manner of God in Craoshivi, and sent down to hada and to the earth and gathered in, both the fallen angels of De'yus and his false Gods, and also the chaotic and foul-smelling spirits, wild and frenzied, and vengeful; and Ahura had them brought to Vara-pishanaha and there treated, and nursed and restored and put to school and to factories, and taught and developed; hundreds of millions of them becoming bright, wise and of great love and power.

3. God sent to Ahura, saying: Greeting to thee in the name of Jehovih. Because of the coming darkness which will soon press upon atmospherea from every quarter, and the trials that will be put upon Gods and angels, let us unite our heavenly kingdoms! Let us bring our plateaux together, and thy kingdom shall be my kingdom, and mine shall be thine; and one of us shall be manager in heaven, and the other shall descend to hada and to the earth, when the great darkness is on.

4. To this Ahura replied: Greeting to thee, God of the heavens of the earth, and with love and most high reverence. There is wisdom in thy design. I will do with thee whatsoever thou demandest, to fulfill this great work.

5. So God, of Craoshivi, and Ahura, brought their forces to bear on their respective plateaux, to unite them. And this was the proceeding, for their places were two thousand miles apart, to the east and south-west; and the one, Vara-pishanaha, seven thousand miles below Craoshivi:

6. For the coming pressure would drive them both down near the earth's surface; to steer Vara-pishanaha to the eastward, would bring one over the other; and to lower the grade of Craoshivi would bring the twain in contact. And the inhabitants of both dominions were so high in power and wisdom that their presence was higher than the place they inhabited. So that the element of the plateaux was all that was required to be moved.

7. To find the power required, and to arrange the ranks for the proceeding, God appointed officers and set them to work, and the officers reported back that the work could be completed in twelve years. And Ahura united with God; and there were engaged in this labor three thousand million angels. And they made a bridge betwixt the two plateaux, and it so connected them that millions of angels could pass and repass objectively whilst the work was going on.

8. Yet God's labors and Ahura's labors in receiving the spirits of the earth, of the Faithists, and of others from the regions of hada, ceased not, lagged not. Their thousands of otevans sailed the heavens along in every way, gathering in the unfortunate.

9. And now that the self-Gods in hada had quarreled amongst themselves and separated, De'yus' blockade was broken of its own accord. His mighty standing army against Jehovih's believers had melted away; and the otevans sped hither and yonder unmolested. And they gathered in many a thousand; yea, tens of thousands, of De'yus' highest raised angels. The lowest would not come; they had been taught to hate with vengeance Jehovih and His worshippers; to look upon all ills as from Jehovih; to look upon all good delights and blessings as the gifts of De'yus, the Lord their God.

10. Suffice it to say, in twelve years' time the great heavens, Craoshivi and Vara-pishanaha, were united and become as one place. And there was a time of rejoicing and delight; great recreation and communion; great rites and ceremonies, and worshipping and rejoicing before Jehovih.

11. Already was the pressure of ji'ay upon the heavens and the earth. Hored was fast falling toward the earth; De'yus' highest raised had already gone; his kingdom was becoming a kingdom of fools and idlers, a most dangerous class when once want and starvation come upon them.

12. De'yus, still stubborn, and, withal, hoping for a change from some cause he saw not, had now no longer time to quarrel with his truant Gods, but from day to day, hour to hour, was kept at the full strain to avert the threatened doom.

13. Meanwhile, the false Gods, his own one-time pupils, were now heaping into his distracted kingdom millions and millions of drujas, who had been taught on the earth that all that was required of them was to call on the Savior, Anubi, and the Lord God, and that when they died they would go straight to glory to dwell on the holy hill of the Lord God. And these poor creatures the self-Gods now applauded, helping them on, saying: Yea, go on; your Savior, Anubi, will open the gate and pass you in. Henceforth, forever, ye shall do nothing but bow to De'yus.

14. And these spirits of darkness, like idiots, were bowing all the time, day and night, doing nothing but bowing, and saying: Blessed Anubi! He can save me! Glory to the Lord our God! Then they would begin again: Blessed Anubi! My Savior! Glory be to De'yus! For this was all they knew; neither would they hear nor see else; they were as wild people; with outbursting eyes, looking for Anubi; looking for De'yus; but bowing incessantly in all directions; millions of them, tens of millions; delirious angels!

15. Anubi gave up his place in consequence, and in fear of them; and his heavenly city was like a house without a keeper, where throngs go in and out, around about, forever shouting: O my blessed Savior, Anubi! Glory be to the Lord God.

16. But Anubi was with the false Lord God, striving to help him find some means of escape or safety.

CHAPTER XLI.

1. Darker and darker, the hadan fields palled before the touch of Jehovih's hand, to try the self-assumed Lord God and his heavenly works. As if an epoch new and terrible had come to one so audacious, who foremost in heaven and earth had sought to banish the worship and the name of the Great Spirit from mortals, and give them instead a heavenly ruler in the image of man.

2. For before this, all nations knew the office of Gods and Lords, and reverenced them as Jehovih's high officers, raised up spirits of the dead, wise and powerful. But now, in five

great divisions of the earth, satan's hadan chief had bound his name in mortals, with threatened penalties, and even death, for mentioning Jehovih's name. And, to put them to the test, made oaths on burning flesh, that whoso would not eat thereof should die.

3. For this was the criterion before the courts that they that refused fish and flesh food, or would not pollute the body by noxious drinks and smoke, intoxicating to the sense, were possessed of Jehovihian worship, and so deserved torture and death.

4. So the names of Lord and God, and Lord God, and De'yus, had now become for a thousand years fixed in mortals' minds as the Creator, a large man sitting on a throne in Hored, his heavenly seat, watched and guarded by his son, Anubi, keeper of the scales, and of the gate to heaven. To make a plausible story of which, the angels, through oracles, and magicians, and priests, and prophets, proclaimed that: In the beginning God created the heavens and the earth, and all things therein and thereon. And he was tired, and rested; and, as if creation was a completed work, left certain laws to run the wonderful machine whilst he sat afar off, looking on; smiling at the pranks of mortals, and their failure to understand him, with a devil and a horrid fire to torture their souls, if they sang not in praise of this compounded, false Lord God.

5. Thus turned he, their false God, the voice of mortals from Him Who is Ever Present, Whose speech hath every soul heard, Whose Presence moveth all things in heaven and earth! The false God turned them to sing and pray to himself, so he should clutch and bind their souls in endless slavery; untaught, half fed; as drudges, to bring into his capital, provender and building stones to glorify him forever.

6. Over Jaffeth, far and wide, this traitor to Jehovih had sealed in stone, and papyrus, and wood, and sacred cloth, his name, Ho-Joss, to suit the Panic voice, as whilst in Vind'yu he made them engrave it Dyaus, to fit the Vedic tongue; and thence in Fonece to suit the higher-spirited race, Adonia-Egad, and go over to Heleste, and, in less distince and bastard Greece, whisper Zeus, saying: These words are watch-words to gain Anubi's ear, and turn the scales for endless paradise. Go ye, slaves, engrave my names; and, in mortal libraries, register my great exploit, of how I created the world!

7. And make me spotless pure, letting sin into the races of men by Osiris' cunning tale of Eve's weakness by fault of the earth. For I am not come like Jehovih's captains, spirits sent to rule men for a season, but a very God of blood and bones, who once, in terrible anger, flooded the earth to drown my disobedient sons and daughters. Make ye them to tremble and draw long breath when my name is spoken, or, by mine own soul, I will hurl heaven and earth into endless chaos!

8. Pressing downward ji'ay came, slowly and surely, the very motion spake as a million tongues, serious, awful. For many, on every side, of the hosts of Anuhasaj were deserting him. As one in a small way may see on a sinking ship, how the expert swimmers, with strong arms, leap into the water boldly and swim for the far-off shore, whilst the helpless, in frantic rage, cluster fast upon the distracted officers, blockading them from doing good. So began the tumult in the fast descending plateau, Hored, which was increased a hundred-fold by the flood of drujas cast upon De'yus' kingdom by his own traitorous false Gods.

9. De'yus' generals and captains first tried music to hold the forty thousand millions to peace and order; but the es'enaurs themselves took fright, and by the million fled, flying down to the earth to Osiris', or Te-in's, or Sudga's kingdoms, and over-flooding mortals

572

with ghostly revelries. Next, by parades, and rites, and great processions, did De'yus' officers seek to divert the panic-stricken millions.

10. Thus for years this maddened God with wonderful strength of will almost held his own, inventing tens of thousands of stratagems. But at last, in the downward course, Hored touched upon the corporeal earth; and suddenly, as if startled by the shock, the frantic millions screamed, and then, alas, all order died.

11. The doors of hell were opened! Anuhasaj's throne and capital, with all their splendor, the maddened mob broke loose to pillage or to destroy. And then rushed in the fault-finders, shouting: Thou lying God, but like a man, who art thou? And thou, Anubi! Deceiving judge! A thousand horrid deaths to thee!

12. But the unlearned drujas knew not who was rank or officer, God or judge, but seized the pale and trembling De'yus and Anubi, and more than a million officers, overpowered them, by ten millions to one, pressed on by the foul-smelling crowd. And now, with blows and kicks and cuffs, on every side began the awful fray. Till stretched as wide as the earth, the countless millions were plunged into hell. Hereupon, to right and left, was now an unceasing combat, and all the hosts of the Lord God were sworn for vengeance against any one they came against.

13. Then came the torturers, casting into the hells most offensive smells and suffocating gases, crammed in the nose and mouth of their victims. No more were the Lord God and Anubi seen, but swallowed up in measureless darkness, where every soul sought nothing good, but labored hard to give unto others excruciating tortures for vengeance sake.

CHAPTER XLII.

1. God in Craoshivi prayed Jehovih what he should do to release De'yus and Anubi; Jehovih answered, saying: My Son, thou shalt first labor for them that desire; whoso courteth darkness deserveth not thy hand. I have proclaimed from since the olden time, warning to them that put Me away; but in their self-conceit they denied My person and power.

2. Wert thou, this day, to deliver from hell De'yus and Anubi, and their thousands of millions of self-torturing slaves, they would but use their deliverance to mock My creation, saying: It lasted not; it was but a breath of wind. For which reason thou shalt not yet meddle with the hells of Hored.

3. In four hundred years I will bring the earth into another dawn of light. Till then, let De'yus and Anubi and their hosts take their course.

4. God inquired concerning Osiris and Te-in and Sudga, and Jehovih answered him, saying: Sufficient unto them is the light they have received. Suffer them also to take their course, for they also shall become involved in hells of their own building.

5. But be thou attentive to My Chosen, the Faithists, in all parts of heaven and earth; not suffering one of them to fall into the hells of my enemies.

6. God acquainted Ahura with Jehovih's words; then Ahura prayed to Jehovih, saying: O Father, grant thou to me that I may go to Osiris, and to Te-in, and to Sudga, to plead Thy cause. Behold, the Lord God is locked up in hell; even high-raised Gods would not find it safe to go to him.

7. Jehovih said: Why, O Ahura, desirest thou to go to Osiris and to Te-in and to Sudga?

Knowest thou not, how difficult it is to alter the mind of a mortal man; and yet these self-Gods are ten-fold more stubborn!

8. Ahura said: I know, I cannot change them; to break this matter of conceit, and all learned men are liable to fall therein, none but Thee, O Jehovih, have power. But these self-Gods were long ago my most loved friends; behold, I will go to them as a father would to a son, and plead with them. Jehovih gave permission to Aura to visit them, the three great self-Gods.

9. So Ahura fitted out an otevan, and with ten thousand attendants, and one thousand heralds, and with five thousand musicians, besides the officers of the fire-ship, set sail for Che-su-gow, Te-in's heavenly place, over Jaffeth. And when he arrived near the place he halted and sent his heralds ahead to inquire if he could have audience with Te-in.

10. Te-in received the heralds cordially, and being informed of their object, sent back this word: Te-in, the most high ruler of heaven and earth sendeth greeting to Ahura, commanding his presence, but forbidding Ahura and his hosts from speaking to any soul in Che-su-gow save himself (Te-in).

11. Ahura received this insulting message with composure, and then proceeded and entered the capital city, the heavenly place of Te-in, where he was met by one million slaves, arrayed in the most gorgeous manner. These conducted him and his attendants to the arena, where Ahura was received by the marshals, who brought him to the throne, leaving the attendants in the arena. Here Te-in saluted on the SIGH OF TAURUS, and Ahura answered in the sign FRIENDSHIP.

12. Te-in signaled privacy, and so all the others fell back, leaving Ahura and Te-in alone. Te-in said: Come thou and sit beside me on the throne. Ahura said: Because thou hast not forgotten me I am rejoiced. And he went up and sat on the throne. Te-in said: Because thou art my friend I love thee; because thou art beside me I am rejoiced. It is more than a thousand years since mine eyes have beholden thee. Tell me, Ahura, how is it with thyself and thy kingdom?

13. Ahura said: As for myself I am happy; for the greater part, my kingdom is happy also. My trials have been severe and long enduring. But of my four thousand millions, more than half of them are delivered beyond atmospherea, high raised; and of the others they grade from fifty to ninety.

14. Te-in said: And for thy more than two thousand years' toil, what hast thou gained by striving to raise up these drujas? Ahura said: This only, O Te-in, peace and rejoicing in my soul.

15. Te-in said: Hereupon hang two philosophies: One seeketh peace and rejoicing by laboring with the lowest of the low; the other, by leading the highest of the high. As for myself the latter suiteth me better than the former. I tell thee, Ahura, all things come of the will; if we will ourselves to shut out horrid sights and complainings, such as the poor druk and the druj indulge in, we have joy in a higher heaven. To me it is thus; sympathy is our most damnable enemy, for it bindeth us to the wretched and miserable. To put away sympathy is to begin to be a great master over others, to make them subservient to our wills.

16. Ahura said: Is it not a good thing to help the wretched? Te-in answered: To help them is like drinking nectar; to make one's senses buoyant for the time being. That is all. They relapse and are less resolute than before, but depend on being helped again.

For which reason he who helpeth the wretched doth wrong them woefully. To make them know their places, this is the highest. For hath not even the Gods got to submit to their places. To learn to be happy with one's place and condition is great wisdom.

17. Herein have thousands of Gods fallen; they helped up the poor and wretched; as one may, in sympathy to serpents, take them into his house and pity them. They immediately turn and bite their helpers. But speak thou, O Ahura; for I have respect to thy words.

18. Ahura said: If a man plant an acorn in a flower-pot, and it take root and grow, one of two things must follow: the growth must be provided against or the pot will burst. Even thus draweth, from the sources around about, the lowest druj in heaven. None of the Gods can bind him forever. Alas, he will grow. All our bondage over them cannot prevent the soul, soon or late, taking root and growing. How, then, can we be Gods over them forever?

19. Te-in said: Thou art a God over them; I am a God over them. Where is the difference? Ahura said: I am not in mine own name; though I am God over them, yet am I not God over them. For I teach them they shall not worship me, but Jehovih. I train them that I may raise them away from me. Neither do my people serve me, but serve the Great Spirit. Thou teachest thy drujas that thou art the all highest, and that they shall be contented to serve thee everlastingly. Thou dost limit them to the compass of thy kingdom. I do not limit my subjects, but teach them that their progression is forever onward, upward.

20. Te-in said: How do we not know but the time will come unto them, and they shall say: Alas, I was taught in error. They told me there was a Great Spirit, a Person comprising all things, but I have found Him not. Will they not then revolt also? Was not this the cause of De'yus' fall? He had searched the heavens to the extreme, but found not Jehovih. Then he returned, and possessed himself of heaven and earth. Although he failed, and is cast into hell, it is plain that his sympathy for drujas caused his fall. From his errors, I hope to guard myself; for I shall show no sympathy for the poor or wretched; neither will I permit education on earth or in heaven, save to my Lords or marshals. When a mortal city pleaseth me not, I will send spirits of darkness to flood it unto destruction. Yea, they shall incite mortals to fire the place, and do riot and death. Thus will I keep the drujas of heaven forever busy playing games with mortals, and in bringing provender and diadems to forever glorify my heavenly kingdom.

21. Ahura said: Where in all the world hath a self-God stood and not fallen? Te-in said: Thou mayst ask of mortals: Where is a kingdom or a nation that stood, and hath not fallen? Yet thou perceivest nations continue to try to found themselves everlastingly. But they are leveled in time. Things spring up and grow, and then fall into dissolution. Will it not be so with ourselves in the far future? Will we not become one with the ever-changing elements, and as nothing, and wasted away?

22. Ahura said: One might say of man and spirits: There were some seeds planted; and many of them rotted and returned to earth; but others took root and grew and became large trees. But yet, is it not true also of the trees that they have a time? For they die, and fall down, and rot, and also return to earth.

23. Ahura continued: Admit this to be true, O Te-in, and that the time may come when thou and I shall pass out of being, doth it not follow that for the time we live we should contribute all we can to make others happy?

24. Te-in said: If by so doing it will render ourselves happy, with no danger to our

kingdoms, then yea, verily. For which reason are we not forced back after all to the position that we shall labor for our own happiness, without regard to others? One man delighteth in art, another in philosophy, another in helping the poor and wretched; and another in eating and drinking, and another in ruling over others; shall not they all have enjoyment in the way of their desires? Shalt thou say to him that delighteth in eating and drinking: Stop thou; come and delight thyself helping the wretched! 25. Ahura said: This I have seen; the intelligent and clean have more delight than do the stupid and filthy; the rich more enjoyment than the poor. As for ourselves, we delight more in seeing the delighted than in seeing the wretched. More do we delight to see a child smile than to hear it cry; but there be such that delight more to make a child cry than to see it smile; but such persons are evil and take delight in evil. Shall we, then, indulge them in their means of delight? Or is there not a limit, as when we say: All men have a right to that which delighteth themselves, provided it mar not the delight of others? 26. Te-in said: Thou hast reasoned well. We shall delight ourselves only in such ways as do not mar the delight of others. Whereupon Ahura said: Then am I not delighted with the manner of thy kingdom; and thou shouldst not practice what giveth me pain. Because thou hast resolved to educate not mortals nor angels, thou hast raised a hideous wall in the face of Gods.

27. Te-in said: This also wilt thou admit: that as we desire to delight ourselves we should look for the things that delight us, and turn away from things that delight us not. Therefore, let not the Gods turn their faces this way, but to their own affairs. 28. Ahura said: Thou art wise, O Te-in. But this I have found; that something within us groweth, that will not down nor turn aside. In the beginning of life we look to ourselves, which is the nature of the young; but when we grow, we take a wife, and we delight to see her delighted; then cometh offspring, and we delight to see them delighted. After this, we delight to see our neighbors delighted; and then the state, and then the whole kingdom. This delight to be delighted groweth within us; and when we become Gods we delight no longer in the delight of a few only, but we expand unto many kingdoms. As for myself, I first delighted in the delight of Vara-pishanaha; but now I delight to see other Gods and other kingdoms delighted. For that, I have come to thee. I fear thy fate. I love thee. I love all thy people, good and bad. Behold, this I have found, that it is an easier matter to suffer a river to run its course than to dam it up; to dam up a river and not have it overflow or break the dam this I have not found. The course of the spirit of man is growth; it goeth onward like a running river. When thou shuttest up the mouth, saying: Thus far and no farther! I fear for thee. I tried this matter once; I was flooded; the dam was broken. I see thee shutting out knowledge from mortals and angels; but I tell thee, O Te-in, the time will come when the channel will be too broad for thee. 29. Te-in said: How shall I answer such great wisdom? Where find a God like unto thee, O Ahura? And yet, behold, the Lord God, Anuhasaj, toiled with thee hundred of years, and learned all these things; yea, he traveled in the far-off heavens, where there are Gods and kingdoms which have been for millions of years. And he came back and renounced the Great Person, Jehovih. He said: All things are not a harmonious whole; but a jumble; a disordered mass, playing catch as catch can.

30. Ahura said: And what hath befallen him? And is here not a great argument? For we behold in all times and conditions and places, in heaven and on earth, wherever people

assume doctrines like unto his, they begin to go down into hell. They flourish a little while, but only as a summer plant, to yield in the winter's blast. For this I have seen for a long time coming against these heavens, even thine, that, as darkness crushed De'yus, so will thy heavenly dominions soon or late fall, and in the shock and fray thou wilt suffer a fate like unto De'yus.

31. Te-in said: For thy wise words, O Ahura, I am thy servant. I will consider thy argument, and remember thee with love. In a thousand years from now I may be wiser; and I may have my kingdom so built up that it will be an argument stronger than words. Hereupon the two Gods brought their argument to a close, and Te-in signaled his vice-Gods and marshals, and they came; and when Ahura and Te-in had saluted each other, Ahura was conducted away from the place of the throne, and after that beyond the capital. The vice-Gods and marshals delivered him to his own attendants, and with them he embarked in his otevan, and set sail for Sudga's heavenly kingdom, over the land of Vind'yu.

CHAPTER XLIII.

1. Sudga, after assuming a heaven unto himself, moved it over the Nua Mountains and called it Hridat, in which place he had eight thousand million angel slaves, after the same manner as Te-in's. Sudga's capital city, Sowachissa, his highest heavenly seat, was modeled after the fashion of Sanc-tu, De'yus' heavenly place in Hored, at the time of its greatest magnificence.

2. The capital house of Sudga was made of precious stones and gems, the work of thousands of millions of angels for many years. And when Hored was pillaged, prior to De'yus' being cast into hell, millions of its most precious ornaments were stolen and brought to Hridat. The streets of Hridat were paved with precious stones; and an arena surrounded the palace on every side, set with crystals of every shade and color, and of every conceivable manner of workmanship. On the borders of the arena stood five hundred million sentinels, arrayed in gorgeousness such as only Gods had looked upon. Inside the line of sentinels were one million pillars of fire, kept brilliant day and night, by the toil of five hundred million slaves. Inside the line of the pillars of fire were one million marshals, so arrayed in splendor one could scarce look upon them. These were watch and watch, with two other groups of one million each, and they stood watch eight hours each.

3. None but the vice-Gods and the high marshals could cross the arena to the palace, walking, but must crawl on their bellies; and for every length crawled, they must kiss the pavement and recite an anthem of praise to Sudga, who now took both names, Sudga and Dyaus. Neither must any one repeat the same anthem twice, but it must be a new anthem for each and every length of the person. For a tall person, a thousand lengths were required, from the line of marshals to the palace, a thousand anthems. So that only the few, as compared to the millions, ever laid eyes on the throne of Sudga. And after they so beheld him on the throne, for they were only permitted to gaze but once on him, and that at a great distance, and amidst such a sea of fire they scarce could see him, then they must re-crawl back again to the place of beginning, again reciting another thousand anthems.

4. Which made Sudga almost inaccessible, and permitted only such as were favored to even look upon him, which with the ignorant is a great power.

5. When Ahura came to the capital and sent word to Sudga who he was, praying audience, Sudga gave orders to admit him, commanding Ahura to walk upright into his presence, along with the vice-Gods. Accordingly, in this manner Ahura came before Sudga, and saluted in Love and Esteem, answered by Sudga in Friendship of Old. The latter at once commanded privacy, and so all others withdrew, and Ahura and Sudga went up and sat on the throne.

6. Sudga said: Because thou hast come to see me I am overflowing with joy. Because I know thou hast come to admonish me for my philosophy and the manner of my dominions, I respect thee. Because thou didst once try to found a kingdom of thine own, and failed, I sympathize with thee; but because thou wentest back on thyself and accepted Jehovih, and so was rescued from thy peril, I commiserate thee.

7. Ahura said: To hear thy gifted tongue once more is my great joy. To know that no misfortune was in store for thee and thy kingdom would give me great delight. Because I love thee, and the people of thy mighty, heavenly kingdom, I have come to admonish thee and plead for Jehovih's sake. As for myself, I have found that to cast all my cares on Him, and then turn in and work hard for others, these two things give me the greatest happiness.

8. Sudga said: Can a brave man justly cast his cares upon another? Was not thyself given to thyself for thyself? If so, thou desirest none to work for thee? If so, how hast thou a right to work for others? If thou prevent them working out their own destiny, wrongest not thou them? Moreover, thou sayest: To cast thy cares on Jehovih, and to work hard for others, these two give thee the greatest happiness: Wherefore, art thou not selfish to work for thine own happiness? For is not this what I am doing for myself in mine own way.

9. Ahura said: Grant all thy arguments, O Sudga, where shall we find the measure of righteous works but in the sum of great results? For you or I to be happy, that is little; for a million angels to be happy, that is little. But when we put two kingdoms alongside, and they be the same size, and have the same number of inhabitants, is it not just that we weigh them in their whole measure to find which of the two kingdoms hath the greatest number of happy souls? Would not this be a better method of arriving at the highest philosophy?

10. Sudga said: Yea, that would be higher than logic, higher than reason. That would be the foundation of a sound theory.

11. Ahura said: And have we not found, both in heaven and earth, that all kingdoms that are overthrown have the cause of their fall in the unhappiness and disaffection of the ignorant. As soon as the masses begin to be in unrest, the rulers apply vigorous measures to repress them, but it is only adding fuel to the fire; it deadeneth it awhile, but only to have it burst forth more violently afterward.

12. Sudga said: Thou reasonest well, O Ahura; go on. Ahura said: How, then, shall we determine the happiness of two kingdoms, in order to determine which hath the greater happiness? Are not revolts evidence of unhappiness? Hear me, then, O Sudga; where, in all the Jehovihian heavens, hath there ever been a revolt? And on the earth, where have the Jehovihians, the Faithists, rebelled against their rulers? Behold, in the far-off etherean heavens, the Nirvanian fields, hath never been any God or Chief environed in tortures. As for my own kingdom, my people will not rebel against me, nor need I fortify myself against disaster.

13. Sudga said: Thou art wise, O Ahura. The only way to judge a kingdom's happiness is by the peace and contentment and civility of its people toward one another, and by the confidence betwixt the ruler and the ruled. He who hath to guard himself liveth on the eve of destruction of his kingdom and himself. And yet, O Ahura, remember this: the Jehovihians of heaven and earth are high raised ere they become such; any one can be a ruler for them, for they know righteousness. But I have to deal with druks and drujas. How, then, canst thou compare my kingdoms with the Nirvanian kingdoms?

14. Ahura said: Alas, O Sudga, I fear my arguments are void before thee. Thou showest me that the line betwixt selfishness and unselfishness is finer than a spider's web. Even Gods cannot distinguish it. And yet, behold, there was a time when I said: I will be a mighty God, and bow not to the Unknown that brought me into being. For this I labored long and hard; the responsibility of my kingdom finally encroached upon my happiness. Long after that I put away all responsibility, and made myself a servant to Jehovih. Then a new happiness came upon me, even when I had nothing that was mine in heaven and earth. This is also unknowable to me; it is within my members as a new tree of delight. This it is that I would tell thee of, but I cannot find it. It flieth not away; it baffleth words, even as a description of the Great Spirit is void because of His wondrous majesty. Such is the joy of His service that even Gods and angels cannot describe it. With its growth we look famine in the face and weep not; we see falling ji'ay and fear not; with the ebb and flow of the tide of Jehovih's works we float as one with Him, with a comprehensive joy.

15. Sudga said: To hear thy voice is joy to me; to not hear thee is great sorrow. Behold, I will consider thy words of wisdom. In thy far-off place I will come in remembrance and love to thee.

16. Thus ended the interview, and Sudga signaled his vice-Gods and high marshal to come; whereat he saluted Ahura in the sign of CRAFT, and Ahura answered him in the sign, TIME.

17. And then Ahura, betwixt the vice-Gods, led by the high marshal, departed, passed beyond the arena, where the vice-Gods and high marshal gave him into the charge of the marshal hosts, who conducted him beyond the line of sentinels, where Ahura joined his own attendants and went with them into his otevan, and set sail for Agho'aden, Osiris' heavenly place, which had been over Parsi'e, but was now moved over Arabin'ya.

CHAPTER XLIV.

1. At this time Osiris' heavenly kingdom numbered thirteen thousand million angels, good and bad. And it was the largest heavenly kingdom ever established on the earth.

2. It was built after the manner of Sudga's; that is to say, modeled after Sanc-tu, in Hored, but more magnificent than Sudga's kingdom, and far larger. The arena-way was five thousand lengths of a man across; so that approaching visitors to the throne must crawl two thousand lengths in order to approach the throne. And they also had to repeat an anthem of praise, or a prayer, for every length crawled, going and coming. And they were, like at Sudga's, permitted to approach only to within a long distance from Osiris; whilst the array of lights around him were so dazzling that scarcely any could look upon him. And they that thus approached were so reverential that their minds magnified Osiris' glorious appearance so much, they verily believed they had looked into the Creator's face,

and saw, of a truth, man was of his image and likeness. And thousands, and even millions, that thus crawled to look upon him, afterward went about in heaven preaching Osiris as the veritable All Highest Creator of heaven and earth.

3. Osiris made his Godhead to consist of three persons: first, himself, as THE FOUNTAIN OF THE UNIVERSE, whose name was UNSPEAKABLE; second, BAAL, HIS ONLY BEGOTTEN SON, into whose keeping he had assigned the earth and all mortals thereon; and, third, ASHTAROTH, HIS VIRGIN DAUGHTER, into whose keeping he had assigned life and death, or rather the power of begetting and the power to cause death with mortals.

4. Osiris was the most cunning of all the self-Gods; for thus he appropriated the triangle of the Faithists; thus appropriated the names and powers of the Lord God, the false (now in hell), for only through Baal and Ashtaroth could any mortal or spirit ever attain to approach the arena of the throne in Agho'aden. And here again, they had to pass the high sentinel, Egupt, before they were entitled to the right to crawl on their bellies over the sacred pavement, the way to the heavenly palace.

5. Only the vice-Gods of Osiris and his chief marshal could walk upright to the capital palace, and they with heads bowed low. And when Osiris was informed of Ahura's coming he sent word that he should come upright, with head erect, but veiled from head to foot. To this Ahura gladly consented; and, being thus veiled by Egupt and handed over to the vice-Gods and the chief marshal, he walked upright till he came to the high arch of the palace; here they halted, and Ahura saluted on the sign OLD TIME LOVE, and Osiris answered in the sign JOY IN HEAVEN. Whereupon Ahura left the vice-Gods and walked near the throne, and Osiris came down, and they embraced in each other's arms, not having seen each other for more than a thousand years.

6. Osiris signaled the vice-Gods and chief marshal to fall back, and they did so, and they ascended the throne and sat thereon, privately.

7. Osiris said: This is a great joy! To meet one's loves, is not this greater, after all, than all the pomp and glory of the Gods? Ahura said: True; but who is wise enough to live to enjoy so cheap a glory? We run afar off; we build up mighty kingdoms, and our places are replete with great magnificence; in search after what? Whilst that which doth cost nothing, love, the greatest good of all in heaven and earth, we leave out in the cold. More delight have I to again look upon thy buoyant face, and hear the music of thy voice, than I ever had in my heavenly kingdom of seven thousand million angels.

8. Osiris said: Is it not so with all Gods, and with mortal kings and queens? They boast of the extent and power of their countless millions; and yet they have not more to love them than would match in numbers their fingers' ends, whom they can take into their arms in the fullness of reciprocity. What, then, are pomp and glory? Are not kings and queens of earth but watch-dogs, to guard the stinking flesh and bones of other mortals? And are not the Gods equally base in their dirty trade of ruling over foul-smelling drujas?

9. Ahura said: It is so. But whence is this great desire to rule over others; to lead them; to be applauded; and to revel in the toil of millions? Would it not be wise for the Gods who understand this, to resign their mighty kingdoms and go along with their loves to feast in the great expanse of the universe.

10. Osiris said: True, O Ahura. But who hath power to do this? Certainly not the Gods. And is it not so with mortals? For thousands of years, have they not been told: Except ye give up your earthly kingdoms, and give up your riches, ye cannot rise in heaven. But,

behold, the rich man cannot give up his riches; the king cannot give up his kingdom. They are weak indeed! As well expect an unhatched bird to fly, as for such souls to be but slaves in our dominions. This do I perceive also, of mine own kingdom, I cannot give it up; because, forsooth, I cannot get the desire to give it up, although my judgment saith it would be the highest, best thing for me.

11. Ahura said: Are not great possessions like unto dissipation? I have seen mortals who admit THE HIGHEST, BEST THING TO DO IS TO LIVE THE HIGHEST, BEST ONE KNOWETH, and straightway go off and pollute the body by eating flesh and drinking wine. They also know the right way, but to attain to the desire to put in practice what one knoweth to be the highest, they have not reached.

12. Osiris said: Yea, all this is dissipation. And if a man give away what he hath, is not that also dissipation? Can it be true, O Ahura, that even as we manipulate mortals, to drive them to war or to make them play peace, to make them destroy their kingdoms and build up others by our angel armies, which they know not of, that we ourselves are ruled over by the Gods in the etherean heavens?

13. Ahura said: It seemeth to me thus, Osiris, that is to say: That the etherean Gods above us rule us, but not in the same way, but by their absence from us when we do unjustly, and by their presence when we do righteously. We rule over mortals by direct action upon them, shaping their destinies by our heavenly wills, and they are often cognizant of our angel servants being with them. But when we cannot appropriate a mortal to do our wills, we withdraw our angels and suffer him to fall into the hands of drujas.

14. Ahura continued: Not that the Gods above us, O Osiris, send evils upon us; but that we foster evils within our own kingdoms which take root, like thorns and nettles in a neglected field, and they grow and environ us. Even this I have seen in thy heavens in the far future. It will come upon thee, O Osiris, and with all thy wisdom and strength thou wilt meet the same fate as De'yus, and be cast into hell.

15. Osiris said: Were I to judge by all the self-Gods who have been before me, I should assent unto thy wise judgment. But hear thou me, O Ahura, for mine is not like any other heavenly kingdom, nor formed for mine own glory only. This, then, is that that I will accomplish:

16. I will cast out sin from amongst mortals, and all manner of wickedness; and I will give them a heavenly kingdom on earth. They shall war no more, nor deal unjustly with one another; nor have suffering, nor immature deaths, nor famines, nor sickness, but peace and love, and righteousness, and good works and nobleness.

17. For I will go down to them in person in time to come; and I will take with me angels high raised, and appoint them unto mortals, and give them corporeal bodies for their pleasure, and they shall be the teachers of man on the earth. And man shall put away all selfishness and deceit, and lust, and lying; and the races of man shall be taught how to beget offspring in purity and wisdom.

18. And in that day I will take back the drujas of heaven and engraft them on mortals and re-raise them up with understanding. Wherefore, O Ahura, though I fortify myself in all this, am I not laboring in the right way?

19. Ahura said: It seemeth to me a dangerous proceeding. I would compare thy plan to that of a teacher who took his pupil into a place of vice to teach him virtue. How can a heavenly kingdom exist amongst mortals, save with celibates? And they cannot people

the world. Is there any other way but by the delight of the lowest passion that man can be born into life? What belongeth to the flesh is of the flesh; the spirit repudiateth the earth.

20. Osiris said: It hath been so said; but I will cast the higher love down into the lower.

21. Ahura said: Why, so thou canst; but, alas, will it remain down, and forever grovel on the earth? I have seen a sweet maiden wed to a vicious husband, and she lifted him not up, but he pulled her down. Will not it be so with the higher love, when thou weddest it to the passions? Behold the manner of the oracles! We appoint high-raised angels to answer the questions of mortals, to lead them to virtue and wisdom; but, alas, mortals come not to the oracles to learn these things, but to learn wickedness, and war, and earthly gain. Will it not be so with thy kingdom founded on earth? Instead of helping mortals up, mortals will pull down the angels to answer them in their most sinful desires and curiosity.

22. Osiris said: Thou hast great reason on thy side, and facts withal to sustain thee. Yet forget not, O Ahura, I shall have a temple built of stone on the earth, and a chamber where I can come and command the kingdom through the mortal king.

23. Ahura said: Behold, my mission is fruitless. I have now visited my three loves, Te-in, and Sudga, and thee. And I cannot turn one, even a jot or tittle. In this I have great sorrow; for I fear the time may come when great darkness will be upon you all.

24. Osiris said: I will consider thy wise words, O Ahura. And though thou now goest from me, my love will follow thee.

25. Hereupon Osiris signaled the chief marshal and the vice-Gods, and they came. Then Osiris and Ahura embraced each other and parted, both saluting in the sign, LOVE FOREVER. Ahura retired even as he came, but backward, the vice-Gods on either side and the marshal leading the way. After they crossed the arena, Ahura was delivered to Egupt, and the chief marshal and the vice-Gods returned to Osiris.

26. Egupt passed Ahura on to his own attendants, who conducted him to his fire-ship wherein they embarked and set sail for his own heavenly place, Vara-pishanaha.

CHAPTER XLV.

1. Jehovih suffered the self-Gods to prosper for more than four hundred years; and Te-in, and Sudga, and Osiris became the mightiest Gods that ever ruled on the earth. Know, then, these things of them, in heaven and earth, whereof the libraries of Jehovih's kingdoms relate more fully that of which the following is a synopsis, to wit:

2. First of Te-in, then Sudga, then Osiris. And of Te-in's heavenly kingdom, two vice-Gods, Noe Jon and Wang-tse-Yot. Chief high marshal, Kolotzka, and under him thirty thousand marshals. Chief general, Ha-e Giang, and under him one hundred thousand generals and high captains. Of these, twenty thousand were allotted to the dominion of mortals in Jaffeth; the others served in heaven, mostly about the throne of Te-in. Chiefly distinguished as Gods on the earth were Te-in's fourteen chief generals: Kaoan-cat, Yam-yam, Tochin-woh, Ho-jon-yo, Wah-ka, Oke-ya-nos, Haing-le, Lutz-rom, Le-Wiang, Thu-wowtch, Eurga-roth, I-sa-ah, To Gow and Ah Shung.

3. These generals were divided into two parts, seven each; and they were allotted equally, of the twenty thousand rank generals deputed to the earth; and these again were allotted each thirty thousand angel warriors.

4. Te-in had said to these fourteen chief generals: When ye come to the earth, and finding

two cities near together, both of which worship other Gods than me, ye shall divide yourselves into two parts; and one army shall go to one mortal city and the other to the other, and by inspiration and otherwise ye shall bring the two cities to war against each other, until both are broken down, or destroyed. After which ye shall inspire another city, that worshippeth me, to come and possess both of those that are destroyed. Better is it to make our enemies kill each other than to kill them ourselves.

5. And such was the mode of warfare by Te-in in that all the land of Jaffeth was subdued unto himself in less than a hundred years. Save the matter of a million Faithists, scattered here and there; and of the Listians who were in the mountains and wildernesses. And great and costly temples were built in all the cities of Jaffeth, and dedicated to Te-in, Creator and Ruler of Heaven and Earth.

6. Now, as to the worshippers of Joss and Ho-Joss, they were not converted but subdued, and they worshipped their God in secret, and made rites and ceremonies whereby they might know one another and the better escape persecution. Many of these rites partook after the manner of the ancient rite of Bawgangad.

7. Of the great cities destroyed in these wars were: Hong We, Chow Go and Sheing-tdo. For Hong We the wars lasted twenty years; and there were slain within the city five hundred thousand men, women and children.

8. The wars of Chow Go lasted forty years, and within her walls were slain three hundred thousand men, women and children. For Sheing-tdo the wars lasted twenty-five years, and there were slain within her walls three hundred thousand men, women and children.

9. In the destruction of Hong-We there were consigned to ashes four hundred houses of philosophy; two thousand four hundred colleges, and twelve thousand public schools. All of which had been made glorious in the reign of Hong, the king of the city. Because he worshipped Ho-Joss, his great city was destroyed.

10. In Chow Go there were destroyed six hundred houses of philosophy and two hundred colleges of Great Learning. Here was the Temple of Jonk, which was dedicated to worship of Joss (God), and which, in building, required twenty thousand men twelve years. It had two thousand pillars of Awana stone, polished; and at the blood altar it had twelve thousand skulls, of which the great king Bak Ho was slaughterer in the name of Ho-Joss. The throne of worship for the king was set with diamonds and pearls; and it had a thousand candlesticks of gold and silver. And the fine silk drapery and fine wool drapery within the temple were sufficient, if spread out, for five hundred thousand men to lie down on and yet not cover up the half of it. And the drapery was painted and embroidered with pictures of battles and wars; and of scenes in heaven. For the ornamentation of which drapery twenty thousand men and women had labored for forty years. All of which were destroyed, together with all the great city and all its riches and magnificence.

11. Sheing-tdo was a city of fashion and splendor, inhabited by the richest men in the world. She had a temple called Cha-oke-king, dedicated to learning, but in fact appropriated to the display of wealth and pageantry. It was round, with a high projecting roof, the eaves of which rested on ten thousand pillars of polished stone. There were four hundred door-ways to enter the temple; but, within each door-way, one came against the square columns of precious stones that supported the roof inside; and to either side of the columns were passage-ways that led into the four hundred chambers within. In

the center of the temple, artificial stalactites, twenty thousand, hung from the roof; these were made of silk and wool and fine linen and painted, and of colors so bright that mortal eye could scarce look upon them, and they were as ice with the sun shining thereon, forming rainbows in every direction. Here came kings and queens and governors of great learning; for here were deposited copies of the greatest books in all the world.

12. Besides the temple of Cha-oke-king, there were seven great temples built to Joss, either of which was large enough for ten thousand men to do sacrifice in at one time. For five and twenty years the people of Sheing-tdo fought to save their great city from destruction, but it fell, and was destroyed, and all the temples with it; by king Bingh it was laid low.

13. Next to these were the following great cities that were destroyed: Gwoo-gee, which had one hundred houses of philosophy and forty colleges for great learning; one temple, with eight hundred polished pillars and two thousand arches; thirty temples of wheat and corn sacrifice; one feed-house, where was stored food for one hundred thousand people in case of famine, sufficient for eight years; and all these, and the libraries of the records of the Gods and Lords of earth, and all things whatever in the city were burnt to ashes.

14. The city of Young-ooh, of two hundred thousand inhabitants, which had seventy houses of philosophy, and thirty-five colleges of great learning, besides many schools; one TEMPLE OF THE STARS, where lectures were given daily to the people to teach them the names and places of the stars and their wondrous size and motion; forty temples of sacrifice, seven of which were large enough to hold all the inhabitants of Young-ooh, the great city. By king Shaing it was laid in ashes, and nothing but heaps of stones remained to tell where the city had been.

15. The city, Gwan-she, which had thirty houses of philosophy, and seventy temples of sacrifice, two Temples of the Stars dedicated to Joss; eighty-five colleges of Great Learning, and also a feed-house, stored sufficiently to feed the city seven years; and there were two hundred thousand inhabitants within the city walls. Twelve years the people of this city fought against the incited plunderers, the warriors under the God Te-in, but were conquered at last, and their city laid low.

16. And the great cities, Ghi, and Owan, and Chong, and Goon, and Ca-On and Jong-wong, and Sow, and Wowtch-gan, and Sem-Sin, and Gee, and Tiang, and Choe, and Doth, and Ah-mai, and Conc Shu, and Guh, and Haingtsgay, and Ghi-oo-yong, and Boy-gonk, all of which had houses of philosophy and colleges of great learning, and public schools, and temples of sacrifice, and feed-houses, and hundreds of thousands of inhabitants. And all these cities were destroyed, and only heaps of stones left to tell where they had been.

17. Besides these, there were more than two thousand cities of less prominence destroyed. And yet, of villages and small cities, so great were they in number which were destroyed, that no man ever counted them.

18. City against city; king against king; man against man; for the inhabitants of Jaffeth were obsessed to madness and war and destruction; almost without cause would they fall upon one another to destroy; for so had Te-in sent his hundreds of millions of warring angels to inspire mortals to destroy all knowledge, and instruction, and learning, and philosophy, and to destroy all trace of all other Gods and Lords, that he alone might reign supreme.

19. And these angels taught mortals how to make explosive powder, and guns to shoot with, more deadly than the bow and arrow; and taught the secret of under-digging a city and blowing it up with explosive powder.

20. So, the fair land of Jaffeth, with its wisdom and great learning, was made as a distracted and broken-up country. In all directions the bones of mortals were scattered over the lands; nor could the land be tilled without digging amongst the skulls and bones of the great giant race of I'huans that once had peopled it.

21. And of those who were not destroyed, one might say: They were a poor, half-starved, sickly breed, discouraged and helpless, badly whipped.

22. And the spirits of the dead were on all the battle-fields, lighting up the dark nights by their spirit-fires, and in the morning and the twilight of evening they could be seen by hundreds and thousands, walking about, shy and wild! But an abundance of familiar spirits dwelt with mortals; took on sar'gis forms, and ate and drank with them, and even did things of which it is unlawful to mention.

23. Thus was Jaffeth won to the God Te-in. Now of Sudga, know ye.

CHAPTER XLVI.

1. Two vice-Gods had Sudga, Brihat and Visvasrij. Next to these, Sudga's heavenly chief marshal Atma, who had four thousand marshals under him, and equally divided amongst them to command, one thousand million heavenly warring angels. Atma had authority over thirty thousand generals and captains, to whom were allotted two thousand million angels.

2. Chief of the heavenly generals were: Shahara, Vasyam, Suchchi, Dev, Nasakij, Tvara, Watka, Shan, Dorh, Hudhup, Nikish, Hajara, Hwassggarom, Viji, Yatamas, Brahma, Goska, Fulowski, M'Duhitri, Yaya-mich-ma, Hijavar, Duth, Lob-yam, Hi-gup and Vow-iska. And these falsely assumed the names of the ancient Gods and Lords of thousands of years before.

3. Sudga had said to them: That my age may be magnified before the newborn in heaven, ye shall also magnify your own names by taking the names of Gods and Lords who are revered in heaven and earth, for all things are free unto you. But into none others do I give privilege to choose the names of the ancients.

4. Sudga then made the following his Private Council: Plow-ya, Vazista, Kiro, Cpen-ista, Visper, E-shong, Bog-wi, Lowtha, Brihat, Gai-ya, Sa-mern, Nais-wiche, Yube, Sol, Don, Mung-jo, Urvash, Cpenta-mainyus, Vazista, and Vanaiti; and to each of them ten thousand attendants.

5. Then Sudga made two great captains, Varsa and Baktu, and he said unto them: Two thousand million angels have I allotted to go down to the earth, to the land of Vind'yu, to subdue mortals and have dominion over them permanently, and I divide the two thousand million betwixt ye twain. But all other angels shall remain in my heavenly kingdom and work for me, and embellish it, and beautify my heavenly cities, especially my holy capital.

6. Now, when ye twain are permanent on the earth, and secured in the temples and oracles, ye shall survey all the lands of Vind'yu, and the cities, large and small, and all the people therein. And, behold, all men shall be subdued unto my two names, Sudga and

Dyaus; and when a city standeth, wherein the people worship any other Gods or Lords, that city shall ye destroy, and all the people therein. City against city shall it be, man against man; for as I am the all highest God of heaven, so will I be the God of earth, and its Lord. And ye twain, in finding two cities to be destroyed, shall divide, one going with his angel warriors to one city, and the other to the other city; and ye shall inspire them against each other unto death; and when they are laid low, ye shall bring into the place, to inhabit it, my worshippers.

7. Thus descended to the earth the two destroying captain Gods, Varsa and Baktu, with their two thousand million angel warriors. And they spread out about over the land of Vind'yu, where were many kingdoms and thousands of cities; and they came to mortals asleep or awake, and inspired them to havoc and destruction, for Sudga's sake.

8. And there were laid in ruins, in twelve years, forty thousand cities, of which thirty-seven were great cities. And chief of these were Yadom, Watchada, Cvalaka, Hoce-te, Hlumivi, Ctdar and Yigam, each of which contained more than one million souls, and some of them two millions.

9. In all of these there were places of great learning, and schools, and temples of sacrifice (worship). In Ctdar the roof of the temple was made of silver and copper and gold; and it had one thousand columns of polished stone, and five hundred pillars to support the roof. The walls were covered with tapestry, painted with written words and histories of heaven and earth, and of the Gods and Lords and Saviors of the ancients. Within the temple were seven altars of sacrifice, and four thousand basins of holy water for baptismal rites. Within the walls of the temple were niches for five hundred priests, for the confession of sins, and for receiving the money and cloth and fruits of the earth, contributed by the penitent for the remission of their sins. Through the central passage within the temple drove the king in his golden chariot, when he came for sacrifice; and the floor of this passage was laid with silver and gold.

10. In the center of the temple floor was a basin filled with water, and the size of the basin was equal to twenty lengths of a man. In the middle of the basin was a fountain throwing up water. And on the east and west and north and south sides of the basin were four pillars of polished stone, with stairs within them; and the tops of these pillars were connected by beams of inlaid wood of many colors, polished finely, which were called the Holy Arch of Suh-hagda. On the summit of the arch was a small house called the Voice of the Oracle, for here sat the king's interpreter of heaven and earth, the reader of visions. And the spirits of the dead appeared in the spray of the fountain, sometimes as stars of light and sometimes in their own forms and features, and were witnessed by the multitude.

11. Within each of the five hundred pillars was a sacred chamber, for benefit of the priests communing with angels. In the east pillar was an opening from top to bottom, a slatway so the multitude could see through the pillar, which was hollow its entire height. This was occupied by te king's high priest or priestess, as the case might be, and this person had attained to adeptship, so that the angels could carry him up and down within the pillar, even to the top thereof, which was equal to fifty lengths of a man. And the multitude thus beheld him ascending and descending.

12. In the west pillar was the library of the temple, which contained a history of its important events for a period of eight hundred years; of the priest and high priests, and of

the kings of the city.

13. Next to the Temple, which was called Tryista, stood the House of Learning, where congregated the wise men and women, skilled in philosophy and music and astronomy and mineralogy. The House was made of polished stone and wood interlocked, and in the front with one hundred and forty columns of polished stone and wood. Within the house were the skins and bones of thousands of creatures, ancient and modern, which wre classified and named; and with these were books of philosophy and history, all of which were free to the public one day in seven. Next to the House of Learning was the Temple of Death, dedicated to all kinds of battles, battles betwixt lions and men, tigers and men, and betwixt lions and tigers, and elephants, and betwixt man and man. And so great was the Temple of Death that its seats could accommodate three hundred thousand men, women and children. The temple was circular, and without a roof over the arena. But the greatest of all buildings in Ctdar was the king's palace, commonly called TEMPLE OF THE SUN. This was also made of polished stone, and on the four sides had eight hundred columns of polished stone; and next to the columns were fifty pillars, on every side connected by arches twelve lengths high, whereon rested a roof of wood and stone; and yet on this was surmounted another row of four hundred columns of polished wood, inlaid with silver and gold, and these were connected to the top by other arches ten lengths high, and on these another roof, and on the top of this a dome covered with gold and silver and copper. From the arena to the dome the height was twenty-eight lengths, and the base of the dome across was sixteen lengths. To enter the temple from the west was a chariot roadway, so that the king and his visitors could drive up into the arena of the palace in their chariots. But as for the interior of the king's palace, a whole book might be written in the description thereof, and yet not tell half its richness and beauty and magnificence.

14. Besides these great buildings there were four hundred and fifty Temples of Darkness, dedicated to the spirits of the dead. These were without any opening save the door, and when the communers were within, and the door shut, they were without light. In the midst of these temples, spirits and mortals congregated, and the spirits taught mortals the art of magic; of making seeds grow into trees and flowers; of producing serpents by force of the will; of carrying things through the air; casting sweet perfumes, and casting foul smells; of casting virus to one's enemy, and inoculating him with poison unto death; of finding things lost, of bringing money to the poor, and flowers and food to the sick; of entering the dead sleep, and of becoming unconscious to poin by force of the will.

15. Nor could any man or woman attain to be a priest in the Temple of Tryista until he mastered all the degrees in the Temples of Darkness.

16. The angels of Sudga decided to destroy this city; and, accordingly, they inspired a war betwixt it and the city of Yadom, which was second unto it in magnificence, and possessed of temples and palaces like unto it also. Yea, but to describe one of these great cities was to describe the other, as to mortal glory. For seven hundred years had these cities lain in peace with each other, half a day's journey apart, on the great river, Euvisij, in the Valley of Rajawichta.

17. And the captain God, Varsa, chose one city, and the captain God, Bactu, chose the other city; and each of them took from their thousand million angel warriors a sufficient number, and inspired the two great cities unto everlasting destruction. Even as mortals

turn savage beasts into an arena, to witness them tear and flay each other, even so sat these captain Gods in their heavenly chariots, witnessing the two great cities in mortal combat. And when one had too much advantage, the angel hosts would turn the tide, or let them rest awhile; then urge them to it again, holding the game in such even balance as would insure the greatest possible havoc to both.

18. Eight years these battles lasted; and hundreds of thousands of men, women and children were slain; and when thus the great cities were reduced, the Gods let loose THE BAND OF DEATH, whose angel office was to carry poison virus from the rotten dead and inoculate the breath of the living; and then in desperate madness make mortals fire their cities, to keep them from falling into other hands. And in eight years the great cities, with their mighty temples, were turned to ruin and to dust; and of the people left, only the ignorant few, starving, helpless wanderers, could tell the tale of what had been.

19. Sudga had said: All knowledge amongst mortals is inimical to the Gods in heaven; therefore I will destroy all knowledge on the earth. And this was the same doctrine maintained by Te-in, God of Jaffeth.

20. In such manner proceeded the captain Gods of Sudga over all the land of Vind'yu, laying low all kingdoms, and cities, and places of sacrifice, and places of learning. And in one hundred years the mighty people of Vind'yu were reduced to beggary, and to scattered tribes of wanderers. The great canals were destroyed, and the upper and lower country became places of famine and barrenness. And in the valleys and on the mountains, in the abandoned fields and in the wildernesses, lay the bones and skulls of millions of the human dead. And lions and tigers came and prowled about in the ruined walls of the fallen temples and palaces. Nor were there left in all the land a single library, or book, or the art of making books, or anything to show what the great history had been.

21. Thus perished the Vedic language, the language of song and poetry, and of great oratory. Save in a small degree, such as was preserved by the remnant of Faithists who had escaped through all these generations, still in secret worshipping the Great Spirit.

22. Hear ye next of Osiris and his dominions, and of Arabin'ya, and Parsi'e, and Heleste:

CHAPTER XLVII.

1. Osiris, the false, on setting up a heavenly kingdom of his own, and dominion over Arabin'ya, and Parsi'e, and Heleste, said: Let Te-in and Sudga pursue their course in destroying; mine shall be in the opposite way.

2. Osiris, the false, said: Three kinds of bad people I have found in heaven and earth: They that are forever finding fault with, and putting down, what others have built up; they are most crafty in argument to find the flaws of others, the inconsistencies, errors and shortness; but there is nothing in them to build up anything in heaven or earth. The next bad man is he who findeth fault not only with all that hath ever been, but with all propositions designed for a new state of affairs. He is as worthless as the shaft of a spear without a head. The third bad man I have found is he who, seeing the faults and errors of others, harpeth not upon them, but plungeth into work with something new and bold, involving himself and others in disaster. And these three have the great multitude, the world, to take care of! I alone am capable of destroying and building up.

3. The non-resistance of the Faithists hath ever made them dependent on the mercy of

their neighbors, in heaven and earth. They must be destroyed, and their doctrines also.

4. In destroying their doctrines, I must give something in the place. I have labored to put away Jehovih and establish the Lord God; now to put away the latter and establish myself as myself would take other hundreds of years. Better, then, is it, that since De'yus is cast into hell, I take the names, Lord God, and De'yus, and Creator, and all such as are acceptable in heaven and earth.

5. Neither will I rob them of their rites and ceremonies, but so add thereunto, that, by the superior glory, they will accept mine.

6. Nor will I abridge mortals of their learning; but, on the contrary, be most exacting and high in aspiration; for by this will I win the approval of the wise and learned.

7. Mortals love idols; therefore I will give them idols. Male and female will I give unto them.

8. Osiris then called Baal, Ashtaroth and Egupt into his heavenly Council chamber, and said unto them:

9. Two idols shall ye inspire mortals to build unto me: and one shall be the figure of a male horse, with a man's head and chest and arms, and he shall point upward, signifying, heavenly rest; and the other shall be the figure of a mare, with the head and breast and arms of a woman. And she shall hold a bow and arrow before her, and behind her a sword and a rose, signifying, for righteousness' sake. And the male idol shall be called Osiris, and the female, Isis.

Plate 90. THE FALSE OSIRIS.   Plate 89. ISIS.

10. For wherein I assert myself creator of all the living, I must show unto men that I am male and female.

11. Which of a truth is the fountain of all that is in heaven and earth, wherein PROJECTION and RECEPTION are the sum of all philosophy.

12. In which ye shall teach that to go forth is Osiris, and to rest in meekness is Isis; for which the ancients used the bull and the lamb.

13. For I was a globe, boundless as to size, and swift as to motion. And I put forth a wing for flying, and a hand for labor, by which are all things conquered and subdued. And beneath the wing I set the Lamb of Peace, as a sign of the flight of the defenseless; but under the hand I set the head of a bull, as a sign of my dominion.

14. And I made heaven and earth with wings flying forth, bearing the serpent and the sun. Square with the world, and circumscribed, have I made all things, good and powerful.

15. And in man's hand I placed the key to unlock the mysteries of the firmament of heaven, and the power, and wisdom, and riches, and glory of the earth. Into his hand I place a club, to slay the lion, or to subdue him.

16. For I am like unto man, having created him in mine own image; and I hold the key of heaven and earth, and dominions over all the inhabitants I created on the earth. I am Tau, I am Sed.

17. I am the light and the life, and the death. Out of myself made I all that live or ever have lived. The sun in the firmament I set up as a symbol of my power. The stars, and the moon, and things that speak not, and know not, are the works of my hand. Without me nothing is, nor was, nor ever shall be.

18. Whoso goeth forth warring for the right is for me, and I am with him. With warriors I am a god of war; with the peaceful I am a lamb of peace. To do, is of me; to not do, is not of me, but of death. An eye for an eye, a tooth for a tooth, blood for blood, mercy for mercy; but force unto all things, with will to conquer, for in these am I manifest unto men.

19. For in the beginning I created the world of mine own force; and this is my testimony, justifying force even with violence when the greater good cometh to the greater number. Hereon hangeth my law; in which any man can understand that had the Faithists fought for righteousness, they would have long since mastered the world and subdued it unto their God.

20. What, then, is the stratagem of Gods, save by some means to reduce men and angels unto oneness in all things? When Osiris had thus addressed the three Gods, he waited for them to speak. Baal said: This is a foundation; we have never had a foundation for men nor angels. Ashtaroth said: This is a head and front to lead the world. Egupt said: The wisdom of the Faithists was in having a direct course.

21. Osiris said: Then will I revise the doctrines of earth and heaven. I will not say this is for De'yus, nor the Lord, nor God, nor Osiris, nor Apollo, nor any other God. But I will give that which all save Jehovihians can accept.

22. For I will allot unto God all things, not defining which God, or what God, but God only; the rest will I manage in Agho'aden, my heavenly kingdom.

23. Go ye, therefore, to mortals, and revise the things of De'yus unto God; and if mortals question of the oracles to know who God is, say ye: He is Osiris, to the Osirians; Apollo, to the Apollonians; Isis, to the Isisians; he is the Creator, the master, the all, out of whom were created all things; he who created man in his own image; who dwelleth on a throne in heaven.

24. But if they question further, asking if he is the ever present, answer them: Nay. And if they say: Is he Jehovih, the Great Spirit? answer them, Nay.

25. For I will not suffer one Faithist to dwell alive on the face of the earth.

Plate 66.
This tablet belonged to the Egyptians in the Mosaic cycle,
And was of the established religion of that day.-- ED.

CHAPTER XLVIII.

1. In Haikwad, in Parsi'e, dwelt king Luthag, a man of great wisdom and kingly power.
His capital city, Sowruts, lay on the border of Fonecea, and had twelve tributary cities,

591

each city being ruled over by a king.

2. And great drouth came upon the regions ruled by Luthag; and, being a king of benevolence, he sent inspectors far and near, to find a country of water and good soil. But alas, they found not what was desired.

3. Luthag consulted the oracles, and behold, the angel, Egupt, came and answered the king, saying: Send thou thy seer and I will lead him. So the king sent for his high seer, and told him the words of the oracle. The seer said: Wherever the God touched thee, suffer thou me to touch also, and perhaps I can hear thy God speak.

4. The seer touched the king in the place, and at once the God spake to him, and he heard. So it came to pass, the God led the seer into Egupt, which at that time was called South Arabin'ya. The seer knew not the country, and he asked the God. The spirit said: Behold, the land of Egupt. Thus was named that land, which is to this day called Egypt.

5. The seer found the land fertile and well watered; and he returned to Parsi'e and informed the king. Thereupon the king commanded his people to migrate to Egupt. And they so went, in the first year fifty thousand, and in the second year one hundred thousand; and for many years afterward an equal number.

6. These things occurred in the seven hundredth year of the reign of De'yus in Hored. And in the space of two hundred years more, behold, the land of Egupt was peopled over with millions of people; for the drouth and famines in countries around about drove them hither.

7. Luthag sent his son to govern the land of Egupt, and he made it tributary to the kingdom of Sowruts. The son's name was Haxax; and when he was old and died, he left the governorship of Egupt to his son, Bakal, who broke the allegiance with Parsi'e and established all of Egupt as an independent kingdom. Bakal's son, Goth, succeeded him; and Goth enriched his kingdom with great cities and temples, and places of learning, and founded games and tournaments. Goth's daughter, Rabec, succeeded him; and was the first queen of Egupt. Rabec still further enriched the great land with cities and places of learning. Thus stood the country at the time De'yus was overthrown in his heavenly kingdom. And now for seventy years the Gods, Osiris, Baal, and Ashtaroth, and Egupt, had not much power with mortals.

8. And during this short period, the shepherd kings migrated into Egupt in vast numbers; and, in sympathy with these, and of kindred faith, were the followers of Abraham, the Faithists, who also migrated rapidly into Egupt.

9. Meantime the kingdom had passed from Rabec to her oldest son, Hwan; and to his oldest son, Naman; and to his oldest son, Sev; and to his daughter, Arma; and to her oldest son, Hotha; and to his oldest son, Rowtsag.

10. And here stood the matter when Osiris resolved to revise the records of mortals and angels as regardeth the history of creation by God; which he did according to his own decrees, which were as hereinbefore stated.

11. So it came to pass that through the oracles, king Rowtsag bestowed upon the libraries of Egupt the history of the creation of heaven and earth, with the origin of sin, and the creation of man, the first of whom was thence after called Adam, instead of A'su, adopting the Parsi'e'an word instead of the Vedic.

12. And these records were the same from which Ezra, three thousand years afterward, made selections, and erroneously attributed them to be the doctrines of the Faithists, who

were called Iz'Zerlites. And the records of the Faithists were not kept, nor permitted in the state records, but kept amongst the Faithists themselves, for they were out-lawed then, even as they are to this day, because they would not adopt the Saviors and Gods of the state.

13. Rowtsag's son, Hi-ram, succeeded him; and Thammas, his son, succeeded Hi-ram. Thammas was a seer and prophet, and could see the Gods and talk with them understandingly. Thammas was succeeded by his daughter, Hannah; and she was succeeded by Hojax, who was a builder on the TEMPLE OF OSIRIS, commonly called the GREAT PYRAMID.

14. In honor of the prophet of De'yus, the first mortal servant of Osiris, whose name was Thoth, Hojax named himself Thothma, which is to say, God-Thoth; for Osiris told Hojax: Thou art the very Thoth re-incarnated; and behold, thou shalt be God of the earth.

15. Thothma could hear the Gods and talk with them understandingly. And to him, Osiris, through his angel servant God, Egupt, gave especial care from his youth up. At the age of sixteen years, Thothma passed the examination in the house of philosophy, and in astronomy and mineralogy. At seventeen he passed THE BUILDER'S SCHOOL and the HISTORIES OF A THOUSAND GODS. At eighteen he was admitted as an ADEPT IN LIFE AND DEATH, having power to attain the dormant state; and to see without his mortal eyes, and to hear without his mortal ears. At nineteen, he ascended the throne, it being the time of the death of his father and mother.

16. For because Osiris desired to use Thothma, he sent his destroying angels, and they inoculated the breath of Hannah and her husband, and they died by poison in the lungs.

17. Osiris, through his servant God, Egupt, thus spake to Thothma, saying: My son, my son! Thothma said: I hear thee, O God, what wouldst thou? Osiris said: Provide thou a dark chamber and I will come to thee. Thothma provided a dark chamber, and then Osiris through his servant God, came to him, saying:

18. Thou hast great wisdom, but thou forgettest thy promise! Thothma said: In what, O God? Osiris said: When thou wert in heaven, thou saidst: Now will I go down to the earth and re-incarnate myself, and prove everlasting life in the flesh. For many years Osiris had told this same thing to Thothma until he believed faithfully he had so been in heaven, and returned, and re-incarnated himself for such purpose.

19. And he answered Osiris, saying: Like a dream it so seemeth to me, even as thou sayest.

20. Osiris asked Thothma what was the greatest, best of all things. Thothma said: There are but two things, corporeal and spiritual.

21. Osiris said: True. What then is wisdom? Thothma said: To acquire great corporeal knowledge in the first place; and in the second, to acquire spiritual knowledge. But tell me, thou God of wisdom, how can a man attain the highest spiritual knowledge?

22. Osiris said: To come and dwell in heaven and see for one's self. Thothma said: How long shall a man sojourn in heaven in order to learn its wisdom? Osiris said: One day; a hundred days; a thousand years; a million years, according to the man.

23. Thothma said: If one could leave the corporeal part for a hundred days and travel in heaven for a hundred days, would it profit him? Osiris said: To do that is to master death. Behold, thou hast already attained to power of the dormant state. To control the course of the spirit; that is the next lesson.

24. Thothma said: Behold, O God, I have attained to the power of the dormant state, even as the magicians who submit to be buried for ninety days. Yea, and I go hence in spirit, and see many things, but my soul is like a breath of wind, and goeth at random.

25. Osiris said: Provide thou me a temple, and I will come and teach thee. Thothma said: How to keep the body so long, that it be not damaged, that is a question? The magicians who have been buried long, and being dug up and resuscitated, find their bodies so damaged that they die soon after.

26. Osiris said: Thou shalt build a TEMPLE OF ASTRONOMY, and dedicate it unto Osiris, Savior of men and angels, God of heaven and earth. And it shall be built square with the world, east and west and north and south. And the observing line shall be with the apex of the Hidan vortex, which lieth in the median line of the variation of the north star (Tuax).

27. In the form of a pyramid shalt thou build it; measure for measure, will I show thee every part.

28. And thou shalt provide such thickness of walls that no sound, nor heat, nor cold, can enter therein; and yet thou shalt provide chambers within, suitable for thyself and for thy chiefs, and thy friends, who are also adepts. For I have also provided the earth unto heaven, and heaven unto the earth; and my angels shall come and dwell for a season on the earth; and my earth-born shall go and dwell for a season in heaven; yea, they shall come to me on my throne and behold the glories I have prepared for them.

29. Nor shall my temple be exclusive, but open unto all who will pursue the philosophies of earth and heaven. For which reason thou shalt build it with the sun, moon and stars; and it shall be a testimony unto the nations of the earth that thou art the highest of all mortals, and first founder of everlasting life in the flesh. For as the angels of heaven can return to the earth and take upon themselves corporeal bodies for a season, so shalt thou master thine own flesh to keep it as thou wilt. For this is the end and glory for which I created man on earth.

CHAPTER XLIX.

1. Osiris then instructed King Thothma to drive out of the land of Egupt all the Faithists, especially the shepherd kings, who could not be made slaves of.

2. Thothma impressed an army of two hundred thousand warriors, and drove off the shepherd kings, putting to death more than three hundred thousand of them. And from the Faithists he took all their possessions, such as houses and lands, and suffered them not to hold any mortal thing in possession; neither permitting them to till the soil, save as servants, nor to engage in any other labor save as servants. And there went out of the land of Egupt, to escape the tyranny of Thothma, three millions of Faithists, including the shepherd kings, the unlearned. And in regard to the Faithists, who remained in the land of Egupt, Osiris, through king Thothma, made the following laws, to wit:

3. Thou shalt not possess any land, nor house, nor ox, nor any beast of burden, nor cow, nor calf, nor shall thy people possess an altar of worship, nor temple, nor place of sacred dance. But a servant and a servant of servants shalt thou be all the days of thy life. But in thy sleeping place and in the sleeping place of thy family thou shalt do worship in thine own way, nor shall any man molest thee therein.

4. Thou shalt not profess openly thy doctrines under penalty of thy blood and thy flesh;

nor shalt thou teach more in the schools or colleges; nor shall thy children receive great learning. And of thy arts, of measuring and working numbers, thou shalt not keep them secret longer, or thy blood be upon thee.

5. And if thou sayest: Behold, the Great Spirit; or Jehovih, the Ever Present, thou shalt suffer death, and thy wife and thy children with thee. And if a man query, to try thee, asking: Who created the world? thou shalt answer: Behold, God! And if he should further ask: Thinkest thou the Creator is Ever Present? thou shalt say: Nay, but as a man that hath finished his labor, he sitteth on his throne in heaven. And if he further ask thee: Where is God? thou shalt answer: On the Mountain Hored, in heaven. And if he still further ask thee: Is the Ever Present a Person? thou shalt say: Nay, the Ever Present is void like the wind; there is but one ruler in heaven and earth, even Osiris, who is Lord the God, Savior of men.

6. Who else but doeth these things shall be put to death; whoso boweth not unto Thothma, my earthly ruler, shall not live, saith God.

7. These laws were entered in the libraries of Egupt, and also proclaimed publicly by the scribes and seers. And yet with these restrictions upon them there remained in the land of Egupt more than two million Faithists.

8. And it came to pass that Thothma began the building of the TEMPLE OF OSIRIS (pyramid), and he impressed two hundred thousand men and women in the building thereof, of which number more than one-half were Faithists. And these laborers were divided into groups of twelves and twenty-fours and forty-eights, and so on, and each group had a captain; but for series of groups of one thousand seven hundred and twenty-eight men and women, there were generals, and for every six generals there was one marshal, and for every twelve marshals was one chief, and these chiefs were of the Privy Council of the king.

9. And the king allotted to every chief a separate work; some to dig canals, some to quarry stone, and some to hew the stones; some to build boats, some to provide rollers, and others timbers, and yet others capstans.

10. Two places the surveyors found stone with which to build the temple, one was above the banks of the great river, Egon, at the foot of Mount Hazeka, and the other was across the Plains of Neuf, in the Mountains of Aokaba. From the headwaters of Egon a canal was made to Aokaba, and thence by locks descended to the Plains of Neuf, and thence to Gakir, the place chosen by the king for the temple to be built.

11. And as for the logs used in building, they were brought down the waters of Egon, even from the forests of Gambotha and Rugzak. These logs were tied together and floated on the water to the place required, where, by means of capstans, they were drawn out of the water ready for use.

12. As for the stones of the temple they were hewn in the region of the quarries. And when properly dressed, were placed on slides by capstans, and then, by capstans, let down the mountain sides, to the water, whereon they were to float to the place required for them.

13. The floats were made of boards sawed by men skilled in the work, and were of sufficient length and width to carry the burden designed. And at the bottom of the floats were rollers, gudgeoned at the ends. Now when a stone was let down from the place of its hewing on to the float, it was ready to be carried to its destination. And when the float

thus arrived near Gakir, ropes, made of hemp and flax, were fastened to the float, and, by means of capstans on the land, the float was drawn up an inclined plane out of the water, the rollers of the float answering as wheels.

14. When all things were in readiness for building the temple, the king himself, being learned in all philosophies, proceeded to lay the foundation, and to give instruction as to the manner of building it.

15. These were the instruments used by the king and his workmen: The gau, the length, the square, the compass, and the plumb and line. Nor were there any other instruments of measure or observation used in the entire building of the temple. And, as to the measure called A LENGTH, it was the average length of a man, after trying one thousand men. This was divided into twelve parts, and these parts again into twelve parts, and so on.

16. After the first part of the temple was laid, the builders of the inclined plane began to build it also, but it was built of logs. And when it was raised a little, another layer of the temple was built. Then again the inclined plane was built higher, and another layer of the temple built; and so on, the inclined plane, which was of wood, was built up even the same as was the temple.

17. The width of the inclined plane was the same as the width of the temple, but the whole length of the inclined plane was four hundred and forty lengths (of a man). Up this inclined plane the floats, with the stones thereon, were drawn by means of capstans and by men and women pulling also.

18. For four and twenty years was Thothma building the temple; and then it was completed. But it required other half a year to take away the inclined plane used in building it. After that it stood free and clear, the greatest building that had ever been built on the earth or ever would be.

19. Such, then, was Thothma's TEMPLE OF OSIRIS, THE GREAT PYRAMID.

20. Jehovih had said: Suffer them to build this, for the time of the building is midway betwixt the ends of the earth; yea, now is the extreme of the earth's corporeal growth; so let it stand as a monument of the greatest corporeal aspiration of man. For from this time forth man shall seek not to build himself everlastingly on the earth, but in heaven. All these things shall be testimony that in the corporeal age of the earth man was of like aspiration, and in the spiritual age of man in an opposite condition of corporeal surroundings; for by the earth I prove what was; and by man prove what the earth was and is at certain periods of time.

CHAPTER L.

1. When the temple was completed, and the king and his four high priests entered into the Holy Chamber, the false Osiris, through his servant God, Egupt, came in sar'gis, and spake unto the king, saying: Here am I, O king!

2. Thothma said: My labor is well recompensed. That thou hast come to me, O Lord my God, I am blessed. Osiris said: Keep holy my chambers; suffer no man, nor woman, nor child, that dwelleth on the face of the earth, to know the mysteries of these, my holies, save and except my adepts. Here layeth the key of everlasting life.

3. Thothma said: How sayest thou, the key of everlasting life? Osiris said: Herein is that which is of good and evil, as I commanded thy forefathers; to eat whereof man shall

become as Gods, and live forever. For this is the triumph of man over death, even for which I created him on the earth.

4. Thothma said: Shall only we five know these things? Osiris said: Nay, verily; else the light of my kingdom would not be full. Behold, thou, how I built the temple! Was it not in the keeping of adepts? So, then, as I have given unto thee to know my kingdom, thou shalt give unto others, not suffering these lights to come, save through my commandments.

5. Now in the second month after the temple was completed, Thothma, the king, having put the affairs of his kingdom in order, went into the HOLY CHAMBER, and thence ascended into the CHAMBER OF LIFE AND DEATH, leaving the four chief priests in the Holy Chamber. And Thothma CAST HIMSELF IN DEATH (dormancy) by swallowing his tongue. Whereupon the priests closed the entrance and sealed the king within.

6. Osiris, through his servant God, Egupt, said unto the priests: One alone shall remain; in quarter-watch shall ye dwell within the Holy Chamber, and I will remain also. And the priests cast lots, and divided the watch in six hours each, unto every day. And Osiris sent Baal to the spirit of Thothma, and took him to Agho'aden, Osiris' heavenly place, showing the spirit unto the glory of the throne, saying: Behold the God of Gods. Thothma said: It is a great glory; lo, mine eyes are blinded by the light of the Lord my God. After this, Baal took the soul of Thothma into a thousand heavenly places in Osiris' kingdom, and showed him the glory thereof.

7. Thothma said unto Baal: Thou angel of God, thou hast shown me, of a truth, God is in the image of man. Nor is there any but one God, who ruleth over all.

8. Baal said: How sayest thou then; who is God? Thothma said: How sayest thou? For behold, his glory was so great I could not look upon him.

9. Then answered Baal, saying: Only angels and mortals; these are the sum of all things. He, thou hast looked upon, was even as thou art; a one-time mortal on a far-off star-world. He attained unto the Godhead, to create a world unto himself, even as thou, who art an adept, canst create flowers and plants and serpents. Thus he came into the void regions of space and created the earth and her heavens, and they belong unto him, for they are his. And in like manner is every star-world, created and ruled by a God like unto thy God, who is Lord of all.

10. Thothma said: O that all people knew these things! O that I may remember them when I am returned to earth. Baal said: More than this shalt thou remember; for I will now take thee to the hells of the idolaters and the Jehovihians. Baal then took the soul of Thothma to the hells of De'yus, and showed him the horrors thereof. But he took him not to the regions of God, in Craoshivi.

11. Now when Thothma had traveled in heaven for thirty days, Baal brought his spirit back to the Chamber of Death, and showed him how to regain his corporeal part, the which he did. And then Baal signaled unto Egupt, and the latter spake to the priest on watch, saying: Behold, Thothma hath returned; go thou and fetch thy brother, and deliver him into the Holy Chamber.

12. And when they came they unloosed the sealing stones and delivered the king into the Holy Chamber, and he was awake from his trance, and remembered all he had seen in heaven, which he related to the high priests who were with him. And both Baal and Egupt came in sar'gis and talked in the Holy Chamber with Thothma and the priests. For one

day the king remained in the Holy Chamber, that his spirit be reconciled to the flesh; and on the next day he and the priests came forth out of the temple and sealed the door thereof, and placed the king's guard in charge, that no man or woman might molest the place. Now Thothma had been in the death trance forty days.

13. The three angels, Egupt, Baal and Ashtaroth, came into the altar in the king's palace that night, and showed themselves to the college students who had attained ADEPT. Baal spake orally before them, directing his words to the king, saying: Behold, I am the angel of God thy Lord, whom thou hast beholden in heaven; I am the same who traveled in heaven with thee. What I speak, I say in the name of the Lord our God, whose servant I am. On the morrow shall thy high priests draw lots, and one of them shall enter the Chamber of Holies, in the Osirian Temple, and do even as thou hast. And after him, behold, another of the high priests shall do likewise; and so on, until the four have had thy experience.

14. And it came to pass that the four priests in turn CAST THEMSELVES IN DEATH, and visited Osiris' heavenly kingdoms, and also many of the hells of De'yus, being led in spirit by Baal or Ashtaroth, Egupt being the guardian God of the temple.

15. When they had thus accumulated the same knowledge of heaven and earth, the five of them were of one mind as to attaining life everlasting in the corporeal body. Osiris said: Behold, I will bring many back who are already dead; and they shall call unto their embalmed bodies and wake them up and inhabit them. Go ye, then, to the root of the matter, and prepare my people, for I will come in person and inhabit the temple ye have built; and my heavenly kingdom shall descend even to the earth. Prepare ye the COLUMN OF STARS!

16. Thothma built a column to the east line of the slat, seven lengths, and the height was thirty-six lengths; of wood and stone built he it, with an opening from the bottom to the top, and the width of the opening was six lengths. In the walls thereof was a winding stairway, and there were windows looking out to the east and west and north and south, that the stars from every quarter might be observed. On the summit of the column were dwelling-places for the seers and mathematicians, with places for the measuring instruments and lenses.

17. When this was completed, Thothma built of wood and stone an external wall across the slat of the temple; and within this wall were stairs also, and these led to the top of the pyramid. This wall was also provided with windows, that the northern stars might be observed.

18. Thothma made an observing column for the sun, and it was provided with lenses of all colors, so that adepts standing at the base of the pyramid could see the sun at every hour of the day, and distinguish the spots and their changes. A gau was set within each of the angles of observation, that the relative position of the sun with northern stars could be determined every day.

19. By these two columns, therefore, Thothma and his mathematicians measured the sun and moon and stars, as to the distances and sizes thereof. And Osiris commanded the king to send into the far-off lands of the earth his wisest mathematicians, to observe the winds of heaven, and the drought upon the earth; and the abundance of the yield of the earth in different regions, in different years and seasons; and to observe famines and pestilences, and all manner of occurrences on the face of the earth. He said unto the king: When thy

mathematicians are returned to thee with their accumulated wisdom, thou, or thy successor, shall examine the sun and the stars and moon, as compared to the things whereof the mathematicians shall relate, one year with another; and three years with another three years, and five with five, and seven with seven, and so on for hundreds of years, and thousands of years.

20. And when thou hast taken in the term of three thousand three hundred years, and compared the sun and moon and stars, as relate to the occurrences of the earth, thou shalt have the key of prophecy for three thousand three hundred years ahead. And thou shalt say of this land and of that land; and of this people and that people, how it will be with them, and thou shalt not err.

21. Thothma, the king, called together his mathematicians, and, according to their grade, chose from amongst them twelve hundred. These he divided into groups of one hundred each; and he gave them a sufficient number of attendants; and he sent them toward all the sides of the world, allotting to them sixteen years each for observation, according to the commandments.

22. And they took with them all kinds of instruments to measure with, besides scribes to make the records of such matters as came before them. And they went throughout Arabin'ya, and Vind'yu, and Jaffeth, and Parsi'e, and Heleste, and Uropa, even across to the western sea; and to the south extreme of Arabin'ya, and to the great kingdoms of the interior, and to the north of Heleste and Parsi'e, and Jaffeth, to the regions of everlasting snow.

23. And in sixteen and seventeen years they returned, save some who died on the journeys. And most wonderful was the knowledge these mathematicians gained. In some countries they found philosophers who had the knowledge required even at their tongues' end. Thothma received them in great pomp and glory, and awarded all of them with great riches.

24. And Thothma had these things rewritten and condensed into books, and named them books of great learning, and they were deposited within the south chamber of the pyramid, where never harm could come to them.

25. And Thothma made it a law, that other mathematicians should travel over the same regions for other sixteen years and make like observations; and after them, yet other mathematicians to succeed them, and so on for three thousand three hundred years. And accordingly, a new expedition started forth. Now during the absence of the first mathematicians, Thothma and his philosophers observed the sun and moon and stars every day, and a record was made thereof, as to the earth in the regions of Thothma's home kingdom. And these observations were reduced to tablets and maps, and a record made of them in Parsi'e'an language, which was the language of the learned. For the Eguptian language of that day was spoken mostly by the unlearned, and was mixed with the Fonecean, a language of sounds.

26. After the mathematicians returned, Thothma and his philosophers examined the whole matter as compared with the maps and tablets of the heavens, and the facts deduced therefrom were written in a separate book and called THE PHILOSOPHIES OF GOD AND HIS SON THOTHMA, KING OF THE EARTH!

27. Copies of this book were made and sent into the lands of Arabin'ya, Vind'yu, Jaffeth, and Parsi'e and Heleste, and Uropa, to the priests of God, but the original book was filed

in the Holy Chamber, in the Temple of Osiris.

28. Thothma applied himself to impart wisdom unto all men. And during his reign he built in the land of Egupt seventy-seven colleges of Great Learning, twelve colleges of prophecy, two hundred houses of philosophy, seven adepteries, and three thousand free schools, and four thousand houses of sacrifice unto Osiris, Savior of men.

29. Three hundred and forty obelisks to God, thirty triumphal arches to De'yus, four thousand oans-nus to the Creator, and these were mounted on pedestals of polished stone, and stood at the street corners.

30. And there were graduated to the rank of adept during Thothma's reign more than four thousand men and three hundred women, all capable of the death trance, and of going about in spirit. And of these over seven hundred were permitted within thirty years to test the cast of the holy chambers in the pyramid. And their spirits were conducted into Osiris' heavenly regions, and sojourned there for many days, and returned to their bodies unharmed. Because of the position of the chambers, there was no action upon their bodies whilst in the swoon.

31. Thus did Thothma prove himself to be one of the wisest and greatest men that ever dwelt on the face of the earth. He believed all things the Gods told him, believed he was Thoth re-incarnated, and believed he would never die as to the flesh.

32. The false Osiris, through his servant God, Egupt, had said to Thothma: This is the manner of heaven and earth, as regardeth man: All men are re-incarnated over and over until perfected to immortal flesh; and in that day man hath so perfected his adeptism he can remain on earth or ascend to heaven, even when he desireth. Hence of all knowledge, adeptism is the greatest.

33. Thothma asked if there were any new creations. Satan prompted Osiris, who said: Nay, thy spirit is old as the earth. At first it was small and round, like a grain of mustard, only it was spirit. And the multitude of these seed comprise the All Unseen. When one of them taketh root in gestation, then is the beginning. And it is born into the world a frog, or an ass, or worm, or lion, or small creeping thing; and it liveth its time and dieth. And the spirit hieth it back again into another womb, and it is born forth a man low as to knowledge, evil as to life. And he liveth a time and dieth again; but again the spirit hieth back to another womb, and it is born forth again, another man, but wiser as to knowledge, and less evil as to life. And this continueth to hundreds of generations and to thousands. But he who hath attained adeptship hath it in his power to call forth out of the earth his own corporeality; he needeth no longer to go through the filth of others.

34. Thothma was wise even in his belief; for when he was growing old, and beholding his flesh sunken, and his eyes growing hollow and dim, and his hands getting withered, he inquired of the Gods, saying: I know thou hast taught me truth, O God. I am weak before thee, as to judgment, and curious in my vanity. Osiris said: Speak thou, O king!

35. Thothma said: By all the force of my will; and by my great learning, I cannot stay the withering of the flesh. If, therefore, I already dry up like a mummy, above the power of my will, how will it be with me when I am further emaciated?

36. Satan prompted Osiris to answer the king, and so he said: Until thou art even more emaciated thou canst not understand the power of thine own soul.

37. With this the king was reconciled, and even at the time he was tottering on his last legs he began to build a new palace, saying: After I have changed this flesh into

immortal flesh, hither will I come and dwell forever. And I shall be surrounded by adepts, wise and faultless. And this shall be the first colony of the kind I will build on the earth. 38. But afterward I will build many colonies of like kind; more and more of them, until I have all the earth redeemed to immortal flesh. For of such shall be my kingdom, and all men and all women on the earth shall own me Lord of all.

39. Nevertheless, with all Thothma's wisdom, and the wisdom of his Gods, he fell on a stone and died suddenly on the day he was one hundred years old.

CHAPTER LI.

1. When Thothma was quite dead the priests carried his body into the temple, fully believing his spirit would return from heaven and transform the body from corruptible into incorruptible flesh to live forever. And they laid the corpse in the place previously designated by the Gods, and sealed it up according to the commands of the false Osiris, Savior of men.

2. Osiris had said: Whoso believeth in me, him will I save unto everlasting life, and though he lose his body, yet again shall he find it, and the corruptible flesh shall be changed in the twinkling of an eye, and become incorruptible unto life everlasting, with the spirit that abideth therein.

3. On the fifth day the priests opened the chamber, for according to the LAWS OF MIRACLES, on that day, the spirit should accomplish the feat; but lo and behold, it came not, and the body still lay cold and dead. But the Gods came in sar'gis and said unto the priests: Seal ye up the body for other five days. And the priests did as commanded; and after that they examined it again, but life had not returned. Again they were commanded to seal it up for other five days, which they did, but life returned not.

4. Houaka, who was now the high priest, inquired of Osiris concerning the matter. And Osiris, through his servant God, Egupt, answered him, saying: Go fetch a young man who is warm in the blood, which is life in the flesh, and he shall be the seventh son of an adept, and know how to CAST HIMSELF IN DEATH.

5. The priests brought Xaian, who was in his twenty-fourth year, and when he came into the Holy Chamber he was bid cast himself in death for benefit of the king's soul. And Xaian thus cast himself, and he was sealed in the chamber of death for five days along with the king's corpse. And in five days the priests brought both bodies into the Holy Chamber, according to instructions. And Osiris came and commanded them to stand around the bodies, and when they had done so, the angels from Osiris' kingdom came and spirited away the body of the king, and they brought back the spirit of Xaian to inhabit the body of Xaian, and put it in possession thereof, making believe it was the spirit of Thothma returned.

6. Houaka said to the Gods: Where is the body of Thothma? Hath it been transformed? And the Gods answered: It hath gone to heaven, and will return after many days. But as to the spirit of the king, behold, he is with thee. And the priests spoke to Xaian, believing it was Thothma. And after three days they came forth out of the temple and recrowned Xaian, Thothma the Second, and they proclaimed it abroad that these things were true, howbeit they knew to the contrary.

7. As to the spirit of Thothma, at the time of death, it was taken to Agho'aden and put

amongst the servants of Osiris' heavenly kingdom, and thus enslaved. So Xaian became king of Egupt.

8. Now, as regardeth the false Gods, Osiris and his confederates, they never tried to reincarnate the spirit of Thothma; but because of the virtues and the wisdom of Thothma, they used him for benefit of Osiris' heavenly kingdom, and to establish Osiris everlastingly on the earth as the all highest God.

9. As to the kingdoms of the land of Egupt, which succeeded Thothma, the inhabitants of the earth already know the chief part. For hundreds and hundreds of years the Eguptians were the most learned people in the world, and especially in a knowledge of the stars, and the sun and moon, and in adeptism and miracles.

10. But woe came unto them; the land became flooded with hundreds of millions of drujas; and as to the people of Egupt, the chief desire was to be able to return in spirit after death and dwell with mortals. And the things which followed are not even lawful to mention.

11. Suffice it, these spirits lost all sight of any higher heavens than to dwell on the earth; they knew no other. And they watched about when children were born, and obsessed them, driving hence the natural spirit, and growing up in the new body of the newborn, calling themselves re-incarnated; and these drujas professed that when they previously lived on earth they were great kings, or queens, or philosophers.

12. And they taught as their master, Osiris, the false, did: That there was no higher heaven than here on the earth, and that man must be re-incarnated over and over until the flesh became immortal. Not all of these spirits drove hence the natural spirit; but many merely engrafted themselves on the same body; and whilst such persons lived, these spirits lived with them and dwelt with them day and night; not knowing more than their mortal companion. And when such person died, behold, the druja went and engrafted itself on another child, and lived and dwelt with it in the same way; and thus continuing, generation after generation.

13. And because of these indulgences many of the spirits came in sar'gis in the families of the Eguptians; eating and drinking with them corporeally; yea, and even doing things whereof no man may speak, whereby dire disease seized upon the flesh of mortals; and their blood and their flesh became inhabited with vermin. The people became idlers and vagrants; the lands were not tilled, and the places of learning became deserted ruins.

CHAPTER LII.

1. Of the land of Egupt, the above sufficeth; and of Parsi'e and Heleste these things are the chief, as regardeth the dominion of Osiris, Baal and Ashtaroth, to wit:

2. Because of the persecutions of Faithists, and shepherd kings, and Listians, these people fled into Parsi'e and Heleste for hundreds of years, and they built cities and established kingdoms.

3. And none of these accepted the Lord, or God, or De'yus, but for the most part worshipped the Great Spirit. Nevertheless, they were not Faithists in purity; for they engaged in war and lived not in communities, with rab'bahs as rulers, but dwelt together after the manner of warriors.

4. To Baal and Ashtaroth was committed the duty of subjugating these people unto Osiris,

Savior of mortals. So Baal and Ashtaroth, finding them stubborn in the worship of the Great Spirit, finally resolved to make them destroy one another, after the same manner as Te-in, in Jaffeth, and Sudga, in Vind'yu; and they asked Osiris for armies of warring angels for that purpose. Osiris gave them the following great angel generals and high captains, to wit:

5. Jah, Apollon-ya, Petoris, Pluton-ya, Hi-ram, Ben, Yube, Ali-jah, Ares, Sa'wang, T'crono, Afro-dite, Argo, Oyeb, Nadar, Abel, Said, Ar-te-mis, Yac-ta-roth, Wab, Josh and Haur; and besides these there were the following deserters from Te-in and Sudga, to wit: Clue, Jon, I-sa-ah, Yam-yam, Luth, Bar, Hote, Ki-dom, Athena, Hira, Oke-ya-nos, Hermes, Posee-ya-don, Ura-na, Hace, T'sodus, Rac-Rom, Mi-kak, Tol, Taes, Wowouski, Sur, Ala-jax and Hesmoin.

6. And Baal and Ashtaroth cast lots for each of the above generals and captains, turn about they chose, until they were divided equally between them. And Osiris gave to Baal and Ashtaroth, each, five hundred million warring angels. And thus armed, they descended to the earth, to the objectionable regions, of Parsi'e and Heleste. In those days these great divisions of the earth were divided into many nations and kingdoms.

7. And a kingdom was not measured according to the land, but according to the number of cities that paid tribute to the central city; though some kingdoms had but one city.

8. These, then, are some of the largest cities that Baal and Ashtaroth determined to destroy, to wit: Su-yan, with five tributary cities; Lakao, with two tributaries; Hangun; with eight tributaries; Waas with three; Lawga, with six; Tol, with six; Sun, with five; Tos, with four; Troy, with six; Abed, with two; Athena, with twelve; Hess, with four; Ituna, with twelve; Fado, with ten; Tuna, with seven; and Wa'ke'at, with seven. And besides these there were many large cities without any tributary cities, which were also doomed to everlasting destruction.

9. The first great cities thus turned to war on each other were Haugun and Lowga; Ashtaroth choosing Haugun and Baal choosing Lowga.

10. These two cities were both of more than four hundred years' standing, and contained each a half million inhabitants, besides their tributary cities. Tojak was king of Haugun; he was the son of Soma, who was the son of Atyis, the necromancer. And of Lowga, Turwea was king; he was the son of Diah, son of Bawn, the philosopher.

11. When Baal and Ashtaroth, with their armies from heaven, came near to these cities, they halted and built a temporary kingdom in the mountains of Zoe.

12. Baal said to Ashtaroth: Behold, thou has had the choice of cities, give thou me the first assault?

13. Ashtaroth said: On thine own terms shall these battles be, and I will beat thee. To it, then; set on Lowga.

14. Baal went to Turwea in his dreams and told him his son was waylaid by the people of Haugun, and, moreover, that Tojak had determined to come upon him and possess the city. When Turwea awoke, he was troubled about his dream, and he inquired of the oracle concerning the matter. Ashtaroth had possession of the oracle, and she answered the king, saying: Thou art of the seed of the Faithists, why fearest thou for a dream? Have a caution of thy dreams; tell not thy son, for this day he goeth on the hunt, and thy words might bring about even that which otherwise might not be. The king went his way, but Ashtaroth sent inspiring spirits to the king, saying: To caution thy son, that would be

wisdom. And the king went and cautioned his son.

15. Ashtaroth then went to Tojak's wife, and gave her a dream that the Prince of Lowga went on a hunt, to all appearances, but came near Haugun for a very different matter, which was no less than the slaying of herself and husband. The queen awoke suddenly, and in fear, and told the king her dream. Tojak said:

16. Foolish woman; it was but the fault of thy diseased blood, which, coursing the heart, gave thee a foolish dream. Tojak dismissed the matter. On the next day, the angels kept inspiring the queen to send her servants to the place of her dreams, to which she acceded; and her servants were armed with spears, and instructed to kill whoso came in their way, as if by accident.

17. Thus it came to pass that Turwea's son was slain. Turwea inquired of the oracle, and was answered by Ashtaroth, saying: Why comest thou to me for comfort; is not thy son dead by thine own fault? I said unto thee: Mention not the matter of thy dream to thy son, for oft it happeneth that telling of a thing bringeth it to pass.

18. Turwea said: I am justly rebuked, O Apollo-ya! But tell me, thou that knowest all things, since one part of my dream hath come true, may not the other part, and, of a truth, Tojak come to possess my kingdom? Ashtaroth said: If I tell thee, thou wilt blab it about, and do nothing in thine own defense. Turwea then made oath to obey the oracle; whereupon she commanded him to march with all his army against Tojak, and suddenly demand satisfaction in ten thousand lives, to balance the loss of the prince.

19. This ended Ashtaroth's part with the city of Lowga; and now she went to Haugun, whilst Baal took charge of Lowga, sending his legions of angels to the people of Lowga, to inspire them with madness because their prince was slain.

20. Ashtaroth, on her part, now assumed control of the oracle in Haugun, and sent her warring angels to the people of the city, advising them of the justice of slaying the prince, because he was come, not on a hunt, but to slay the king and queen. And Ashtaroth, further, told the king, Tojak: Try thou me as to my truthfulness: Behold, in two days the warriors of Turwea will be at thy city's gates; be thou ready for them and drive them hence, or lo, thy city wall will be reduced to dust and ashes.

21. Of course the prophecy of Ashtaroth came true, and Tojak now believed he was in the protection of the Gods. The queen said unto him: A matter of weight is on my mind, O king: I commanded my servants to slay the prince, for the Gods showed it to me that only by this could thy life and mine be preserved.

22. The king, Tojak, justified the queen, saying: Thou hast been the preserver of my life and thine.

23. Baal, God of Lowga, thus marched the mortal armies against the city of Haugun, whilst Ashtaroth marched the armies of the latter place to battle against them.

24. And thus, as mortals play a game with sticks and pegs, so played this God and Goddess a game with these mortals of these two great cities; played give and take to see the battles lost or won; and they used their legions of angels to inspire the mortals on, or to make them at times turn and flee. And whilst the Gods rested, amusing themselves by feasting and by talking over the sport of mortal death, the two great cities would also gain a little rest, but only to renew the bloody work.

25. For four years the gods and angels kept these two mortal cities at war; and though they lay a day's journey apart, all the way was strewn with the bones of the slain. And in

four years they were reduced to dust and ashes; and as to the people of the last year, for the most part, they were inoculated with the poisoned air of the dead, and they died also. And yet it came to pass, Baal beat Ashtaroth in the battle of death, for he caused all his people to be slain, whilst yet a few of Ashtaroth's remained.

26. Thus did Baal and Ashtaroth pursue the other great cities of Parsi'e and Heleste. And the time of the destruction of any two or three cities varied from two years to ten years. For the destruction of Athena and Troy it required twelve years. And for the destruction of Ituna and Fado it required eleven years. Betwixt Su-gun and Lakao it required two years to bring them to war. Betwixt Athena and Troy it required three years to bring them to war. Two hundred vampires, angels of lust, were set upon a prince of Troy, and in desperation he was driven to kidnap an Athenian princess, who was led to exposure by Baal's angel hosts. In this great battle Ashtaroth won the game, having succeeded in having the whole of the Trojans destroyed.

27. In the war betwixt Tos and Sun, which lasted nine years, it was an even game, for both cities were entirely destroyed and all the people in them, and also their tributary cities as well. But the city of Tol was destroyed within itself, for there was no city near enough to war upon it. The angels brought virus from the dead of other regions, and inoculated the breath of the people of Tol, and their flesh festered, and they died of themselves without war.

28. The whole time of destruction was one hundred and sixty years; and after that Parsi'e and Heleste were wasted and desert, and wild beasts coursed the country far and near.

29. Osiris had said: I will make the land of Egupt the greatest country in the world; I will have the place of my dominion near at hand. Satan had said to Osiris: If thou destroy not Parsi'e and Heleste, behold, Baal and Ashtaroth will rebel against thee, choosing these lands for their own kingdoms.

30. But both satan and Osiris, who now falsely styled himself God of heaven and earth, were powerless to prevent the march of Jehovih's hand. For as He gave liberty unto all His creatures, and as Osiris had fostered the idea of being sole ruler of earth and heaven, even so the seed of his own sowing took root in Baal and Ashtaroth. And they formed a compact with each other and seceded from Osiris after all. And in order to determine what share of the earth should be theirs, a war in heaven ensued between the three Gods, and Te-in and Sudga joined in also.

CHAPTER LIII.

1. Jehovih had said: I created man blank, as to good and evil, and gave him liberty: And I gave liberty also to the spirits of the dead. But these spirits set themselves up as Gods; and to glorify themselves used mortals in their own way. For they found that mortals could be turned to good or evil, to war or to peace, to virtue or to lust, according to the inspiration of the angels watching over them.

2. But in this I provided a remedy also, and without abridging liberty, which was, that the Gods, in contention for mortal souls, should fall out and ultimately destroy their own heavenly kingdoms, wherefrom angels and mortals should escape from bondage.

3. And this was so. Te-in and Sudga and Osiris, even whilst their wars and machinations were going on with mortals, were scheming for mastery in hada, each to overthrow the

others, and involve them in ruin. And it thus came to pass that a triangular war ensued in these two heavens, in which upward of ten thousand millions of warring angels were engaged hundreds of years. For, as mortals engage in corporeal warfare, so do angels engage in es'sean warfare. For though they cannot kill one another, they can bind and enslave and cast one another into hells, and surround them with never-ending fire, so they cannot escape. And the warring Gods send their armies forth to make captives of their enemies, who, when seized, are either made subjects of, or else cast into torments. And these armies of warring angels, hundreds of millions strong, go into the kingdom of another God, and out of suburban districts, carrying hence the subjects, with all their acquisitions. And yet at times these raiding armies venture too far, and are themselves captured and cast into torments. So that Gods in hada wall their kingdoms round with standing armies, even as they have taught mortals to defend themselves. And their enemies seek to invent means to break these armies through, and go in and plunder and destroy.

4. In times of which madness no voice from Jehovih's angels can gain an attentive ear amongst them; even the same as when mortal kings are at war, for one to say to them: Behold, Jehovih is All Peace! They will even curse Jehovih and peace, so do the fighting angels threaten and curse if one of Jehovih's holy ones interpose in peace and love.

5. As like a burning fever or canker worm that needeth run its course, before a healing balm availeth good, so Jehovih permitteth the Gods to pursue their reign, till, helpless, they fall, environed in the harvest they sowed. For a time cometh to every man and woman born, on earth or in heaven, when sore disaster, if nothing else, will cast him helpless in agony, to make him own the Mighty Power Who created him; and make him supplicate in pity for some helping hand to lead him safely to the All Person's pleading Voice. Then he is ready to listen; to turn from Gods, and Lords, and Saviors, and Sons who profess to save; and to stand upright before the Father, and learn to know Him, and willingly learn peace, love, reason and truth.

6. Jehovih hath said: In every soul I made a door, and in this My Light shineth. Herein My Voice speaketh; but they turn away, and go after them that speak to the external ear; a serpent biteth them, and they are cast in poison and in death!

7. Man on the earth hath said: I will not heed Thy still small voice, O Jehovih, which speaketh to the soul; I will obey the king, that leads on to war, and with loud noises and violent oaths pursueth death-dealing as a virtuous trade. Not Thou, O Jehovih, shall be my master, but their king, who hath great pageantry. Behold, I will stand in his great armies, or be led on to death, even as the king willeth me; for he is my Savior and my defense. His Gods shall be my Gods; his Lords my Lords; his Savior my Savior; by blood and heroic butcheries will I prove my loyalty.

8. And even so hath thousands of millions of angels in hada said: Not the still small voice of my soul will I obey; but yonder gaudy God, whose sacredness is so great none can approach him but by crawling on their bellies! He shall be my Lord and Savior; his battles shall be my battles; to feed the hells of hada with his enemies shall be my trade.

9. Jehovih hath said: Even to them that choose darkness and evil have I given liberty also; for they shall learn by experience, in time to come, that all these guides and leaders, be they kings, or Gods, or Lords, or Saviors, are but snares, from whom, soon or late, they must turn in order to rise out of the hells they have built for others. For, because they put

Me afar off, or denied My Person, or called Me Void like the wind, I cut them not off; but they cut themselves off from Me, and thus fell into torments.

10. For I am as near to the corporean as to the es'sean; let them, then, disown their kings and Gods, and whoso hath a kingdom to glorify; and they shall espouse Me, for I am Ever Present. For this, all people shall do, either on earth or in heaven. My kingdoms are not by violence or by war, but by liberty to every soul; and whoso practiceth peace and love, and liberty unto others, are My chosen. They are on the way of everlasting resurrection.

CHAPTER LIV.

1. About the time Baal and Ashtaroth had destroyed the inhabitants of the earth in Parsi'e and Heleste, they applied to Osiris, demanding promotion to separate kingdoms of their own. They said:

2. Thou knowest of a truth that for sake of confederacy we merged our own kingdoms into thine; to make thee powerful against the wars of Te-in and Sudga in heaven. And to do thy will we have laid desolate the mortal kingdoms of Parsi'e and Heleste. For which things thou didst promise us in the start we should have great kingdoms in heaven.

3. Now behold, heaven is but one vast scene of war! And this also do we perceive, that the mighty contests are without any prospect of an end. As these heavenly wars raged hundreds of years ago, even so do they this day. Yea, the heavenly forces are becoming less disciplined and less scrupulous from year to year.

4. By evidence of which it is plain that thy heavens, and Te-in's, and Sudga's, will soon or late be cast into interminable hells. To prevent which, we ask of thee, our God, go give us each a section to ourselves, and we will subdue the places and govern them in our own way.

5. Osiris answered them, saying: Of all the Gods, who but I hath done a hand's turn to raise mortal subjects to a higher plane? Te-in's course was destruction; so was Sudga's. And by much importuning ye twain persuaded me to have the mortals of Parsi'e and Heleste destroyed. And now, in the time when most of all we should be united, ye importune me to have my great kingdom disruptured and divided. Perceive ye not that we have the balance of power in our favor? And also, that if in these troublous times ye espouse new kingdoms, we will all be at the mercy of Te-in and Sudga.

6. For which reason I beseech you both to postpone the matter till we have driven our enemies from our doors. Let us be faithful to the confederacy.

7. Now in this affair Baal and Ashtaroth came not to Osiris in person, but sent messengers, as if they were ashamed of their own proposal. And yet, on the other hand, Osiris invited them not to his kingdom.

8. Ashtaroth said to Baal: See what Osiris hath done! He taketh us for children; giving us sweet promises if we will but keep right on serving him. I tell thee, Baal, thou mayst serve Osiris; but from this time forth I am none of his! Behold, I will mark out a kingdom of mine own, and I will establish it and rule it in mine own way. Moreover I will send word to Te-in and Sudga; and if Osiris balk me, they shall know his vulnerable points.

9. Baal said: Even so will I; and I will establish a kingdom alongside of thine, and if our enemies attack us we can the better defend ourselves.

10. So said, so done. And Baal marked out for his heavenly kingdom over Heleste and

north-western Arabin'ya; and Ashtaroth marked out for her heavenly kingdom over Parsi'e and north-eastern Arabin'ya. And the twain no sooner chose their generals and captains, and founded their heavenly thrones, than they sent word to Osiris and to Te-in and to Sudga.

11. A general dismemberment of these mighty kingdoms took place. In Osiris' heaven there revolted one Kabbath, who took the name Thammus. He was a general, whom tens of thousands of angel officers delighted to serve. He marked out his heavenly place over western Egupt, and established his throne and officers, and had himself proclaimed to mortals through the oracles as THE ONLY SON OF THE GREAT SPIRIT, THE SAVIOR OF MEN.

12. Teos-judas also revolted from Osiris, and established a heavenly kingdom over south Arabin'ya (Africa). Besides these there were: Marcus, Delos, Acta, Hebron, Debora, Julta, Wab, Thais and D'nor, great generals and captains in Osiris' heavenly kingdom, all of whom revolted and began setting up heavenly kingdoms of their own.

13. And in Sudga's heavenly kingdom more than one thousand generals and captains revolted and began to establish heavenly kingdoms of their own. Of these the most prominent were: Judsa, Vishnu, Eorata, Chrisna, Histaga, Vivaulias, Hiras, Haroyu, Ahhoma, V'ractu and Tiviressa.

14. And in Te-in's heavenly kingdom more than eight hundred generals and captains revolted, and established kingdoms of their own. Of these the most powerful were: Chong, Ho-Tain, Dyut, Cow, Ghan, Su-Lep, Djhi, Hiss, Me Lee, Wang, Hop-jee and Kaab.

15. And all the revolted ones called themselves Gods or Lords or Saviors, and endeavored to establish an earthly habitation as well. And all of them took with them millions and millions and tens of millions of angel followers; and some of them had more than a hundred million subjects to start with.

16. So anarchy began to reign in hada. Order was broken down; warfare was divided in a thousand ways, and neither angels nor Gods could more discover what this war or that war was about, save to inflict torments on others. And so great was the conflict that over more than half the earth all the lowest heaven was but one continuous succession of knots and hells. To inflict pain and disorder and destruction was the work of twenty thousand million angels in darkness; war, war, war; hell, hell, hell!

17. And now, alas, over all the earth where war had reveled hundreds of years, were thousands of millions of spirits in chaos, not knowing in fact they were in the spirit world, but still battling against all who came along, to the left and to the right, before and behind, screaming, bawling with madness, striking out in madness, in unceasing agony, in an unending nightmare of madness.

18. And from the mighty hosts of darkness, the drujas, deep born in darkness, now pestering the people on earth, were hundreds of millions of familiars taking to fetalism! Vampire spirits who suck the blood and the flesh of mortals till the brain and heart are wild and mad! Till the mortal is driven to nameless deeds of horrors, desperate with the foul obsession. Spirits who bring poison and horrid smells to afflict mortals with; spirits who delight to feed on the flesh of mortals which is corrupted with scabs and running sores. Spirits that teach re-incarnation and lust as the highest, most exalted heaven.

19. And now the mighty hosts of Anuhasaj, alias De'yus, the Lord God, the false, broke in on every side, and spread here and there for foulness and for fuel to feed their thousands

of hells.

20. And these in remembrance of Osiris' hated name and treachery went for his great kingdom, followed by thousands of millions of angels, desperate with long-continued slavery, roused for deeds of vengeance. Forth into his capital, Agho'aden, they rushed, beating down the pillars of fire and high archways and rushing into the throne of Osiris, seized him and his vice-Gods and high marshals and dragged them off and cast them into foul-smelling hells, hideous with the wail and roar of maniacs and tantalizing drujas, and with kicks and blows and poundings covered them up in foul darkness, heaped deep and smothering in suffocating gases.

21. Then off ran other legions for Te-in and his high officers, and to pillage his kingdom also. And him and them they seized and bore off in triumph to equally horrid hells. And then others for great Sudga ran, even more desperate for vengeance sake; and him they also caught, despoiling his mighty kingdom and cast him into hell.

22. And for many of the lesser Gods they ran, and broke them down utterly, and cast them into hells. Only two Gods of the past days in these regions escaped, Baal and Ashtaroth, who fled to save themselves for a more opportune season to carry out their wicked schemes.

CHAPTER LV.

1. Of the self-Gods of Uropa, and North and South Guatama, little need be said. They established weak heavenly kingdoms and succeeded in inciting mortals to war, but to no great destruction. Their heavenly kingdoms were for the most part failures; their thrones were poor and dilapidated almost from the start.

2. Of these great divisions of the earth mortals were too scattered and few to be profitable for false Gods. In Guatama they had not forgotten the lessons of I'tura, the false God who had ruined their forefathers. They were wary, and for the most part preserved their allegiance to the Great Spirit.

3. This much, then, of evil; now know ye of the good and faithful, and of the changes of earth and heaven.

4. By the pressure of ji'ay, Craoshivi had descended near the earth, and some places bordered upon it. Darkness had overspread the land of the earth in some regions for seven hundred years, so that the sun shone not, save as a red ball of fire. And nebula fell in many places to a depth of three lengths, so that even the places of the great cities of the earth, which had been destroyed, were covered up, and it was like a new country.

5. The which was beneficial to Jehovih's angels, in assisting them to deliver hosts of the chaotic spirits, whose mortal part fell in dread war. For such was the labor of the true God in Craoshivi, Son of Jehovih, and of his hosts of upraised angels. To gather in from every quarter of earth and her heavens the fallen victims of the self-Gods; to restore them to reason and to happier and holier scenes; and to teach them righteousness and good works.

6. Jehovih had said to God, His Son: Because one man can not lift up the whole world he shall not grieve, nor cease doing what he can. For his glory lieth in exerting himself to the full.

7. Because the self-Gods have come against thee, they are against Me also; because they have espoused to be Creators, and thus proclaimed themselves for their own glory, they shall have their fill. Before these times, the false Gods were content to proclaim their own

names; but lo and behold, they have made the Lord God as the Creator, and set him up as a man, on a throne, to worship him!

8. And Te-in, and Sudga, and Osiris, too! All of woman born, and knowing My breath upon them. Sufficient is it for thee, My Son, to gather in the afflicted and distressed, and restore them and deliver them in light and truth. Keep thou thy schools and colleges in heaven; and thy nurseries and hospitals, and factories, and thy fleets of swift-flying otevans and airavagnas. And send thou thy faithful volunteers, and make the afflicted to rejoice and hold up their heads in great joy.

9. But to them that will not hear; and to them that curse thee and Me, seeking to destroy Me for their own glory, be thou silent. My hand is upon them. My ji'ay'an shower covereth earth and heaven. In their own game shall they cast themselves in darkness and destruction.

10. And all the while the self-Gods were at their evil deeds, the Faithists, Jehovih's angels, worshippers of the Ever Present, All Person, coursed the heavens along in their fire-ships, calling in the persecuted children of Jehovih. Calling loud and cheerfully through the heavens of the evil Gods, and over the kingdoms of the earth; calling in these words:

11. Come! Come! The Father's kingdom is free! Come! Come! In peace and quietness thou shalt be thine own master! Behold, the Father's places rise higher and higher! Not downward, to the lower kingdoms, nor to the earth, nor to re-incarnation, the invented tale of drujas; but upward to wisdom, goodness, love and happiness.

12. Because ye have put away the All Person, ye have fallen in the mire; ye have closed your eyes to yonder higher heaven. Come, O ye that are in bondage! Cut loose from all! Fly to Him Who brought ye forth to life! Disown the world! And self! And all the Gods and Saviors! Lords and kings! Be Jehovih's! Sworn to peace and love! To good works and righteousness!

13. Come! Come! Our otevans are free! Our airiavagnas full of comfort. O Come and be our loves! Be fellows, one with Jehovih.

14. And they gathered in millions and thousands of millions! For hundreds and hundreds of years they labored in the distracted regions of hada; toiled and toiled till wearied and prostrate, tens of thousands of times; then rested awhile, invigorated for more energetic work.

15. But not alone nor unseen, these toiling millions, hundreds of millions of Jehovih's angels, faithful Sons and Daughters. For the labor built up their own spirits to be as very Gods and Goddesses in noble endurance. Which was written in their fair faces, so the high-raised messengers of far-off heavens, traveling past, beheld Jehovih's soul in them. And so bore the news to other worlds of the darkness of the earth and her evil Gods, and of the faithful, struggling hosts of Jehovih in their up-hill work.

16. And now the earth and her heavens crossed the boundaries of the ji'ay'an forests, and rolled slowly towards the homes and dominions of other etherean Gods.

END OF THE BOOK OF WARS AGAINST JEHOVIH.

Made in the USA
Las Vegas, NV
07 March 2024

86839124R00345